# The Cambridge Dictionary of Human Biology and Evolution

The *Cambridge Dictionary of Human Biology and Evolution* (*CDHBE*) is an invaluable research and study tool for both professionals and students covering a broad range of subjects within human biology, physical anthropology, anatomy, auxology, primatology, physiology, genetics, paleontology, and zoology. Packed with 13,000 descriptions of terms, specimens, sites and names, *CDHBE* also includes information on over 1000 word roots, taxonomies and reference tables for extinct, recent and extant primates, geological and oxygen isotope chronologies, illustrations of anatomical landmarks, bones and muscles, and an illustration of current hominid phylogeny, making this a must-have volume for anyone with an interest in human biology or evolution. *CDHBE* is especially complete in its inventory of archaeological sites and the best-known hominid specimens excavated from them, but also includes up-to-date information on terms such as *in silico*, and those relating to the rapidly developing field of human genomics.

Larry L. Mai is Associate Professor in the Departments of Anthropology and Biological Sciences at California State University, Long Beach.

Marcus Young Owl is Professor in the Departments of Anthropology and Biological Sciences, also at California State University, Long Beach.

M. Patricia Kersting is an editor at the Audio-Digest Foundation in Glendale, California.

# The Cambridge Dictionary
## of Human Biology and Evolution

LARRY L. MAI
*California State University, Long Beach*

MARCUS YOUNG OWL
*California State University, Long Beach*

M. PATRICIA KERSTING
*Audio-Digest Foundation, Glendale, California*

**CAMBRIDGE**
UNIVERSITY PRESS

CAMBRIDGE UNIVERSITY PRESS
Cambridge, New York, Melbourne, Madrid, Cape Town, Singapore, São Paulo

CAMBRIDGE UNIVERSITY PRESS
The Edinburgh Building, Cambridge CB2 2RU, UK

Published in the United States of America by Cambridge University Press, New York

www.cambridge.org
Information on this title: www.cambridge.org/9780521662508

First published 2005

Printed in the United Kingdom at the University Press, Cambridge

*A catalogue record for this book is available from the British Library*

ISBN-13 978-0-521-66250-8 hardback
ISBN-10 0-521-66250-8 hardback

ISBN-13 978-0-521-66486-1 paperback
ISBN-10 0-521-66486-1 paperback

# Contents

# Preface

Human biology is a diverse and multidisciplinary field that includes or borrows from anthropology, anatomy, auxology, evolutionary biology, genetics, geology, physiology, and zoology. In our studies of human biology we found that medical or general biology dictionaries often did not define many terms used in non-clinical human biology. This was especially true of the core terms used in physical anthropology and primatology. We have attempted to bridge that gap with this work.

This compilation is intended to define and elaborate on the more important terms used in human biology and evolution. For readers with little background in these subjects, it identifies and provides definitions of core terms most frequently used in these areas. In addition, we have attempted to define, and occasionally annotate or expand on, subjects of interest to advanced students and professionals, such as fossil specimens, paleontological sites, and primate genera.

**Rationalization of entries**

Terms: individual entries were selected by compiling lists of terms from glossaries and indices found in major textbooks and best-selling or classic works on relevant subjects. Approximately 30 000 terms were ranked with respect to ubiquity; the least frequent terms were then culled to leave a manageable body of about 13 000 terms. Occasionally, a neologism (e.g. genomics) was included when it was deemed that such terms would be useful in the future.

The 1000 most common terms are preceded in this dictionary by the symbol ‡. We hope that students will find these pointers useful.

Similarly, short biographies were included for individuals that have been most frequently mentioned in introductory textbooks. The editors apologize for any inadvertent omissions, and would appreciate suggestions in this area.

Please send comments, corrections and/or additions to lmai@csulb.edu or youngowl@csulb.edu.

Note that all terms apply to the human species by default, unless a primate is specifically mentioned.

**Cross-referencing**

Bold terms in the body of a definition refer to an entry elsewhere in the dictionary. In the following entry, for example,

‡ **matriline:** pertaining to the lineal descent of anything passed from a mother to her offspring, such as access to territory or other resource, social status within a dominance system, or specific genes that display a pattern of **maternal inheritance** such as those contained in **mitochondrial DNA**; matrilineal. Aka uterine descent, matrilinear inheritance. See **hologyny**. *Cf.* **patriline** and **holandry**.

the reader is referred to the entries *maternal inheritance, mitochondrial DNA* and *hologyny* for related or supplementary material, and to the terms *patriline* and *holandry* for contrasting material.

**A note on taxonomy**

The fundamental unit of taxonomy is the species. The species name is always accompanied by its genus (although the genus may be abbreviated). These two terms form a binomen. The binomen is often followed by the authority when first presented in a publication. The authority is the name(s) of the author(s) who first described the species. That authority will forever follow the species name, even though the genus may change. For example, the original common description of the chimpanzee was by J. F. Blumenbach:

*Simia troglodytes* Blumenbach, 1775

Later a new genus name was accepted and a new authority for the genus was established, *Pan* Oken, 1816. However, the species name for the common chimpanzee remained the same. The original authority is retained, but is now enclosed by parentheses, thereby noting that there has been a change in the genus name. Thus,

*Pan troglodytes* (Blumenbach, 1775)

To be valid, a proposed taxonomic name for a living species must be examined and approved by a board of the International Commission on Zoological Nomenclature (ICZN). In the case of fossil species, the use of the species name in a subsequent publication by another author(s) validates a new species' name.

Appendixes 1 and 2 provide taxonomies of living and extinct primates. These are not formal taxonomies, but are intended to provide the reader with lists of species' names that have been used consistently in the literature, although not all are universally accepted.

# Acknowledgements

The authors thank the following individuals who participated in the production of this dictionary.

- Our acquisitions editors at Cambridge University Press, Tracey Sanderson and Dr Maria Murphy; our copy editor, Lynn Davy and our production editor, Jayne Aldhouse.
- Several anonymous reviewers who provided useful feedback with respect to both content and format.
- Our constant and inexhaustible sources of arcane factoids, Wendy Culotta and Peggy Moyer.
- P. A. Perkins for the superb anatomical illustrations in Appendix 7.
- The many students who provided feedback, but most especially to Candace Parrish McGowan, Denise Cucurny, Eilene Cruz, Torrey Palovchik, and Egon Trujillo.

Finally, we acknowledge and deeply appreciate the patience and forbearance of our colleagues, families and friends, especially Janine Bernor Mai and Rolaine Young Owl.

# Word roots

a-: not, without, negating
ab-: away from
abdom(in)-: abdomen, belly
-able: capable (of)
ac-: to, toward
acet(o)-: vinegar
acid-: sour, bitter, sharp
acous-: hearing
acro-: tip; top; height
act-: do, drive, act
acti(no)-: radius
acu-: needle; sharp
ad-: to, towards
aden(o)-: gland
adip(o)-: fat
aer-: air, atmosphere; gas
aesthe-: perceive, feel
af-: to, toward
-agogue: away, leading
agglutin: glue together
-agra: acute pain
alb-: pale, white
alg-: pain
-alis: of, belonging to
all(o)-: other, different
alve(ol)-: socket, channel
ambi-: both; surround
amph-: both, two
amyl(o)-: starch
an-: up; back; not
ancyl(o)-: crooked, bent
andr(o)-: man, male
ang-: vessel
ankyl(o)-: bent; fusion
ante-: before
anthrop(o)-: human, Man
anti-: against, opposite
antr(o)-: cavern
-anus: belonging to
ap(ic)-: toward; tip
-aph(e)-: touch
apo-: derived from
append(ic)-: attach

aqua-: water
arachn-: spider
arch-: first; origin; ancient
-aris: pertaining to
arteri(o)-: artery; wind pipe
arthr(o)-: joint
arti-, art-: art
artic(ul)(o)-: joint
as-: to, toward
-asia: pathological state
-asis: condition, state (of)
at-: to, toward
-atus: provided with
audi-: hearing
aur-: ear; gold
austr-: south, southern
aut(o)-: self
aux-: grow, enlarge
axo-: axis; axle
axill-: armpit
ba-: walk, stand
bacill-: rod, little stick, wand
bacteri(o)-: staff, cane
ball(o)-: throw
bar-: heavy; pressure
bas-: base, foundation
bi-: two, twice; between
bili-: bile; anger
(-)bio(-): life, living
biocenos-: compound prefix refer-
    ring to living organisms in a
    shared environment (is com-
    posed of two stems)
(-)blast(o)(-): bud, embryo
blep(o)-: looking, seeing
blephar-: eyelash
bol(o)-: throw
brachi(o)-: arm
brachy-: short
brad-: slow
brom(o)-: stench; oats; food
bronch-: windpipe
bryo-: be full of life; moss

bucc-: cheek
cac-: bad, ill
calcan(e)-: heel
calc(i)-: heel; limestone; lime
calor(i)-: heat
canc-: crab; ulcer; cancer
capit-: head
caps-: container, box
carb-: coal, charcoal
carcin-: crab; ulcer; cancer
card-: heart
cary(o)-: nut; kernel; nucleus
cat-: down, lower; against
caud-: tail
cav-: hollow
cec-: blind
celo-, -cele: tumor; cavity
cell-: small room; granary
cen(o)-: common; empty; new
(-)cent(e)(-): puncture, prick
centi-: hundred; hundredth
centr-: point, center
(-)cephal(-): head
cept-: take, receive
cer-: wax
cera-: horn
cereb-: brain
cervi-: neck
chamae-: dwarflike; low
chancr-: crab; cancer
cheil(o)-: lip; edge; claw
cheir(o)-, chir(o)-: hand
chiasm-: cross-shaped
chlor(o)-: green
chol-: bile; anger
chondr(o)-: cartilage; grain
chord-: string, cord, gut
chori-: membrane; skin
chrom-, chromat(o)-: color
chron-: time
chy-: pour; juice
-cid(e), -cidal: cut, kill
cili(o)-: eyelid; eyelash; hairlike

cine-: movement
cingul-: girdle; belt
-cipient: receive, receptor
circum-: about, around
(-)cis(-): near side of
clad-: branch, offshoot
(-)clas(-): break, fragmented
cleav-: divide
clin(o)-: bend, incline, slope
clu-: shut, close
co-: with, together
cocc-: berry, grainlike
(-)coel(-): swelling, cavity
-coid: like
col-: with, together
colo(n): colon, limb
colp(o)-: hollow; womb
com-, con-: with, together
contra-: against, opposite
copr(o)-: feces, dung
cor-: with, together
corn-: animal horn; hard
coron-: crown; crow
corp-: body
cort-: bark, rind
cost(a)-: rib
crani-, -cranic: skull; helmet
cre-: meat, flesh
-cresc: growth, increase
cret-: chalk; separate; grow
crin(o)-: separate off; secrete
cross(o)-: at right angles
crur(a)-: shin, leg
crux-: at right angles; cross
cry(o)-, crym(o)-: cold, frost
crypt(o)-: hidden, concealed
cult-: tend, plow; worship
cune(i)-: wedge
cusp-: point, apex
cut-: skin, surface
cyan-: blue
cycl(o)-: circle, cycle
cyst(o)-: sac, bladder,
cyt(o)-, -cyte: cell
dacry-: tear
dactyl(o)-: finger, toe
de-: down, lack of, from, out
dec(a)-: ten
demi-: half or lesser
dendr(o)-: tree, treelike
dent-: tooth
derm-: skin
desm-: band, ligament
dext-: to the right
di-: twice, two, double

di(a)-: through, completely
didym(a)-: twin; double; testis
digit-: finger, toe
dipl-: double, twice, twin
dis-: reversal; separation
disc-: plate, disk
dist-: distant
dolicho-: long
-donto-: tooth
dors(o)-: back
drom-: running; race course
-ducent: lead, conduct
duc(t)-: lead, conduct; carry
dur-: hard
dyn-: power
dys-: bad; ill; difficult; enter
e-: from, without, other than
ec-: out, outside
(-)ech(-): have, hold, be
eco-: house, dwelling
ecto-: out, outside, external
-ectomy: surgical removal
ede-: swelling; genitals
electr-: amber; electricity
-ellus: diminutive; small
(-)em(-): in; within; blood
-emia: state of the blood
en-: in, within
encephal(o)-: brain
end(o)-: inside, within
-ens: belonging to (a locality)
enter(o)-: intestine
ep(i)-: upon, beside, above
equi-: equal to; horse
erg(o)-: work, deed
erythr(o)-: red
eso-: inside, within, inward,
esth-: perceive; clothe; eat
ethm-: sieve
eu-: well, good, normal, easily
ex(o)-: outside, outward
extra-: outside of, beyond
faci-: face
-facient: making, causing
-fact-: make
fasci-: band; bundle
febr(i)-: fever; boil
-fect-: make
-ferent: bear, carry
ferr(o)-: iron
fibr-: fiber
fil-: thread
fili-: son, daughter
fiss-: split, cleft
flagell-: whip

flav-: yellow
-flect-, (-)flex-: bend, divert
flu-: flow
for-: door, opening
fore-: before
-form: shape, resembling
fract-: break
front(o)-: forehead, front
-fug: flee, avoid; banish
funct-: perform, serve
fund-: pour; alkaline
furc-: fork
fus-: pour; spindle
gala-: milk
gam-: marriage
gangli-: swelling, knot
gast-: stomach
gelat-: freeze, congeal
gemin-: twin, double; coupled
gen(o)-, -gen: originate; race
-gene, -genic, -geny: origin
geo-: earth
germ-: bud; seed
gera-: old age
gest-: bear, carry
giga-: giant
gland-: acorn
glen(o)-: pit, socket
-gli: glue
gloss-: tongue
glott-: tongue; language
gluc-: sweetness
glutin-: glue
glyc-: sweet
(-)gnath(-): jaw
gnos-: know; knowledge
gon-: produce; seed; angle
-gony: seed; offspring
grad-: walk; slope
gram-: grass
-gramm: scratch, write
gran-: grain, seed
(-)graph-: write, record
grav-: heavy; pregnancy
gymn-: naked, exposed
gyn-: woman, female
gyr-: ring, circle
haem-: blood
halo-: salt; breathe
hapl(o)-,: simple, single
hapt(o)-: touch; fasten
hect(o)-: hundred
helco-: sore, ulcer; suck
helic(o)-: spiral
helio-: sun

hem-: blood
hemi-: half
hen(o)-: one; year
hepa-: liver
hept(a)-: seven
hered-: heir; inherit
heter(o)-: other, different
hex(a)-: six
hidro-: sweat
hist(o)-: tissue, web
hod(o)-: road, path
hol(o)-: whole, entire
homeo-: same; constant
horm-: impetus, impulse
hyal(o)-: glasslike
hydat-, hydr-: water
hygr(o)-: wet; moist
hyl-: wood; matter
hyper-: above, beyond
hyp(o)-: under, below
hypn(o)-: sleep; hypnosis
hyps-: high
hyster(o)-: uterus; lower; latter
-ia: state, condition
iatr-: physician; medicine
-id: form, shape; condition
idi-: small; peculiar to
il-: not; without; in
ile(o)-: intestine; twist; roll
ilia-: flank, loin
im-: in, within; not
immun-: safe, free, exempt
in-: in, within; not
infra-: beneath, below
insul(a)-: island
inter-: between
intr(a)-: inside, within, during
-inus: like
-ion: go, enter; small
ir-: in, within; not
iri-: rainbow; iris (of the eye)
isch(o)-: suppress
ischi-: hip
-iscus: less than or smaller
-ism: belief; process; state of
iso-: equal, same, uniform
-itis: inflammation
jact-; ject-: throw
jejun(o)-: empty; hungry; dry
jug(o)-, junct-: yoke; join
juxta-: near, beside
kary(o)-: nucleus, nut, kernel
kerat(o)-: horn
kilo-: thousand
kine-: movement; moveable

labi-: lip
lacr-: tears
lact-: milk
lal-: speech
lapar(o)-: loin, flank; abdomen
laryng-: windpipe; gullet
lat(i)-: wide
later-: to the side
lent-: thick, slow
lepi-: scale, flake
leps-: take, sieze
lept-: slender
leuc(o)-, leuk(o): white
lien-: spleen
liga-: tie, bind
limn-: swamp, marsh; lake
lingu(a)-: tongue
lip(o)-: fat; leave; lack
lith-: stone, calculus
loc-: place
log(o)-: discourse, words
-logy: study of
lumb-: loin; lower back
lut-: yellow; mud
ly(o)-: dissolved; loose
lymph-: water; nymph
-lys: dissolve; loose; solution
macr(o)-: long; large
mal-: bad, abnormal; ill
malac-: soft
mamm-: teat; breast
man(u)-: hand
mani-: mental aberration
mast(o)-: breast; nipple
medi-: middle
mega-: great, large
mel(o)-: limb, member; cheeks
melan(o)-: black; dark
men(o)-: month
menin-: membrane
ment-: mind, chin
mer-: part
mes(o)-: middle, intermediate
met-: after; beyond; change
(-)metr-: measure; uterus
micr(o)-: small
mid-: middle
mill-: one thousand
miss(i)-: send
mito-: thread
-mittent: sending
mnem-: remember
mon-: one, single
(-)morph(-): form, shape
mot-: move

mu-: change
multi: many, much, several
my(o)-: muscle; mouse
myc-: fungus, fungal
myel-: marrow; spinal cord
myx-: mucus, slime
narc-: numbness, stupor
nas-: nose
ne(o)-: new, recent, immature
necr(o)-: death; dead
nephr-: kidney
neur-: nerve; cord
nod-: knot
non-: not; nine
nos(o)-: disease
noth(o)-: spurious; a mongrel
noto-: back
nuc(le)-: nut, kernal; nucleus
nutri-: nourish, nourishing
nyc-: night
ob-, oc-: inversely, against
ocul-: eye
-od-, -ode: road, pathway
odont(o)-: tooth, toothlike
-odyn: pain, distress
-oid: form; resembling
-ol: oil; alcohol
ole-: oil; olive
olecran(o)-: elbow
olig(o)-: few, small, deficient
-(o)logy: discourse or study
-oma: tumor
omni-: all, everywhere
omphal-: umbilicus, navel
onc(o)-: mass, tumor, swelling
onych(o)-: claw, nail
oo-: egg, ovum
ophthalm(o)-: eye
opt-: see, vision, sight
or-: mouth
orbi-: circle
orchi-: testis, testicle
organ(o)-: instrument; organ
orth-: straight, normal, exact
-ory: pertaining to; effect of
-os, -osus: full of; prone to
oss-, ost-: bone
ot-: ear
ov-: egg
oxy-: sharp, quick, sour; acid
pach(y)-: thick
pagi(o)-: fix, make fast
pale(o)-: old, ancient
pan-: all; general, global
par(a)-: beside, parallel

-parous: producing; birthing
partum-: bear, give birth to
path(o)-, -pathy: disease
pec-: fix, make fast; comb
ped(o)-, pedi-: child; foot; soil
pell-: skin
-pellent: drive
pelv-: basin, bowel
pen(e)-: need, lack; almost
pend-: hang down
-penia: deficiency
pent(a)-: five
pep-: digest; cook
per-: through, completely
peri-: around, surrounding
pet-: seek, tend toward
petr-: rock, stone
pex-, -pexy: fix, make fast
pha-: say, speak
phac-, phak-: lentil; lens
phag-: eat, swallow
-phagous: eating, feeding on
phan-: show; appear
pharm(ac)-: drug; toxin
pharyn-: throat, pharynx
phen-: show, be seen
pher-, phor-: bear, carry
(-)phil(-): like, love, affinity for
phleb(o)-: vein, blood vessel
phleg-, phlog-: burn, inflame
(-)phob(-): fear, dread
phon-: sound
phor-: show; carry, move
phot(o)-, phos-: light
phragm, phrax-: fence, wall
phren-: mind; heart
phthi-: decay, waste away
phy-: beget, bring forth
phyc-: seaweed
phyl-: race, tribe, kind
phyla-: guard
phyll(o)-, -phyll: leaf
phys-: blow, inflate; nature
pico-: one trillionth
pil(i)-: hair
-pithecus: simian; ape
pituit-: phlegm
placent-: flat cake; placenta
plas-: form; mold; shape
plasm-, -plast: mold, form
plat-: broad, flat
(-)pleg(-): blow, stroke
pleo-: more
plesi(o)-: near
pletho-: fill

pleur-: rib, side
plex-: strike; network; plait
plic(o)-: fold
plio-: more
(-)pne(-): breathe; lungs; air
pod(o)-: foot
(-)poie(-): make, produce
poikilo-: variable, various
pol(i)-: axis of a sphere
poly-: many, much
pont(i)-: bridge
por-: passage; stone; pore
posit-: put, place
post-: behind in time or place
pre-: before in time or place
press-: stress, strain
prim-: first
pro(s)-: before in time or place
proct(o)-: anal or rectal region
prosop(o)-: face
proto-: first, earliest form of
pseud(o)-: false
psych-: soul, mind; thought
psychr(o)-: cold
pto-: fall
pub(er)-: adult
pulmo(no)-: lung
puls-: drive; stroke; beat
punct(i)-: prick, pierce
pur(i)-: pus
py-: pus
pyel(o)-: trough; basin
pyl(o)-: door, orifice
pyr(i)-: fire, heat, fever
quadr-: four, fourth, fourfold
quasi-: almost; nearly; like
quin-, quinque-: five, fifth
rachi-: spine
radi-: rays; radius; spoke
re-: back; again
rect-: straight
ren-: kidney
ret-: net
retr(o)-: backwards, behind
rhag-: break, burst, cracked
(-)rhaph(-): suture, seam
rhe(o)-: flowing, current
rhexi-: break, burst, rupture
(-)rhin(o)(-): nose
rhiz(o)-: root
rota-: wheel
-rrhage, -rrhea: flow
rube-, rubi-, rubr-: red
saggit: arrow
salpin-: trumpet; tube

sangui-: blood
sarc-: flesh
schist(o)-: split, cleft
schiz(o)-: split, cleft, divide
scler(o)-: hard
scop-, -scope, -scopy: look at
(-)sect(-): cut, cutting
semi-: half, partly
sens(i)-: perceive, feel
sep-: rot, decay; infect
sept-: seven; fence
ser-: whey, watery substance
serrate-: saw-edged
sex(a)-: six
sial-: saliva
simi: ape
sinu-: hollow, fold
-sis: process, action
sit-: food; place, location
solut-, -solv-: loose, dissolve
soma-, -some: body
spas-: draw, pull
spectr-: presence; apparition
sperg-: scatter
sperm-: seed
sphen-: wedge
spher-: ball, globe, round
sphin-: draw tight, constrict
sphygm(o)-: pulse
spin(i)-: thorn
spir(o)-: breathe; coil
splanchn-: viscera
splen-: patch
spor-: seed, spore
squam-: scale
sta-: make stand, stop
stal-: send
staphyl(o)-: cluster of grapes
stea-: fat
sten(o)-: narrow, constricted
ster-: solid; three dimensional
sterc-: feces, dung
sthen-: strength
stol-: send
stomat-: mouth, orifice
-stomy: surgical opening
streph(o)-: twist
strict-: draw tight, compress
-stringent: draw tight
stroph-: twist; cord
struct-: pile up (against), build
sub-, suf-, sup-: under, below
super-, supra-: above, beyond
sutur-: sew; stitch; seam
sy(l)-, sym-, syn-: join, together

ta-: stretch, put under tension
tac-: order, arrange
tach-: swift, rapid, speed
tact(i)-: touch
tapein(o)-: flat; low
taph-: grave, burial
tax-, -taxis: order, arrange
tect-, teg-: cover, roof
tele(o)-: at a distance; end
tempor-: time, timely; temple
ten-: hold; stretched
ter-: thrice, three
test-: shell; oyster
tetr-: four
thec-: repository, case, sheath
thel(i)-: nipple
the(o)-: put, place; god
therap-: treatment; serve
therm(o)-: heat; summer
thero-: wild animal; wolf
thi-: sulphur
thora(co)-: chest
thromb(o)-: clot

thym(o)-: soul, emotions
thyr(eo)-: shield
tme-: cut
toc(o)-: childbirth
(-)tom(-): cut, slice; layer
ton(o)-: stretch; tone
top(o)-: place, position
tors-: twist
toxic-: poison
trache-: windpipe
trachel(o)-: neck
tract-: draw, drag
trans-: across, over
trauma(to)-: wound
tri-: three, third
trich(o)-: hair
trips(i)-: rub
triplo-: three; triad
(-)trop(-): turn, change, rotate
(-)troph(-): food, nourishment
tuber(i)-: swelling, node
tych-: chance
typ-, -type: type; image

typh(o)-: fog, stupor
typhl(o)-: blindness
ultr-: beyond, excess
un-: not; one
ur(o)-, uron(o)-: urine; tail
-uria: diving bird; urine
vacc(i)-: cow
vagin(o)-: sheath
vas-: vessel, duct
verm(i)-: worm
vers, verti-: turn
vesic(o)-: bladder; blister
viscer-: organ
vit(al)-: life
vor-, -vore: eating, feeding
vuls-: pull, twitch
xanth(o)-: yellow, blond
xen-, -xene: alien; strange
xer(o)-: dry
-yl-: matter, substance
zo-, -zoic, -zoite: animal
zyg(o)-: yoke, union
zym(o)-, -zyme: fermentation

# Abbreviations

| | |
|---|---|
| 1°, 2°, etc. | primary, secondary, etc. |
| 3-D | three-dimensional |
| ACLU | American Civil Liberties Union |
| aka | also known as |
| AMH | anatomically modern human |
| Ar/Ar | argon–argon dating technique |
| BCE | Before Common Era |
| BP | (years) before present |
| bp | base pair(s) |
| by | billions of years |
| bya | billions of years ago |
| CDC | US Centers for Disease Control and Prevention |
| CE | Common Era |
| cf. | compare |
| DOE | US Department of Energy |
| esp. | especially |
| FBI | Federal Bureau of Investigation |
| IgM, etc. | immunoglobulin M, etc. |
| IQ | Intelligence Quotient |
| K/T | Cretaceous–Tertiary boundary |
| ky | thousands of years |
| kya | thousands of years ago |
| my | millions of years |
| mya | millions of years ago |
| SI | Système International d'Unités |
| TL | thermoluminescence dating technique |
| U/Th | uranium–thorium dating technique |
| U-series | uranium series dating technique |

# The Cambridge Dictionary

## of Human Biology
## and Evolution

**A.** *n* **dates:** see Oakley's dating series in box below.

**AAA:** abbreviation for several societies of interest to **human evolutionary biologists**, including the **American Anthropological Association** and the **American Anatomical Association.**

**A antigen: epitope** that specifies the A in the **ABO blood group.** It consists of four precursor sugars attached to glycoproteins of the cell membrane, aka **H substance,** plus a specific fifth terminal sugar, N-acetylgalactosamine, that is attached by an enzyme.

---

**Oakley's absolute dating series**

**A.1 date:** highest of **Oakley's** hierarchical levels of **absolute dating,** the direct dating of a specimen, e.g. by measuring the radiocarbon activity of a bone itself.

**A.2 date:** one of **Oakley's** hierarchical levels of **absolute dating,** dating derived from direct determination by physical measurement of the age of the sediments containing the fossil specimen.

**A.3 date:** one of **Oakley's** hierarchical levels of **absolute dating,** the correlation of a fossil-bearing horizon with another deposit whose age has been determined directly by A.1 or A.2 methods. See **biostratigraphy.**

**A.4 date:** lowest of **Oakley's** hierarchical levels of **absolute dating,** estimating an absolute age on the basis of some theoretical consideration, such as matching climatic fluctuations observed in strata with astronomically derived curves of effective solar radiation, or matching terrestrial glacial and interglacial episodes with the known marine paleotemperature or **oxygen isotope stage.**

(Cf. R.*n* dates)

---

This enzyme differs from its homologue that attaches the B-specific sugar by one amino acid substitution. See **B antigen** and **O null allele.**

**AAFS:** see **American Academy of Forensic Scientists.**

**AAPA:** see **American Association of Physical Anthropologists.**

**abaxial:** on the opposite side of, or facing away from, the axis of a structure or an organism.

**Abbeville:** archaeological site found in 1830 in the French Valley of the Somme, possibly dated to the first interglacial (= **Pleistocene** deposits) described by **Boucher de Perthes** in 1847; one of the first historical cases of **artifacts** of arguable antiquity; used as proof of the existence of early humans contrary to the story contained in Genesis. Through the early twentieth century the term **Abbevillian** was applied globally to the most ancient tool deposits; **Oakley** lumped both **Oldowan** choppers and **Acheulean** choppers under this term. Aka Port du Bois, Menchecourt-les-Abbeville.

**Abbevillian tool tradition:** term that refers to pre-Acheulean stone-tool assemblages found in Europe; among the artifacts are crude **bifacial tools** constructed with a **hammerstone** rather than a softer striking instrument (as in **Acheulean**). Aka **Chellean.** See **Oldowan.**

**abdomen:** portion of the body between the thorax and the pelvis.

**abdominal cavity:** space within the body between the **respiratory diaphragm** and the **pelvic inlet** in which the abdominal viscera are contained; abdomen. Cf. **coelom.**

**abdominal circumference: anthropometric** measurement; distance around the **torso** measured with a tape measure placed at the level of the greatest anterior extension of the **abdomen** in the horizontal plane, normally the **umbilicus,** passed horizontally around the body. The measurement is taken after a normal expiration. Used for various body indices pertaining to adipose distribution. Cf. **waist circumference.**

**abdominal skinfold: anthropometric** measurement; skinfold measured about 3 cm lateral to the **umbilicus.** Used in combination with other **skinfold measurements** to estimate body composition. See **skinfold thickness.**

**abductor:** muscle or muscle group that moves a body part away from the mid-line; aka levator. Cf. **adductor.**

**abductor pollicis brevis: intrinsic muscle** of the hand; it originates from the **scaphoid** and **trapezium** and inserts into the lateral surface of metacarpal I. Its action is to abduct the thumb; one of the thenar group of muscles. Cf. **adductor pollicis.**

**abductor pollicis longus:** muscle that acts on the hand; it originates from the posterior surface of the **radius** and **ulna** and inserts into the base of metacarpal I. Its action is to abduct and extend the thumb.

**Abdur Reef:** archaeological site near Abdur along the Bari Coast in Eritrea on the coast of the Red Sea, dating to 125 kya (U/Th). The elevated reef contains artifacts including bifacial hand-axes, blade tools and sharpened obsidian flakes found among shellfish remains and animals bones deposited on an uplifted reef system. Aka Abdur Limestone Site.

**aberrant:** 1. a departure from the norm; an anomaly or aberration. 2. in genetics, an individual phenotype that exhibits atypical characteristics due to the influence of the environment rather than from genetic factors.

**ABH blood group** (ABH): a **polymorphism** found in many organisms and determined by the presence or absence of A, B, and/or H **antigens** found on cell membranes such as erythrocytes. In humans, this system has been modified and is named the **ABO blood group.**

**abiotrophy:** 1. general term denoting degenerative changes of tissue due to genetic causes. 2. deterioration of the body.

**abnormal:** 1. not normal. 2. departing from the usual structure, position, or condition. Abnormality.

**abnormal hemoglobins:** any of the **hemoglobin alleles** other than hemoglobin A; most are causes of **hemoglobinopathies,** such as **sickle cell anemia** and **thalassemia.**

‡ **ABO blood group:** **polymorphism** based on the presence or absence of two **antigens** ($I^A$ and $I^B$) found on the cell membrane of **erythrocytes** (red blood cells); the antigens are also found on other cells. The 'O' factor is an absent or 'null' **allele,** not an antigen. See **H substance.**

**ABO disease association:** any abnormal condition correlated with an allele or genotype of the ABO blood group. A number of diseases are associated with the presence of each of the A, B and O alleles in the ABO blood group; among the more prominent are salivary gland tumors (type A), ulcers (type O), and certain infant diarrheas (types A and B).

**ABO hemolytic disease of the newborn** (HDN): destruction of the **erythrocytes** of a **fetus;** a maladaptive condition roughly twice as common as the **Rhesus incompatibility** form of **HDN,** but almost always clinically milder in its manifestation. Caused by some of the smaller anti-A or anti-B **antibodies** in a mother's immune system penetrating the **placental membranes.**

**ABO incompatibility:** lowered probability of conception owing to the genotypes in the ABO blood group possessed by potential parents. In populations that maintain all three alleles, it has been suggested that type O mothers produce fewer offspring than expected when the fathers are either type A or type B; this may be due to the presence of either antibodies in the mother's vaginal secretions (that could agglutinate sperm), or certain smaller classes of maternal anti-A and anti-B antibodies that could pass through the placenta and affect the development of the fetus.

**aboriginal:** indigenous; native to; original biological species or populations inhabiting a particular geographical region, particularly referring to groups antecedent to later colonizers. In reference to humans, this term has been applied most often to the original inhabitants of Australia; aborigine. Cf. **indigenous, autochthonous.**

**abortion:** 1. arrest of a process or disease before completion. 2. interruption of pregnancy before the fetus has attained a stage of viability, usually before the 24th gestational week. There are two classes: an *induced abortion* is the termination of a pregnancy, often for medical reasons, by means other than those causing spontaneous abortion (aka clinical abortion, therapeutic abortion, feticide). A *spontaneous abortion* is the natural termination of a pregnancy before the **fetus** can survive outside the uterus (between 0 and 20 weeks); occurs in about 30% of first pregnancies, frequently so early that a woman is not aware that she was pregnant, and is most often due to chromosomal errors (50–60%); sometimes applied to a specific period of **gestation,** such as during the first 20 weeks of **pregnancy** (aka early fetal death). See **miscarriage** and **stillbirth.**

**Abri Pataud:** archaeological site found in 1949 near Les Eyzies in the Vézère River Valley, Dordogne, France, dating from 34 kya and persisting for over 14 ky; excavated by H. Movius; contains over 25 000 Aurignacian II artifacts including burins, an engraving tool for working antlers, a venus figurine in relief on stone, and hominid remains from at least two individuals, including a young female attributed to *Homo sapiens.* Of 30 crates of animal bones excavated, about 30% of all prey appear to have been reindeer. Aka Pataud.

**Abri Suard:** archaeological site found in 1870 in the La Chaise cave area, western France, dated to 200–100 kya; contains hominid remains from several individuals including an incomplete 1050 cm³ **calotte** assigned to the archaic **Neanderthal** group. Aka Suard.

**Abrigo do Lagar Velho rockshelter:** archaeological site found in 1998 in the Lapedo Valley, north of Lisbon, Portugal, dated to 24.5 kya (radiocarbon), that contains **Gravettian** artifacts. The fossil hominid remains include a nearly complete skeleton of a child (**Lagar Velho 1**) attributed to either *Homo sapiens* or *H. neanderthalensis.* Among the artifacts collected were charcoal, stone tools, pierced deer canines and fossilized red deer bones and horse teeth. Aka Lagar Velho. This find has been interpreted by some as indicative of gene flow between Neandertals and **AMHs,** and in support of the **multiregional continuity model.** See **pierced mammal teeth** and **last of the Neandertals.** Cf. **Mezmaiskaya Cave.**

**abris:** French for **shelter;** rockshelter is 'abris sous roche'.

*Absarokius* **Matthew, 1915:** poorly known tarsiiform belonging to the subfamily **Anaptomorphinae**, family **Omomyidae**. Found in early to middle **Eocene** deposits from the Rocky Mountain region of North America. Three to seven species, two of which may be in an ancestor – descendant relationship; *Tetonius homunculus* is suggested as an ancestor for at least one species. Dental formula: 2.1.3.3/2.1.3.3 or 2.1.3.3/2.1.2.3, depending on the species. *Absarokius* differs from other anaptomorphines in the enlargement of the third and fourth premolars and in thickening of the **mandible**, suggesting a diet of hard morsels. Body mass estimates range from 130 to 500 g. Synonym for *Anaptomorphus*. See Appendix 1 for taxonomy.

**abscess:** localized collection of pus in a cavity due to the accumulation of **white blood cells**; often due to infections caused by *Staphylococcus bacteria* in skin and other tissues.

‡ **absolute dating (technique):** any of the methods that provide an estimate of a specific date or age in solar years, subject to probabilistic limits, from material recovered from an archaeological or paleontological site. Common absolute techniques include **dendrochronology, radiocarbon dating** (see **carbon 14**), and **potassium – argon dating**. Aka chronometric dating. See **dating techniques.**

**absolute geological time:** scale established by geophysicists that is defined by time in years ago, thousands of years ago (**kya**), and millions of years ago (**mya**); the time scale is derived by using **absolute dating techniques** that depend upon the regular decay of unstable elements into stable daughter products. The absolute geological time scale of the earth currently extends back over 4.5 billion years (**by**) of earth history. Aka the **geological time scale.** See Appendix 4.

**absolute risk:** probability that an organism will experience a certain event, such as a disease; risk is calculated on the basis of test results and/or the occurrence of the event in relatives.

**absorption:** process by which a substance passively enters a body membrane.

**acatalasia:** genetic disorder marked by deficiency of the enzyme catalase; manifestations range from mild (ulcers in tooth sockets) to severe (recession of tooth sockets with gangrene of the gums). Two principle forms of acatalasia have been identified: (a) Japanese type, and (b) Swiss type. Aka acalalesemia.

**acaudate:** without a tail, as in the great apes; acaudal.

**accelerating differentiation:** after isolation of populations due to differences accrued at a few loci, the rapid increase of differentiation at many loci resulting in broad geographic radiation.

**accelerator mass spectrometry** (AMS): method of counting single radiocarbon atoms that is much more accurate than counting radioactive decay (conventional **radiocarbon dating**); AMS allows dating based upon very small samples (such as a speck of wood), and also extends the useful range of the technique back to almost 100 kya.

**acceptor stem:** that region of a **tRNA** molecule to which a specific **amino acid** is attached in an enzymatic reaction, which loads the tRNA prior to the **genetic translation** step of polypeptide synthesis.

**accessory olfaction system** (AOS): special sensory cells in the vomeronasal organ of the nose plus their connections to the brain. The AOS is distinct from the sense of smell, which is part of the main olfactory system. The AOS receives social and sexual signals in the form of pheromones from other members of the same species.

‡ **acclimation:** short-term **plasticity** of individual phenotype; **somatic** physiological response by individuals to environmental pressures. See **developmental acclimation**. Not to be confused with **evolution** or **genetic adaptation**. Cf. **acclimatization**.

‡ **acclimatization:** phenotypic **plasticity** in an organism that enables it to make physiologic changes that reduce the strain caused by stresses from environmental factors. Acclimatization may be short-term (see **acclimation**) or long-term (see **developmental plasticity**). It has been suggested that the ability to respond physiologically to the environment is partly genetic but requires environmental interaction to be expressed. Verb: acclimatize.

**accommodation:** 1. responses by an organism to environmental stress that are not wholly successful because, even though they favor survival of the individual, they also result in significant losses in some important functions. 2. alteration in the convexity of the lens of the eye to increase visual acuity.

**accretion model:** scheme in which fossil hominids formerly termed **archaic** or **transitional form** are further segregated into Stage 1, the early pre-Neandertals (e.g. **Mauer** and **Petralona**); Stage 2, the pre-Neandertals (e.g. **Steinheim, Swanscombe,** and **Atapuerca**); Saale – Eem Stage 3, the early Neandertals (e.g. **Biache**); and Weichsel Stage 4, the 'classic' Neandertals (e.g. **La Chapelle** and **La Ferrassie**). This model is assumed by some to represent a temporal series of a single isolated gene pool.

**accretionary growth:** multiplication of components in an organ or tissue without qualitative functional change.

**acculturation:** nearly symmetrical increase in the similarity of two autonomous cultural systems, and the lessening of culture distance between them; one of the possible outcomes set in motion by the meeting of the two systems. Cf. **assimilation.**

**acculturation model:** proposal advanced to explain the 10 ky temporal overlap of **Neandertals** and **Cro-Magnons** in central and southern Europe in which transitional tool industries such as the **Châtelperronian** result from the interaction between Neandertals and anatomically modern 'invaders' bearing an **Aurignacian tool tradition**. According to this model, the development and use of decorated bone objects and body ornaments by Neandertals was the result of borrowed or mimicked culture rather than of independent invention.

‡ **accuracy:** 1. freedom from error. 2. degree of conformity of a measured quantity to the true value of what is being measured, where the true value is represented by a standard.

**acentric chromosome:** chromosome fragment that lacks a centromere.

**acentric primate group:** terrestrial primates that flee into trees when confronted with danger. Cf. **centripedal primate group**.

**acetabulocristal buttress:** thickening of the hip bone between the **acetabulum** and the iliac crest. Found in bipedal **hominids** but not in pongids. One of the necessary modifications that led to **habitual bipedalism**.

**acetabulum:** cup-shaped socket formed from the junction of the **ilium**, **ischium**, and **pubis** on the **coxal bone**. The acetabulum is on the lateral surface and receives the head of the femur with which it forms a **ball-and-socket joint**. In female humans this structure is often oriented anteriorly, whereas in males it is more lateral. Adjective: acetabular.

**acetylcholine:** ubiquitous **neurotransmitter** that is involved in the transmission of signals at nerve **synapses**.

**Aché:** foragers or hunter-gatherers in modern-day Paraguay who have survived with a subsistence lifestyle in small-scale societies into the twenty-first century.

‡ **Acheulean tool tradition:** stone-tool technology characterized by large, pointed, almond-shaped bifacial tools called **hand-axes** and **cleavers**, whose exact purpose is unknown. Smaller **flake tools** were also present, but in lesser numbers. Acheulean tools range in time from 1.5 mya to 200 kya; widespread in the Old World. The Acheulean industry gets its name from **St. Acheul**, a site in France. In African sites, where Acheulean tools are often found at sites with **Developed Oldowan** tools at the same level, the hand-axes are usually found near sources of water such as stream channels.

**Achilles tendon:** see **calcaneal tendon**.

**achondroplasia** (ACH): a congenital, **autosomal dominant** form of dwarfism that results from a failure of cartilage to be converted into bone in the epiphyseal disks. ACH affects mainly the long bones by causing rhizomelic shortening, but may also cause trident hand, frontal bossing and mid-face hypoplasia; the cranial base may distend, causing the cranium to become enlarged. The defective gene is a fibroblast growth factor receptor. Cf. **hGH-resistant dwarfism** and **pituitary dwarfism**.

**achromatopsia:** see **color blindness**.

**acidic protein:** any of certain classes of protein that coat a **DNA** molecule, binding to specific regions, and involved in **genetic regulation**.

**acidity:** 1. the quality or state of being acid measured as the concentration of free, unbound hydrogen ions in a solution. The higher the $H^+$ concentration, the greater the acidity and the lower the pH; an acid has a pH less than 7.0. 2. the acid content of a fluid.

**acquire:** to develop after birth. Adjective: acquired. Cf. **congenital**, **hereditary**.

‡ **acquired characteristic:** refers to the outdated Lamarckian concept of **transformism**, in which phenotypic modifications arise solely through environmental influences on the developmental processes of an organism; some proponents believe that such characters can be passed on to the next generation, now largely discredited. Aka use inheritance, use – disuse, and **soft inheritance**. See **adaptation**, **Baldwin effect**, **evolution**, **Lamarckism**, and **Lysenkoism**.

**Acquired Immune Deficiency Syndrome:** see **AIDS**.

**acquired immunity:** immunity to a specific pathogen acquired after birth owing to exposure by either natural or artificial means. Immunity results from the activation of specific B cells or T cells exposed to the pathogen's antigens. This exposure results in the production of antibodies and memory cells. Aka acquired defense.

‡ **acrocentric chromosome:** chromosome in which the **centromere** is very near one end so that the short arm is very small or minute and the long arm is much longer.

**acrocephaly:** condition of being high-headed, such that the height of the skull is at least 98% of the breadth.

**acrocranic index:** in reference to the **cranial breadth – height index**, with an index of 98.00 or greater; such an individual is considered to have a high skull.

**acrodont:** having rootless teeth attached to the **alveolar ridge** of the jaws, e.g. human **deciduous dentition**.

**acromegaly:** form of gigantism often confused with several similar disorders of which acromegaly is a feature; it is genetically heterogenous. Familial acromegaly is characterized by continued growth after a normal adolescent growth spurt, resulting in coarseness of features, and is due to overproduction of human growth hormone (hGH) secondary in the majority of cases to an hGH-secreting pituitary adenoma (aka familial somatotrophinoma). This condition is also obvious in skeletal remains; see **paleopathology**. Cf. **gigantism**.

**acromelic shortening:** congenital condition in which the most distal portions of a limb, i.e. the hands or the feet, are shortened. Cf. **rhizomelic shortening, mesomelic shortening.**

**acromial:** pertaining to the shoulder region.

**acromio-cristal index: bicristal breadth** multiplied by 100 and divided by the **biacromial breadth.**

**acromion:** tip of shoulder that results from the lateral extension of the scapular spine.

**acromion process:** dorsal platelike extension of the scapular spine that articulates with the clavicle; the acromion process provides sites for attachment of the muscles of the upper limb and chest.

**acrosome:** dense structure covering the anterior half of the head of a spermatozoon that contains hyaluronidase, an enzyme that aids the penetration of the **zona pellucida** by the sperm during fertilization. See **capacitation.**

*Acrossia lovei* Bown, 1979: anaptomorphine from middle **Eocene** of North America. Not recognized by all authorities; some include *Acrossia* in *Absarokius*. Most notable features are enlarged central incisors and relatively reduced size of the canines forming a scooplike arrangement suggestive of a **gummivorous** adaptation, although the cheek teeth are suggestive of **frugivory**. See Appendix 1 for taxonomy.

**ACTH:** abbreviation for **adrenocorticotropic hormone.**

**actinic ray:** short-wavelength light that produces photochemical effects, such as **ultraviolet light.**

**actinomycosis:** disease in humans characterized by systemic soft tissue lesions and drainage sinuses, but that may progress to cartilage and bone. Affects males twice as often as females. Caused by two types of bacillus, *Actinomyces israelii* and *Arachnia propionica*. This condition is of interest to osteologists because it leaves its signature on the vertebral column, the coxals, and bones of the hand.

**action:** 1. movement by the whole body. 2. particular effect of a specific **skeletal muscle** or muscle group when it contracts. 3. performance or function of any organ or part.

**active:** capable of functioning or changing; requiring energy. Cf. **passive.**

**active immunity:** resistance to infection acquired by contact with microorganisms, their toxins, or other antigenic material such as by **inoculation**. Cf. **acquired immunity.**

**active metabolism:** any metabolic activity that generates additional heat as a byproduct of the additional energy requirements of muscular work.

**active site:** that portion of a protein that is required for normal function, such as the substrate-binding region of an enzyme or antigen-binding part of an antibody.

**activity:** 1. condition of being active. 2. release of energy by nerve tissue. 3. intensity of a radioactive element.

**activity budget:** amount of energy available for foraging and feeding, movement, reproduction, and other activity beyond **basal metabolism**. Primates on a low-quality diet, such as **folivores**, are typically not very active owing to the lack of energy for their activity budgets.

**activity period:** time of day when an animal is most active, especially in terms of **foraging**; e.g. **diurnal, nocturnal, crepuscular.**

**actual extinction:** physical extinguishment of a species or germ line; actual extinctions occur during episodes of **mass extinction**, or when a species is competitively excluded from a niche, etc. See **pseudoextinction.**

**actualistic study:** in archaeology, the study of the products and processes of present cultures as a key to the past.

**acuity:** sharpness, clarity, or distinctiveness, usually in reference to a sense.

**acute:** sudden; often severe, and short-lived; e.g. an acute illness.

**acute mountain sickness:** condition caused by exposure to high altitude in which symptoms appear in a few hours that include fatigue, dizziness, breathlessness, headache, nausea, vomiting, insomnia, impairment of mental capacity and judgment, and prostration. Not persistent; during **acclimation** the body makes several physiological adjustments in breathing rate and red cell mass, and these symptoms abate. Cf. **altitude sickness, chronic mountain sickness.**

**acute promyelocytic leukemia** (APL): malignant proliferation of white blood cell precursors; see **leukemia**. APL is due to the abnormal transcription of a fusion protein precipitated by a characteristic **translocation** of chromosomes 15 and 17 (t15;17) that causes a **position effect** when the gene for the retinoic acid receptor is located near an **oncogene.**

**acute radiation:** certain amount of radiation received within a brief period. Cf. **chronic radiation.**

**AD:** 1. abbreviation for the (Latin) phrase *anno Domini*; since the birth of Christ. Used to indicate that a time division falls within the Christian era. Replaced by **CE** in some academic contexts. Cf. **BC** and **BCE**. 2. abbreviation for **autosomal dominant.**

**Ad Dabtiyah:** archaeological site found in 1987 in Saudi Arabia, faunal remains from which date to 17–16 mya. **Hominoid** remains include fragments of *Heliopithecus* (cf. *Afropithecus*).

*ad interim* (ad. int.): (Latin) term used taxonomically to mean provisionally or temporarily; e.g. a new fossil may be classified *Homo habilis ad int.*, meaning that it appears that this fossil best fits into *Homo habilis*, but it may later be put into another or a new species.

**ad libitum** (ad lib.): (Latin) at pleasure; applied in science when no constraints are placed on the experimental subject. In *ad libitum* sampling there are no set procedures as to what is recorded or when it is recorded. In primate behavior studies in which no constraints are placed upon when or what is recorded, the observer records any relevant behavior that is visible during observation. This technique is prone to bias in favor of conspicuous behavior or individuals. Aka haphazard sampling, convenience sampling. Cf. **behavior, focal sampling, scan sampling.**

**ADA:** acronym for **adenosine deaminase.**

‡ **Adapidae:** family of prosimians known from the Eocene and early Oligocene of Europe and Asia; systematics in flux, but currently about five adapid genera are recognized; origins and phylogenetic relationships uncertain. Adjectives: adapid, adapoid. Earlier taxonomies included the notharctids (**Notharctidae**)(as a subfamily) within the adapids, which was a much larger group. See **Adapinae** and Appendix 1 for taxonomy.

**Adapiformes: infraorder** of primates proposed by **Szalay** and Eric Delson that would include all of the lemur-like primates of the **Eocene.**

**Adapinae:** subfamily of prosimians belonging to the adapoid family **Adapidae.** Adjective: adapine. Known from the late Eocene to early Oligocene; five genera and twelve species. Recent revision of the adapoids has resulted in this subfamily being reduced in size as well as becoming the only subfamily of the adapids. All members are characterized by a molarized fourth premolar that is equipped with shearing crests. Dental formula variable over time. Unlike modern prosimians, the mandible is fused. Body mass estimated to range between 600 g and 4 kg for the included genera. Analysis of the limb bones led some workers to suggest that the adapids employed a slow methodical climbing locomotion similar to extant lorisoids (**Lorisoidea**), but others think that there was more diversity of locomotor behavior in this group. See Appendix 1 for taxonomy.

*Adapis* **Cuvier, 1821:** well-known genus of primate from the late Eocene to early Oligocene of western Europe and China belonging to the adapoid subfamily **Adapinae;** four to five species; first fossil primate described (by G. Cuvier, 1821), although its affinities were not recognized at the time. Possesses some lemurlike characteristics, which include an inflated **auditory bulla** with a free tympanic ring and some dental similarities; however, unlike modern lemurs,

*Adapis* has a fused mandible. Estimated body size of the species around 1.5 kg. Small orbits suggest diurnality. Dental formula: 2.1.4.3/2.1.4.3; shearing crests on cheek teeth suggests **folivory.** Appears to have become extinct during the **Grande Coupure** (c. 38 mya). According to Gingerich, *Adapis* shows evidence of sexual dimorphism; if so, this would be the earliest appearance of this characteristic among the primates. See **Leptadapis** and Appendix 1 for taxonomy.

**Adapoidea:** superfamily of prosimians that consists of the families **Adapidae, Notharctidae,** and **Sivaladapidae** that are found from the Eocene to the Miocene. Adapoids are considered the most primitive **euprimates.**

*Adapoides troglodytes* **Beard, Qi, Dawson, and Li, 1994:** adapoid **prosimian** from the Eocene of China assigned to the adapid subfamily **Adapinae;** **monotypic.** Prior to the recovery of this fossil, adapids were known only from Europe, although there is no evidence that they originated there; the discovery of *Adapoides* suggests to some workers that the adapids migrated to Europe from Asia. Body mass estimated at 500 g. See Appendix 1 for taxonomy.

**adaptation:** 1. adjustment. 2. any alteration in structure or function by which an organism becomes better fitted to survive and reproduce in a given environment. See **biological adaptation, behavioral adaptation, functional adaptation, genetic adaptation, insulative adaptation, metabolic adaptation,** and **sociocultural adaptation.** Cf. **preadaptation** and **postadaptation.**

**adaptationist classification:** proposed classification of organisms using shared **adaptations** as data, rather than cladistic or phenetic similarity. Mayr proposed the use of such a method to define **paraphyletic** higher taxonomic groups, such as birds, which evolved rapidly from a common ancestor after achieving an **adaptive breakthrough.**

**adaptationist program:** perspective among some evolutionary biologists in which all characters are viewed as being optimized in adapting a species to its environment. Researchers using this approach attempt to determine the adaptive significance of species characters. The term was introduced in a discussion by **Gould** and **Lewontin** in 1979. See W. D. **Hamilton,** G. C. **Williams,** E. O. **Wilson,** and R. **Dawkins.**

**adaptedness:** state of the current **fitness** or functional superiority of one phenotype or genotype over another, as a result of past selection.

**adaptive:** describes any trait that has arisen by the evolutionary process of adaptation; the trait may be anatomical, physiological, or behavioral.

**Adaptive Behavior Scale:** index of the range of adaptive behavior patterns measured in an organism or society.

**adaptive breakthrough:** evolution of a way of life radically different from that of a recent common ancestor, which sometimes results in a perceived **paraphyletic** higher taxonomic group, such as birds, which then evolved rapidly from a common ancestor after achieving flight. The phrase could apply as well to certain **hominids** which, because of increased **encephalization**, are classified in the genus *Homo* rather than as **australopithecines**.

**adaptive capacity:** environmental tolerance of an organism as determined by its genetic endowment.

**adaptive complex:** suite of biological traits (including behaviors) that enable a phylogenetic lineage to occupy a particular **ecological niche**.

**adaptive evolution:** see **adaptation**.

**adaptive hormone:** any substance secreted within the body during adaptation to unusual circumstances, e.g. **adrenocorticotropic hormone** or the **corticoids**.

**adaptive immunity:** immune response that develops after exposure to a foreign antigen.

**adaptive landscape:** sinuous topographical graph of the average fitnesses of small, subdivided, and isolated populations in relation to the frequencies of the genotypes residing in it. Peaks in such a landscape (**multiple-peaked fitness surfaces**) correspond to genotypic frequencies at which the average fitness is high; valleys to genotypic frequencies at which the average fitness is low. Proposed by Sewall **Wright**. Aka adaptive topography, fitness surface, surface of selective value. See **shifting balance theory**.

**adaptive mechanism:** any device, idea or process that increases an organism's chances for survival, e.g. **mechanisms of culture change** and **mechanisms of evolution**.

**adaptive niche:** see **ecological niche**.

**adaptive prediction:** theoretical relationship between certain morphs and environmental variables; if a trait is an adaptation to an external condition, then the value of that condition should predict morphology. **Bergmann's rule**, predicts, for example, that organisms with adaptations for high average annual temperature should be found nearer to the equator than organisms with adaptations to low temperatures.

‡ **adaptive radiation:** biologic evolution in a group of related species that is characterized by spreading into different environments and by **divergence** of structure, e.g. the 14 species of finch in the **Galápagos archipelago**, and hundreds of Hawaiian fruit fly species (the 'Hawaiian radiation').

**adaptive strategy:** 1. totality of mechanisms possessed by a taxon that help it survive in an environment. 2. technological, ecological, demographic and economic factors that define human behavior from a research perspective.

**adaptive trait:** see **adaptation** and **adaptive**.

**adaptive value:** reproductive success of an individual as measured by the mean value of its offspring with respect to a particular character. See **fitness**.

**adaptive zone:** environment of previously unexploited **ecological niches** that becomes available to evolutionary opportunistic taxa; often results in an **adaptive radiation**.

**additive:** 1. effect of any element in a summation. 2. substance added to another material. 3. synergistic effect.

**additive genetic effect:** contribution an allele makes to the phenotype independent of the identity of other alleles at the same or different loci. Aka additive effect. See **heritability**.

**additive genetic variation** ($V_{ga}$): proportion of the **total phenotypic variance** of a quantitative trait due to genes that will actually be inherited in offspring. See **heritability**.

**additive genotype fitness:** hypothetical case where fitness is the sum of a number of factors, such as the activities of the members of a family of digestive enzymes.

**additive hypothesis:** in molecular taxonomy, a proposal that parallelisms and convergences are randomly distributed among the taxa in any analysis.

**additive model:** model of **heritability** in which the **total phenotypic variance** of a quantitative trait is partitioned into several genetic and environmental subcomponents.

**additive technology:** processes in which manufactured artifacts take form by the addition of materials to the original mass, such as ceramic production or basket making. Cf. **subtractive technology**.

**adductor:** muscle that moves a limb or structure toward the mid-line; aka depressor. Cf. **abductor**.

**adductor pollicis: intrinsic muscle** of the hand; originates from the **trapezium**, **trapezoid**, **capitate**, and **metacarpals** II–IV, and inserts into the medial surface of proximal **phalanx** I. Its action is to adduct and oppose the thumb; one of the thenar group of muscles.

‡ **adenine** (A): one of the **purine** nitrogenous bases that composes **DNA** and **RNA**; composed of two carbon–nitrogen rings. Adenine bonds with thymine in DNA and with uracil in RNA (see **base pairing rule**); it is also a major component of other molecules such as **adenosine triphosphate**.

**adeno-associated virus** (AAV): any one of a group of defective spherical DNA viruses frequently isolated from tonsillar tissue that can replicate only in the presence of **adenoviruses**. No disease has been associated with AAV in humans. When not replicating it is integrated into the host chromosome. AAV is most notable as a proposed vector for human gene transfer experiments.

**adenohypophysis:** anterior portion of the **pituitary gland**, and which secretes most of its **hormones**, including **growth hormone**. See **pituitary gonadotropic hormones**. Cf. **neurohyphophysis**.

**adenoma:** tumor or growth located in glandular tissue.

**adenomatous polyposis of the colon, familial** (FAP): one of the two most common forms of hereditary colorectal cancer. FAP is an autosomal dominant found in adolescents who present with abdominal pain, diarrhea and rectal bleeding. A carpet of precancerous growths, usually in the colon, progresses to colorectal **cancer**. The mutant gene is adenomatous polyposis coli (APC); about 740 different mutations in this gene have been identified with simultaneous **loss of heterozygosity** or mutation to the *p53* **tumor suppressor** gene. There is some evidence for a **paternal age effect**. Aka familial polyposis of the colon (FPC). Cf. **colon cancer, hereditary nonpolyposis**.

**adenosine deaminase** (ADA): an enzyme that converts adenosine to inosine in the purine salvage pathway, and is essential to the production of T cells and B cells in the immune system. The ADA gene is located on **HSA** 20q13.1. Some 95% of the ADA **cistron** consists of introns; the 12 exons have a final translation length of 1500 base pairs. Cf. **purine nucleoside phosphorylase**.

**adenosine deaminase deficiency:** an autosomal dominant condition, one of the primary immunodeficiency diseases (PIDs) characterized by skeletal and neurological abnormalities; frequent infections, fatal if untreated. Death usually occurs by the age of 7 months owing to infection. ADA deficiency accounts for about 15% of all **severe combined immune deficiency** (SCID) cases. There are no T cells, and B cells do not produce antibodies. An ADA-deficient SCID girl was selected as the first person with a genetic disorder to be treated by **somatic gene therapy**, using a viral vector, in September 1990. Cf. **agammaglobulinemia**.

**adenosine triphosphate:** see **ATP**.

**adenovirus** (AV): any member of a group of spherical DNA viruses that infect several mammalian species, including humans; some are oncogenic.

**adenylate kinase** (AK): an enzyme that releases energy within cells; in humans, two common alleles are known, AK-1 and AK-2. AK is of historical significance because it is linked to both the ABO blood group locus and the Nail Patella locus; this linkage group is one of the first discovered, now known to reside on chromosome 9q.

**adiacritic:** pertaining to the condition in which no member of a race or breed is recognizable as such by an expert. Cf. **typology, microdiacritic,** and **mesodiacritic**.

**adipocyte:** fat cell.

**adipometer:** anthropometric instrument used for measuring skinfold thickness in order to estimate the amount of subcutaneous fat.

**adipose tissue:** specialized connective tissue that stores **fat**; in humans much of this tissue is found in the **subcutaneous layer** of the skin. It is also found in spaces between muscles, behind the eyes, around the kidneys, in some abdominal membranes, on the surface of the heart, and around certain joints.

**adiposis:** corpulence or **obesity**; an excessive accumulation of body fat.

**adiposity:** amount of body fat; state of being fat. Often used in reference to excessive **obesity**, esp. in medicine.

**adjustment:** physiological or behavioral response of an organism to change in its environment, without regard to whether the change is beneficial to the organism. See **accommodation**.

**admixture:** term used for interbreeding between races; in humans, **miscegenation**; in evolutionary terms, **gene flow**.

**adolescence:** another term for the **adolescent stage**.

**adolescent:** see **adolescence**. Cf. **juvenile** and **adult**.

‡ **adolescent growth spurt** (AGS): a rapid increase in **stature** during **adolescence**. It occurs at the same developmental stage in all primates regardless of the age of the individual in years. See **hypertrophy, hyperplasia** and **life-history variable**.

‡ **adolescent stage (or period):** interval in the human **life cycle** preceeding **adulthood** that is characterized by the **adolescent growth spurt** in height and body mass, fusion of the epiphyses of the long bones, development of secondary sexual characteristics, continuation or completion of adult tooth eruption, sociosexual maturation, and intensification of interest in and practice of adult social roles. The stage commences at **puberty** and lasts five to eight years; aka adolescence.

**adolescent sterility:** physiological state in adolescent females that begins with menarche and ends with the onset of regular ovulatory cycles.

**adontia:** lack of tooth bud development; see **ectodermal dysplasia**. See also **hyperdontia, hypodontia**.

**adoption:** shared welfare of offspring by individuals other than biological parents; a behavior found in many species. Contrasts with strict biological or genetic modes of defining human relationships.

**adrenal:** 1. located near the kidney. 2. pertaining to the **adrenal gland**; adrenogenic.

**adrenal cortex:** outer layer of the **adrenal gland**; secretes mainly **cortisol** and other **glucocorticoids, aldosterone**, and **androgens**.

**adrenal gland:** paired **endocrine gland** located superior to each kidney in most vertebrates; a composite organ that consists of the **adrenal medulla** and the **adrenal cortex** of differing embryonic origin that function to secrete several 'stress' **hormones**. Aka suprarenal gland, epinephric gland, third gonad.

**adrenal hypoplasia, primary:** heritable disease characterized by delay or absence of puberty, possible mental retardation, and possible death at puberty without hormonal supplementation. Caused by mutations in genes that disrupt the adrenal glands and by hormone deficiencies.

**adrenaline:** alternative name for the hormone and neurotransmitter **epinephrine**; produced by the adrenal **medulla** of the kidney. Adrenaline initiates actions similar to those initiated by sympathetic nervous system stimulation (andrenergic stimulation) in the heart, bronchioles and blood vessels.

**adrenal medulla:** soft center of the **adrenal gland**; secretes mainly **epinephrine** and **norepinephrine**.

**adrenarche:** period when secretion of the adrenal androgen hormones begins; has been suggested to be involved with the mid-growth spurt that occurs in children between the ages of six and eight. See **androgen** and **mid-growth spurt**.

**adrenergic:** pertaining to nerve fibers of the sympathetic nervous system that, upon stimulation, release the chemical transmitter norepinephrine (and possibly epinephrine) at their post-ganglionic endings; any compound that acts like norepinephrine or epinephrine.

**adrenocortical hormones:** steroids produced by the adrenal cortex, including **estrogens, androgens, progesterone**, and the **glucocorticoids**.

**adrenocorticotropic hormone** (ACTH): a polypeptide secreted by the anterior **pituitary gland**; it controls secretion of certain **hormones** called adrenal **androgens** (e.g. **cortisol**) that originate in the **adrenal cortex**, and assist in the breakdown of fats. Aka adrenocorticotropin, corticotropin.

**adrenocorticotropin:** see **adrenocorticotropic hormone**.

**adrenogenital syndrome:** condition resulting from a hereditary defect in the **adrenal glands** in which a nonfunctioning enzyme in a metabolic pathway is produced, causing the accumulation of testosterone-like breakdown products that cause affected females to exhibit masculine characteristics and to develop rudimentary male sex organs.

**adrenoleukodystrophy** (ALD): characterized by dementia, seizures, paralysis, loss of speech, deafness, and blindness; neonatal death is usual, and inevitable by age 3. Variable symptoms: the X-linked form is less severe than the neonatal autosomal recessive form. The defect is in the ALD membrane transport protein; adrenal insufficiency causes an excess of long-chain fatty acids. Maps to Xq 28. The condition is associated with **HLA** DR3 and increases the relative risk of ALD to 6.3×. ALD is rare, incidence 1:100 000. Aka Addison disease.

**adrenomegaly:** enlargement of the adrenal glands.

**adrenosterone:** androgenic **steroid** present in the **adrenal cortex**. See **androgen**.

**adrenotropin:** 1. see **adrenocorticotropic hormone**. 2. see **corticotropin**. Also spelled adrenotrophin.

**adulation:** transfer of the appearance of a trait from a late to an earlier stage of development. Cf. **neoteny**.

**adult:** in mammals, including humans, an individual that has reached full growth in height or length; note that reproductive **adulthood** can occur before full body size is reached. Cf. **adolescent**.

**adult body size:** mass or dimension of an organism during maturity. Cf. **body size**.

**adult dentition:** set of teeth in mammals that replaces the **deciduous dentition**; in most mammals the adult set consists of incisors, canines, premolars, and molars. The larger adult dentition fits the growing adolescent, and later adult, jaw. Aka permanent teeth, **replacement dentition**, adult teeth.

**adult form:** in genetics and physiology, the form of a molecule that is present in the adult, as opposed to forms present in the embryo, fetus, or other developmental stage. The **hemoglobin** molecule, for example, is found in three forms during the corresponding stages of development: embryonic, fetal, and **adult hemoglobin**.

**adult hemoglobin:** umbrella term for three forms of **hemoglobin** found in the **erythrocytes** of adult humans that are metabolically active in the late fetal stages of development through adulthood. The majority consists of **hemoglobin A** (aka the major fraction) and about 2% is **hemoglobin A$_2$**, the minor fraction; a very small percentage consists of the so-called fetal fraction, which, however, is not quite identical to **fetal hemoglobin** in that the fraction circulating in normal adults has an amino acid substitution at position 136 in the γ chain compared with the normal fetal form. Cf. **embryonic hemoglobin**.

**adult polycystic kidney disease:** see **polycystic kidney disease, adult**.

**adulthood:** interval of maturity that commences at about age 20 years. The stage in the human **life cycle** between **adolescence** and **senescence**; the prime of adulthood lasts until the end of child-bearing years and is a period of homeostasis in physiology, behavior and cognition. Cf. **middle age**.

**adult teeth:** see **adult dentition**.

**advanced:** see **derived**.

**advanced age:** state of living into post-reproductive life; living after the majority of one's birth cohort has already expired. See **maturity, senility**.

**advanced parental age effect(s):** increase in the frequency of a human trait when either the mother is over about 35 years of age (see **Down syndrome** and **dizygotic twins**), or the father is over about 50 years of age (see **Marfan syndrome** and other **collagen diseases**). See **maternal age effect** and **paternal age effect**.

**adventive:** in reference to an organism not native to a particular region. Aka exotic; alien; introduced.

*Aedes:* genus of mosquito (family Culicidae) that contains over 700 species and that is a potential vector of yellow fever and malaria; e.g. *Aedes aegypti*.

‡ *Aegyptopithecus* Simons, 1965: extinct genus of largest and best known of the **haplorhines** of the **Oligocene epoch** (c. 34–33 mya); recovered from the **Fayum Depression**, Egypt; member of family **Propliopithecidae**. Completely **anthropoid** in characteristics such as closed **orbits**, fusion of frontal and mandibular bones. Highly **sexually dimorphic**; **sagittal crest** and long canines present in males. Small orbits indicate **diurnal** habits. Brain size about 30 cm³, and comparable with that of extant prosimians. Elongated maxilla; dental formula: 2.1.2.3; dentition suggests **frugivory**. Estimated body mass 6–8 kg. **Monotypic**; the only known species is *A. zeuxis*, which has affinities with both monkeys and apes; it could be ancestral to one or both of these groups. Some authorities now include *Aegyptopithecus* in **Propliopithecus**. See Appendix 1 for taxonomy.

**aeolian:** alternative spelling of eolian.

*Aeolopithecus* Simons, 1965: genus of the fossil primate family **Propliopithecidae**, an **anthropoid** from the **Oligocene epoch**. Synonym: *Propliopithecus*, which is accepted now by most authorities. Recent considerations of **sexual dimorphism** within *P. chirobates* has removed this genus as a valid taxon. See *Propliopithecus*; See Appendix 1 for taxonomy.

**aerobic capacity:** highest rate at which an individual is capable of utilizing **oxygen**. See **aerobic endurance**.

**aerobic endurance:** length of time that an organ, particularly muscle tissue, can continue to use **oxygen** in metabolic pathways. See **aerobic capacity**.

**aerobic power: aerobic capacity** divided by body mass.

**aestivation:** see **estivation**.

**Aethiopian:** early ethnic term, dating from antiquity, meaning 'person with a burnt face'. Used by Homer, Xenophanes, Scylax of Caryanda, and Herodotus. See **Ethiopian**.

**aetiology:** see **etiology**.

**Afalou man:** AMH fossil found in North Africa, and similar to **Cro-Magnon**.

**Afalou-Bou-Rhommel:** Upper Pleistocene rockshelter found in 1928 near Bugia in Algeria, dated to 15–8 kya, that contains artifacts identified as Oranian (= Capsian) and closely related to **Aurignacian**. Hominid remains include at least 50 skeletons comparable in morphology to **Cro-Magnon** in Europe (i.e. *Homo sapiens*). All the individuals had experienced dental mutilation. Aka Afalou-Bou-Rhummel, Mechta-el-Arbi. The artifacts are aka Ibero-Maurusien.

**Afar depression:** region in Ethiopia; the west central Afar sedimentary basin contains several hominid-bearing sites (e.g. **Hadar, Belohdelie, Maka**) that date to earlier than 2.9 mya, and possibly as far back as 3.6 mya.

**Afar hominids:** see entries beginning with **NME**.

**Afar Locality** (AL): any site located in the Afar Depression of Ethiopia. Thus AL-288 is the specification for the site where the **australopithecine** known as '**Lucy**' was found (field number **NME AL-288-1**) in 1974, **NME AL-333** where the '**first family**' was found in 1975, and so forth.

**Afar triangle** or Afar region: see **Afar depression**.

*afarensis* **nomen debate:** difference of opinions concerning the attribution of fossils found at **Laetoli** and **Hadar**; one group (led by Mary **Leakey**) felt that these early pre-habilines should be placed in the genus *Homo*, while another (**Johanson, White,** and others) erected the taxon *Australopithecus afarensis* for these specimens. The first group felt that the new taxon contained more than one species and that, as the **holotype** had come from Laetoli and not the **Afar triangle**, the selection of the specific nomen was itself inappropriate. **Tobias** had suggested sub-specific taxa to resolve the issue (*A. africanus aethiopicus* for Johanson's Ethiopian fossils, and *A. A. tanzaniensis* for Leakey's), but Johanson presented his description first, thus establishing priority.

**affection:** expression of emotions, feelings or mood indicating tenderness, one of the emotions mediated by the **limbic system**.

**affective disorder:** any of a group of similar behavioral disorders pertaining to feelings; alternation between manic and depressive behavior is called **bipolar affective disorder**, whereas the experience of depressive bouts alone is called **unipolar disorder**. See **psychiatric disorder**.

**afferent:** towards a reference point; for example, afferent nerves conduct impulses towards the **central nervous system**.

‡ **affiliative:** pertaining to persistent amicable relations between individuals.

**affinitive behaviors:** see **alliances, cooperation, food sharing, grooming, reciprocity.**

**affinity:** with reference to the degree of evolutionary relationship between organisms.

**afibrinogenemia:** genetic anomaly caused by an absence of **fibrinogen** in which the blood does not clot normally.

**afoveate:** lacking the **fovea centralis** of the retina.

**Aframonias Simons, Rasmussen, and Gingerich, 1995:** adapoid prosimian from the late Eocene of Africa, belonging to the notharctid subfamily **Cercamoniinae; monotypic.** Estimated body mass around 1.5 kg. See Appendix 1 for taxonomy.

**African collision event:** contact of Africa with Eurasia as the result of plate movement; as the African continental plate surged northward it collided with Eurasia, subducting that continent and raising the early Alps, beginning 17 mya. This established the first recent land bridge between Africa and Eurasia across which floras and faunas could be exchanged, and providing a means by which African primates could invade Eurasia.

**African Eve model:** see **mitochondrial 'Eve'.**

**African Genesis:** book written by playwright turned popular science writer Robert **Ardrey.** Ardrey had visited Raymond **Dart** in the mid-1950s at a time when Africa was not accepted as a likely geographical area for **human origins,** Asia being preferred. *African Genesis* fired the popular imagination of the public and gave support to **Dart's** and (later) Louis **Leakey's** assertions that Africa was the 'birthplace' of the human species. Ardrey also proposed that early hominids were 'killer apes', were territorial, and had a social stratification based on the male dominance hierarchy.

**African monogenesis:** see **out of Africa II.**

**African Negro:** see **Nilotic Negro.**

**Africanthropus helmei Dreyer, 1935:** see **Florisbad** skull.

**Africanthropus njarasensis Weinert, 1940:** nomen for fossils found in 1935 at Njarasa near Lake Eyasi in Tanganyika (now Tanzania), including parts of a cranium and maxilla, and an occiput and other fragments of a second individual found by Ludwig Kohl-Larsen. These specimens are often compared to both *Homo erectus* and the **Neandertals.**

**Afro-European sapiens hypothesis:** variant of the **mitochondrial 'Eve'** or **'out of Africa'** model of **AMH** dispersion from Africa to Europe and elsewhere.

**Afropithecus Leakey and Leakey, 1986:** enigmatic genus of fossil ape of the early **Miocene** (18–16 mya) found at **Kalodirr Riverbed,** Northern Kenya, and in Saudi Arabia; the phylogenetic relationship to other **hominoids** is uncertain. Monotypic; *A. turkanensis* has some unique traits, such as a very long snout, not seen in other hominoids, and has a **mosaic** of other features found in diverse ape groups. This mosaic pattern includes thick molar **enamel** and large **procumbent** central incisors that it shares with the large Miocene Asian apes; other facial features resemble those of the African apes. It also has many characteristics reminiscent of the Oligocene African anthropoid **Aegyptopithecus.** Description of this ape in the 1980s expanded the view of Miocene ape diversity.

**Afrotarsius Simons and Bown, 1985:** tarsiiform genus from early Oligocene of the **Fayum Depression** in Africa. This is the only tarsiiform known from Africa. Body mass estimated at 100 g. The preserved dentition consists of the three lower molars and parts of the lower third and fourth premolars. *A. chatrathi* has affinities with the microchoerines of Europe and with the modern tarsiers; some authorities suggest that it be placed in the family **Tarsiidae.** The importance of this fossil is that it expands the known range of fossil tarsiers.

**afterbirth: placenta** and associated membranes expelled from the uterus after delivery of an infant. Whereas some societies consider the placenta to be sloughed or discarded tissue, others have elaborate rituals regarding its disposal.

**agammaglobulinemia** (XLA): an X-linked recessive disorder, one of the heritable primary immunodeficiency diseases (PIDs), characterized by lack of mature B cells associated with IgM heavy chain rearrangements. Onset is in the third decade, and affected individuals cannot synthesize certain antibodies. There are several modalities. The most common defect is caused by mutations in the Bruton-type tyrosine kinase gene (BTK), an essential regulator in B cell development. **X-linked severe combined immune deficiency** is a more severe form; yet another X-linked (Swiss) type also exists. **Adenosine deaminase deficiency** is an autosomal dominant form; the remaining forms are either autosomal recessive forms, or of unknown etiology. Cf. **severe combined immune deficiency syndromes.**

**agar:** polysaccharide extract of seaweed used in cell culture and electrophoresis.

**agarose:** polymer fractionated from **agar,** useful as a medium in **electrophoresis** because few molecules bind to it.

**agarose gel electrophoresis:** method of sorting DNA fragments by size. See **electrophoresis.**

**Agassiz, Jean-Louis Rodolphe** (1807–73): Swiss-born US geologist and zoologist trained by **Cuvier.** Founded the Museum of Comparative Zoology (1859) while at Harvard University (1847–73). Agassiz constructed lasting hypotheses regarding the dynamics of **glaciation** and the **Ice Age,** and was also well known for his study of fossil fish. Because he criticized **Darwinism** as 'unscientific' and 'mischievous' and tried to discredit Asa **Gray**, Agassiz was abandoned by his students, including his marine biologist son, in favor of Darwinism. Agassiz embraced **racism** and **polygenism**, and supported Cuvier's theory of **catastrophism**.

**age:** 1. chronological status of an individual measured in arbitrary local units; such units may be internal (generational, as with the growth stages of childhood, adolescence, adulthood...), or external and cyclical, such as lunar, solar, or, even rarer, dependent upon the cyclical blossoming of certain local plants, and so forth. 2. a recognized historical interval such as the Elizabethan age or geological period such as the **Age of Mammals**.

**age and area hypothesis:** early notion, advanced primarily by Wissler in anthropology, then Willis in biology, that a trait diffuses outward from its point of origin at an equal rate such that the distance of a trait from its origin can be taken as an indication of its age; strongly criticized by **Wright** in the 1940s. Aka age area. See **diffusionism**.

**age at menarche:** age at which a human female experiences her first menstrual period.

**age class:** demographic category consisting of individuals in a population of a particular age. See **age-graded group** and **age cohort**.

**age cohort:** individuals who share demographic variables. See **age set, age grade**.

**age-dependent penetrance:** increasing likelihood of manifesting signs or symptoms of a **genetic disorder** with increasing age.

**age-dependent selection:** selection in which fitness varies as a function of an individual's age.

**age determination:** procedure in which the age at death of a specimen is estimated from established criteria such as suture closure on skeletal specimens or corpus albicans count on a contemporary human female. In osteological specimens, the estimation of age at death is based on such features as development of growth centers and epiphyseal closure, eruption and wear on dentition, and assessment of the amount of fusion of cranial sutures. Age determination is more reliable for subadults than for adults.

**age grade:** series of formal, fixed ranks through which all members pass; members may constitute either **age classes** or **age sets**. See **age system**.

**age-graded (play) group:** cohort of children of a particular age range in which the older individuals serve as custodians of the younger children and socialize them in the ways of the society; an institution in many primate societies. Age-graded play groups enable adults to focus on other activities such as **subsistence**.

**Age of Glaciers: Pleistocene** epoch covering the most recent 1.8 my of the earth's history. Aka the **Ice Age**.

**'Age of Omics':** label first used in 2001 to describe the rapid development of the multilayered and epigenetic aspects of genomic architectures in the many organisms that have been sequenced. The term refers to information gleaned from studies in genomics, proteomics, transcriptomics, pharmacogenomics, toxicogenomics, etc.

**Age of Mammals:** see **Cenozoic era**.

**age of weaning:** chronological age of an infant at weaning; one of the intervals in biology that is known as a **life-history variable**.

**age polyethism:** regular and predictable change of labor roles by members of a society as they age.

**age set:** formally established group of persons of about the same age, whose members may advance through **age grades** and other passages marked by ritual or status activities at each level.

**age–sex structure:** measure of the demographic composition of a population in terms of the number of males and females at different ages.

**age-specific mortality:** death rate for a particular age cohort within a population, calculated by dividing the number of deaths in the cohort by the total number of individuals who reach the age class in question. Aka age-specific death rate.

**age-specific vital rate:** demographic index expressing the ratio between the number of events (such as births, deaths, migrations) and the number of individuals within the different age and sex cohorts; individuals within a cohort are considered to be at greater or lesser risk for such an event occurring within a specific time period.

‡ **age structure:** number or percentage of individuals in a particular age interval; the composition of a population expressed in age intervals. See **life table**.

**age system:** any scheme that subdivides a larger temporal interval, such as the **geological time scale, age grades**, the Victorian age, or the **three-age system**.

*Ageitodendron matthewi* **Gunnell, 1995:** genus of tarsiiform primate from the middle Eocene of North America, belonging to the omomyid subfamily **Omomyinae; monotypic**. Estimated body mass around 1 kg. See Appendix 1 for taxonomy.

**agemate:** see **cohort**.

**agenesis:** absence, failure, or defective development of structures.

**agenitalism:** lack of gonads and secondary sexual characters in an individual.

**agent:** 1. any power, principle, or substance that is capable of producing a physical, chemical, or biological effect. 2. in **epidemiology**, an etiologic agent is the organism or substance ultimately responsible for a morbid condition or **disease**. 3. in evolutionary studies, an agent of change can be any of the forces or **mechanisms of evolution.**

**agent of selection:** any factor that causes individuals with certain phenotypes to have an average higher fitness than individuals with other phenotypes in a specific environment.

*Agerinia* **Crusafont-Pairo and Golpe-Posse, 1973:** adapoid prosimian from the middle Eocene of Asia and Europe belonging to the notharctid subfamily **Cercamoniinae;** two species; only known from isolated teeth and fragments of jaw with teeth. Dental formula unknown; known dental morphology suggests **faunivory.** See Appendix 1 for taxonomy.

‡ **agglutination:** clumping together or bridging of cells caused by the attraction of antibodies and **antigens,** as in the case of red blood cell antigens with specific antibodies. Verb: to agglutinate.

**agglutinin:** antibody that causes **agglutination** of red blood cells.

**agglutinogen:** antigen that produces **agglutination** when mixed with blood from another individual or group.

**aggregation:** group of **conspecifics** beyond a mated pair or family, that occupy the same area, but do not cooperate or function as a unit; not a true society.

**aggression:** hostile physical act or threatening behavior to defend or attack territory, social units, or dominance. Some anthropologists argue that the category should include self-injury as well as psychological suffering (ostracism).

**agile gibbon:** vernacular for *Hylobates agilis;* aka dark-handed gibbon.

**agile mangabey:** vernacular for *Cercocebus galeritus.*

‡ **aging:** biologic process marked by the decline of bodily function and individual adaptability (see **entropy**) that commences at conception and proceeds until the death of an individual. Aging is variously described as the end of growth, or the increasing probability of mortality with time. Aging is universal, progressive, deleterious, and intrinsic. See **senescence, Hayflick limit, longevity,** and **telomere.**

**aging of populations:** phenomenon that, as populations modernize, life expectancy increases, leading to demographic shifts such as an increasing proportion of elderly in a population.

**aging, theories of:** senescence theories fall into two general categories: (1) aging and death results from wear and tear on an organism (e.g. **exhaustion theory of aging**), or (2) see **genetic theories of aging** (e.g. **Hayflick limit**).

‡ **agonistic behavior:** behavior or activity connected to any type of fighting; agonism.

**agonistic buffering:** use of third parties, such as infants, by adults of social species to restrain **aggression** by other adults; observed among some species of monkey.

**agouti pattern:** hair in which there is an alternating light and dark banding that provides a speckled appearance to the **pelage.**

**agranulocytes:** group of so-called nongranular white blood cells that contain nonspecific (azurophilic) granules; it includes the lymphocytes and the monocytes and normally constitutes from 37% to 42% of the total white blood cell population. Aka agranular leukocytes.

**agriculture:** deliberate domestication, growth, harvesting and storage of plants; **swidden agriculture** is considerably simpler than **horticulture** and **sedentary** farming, which are characterized by increasing use of devices for crop irrigation; the term is sometimes used to include the raising of animals. See **domestication.** Cf. **nomadic pastoralism.**

**Agta:** foragers or hunter – gatherers in the modern-day Philippines who have survived with a subsistence lifestyle in small-scale societies into the twenty-first century.

‡ **AIDS:** Acquired Immune Deficiency Syndrome, a clinical condition caused by the suppression of the human **immune system** due to the agency of the **human immunodeficiency virus** (HIV). The **syndrome** includes an **AIDS-Related Complex** (ARC) of early symptoms, plus chronic opportunistic infections, which are able to challenge the body because the affected person's deficient immune system can no longer ward them off. Until the discovery of potent drug combinations ('cocktails'), AIDS was usually fatal within 10–13 years. The clinical criteria of the **CDC** requires laboratory confirmation of HIV infection in persons who have a CD4+ **lymphocyte** (T4 helper cell) count of <200 cells ml$^{-1}$ or who have an associated clinical condition (a **neoplasm** or AIDS-related opportunistic **infection**). The clinical test for AIDS involves the detection either of the virus itself (antigen test), or of **antibodies,** which appear about two months after exposure (antibody test); the presence of AIDS-specific antibodies classifies an individual as AIDS **seropositive.** Testing for the AIDS antibody began in April 1985; testing for the antigen began in 1996. Aka Acquired Immunodeficiency Syndrome, HIV disease. See **chemokine (C-C) receptor 5.**

**AIDS-Related Complex** (ARC): set of early-onset symptoms that presage the formal onset of **AIDS,** including fevers of unknown origin, night sweats, weight loss, fatigue, and an increase in the incidence of opportunistic infections.

**Ailuropoda–orang fauna:** fossil assemblage found in the 1930s in Hong Kong drugstores by

G. H. R. von **Koenigswald** that included teeth of *Gigantopithecus*, orangutans, giant pandas (*Ailuropoda*), tapir, bear, rhinoceros, and a primitive species of elephant. Later finds *in situ* confirmed that these were contemporary Middle Pleistocene fauna.

**Ain Mallaha:** archaeological site located in northern Israel, dated to 12.5–10.5 kya, and that contains **Natufian** artifacts and evidence for domestication of the dog by a well-documented burial of an **AMH** female with her dog. The site has several village-like structures indicative of sedentism.

**Ainu:** 1. **ethonym** for an indigenous people of the northernmost Japanese archipelago on the island of Hokkaido, traditionally characterized as having **Caucasoid** or **Australoid** features such as light skin color and body hair, and thought to be descended from an ancient proto-Nordic stock. Aka Ainuids. 2. the language spoken by these people.

**airorryhnchy:** condition in which the face is tilted towards the **cranium**. This is said to be the case in *Alouatta* and *Pongo*.

**AIS:** see **androgen insensitivity syndrome** and **testicular feminization.**

**AJHB:** see *American Journal of Human Biology.*

**AJP:** see *American Journal of Primatology.*

**AJPA:** see *American Journal of Physical Anthropology.*

**aka:** abbreviation for 'also known as'.

**AL:** 1. abbreviation for **Afar Locality**; see **NME** and **NME AL** for specific fossils. 2. (Latin) for *Anno Lucis*, in the Year of Light; after 1650, Freemasons adopted Archbishop Ussher's conclusion that the **Special Creation** had occurred in 4004 BC, and that Ussher had published his conclusions in AL 5654.

**alanine** (Ala): an **amino acid** of the pyruvic acid family; one of the twenty building blocks of **proteins.**

**alare, alarae** (al): 1. generally in reference to the lateral wings of the **nasal aperture.** 2. paired osteologic landmark of the facial skeleton; lateralmost point of the nasal aperture. See Appendix 7.

**alarm response:** 1. in behavior, a warning given by an individual to its **conspecifics.** In primates this signal may be a **call** or a visual **sign.** 2. in physiology, an immediate and energy-costly physiologic response to an environmental change, e.g. **sweating** or **shivering thermogenesis** in response to temperature change.

**ALA-VP-2/10:** see *Ardipithecus ramidus kadabba.*

**Alaya:** see *Ardipithecus ramidus kadabba.*

**albedo:** ratio of the light reflected by a surface to that received by it.

**albinism:** refers to any one of several inherited conditions in animals and plants. In humans, albinism is usually caused by an autosomal recessive allele (see OCA1, below) that blocks a step in the production of the pigment melanin by failure to produce an enzyme essential to the process; associated with a lack of the pigment in skin, hair, eyes and/or other tissues (amelanic melanocytes). The most important forms are (1) **albinism, ocular, type I, X-linked** (OA1), an X-linked form, in which only the eyes lack pigmentation; females are more severely affected than males. A second form of X-linked OA also exists (OA2). See **Hermansky–Pudlak syndrome.** (2) **albinism, type I, oculocutaneous, tyrosinase negative** (OCA1), complete or 'classic albinism', in which absence of melanin affects the eyes, hair, skin, and hearing. Affected individuals also lack stereoscopic vision as a result of misrouting of optic nerve fibers; they are often also cross-eyed and blind. The impaired protein is tyrosinase. Most OCA1 individuals are compound heterozygotes; aka tyrosinase-negative albinism. Affects at least 1 in 20 000 children worldwide. (3) **albinism, type II, oculocutaneous, tyrosinase positive:** in OCA2, functional tyrosinase is present; two phenotypes occur, those with and those without freckles. Sequelae include skin cancer and gross visual impairment. Some pigment is present at birth but lost during childhood. Cause is a deletion in the P protein, which encodes a melanosomal membrane protein. Matings between OCA1 and OCA2 individuals produce double heterozygotes that are unaffected (aka P-gene related OCA2, tyrosinasepositive albinism). This form is common among Nigerian Ibos, the Bantu of South Africa, and African-Americans. (4) **albinism, type III, oculocutaneous, tyrosinase positive:** in autosomal recessive OCA3, functional tyrosinase is present; affected individuals are less sensitive to sunlight than OCA1 or OCA2. Freckled skin and reddish hair may be present. The defect seems to be a nonsense mutation in tyrosine hydroxylase that reduces but that does not entirely eliminate enzyme activity. There are about a dozen other forms of albinism.

**albino:** individual that exhibits a **melanin** deficiency; albinos are found in all human populations, as well as among most animal and plant species. See **albinism.**

**Albright syndrome:** one form of the bone disease **fibrous dysplasia** in which there is an endocrine disturbance that leads to dermal pigmentation, early puberty, and cessation of growth. Aka Albright–McCune Sternberg syndrome, McCune–Albright syndrome. Formerly called Albright's disease.

**albumin:** water-soluble protein found in many foods as well as **serum albumin** in human blood, synthesized and secreted by the liver, and mapped to HSA 4q; utilized by V. **Sarich** and A. C. **Wilson** to create one of the first **molecular clocks.** See **alpha globulins.**

**alcelaphine:** any member of the tribe Acelaphini, medium to large-sized antelopes (hartebeests, yopis, wildebeests).

**alcohol dehydrogenase** (adh): an enzyme present in most organisms that breaks down products (alcohols) which are the result of fermentation, usually as a normal part of the digestive process. The oxidized products include aldehydes and ketones.

**aldosterone:** mineralocorticoid **hormone** secreted by the **adrenal cortex**, the principal electrolyte-regulating **steroid**; promotes sodium retention and potassium excretion in the kidneys, and the secondary retention of water.

**alert face:** primate facial expression in which the eyes are wide and the lips may part in response to a novel object or situation.

**Aleutian: ethonym** for an **autochthonous** people that inhabit the Aleutian Island chain in northwest North America. Aleuts are a subsistence people who speak languages related to those of the **Arctic Inuit**. See **Native American.**

*Algeripithecus* **Godinot and Malboubi, 1992:** parapithecoid from the Eocene of Algeria; one species described; known from three isolated teeth. Phylogenetic relationships uncertain with some researchers stating that the affinities lie with the propliopithecines while others think that it belongs with the oligopithecines. Estimated body mass around 200 g. See Appendix 1 for taxonomy.

**algorithm:** 1. procedure for solving a mathematical problem in a finite number of steps. 2. broadly, any step-by-step procedure for solving a certain type or class of problem.

**alignment:** longitudinal positioning of a limb or bone.

**alike in state:** refers to identical alleles inherited from parents who are not closely related.

**alimentary:** pertaining to food or nutrition. Noun: alimentation.

**alimentary canal or tract:** tubular portion of the digestive system that begins with the mouth and ends with the anus. See **gastrointestinal tract.**

**alisphenoid bone:** portion of the sphenoid bone forming part of the lateral wall of the cranium; alternative term for the greater wing of the sphenoid.

**alive:** 1. having life or living; not dead or lifeless; surviving. 2. pertaining to an entity capable of metabolism, reproduction, and adaptation. See **life.**

**alizarin staining:** use of red alizarin to measure current bone growth. Because nongrowing bone tissue remains white in the presence of red alizarin, only currently calcifying tissues take up the stain, and indicates which tissues are growing at a particular developmental stage.

**alkaline:** pertaining to, containing, or having the reaction of an alkali (base); having an $H^+$ concentration lower than that of pure water, i.e. possessing a pH greater than 7.0. Cf. **acid.**

**alkaloid:** any of a class of compounds produced in plant tissues that are distasteful, toxic and/or poisonous to herbivores; many also exhibit a pharmacological action, as in caffeine, cocaine, nicotine, morphine and **quinine.**

**alkaptonuria:** autosomal recessive caused by defects in the enzyme homogentesic acid oxidase (HGO) that normally breaks down homogentesic acid (alkapton); results in the relatively benign excretion of high levels of alkapton, which causes urine to turn black upon exposure to air, especially when allowed to stand; black pigmentation of cartilage and collagenous tissues is also a feature. Most people with alkaptonuria also develop arthritis. This trait was the first ever discovered to be the result of a **metabolic block** and (among others, such as **albinism**) resulted in Sir Archibald **Garrod**'s book *Inborn Errors of Metabolism* (1909).

**allantois:** membranous sac outside the body of the **embryo** that develops out of the yolk sac. In **oviparous** animals it serves as a waste repository, but in mammals it functions in the formation of blood cells during the embryo stage. Later the blood vessels of the allantois become the umbilical blood vessels. The allantois also contributes to the formation of the urinary bladder. See **angiogenesis.**

**Allee principle:** concept that there is an intermediate number of individuals that represents the optimal size of the population; too few and individuals cannot find mates, too many and there is competition for resources.

‡ **allele:** particular form or variant of a **gene**, distinguishable from alternative forms at a single genetic locus which they occupy, one at a time. In humans, for example, there are three alleles in the **ABO blood group** system. Variations include allelic, allelism, allelomorph, allelomorphic series.

‡ **allele frequency** ($p, q, r$): percentage or proportion of a particular form of a gene in relation to the total of all forms at a particular **locus** in a **deme** (for example, A = $p$ = 0.3, B = $q$ = 0.2, O = $r$ = 0.5, in the three-allele human **ABO blood group** system); also, the probability of **sampling** an **allele** at random from such a population.

**allelic exclusion:** process by which one of two alleles is expressed in a diploid cell; the second allele is excluded from expression. Cf. **parental imprinting.**

**allelomorph:** see **allele.**

**allelotype:** genetic composition of a population. In practice, a tabulation of all variable genetic information that characterizes a population.

*Allenopithecus* **Lang, 1923:** monotypic catarrhine genus to which the swamp monkey belongs; inhabits forests of central and western Africa. **Terrestrial** or **semiterrestrial; diurnal. Sexually dimorphic** in mass: males average 7 kg, females 3 kg. Natural history poorly known. Dental formula 2.1.2.3. Diet probably **frugivory**. See Appendix 2 for taxonomy and Appendix 3 for species.

**Allen's galago (bushbaby):** vernacular for *Galagoides* (= *Galago*) *alleni*.

‡ **Allen's rule:** tenet that extremities (e.g. legs, ears and tails) of polytypic and **homeothermic** species tend to be shorter in colder climates than in warmer ones, thereby reducing the surface area of the body. In humans, for example, equatorial peoples such as **Nilotics** have long and slender arms, whereas arctic peoples such as the **Inuit** possess shorter arms and legs. This tendency is correlated with the need to conserve heat in colder climates and to radiate heat in warmer climates. See **thermoregulation** and **crural index**.

**Allen's swamp monkey:** vernacular for *Allenopithecus nigroviridis*.

**allergen:** any substance that stimulates an allergic response in the body; allergic reactions are markedly specific and usually require only minute amounts of the allergen. Adjective: allergenic.

**allergic rhinitis:** inherited condition characterized by chronic runny nose and itchy eyes. Exhibits evidence for **genomic imprinting**.

**allergy:** acquired, altered reactivity to a substance that can result in pathologic reactions upon subsequent exposure to that particular substance; antibodies are generally of the IgE class. Aka hypersensitivity.

**Allia Bay:** archaeological site found in 1982 in East Lake Turkana, Kenya, dated to 4.1–3.9 mya. The hominid remains, 12 specimens, include fragments attributed to *Australopithecus anamensis*. Postcranial remains are indicative of bipedalism, yet jaw fragments possess characteristics that are very ape-like, including parallel tooth rows. Site paleoenvironment was lakeside forest in arid region. See **Kanapoi**.

**alliance:** association between individuals or social groups for some mutual **benefit**.

**alloantibody:** antibody from one individual that reacts with an antigen present in another individual of the same species. Anti-A, for example, is an alloantibody of the A antigen in the human ABO blood group.

**alloantigen:** antigen from one individual that reacts with an antibody present in another individual of the same species. A, for example, is an alloantigen of the anti-A antibody in the human ABO blood group. Aka homologous antigen, isoantigen.

*Allocebus* Petter-Rousseaux & Petter, 1967: monotypic **prosimian** genus to which the hairy-eared dwarf lemur belongs; believed to have been extinct until a German naturalist photographed an individual in a remote region of Madagascar in the late 1980s. Body mass probably between 60 and 100 g. Natural history

virtually unknown. Population densities low. Appears to hibernate from May to October. See Appendix 2 for taxonomy and Appendix 3 for species.

**allochemical:** any substance produced by a plant to defend itself from predators. Allochemicals may be toxic, disruptive to metabolism, or inhibit digestibility. Evolutionarily these plant defensive chemicals appear to be directed against insects, whereas physical structures such as thorns are directed against vertebrate herbivores. Aka secondary compound, plant defensive chemical. See **alkaloid**.

**allochronic speciation:** split of a species into two species owing to a difference in timing of their breeding seasons.

**allochthone:** any organism that evolved in a geographical region other than the area where it is currently found; organism that dispersed from the geographical area where it evolved. For example, lemurs appear to have evolved in North America and Europe, but are only found in Madagascar today. Adjective: allochthonous. Cf. **autochthone**.

**allocortex:** any primitive, unlaminated portion of the cerebral cortex such as the olfactory cortex.

**allogamy:** fertilization by the union of the ovum of one organism with the **spermatozoon** from another. Aka cross-fertilization.

**allogeneic:** relating to genetically different mammals produced by normal genetic recombination of outbred lines. Cf. **syngeneic**.

**allogenic:** pertaining to genetically similar individuals of a single species; **allogeneic**.

**allograft:** transplantation procedure in which both the donor and the graft recipient are members of the same species. Cf. **xenograft**.

**allogrooming: grooming** performed on another individual. See **autogrooming**.

**allomarking:** act of applying an odorous substance, such as glandular secretion or urine, to a social partner.

‡ **allometry:** 1. relative growth of a part in relation to another part or to the entire organism. 2. the study of such relationships, such as **brain size** and **body size**, or **basal metabolic rate** and **longevity**. 3. Any relationship of size between two body parts $y$ and $x$ that can be expressed by the **power formula** $y = c + bx^a$, where $c$, $b$ and $a$ are parameters, the **intercept**, the **slope**, and an exponential term, respectively. Allometry frequently employs **regression** methods to express the relationship between **variables**. Adjective: allometric. Aka heterauxesis, heterochrony. Cf. **correlation**. See J.S. **Huxley, interspecific allometry,** and **intraspecific allometry**.

**allomother:** female that participates in the rearing of an infant other than her own. See **alloparenting**.

**allonurse:** female that is not the mother, but allows an infant to suckle (nurse).

**alloparapatric speciation:** proposal that some new species emerge from geographically isolated (**allopatric**) populations but later become **parapatric** (contiguous) in regions where limited **hybridization** may occur.

‡ **alloparenting:** common behavior in many primate species in which individuals other than the parent(s) hold, carry, and in general interact with infants. See **allomother**.

**allopatric:** pertaining to two populations that are separated from each other; isolation.

**allopatric hybrid zone:** see **hybrid zone**.

**allopatric model:** proposal that speciation occurs after populations become isolated and subsequently diverge owing to the independent action of **natural selection** and **genetic drift**.

**allopatric populations:** breeding populations that occupy separate, disjunct geographical areas.

**allopatric race:** see **geographical race**.

**allopatric speciation:** gradual emergence of a reproductively isolated new **species** from a former population owing to **geographical isolation**; aka geographic speciation. Cf. **sympatric speciation**. See **Mayr, Ernst**.

**allopatry:** pertaining to a state of absence of overlap in the geographical range of two **demes** or **species**; mutual exclusivity, as opposed to **sympatry**. Cf. **gene flow**. Allopatry effectively prevents populations from sharing genes as long as they remain separated.

**alloploid:** fertile hybrid arising from the combination of two or more sets of chromosomes from different ancestral species. Aka allopolyploid.

**alloprocoptic selection:** form of selection in which matings of allelic homozygotes (e.g. AA × aa) tend to produce more surviving offspring, on average, than other possible matings. See **hybrid vigor**.

**allotype:** in **sexually dimorphic** species, a **type specimen** representing the opposite sex of the **holotype**.

**allozygous:** referring to two alleles at the same chromosome **locus** that are different or at least whose identity is not due to common descent. Cf. **autozygous**.

**allozyme:** distinct form of an enzyme, encoded by different alleles at the same genetic locus, and detectable by **electrophoresis**. Cf. **isozyme**.

**alluvium:** sand, gravel and soil that have been deposited by flowing water.

*Alouatta* Lacépède, 1799: **platyrrhine** genus to which the howler monkeys belong. Most workers recognize six **allopatric** species in South and Central America ranging in body mass from 4 to 11 kg. **Sexually dimorphic** in body mass, **pelage** color, or both. Arboreal. Diurnal. Dental formula: 2.1.3.3/ 2.1.3.3. **Folivorous**, with fruit supplements. **Hindgut fermenters**. Possess a **prehensile tail**. A distinctive feature of these monkeys is their loud roar, which advertises their territories, made possible by a modified and enlarged hyoid. There is no agreement on the placement of **Alouatta** within the **ceboids**. A subfamily **Alouattinae** (Trouessart, 1897) is recognized, but is included among the family **Cebidae** or the family **Atelidae** depending on the authority. See Appendix 1 for taxonomy.

**Alouattinae:** subfamily of the **platyrrhine** family **Cebidae** that consists of the genus *Alouatta*; howler monkeys. Some workers recognize the howlers as belonging to a separate family, the Alouattidae. See Appendix 2 for taxonomy, Appendix 3 for living species.

**alpha:** 1. the first letter of the Greek alphabet (A, α), which also usually denotes the first member in a series or set. 2. term that refers to the highest-ranking individual within a **dominance hierarchy**; others of lesser rank in the hierarchy may include beta individuals, gamma individuals, etc.

**alpha$_1$-antitrypsin** (AAT): plasma protein produced primarily in the liver that inhibits the activity of elastase, **trypsin**, and other proteolytic enzymes. Also written α$_1$-antitrypsin. Aka alpha$_1$-proteinase inhibitor. See **alpha$_1$-antitrypsin deficiency**.

**alpha$_1$-antitrypsin deficiency** (AATd): condition in which elastase accumulates in the lungs owing to deficiency of **alpha$_1$-antitrypsin**, a heritable **recessive** genetic defect. Deficiency of this protein is associated with the development of **emphysema**.

**alpha decay:** radioactive decay in which the nucleus of the parent atom loses a positively charged alpha particle (two protons and two neutrons, the nucleus of a helium atom) decreasing its atomic number by two.

**alpha diversity:** species diversity within a habitat or community of organisms.

**alpha female:** dominant female in a primate group. There is a dominance hierarchy in multi-female primate troops. If the troop is also multi-male, the dominant female may or may not be a partner or consort of the **alpha male**.

**alpha fetoprotein** (AFP): protein found normally in amniotic fluid that indicates, by both presence and concentration, an increased probability of certain fetal defects. High AFP values are associated with congenital anomalies such as neural tube defects; low AFP can be a sign of **Down syndrome**. AFP is structurally related to **serum albumin**.

‡ **alpha globin chain** (α Hb): one of two **polypeptide chains** that compose the **tertiary structure** of several forms of **hemoglobin**. In humans, the alpha globin chain consists of 141 amino acids, transcribed and translated from a **cistron** on chromosome 16. A total of four chains are required for the completion of a functional molecule: two alpha chains, and two **beta globin chains**. Aka alpha globin.

**alpha globulins:** serum proteins consisting of **polypeptides**. Functions largely unknown, although they appear to alter binding sites for **neurotransmitters** in the human brain. Two electrophoretic fractions exist: $\alpha_1$ globulin contains the 'good' type of cholesterol, high-density lipoprotein (**HDLs**); and $\alpha_2$ globulin contains **haptoglobin**. See **albumin** and **globulins**.

**alpha karyology:** determination of chromosome numbers and approximate sizes. The first analytical level of **karyology**.

**alpha lactalbumin:** milk-specific protein evolved from lysozyme and necessary for the synthesis of lactose.

**alpha level** ($\alpha$): in statistics, the probability of incorrectly rejecting the **null hypothesis** when such a hypothesis is tested. See **Type 1 error**.

$\alpha_m$: see **ratio of male to female mutation rates**.

**alpha male:** dominant male in a primate group.

**alpha satellite:** essential portion of the **centromere** that consists of a repeated 171-base DNA sequence.

**alpha** (or $\alpha$-) **thalassemia:** see **thalassemia**.

**alpha waves:** electrical activity emanating from the parietal and occipital lobes of the cerebral hemispheres, normally detected as rhythmic oscillations of about 10–12 cycles per second when a person is awake and relaxed but with eyes closed. See **electroencephalogram**. Aka alpha rhythm.

**alpine:** 1. strictly defined, in reference to the habitats and organisms (including, in the past, humans) found in the European Alps. See **Alpine**. 2. used in reference to environments and organisms found between the tree line and the snow line of mountains.

**Alpine:** ethonym for one of the European races of Lapouge (**European**, Alpine, and *Homo contractus*), a taxon not considered valid today. Physically, Alpines were hybrids, with round heads, stocky bodies, and had medium European skin complexions; this **race** was alleged to have dull intelligence, and to be stubborn and miserly. Geographically, Alpines were distributed from Switzerland through to the Balkans.

**Alpine glacial sequence:** older standard glacial sequence for the **Pleistocene**, proposed in 1909 by A. Penck and E. Brückner. See **Günz, Mindel, Riss**, and **Würm** glacial maxima, and **Günz–Mindel** (Cromerian), **Mindel–Riss** (Holstein), and **Riss–Würm** interglacials (or **interstadials**). The quadrate Alpine sequence has recently been modified and extended as the **Emiliani–Shackleton glacial sequence**.

**alpine tundra:** located today in the arctic, any treeless area with low-growing vegetation and permanently frozen ground below the surface. The surface soil supports lichens and mosses. During the **Pleistocene**, tundra conditions were found much nearer the equator owing to the encroachment of **glaciers**.

**Alport syndrome:** heritable, X-linked recessive condition characterized by deafness and inflamed kidney tubules, due to abnormally formed collagen. Similar symptoms are also caused by autosomal modes of inheritance.

**ALS:** see **amyotrophic lateral sclerosis**.

**Altamira Cave:** archaeological site found in 1869 in the Cantabrian region of northern Spain, dated to 14 kya, and that contains artifacts, faunal assemblages, and elaborate wall decorations.

**Altamura:** archaeological site found by spelunkers in 1993 near Altamura, Italy, dated to an estimated 500 kya. Contains unexcavated hominid remains including the complete skeleton of an adult male coated by calcium nodules and partly obscured by stalactites. Originally attributed to *Homo neanderthalensis* but more recently considered by some researchers to be *Homo heidelbergensis*.

***Altanius orlovi* Dashzeveg and McKenna, 1977:** fossil species from the late **Paleocene** and early **Eocene** of Mongolia. Based on characteristics of the lower back premolar (P4) it has been referred to as a tarsiiform provisionally assigned to the **Omomyidae**, although this affinity has been questioned. Other authors suggest it belongs with the anaptomorphines (**Anaptomorphinae**). *A. orlovi* is known only from a single right mandibular fragment that contained the lower fourth premolar and the three lower molars. If *A. orlovi* is a tarsiiform, it is the oldest Asian representative of that taxon. Very small, with an estimated body mass of 30 g. The dentition suggests an **insectivorous**, a **nectarivorous**, or a **gummivorous** diet.

**altered proteins theory of aging:** intracellular, stochastic model of aging in which the major premise is that there are time-dependent post-translational changes in molecules that result in conformational changes in structural molecules, and that decrease enzyme activity and cell efficiency. See **prion protein, Alzheimer disease**, and **racemization**. Aka protein changes theory.

**alternative hypothesis** (HA): hypothesis offered as an explanation if a corresponding **null hypothesis** fails. Aka the **operational hypothesis**. See **hypothesis testing**.

**alternative splicing:** different patterns of **exon** splicing of a transcript, resulting in production of peptides that differ in amino acid sequence. Variants of a protein (isoforms) can thus be produced from a single gene. Aka differential splicing, exon shuffling.

**altitude:** vertical distance above sea level; used in adaptation studies, the term usually refers to exceptionally high altitudes where populations have adapted to cold temperatures, increased UV radiation, and relative hypoxia.

**altitude sickness:** distress brought about by exposure to high altitude, where there is less oxygen per cubic centimeter of air, causing **hypoxia** and consequent lowering of arterial oxygen content; also caused by respiratory alkalosis. See **acute mountain sickness, subacute mountain sickness,** and **chronic mountain sickness.**

‡ **altitude thorax:** expanded thorax that produces a barrel-shaped chest in individuals who inhabit high altitude during their growing years. This expanded thorax allows for larger lungs and more efficient respiratory ventilation in environments with lower atmospheric pressure.

**altitudinal race:** see **physiological race.**

**Altmann, Jeanne** (1940–): US primatologist. J. Altmann was trained in mathematics as an undergraduate; her Ph.D. (Chicago, 1979) reflected a strong interest in research design and female social organization. J. Altmann began a long field collaboration with her husband S. A. **Altmann** that has included field studies of baboons at what is now Amboseli National Park in Kenya. Author of 'Observational study of behavior: Sampling methods' (*Behaviour,* **49:** 227, 1974); this paper is one of the most cited papers in primatology, and was instrumental in causing primatologists to rethink field research methods. J. Altmann is known for a focus on primate demography and nonexperimental research design. She was among the first to suggest that females should be a focus of research and that primatologists had underestimated the genetic contribution of females to future generations.

**Altmann, Stuart A.** (1930–): US zoologist and primatologist. S. A. Altmann took a master's degree with UCLA bird ecologist George A. Bartholomew and a Ph.D. in behavioral ecology with E. O. **Wilson** at Harvard, and did field research in the Cayo Santiago rhesus populations, then conducted a census of the Barro Colorado howler populations; both works had a communications-oriented approach. He and his wife Jeanne began a field collaboration in the 1950s that included one of the longest ongoing field studies of baboons at Amboseli National Park, Kenya. S. A. Altmann was instrumental in introducing American and European researchers to the work of Japanese primatologists (see **potato-washing behavior** and **rice-washing behavior**), and arranged for the translation of several papers that were published in western journals. The result of this collaboration was *Japanese Monkeys* (1965), co-edited with K. **Imanishi.** S. A. Altmann was one of the early promoters of mathematical models of behavior and ecology, and was active into the twenty-first century at his long-term site in Kenya, where he studied foraging behavior.

**altricial:** pertaining to species characterized by small litters, long gestation, and slow development, that are less developed at birth, and that exhibit a marked delay in the attainment of independent self-maintenance; hence, an increased dependency upon parents, a condition found in primates, especially humans. Said of *K***-selected species.** Cf. **precocial.**

‡ **altruism:** social interaction with a **cost** to self or one's individual **fitness,** for the **benefit** of a recipient(s), whose fitness is increased; selfless behavior within a species. According to E. O. **Wilson** and others, altruism may be either rational, conscious, or conscious and influenced by emotion. One of three classes of cost–benefit behaviors in the theory of **sociobiology** (the others are **selfishness** and **spite**). Altruism is a central problem of both sociobiology and **Darwinism.** See **behavioral ecology** and **limbic system.** Cf. **reciprocity** and **nepotism.**

**Alu sequence:** name for a characteristic 281 base sequence of DNA recognized by the restriction endonuclease *Alu*1. It is very common: about 5–10% of human DNA consists of the Alu sequence, or about 300–500k copies in the nuclear genome; it appears to be untranscribed DNA. Because it is polymorphic, it can be used for phylogenetic studies. The sequence had been proposed as an example of **selfish DNA.** Aka alu family, alu element. See **SINE.**

**alvar:** chemical substance used to harden bones recovered from an archaeological excavation so that they can be removed and handled without breakage.

**Alvarez theory:** see **asteroid impact model.**

*Alveojunctus minutus:* **Paleocene** species found in North America and belonging to the controversial fossil family **Microsyopidae,** suborder **Plesiadapiformes.** See Appendix 1 for taxonomy.

**alveolar:** of, relating to, or constituting: 1. an alveolus. 2. the part of the jaw where the teeth arise. 3. an air sac of the lungs.

**alveolar arch:** see **dental arcade.**

**alveolar border:** superior border of the **mandible** that contains the **dental alveoli** that bear the lower teeth.

**alveolar point:** landmark at the center of the alveolar margin of the upper jaw mid-way between the central incisors.

**alveolar process:** inferior border of the **maxillary bone** that projects down and contains the **dental alveoli** that bear the upper teeth. See **alveolar border, dental arcade.**

‡ **alveolar prognathism:** forward projection of that part of the mandible and/or maxilla that contains the teeth; results from the large size of teeth, roots, or both. See **prognathism.**

**alveolar ridge:** area directly to the rear of the upper teeth.

**alveolare** (ids): single craniometric landmark of the facial skeleton; mid-sagittal point of the maxillary alveolar arch, inferior to the **nasal septum,** between the upper central incisors. This is the lowest land-mark used for the measurement of facial height. See Appendix 7.

**alveolo-condylian plane** (CA): see **Broca horizontal**.

**alveolon** (alv): single osteologic landmark of the **hard palate**; point where a **coronal** line drawn from the alveolar ridges intersects the mid-sagittal point of the most posterior portion of the hard palate. See Appendix 7.

**alveolus:** general anatomical term used to designate a small saclike structure. 1. a dental alveolus is one of the cavities in the alveolar process of the mandible or maxilla in which the roots of the tooth are held by the fibers of the periodontal ligament. 2. a pulmonary alveolus is one of the polyhedral outpouchings along the walls of the alveolar sacs and alveolar ducts through the walls of which alveolar gas and pulmonary capillary blood gas are exchanged. Plural: alveoli, alveolae.

**Alzheimer disease** (AD): or 'presenile dementia', so-called by Alois Alzheimer in 1907 when he described a disability that affected the middle-aged and eld-erly; a progressive form of mental disease occurring in middle age or later, characterized by intellectual deficit and loss of short-term memory. AD is with characteristic changes in and near nerve cells, and with an increase in the amounts of certain gummy brain proteins, the beta- and tau-**amyloids**. Intraneuronal tangles of neurofibrils are also a fea-ture. At least eight variants have been mapped to var-ious human chromosomes. AD is twice as common in women as in men, and (in 2003) is the fourth leading cause of death in American adults. A clinical variant, familial Alzheimer disease (FAD), early onset, manifests in the fifth or later decades of life, but only 5–10% of Alzheimer cases are inherited. Aka Alzheimer's dementia, presenile dementia. Cf. **Parkinson disease.**

**a.m.** or **AM:** abbreviation for anatomically modern; used to refer to a fossil that falls within the range of variation of an existing species, e.g. anatomically modern humans (**AMH**).

**amalgamation:** 1. a mix or blend. 2. see **racial amal-gamation.**

**amaurotic idiocy:** see **infantile amaurotic idiocy.**

**ambidextrality:** 1. state of having symmetrical parts or members and equally efficient use of parts on either side with equal skill; ambidextrous. 2. commonly, being equally skilled with both hands. Cf. **dextrality** and **sinistrality.**

**ambient:** pertaining to the prevailing conditions of the environment surrounding an organism or research equipment.

**ambient temperature** ($T_A$): temperature of the envi-ronment immediately surrounding an organism or

research equipment; usually refers to the air or water immediately surrounding a body.

**ambiguous:** poorly defined such that an open inter-pretation can be made; uncertain; equivocal. Noun: ambiguity.

**ambiguous genetic code:** refers to a codon that pro-duces more than one product.

**ambiguous genitalia:** compromised sexual develop-ment due to a variety of causes, both environmental and genetic. Among the approximately forty genetic conditions that have ambiguous genitalia as a major feature are partial and/or complete **androgen insensi-tivity syndrome, congenital adrenal hyperplasia** (several varieties), **male** and/or **female pseudoher-maphroditism**, and hermaphroditism (see **hermaph-rodite**) Some researchers estimate the frequency at between 1 and 2% of all live births. Aka syndromes of abnormal sex differentiation.

**ambisexuality:** having characteristics of, or affecting, both sexes. Adjective: ambisexual.

**Amboseli National Park:** research site located in Kenya where long-term field studies of yellow baboons (**Papio** *cynocephalus*) and vervet monkeys (**Chlorocebus** *aethiops*) have been conducted for decades. Primatologists who have conducted field research at this site include: S. A. **Altmann**, J. **Altmann**, T. T. Struhsaker, D. Cheney, R. Seyfarth, G. Hausfater, D. G. Post, M. D. Hauser, and J. E. Philips-Conroy.

**Ambrona:** archaeological site found in the 1960s in cen-tral Spain, dated to 700–500 kya (Middle Pleistocene), painstakingly excavated by F. C. **Howell**, and that contains Acheulean artifacts which indicated that their makers preferentially used their right hands when manufacturing tools. It has been argued that this site also contains evidence for the controlled use of fire, as bones of 30–35 'wooden elephants' appear to have been charred. Aka Torralba and Ambrona (two distinct sites, however).

**ambulatory:** possessing limbs that enable walking about. Noun: ambulation. See **locomotion.**

**Ameghino's autochthonous thesis:** proposal by Argentinean paleontologist F. Ameghino, advanced in the 1930s, that Native Americans arose and evolved from basal New World primates. Little evidence sup-ports this idea, and it was discarded by the 1960s. The term 'ameghinoi' has come to refer to any fossil of dubious provenance or authenticity.

**ameiosis:** type of cell division in which gametes are formed without reduction in chromosome number.

**amelia:** congenital condition resulting in the absence of a limb or limbs.

**amelification:** see **amelogenesis.**

**ameloblast:** specialized cell that forms tooth **enamel.**

**amelogenesis:** process through which dental **enamel** is formed, involving the **biomineralization** of **hydroxyapatite** within a self-assembled **amelogenin** structural matrix. Aka amelification.

**amelogenesis imperfecta** (AIH1): heritable, X-linked recessive condition characterized by abnormal soft and white tooth enamel, due to defects in the **amelogenin** gene, and that has a homologous locus in the Y chromosome.

**amelogenin:** enamel matrix protein formed in the juvenile stage of a mammal as part of **amelogenesis**. Homologous amelogenin is found on both the X (AMELX) and Y (AMELY) chromosomes, and is useful for **molecular sex determination**. Functionally orthologous amelogenin **exon** 2 is found in a wide variety of biomineralizing organisms, dating the genesis of this sequence to well over 500 mya. Amelogenin is also suspected to contribute to **enamel thickness** and to be one of the polygenes that contributes to **sexual dimorphism**.

**amenorrhea:** absence or arrest of **menstruation**.

*Ameranthropoides loysi* **Montandon, 1929:** mistaken example of **early man in the New World**, an 'anthropoid' from Venezuela that was photographed, but the bones of the animal hunted by F. de Loys have since disappeared.

**American:** eighteenth-century name for the indigenous peoples of the Americas. One of the five often-cited racial varieties recognized by **Blumenbach** (1790); the others were **Ethiopian**, **Malayan**, **Mongolian**, and **Caucasian**.

**American Academy of Forensic Sciences** (AAFS): professional society dedicated to the application of science to the law; membership includes physicians, criminalists, toxicologists, attorneys, dentists, physical anthropologists, document examiners, engineers, psychiatrists, and educators who practice and perform research relating to **forensic science**.

**American Anatomical Association** (AAA): parent organization from which the **American Association of Physical Anthropologists** was formed. The AAA has declined in recent years and currently has only about 500 members.

**American Anthropological Association** (AAA): largest and oldest active major anthropological organization in North America. Primarily represents the social science branch of **anthropology** (only about 15% of the **AAPA** hold concurrent membership). Evolved from the Washington (DC) Anthropological Association. In addition to divisions containing units of interests to cultural anthropologists, there are today (2003) major units for the **Archaeology** Division, the Biological Anthropology Division, and the Society for **Medical Anthropology**, among others.

*American Anthropologist:* journal that commenced publication in January 1888 as an organ of the Anthropological Society of Washington, DC. Currently the official journal of the **American Anthropological Association**.

**American Association of Physical Anthropologists** (AAPA): society founded in 1931 at the annual meetings of the **American Anatomical Association**. The AAPA is devoted to the study of **human biology**, including **human evolution** and human biological **variation**. The AAPA was heavily anatomical in its original orientation; its current members conduct research in **physiology**, **genetics**, **adaptation**, **growth and development**, and primate **morphology** and **behavior**, as well as other areas of interest to **human evolutionary biologists**. This is the largest society of human evolutionary biologists in North America, with approximately 1500 members. The official journal of the AAPA is the *American Journal of Physical Anthropology*.

**American Board of Forensic Anthropologists** (ABFA): professional certifying board for physical anthropologists specializing in **forensics**.

**American Historical School:** the approach of Franz **Boas**, termed historical particularism. Although he never established a formal 'school' of anthropology, Boasian anthropology nevertheless exists in terms of the influence of the man and his students, who included Alfred Kroeber, Margaret Mead, Ruth Benedict, Edward Sapir, Melville Hershkovits, Robert Lowie, A. Irving Hallowell, M. F. Ashley **Montagu**, Ruth Bunsel, Paul Radin, and Leslie Spier.

**American homotype:** proposal in 1842 by S. G. **Morton** that an average **type** of **American Indian** existed; this **typological race concept** was carried forward by A. **Hrdlička** a century later, and lost momentum only in the latter part of the twentieth century.

**American Indian: ethonym** for some of the indigenous peoples of North America, especially those in the continental USA. The term resulted from the erroneous belief held by Europeans during the first decade after contact that the Indies could be reached by sailing directly across the Atlantic Ocean. Cf. **Native American**.

*American Journal of Human Biology* (AJHB): official journal of the Human Biology Association (formerly the Human Biology Council). First published in 1989, it presents research conducted in the interdisciplinary field of human biology.

*American Journal of Physical Anthropology* (AJPA): founded in 1918 by Aleš **Hrdlička** as the official organ of the newly formed **American Association of Physical Anthropologists**, it is currently published by Wiley–Liss (John Wiley and Sons), New York.

***American Journal of Primatology*** (AJP): journal devoted to the study of primate biology; the official journal of the **American Society of Primatologists**, first published in 1976. The current publisher is Wiley–Liss (John Wiley and Sons), New York.

**American Mongol:** Mongoloid subgroup found among some Native American groups, such as the Pueblo.

**American polygenist school:** idea of plural origins of the species ***Homo sapiens*** held in the early nineteenth century. One group, exemplified by S. G. **Morton**, rationalized a form of scientific **racism**, while a second group, of which J. C. Nott and G. R. Gliddon were representative, approached the problem using both anthropological theory and socioeconomic ideas. Both groups, however, were strict supporters of **polygenism**.

**American School of Anthropology:** influential group of mid-nineteenth century orthodox physicians and biblical scholars whose research led them to believe that **evolution** could not have occurred within the time frame allowed since the biblical **Special Creation**; that variation among 'human types' was too great to be explained by historical or climatic influences, and therefore the **races** (even species) of humans must have been created separately; hence these scholars were also known as **polygenists**. Among the more prominent were Samuel **Morton**, Josiah Nott, and George Gliddon.

‡ **American Sign Language** (Ameslan, ASL): a language of gestures used by deaf people in the USA. ASL is a legitimate **language** and has not only vocabulary, but also grammar and the other aspects of any language (with the exception of spoken words). ASL is unique to the American deaf community; other countries have their own sign languages. Some studies of ape language and cognition utilize subsets of ASL. See **pasimology**.

**American Society of Primatologists** (ASP): organization founded in 1977 as an American affiliate of the **International Society of Primatologists**; its first meeting was held in Seattle, WA (USA) in 1977. By 1982 its scientific organ, the ***American Journal of Primatology***, had commenced publication. The ASP has approximately 750 members. More than half of the membership specialize in some aspect of behavior and the largest academic disciplines represented in the ASP are anthropology, psychology, and zoology, respectively.

**American trypanosomiasis:** see **Chagas' disease**.

**Amerind:** 1. anthropological term (**ethonym**) denoting an **American Indian**. 2. a language family proposed by linguist Joseph Greenberg that includes all indigenous languages of the Americas.

**Amerindian: ethonym** used by anthropologists to designate the indigenous peoples of the Americas; aka American Indian, Native American, **Amerind**.

**Ames test:** bioassay developed by Bruce Ames and others for identifying mutagenic compounds; utilizes *Salmonella typhimurium*.

**Ameslan:** see **American Sign Language**.

‡ **AMH:** anatomically modern human; comparable to living humans in all structural aspects; ***Homo sapiens sapiens***.

‡ **amino acid:** one of twenty unit molecules that are the common building blocks of **polypeptides** or **proteins**, arranged in a specific order by each gene, called the sequence. In living organisms, amino acids are **levorotatory** molecules, containing both an amino group ($-NH_2$) and a carboxyl group ($-COOH$). Amino acids occur naturally in plants and animals. In fossils and some low-turnover living tissue (bone, tooth enamel), L- forms slowly **racemize** into **dextrorotatory** molecules at specific rates. See **amino acid racemization** and **protein synthesis**.

‡ **amino acid racemization** (AAR): nonradiometric dating technique in which the ratio of an L-amino acid to its D-amino acid is measured; fossil material can be dated directly. After the death of an organism, the **proteins** break down into free amino acids. In life proteins contain L-**amino acids**, but after death these slowly invert into D-**amino acids**, a process called **racemization**; different **amino acids** have different conversion rates. Amino acid racemization includes periods that range from a few hundred years to several hundred thousand years; however, amino acid racemization rates are very sensitive to temperature and pH. If these factors significantly influence the rates, the dates obtained can be unreliable. Aka amino acid dating.

**amino acid replacement:** substitution of one **amino acid** for another, creating variation in the amino acid sequence of a protein.

‡ **amino acid sequencing:** molecular technique in which amino acid sequences in proteins are mapped; these sequences can then be compared between species to deduce evolutionary relationships.

**amino acid substitution: mutation** that involves the substitution, insertion or deletion of one or more amino acids in a polypeptide chain.

**amino group:** chemical group ($NH_2$) found in amino acids and at one end of a polypeptide chain.

**aminoaciduria:** presence of an amino acid(s) in the urine in abnormal quantity, usually due to a metabolic defect.

**Amish culture:** Americans of German descent, an Anabaptist sect, residing primarily in Pennsylvania, all descended from about 200 original immigrants, who dress plainly and shun innovation and technology.

Several genetic traits are found in this population at high frequency, owing to the **founder effect**. Aka Old Order Amish.

**amitosis:** direct division of a cell simply by elongation and division of the nucleus and cytoplasm into two new cells, unlike the ordinary process of cell reproduction **(mitosis)**.

**amity–enmity complex:** Herbert **Spencer's** term for the perceived duality of the nature of animals to form friendships with some individuals and to behave agonistically toward others.

**Ammon's law:** generalization that there is a correlation between stature and the shape of the cranium; specifically, that there is a negative correlation between stature and the **cephalic index**. The correlations are modest, and applicable only to males from a homogenous population.

**amniocentesis:** procedure performed on pregnant women introduced in 1952, a method of sampling **amniotic fluid** that surrounds the developing fetus. The procedure involves the insertion of a hollow needle into the uterus and the withdrawal of fluid and suspended fetal cells. Cultured cells are used for the diagnosis of potential genetic and **cytogenetic disorders** in the **fetus**. The test is usually performed during the 15th or 16th week of a pregnancy.

‡ **amnion:** extraembryonic membrane that envelopes the developing **fetus** and that fills with **amniotic fluid**; develops about the 7th day after conception. Amniotic fluid cushions the developing embryo. Aka amniotic membrane.

**amniotes: clade** that includes reptiles, birds and mammals; these all develop through an embryo that is enclosed within an **amnion**, which is probably an adaptation for breeding on dry land.

**amniotic cavity:** fluid-filled space enclosed by the **amnion**, located between the uterine lining and an early embryo.

**amniotic egg:** hard-shelled reptilian egg.

**amniotic fluid** (Amf): fluid contained within the amniotic cavity that surrounds the developing **fetus** in a pregnant female. It is this watery fluid, which contains fetal cells, that is obtained during **amniocentesis**.

**amoebiasis:** common **protozoan** disease caused by infection with *Entamoeba histolytica*; of Old World origin (tropical) and associated with poor sanitation and health practices. Inflammation caused by ingesting food or water contaminated with cysts of the amoeba which release in the intestines, and can progress to abscesses in the liver and other organs. Aka amoebic dysentery.

**amorph:** mutant allele that has no detectable phenotypic effect that is different from that of the wild-type allele; all **recessive alleles** are amorphs.

**amorphous:** without shape or structure.

**amphiarthrotic joint:** joint that allows only a slight degree of movement. A **syndesmosis** between the distal ends of the **tibia** and **fibula** would be an example of such a joint. See **joint**.

**amphicone:** buccal cusp of a premolar tooth produced by developmental fusion of the metacone and paracone.

**amphimictic population:** population that has freely crossing and fertile descendants.

*Amphipithecus mogaungensis* **Colbert, 1937:** fossil primate from the late **Eocene** (44–40 mya) of Burma, recovered in 1923. The **holotype** consists of a left mandibular fragment that contains the third and fourth premolars, plus the first molar. Systematics are contentious owing to **mosaic** of **primitive** and **derived** traits. Some researchers think that *Amphipithecus* is an adapid, others consider it a transitional form between adapids and higher primates, and yet others think it is an early **anthropoid**. Even an omomyid affinity has been suggested. *Amphipithecus* has deep, fused **mandibles**, which is a characteristic of the adapids as well as of higher primates. The anthropoid character is the low-crowned molars, and suggests **folivory**. Body mass estimate 9 kg. See Appendix 1 for taxonomy.

**amphixenosis:** transmissible disease of vertebrates caused by any microorganism that can inhabit either humans or animals as its maintenance host. Cf. **anthropozoonosis, zooanthroponosis**.

**amplification:** see **gene amplification**.

**amplitude:** in behavioral studies, the magnitude of behavioral change, i.e. the maximum range of behavior observed.

**Amud Cave:** archaeological site found in 1959 in Wadi Amud, north of the town of Tiberias, near Haifa, Israel, dated to 50–27 kya, and that contains **Levallois–Mousterian** tools and intentionally buried hominid remains, including the skeleton of a 25 year old male (**Amud 1**). Part of the Near Eastern **Neandertal** group (see **Near Eastern fossil groups**), with closest affinities to **Shanidar** and **Tabūn**. Remains of about 15 individuals have been attributed to *Homo neanderthalensis*. Dating of the cave is controversial, as pottery from higher levels has been mixed with the Middle Paleolithic levels. Aka Wadi Amud, 'Valley of the Pillar'; not the same cave as **Zuttiyeh**, which is sometimes also called Wadi Amud.

**amygdala:** 1. term used to designate an almond-shaped structure, e.g. an amygdaloid **Acheulean handax**. 2. one of two ovoid masses of gray matter located in the front part of the temporal lobe of the brain in the roof of the terminal portion of the inferior horn of the lateral ventricle. The amygdala is involved with human

---

**Some fossil hominids from Amud Cave**

Amud 1: field number for a hominid intentionally buried in **Amud Cave**; the skeleton of a 25 year old male found in 1961. The skull of this individual was incomplete and was reconstructed using corresponding material from **Shanidar**. At 1740 cm$^3$, cranial capacity is the largest of any known fossil hominid. Remains attributed to *Homo neanderthalensis*.

Amud 7: field number for a hominid intentionally buried in **Amud Cave**; the well-preserved partial skeleton of a child found in 1961 and excavated by Yoel Rak in 1992. Although ostrich shell and a red deer maxilla 'grave gifts' were also recovered, the intentionality of the deposit has been challenged. Remains attributed to *Homo neanderthalensis*.

---

moods and emotions. Aka amygdaloid nuclear complex. Plural: amygdalae. Adjective: amygdaloid.

**amylase:** enzyme secreted by the **salivary glands** and pancreas that functions to begin the conversion of starch and glycogen into **disaccharides** during **digestion**.

**amyloidosis, type I:** autosomal dominant condition characterized by cerebral hemorrhaging in older adults, and featuring build-up of a fibrillized, gummy protein, amyloid, owing to mutations that cause misfolding in **transthyretin** (TTR). One of at least seven varieties of amyloidosis (the TTR amyloid diseases); most are related to specific mutations in the TTR protein. Aka familial amyloid neuropathy (FAP), Dutch variety amyloidosis. See **protein misfolding disorder**.

**amyloids:** accretions of fibrous, gummy secretions in the brain and other tissues. Up to 25% of these plaques consist of misfolded proteins. See **protein misfolding disorder**.

**amyotrophic lateral sclerosis, familial** (FALS, ALS): an autosomal dominant neurological condition characterized by an asymmetrical, progressive deterioration of cells in the brain stem and spinal cord; paralysis and death are inevitable. Manifests by the fifth decade of life. The defective gene is SOD1 (**superoxide dismutase** 1); Aka Lou Gehrig's disease.

‡ **anabolism:** synthesis and build-up of organic molecules, mainly **proteins**, through the expenditure of energy; the metabolic conversion of food into **tissue**. Adjective: anabolic.

**anaerobic:** in the absence of free oxygen.

**Anagalidae:** family of fossil tree shrews erected by Simpson in 1945. These are Paleocene animals previously included among the primates, but removed with the other tree shrews and placed into the order Scandentia.

‡ **anagenesis:** accumulation of changes in a single ancestor–descendant lineage through time without branching; linear evolution, sometimes interpreted as '**progressive**' **evolution**; **phyletic gradualism**. Adjective: anagenetic. Aka single-line evolution, virtual evolution. Cf. **cladogenesis** and **catagenesis**.

**anagenetic speciation:** transformation along one lineage without branching, or **cladogenesis**. Aka phyletic speciation, successional speciation. See **pseudoextinction**.

**anal gland:** see **anogenital scent gland**.

**analog:** synthetically produced chemical variant of a natural compound; certain analogs possess significantly improved therapeutic properties in specific applications, over the natural compound. Also spelled analogue.

‡ **analogy:** presence of a **trait** in two different, very distantly related, organisms, in both of which the trait serves a similar function; e.g. the wings of butterflies as compared to the wings of birds. Adjective: analogous. Cf. **homology**.

**analysis:** in statistics, the separation of a whole into its perceived constituent **elements** to study the relationship of those parts to each other and to the whole. The elements are often **quantified** as numbers or categories. Cf. **synthesis**.

**analysis of variance** (ANOVA, AOV): statistical procedure by which two or more populations can be compared; i.e. the sample means can be tested to see whether they could have been obtained from **populations** with the same parametric **mean**. Used to partition the sources of **variability**. ANOVA is one of the most widely used statistical techniques in biology.

‡ **anaphase:** stage in **cell division** during which the **centromeres** separate and the daughter chromosomes or chromatids begin to separate (**disjunction**). In **mitosis** there is one such stage and in **meiosis** there are two, **anaphase I** and **anaphase II**.

**anaphase I:** in **meiosis**, the stage of the **cell cycle** when the **homologous chromosome** pairs separate, reducing the number of chromosomes in each new cell by half.

**anaphase II:** in **meiosis**, the stage of the **cell cycle** when the **centromeres** separate and the **homologous chromatids** are pulled to opposite poles of the **spindles**, reducing the chromatid complement to the final **haploid** count. Aka **equational division**.

**anaphase lag:** failure of a chromosome to migrate to either spindle pole following **metaphase** in **mitosis**; results in the resorption and loss of the chromosome in an **aneuploid** daughter cell.

**Anaptomorphinae:** extinct subfamily of the Eocene **prosimian** family Omomyidae that includes approximately 19 genera; recovered primarily from North American deposits, but also known from Europe and Asia; most primitive omomyid group. Small body size (under 500 g); dentition suggestive of **frugivory** with insect supplements. Adjective: anaptomorphine. See **Omomyidae** and Appendix 1 for taxonomy.

*Anaptomorphus* **Cope, 1879:** genus of fossil tarsiiform from the middle **Eocene** of the Rocky Mountain region of North America, known from jaws and teeth. Assigned to the family **Omomyidae**, subfamily **Anaptomorphinae**. Three recognized species. Dental formula: 2.1.2.3; has small anterior dentition and relatively large molars suggestive of a **frugivorous** diet with insect supplement. Body mass estimated between 150 and 500 g, depending on the species. See Appendix 1 for taxonomy.

*Anasazia* **Van Valen, 1994:** archaic mammal known from the middle Paleocene? of North America belonging to the **Plesiadapiformes** family **Palaechthonidae; monotypic.** *A. williamsoni* is known only from mandibular and dental remains; type specimen confiscated from a commercial collector and provenance not preserved. Mandibular remains indicate the incisor was reduced in size, uncharacteristic of a plesiadapid. Dental formula unknown. See Appendix 1 for taxonomy.

**anastomosis:** interconnecting aggregation of blood vessels or nerves that forms a network plexus. Plural: anastomoses.

**anataxic processes:** recycling processes, such as erosion, whereby bones and artifacts are uncovered and exposed to forces of attrition.

**anatomical age:** see **skeletal age.** Cf. **dental age, physiological age** and **chronological age.**

**anatomical direction:** orientation; refers to terms that allow anatomists to explain where a structure is in reference to another structure, such as **proximal** and **distal.** Anatomical directions are made in reference to the **anatomical position.**

**anatomical grade scale:** qualitative gradient commonly used to evaluate degrees of manifestation of a feature: (1) absent or none, (2) slight, (3) moderate, (4) marked, (5) extreme.

**anatomical position:** reference standard used in human anatomy, in which a human is seen as standing erect, feet together, with the palms of the hands facing the observer and the thumbs pointing away from the body. This position is the reference for any **anatomical direction,** regardless of the actual position of the specimen.

**anatomical sex:** gender of an individual as summarized by **genetic sex, chromosomal sex, gonadal sex,** and **phenotypic sex,** which are normally a continuum resulting in one of the two mammalian sexes, **female** or **male.**

‡ **anatomically modern human:** see **AMH.**

**anatomy:** 1. discipline that studies the structure of humans and other organisms. For a century-and-a-half **physical anthropology** was a minor subfield of human anatomy. Currently the discipline is undergoing a name change in many academic departments, frequently being called cell and structural biology. 2. structure of an organism or any of its parts, as revealed by dissection. Cf. **morphology.**

**ancestor:** individual, population or species that is a direct progenitor of another; one or more generations in the past.

‡ **ancestral:** pertaining to any primitive character state present or assumed to have been present in an ancestor. Cf. **derived.**

**ancestral homology:** with respect to a given set of species, a trait or character common to all species within the set of interest, and present in outgroups as well, implying that the trait evolved in a species that lived before the common ancestor of the set of interest. Cf. **derived homology.**

**ancestral population:** population that gives rise to one or more descendant populations.

**ancestral suite:** set of behavioral traits proposed by Harvard anthropologist Richard W. Wrangham as a way of inferring the social organization and behaviors of the common ancestor of early hominids.

‡ **ancestral trait, character or feature:** primitive character state present or assumed to be present in an ancestor. See **plesiomorphy** and **symplesiomorphy.**

*Anchomomys* **Stehlin, 1916:** genus of fossil adapid, subfamily **Adapinae,** from the **Eocene** (*c.* 38 mya) of western Europe. Two to three species are recognized (*Huerzeleris quercyi* is considered the third species by some authorities). Small; body mass estimates range from 120 to 250 g. Dentition and size suggestive of **insectivory;** dental formula 2.1.4.3. Some researchers suggest that *Anchomomys* is a **lorisoid.** See Appendix 1 for taxonomy.

**ancient DNA:** any **DNA** fragment recovered from a **fossil.**

‘**ancient human life cycle’ hypothesis:** argument by A. E. Mann that the human life cycle is ancient, based on evidence from the fossil record, and that **australopithecine** rates of growth and development resembled that of humans, rather than apes.

**Andaman Islander: ethnonym** for an indigenous people of Asia; the Andamans are a pygmoid group. Andaman Island is located south of Myanmar (formerly Burma) in the Bay of Bengal. It was reported by contact anthropologists that the Andaman peoples had no device for making fire. Aka Andamanese, Andaman.

**Andamanese:** family of languages spoken by the **Andaman Islanders**.

**Andean night monkey:** vernacular for *Aotus miconax*.

**Andean titi monkey:** vernacular for *Callicebus oenanthe*.

**Andersen disease: glycogen storage disease.**

**Andersson, Johan Gunnar** (1874-1960): Swedish mining expert and amateur paleontologist. Funded by the Swedish China Research Committee shortly after World War I, he discovered the **Zhoukoudian** (then Choukoutien) site in 1918, and oversaw paleontological excavations near Beijing (Peking) in the 1920s. Although many were lost *en route*, Andersson sent so many fossil specimens to Professor Wiman at Sweden's Uppsala University that they have not yet been completely described.

**androcentric:** male-centered; from the perspective of the male sex. Cf. **gynocentric**.

**androcentric models of evolution:** male-centered models in paleoanthropology. Include: '**killer ape' hypothesis**, the '**man the hunter' hypothesis**, and the **provisioning monogamist hypothesis**. Cf. **gynocentric models of evolution**.

**androcentrism:** theory attributed by feminists to male scholarship; asserts that male values are taken as the norm, and then explains female values or practices as deviations from, or unsuccessful aspirations towards, male practices.

**androgen:** any **steroid** substance in a class of **gonadotropins** secreted at higher levels in males than in females and consequently often referred to as the male **hormones**. Androgens are involved with the growth and stimulation of the sexual organs and are responsible for male sexual characteristics. The most abundant androgen is **testosterone**. Aka male gonadal hormone.

**androgen insensitivity syndrome** (AIS): an X-linked developmental anomaly in which a chromosomal XY male embryo with testicular tissue does not respond to androgens (both testosterone and DHT are present) and the individual thus appears phenotypically female. Testes are undescended, and spermatogenesis is absent. AIS is caused by microdeletions in the gene for the androgen receptor. There are two clinical classes: complete (CAIS) and partial (PAIS). CAIS individuals possess what has been described as the 'supermodel' phenotype: affected individuals are tall, highly symmetrical and phenotypically 'attractive' females with micromastia, have little pubic hair ('hairless pseudofemale'), and lack menstruation owing to a blind vagina. Aka testicular feminization (TF), androgen resistance syndrome, Lubs syndrome. AIS is the most common form of **male pseudohermaphroditism**. AIS is about 1.5 times more common than **male pseudohermaphroditism** with **gynecomastia**.

**androgen receptor:** protein belonging to a class of steroid receptors with zinc finger domains and an androgen-binding domain. The gene itself maps to the middle of the X chromosome. Some mutations in this gene cause **androgen insensitivity syndrome**.

‡ **androgenic hormone:** masculinizing hormone, e.g. **androsterone** or **testosterone**. See **androgen**.

**androgenization:** process in which a female acquires male characteristics; this may be present at birth or acquired later in life; aka virilization.

**androgyny:** in anthropometry, the degree to which one sex has bodily forms characteristic of the other.

**andromedullary hormones:** substances secreted by the **adrenal medulla**, e.g. **epinephrine** and **norepinephrine**.

**androsterone:** an **androgen** degradation product; in some species it exerts weak androgen-like effects.

**androtype:** in taxonomy, a type specimen that is a male. Cf. **gynetype**.

**anemia:** 1. reduction in total blood hemoglobin. 2. insufficient **red blood cell** production, which is often due to severe iron deficiency, but may also be due to loss of, or defective, **erythrocytes**; any imbalance between the loss of erythrocytes and the ability of the body to replace them. 3. a state of malnutrition in strict vegetarians caused by a reversible deficiency (**avitaminosis**) of **vitamin B$_{12}$**. The primary cause is a deficiency of cyanocobalamin, required for **DNA** synthesis (esp. carbon bonding).

**anemia, sickle cell:** see **sickle cell disease**.

*Anemorhysis* **Gazin, 1958:** genus of fossil primate assigned to the family **Omomyidae**, subfamily **Anaptomorphinae**. Known from the early **Eocene** of North America. five recognized species. Known from jaws and teeth; dental formula: 2.1.3.3. Body mass estimate 70–180 g. See Appendix 1 for taxonomy.

**anencephaly:** neural tube defect characterized by an open cranium, accompanied by degrees of absence of the brain and spinal cord.

**aneuploid:** description of cells with fewer or more **chromosomes** than the basic **diploid number** characteristic of the species in question; 44, 45, 47, and 48 would all be aneuploid counts for humans, where the modal diploid number is $2N = 46$. Noun: aneuploidy. Humans with **Down syndrome** have 47 chromosomes and are aneuploid. See **euploid** and **chromatid**.

**Angel, John Lawrence** (1915–86): British-born US anatomist, paleopathologist; student of Kluckhohn, Coon and Hooton at Harvard; affiliated with the Jefferson Medical College (Philadelphia) and later with the Smithsonian. Interested in the skeletal biology of aging, Angel was an expert on the pathologies in the **Terry** collection, and was a regular forensic consultant to the FBI and US Navy.

**Angelman syndrome** (AS): uncommon autosomal dominant, heterogenous condition characterized by seizures, mental impairment and growth retardation, a protruding tongue, floppy muscle tone, large jaw, an inability to talk, and excessive and inappropriate laughter. AS is caused by a small deletion in chromosome 15, inherited maternally. The ubiquitin ligase gene (*UBE3A*) has been implicated. Exhibits evidence for **genomic imprinting**. Aka 'happy puppet' syndrome, Prader–Willi/Angelman syndrome. See **Prader–Willi syndrome.**

**angioblast:** 1. embryonic tissue from which blood vessels and blood cells are formed. 2. any vessel-forming cell.

**angiogenesis:** generation of new blood vessels.

**angiosperm:** vernacular for a plant that produces flowers and has sexual organs with seeds enclosed in an ovary, a true seed vessel; the angiosperms displaced most fern-like plants during the **Cenozoic era**, beginning 65 mya, although they existed during the **Mesozoic**. See **fruit** and **nut**. Cf. **gymnosperm.**

**angiosperm radiation hypothesis:** hypothesis proposed by Robert Sussman that posits that many primate traits are the result of coevolution with **angiosperms**, in which many early primates exploited the products of these plants in low-light canopy conditions; **binocular vision, color vision** and grasping hands were selected for observing and manipulating fruiting plants; some early primates are speculated to have served as pollinators. Aka pollinator hypothesis, terminal branch-feeding hypothesis.

**angle of the cranial base:** angle between the basiocciput and the body of the **sphenoid.**

**Anglian glaciation:** second major glaciation of the Pleistocene in the British Isles sequence; see **Mindel glaciation.**

**Angolan (black-and-white) colobus monkey:** vernacular for *Colobus angolensis.*

**ångström unit** (Å): unit of measurement equal to one hundred millionth of a centimeter ($10^{-10}$ m).

**angular gyrus:** center for the integration of auditory, visual, and somasthetic information located at the junction of the parietal, temporal and occipital lobes of the brain, just posterior to **Wernicke's area.**

**angular process:** posterior ventral projection of the mammalian **mandible** where the ascending **ramus** and mandibular body meet. The medial **pterygoid muscle** attaches to its medial side and the **masseter muscle** attaches to its lateral side. This structure is present in some of the **prosimians**, but in most primates has been replaced by the **mandibular angle.**

**angular torus:** bony marking resulting from enlargement of the posterior superior **temporal line** as it approaches the mastoid angle on the **parietal bone** on some *Homo erectus* crania.

**angwantibo:** vernacular for *Arctocebus calabarensis.*

**anilingual diameter:** transverse diameter of a tooth, from buccal to lingual.

**animal:** any member of the animal kingdom. See **Animalia.**

**animal–hominid threshold** (AHT): older term for the point at which an ancient ape 'stands up', begins using tools, and has brain expansion, in accordance with Darwin's **tool-feedback hypothesis**. Used in a linear fashion that is no longer accepted.

**animal language hypothesis:** allegation that some nonhuman species can communicate with humans using a true language, such as English or **American Sign Language**. Experiments with parrots and chimpanzees have been provocative, but many scientists remain skeptical of such reports. See **pasimology.**

**animalculism:** form of the **Preformation Doctrine**, which stated that a complete organism was dormant in the semen of the male, and that growth was started by fertilization. Aka spermism. Cf. **ovism.**

**animalculist:** proponent of **animalculism.**

**Animalia:** taxonomically, one of the five (some say six) kingdoms of life. Animals are multicellular and are capable of movement in some part of their life cycle; muscles and nervous systems (including sensory specializations) are unique to animals; animals are **heterotrophs**, i.e. they must consume other organisms because they cannot synthesize their own food. See phylum **Chordata.**

**anisogamy:** 1. fusion of two gametes of unequal size. 2. condition in which the female **gamete** (**ovum**) is larger than the male gamete (**sperm**); heterogamy. Cf. **isogamy.**

***Ankarapithecus*** Ozansoy, 1957: fossil genus of **hominoid** from late **Miocene** (9.8 mya) of Turkey. Now grouped with *Sivapithecus*, *Ankarapithecus* had a mosaic of gorilla-like and orang-like features. Aka *Sivapithecus meteai*. See Appendix 1 for taxonomy.

**ankle bone:** see **tarsal** bone.

**ankle breadth: anthropometric** measurement of distance between the medial **malleolus** of the **tibia** and the lateral malleolus of the **fibula** as measured with either spreading calipers or sliding calipers; the subject stands with feet separated and weight evenly distributed. Used for studies of body frame size and skeletal mass. Aka bimalleolar breadth.

**ankle circumference: anthropometric** measurement of distance around the ankle as measured with a tape measure placed at the narrowest portion of the calf just proximal to the two **malleoli** and passed horizontally around the ankle. Used in estimations of body frame size and in **human engineering**, especially in producing footwear products.

**ankylose:** to fuse. Fused **mandibles** in the tarsioids and anthropoids are ankylosed mandibles.

**ankylosing spondylitis:** pathological condition in which the synovial joints of the axial skeleton and the cartilaginous joints of the vertebral column ossify, caused by an autosomal gene located on chromosome 6p. Certain HLA haplotypes predispose individuals to this condition, e.g. B27.

**ankylosis:** pathological condition in which joints stiffen owing to the formation of scar tissue through disease, injury, or surgical procedure; the affected joint may eventually ossify. Adjective: ankylosed.

**anlage:** 1. any embryonic structure; **primordium**. 2. **predisposition** (1).

*Annals of Human Biology*: journal founded in 1954 as a venue for growth and development, and acclimation and adaptation research. Also well known for classic publications in population biology and population physiology.

**annidation:** adaptation of an inferior mutant **genotype** that is able to occupy an existing **niche** not available to the parent, and that by means of the **mutation** has a high **fitness** in the new environment. One of the **mechanisms of evolution**.

*anno Domini*: see **AD**.

**annual cycle:** reoccurrence of behavior or physiological functions that follows a twelve-month interval.

*Annual Review of Anthropology* (ARA): yearly series that commenced publication in 1972 and that contains essays on the state of the art in those areas of anthropology of current interest, that reflect the principal ways that anthropologists conceptualize their discipline, and that properly cover the important subfields of the discipline. The ARA has become increasingly important as the volume of literature in each subfield has exceeded manageable limits.

**annular:** ringlike.

**anogenital scent gland: exocrine gland** that opens just inside the anus or on either side of it and usually secretes an odoriferous substance. The secretions of these glands are used for attracting mates, marking territories, and, in some mammals, for defense. Found in many mammals, including some of the **prosimians, tarsiers,** and **platyrrhines.** See **caudal gland** and **scent gland**. Aka anal gland, anal sac, circumanal glands.

‡ **anomaly:** anything that is a departure from the norm or the usual; aberration.

**anonymous DNA segment:** piece of DNA of unknown gene content that has been localized to a chromosome.

**anonymous marker:** segment of cloned DNA of unknown function used as a reference point for DNA mapping.

*Anopheles*: genus of mosquito (family Culicidae) that is a potential **vector** of **malaria**; e.g. *Anopheles gambiae*. At least 54 malaria-carrying species have been identified; only females transmit the agent of malaria, *Plasmodium*.

**anorexia:** lack of, or loss of, appetite.

**anorexia nervosa:** mental condition in which an individual suffers loss of appetite and systematically ingests little food (usually in the presence of adequate resources); characterized by progressive emaciation and **amenorrhea** in females.

**anosmia:** inability to detect by smell certain musk-like sexual odors; any of several autosomal recessive polymorphisms that may be caused by deletions due to unequal crossing-over. There are several modes of anosmia; aka smell blindness.

**ANOVA:** see **analysis of variance**.

‡ **anovulatory:** pertaining to the absence of ovulation.

**ansa coli:** colonic loop; a number of corkscrew-like spirals in the long **colon** of prosimians.

**antagonist:** that which opposes. 1. a chemical substance that blocks the ability of a given **agonist** to bind to its molecular target so as to prevent or reduce a biological response. 2. a muscle whose action opposes the action of another muscle.

**antagonistic pleiotrophy:** state when a gene has a positive effect on fitness when expressed at one time of life, but a negative effect when expressed at another time or developmental stage. See **pleiotrophy**.

**antebrachium:** forearm; that region between the **carpals** and the elbow joint. Adjective: antebrachial.

**antecubital:** pertaining to the region directly in front of the elbow.

**antediluvian:** early nineteenth century term used to label any 'very old' artifact or bone fragment thought to have come from times before the Biblical flood, such as antediluvian man. Cf. **Celtic**.

**ant-dipping:** behavior that involves the use of a stick to obtain insects for food. See **termite stick** and **probe-using behavior**.

**anteflexion:** sharp curve or angle.

**antemolar dentition:** all the teeth forward of (mesial to) the **molars**, i.e. the **incisors, canines** and **premolars**.

**antemortem:** before death; refers to injuries, pathologies, or any other phenomenon on a fossil or skeleton that occurred before that individual died; see **perimortem** and **postmortem**.

**anteneandertal:** term used by some paleoanthropologists to refer to any of a number of fossil hominids found in a European group of sites (**Biache**,

Ehringsdorf, Fontéchevade Cave, La Chaise, Montmaurin, Pontnewydd, Sima de los Huesos at **Atapuerca**, **Steinheim**, and **Swanscombe**) that possess few erectine characteristics, and many of the **synapomorphic** features seen in a more exaggerated manifestation in later European Neandertals. Aka pre-Neandertalers.

**antepenultimate glaciation:** second glaciation of the Pleistocene epoch; see **Mindel glaciation.**

**anterior:** anatomical term of orientation meaning towards the front. In humans anterior is often synonymous with **ventral.** Cf. **posterior.**

**anterior commissure:** fibers that connect the neurons and gyri of one cerebral hemisphere with another located inferior to the septum pellucidum and superior to the thalamus.

**anterior iliac spine:** in hominids, one of two bony projections at the ventral edge of the **ilium** to which superior and inferior muscles are attached.

**anterior inferior iliac spine:** protrusion of the anterior **coxal bone** below the greater sciatic notch and superior to the lesser sciatic notch; it serves as a site of attachment for the straight head of the rectus femoris, a muscle important in erect bipedal locomotion and unsupported erect standing. A well-defined iliac spine indicates development of this muscle and suggests bipedalism.

**anterior pillar:** one of the two vertical columns of bone on either side of the **nasal aperture** in the faces of some **australopithecines**; it apparently developed to offset the large chewing stresses of massive jaws and teeth.

**anterior pituitary:** frontal lobe of the **pituitary gland.** Aka adenohypophysis.

**anterior pituitary hormone:** any polypeptide secreted by the anterior lobe of the **pituitary gland**, including **growth hormone, thyrotropin, prolactin, follicle-stimulating hormone, luteinizing hormone,** and β-lipotropin.

**anterior trunk length:** measured in a standing position, the **suprasternal height** minus the **symphysion height.**

**anterocone:** small cusp on the front of the incisors in some **plesiadapiforms.**

**anteroposterior:** from front to back.

**anthracothere:** member of the family Anthracotheriidae, an extinct group of large, hippo-like ungulates.

**anthropic:** pertaining to humans as animals among other animals in nature, especially before the beginnings of culture.

**anthropic hypothesis:** any proposal that collections of bones, stones, etc., are specifically the result of human activity, rather than due to nonhuman taphonomic processes.

‡ **anthropocentric:** viewing other organisms from the perspective of humans for example, attributing human motivations to animal actions.

**anthropocentric view of nature:** perspective that nature exists for the benefit of humans, who are seen as central, the highest form of life. In this view, other life forms exist to serve humans. See **anthropocentrism.**

**anthropocentrism:** any human-centered theory or point of view.

**Anthropogene:** term used mainly in the Russian literature referring to the last three periods of the **Cenozoic era**, corresponding roughly to the **Pleistocene**, a time when humans appear in the fossil record. Aka Quaternary.

‡ **anthropogenic:** of, relating to, or influenced by, any activity of humans. Noun: anthropogenesis.

**anthropogenic selection:** mode of biological **selection** in which the **agent** of **differential reproduction** or **differential mortality** is human. Called **domestic selection** in Darwin's time in the mid-nineteenth century. The term 'anthropogenic selection' was coined to supplement the older term **relaxed selection.** Relaxed selection was applied to any cultural buffering of **natural selection**, whereas anthropogenic selection is suggested for cases in which **DNA** has undergone 'domestication', i.e. been manipulated to serve human ends. Aka **directed evolution, directed molecular evolution.**

**anthropogenic unit:** time-stratigraphic horizon in an archaeological site that has accumulated as a result of human or hominid cultural activity, rather than to natural sedimentation, etc.; see, for example, **midden.**

‡ **anthropogeny:** scientific study of humankind's origin and development (anthropogenesis), both individual and racial.

**anthropogeography:** study of the relationships between humans and the environment.

‡ **anthropoid:** vernacular for any member of the primate suborder **Anthropoidea**. In Europe, however, this term usually refers to the anthropoid apes, the other members of the Anthropoidea being referred to as simians.

‡ **Anthropoidea Mivart, 1864:** primate suborder that includes all **monkeys** and **hominoids**. See **Haplorhini.** See Appendix 2 for taxonomy, Appendix 3 for species.

**anthropological genetics:** 1. synthesis of anthropology and population genetics in order to study the interactions between culture and **allele frequencies.** 2. Use of genetic techniques to reconstruct the past, including the use of **DNA sequences** to reconstruct likely phylogenetic or genealogical relationships among populations; aka gene genealogy, genetic genealogy. See **mitochondrial DNA** and **Y**

chromosome DNA. 3. The use of archaeological samples, including **ancient DNA**, to achieve these goals. Aka archaeogenetics, archaeological genetics.

**Anthropological Society of London** (ASL): formed in 1863 as a competitor to the older **Ethnological Society of London**, chaired with a singular vision by James Hunt, who felt that ethnology was 'too confined a term {and} no other word than anthropology could embrace the whole science of man'. Two years after Hunt's death in 1869, the two societies met together, and were officially merged by 1884 into the Anthropological Institute of Great Britain and Ireland.

**Anthropological Society of Washington** (ASW): secular institution serving the Washington, DC, area, founded in 1879. Its first journal was *Transactions* (1881–8), which was succeeded by the *American Anthropologist* in 1888.

**anthropologist**: scientist in the field of **anthropology**.

‡ **anthropology**: scientific study of the **culture, biology, evolution**, and **behavior** of humans, their ancestors, and their evolutionary relatives, the nonhuman **primates**. Anthropology is divided into subfields: biological or **physical anthropology** is the life-science branch, whereas cultural anthropology is the social science branch. **Archaeology** and linguistic anthropology are the other two traditional subfields. Exact definitions vary significantly from one learning institution to another; in the Old World the term is generally limited to **physical anthropology**.

‡ **anthropometer**: anthropometric instrument for measuring height of the individual or of body regions such as the limbs or trunk. An anthropometer usually consists of four graduated tubes that are attached to one another. Usually there is a top piece with metal flaps that enables the measurer to obtain a level reading.

**anthropometric**: pertaining to the measurement of the size and proportions of the body and its component parts (**anthropometry**).

**anthropometric landmark**: see **craniometric landmark**.

**anthropometry**: measurement of body features. Adjective: anthropometric. Most commonly used to mean the description of the human body, skull and face, but may include comparison with other species, usually **primates**. Raw measures are often transformed into indices and used to describe and understand **functional anatomy**. See **transformation** and **index**.

**anthropomorph**: apelike animal; this term is used in primate paleontology when it is desirable to avoid taxonomic bias inherent in reference to living ape groups such as **pongid** or **hominid**.

**Anthropomorpha**: defunct term coined by **John Ray** and utilized by **Linnaeus** and his students from 1735 to 1758 to describe the order that contained the human-shaped animals *Homo troglodytes*, *Lucifer aldovandii*, *Satyrus tulpii*, and *Pygmaeus edwardi*, four creatures who were then candidates for variants of humanity. The term was replaces by Primates in 1758.

**anthropomorphism**: interpretation of animal behaviors in terms of human motivation, such as the notion that a mother dog cares for pups because she loves them. Adjective: anthropomorphic.

**anthropopathism**: ascription of human emotions to objects, or to an environment.

**anthropophagy**: see **cannibalism**.

*Anthropopithecus erectus* **Dubois, 1892**: original **binomen** presented by **Dubois** for the **Trinil 2** material, which he first believed to be a variety of chimpanzee. Dubois changed the genus nomen to *Pithecanthropus* in 1894. See *Homo erectus* and G. **Mortillet**.

**anthroposcopy**: 1. archaic term for **anthropometry**. 2. visual examination and reportage by eye of physical traits that cannot be exactly measured, e.g. eye color. See **physiognomy**.

**anthroposociology**: movement in late nineteenth century France, led by LaPouge, that sought to identify traditional French racial history with long-headed **types** of people (**dolichocephalic**); Lapouge greatly influenced the racial thinking of the German O. Ammon and the American economist C. Closson.

**anthropozoonosis**: any disease of humans acquired from other vertebrates that harbor pathogenic organisms, e.g. **trichinosis**, rabies, etc. Cf. **zooanthroponosis, amphixenosis**.

**anthrozoology**: study of the relationships between humans and domesticated and/or feral animals.

**antibiosis**: any association of two organisms whereby one is affected detrimentally.

‡ **antibody** (Ab): an **immunoglobulin** molecule found in blood plasma and other tissues that has a specific amino acid sequence, synthesized by lymphoid series cells in response to the specific **antigen** that induced its synthesis; antibodies are multisubunit **proteins** consisting of several **haptens**.

**antibody-mediated immunity**: see **immune response**.

**antibody, theories of**: see **clonal selection theory, germline theory of antibody diversity, selective theory of antibody diversity**, and **side-chain theory**.

**anticipation**: phenomenon whereby a genetic disorder becomes increasingly severe from one generation to the next; characteristic of triplet repeat expansion disorders.

**anticlinal vertebra**: thoracic vertebra that is transitional between the anterior thoracic vertebrae, which have anterior facing spinous (neural) processes, and the posterior thoracic vertebrae, which are directed **caudally**. Marks the mid-point between the front and rear muscles of the back on a **pronograde** animal such as the jumping primates.

**anticoagulant:** any substance that inhibits or prevents blood coagulation, such as heparin.

‡ **anticodon:** specific sequence of three nucleotides in **transfer RNA** (tRNA) that is complementary to the **codon** in messenger RNA (mRNA) that specifies the amino acid; for example, the anticodon UUU is complementary to the mRNA codon AAA. Cf. the **wobble hypothesis**.

**anticodon loop:** that region of a **tRNA** molecule that contains the **anticodon**, a three-base sequence complementary to a relevant **codon** in mRNA.

**anti-Darwinism:** any proposal that specifically negates **natural selection** or **sexual selection** as a viable mechanism. An anti-Darwinism view need not be anti-evolutional. See **anti-evolutionism**.

**antidiuretic hormone:** see **vasopressin**.

**anti-evolutionism:** any proposal that specifically negates **evolution** as a viable mechanism of long-term organismal change. Adjective: anti-evolutionary. Cf. **anti-Darwinism**.

‡ **antigen:** any of a variety of nonself **proteins** or cell-surface **polysaccharides** that, having gained access to a body's tissues, is capable of inducing a specific **immune response**, i.e. the production of a specific **antibody** or specifically sensitized T-lymphocyte.

**antigen binding site:** region of an antibody molecule that includes the **idiotype**, where foreign antigens bind and composed of the variable regions of the H chain and L chain of the **antibody**. Aka antigen combining site.

**antigen processing:** macrophage's presentation of a foreign antigen on its surface, next to an HLA self antigen; this combination signals the immune system to respond.

**antigen receptor:** receptor on the surface of the cells of the immune system that permits recognition of antigens.

**antigenic drift:** genetic mutation causing a minor change in the outer protein coat of a virus.

**antigenic shift:** genetic mutation causing a major change in the outer protein coat of a virus.

**antigenic site:** portion of a protein that is recognized by the **immune system**, and that causes an immune response. Aka epitope, antigenic determinant.

**antihelix:** inward-curving ridge of skin-covered cartilage that runs parallel to the helix, or outer rim, of the auricle of the ear.

**antihelminthic:** substances, such as **allochemicals** in plants, that have antiparasitic properties. Chimpanzees are known to consume plants with antihelminthic properties.

**antihemophilic globulin:** plasma protein that is deficient in the condition **hemophilia A** and that results in a compromise of the blood clotting mechanism. Aka factor VIII.

**antihistamine:** any chemical that blocks **histamine** action.

*Antillothrix* **MacPhee, Horovitz, Arrendondo, and Jimenez Vasquez, 1995:** Hispaniolan monkey; **monotypic, platyrrhine** genus; *A. bernersis* is the sole species; recently **extinct**. Materials recovered from deposits in the Dominican Republic and Haiti dated to 10–4 kya; known mainly from teeth. Dental formula: 2.1.3.3; diet probably included fruits and seeds. See Appendix 1 for taxonomy.

**antilopine:** member of the tribe Antilopini; small to medium-sized antelopes, including springboks and gazelles.

**antimitotic:** any agent that arrests **mitosis**.

**anti-Müllerian hormone:** see **Müllerian-inhibiting hormone**.

**antimutagenic agent:** any of the materials and techniques that protect cells from the mutation-inducing effects of radiation.

**antiparallel:** describes a head-to-tail arrangement of the two complementary halves of the DNA double helix; 3′ to 5′. See **3′-end** and **5′-end**.

**antiparallel transcription:** production of an opposite-sense nucleotide sequence. See **antisense DNA/RNA**.

**antiquarianism:** study of antiquities, usually by an amateur (an antiquarian) who studies archaeology as a hobby.

**antisense DNA/RNA:** any nucleotide sequence that is complementary to its sense strand. Antisense strands are produced either by antisense genes or by **antiparallel transcription**.

**antisense technology:** technique that stops the expression of a particular gene by binding a section of complementary RNA to **sense RNA** that is active during transcription of the gene.

**antiserum:** blood serum containing agglutinins (**antibodies**) to a particular **antigen**. Plural: antisera. Antisera are used to identify blood types. They are prepared either by inoculating an animal with the antigen in question, which then develops an immune reaction resulting in antibodies which are then harvested, or by harvesting antibodies from animals or people who have had contact with the antigen.

**antisocial factor:** any selection pressure that tends to inhibit or to reverse social evolution.

**antler sleeve:** portion of a **composite tool** fashioned from an antler; Upper Paleolithic **artifact**, dated to less than 18 kya (post-glacial maximum) found in a broad belt across Europe and the western Ukraine; the sleeve served as a mount for flint gouges.

**antler tool:** implement made from a **deciduous** horn of a member of the deer family.

**antrum:** cavity, chamber. Plural: antra. Often used in reference to the sinuses of the **cranium**, but antra are present in other structures as well, such as the lower stomach and the ovarian follicle.

**Anubis baboon:** vernacular for *Papio anubis.*

**anus:** inferior opening of the alimentary canal; end of the digestive tract through which waste products are eliminated. Cf. **mouth.**

**anvil:** any solid block or surface on which blows are struck.

**anvil stone:** rough stone upon which other **lithics**, food (e.g. nuts), or skins are placed and reduced or softened with a stone hammer. The use of a hammerstone to crush a bone on an anvil leaves a distinct fracture signature on the object bone.

**anvil technique:** method of manufacturing a stone tool in which a **core** is swung down forcefully against a large, stationary **anvil stone.**

**Anyathian:** pertaining to a **chopper-chopping tool industry** found in present-day upper Burma that flourished between the second and third glacial periods.

**aorta:** main systemic artery in vertebrates that arises from the left ventricle of the heart.

**Aotinae Poche, 1908: monotypic** subfamily to which *Aotus*, the owl (night, douroucoli) monkeys belong.

**Aotus Illiger, 1811: platyrrhine** genus to which the owl monkeys belong; aka night monkeys, douroucoulis. This genus has recently undergone a systematic revision; as many as ten species recognized in two species groups. Range from Panama through the Amazon to the Chaco of Argentina. Vary in body size from 800 to 1200 g. Not **sexually dimorphic. Arboreal**; found in upper canopy of dense forests; occupy dry shrub in the Chaco. The only **nocturnal** anthropoid. Arboreal **quadrupeds** and leapers. Dental formula: 2.1.3.3/ 2.1.3.3. **Frugivorous** with leaf and insect supplements. **Monogamous.** Solitary individuals give owl-like hoots. See Appendix 2 for taxonomy, Appendix 3 for living species. See *Aotus* **species groups.**

**Aotus species groups:** clusters of *Aotus* species based on the possession of primitive or derived traits. The genus contained two recognized species until a recent revision that has resulted in at least ten species. The gray-necked group is considered to be more primitive and contains animals with a dull **pelage** and yellow underparts; this group is composed of *A. trivirgatus, A. lemurinus, A. brumbacki, A. hershkovitzi,* and *A. vociferans.* The more derived red-necked group is composed of animals that are more brightly colored and includes *A. micronax,*

*A. nigriceps, A. nancymaae, A. infulatus,* and *A. azarai.* There are workers who still think there may not be more than three species. Molecular systematics may elucidate this situation within the next few years.

**apartheid:** in South Africa, segregation of, and discrimination against, people of color, especially Africans.

**Apatemyidae:** Insectivoran family from the **Paleocene** that was formerly proposed as the progenitor of the primate order; apatemyids. These archaic mammals were gnawers that possessed traits that some workers think were convergent with the modern **aye-aye** and some of the marsupial phalangers.

**apatite:** phosphate crystal containing fluorine, found in bone tissue and tooth enamel. See **hydroxyapatite.**

‡ **ape:** nonhuman member of the **Hominoidea** characterized by a broad sternum that stabilizes the thoracic cage and dorsal scapulae that increase the range of shoulder motion, permitting climbing by **suspensory locomotion,** and by the absence of a tail. See the **extant** ape genera *Hylobates, Pongo, Gorilla, Pan,* and *Homo.*

**'ape-man':** vernacular for any **fossil** of a pre-human **hominid** such as a **Neandertal** or an **australopithecine.** Aka affennmensch.

**apelike:** resembling an ape; possessing qualities more like those of a pongid than like those of either a hominid or a monkey.

**aperture:** gap, open space, or hole. In **osteology,** the orbit is called the **orbital aperture;** the mouth, the oral aperture; and the nose, the nasal aperture.

**apex:** 1. tip or extremity; e.g. apex of a tooth root. 2. (ap) craniometric landmark; most superior point of the cranium opposite the **porion;** a line from the apex to the porion is at 90° to the **Frankfort Horizontal.** See Appendix 7 for an illustration of craniometric landmarks.

**apex carnivore:** meat-eater that is at the top of the food pyramid, e.g. **Neandertals.**

**Apgar score:** standard that assesses the physical state of a **neonate.**

**aphasia:** speech and/or language disorder caused by damage to specific language areas of the brain, and not due to mental retardation nor muscular weakness. See **Wernicke's area** and **motor speech area.**

**apical:** toward the apex or tip of a conical or pointed structure such as a tooth root; closer to the apex relative to some reference point.

**apical abscess cavity:** cavity formed in the bony tissue associated with a **dental alveolus** due to erosion of tissue by necrotic liquefaction; this cavity forms at the tip of the dental root.

**apical crushing activity:** 1. mastication of food primarily on the top of a tooth. 2. the use of canines in a crushing, as opposed to a shearing, role; often said of the 'premolarized' canines of **Paranthropus**.

**apical foramen:** opening in the proximal end of a **root canal** through which blood vessels and nerves pass to enter the **pulp cavity** of a tooth.

**apical wear:** any attrition from the apex of a tooth.

**Apidima Cave:** an archaeological cave site found in 1978 in South Peloponnese, Greece, dating to *c.* 300–100 kya (middle to upper Pleistocene), and containing some 30,000 artifacts in two layers: a middle paleolithic with hominid remains from two individuals (Apidima 1 and Apidima 2) assigned to *Homo neanderthalensis* (other workers favor *H. heidelbergensis*); and an upper assemblage dated to 30–20 kya and that contains the remains of 4–6 **AMHs**. Aka Taenarius man.

‡ *Apidium* **Osborn, 1908:** well-known genus of **fossil anthropoid** that belongs to the infraorder **Parapithecoidea**, family **Parapithecidae**, from the **Oligocene** of the **Fayum Depression**, Egypt. Contains two species. Anthropoid traits include fused mandibular and frontal bones and relatively small enclosed orbits. This last trait suggests **diurnal** activity. Dental formula: 2.1.3.3; small incisors and low, rounded cusps on molars suggest **frugivory,** but the thick enamel on the molars point to seeds as part of diet. *Apidium* had **sexually dimorphic** projecting canines of intermediate size, suggesting **polygynous** social groups (based on similar data from living mammals). Distally, the tibia and fibula of the lower leg were joined by a fibrous connection for about 40% of the length; this condition is unusual among extant higher primates and suggests a **leaping adaptation,** although more in the way that **New World monkeys** leap. *Apidium* has a relatively long hindlimb compared to the forelimb. See Appendix 1 for taxonomy.

*Apidium moustafai* **Simons, 1962:** smaller and geologically older of the two species of fossil *Apidium*. Known principally from jaws and teeth. Body mass estimate around 850 g. Some researchers consider *A. moustafai* to be the ancestor of *Apidium phiomense*.

*Apidium phiomense* **Osborn, 1908:** larger and geologically younger of the two species of *Apidium*. Known from a large number of specimens, mostly postcranial. Body mass estimated at 1.3 kg. Some researchers consider *A. phiomense* to be the descendant of *Apidium moustafai*.

**aplasia:** complete or partial failure of a tissue or an organ to develop.

**apnea:** cessation of respiration due to temporary elimination of carbon dioxide from the blood. See **SIDS**.

‡ **apocrine sweat gland:** type of sweat gland that is associated with a hair follicle, found in greatest concentrations in the axilla, groin, and around the nipples. Apocrine glands become active at puberty; they respond during emotional stress or sexual arousal. Their secretions are sebaceous, i.e. rich in **lipids** and **proteins** and other parts of the secreting cells. Cf. **eccrine sweat gland**.

**apolipoprotein:** protein section of a **lipoprotein**.

**apomorph:** 1. structural feature found in an evolving lineage that is distinct from that of the ancestral line. Adjective: apomorphic, apomorphous, aka derived. See **derived trait** and **synapomorphy**. 2. any new morphological, chromosomal or molecular feature that has appeared in an evolving lineage that may indicate a **node** of divergence, or branch; see **cladogenesis**.

**aponeurosis:** fibrous sheetlike or flat tendon that attaches a muscle to other structures. Plural: aponeuroses.

**apophysis:** projection formed directly on an anatomical structure.

**apoptosis:** death of cells or cell lines that is normal in **growth, development,** and **aging**. Aka programmed cell death.

**apoptosis theory of aging:** intracellular, systemic model of aging in which the major premise is that either cellular mechanisms that induce or carry out **apoptosis** become less efficient with the age of an organism, or gene-based damage to the mechanism results in an inappropriate increase in apoptosis.

**apostatic:** describes a phenotype that differs greatly from the norm of a species. This excludes such individuals from the search image of predators.

*a posteriori* (Latin): from the one behind; an argument from effect to cause, usually based upon actual observation or experimental data; **induction**. Cf. *a priori*.

**appeasement:** social **behavior** in which an animal 'surrenders' to another of its species in such a way as to avoid aggression from the **conspecific**. In some monkeys this may take the form of presenting the rump to the dominant animal. Appeasement serves to prevent any further injury to the submissive animal as well as helping to maintain the **dominance hierarchy** of the **society**.

**appendage:** any part, secondary in size and function, attached to a larger structure. Adjective: appendicular. For example, the **appendix** is an appendage of the **cecum**, and the hand is an appendage of the arm.

**appended genetic program:** matrix of gene activities including structural, control, and regulatory genes that can be expanded, reduced or changed without affecting the **backbone genetic program**.

‡ **appendicular skeleton:** bones of the limbs and the limb girdles that anchor the limbs to the **axial skeleton**.

**appendix, vermiform:** see **vermiform appendix**.

**apperception:** comprehension of new information based on previous knowledge and experience.

**applied anthropology:** use of anthropology outside the university to provide information to indigenous peoples, influence policy, and/or intervene directly in human affairs; some now prefer the label practising anthropology. See **medical anthropology, demography,** and **diet**.

**applied archaeology:** site conservation archaeology.

**applied physical anthropology:** field that utilizes techniques and concepts of physical anthropology in a non-academic setting. Areas where applied physical anthropology is used include clinical **anthropometry**, the clothing industry, the military, health clubs, biotechnology, and genetic counseling.

**appositional growth: bone remodeling** process in which a bone increases in width, and hence size, owing to **osteoblasts** depositing new matrix on the superficial surface of the bone and **osteoclasts** resorbing bone matrix from the inner surface of the bone.

*a priori* (Latin): from the one before; an argument from cause to effect, i.e. validity is independent of observation. Any argument from a general law to a particular instance. Reasoning that deduces consequences from axioms presumed to be true without verification by personal experience; **deduction**. Cf. *a posteriori*.

*a priori* **method:** method of compensation in pooled familial genetic data, based on the likelihood that more than 1/4 of the children of heterozygous parents will exhibit a homozygous trait when the familial **propositi** are homozygous offspring.

**aptitude for culture:** potential for adaptation to the natural environment by learning. See **protoculture, primate culture,** and **culture**.

**aquatic theory of human evolution:** controversial idea that humans evolved through a semi-aquatic phase; invoked to explain bipedalism, hairlessness, body fat distribution, genital anatomy, and the 'instinct' for swimming exhibited at birth. Espoused by M. Westenhöfer in 1912, later promoted by A. C. Hardy and most recently by Welsh screenwriter Elaine Morgan; viewed with skepticism among evolutionary biologists. Aka aquatic ape hypothesis, river ape hypothesis.

**Ar/Ar:** see **argon–argon dating**.

**ARA:** see **Aramis**.

**ARA-VP:** abbreviation for **Aramis** Vertebrate Paleontology, Ethiopia.

**arachidonic acid** (AA): one of the long-chain polyunsaturated **essential fatty acids** required for growth of the liver, adrenal glands, and brain structures; sources are predominantly in the marine food chain. Researchers have suggested that arachidonic acid and **docosahexaenoic acid** were substances critical for increased encephalization in **hominid** lineages. Aka omega-6 fatty acid.

**arachnodactyly:** condition in which the hands and fingers are abnormally long and thin. One of the signs of **Marfan syndrome**. Aka spider fingers.

**arachnoid pits:** see **Pacchionian depressions**.

**Aragai:** see **Rondinin**.

**Arago:** archaeological site found in 1964–71 in the Verdouble Valley near Tautavel village, Pyrénées-Orientales, France, dated to >400 kya (**Riss** or **Mindel glaciation**?). Contains artifacts assigned to the **Tayacian** and Middle **Acheulean**, and 60 specimens of hominid remains from at least seven individuals, including a 1160 cm³ skull (which may be a composite of two individuals: XXI and XLVII). Assigned to the earlier archaic group *Homo cf. erectus*. Aka La Caune de l'Arago, Tautavel man.

**aragonite:** with **calcite**, one of the two common carbonates of calcareous (chalky) skeletons; aragonite disappears almost completely from older fossils, whereas calcite may be replaced by silica or pyrite, a process known as **permineralization**.

**Arambourg, Camile** (1885–1969): Algerian-born French agronomist and vertebrate paleontologist. He described several Miocene vertebrates in Northern Africa, and Plio-Pleistocene hominid remains from **Ternifine**, Algeria (1954); worked in the Omo region in Ethiopia (1932–4), and later described the first geological sequence for the Lower **Omo Valley** (1967–9).

**Aramis** (ARA): archaeological sites found in 1992 and 1993 in the **Middle Awash** River valley region near **Hadar**, Ethiopia, dated to just less than 4.4 mya. The sites (1, 6 and 7) contain *Canthium* seeds and fossil **colobines**, suggesting the paleoenvironment was possibly a closed, densely wooded habitat on a broad alluvial plain, inhabited by kudus and arboreal monkeys. The site also yielded fragmentary hominid remains of from 17–40 individuals (e.g. **ARA-VP 6/1**; see box), including those attributed to *Ardipithecus (*Cf. *Australopithecus) ramidus*.

---

**Some fossil specimens from Aramis**

ARA-VP 6/1: field number for ten teeth presumed to be from one individual, attributed to *Ardipithecus (*cf. *Australopithecus) ramidus*.

ARA-VP 7/2: field number for a humerus, radius and ulna presumed to be from one individual, attributed to *Ardipithecus (*cf. *Australopithecus) ramidus*.

*Arapahovius gazini* **Savage and Waters, 1978:** genus of tarsiiform primate from the early Eocene of North America, belonging to the omomyid subfamily **Anaptomorphinae**; two species; known from tibia, calcaneum, astragalus, cuboid, and navicular bones. Estimated body mass ranges from 100 to 300 g. See Appendix 1 for taxonomy.

**Arashiyama:** research site located in Japan where long-term field studies of Japanese macaques (*Macaca fuscata*) have been conducted for decades. Primatologists who have conducted field research at this site include: K. **Imanishi**, J. Itani, S. Kawamura, and Y. Takahata.

**Arashiyama West:** Primate Research Station established at LaMoca, Tx (USA) in 1972; contains a troop of Japanese macaques (*Macaca fuscata*) studied previously by S. Kawamura and others for 18 years in Japan and then relocated to the USA. Primatologists who have conducted field research at this site include: C. Bramblett, L. M. Fedigan, and L. Wolf.

**Arber's law:** rule that any structure disappearing from a lineage during the course of evolution will never be regained by the descendants of that phylum; Aka irreversibility rule. Cf. **Dollo's law.**

**arbitrary:** as defined by G. G. **Simpson**, describes the inclusion of organisms within the same taxon even though there are internal traits not shared by all members of the same taxon; or, the exclusion of organisms from a taxon even though these organisms share external traits with the other members of the taxon.

**arbitrary level:** in archaeology, a basic vertical subdivision of a square; used only when 'natural' stratification is not obvious.

‡ **arboreal:** living in trees; pertaining to life in the trees.

**arboreal grasper hypothesis:** model of **primate origins** proposed by Bloch and Boyer in which the **Carpolestidae** are linked to or included in the Order **Primates** because they possessed long limbs and an opposable **hallux** with a nail.

**arboreal quadrumanualism:** see **quadrumanualism.**

**arboreal quadrupedalism:** walking on the horizontal surface of tree branches on all four limbs. Arboreal quadrupedal primates differ from terrestrial quadrupedal primates by having shorter limbs, by walking with flexed limbs, by having more grasping ability in the fore and hind paws, and by having longer tails used to balance on an uneven surface.

‡ **arboreal theory of primate evolution:** proposal, originally by T. H. **Huxley** but popularly associated with G. E. **Smith** and F. W. **Jones**, that many primitive features of primate anatomy such as **stereoscopic vision** and **prehensile hands** and feet first evolved as a suite of adaptations to life in the trees.

Cf. **pollinator hypothesis** and **visual predation model.**

**arc:** bowed shape; curved line or structure.

**ARC:** see **AIDS-Related Complex.**

**arcade:** curve or arch in a structural feature; for example, the human tooth row is also referred to as the **dental arcade.**

**Arcadianism:** tenet that humans are an integral part of nature and should have an innate reverence for it because of its beneficence.

**arch:** in anatomy, any vaulted or bowlike structure.

**Archaea:** kind of cell recently assigned its own **Domain**; the Archaea have features in common with **prokaryotes** but differ from them significantly in 16S RNA sequences and membrane-bound lipid molecules. Previously known as Archaebacteria, they include many of the extreme halophilic and hyperthermophilic organisms known to science. The Archaea are expected to have a significant impact on **biotechnology**. Cf. **Bacteria** and **Eukarya.**

**archaeofauna:** assemblage of animal remains recovered from a single archaeological context.

**archaeogenetics:** see **anthropological genetics.**

*Archaeoindris* **Standing, 1908:** monotypic genus of extinct **subfossil Malagasy prosimians** belonging to the **Palaeopropithecidae**; *A. fontoynonti* known only from central Madagascar in deposits dated at 8 kya (suggesting its extinction was not due to human intervention). Largest of the subfossil lemurs, weighing between 160 and 200 kg, the size of an adult male gorilla. Little known about postcrania, but it is probable that *Archaeoindris* was terrestrial; probably diurnal. Dental formula: 2.1.2.3/1.1.2.3; diet presumed to be **folivory**. See Appendix 2 for taxonomy, Appendix 3 for living species.

*Archaeolemur* **Filhol, 1895:** genus of extinct **subfossil Malagasy prosimians** belonging to the **Archaeolemuridae**; two species, *A. majori* and *A. edwardsi*. Recovered from sites throughout Madagascar dating between 2850 and 1000 BP. Terrestrial; diurnal; quadrupedal. Body mass around 22 kg. Dental formula: 2.1.3.3/1.1.3.3; molars are **bilophodont**, the first premolar is **caniniform**, and the premolars form a shearing edge; incisors and canines reduced, face shortened; diet unknown, but dentition is suggestive of **granivory** with fruit supplements. See Appendix 2 for taxonomy, Appendix 3 for living species.

**Archaeolemuridae Major, 1896:** family of **subfossil Malagasy prosimians** that are closely allied to the **Indriidae**. Some authorities give this group subfamily status within the Indriidae; two genera. They appear to have become extinct about 1 kya, possibly due to human activities. These prosimians were larger than any living indriids, although not the largest of the subfossil Malagasy lemurs, and are considered the ecological equivalent of baboons, hence the common name baboon lemurs. They have dental and skeletal features convergent with Old World monkeys. See Appendix 1 for taxonomy. See *Archaeolemur* and *Hadropithecus*.

**Archaeolemurinae:** subfamily of two genera within the **prosimian** family **Indriidae**. Many workers recognize these genera of **subfossil Malagasy prosimians** as a separate family, **Archaeolemuridae**.

**Archaeolithic:** pertaining to the **Mesolithic – Upper Paleolithic** of France.

**archaeological context:** artifacts, features and residues found in the archaeological record.

**archaeological genetics:** see **anthropological genetics**.

**archaeological period:** any of several horizons or stages in a cultural sequence, derived from prehistoric evidence.

**archaeological site:** any concentration of **artifacts**, **features**, or **ecofacts** manufactured or modified by humans or their ancestors.

**archaeological survey:** exploration, sampling, and mapping of a potential site.

‡ **archaeology:** subfield of **anthropology** that focuses on past cultural variation in prehistoric and some historic populations through an analysis of material remains; literally, the 'science of the old'. Historically, in the Old World, the term 'archaeology' was generally restricted to **civilizations** that had writing, and the term '**prehistory**' was applied to cultures that antedated these **civilizations** or to so-called 'precontact' **cultures**. American archaeologists use the term much more loosely; sometimes spelled *archeology* in the USA, especially when referring to **processual archaeology**.

**archaeomagnetism:** see **paleomagnetism**.

**archaeozoology:** discipline that studies the animal collections recovered from archeological sites in order to deduce environmental features of the site as well as to provide indications of which animals were living with or around the human archeological population. Also referred to as zooarchaeology. See **faunal analysis**.

**archaic:** 1. marked by the characteristics of an earlier period; antiquated. 2. in linguistics, describes any term used rarely in present-day language. 3. in paleontology, refers to any specimen that possesses many traits of a **type specimen**, but a few traits found in an earlier species or specimen, as well.

‡ **archaic form:** fossil that is thought to have both primitive and derived features; not fully either one form or another, but rather exhibiting traits from two different species, such as *Homo erectus*/*H. sapiens* or Neandertal/modern. The term tends to be used by researchers who prefer the **monophyletic hypothesis** of modern **human origins**, as opposed to the use of **transitional forms**. See **polyphyletic hypothesis**.

‡ **archaic *Homo sapiens*:** earliest fossil forms of *Homo sapiens*, possibly including, but not limited to, **Neandertals** that postdate *Homo erectus*, but antedate **AMHs**. Dates for archaics range from about 400 kya to 32 kya. Archaics possessed a nearly human-sized brain but retained certain primitive features of the skull such as a lower cranial height and a mosaic of other **primitive** and **derived** features. Commonly divided into an **earlier archaic group** and **later archaic group**.

**archaic primate:** term previously used to refer to the **Plesiadapiformes**, considered an infraorder of the primates; currently, the plesiadapiforms are placed in a separate order and are now more commonly referred to as archaic mammals. Cf. **higher primate**.

**archanthropic:** pertaining to a **paleoanthropic** or **neanthropic** hominid.

*Archanthropinae* **Broom, 1950:** defunct subfamily erected by R. **Broom** to include specimens from **Makapansgat** then attributed to the species *Australopithecus prometheus*.

**archean apex chert:** rocks in Western Australia dated to 3.465 bya, containing fossil filamentous microbes, already cellular, and thus thought to be descended from a long line of previously evolved organisms.

**Archean Era:** geologic time interval that spans the first 2.1 bya since the earth was completed, i.e. from 4.6 to 2.5 bya. Aka Archean Eon.

**archepallium:** area located dorsally and medially on the reptilian cerebral cortex. The older, original part of the cortex; sometimes divided further into a paleocortex and archicortex. In mammals this area is greatly reduced and becomes synonymous with the **hippocampus**. It serves as a relay center between the olfactory bulbs and olfactory lobe. One of G. Elliot **Smith's** tripartite divisions of the **pallium**, now called the allocortex. Aka archipallium. Cf. **mesopallium** and **neopallium**.

**archetype:** nineteenth century concept promoted by Richard Owen and others in which members of each species were visualized as varying slightly about a Platonic ideal type, or morphotype, now generally discounted.

**archipallium:** see **archepallium**.

**Archonta McKenna, 1975:** grandorder (some refer to it as a **cohort**) that includes the mammalian orders **Primates, Chiroptera, Dermoptera**, and **Scandentia**. These Orders are considered to be derived from a common mammalian ancestor that diversified during the **Paleocene**. Adjective: Archontan.

*Arcius* **Godinot, 1984:** archaic mammal from the early Eocene of Europe belonging to the **Plesiadapiformes** family **Paromomyidae**; three species recognized. Small-bodied forms with estimated body mass around 80 g. See Appendix 1 for taxonomy.

**Arctic Inuit:** foragers or hunter-gatherers in modern-day Canada who have survived with a subsistence lifestyle in small-scale societies into the twenty-first century. The word literally means 'the people', and is the Inuit name for themselves. NonInuit outsiders previously used the term Eskimo.

**Arctic Mongol:** Mongoloid subgroup found in northeast Asia and the Arctic.

**Arctic Ocean spillover model:** theory that the **mass extinction** events at the Cretaceous–Tertiary (K/T) boundary occurred about 65 mya because of a chain of ecological events triggered by the passage of colder, less salty water from the Arctic out into the North Atlantic; one of but several competing models proposed to explain K/T extinctions.

**Arctic period:** earliest stage of the **Blytt–Sernander classification**, dated to about 14–10 kya, characterized by tundra vegetation and by cold, late-glacial conditions.

*Arctocebus* **Gray, 1863:** monotypic **prosimian** genus to which the angwantibo (*A. calabarensis*, the golden potto) belongs; found in west central Africa; body mass around 300 g; **nocturnal; arboreal;** mostly insectivorous; slow methodical climbers; **noyau.** The second digit is reduced and the **pollex** is 180° from digit 3, providing for a powerful vice-like grip; circulatory adaptations in the limbs provide an ample oxygen supply that prevents lactic acid build-up. See Appendix 2 for taxonomy and Appendix 3 for species.

*Arctodontomys:* archaic mammal from the early Eocene of the Rocky Mountain region of North America belonging to the **plesiadapiform** family **Microsyopidae**; consists of three species; some authorities assign these species to the order Insectivora. Estimated body mass for these species ranges from 250 to 500 g. See Appendix 1 for taxonomy.

**arcuate fascicularis:** fiber tract that connects the **motor speech area** directly to **Wernicke's area.**

**arcuate line:** ridge of bone on the auricular surface of the **coxal bone** that, with the sacral promontory helps to form the pelvic brim. See **pelvic inlet.**

**arcuate nucleus:** small mass located between the **hypothalamus** and **pituitary gland** consisting of gray matter, and that regulates the release of reproductive hormones secreted from the pituitary.

**arcuate sulcus:** transverse cleft in the frontal lobes of **higher primates**; it separates the motor areas from the prefrontal association areas.

**Arcy-Renne:** archaeological site found in north central France, dated to about 34 kya, and that contains **Châtelperronian** artifacts and hominid remains including a few teeth assigned initially to *Homo neanderthalensis*. Aka Grotte du Renne ('reindeer cave'); one of the **Arcy-sur-Cure** cave complex sites in the Paris basin.

**Arcy-sur-Cure:** archaeological site found in Burgundy, north central France, dated to about 36 kya, and that contains **Châtelperronian** artifacts including decorated bone objects and body ornaments. Evidence of a campsite and hut construction. The ornament-containing stratum overlies a deeper and clearly **Mousterian** horizon that dates to 45 kya. The hominid remains include specimens originally attributed to *Homo neanderthalensis*; conflicting recent analyses of the inner ear suggest that the remains may be *Homo sapiens*. Aka **Grande Grotte**; one of a group of caves that includes **Arcy-Renne.**

*Ardipithecus kadabba* **Haile-Selassie, Suwa, and White, 2004:** provisional species of fossil **hominid** dating from 5.8–5.6 mya. Six specimens were recovered in 2002 from **Asa Koma Locality 3**, in the Middle Awash region of Ethiopia; the holotype is ASK- VP-3, and consists of six isolated teeth. *A. kadabba* has a **canine–third premolar honing complex** that approximates that of extant and fossil apes, and is thereby distinct from *A. ramidus*. Specimens described in 1961 from *Ardipithecus ramidus kadabba* are now referred to this new species. *A. kadabba* may be sufficiently similar to *Orrorin tugenensis* and *Sahelanthropus tchadensis* to warrant the latter's collapse into a single genus, *Ardipithecus*.

‡ *Ardipithecus ramidus {ramidus}* **White, Suwa and Asfaw, 1994:** provisional species of fossil **hominid** dating from 4.4 mya. Over 40 specimens representing at least 17 individuals were recovered from **Aramis**, Ethiopia, in 1992–3; an undescribed specimen is said to be 40% complete. More specimens continue to be found. *A. ramidus* is very primitive, with large canines, **sectorial premolars**, and thinly enameled molars. Cranial capacity is presumed to be very small. Nevertheless, *A. ramidus* has a number of anatomical features (including pelvic morphology) that indicate **bipedalism**. Some researchers think that *Ardipithecus* may be the stem species for all later hominids. The validity of the nomen *Ardipithecus* is currently under review and some workers place these specimens in the taxon *Australopithecus ramidus*. Since the 2001 finds at **Alaya**, however, these younger specimens are viewed by some as subspecific material (*Ardipithecus ramidus ramidus*), and congeners to the older *Ardipithecus ramidus kadabba*.

**Ardrey, Robert** (1908–80): author and screenwriter; known for his interpretation of behavior and the fossil record in works such as *African Genesis* (1961) that promulgate Dart's **'killer ape' hypothesis**.

**area cladogram:** branching diagram (**phylogeny**) for a set or **species** (or other taxa) showing the geographic areas they occupy. According to the **vicariance model**, the branching diagram represents the history of range splits in the ancestry of the taxa, probably driven by geological processes such as **plate tectonics**.

**area subcallosa:** see **motor speech area**.

**arena:** see **lek**.

**areola:** 1. portion of the eye iris that surrounds the pupil. 2. pigmented circular area that surrounds a nipple, pustule, or vesicle; see **mammary areola**. 3. space or pore in a tissue. 4. decorative tile or earthenware. Plural: areolae.

**arete:** 1. archaic (Greek) term for human excellence or perfection. 2. ridge between the flaked surfaces of a flint artifact.

**Argentine hemorrhagic fever** (AHF): a hemorrhagic fever caused by the Junin **RNA virus** and transmitted by contact with the excreta of vesper mice (*Calomys musculinus* or *C. laucha*). The virus is deposited into maize farmers' homes in urine when the rodents' natural grassland habitat is cleared and maize is planted. AHF is a significant disease in South America. Clearing of the pampas for the exclusive use of maize planting has expanded the rodents' range. The use of herbicides drastically reduced the natural weeds, and this in turn reduced the local snake populations and favored rodent overpopulation.

**arginine** (Arg): an essential **amino acid**; one of the twenty building blocks of **proteins**. Arginine is derived from the digestion or hydrolysis of protein.

**argon:** colorless, odorless, gaseous element that constitutes about 1% of the earth's atmosphere. Relative atomic mass 39.6.

**argon–argon dating** (Ar/Ar): a **chronometric dating** method based on the half-life of radioactive argon that can be used with very small samples, and is more accurate than **potassium–argon dating**.

**argument from design:** component of **natural theology** which stresses that animal adaptations are perfect for their environments and that these adaptations are evidence for design by a special creator. Aka **Grand design; Paley's watchmaker argument**.

**aristogenes:** good or purposeful genes; see **eugenics**.

**Aristotle** (384–322 BC): scientist, philosopher, and tutor to Alexander the Great who financed a Great Zoological Expedition that provided many **taxa** for study. Aristotle provided the first systematic scheme of nature, with humans at the top of a crude 500-species *Scala Naturae*, i.e. a teleological scheme constructed upon the **phenetic principle** of classification. His scheme was refined into a utilitarian medieval product that was developed by Leibniz into the **Great Chain of Being** in the seventeenth century. Aristotle distinguished between the individual, the species, and the genus (although he meant by genus what modern taxonomists mean by **class**, i.e. birds vs. fishes). He supported the idea of **geocentricity**. He described the 'barbary ape' (*Macaca sylvanus*), not as a **hominoid**, but as a monkey. He commented on Aethiopian–white matings, noting that on continued mixing the descendents were no longer **Aethiopian**.

**Arlington Springs:** archaeological site found about 1960 in Arlington Canyon on Santa Rosa Island near Santa Barbara, CA (USA), dated to 13–10.9 kya; contains hominid remains including two femora of a Paleo-Indian female assigned to *Homo sapiens*.

**arm circumference: anthropometric** measurement; distance around the upper arm as measured with a tape measure placed at the mid-point between the **acromion process** of the scapula and the **olecranon process** of the ulna; the tape is passed horizontally around the arm. Used to help determine protein mass and energy stores in adults.

**arm length:** with the arm outstretched, the distance between the longest finger tip and the **acromial point**.

**arm span: anthropometric** measurement; distance between the tips of the third (middle) finger of the left hand and the tip of the third finger of the right hand when both arms are outstretched laterally and maximally at the level of the shoulders. Aka fathom.

**Armelagos, George J.** (1922–): US biomedical anthropologist at Massachusetts (Amherst) and Emory Universities. Interests include skeletal biology, paleopathology, demography and epidemiology; president, AAPA (1987–9). Author of *Bibliography of Human Paleopathology* (1971). Co-author (with Mark N. Cohen) of *Paleopathology and the Origins of Agriculture* (1984); co-author (with A. C. Swedlund) of *Demographic Anthropology* (1976); co-editor (with Swedlund) of *Disease in Populations in Transition* (1990).

**Armenoid:** archaic racial designation or **ethnym** for Armenians (West Asian Highlanders). Armenoids were characterized by hairy bodies and **dolichocephaly**. Another characteristic was a flattened **occipital bone**; later it was recognized that this characteristic was due to bone modeling from cradle boards.

**arrested development:** ethnocentric idea associated with nineteenth century concepts of unilineal evolution, which attempted to explain cultural diversity, i.e. 'lower' cultural stages (hunting and gathering), as either environmental poverty or an inherent racial inferiority which inhibited any further 'advancement' of people possessing that cultural state.

**Arsuaga, Juan Luis** (1959–): Spanish paleontolologist at Complutense University in Madrid and co-director since 1991 of excavations at Sierra de **Atapuerca**. Arsuaga collaborates at numerous sites, including **Sima de los Huesos, Gran Dolina**, and the **Abrigo do Lagar Velho rockshelter**. Winner of the Premio Principe de Asturias prize (1997). Author of *The Neanderthal's Necklace* (2001).

**art:** aesthetic embellishment of objects, dwellings, and/or the human body. Art is of significance to the study of human prehistory because embellishment seems to be a feature primarily of **AMHs** (see the **Aurignacian**), although some researchers maintain that the **Neanderthals** were capable of art (see the **Châtelperronian**). Cf. **cave art.**

**artefact:** see **artifact.**

**arteriole:** small vessel that carries blood from an artery to the the capillary network. Cf. **venule.**

**arteriosclerosis:** hardening of the arteries; a cerebrovascular disease in which the walls of blood vessels become fragile and susceptible to aneurysm or rupture.

**artery:** blood vessel that conducts blood away from the heart. Arterial blood is generally oxygenated, but not in all cases (e.g. pulmonary artery). Cf. **vein.**

**arthrology:** study of joints.

**articular:** pertaining to a joint (or **articulation**).

**articular capsule:** double-layered sac of tough fibrous tissue attached to the ends of bones that form a joint.

**articular cartilage:** thin layer of **hyaline cartilage** that covers the articular surfaces of bones in a **synovial joint**; helps resist wear and reduces friction when there is movement at the joint.

**articular modification:** changes in joints as a result of pathological conditions.

**articular process:** structure with an articulating surface found on vertebrae; there are superior and inferior articular processes and they join a vertebra with other vertebrae that are immediately above and below.

**articular surface:** pertaining to the smooth surface of a joint (or **articulation**).

**articulate:** 1. to connect or join (in reference to the connection between two bones). 2. to enunciate speech clearly and distinctly.

**articulation:** 1. area where two or more bones join or contact one another; a joint. Articulations are classified either by tissue type (see **fibrous joint, cartilaginous joint, synovial joint**) or by degree of motion (see **amphiarthrotic joint, diarthrotic joint, synarthrotic joint**). 2. in dentistry, the contact relationship of the **occlusal surfaces** of the teeth while in action.

**articulator:** organ, especially a vocal organ, that can be moved and that can assume a number of positions.

‡ **artifact:** human-made object; the preserved material remains and evidence of human or hominid cultural behavior. Owing to **differential preservation**, the very oldest known artifacts are made of stone. Cf. **life history artifact.** Also spelled artefact.

**artifact, sociotechnic:** tool used primarily in the social subsystem.

**artifact, technomic:** tool used primarily to cope with the physical environment, with variability explained largely in environmental or ecological terms.

**artificial classification:** any **classification** system in which the members of a group resemble each other in the defining characters only, and show no similarity in nondefining characters, such as the classification of all two-eyed organisms into a single taxon. See **folk taxonomy.**

**artificial deformation:** see **cranial deformation** and **dental mutilation.**

**artificial insemination:** assisted reproductive technology in which sperm is introduced into a woman's reproductive tract near the cervix; this takes place without sexual intercourse. This technique is also used with domestic and zoo animals. Cf. *in vitro* **fertilization.**

**artificial manipulation:** in behavioral studies, a situation in which the researcher takes control of the variables and manipulates them in the laboratory or field. In this type of study every effort is made to model nature. An example is the placement of a mechanical leopard near chimpanzees to see their response.

**artificial selection:** breeding controlled by humans to alter the genetic characteristics of a domestic **population** based on the perceived value of those inherited **characters.** The current forms of most domesticated plant and animal species are the result of centuries of artificial selection. Experiments using this mechanism are one method of studying and understanding the evolutionary process. See **Darwin's** view of **domestic selection;** also **sexual selection, assortative mating, anthropogenic selection, 'relaxed' selection,** and **directed evolution.**

**artificial selection experiment:** trial or series of trials in which an experimenter permits individuals with certain genotypes or phenotypes to reproduce but not others. Such experiments can be used to estimate the **heritability** of a trait if subpopulations exhibit trait divergence in response to selection.

‡ **Artiodactyla:** order that contains the even-toed hoofed mammals; this order contains 194 species and includes swine, camels, deer and cattle. Artiodactyls are important to hominid evolution because they became important food sources; after **domestication,** many varieties were produced within each of several species as humans learned to manipulate the

heritability of desired traits. Darwin called this process **domestic selection**. Cf. **Perissodactyla**.

**Aryan: ethonym** pertaining to ancient Indo-Iranian peoples, a group of linguistically related tribes who invaded present-day India *c*. 1.8–1.5 kya. This label later came to mean Indo-Europeans in general, and still later was transformed and associated with **Aryanism**.

**Aryan migration hypothesis:** proposal by A. A. **Retzius** that early Europeans were **brachycephalic**, and that a **dolichocephalic** people, the **Aryans**, had invaded Europe at a later date, thus not all Indo–Europeans were descended directly from Aryans.

**Aryan superiority myth:** idea that **Aryans** were the highest breed of humans and that other human stocks were somehow degraded or unhealthy. Because the term 'Aryan' itself refers to a morphologically heterogenous group of tribes that had in common a language group, the later attempt to equate the linguistic stock to a homogenous morphological race and culture found little support among anthropologists.

**Aryanism:** philological term linking most European, Iranian and Indian languages into a common language family, Indo-European; early scholars supposed the geographical focus to have been Bactria or the Hindu Kush; those supporting a biblical chronology suggested eastern Turkey because of the site of Mount Ararat, near Armenia and Iran; **Retzius** and other **craniometrists** suggested that 'true' Aryans had been **dolichocephalic**, a theme continued by **Virchow** and de **Gobineau**; American economist Theodor Poesche first suggested in 1878 that Aryans were Nordic.

**Asa Koma Locality 3:** site in the Middle Awash region of Ethiopia from which the holotype of *Ardipithecus kadabba* was recovered.

**ascending colon:** first portion of the **colon** that begins at the **cecum**, moves upward against the posterior abdominal wall, and turns sharply to the left just inferior to the liver.

‡ **ascending ramus (of the mandible):** in anthropology, usually refers informally to the vertical portion of the jawbone, or **mandible**. Aka **mandibular ramus**.

**ascending ramus height** (go–cdl): **craniometric** measurement; vertical distance from the **gonion** to the **condylion laterale** as measured with spreading calipers or a **mandibulometer**. See Appendix 7 for an illustration of the landmarks used.

**ascertainment:** method by which an investigator becomes aware of a **propositus**; a sampling method.

**ascorbic acid:** see **vitamin**.

**ascorbic acid deficiency:** condition of **avitaminosis** caused by a lack of **vitamin C**. See **scurvy**.

**aseptic necrosis:** pathological cell, tissue, or organ death in the absence of infectious agents.

**asexual:** without sex.

**asexual reproduction:** reproduction in which the individual is produced from one parent and is genetically identical to that parent; the individual is not produced by the fusion of gametes. Common in unicellular organisms, some plants; also occurs in simple animals through budding, and in more complex animals through **parthenogenesis** (e.g. social insects, whip-tailed lizards). Cf. **sexual reproduction**.

**Ashkenazim:** Jewish **deme** of Eastern European origin, a Yiddish-speaking division of the Hebrews. Aka Ashkenazi Hebrews.

**Ashley Montagu, M. F.:** see Montagu, M. F. Ashley.

**Asian australopithecines:** see *Meganthropus paleojavanicus* and *Homo modjokertensis*.

**Asian origin hypothesis:** version of the **monophyletic** or single origin hypothesis that proposes Asia as the center of a recent radiation of **AMHs**; cf. the **out of Africa II** hypothesis and the **multiregional continuity model** of **human origins**.

**Asiatic Primate Expedition, 1937:** scientific endeavor to Siam (now Thailand) mounted in 1937 and sponsored jointly by Harvard, Columbia and Johns Hopkins Universities. Thailand was then a focal area for **gibbons**. The co-directors were Charles R. **Carpenter**, who studied the pattern of boundaries of hylobatid social organization; Adolph **Schultz**, who studied anatomy and morphology; and Harold J. Coolidge, Jr. (the initiator of the project), who studied social organization. Sherwood **Washburn**, then a graduate student, was also a member. One group also studied **orangutans** in northern Borneo. The team collected and dissected specimens, and conducted behavioral observations for four months in the Thai rain forests. This was the last major field study of primates until the 1950s, and was important because several members of the expedition would have a significant impact on primatology in the 1950s.

*Asiomomys* **Beard and Wang, 1990:** tarsiiform primate from the early Eocene of China, belonging to the omomyid subfamily **Omomyinae**. Monotypic; *A. changbaicus* is described as very similar to the North American *Stockia*. Body mass estimated at around 500 g. See Appendix 1 for taxonomy.

**A site:** section in a **ribosome** that holds an incoming **amino acid** as it is released by a **transfer RNA** molecule, and where that amino acid is bound to others as part of a growing peptide chain. Cf. **P site**.

**ASL:** 1. see **American Sign Language**. 2. see **Anthropological Society of London**.

**asparagine** (Asn): an **amino acid**; one of the twenty building blocks of **proteins**. Found in nature in asparagus shoots and other plants.

**aspartic acid** (Asp): an **amino acid**; one of the twenty building blocks of **proteins**. Found in sugar cane and sugar beet molasses.

**Asperger's syndrome:** mild form of **autism** characterized by 'mind-blindness', or an inability to read common nonverbal cues involving kindness, love, or anger; those affected lack empathy skills. Considered a highly functional modality of autistic behavior; affected individuals have normal or above-normal intelligence, and may display savantism (a specific skill ability). Aka 'nerd' syndrome.

**aspermia:** absence of sperm that results in male infertility.

**Assamese macaque:** vernacular for *Macaca assamensis*.

**assay:** laboratory test performed to measure the activity of a substance against a certain target; it must maintain a certain minimal level of biological activity to be considered for animal or clinical testing or, later, for marketing. Aka biological assay, chemical assay.

**Asselar Post:** archaeological site found in 1927 in the central Sahara 400 km northeast of Timbuktu, Mali, dated to the Upper Pleistocene or **Holocene** (*c.* 7 kya), and that contains a fossil skeleton with **Nilotic** affinities attributed to *Homo sapiens,* comparable to modern Bantus and Hottentots.

**assemblage:** 1. any set or aggregation of **artifacts, fossils** or other remains collected at a hominid **site**. 2. material evidence used in support of **hypotheses** concerning the culture (or cultures) that inhabited it. Similar terms include **industry, culture**, and **tradition.** 3. congregation of two or more species.

**assembly:** coalescence of a community of primates for social activities.

**assimilation:** asymmetrical increase in the similarity of two cultures. Cf. **acculturation.**

**assimilation efficiency:** refers to the total **absorption** of **nutrients**, calculated by dividing the total amount of **feces** recovered by the total amount of dehydrated food ingested, and subtracting from 1.

**assimilation model of human origins:** variant of the **hybrid models of human origins**; accepts an African origin for **AMH**s but disallows replacement or significant migration. Supports local speciation of AMHs as the result of **orthogenesis**, but allows for gene flow and changing environmental pressures. Advocated by F. H. Smith and E. **Trinkaus.**

**assisted reproductive technique:** any procedure that helps couples who experience **infertility** to conceive and deliver **viable** young.

**associated find:** method of contextualizing objects by considering the context in which they are discovered. If the association is undisturbed, an object, such as a cranium, found in direct stratigraphic association with artifacts belonging to, for example, the **Mousterian tool tradition**, is inferred to be contemporary with those tools. See **association** and **provenance.**

‡ **association:** 1. context in which an **artifact** is found, and its relationship to other such artifacts; **provenance.** See **principle of association.** 2. in biology, a mixed species group of primates that forage or travel together. Cf. **polyspecific association.**

**association cortex:** in sequential models of cortical processing, those frontal, temporal, or parietal areas of cortex (not devoted to sensory or motor function) where higher-order (associative) processes such as memory, reasoning, judgment, and emotions are involved.

**association fibers:** fiber tracts within the **white matter** of the **cerebrum** that conduct impulses between neurons within each hemisphere; association fibers do not cross the **corpus callosum.**

**association neuron:** nerve cell located completely within the **central nervous system.** Association neurons convey impulses in an arc from sensory to motor neurons. Aka internuncial neuron.

‡ **assortative mating:** nonrandom mating. **Endogamy** is termed **positive assortative mating**, whereas **exogamy** is termed **negative assortative mating**; one of the systematic forces or **mechanisms of evolution.** See **sexual selection.**

**association study:** comparison of the genetic variation in the **haplotypes** of people who have a particular genetic condition against a panel of unaffected people.

‡ **assortment:** (usually) random distribution of whole **chromosomes** to the cell poles during anaphase I of meiosis, and of sister **chromatids** during anaphase II of meiosis, and the single anaphase of mitosis, resulting in the **segregation** and recombination of genes. See **independent assortment.**

**Astaracian:** the European land-mammal age (middle **Miocene**, approximately 14–13 mya).

**asterion:** external landmark on the skull at which the lambdoid, parietomastoid and occipital sutures converge.

**asterionic bone: sutural bone** that develops at the **asterion** of the cranium.

**asterionic notch:** indentation formed at the **asterion** on the cranium of *Paranthropus*, presumably because of chewing stresses; this trait is also found in some of the great apes and *Australopithecus afarensis*.

**asternal ribs:** ribs number 8 through 10 in the human; these ribs do not join to the **sternum** directly, but are attached by cartilage. Aka false ribs.

‡ **asteroid impact model:** theory that the **mass extinction** event(s) that occurred at the **Cretaceous– Tertiary boundary** about 65 mya resulted from

sudden climatic changes induced by collision of the earth with an asteroid, meteorite or comet; one of several models competing to explain the **K/T** mass extinctions. Aka **Alvarez theory.**

**asthenosphere:** layer of the earth located directly below the **lithosphere**. The asthenosphere begins about 70 km below the earth's surface, and extends to a depth of about 200 km. Also spelled athenosphere.

**asthma:** heterogenous atopic disorder of airways and lungs characterized by reversible inflammatory obstruction, breathing difficulties, wheezing, and hypersensitivity. An autosomal dominant susceptibility region has been identified: cytokine genes are known to regulate IgE production, resulting in various severities of allergic diseases; the IgE adrenergic receptor gene is strongly linked to maternal smoking during pregnancy. The **CCR5 co-receptor** locus apparently also attenuates the severity of asthma. The trait also exhibits evidence for **genomic imprinting**. It has been suggested that asthma is found most frequently in individuals with hyperresponsive IgE due to an indigenous parasite load, and who then remove to regions where parasite load is low. See **chronic obstructive pulmonary disease.**

**astragalus:** main bone of the mammalian ankle, referred to as the **talus** in primates.

**astrobiology:** 1. discipline that searches for life beyond earth; heavily dominated by physical scientists. Astrobiologists do not limit themselves solely to the search for life, but also look for such things as prebiotic molecules in interstellar space, solar systems in the process of forming, and mature planets orbiting other stars. Cf. **exobiology.** 2. specific **anthropic** subtheory associated with Rhawn Joseph, who proposed that 'genetic seeds' encased in stellar debris have bootstrapped life in many locations throughout the universe. The Joseph subtheory is specifically anti-Darwinian.

**astrokinetic:** relating to the movements of the centrosome in a dividing cell.

**astronomical cycles:** daily, weekly, monthly, seasonal and annual rhythms that influence behavior and, in particular, patterns of **reproduction** and **growth and development.** Incremental lines of cyclic tissue growth are ubiquitous in tree trunks, shells, and skeletons; see **dendrochronology, stria of Retzius,** and **perikymata,** for example. The morbid disruption of normal metabolism can disturb growth rhythms; see **Harris lines** and **neonatal line.**

**astrosphere:** group of fibrillar cytoplasmic rays that extend outward from the **centrosome** and centrosphere of a dividing cell. Aka aster, attraction sphere.

**asymmetrical reproductive strategies:** tendency in most species for males to exhibit higher variance in **reproductive success** than females, for males to copulate more frequently and with more partners than females, and for females to be more discriminating than males in choosing their partners.

**asymmetry:** the state of not being identical on either side of a mid-line. Cf. **bilateral symmetry.**

**Atapuerca:** archaeological site(s) found in 1899 and located in the Sierra de Atapuerca, a few miles east of Burgos in north central Spain. Excavated intensely since 1984, one site, the **Sima de los Huesos** ('Pit of Bones'), has yielded remains of at least 33 individuals assigned provisionally to archaic *Homo* group status, and dates to about 300 kya; a second occupation cave site a few hundred meters away, the **Gran Dolina,** has produced pre-Acheulean tools and the remains of at least four individuals, and dates to about 800 kya. Aka Cuerva Mayor, Galeréa. See Juan Luis **Arsuaga.**

---

**Some fossil hominids from Atapuerca**

**ATD6-69:** fossil hominid discovered at **Atapuerca**, Spain, dating to >780 kya. Specimen consists of the partial face of a juvenile attributed to *Homo antecessor*.

**Atapuerca 5:** fossil hominid recovered from the 'pit of bones' (**Sima de los Huesos**) at **Atapuerca**, Spain, dating to 300 kya. Specimen consists of the cranium of an adult with a cranial capacity of 1125 cm$^3$; attributed to archaic *Homo sapiens* cf. *heidelbergensis*.

---

**atavism:** 'throwback', or the reversion to an earlier type; the reappearance of a trait that has been absent for several generations; misapplied by Lombroso and others to explain 'criminal types'. A pre-genetic concept that is rarely invoked today, as such phenomena are better explained by **mutations** or **recessive** alleles.

**atavistic regression:** return to a more primitive or infantile pattern of behavior.

**ataxia telangiectasia** (AT): autosomal recessive condition characterized by poor muscle coordination, involuntary eye movements, capillary dilation in eyes and skin, sensitivity to light (radiosensitivity), immune defects, and susceptibility to infections and cancer (9× normal controls); chromosome breakage is a feature. Onset in the first decade of life. AT is a heterogenous condition with at least two distinct subtypes. The causal agent is believed to be a gene (*ATM*) involved with DNA processing and repair. Several hundred SNP mutants have been reported. Aka Louis–Barr syndrome.

*Ateles* É. Geoffroy, 1806: ceboid genus to which the spider monkeys belong. Most authorities recognize four **allopatric** species; some workers think that there is only one species with 16 **subspecies**. Found in Central and South America where it prefers evergreen tropical rain forest. Ranges in body mass from 6 to 14 kg; nonsexually dimorphic to the extent that the female has an elongated **clitoris** that is sometimes mistaken for a **penis**. Arboreal; possesses **prehensile tail**; diurnal; capable of a variety of **locomotor patterns: arboreal quadrupedalism**, semibrachiation, climbing, and **bipedalism**; thumb reduced to tubercle. Dental formula: 2.1.3.3; **frugivorous,** but in some seasons switch to heavy leaf diet. Mixed-sex social organization; troops that fission into smaller foraging units and fuse back into the larger troop. See Appendix 2 for taxonomy, Appendix 3 for living species.

Atelidae Rosenberger, 1977: family of ceboids that includes the larger-bodied New World Monkeys, namely the spider, woolly, and woolly spider monkeys, and howlers; some workers also include the sakis, bearded sakis, and uakaris. Not all authorities recognize this family and the monkeys in this group are often treated as a subfamily of the **Cebidae** or, in the case of the howlers, separated out as another distinct family. See Appendix 2 for taxonomy, Appendix 3 for species.

Atelinae Gray, 1825: subfamily of either the family **Cebidae** or the family **Atelidae**, depending on the taxonomic scheme being used. This subfamily consists of the spider, woolly, and woolly spider monkeys; the howlers are also sometimes included. See Appendix 2 for taxonomy, Appendix 3 for species.

ateliosis: growth abnormality caused by malfunction of the **pituitary gland** and characterized in the adult by a childish face and voice and **dwarfism**. Aka infantilism, ateleiosis.

Aterian: North African tool tradition characterized by tanged projectile points, which some say dates to >70 kya (based on a sequence at Bir Tarfawi in the Egyptian Sahara); but French scholars disagree, citing the technology as <40 kya. See **Dar-es-Soltane II.**

atherosclerosis: deposition of hard, lipid-containing plaques in the interior walls of arteries, and thickening of arterial walls with abnormal smooth muscle cells; results in narrowing of vessel lumen. Aka hardening of the arteries.

*Atlanthropus* Arambourg, 1954: generic term assigned to a group of North African Pleistocene hominids; named after a range of mountains in North Africa, the Atlas Mountains; Atlanthropine. Most workers assign these fossils, such as **Ternifine,** to *Homo erectus.*

atlanto-axial joint: **condyloid joint** between the first and second **cervical vertebrae** (i.e. the atlas and the axis) that allows rotation of the head.

Atlanto-Mediterranean: older **ethonym** for a hypothetical **autochthonous** people of western Europe, a Mediterranean group with tall stature and white to ruddy skin color.

atlanto-occipital: pertaining to the articulation between the occipital condyles of the skull and the first cervical vertebra (or atlas).

atlanto-occipital joint: condyloid junction between the first **cervical vertebra** (the atlas) and the **occipital bone** that permits flexion, extension, abduction, adduction, and circumduction.

atlanto-odontoid: pertaining to the articulation between the odontoid process of the second vertebra (or axis) and the fovea dentis of the first cervical vertebra (or atlas).

atlas: first **cervical vertebra** that articulates with the **occipital condyles** of the skull.

‡ atlatl: Central American term for **spearthrower.**

atmosphere: 1. mantle of gases surrounding the earth and some other planets. The earth's atmosphere at sea level is about 78% nitrogen, 21% oxygen, 0.5% carbon dioxide, and 0.5% inert gases. 2. a unit of air pressure.

atmospheric oxygen concentration: proportion of oxygen in the atmosphere relative to particulate matter and, especially, other gases such as carbon dioxide. In the **fossil record**, at the time when photosynthetic organisms seem to have radiated, there was an increase in the oxygen concentration of the earth's atmosphere. Gas ratios are affected by the relative proportions of photosynthetic organisms and **herbivores**, which increase and decrease atmospheric oxygen, respectively.

atmospheric pressure: see **barometric pressure.**

atocia: sterility in the female.

atomistic: inheritance, an approach in which the entities controlling heredity are distinctly particulate, permanent, and capable of independent action; **Mendelian inheritance**, for example, is atomistic because it postulates that inheritance is controlled by factors now called **genes**. Cf. **pangenesis.**

atopy: denoting an allergy characteristic of humans and tending to be inherited; e.g. hay fever, asthma.

ATP: adenosine triphosphate, the stable, phosphorylated adenine–ribose molecule that stores energy in its highly charged bonds to be later released during cellular activities.

atresia: decrease in the number of viable germ cells found in female mammals as they age; from an initial 500 000 or so, most females are born with about 50 000 in each ovary, but fewer and fewer of these are capable of completing meiosis normally as the female ages; human females ovulate only about 450–500 times during their reproductive life.

**atrichia:** congenital or acquired condition characterized by a loss or absence of hair.

**atrophic spots:** areas of bone that show evidence of **atrophy**. Atrophic spots are often translucent.

**atrophy:** 1. wasting action on a structure, such as an organ, tissue, appendage, that causes withering away. 2. To decrease in size. Adjective: atrophic.

**attachment behavior:** 1. bonding of an infant with its mother through a series of physical and psychological cues. 2. a set of physical and psychological cues and responses that bond an infant with one of its caretakers.

**attenuation:** reduction; weakening by dilution.

**attribute:** 1. inherent characteristic, key, or an accidental quality that distinguishes one object or organism from another. 2. an object closely associated with or that belongs to a specified individual. Aka **trait, character**.

**attrition:** wearing away of a structure by friction or rubbing; abrasion.

**attrition strategy:** description of the interaction of morbidity and **mortality** that together offset the **fertility** of a population. Various attrition strategies ensure that a population will survive each generation and yet not tax the **carrying capacity** of the environment in which it exists.

**attritional age profile:** fossil demographic profile in which an estimate of the structure of the population ages takes into account routine mortality factors.

**atypical:** differing from the normal or usual type; not typical.

**audiogram:** graph, chart or table indicating hearing level for pure tones as a function of frequency; result of a hearing test using an audiometer.

**audiology:** field of medicine that investigates and treats hearing disorders.

**audiometry:** measurement of hearing abilities by an audiometer.

**auditory:** pertaining to the sense of hearing or to the organs and structures associated with hearing. Noun: audition.

‡ **auditory bulla:** protective bony housing for the middle ear cavity and the **auditory ossicles** contained within; found only in mammals. In primates it is formed by the petrosal portion of the **temporal bone**; used as an important diagnostic trait in early primates. Aka tympanic bulla, bulla tympani.

**auditory cortex:** region of the cerebral cortex that receives nerve fibers from the auricular apparatus; occupies the transverse temporal gyri and the superior temporal gyrus.

**auditory exostosis:** bony projection that develops in the **external auditory meatus**; canal of the temporal bone. In rare cases, may occlude the auditory canal completely. Aka auditory tori.

**auditory meatus:** see **external auditory meatus**.

**auditory ossicle:** any of the three bones of the **middle ear** that transmit vibrations to the inner ear, the incus, malleus, and stapes.

**auditory system:** those structures in the ear that enable or support hearing and the central connections to the brain responsible for the sense of hearing.

**auditory tube:** bony and cartilaginous tube that connects the middle ear cavity with the back of the throat. It functions to equalize pressure on either side of the **tympanic membrane**. Aka Eustachian tube.

**auger:** tool used by archaeologists for digging test holes.

**augmented distance:** estimate of the total number of fixed nucleotide substitutions separating any two nucleic acid distances, a correction required because a phylogenetic tree is not equally dense. Cf. **phylogenetic density**.

**August Krogh principle:** observation made by A. Krogh in 1929 that for many, if not most, questions about nature there are species of choice because they are more easily studied or have some other desirable characteristic.

**aunt:** 1. a sister of one's mother or father; a kinship term that identifies a genealogical or fictive degree of relationship in a **nuclear family** or **extended family**. See **father, mother, brother, sister, uncle, cousin**. 2. female primate, usually a juvenile, who assists a mother in caring for her offspring; this behavior is called aunting.

**auricle:** 1. the outer ear of a human; this is referred to as a **pinna** in other mammals. 2. any ear-like lobed appendage, as related to the atria of the heart. 3. the sacro-iliac articulation. Adjective: auricular.

**auricular head height:** projected **vertex–tragion** distance as measured by subtracting the height of the tragion above the floor from a subject's stature.

**auricular height** (po–b): **craniometric** measurement; height from the **porion** to the **bregma** with the skull in the **Frankfort horizontal** and measured with a head spanner. Cf. **porion–bregma height**. See Appendix 7 for an illustration of the landmarks used.

**auricular point:** landmark at the top of the orifice of the ear.

**auriculo-orbitale** (ao): see **Frankfort horizontal**.

**Aurignac:** archaeological site found in 1852 in Haute Garonne, France, dated to perhaps 15 kya, which contained incised artifacts and fossil **hominids**, including the remains of at least 17 individuals, and the engraved bones of **extinct** animals; the bones were later interpreted as **Neolithic** (= **Holocene**) and intrusive into the layer containing the extinct fauna.

The skeletal remains were reburied in a local Christian cemetery. Type site for the **Aurignacian.**

‡ **Aurignacian tool tradition: Upper Paleolithic** culture period dating in Europe from about 43 to 15 kya that also includes art objects, and that is usually diagnostic of **AMHs**, especially the **Cro-Magnon** people. The tool kit may contain flint side and end scrapers, tips, blades, and bladelets indicative of composite tools, as well as bone and ivory implements such as awls and spear points. The earliest example is found in **Bacho Kiro Cave** and dates to 43 kya. Early Aurignacian sites in Spain, Bulgaria and Russia date to 43 kya; dates in France are in the range *c.* 40–30 kya. Aka Sebilian. See **Aurignac.** Cf. **Gravettian.**

**aurochs:** extinct Pleistocene **bovid**, the European bison, *Bos primigenius*.

**Aurora stratum:** primary fossil-bearing stratum at the site of **Gran Dolina.** Aka TD6.

**Australo-African roots hypothesis:** controversial proposal by Brazilian anthropologist Walter A. Neves that putative early sites in South America (Lapa Vermelha IV, Santana do Riacho 1, Serra da Capivara) contain skeletal material that is revealed by multivariate studies to have an affinity to either **Australoid** or African material, but not to Asian or Native American populations.

**Australoid:** ethnym used in the past to denote one of the 'races' of humanity. Australoids included the indigenous peoples of Australia; it also included peoples that physically resembled the native Australians such as the aboriginal peoples of New Guinea and Melanesia, the '**Negrito**' pygmies of Indonesia and Southeast Asia, and some of the native peoples of Southeast Asia and India.

‡ **Australopithecinae Gregory and Hellman, 1938:** one of two proposed subfamilies of the family **Hominidae,** the other being the **Homininae;** many researchers, however, do not consider the family Hominidae as warranting subfamilies. Contains the fossils that carry the sobriquets 'ape-man', 'man-apes' and 'near men'.

‡ **australopithecine:** referring generally to any species in the genera *Australopithecus* or *Paranthropus*; 'man-apes' of the **Plio-Pleistocene** who were **bipedal** and dentally similar to humans, but whose **brain size** was not much larger than modern **apes**; that is, they lacked the **encephalization** characteristics of the genus *Homo*. In the formal sense, a member of the subfamily **Australopithecinae** of the family **Hominidae.**

*Australopithecus* **Dart, 1925:** formal genus nomen of the 'man-apes' including, for example, *Australopithecus africanus* from South Africa and possibly also from East Africa. The genus includes **hominids** that were capable of a form of **bipedal locomotion,** had a relatively small **brain size,** large face, and large but human-like teeth. Literally, 'Southern ape'. See box for species and Appendix 1 for taxonomy.

---

**Species within the genus *Australopithecus***

*Australopithecus aethiopicus* Walker, Leakey, Harris and Brown, 1986: see *Paranthropus aethiopicus*.

*Australopithecus afarensis* Johanson, White and Coppens, 1978: 'southern man-ape from the Afar'; early **hominid** species that existed 4–3 mya and is known only from East Africa. This species was recognized with the recovery of **NME AL-288-1** ('Lucy') in 1974. The type specimen, however, is **LH-4**, a partial adult mandible from **Laetoli**. *A. afarensis* has a mosaic of nonhominid and hominid traits. The pelvis is hominid-like and indicative of some form of **bipedalism**. The arms relative to the legs are longer than in modern humans. Toe and finger bones are curved and other features of the **manus** and **pes** are pongid-like, suggesting to some authorities that the species was partly **arboreal**. Incisors and canines are large, with **diastemata** between upper canines and incisors and between lower canines and premolars. Tooth rows are parallel, with thickly enameled molars. Brain is small, with mean cranial capacity around 415 cm³. The skull is **pneumatized**. Body size estimate: females 105 cm in height and 30 kg in mass, males 150 cm in height and 50 kg in mass. *A. afarensis* is one of the most **sexually dimorphic** primate species known, leading some workers to propose that the collection of fossils currently assigned to *A. afarensis* may represent more than one species. See *afarensis* **nomen debate**.

*Australopithecus africanus* Dart, 1925: first species of *Australopithecus* discovered, and described by Dart in 1925; found only in South Africa (some researchers had attributed certain fossils from East Africa to *A. africanus*, but on reconsideration, those fossils were moved into different taxa). *A. africanus* was the primary species among the 'gracile' australopithecines until discoveries in the 1970s. Members of *A. africanus* were fully **bipedal**. They had large cheek teeth relative to the anterior dentition, with a reduced **canine**. The species lacks the occipital and sagittal crests characteristic of **robust** australopithecines. The face is less prognathic than in other *Australopithecus* species. Mean cranial capacity is about 440 cm³. The skull is **pneumatized**. Body mass estimate 46 kg. Height 115–138 cm. Found in geological strata dated 3–2 mya. (cont. overleaf)

---

**Species within the genus *Australopithecus* (*cont.*)**

*Australopithecus anamensis* Leakey, Feibel, McDougall and Walker, 1995: provisionally named species of *Australopithecus*, first recognized in 1995 after 21 specimens were recovered in 1993–4 at **Allia Bay**, Kenya. This species has a **mosaic** of traits shared between *Ardipithecus* and *Australopithecus afarensis*. The dental apparatus is very primitive, except in having thickly enameled molars. **Postcrania** suggest **bipedalism**. Body mass estimate 50 kg. **Radiometric dating** indicates that this species lived 4.2–3.9 mya. See **Kanapoi**.

*Australopithecus bahrelghazali* Brunet, Beauvilain, Coppens, Heintz, Moutaye, and Pilbeam, 1996: **hominid** species that existed between 3.5 and 3.0 mya, known only from site KT 12 near Yayo in Chad (central Africa). This species was recognized with the recovery of a partial **maxillary bone**, one **premolar**, and an adult **mandible** possessing thickly enameled teeth; Aka KT 12-H1. This material was originally described as comparable to *A. afarensis*. *A. bahrelghazali* is significant because it is the first Pliocene hominid found outside the East African Rift Valley. It is described as possessing a more vertical **mandibular symphysis** and overall is more **gracile** than the contemporary *A. anamensis* or the earlier *Ardipithecus ramidus*; its discoverers suggest that it is the ancestor of the **gracile** clade and probably of modern humans.

‡ *Australopithecus (= Zinjanthropus) boisei* Leakey, Tobias and Napier, 1964: see *Paranthropus boisei*.

*Australopithecus capensis* (Oakley, 1964): see *Telanthropus capensis*.

*Australopithecus crassidens* (Oakley, 1954): see *Paranthropus crassidens*.

*Australopithecus garhi* Asfaw, White, Lovejoy, Latimer, Simpson and Suwa, 1999: provisional **hominid** species described from materials (representing three individuals) recovered from the **Middle Awash** from the **Bouri formation**, Ethiopia. Dating indicates this species lived around 2.5 mya. BOU-VP-12/130 is the type specimen. Leg bones indicate **bipedalism**, but the arms, relative to the legs, are long in comparison to modern humans; height for one individual estimated at 140 cm. Small brain (estimated at 450 cm$^3$ from one individual) and larger molars than found in the robust *Australopithecus* clade; maxillary **prognathism** with **procumbent** incisors reminiscent of *Pongo*. Slightly **parabolic dental arcade**. Scored animal bones bearing marks from stone tools were recovered with this species; this is considered the earliest evidence for deliberate **butchering** of animals by hominids.

‡ *Australopithecus habilis* (Wood and Collard, 1999): see *Homo habilis*.

*Australopithecus prometheus* Dart, 1948: 'southern fire-making ape'; fossil species proposed from material recovered at **Makapansgat**, South Africa. Species nomen was proposed because **Dart** believed he had found evidence of fire use by these **hominids**. Junior synonym of *A. transvaalensis*, now subsumed under *A. africanus*. See **controlled use of fire**.

*Australopithecus ramidus* White, Suwa and Asfaw, 1994: see *Ardipithecus ramidus*.

*Australopithecus robustus* (Broom, 1938): see *Paranthropus robustus*.

*Australopithecus transvaalensis* Broom, 1936: fossil **hominid** species proposed from fragmentary material recovered at **Sterkfontein**, South Africa. Broom transferred this material to a new genus, *Plesianthropus*, in 1938. The most prominent specimen among *Plesianthropus* is **Sts 5** ('Mrs. Ples'). Material now subsumed under *A. africanus*. Synonym: *A. prometheus*.

---

***Australopithecus garhi* dietary hypothesis:** hypothesis put forth by **T. White** that *A. garhi*, a **bipedal**, small-brained, large-toothed **hominid**, began eating animals *c.* 2.5 mya; that the higher-quality diet resulting from animal consumption led to an increase in brain size and a decrease in molar size; and that these two changes cascaded into other modifications of the skull. This hypothesis suggests that *A. garhi* is the ancestor of ***Homo***. See **vegetarian dietary hypothesis**.

‡ **autapomorphy:** referring to a unique, **derived** character that defines a species (or its demes) within a **monophyletic group**, and that arose for the first time in that singular group. Autapomorphs are not shared with **sister groups** or with a most recent common ancestor. Adjective autapomorphous or autapomorphic.

**autecology:** study of the relationship between individual organisms or species with their environment.

**autistic disorder:** developmental disorder characterized by failure to understand stimulation; features impairment of reciprocal social interaction and communication, and ritualized patterns of behaviors and interests; it affects boys 4× more than girls. Often involves some degree of mental retardation and limited verbal skills. Autistic boys have been shown to possess only half as much of the hormone **oxytocin** as their peers; onset from infancy to age 3. Risk in an affected sibship is $75\times$ that of normal controls. A putative autosomal recessive factor has been nominated. Aka Autism spectral disorder. Cf. **Asperger's syndrome.**

**autoantibody:** antibody produced in and that reacts to an **autoantigen** present in the same individual.

**autoantigen:** antigen that induces the production of **autoantibodies.**

**autocatalysis model:** model proposed by E. O. **Wilson** (1975) for the increased rate of **cultural evolution** after certain biological traits had evolved in **hominids.**

**autochthonous:** pertaining to an aboriginal organism, or group of organisms, that evolved in the geographical area where they are still found; native. Noun: autochthone. Cf. **allochthonous.**

**autochthonous semi-legendary concept:** perception among human groups that each originated in the place it currently occupies and was created by its local god(s); a latent, implicit form of **polygenism.**

**autocrine:** of or pertaining to a **hormone** that binds to receptors on, and affects the function of, the cell type that produced it. Cf. **exocrine** and **paracrine.**

**autocrine hypothesis:** idea that cancerous cells both produce, and respond to, growth factors, unlike normal cells.

**autogenesis:** see Lamarckism.

**autogenetic evolution:** referring to theories of evolution which hold that organisms are inherently self-evolving and that there are orienting qualities of evolution present within the organism.

**autograft:** tissue transplant from one part of a person's body to another part; self graft. Cf. **allograft, xenograft.**

**autogrooming:** self **grooming**; grooming one's own body. Cf. **allogrooming.**

**autoimmune diseases:** group of conditions, including **rheumatoid arthritis** and **systemic lupus erythematosis**, that arise when the **immune system** mistakenly recognizes the body's own tissues as foreign and produces **antibodies** against itself.

**autoimmunity:** inappropriate immune attack against one's own tissues.

**autologous:** related to or derived from the subject itself.

**automarking:** act of a primate applying an odorous substance to itself for the purpose of communication; for example, in some cercopithecine species females apply urine to their tails when they enter **estrus** in order to advertise their state to males. In nonprimate fields of **ethology** this is usually referred to as self-marking. Cf. **allomarking.**

**automimicry:** 1. a form of **mimicry** within some species such that a palatable morph resembles an unpalatable morph; the mimic morphs have not ingested the requisite toxins yet are avoided by predators. Aka **Batesian mimicry**, intraspecific mimicry. 2. the imitation by one sex or life stage of communication in another sex or life stage of the same species; e.g. the imitation by the males of some monkey species of female sexual signals, which they appear to employ in appeasement rituals.

**autonomic:** self-controlling or functionally independent, e.g. an involuntary physiological response such as **sweating.**

**autonomic nervous system** (ANS): a functional subdivision of the nervous system, part of the **central nervous system**, with controlling centers in the brain. The peripheral portions of the ANS are composed of two elements, the **parasympathetic division** and the **sympathetic division.**

**autopolyploidy:** the state of having multiple sets of chromosomes of the same species: autodiploidy, autotriploidy, autotetraploidy, etc. Adjective: Autoploid.

**autoradiography:** 1. a method of using radioactive molecules to identify their location after they have become fixed at some location in a cell, by producing a photographic image. 2. in DNA analysis, the placement of a final membrane containing a **DNA fingerprint** (or other outcome from **electrophoresis**) against X-ray film, where it is photographed. Aka autorad.

**autosomal dominant:** used of a dominant allele located on an **autosome**. See **dominant pattern of inheritance.**

**autosomal inheritance:** mode of inheritance of the **autosomes**, in which each parent normally contributes one homologue of each pair of autosomal **chromatids** in each **gamete.**

**autosomal recessive:** used of a recessive allele located on an **autosome**. See **recessive pattern of inheritance.**

‡ **autosome:** any **chromosome** or **chromatid** in an individual that is not involved in **sex determination**; there are normally $2N-2$ autosomes in humans and other heterogametic species (the **diploid number**, $2N$, less the two **sex chromosomes**). See **heterogamy, karyotype.** Cf. **heterosome.**

**autotroph:** organism capable of synthesizing its own nutrients by the conversion of simple compounds to carbohydrates and proteins. Aka producer, self-feeder. Cf. **heterotroph.**

**autozygous:** referring to two **alleles** at the same genetic **locus** that are identical owing to descent from a recent common ancestor. Cf. **allozygous.**

**auxology:** the study of human physical and physiological growth and development. The parent organization is the International Association of Human Auxologists. See **Tanner**.

*Avahi* Jourdain, 1834: **prosimian** genus to which the woolly lemur(s) belong; may contain one or two species. Inhabits forests of eastern and northwestern Madagascar; **nocturnal; arboreal;** primary locomotion is leaping; body mass ranges between 600 and 1000 g. Dental formula in dispute, either 2.1.2.3/ 2.0.2.3 or 2.1.2.3/1.1.2.3. Proponents of both formulae agree there are 30 teeth and that there are only 4 teeth in the **dental comb**. Folivorous; digestive adaptations include enlarged **salivary glands** and rudimentary sacculated stomach. Live in monogamous groups. See Appendix 2 for taxonomy and Appendix 3 for species.

**available space theory:** adapted from botany, the proposal that a new **tooth bud** arises only when a certain minimum space has become available for it to germinate. Cf. **field theory**.

*Avenius amatorum:* archaic mammal from the early Eocene of Europe belonging to the plesiadapiform family **Microsyopidae; monotypic;** some authorities assign this genus to the order Insectivora. Estimated body mass around 8 g; if this organism is related to the primates, it would be the smallest one known. Small body size and dentition suggests **insectivory**. See Appendix 1 for taxonomy.

**average mutation rate:** for pedagogical purposes, a mutation rate of $1 \times 10^{-5}$ is often cited. See **mutation rate**.

**Aves:** taxonomic class to which birds belong.

**avitaminosis:** any condition due to a deficiency of one or more essential dietary **vitamins**, e.g. **scurvy**. Plural: avitaminoses.

**avulsion:** 1. forcible tearing away of a part or structure, e.g. **tooth avulsion**. Aka evulsion. 2. sudden erosion of soil.

**Awash:** research region located in Ethiopia where long-term field studies of olive baboons (*Papio anubis*), hamadryas baboons (*Pa. hamadryas*), and olive–hamadryas baboon hybrids have been conducted for decades. Primatologists who have conducted field research at this site include: F. P. G. Aldrich-Blake, J. H. Crook, U. Nagel, J. E. Phillips-Conroy, C. J. Jolly, and L. A. Fairbanks.

**awl:** pointed **tool** used to punch holes in skins, wood, or other materials; made out of stone or bone by prehistoric humans. Awls became more common during the **Upper Paleolithic**.

**awn:** guardhair; **hair** that is sensitive to touch and can warn the animal of danger. Among the **primates** these structures are found associated with the 'neck shield' of *Perodicticus potto*.

**ax:** stone, and later, metal cutting tool. In most cases it is perforated so the it can be attached to a handle. The ax evolved from the pear-shaped **coup-de-poing** or **hand-axe** to a flatter, oval object with straight edges, and from a piercing or cutting function to the ax intended to strike a crushing blow. Also spelled axe.

**axial:** of or pertaining to an axis.

**axial precession:** systematic wobble of the earth on its N–S rotary axis.

‡ **axial skeleton:** portion of a skeleton located on or near its mid-line: bones of the **cranium**, **vertebral column**, and the **ribs** and **sternum**. Cf. **appendicular skeleton**.

**axillary:** pertaining to the armpit (axilla). The axillary region is where **physical anthropologists** determine the **skin color** of individuals in human populations because it is the area least affected by environmental conditions such as sunlight.

**axillary chest girth:** circumference of the chest as measured across the axillary fossae (under the armpits). Readings taken during inspiration and expiration, then averaged.

**axillary hair:** clumped body hair in the axillary region (armpit) that develops during puberty.

**axis:** the second **cervical vertebra**. Aka the epistropheus Cf. **atlas**.

**axis of leverage:** path followed by the central vector of weight stress as it passes through the distal metatarsals during forceful leverage.

**axon:** elongated process of a nerve cell that transmits an impulse away from the cell body of a **neuron**.

*Aycrossia lovei* Bown, 1979: see *Acrossia lovei*.

**aye-aye:** vernacular for *Daubentonia madagascariensis*.

**Aymara deformation:** form of circular deformation of the cranium resulting in **macrocephaly**; particularly common among the Aymara people that live near Lake Titicaca, Peru.

**azacytidine:** drug useful in cancer therapy that has also been used experimentally to promote expression of hemoglobin F genes. Aka 5-azacytidine. Cf. **hydroxyurea**.

**Azara's night monkey:** vernacular for *Aotus azarai*.

*Azibius treki* Sudre, 1975: adapoid **prosimian** known from the late **Eocene** of North Africa; phylogenetic relationship unknown and assigned to a family *incertae sedis*; **monotypic**. Known only from a single jaw with three teeth. Estimated body mass around 120 g. See Appendix 1 for taxonomy.

**Azilian culture:** transitional culture area of the **EpiPaleolithic era** in France that succeeded the **Tardenoisian–Magdalenian** and preceded the **Neolithic**, and characterized by a relatively meager stone tool tradition with round scrapers and points, poorly made angle gravers, and crude stag antler harpoons. Representational art is absent; pebbles with painted dots are typical. See **Azilians** and the type site for this culture, **Mas d'Azil.**

**Azilians: ethonym** for a **Mesolithic** people or culture considered to be descended from the Franco-Cantabrian Magdalenian culture of the late upper Paleolithic. The Azilians occupied western Europe and were a hunting and fishing culture that used harpoons, lived in small isolated communities, and inhabited caves. Azilian technology and art is considered to be poor in comparison to the Magdalenians; Azilian art was much more abstract than the art of the **Magdalenians.** Azilian culture existed from *c.* 11.5 to 9.5 kya. See **Mas d'Azil.**

**azygous:** unpaired.

$b_0$: abbreviation for **intercept**.

***Babakotia*** **Godfrey, Simons, Chatrath, and Rakotosaminimanana, 1990: extinct subfossil Malagasy prosimian** genus belonging to the family Palaeopropithecidae; *B. radofilai* is the only recognized species. Material recovered from a site in far northern Madagascar. Arboreal; diurnal; forelimbs longer relative to hindlimbs; curved **phalanges** on fore paw; reduced hind paw, all of which suggest suspensory locomotor adaptation. Body mass estimated to be between 15 and 20 kg. Dental formula: 2.1.2.3/1.1.2.3 or 2.1.2.3/2.0.2.3; dental adaptations suggestive of **folivory**. See Appendix 2 for taxonomy, Appendix 3 for living and recently extinct species.

**babakoto:** Malagasy vernacular for ***Indri indri.***

**baboon:** vernacular for large, terrestrial, sexually dimorphic cercopithecine monkeys of Africa. See ***Papio***, ***Mandrillus***, and ***Theropithecus***.

**baboon lemur:** vernacular for the two genera belonging to the recently **extinct subfossil Malagasy prosimian** family **Archaeolemuridae**.

**BAC:** bacterial artificial chromosome; an artificial chromosome, created from modification of the fertility factor of *E. coli* plasmids, which allows incorporation of up to 330 kb of foreign (such as human) DNA.

**Baccinello:** paleontological site found in 1956 in Italy, dated to the late **Miocene**, and that contains hominoid remains including six individuals attributed to *Oreopithecus*.

**bachelor:** in mammalogy, a reproductive age male that is unattached to a group that has reproductive age females or, in cases of **noyau** or **monogamy**, a single reproductive age female. A bachelor may also be an older male that has been displaced from a mixed-sex group.

**bachelor herd:** in **primates** and other mammals, a group of **bachelors** that are unattached to a group that has reproductive age females. Bachelor herds often originate from mixed-sex groups or **one-male units**. Aka bachelor gang.

**Bacho Kiro cave:** archaeological site found in Bulgaria, dated to 32.7 kya ($^{14}$C, perhaps as old as 47.5 kya), and that contains Early Upper Paleolithic artifacts (**Mousterian** or **Aurignacian**) and very fragmentary hominid remains including jaw and tooth fragments assigned variously to either *Homo neanderthalensis* or *Homo sapiens* by various researchers.

**bacillary dysentery:** infectious disease of the digestive tract caused by a gram-negative bacillus *Shigella dysenteriae* and three other species. Symptoms include intestinal pain and diarrhea; the stool contains blood and mucus.

**back:** 1. posterior portion of the thorax. 2. stone tool with a blunted edge produced by secondary flaking, aka *à dos rabattu*.

**back mutation** (v): a heritable change in a mutant gene resulting in a reversion that has regained the enzyme or function that was lost with a former **forward mutation**; the average rate of reverse mutations is about $1 \times 10^{-9}$ gametes per generation. Aka reverse mutation.

**backbone:** 1. see **vertebral column** and **vertebra**. 2. phosphate groups and 5-carbon sugars that bond to form the vertical structure of **DNA**; pairs of **nitrogenous bases** form the horizontal structures.

**backbone genetic program:** matrix of gene activities including structural, control, and regulatory genes critical to the basic developmental plan of an organism. Cf. **appended genetic program**.

**backcross:** 1. the crossing of a **heterozygote** with one of its parents. 2. in experimental genetics, a mating between a heterozygote and a homozygote.

**background extinction:** extinction that occurs during normal times, as opposed to those which are part of extraordinary **mass extinction** events; the constant low rate of extinction, as distinct from the five mass extinctions; the normal, or background, extinction rate.

**background genotype:** genotype of an organism that is not responsible for the phenotype; the unexpressed genotype.

**background radiation:** mutagenic, carcinogenic and teratogenic radioactivity from both cosmic and terrestrial sources that constantly bombards all organisms. Background radiation averages 0.5–1.0 microcoulombs per kilogram (2–4 milliroentgens) per week, and 77.5 μc kg$^{-1}$ (300 milliroentgens) per week is considered the maximum permissible dose.

**Baco Kiro:** see **Bacho Kiro cave**.

**Bacsonian:** pertaining to a stone industry of Indo–China characterized by a stone ax with a ground cutting edge similar to that found in Australian sites.

**Bacteria:** one of the three basic kinds of life assigned its own **Domain**; the other two are the **Eukarya** and the **Archaea**. See also **bacterium**.

**bacterial artificial chromosome:** see **BAC**.

**bacterial diseases:** diseases of animals, especially humans, caused by or facilitated by **bacteria**; examples are **cholera**, **bacillary dysentery**, and **bubonic plague**.

**bacteriophage:** any member of a class of viruses that specialize in attacking bacteria. Most phages destroy their bacterial host; some, however, incorporate their DNA into that of the host and remain dormant. Bacteriophages have become important tools in **genetic engineering**. Aka phage.

**bacterium:** any microorganism in the order Eubacteriales. Plural: bacteria. Bacteria have a well-defined cell wall, can reproduce without the requirement of a host cell, and can be classified according to shape: spherical (coccus), rod-shaped (bacillus), and spiral (spirillum and spirochete). In humans, diseases caused by bacteria are the most common mode of fatal **infectious disease** in developed countries, and a leading cause in underdeveloped countries; bacterial. See **syphilis**, and **bacterial diseases**.

**baculum:** rod-like bone found in the penis of some mammals, including many primates. Some female primates have a bony structure in the clitoris that is reminiscent of, but smaller than, the male baculum. Aka *os penis*.

**Badegoulian:** early (*c.* 16 kya) **Magdalenian**-like culture of central France that placed an emphasis on blades and burins; aka Magdalenian 0 and Magdalenian I.

**badlands:** landscape in which intermittent streams and flash flood channels have created a complex, cross-cut topography.

**Baer, Karl Ernst Ritter von** (1792–1876): Estonian anatomist and embryologist, first at Königsburg, and after 1834 a member of the St. Petersburg Academy of Sciences; discovered **eggs** in mammalian reproductive systems (1827). Von Baer accepted **Darwinism** with reservations; on craniometric grounds he argued for six **races**, that none could be considered either inferior or superior, and that all were derived from a single stock.

**Bahr el Ghazal:** region containing several archaeological sites found in 1960 in the Borkou–Ennedi–Tibesti Province near Koro Toro (KT) in northern Chad, dated to 3.5–3.0 mya, and that contains hominid remains, including a partial mandible attributed to *Australopithecus bahrelghazali* from site KT 12. Paleoenvironment was a lakeside forest with patchy grass arenas. In Arabic, the name means 'river of the gazelles'. The most notable of at least 17 sites. Aka Koro Toro, **Yayo**.

**BAIB:** see **beta-aminoisobutyric acid**.

**Bailongdong Cave:** archaeological site found in 1975 near Bailongdong in Yunxi county, Hubei province, China, dated to about 30 kya, and that contains a late Pleistocene fauna. Hominid remains include isolated teeth assigned to *Homo erectus*. Aka Yunxi, Bailiandong.

**Baker, Paul Thornell:** (1927–) US adaptation physiologist at Penn State; initiated the high-altitude research site at Nuñoa, Peru (1962–76). At the Samoan Migrant Health Project (1975–86) he studied the effects of adaptation and modernization. He mentored 25 Ph.D. students and retired in 1987.

**balance hypothesis:** idea that **parasitism** is based on an equilibrium between the host's ability to provide substances that both promote and inhibit growth of the parasite.

**balance school:** genetic perspective developed by T. **Dobzhansky** that recognizes that **genetic variation** and **polymorphism** are necessary to produce an adaptive **population**. In this model, the ideal **genotype** is **heterozygous** rather than homozygous, as prescribed by the opposing **classical school of genetics**. Aka balance model.

**balanced genetic polymorphism:** see **balanced polymorphism**.

**balanced load:** see **segregational load**.

‡ **balanced polymorphism:** state in which a population is usually maintained at **equilibrium** values by a selective superiority of the **heterozygote** over either class of **homozygote**. Characterized by changes in **genotype frequencies** due to **selection** against both homozygote classes but does *not* result in changes in **allele frequencies** between generations. One of the alleles is usually **deleterious** in the **recessive** homozygous genotype, as in **sickle cell anemia**. Rarely, this state is also achieved by selective superiority of both homozygote classes.

**balancing selection:** see **stabilizing selection**.

**balancing side:** side of the mouth where no tooth contact takes place during chewing. Cf. **working side** and **occlusion**.

**bald-faced saki:** vernacular for *Pithecia irrorata*.

**bald (-headed) uakari:** vernacular for *Cacajao calvus*.

**baldness:** lack of natural hair covering on the pate of the head; see **male pattern baldness**.

**Baldwin effect:** hypothesis that an advantageous phenotypic trait can appear in a few individuals in response to environmental factors; an individual could, in the absence of such factors, become endowed with the advantageous trait by mutation and the gene responsible would then spread through the population. A controversial hypothesis. See **organic selection theory**. Aka genetic assimilation, the Baldwin–Morgan–Osborn hypothesis.

**ball-and-socket joint:** type of **synovial joint** in which a round head articulates with a cup-shaped cavity in the bone it joins with; freely movable joint that allows a wide range of motions including rotation. Aka spheroidal joint, enarthrosis.

**bamboo:** rapidly growing, fibrous, and extremely strong (by mass) tubular grass indigenous to Asia. Researchers have shown that the natural distribution of bamboo (before it was transported worldwide by colonials) coincides closely with the distribution of the simple non-Acheulean chopper and flake tool distributions of Middle Pleistocene Asian hominids. This has been invoked to explain the lack of need to develop more complex tools in Asia during the **Pleistocene**. See **nonlithic model**.

**bamboo forest:** thick clumps of **bamboo**, usually along river banks of lowland tropical rain forests. At one time bamboo forests were more widespread in Madagascar, Africa, and Asia. It is the habitat of the primate genus *Hapalemur*. See **forest**.

**bamboo lemur:** one of the vernaculars used for the genus *Hapalemur*.

**band:** 1. term applied to groups of certain social mammals, including humans (see **band societies**). In humans, band size is often between 25 and 35, and is usually composed of closely related individuals. 2. in genetics, an alternating horizontal stripe on a chromatid that has been treated with trypsin or other proteolytic enzyme; after **banding**, certain bands indicate the presence of **heterochromatin**, whereas others indicate **euchromatin**. See **C-banding, G-banding Q-banding, and R-banding**

**band society:** group of humans, usually not exceeding 25 individuals, that organize on a seasonal basis for the purpose of subsistence. Aka campsite community.

**banded leaf monkey:** vernacular for *Presbytis melalophos*.

**banding (pattern):** staining of chromosomes to make characteristic cross bands visible, thus facilitating identification of chromosome pairs, allocation of phenotypic features to the specific chromosome segment, and classification of clinical syndromes. See **chromosome banding technique, chromosome banding designation, G-banding, Q-banding, and R-banding.**

**Banks, Joseph:** (1743–1820) British botanist, President of the Royal Society (1778–1820); one of the great patrons of natural science and also a scientist in his own right. Banks was the companion of Captain James Cook on a voyage of circumnavigation (1768), and also explored Newfoundland and Iceland. Banks was the author of the policy that placed naturalists on board British naval vessels, and which thus impacted the lives of Charles **Darwin**, Daniel Solander and many other young men of the nineteenth century.

**Bañolas:** archaeological site found in 1887 in Gerona, Spain, dated to 45–40 kya (U–series), and that contains hominid remains, including a mandible attributed to *Homo* cf. *neanderthalensis*. Researchers have reported that the mandible exhibits evidence of toothpick use. Aka Banyolas.

**banquet feeder:** term used by a few authors in reference to colobines (**Colobinae**) that forage in a small area and fill their **sacculated stomachs** with leaves. Cf. **smorgasbord feeder**.

**B antigen:** **epitope** that specifies the B in the **ABO blood group**. It consists of four precursor sugars attached to glycoproteins of the cell membrane, aka **H substance**, plus a specific fifth terminal sugar,

galactose, that is attached by an enzyme. This enzyme differs from its homologue that attaches the A-specific sugar by one amino acid substitution. See **A antigen** and **O null allele**.

**Banyolas:** see **Bañolas**.

**Bapang Formation:** revised name proposed for the **Kabuh Formation** in central Java, a member of the Kendeng Group. The geological age of the formation has recently been estimated to be 1.6–1.0 my.

**Baradostian:** tool industry, centered in Iraq, which emphasized blades and a high predominance of **burins**; dated at 34–29 kya.

**barbarism:** 1. vernacular for any culture that has no written language but practices horticulture. 2. in outmoded studies of **unilineal evolution**, the cultural stage that succeeds **savagery** and precedes **civilization**.

**Barbary macaque:** vernacular for *Macaca sylvanus*; formerly referred to as the Barbary 'ape'.

**bare-eared marmoset:** vernacular for *Callithrix argentata*.

**bare-faced tamarin:** vernacular for *Saguinus bicolor*.

**bare-faced tamarin section:** division of the genus *Saguinus* based on the presence or absence of facial fur, and other **pelage** patterns. Not a subgenus. The bare-faced tamarin section consists of two groups. The major distinguishing features are a densely furred crown, but a naked face. The *S. bicolor* group consists of *S. bicolor* only. The *S. oedipus* group consists of *S. oedipus* and *S. leucopus*, which are distinguished from the *S. bicolor* group by body pelage features.

**bared-teeth display:** see **fear grin (grimace)**.

**Baringo:** 1. one of the fourteen districts in Rift Valley Province, Kenya. 2. a lake in the Baringo district. 3. an archaeological region identified in 1966 near Lake Baringo, with twelve different fossiliferous units. Hominid fossils have been recovered from the **Ngorora, Lukeino, Chemeron, Chemiogut, Chesowanja,** and **Kapurthin** sedimentary formations. Often used with specific reference to an archaeological site found in 1966 near Lake **Baringo**, Kenya, dated to 500–200 kya, and that contains **Acheulean** artifacts at a **living site** and hominid remains, including two partial mandibles attributed to **archaic** *Homo sapiens*.

**barium:** trace dietary **element**; a **stable isotope** used in determining nutritional states of prehistoric populations; see **paleonutrition**.

**barometric pressure:** pressure of the earth's atmosphere as measured by a barometer; i.e. 760 mmHg at sea level and at a depth of 10 m in sea water. Aka atmospheric pressure.

**baroreceptor:** cluster of neuroreceptors stimulated by pressure changes that monitor blood pressure.

**Barranc de Can Vila 1** (BCV1): type locality near the

village of Els Hostalets de Pierola near Barcelona in Catalunya, Spain, site of the discovery of *Pierolapithecus catalaunicus*.

**Barranco León** (BL5): see **Orce Ravine**.

‡ **Barr body:** sex chromatin; darkly staining, inactivated **X chromosome** in a squamous epithelial cell. Technically, this **heteropycnotic** mass is an inactivated **chromatid**, not a chromosome. See **X inactivation**.

**barrel-shaped incisor: incisor** in which there are lingual extensions of the enamel from the **mesial** and **distal** borders that touch and give the appearance of a small distorted premolar. See **shovel-shaped incisor**.

**barrier:** 1. as used in biology, any obstacle to reproduction between populations or species, e.g. geographical barriers such as bodies of water, deserts, or mountains that separate populations and prevent breeding. Other barriers to reproduction include structural barriers (e.g. male **intromittent organs** that do not fit the reproductive organs of females of other species), behavioral barriers (e.g. differences in courtship rituals or activity cycles) and, in humans, social and cultural barriers. 2. In physiology, a barrier that limits movement between entities; e.g. the **blood–brain barrier**.

**Barro Colorado Island** (BCI): research site located in Lake Gatun, Panama, where long-term field studies of howler monkeys (**Alouatta** sp.) have been conducted since 1931. Primatologists who have conducted field research at this site include: C. R. **Carpenter**, K. Milton, and D. D. Colwell.

**bartonellosis:** infectious disease caused by a rickettsial organism, *Bartonella bacilliformis*; Rickettsiales. Endemic in the Peruvian highlands, where the sand fly *Phlebotomus verrucarum* serves as the **vector**. Reservoirs of infection include arboreal rodents and New World monkeys. After resolution of the acute stage, persistence may result in lesions known as verrugas peruana. Of New World origin, but later exported into the Old World, where the **disease reservoir** now includes gerbils. Aka Oroya fever, Carrion's disease. See **leishmaniasis**.

**basal forebrain:** region of the **limbic system** that regulates human emotion through connections to the **prefrontal cortex**; consists of the **ventral striatum**, the **ventral pallidum** and the **nucleus accumbens**.

**basal ganglion:** mass of bilateral nerve cell bodies located deep within a **cerebral hemisphere** of the brain. Among other functions, the basal ganglia function to initiate and control smooth muscle movement by processing dopamine; failure of dopamine to reach the basal ganglia can result in loss of muscle control.

**basal group:** smaller of two sister groups; the **outgroup** used when studying relationships among members of the larger clade.

**Basal Member:** oldest Member in the **Hadar Formation**.

‡ **basal metabolic rate:** see **BMR**.

**basal metabolism:** minimum energy requirements of an animal at complete rest, usually measured as oxygen turnover; aka **basal metabolic rate**.

**basalt:** dark, fine-grained igneous rock of a lava flow that is important in evolutionary studies because it can be used for **radiometric dating**.

‡ **base:** in biochemistry, an alternative term for a nitrogenous **nucleotide** (joined with a backbone sugar and phosphate); the fundamental building blocks of both **DNA** (adenine {A}, cytosine {C}, guanine {G}, thymine {T}) and **RNA** (where uracil {U} is substituted for thymine). A and G are **purines**; C, T, and U are **pyrimidines**.

**base analogue:** any purine or pyrimidine that differs in chemical structure from those normally found in **nucleic acids** (A, T, G, C, U) and that is incorporated into nucleic acids (DNA, RNA) in place of the normal base, causing a **mutation**.

**base camp:** central location within a **home range** to which a **troop** or **band** returns with regularity.

**base excision repair:** removal of five or fewer nucleotides in DNA in order to repair damage caused by reactive oxygen molecules.

**base pair** (bp): 1. in **DNA**, two bonded nitrogenous bases; a purine is always paired with a pyrimidine, in the absence of mutation. 2. a unit of size for measuring the width of DNA, equivalent to the length of one pair of complementary nucleotides on opposing strands of DNA.

‡ **base-pairing rule:** in double-stranded DNA, **adenine** normally bonds with **thymine** (A–T) and **cytosine** normally bonds with **guanine** (C–G), producing molecular pairs with equal dimensions. Aka principle of complementarity. See **Chargaff's rules**.

**basement membrane:** thin sheet of extracellular substance to which the basal surfaces of membranous epithelial cells are attached; Aka basal lamina.

**basic invention:** original concept and its application to material or cognitive culture. See **invention**.

**basic rank:** position an individual holds within a social hierarchy when there is no interference by other group members. Cf. **dependent rank**.

**basicranial:** of or pertaining to the **basicranium**, the base of the skull.

**basicranial flexion:** condition in which the bones on the floor of the cranium form an arch; the flexed condition is found in certain species of the genus *Homo*, but not in **australopithecines**.

**basicranium:** region of the cranium that is composed of the **ethmoid**, **sphenoid**, petrous and mastoid portions of the **temporal bone**, as well as a part of the **occipital bone**. The basicranium forms the floor of the cranium and develops through **endochondral ossification**. Aka viscerocranium, basocranium. See **cranium.**

**basilar:** 1. of, or pertaining to, or positioned near the base. 2. in anatomy, refers to a suture on the base of the cranium between the **occipital** and **sphenoid** bones.

**basilar membrane:** membrane of the mammalian inner ear that separates the two cochlear canals, the scala vestibuli and scala tympani; the organ of Corti, the structure that contains the auditory hairs, is located on the internal surface of this membrane.

**basilar suture:** articulation between the **occipital** and **sphenoid** bones. See **basioccipital synchondrosis.**

**basin:** shallow area on a **molar** tooth between the **cusps.**

**basioccipital synchondrosis:** region of the basal portion of the skull where the **sphenoid** and **occipital bones** articulate. This suture is considered one of the most consistent fusion events of the skull and is useful in **age determination** of young individuals. Aka basilar structure.

**basion** (ba): craniometric landmark on the external inferior surface of the cranial base at the midpoint of the anterior border of the **foramen magnum.** Used to measure the height of the skull. See Appendix 7.

**basion–alveolar length** (ba–ids): **craniometric** measurement; distance from the **basion** to the **alveolare** measured with sliding calipers. See Appendix 7 for an illustration of the landmarks used.

**basion–nasion length** (po–b): **craniometric** measurement; height from the **nasion** to the **bregma** measured with spreading calipers. See Appendix 7 for an illustration of the landmarks used.

**basion–porion height** (ba–po): **craniometric** measurement; distance from the **basion** to the **porion** measured by coordinate calipers. See Appendix 7 for an illustration of the landmarks used.

**basion–prosthion length:** cranial measurement, the distance from the **basion** to the **prosthion;** Aka the basion–prosthion line.

**basionym:** initial name for a **taxon** that is replaced because of a shift in the rank or position of that taxon; nevertheless, the basionym's stem is retained in the name of the new taxon. Alternative spelling: basinym.

**basophil:** polymorphonuclear granular **leukocyte** that readily stains blue with basophilic dye; basophils enter tissues and become **mast cells.** Basophils constitute less than 1% of total blood volume, and secrete **heparin** and **histamine.**

**Basque: ethnym** for people of the Pyrenees region of France and Spain, distinct from other European populations, based on a high frequency of the Rh− allele and distinctive language. L. L. **Cavalli-Sforza** has suggested that the Basque-speaking people are the descendants of the original **AMHs** (i.e. **Cro-Magnon**) to occupy Europe. See **Rhesus blood group.**

**Bass, William M.** (1928–): US skeletal biologist and forensic osteologist who has identified over 300 crime and accident victims. Trained by Charles **Snow** at the University of Kentucky (MA) and Wilton M. **Krogman** at the University of Pennsylvania (Ph.D.). Faculty member at the University of Kansas (1960–71) and University of Tennessee (1971–present); author of *Human Osteology: Laboratory and Field Manual of the Human Skeleton* (1971), a standard work.

**bastard:** 1. an illegitimate child. 2. in anthropology, any half-breed, half-blood, or **shadow child**, especially any regional cluster of such individuals as the result of warfare, displaced peoples, and/or colonization.

**Bateman's principle:** proposition that in most **polygamous** species some males will produce more offspring than others; variance in reproductive success will thus be greater among males than among females. See **sexual selection.**

**Bates, Henry Walter** (1825–92): natural historian; with only £100 between them, Bates and Alfred Russel **Wallace** embarked for South America in 1848, navigating up the Amazon at least 1000 miles. Bates is best remembered for his hypotheses concerning interspecific mimicry (**Batesian mimicry**). Author of *The Naturalist on the River Amazons* (1863).

**Batesian mimicry:** kind of mimicry in which a nonpoisonous species (the Batesian form) mimics a poisonous and conspicuous species, such as when certain butterfly species mimic distasteful, unrelated species, and they thus become less susceptible to predation by birds. Aka pseudoaposematic coloration. Cf. **Müllerian mimicry.**

**Bateson, William** (1861–1926): English embryologist at Cambridge and later one of the founders of **genetics** after the rediscovery of Gregor **Mendel's** work. Co–discoverer of **linkage.** Author of *Material for the Study of Variation* (1894) and *Mendel's Principles of Heredity* (1908).

**bâton percé: Magdalenian** antler artifact that usually has a hole that runs through it. Frequently, these tools are engraved with images of animals. The actual purpose of a baton tool is unknown, although it has been suggested that it was used to straighten spear shafts. Known as a bâton de commandement in the older literature.

**Bau de l'Aubesier:** archaeological site in southeastern France, dated to 200–175 kya (thermoluminescence), and that contains Mousterian artifacts and hominid remains from at least 11 individuals assigned to *Homo* cf. *neanderthalensis.* A mandible (Aubesier 11), with extremely worn teeth and periodontal disease resulting in premortem tooth loss, has been interpreted as a sign of care-giving in Neandertals, since this individual is presumed to have been incapacitated for several months.

**Bauplan:** structural plan; **archetype**; morphotype; the generalized ancestral body plan of a taxon, lineage or phylum; e.g. the bauplan of vertebrates.

**Baventian glaciation:** early major glaciation of the Pleistocene in the British Isles sequence; see **Donau glaciation.**

**bay region theory:** hypothesis that chemical **carcinogenesis** involves a specific 'hollow' structural element (a diol epoxide) of certain polynuclear aromatic hydrocarbons, that visually resembles an aquatic bay.

**Bayley scale:** psychomotor test commonly used on newborn infants to children of about two years of age that measures development. Developed by psychologist Nancy Bayley, it has two components: one measures cognitive and perceptual development and the other, motor development.

**BC:** before Christ; refers to dates before the birth of Christ, put at AD 1. To determine how many years ago a BC date is, the number of years since **AD** 1 must be added to the BC date. See **BCE.**

**BCE:** before the common era; a modern means of referring to dates. BCE is used the same way as BC. See **BC** and **BP.**

‡ **B cell:** white blood cell (**lymphocyte**) that originates and matures in the marrow of bones. B cells secrete antibodies in response to antigens displayed on other immune system cells such as **macrophages**. Aka B lymphocyte. Cf. **T cell.**

**BCV1:** type locality of **Barranc de Can Vila** near the village of Els Hostalets de Pierola near Barcelona in Catalunya, Spain, site of the discovery of *Pierolapithecus catalaunicus.*

**B-DNA:** common form of **DNA** characterized by a right-handed helical conformation. Cf. **Z-DNA.**

**Beagle, HMS:** British Royal Navy surveying vessel on which Charles **Darwin** traveled around the world collecting **biota**. Darwin's voyage on the *Beagle* (1831–6) was a turning point in his life and for subsequent developments in biology.

**beanbag genetics:** popular synonym for **population genetics** or **particulate inheritance.**

**bear cult:** inference of human ritual associated with certain hominid groups, especially European **Neandertals**, who apparently stacked the skulls and post-cranial bones of cave bears almost geometrically at sites such as Dragon's Lair in Austria, giving an impression of interest or investment in such species.

**bear howler:** vernacular for *Alouatta arctoidea.*

**bear macaque:** vernacular for *Macaca arctoides.*

**bearded saki:** vernacular for the genus *Chiropotes*; consists of two species.

**Becker muscular dystrophy** (BMD): see **muscular dystrophy, Becker type.**

**Beckwith–Wiedemann syndrome:** inherited genetic condition characterized by an enlarged tongue, umbilical abnormalities, hypoglycemia, and a high risk of adrenal and kidney cancer. Exhibits evidence for **genomic imprinting.**

**becquerel** (Bq): unit of radioactivity that replaces the curie (Ci); radioactivity of a material decaying at the rate of one disintegration per second.

**bed:** in geology, a small, distinct **rock unit** that is identifiable by the field observer.

**Beddoe, John** (1826–1911): English physician. Studied hair and eye color among the Irish in 1861, and assumed these variants to be important racial markers; developed an 'index of nigrescence' to measure the ratio of light- to dark-haired individuals in a population. Conducted major anthropometric survey of Great Britain, published as *The Races of Britain: Contribution to the Anthropology of Western Europe* (1885) and conducted a second survey in Europe in 1891. Probably the first person to survey geographical regions in anthropometric detail.

**bedrock:** broad term that refers to rock underlying upper, unconsolidated materials. Cf. **soil.**

**Beestonian glaciation:** first major glaciation of the Pleistocene in the British Isles sequence; see **Günz glaciation.**

‡ **before present:** see BP. Cf. **BCE** and **CE.**

**before the common era** (BCE): see **BCE.** Cf. **BC** and **BP.**

‡ **behavior:** 1. any observable action or reaction by an organism in response to a stimulus. 2. the sum total of all activities of an organism in response to its **environment**, including **locomotion, foraging, mating behavior**, etc. See **primate behavior.**

**behavior–brain–gene approach:** method of deducing the relationships of disorders with a complex **etiology**, especially behavioral disorders, by examining a system with a 'top-down' model, i.e. from an abnormal condition or behavior, to its set of physiological conditions, to its genetic component and perhaps even specific gene(s). Examples are **schizophrenia, mood disorder**, and **autistic disorder.** Cf. **gene–brain–behavior approach.**

**behavior coding:** converting behavioral observations into **quantitative** categories.

**behavior genetics:** study of the patterns of inheritance of certain behavioral phenotypes. Behaviors in humans that exhibit a tendency to cluster in families include Huntington disease, mood disorders, schizophrenia, and Gilles de la Tourette syndrome. The genetic components in these cases may exhibit single-gene effects, but are most often subtle and multifactorial.

**behavior sampling:** sampling technique used in primate behavior studies in which the observer watches the entire group of animals and records each instance of a particular type of behavior with the details of the interactions that took place. This technique has the advantage that rare behaviors that might be missed, such as copulations or fighting, are more likely to be observed than by either **focal sampling** or **scan sampling**. Cf. *ad libitum* sampling.

**behavioral:** of or pertaining to behavior.

**behavioral adaptation:** behavioral response that adds to an individual's or species' fitness. A behavioral adaptation is the fastest way to respond to changing conditions.

**behavioral assessment:** argument that every organism is able to evaluate and make a choice as to what strategy it will pursue under any given circumstance; presumably, the individual will behave in the manner most optimal for itself.

**behavioral barrier:** reproductive isolating mechanism that prevents mating between two **allopatric** species or subspecies, owing to a difference in courtship behavior. Aka behavioral isolation; ethological isolation.

**behavioral biology:** discipline within biology that studies all aspects of behavior including those behaviors resulting from genetic, physiological and ecological influences; replaces the previous fields of **ethology** and comparative psychology. See **evolutionary psychology**, **behavioral ecology**, and **sociobiology**.

**behavioral drift:** changes in behavior that have no consequences for survival.

**behavioral ecology:** approach to the science of **ethology** in which certain **behaviors**, such as biological **altruism**, are proposed to have evolved, or can at least be modeled, by mechanisms such as **natural selection**, through the addition of concepts like **kin selection** and **group selection**. See **Robert Hinde**. Cf. **Standard Social Science Model**.

**behavioral evolution:** A. Irving Hollowell's term for a 'conjunctive' approach to **human evolution**, taking into account the organic, psychological, social, and cultural dimensions of the evolutionary process 'as they are related to underlying conditions that are necessary and sufficient for a human level of existence'. One of a group of terms describing a new sympathy for evolutionary aspects of behavior, after certain anthropologists 'rediscovered' **Darwin** in the 1970s.

**behavioral genetics:** discipline that studies the relative contributions of genes and environments underlying individual differences in behavior; see **nature–nurture controversy**.

**behavioral heterogeneity:** existence of many alternatives to each type of human behavior within any human population.

**behavioral phylogeny:** approach in which the evolution and taxonomic relationship of behaviors is studied. This type of study is conducted by observing the behavior of living species; shared behaviors are presumed to be derived from the common ancestor.

**behavioral reconstruction:** extrapolation of the behavior habits of an extinct species based on physical evidence as well as on the behavior of living species that are closely related or occupy an ecological niche, presumed to be similar.

**behavioral scaling:** pertaining to the diversity and strength of a behavior that can be used as a successful **adaptation** as conditions change by the same society or the same individual.

**behaviorism:** psychological theory of animal behavior that rejects genetically based explanations and introspection, and holds instead that actions can be explained entirely as responses to stimuli. Proposed by American psychologist John Watson (1878–1958), it has largely been supplanted by **ethology** except in clinical and educational psychology. Also spelled behaviourism.

**Behrensmeyer, Anna K.** (1948–): US paleobiologist at the Smithsonian Institution (NMNH). Member of the Second Rudolf Expedition (1969); published on the fossil assemblages east of Lake Rudolph, now **Lake Turkana**; the **KBS tuff** is named for her. Interests include geology, **taphonomy**, and the paleoecology of Africa and Pakistan; often referred to as the 'mother of taphonomy'. Co-author (with A. P. Hill) of *Fossils in the Making* (1980); co-editor of *Terrestrial Ecosystems Through Time* (1992).

**bejel:** form of **syphilis** contracted without sexual contact, characterized by lesions of the skin, mucous membranes and bones; caused by a spirochete, *Treponema pallidum endemicum*. Infects mainly children; endemic in the arid countries of the Middle East, North Africa, and Eastern Mediterranean. Aka nonvenereal syphilis, endemic syphilis. See **nonvenereal treponematoses**.

**BEL-VP-1/1:** see **Belohdelie**.

**belief systems:** ideas taken on the basis of faith, and that cannot be tested in the scientific sense. Closed systems of ideology, e.g., religions, philosophies, ethical beliefs, and moral beliefs. Some anthropologists argue that the 'philosophy of science', although internally consistent and rigorous, should also be viewed as a belief system.

**bell curve:** see **normal distribution**.

**Belohdelie:** archaeological site found in 1981 in the Afar basin along the **Middle Awash** River, Ethiopia, dated to > 4.0–3.8 mya, and that contains hominid remains, including a fragments of a frontal bone (BEL-VP-1/1), considered too fragmentary for a secure attribution; *sp. indet.*

**beloid:** of or pertaining to a cranium that when viewed from above is narrow in front and broad at the back.

**bends:** pain in the joints and muscles produced by liberation of gas bubbles in the tissues due to rapid ascent from an environment of high pressure; limbs are maintained in a semiflexed position (hence the name). Aka caisson disease.

**benefit:** potential gain of **fitness** to an individual associated with any particular behavior.

**Beni titi:** vernacular for *Callicebus* olallae.

**benign:** not **malignant.**

**Bennet movement (shift):** slight lateral movement of the mandibular **condyles** during chewing.

**Benninghof's lines:** small cracks and splits that radiate from a hole made in a dried cranium by piercing it with an awl. The lines indicate forces of pressure, torsion and stress, and follow a general pattern of tension created by chewing. A later application of this methodology was known as the split-line and stresscoat technique.

**bent-hip gait:** see **bent-knee gait.**

**bent-knee gait:** type of **bipedal locomotion** that the earliest hominids (genus *Australopithecus*) are presumed to have used. In a bent-knee gait, the knee is flexed, rather than locked in extension as in modern humans. This type of locomotion is seen in living **chimpanzees** when they attempt to walk bipedally. Aka bent-hip bent-knee gait. See **striding gait.**

**bentonitic clay:** clay formed from decomposed volcanic ash, important because it can be dated by **radiometric dating.**

**benzo(a)pyrine:** carcinogen found in tobacco, that causes a specific mutation in the *p53* **tumor suppressor** gene.

**Berber: ethonym** for pre-Arab people of North Africa who speak a language that is a subfamily of the Afro-Asiatic language family. The geographic distribution of the Berber language is now fragmented, ranging from the Canary Islands (before AD 1500) to western North Africa to Egypt. Berbers are presumed to be descended from Eurasian peoples who entered North Africa about 15 000 BP.

**Berg Aukas:** archaeological site found in Namibia that 1. is dated to *c.* 13 mya (middle **Miocene**), and that contains fossil hominoids attributed to *Otavipithecus*. 2. is dated to the middle **Pleistocene**, and that contains a fossil hominid femur comparable, owing to its robusticity, to that of European Neandertals.

‡ **Bergmann's rule:** tenet that among polytypic and **homeothermic** species (a) of similar shape, that larger individuals lose heat less rapidly than smaller, and (b) of similar size, that individuals with a linear shape lose heat more rapidly than individuals with a nonlinear shape; the consequence is that populations in colder environments tend to be larger and stouter, on average, than those in mild climates.

**beriberi:** state of **malnutrition** caused by a reversible deficiency (or **avitaminosis**) of **vitamin B$_1$**. In the infantile forms there is involvement of the heart and **gastrointestinal tract**, usually fatal unless vitamin supplemented. In the adult onset form there are two primary types, dry and wet. The symptoms of the dry type include symmetrical, ascending neuritis (weakness of lower limbs, progressing upward) with increasing skin sensitivity. In the wet type there is heart failure and edema. Both types can be fatal. The primary cause is a deficiency of **thiamine** (vitamin B$_1$), which is required for carbohydrate metabolism, and essential for the breakdown of pyruvic acid. Beriberi is common in Asia where the milling process, or rice polishing, removes the fuzzy surface of the grain, where thiamine is located. Feeding humans and test animals (e.g. chickens) affected with beriberi with a concentrate made from rice polishings reverses the clinical symptoms. Although first described in SE. Asia in the nineteenth century, it was 1912 before Casimir Funk showed that beriberi in pigeons could be cured by the above process; in similar experiments he showed the reversibility of several such conditions, coining the term 'vitamines' (**vitamins**) for the deficient substances. The condition was described in Pacific fishermen in the twentieth century, when they subsisted on raw fish (sushi) that contains an enzyme that binds with and inactivates thiamine. Thiamine is abundant in pork meat and the coats of cereal grains.

**Beringia:** continent-sized former land bridge spanning the Bering Strait between present-day Alaska and Siberia; formed during the **Cretaceous period.** It persisted into the early **Tertiary**, and was exposed intermittently during **glacial maxima** of the **Pleistocene epoch.** Currently under the Bering Sea, this former **land bridge** permitted exchanges of **biota** including the **migration** of humans from Asia into North America. During the last great glacial period this land bridge was about 1200 miles wide. Aka Bering land bridge.

**Beringian walk theory:** proposal that **AMHs** dispersed into the New World across **Beringia** over many generations.

**Bermuda rules:** guidelines used by the international consortium sequencing the human genome that resulted in the publication of the human genome in the public domain.

**Bernhardt's formula:** specification for determining the ideal mass in kilograms of an adult human, given as {height (in cm) × chest circumference (in cm)}/240.

*Berruvius* **Russell, 1964:** poorly known, very small (estimated body mass 20 g) microsyopid from the late **Paleocene** – early **Eocene** of Europe. Two species. Appears to be most closely related to *Navajovius*. Dentition and small size suggest **insectivory**. Some authorities think that the **Microsyopidae** are not primates, but that their affinities lie with the **extant** bats. See **Chiroptera**.

**best-fit line:** in a scatterplot, the line that most accurately represents the trend of the data. Typically, best-fit lines are estimated by **least squares regression**.

**bet hedging:** model developed by Schaffer and considered to be an alternative **hypothesis to _r_-selection** and ***K*-selection**. Bet hedging predicts that when there is high juvenile mortality in a fluctuating environment, longer-lived, slower-reproducing individuals will be favored, while in situations where there is high adult mortality, short-lived, rapidly reproducing individuals will be favored.

**beta:** the second letter of the Greek alphabet (see appendix 10); usually denotes the second item in a series or set.

**beta-aminoisobutyric acid** (BAIB): amino acid that is normally excreted in small amounts in the urine. This has been used as a **genetic marker** by population geneticists because the amount excreted varies in different populations. This trait is inherited as a simple Mendelian **recessive pattern of inheritance**, with homozygous recessive individuals being the highest excretors of BAIB.

**beta amyloid** (Aβ): one of several proteins that accumulate in the brain tissue of people with **Alzheimer's disease**. See **tau amyloid** and **prion protein**.

**beta decay** (β): radioactive decay in which the nucleus of an **isotope** emits an electron and one of its neutrons turns into a proton.

**beta diversity:** measure of the rate and degree to which species composition changes along a gradient from one environment to another.

**beta galactosidase:** enzyme that catalyzes the hydrolysis of lactose into galactose and glucose.

‡ **beta globin chain** (β Hb): one of two **polypeptide chains** that compose the **tertiary structure** of **adult hemoglobin**. In humans, the beta globin chain consists of 146 amino acids, transcribed and translated from a **cistron** on chromosome 11p. A total of four chains are required for the completion of a complete molecule: two beta chains, and two **alpha globin chains**. Aka beta globin.

**beta globulins:** serum proteins consisting of **polypeptides** including **complement** C3 (def. 2), plasminogen, **transferrin**, and **lipoproteins**. See **globulins**.

**beta karyology:** determination of chromosome numbers and arm lengths and the identification of the **sex chromosomes**. The second analytical level of **karyology**.

**beta level** (β): in statistics, the probability of accepting a **null hypothesis** when it is in fact false. See **Type 2 error**.

**beta thalassemia:** see **thalassemia**.

**beta thegosis:** a pattern of dental wear in which the facet becomes parallel to the enamel prisms. See **thegosis**.

**beta waves:** electrical activity emanating from the frontal lobes of the cerebral hemispheres, normally detected as rhythmic oscillations of about 13–25 cycles per second. Beta waves are correlated with responses to normal stimuli and are indicative of visual and mental activity. See **electroencephalogram** and **brain waves**. Aka beta rhythm.

**Betche-aux-Rotches Cave:** see **Spy Caves**.

**Bhudas:** inbred community in Hyderabad, India, in which there exists a high frequency of hereditary **adontia**, baldness, and sensitivity to heat. Aka the 'toothless men of Sind'. See **ectodermal dysplasia**.

**Biache:** archaeological site found in Europe, dated to 175 ± 13 kya (TL), and that contains Middle Paleolithic artifacts and hominid remains including the rear portion of a gracile, 1200 cm³ cranium (female?) possessing an **occipital bun**; teeth (possibly from a male); assigned to either *Homo neanderthalensis* or the younger 'anteneandertal' or archaic *Homo sapiens* group. Aka Biache-Saint-Vaast.

**biacromial breadth: anthropometric** measurement of shoulder width; distance between the left and right **acromion processes** of the scapula as measured with an **anthropometer**; the subject stands while the measurer locates the most lateral borders of the acromion processes and makes the measurements across the back of the individual. Used in body frame indices, **somatology**, and **human engineering**. Aka biacromial diameter.

**biallelic expression:** genotype in which both of two alleles is expressed in a heterozygote; symmetrical, Mendelian expression. Cf. **monoallelic expression**.

**bias:** 1. a systematic error in data collection that is caused by an inherent problem in the sampling technique. 2. an error that is introduced because of the expectations of the researcher, whether conscious or unconscious. Aka experimenter bias.

**bias of ascertainment:** selection of individuals for study by virtue of their possession of a certain trait; this bias inflates the estimate of the frequency of that trait in the study population.

**biased learning:** suggestion that learning abilities have evolved in the same way that physical traits have evolved.

**biased sample:** any sample selected in such a way that some members of the population are more likely to be selected than others.

**biasterionic breadth:** width of the skull on the chord between the left and right **asterion**.

**biblical races:** traditional names for groups of people classified according to either religion (idolators, infidels, etc.) or location (Palestinians, land of Nod, etc.). The term 'people' specifies those who 'huddle together'. See **folk taxonomy**.

**bicentric:** condition in which a taxon has two centers of evolution or distribution.

**biceps brachii:** muscle that moves the forearm. The short head of the biceps brachii originates from the **coracoid process**, and the long head originates from a tubercle above the glenoid cavity; they insert by a common tendon into the radial tuberosity. Its action is to flex the forearm at the elbow and to rotate the hand laterally.

**biceps skinfold: anthropometric** measurement; skinfold located and measured over the belly of the **biceps brachii** muscle as measured with skinfold calipers. Used in combination with other **skinfold measurements** to estimate total body fat. When combined with **triceps skinfold**, it can be used to calculate muscle and bone cross-sectional area. See **skinfold thickness**.

**bicipital:** 1. in reference to an anatomical structure that has either two heads or two points of origin. 2. in reference specifically to the biceps muscle (**biceps brachii**).

**bicondylar breadth** (cdl–cdl): **craniometric** measurement; distance between the left and right **condylions** as measured by sliding calipers. See Appendix 7 for an illustration of the landmarks used.

**bicornuate uterus:** structural type of mammalian uterus in which there is a single **cervix** and the two uterine horns are fused for part of their length. Among the primates this type of **uterus** is found in the **prosimians**. See **simplex uterus**. Alternative spelling: bicornute.

**bicristal breadth:** maximum linear distance between the iliac crests of a specimen. Cf. biiliac breadth, **pelvic breadth**. Aka bicristal diameter.

**bicuspid tooth:** tooth that has two **cusps** on the occlusal (chewing) surface. In primates bicuspids are normally **premolars**.

**bidirectional replication:** synthesis of DNA that occurs in both directions from the center of origin.

‡ **bifacial flaking:** act of removing flakes from both sides of a stone tool. See **bifacial tool**.

‡ **bifacial tool:** stone tool on which both sides have been worked. The result is a more efficient and symmetrical tool. A common biface is the **hand-ax** of the **Acheulean** tradition; bifacial.

**bifid:** divided into two equal parts by a medial cleft; forked; e.g. bifid spinous process of a cervical vertebra. Noun: bifidity.

**bifurcate:** to split into two branches. See **node** and **clade**.

**'Big Five' mass extinctions:** mass extinctions that occurred at or during the (1) end-Ordovician, (2) late Devonian, (3) end-Permian, (4) end-Triassic, and (5) Cretaceous–Tertiary. See **K/T**.

**big game:** large **Pleistocene** animals such as mammoths, woolly rhinos, cave bears, and aurochs; **megafauna** thought to have been hunted by **hominids**.

**big game hunting hypothesis:** suggestion that **Middle Paleolithic** peoples were capable of individual kills of **big game**. Some researchers propose that herds were driven over cliffs or into bogs, possibly with the aid of fire, as a more reasonable interpretation of **megafauna** extinction.

**big toe:** see **hallux**.

**bigamy:** state of having more than one husband or wife while an undivorced prior spouse is still living. See **polygamy, polygyny, polyandry**.

**bigeneric:** referring to a hybrid obtained by crossing individuals that are members of different genera. Aka multigeneric.

**bigonial breadth** (go – go): **craniometric** measurement; distance between the left and right **gonion** as measured with sliding calipers. Aka bigonial diameter. See Appendix 7 for an illustration of the landmarks used.

**biiliac breadth:** measurement of pelvic width. Biiliac breadth is measured from the most lateral projection of the right ilium to the most lateral projection of the left ilium. Aka biiliac diameter, biiliac depth. See **pelvic breadth**.

**bilaminar:** consisting of two layers.

**bilateral:** in reference to left and right sides of an organism, organ, or region.

**bilateral symmetry:** proportionality in which a division down the **midsagittal** plane would divide the body into right and left halves that are near mirror images; a characteristic of vertebrates.

**bile:** a yellow or greenish viscid alkaline fluid that is secreted by the liver and passes into the duodenum, from where it aids in the digestion and absorption of fats.

*Bilharzia:* former genus of trematode, now *Schistosoma*. See **schistosomiasis**.

**bilharziasis:** synonym for **schistosomiasis**; Aka bilharziosis.

**bilious:** 1. biliary. 2. of, pertaining to, or characteristic of biliousness. 3. formerly, of or pertaining to a temperament characterized by a quick, irritable temper. 4. of or pertaining to one of Galen's four types of human temperament, classified on the basis of the theory of humors. See **lymphatic, melancholic**, and **sanguineous**.

**bilirubin:** a yellow-orange bile pigment mainly formed from the breakdown of **hemoglobin** in reticuloendothelial cells, but also formed by breakdown of other heme pigments. High concentrations of bilirubin in tissues may result in jaundice.

**bilirubin diglucuronide:** see **conjugated bilirubin**.

**biliverdin:** a green bile pigment formed from the oxidation of **bilirubin.**

**bilophodonty:** condition found on molar teeth in which **mesial** and **distal** pairs of cusps form transverse ridges, or lophs, and characteristic of old world monkeys. Adjective: bilophodont. Aka two-crested tooth.

**bilou:** vernacular for *Hylobates klossii.*

**Bilzingsleben:** nineteenth century archaeological site that was reworked in 1927, 1974–7, and the 1990s, located near Erfurt, East Germany, dated to about 230 kya (Th/U), and that contains chopper-like artifacts, chisels and knives (a **microclactonian** flake industry). Hominid remains include a **taurodont** molar (1927), many cranial fragments (supra-orbital torus, sharp nuchal angle, thick bones, possibly male), and a mandible (E7), all attributed to the 'older' archaic *Homo* cf. *erectus* group. Aka Steinrinne Quarry.

**Bimana:** older classificatory term for organisms that use two limbs.

**bimanual:** with the use of two hands.

**Bimanus:** one of two orders erected by **Blumenbach** into which he classified the **primates;** humans alone were placed in Bimanus while the rest of the primates were classified as Quadrumana. This dramatic separation of humans from apes has not been supported by subsequent evidence, and these taxa have been dropped.

**bimorphic art:** aesthetic embellishment of small stones during the **Upper Paleolithic.** The designs were based on organic forms.

**binary:** 1. involving two. 2. a number system to the base 2.

**binary nomenclature:** see **binomial nomenclature** and **binomen.**

**binary trait, character** or **feature:** any character or trait with only two states; in taxonomic studies, such characters are recorded as being either present ($+$) or absent ($-$), while quantitative differences are ignored. Aka all-or-none trait.

**binaural hearing:** perception of sound waves by two ears.

**Binford, Louis R. ('Lou')** (1930–): US archaeologist and prehistorian at Southern Methodist University. Known for various heuristic theoretical and philosophical views, e.g. advocate of 'new' archeology (**processual archaeology**) and ethnoarchaeology. Co-author of *New Perspectives in Archaeology* (1968, with Sally R. Binford), *Bones* (1981), and *In Pursuit of the Past* (1983).

‡ **binocular vision:** sight that results from having eyes on the front of the head and that produces an overlapping visual field without **diplopia.** Binocular vision is a prerequisite for **stereoscopic vision.**

**binom:** taxon that is clearly characterized morphologically but poorly defined in terms of biosystematic data.

‡ **binomen:** two names, usually Latinized, that are used to identify an organism, namely the genus and the species; **binomial nomenclature. Linnaeus** was the first to use binomens routinely (*c.* 1758). See **trinomen.**

**binomial:** in mathematics, any algebraic expression containing two terms, such as $(p + q)$.

**binomial experiment:** test consisting of $n$ identical and independent trials, each of which can result in only one of two outcomes, the probability of one of which is $p$ and the other is $(1 − p) = q$.

‡ **binomial nomenclature:** name assignment system devised by **Linnaeus** whereby each species is assigned two names, a generic and a specific name, or the **genus** and **species** designations, respectively; in humans, e.g., *Homo sapiens.* See **binomen** and **trinomen.**

**binomial theorem:** 1. expansion of an expression containing two terms. 2. general result that yields the expansion to the $n$th power of a **binomial** as a polynomial, or $(p + q)^2$; i.e. by multiplying a binomial by itself $n$ times. In the following case the binomial $(p + q)$ is expanded to three terms when the binomial is squared: $(p + q)^2 = p^2 + 2pq + q^2$.

**bioacoustics:** study of the production and reception of sound by animals. In many cases this requires special technology that can detect high or low sound frequencies beyond the **hearing range** of the human ear. Bioacoustical research can also involve the generation of sound by the researcher to observe animal responses, as has been done with vervet monkeys.

**bioanthropology:** see **biological anthropology.**

**bioarchaeology:** interpretation of behavior from the human skeletal remains found in an archaeological context.

**biobank:** repository of large numbers of DNA samples, together with genealogies and the health histories of the donors. Examples in the public sector include: the UK biobank, CARTaGENE (Canada), GenomeEUtwin. Private sector ventures are owned by deCODE genetics and the Genomics Collaborative.

**biocenose:** natural assemblage of organisms; sometimes erroneously used as a synonym for ecosystem, but a biocenose does not include the abiotic elements included in an ecosystem; aka biocenosis.

**biochemical evolution:** evolution of organisms at the molecular level; **molecular evolution.**

**biochemical pathway:** stepwise conversion of one substrate to another through the use of enzymes.

**biochemistry:** science concerned with the composition and interactions of organisms. See **chemistry** and **organic.**

**biochrome:** substance that adds coloration to plant and animal tissue. Biochromes include such **pigments** as melanin, heme, and carotene.

**biochron:** total temporal duration of a given taxon or biostratigraphic unit. Cf. **chron.**

**biochronology:** establishment of a sequence of biological events using either biostratigraphic or paleontological methods.

**bioclast:** any fossil fragment.

‡ **biocultural:** pertaining to a recurrent interaction between the biology of human development and the sociocultural environment. Not only does the latter influence the former, but human developmental biology modifies social and cultural processes as well. Refers to patterns of **behavior** rather than to patterns of thought. Cf. **biosocial.**

‡ **biocultural approach:** method of understanding humans that considers both biological and cultural components of a phenomenon or **adaptation.**

‡ **biocultural evolution:** interaction between biology and culture during **human evolution** and **adaptation.**

**biocultural feedback model:** model developed by S. **Washburn** proposing that culture accelerated the adaptive process in early hominids, and that genes that support its development were advantageous and thus selected, which then allowed for additional cultural adaptation, and so forth. See **autocatalysis model, gene–culture coevolution.** Cf. Darwin's **tool-feedback hypothesis.**

**biodemography:** study of populations that combines both ecology and population genetics.

**biodeterminism:** see **biological determinism.**

**biodistance:** biological distance. Any of various methods that generate relative distance measures between individuals or populations, using either metric or nonmetric variables. One such common measure is the **Mahalanobis distance.** See **genetic distance.**

**biodiversity:** any measure or method of describing species richness, ecosystem complexity, and genetic variation.

**biodynamics:** science concerned with energy as it relates to living organisms and their environment.

**bioeconomics:** processes in which members of a species or population cooperate, benefiting the group. For example, penguins huddle together in order to share body heat with one another; East African hunting dogs work together to improve both the size of game captured and the efficiency of the hunt.

‡ **bioenergetics:** field of **ecology** that examines **energy** flow through ecosystems.

**bioethics:** study of behaviors and policies concerning biological materials such as organ transplants, induced **abortion** and life termination, artificial insemination and sex selection, the use of embryonic tissue in research, and the engineering of genomes, among others.

**biogenesis:** 1.theory that life comes only from the reproduction of living things, and that species can reproduce offspring only of the same species.

Adjective: biogenic. Proposed by T. H. **Huxley** in 1870 to counter lingering belief in **spontaneous generation.** 2.synoym for **biosynthesis.**

**biogenetic law:** Haeckel's nineteenth century 'law', which asserted that 'ontogeny recapitulates phylogeny'; that embryological stages reflect completely the phylogenetic stages through which more thoroughly evolved organisms have passed. Viewed today as too simplistic, the original notion was based on observations such as 'gill slits' and tails that appear in early stages of mammalian development. Aka biogenic law, recapitulation.

**biogenetics:** any process that alters the genome of a living cell and that does not involve the normal recombination and transmission of genetic information either sexually or asexually; **genetic engineering.** The human manipulation of the genome in a living cell that alters the products and functions of that cell. See **biotechnology, genomics,** and **proteomics.**

**biogenic carbonate:** sediment or rock produced by the direct action of organisms. Such sediments are characterized by significant amounts of calcium, magnesium and iron.

**biogeny:** obsolete term coined by E. **Haeckel** for biological evolution that included both **ontogeny** and **phylogeny.**

**biogeocenosis:** term used in the Soviet and Central European literature that is equivalent to the term **ecosystem.**

**biogeochemical cycle:** movement of chemical elements from organisms to the physical environment and back into organisms in more or less circular pathways.

**biogeochemist:** 1. chemist who investigates the environmental influences on the earth's isotopic compositions. 2. one who studies the dietary incorporation of inorganic atoms into the tissues of living organisms. Biogeochemistry is of interest to **archaeologists** and **physical anthropologists** because different proportions of incorporated isotopes reflect dietary patterns, even in fossils. See **paleonutrition.**

**biogeographical barrier:** geographical obstacle such as a body of water, desert, mountain range, or habitation zone that prevents the migration of a species.

**biogeographical region:** area characterized by a distinctive **flora** and/or **fauna;** aka province, biome.

**biogeography:** study of the geographic distributions of living organisms.

**bioinformatics:** storage and retrieval of information about genes in computer databases, including the sequences, function(s), and genealogical relationships among gene families and functional homologues. Aka biological computing.

**biolinguistics:** examination of language processes and

language acquisition, with particular emphasis on neurophysiological and genetic factors.

**biologic:** of or pertaining to life or living organisms; biological.

‡ **biological adaptation:** 1. the development or enhancement of structural, physiologic, or behavioral characteristics that improve chances for survival and reproduction in a given environment. 2. any trait that so develops or enhances an individual's survival relative to others without the trait. See **adaptation**.

**biological altruism:** see **altruism**.

**biological amplification:** concentration in a food chain of a given substance such that the substance increases in concentration in organisms at each trophic level as it moves up the chain. Aka **biological magnification**.

‡ **biological anthropology:** subfield of anthropology, also referred to as **physical anthropology**, that focuses upon the biological aspects of human **adaptation** and **evolution**, human ancestors, the relationship of humans to other organisms, and patterns of biologic **variation** within and among human **populations**; studied by biological anthropologists. Biological anthropology arose in reaction to the traditional interest of **race** and typology of pre-1950s physical anthropology, and is sometimes referred to as the 'new physical anthropology'. Biological anthropologists emphasize hypothesis testing and field experimentation. One of the results was the incorporation of primatology from zoology. Some workers consider biological anthropology to be that part of the life science branch of anthropology that studies genetics and genetic influences on behavior. See **human evolutionary biology**.

**biological clock:** internal mechanism by which organisms provide the observable highly dependable timing for their overt physiological and behavioral rhythmic patterns that, in nature, correlate with external photoperiodic, seasonal, and geophysical periods. See **circadian rhythm**.

**biological death clock:** see **programmed aging**.

‡ **biological determinism:** attribution of certain behaviors to particular human **races** or **ethnic groups**, behaviors that exist presumably because of some inheritance pattern. See **racial determinism**.

**biological diversity:** 'the variability among living organisms from all sources including, *inter alia*, terrestrial, marine and other aquatic ecosystems and the ecological complexities of which they are part; this includes diversity within species, between species and of ecosystems', according to the Convention on Biological Diversity.

**biological equivalence:** use of analogy to describe behavior or physical traits that are perceived to exist in different, unrelated organisms.

‡ **biological evolution:** 1. change in a **lineage** of an organism through time (É. **Geoffroy Saint-Hilaire**, 1831); **transformism**. 2. descent with modification (**Darwinism**, 1859). 3. the **transformation** of the form and mode of existence of an organism in such a way that descendants differ from their predecessors. 4. change in a population's **allele frequencies** between generations (this also called the **operational definition** of **neo-Darwinism**).

**biological fitness:** see **fitness**.

**biological magnification:** see **biological amplification**.

**biological marker:** molecule found on a tumor cell and not normally found in the same conditions or in the same amount on a normal cell.

‡ **biological population:** group of interbreeding organisms coexisting within a limited geographic range, the extent of which is proportional to their mode of **locomotion**, so that members have the opportunity to make contact with many other members during a lifetime. See **deme**.

**biological races: sympatric** populations within a species that differ biologically but not morphologically and in which interbreeding is inhibited by different behavioral cycles, or by food or host preferences; **varieties**. See **race** and cf. **geographical race**.

**biological reduction:** form of **reductionism** that treats social and/or cultural phenomena as simple expressions of basic biological needs or drives.

**biological role:** way in which an organism uses a particular structure in its adaptation to its environment; the relationship between form and function and the environment.

‡ **biological species concept** (BSC): a set of interbreeding forms; adult individuals who produce viable and fertile offspring are valid members of the same biological species.

**biological theory of evolution:** see **evolutionary theory**.

**biological time scale:** sequence based on the evolutionary record provided by lineages such that the relative order of species in succession provides a record of events in geological time.

‡ **biology:** study of life.

**biomass:** sum of the masses of the living organisms in a particular species, habitat or geographic area.

**biome:** large terrestrial ecosystem that occurs in major regional or subcontinental areas.

**biomechanics:** field within the life sciences that studies the physics of motion and complex processes in organisms. Adjective: biomechanical.

**biomedical anthropology:** study of human **health, epidemiology, paleonutrition, nutrition, disease, aging**, and **physiology**. See **medical anthropology**.

**biometricians:** loosely affiliated group of mathematicians who develop techniques for the quantification of **complex characters**. Among the techniques developed are **regression** and **correlation**. See, for example, **Pearl** and **Pearson**.

**biometry:** field within the biological sciences that applies statistical methods to the investigation of biological observations and phenomena; aka biometrics. See **anthropometry**.

**biomineralization:** fixation of crystals such as **hydroxyapatite** in **hard tissue** by molecular mechanisms such as **amelogenesis**.

**biomolecular archaeology:** see **anthropological genetics**.

**biomorph:** any representation of a living organism, such as a painting of a human or animal.

**bion:** any living organism.

**bionomics:** study of relationships between an organism and its environment; an older term for **ecology**.

**biophysics:** study of physical laws governing the activities of living organisms.

**biorbital breadth:** distance from the center of the lateral border of one eye socket (**orbit**) to the other.

**bioremediation: anthropogenic** use of the natural (or engineered) mechanisms that remove toxins from an environment.

**biorhythm:** 1. periodic fluctuation or variation of a biological process as a function of time. See **circadian rhythm** and **biological clock**. 2. unsupported proposal that three cycles are set into action upon the birth of a human: a physical cycle of 23 days, an emotional cycle of 28 days, and an intellectual cycle of 33 days.

**bioseries:** sequence of changes in a heritable character through time.

**biosocial:** pertaining to the interaction or combination of biological and social factors that contribute to a phenomenon. This is a hybrid term that dates to the late nineteenth century and, in anthropology, is linked to **social Darwinism**. The more recent term **biocultural** is used with increasing frequency.

**biospace:** see **realized niche**.

**biospecies:** see **biological species concept**.

‡ **biosphere:** 1. substrate in which living organisms exist, and that includes the **atmosphere, lithosphere**, and hydrosphere. 2. total geographic range inhabited by living forms; the entire network of life on the planet; aka ecosphere.

**biostasis:** property of organisms that exhibit no adaptational changes in the face of environmental fluctuation.

**biostratigraphic unit:** stratum defined by one or more characteristic fossils.

‡ **biostratigraphy:** collation or correlation of otherwise undatable rocks by using **index fossils** such as pigs and antelopes contained in a fossilifer-

ous stratigraphic sequence. See **A.3 date** and **faunal correlation**.

**biostratinomy:** study of the relationship of fossils and the environments in which they existed.

**biosynthesis:** genesis of organic compounds by the action of living organisms; aka biogenesis.

**biosystematics:** study of the evolution and taxonomy of living organisms. Modern biosystematics utilizes knowledge from population genetics, including the extent of variation, hybridization potentials, competition and mating strategies. Aka genonomy.

**biota: flora** (plants) and **fauna** (animals), usually used with reference to a particular region or environment. This term does not include other life forms such as microbes. Adjective: biotic. Aka bios.

**biotechnology:** industrial development of commercial products as the result of a biological process such as fermentation. The development process may utilize intact organisms (e.g. bacteria or yeast) or natural substances (e.g. enzymes) extracted from such organisms.

**biotelemetry:** method of registering the location, movements, and activities of primates that have been fitted with a transmitter; aka radio telemetry or radio tracking.

**biotic baggage:** see **invisible biotic baggage**.

**biotic environment:** organisms living in an ecosystem.

**biotic index:** use of organisms as indicator species to assess an environment.

**biotic potential:** maximum growth potential of a population under optimum conditions, expressed as a rate.

**biotic pyramid:** model of an ecosystem that resembles a triangle with photosynthetic and primary producers at the base and with consumers and parasites increasing at each **trophic level** toward the apex of the pyramid.

**biotinase deficiency:** heritable, autosomal recessive condition characterized by mental retardation, seizures, skin rashes, and loss of vision, hearing, and hair; fatal if untreated. Caused by an inability to metabolize the vitamin biotin.

**biotope:** minimum defined region with a unique set of environmental characteristics. See **ecological community**.

**bioturbation:** mixing of sediments through the action of burrowing organisms.

**biotype:** 1. group of organisms that share the same **genotype**. 2. physiological race identical in morphology, but differing in physiological and biochemical characteristics. 3. a constitutional type from Pende's **biotypology** that incorporates structure, physiological, and psychological factors in evaluating the characteristics of an individual person.

**biotypology:** movement founded in 1920 and later defined by its founder, Nicola Pende, as the science that studies the individual human as an integrated whole or the psychosomatic unity of the individual, i.e. the morphological, physiological, and psychological characteristics of individual human beings. Biotypology has a long history, especially in France. Most such classifications had three or four types. Biotypology has generally been discarded in favor of theories that stress continuous human variation rather than **types** or categories, and for hypotheses that appreciate both **acclimatization** and **genetic adaptation** to environmental variables. See **morphological types**. Cf. **somatology**.

**biozone:** complete geographical distribution of a particular fossil **taxon** within a particular geological time period.

**biparietal:** of or pertaining to the two walls of the skull, the **parietal bones,** taken together.

**biparietal breadth: cephalometric** measurement performed on living humans; maximum distance between the left and right parietal eminences as measured with spreading calipers. Similar to the **craniometric** measurement **maximum cranial breadth.** Aka head breadth, biparietal diameter.

**biparity:** 1. having produced only one previous **litter** or brood. 2. producing two offspring in a single litter or brood; producing **twins.** This is the usual condition in some **prosimians** and among most of the callitrichids. Adjective: biparous, ditokous. See **parity.**

‡ **biped:** terrestrial vertebrate that moves about on two legs. Among extant bipeds are the birds and humans. Adjective: bipedal. See **habitual bipedalism.**

**bipedal:** referring to a **biped, bipedalism, habitual bipedalism,** or a **bipedal gait.** Adverb: bipedally.

**bipedal gait:** walking habitually on two legs, as in humans and ground birds. See **bent-knee gait** and **striding gait.** Aka bipedal locomotion.

‡ **bipedalism:** mode of **locomotion** using only the **hindlimbs.** Limbs are used in an alternating rather than a parallel pattern (as in kangaroos); efficient bipedalism is further characterized by a **striding gait,** as in humans.

**bipolar affective disorder:** see **major affective disorder.**

**bipolar technique:** method of tool making in which a core is placed upon another rock, called the **anvil,** and the core is then struck with a hammerstone.

**biporionic breadth** (POB): chord length measured from the top of one external ear to the other.

**biramous:** having two branches.

**Birdsell, Joseph B**. (1908–94): US anthropologist and genetic ecologist; spent several field seasons in Australia with Australian biologist and anthropologist Norman B. Tindale (1900–93). Birdsell coined the term **gene flow** to account for the clinal distribution of traits such as **tawny hair** in the western desert. Known for his estimation of the number of major migrations

that peopled continents by examination of the spatial clustering of phenotypes; this resulted in the '**trihybrid' hypothesis** of the peopling of both Australia and the Americas. Author of *Microevolutionary Patterns in Aboriginal Australia* (1993).

**birth:** 1. act of being born. 2. bringing forth of offspring, as in childbirth; **parturition**. In studies of development and growth, an event in the human **life cycle** that occurs at about 36–38 weeks post-conception that is marked by a decreased dependency of offspring on the mother for oxygen, heat, and the removal of waste products, but a continued dependency for many other factors necessary for continued growth and survival. See **altricial** and **precocial**. Cf. **death**.

**birth canal:** passageway in female mammals through which the fetus is expelled during **birth**; consists of the cervix, vagina, and vulva. Because it receives the penis and sperm, the birth canal (as the vagina) is also the female mammal's organ of copulation.

**birth dearth:** lower fertility rate among certain groups or subpopulations within a population.

**birth defect:** any congenital anomaly present in a newborn. Birth defects may be due to the fetal environment, as in **fetal alcohol syndrome**, but are often due to a developmental problem that is genetic in nature, such as a **major chromosome anomaly**. About 3% of all babies are born with some clinically significant birth defect.

**birth-flow:** model that describes the birth frequencies in animals that give birth throughout the year. Cf. **birth-pulse**.

**birth-pulse:** model that describes birth frequencies in animals for which there are clearly defined **birth seasons**. Cf. **birth-flow**.

**birth rate:** proportion of births in a given place and time, usually expressed as a quantity per 100 000 of population.

**birth season:** period of time during which the females of a species or population give birth. In primates this may occur twice a year (especially in prosimians) or once a year (especially in anthropoids). The birth season usually occurs at that time of the year when resources are most abundant. Aka birthing season.

**birth synchrony:** condition in which reproductive females in a population all give birth at the same time. There are various explanations for this including: effects of individual's **pheromones** on all females; producing large numbers of offspring and flooding the environment so that the chances of any one young being taken by predators is reduced; or simply being born at the optimal time for resources in the environment. See **breeding season**.

**birth weight:** body mass of a neonate at parturition. Humans, among primates, are unusual in being heavy relative to maternal mass.

**birthmark:** see **hemangioma**.

**bisexual:** 1. pertaining to a population or cohort that contains both males and females. 2. pertaining to an individual possessing genitalia of both sexes (hermaphroditic). 3. pertaining to a functional male or female that has sexual relations with either sex. Cf. **unisexual**.

**bisexual group:** see **multi-male/female group**.

**Bishop, Walter William** (1931–77): British geologist; co-organizer of the East African Geological Research Unit and director of several other East African surveys. His students located many of the early hominoid sites in East Africa, including **Chemeron** and **Chesowanja**. Editor of *Geological Background to Fossil Man* (1978).

*Biston betularia*: species binomen for the **peppered moth** involved in the studies of **industrial melanism**.

**bit:** basic **quantitative** unit of information in a medium of communication; specifically, the amount of information required to control, without error, which of two (binary) equiprobable alternates is to be chosen by the receiver.

**bite:** 1. to cut or wound with the teeth. 2. closing the jaws and bringing the anterior teeth into closer proximity. 3. in nutritional ecology, the amount of plant tissue that a mammal removes during one closure of the jaws.

**bite force:** power exerted during the closure of the jaws resulting from contraction of muscles used in chewing.

**bite mark:** particular pattern made by the anterior dentition when biting into an item.

**bitrochanteric breadth: anthropometric** measurement; the distance between the left and right **greater trochanters** of the femurs as measured with an **anthropometer**. This measurement can be obtained from either the subject's front or back. Used for body frame indices and for **human engineering**.

**bitypic:** refers to a taxon with only two principal taxa in the subordinate taxa, as a genus composed of only two species. Cf. **monotypic**.

**bivalent:** structure formed by a pair of synapsed homologous chromosomes during **prophase** I of **meiosis**. See **synapsis**.

**bivariate analysis:** simultaneous **analysis** of two **variables**.

**biverbal:** pertaining to a name containing two words but that is not a **binomen**.

**bizygomatic breadth** (zy–zy): **craniometric** measurement; maximum width between the left and right **zygions** as measured by spreading calipers. Aka facial width, bizygomatic diameter. See Appendix 7 for an illustration of the landmarks used.

**BK:** (Peter) Bell's **Korongo** at **Olduvai Gorge**.

**black-and-red tamarin:** vernacular for *Saguinus nigricollis*.

**black-and-white colobus:** vernacular for *Colobus guereza*.

**black-and-white ruffed lemur:** vernacular for *Varecia variegata variegata*.

**black (-bearded) saki:** vernacular for *Chiropotes satanas*.

**black-bellied spider monkey:** vernacular for *Ateles marginatus*.

**black-capped capuchin:** vernacular for *Cebus apella*.

**black-chested moustached tamarin:** vernacular for *Saguinus mystax*.

**black colobus:** vernacular for *Colobus satanas*.

**black (-crested) mangabey:** vernacular for *Cercocebus aterrimus*. This vernacular is also sometimes applied to *C. albigena*.

‡ **Black, Davidson** (1884–1934): Canadian physician attached to the British consulate as Professor of Anatomy at Peking Union Medical College in the 1920s and 1930s; he secured **molar** teeth from Austrian paleontologist Otto Zdansky (1894–1955) from among which Black was able to identify a **hominid** tooth in 1927 which possessed an 'abnormal' root structure; he called the new species *Sinanthropus pekinensis*. Through inquiry, Black located the source of the teeth in the 'Hills of the Dragons', or Choukoutien (now **Zhoukoudian**). See *Homo erectus*.

**black death:** see **bubonic plague**.

**black-faced lion tamarin:** vernacular for *Leontideus chrysopygus* (= *caissara*).

**black gibbon:** vernacular for *Hylobates concolor*.

**black-handed spider monkey:** vernacular for *Ateles geoffroyi*.

**black-headed marmoset:** vernacular for *Callithrix nigriceps*.

**black-headed night monkey:** vernacular for *Aotus nigriceps*.

**black (-headed) uakari:** vernacular for *Cacajao melanocephalus*.

**black howler:** vernacular for *Alouatta caraya*; previously included in *A. pigra*.

**black lemur:** vernacular for *Eulemur* (= *Lemur*) *macaco*.

**black mangabey:** general vernacular for species belonging to the catarrhine genus *Lophocebus* and the specific vernacular for *L.* (= *Cercocebus*) *aterrimus*.

**black saki:** vernacular for *Chiropotes satanas*.

‡ **'black skull':** sobriquet for the hyper-robust, **edentulous** hominid cranium designated **KNM-WT 17000**. Found by Alan **Walker** in 1985 at **Lomekwi locality** I, West Lake Turkana, Kenya, this specimen caused a re-evaluation of previous **hypotheses** regarding early **australopithecine** evolution. The 'black skull' has robust affinities and is called *Paranthropus* (=*Australopithecus*) *aethiopicus* by some researchers, based on its early date (2.5 mya) and elongated face,

although others place it with **P. boisei**. A key feature of this **hominid** is that it has a very small **cranial capacity**, estimated at 410 cm³. The dark color of the bones is due to the manganese in the deposits where the skull was buried. Aka Nachukui.

**black spider monkey:** vernacular for **Ateles** *paniscus*.

**black-tailed marmoset:** vernacular for **Callithrix** *melanura*.

**black tufted-ear marmoset:** vernacular for **Callithrix** *penicillata* (= *kuhli*).

**Blackman curve:** model proposed by British biologist F. F. Blackman that is essentially an application of Liebig's earlier **law of the minimum**; specifically, Blackman proposed that insufficiency of some critical nutrient will retard growth even in the presence of adequate other resources.

**blackwater:** describes Amazonian waterways that are colored dark brown from the eroded organic material that is washed into them. These streams and rivers are nutrient-poor and originate from areas with leached out soils. See **igapo forest**. Cf. **whitewater**.

**'black water fever':** see **malaria**.

**bladder:** any anatomical structure that serves as a receptacle for fluids or gas such as the urinary bladder or the swim bladder in fish.

‡ **blade: flake artifact** with a minimum 2 : 1 aspect ratio, giving it a long parallel-sided appearance, that has been struck from a specially prepared core. A common **Upper Paleolithic** tool. See **Levallois**.

**blank:** intermediate manufacturing stage in the production of stone tools; an unfinished tool.

**blank leaf:** layer of stalagmite or other material deposited at a site during a time when humans did not inhabit the site, such that it clearly separates habitation horizons.

**blank tablet (or slate):** see *tabula rasa*.

**blastocyst:** fluid-filled sphere formed by the earliest divisions of cells after **fertilization** that is ready for **implantation** in the uterine wall of mammals. Aka preimplantation blastocyst.

**blastocyst cavity:** fluid-filled cavity in the hollow sphere of cells succeeding the **morula** stage, and before **implantation** in the uterine wall. The cavity contains the **embryoblast**.

**blastogenesis:** 1. reproduction via a budding process. 2. **embryogenesis** through the stages of cleavage and germ-layer formation.

**blastogenic:** pertaining to characters that are hereditarily transmitted.

**blastomere:** early embryonic cell formed as the result of **cleavage**.

**blastula:** early stage of prenatal development between the **morula** and **embryonic stage**.

**blastulation:** formation of the **blastula** during embryogenesis.

**bleeder's disease:** see **hemophilia**.

‡ **blending inheritance:** hypothesis that heritable factors mix and are subsequently passed on intact to offspring in the new, blended form; aka **pangenesis**. Now disproven; one of the missing elements that makes such a scheme impossible is the absence of a **reduction division** step in the process.

**blighted ovum:** early embryo whose development has ceased.

**blind:** 1. unable to see. 2. to deprive of sight. 3. cover from which an observer can watch animals without being seen; this allows animal behavior to be observed with as little disturbance as possible. Aka **hide**. Once animals become **habituated** to human presence, blinds are usually unnecessary.

**blind experiment:** test in which the individual making the measurements does not know which treatment a subject has received; this is done to prevent preconceived notions from influencing the results of the experiment. See **Clever Hans effect**. Cf. **double blind experiment**.

**blind spot:** see **optic disc**.

**'blitzkrieg' human-induced extinction model:** recent proposal that the extinction of 46 species of Australian large mammal within a few centuries *c.* 46 kya was due to overhunting by Australian aboriginals who had arrived from Asia via the **Sahul Shelf** at about the same time. Aka anthropogenic overkill hypothesis, anthropogenic ecosystem disruption model. See **megafauna**; cf. **Pleistocene extinction hypotheses**.

**block-on-block technique:** production of large, thick flakes of rock by swinging a core against the edge of a larger, stationary stone or boulder.

**Blombos Cave:** archaeological site found in 1991 near Still Bay (Stillbaal) in the southern Cape, South Africa, and is dated to >100 kya (min. 70 kya). In its lower levels, the site contains Middle Stone Age hearths and artifacts such as silk red stone blades, perforated tick shells for personal adornment (c. 75 kya), and awls indicative of clothing manufacture. Evidence for marine exploitation includes fishbones. Red ochre was employed in ritual use and incised with symbols.

‡ **blood** (B): fluid connective tissue that circulates throughout the **cardiovascular system** to transport substances throughout the body, including oxygen. In general anthropology, the term has acquired a cultural elaboration such that its meanings extend well beyond those of mere **serology**. See for example, **blood royal**.

**blood alcohol content** (BAC): proportion of blood that consists of alcohol, measured as a percentage of volume, such as 0.08%. BAC is estimated as 0.038 per 45 kg (100 lbs) of body mass per drink equivalent (minus 0.015 times the number of hours since consumption).

**blood bank:** location such as a hospital where blood and blood products are stored.

**blood–brain barrier** (BBB): structural arrangement of capillaries, connective tissue, and specialized neuroglial cells that selectively determine which substances can move from the plasma of the blood to the extracellular fluid of the brain, while inhibiting others; Cf. **semipermeable membrane.**

**blood count:** 1. number of red or white blood cells per cubic millimeter of whole blood. 2. determination of such a number.

‡ **blood group:** generic term for a series of inherited **antigens** embedded in the plasma membrane of blood cells and used as genetic markers. See **ABO blood group, Rhesus blood group, MN blood group.** Other blood groups include **Diego, Duffy, Lutheran,** and **Kell.**

**blood group incompatibility:** condition in which cells of a fetus are attacked *in utero* by the immune system of its mother. Incompatibility results from maternal antibodies made to fetal antigens. **ABO incompatibility** and **Rhesus incompatibility** are the most common, but the condition occurs in rarer blood groups as well; see, for example, **Diego blood group.**

**blood grouping:** classification of blood samples according to their **agglutination** characteristics.

**blood platelet:** see **thrombocyte.**

**blood royal:** belief that individuals in royal lineages possess a special and qualitatively 'pure' blood. In many societies, maintenance of the purity of royal bloodlines has led to marriage rules that forbid persons of pure blood from mating with outsiders.

‡ **blood type:** phenotypic chemical signature specific to an individual in a certain **blood group.** One may be blood type 'A' in the ABO system, ' + ' in the Rh system, 'N' in the MN system, and so forth.

---

### Blood group factors and deficiencies

At least 13 molecules, called 'factors', are required for normal blood coagulation. Heritable deficiencies are documented for all but one (factor III). Only factors VIII and IX are X-linked. Some of the most common blood group factors and deficiencies are:

**factor V Leiden thrombophilia:** the factor V Leiden mutation predisposes individuals to venous thrombosis (blood clots in limbs). Heterozygotes have lowered levels of Factor V but never exhibit abnormal hemorrhaging. The gene is an autosomal recessive.

**factor VIII:** one of the proteins required for normal blood clotting; the gene for factor VIII (HEMA) is located on the X chromosome. A deficiency in this product can cause **hemophilia A,** 'classic' hemophilia. A genetically engineered (recombinant) gene product has been available since the 1980s.

**factor IX:** one of the proteins required for normal blood clotting; the gene for factor IX (HEMB) is located on the X chromosome. A deficiency in this product can cause **hemophilia B,** AKA Christmas disease.

**factor XI deficiency:** heritable, autosomal recessive condition characterized by excessive bleeding during an injury or surgery, and caused by a mutation in the gene that codes for the protein portion of a plasma glycoprotein, and that interferes with the normal formation of blood clots.

Combinations of deficiencies, such as factor VIII & IX combined deficiency, have also been reported.

---

**blood vessel:** see **artery, vein, arteriole, venule, capillary.**

**Bloom syndrome** (BLM): **autosomal recessive** pre- and post-natal growth deficiency characterized by dwarfism, sun sensitivity that results in skin rashes, dilated capillaries, impaired immunity, increased risk of cancer, and chromosomal instability. Death before age 50; usually much sooner. A DNA excision–repair disorder in which a DNA ligase gene is defective and slows DNA replication. Exhibits evidence for somatic recombination.

**blot:** 1. to soak up or remove. 2. in biotechnology, to transfer a specific sample from a discriminating gel that has served to isolate the sample. See **Southern blot analysis, western blot analysis, northern blot analysis, zoo blot,** and **electroblotting.**

**blue baby:** neonate with cyanosis, a bluish discoloration caused by any of several congenital conditions; discoloration caused by excess reduced (deoxygenated) **hemoglobin.**

**blue monkey:** vernacular for *Cercopithecus mitis.*

**Blumenbach, Johan Friedrich** (1752–1840): German anatomist, craniologist and 'founder of anthropology'. Although he compared crania only by eye, in 1790 he defined five nonhierarchical human **varieties,** which he termed **Ethiopian, Malayan, American, Mongolian** and **Caucasian;** the latter was the result of the examination of a single skull from the Caucasus Mountains near the Black Sea. Blumenbach was the first to create a typology based solely on **morphology;** his de-emphasis of behavioral attributes was a departure from earlier taxonomists such as

**Linnaeus**. A biblical **monogenist**, Blumenbach held that **human variation** was accounted for by **degenerative** adaptive responses to varied environments, and that variations in skin color, stature and body proportions had no absolute value, but merge gradually into one another, thus, that classification into human races is arbitrary.

**Blumenschine scavenging theory:** see **scavenging opportunity theory**.

**Blytt–Sernander climatic classification:** alternative classification of Pleisto-Holocene climate based upon palynology and plant fossils. Periods of this scheme include the Arctic, Preboreal, Boreal, Atlantic, Subboreal and Subatlantic periods; these cover roughly the past 14 ky of geological time.

**BMI:** abbreviation for **body mass index**.

‡ **BMR:** basal metabolic rate, the lowest level of energy required for basic maintenance of an organism; aka basal metabolism. The rate at which metabolic reactions occur when the individual is awake but resting, is not thermally stressed, and is fasting (eliminating the thermal effects of food; in humans this is twelve hours after the last meal). Basal metabolic rate is generally measured as amount of **oxygen** consumed or **carbon dioxide** produced.

**Boas, Franz** (1858–1942): US physicist (Ph.D.), ethnologist, the 'father of American anthropology'; known for careful use of Kwakiutl informants in the American northwest; also known for a pioneering study of the inheritance of the **cephalic index** (CI) in American immigrants, in which he showed that offspring possessed CIs substantially different from those of their foreign-born parents (1912), thus undermining the supposed high **heritability** of the CI and its habitual use as a **race marker**. Remembered for the **cultural relativism** embodied in his historical particularism.

**Boasian anthropology:** see **American Historical School**. Aka historical particularism.

**Bodo:** archaeological site found in 1976 in the Afar region of Ethiopia, dated to >300 kya, and that contains **Acheulean** artifacts. Hominid remains include a 1300 cm³ cranium with a massive **double-arched supra-orbital torus**, and possessing cut marks suggestive of defleshing, **cannibalism**, or scalping; a humerus from a smaller individual suggests extensive **sexual dimorphism**. Attributed to the **archaic *Homo sapiens*** group; considered by some anatomists to be an anomalous variant.

***Bodvapithecus altipalatus* Kretzoi, 1975:** see ***Sivapithecus***.

**body:** 1. the complete organism. 2. largest part of an organ, such as a vertebral body, sternal body, etc.; aka *corpus*. 3. part of a cell, such as a neuron, where the nucleus and most of the cytoplasm is present.

**body bubble:** space around an organism that an individual defines as its private space; aka personal territory; entry into the bubble is usually by invitation, otherwise the individual experiences a sense of violation. See **individual distance**.

**body build:** morphology or shape of a body including proportions of different regions relative to one another. See **somatotype** and **somatology**.

**body composition:** make-up of the body in terms of the absolute and relative amounts of adipose tissue, muscle mass, skeletal mass, internal organs, and other tissue.

**body fat and fertility hypothesis:** proposal by R. Frisch that cross-cultural studies indicate a relationship between body fat content and the onset (or maintenance) of **menstruation**; especially, that menstruation ceases when body fat falls below predictable thresholds.

**body form:** shape of the human body. See **somatotype** and **somatology**.

**body fullness index:** mass divided by the cube of stature, then multiplied by 100. This index separates individuals by age and sex.

**body language:** information contained in nonauditory signals such as gesture, expression, posture, **proxemics**, etc.

**body mass:** mass (usually in kilograms) of an individual soma, or whole body of an organism. Interspecific body mass is highly correlated with several **life history variables**. Often used synonymously (although incorrectly) with **body weight**.

**body mass index** (BMI): mathematical indication of the relative weight-for-height of a person. BMI is calculated in several ways; one is {mass in kg/(height in m)²}. High BMI scores indicate greater weight-for-height, or people with a relatively small surface area for height, and potentially greater body fatness. Low BMI scores indicate the opposite result and effect. This index was developed by the Belgian astronomer Quetelet in 1870. Aka Quetelet's index.

**body segment:** 1. division of the body into regions, or body regions into components. Gross segments are the head, neck, trunk, upper limbs, and lower limbs. Most of these segments can be further subdivided: for example, the lower limbs consists of the thigh, lower leg, and foot. 2. one of the regions of the body in relation to the ancestral muscle arrangements in vertebrates. Vertebrate segmentation is limited (for example, the skin is not segmented) and the segmented arrangement is principally of the trunk muscles, skeleton, and nervous system.

**body segment analysis:** anthropometric analysis of the relationship between various body regions in the human.

**body size:** mass or defining dimension of an organism. Body size is correlated with singular body components (see **allometry**) as well as with many ecological variables. See **adult body size** and **neonatal body size.**

**body temperature:** temperature of the body. See **normal human body temperature, lower critical temperature, hyperthermia, hypothermia,** and **normothermia.**

**body weight:** see **body mass.** Cf. **neonatal body weight.**

**bog:** wet, spongy ground with soil composed primarily of decayed plants (peat). A superficial stratum with low mineral content but high in organic nutrients; usually supports mosses, shrubs and sedges, and is a typical feature of formerly glaciated basins.

**bog person:** mummified remains of a person buried in a **peat bog.** This type of mummification occurs in cold climates. The peat environment is acidic and low in oxygen; this is a natural antibiotic environment. Individuals preserved in peat often have tanned skin and a reddish hue to hair, owing to peat acidity. The most prominent example is Tollund Man, a male found in Denmark who had been executed some 2400 years ago.

**Bogu:** archaeological site found between 1988 and 1996, in the **Bose Basin** of the Guangxi Zhuang Autonomous Region of China, dated to 803 kya (based on associated tektites), and that contains many **mode 2** large cutting tools similar in complexity to those assigned to the **Acheulean tool tradition** at sites located west of **Movius' line.**

**bolas stones:** round quartzite balls recovered at **Olorgesailie** and other East African prehistoric sites dating from 1.8 mya to 40 kya; a fanciful early interpretation that the balls were a primary hunting tool (bolas) has been revised by later archaeologists who showed that, when used as a **hammerstone,** repeated strikes turn such a rock into a round ball or spheroid. See **by-product hypothesis.**

**Bolivian black howler:** vernacular for *Alouatta sara.*

**Bolivian gray titi:** vernacular for *Callicebus donacophilus.*

**Bolivian squirrel monkey:** vernacular for *Saimiri boliviensis.*

**bolus:** masticated mass of food held together by saliva that is swallowed from the oral cavity into the pharynx.

**bomb calorimeter:** see **calorimeter.**

**Bombay phenotype:** rare but informative variant of the **ABO blood group** in which affected individuals cannot make the **H substance** precursor protein needed by the A and B antigens and the null O allele; individuals with this phenotype are homozygous recessive (hh) but appear to be blood type O. They also make a unique anti-H antibody. First discovered in Bombay, India. A classic case of **epistasis.** Aka Bombay blood group.

**bond:** close relationship developed between two or more individuals; a bond observed consistently in mammals is between mother and offspring. In social **primates** bonds may be extended to other members of the group. See **pair bond.**

**bonding:** process of forming a **bond.**

‡ **bone:** solid, rigid, ossified connective tissue forming the skeletal system.

**bone bed:** geological stratum that is rich in fossil fragments. Cf. **shell bed** and **midden.**

**bone black:** carbon black pigment used in prehistoric times made by burning animal bones in a closed container.

**bone breaking:** act of bashing in or breaking open bones to obtain cryptic nutrients. Some paleontologists believe that bone breaking behavior was characteristic of early hominids, and may have spurred a connection between the available tool and the later cutting task.

**bone density:** mass of bone relative to volume; variation in bone density is due to several factors including thickness of compact (or cortical) bone and the mineral content of the bone. Humans vary geographically with respect to bone density.

**bone fracture pattern:** a characteristic set of marks, consisting of pits and percussion marks, on a bone that has been deliberately broken by tool-using hominids. These marks result from the force of the hammer blow and the underlying anvil stone as the bone is crushed between them. Such marks are often repeated several times in a line along the shaft of a bone, and it is believed that they can be distinguished from the marks left when the bone is broken by natural forces.

**bone fragment frequencies:** in reference to the occurrence of particular animal species at archeological sites.

**bone growth:** see **appositional growth, endochondral bone, epiphyseal disk, intramembranous bone.**

**bone marrow:** see **red marrow** and **yellow marrow.**

**bone nitrogen content:** see **nitrogen test.**

**bone remodeling:** normal process in which bone tissue **deposition** and **resorption** occur simultaneously, controlled mainly by endocrin factors emitted by **osteoclasts** and **osteoblasts.** Bony tissue is replaced throughout life (10% annually); those bones that bear weight have a higher rate of bone remodeling. Bone remodeling can add bony tissue in the form of various muscle markings when tension is applied to that part of the skeleton and is the process that heals fractured bones. **Osteoporosis** is a form of abnormal bone remodeling.

**bone resorption:** see **resorption.**

---

**Some hominids found at Border Cave**

These specimens are from the horizons dated to > 90 kya and are attributed to anatomically modern *Homo sapiens*. see **AMH**.

Border Cave 1: field number assigned to a cranium.

Border Cave 2: field number assigned to a mandible.

Border Cave 3: field number assigned to an infant's skeleton.

---

**bone thickness:** see **cortical bone thickness.**

**bone tool:** artifact or implement made from bone, usually animal bone.

**bonelet:** alternative name for any of the three **auditory ossicles.**

**bonnet macaque:** vernacular for *Macaca radiata.*

**bonobo:** vernacular for *Pan paniscus.*

**bonobo hypothesis:** 1978 proposal by Adrienne **Zihlman** and others that **bonobo** morphology and **social organization** make a good interpretive model for explaining early hominid morphology, and for speculating about the behavior of fossil **hominids.**

**bony landmark:** see **landmark.**

**bony orbit:** see **orbit.**

**bony palate:** any wall of bone.

**bony thorax:** portion of the **thorax** that includes the ribs, sternum, and thoracic vertebrae; also referred to as the **thoracic cage,** but see that term for a more precise definition.

**booted titi:** vernacular for *Callicebus calligatus.*

**bootstrap value:** in phylogeny construction, an estimate of the strength of the evidence that a particular node in a tree exists; values range from 0% to 100%, with higher values representing greater probability.

**Border Cave:** archaeological site found in 1940 in North KwaZulu and Swaziland, Africa, and dated to 110–90 kya (**ESR,** 141–42 kya; controversial). Contains **Levallois** artifacts of **Middle Stone Age** (**Howiesons Poort**); hominid remains (see box) include a partial 1507 cm³ male cranium, 2 adult mandibles, and a partial infant skeleton (grave was shallow and may have been intrusive from the 80 kya level). Some material was removed by a farmer for use as fertilizer before scientific excavation began. The early date for these fossils, now generally agreed to be AMHs, has led to the proposal that *Homo sapiens* evolved only once, in Africa, during the **Pleistocene,** and then spread to Europe and elsewhere at later times. See the **monophyletic hypothesis** and the **Afro-European** *sapiens* **hypothesis.** Cf. the **polyphyletic hypothesis.**

**Bordes, Francois** (1919–81): French prehistorian; standardized Paleolithic tool typology, introduced quantitative classification methods (*système Bordes*), and personally learned and illustrated manufacturing techniques. Excavated Combe-Grenal and Pech de l'Azé in the Dordogne. Editor of *The Origins of Homo sapiens* (1972).

**boreal:** pertaining to the climate of the cooler regions of the northern hemisphere consisting of the coniferous zone and **taiga** (lichen woodland).

**boreal forest:** zone of **forest** that encircles the arctic between the arctic–subarctic tundra of the north and the hardwood forests and steppes of the temperate zone; aka **taiga.**

**Boreal period:** stage of the **Blytt–Sernander classification,** dated to about 9–7.5 kya, characterized by pine and hazel vegetation and by relatively dryer and warmer conditions than the **Preboreal period.**

**Bornean orangutan:** vernacular for *Pongo pygmaeus pygmaeus.*

**Bornean tarsier:** vernacular for *Tarsius bancanus.*

**Bose Basin:** archaeological region found between 1988 and 1996, in the Guangxi Zhuang Autonomous Region of China, and dated to 803 kya (based on associated tektites); several sites containing many **mode 2** large cutting tools similar in complexity to those assigned to the **Acheulean tool tradition** at sites located west of **Movius' line.** Sites include **Hengshandao, Yangwu, Bogu, Xiaomei,** and **Gaolingpo.**

**Bose Basin LCTs:** any of the **large cutting tools** found in sites located in the **Bose Basin** of southern China.

**Bosman's potto:** vernacular for *Perodicticus potto.*

**boss:** protuberance or eminence, e.g. parietal boss.

**bottleneck** or **bottleneck effect:** see **population bottleneck.**

**bottleneck-colonization model:** corollary to the **out of Africa II** hypothesis. According to this model all modern humans are descended from a single population that existed in central Africa 300–200 kya. Differences that exist between modern human populations are the result of drift; similarity between modern inhabitants of regions and middle Pleistocene populations that inhabited the same regions is the result of convergence and adaptation to conditions in that particular region, and not because of an ancestral–descendant relationship.

**Boucher de Perthes, Jacques** (1788–1868): French customs official stationed at Abbeville, and amateur prehistorian; published a study in 1836 of 'antediluvian' flint tools found in the Somme River gravels that were apparently contemporary with the bones of strange and extinct animals. In 1838, he suggested that humans might have developed over hundreds of thousands of years. Aka Boucher de Crèvecoeur de Perthes.

**Boule, Pierre Marcellin** (1861–1942): French paleontologist. In 1908–12, excavated the rockshelter at **La Chapelle-aux-Saints**, including its **Mousterian** tools and **neandertaloid hominid** remains (1912). Boule also reconstructed the arthritic 'Old Man of La Chapelle' as if he were a clinically normal **type specimen** for a new species, and the result was a popular image of a hirsute, short, robust, hunched-over **cave man** with a massive **supra-orbital torus**, a stereotype that still survives in the public mind. Proposed the **presapiens hypothesis**. Author of *Les Hommes Fossiles* (1921).

**bound ribosome:** term used to describe a **ribosome** while attached to the endoplasmic reticulum; aka bound polysome.

**boundary lubrication:** reduction of friction during movement of a joint as a result of the presence of mutually repellant and opposing surfaces during movement.

**Bouri formation** (BOU): 1. a geological formation located near the village of Bouri, in the **Middle Awash**, Afar rift region of Ethiopia, with three members (Hata, Dakanihylo, Herto) consisting of fossiliferous sediments spanning from at least 2.5 mya to 154 kya. 2. archaeological site found in 1990 in the Hata member, dated to 2.5 mya, that contained evidence of butchery of a three-toed horse and an antelope (cut and percussion marks), and hominid remains recovered in 1997, the type specimen for *Australopithecus garhi*, BOU-VP-12/130. 3. archaeological site found in 1997 in the Dakanihylo member, dated to *c.* 1.0 mya, that produced the **Daka hominid**, BOU-VP-2/66. 4. archaeological site found in 1997 in the Herto member, dated to *c.* 160–154 kya, that produced the **Herto hominids**, including BOU-VP-16/1, the type specimen of *Homo sapiens idaltu* subsp. nov.

**bout:** 1. period, as in a bout of illness. 2. episode during which a repetitive behavior is observed and recorded.

**BOU-VP:** Bouri Vertebrate Paleontology, Ethiopia.

**BOU-VP-2/66:** field number of the **Daka hominid**.

**BOU-VP-12/130:** field number of the type specimen for *Australopithecus garhi* from the **Middle Awash**; consists of a partial cranium and maxilla with teeth, and has an estimated cranial capacity of 450 cm³. The specimen is dated at 2.4 mya. See **Bouri formation**.

**BOU-VP-16/1:** field number of the type specimen for *Homo sapiens idaltu* from the Herto member of the Bouri formation, **Middle Awash** region of Ethiopia; consists of a partial cranium with dentition that has an estimated cranial capacity of 1450 cm³. The specimen is dated at 160-154 kya. See **Herto hominids**.

**bovid:** member of the mammalian family Bovidae (order Artiodactyla), the cloven-hoofed ungulates, usually taken to include goats, sheep, antelopes, and deer. Cf. **bovine**.

**bovine:** member of the subfamily Bovinae. 2. pertaining to cattle, bison and buffalo. Cf. **bovid**.

**bovine spongiform encephalitis** (BSE): one of the **transmissible spongiform encephalopathies** of animals alleged to be caused by a **prion protein**; transmitted by direct ingestion or contact with infected brains. Aka bovine spongiform encephalopathy, 'mad cow disease'. See **Creuzfeldt–Jacob disease, new variant**.

**bowel:** intestines; see **small intestine**, **large intestine**.

**bowleg:** leg alignment in which there is an outward bowing of the bones, as in **rickets**. See **valgus**.

**Boxgrove:** archaeological site found in 1983 near Sussex, southern England, dated to 500–400 kya, containing **Acheulean** artifacts and hominid remains including a tibia (Boxgrove 1) assigned to the **earlier archaic *Homo sapiens*** group. Also at the site are the bones of rhinoceros, elephant, and horse, several of which exhibit cut marks that have been interpreted as indicative of hominid defleshing behavior. A notable refitting study from several thousand flakes yielded a large flint nodule from which a **hand-ax** had been fashioned.

‡ **BP:** abbreviation for 'Before Present', the internationally accepted standard for designating past dates; the 'present' originally was set arbitrarily at the year 1950, when **radiometric dating** became common, but the new reference year is now 2000; the date 3000 years BP thus means 3000 years before CE 2000. See **BCE** and **CE**.

**Brace, C. Loring, IV** (1930–): US odontometrician and anatomist; since the 1950s, Brace has provided contrapuntal, and pithy publications that taught as well as entertained; also author of the **probable mutation effect**, an **hypothesis** concerning alleged **Plio-Pleistocene** hominid dental reduction, a form of **relaxed selection**. Although supportive of the **Neandertal phase of man hypothesis**, he also stressed the role of **gene flow**, and that **race** is an arbitrary taxonomic construct. Brace also argued, on odontometric grounds, that *Homo habilis* is an invalid taxon. Author of *Refocusing on the Neanderthal Problem* (1962).

**brachial:** of or pertaining to the arm; for example, brachial blood vessels serve the arm.

**brachial index:** ratio of the length of the forearm (the **radius**) divided by the length of the upper arm (the **humerus**), × 100. Because Neandertals possessed relatively short forearms, this index is one of the criteria used to differentiate that group from **AMHs**.

**brachial plexus:** network of nerve fibers that arise

from spinal nerves and supply the torso and upper limbs.

**brachial tissue:** the tissue (e.g. muscle, skin, connective tissue, nervous tissue, etc.) that makes up the arm.

**brachialis:** muscle that moves the forearm. The brachialis originates from the anterior shaft of the **humerus** and inserts onto the coronoid process of the **ulna**. Its action is to flex the forearm at the elbow.

‡ **brachiation:** form of **locomotion** found in some **arboreal** primates in which an animal moves arm over arm while suspended below branches. Among the mammals only the hylobatids are true habitual brachiators; spider monkeys are semibrachiators, whereas the great apes have the anatomy for potential brachiation but do not routinely display the behavior.

**brachium:** upper arm or forelimb from the shoulder to the elbow.

‡ **brachycephalic:** pertaining to **brachycephaly**. Aka brachycranic.

**brachycephalization of man hypothesis:** series of arguments that try to explain why **hominid** cranial morphology has changed from **dolichocranic** to **brachycranic** (or brachycephalic) over time, first appearing in Europe during the Mesolithic but in Asia much earlier. **Weidenreich** was one of the workers who proposed a hypothesis to explain this matter.

**brachycephaly:** having a relatively 'short', broad or round head, with a **cranial index** of between 80.00 and 84.99. Adjectives: brachycranic, brachycephalic. Applied to skeletal material rather than to living humans. Cf. **dolichocephaly, mesocephaly.**

**brachycolic:** pertaining to a short colon, of up to 150 cm.

**brachycormic:** in reference to the **cormic index**, with an index of 50.90 or less; such an individual has short limbs in relation to trunk size. All humans are brachycormic in infancy. The most brachycormic human populations are found in the Far East and the Arctic region of North America. Cf. **brachyskelia**. See **metriocormic, macrocormic.**

**brachycranic:** pertaining to **brachycephaly**. Aka brachycephalic.

**brachydactyly:** congenital genetic condition in humans caused by an **autosomal dominant** allele that results in the shortness of fingers, toes, or both.

**brachydont:** describes teeth characterized by low crowns, deep and well-developed roots, and narrow root canals. This is the condition found in humans and other primates.

**brachymeiosis:** meiosis characterized by suppression of the second division.

**brachymetatarsia:** condition characterized by abnormally short **metatarsal** bones.

**brachyphalangy:** see **brachydactyly.**

**brachyskelia:** in reference to **Manouvrier's index**, with an index of 84.90 or less; such an individual has short limbs in relation to trunk size. All humans are brachyskelic in infancy. Cf. **brachycormic**. See **mesatyskelia, macroskelia.**

**brachystaphyline:** with reference to the **palatal index**, with an index of 85.00 or greater; such an individual is considered to have a broad or wide palate.

*Brachyteles* **Spix, 1823:** monotypic **platyrrhine** genus to which the woolly spider monkey or muriqui belongs; restricted to coastal forests of southeastern Brazil. **Diurnal; arboreal** quadruped with **prehensile tail**; also brachiates. Thumb vestigial. Largest of the New World primates; slight **sexual dimorphism** in body size. Body mass ranges from 7.5 to 15 kg. Dental formula: 2.1.3.3. Diet principally folivorous with fruit supplements. Mixed-sex social groupings. Nonterritorial. Females have enlarged **clitoris** that resembles a penis. Mating is promiscuous. Males have large testicles; it has been suggested that males compete for reproductive success via **sperm competition**. See Appendix 2 for taxonomy and Appendix 3 for species.

**brachyuranic:** pertaining to an **external palatal index** of more than 115.00.

**bradyauxesis:** growth in which a part or organ of interest grows slower than the organism as a whole. See **heterauxesis** and **allometry.**

**bradycardia:** abnormally slow heart rate; a rate less than 60 beats per minute in a resting human adult subject.

**bradygenesis:** slowed phylogenetic development; aka bradytely.

**bradytely: Simpson's** term for a rate of evolution that is slow. Adjective: bradytelic.

‡ **brain:** enlarged superior portion of the **central nervous system** located in the cranial cavity of the skull, which consists of a convoluted mass of **gray matter** and **white matter** that serves to control and coordinate thought and movement. Its tripartite structure consists of the **prosencephalon, mesencephalon, and rhombencephalon**. Individual structures include the **cerebrum, cerebellum, corpus callosum, hypophysis, vermis, spinal cord, medulla oblongata, and pons.**

**brain case:** see **cranium.**

**brain cast:** see **endocranial cast.**

**Brain, Charles Kimberlin ('Bob')** (1931–): zoologist, taphonomist at the Transvaal Museum (Pretoria), South Africa. Brain was a primary investigator at **Swartkrans** after the mid-1950s. One of the early advocates of **taphonomy**, especially with respect to weakening of the **'killer ape' hypothesis** and re-examination of the putative **osteodontokeratic** culture. He also pioneered studies demonstrating a relationship between bone strength and taphonomic event survival. Author of 165 scientific articles and *The Hunters or the Hunted?: An Introduction to African Cave Taphonomy* (1981), in which he suggested — after a two-decade study — that the **Swartkrans** hominids were hunted by leopards; aka the leopard hill hypothesis.

**brain expense:** energy, or caloric cost, required for **brain metabolism.**

**brain lateralization:** asymmetry of the cerebral hemispheres, especially in higher primates and most of all in the **Hominidae**. Lower Pleistocene tools found at **Koobi Fora** suggest that lateralization of the hominoid brain has an early history, as most of the tools were manufactured by striking a target with a hammerstone held in the right hand. See **hand preference.**

**brain mass:** mass (usually in grams) of the **central nervous system** that is contained within the **cranium**. Interspecific brain mass is highly correlated with several **life history variables**, and accurately predicts both **gestation length** and **maximum life span potential** in mammals. Often used synonymously (though incorrectly) with brain weight. See **brain size.**

**brain metabolism:** sum of the synthetic and degradative chemical activities that occur in the brain. An adult human brain weighs about 1.5 kg (3–3.5 lbs) and is composed of an estimated 100 billion neurons. Over 200 known neuropeptides facilitate neurotransmission. The high metabolic rate of the human brain requires that it receive about 20% of the total resting cardiac output although it accounts for only 2% of the total body mass; interruption of this flow for 10 seconds results in unconsciousness. These vascular needs are supplied by the paired internal carotid and vertebral arteries that unite at the **cerebral arterial circle**. The hominid, and especially human, brain generates excess heat that must be transferred to other tissues, and its **thermoregulation** and **homeostasis** is of ongoing concern to human biologists.

‡ **brain size:** estimate of either **brain mass** or brain volume (**endocranial volume**).

**brainstem:** portion of the **brain** consisting of the **medulla oblongata, pons,** and **midbrain**; located between the spinal cord and forebrain.

**brain volume:** see **brain size** and **endocranial volume.**

**brain waves:** summations of electrical activity in the brain, termed action potentials, that can be detected by an **electroencephalogram**. There are four common modes of activity; alpha waves, **beta waves**, theta waves, and **delta waves.**

**brain weight:** see **brain mass.**

*Bramapithecus* **Lewis, 1934:** genus of **hominoid** later referred to *Ramapithecus*. *Bramapithecus* consisted of a maxilla, which was later found to match the mandible of the **holotype** for *Ramapithecus*. *Ramapithecus* was subsequently referred to *Sivapithecus*.

**branch:** 1. any division or subdivision of a stem or axis. 2. in taxonomy, a line connecting a **node** with a terminal taxon; a line connecting any two nodes; any lineage in a **phylogram, dendrogram,** or **cladogram**. 3. grouping of animals according to Cuvier (archaic).

**branch swapping algorithm:** any procedure that adds, subtracts, or interchanges lineages in a classificatory tree; the aim of the procedure is to produce a set of alternative trees, each of which reflects equally the data used to generate the set. See **PAUP** and **PHYLIP**. Cf. **maximum parsimony hypothesis.**

**branching evolution or pattern:** see **cladistics** and **cladogenesis.**

*Branisella boliviana* **Hoffstetter, 1969:** earliest **platyrrhine** from the late **Oligocene** (*c.* 27 mya) of Bolivia. Four specimens recovered, consisting of molars, premolars, mandible and maxilla. There is an incomplete set of dentition with 3 molars and 3 premolars, and presumed dental formula is 2.1.3.3; cusp patterns suggest **frugivory**. Short face; mandible shallow, suggestive of the parapithecids. Body mass estimate 1 kg. Relationship to later platyrrhines is ambiguous, although the recovered material is reminiscent of cebids like *Saimiri* or *Aotus*. Nevertheless, *Branisella* also has some omomyid features. See Appendix 1 for taxonomy.

**Branisellinae Hershkovitz, 1977:** monotypic subfamily (*Branisella boliviana*) of Oligocene **platyrrhines**. Many authorities disregard the subfamily distinction and place *Branisella* in the Superfamily **Ceboidea** or *incertae sedis*. See Appendix 1 for taxonomy.

*Brassica:* genus of plants that includes the species *Brassica oleracea*. Also includes the human food plants cabbage, kale, Brussels sprouts, cauliflower, broccoli, and kohlrabi. See **PTC**.

**Bräuer, Günter** (1949–): physical anthropologist at the Institut für Humanbiologie, University of Hamburg; analysed sites containing African archaic *Homo* and early **AMHs**, and in 1982 was the first to propose a non-Eurocentric model of **human origins**, an 'out of Africa' hypothesis. Bräuer's version was later termed the **hybridization and replacement model** to distinguish it from the **out of Africa II model** proper. Recipient of the prestigious Rudolf Martin Prize. Co-editor (with F. H. Smith) of *Continuity or Replacement: Controversies in Homo sapiens Evolution* (1992).

**Brazilian barefaced tamarin:** vernacular for *Saguinus bicolor*.

**BRCA**: abbreviation for **breast cancer** and ovarian cancer susceptibility gene(s).

**breadth** (b): width.

**breadth of the foramen magnum: craniometric** measurement; maximum internal width of the **foramen magnum** perpendicular to its length. Aka foraminal breadth.

**breakage and reunion model:** proposal that genetic recombination involves the physical breakage and exchange of parts of the chromosomes and the reunion of the broken pieces. Aka break and exchange model.

**breakthrough:** homozygous recessive genotype, usually lethal, that survives a crisis. Aka escaper.

**breast:** 1. chest region. 2. in humans, the organ of milk secretion, well developed in the female, rudimentary in the male.

**breast cancer, familial, Type 1** (BRCA1): autosomal dominant condition characterized by tumors in female breast tissue. Onset usually in the fourth decade. It is the most common form of cancer among American women, with about 44 000 female (vs. 300 male) deaths annually. The chance of contracting BC are about 13% overall; only about 5–10% of all breast cancers cases are familial, but the penetrance is high: between 80 and 90% with the gene are at high risk. The defective susceptibility gene is *BRCA1*, a transcription factor gene. At least three more related genes have also been mapped: *BRCA2*, *BRCA3*, and *BRCA4*. One of the features of these cancers is a characteristic **loss of heterozygosity** (LOH) in chromosomal regions contiguous with the affected gene. The possession of a *BRCA1* gene (but not of *BRCA2*) also increases the probability that a woman will develop ovarian and/or cervical cancer during her lifetime. These *BRCA* genes normally function to repair radiation-induced breaks in double-stranded DNA. In some breast sarcomas, tumor-generated MDM-2 proteins inhibit the effects of the *p53* **tumor suppressor** gene, permitting additional tumor growth. Although men account for only about 1 of every 150 cases of familial breast cancer, they can pass on susceptibility mutations to daughters.

‡ **breast milk:** white or yellowish secretion of the mammary glands of female mammals, primarily for the nourishment of offspring; milk contains protein, sugar, lipids, and certain antibodies that provide **passive immunity**. See **colostrum**.

**breastbone:** vernacular for **sternum**.

**breast milk substitute:** any product used to replace mother's milk, whether it is suitable or not.

**breath:** 1. inspired air and expired air from the lungs. 2. one cycle of inspiration and expiration.

**breathing:** movement of air into and out of the lungs; ventilation.

‡ **breccia:** conglomerate of angular stone, sand and bone embedded by the action of a precipitating cement (often **limestone**); found in several South African fossil **hominid** sites, such as **Taung**. Aka osseous breccia.

**breed:** 1. to produce offspring by hatching or gestation. 2. to propagate sexually and usually under controlled conditions. 3. a group of animals or plants presumably related by descent from common ancestors and visibly similar in most characteristics; especially, such a group under the influence of humans and differentiated from the wild type. 4. a number of persons of the same stock. 5. class; kind.

**breeding:** 1. the act of reproduction. 2. the improvement of stock by selective matings, especially in animal husbandry. 3. individual heritage or lineage. See **domestic selection**.

**breeding biology:** see **reproductive biology**.

‡ **breeding isolate:** deme that is socially or geographically isolated from other **demes** within a **species**.

**breeding out:** maintenance of genetic variability in domesticated plants and animals by the regular practice of using unrelated specimens brought in from outside a known lineage.

**breeding population:** group of organisms that tend to choose mates from within the group; cf. **deme**.

**breeding season:** period of time when the females of a species or population come into synchronized **estrus**, producing synchronized birth of offspring. This may occur twice a year among the **prosimians**, but usually only once a year among the higher primates; humans do not have a breeding season. See **birth synchrony** and **birth season**.

**breeding size:** number of viable individuals in a population of breeding age, and actually reproducing in a given generation or cohort; aka breeding population size. Cf. **effective breeding population**.

**breeding system:** mode or pattern of interbreeding within a **deme**.

**breeding true:** see **true breeding**.

**breeding value:** reproductive success of an individual as measured by the mean value of its offspring with respect to a particular character. See **fitness**.

**bregma** (b): craniometric landmark; point where the coronal and sagittal sutures intersect mid-sagittally. See Appendix 7 for an illustration of craniometric landmarks.

**Brelich's snub-nosed monkey:** vernacular for *Rhinopithecus* (= *Pygathrix*) *brelichi*.

**Breuil, Henri Édouard Prosper** (1877–1961): French Abbé and prehistorian; ordained 1897. An interest in Paleolithic art and prehistoric archaeology led to his contributions in both areas. Professor at the National Museum of Natural History (1910–) and College de France (1929–47). Breuil proposed that the people who painted the animals and symbols in European caves believed that they exercised ritual control over predators and prey. Breuil also reclassified the extant Paleolithic industries into a form recognizable today, and in which the importance of the **Aurignacian** was emphasized.

**bridge:** 1. any spanning or transitional structure, e.g. bridge of the nose. 2 see **land bridge.**

**bridging argument:** in archaeology, logical statements that link the static data to the past dynamics that produced them; observations of contemporary circumstances are generally required to make sense of such linkages.

**Brinton, Daniel Garrison** (1837–99): US anthropologist; among the first anthropologists in America and one of the first five to work in physical anthropology. Brinton was affiliated with the University of Pennsylvania museums; a specialist in native American origins, Brinton was one of those who, in *Races and Peoples* (1890), denied the Asiatic origin hypothesis for Native Americans.

**bristlecone pine:** see **California bristlecone pine.**

**Britten–Davidson model:** proposal for nuclear **genetic regulation** in eukaryotic cells that involves sensor genes that promote production of a specific activator RNA which binds to the **receptor** site of a **structural gene.** Cf. **Jacob–Monod model** for prokaryote version.

**brittle bones:** see **osteogenesis imperfecta.**

**broad-nosed bamboo (or gentle) lemur:** vernacular for *Hapalemur simus.*

**broad ramus:** vertical portion of the **mandible** behind the teeth where certain large chewing muscles attach; relatively wide (from front to back) to accommodate attachment of those muscles. A diagnostic feature of primates, including early hominids. See **mandibular ramus.**

**Broca horizontal** (CA): plane of orientation for viewing the profile of the skull. This plane extends from the alveolar point (between the two medial upper incisors) to the lowermost point of the occipital condyle while the skull is resting on a horizontal plane. The **Frankfort horizontal** is favored by most workers over the Broca horizontal. Aka Broca plane.

**Broca, Pierre Paul** (1824–80): French surgeon, anatomist, racial craniometrician, founder of neuroanatomy; proved localization of brain functions by identifying the eponymous speech center (1862), the 'limbic lobe' (1878), and homologous olfactory centers in both humans and nonhuman primates (1879). His anthropological work included the creation of an **orbital index;** founder of the Société d'Anthropologie (1859) and the Ecole d'Anthropologie (1876). A moderate Darwinian, he was a **polygenist** who elaborated on the American S. G. **Morton's** version of primordial

racial **typology**, while warning, however, against the **reification** of **races**, as did his student **Topinard.**

**Broca plane:** see **Broca horizontal.**

‡ **Broca's area:** see **motor speech area.**

**Broken Hill:** see **Kabwe.**

**bronchial:** of or pertaining to the **bronchi** of the lungs.

‡ **bronchus** (plural **bronchi**): one of the two main branches (primary bronchus) of the trachea that leads to the lungs or any of the pulmonary branches (secondary bronchi); composed of cartilage.

**brood:** set of young animals that are being cared for by adults.

**brood parasite:** individual, usually from another species, that exploits parental care from individuals other than its parents, usually at the expense of the natural offspring.

‡ **Broom, Robert** (1866–1951): Scots-born South African physician and mammal anatomist; in 1938 it was Broom who located and, with John **Robinson**, described *Paranthropus robustus* (= *Australopithecus robustus*), the second species of **australopithecine** then known from South Africa. Broom had received earlier acclaim for his paleontological work on mammal-like reptiles and had been awarded the Medal of the Royal Society for this work. Author of more than 450 papers and monographs.

**brother:** male in a **sibship**; a kinship term that identifies a genealogical or adopted degree of relationship in a **nuclear family** or **extended family.** See **father, mother, sister, uncle, aunt, cousin.**

**brow ridge:** superciliary arch, a ridge of bone above the eye orbit. Brow ridges are most noticeable in the fossil **erectines** and **archaic** *Homo sapiens.* In *Homo erectus*, brow ridges consist of compact bone, but in later stages of human evolution (e.g. **archaics**) the ridge contained a **frontal sinus.** The brow ridge is often more pronounced in males, and can be used in **skeletal sexing.** See **supra-orbital torus.**

**brow-ridged langur:** general vernacular for colobine monkeys belonging to the genus *Trachypithecus*; aka leaf-monkeys.

**brown capuchin:** vernacular for *Cebus apella.*

**brown-headed spider monkey:** vernacular for *Ateles fusciceps.*

**brown-headed tamarin:** vernacular for *Saguinus fuscicollis.*

**brown howler:** vernacular for *Alouatta fusca.*

**brown lemur:** vernacular for *Eulemur (= Lemur) fulvus.*

**Brownian movement:** continuous movement of microscopic particles suspended in a fluid resulting from molecular bombardment; used metaphorically in both **population genetics** and **chaos theory** as an example of random movement that can be described mathematically. Aka Brownian motion.

**Brownian system:** comprehensive medical system proposed in 1780 by Scottish physician John Brown (1735–88) that the functions and life of an organism are the aggregate of the constant responses of an organism to its environment. One of the systems of medicine that balanced opposing forces, health for Brownians was a balance between stimulating impressions and the body's responses to them; inadequate stimuli created the conditions for disease, and balance could be restored by prescriptions of brandy, spicy food, opium, soup, musk and camphor.

**browse:** 1. to feed on plants. 2. the non-reproductive parts of plants that is edible and is available to browsing animals.

**browsers:** animals such as giraffes, rhinos, some bovids, etc., that ingest food primarily by nibbling at the non-reproductive parts of woody plants. Owing to their predominantly $C_3$ **vegetation** consumption, browsers have a decreased $\delta^{13}C$ ratio ($^{13}C : ^{12}C$) ratio. Aka $C_3$ **consumers.** See **carbon isotope analysis.**

**Brues, Alice Mossie** (1913–): geneticist, forensic anthropologist; a student of E. A. **Hooton,** Brues made significant contributions to the knowledge of inheritances of polygenic traits. The 1954 paper on selection and polymorphism in the ABO blood group was an instant classic. President, **AAPA** (1971–73); author of *People and Races* (1977).

**Brumback's owl monkey:** vernacular for *Aotus brumbacki.*

**Brunhes normal epoch:** extended geological interval (a **chron**) dating from about 780 kya to the present, in which the polarity of the earth's magnetic field has not changed significantly, and is therefore termed 'normal'. See **paleomagnetism.** Cf. **Matuyama reversed epoch.**

**bubas:** see **yaws.**

**bubonic plague:** major form of **plague,** a severe acute or chronic bacterial infection caused by a bacillus, *Yersinia pestis,* and which occurs both endemically and epidemically worldwide. Bubonic plague is typically characterized by abrupt onset of fever, chills, weakness, and headache, followed by pain, tenderness, and swollen and sometimes suppurating regional lymph nodes (buboes). Historically, one of the original hosts was the black rat indigenous to India (*Rattus rattus*). It has been suggested that the observed **cline** for the B blood group allele across Europe can be accounted for by the bubonic plague **pandemic** in the fourteenth century CE, with individuals possessing anti-A **antibody** surviving more frequently than those without it. Aka black death, rat fever, glandular plague, 'Pestis fulminans'. A milder form of bubonic plague is known as 'Pestis minor'.

**buccal:** pertaining to the cheeks.

**buccal gland:** one of paired serous and **mucus** glands on the inner surface of the cheek., Aka glandulae buccales.

**buccal phase:** sequence during chewing in which the teeth on the masticating (chewing) side make lateral contact on the way to central **occlusion.** first sequence of the **power stroke** of the **masticatory cycle;** aka phase 1.

**buccal pouches:** see **cheek pouches.**

**buccal smear:** mounted and stained preparation of cells sampled from the lining of the mouth.

**buccal surface:** in reference to teeth, the surface that faces the cheek.

**buccinator:** muscle of facial expression. The buccinator originates on the **maxillary** bone and the **mandible** and inserts into the **orbicularis oris** muscle. Its action includes compressing the cheeks (as when blowing), drawing the corner of the mouth laterally, and holding food on the teeth during **mastication.**

**buccolingual:** pertaining to the two sides of a tooth: the cheek (buccal) side of a tooth and the tongue (lingual) side. Often used to reflect the distance (width or diameter) between the two sides.

**bucco-occlusal:** pertaining to the chewing surface of a tooth that is on the side bordering the cheek.

**disto-occlusal:** pertaining to the chewing surface of a tooth that is on the side bordering the tongue.

**Buckland, William** (1784–1856): UK geologist, catastrophist; author of *Geology and Mineralogy Considered with Reference to Natural Theology,* published complete with a foldout chart of extinctions due to catastrophes (see **catastrophism**). An early teacher of **Lyell** and Murchison at Oxford, he fell intellectually farther behind and was eventually spent, resorting to reconciliation of new geological observations with biblical passages. Studied some of the then-earliest fossils in England; for an example of his interpretation, see **Paviland Cave** (Goat's Hole).

**bud:** 1. germinal tissue; resembling a plant bud, as in a tooth bud. 2. in demography, to undergo **fission.**

**Buda industry:** collection of artifacts that consists of microlithic variants of pebble and chopper tools; found in association with the **Vertesszöllös** hominid remains.

**budding:** 1. in biology, asexual reproduction in which a more or less complete new organism grows from the body (cells) of a parent organism. 2. in **demography,** the division of a population by fission; that is, some of its members 'bud off' to form a new colony or village. See **fission–fusion society.**

**Buettner-Janusch, John** (1924–92): US physical anthropologist, primatologist, student of J. N. Spuhler; director of the Duke Primate Center (1965–73), where he initiated studies of the comparative serology of primates, for which he was recognized internationally. Author of *Origins of Man* (1966).

**buffer:** 1. reduction of an impact or the effect of an agent. 2. protection of a system from change by some external agency. 3. substance that stabilizes the pH of a solution.

**buffer species:** any alternative food source for a predator that diminishes the effect the predator has on its primary prey species.

‡ **buffered evolution:** adjustment to selective pressures through use of physiological and/or behavioral adaptive strategies to environmental stressors.

**buffered populations: demes** interacting such that the density of each is maintained within certain limits.

**buffering system:** system that prevents changes in the environment from exerting direct influence on the state of certain of its elements.

‡ **Buffon, de, Compte Georges-Louis Leclerc** (1707–88): French naturalist. Applied Newtonian methods to plant physiology and eventually became director of the Jardin du Roi in Paris. His 44-volume *Histoire naturelle* was modeled after **Aristotle**'s works and contained material of biological interest as well as reports of several experiments that questioned the age of the earth. With Immanuel Kant, he was among the first to suggest that the evidence showed that the earth was of extremely old age. First to define **species** in terms of reproductive barriers. Cf. **Ussher.**

**buffy-headed marmoset:** vernacular for *Callithrix flaviceps.*

**buffy layer:** thin layer of **white blood cells** found below the **plasma** and resting upon the uppermost compacted **red blood cells** after whole blood has been centrifuged. Aka buffy coat.

**buffy saki:** vernacular for *Pithecia albicans.*

**buffy tufted-ear marmoset:** vernacular for *Callithrix aurita.*

**Buhunician tool tradition:** Upper Paleolithic 'transitional' tool industry found in Moravia in the western Ukraine and thought by some to have been created as **Neandertals** modified (or mimicked) technology borrowed from the **Aurignacian** of **AMHs**, but thought by others to precede the latter industry. Found at about 38 kya. Cf. **Uluzzian, Szeletian** and **Châtelperronian.**

**Buia:** archaeological site found in 1995–7 in the Danakil desert, Eritrea, and dated to 1 mya. In addition to faunal remains, the site yielded some **Acheulean**-like tools; hominid remains included an early complete cranium, some isolated teeth, and a partial pelvis, all attributed to *Homo ergaster (=erectus).*

**bulb of percussion:** bulge or swelling just below the **striking platform** on the core side of a flake, representing the energy waves of the striking blow as they spread into the **core** of a stone tool; one of the diagnostic features that archaeologists use to distinguish

a stone **tool** from a naturally occurring **geofact.** Aka percussion bulb, semicone of percussion.

**bulbar scar:** small, paper-thin, often crescent-shaped scar left within the **bulb of percussion** after a flake has been removed from a core with a hammerstone; one of the diagnostic features that archaeologists use to distinguish a stone **tool** from a naturally occurring **geofact.** Aka éraillure.

**bulbourethral glands:** pair of glands that secrete a viscous fluid into the male urethra during sexual excitement. Aka Cowper's glands.

**bulimia:** eating disorder in which the affected individual consumes large amounts of food and purges the stomach by vomiting.

**bulla:** Latin term meaning bubble or spherical, e.g. ethmoidal bulla. See **auditory bulla.**

**Buluk:** archaeological site found in 1973 in northern Kenya, dated to >17 mya, and that contains a **hominoid** partial mandible found by Meave **Leakey** in 1983 and attributed to *Sivapithecus*; later reclassified as *Afropithecus.*

**bun:** see **occipital bun.**

**bunodont:** condition of cheek teeth in which there are low rounded cusps, as in humans.

**bunolophodont:** condition in which rounded **cusps** on **molars** are united by ridges.

*Bunopithecus* Matthew and Granger, 1923: synonym for *Hylobates hoolock*; also suggested as a subgenus of *Hylobates*, of which the only member of this subgenus is *H. hoolock* (see **gibbons**).

**Burgi tuff:** Pleistocene volcanic deposit at **Koobi Fora**, Lake Turkana, dated by K/Ar to 3.0–1.9 mya. The fossiliferous Upper Burgi Member has a date of 1.89 mya.

**burial:** 1. in modern practice, the intentional interment of a human body. 2. controversial term applied in some cases when a nearly complete, articulated **skeleton** is excavated at an **archaeological site**; some have suggested that the term 'nearly complete skeleton' be applied, in order to avoid confusion with modern practice; common **skeletal positions** include **contracted, flexed**, semi-flexed, and **extended burial position**(s). See **grave.**

**burial mound:** see **funeral mound.**

**burial shaft:** very deep **grave.** In some cultures, burial shafts are 24 m deep.

‡ **burin: Upper Paleolithic** stone **tool** with a sharp edge that is used to cut and engrave bone, wood, horn, or soft stone; aka stone chisel, burin en-bec-de-flûte.

**burin technique:** method developed by Upper Paleolithic peoples for removing a small facet of stone from the side of a flake, in which the blow is delivered on the same plane as the flake.

**Burkitt lymphoma** (BL): endemic BL is a malignant form of lymphatic cancer that develops in the jaws and face bones of children, found predominately in central and subequatorial Africa in the same regions as endemic malaria. In Africa, the tumors are associated with infection by the mosquito-borne Epstein–Barr virus (EBV), a form of herpesvirus, which causes chromosome translocations that involve the *c-myc* proto-oncogene normally located on chromosome 8. No EBV has been detected in European or American BL patients. The most common translocation is t(8; 14). The *Myc* gene normally functions to control cell growth and proliferation, but at its new position next to a highly expressed antibody gene on chromosome 14, this function of *Myc* is altered and it is over-expressed, becoming an oncogene. Other EBV-precipitated cancers include nasopharyngeal carcinoma and **Hodgkin disease**. Cf. the **Philadelphia chromosome**.

**bursa, bursae:** synovial fluid-filled sacs associated with some **synovial joints** and lined by **synovial membrane**. These sacs are often located between bone and skin and offer protection to the underlying structures and assistance in the movement of tendons that slide over bone or other tendons.

**bursitis:** inflammation of a **bursa**.

**Burt, Cyril Lodowic** (1883–1971): British psychologist and psychometrician; his work was focused in two areas: multivariate statistics and the genetics of intelligence. In the first, Burt succeeded and thus inherited work involving Spearman's statistical work. The second area proved the more controversial; through a series of **twin studies** (1943–6), Burt estimated the **heritability** of **intelligence** to be >0.70, a finding that led him to conclude that environment had less to do with general intelligence than did one's genetic constitution. Shortly after Burt's death he was accused by the medical correspondent to the (London) *Sunday Times* of falsifying data used in the twin studies. Since then, scientists have published opinions on both sides of the affair. Although Burt's name has not been cleared, a study of **twins** reared apart has been completed in Minnesota that reported an equally strong heritability for IQ, using a much larger sample.

**Busch theory:** theory of cancer proposed by American physician/biochemist Harris Busch which states that there are three stages of cancer causation: initiation, promotion, and acceleration. Certain segments of DNA are carcinogenic, according to this theory, and are normally suppressed, but if released they produce carcinogenic RNA.

**bushbaby:** vernacular for the four **prosimian** genera belonging to the family **Galagidae**. See *Galago*, *Galagoides*, *Otolemur*, and *Euoticus*.

**Bushman: ethonym** applied to peoples who live in marginal areas, i.e. the 'bush'. The term is best known in its application to the **Khoisan**-speaking peoples of the Kalahari in southern Africa, and the indigenous people of Australia. See **Hottentot**.

**Bushman canine:** 'premolariform'-shaped **canine** denoted by a hypertrophied mesial lingual ridge coalesced with **tuberculum** dentale, and a distally positioned lingual **sulcus**.

**bushmeat:** term used for meat that is obtained from wild mammals hunted in areas previously inaccessible to most hunters. Primates make up a portion of the bushmeat trade; it especially affects gorillas and chimpanzees, and is a serious problem for primates, in general, in western Africa.

**bushy lineage:** any **paraphyletic group** or lineage; a lineage that is evolving away from an ancestor so rapidly that several similar **taxa** may exist at the same time. The **hominid** lineage may represent an example.

**butchering:** behavior in which meat is extracted from animals through the use of tools; as distinct from the strictly English definition, which includes killing the animal, butchering by early hominids may result from scavenging behavior: when early hominids developed tool technology that enabled them to butcher animals it marked an adaptive change in our evolution. Aka butchery.

**butchering site:** archaeological location where primary bone **disarticulation** occurred, and where tissues of an animal were harvested, often the **kill site**.

**butchery, evidence of:** any sign that an organism has been defleshed. Such signs include striations made by defleshing tools, characteristic fractures produced by, for example, hammerstones or anvils (or both), certain patterns of bone removal and deposition, and burn marks.

**button scurvy:** alternative name for nonvenereal **syphilis**.

*Buxella* Godinot, 1988: adapoid prosimian from the middle Eocene of Europe belonging to the **notharctid** subfamily **Cercamoniinae**; two species. Estimated body mass around 600 g. See Appendix 1 for taxonomy.

**Bwindi mountain gorilla:** see *Gorilla gorilla*.

**byproduct hypothesis:** proposal that early stone tools are highly variable, the result of rather haphazard tool manufacture, primarily byproducts of making flakes, rather than the end product of a **mental template**. See **bolas stones**.

**byte:** quantitative unit of information in a system of communication, consisting of several **bits**.

**C:** abbreviation for (1) **centigrade scale**; (2) **Celsius scale**; (3) **constant region**; (4) **canine**; (5) **carbon**; (6) **consumption**; (7) **cytokine**; (8) **kilocalorie**.

**c.:** abbreviation for *circa* (Latin) meaning about, approximately.

**CA:** 1. acronym used by some authors standing for common ancestor. 2. abbreviation used for the **Broca horizontal** of skull profile orientation.

**C₃ consumers:** animals classified as frugivores and browsers of **C₃ vegetation**, including giraffids, rhinocerotids, many **primates**, and some bovids. See **stable isotope analysis** and **carbon isotope analysis**.

**C₃ photosynthetic pathway:** set of reactions during diurnal **photosynthesis** in which a specific enzyme (Rubisco) uses carbon atoms from $CO_2$ to produce a three-carbon compound ($C_3$); this occurs in a single chloroplast. Plants that utilize this process are at risk of losing carbon through photorespiration. More than 95% of the earth's plant species can be characterized as **C₃ vegetation**. Cf. **C₄ photosynthetic pathway**. See **carbon isotope analysis**.

**C₃ vegetation:** evolutionarily older trees, fruits, bushes, shrubs, and forbs that discriminate against the heavy $^{13}C$ **isotope** during fixation of $CO_2$ by fixing carbon in a three-carbon compound in the **C₃ photosynthetic pathway**. $C_3$ plants have a relatively low $\delta^{13}C$ ratio ($^{13}C : ^{12}C$ ratio). Used in dietary analysis to identify **C₃ consumers**. See **carbon isotope analysis**.

**C₄ consumers:** animals classified as **grazers** of **C₄ vegetation**, including equids, suids, and some bovids. See **stable isotope analysis** and **carbon isotope analysis**.

**C₄ photosynthetic pathway:** set of reactions during diurnal **photosynthesis** in which a specific enzyme (PEPC) uses carbon atoms from $CO_2$ to produce an initial four-carbon compound ($C_4$) that is later refixed as a $C_3$ compound; this requires two different chloroplasts. Plants that utilize this process are at lower risk of losing carbon through photorespiration. Less than 1% of the earth's plant species can be characterized as **C₄ vegetation**. The $C_4$ pathway is thought to be a more recent adaptation than the older **C₃ photosynthetic pathway** and **CAM photosynthesis** pathway, and a selective response to the relatively low atmospheric concentrations of $CO_2$ that have prevailed during the **Cenozoic epoch** of the earth's history. See **carbon isotope analysis**.

**C₄ vegetation:** recently evolved tropical grasses and sedges found in warm, herbaceous ecosystems that utilize the **C₄ photosynthetic pathway** and thus discriminate less markedly against the heavy $^{13}C$ **isotope** during fixation of $CO_2$. $C_4$ plants have a relatively high $\delta^{13}C$ ratio ($^{13}C : ^{12}C$ ratio). Used in dietary analysis to identify **C₄ consumers**. See **carbon isotope analysis**.

*Cacajao* **Lesson, 1840**: **platyrrhine** genus to which the uakari monkeys belong; two to three species recognized; found in upper Amazon basin of southern Venezuela, eastern Peru and eastern Colombia, where they prefer the canopy and middle levels of flooded primary forests. Diurnal; **arboreal quadrupeds** that rarely descend to the ground; the only short-tailed platyrrhines (1/3 of body length or less). These are the largest pithecines, ranging in body mass from 2.8 to 4.1 kg, with males larger than females; species comparable in size. Natural history poorly known. Dental formula: 2.1.3.3; appear to be **frugivorous** and **granivorous**. Face bare; adult males have well-developed **temporalis muscle** that forms a bulge on the head. Live in troops, usually 20–30 individuals but sometimes up to 100 mixed-sex individuals; these troops undergo **fission** into smaller foraging groups; believed to be **polygamous** and **fission–fusion society**. See Appendix 2 for taxonomy, Appendix 3 for living species.

**cache:** deliberate storage of food or materials at a hidden location for future use. Noun: caching. According to Potts, early humans may have been caching **tools** or raw materials at **Olduvai Gorge**.

**cachexia:** chronic condition characterized by weight loss and catabolism, resulting from a malignant disease, malnutrition, or long-term emotional stress.

**cacogenesis:** state of being incapable of hybridization.

**cacogenics:** study of the effects of bad heredity. See **eugenics**.

**Cactus Hill:** archaeological site found in 1993, on the Nottoway River near Richmond, VA, dated to 15.1 and 10.9 kya (the 15.1 date is provisional, as are even earlier estimates of 18 kya), and that contains artifacts of the **Clovis** type in the younger level and 'non-Clovis' stone points and other implements in the deeper level. The site is thus a viable candidate for a pre-Clovis site, raising the possibility that seagoing Europeans settled eastern North America. See the **Solutrean/Clovis similarity hypothesis**.

**CAD:** computer assisted design system. A technique that triangulates three digitized data points $(x, y, z)$ in a computed 3-D space. CAD systems facilitate the quantitative comparison of **organs**, such as the brain, across species, or the modeling of growth changes, such as **craniofacial growth**, for a single individual.

**cadaver:** dead body; corpse.

**caecotrophic pellets:** soft feces, produced in the cecum, of some mammals that ingest a high-cellulose diet. The pellets are ingested (a process referred to as refection or **coprophagy**) as they are eliminated, providing additional time for symbionts to break down cellulose. It has been proposed that one primate, **Lepilemur**, is a coprophage, suggesting caecotrophic pellets may be ingested.

**caecum:** see **cecum**.

***Caenopithecus lemuroides* Rutimeyer, 1862:** adapoid **prosimian** known from the late Eocene of Europe, belonging to the notharctid subfamily **Cercamoniinae; monotypic;** known from jaws and teeth; this was the first fossil primate described that was considered to be lemurlike. Fused mandibular symphysis. Estimated body mass around 3 kg. Dental formula extrapolated to be: 2.1.3.3/1.1.3.3; dental morphology suggests **folivorous** adaptation similar to living indriids. See Appendix 1 for taxonomy.

**cafe-au-lait spots:** spots of abnormal skin pigmentation that are found on many individuals with neurofibromatosis.

**cage effects:** in behavioral studies, a **bias** of nonindependence in behavior among animals kept together in the same environment.

**cal:** abbreviation for **gram calorie**.

**Cal:** abbreviation for **kilocalorie**.

**calcaneal tendon:** large and strongest tendon in the human; formed by the union of the tendons from the gastrocnemius and soleus muscles; the calcaneal tendon inserts into the **calcaneus**. Aka Achilles tendon.

**calcaneus:** largest of the **tarsal** bones that forms the base of the heel; articulates superiorly with the **talus** and anteriorly with the other bones of the **tarsus**. Much of the weight of the body is transferred to this bone; it also serves as a site of attachment for the intrinsic muscles that move the foot. Alternate spelling: calcaneum.

**calcareous:** 1. pertaining to chalk or **limestone**; rich in calcium carbonate. 2. pertaining to plant species that grow on or have an affinity for chalky soil.

**calcarine fissure:** characteristic groove on the medial surface of each **occipital lobe** of the primate brain. See **visual cortex**.

**calcific:** pertaining to the **calcification** process.

**calcification:** process of mineral deposition, usually calcium, in tissues of the body. Regular sites of calcification include the **skeleton** and **dentition**.

**calcite:** 1. **calcium carbonate**, a common mineral form of **limestone**, a rock that possesses an internal crystal face that produces a preferential cleavage plane and that makes it difficult or impossible to control fracture and to produce a sharp-edged tool. 2. with **aragonite**, one of the two common carbonates of calcareous (chalky) skeletons; aragonite disappears almost completely from older fossils, whereas calcite may be replaced by silica or pyrite, a process known as **permineralization**.

**calcitonin:** hormone secreted by the **thyroid gland** that lowers **calcium** ion and phosphate concentrations in blood, inhibits bone resorption (decalcification), and acts as an antagonist to **parathyroid hormone**.

**calcium** (Ca): silvery, moderately hard metallic element. Calcium (with phosphate and carbonate) gives bone most of its structural properties, and is essential to many physiological processes. See **hydroxyapatite**.

**calcium carbonate** ($CaCO_3$): white powder found in nature as **calcite**, chalk and limestone; used in the manufacture of lime and cement. The major component of marine shells and a common precipitate of sea water.

**calcrete:** desert soil cemented with **calcium carbonate** (**calcite**).

**caldera:** 1. large basinlike depression formed as the result of violent volcanic activity. 2. the most severe mode of volcanic eruption. The most recent example — the **Toba eruption** — occurred on the island of Sumatra 74 kya, and is an example of an **ultra-Plinian eruption**. Calderas are large, flat depressions that eject large volumes of rhyolite into the atmosphere, followed by a collapse of the central part of the volcano; the intensity of the eruption is further enhanced if the caldera is located on an island and seawater then rushes into the cone.

**calendar:** any of a number of techniques that reckon sequences of days, number of days in a lunar month and/or solar year, etc.

**calf circumference: anthropometric** measurement; distance around the lower leg as measured with a tape measure placed at the position determined to produce the maximum circumference and passed horizontally around the calf. Used to help determine body composition in adults.

**calf length: anthropometric** measurement; distance between the knee joint and the tip of the medial **malleolus** of the tibia as measured with an **anthropometer**. Used in studies of body proportions and in various areas of **human engineering**.

**calibration:** 1. in geology, the assignment of an absolute date to at least one point on a relative **stratigraphic column**. 2. among dating systems, the crossreferencing and reconciliation of results obtained by one technique with those of another, such as **radiocarbon dating**, and **dendrochronology**.

**Calico Hills Early Man site:** highly controversial archaeological site located in an alluvial fan on the shore of **Pleistocene** Lake Manix, now in the Mojave Desert of southern California, thought by some to date to 200 kya, and that contains lithic artifacts interpreted by some as being choppers or chopping tools. Other archaeologists interpret the lithics at the site as **geofacts**.

**California bristlecone pine:** cone-bearing pine found in the southwestern USA; one of the longest-lived species on record, reaching an indiidual age of 4700+ years. The overlapped **dendrochronology** record for the region is 9400 years.

Aka hickory pine, *Pinus aristata*. See **radiocarbon dating**.

**caliper:** instrument used to take precise measurements.

**caliper wear:** erosion of bone or enamel from excessive use of **anthropometric** instruments on skeletal specimens; can lead to erroneous readings on future measurements.

**call:** see **call system** and **vocalization**.

**call system:** scheme of animal **communication** relying on a fixed repertoire of sounds, each of which signals a specific meaning. Calls are varied in pitch and intensity only; they cannot be combined and recombined to create new meanings, thus making a call system a closed system.

**Callicebinae:** **monotypic** subfamily of the **platyrrhine** family **Cebidae**. *Callicebus* is the sole genus and these monkeys are commonly known as titis. See Appendix 2 for taxonomy, Appendix 3 for living species.

*Callicebus* **Thomas, 1903: platyrrhine** genus to which the titi monkeys belong; consists of 3–13 species, depending on authority. Systematics in flux; molecular evidence supports a smaller number of species. Distributed from Columbia and Venezuela through much of Brazil, with several of the species **sympatric.** Diurnal. **Arboreal quadrupeds** and leapers. Body mass ranges from 800 to 1600 g. Not **sexually dimorphic**. Dental formula: 2.1.3.3. **Frugivorous**. Live in territorial **monogamous** family units; **territories** delineated by song. Known for intertwining of tails between the male and female. See Appendix 2 for taxonomy, Appendix 3 for living species.

*Callimico* **(Miranda-Ribeiro, 1912):** monotypic **platyrrhine** genus to which Goeldi's marmoset or monkey belongs. Ranges through the upper Amazon of southern Columbia, Ecuador, Brazil and southwestern Bolivia; aboreal; diurnal. Quadrupedal leapers. Body mass: 393–505 g. Dental formula: 2.1.3.3; **frugivorous**, with insect supplements. Most authorities place this genus among the **Callitrichidae**, and it shares many features including small size and claws. However, unlike the other callitrichids, it only gives birth to single infants and has three molars. Some workers place this species in a monotypic family, Callimiconidae. Believed to live in mixed-sex groups of up to eight individuals. See Appendix 2 for taxonomy and Appendix 3 for species.

**Callimiconinae:** subfamily of the **Callitrichidae** erected by Simpson in 1945 that consists of the enigmatic genus *Callimico*. This subfamily is not widely accepted.

*Callithrix* **Erxleben, 1777: platyrrhine** genus to which the true marmosets belong. Recent taxonomic revisions produced up to seventeen species. However, not all workers agree with these revisions; some see three

highly diverse species (*C. argentata*, *C. humeralifera*, and *C. jacchus*), with subspecies. This interpretation is primarily supported by molecular genetics. Found in tropical rain forests south of the Amazon River in Brazil and eastern Bolivia. Diurnal. **Arboreal quadrupeds** who employ leaping. Digits have secondary claws (**tegulae**). Body mass ranges from 210 to 454 g. Dental formula: 2.1.3.2; enlarged incisors used for gnawing through bark; **frugivorous**, with insect supplements. **Gummivorous** during particular seasons. Social units said to be **monogamous** families, but some workers have disputed this. Birth of **dizygotic twins** is the norm. See Appendix 2 for taxonomy, Appendix 3 for living species.

*Callithrix* **species groups:** clusters of marmoset species based on closeness of relationship. The systematics of *Callithrix* is in flux, with recent revisions producing as many as 17 species. However, some workers prefer a smaller number of *Callithrix* species, with the understanding that these species contain highly variable subspecies or populations that do not deserve species recognition. Molecular evidence appears to support this view. Consequently, the marmosets can be grouped into three clusters, the silvery marmoset, the tassel-ear marmoset, and the tufted-eared marmosets, that may eventually be collapsed into a smaller number of species. See Appendix 2 for taxonomy, Appendix 3 for living species.

‡ **Callitrichidae: platyrrhine** family of ceboids consisting of five genera; marmosets and tamarins. Adjective: callitrichid. Geographical range from Panama into the Amazon Basin of South America. Small-bodied forms (less than 750 g); arboreal; possess **tegulae**. Formerly spelled Callithricidae. See Appendix 2 for taxonomy, Appendix 3 for living species.

**Callitrichinae:** subfamily of the **platyrrhine** family **Cebidae** used by some workers as an alternative to the separate family **Callitrichidae**.

**callosity:** build-up of cells or tissue along the surface of the **epidermis** in response to friction or wear at that site; hyperkeratinized skin cells. Often called a **callus** (2).

**callus:** 1. mass of tissue that develops at the site of a fracture. Initially the callus is composed primarily of cartilage (and is referred to as a cartilaginous or soft callus) and is gradually replaced by bone (termed a bony callus). The bony callus is sculpted into the shape of the original bone through **bone remodeling**. 2. commonly used term for a skin **callosity**.

**callus pads:** see **ischial callosities**.

**caloric equator:** latitude near the earth's **equator** at which there is minimal fluctuation of solar radiation. The caloric equator is the zone of most intense radiation, highest average temperature, and minimum seasonality. See **ultraviolet radiation**.

**calorie:** 1. in chemistry, the amount of heat required to raise the temperature one gram of water by one degree centigrade; see **gram calorie**. 2. in human nutrition, Calorie (with a capital C) represents a **kilocalorie**, or one thousand calories.

**calorimeter:** instrument used to measure the heat content of foods. A bomb calorimeter does this by having a compartment where the food is placed and ignited. The temperature of a surrounding water jacket is measured to obtain the number of calories in the food. The measurement process is called calorimetry.

‡ **calotte:** uppermost portion of a dome, as in the **skull** cap, or bones of the **cranial vault**; the **calvaria** minus the basal portions. See **calva**.

‡ **calva:** older term sometimes used for **calotte**; the top of the skull or braincase, usually lacking the base.

‡ **calvaria:** superior portion of the **skull**, i.e. the skull without the **mandible** or upper facial skeleton. Plural: calvariae. An often used but incorrect spelling is calvarium. Cf. **calotte**.

**Calvin cycle:** see **C₃ photosynthetic pathway.**

**calyx:** funnel-shaped structure. Plural: **calyces.**

**CAM:** see **cellular adhesion molecule.**

**CAM photosynthesis:** Crassulacean acid metabolism (CAM), a type of nocturnal/diurnal photosynthesis that occurs in succulents and that is useful in **carbon isotope analysis**. CAM plants are found in arid regions and are at low risk of losing carbon through photorespiration. Less than 3–4% of the earth's plant species can be characterized as CAM plants. Cf. **C₄ photosynthetic pathway.**

**cambium:** part of a deciduous tree that lies between the bark and the old wood, and that forms the tree's annual growth ring. See **dendrochronology.**

**Cambrian explosion:** advent of multicellular organisms and the proliferation of over 100 different **phyla**, all within a span of 70 my in the **Cambrian period.**

‡ **Cambrian period:** oldest period of the **Paleozoic era**, lasting from approximately 570 to 500 mya. See **Cambrian explosion.**

**Caminade Est:** archaeological site located in the Dordogne department, France, and dating to 37 kya; contains both **Mousterian** (level M3) and **Aurignacian** (level G) artifacts and hominid remains from the Mousterian level assigned to *Homo* cf. *neanderthalensis*.

**Camin–Sokal hypothesis:** special case of the **maximum parsimony hypothesis**, which states that back mutations to prior evolutionary character states are not permitted. See **Dollo's law.**

**camouflage coloration:** color pattern, generally of the **pelage**, that allows a primate to blend in with its surroundings, making it difficult for predators or prey to detect the animal; color pattern that facilitates concealment. It has been suggested that 'black' **skin color** in humans functions as camouflage in primary tropical rain forests.

**cAMP:** cyclic adenosine monophosphate, a synthetic product of **ATP** and a mediator of hormone action in mammals; the enzyme adenyl cyclase normally converts ATP to cyclic AMP. Aka genetic regulator. Certain forms of cAMP have been implicated in susceptibility to rapid behavioral changes (in *Drosophila*) after consuming alcohol.

**Campbell, Bernard Grant** (1930–): British physical anthropologist at Cambridge and UCLA. Known for thoughtful contributions to fields of human ecology and evolution; associated with the **Spectrum hypothesis**. Author of *The Nomenclature of the Hominidae* (1965), *Human Evolution: An Introduction to Man's Adaptations* (1966), and *Human Ecology* (1983); editor of *Sexual Selection and the Descent of Man* (1972).

**Campbell's guenon:** vernacular for *Cercopithecus campbelli* (= *mona*).

**Camper, Petrus (Peter)** (1722–89): Dutch physician and draftsman, who developed the **facial angle** to measure degrees of **prognathism**, *c.* 1791. Described what he believed to be a graded relationship among humans and apes. Was among the first anthropometrists to define **norma lateralis** (auriculospinalis). Camper was a biblical monogenist who held that there were four natural divisions of humans, and agreed with **Buffon** that these were due to climate, food, and customs.

**Campignian:** transitory cultural stage of the late **Mesolithic** that bridges from the **Paleolithic** to the **Neolithic**; sites known from Mesopotamia, the Levant, and Europe. Characteristic 'factory sites' are located near sources of flint ('mines') and artifacts consist almost entirely of flint tools and waste comprising cores, flakes, and thick blades, as well as roughed out and/or fully finished biface axes, adzes, chisels and picks. Arrowheads and sickle blades are rare or absent. Because the artifacts are relatively large and coarse, the sites have also been described as 'Heavy Neolithic'. Aka proto-Neolithic. Cf. **Natufian** and **Capsian.**

**camptodactyly:** inherited autosomal dominant condition characterized by palmward bending of an immobile finger, usually the fifth. Cf. **clinodactyly.**

**campsite community:** group organized at the level of the **band.**

**canal:** anatomical term that denotes a tubular duct or channel, e.g. the auditory canal.

**canaliculi:** microscopic channels, such as the minute canaliculi associated with the osteonic (Haversian) canals of bone. Singular: Canaliculus. See **canal.**

**canalization:** alleged tendency of developmental pathways to converge on a standard organismal phenotype in spite of genetic or environmental disturbances; a proposed buffering system which theoretically reduces potential phenotypic variation. Aka **canalizing selection.**

**canalizing selection:** selection for phenotypes that are largely unaffected either by fluctuations in the environment or by genetic variability. See **canalization.**

**cancellous bone:** bone tissue that occupies the interior of **flat bones** and the **epiphyses** of **long bones**; characterized by a lattice framework of struts. The struts (**trabeculae**) of cancellous bone are integral in reducing bone weight; space between the trabeculae is filled with **red marrow**; the **osteocytes** are embedded in the trabeculae. Adjective: cancellated. Aka spongy bone.

**cancer:** any of a large class of disorders resulting from loss of cell cycle control; cancer means 'crab', the characteristic morphology of cells as they proliferate outward from a center of origin.

**cancer, theories of:** current evidence suggests that **cancer** results from a complex interaction of carcinogens and the accumulation of several point **mutations** in cancer-causing genes. Some cancer genes are **oncogenes** that alter the **cell cycle**; others are **tumor suppressor genes** that normally check or restrain **cell division**. See **oncogene hypothesis, chromosome theory of cancer, epigenetic reprogramming, two-hit hypothesis,** and **loss of heterozygosity.** Other factors that increase susceptibility to carcinogenesis include nutritional status, age, stress, and immunologic competence. See specific cancer and tumor types, e.g. **colon cancer, melanoma, neoplastic disorder.**

**candelabra model:** conservative version of the **trellis model** of **hominid evolution**, with little or no interregional **gene flow**; see the **multiregional continuity model**; aka the **polyphyletic hypothesis** of modern **human origins.**

**candidate gene:** gene thought to be involved in a specific genetic trait or disorder on the basis of mapping information or physiological evidence.

‡ **canine** (C): one of four types of tooth found in **heterodont** mammals; a conical tooth in the front of the mouth (between the lateral **incisor** and first **premolar**) that serves in puncturing and grasping; in most mammals the canines are longer than other teeth. Aka eye tooth or cuspid. See **teeth** and **molar.**

**canine diastema:** condition in which there is a gap between the upper canine and the **lateral incisor** and on the mandible between the canine and the first premolar. Canine diastemata serve to accommodate the projecting canines of the opposite jaw. See **diastema.**

**canine fossa:** depression or slight concavity in the **alveolar process** of the maxilla just behind the

**canine jugum**; in hominids, this feature is the result of reduction in the size of the canine root.

**canine jugum:** vertical ridge in the **alveolar process** of the maxilla caused by an enlarged canine root. Plural: canine juga.

**canine–third premolar honing complex** (C/P3): condition due to sharpening of the distal edge of the upper canine against the mesiobuccally extensive buccal crown surface of the lower third premolar. Aka functional honing.

**caniniform:** in reference to a tooth that resembles a canine tooth; canine-like; when present in primates, such a tooth is usually an incisor or a premolar that resembles a canine tooth.

**Can Llobateres:** archaeological site found in the 1990s in the Valles Peredes, Spain, dated to *c.* 9.5 mya, and that contained fossil hominoids, including an extraordinarily complete partial skeleton attributed to *Dryopithecus laietanus.*

**Cann, Rebecca L.:** US molecular biologist at Hawaii; with mentor and later Berkeley colleague A. C. **Wilson,** Cann calibrated a '**molecular clock**' using **mitochondrial DNA.** They obtained samples representing humans from most of the regions of the world and compared **DNA sequences** from a specific region of mtDNA; the degree of variation was so small that their conclusion was that all **AMHs** shared a common ancestor less than 200 kya, who was dubbed **mitochondrial 'Eve'.** As the deepest clades appeared to be in Africa, this soon became known as the '**mitochondrial Eve**' hypothesis. The Cann, Stoneking and Wilson paper, 'Mitochondrial DNA and human evolution', *Nature* **325:** 31 (1987), is one of the most frequently cited in recent decades. Cf. the **multiregional continuity model.**

**cannibalism:** eating **conspecifics.** Cannibalism is known among modern humans in extreme conditions (starvation from war or a survival situation); it is rare, and gustatory cannibalism is even rarer. There is speculation that some ancient humans practised cannibalism. Aka anthropophagy.

**canonical sequence:** highly conserved (archetypical) **DNA sequence** found in some chromosomal regions, such as boxes or *Hox* genes, where the sequence is the same in virtually every species owing to the critical function performed by the sequence, such as an attachment site.

**canopy:** layer of foliage above the ground; forest foliage that is horizontally continuous and usually distinct from other vertical layers. Cf. **understory.**

**cant:** behavior by prosimians in which they support themselves with their hind paws in order to free the fore paws for activities such as catching insects.

**canthus:** 1. term referring to the inner angle of the eye. 2. angle formed by the meeting of the upper and lower eyelids. See **inner epicanthus** and **outer epicanthus**.

*Cantius* (= *Pelycodus*) **Simons, 1962:** adapoid **prosimian** from the early Eocene of North America and Europe, belonging to the notharctid subfamily **Notharctinae**; ten known species; most primitive adapoid. Previously included within *Pelycodus*, which some authorities still recognize; one of the distinctions between *Cantius* and *Pelycodus* is geographical location, the former being found in the more northern latitudes of North America. Appears to be the ancestor of *Notharctus*. Dental formula: 2.1.4.3/2.1.4.3; dental morphology suggests **frugivory**; some species exhibit sexual dimorphism in canine size. Body mass estimated to range from 1 to 3 kg. One of the three adapoids with an unfused **mandibular symphysis**, a condition found in the living prosimians. See Appendix 1 for taxonomy.

**cap:** modified guanine nucleotide that is attached to the 5′ end of eukaryotic **mRNA** molecules.

**capacitation:** physiological changes that activate sperm after they have entered the female reproductive tract. These changes include a weakening of the acrosomal membranes surrounding a sperm, after which hydrolytic enzymes are released; these enzymes enable sperm to penetrate the protective coverings surrounding the **oocyte**. Capacitation requires from six to eight hours after entrance into the **uterine tube** for completion. Adjective: capacitated. Aka sperm capacitation.

**capacity:** 1. maximum potential amount. 2. volume of a cavity or receptacle. 3. measure of ability.

**capillary:** microscopic blood vessel that connects an arteriole and a venule; the functional unit of the **circulatory system**.

**capillus:** long, thick, coarse hair found on eyebrows, scalp, beard, and fingers. Aka terminal hair.

**capitate:** 1. anatomical term meaning headlike. 2. name of the largest of the **carpal** bones; see **capitate (of wrist)**.

**capitate (of wrist):** medial and largest bone of anterior row of the **carpus**. In the past it has also been known as the *os capitum*, *os magnum*, or *os maximum*.

**capitulum:** 1. headlike structure. 2. lateral ball-like structure of the humeral trochlea that articulates with the **radius** of the forearm.

**Capoid:** obsolete term (**ethnym**) used for a human race that included the Khoisan **!Kung** and Hottentot peoples of sub-Saharan Africa. See **Congoid**.

**capped langur:** vernacular for *Trachypithecus pileatus*.

**capping:** addition of a methylated guanine nucleotide to the 5′ end of **pre-mRNA**.

**Capsian culture:** transitional Epipaleolithic culture area in north Africa, i.e. the **Aurignacian** in Africa.

The type site is el-Mekta. The Capsian followed the **Campignian**.

**captive setting:** enclosed area in which primates can be observed; such areas range from cages to fenced areas of several hectares or more.

**capuchin monkey:** vernacular for any of the four **platyrrhine** monkey species belonging to the genus *Cebus*.

**caput:** pertaining to a head or headlike structure. Plural: capita.

**Carabelli's cusp:** supernumerary cusp on the **lingual** surface of an upper molar tooth crown. Variations may be expressed as a pit, a groove, pit and groove together, or a tubercle. It is common in populations of southwestern American Indians.

**Carabelli's pit and groove:** see **Carabelli's cusp**.

**carbohydrate:** organic compound composed of carbon, hydrogen and oxygen, and synthesized by plants; the principal nutrient source for most animals. The general formula is $C_n(H_2O)_n$, where *n* is any whole number; includes sugars, starches, chitin, steroids and cellulose.

**carbohydrate metabolism:** process of **catabolism** of complex carbohydrates into simpler sugars and their metabolites, a process that typically requires pathways with about ten catalytic steps. Among the better-known conditions resulting from defective enzymes required to complete these processes are galactosemia, Von-Gierke disease, Pompe disease, Forbes Disease, Andersen disease, fructosuria and pentosuria, all X-linked or autosomal recessive diseases. Aka the **glycogen storage diseases**. See **citric acid cycle**.

**carbon** (C): an **organic** element; together with **oxygen**, **nitrogen**, and **hydrogen**, carbon is an essential element of living cells, including those of **primates**.

**carbon 12** (¹²C): normal isotope of carbon that consists of 6 neutrons, 6 protons, and 6 electrons, an element found in virtually all living things. See **carbon 14** and **radiocarbon dating**.

**carbon 13** (¹³C): stable **isotope** of carbon that consists of 7 neutrons, 6 protons, and 6 electrons. See **stable isotope analysis**, **carbon 12** and **carbon 14**.

‡ **carbon 14** (¹⁴C): unstable **isotope** of carbon that consists of 8 neutrons, 6 protons, and 6 electrons, and which decays stochastically into nitrogen (¹⁴N), the stable element from which carbon 14 was derived, with an empirical **half-life** of 5568 years. See **radiocarbon dating**, **carbon 12**, **carbon 13**, and **accelerator mass spectrometry**.

‡ **carbon 14 dating:** see **radiometric dating**.

**carbon assimilation:** incorporation of inorganic carbon present as carbon dioxide, including a small proportion of radiocarbon, into organic compounds during photosynthesis. This is the initial step in the movement of carbon up the **food chain**.

**carbon cycle:** recurrent binding of carbon dioxide during **carbon assimilation** into organic compounds, its movement through the food chain, and its release as inorganic carbon dioxide into the atmosphere by respiration and/or decomposition.

**carbon dioxide** ($CO_2$): colorless, odorless gas formed by the oxidation of carbon, the byproduct of **respiration** in animals.

**carbon film:** thin layer of carbon found in some **sedimentary rocks**, the remains of past life.

**carbon isotope analysis:** technique applied to bone protein (**collagen**) or bone carbonate, measured as a ratio of carbon 13 ($^{13}C$) to carbon 12 ($^{12}C$), which yields a value expressed as $k\times^{13}C$ per mil that can be compared to the international carbohydrate standard. See **stable isotope analysis.**

**carbonate** ($^*CO_3$): sediment derived from the precipitation of calcium ($CaCO_3$), magnesium ($MgCO_3$), or iron carbonates ($FeCO_3$) from either inorganic or organic sources; examples are **limestone** and **dolomite.**

‡ **Carboniferous period:** period of the **Paleozoic era**, lasting from approximately 345 to 280 mya; formation of widely distributed fern-filled swamps, from which the majority of the earth's known coal deposits were formed. Aka the Age of Vegetation. Fossil amphibians are common from this period.

**carbonization:** process of chemical action on postmortem tissues that further reduce a **fossil** to a thin film of carbon during **permineralization**, during which the form of the original is usually lost. See **diagenesis.**

**carboxyhemoglobin** ($HbCO_2$): compound formed by the union of carbon dioxide to amino group binding sites on hemoglobin molecules. Cf. **oxyhemoglobin.**

**carboxyl group:** chemical group (-COOH) found in **amino acids** and at one end of a polypeptide chain.

‡ **carcinogen:** any agent capable of producing a somatic mutation that transforms a cell line into a malignant form of **cancer**; typically, carcinogens are radiation or chemicals. Adjective: Carcinogenic. See **mutagen** and **teratogen.**

**carcinogenesis:** see **cancer, theories of.**

**cardiac:** positioned near or pertaining to the heart; e.g. the cardiac sphincter of the stomach.

**cardiac cycle:** one contraction–relaxation sequence of the heart.

**cardiogram:** graphic tracing made by the stylus of a **cardiograph.**

**cardiograph:** device used in the diagnosis of **cardiovascular disease** that detects and records differences in galvanometric potential caused by heart actions. Aka electrocardiograph.

**cardiology:** field of medicine that investigates and treats **cardiovascular disease.**

**cardiovascular disease:** disease or syndrome that affects the heart and blood vessels; a common example is **hypertension.**

**cardiovascular system** (C/V system): physiological system consisting of the heart, the blood vessels, and the blood. The C/V system is involved with transportation and communication within the body. Its major function is the transportation of gases, nutrients, and certain body cells such as **leukocytes.**

**caries:** see **dental caries.**

**Carnivora:** 1. mammalian **order** that includes dogs, cats, bears, racoons and their relatives, weasels, and other mammals that possess carnassial teeth. 2. members of the order Carnivora.

**carnivoran:** member of the mammalian order **Carnivora**, the true carnivores. Not all meat-eaters are members of Carnivora.

**carnivore:** 1. any animal that eats flesh. 2. member of the order **Carnivora.**

‡ **carnivory:** the condition of eating flesh. In the strictest sense, carnivores consume only terrestrial vertebrates. See **faunivory, insectivory, piscivory.** See also **diet.**

**carotene:** yellowish-orange pigment obtained in the human diet from plants. Carotene contributes to the color of skin pigmentation and is a precursor of vitamin A. Not to be confused with the protein found in the epidermis, **keratin.** See **skin color** and **coloration.**

**carotid sinus:** enlargement at the base of the internal carotid artery as it arises from the common carotid artery. The carotid sinus contains baroreceptors that help regulate blood pressure, and carotid bodies containing chemoreceptors that are involved with circulatory and respiratory regulation.

**carpal:** of or pertaining to the wrist. The term carpals is often used to refer to the bones that comprise the wrist.

**carpal gland:** glandular tissue or a horny spur on the wrist and distal forearm of some prosimians; a **scent gland** used for marking. Found in *Lemur* and some *Eulemur* species.

**carpal joint:** see **carpometacarpal joint.**

‡ **Carpenter, Clarence Ray** (1905–75): US comparative psychologist and pioneering primatologist at Penn State; considered by many to be the founder of modern field primatology. Carpenter made early (1930s–1940s) observations of free-ranging howler, gibbon, and macaque populations in their natural habitats that are now considered classic field studies. He was a co-director of the **Asiatic Primate Expedition** of 1937. He made arrangements while on this trip to import 500 **rhesus macaques** from India to the **Cayo Santiago Island** Rhesus Colony in Puerto Rico. He later became a pioneer in instructional television and played a key role in the passage

of the National Education Act (Title VII) that prohibits discrimination. He was President of the Association for Higher Education, 1965–6. He retired in 1970, but remained active until his death.

***Carpocristes:*** archaic mammal from the late Paleocene – early Eocene of North America and eastern Asia belonging to the **plesiadapiform** family **Carpolestidae**; three known species; the most **derived** of the **Carpolestidae**, although very small (estimated body mass 18–50 g). See Appendix 1 for taxonomy.

***Carpodaptes*** Matthew and Granger, 1921: archaic mammal from the late Paleocene of North America, belonging to the **plesiadapiform** family **Carpolestidae**; three known species. Believed to have evolved from *Elphidotarsius* and to have given rise to *Carpolestes*. Dental formula: 2.1.3.3/2.1.2.3; lower premolar bladelike (**plagiaulacoid dentition**) and enlarged compared with its *Elphidotarsius* predecessor; diet probably a high-energy food. Body mass of the species between 50 and 100 g. See Appendix 1 for taxonomy.

***Carpolestes*** Simpson, 1928: archaic mammal from the late Paleocene – early Eocene of North America, belonging to the **plesiadapiform** family **Carpolestidae**; two known species; previously included in *Carpodaptes*, which appears to be the ancestor of this genus. Dental formula: 2.1.3.3/2.1.2.3; lower premolars bladelike with upper **plagiaulacoid dentition**; diet probably high-energy food. Body size of the species between 90 and 150 g, representing an increase in size from the earliest carpolestids. See Appendix 1 for taxonomy.

**Carpolestidae:** family of archaic fossil mammals belonging to the order **Plesiadapiformes**. Adjective: carpolestid. Known from the middle Paleocene and early Eocene; predominantly a North American taxon, but there have been recent recoveries from eastern Asia. Five genera of small-bodied forms are known, ranging from 20 g to 150 g. Known only from dentition. Each genus is temporally restricted and a sequence is produced that leads workers to state that earlier genera evolved into genera that come later. Dental formula varies over time; procumbent incisors; specialized premolars, the lower fourth premolar is large, bladelike, and multicusped, upper third and fourth premolars are large and butcher-block, reminiscent of the **Mesozoic** multituberculate mammals (i.e. **plagiaulacoid dentition**); dentition and body size suggestive of a high-energy diet, such as insects, seeds, nuts, or high-calorie and easily digested fruit (such as berries). See Appendix 1 for taxonomy.

**carpometacarpal:** of or pertaining to the bones that make up the wrist and the body of the hand. To the lay observer these are the bones of the hand (the wrist of popular conception is actually the **distal** ends of the **radius** and **ulna**).

**carpometacarpal joint:** **articulations** formed between the **carpals** and the **metacarpals** of the hand or forepaw.

**carpus: wrist;** the eight bones of the wrist as a whole; proximal portion of the hand.

‡ **carrier:** 1. an individual who harbors the agent of an infectious disease without manifesting symptoms. 2. a **heterozygous** individual possessing one copy of a **recessive** allele or chromosomal structural defect that is not fully expressed because of the presence of a normal allele on the **homologous chromosome**. 3. a substance in a cell that can temporarily bind with other molecules.

**carrier screening:** see **genetic screening**.

**carrying angle:** angle made by the axes of the arm and forearm when the forearm is extended. Aka cubital angle.

**carrying behavior:** transportation of materials from one location to another. This behavior is observed among many animal species which transport nesting material, food, or young. Humans are able to carry objects in their hands and arms. The invention of carrying containers enabled ancient humans to move away from vital resources such as water; it is thought by some researchers that humans may have transported water in either animal bladders or gourds.

‡ **carrying capacity** (*K*): the largest number of organisms of a particular species that can be maintained indefinitely in a given part of the environment.

**cartilage:** semi-rigid, but elastic, type of connective tissue characterized by cells located within cavities called **lacunae**, which are separated from each other by a semisolid matrix; found at joints, the nose, **auricles,** and the respiratory framework. The skeleton of immature individuals contains cartilage that will ossify with maturation. See **endochondral bone**.

**cartilaginous:** of or pertaining to a tissue or structure composed of **cartilage**.

**cartilaginous joint:** articulation in which the bones joined are connected by either hyaline cartilage or fibrocartilage, lack a joint cavity, and permit little movement between the bones. See **synchondrosis, symphysis.** See also **joint**.

‡ **cartilaginous** or **cartilage model:** first stage in **endochondral bone** development; masses of hyaline cartilage in the form of the future bony structures.

**cartilaginous ossification:** see **endochondral ossification**.

**cascade testing:** mode of screening for **carriers** of a genetic trait by testing relatives of an individual known to be affected.

**case:** 1. an instance. 2. a particular occurrence of a disease.

**case–control study:** method used in epidemiology in which people with a certain condition (the cases) are paired with others without the condition but otherwise matched as closely as possible (the controls), and both groups are then followed.

**cast:** 1. any structure formed within a cavity, especially a mould of an organism during **permineralization**. See **endocast**. 2. a facsimile or copy of an original fossil or other specimen, such as an **endocranial cast**.

**Castle–Hardy–Weinberg law:** see **Hardy–Weinberg equilibrium principle**.

**Castle, William Ernest** (1867–1954): population geneticist at Harvard, who derived an early, incomplete formulation of what later Hardy and, independently, Weinberg, were to show was the **binomial theorem**. Performed classic selection experiments on hooded rats; mentor of Sewall **Wright**; author of *Genetics and Eugenics* (1916). See **Hardy–Weinberg equilibrium principle**.

**castrate:** to remove or disable the **gonads**. Noun: Castration.

**casual society (or group):** temporary fluid group formed within a primate society that may groom, play, forage, or perform other activities together, with the membership changing as individuals join and leave the group.

**CAT:** computer-assisted tomography, a radiographic technique that can display virtual 'slices' taken through bones or skulls that will show the shape and extent of internal cavities. CAT scans are used in human paleontology to observe structures not accessible in conventional observation. Aka CT scanning.

**cat-cry syndrome:** see **cri-du-chat syndrome**.

**CAT scanning:** computer assisted tomography scanning, a technology in which an X-ray emitter is positioned between the body region that is being examined and an X-ray detector positioned on the opposite side. Because different organs absorb X-rays differently, a computer associated with the detector can record virtual 'slices' taken through bones or skulls that indicate the shape and extent of internal cavities. Software then produces an integrated three-dimensional image of the subject tissue. CT scans are used in human **paleontology** to observe internal structures of fossils not accessible by conventional observation. Aka CT scanning.

**catabolism:** breakdown of organic molecules, which releases energy. Adjective: catabolic. Cf. **anabolism**.

**catagenesis:** regressive evolution; evolution characterized by an increasing dependency upon the environment, including loss of control over environmental variables. Adjective: catagenetic. Cf. **anagenesis**.

**catalase:** enzyme that oxidizes hydrogen peroxide in tissues, thus preventing the accumulation of other peroxides. See the **free radical theory of aging**.

**catalog of behavior:** list of all of a species' behavior. When it is believed that all of the behavior that the animal is capable of performing (i.e. the **repertoire**) has been observed and recorded, the catalog becomes referred to as the **ethogram** for that species.

**catalysis:** process by which a substance (a catalyst) accelerates a reaction without itself being consumed in the overall course of the reaction.

**catamenial:** monthly; occurring once a month.

**cataract:** abnormal opacity of the lens of the eye.

‡ **Catarrhini:** one of two possible infraorders of the suborder **Anthropoidea**; contains the Old World monkeys, apes, and hominids. Catarrhine monkeys have narrow noses and fewer premolars than the **Platyrrhini**, and never have a tail that is prehensile; includes monkeys from Africa and Asia; aka **Old World monkey**.

**catastrophe theory:** branch of mathematics that analyzes the nature of sudden and discontinuous change in a phenomenon that is produced by regular and continuous change in the factors that control the behavior of that phenomenon.

‡ **catastrophism:** view that the earth's geology is the result of a series of cataclysmic events: the view espoused by **Cuvier** *c.* 1810. In more modern terms, the **hypothesis** that the fossil record can be explained by repeated catastrophes followed by repopulation by new and different organisms from outside areas.

**catch-down growth** or **period:** slowing of growth by regulatory hormones after a period of abnormal acceleration of growth in a child.

‡ **catch-up growth** or **period:** period of recovery during which a child who has experienced delayed growth because of **malnutrition, undernutrition**, emotional **stress** or **disease** can increase stature up to the maximum of her or his genetic potential.

**catechol-*O*-methyltransferase** (COMT): dopamine-degrading enzyme with 'fast' and normal alleles. The 'fast' variant degrades dopamine quicker than the normal allele. Rapid dopamine degradation interferes with prefrontal cortex tasks such as number memory, card sorting and color matching. Typically, schizophrenics are impaired with respect to such tasks, exhibit increased prefrontal cortex activity during such tasks (owing to dopamine degradation), and are members of **schizophrenia**-prone families that are more likely to have the 'fast' COMT allele segregating in those pedigrees.

**catecholamine:** one of a group of biogenic amine compounds derived from catechol and that have sympathomimetic action; examples include **epinephrine**, norepinephrine, and **dopamine**. The chemical derivatives are **hormones** and **neurotransmitters.**

**category:** 1. a division in any field of knowledge. 2. a clearly specified group or level in a hierarchical classification.

**cathemeral:** describes an activity cycle in which the animal may be active at any time during the day or night.

*Catopithecus browni* **Simons, 1989:** catarrhine genus from the late Eocene and early Oligocene of North Africa, belonging to the family **Propliopithecidae; monotypic;** known from skulls, jaws, and some limb bones. Phylogenetic relationships uncertain except that it is an **anthropoid;** it has some adapid traits, which have generated a debate regarding anthropoid origins, previously considered to be from the omomyoids. Small orbits indicate **diurnal** activity. Estimated body mass around 1 kg. Dental formula: 2.1.2.3; anterior dentition is anthropoidlike, while cheek teeth are a mosaic of anthropoid and adapid traits; dental morphology suggests a mixture of **frugivory** and **insectivory** as the diet. **Postcranial** remains suggest **arboreal quadrupedalism** with little leaping or clinging ability. See Appendix 1 for taxonomy.

**Cattell's paradox:** apparent contradiction between two observations: (1) people with high IQs tend to produce fewer children than people with lower IQs; (2) average intelligence does not decline with successive generations. See **IQ.**

**Caucasian:** 1. eighteenth century name for the indigenous peoples of Europe and Asia Minor; one of the five often-cited racial varieties recognized by **Blumenbach** (1790); others were **Ethiopian, Malayan, American,** and **Mongolian.** 2. any of 300 languages spoken by people in the region of the Caucasus mountains.

**Caucasiocentrism:** belief that lightly melanized peoples are superior to people of color. Few, if any, anthropologists think that there is support for such a belief.

**Caucasoid:** of or pertaining to **Caucasian;** typological racial categories such as this **ethonym** are rejected by many, if not most, human biologists and anthropologists.

**cauda equina:** lower extension of the spinal cord where the roots of spinal nerves have a tail-like appearance.

‡ **caudal:** in reference to the tail region, or proximity, of a vertebrate; caudally, toward the tail. For example, caudal vertebrae are the vertebrae that make up the tail in primates. Caudal is used synonymously with inferior in human anatomy.

**caudal gland:** cutaneous glandular area associated with the base of the tail. A subcaudal gland is found below the base of the tail; a supracaudal gland is positioned above the tail root. *Aotus* is an example of a primate with such a gland.

**caudal remnant:** see **coccyx, caudal vertebra.**

**caudal vertebra:** vertebra of the primate tail. The number of caudal vertebrae is variable between primate species, but a usual number is 25 (range 2–33).

**caul:** part of the **amnion** sometimes covering a child's head at birth.

**causal principle:** in philosophy, the principle that every event has a cause, that a specific cause has a specific effect, and/or that a particular cause has at least as much reality as a particular effect.

**causal theories:** any theory that analyzes a concept in terms of causation; that **evolution,** for example, is caused by certain **mechanisms.**

‡ **Cavalli-Sforza, Luca Luigi** (1922–): Italian-born population geneticist, anthropologist; early career devoted to human **population genetics,** especially **pedigree analysis** in insular Italian valleys; concerned with the co-evolution of genes, language and culture, and especially the spatial dispersion of domesticated varieties of **wheat** and its dispersion with the **migration** of humans. Later, at Stanford, was concerned with sampling human **biodiversity.** Was influential in the careers of both Mary-Claire **King** and Mark Skolnick. Co-author of several monumental works, including *The Genetics of Human Populations* (1971), *African Pygmies* (1986), and *The History and Geography of Human Genes* (1994).

**cave art:** aesthetic embellishment of cave walls in southern France and northern Spain during the **Upper Paleolithic.** See, for example, **Lascaux.** Cf. **rock art.**

**cave breccia:** sediments such as rocks, bones, and guano that have collected as debris within a cave and have subsequently become cemented into a solid mass by the action of **calcium carbonate** solutions that have dripped from the cave roof. See **stalactite,** and **breccia.**

**cave dweller(s):** vernacular for the denizens of caves, particularly during the Pleistocene epoch, and especially in the northernmost latitudes; aka cave man. See **Neanderthals.**

**cave man:** vernacular for a denizen of caves, hypothetical early human(s) who dwelled in caves, particularly during the **Pleistocene epoch** and especially in the northernmost latitudes. Archaeological evidence supports the idea that **Neandertals** and Upper Paleolithic peoples probably lived under **rockshelters,** however, rather than deep in caves *per se*. Some **cave paintings** are nevertheless found deep within cave systems, such as at **Altamira.** Aka cave dweller, troglodyte.

**caviomorph:** member of the mammalian suborder Caviomorpha (Rodentia). Includes South American rodents such as guinea pigs and porcupines.

**cavity:** hollow space contained within a structure; a **sinus.**

**Cayo Santiago Island:** research site located off the coast of Puerto Rico where long-term field studies of rhesus monkeys (*Macaca mulatta*) have been conducted for decades. More than 500 monkeys were imported from India to the site by C. R. **Carpenter** in 1938. Primatologists who have conducted field research at this site include: Carpenter, J. **Buettner-Janusch,** J. E. Buikstra, J. M. Cheverud, R. G. Rowlins, M. J. Kessler, P. Marler, Ch. H. Southwick, F. B. Berkovitch and C. J. DeRousseau. The site later became part of the Caribbean Primate Research Center.

**C-banding:** one of the methods of creating identification bands on individual chromosomes after treatment of the metaphase plate with alkali and controlling hydrolysis in a buffered salt solution. See **chromosome banding technique.**

**cc:** see **cubic centimeter.**

**CCR5 co-receptor:** see **chemokine (C-C) receptor 5.**

**CD4 co-receptor:** co-receptor on helper T cells to which the **HIV** 'docks' and binds before invasion of the cell. See **chemokine (C-C) receptor 5.**

**CDC:** US Centers for Disease Control and Prevention, based in Atlanta, GA. The centers are involved with basic disease-related research, the collection and cataloging of samples of organisms, with the maintenance and distribution of incidence and prevalence rates, and with the dissemination of current information. When necessary, the CDC employs intervention and containment procedures.

**cDNA:** complementary DNA; **DNA** transcribed from a specific RNA by the enzyme **reverse transcriptase.** When created synthetically, cDNA lacks **introns** as it is a complement to edited **mRNA** and can be inserted into expression **vectors** to synthesize foreign proteins in cells. See **genetic engineering.**

**cDNA library:** complementary DNA library; a set of cDNAs constructed from mRNA templates obtained from a particular cell type and that define the gene expression of that cell type.

**CE:** common era; a modern means of referring to dates. CE is used in the same way as **AD.** See **BCE** and **BP.**

‡ **Cebidae:** family of the **platyrrhine** superfamily **Ceboidea,** consisting of eleven **extant** genera and three recently **extinct** genera. Adjective: cebid. A diverse group of New World monkeys. Some workers break this family into two or more separate families. Geographic range from Mexico to southern South America; diurnal; arboreal; large; body mass, ranging from approximately 1 kg to 10 kg. Dental formula: 2.1.2.3. See Appendix 2 for taxonomy, Appendix 3 for living species.

**Cebinae:** subfamily of the **platyrrhine** family **Cebidae,** consisting of the genera *Cebus* and

*Saimiri*; capuchins and squirrel monkeys. Adjective: cebine. See Appendix 2 for taxonomy, Appendix 3 for living species.

‡ **Ceboidea: platyrrhine** superfamily. The number of families contained within the ceboids varies with author. Adjective: ceboid. See Appendix 2 for taxonomy, Appendix 3 for living species.

*Cebuella* Gray, 1865: monotypic **platyrrhine** genus to which the pygmy marmoset belongs. Ranges from southern Colombia through the Amazon regions of Ecuador, Peru, western Brazil and Bolivia, where it prefers primary rain forest. **Diurnal. Arboreal** quadruped that employs leaping. Smallest of the **anthropoids;** body mass 70–141 g. Dental formula: 2.1.3.2; **gummivorous** with fruit and insect supplements. **Monogamous;** gives birth to **dizygotic twins.** Some workers think that DNA evidence suggests that this species should be placed in the genus *Callithrix.* See Appendix 2 for taxonomy and Appendix 3 for species.

*Cebus* Erxleben, 1777: **platyrrhine** genus to which the capuchin monkeys belong, consisting of four species; aka organ-grinder or ring-tail monkeys, sapajou. Capuchins are generally divided into two groups: tufted and untufted. Widely distributed from Central America into South America on both sides of the Andes and as far south as Paraguay and Argentina; some species **sympatric** on certain parts of this range. Diurnal; **arboreal quadrupeds** with a semi-**prehensile** tail and **opposable thumb.** Range in body mass from 1 to 4 kg. Dental formula: 2.1.3.3; diet varied, but principally **frugivorous.** Troops of 6–50; more females, but dominated by an older male; **polygamous** mating pattern; often found in association with squirrel monkeys (genus *Saimiri*). See Appendix 2 for taxonomy, Appendix 3 for living species.

**cecum:** pouchlike portion of the large intestine that connects to the small intestine. In humans, the cecum is greatly reduced in size, but in some primates that consume a high-fiber diet this is a large structure that serves as a site where symbionts breakdown the food. Also spelled caecum.

**ceiling effect:** result of a behavior test or experiment that allows the subjects to easily obtain the maximum score, obscuring differences between the subjects. Cf. **floor effect.**

**Celebes black macaque ('ape'):** vernacular for *Macaca nigra.*

**Celebes macaque:** vernacular for *Macaca maura.*

**Celebesian tarsier:** vernacular for *Tarsius spectrum.*

**celiac disease:** gastrointestinal disorder due to a food intolerance to gluten, a protein found in wheat. The affected individual is unable to properly absorb nutrients as the result of partial atrophy of the gut mucosa. Also spelled coeliac disease. See **HLA DR3.**

‡ **cell:** smallest living biological functional and structural unit of an organism that displays the properties of growth, metabolism, energy cycles, and reproduction. Adjective: cellular. See **eukaryotes** and **prokaryotes.**

**cell culture:** growth or maintenance of **cells** in a specific nutritional medium *in vitro*, or outside of their normal growing environment, including single cells; in cell cultures, the cells are no longer organized into tissues. In biotechnology applications, host cells containing recombinant DNA are grown in cell cultures.

**cell cycle:** life events of an individual cell, from mitosis to mitosis. In most proliferating **somatic cells,** the cell cycle consists of four phases: mitotic phase, **gap 1 phase** (G1=growth1), **S phase** (S=synthesis), and **gap 2 phase** (G2=growth2). The last three occur during **interphase,** the mitotic stage consists of four additional subphases. In some cell types, the **G1 phase** may be quite protracted. Arrest of the cell cycle is an important feature of many organisms, including humans.

**cell division:** reproduction of **somatic cells** by **mitosis,** or the production of **gametes** from primordial **germ cells,** by **meiosis.** In mitosis, five main stages occur: **interphase, prophase, metaphase, anaphase,** and **telophase;** in meiosis, additional stages occur.

**cell doubling time:** time required for a population of cells to double in number. Cf. **cell generation time.**

**cell furrow:** during cell division, a constriction in the cell membrane that forms at the point of cytoplasmic cleavage during **anaphase.**

**cell fusion:** experimental conjugation of cells from different species — such as humans and mice — to produce hybrid cells that are grown *in vitro* on a special growth medium that selects for hybrids. Loss of any human chromosome from the hybrid culture results in locating the gene for a particular enzyme on that chromosome.

**cell generation time** (Tg): time required for a cell to complete one growth cycle. See **cell doubling time.**

**cell, germ:** see **germ cell.**

‡ **cell-mediated immunity** (CMi): specific immune response conducted by antigen-sensitized **T cells.** Aka cellular immunity. See **cytokine, lymphokine.**

‡ **cell membrane:** external, living boundary of an animal **cell.** A differentially selective, filmlike structure made up of fatty lipid and protein molecules, which surrounds an entire cell. Aka plasma membrane.

**cell migration:** movement of cells within the body of an **embryo** during development.

**cell mosaic:** any organism that possesses genetically different cell lines; this can arise through mutation or can be induced experimentally.

**cell senescence:** see *in vitro* **senescence.**

**cell-surface antigen:** heritable factor that is used for identification, such as a blood group antigen or a histocompatibility antigen; combinations of these factors give rise to the cellular uniqueness of every individual, with the exception of **identical twins.**

**cell theory:** theory which states that the **cell** is the fundamental unit of all living things, and that all plants and animals are composed of cells.

**cell theory of aging:** see **Hayflick limit.**

**cellular:** pertaining to, resembling, derived from, or composed of cells.

**cellular adhesion molecule** (CAM): any of the proteins that promote cell contact, thus permitting cellular interactions.

**cellular immune response:** group of immune response functions carried out by whole cells rather than by antibodies in the blood serum. It is dominated by **T cells** that release **cytokines** to stimulate and coordinate an immune response to foreign **antigens,** intracellular viruses and cancer cells. Cf. **humoral immune response.** Aka cell-mediated immune response, cellular immunity, delayed hypersensitivity.

**cellular immunity:** immune response functions carried out by whole cells rather than by **antibodies** in the blood serum.

**cellular respiration:** aerobic process by which energy-rich **ATP** is produced from compounds such as glucose; occurs within the **mitochondria** of a cell.

**cellulite:** colloquial term for fat deposits and fibrous tissue in the human body that causes the overlying skin to present a dimpled pattern.

**Celsius scale** (C): see **centigrade scale.**

**celt:** stone or metal ax or adze.

**Celtic:** 1. early nineteenth century term (= **ethonym**) used to label any artifact or bone fragment thought to have come from pre-Roman times in Europe. 2. of the Celts or their language family. 3. pertaining to the people of Ireland. Aka Keltic.

**cementation:** binding of deposits by lime and similar materials, forming **breccia** and other stratigraphic units.

**cementoblast:** specialized cell that produces **cementum.**

**cementocyte:** matured **cementoblast** that has enclosed itself in a matrix of **cementum.**

**cementum:** bonelike material that fastens the root of a tooth into the **dental alveolus.**

**cenancestor:** most recent common ancestor of all living organisms (excluding viruses).

**cenogenesis:** emergence of an evolutionary novelty early in **ontogeny.** Term coined by **Haeckel;** also spelled caenogenesis.

**cenospecies:** set of species capable of limited hybridization and therefore limited genetic exchange; also spelled coenospecies.

‡ **Cenozoic era:** that portion of the earth's history covering the past 65 million years ('recent life'); the third era of the **Phanerozoic** eon, also known as the **Age of Mammals.** The first true **primates** appeared during the early Cenozoic. See **epoch** and Appendix 4.

**census:** periodic enumeration of organisms within a given social or political unit, usually with additional **vital statistics.**

**centenarian:** in the human life cycle, referring to a person who has lived 100 years or longer.

**center:** 1. a source. 2. a pivot point. 3. the middle of an organ or structure, the core. 4. a specialized region where a process such as ossification begins. 5. a functional collection of neurons. 6. an agency designed to serve a community.

**center and edge model:** older label for a model attempting to explain the position of the **Neandertals,** proposed by Alan **Thorne** and Milford **Wolpoff,** now better known as the **multiregional continuity model.**

**center of dispersal:** area from which a population spreads; see **center of origin.**

**center of endemism:** biome that serves as a source from which colonizing species disperse and which helps to explain current distribution of **biota.** For example, expansion of pioneering tropical rain forest species enabled primates to expand their range; later, climate changed, forests contracted leaving gaps between them, but primates were established in other geographical areas. Cf. **endemic center.**

**center of gravity:** center of the body's total distribution of mass; functionally, this is the point that must be supported in order for balance to be achieved.

**center of origin:** argument that a region where the greatest diversity in a species occurs is also the region where the species evolved; the center of greatest diversity is the center of origin. Proposed by Russian geneticist Nikolai Vavilov (1887–43), but too many exceptions have been noted to make the principle a rule. Aka area production theory, Vavilov center, Ludwig effect.

**Centers for Disease Control and Prevention:** see **CDC.**

**centigrade scale** (C): denoting a temperature gradient that indicates the freezing point of water at 0 °C and the boiling point at 100 °C under atmospheric pressure at sea level. Aka Celsius. Cf. **Fahrenheit scale.**

**centimorgan** (cM): unit of genetic distance on a chromosome corresponding to 1% recombination. See **morgan unit.**

**Central American land bridge:** strip of land between North and South America that permits north–south dispersion of terrestrial species and prevents east–west dispersion of marine species. The current bridge has existed only from Plio-Pleistocene times; a previous Mesozoic bridge is now an archipelago in the Caribbean, owing to **continental drift**; no bridge existed during much of the **Tertiary.**

**Central American spider monkey:** vernacular for *Ateles geoffroyi.*

**central canal:** elongated longitudinal channel in the center of an **osteon** in bone tissue that contains branches of the nutrient vessels and a nerve; Aka Haversian canal.

**central dogma:** concept in modern biology that genetic information proceeds in only one direction, from **DNA** to **RNA** to **protein.** Thus, a change in a protein sequence cannot directly cause a subsequent change in the **DNA sequence.** Few exceptions are known, but see the **provirus hypothesis.** Cf. **Lamarckism** and **Bladwin effect.**

**central incisor:** most medial **incisor.**

**Central Negrillos:** traditionally, one of the three geographic divisions of **Negrillo** peoples in Africa. Included in this group are the Batwa, Bacwa, and Batemba.

‡ **central nervous system** (CNS): that part of the **nervous system** that is condensed and centrally located, e.g. the **brain** and **spinal cord** of vertebrates. The CNS functions to integrate sensory input information and motor output. Cf. **peripheral nervous system.**

**central place:** any locality where **hominids** aggregate or seem to have aggregated in the past. See **home base** and **butchering site.** The term derives from descriptions of more recent settlement patterns as proposed in 1933 by German geographer Walter Christaller.

**central sulcus:** transverse groove across the top of the **cerebral cortex**, separating the somatic sensory area from the somatic motor area.

**centrale:** carpal bone that is fused with the **scaphoid** in humans.

**centric fusion:** see **Robertsonian translocation.**

**centric occlusion:** 1. point of contact of teeth at rest when the cusps of upper teeth fit into the basins present on lower teeth. 2. contact point of the teeth when the **mandible** is centered relative to the **maxillary bone.**

**centrifugal:** as used in organismic biology, movement away from a center.

**centrifugal speciation:** origin of new species through isolation of small populations on the periphery of larger ones during periods of population decline. Cf. **parapatric speciation** and **peripatric speciation.**

‡ **centriole:** cellular organelle that organizes the spindle apparatus during **cell division**; it can reproduce itself and usually displays **paternal inheritance.** See **centrosome.**

**centripedal primate group:** a group of terrestrial primates (e.g. savanna baboons) that cannot flee into trees when confronted with danger and in which protection comes from the members of the troop itself. Cf. **acentric primate group.**

**centripetal fat distribution:** condition in which fat is concentrated in the central areas of the body's trunk.

‡ **centromere:** region of constriction in each **chromosome** or **chromatid** with which the traction **spindle fibers** become associated during **meiosis** and **mitosis.** The location of the centromere determines whether chromosomes are termed **acrocentric chromosome, metacentric chromosome, submetacentric chromosome** or **telocentric chromosome.** Aka kinetochore. See **chromosome structure.**

**centromere paradox:** observation that **centromeres,** which exhibit a chromatin-based inheritance mechanism, consists of highly conserved chromosome segregation machinery, but rapidly evolving centromeric **chromatin** that may impact reproductive isolation.

**centrosome:** dense body that contains a pair of organelles (**centrioles**) that lie just outside the **nuclear envelope** of animal cells and that organize the **spindle.**

**centrum:** older name for the body of a **vertebra.**

‡ **cephalic:** pertaining to the head. See for example, **cephalic index.**

**cephalic index:** measure of cranial shape defined as the total length of the skull (*l*) divided by its maximum width (*w*),multiplied by 100, i.e. $(l/w) \times 100$.

**cephalometric:** relating to measurement of the living head as opposed to the skull. Cf. **craniometry.**

**cephalometry:** field of physical anthropology and human biology that applies statistical measurements to the investigation of the living human face and head. See **cephalometric.**

**cephalotaphy:** preservation or burial of a body without the head.

**Ceprano:** archaeological site found in 1994 near Ceprano, 80 km southeast of Rome, Southern Latium, Italy, that dates to 900–700 kya, and contains archaic Mode 1 Paleolithic artifacts and hominid remains including an incomplete adult calvaria originally referred to **Homo erectus** or **H. ergaster,** although others seek either a new taxon, **H. cepranensis,** or referral to **H. antecessor.**

**Cercamoniinae** (= **Protoadapinae**): subfamily of prosimians belonging to the adapoid family **Notharctidae**; known from the early Eocene to the early Oligocene; predominantly a European taxon with a few later representatives in Asia, Africa, and one from North America; approximately 18 genera of small to medium-sized forms ranging from 200 g to 4 kg. Dental formula: 2.1.4.3/2.1.4.3 or 2.1.3.3/2.1.3.3; body size and dentition suggest **frugivory** in the larger genera. Fused **mandibular symphysis.** Known postcrania indicate leaping abilities as well as slow quadrupedalism and climbing. Cercamoniines comprised a sizable portion of the European fauna. See Appendix 1 for taxonomy.

**Cercamonius** (= **Protoadapis**) **brachyrynchus Gingerich, 1975:** adapoid **prosimian** from the late Eocene of Europe belonging to the notharctid subfamily **Cercamoniinae; monotypic.** Known from a left mandibular fragment recovered early in the twentieth century; consequently, some workers retain this species in *Protoadapis*. Estimated body mass around 4 kg. Dental formula uncertain, but has three lower premolars rather than four as in many cercamoniines; fused **mandibular symphysis.** See Appendix 1 for taxonomy.

**cercaria:** free-swimming larval form of the blood fluke that penetrates human skin and results in the disease **schistosomiasis.** Plural: cercariae.

**Cercocebus É. Geoffroy, 1812:** cercopithecine genus to which the mangabeys belong. There are four species with an estimated five **subspecies.** Distributed in varied types of forest of western and central equatorial Africa. Arboreal; diurnal; **quadrupedal.** Body mass from 3 to 12 kg; **sexual dimorphism** in body size. Dental formula: 2.1.2.3; **frugivorous.** Possess **cheek pouches** for storing food. Lives in bands of 10–20 individuals, including both mixed-sex groups and **one-male units.** Recent taxonomic revision based on morphology, biochemistry, and ecology resulted in the black mangabeys being moved to the genus **Lophocebus.** Evidence suggests that *Cercocebus* shares ancestry with **Mandrillus** whereas **Lophocebus** is more closely related to **Papio** and **Theropithecus.** See Appendix 2 for taxonomy, Appendix 3 for living species.

‡ **Cercopithecidae:** catarrhine family, consisting of the subfamilies **Cercopithecinae** and **Colobinae.** Adjective: cercopithecid. This family first appeared in the fossil record during the Miocene. See Appendix 2 for taxonomy, Appendix 3 for living species.

**Cercopithecinae:** subfamily of the catarrhine family **Cercopithecidae,** consisting of approximately 9 genera and 54 species, and that includes the baboons, macaques, vervets, and guenons. Adjective: cercopithecine. Widely distributed group that ranges from western Africa into the islands of Southeast Asia. Cercopithecines are medium-sized species with few exceptions. See Appendix 2 for taxonomy, Appendix 3 for living species.

‡ **Cercopithecoidea:** one of the two superfamilies belonging to the infraorder **Catarrhini;** Old World monkeys. One living family and two subfamilies. Widely distributed and highly successful group of

monkeys. Adjective: cercopithecoid. See Appendix 2 for taxonomy, Appendix 3 for living species.

**Cercopithecoides Mollett, 1947:** genus of **colobine** monkeys known from the Pliocene of Africa; two species. Estimated body mass ranges from 15 to 35 kg. **Sexual dimorphism** appears to be present in canine size only. Dental formula: 2.1.2.3. **Postcrania** strongly suggestive of a terrestrial adaptation. Based on molars with bulbous cusps, limb structure, and its recovery from savanna environments, it has been suggested that this monkey was a terrestrial forager that consumed soft gritty morsels rather than the **folivorous** diet of extant colobines. See Appendix 1 for taxonomy.

**Cercopithecus Linnaeus, 1758:** catarrhine genus of the guenons consisting of about 20 species (although this number is in flux) and numerous **subspecies** (see box below); some subspecies **sympatric.** Distributed throughout Africa in forested environments. Mostly large monkeys, ranging in body mass from 1.8 to 12 kg. Noted for their diversity in **pelage** color and markings. **Sexually dimorphic** in body size and canine teeth. Dental formula: 2.1.2.3; primarily **frugivorous.** Sympatric species often found in **association. One-male unit** is a common social group. See Appendix 2 for taxonomy, Appendix 3 for living species.

**cerebellar cortex:** outer layer of the **cerebellum.**

---

### Species groups within the genus *Cercopithecus*

*Cercopithecus* species groups are clusters of guenon species that are considered so closely related that they may not be separate species. The genus *Cercopithecus* contains at least 20 different species. However, many researchers feel that some of these species may actually be **subspecies** of other species, and lump them with close forms into eight species groups. These groups are the *C. cephus* group (5 species), *C.* (= *Chlorocebus*) *aethiops* group (1 species, but 21 subspecies), *C. diana* group (3 species), *C. neglectus* group (1 species), *C. hamlyni* group (1 species), *C. l'hoesti* group (2 species), *C. mitis* group (2 species), *C. mona* group (5 species). See *Cercopithecus*, **Chlorocebus**, **lumper**, and **splitter**.

*Cercopithecus cephus* group: consists of *C. cephus*, *C. ascanius*, *C. erythrogaster*, *C. erythrotis*, and *C. petaurista*. Some workers think these five species represent one **polytypic** species, whereas others think that the subspecies contained within these five species may be separate species.

*Cercopithecus diana* group: consists of *C. diana*, *C. dryas*, and *C. salongo*.

*Cercopithecus l'hoesti* group: consists of *C. l'hoesti* and *C. preussi*. Many researchers think that the subspecies contained within these two species may be separate species in their own right.

*Cercopithecus mitis* group: includes *C. mitis* and *C. nictitans*. Many researchers think that the subspecies contained within these two species may be separate species in their own right.

*Cercopithecus mona* group: consists of *C. mona*, *C. campbelli*, *C. denti*, *C. pogonias*, and *C. wolfi*. These forms are sometimes placed in *C. mona* as **subspecies**.

---

**cerebellar hemisphere:** one of two bilateral hemispheres of the **cerebellum.**

**cerebellar peduncle:** structure within the mid-brain or **mesencephalon** consisting of three paired cylindrical structures containing an aggregation of ascending and descending fiber tracts that support and connect the **cerebrum** to structures in the hindbrain; e.g. the **cerebellum.**

‡ **cerebellum:** structure within the hindbrain or **rhombencephalon** that functions to maintain balance and motor coordination. After the **cerebrum,** it is the second largest structure of the brain. See **metencephalon.**

**cerebral aqueduct:** channel containing **cerebrospinal fluid** that connects the **third ventricle** with the **fourth ventricle** of the brain. Aka aqueduct of Sylvius, mesencephalic aqueduct.

**cerebral arterial circle:** arterial vessel located on the ventral surface of the brain around the pituitary gland. Aka circle of Willis.

‡ **cerebral cortex:** convoluted outer layer of the **cerebrum** composed of gray matter. The cerebral cortex consists of millions of closely packed neurons and contains regions associated with learning and cognition.

**cerebral dominance:** see **brain lateralization** and **dominant hemisphere.**

**cerebral gyri:** convex portion of the **convolutions** of the **cerebral cortex,** separated by the **cerebral sulci.**

**cerebral hemisphere:** one of the two lateral halves of the **cerebrum.**

**cerebral peduncles:** paired bundle of nerve fibers along the ventral surface of the mid-brain that conduct impulses between the **pons** and the cerebral hemispheres.

**cerebral Rubicon:** hypothetical dividing line between the smallest known brain size of **AMHs** (about 885 cm³) and the largest known brain size of a great ape (about 650 cm³). A. **Keith** set the Rubicon at 750 cm³, F. **Weidenreich** at 700 cm³, and H. **Vallois** at 800 cm³. Aka mental Rubicon.

**cerebral skull:** portion of the skull that excludes the mandible, i.e. the **cranium.**

**cerebral sulci:** divisions between the **cerebral gyri** on the surface of the **cerebral cortex.**

**cerebretonia:** sensitive and introverted personality, associated with **ectomorphy** in Sheldon's system of constitutional typology.

**cerebrospinal:** of or pertaining to the brain and the spinal cord.

**cerebrospinal fluid** (CSF): clear, lymphlike fluid that forms a protective cushion around and within the **central nervous system** and fills the ventricles and subarachnoid space; it also buoys the brain. Cerebrospinal fluid is produced by the choroid plexus of the brain.

**cerebrotype:** standardized volumetric fractions of the principal morphological divisions of the mammalian brain for a species, i.e. **telencephalon, diencephalon, mesencephalon, medulla,** and **cerebellum.** Subcomponents of the telencephalon include the neocortex, hippocampus, schizocortex, septum, piriform cortex, olfactory bulb and striatum.

‡ **cerebrum:** area of the mammalian forebrain in both cerebral hemispheres united by the corpus callosum, and that consists of the outermost layer of brain cells whose function is associated with higher forms of memory, learning and intelligence. It also controls instinctual and limbic (emotional) functions. In higher primates the **cerebral cortex** has expanded to cover the entire brain, and is the largest portion of the **central nervous system.** See **telencephalon** and **limbic system.**

**ceremony:** complex social behavior that has a constant form and is repeated nearly the same each time it is performed; ritual behavior, e.g. begging, patterns of courtship, or greeting ceremonies among chimpanzees.

**cerumen:** wax-like substance secreted by glands that line the external ear canal. The functional purpose of cerumen may be to trap insects that enter the ear. Cerumen is inherited as a simple Mendelian trait and is polymorphic with a yellow waxy variety (dominant) and a gray dry variety. Frequencies of the two varieties of cerumen vary in human populations. Aka earwax.

**ceruminous gland:** specialized integumentary gland that secretes **cerumen** into the external auditory canal.

‡ **cervical:** pertaining to the neck region or a necklike structure, e.g. the cervical vertebrae.

**cervical curvature:** convex anterior (secondary) curvature of the vertebral column corresponding to the region of the cervical vertebrae; one of the four curvatures of the **vertebral column** that help distribute the body's weight over the center of gravity and provide resiliency.

**cervical ganglion:** cluster of postganglionic nerve cell bodies located in the neck near the cervical vertebrae.

**cervical line:** demarcation between the crown and the root at the neck of a tooth.

**cervical plexus:** network of spinal nerves formed by the anterior branches of the first four cervical nerves.

**cervical rib:** accessory pair of **ribs** that originate in the cervical region, are found in less than 1% of **AMHs,** and can cause nerve and artery problems. Aka neck rib. See **vestigial trait.**

**cervical vertebrae:** first seven **vertebrae** of the mammalian **vertebral column;** the vertebrae of the neck. See **atlas** and **axis.**

**cervix:** necklike structure, e.g. the cervix of a canine or the cervix of the **uterus.** Adjective: cervical.

**Cf., Cfr.:** see *confer.*

**C-factor paradox:** conundrum that many eukaryotic organisms contain more DNA than appears to be necessary; may be explained by **selfish DNA.**

**CFTR:** see **cystic fibrosis transmembrane regulator.**

**chacma baboon:** vernacular for *Papio ursinus.*

**Chagas' disease:** uncommon **protozoan** disease caused by infection with *Trypanosoma cruzi* and transmitted by the bite or feces of an infected species of bloodsucking bug (the 'kissing bug'). Of New World origin, primarily Brazil. Symptoms in adults include fever, gastrointestinal complications and possible cardiomyopathy; Charles **Darwin** recorded having been bitten by a kissing bug in South America, and there has been some speculation that the pattern of his later illness was compatible with this disease. Aka American trypanosomiasis.

**Chagnon, Napoleon** (1938–): US biocultural anthropologist at UCSB. Chagnon was an anthropologist with J. V. **Neel**'s multidisciplinary expeditions to Venezuela, and has spent several cumulative years among the **Yanomamö** since 1964. Chagnon published descriptions of the lifeways of these people, with particular emphasis on demographic dynamics. This culminated in *Yanomamö: Fierce People* (1968), and became required reading in introductory classes; supplemented by Chagnon's films on the same themes, he became a high-profile authority on human warfare. In the 1990s Chagnon's interpretations of Yanomamö warfare came to have a **sociobiological** emphasis, and he and his colleagues, including Neel, came under severe criticism from cultural anthropologists. The issues surrounding their fieldwork remained contentious and unresolved in 2004. Chagnon was instrumental in founding the Yanomamö Survival Fund. He was co-editor (with W. I. Irons) of *Evolutionary Biology and Human Social Behavior: An Anthropological Perspective* (1979).

**chain of being:** see **Great Chain of Being** and *Scala Naturae*.

**chain termination codon:** one of three **codons** that specifies the end of translation and that does not code for an amino acid. They are UAG, UAA, and UGA. Aka **stop codon**.

**chalcedony:** waxy, translucent **cryptocrystalline siliceous rock**; a material often quarried for use in making **stone tools**. Both **chert** and **flint** are opaque varieties of chalcedony. The red variety is called carnelian and the yellow is called jasper.

**chalcedony tool:** any implement made from **chalcedony**.

*Chalicomomys* **Beard and Houde, 1989:** archaic mammal known from the early Eocene of North America belonging to the **plesiadapiform** family **Micromomyidae**; **monotypic**. Small body size, estimated at 12 g, strongly suggestive of **insectivory**. See Appendix 1 for taxonomy.

**challenge:** in immunology, exposure to an antigen after specific immunization.

**challenge display:** highly emotive exhibition of aggression performed by one male directed towards another.

**chalone:** substance that inhibits cell division and is synthesized by mature cells of the tissue upon which it acts.

**chamaeconchic:** in reference to the **cranial index**, with an index of between 80.00 and 84.99; such an individual is considered to be round-headed.

**chamaecranic:** in reference to the **orbital index**, with an index of 75.99 or less; such an individual is considered to have wide orbits.

**chamaedont:** pertaining to teeth with low crowns.

**chamaeprosopic:** pertaining to a person with a short, broad face.

**chamaerrhinic:** in reference to the **nasal index**, with an index between 51.00 and 57.99; such an individual is considered to have a wide **nasal aperture**. An earlier approach referred to this type as platyrrhinic, with an index of 53.00 or greater. Aka broad-nosed.

**Chambers, Robert** (1802–71): publisher, writer and amateur geologist. Chambers was the anonymous author of *Vestiges of the Natural History of Creation* (1844).

**chance:** 1. absence of cause or design. 2. luck or fortune. 3. a numerical possibility or probability of an occurrence.

**chance mummification:** see **mummification**.

**chance variation:** in the nineteenth century, the irregular appearance of **sports** (mutations) in populations of organisms.

**Chancelade:** archaeological site found in 1888 near Periguex in the Commune of Chancelade in the Dordogne Valley, France, dated to 18–12 kya, and that contains **Magdalenian** artifacts and hominid remains, including the flexed burial of a nearly complete skeleton attributed to *Homo sapiens* Cf. **Cro-Magnon**. The skeleton has been regarded as having features similar to those of modern **Artic Inuit**. Aka Raymonden Rockshelter.

**change:** in biology, a definite and continuous process of adaptation, usually accompanied by an increase in differentiation; **evolution**.

**chaos theory:** organizing set of hypotheses that propose that there exists a regularity in phenomena that appear to be random; such patterns have been termed chaotic behavior.

**chaperone proteins:** auxiliary polypeptides that stabilize sections of a partly folded protein during its formation.

‡ **character:** 1. any variable feature or property of an organism that can be used for comparative purposes; aka characteristic. 2. observable feature of a developing or fully developed individual, such as a tooth cusp, a molecular sequence, a rate of metabolism, or a psychometric attribute. In genetics, characters influenced by only one gene are called **oligogenic traits**; those influenced by two or more are called **polygenic** characters. Aka morph, **trait**, phene.

**character displacement:** pattern observed in some closely related populations, in which certain traits are more exaggerated or divergent where the ranges of the populations overlap. Increased difference between two closely related **species** where they live in the same geographic region; explained by the relative influences of intra- and interspecific **competition** in **sympatry** and **allopatry**. See **niche divergence**.

**character divergence:** Darwin's term for differences developing between two or more related species in their geographic region of coexistence, owing to the selective effects of competition.

**character stasis:** constancy of a phenotypic character within a lineage over time.

**character state:** 1. scoring of the presence or absence $(+/-)$ of a character, regardless of size variations. 2. assessment of a morphological **trait** as either **primitive** or **derived**.

**character weighting:** assignment of more or less importance to certain **traits** over others when using them to infer evolutionary relationships. For example, brain size increase is often considered more important than other **hominine** adaptations.

**characteristic fossil:** fossil diagnostic for a given stratigraphic unit or temporal period; aka **index fossil**, diagnostic fossil.

**characteristic species:** see **index species**.

**Charcot–Marie–Tooth disease** (CMT): set of related conditions characterized by progressive loss of feeling in arms and legs, and progressive limb atrophy; CMT is caused by mutations in a peripheral myelin protein gene (*PMP22*). CMT is heterogenous; there is an autosomal dominant (CMT 1), an autosomal recessive, and an X-linked form (CMTD2), each of which has several types and subtypes. CMT is also associated with a similar condition, Dejerine Sottas syndrome (DSS). CMT is the most common inherited peripheral neuropathy, and is found worldwide.

**Chargaff's rules:** observation that (1) the measured ratios of A : T and G : C in **DNA** both approached 1 : 1; and (2) that the number of **purines** (A + G) equals the number of **pyrimidines** (T + C). Aka Chargaff's ratios.

**charged tRNA:** transfer RNA to which an appropriate amino acid is attached.

**Chari tuff:** Pleistocene volcanic deposit at **Koobi Fora**, Lake Turkana, dated by K/Ar to 1.39–1.2 mya (upper layers as recent as 600 kya).

**charismatic animals:** in conservation biology, animals that elicit great emotional support from the lay public for conservation measures to preserve them, e.g., gorillas, pandas, elephants, and lions.

**Châtelperron point:** small knife blade with flaked blunting of one edge, characteristic of the **Aurignacian tool tradition**. Aka backed blade.

‡ **Châtelperronian tool tradition:** Upper Paleolithic 'transitional' tool industry found in France and northern Spain and thought by some to have been created as **Neandertals** modified (or mimicked) technology borrowed from the **Aurignacian** of **AMHs**, but thought by others to precede the latter industry. Found at about 35–29 kya in at least three French sites: **Arcy-sur-Cure**, **Roc de Combe**, and **Saint Césaire**; an early form of the **Perigordian**. Cf. **Uluzzian**, **Szeletian** and **Buhunician tool traditons(s)**.

**cheater:** in the sociobiological literature, referring to an individual that has not reciprocated or returned an **altruistic** act.

**check sheet:** tool used in behavior studies in which columns and rows of a list of possible observations are put on paper and may be quickly checked off with a pencil as they occur; other aspects of the check sheet may include the number of times a behavior is performed and the time span between observations. Modern check sheets have been incorporated into computer technology.

**checkpoint:** any part of the cell cycle when a certain protein controls the cellular processes.

**checks and balances system:** pertaining to a mode of physiological control in which two separate components, one stimulatory and the other inhibitory, attenuate the behavior of a system. Heart rate, for example, is stimulated by the **sympathetic division** and inhibited by the **parasympathetic division** of the **autonomic nervous system**. See **feedback**.

**Cheddar Gorge Man:** relatively complete skeleton found in 1903 in the caves of Cheddar Gorge in southwest England. The skeleton of the 23-year-old man was dated at 9 kya, showed signs of a violent death, and was buried with Mesolithic artifacts. Oxford scientists extracted **mtDNA** from a tooth cavity of the fossil and in 1997 matched the sample to a history teacher living in present-day Cheddar village.

**Chédiak–Steinbrinck–Higashi syndrome:** heritable autosomal recessive condition characterized by decreased hair and eye pigmentation, and a tendency toward infections and lymphomas; a defect of lysosome formation. There are analogous conditions in several animal species.

**cheekbone:** vernacular for **zygomatic bone** or malar bone.

**cheek flange:** flap on the side of the male **orangutan** face composed of fibrous tissue; bilateral cheek flanges enlarge the male's face and are believed to enhance a male's aggressive display.

**cheek pouch:** one of a pair of sacs on either side of the face opposite the cheek teeth that are formed from the adjacent oral membrane; these pouches are used to store and carry food items temporarily; facial musculature assists in emptying these sacs. Cheek pouches are common among rodents, but among primates they are found only in the **Cercopithecinae**; these structures contain the carbohydrate digestive enzyme amylase and cercopithecines appear to force chewed food into the cheek pouches before swallowing. Aka buccal pouches.

**cheek pouch monkey:** term sometimes used for the **Cercopithecinae**, who possess a **cheek pouch**.

‡ **cheek tooth:** one of the **postcanine teeth**, i.e. the **premolars** and **molars**. In primates the cheek teeth are used for pulping, crushing, or pulverizing.

**cheilion:** most lateral point of the lips.

**cheiloscopy:** observation and analysis of the lines and wrinkles of the lips. These lip marks are considered to be unique to each individual and can aid in identification.

**cheiridia:** rays; used in reference to the bones of the paws or foot and hand.

**Cheirogaleidae: prosimian** family to which dwarf and mouse lemurs belong, consisting of five genera and eight species confined to the island of Madagascar. Adjective: cheirogaleid. See Appendix 2 for taxonomy, Appendix 3 for living species.

*Cheirogaleus* **É. Geoffroy, 1812: prosimian** genus to which the dwarf lemurs belong; located throughout Madagascar. There are two recognized species. Small (body mass 150–600 g), **nocturnal** (possess **tapetum lucidum**); **arboreal quadrupeds**. Dental formula:

3.1.3.3; predominantly **frugivorous. Dental comb** present; **grooming claw** on second digit of hind paw. A characteristic of dwarf lemurs is their thick tails, in which fat is stored and used during seasonal **torpor** during the dry southern winter of Madagascar. During the day and during **hibernation**, individuals form 'balls' of several animals for heat conservation and congregate in sleeping '**dormitories**' in hollow trees; however, during their active cycle they are **noyau** and the females have home ranges that are overlapped by the male home ranges. See Appendix 2 for taxonomy, Appendix 3 for living species.

**cheironym:** unpublished scientific name; manuscript name under consideration.

**cheirotype:** type specimen as designated by its **cheironym.**

**chelation:** way in which metals bind to certain molecules, such as proteins. **Heme** is an iron chelate, and the porphyrin ring is a magnesium chelate.

**Chellean:** pertaining to crude **Lower Paleolithic** bifacial **choppers** and **hand-axes** found in sites that date to the basal **Pleistocene** of Europe; archaic cultural stage named after a French site (Chelles-sur-Marne) where such tools were first discovered in 1847. Now called **Abbevillian.**

**Chellean Man:** paleontologist Louis **Leakey**'s name for the fossil hominid that he and Mary **Leakey** pursued for over 30 years at **Olduvai Gorge**, the alleged maker of the '**Chellean**' tools (actually **Acheulean**, as the Chellean tradition is restricted to Europe). Leakey found what he believed to be this Man in December, 1960; see **OH 9** and site **LLK II.**

**Chemeron:** archaeological site found in 1965 near west Lake **Baringo** in the **Tugen Hills**, Kenya, dated to 2.5–1.5 mya, and that contains hominid remains, including a temporal fragment (KNM-BC 1) of genus *Homo* sp. *indet.*; originally referred only to the **Hominidae.** A few researchers prefer the attribution *Australopithecus* cf. *boisei*. See **Mabaget** and **Baringo.**

**Chemeron Formation:** sedimentary unit in the Lake **Baringo** region of Kenya. A younger segment is dated to 2.5–1.5 mya. Paleoenvironment reconstruction, from faunal lists, suggests a lake or lake marginal regime. An older segment at Tabarin is dated to 4.48–4.41 mya, and contains the Tabarin mandible fragment (KNM-TH 13150).

**chemical maturity:** levels of body potassium and bone mineralization in an individual relative to the standard adult values.

**Chemiogut:** archaeological site found in 1970 near East Lake **Baringo**, Kenya, dated to 1.25 mya, and that contains hominid remains, including a cranial fragment assigned to *Australopithecus* (= *Paranthropus*) *boisei* (KNM-CH 304).

**Chemiogut Formation:** sedimentary unit in the Lake **Baringo** region of Kenya, dated to 1.24 mya.

**chemistry:** science concerned with the composition and interactions of matter. See **biochemistry** and **organic.**

**chemokine (C-C) receptor 5** (CCR5): identified as a co-receptor for the human immunodeficiency virus-1 (**HIV**-1). The other major receptor is the **CD4 co-receptor.** The co-receptors are found on the plasma membrane of CD4+ T cells. A 32 base pair deletion (designated $\Delta32$) in the gene results in a frameshift and premature termination of mRNA translation. The resulting product cannot be utilized by the HIV-1, and is at least partly responsible for long-term survivorship in HIV-1-exposed individuals. Almost 20 mutations in the CCR5 receptor, including $\Delta32$, confer immunity or variable resistance to HIV-1 penetration of CD4+ T cells, with homozygotes being at an advantage relative to heterozygotes. The CCR5 co-receptor also attenuates the severity of **asthma** and **rheumatoid arthritis.**

‡ **chemoreceptor:** neuroreceptor that is stimulated by presence of chemical molecules.

**chemotherapy:** use of drugs in the treatment of disease. Adjective: chemotherapeutic.

**Chenggong:** archaeological site found in 1985 near Longtanshan, Chenggong County, Yunnan Province, China, dated to about the middle or early late **Pleistocene** and that contains artifacts described as **paleoliths.** Fossil hominid remains include a human tooth attributed to *Homo erectus*. Other teeth are attributed to *Homo sapiens*. Aka Longtanshan.

**Chenjiawo (Lantian 1):** archaeological site found in 1963 near Chenjiawo, in **Lantian** County, Shaanxi Province, China, dated to 1.15 mya–500 kya, and that contains large quartz chopping tools, cores and flakes. Hominid remains include a chinless adult mandible (Lantian 1, probably female), attributed to *Sinanthropus lantianensis* (= *Homo erectus*). Aka Ch'enchiawo, Lantian 1. See **Gongwangling Hill** for the Lantian 2 calotte.

**cherry-crested mangabey:** vernacular for *Cercocebus torquatus*.

**chert:** impure **cryptocrystalline siliceous rock** found in sedimentary limestone; often used in **stone tool** manufacture, as at **Olduvai Gorge.** Because chert tends to splinter, forming flat fractures, it forms cruder tools than those made of **flint.** Its primary component is silica, and it is considered an opaque variety of **chalcedony.**

**chert tool:** any implement made from **chert.**

**Chesowanja:** archaeological site found in 1970 near East Lake **Baringo**, Kenya, dated to >1.34 mya, and that contains hominid remains including a cranial fragment attributed to *Australopithecus* cf. *boisei* (KNM-CH 1) and a fragmentary molar (KNM-CH 302).

**Chesowanja Formation:** sedimentary unit in the Lake **Baringo** district of Kenya, dated to 1.42 ± 0.07 mya.

**chest-beating display:** ritualized communicative behavior among male gorillas that involves standing bipedally and pounding air sacs contained within the chest making a loud booming sound, in response to interlopers.

**chest breadth: anthropometric** measurement; distance between the left and right sixth ribs on the mid-axillary line as measured with **spreading calipers.** Used for indexes of growth in children and adolescents and for **human engineering.**

**chest circumference: anthropometric** measurement; distance around the chest; a tape is placed under the arms and passed along the horizontal plane at the level of the fourth costo-sternal joint; the measurement is taken after a normal expiration. Used for indexes of body frame size; in infants, chest circumference is used for nutritional assessment.

**chest depth: anthropometric** measurement; distance between the **sternum** at the fourth costosternal joints and the spinous processes on the same horizontal plane as measured with **spreading calipers.** Used for indexes of growth in children and adolescents and for **human engineering.**

**chest expansion:** dimension that is the difference between maximum chest girth at inspiration and minimum girth after expiration of the lungs.

**chestnut-bellied titi:** vernacular for *Callicebus calligatus.*

**Chetverikov, Sergei S.** (1880–1959): Russian geneticist; author of a 1926 paper which, taken with those of **Fisher, Haldane** and **Wright** *c.* 1930, led to the **modern synthesis** of genetics and evolutionary theory. Chetverikov was imprisoned after 1929 for his support of **Mendelism** rather than **Lysenkoism.**

**chevron bone:** small V-shaped bone that forms the hemal arch of a **caudal vertebra.**

**chewing:** see **mastication.**

**Chi Ku Shan:** see **Chicken Bone Hill.**

**chi-square test** ($\chi^2$): statistical test for the degree of difference between a set of observed values or frequencies and its corresponding set of expected values or frequencies generated by the hypothesis being tested, and that utilizes the $\chi^2$ statistic. A goodness-of-fit test for one variable, or a test of independence for several variables. Aka chi-squared test.

**chiasma:** 1. crossing of nerve tracts from one side of the **central nervous system** to the other; aka chiasm. 2. The physical location of cross-overs in intimately synapsed homologous chromosome pairs which, only in **meiosis,** lasts from late prophase up to early **metaphase.** Plural: chiasmata.

**chiasma interference:** either more or less frequent formation of **chiasmata** between homologous chromosomes than can be explained by chance.

**chiasmatype hypothesis:** hypothesis in genetics that crossing over between nonsister chromatids results in the formation of chiasmata; proposed by cytologist F. A. Janssens (1843–97) in 1909, the concept is still held in the general case to be nonfalsifiable.

**Chicken Bone Hill:** Chi Ku Shan; local name in 1918 for the archaeological site known today as **Zhoukoudian.** So named because of the red clay found there full of the hollow bones of fossil birds.

**Chicxulub structure:** putative crater off the Yucatan peninsula of Mexico of late **Cretaceous** age, thought to be the major impact site implicated in the **asteroid impact model** of K/T extinctions.

**chignon:** 'bunning' or elongation of the occipital region. Characteristic of Neandertals. See **occipital bun.**

**chilblain:** condition resulting from excessive exposure to cold temperature, marked by inflammatory swelling of hands and feet accompanied by severe itching and burning sensations, and sometimes ulceration; usually affects individuals with a history of cold limbs in summer as well as in winter. Aka pernio.

**child:** young person between the stages of **infancy** and **adolescence.** See **childhood.**

**childbearing age:** in females, the period during which the reproductive system is fully functional.

‡ **childhood:** stage in the human **life cycle** that succeeds **infancy** and precedes the **juvenile growth stage.** The childhood stage usually begins at weaning (between the ages of one and three in many cultures) and lasts until the age of about ten years. During this interval children are still dependent upon adults for food and other resources, including intensive care. Childhood is characterized by greater neurological development and less physical development. See **child.**

**childhood growth period:** stage in the growth of human children that occurs between the end of infancy and the start of the **adolescent growth spurt,** usually about the ages of 2–10 years; characterized by rapid neurological development but slow physical growth and development.

**Childe, V. (Vere) Gordon** (1892–1957): Australian archeologist, prehistorian at the University of London. Proponent of a version of cultural evolution termed **unilineal evolution,** with an emphasis upon technological innovation, an approach that gives rise to historical narratives. Also proposed the **Neolithic Revolution hypothesis** to explain the origins of agriculture. Author of *Man Makes Himself* (1951) and *What Happened in History* (1942).

**chill:** sensation of coldness ranging from moderate to severe, sometimes accompanied in the latter range by shivering and fever.

**chimera:** 1. any hybrid structure not commonly found in nature. In chemistry, chimeras are often used as tools to elucidate protein structure and function. 2. an entire organism consisting of amalgamates of cells from more than one **zygote**; Cf. **mosaic**. See **chimeric twins** and **freemartin effect**. 3. sometimes used to describe the mistaken attribution of specimens from more than one individual, or even species, to the same individual **fossil**, as in the case of **Piltdown**.

**chimeraplasty:** anthropogenic use of DNA repair processes to repair a mutation; used in **biotechnology**.

**chimeric gene:** natural hybrid **cistron** produced by the fusion of two formerly separate functional elements, such as the *Tre2* gene that influences testicular cell proliferation, and found only in members of the **Hominoidea**.

**chimeric twins:** usually, blood group **chimeras**. **Fraternal twins** whose blood contains cells derived from its twin, as well as its own, are homologous chimeras, whereas **identical twins** are isologous chimeras.

‡ **chimpanzee:** vernacular for *Pan troglodytes*, but see **bonobo**. Vernacular taken from the native Zaire term *kimpenzi* for the **bonobo** or pygmy chimpanzee.

**chin:** vernacular for the **mental protuberance**; the knob of bone protruding from the mid-line of the **mandible**, found only in *Homo sapiens*.

**Chinese:** 1. **ethonym** for the **autochthonous** peoples of central and eastern mainland Asia. 2. a subfamily of the Sino-Tibetan family of languages.

**Chinese white-cheeked gibbon:** vernacular for *Hylobates leucogenys*.

**Chipetaia lamporea:** tarsiiform primate from the middle Eocene of North America. Body mass around 1 kg. See Appendix 1 for taxonomy.

**Chirogaleus samati Grandidier, 1868:** synonym for *Cheirogaleus medius*.

**Chiromyoides Stehlin, 1916:** archaic mammal of the late Paleocene and early Eocene of Europe and North America belonging to the family **Plesiadapidae**, composed of five species. Hypothesized to be descended from a *Plesiadapis* species. Dental formula: 1-2.0-1.3.3/1.0.2.3; there is uncertainty regarding the upper incisors and canine; there is also dental reduction through time. The incisors are robust, the mandible stout and deep, and the muzzle shortened; these adaptations have suggested to some that this animal filled a niche similar to the aye-aye (*Daubentonia*) and used its incisors to gnaw away at the bark of trees. Body size estimated to be between 150 and 300 g. See Appendix 1 for taxonomy.

**Chiropotes Lesson, 1840:** **platyrrhine** genus to which the bearded sakis belong; two species. Found in mature rain forests of central and northwestern Brazil and the Guianas, where they occupy the upper canopy. Diurnal; arboreal **quadrupeds** without a **prehensile** tail. Range in body mass from 2 to 4 kg; slight **sexual dimorphism** in body size; males have well-developed **temporalis muscle**s, which form bulge on head. Pink face, long rounded beard that emanates from cheeks and chin. Dental formula: 2.1.3.3; **frugivorous** and **granivorous**. Live in mixed-sex **troops** of up to 25 individuals. See Appendix 2 for taxonomy, Appendix 3 for living species.

**Chiroptera:** mammalian **order** to which the bats belong; subdivided into two subclasses, the small **Microchiroptera** and the larger **Megachiroptera**; one of the four orders within the grandorder **Archonta**.

**chiropteran:** bat; member of the mammalian order **Chiroptera**.

**chisel:** tool used for engraving, and which has a narrow blade. The chisel was developed in **Mousterian** times. Aka chiseau, burin-chiseau.

**Chlorocebus Gray, 1870:** monotypic catarrhine genus to which the savanna guenons belong. Taxonomy equivocal; some workers group the 21 subspecies into 4 separate species. Distributed from western to eastern and southern equatorial Africa and often found in savanna, but habitat variable. Terrestrial, but sleep in trees. Diurnal. Quadrupedal. Dental formula: 2.1.2.3; **frugivorous**. Slight **sexual dimorphism**: males weigh around 4 kg, females 3 kg. Troop size ranges from 5 to 200 animals. Females are the **resident sex**. See Appendix 2 for taxonomy, Appendix 3 for living species.

**chlorophyll:** group of green pigments in plants that is essential for the process of **photosynthesis**.

**chloroplast:** subcellular organelle containing **chlorophyll**, which transforms the energy in sunlight into the energy of chemical bonds by the process of **photosynthesis**.

**Chlororhysis Gazin, 1959:** genus of tarsiiform primate from the early Eocene of North America belonging to the **omomyid** subfamily **Anaptomorphinae**; two species; poorly known, but appears to be among the most primitive anaptomorphines. Estimated body mass around 160 g. Dental formula: 2.1.3.3/ 2.1.3.3; some workers suggest *Chlororhysis* was **insectivorous,** but not necessarily exclusively; some of the dentition attributed to this genus may actually belong to another organism. See Appendix 1 for taxonomy.

**choice test:** experiment in which an animal is presented with several objects or other animals (either **conspecifics** or different species, depending on what is being tested) either simultaneously or in succession, and observations are recorded, compiled, and analyzed to determine subject preference.

**cholera:** acute infectious form of enteritis caused by the enterotoxin choleragen produced by a bacillus, *Vibrio cholerae*, in the human small intestine, where it causes abnormal secretion of fluids from the mucosal surface. In severe cases, cholera is manifested by severe, painless, watery diarrhea with the passing of rice-water stools, which are diagnostic, resulting in dehydration, saline depletion, acidosis, shock, effortless vomiting, muscle cramps, and a characteristic faint, high-pitched voice. Cholera is spread by feces-contaminated water and food. Mortality is 70% in untreated cases. Cholera has been implicated as a potential cause of the **cystic fibrosis** polymorphism.

**cholesterol:** a white, waxy, crystalline organic eukaryotic sterol that in higher animals is the precursor of bile acids and **steroid** hormones and is a key component of cell **membranes**, mediating their fluidity and permeability. Most cholesterol is synthesized by the **liver** and other tissues, but some is absorbed from dietary sources, with each kind transported in plasma by specific **lipoproteins**. Cholesterol is a universal tissue constituent present in all animal fats, oils, bile, brain tissue, blood, plasma membranes, and egg yolk, and can accumulate or deposit abnormally, as in some gallstones.

**chondrification:** cartilage formation or conversion.

**chondriome:** collection of mitochondria in a cell's cytoplasm; part of a cell's **plasmon**. Cf. **genome**.

**chondroblast:** cell that produces cartilage.

**chondroclast:** large multinucleated cell that resorbs cartilage.

**chondrocostal:** of or pertaining to the cartilages of the ribs; aka costochondral.

**chondrocranium:** that portion of the adult **cranium** that is derived from the prenatal cartilaginous cranium, and formed by **endochondral ossification**. Cf. **desmocranium**.

**chondrocyte:** cartilage cell; cell embedded in matrix that it secretes.

**chondrodysplasia:** inherited, autosomal recessive condition characterized by deformed joints and stunted growth, and caused by a mutation in one of the genes important in collagen formation.

**chondrogenesis:** formation of cartilage. Aka chondrosis.

**chondrogenic:** facilitatiing of the formation of **cartilage**.

**chondroitin:** nitrogenous polysaccharide that is a component of cartilage in the form of chondroitin-sulfuric acid.

**chondrosarcoma:** rapidly growing cartilaginous tumor; see **sarcoma**.

‡ **chopper:** large, roughly formed stone tool, large, and usually circular. A generic term used to describe any heavy polyhedral tool that is not shaped like an ax, blade, etc.

**chopper** or **chopping tool industry:** crude chopping tool tradition found east of **Movius' line**, especially in the later Lower Paleolithic of Asia at sites such as **Zhoukoudian**; sometimes used as a synonym for **developed Oldowan**.

**chord:** standardized method in **anthropometry** for obtaining a straight line measurement from a curved surface.

**chord distance:** graphical representation of the relationship between two populations based on a **genetic distance** measure calculated from gene frequencies or other population data.

‡ **Chordata:** phylum of the Animalia that contains the vertebrates. Chordates are characterized by a **notochord** at some stage of life, a single dorsal hollow nerve cord, and pharyngeal slits. Approximately 42 500 species, including those contained within the subphylum **Vertebrata**.

‡ **chordate:** bilaterally symmetrical animal characterized by distinct head–tail, side-to-side, and top–bottom axes; trunk musculature is paired; possesses either a rodlike or a segmented backbone.

**chorea:** any nervous disorder characterized by involuntary muscle action, as in **Huntington disease**, **Parkinson disease**, and **essential tremor**.

**chorematic index:** measure of closeness of the greater sciatic notch to the auricular point in a pelvis; used to distinguish male from female pelves in hominids.

**chorioallantoic placenta:** placenta that is composed of two membranes. The outer membrane is the chorion and the inner membrane is the highly **vascularized** allantois. This form of placenta is found in the **metatherian** bandicoots and most **eutherian** mammals, but not rodents and primates, who possess a **chorionic placenta**.

**chorion:** extraembryonic membrane that contributes to the formation of the **placenta**. It surrounds the **amnion**. Adjective: chorionic.

**chorionic–allantoic placenta:** kind of placenta in which portions of the **allantois** fuse with the chorion; lacking an **umbilical cord**. Found in most mammals, but not rodents and primates, which have a **chorionic placenta**.

**chorionic gonadotropin** (CG): protein hormone secreted by the blastocyst and **placenta** that affects sexual development while *in utero* as well as maintaining the activity of the **corpus luteum** during the **first trimester** of pregnancy; also thought to promote steroidogenesis in the fetoplacental unit and to stimulate fetal testicular secretion of testosterone. Aka human chorionic gonadotropin.

**chorionic placenta:** kind of placenta with a direct connection between the **chorion** and the fetus via the **umbilical cord**; found in rodents and primates. Cf. **chorionic–allantoic placenta.**

**chorionic somatomammotrophin** (hCS): a polypeptide **hormone** secreted by the **placenta** that enters the maternal circulation and disappears from the circulation immediately after delivery. It has growth-promoting activity, is immunologically similar to **growth hormone**, and inhibits maternal **insulin** activity during pregnancy. Aka human placental lactogen.

**chorionic villi:** fingerlike growths that extend from extraembryonic membranes to implant into the uterine wall.

**chorionic villus sampling** (CVS): method of sampling fetal **chorionic** cells by insertion of a catheter through the mother's vagina and into the uterus. Used in the diagnosis of possible biochemical and **cytogenetic disorders** in the **embryo**, and usually performed in week 8–12 of a pregnancy. The chorionic villus is descended from the fertilized ovum. CVS presents a slightly higher risk to the fetus than **amniocentesis**. Aka chorionic villus biopsy.

**choriovitelline placenta:** placenta composed of a chorion and a yolk sac. This form of placenta is found among the **metatherian** mammals, with the exception of the bandicoots.

**chorography:** study of large regional events.

**choroid:** vascular, pigmented middle layer of the wall of the eye.

**choroid plexus:** mass of vascular capillaries from which cerebrospinal fluid is secreted into the ventricles of the brain.

**Chorora Formation:** middle **Miocene** geological unit in the **Afar triangle**, sampled in 1975–7; has yielded vertebrate remains but as yet no fossil primates.

**chorus:** any group of primates that **call** in unison.

**Chou K'ou Tien:** district about 50 km southwest of Peking (Beijing), China; see **Zhoukoudian.**

**Choukoutien:** obsolete spelling of **Zhoukoudian.**

**Christmas disease:** see **hemophilia.**

**chromatid:** either one of two distinct longitudinal subunits of a **chromosome**. The two identical **sister chromatids** share a common centromere and constitute a whole chromosome. Humans normally have the species-specific **diploid** number of 23 pairs of chromatids ($2N = 46$) in nondividing **somatic** cells, and the **haploid** number of 23 unpaired chromatids ($N = 23$) in mature sex cells or **gametes**. Aka unreplicated chromosome. See **mitosis** and **meiosis.**

‡ **chromatin:** latticelike molecular conjugation of DNA, RNA, **histones**, and **nonhistone proteins** that forms the physical backbone of a **chromosome** or **chromatid**. Originally defined as that portion of a cell nucleus which 'stained well'. See **sex chromatin.**

**chromatin modification:** **epigenetic** changes to molecules that chaperone DNA, without an actual change in a DNA sequence. See for example, **DNA methylation** and **histone modification**. See also **chaperone proteins.**

**chromatin negative:** having no **Barr body** in the nucleus of a cell.

**chromatin positive:** having one or more **Barr bodies** in the nucleus of a cell.

**chromatin remodeling:** a transient change in **chromatin** accessibility.

**chromatography:** any of a diverse group of techniques used to separate mixtures into their constituents through differential migration and absorption by a solid such as a column of silica (column chromatography) or a strip of filter paper (paper chromatography). One common use in human biology is the isolation of peptide fragments along a filter paper after digestion by a proteolytic enzyme (such as trypsin) of the original protein.

**chromatophilic substance:** membranes with attached ribosomes found within the cell body of a neuron; analogous to the rough **endoplasmic reticulum** of other cells. Aka Nissl body.

**chromoblast:** embryonic pigment cell.

**chromodomain:** highly conserved sequence **motif** that yields proteins that are components of large macromolecular **chromatin** complexes and/or **chromatin remodeling.**

**chromomeres:** irregularly spaced, nodule-like enlargements aligned serially on **chromonemata** or **chromosomes.**

**chromonema:** coiled filament consisting of histone proteins and DNA, which extends the entire length of a **chromatid** in its attenuated, threadlike state. Plural: chromonemata.

**chromoprotein:** any compound, such as hemoglobin, composed of a pigment and a simple protein.

**chromosomal aberration** or **mutation:** change in the normal number or structure of chromosomes while visible under a microscope; see **major chromosome anomaly.**

**chromosomal anomalies, major:** see **MCA.**

**chromosomal chimaera:** any **mosaic** individual consisting of clones of cells constituted by numerically or structurally different chromosomes.

**chromosomal imbalance:** condition in which the normal balance of an organism's chromosomes and genes has been upset by the addition or subtraction of a full set of chromosomes, segments of chromosomes, or single chromosomes. See **polyploidy, translocation,** and **trisomy.**

**chromosomal incompatibility:** failure of phenotypically similar, sympatric populations to produce viable and fertile offspring owing to numerical or structural differences between the populations. See **stasipatric speciation.**

**chromosomal inheritance:** transmission of traits between generations owing to genetic factors located on nuclear chromosomes; aka **Mendelian inheritance.** Cf. **cytoplasmic inheritance.**

**chromosomal inversion:** see **inversion.**

**chromosomal mechanism:** 1. any normal process involving a chromosome(s) or chromatid(s), such as **recombination.** 2. any abnormal process involving a chromosome(s) or chromatid(s) that results in **aneuploidy,** disrupts **linkage groups,** and/or affects the **fecundity** or **fertility** of an organism.

**chromosomal mosaicism:** unusual condition in which some of an individual's cell lines have a certain **major chromosome anomaly,** while other cell lines are normal; see **chromosomal chimaera.**

**chromosomal polymorphism:** occurrence of a chromosome in two or more alternative structural forms within a **breeding population.** Aka a chromosomal heteromorphism. Analogous to **genetic polymorphism.**

**chromosomal sex:** determination of gender. In mammals, the male is usually the **heterogametic sex** (XY) and the female the **homogametic sex** (XX). Thus, males carry the **sex-determining** chromosome, which is actually a gene or a few genes (e.g. **TDF gene** or **SRY gene**) usually located on the **Y chromosome.** The SRY gene can rarely become **translocated** to its segregation partner, the **X chromosome.** For this reason, some rare XX individuals can be phenotypic males in future generations.

**chromosomal species:** one of the mechanical determinants of the reproductive species; all individuals with the same **diploid number** and **chromosome structure** are members of this set (i.e. the linear arrangements of genes on **chromosomes** are also identical). Phenotypically similar individuals that are either **aneuploid** or have structural rearrangements of chromosomes, although perhaps chosen as mates, could experience meiotic problems that result in a **reproductive barrier.**

**chromosomal sterility:** infertility in a viable hybrid owing to numerical or structural differences between parental chromosomes, as in the **mule** (1).

**chromosomal variation:** deviation from the modal diploid number of **chromosomes** within a species.

‡ **chromosome:** transient pair of **sister chromatids** (identical strands of **DNA**) joined by a **centromere** and which have temporarily condensed to facilitate **segregation** during cell division. Usually found in the **nucleus** of a dividing **eukaryote** cell. A chromosome contains the genetic material (**DNA**) that is passed from parents to offspring. Because chromosomes are distinctly visible only during cell division,

reference is commonly made to 'the **diploid** number of chromosomes' rather than to the strictly correct number of **chromatids,** which are the units permanently present as **chromatin** in nondividing cells. Aka replicated chromosome. See **mitosis, meiosis,** and **mitochondrial chromosome.**

**chromosome band:** part of a chromosome that is distinguishable from its adjacent segments by a difference in staining intensity. See **euchromatin** and **heterochromatin.**

**chromosome banding designation:** species-specific convention for the identification of banded chromosomes. In humans, each homologous pair of chromosomes is assigned a sequential number (HSA 1, HSA 2, etc.), and the bands on the short (p arm) and long (q arm) arms are each numbered from the centromere (pcen) to the terminus (pter) at the telomere. The numbering scheme is hierarchical, with major portions (1, 2, etc.) further subdivided into one or two more tiers (e.g. 1q24.2). This nonsequential scheme allows for additional band assignments as banding techniques evolve.

**chromosome banding technique:** any of several methods that treat and then stain chromosomes, producing horizontal bands of characteristic lengths that are numbered sequentially from the centromeres to the telomeres of each arm. The most common techniques are **C-banding, G-banding, Q-banding** and **R-banding.** Cf. **chromosome painting.**

**chromosome bridge:** bridge formed by an abnormal chromosome with two **centromeres,** which is thus pulled toward opposite poles during **cell division.**

**chromosome evolution:** the accumulation of **chromosome mutations** in a lineage. Such mutations may alter genomic content by altering **synteny** and/or producing one or more **position effect**(s) that may result in **reproductive isolation** even in the presence of little phenotypic change.

**chromosome imprinting: epigenetic** process by which one of two homologous chromosomes or regions becomes altered, and performs differently during a subsequent stage of development.

**chromosome jumping:** means of DNA cloning in which one cloned segment is used to identify another located a long distance away on the same chromosome.

**chromosome map:** graphic representation in linear form of a **chromosome** in which the **genes** or **genetic markers** belonging to a particular **linkage group** assigned to that chromosome are plotted according to their relative distances (in **Morgan units**) from other markers.

‡ **chromosome mutation:** any change in **chromosome structure** and/or **chromosome number.** A **standard karyotype** for each species is used for comparison. Among the more common chromosome mutations are

**deletion, fusion, dissociation** (fission), **inversion**, and **translocation**. In primates, **chromosome evolution** via such mutations is one of the major modes of establishing **reproductive barriers** between species or **demes** that may otherwise be genetically similar, such as the Bornean and Sumatran orangutan populations. Aka chromosome aberration and chromosome anomaly. See **major chromosome anomaly, aneuploidy, triploidy** and **polyploidy.**

**chromosome number:** a count of chromosomes or chromatids, usually either the standard **diploid number** of chromosomes or the standard **haploid number** of chromatids in an individual displaying **euploidy** for a species. Alternatively, the count in an individual with **aneuploidy.** See **nombre fondamental.**

**chromosome painting:** technique for staining whole **chromosomes**, based on hybridization with fluorescent labeled **DNA sequences** complementary to DNA on each chromosome. Allows very specific identification of chromosomes in a **karyotype.** See **chromosome banding designation** and **chromosome banding technique.**

**chromosome-specific sequence:** DNA sequence that is unique to a specific chromosome and that contains the genes found only on that chromosome. In contrast, much of the DNA on a chromosome appears to be found in several or all chromosomes; centromeric DNA, telomeric DNA, and certain repetitious DNAs make up this second group.

**chromosome structure:** length of **DNA** that consists of a interspersed sequence of functional units called **genes**, which are organized into **linkage groups**, the tightness of which is dependent upon the **recombination fraction.** The DNA is complexed within **chromatin.**

**chromosome theory of cancer:** theory that cancer is caused by abnormal chromosomes that result from chromosomal mutations that occur during mitosis, attributed to German cytologist Theodor Boveri (1862–1915). Although the discovery of the **Philadelphia chromosome** in 1960 lent some support to this hypothesis, recent efforts to identify the causes of cancer have focused on mutations in DNA such as the *p53* **tumor supressor** gene.

**chromosome theory of heredity (or inheritance):** hypothesis that principles of inheritance can be understood if genes are located at specific sites on chromosomes and that the behavior of chromosomes during **meiosis** is the physical explanation for **Gregor Mendel**'s observations. Proposed in 1902 by Walter Sutton (1877–1916), this idea is still held to be nonfalsifiable.

**chromosome theory of inheritance:** hypothesis that **genes** are carried on **chromosomes** and that the behavior of chromosomes during **meiosis** is the physical explanation for **Gregor Mendel**'s observations on the **segregation** and **independent assortment** of 'factors' (**genes**).

**chromosome walk:** technique of overlapping short pieces of sequenced DNA in a chromosome in order to characterize the entire length.

**chron:** 1. designated unit of time. 2. a magnetic reversal of relatively long duration, often interspersed with a shorter reversal(s) called a **subchron.** Cf. **biochron.** See **paleomagnetism.**

**chronic:** constant or habitual; inveterate.

**chronic disease:** any slowly progressing and persistent **disease** or condition.

**chronic exposure:** continuous or frequently recurring long-term exposure, often to low concentrations or levels of some agent.

**chronic malnutrition:** impairment of health and physiological function resulting from the failure of the individual to obtain all the essential nutrients in proper amounts and balance over an extended period of time.

**chronic mountain sickness:** condition of natives or long-term residents of high altitude characterized by a loss of tolerance to **hypoxia** in a previously acclimatized person, lowered **ventilation rate**, and a profound increase in secondary **polycythemia**; symptoms include changes of color, fatigue, headache, episodic stupor, anorexia, nausea, vomiting, and compromised visual acuity. Cf. **acute mountain sickness, altitude sickness.** See **acclimatization.**

**chronic myeloid leukemia** (CML): chronic **leukemia** of the myelogenous type, occurring mainly between the ages of 25 and 60 years, usually, but not always, associated with a unique chromosomal anomaly such as the **Philadelphia chromosome.** The major clinical manifestations are related to abnormal, excessive, unrestrained overgrowth of **granulocytes** in the bone marrow. Exhibits evidence for **genomic imprinting.** Aka chronic granulocytic leukemia, chronic myelocytic leukemia, chronic myelogenous leukemia.

**chronic obstructive pulmonary disease** (COPD): long-term airway obstruction that results from **emphysema**, chronic bronchitis, **asthma**, or a combination of these conditions.

**chronic radiation:** any amount of radiation received in small quantities over a long period.

**chronobiology:** 1. study of biological rhythms. 2. study of the duration of life and ways of prolonging it. See **gerontology.**

**chronocline:** gradual change in a trait or traits over long units of geological time. See **cline.**

**chronogenesis:** sequence of fossil organisms in stratified rock.

*Chronolestes simul* **Beard and Wang, 1995:** poorly known archaic mammal of the early Eocene of Asia, belonging to the **plesiadapiform** family **Carpolestidae; monotypic.** Earliest member of this family. See Appendix 1 for taxonomy.

**chronological age:** 1. length of existence. 2. in many societies, current duration of life as reckoned in solar years. Cf. **skeletal age, dental age, physiological age,** and **anatomical age.**

**chronology:** study of a sequence of related events, such as a chronology of events relating to biology, **evolution, geology,** and/or physical anthropology (see Appendix 5 for such a chronology). Cf. **relative dating** and **absolute dating.**

‡ **chronometric dating:** see **absolute dating.**

**chronospecies:** 1. successive species in an anagenetic lineage that are assigned ancestor/descendant status in a stratigraphic unit; paleospecies. 2. a group of fossils whose justification as separate species is based on a distance of time rather than of morphology. 3. any species found in more than one temporal stratigraphic unit.

**chronostratigraphy:** study of the dating and age relationships of rock strata.

*Chumashius balchi* **Stock, 1933:** genus of tarsiiform primate from the late Eocene of North America belonging to the subfamily **Omomyinae; monotypic;** one of the more primitive omomyines. It has been suggested that *Chumashius* is the ancestor of **Omomys,** although it is more likely that they both share a common ancestor to which *Chumashius* is closer. Estimated body mass around 300 g. Dental formula: 2.1.3.3/2.1.3.3; known dental morphology very similar to that of the living **callitrichids,** suggesting **insectivory** and, perhaps seasonal, **gummivory** for *Chumashius.* See Appendix 1 for taxonomy.

**chyle:** milky fluid composed of lymph and digested fat, adsorbed into the lymphatic capillaries (lacteals) from the intestine during digestion. Chyle is transported by the thoracic duct to the left subclavian vein, where it becomes mixed with the blood.

**chyme:** mass of partly digested food that passes from the pylorus of the stomach into the duodenum of the small intestine.

**chymotrichous:** pertaining to one who has wavy hair.

**CI:** abbreviation for 1. **cranial index.** 2. **confidence interval.**

**cicatrisation:** deliberate scarification of a body for aesthetic reasons; also spelled cicatrization.

**cicatrix:** tissue that develops at a wound site; scar.

**cilia:** microscopic hairlike appendages on the free surface of certain cells that serve either as a means of locomotion or to move material past the cell; in human females, cilia line the **uterine tubes** and facilitate the transport of ova.

**ciliary body:** portion of the choroid layer of the eye that secretes aqueous humor. It contains the ciliary muscle.

**cinchona bark:** Peruvian Indian remedy for **malaria** and other fevers; named for the wife of a Viceroy of Cinchon who was dramatically cured of a fever; introduced into Europe by Jesuits about 1630 CE; **quinine** identified as an active ingredient in 1820; Linnaeus named the genus *Cinchon* and several species, all from South America; transplanted to Africa and southeast Asia primarily by the East India Company. Extract first given as a tea; later mixed with chocolate, tonic water or other media. Other constituents include quinidine.

**cincona:** see **cinchona bark.**

**cingulate cortex:** transverse connection located above the **corpus callosum;** part of the **limbic system.**

**cingulate gyrus:** extensive circuitry within the **limbic system** that is involved with the regulation of maternal behaviors such as nursing, play behavior, and infant-rearing skills. Also involved in the regulation of pain and attention.

**cingulid:** ridge that surrounds the base of an upper tooth crown; always found above the enamel–dentin junction. Cf. **cingulum.**

**cingulum:** 1. ridge that surrounds the base of a lower tooth crown; always found above the **enamel–dentin junction.** Plural: cingula. Cf. **cingulid.** 2. tract of association nerve fibers in the brain that connects the callosal and hippocampal gyri.

*circa:* see **c.**

**circadian rhythm:** cycles of metabolic activity and behavior that occur within a 24 h pattern. This daily rhythmicity includes hunger, wakefulness, and sleeping. Some circadian rhythms are influenced by the cycle of light and darkness throughout the year; however, when humans or animals are isolated from the outside environment circadian rhythms remain fairly intact. The mechanism that controls circadian rhythm is the endogenous **biological clock.** Cf. **infradian rhythm, ultradian rhythm.**

**circannual rhythm:** annual cycle of behavior that is independent of environmental factors.

**circaseptan:** time period of around seven days (related to growth-rate periodicities).

**Circeo Cave Complex:** archaeological site found in 1939 in a cave on Monte Circeo, 100 km south of Rome, Italy, dated to *c.* 70 kya, containing artifacts and hominid remains including a cranium (Circeo I) and fragmentary mandible (Circeo II), both attributed to *Homo neanderthalensis,* with a cranial capacity of 1500 cm³. The individual may have been intentionally 'sacrificed', then portions buried. Aka

Monte Circeo; Grotta Guattari (Guattari Cave) is also part of this complex.

**circle of Willis:** see **cerebral arterial circle**.

**circulation:** 1. act of moving or flowing in a circle or circuit. 2. movement of the blood through bodily vessels. 3. movement of substances through a circumscribed set of organs and tissues, e.g. placental circulation, fetal circulation, **lymphatic drainage**.

**circulatory system:** system of organs and tissues that move blood and lymph through the body, consisting of the heart, blood, blood vessels, lymph, lymphatic vessels, and lymph glands.

**circumanal gland:** see **anogenital scent gland**.

**circumaustral:** pertaining to distributions around high latitudes of the southern hemisphere.

**circumboreal:** pertaining to distributions around high latitudes of the northern hemisphere.

**circumduction:** movement of a body part so that the **distal** end follows the path of an arc; this movement is only possible for limbs attached to a **ball-and-socket joint**.

**circumpolar:** pertaining to distributions around the north or south polar regions.

**circumpubertal years:** age period that surrounds the development of the reproductive system.

**circumstantial evidence:** collateral evidence from which a case may be logically and reasonably inferred.

**cis phase:** see **coupling linkage**.

**cis–trans:** referring to the arrangement of two nonallelic mutations on a given homologous chromosome pair that can be either on the same chromosome (cis) or one on each chromosome (trans). See **coupling linkage** and **repulsion linkage**.

**cistron:** term synonymous with functional gene; a length of DNA that, when transcribed into **hmRNA** and edited into **mRNA**, will be translated into a **gene product** that will perform a single function or form part of a structure. Aka transcription unit, split gene, coding strand. Cf. **pleiotrophy**.

**CITES:** see **Convention on International Trade in Endangered Species of Wild Fauna and Flora**.

**citric acid cycle:** series of chemical reactions in which food metabolites are oxidized, resulting in the production of high-energy storage molecules of **ATP** and the by-products of heat, water, and carbon dioxide. This process takes place in the **mitochondria** of the cells; Aka Krebs cycle, tricarboxylic acid cycle.

**CIVD:** abbreviation for **cold-induced vasodilation**.

**civilization:** 1. level of cultural organization characterized by some researchers as a society with internal social hierarchies, craft specialization, and cities with large populations, and possessing methods of reckoning, mathematics, and time-displaced communication. 2. stage of evolutionary development

proposed by **unilineal evolutionists** that succeeded both **savagery** and **barbarism**.

**CJD:** abbreviation for **Creutzfeldt–Jakob disease**.

**Clactonian assemblage:** lower Paleolithic flake tool tradition of northwest Europe; the type site is **Clacton-on-Sea**, in Essex, England.

**Clactonian flake:** flake with a nonfaceted striking platform and that has an angle of 120° to the main surface.

**Clacton-on-Sea:** archaeological site in Essex, England, dated to *c*. 400 kya, and that contains concave scrapers, cores and flakes with retouched edges, and a preserved fire-hardened yew-wood spear point; type site for the **Clactonian** flake culture. Aka Claxton.

‡ **clade:** species or set of species representing a distinct branch in a phylogenetic tree; a delimited monophyletic unit formed by **cladogenesis**, i.e. that group consisting of all the species descended from a single **common ancestor**. Synonymous with **monophyletic group**.

**cladism:** classification by means of shared derived characters; see **phylogenetic systematics**.

**cladistic affinity:** degree of recency of common ancestry; Cf. **patristic affinity**.

**cladistic analysis:** process of grouping taxa into sets based upon the possession of shared, derived features held in common by related groups.

**cladistic species concept:** species defined as the members of an evolutionary lineage between two branch points. If the **biological species concept** is applied temporally, it can lead to arbitrary divisions of a lineage.

‡ **cladistics:** see **phylogenetic systematics** and W. **Hennig**.

‡ **cladogenesis:** splitting of a lineage into two distinct lineages; **speciation**; branching, dendritic evolution, as opposed to **anagenesis**.

‡ **cladogram:** branching diagram or species tree derived through **cladistic analysis**, in which the derivation of a most probable order of **nodes** in a branching pattern is given priority over branch lengths. A genealogy is often assumed. Cladograms may be either rooted (bushy) or unrooted (neticular). Cf. **phenogram, dendrogram, phylogenetic tree**.

**clan:** 1. an exogamous, unilineal descent group, usually a **matriline**; clan members consist of remembered **lineages** that trace descent from a hypothetical common ancestor. Cf. **gens**. 2. term used for **bachelor herds** among hamadryas baboons (*Papio hamadryas*); it is felt that these clans may consist of related individuals.

**clandestine:** 1. concealed or private. 2. referring to evolutionary change not manifested in the adult stage of an organism. 3. referring to a character present in the embryonic form of an ancestral species that manifests in the adult form of a descendant species.

**Clark, John Desmond** (1916–2002): English-born US anatomist, educated at Cambridge. Prehistorian of Africa at UC Berkeley (1961–86). Clark worked in Zimbabwe (then Rhodesia, Africa) in 1938, as curator of the David Livingstone Museum. He was the discoverer of the **Kalambo Falls** site in 1953. Often in the field, he worked the Middle Awash on several occasions. He was among the first to involve Africans in excavation and research methods. He is remembered for his extensive knowledge of lithic industries of all archaeological time periods. He also excavated in India, and in the Nihewan Basin near Beijing in the 1980s. Author of 300 scholarly papers and 18 books including *Atlas of African Prehistory* (1967) and *The Prehistory of Africa* (1970); co-editor of *Kalambo Falls* (vol. 3, 2001).

**Clark, Wilfred Edward Le Gros** (1895-1971): British physician and functional anatomist (Oxford); known for early descriptions of the tree shrew (*Tupaia*, which he considered a primate) and the tarsier (*Tarsius*) while in Borneo (now Sarawak); compared the known fossil primates to extant species, and believed in viewing the total morphological pattern when considering adaptations and when attributing a **fossil** to a **taxon**; probably the first major scientist to support **Dart's** view that **australopithecines** are **hominids**, at the first Pan-African Congress in 1947. Supported the **arboreal theory of primate evolution**; considered by some to be the first **primatologist**; involved in the exposure of the **Piltdown** fraud; critic of the *Homo habilis* taxon; Viking Fund medallist (1955).

**clasp reflex:** paw grasp reflex present in most arboreal mammals, including primates. It appears to be associated with clinging onto the mother while she carries the infant during travel. It is also present in human infants and has been cited as a vestigial behavior. See **clinging infant.**

‡ **class:** in the hierarchical system of classification of organisms, the category below the **phylum** and above the **order**; a grouping of similar, related orders. See class **Mammalia.**

**classic:** 1. standard, model, or guide. 2. in paleontology, any specimen that closely resembles a **type specimen.**

**Classic Mongol:** Mongoloid subgroup found in Central Asia, Northern China, and Mongolia. Aka Mongol, **Mongoloid.**

**'classic' Neandertal:** in reference to the Middle Pleistocene European populations of *Homo neanderthalensis* that show the most extreme **neandertaloid** features such as heavy brow ridges, elongated skull, **occipital bun** and, historically, bowed femurs. It was later recognized that malformations of the postcrania were due to degenerative disease.

**classical archaeology:** study of Old World (Greek and Roman) civilizations.

**classical conditioning:** form of learning in which a previously neutral stimulus becomes a conditioned stimulus when presented together with an unconditioned stimulus. For example, in Pavlov's experiments, a bell was rung (neutral stimulus) simultaneously with the presentation of food (unconditioned stimulus) to a dog. After the dog had learned to associate the ringing of a bell with the presence of food, it would salivate every time a bell was rung, whether or not food was present: the dog had become conditioned to the ringing of the bell. Cf. **operant conditioning.**

**classical hypothesis:** proposal that humans are predominantly homozygous at most loci and that this degree of homozygosity produces predominantly normal phenotypes.

**classical school of genetics:** aggregate of scholars typified by H. J. **Muller** who argued for the importance of mutation, of directional selection, and the reduction of polymorphism in natural populations by natural selection. Cf. **balance school.**

‡ **classification:** arrangement of things into hierarchical classes (sets) based upon shared characteristics or perceived similarity. Modern scientific classifications are generally Linnaean. See **taxonomy.** Cf. **folk classification.**

**classification of odors:** taxonomy of olfactory sensations. The well-known schemes are those proposed by Linnaeus (1752), Zwaardemaker (1895), and Henning (1915).

**classification of primates:** arrangement of extant or living (and sometimes **fossil**) **primates** into a hierarchical scheme, based upon shared characters or perceived similarities. See Appendix 2 for an example of a **classification** of living primates.

**classification of races:** see **racial classification.**

**clast:** individual constituent of a rock.

**clastic:** having a tendency to crumble, break or divide; e.g. pyroclastic rock.

**clastogen:** any substance that causes defective chromosomes.

‡ **clavicle:** one of a pair of S-shaped bones of the mammalian **pectoral girdle**; these bones connect the shoulder to the **axial skeleton** and brace the **scapulae.** Clavicles are considered a **primitive trait**; many mammals have lost this structure and retention in primates is believed to be associated with an arboreal lifestyle. Animals with a clavicle are described as claviculate. Aka key or collar bone.

**claviform:** pertaining to a clublike shape; clavicular.

**claw:** sheath formed from keratinized epidermal cells located at the tips of the **distal phalanges**; claws are usually sharp, curved and pointed. Claws are found on some of the digits of **prosimians**; claws secondarily derived from nails (**tegulae**) are found on digits 2–5 among the **Callitrichidae**. Aka falcula.

**claw climbing:** locomotion in trees in which claws are dug into vertical trunks or branches to keep the animal moving forward; this is considered to be the ancestral condition in primates.

**cleavage:** refers to a series of mitotic cell divisions of the zygote that result in **blastomeres**, each of which becomes progressively smaller with each succeeding cleavage division.

‡ **cleaver:** large bifacial tool similar to a **hand-ax** but with an oblique cutting edge; found in both **Acheulean** and **Mousterian** sites.

**cleft:** fissure.

**cleft palate:** opening in the roof of the mouth caused by failure of the palatal bones to close and fuse. A multifactorial congenital condition with a partial X-linked pattern of inheritance.

**cleidocranial dystosis:** genetic disorder characterized by lack of **clavicles** and abnormalities of the face and cranium.

**Clever Hans effect:** condition in which an animal may perform a behavior because it is given an unconscious cue by a human observer. Clever Hans was a horse that was reputed to perform arithmetic, but actually responded to visual signs unwittingly supplied by his handler. Ape language studies have been criticized as possessing a Clever Hans effect.

**climacteric:** transition from the reproductive to the post-reproductive phase of life; **menopause** is one of the central events in a female, or normal diminution of sexual activity in a male.

**climate:** long-term weather conditions for a given time and place such as the **Cenozoicera**. See the individual epochs: **Paleocene, Eocene, Oligocene, Miocene, Pliocene, Pleistocene,** and **Holocene.** Direct evidence for these climatic patterns and changes comes from marine sediments (deep-sea drilling cores) and **palynology** (pollen studies).

**climate forcing model:** 1. any hypotheses that attempts to relate global climatic changes with apparently associated environmental and ecological changes. 2. specifically, E. S. **Vrba's habitat hypothesis.** See **evolutionary pulse theory.**

**climatic:** pertaining to climate.

**climatic rule:** any principle describing a trend or relationship correlating animal or plant morphology with a climatic state or gradient; aka ecogeographical rule. See **Allen's rule, Bergmann's rule, Cope's law, Dollo's law, Gloger's rule, heart weight rule, Hopkin's bioclimatic law,** and **Rensch's laws.**

**climax:** 1. highest, most intense. 2. phase of a succession in which the nutrient cycling system has achieved a mature and balanced state, or **equilibrium.** 3. orgasm.

**clinal distribution:** geographical range of a phenotypic or genetic characteristic. See **cline.**

‡ **clinal variation:** variation in the values of a character in space; a **cline.**

**cline:** geographic gradient in the frequency of an **allele,** in the average value of a metric **character,** in pelage color, etc., usually as the result of some causal environmental agent. Adjective: clinal. See J. S. **Huxley.**

**clinging infant:** primate young that grasps its mother's fur while being transported on the mother's back or belly.

**clinging reflex:** see **clasp reflex.**

**clinical:** 1. pertaining to the observation of a condition, malady or disease. 2. relating to a clinic.

**clinocephaly:** pathological condition in which there is premature closure of the skull, forming a concavity on the superior aspect of the skull and a saddlelike appearance in profile.

**clinodactyly:** inherited autosomal dominant condition characterized by a shortened and radially curved fifth finger. Cf. **camptodactyly.**

**clitoridectomy:** surgical operation in which the **clitoris** is removed.

**clitoris:** small, erectile structure in the vulva of the female; homologue of the **glans penis** of male mammals. In some mammals, including primates, the clitoris is supported by a small bone, the *os clitoris.* Cf. **baculum.**

**clivus:** convexity; downward sloping surface.

**cloaca:** chamber that contains the common opening for the gastrointestinal, urinary, and reproductive tracts; the cloaca receives discharges from all three of these systems. Only monotremes, among the mammals, possess a cloaca.

**clock:** 1. device made for estimating time. 2. see **biological clock.** 3. see **molecular clock.**

**clock calibration:** setting of a **molecular clock** in geological time by referencing a **node** or **common ancestor** branch point at a securely dated event such as a **vicariance** event, e.g. the last possible time that certain African and South American rodent populations could have shared a common ancestor before the breakup of **Gondwanaland** that formed the present southern continents.

**clock theory:** see **programmed aging.**

**clonal selection theory:** hypothesis that antibodies form because of continual mutations in the antibody-producing genes, leading to a large pool of pre-existing potential antibodies; that immunity is acquired when a particular antibody is selected in response to a specific antigen and thus undergoes rapid clonal proliferation, while those less useful antibody variants die out. Proposed in 1957 by N. K. Jerne and F. M. Burnet (1899–1985).

‡ **clone:** 1. individual derived mitotically (asexually) from a single parent. Adjective: clonal. Any individual that is genetically identical to its parent or to other individuals that are genetically identical to the same parent. Clones are usually derived from **totipotent** embryonic cells before cell specialization has occurred, although recent attempts (*c.* 1998) to clone offspring from adult mammalian cells have met with some success. See **specialized cell**, **restriction**, **twins**, and **asexual reproduction**. 2. duplicated DNA. 3. in cell culture, a population of cells derived mitotically from a single cell.

**cloning:** 1. creation of a collection of genetically identical individuals that have been derived from, and are identical to, a single parent; aka whole organism cloning. 2. in **biotechnology**, cloning usually involves growing genetically identical **cloning vectors** or host cells — usually bacteria, yeast, or nonhuman mammalian cells grown in culture — which all contain the same piece of inserted **recombinant DNA**, including the target **gene**. See **genetic engineering**.

**cloning vector:** 1. any length of DNA into which one or more fragments of DNA (the **clone**) are inserted *in vitro* through the use of **restriction enzymes** and **ligases**. 2. any gene carrier such as a plasmid, phage, or **cosmid**. Aka cloning vehicle.

**close affinity hypothesis:** view that humans and apes are closely related, in contrast to **Blumenbach's** separation of humans and nonhuman primates into completely different orders (**Bimanus** and Quadrumana, respectively). Thomas Henry **Huxley** suggested that humans and apes shared a recent **common ancestor**, a nineteenth century view championed also by **Darwin** and **Haeckel** but few others. In the early twentieth century, **Schultz** recognized close embryological similarities, as did Le Gros **Clark**, based on comparative anatomy. Later, **Gregory** and then **Washburn** supported this proposal, then still a minority view. The molecular studies of M. **Goodman**, A. C. **Wilson**, V. **Sarich** and R. **Cann** suggested an even closer genealogical relationship; the close affinity hypothesis is now the dominant view of relationships among the higher primates.

**close-packed joint:** position of a joint when all the articular surfaces are as close together as possible.

**closed find:** archaeological context in which a particular horizon is undisturbed, from which it is inferred that the objects located there were deposited at the same time. See **associated find**.

**closed group:** primate social group that excludes **conspecifics** that are not members of the social unit; the members of this group can recognize each other individually and there is usually a **hierarchy** associated with the group. This type of closed group found in primates is actually an **individualized group** as opposed to the anonymous closed groups found in insects or many rodent species.

**closed population:** any population that undergoes no introgression of genetic variation, usually a geographically isolated population, and where the only source of genetic input is by mutation. Cf. **open population**.

**closed system:** any entity that is isolated from its surroundings such that no exchange with similar entities occurs. Examples are an insular **deme** or isolated population, a closed **paradigm**, etc. Cf. **openness**, **gene flow**.

**closing stroke:** first sequence of the **masticatory cycle** in which the jaws move from an open position to a closed position with the teeth approaching **occlusion**. See **power stroke**, **opening stroke**.

**clotting factor:** see **factor VIII** and **factor IX**.

‡ **Clovis:** archaeological site found in 1929 near Clovis, New Mexico, dated to 11.5–9 kya, and that contains artifacts known as 'fluted points' of the **Clovis tool tradition**, and associated mammoth and bison remains. Various other New World kill sites are also termed 'Clovis sites'.

‡ **Clovis tool tradition:** currently the earliest extensive tool tradition known for the New World. The **Clovis** tradition is characterized by large, long, bifacially flaked and fluted points, and is represented at a cluster of sites. This tradition dates from >10 kya, and Clovis points are associated with mammoth kills by Paleo-Indians. Cf. **Solutrean** points.

**club:** tool with a pointed or knobbed end, often used as a weapon.

**clumped dispersion:** in ecology, pattern of spatial distribution of individual members of a species within their geographic range. A clumped dispersion refers to groups of individuals concentrated together in particular areas and absent from other parts of the range. This is the case for those primate species that are not **noyau**. Cf. **random dispersion**, **uniform dispersion**.

**cluster-of-differentiation antigen:** any self-antigen capable of recognizing foreign antigens carried on macrophages, and that sends an appropriate alert to the immune system, e.g. CD4.

**cm³:** see **cubic centimeter**.

**CNS:** abbreviation for **central nervous system**.

**CO₂:** see **carbon dioxide**.

**CO₃:** see **carbonate**.

‡ **coadaptation:** 1. evolution of two or more mutually advantageous **adaptations** in interactive species. 2. a process of harmonious integration of collaborating **genes**, such as the several genes involved in a sequential **biochemical pathway**; **neutral mutations** in coadapted systems may be suppressed by **selection** because so many dependent **loci** are affected, but an advantageous **mutant** at any one

locus could permit optimizing mutations to cascade through the system as other loci accommodate to the original advantageous mutant.

**coagulation:** 1. clotting; the conversion of a fluid into a jellylike solid, e.g. blood coagulation. Verb: to coagulate. 2. a clot.

**coalescence theory:** proposition that all alleles at a locus in any extant population have descended from a single ancestral allele to which they coalesce at some calculable time in the past.

**coalition:** temporary alliance between members of a primate society to confront an animal of higher **rank** which at least one member of the coalition could never challenge alone in agonistic encounters. Coalitions may be same-sex or mixed-sex.

**coalition rank:** rank attained by one or more individuals when they are part of a **coalition** of other animals. See **rank, basic rank, dependent rank.**

**coancestry, coefficient of:** measure of the probability that two homologous alleles found in two individuals are identical by descent. Cf. **coefficient of inbreeding.**

**coarse-grained environment:** environment where the resource patches are large enough that the individual organism can distinguish and choose from among the patches. See **fine-grained environment.**

**coarse-grained exploitation:** consumption of resources disproportionately to the environmental abundance of those resources. Cf. **fine-grained exploitation.**

**coarse-grained resource:** consumable harvested by predator species in a different proportion than its abundance in the environment. Cf. **fine-grained resource.**

**coarse-grained species:** coexisting, morphologically dissimilar species that utilize different resources in a habitat. Species with limited homeostatic mechanisms and low behavioral plasticity and mobility. Cf. **fine-grained species.**

**Cobb, William Montagu** (1904–90): US physician and physical anthropologist; trained at the Howard University Medical School (M.D., 1929), and at Western Reserve University, where he received a Ph.D. under T. Wingate **Todd** (1932). He founded the Laboratory of Anatomy and Physical Anthropology at Howard University. Cobb was the author of more than 1000 scholarly publications, many on human craniofacial variation, on race, and on integration in medicine. He was the president of the **AAPA** (1957–9), of the NAACP (1976–82), and of numerous other organizations.

**cobble:** in various classification systems, a particle of sediment about $130 \pm 70$ mm in diameter, larger than either a **stone** or a **pebble.** Cf. **rock.**

**cobble tool:** implement made from a **cobble,** as in the **Oldowan tool tradition.**

**coccidioidomycosis:** respiratory infection caused by spores of a unicellular fungus, *Coccidioides immitis*. Of New World pre-Columbian origin, now distributed throughout the southwestern USA and Central and South America. Symptoms include a persistent fever, and possibly a dry cough, sore throat, headache, and an itchy rash. The pulmonary form usually heals spontaneously in a few weeks; rarely, it progresses to a disseminated form that produces abscesses throughout the body and carries a mortality of up to 60%. Aka valley fever, San Joaquin Valley fever.

**coccyx:** four vertebrae that are fused in the adult human; inferior to the **sacrum;** frequently fractured during childbirth; these are the **vestigial** remnants of the **caudal vertebrae.**

**Cockayne Syndrome** (CKN): autosomal recessive disorder characterized by short stature, sensitivity to light, and the appearance of premature aging. In type I, onset is after one year, progressive; type II is congenital. Either of two genes is mutated (CSA or CSB); also involves excision-repair cross-complementation group 8 (ERCC8). Mutations compromise normal transcription-coupled repair during DNA replication.

**codin:** unit of three nucleotides in DNA that is transcribed into a **codon.** Aka **triplet.**

**coding regions:** portions of DNA that result in transcription and translation, and that result in a polypeptide chain.

‡ **codominant:** pertaining to **alleles** at a genetic **locus** that are neither **completely dominant** nor completely **recessive** (the effect of one gene product is not definitively 'masked'); instead, the gene products of both are expressed phenotypically. Aka incomplete dominance, semidominance.

‡ **codominant pattern of inheritance:** in **Mendelian genetics**, a system of inheritance in which, when one **allele** of any ancestral homozygote mutates to form a new **heterozygote**, the phenotype of that heterozygote is distinguishable from both the ancestral and subsequent new homozygote. In such cases, the ancestral **homozygote** is termed AA, and the *de novo* heterozygote is termed AB, with B now used to symbolize the new codominant **mutant** and BB the other homozygote. The **phenotype** of the distinguishable heterozygote is intermediate. In humans, the A and B alleles in the ABO blood groups interact in a codominant fashion. See **dominant pattern of inheritance, recessive pattern of inheritance,** and **incomplete dominance.**

‡ **codon:** smallest combination of **bases** in a **polynucleotide** that determines that a certain **amino acid** will be inserted at a specific position into a **polypeptide** chain; consists of three contiguous **nucleotides** called a triplet. By convention, a codon refers to an **mRNA** reading frame, whereas a **triplet** refers to a

reading frame in **DNA**. Cf. **anticodon** and **stop codon**.

**codon-restriction theory:** proposal that as cells age they lose the ability to translate mRNA accurately. Not generally accepted by cell biologists. Cf. **error catastrophe theory of aging**.

**codon usage bias:** nonrandom distribution of codons in a **DNA sequence**.

**coefficient:** 1. quantity placed before another prior to multiplication when one is unknown, as in 3*x*. 2. any value that is constant for a given instance, that is one of the properties of that instance, as in **coefficient of inbreeding**. 3. any constant, as opposed to a variable.

**coefficient of cephalization:** see **Dubois' coefficient of cephalization**.

**coefficient of coincidence:** proportion of the observed number of **double crossing over events** to the number expected from the random combination of single crossovers among a set of linked genes; a measure of the intensity of **chiasma interference**.

**coefficient of inbreeding** (*F*): the probability that like alleles are derived from a common ancestor; in first cousins (third-degree relatives) the coefficient is higher (1/16) than in second cousins (1/64) (or fourth-degree relatives).

**coefficient of kinship:** symbolized by $F_{ij}$ or $f_{ij}$, the probability that a pair of alleles (i, j) drawn at random from the same locus in two individuals are identical by virtue of common descent. Aka coefficient of consanguinity.

**coefficient of linkage disequilibrium** (*D*): calculated value that quantifies the degree to which genotypes at one locus are nonrandomly associated with genotypes at another locus.

**coefficient of relatedness** (*r*): probability that **alleles** at any particular locus in two individuals are identical by descent. In closely related people *r* is predictably high, such as third-degree relatives (first cousins, *r* = 1/8), second-degree (grandparents and grandchildren, *r* = 1/4), and first-degree relatives (parents and their offspring, or siblings, *r* = 1/2). In **identical twins**, *r* = 1. Aka Wright's inbreeding coefficient, panmictic index, coefficient of relationship.

**coefficient of reliability:** quantitative indicator of the error associated with any particular type of measurement.

**coefficient of selection** (*s*): relative proportion of the reduction of gametic contribution to the next generation of a parental genotype compared to a reference genotype (with the highest fitness and that has a selection coefficient of zero). The coefficient of selection ranges in value from zero to one, and is the inverse of the **fitness** of a genotype, i.e. with *s* = 0.10, fitness is 1−*s*, or 0.90. Aka selection coefficient.

**coefficient of variation** (CV): a statistical measure of the amount of variation in a population for a particular trait; because of the way it is calculated as ({$\sigma \times$ 100}/$\bar{x}$; see **mean**, as a ratio, it is independent of trait size. A CV greater than 10 (some use 8.5) is suggestive of the presence of more than one **species** in a sample.

**coeliac disease:** see **celiac disease**.

**coelom:** body cavity of the **embryo**, which in adults is the **abdominal cavity**.

**coenzyme:** nonprotein organic compound produced by living cells, a **cofactor** that transfers atoms or small molecular fragments during a reaction; like the enzyme, it is not consumed by the reaction and may be reused. See, for example, **thiamine, riboflavin**.

‡ **coevolution:** 1. **evolution** of two or more closely associated **species** in which each species exerts reciprocal pressures on the other(s). 2. interaction of molecules of interrelated function (e.g. an enzyme series in a **biochemical pathway**) such that evolution in one molecule impacts the potential for evolution in one or more of the others. 3. theory of **cultural evolution** that attempts to explain changes in social systems in a nonlinear way, by a process of mutual selection among components; thus, the development of domestication systems affected the development of agriculture, and vice versa.

**coevolution hypothesis:** proposal that sexual reproduction, and the diversity of genotypes it produces, is favored by the evolutionary interaction between a species and the other species in its ecosystem that it exploits or that exploit it.

**cofactor:** substance that participates, along with an enzyme, in a chemical reaction.

**cognitive ecology** (CE): emerging theoretical focus that attempts to understand the cognitive traits and neuronal processes that contribute to information acquisition, optimization of tasking and decision-making, and especially the estimation of the degree to which certain mechanisms are the product of adaptive evolutionary change. Comparative approaches attempt to provide information about perceptual constraints that act as delimiters on the natural world, and thus affect an animal's fitness. CE has theoretical links to **sociobiology, evolutionary psychology**, and **behavioral ecology**. Cf. **social intelligence hypothesis**.

**cognition:** in humans, refers to mental processes such as consciousness and self-awareness as well as other mental functions such as motivation, learning, planning, memory and other analytical aspects of thinking. It has become an important area in primate studies including laboratory and field language studies. However, it remains controversial within biology because there is a historical prejudice against 'animal thinking' in scientific studies, including the concern of **anthropomorphism**.

**cognitive archaeology:** study of past mental processes as inferred from the archaeological record.

**cognitive ethology:** field within **ethology** that studies animal intelligence.

**cognitive map:** concept in behavioral biology that refers to an animal's ability to learn locations, distances, and routes in a three-dimensional environment. This concept was proposed by Edward Tolman in 1930 as an explanation for the learning process in rats that run mazes. Cognitive mapping has been applied to many organisms, including primates, and to bird navigation.

**cohort:** 1. category within a taxonomic hierarchy consisting of a group of orders and, as such, a rank between a **class** and **order**. The grandorder **Archonta** is referred to as a cohort by some workers. 2. group of individuals who entered a population during the same period of time. See **age-class, age-graded group**.

**Coiba mantled howler:** vernacular for *Alouatta coibensis*.

**coitus:** coition; see **copulation**.

**colchicine:** alkaloid chemical that disrupts the **mitotic spindle**; used to collect cells suspended by **metaphase arrest** for chromosome analysis.

**cold-blooded:** see **poikilothermic**.

**cold-induced vasodilation** (CIVD): **vasodilation** that follows **vasoconstriction** in peripheral areas of the body after exposure to cold. This may represent a compromise in which heat is conserved through initial vasoconstriction, but the skin is kept warm through periodic vasodilation, preventing frostbite. Cold-induced vasodilation occurs among peoples, such as the **Sami** and (Arctic) **Inuit**, of northern latitudes. Aka hunting response.

**cold stress studies:** in adaptation physiology, the study of the adaptations of indigenous peoples to the stress of cold temperatures on their development and growth.

**coldward march of civilization:** doctrine that the techniques characteristic of civilization arose in colder climes owing to higher metabolic requirements and natural food storage conditions.

**collagen:** any of a group of twelve or more major connective tissue proteins. The body deposits collagen in wounds as part of the healing process; it is one of the major structural components of normal skin, cartilage, membranes, arteries, etc. Collagen is a long, three-stranded protein that forms a triple helix; individual collagen fibers bundle together into rope-like structures that provide sites for the deposition of mineral calcium phosphate.

**collagen diseases:** group of abnormal conditions that affect connective tissues and/or blood vessels, and that

may include deposition of excess or abnormal material. Examples are **rheumatoid arthritis**, scleroderma, and **systemic lupus erythematosus**. Aka connective tissue disorders. See **autoimmune diseases**.

**collared brown lemur:** vernacular for the brown lemur **subspecies** *Eulemur fulvus collaris*; found in the far southeastern forests of Madagascar.

**collared titi:** vernacular for *Callicebus torquatus*.

**collateral kin:** siblings of a lineal ancestor and their kin (such as cousins, uncles and aunts, etc.).

**collateral type:** any specimen other than the **primary type** used to extend the description of a species.

**collateral vascularization:** see *rete mirabile*.

**collecting economy:** mode of human existence predicated upon gathering of wild plant foods.

**collective group:** in taxonomy, a taxon at the genus level, composed of uncertain species, that is treated as a genus without a type species.

**Colobinae:** subfamily of Old World monkeys that have evolved anatomical specializations in their teeth and in a large sacculated stomach for consuming a diet primarily of leaves. Adjective: colobine.

*Colobus* Illiger, 1811: catarrhine genus to which the colobus monkeys belong; four to seven species depending on authority; some workers form up to three **subgenera**. Occupy variable types of forest in west, central, and eastern Africa, as well as Zanzibar; with few exceptions, this is a highly arboreal group that rarely comes to the ground; **diurnal**; **quadrupedal**, also employ leaping and semibrachiation; thumb absent or reduced to small **tubercle**. Body mass ranges from 7 to 23 kg; **sexually dimorphic** in body size and canines. Dental formula: 2.1.2.3; large **sacculated stomach** that contains an alkaline environment adapted for **folivory**; generally, molar teeth have high cusps and sharp crests for shearing leafy material; some species are extreme dietary specialists, relying on only a few plant species. Social organization diverse, ranging from **one-male unit** to **troops** of 80 animals. See Appendix 2 for taxonomy, Appendix 3 for living species.

**colon:** portion of the **large intestine** that extends from the **cecum** to the **rectum**.

**colon cancer, hereditary nonpolyposis** (HNPCC): cancer caused by mutations that occur in DNA repair genes. There are two major varieties, type I and type II. In type I colorectal cancer, the affected gene is *MLN1*, an autosomal dominant (aka familial colon cancer, type 1, FCC1). Type II, also an autosomal dominant, is caused by multiple mutations in genes at up to 13 loci. **Loss of heterozygosity** is a feature at these loci. Aka colorectal cancer (CRC), familial colon cancer type 2 (FCC2).

**colonization:** successful invasion of a new habitat by a species.

**colony fission:** multiplication of colonies by the departure of one or more reproductive forms from the parental colony or nest, leaving behind comparable units to perpetuate the parent colony. Aka fission society.

**colony stimulating factors:** cytokines that stimulate lymphocyte production in the bone marrow.

**coloration:** appearance as to color; **epigamic** coloring. See **pelage**.

**color blindness:** hereditary inability to distinguish one or more colors in the environment, independent of the ability to distinguish light, shape and form. Either red or green color blindness is the most common form of partial color blindness; both are rare, and owing to an interaction of recessive allele(s) at two loci (deutan and protan), both loci are on the X chromosome; mutations produce quantitatively defective opsins in the retina of the eye. A red-blind individual has **protanopia** and cannot produce the pigment erythrolabe. A green-blind individual has **deuteranopia** and cannot produce the pigment chlorolabe. A blue-blind individual has **tritanopia** and cannot produce the pigment cyanolabe: this is a much rarer form (aka blue opsin defect). **Achromatopsia**, the inability to discriminate among all colors of the rainbow (complete colorblindness) is sometimes found combined with other conditions such as myopia and cataracts. About 8% of the male and 0.4% of the female US population is affected. Roughly 75% of colorblind males have a defect in green opsin, while 25% have a defect in red opsin. See **tritanopia** and **complete color blindness**.

**color vision:** in reference to a species, the ability to discriminate between differences in colored stimuli or between colored and white stimuli; this discrimination must not be due to intensity (brightness) of the stimuli. To perceive color, two or more types of visual receptor, each of which is maximally sensitive to a different wavelength, are necessary. There are three types of primate **cone** that overlap one another, but are maximally sensitive at wavelengths of 440, 535, or 566nm, respectively. See **monochromatic vision, dichromatic vision, trichromatic vision**.

**colorimetry:** procedure in chemistry in which the color of a solution is observed against a standard when chemicals are added to it, e.g. in a titration.

**colostrum:** sticky secretion from female breasts that occurs just before and after childbirth. It is high in protein, low in carbohydrate and fat, and contains maternal antibodies. Aka foremilk.

**colugo:** vernacular for extant members of the mammalian family **Cynocephalidae**, order **Dermoptera**, a taxon closely related to the order **Primates**.

**colour:** see entries under **color**.

**Comas, Juan** (1900–79): Spanish-born Mexican physical anthropologist; studied in Geneva and held various teaching and institute positions in Mexico, including as head of the Anthropology Section at the National University of Mexico after 1955. He is remembered as a teacher, bibliophile and prolific journal editor, but also published 150 scholarly papers, many on the fallacies of racism, especially scientific racism. Author of *Manual of Physical Anthropology* (1957; English transl. 1960), and *Introducción a la prehistoria general* (1962).

**combed DNA color bar coding:** technique that stretches out DNA strands on treated glass and visualizes their structure using fluorescent molecular probes; it was developed in 1994 and subsequently patented by Aaron Bensimon at the Institut Pasteur (Paris).

**Combe-Grenal 1,2:** archaeological site found in 1815 (reworked in 1927) located in the Dordogne Valley in southwest France, dated to 68–37 kya, and excavated by the Abbé Henri **Breuil** and Francois Bordes. It contained 14 000 typical scrapers, notched saws, backed blades and denticulate **Mousterian** artifacts, 60 000 flakes, and hand-axes; fragmentary hominid remains referred to *Homo neanderthalensis*. The very lowest levels contain **Acheulean** artifacts dated to 113–105 kya.

**combined description:** description of a new **monotypic** genus such that the description serves for both the genus and the single species within it.

**commensalism:** 1. symbiotic association in which one species (the commensal) is benefited while the other (the host) is not affected. 2. state of living or eating benignly together.

**comminuted:** fragmented into small pieces; often used in reference to a fractured bone.

**common:** 1. shared, as in a **symplesiomorphy**. 2. united, as by a **common ancestor**. 3. widely known, familiar, or commonplace, e.g. the **common chimpanzee**. 4. in epidemiology, having a frequency of greater than 1 in 1000.

‡ **common ancestor** (CA): progenitor of any pair or set of more recent individuals, populations, species or higher taxon; the progenitor is identified by possession of **plesiomorphic** characters common to most if not all descendant taxa.

**common black lemur:** vernacular for *Eulemur macaco macaco*.

**common brown lemur:** vernacular for *Eulemur fulvus fulvus*.

**common chimpanzee:** vernacular for *Pan troglodytes*. Cf. **bonobo**.

**common cold:** respiratory rhinovirus infection characterized by sneezing, sore throat, coughing, and inflammation of nasal tissues. Caused by any of more than 100 RNA rhinoviruses, which are also found in chimps and gibbons. Many other viruses also precipitate 'colds'. These viruses had a worldwide pre-Columbian distribution.

**common descent:** concept that derived species share a common evolutionary ancestry; Aka propinquity. Attributed to Charles **Darwin.**

**common era:** see **CE.** Cf. **BCE** and **BP.**

**common gray langur:** vernacular for *Presbytis entellus.*

**common integrative area:** area of the cerebral cortex that collects sensory input from other areas and allows the analysis of input in the light of past experiences.

**common marmoset:** vernacular for *Callithrix jacchus.*

**common name:** see **vernacular.**

**common slow loris:** vernacular for *Nycticebus coucang.*

**common squirrel monkey:** vernacular for *Saimiri sciureus.*

**common woolly monkey:** vernacular for *Lagothrix lagothricha lagothricha.*

**communal:** group-living; describes species that live in a group and cooperate in such things as establishing and defending a living space. This cooperation does not apply to care-giving to offspring.

**communicable disease:** disease capable of being transmitted from one person to another; any **infectious disease** with host-to-host transmission.

‡ **communication:** 1. action on the part of one organism that alters the probability pattern of **behavior** in another organism in an adaptive fashion. See **symbolic communication** and **vocalization.** 2. In genetics and biology, the expression of chemical messages from one tissue to a target tissue.

**community:** social group of any size whose members live together in a specific locality; see **campsite community, village** and **ecological community.**

**community ecology:** field of study within ecology that studies the processes that influence the structure (composition) and function (interaction) of an **ecological community.**

‡ **compact bone:** dense tissue in which cells are arranged around **osteonic canals;** compact bone makes up the surface of bones. Aka cortical bone, dense bone. Cf. **cancellous bone.**

**compaction:** process of producing a compact ball of 12 or more **blastomeres** that form as the cells of a preimplantation **zygote** reduce in size and change shape and form a **morula.**

**comparative anatomy:** discipline within zoology that studies the differences and similarities between species or higher taxonomic groups. Although anatomists dissected other vertebrates since the time of the ancient Greeks, many consider Georges

Cuvier to be the founder of comparative anatomy; by its approach comparative anatomy is evolutionary in nature and was used by **Darwin** as evidence for descent with modification. The use of comparative anatomy is vital when reconstructing **fossil species** from fragmentary remains.

**comparative approach:** method used by anthropologists that compares populations to determine common and/or unique behaviors or biological traits.

**comparative biology:** study of patterns among more than one species.

**comparative method:** study of adaptation through the comparison of many species, the goal of which is to test hypotheses about adaptation.

**comparative odontology:** see **odontology.**

**comparative psychology:** discipline that studied animal behavior. This was an American school as opposed to the European-derived discipline of **ethology** and had a different approach, foremost being associated with psychology departments rather than zoology departments. Known for its research regarding rat mazes, it did have representatives in primatology, one of the most prominent being Clarence **Carpenter.**

**compass gait:** hypothetical walking motion used as a model for studies of human **bipedal locomotion** and named after the (two-legged) drafting compass. In the compass gait the knee and ankle are fixed, the hip is capable of flexion and extension, and the center of gravity is displaced to the sides and to the front and the back. This model is used for analysis of theoretical bipedalism of early hominids and for comparison with modern human bipedalism, which is not a compass gait.

‡ **competition:** 1. simultaneous seeking of a scarce, essential environmental resource. 2. symbiotic association in which the growth or survival of one of a species populations is adversely affected in instances in which a community resource is in short supply. See **contest competition, direct competition, intrasexual competition, local mate competition, local resource competition, male-male mate competition, scramble competition, sibling competition,** and **sperm competition.**

**competitive exclusion principle:** tendency for two organisms of similar adaptive levels not to be found occupying the same vicinity, since **competition** leads inevitably to extinction or to divergence of the less effective competitor.

**complacent tree ring:** in **dendrochronology,** an annual growth ring on a tree in which the width is approximately the same as that of other rings on the tree. Cf. **sensitive tree ring.**

**complement:** 1. part of a complete unit; used to describe the **haploid number** of 23 chromatids in a human gamete, for example, which, when combined with another gamete also containing 23 chromatids provided by the opposite sex (during **fertilization**), produces a complete **diploid** zygote. 2. in serology, a group of components present in fresh normal serum which take part in some antigen–antibody interactions, destroy microbes and attack transplanted tissue; see **microcomplement fixation**.

‡ **complementarity:** 1. forming a full quantity. 2. exclusive distribution of skills in the cerebral hemispheres such that if language is represented in one hemisphere, some nonlanguage skills are represented in the other. 3. in zoogeography, phenomenon in which animals occupy niches that are filled elsewhere by animals from different taxa. This particularly applies to Madagascar and the primate fauna there.

‡ **complementarity, principle of:** see **base-pairing rule**.

**complementary base pairing:** process during which specific purine bases are matched with specific pyrimidine bases. See **base pair** and **base-pairing rule**.

**complementary DNA:** see **cDNA**.

**complementary DNA library:** see **cDNA library**.

**complementary gene:** one of two or more nonallelic factors that contribute to a single phenotype, as stature in humans; see **polygenic trait**.

**complementary resource:** two or more resources that interact with one another synergistically; this means that less of each individual resource is needed than if only one were utilized.

**complementation:** situation in which a phenotypically normal individual inherits two defective alleles, one from each parent, for a similar genetic abnormality; indicates that the mutant alleles in the parents were at different loci. A common situation in the many genetic forms of **deafness**.

**complete antibody: agglutinin** that reacts with its specific antibody, causing **agglutination** of red blood cells in a saline medium.

**complete color blindness:** rare, total inability to distinguish colors in the environment; see **color blindness**.

**complete competitors:** two species that occupy the same ecological niche. This is extremely rare; in actuality there are usually subtle differences. It violates the **competitive exclusion principle**.

**complete linkage:** condition where two genetic loci on the same chromosome fail to recombine after repeated generations of crossing over; they are always transmitted together into a gamete. See **haplotype**.

**complete protein:** food source that contains all of the **essential amino acids** needed to maintain human body tissues and promote normal growth and development. Complete proteins are found in animal

sources. See **incomplete protein**, **partially complete protein**.

**completely dominant:** describes an allele that wholly masks the expression of its alternative allele. Cf. **incomplete dominance, codominant**.

**completely penetrant:** in genetics, refers to a situation in which the frequency of the expression of a genotype is 100%. See **penetrance**.

**complex:** group of anatomical structures that are integrated in a function that they perform.

**complex organism:** 1. individual composed of many **organ** systems. 2. loosely, any species that occupies a 'higher' trophic level in an ecosystem. 3. macroorganism.

**complex society:** human social group in which social stratification is present, often based on nonkinship criteria, and access to power is restricted to members of the ruling class; power is enforced through rules and sanctions. Complex societies have some form of centralized control over food production, nonfood-producing specialists, and long-distance trade routes. Some workers consider complex society to be synonymous with stratified society, state, or civilization.

**complex trait, character** or **feature:** feature whose final form or manifestation is influenced by both its genetic constitution and environmental factors. See **polygenic trait** and **multifactorial trait**.

**component:** any culturally homogenous **time-stratigraphic unit** within an archaeological site.

‡ **composite cell:** hypothetical **cell** used for teaching or illustrative purposes. A composite cell is generalized and contains structures known from real, specialized cells; not all cells have the **organelles** represented in a composite cell nor do they necessarily have the same proportions of organelles. Aka generalized cell.

**composite life table:** life table prepared from data obtained by using time-specific and age-specific methods.

**composite measure:** in behavior studies, combining the measurements of several behaviors into a single entity, i.e. the composite measure.

**composite race:** race that is a stable blend of two or more primary races and that represents combinations of features from the different racial stocks involved. Stabilization is often due to the geographic region in which the blend occurred.

**composite signal:** signal composed of two or more simpler signals.

**composite tool:** any implement constructed of two or more materials; for example, a point hafted to a shaft with a fibrous binding and perhaps cemented with pitch or tar.

**composites:** herbs, such as ragweed and sagebrush, belonging to the plant family compositae (Asteraceae).

**compound heterozygote:** individual with two different mutant alleles at a locus.

**compression:** 1. transition to an environment of higher pressure, as in diving or a hyperbaric chamber. 2. process of fossilization in which organic remains are flattened by the weight of overlying strata. 3. decrease of niche width owing to interspecific **competition**.

**computer-assisted design system:** see **CAD**.

**computer-assisted tomography:** see **CAT**.

**computer simulation:** use of a computer to **model** some complex, dynamic behavior or system; useful for examining individual **variables** to determine how they affect the overall system.

**concealed ovulation:** discharge of an ovum from an ovary for fertilization without any obvious signs that the female is reproductively receptive. This is a characteristic of humans and unusual among primates, although this trait is not unique to humans. See **life-history variable**.

**concentration:** 1. quantity of a specified substance per unit amount of another substance. 2. any preparation in which the strength of a substance has been increased by evaporation. 3. the act of concentrating, as in focusing on one subject.

**concept of multiple origin:** hypothesis advanced by evolutionary thinkers of the nineteenth century that every human group contains within itself the possibility of being the origin of the essentials of civilization.

**conception:** see **fertilization**.

**conceptual model of early hominid behavior:** model that extrapolates early **hominid** behavior based on modern primate behavior and principles from behavioral ecology and evolutionary theory.

**conceptus:** product of conception. Aka **fertilized ovum** and **zygote**.

**concerted evolution:** tendency for different genes in a gene family to evolve in concert; each locus comes to have the same genetic variant.

**conchoidal fracture:** smooth, undulating surface of a stone tool at the site of fracture on both the core and the flake, reminiscent of the surface of a bivalve shell. One of the diagnostic features of the **percussion flaking** technique.

**concomitant mortality:** death that occurs during exposure to an agent; cf. **consequential mortality** and **delayed mortality**.

**concordant trait, character,** or **feature:** shared, derived character(s) that is present in two specimens; said of a matched group or pair (such as **twins**) when both possess a character state owing to homology; concordance. Cf. **discordant trait**.

**Concorde fallacy:** argument that if an individual has invested greatly in an offspring or some other object such as a nest, it will continue to invest in it rather than abandon the project, even if the continued costs will outweigh the benefits. The term has its origins in the now defunct Concorde supersonic transport, aircraft, beset with problems, and the reluctance of the nations involved in its development to abandon the project because of the costly investment already made.

**condensation:** increased rate of phylogenetic **development** and **growth**, owing either to acceleration of all developmental stages or to elimination of specific stages in **ontogeny**; thus, descendant lineages pass through all or the remaining stages of development in a shorter time than their ancestors.

**conditional mutation:** allele that is expressed only within a certain range of environmental conditions.

**conditional strategy:** behavioral capacity to be flexible as conditions change and to make adaptive responses; ability to use different tactics under different environmental conditions.

**conditioned reflex:** see **conditioning**.

**conditioning:** the process of acquiring, developing, educating, establishing, learning, or training new responses in an individual; used to describe both respondent and operant behavior. In both usages, it refers to a change in the frequency or form of behavior as a result of the influence of the environment. See **classical conditioning** and **operant conditioning**.

**conduction:** transfer of heat between two solid objects during physical contact, i.e. collisions of adjacent molecules. Conduction is one of the processes utilized by mammals for thermoregulation; heat is transferred to the skin and, in humans, removed by evaporation of sweat.

‡ **condyle:** 1. any rounded projection on a bone, usually for articulation with another bone. 2. any rounded eminence. Adjective: condylas.

**condylion (laterale** or **mediale):** osteologic landmark(s) on the **mandibular condyle**. The lateral condylion (condylion laterale, cdl) is the most lateral point of the condyle; the medial condylion (condylion mediale, cdm) is the most medial point of the condyle. See Appendix 7 for an illustration of craniometric landmarks.

**condyloid joint:** type of **synovial joint** in which the ovoid **condyle** of one bone fits into the elliptical cavity of the bone it joins with; permits all movements except rotation. Aka ellipsoidal joint.

**condyloid process:** generally in reference to the posterior branch of the **mandibular ramus** that bears the **mandibular condyles**.

**cone:** 1. see **cone cell**. 2. polished stone object, usually made of hematite.

**cone cell:** one of the two types of photoreceptor embedded in the retina of the eye; cones are sensitive to colored light. The retina of the human eye contains about three million cones per eye. Cones are modified neurons and are found only in the eyes. Cf. **rod cell.**

**cone pigment gene:** any of several genes that code for the **opsin** pigments that are responsible for **color vision.** See also **color blindness.**

*confer:* (cf. cfr.). 1. (Latin) confer, compare. 2. may appear in a taxonomic name when the affinity of the specimen in question is uncertain, but it compares favorably with the specimen referred to; e.g. *Homo* cf. *habilis.*

**confidence interval** (CI): indication of the statistical certainty of an estimate. In theory, if an experiment is done repeatedly, the confidence interval will include the actual value 95%–99% of the time.

**conflict area:** area of overlap in adjoining territories; this becomes an area of dispute when both residents or resident groups are in it at the same time. Cf. **overlap area.**

**conflict behavior:** strife within an individual animal regarding two incompatible inclinations that are both strongly stimulated, such as attacking and fleeing during a territorial dispute. See **displacement activity, redirected behavior, intention movement.**

**conformation:** quaternary **structure** of a molecule, its shape or topology.

**confounding factor:** unanticipated effects from a variable other than the one being studied.

**confused name:** see *nomen confusum.*

**confusing coloration:** markings on the **pelage** that can distract a predator; some markings are believed to present an optical illusion such as making the animal appear larger.

**congealed karyotype:** vernacular term used to describe an individual or species that has far fewer chromosomes than closely related species, while maintaining an equivalent amount of DNA and close molecular relatedness. Usually due to a series of centric fusions or **Robertsonian translocations.**

**congeneric:** describes organisms belonging to the same **genus** (congeners).

**congenital:** describes phenotypic character or condition recognizable at, and usually before, birth. The term usually refers to hereditary or inborn conditions that are most often harmful, but not all congenital defects are genetic.

**congenital adrenal hyperplasia** (CAH): any one of half a dozen enzyme deficiencies that causes male sex hormones to accumulate abnormally in tissues. In 90% of cases, the deficient enzyme is 21-hydrolase, an autosomal recessive gene; the result is a highly polymorphic system with multiple alleles and four genotypic combinations. (1) In the salt-wasting form, shock and death occur within a few weeks of birth. (2) Early-onset 46,XX congenital virilizing adrenal hyperplasia (CVAH) is a simple masculinizing form in which females have normal internal reproductive organs but enlarged clitorises, and males have enlarged penises and experience precocious puberty. (3) In the more common late onset form, profound masculinization of females occurs at puberty. (4) In the cryptic form, there are no phenotypic symptoms but enzyme and hormone concentrations are elevated. Enlarged adrenal glands are a feature in all cases. Certain HLA haplotypes predispose individuals to this condition: B47 increases the relative risk by 15×.

**congenital anemia:** hereditary childhood disease characterized by a fatal reduction in the number of **erythrocytes.** Aka hypoplastic anemia.

**congenital atrichia:** rare form of hereditary human hair loss shortly after birth, characterized by the complete shedding of hair coupled with papular skin lesions. Aka inherited congenital atrichia. See **human hairless gene.**

**congenital dermal melanocytosis:** macular blue-gray pigmentation, usually in the sacral area of normal infants, due to the entrapment of melanocytes in the **dermis** during development. Commonly called the sacral spot, Mongolian spot or Mongoloid birthmark because of its high frequency in Asian populations (90%), but it also occurs in high frequency in East Africa (80%), Native Americans and Hispanics (45%), and other groups of humans. It is present at birth and typically disappears within four years.

**congenital generalized hypertrichosis:** see **hypertrichosis.**

**conglomerate:** sedimentary rock consisting of older, rounded pebbles (clasts larger than 2 mm) embedded in a younger cement; aka puddingstone.

**Congoid:** obsolete **ethonym** used to denote a 'race' of humans that consists of all sub-Saharan Africans, including the pygmy peoples of central Africa, with the exception of the Khiosan. Aka Negroid. See **Capoid.**

**coniferous:** pertaining to certain drought-resistant **gymnosperms,** the cone-bearing trees: the conifers (redwoods, pines, firs, spruces), evergreen trees and shrubs. See **evergreen forest.** Cf. **deciduous forest.**

‡ **conjoined twins:** identical **twins** who fail to separate completely during the first two weeks after conception. Conjoined twin incidence is about 1.3 : 1 000 000. Colloquially, known as Siamese twins.

**conjoining:** in archaeology, the reassembly of flakes and cores into an original **cobble** such that a blow-by-blow sequence of flake removal can be ascertained.

**conjugation:** temporary union of two bodies, such as 1. exchange of genetic material between unicellular organisms. 2. the intimate association of **homologous chromosomes.** 3. during coitus.

**connectedness:** number and direction of communication links within and between societies.

**connective tissue:** one of the four basic types of tissue; characterized by cells surrounded by an acellular matrix and, in some connective tissues, by extracellular fibers. It functions in binding structures together, forming framework and capsules for organs, storing energy, and carrying substances. Types of connective tissue include bones, cartilage, adipose tissue, blood, and loose and fibrous connective tissue.

**connective tissue disorders:** see **collagen diseases.**

**consanguineous mating** or **marriage:** mating in which the mates share some part of their ancestry, raising the possibility of transmitting hereditary traits inherited from the common ancestor to their offspring; mating between 'blood relatives'.

**consanguinity:** kinship, relationship by blood. Any close genetic relationship due to descent from a **common ancestor. Darwin**'s term for this concept was 'propinquity'. Colloquially applied to blood relatives who have **offspring.** Adjective: consanguineous.

**conscious:** aware, awake; knowingly performing actions. Noun: consciousness.

**consensus sequence:** common nucleotide sequences in sites at which RNA transcription is originated or introns are excised from **pre-mRNA.**

**consequential mortality:** death that occurs during a recovery period following exposure to an agent. See **concomitant mortality** and **delayed mortality.**

**conservation:** 1. in ecology, measures and management that lead to the preservation, restoration, or maximization of natural resources. 2. in taxonomy, a procedure to retain a taxonomic name (conserved name) that would be unavailable because it violates the **International Code of Zoological Nomenclature.**

**conservation archaeology:** recent movement in archaeology that views sites as nonrenewable resources.

**conservation biology:** field of endeavor that studies ways to preserve biological diversity. Conservation biology is a multidisciplinary field and includes individuals trained in law, economics, and many other fields outside biology.

**conservative:** 1. describes an existing condition. 2. describes gradual rather than abrupt change. 3. said of an organism that retains most of the morphological characteristics of its ancestors; e.g. the chimpanzee, which appears to have changed little physically in three million years when compared with humans.

**conservative change:** substitution of one amino acid for another with similar chemical properties, and thus with little or no effect on the structure and function of the protein. See **degenerate codons** and **neutral mutation.**

**conservative replication:** early model of DNA replication that results in one daughter molecule consisting of both old strands, and one consisting of two newly synthesized strands; now discarded in favor of the **semiconservative replication** model.

**conservative trait, character** or **feature:** trait that has changed very little over evolutionary time; such a trait may actually be resistant to change.

**conserved domain:** evolutionarily **conservative** structural unit within the amino acid sequence of several proteins characterized by a specific modular function. Molecular **domains** are combined in various arrangements to produce proteins of unique function; conserved domains are modules that are frequently reused during the process of evolution.

**consistency:** ability to obtain the same results with repeated measurements of an object.

**consortium:** collection of individuals found living together in natural association, especially groups of different phyla, as might be found on a savannah, for example.

‡ **consortship:** temporary relationship between one adult male and an **estrus** female (known as a consort pair) in a **polygamous** primate society, that involves interactions such as grooming, parallel feeding, and sexual behavior. The pair bond dissolves after the estrus period is over.

‡ **conspecific:** belonging to the same species.

**conspecific killing:** members of the same species killing one another. One form of this behavior is **infanticide.**

**constant:** quantity that under specified conditions does not vary with conditions in the environment.

**constant region** (C): the region(s) in an **antibody** of an H and/or L chain closer to the C-terminus, that is invariant within a given class of antibody.

**constitution:** physical character of an organism, i.e. strength, health, temperament. See **biotypology.**

**constitutional mutation:** mutation found in every cell in an individual, indicating that it was inherited; aka germline and familial mutation.

**constitutional typology:** set of hypothetical personality modes that correspond to certain morphological characteristics such as body build. **Lombroso** constructed a typology that putatively accounted for habitual criminals. In 1921, the German psychiatrist Ernst Kretschmer postulated asthenic, pyknic, athletic, and dysplastic types. In 1940, W. H. **Sheldon** identified ectomorphy, mesomorphy, and endomorphy. Most scholars remain skeptical of the utility of such typologies.

**constraint:** any factor that tends to slow the rate of adaptive evolution or to prevent a population from evolving the optimal values of a trait. See, for example, **phylogenetic constraint.**

**constructional morphology:** school that proposes that an organism's final morphology is explained by a complex combination of phylogenetic history, considerations of functional morphology, and limitations imposed by the chemistry and architecture of the organism.

**consultand:** individual (not necessarily affected) who presents for **genetic counseling** and through whom a family with an inherited disorder comes to medical attention. Cf. **proband.**

**consumer:** organism that obtains food directly from producers; aka **heterotroph.** Cf. **autotroph.**

**consumption** (C): in ecological genetics, C = P + R + FU, where P is production, R is respiration, and FU is rejecta; a measure of the total intake of food and other energy taken in by a trophic unit per unit time.

**contact behavior:** huddling or touching of bodies between two or more primates; this behavior is particularly prominent in those primate species in which the infant clings to the mother's fur. See **clinging infant.**

**contact inhibition:** property of cells that inhibits **cell division** when cells are in close contact.

**contact stratum:** topmost layer of an archaeological site.

**contagious disease:** infectious condition transmitted by a **fomite,** by a **vector,** or by direct physical contact between an infected and an uninfected individual.

‡ **contemporaneous:** living or having lived at the same time; contemporary.

**contest competition:** form of **competition** in which some members of the population obtain a larger share of resources, while unsuccessful competitors do not obtain sufficient resources for survival and reproduction. Cf. **scramble competition.**

‡ **context:** 1. circumstance, facts, events, or objects that precede or succeed something of interest. 2. in archaeology, the situation in which an artifact is found; **archaeological context.** 3. see **epistasis.**

**contextless artifact:** cultural element with no **provenance** because it was discovered and removed by an amateur, discovered and removed accidentally, or transported by weathering agents from its place of origin.

**contig:** length of a mapped segment of a chromosome, expressed in **kilobases** or **megabases.**

**contig mapping:** process of mapping segments of a chromosome by sequencing or characterizing small segments and by connecting each with adjacent segments by identifying overlapping (identical) zones. Aka the **shotgun approach** to sequencing. This is the same mental algorithm as is used in **dendrochronology.**

**contiguous:** characterized by tangent but nonoverlapping boundaries, as with some territories.

**continent:** one of the (usually eight) main land masses on the earth, each usually associated with a continental plate: Africa, Antarctica, Asia, Australia, Europe, Greenland, North America, and South America. Cf. **plate tectonics.**

**continental bridge hypothesis:** proposal that **continents** used to span the areas where oceans exist today, and formed bridges between what are today's separated land masses. Largely replaced by the **continental drift theory.** Some **land bridges** seem to have existed owing to **eustatic** fluctuation in sea levels.

**continental crust:** portion of the earth's **crust** that includes both the **continents** and the **continental shelves.**

‡ **continental drift theory:** proposal originally based upon similarity of coastline shapes of the circum-Atlantic continents that land masses move independently over the earth's surface. Proposed in 1912 by meteorologist Alfred **Wegener,** the theory was virtually proved in the 1960s when deep-sea cores from the drilling vessel *Glomar Challenger* showed that the floor of the Atlantic ocean is symmetrical in both composition and age on both sides of the mid-Atlantic ridge. The original concepts have been subsumed by **plate tectonics.** Aka Gondwanaland hypothesis, sea-floor spreading.

**continental shelf:** sea bed found at the edge of a continental margin. The shelf usually slopes gradually away from the shoreline to a depth of 200 m, marking a submerged former shoreline, and where an abrupt steepening indicates the edge of the continental slope.

**contingency:** evolutionary concept that later stages of the evolution of any taxon are dependent on the earlier stages in that group's history. See **historicity, evolutionary constraint.**

**contingency table:** arrangement of data in two or more rows and columns in which observations are classified according to two variables; often constructed prior to execution of, for example, a **chi-square test.**

**continuous estrus:** condition in which females are sexually receptive to males throughout the year and can achieve conception at any time during the year.

**continuous random variable:** element, character or **trait** described by a continuous series of infinitely small steps; having a continuous spectrum of values from one given extreme to the other; quantitative rather than qualitative variation. Aka scale variable.

**continuous recording:** behavioral observation recording rule in which all instances of a behavior are recorded as they occurs, with the time when an event occurred noted.

‡ **continuous trait, character, or feature:** physical **character** that exhibits measurable and continuous

metric gradation between two extreme population values; in humans, such a character is **stature**. Continuous traits are usually expressions of both environmental and genetic factors, the latter being the combined action of several loci (see **polygenic**). Aka metric variation. Cf. **discrete trait** and **discontinuous variation**.

**continuous variation:** see **continuous trait**.

‡ **continuum:** 1. gradient of relationships that fall along an integrated line; often used in reference to a biological continuum of all life on the planet. 2. scale of an environmental gradient based upon changes that occur in the physical characteristics of an **ecological community**'s composition.

**contracted burial position:** common method of placing a body in a grave during ancient interments. The body is placed on one side with the limbs markedly flexed and with the knees drawn up to the chin. See **burial** and **grave**.

**contraction:** shortening or tensing; often in reference to the forceful shortening of muscle cells.

**contradiction and induction, method of:** see **method of contradiction and induction**.

**contralateral:** refers to a structure that is on the opposite side; the contralateral structure may be working together with its counterpart. See **ipsilateral**.

**control:** in primate sociobiology, the intervention by one or more individuals to reduce or alter aggression between other members of the group.

**control group:** in experimental design, a reference group that provides a basis for comparison with an **experimental group**. The control group is exposed to all the conditions affecting the experimental group, except one: the potential causative variable.

**controlled use of fire:** physical evidence of controlled combustion found in direct association with early humans. Many confirmed hearths are associated with the **Mousterian tool tradition** and later sites; the controlled use of fire at early sites has been systematically challenged or refuted, but see **Ambrona**, **Clacton-on-Sea**, **Ehringsdorf**, **Lazaret**, **Makapansgat**, **Torralba**, and **Zhoukoudian**.

**controlling factor:** any factor whose effect becomes more pronounced or severe when populations become more dense.

**conule:** eminence on the crown of a tooth that is smaller than a **cusp**; secondary cusp, used synonymously with **cuspule**.

**conus medullaris:** caudal, tapering portion of the spinal cord.

**convection:** heat exchange between an object and a gas or liquid.

**Convention on International Trade in Endangered Species of Wild Fauna and Flora** (CITES): international organization established to help in the effort to regulate importation of threatened and endangered animals and plants.

**conventional behavior:** any behavior by which members of a population reveal their presence and allow others to assess the density of the population (V. C. Wynne-Edwards). A more elaborate form of such behavior is referred to as an epideictic display.

**convergence:** 1. approaching or inclination toward a common point. 2. in evolution, similarity not due to descent. See **convergent evolution**. 3. in organisms with **stereoscopic vision**, movement of the eyes to focus simultaneously on a near object.

**convergence flexion:** ability of some mammals, particularly primates, to splay the five **digits** out and to bend them together in a convergent manner so that they can grasp objects.

**convergent dental arcade: alveolar** row in which the molars and premolars converge towards the midline and the anterior dentition as the progression moves from back to front, forming a V-shaped arcade. Characteristic of some early **hominids** and other primates, particularly Malagasy **prosimians**. Cf. **parabolic dental arcade**, **parallel dental arcade**.

‡ **convergent evolution:** process of independent evolution of structural or functional similarity in two or more unrelated (or very distantly related) lineages or forms owing to adaptation to similar environments, not genotypic similarity. The independent development of flight in both birds and insects is an example of convergent evolution. Often confused with **parallel evolution**. See **analogy**. Cf. **homoplasy**.

**conversion:** see **gene conversion**.

**convolution:** folding in or twisting of tissue upon itself that results in an elevated area separated by a depressed area or a groove on a structure's surface, e.g. in the primate brain. See **cerebral gyri** and **cerebral sulci**.

**Cooley's anemia:** see **thalassemia**.

**Coolidge effect:** effect of a novel female or new setting on the sexual activity of a male. A male loses interest in a female following copulation, but can be sexually aroused by another female or by the same female in a different surrounding. The Coolidge effect attributes this to the novelty of the situation, in contrast to the **sociobiological** explanation, which is that the male regains sexual interest in order to produce offspring with an unfertilized female.

**Coon, Carlton Stevens** (1904–81): anthropologist, teacher, Professor at Harvard University (1928–48); with **Hooton**, Coon educated the second and third generations of physical anthropologists in America. President, **AAPA** (1961–3); Viking Fund medallist (1951). Coon supported **Weidenreich** on the **Neandertal** question, advocating the **trellis model** of **hominid evolution**, and viewed humanity as composed of deeply rooted, regionally homogenous **races**, i.e. as a **polytypic** species. Author of *The Races of Europe* (1939) and *The Origin of Races* (1962).

**cooperation:** behavioral relationship in which two or more individuals act together for a mutually beneficial result; most activities in human societies presume some form of cooperation, from food market exchanges to political activities. Most behavioral biologists do not use the term cooperation for animal activities, although in some cases, such as baboon group hunting, this term is used. See **mutualism, altruism.**

**cooperative trait, character,** or **feature:** behavior that incurs a benefit to both an actor and recipient, measured as a quantitative increase in reproductive success. Aka cooperative act or behavior. See **altruism.**

**coordinate caliper: sliding caliper** that has a movable coordinate arm attached to it for measuring depths below or elevations above two points.

**coordination:** interaction within a group directed toward a common goal; this may be done without any leadership being exerted on the individuals in the group (especially in nonhuman animals) or from a central authority (especially among humans).

**Cope, Edward Drinker** (1840–97): US paleontologist; known for his competitive harvesting of equid fossils from the American Mid-west, Cope is less well known for the Eocene primates he excavated and described; also well-remembered for his neo-Lamarckism and the exposition of **Cope's laws**, but less so for the obscure but important fact that he was the first scientist to use the word **evolution** in the title and text of an English-language publication (1868); later also owner–editor of the successful journal *The American Naturalist*.

**Copelemur** (= *Pelycodus*) **Gingerich and Simons, 1977:** adapoid **prosimian** from the early Eocene of North America belonging to the notharctid subfamily Notharctinae; five species; poorly known. Previously included within *Pelycodus*, from which this genus may have evolved. Unfused **mandibular symphysis.** Dental formula: 2.1.4.3/ 2.1.4.3; differs from *Pelycodus* in that the teeth are smaller, molars have taller crests, and the fourth lower premolars have a well-defined **metaconid**; it has been suggested that this primate was a specialized **insectivore.** Body mass estimated to range from 1 to 3.5 kg (which would not be consistent with insectivory). See Appendix 1 for taxonomy.

**Copernican revolution:** change in the world view from **geocentricity** to **heliocentricity** since the sixteenth century; i.e. recognition that the earth revolves around the sun, and not the reverse. See **paradigm shift.**

**Copernicus, Nicolas** (1473–1543): Polish scientist, astronomer; promulgated the now accepted theory of **heliocentricity.**

**Cope's laws or rules:** nineteenth century observations by **Cope** 1. that a species' survival is related to the degree of its maintenance of generalized adaptations; conversely, that specialization is maladaptive. Aka law of the unspecialized. 2. that phyletic lineages tend to be founded by organisms of relatively small size, and that successive organisms tend to increase in size through time. This latter phenomenon is currently thought to be explained by climatic shifts as well as by corresponding responses of organisms along a continuum from *r*-**selected species** to *K*-**selected species.**

**coppertail monkey:** vernacular for *Cercopithecus ascanius*.

**coprolite:** fossilized **feces.** Coprolites can provide important information about a fossil species, such as its diet.

**coprolith:** abnormal hard mess of **feces.**

**coprology:** study of animal feces.

**coprophagy:** ingestion of feces. In some small, herbivorous mammals this can be the reingestion of their own feces; these mammals have guts that are too short to allow complete breakdown of cellulose by **symbionts.** Such animals typically have a relatively large **cecum** where symbiotic microbes break down cellulose; this process continues as the nutrients are reingested and begin to be absorbed at the lower end of the small intestine. Common among voles and rabbits; among primates only *Lepilemur* has been suggested as a coprophage. Aka refection, caecotrophy. See **caecotrophic pellets.**

**copulation:** joining together, i.e. the sexual union of organisms; the sex act, or intercourse; in a broader sense, behaviors (in animals) potentially leading to insemination and **reproduction.**

**copulin:** substance that is a metabolite of sex hormones, exuded by genital skin and sebaceous glands, and that some researchers believe acts as a powerful **pheromone** and is important in initiating sexual behavior in many mammals, including primates.

**copying error:** induction of a **mutation** during cell division by the failure of the gene copying mechanism, **DNA replication.** Aka copy error.

**Coquerel's dwarf lemur:** vernacular for *Mirza coquereli*.

**coracoid:** crow-like; used to describe anatomical structures that have a bird-like appearance; e.g., **coracoid process** of the **scapula.**

**coracoid process (of the mandible):** anterior projection of the ascending ramus of the **mandible** that resembles a crooked little finger or beak. It serves as a site of attachment for the temporal muscle.

**coracoid process (of the scapula):** anterior projection of the **scapula** that resembles a crooked little finger or beak. It serves as a site of attachment for chest and arm muscles.

**cord blood:** blood obtained from the **umbilical cord**.

**cordate:** heart-shaped.

‡ **core:** 1. mass of stone from which **flakes** have been removed; sometimes a core is the relict of tool-making, but may itself also be shaped and modified to serve as a **tool** in its own right. See **core tools**. 2. portion of the interior of the earth from the center to the **mantle**, the source of the earth's **magnetic field**.

‡ **core area:** that portion of a **home range** or **territory** used most intensively by a social group of animals, generally including the most vital resources such as favored sleeping areas and **foraging range**.

**core industry:** set of related stone tools that consist predominantly of cores.

**core population:** one or more populations of the **metapopulation** that is stable in population size. Cf. **satellite area**.

**core tool:** mass of stone from which **flakes** have been removed, e.g. the **Acheulean** hand-ax (probably a core from which flakes were removed as needed), and the **Levallois** core.

**Cori disease:** glycogen storage disease (III).

**corium:** portion of skin underneath the **epidermis**. The corium is the part of the skin that is chemically treated during the tanning process. Aka **dermis**.

**cormic index:** ratio of **sitting height** to **stature**; sitting height divided by total height and multiplied by 100. This index exhibits population variation, being highest in Africans and African-derived populations, intermediate in Europeans, western and southern Asians, and lowest among Far Eastern populations and American Indians. Used especially in **human engineering** for spatial utilization designs and clothing. See **brachycormic, metriocranic, macrocormic**. Cf. **Manouvrier's index**.

**cornea:** transparent anterior portion of the fibrous surface of the eye.

**corneum:** see **stratum corneum epidermis** and **stratum corneum unguis**.

**cornification:** see **keratinization**.

**cornu:** hornlike projection.

**corona radiata:** cells that surround the zona pellucida of the **secondary oocyte**.

**coronal:** pertaining to a crown, garland or wreath.

‡ **coronal plane:** anatomical plane that divides a body into anterior and posterior halves, parallel to the **coronal suture**. Aka frontal plane.

‡ **coronal suture:** articulation between the frontal bone and the parietal bones.

**coronary circulation:** in reference to the blood vessels that supply and drain the heart.

**coronoid:** beak-like; e.g. **coronoid process** of the **mandibular ramus**.

**coronoid fossa (of the humerus):** depression on the anterior side of the **distal** end of the **humerus**, above the **trochlea**, that receives the ulnar **coronoid process** when the elbow is flexed.

**coronoid process:** 1. generally, in reference to the anterior branch of the **mandibular ramus** that serves as a site of attachment for chewing muscles. 2. inferior and anterior portion of the **trochlear notch** of the **ulna** that fits into the **coronoid fossa** of the **humerus** when the elbow is flexed.

**coronolateral sulcus:** in the brain, a groove running longitudinally along the lateral side of the cortex; found typically in many prosimians.

**corpora quadrigemina:** structure in the dorsal portion of the **mid-brain** concerned with visual and auditory reflexes. Four paired bilateral elevations constitute the **superior colliculi** (superior pair concerned with visual reflexes) and the **inferior colliculi** (inferior pair concerned with auditory reflexes).

**corporeal:** of or pertaining to the body.

**corpulence:** fatness; fleshiness.

**corpus:** body, e.g. **corpus callosum** of the primate brain.

**corpus callosum:** thick collection of nerve fibers that connects the two cerebral hemispheres; consists of white matter.

**corpus luteum:** mass of yellowish glandular tissue remaining at the site of an erupted follicle after **ovulation**; source of the hormone **progesterone** but degenerates if no **implantation** occurs.

**corpus luteum hormone:** see **progesterone**.

**corpuscle:** 1. small body or mass. 2. a cell capable of moving freely in the body. 3. an encapsulated sensory end organ, such as a Pacian corpuscle.

**correlated progression:** proposal that traits are interrelated, that character complexes evolve interactively, and thus that certain evolutionary changes in a phenotype cannot be realized until others have occurred.

**correlation:** mutual relation of two or more things or parts. In statistics, an association between the **dependent variable(s)** and the **independent variable(s)**.

**correlation coefficient** ($r$): in statistics, an indicator of the strength of an association between the **dependent variable** and the **independent variable**(s); the value of $r$ can range from $-1$ to $+1$.

**corridor:** connection between land masses or one defined by geological terrain and through which organisms may disperse or migrate, as in the ice-free corridor in North America during the late Pleistocene.

**cortex:** 1. outer layer of an organ or structure; cortical. 2. in the **cerebrum** of the human brain, the highly convoluted expansion of the neopallium, the **gray matter** that contains centers of consciousness and rational thought. 3. the outer rind of a cobble or **core** possessing the ancient patina or weathering surface;

one of the diagnostic features that archaeologists use to distinguish a stone **tool** from a naturally occurring **geofact**.

**cortical asymmetry:** nonidentical left and right hemispheres of the brain. Cortical asymmetry is typical of humans and, to some extent, the great apes. In fossil **endocasts**, a pronounced **left-occipital–right-frontal petalia pattern** is considered indicative of the asymmetry peculiar to the hominids. See **brain lateralization**.

**cortical bone:** see **compact bone**.

**cortical bone thickness:** measurement of the layer of **compact bone**, usually in long bones. Cortical bone thickness varies within the same bone (e.g. lateral vs. medial sides) and reflects such factors as weight-bearing and stress on the bone due to size and force of muscles.

**corticoid:** see glucocorticoid.

**cortical evolution:** see **radial unit model of cortical evolution**.

**cortisone:** a natural **glucocorticoid** that is metabolically convertable to cortisol. The human **adrenal cortex** secretes only minute amounts; most that is found in peripheral plasma is formed from cortisol by a reversible reaction. Cortisone functions to regulate carbohydrates during the conversion of fat, protein, and lactate into **glucose**, primarily in the liver (gluconeogenesis).

**cosmic teleology:** belief that the universe (and its components) is directed toward a final objective or goal, such as perfection.

**cosmid:** large **cloning vector** consisting of a plasmid with sequences that allow packaging in a lambda phage head; used for cloning large DNA segments to be amplified and sequenced.

**cosmogenic radionuclide dating:** absolute **radiometric dating** technique based on the fact that unstable molecules are constantly produced in quartz crystals located on the earth's surface by exposure to atmospheric cosmic rays; if the quartz is suddenly buried at depths greater than 20 m this production ceases. Useful molecules produced in this way include $^{26}$Al (aluminum-26) and $^{10}$Be (beryllium-10) with known rates of decay.

**cosmogony:** any society's belief about the beginnings and the composition of the world or universe, and that contains a local variant of a **creation myth**.

‡ **cosmology:** 1. in physical science, study or scheme of the origin and general structure of the universe, including its elements and laws, and especially the properties of space, time, causality, freedom, and meaning. 2. see **cosmogony**.

**cosmopolitan medicine:** ethnomedical system that holds to an organic, germ theory of disease, that stresses the values of technology and control over the environment, and employs healers aligned in hierarchical tiers. Aka Western medicine.

**cost:** potential loss of **fitness** to an individual associated with any particular behavior. See **cost–benefit analysis**. Cf. **benefit**.

**costa, costae:** see **rib**.

**cost–benefit analysis:** approach used in behavioral ecology in which behavior is examined based on the net potential loss (**cost**) or potential gain (**benefit**) associated with any particular behavior, and that affects **inclusive fitness**.

**cost of selection:** number of genetic deaths (i.e. non-replication of the predominant **allele** by **homozygotes** or **heterozygotes** for the allele) required to change an **allele frequency** from 0.0 to near 1.0. It is estimated that this requires deaths that equal about 30 times the size of the population, assuming that population size is stable. This can happen quickly if only a very few **loci** are involved, or more slowly for a larger number of loci. Aka cumulative substitutional load. Cf. **Muller's ratchet**.

**costal cartilage:** cartilage associated with the ribs.

**costotransverse:** between the left and right ribs of the body.

**Cot value:** parameter used to measure renaturation of DNA, given as the original concentration of DNA × time. Cot + is the Cot required to proceed to half completion of the reaction; highly repetitive **DNA sequences** renature at low Cot values, whereas unique sequences renature at high Cot values.

**coterie:** 1. male, several females, and their offspring. 2. group of animals that defend a territory against outside groups.

**cotransduction:** simultaneous activation of two or more genes, usually when the activated sequence contains two or more genes.

**Cottevieille-Giraudet theory, the:** proposal in 1928 by R. Cottevieille-Giraudet that at least some peoples later identified as Native Americans may have originated in Europe, rather than solely by a Bering Strait or other western point of entry. Specifically, he reaffirmed the earlier observations by Hamy, Quatrefages, G. Saint-Hilaire and Deniker that there are resemblances between members of the tribes of northeastern America and Upper Paleolithic Europeans such as **Cro-Magnon**. This hypothesis has recently been revived; see **Solutrean–Clovis similarity hypothesis** and **haplotype X**.

**cottontop tamarin:** vernacular for *Saguinus oedipus*.

**cotwin:** one of a pair of **twins**; used to distinguish individual twin pairs from many such pairs, especially during a research study.

**cotwin control study:** administration of different treatments to **identical twins** to study the effects on development while controlling for genetic background.

**cotyloid:** see **scaphoid**.

**cotype:** former term for each specimen in a series, in the absence of a formally designated **holotype**; syntype.

**counterselection:** arguably, any maladaptive event, such as war, that culls those vigorous and healthy individuals who would have reproduced.

**counteracting selection:** operation of selection pressures on two or more levels of organization, e.g. on the individual, family and population, in such a way that certain genes are favored at one level but disfavored at another; aka antagonistic selection. Cf. **reinforcing selection**.

**countershading: pelage** pattern in mammals in which the ventral surface of the body and the insides of the legs are pale, while the back is dark. The back is usually in light and if the undersides were the same color they would be seen as darker; by countershading, the mammal form is obscured and less conspicuous. This pattern is almost universal among mammals (including primates).

**coup-de-poing:** simply flaked, triangular stone **tool**, one of the earliest formal instruments; probably used for a variety of purposes. Aka **hand-ax** (or hand axe), fist ax, Beil, Faust Keil.

**coupling linkage:** in a dihybrid cross, the presence of both dominant alleles on one chromosome, and the presence of both recessing alleles on the other, e.g. AB/ab. Cf. **repulsion linkage**.

**courtship:** patterns of behavior that signal intention or initiate mating; not all such behavior results in **copulation**. Courtship functions to bring the sexes together in those species that are **noyau**, relaxes the inclination to attack or flee, synchronizes both partners for mating, and prevents interspecific breeding. Aka courtship ritual.

**cousin:** child of an aunt or uncle; a kinship term that identifies a genealogical or adopted degree of relationship in a **nuclear family** or **extended family**. See **father, mother, brother, sister, uncle, aunt**.

**covariance:** expected value of the product of the deviations of two random variables from their respective means.

**covariation:** any systematic relationship between variables.

**covarions:** codons that could change an amino acid during transcription of mRNA without a serious deleterious effect, owing either to the **redundancy of the genetic code** or to the functional similarity of the two amino acids. See **neutral theory of molecular evolution**. Cf. **varion**.

**covering laws:** explanation of a phenomenon as a particular example of an existing law that 'covers' similar phenomena. A covering law suggests an outcome or a particular relationship between two sets of evidence, especially as described by Carl Hempel in *Aspects of Scientific Explanation* (1965).

**covolo:** small **rockshelter**.

**Cowper's glands:** see **bulbourethral glands**.

‡ **coxal bone:** one of a pair of bones that form half the **pelvic girdle**; this bone is composed of three bones, the ilium, ischium, and pubis, that fuse into the single coxal bone. Previously referred to as the innominate, now considered to be an incorrect usage.

**coxal joint: ball-and-socket joint** formed between the **femur** and the **acetabulum** of the **coxal bone**. This articulation permits flexion, extension, adduction, abduction, and circumduction of the leg.

**CpG doublet:** adjacent sequence of **cytosine** and **guanine** nucleotides along a sugar-phosphate backbone, reading from the 5′ toward the 3′ end of DNA. A series of such doublets is called a **CpG island**; because of the **base pairing rule**, the islands form a short **palindrome** and are often sites of **DNA methylation** (at cytocine): 5′…CpG CpG…3′ 3′…GpC GpC…5′.

**CpG island:** 'CG-rich' regions of a genome; portions of a genome that contain more than 55% cytosine and guanine that in over 60% of cases indicate the 5′ end of a gene. See **CpG doublet**.

**crab-eating macaque:** vernacular for *Macaca fascicularis*.

**cradle board head:** see **plano-occipitaly**.

‡ **cranial:** helmetlike; pertaining to that portion of the skull that encloses the brain, i.e. the **cranium**.

**cranial amulet:** charm made from the trepanned portion of a human cranium, and usually believed to have certain magical properties.

**cranial base:** see **basicranium**.

**cranial base flatness index:** ratio that provides for a comparison of cranial vault heights; basion–porion height divided by basion–bregma height and multiplied by 100. This index identifies low cranial vaults (ratios around 13.70) and high cranial vaults (ratios around 18.40).

**cranial breadth–height index:** ratio of cranial height to cranial width; **cranial height** divided by **maximum cranial breadth** multiplied by 100. Aka height–breadth index. See **tapeinocranic, metriocranic, acrocranic**.

‡ **cranial capacity:** estimate of the volume of the brain case, usually measured directly by determining the **endocranial volume**; an approximation of **brain** mass. See **cubic centimeter** and **endocranial volume**.

**cranial–caudal gradient:** developmental condition in which the head is larger than the tail in immature individuals; seen in most organisms, including humans.

**cranial cavity:** hollow space surrounded by the bones of the cranium. In life this area contains the brain;

thus, it is possible to obtain a volumetric measurement of the brain in a nonliving individual.

**cranial deformation:** artificial remodeling of the shape of the infant **cranium**, often due to unintentional cultural factors such as cradle boards, or carrying straps, or to intentional modification by binding the head with tight wrappings or other methods that apply pressure to the area that is being deformed. Known from every continent except Australia. Cf. **dental mutilation** and **natural cranial deformation.**

**cranial fossa:** one of three depressions in the floor of the cranium. The anterior cranial fossa lies above the **orbits** and is composed of portions of the ethmoid, sphenoid, and frontal bones; in life it receives the frontal lobe of the brain. The middle cranial fossa is located behind the orbits and is composed of parts of the sphenoid and temporal bones; it houses the temporal lobe of the brain. The posterior cranial fossa is the largest and deepest fossa and extends from the dorsum sella of the sphenoid to the floor of the occipital bone. It is also composed of parts of the temporal and parietal bones. In life it receives the occipital lobe and cerebellum of the brain; the **foramen magnum**, which transits the spinal cord, is also in this fossa. Plural: cranial fossae.

**cranial height** (ba-b): **craniometric** measurement; distance from the **basion** to the **bregma** as measured with sliding calipers. Aka cranial vault height. See Appendix 7 for an illustration of the anatomical landmarks used.

**cranial index:** ratio of cranial width to cranial length; **maximum cranial breadth** divided by **maximum cranial length** multiplied by 100. See **dolichocranic, mesocranic, brachycranic, hyperbrachycranic.**

**cranial landmark:** see **craniometric landmark.**

**cranial length–height index:** ratio of cranial height to cranial length; **cranial height** divided by **maximum cranial length** multiplied by 100. This index is applied to skeletal populations. Aka height–length index. See **chamaecranic, orthocranic, hypsicranic.**

**cranial module:** index that provides a numerical assessment for the size of a skull; cranial length + cranial height + cranial breadth divided by 3.

**cranial suture closure:** pertaining to the contact and fusion of the articulations (sutures) of the skull that begins in early childhood. Degree of cranial suture closure is used for age estimation in archaeological populations.

**cranial vault:** arched portion of the **cranium**; the **calotte.**

**craniofacial evolution:** changes in the proportions of the face to the rest of the skull over evolutionary time in a phylogenetic line.

**craniofacial growth:** growth in the skeletal elements of the face and skull.

**craniology:** science dealing with variation in shape, size and proportion of the skull, especially among *Homo sapiens*. Historically, particularly in the nineteenth century, craniology was used to compare different human populations, especially in terms of **cranial capacity**, and by inference, intelligence.

**craniometric:** pertaining to the measurement of the human **cranium**. See **craniometry.**

**craniometric landmark:** feature found consistently on skulls that is used as a reference point for measurements of the skull. Craniometric landmarks were developed for use on modern human skulls, but many can be applied to fossil species and other primates; however, not all of the landmarks developed for modern humans are present on earlier hominid species. Sometimes referred to as **anthropometric landmark**. See Appendix 7.

**craniometric measurements:** standard measures of the cranium. Some 282 or more measures have been defined, and at least 108 indices have been created. Cf. **osteometric measurements.**

**craniometry:** field of study that performs measurements on the human skull. See **craniometric landmark.**

**craniophor:** scaffold-like instrument used to hold a skull in any desired position as it is studied.

**craniorhachischisis:** congenital condition in which there is incomplete closure of the skull and vertebral column.

**cranioscopy:** archaic; older term for **craniometry**. See **anthropometry.**

‡ **cranium:** inconsistently applied term whose variations include: 1. portion of the skull that includes the bones that surround the brain case; this is referred to as the **neurocranium** by some. 2. skull without the **mandible** or **hyoid**; the term **skull** is often used interchangeably with cranium. 3. as sometimes used in comparative anatomy (including primate comparative anatomy), the skull which is composed of a neurocranium, **basicranium**, and **splanchnocranium**; i.e. this approach defines the cranium as the skull. Plural: crania. Aka brain case. Cf. **calvaria.**

*Craseops sylvestris* **Stock, 1934:** archaic mammal of the late Eocene of the Rocky Mountain region of North America, belonging to the **plesiadapiform** family **Microsyopidae; monotypic;** some authorities assign this genus to the order Insectivora. Dental formula uncertain. Estimated body mass around 2 kg. See Appendix 1 for taxonomy.

**crash:** to collapse or fall suddenly; see **population crash.**

**created types:** see **fixity of species** and **polygenesis.**

**creatine:** nitrogenous compound found primarily in muscle tissue; see **creatinine**. Aka creatin.

**creatinine:** compound originating primarily in muscle tissue, a waste product derived from **creatine** metabolism and excreted in urine.

**creatinine coefficient:** ratio of creatinine to body mass during a 24 h period, used to estimate **obesity**.

**creation myth:** story of the beginning of the world and the creation of the first of one's own people. All cultures have ethnocentric creation myths that are strongly believed and thought to be mutually exclusive. See **cosmogony** and **ethnocentrism**.

**creation science** (CS): see **scientific creationism**.

**Creationism:** idea that the earth and its inhabitants came about literally as described in the first chapter of Genesis in the Bible, in six natural days. Scientists who have been strong supporters included Voltaire and **Linnaeus**. Aka fundamentalism.

**creative evolution:** modified view of evolution in which the French philosopher Henri Bergson proposed an *elan vital* that provided for **progressive evolution** and was thus a blend of **natural selection** and a **teleological** element that explicitly provided for religion.

**crenulation:** wrinkled appearance (secondary folding) of enamel on the **occlusal surface** of the teeth of some species of mammal; consistently found in molar teeth of the modern orangutan (***Pongo pygmaeus***); also known from **australopithecine** and **pithecanthropine** teeth. Aka enamel wrinkling.

‡ **crepuscular:** describes an activity cycle in which an animal is active during the periods of low light, i.e. twilight and dawn.

**crescent:** crescent-shaped bifacially flaked stone tool generally restricted to the American Paleo-Indian period and usually found near extinct Pleistocene lakeshores. Such tools may have been used for hunting large shorebirds.

**Creswellian:** late Paleolithic tool industry of Britain that existed from 12 000 to 8000 BP. Characterized by blades, awls, shouldered points, and uniserial and biserial harpoon points.

**crest:** 1. ridge or prominent feature, such as a ridge of tissue or tuft of hair. 2. osteologic landmark that is a thickened, ridgelike projection of bone for the attachment of muscle, e.g. **sagittal crest**. Cf. **sagittal ridge**. 3. any design, decoration, or identifying mark.

**crested gibbon:** vernacular for *Hylobates concolor*.

**crested mangabey:** vernacular for *Cercocebus galeritus*.

**Cretaceous period:** most recent period of the **Mesozoic era**, lasting from approximately 136 to about 65 mya; characterized by final rifting between South America and Africa; a **mass extinction** event defines the terminal Cretaceous. Fossil plants include ancestors to the **Angiosperms**; dinosaurs are the dominant terrestrial animal, and birdlike fossils are also found in this period.

‡ **Cretaceous–Tertiary boundary** (K/T): in geology, the boundary between the strata of the **Mesozoic era** (the Age of Reptiles) and those of the later **Cenozoic era** (the Age of Mammals); this boundary is dated to approximately 65 mya. See **chicxulub structure**.

**cretinism:** mental and growth retardation in infants resulting from **iodine** deficiency in the mother during pregnancy, or deficiency of thyroid hormones in other cases. Hereditary cretinism is accompanied by goiter and deafness, and can be caused by any of several autosomal recessive genes.

**Creutzfeldt–Jakob disease** or **syndrome, familial** (fCJD): in humans, a slow but fatal heritable degenerative disease of brain tissue caused by two simultaneous conditions: mutation from aspartic acid to asparagine at position 178 in the **prion protein**, and methionine homozygosity at position 129. A related heritable condition, **familial fatal insomnia** (FFI), like CJD, is caused by valine homozygosity at position 129. See **Creutzfeldt–Jakob disease, new variant**.

**Creutzfeldt–Jakob disease, new variant** (nvCJD): fatal degenerative disease of the human brain, sporadic and nonfamilial, now recognized as one of the **transmissible spongiform encephalopathies** (TSEs). In March 1996 a new variant of CJD in Great Britain was linked to exposure through the consumption of beef infected with **bovine spongiform encephalopathy**, or 'mad cow disease'. About 85% of all CJD cases are now recognized as nvCJD and are associated with **methionine homozygosity** in the **prion protein**. See **Creutzfeldt–Jakob disease, familial**, and **Creutzfeldt–Jakob disease, sporadic**.

**Creutzfeldt–Jakob disease, sporadic** (sCJD): occurrences of symptoms of CJD in an isolated patient with no family history of fCJD, nor history of living or traveling in a region where it might be transmitted as **nvCJD**. sCJD is associated with valine homozygosity at position 129 of the **prion protein**.

**cribiform plate:** region of the ethmoid bone on either side of the **crista galli** that connects the two lateral masses; it forms a portion of the roof of the nasal cavity and contains the olfactory foramina through which olfactory nerves pass.

**cribra orbitale:** pathological condition in which laminar bone in the orbital roof becomes porous; this results in an increase of **cancellous bone** and an increase in thickness of the orbital plate; the spaces within the cancellous bone are filled by a net of vascular tissue from the **diploe** to the region of the orbit. Aka usura orbitae, hyperostosis spongiosa orbitae, cribra orbitalia.

**Cricetinae:** hamsters; subfamily of the rodent family Muridae (the largest mammalian family, with 1336 species). Distributed in Europe and central and western Asia. Given family status by some authors and in historical texts. Cricetinines are important index animals used by primate evolutionary biologists.

**Crick, Francis Henry Compton** (1916–2004): molecular biologist at the Cavendish Laboratory in Cambridge; Nobel laureate. In 1953, working with James **Watson** and using data collected by R. **Franklin** and M. Wilkins, Crick deduced the structure of DNA, and participated in subsequent efforts to determine the **genetic code**. Late in his career, Crick was president emeritus of the Salk Institute for Biological Studies, favored an extraterrestrial origin for life on earth, and sought the neuroscientific basis of consciousness.

**cri-du-chat syndrome:** congenital syndrome marked by profound physical deformity (low-set ears, facial disproportion, microcephaly, wide-set eyes), profound mental retardation, and a shrill vocalization in infancy that sounds like a cat's cry. Cause is a deletion in chromosome 5. Most affected individuals are aborted spontaneously or die in the first year of life, but some live into adulthood. Aka cat's cry syndrome, 5p-syndrome.

**criss-cross inheritance:** the transmission of sex-linked traits from a parent of one sex to progeny of the opposite sex.

**crista:** 1. the folded, inner membranes of a **mitochondrion** that contain the molecules engaged in energy formation. 2. crest or ridge present on the **occlusal surface** of an upper tooth. This term frequently has an additional descriptive name added to it, as in entocrista. Cf. **cristid**.

**crista galli:** superior portion of the ethmoid bone, which anchors membranes that enclose the brain.

**crista obliqua:** enamel crest on the upper molars of **hominoids** that bridges the **protocone** and **metacone**.

**crista orbitalia:** condition resulting from iron-deficiency **anemia**, which manifests as a thinning of the outer table of bone, exposing the porotic bone underneath; evidence of paleonutritional **stress** in prehistoric skeletons. See **paleonutrition** and **porotic hyperostosis**.

**cristid:** crest or ridge present on the **occlusal surface** of an lower tooth. This term frequently has an additional descriptive name added to it, as in entocristid. Cf. **crista**.

**cristid obliqua:** ridge of enamel on the lower molars running obliquely from the hypoconid to the back of the trigonid.

**cristodont:** condition found in teeth with distinct crests on the crown.

**criterion:** standard upon which a decision may be made.

**criterion variable** (g): See **dependent variable**.

**critical function:** trait that is absolutely necessary for the continued survival of an organism during a season or a short period of time, even though this feature is not necessary the majority of time, such as the specialized dentition of a facultative **gummivore** that may eat gums for only a few weeks or months out of the year.

**critical period:** 1. time during development of an organism when a system is most readily influenced by environmental factors. 2. time when the embryo is most susceptible to the effects of **teratogenis**; in humans, developmental weeks 2–9; aka sensitive developmental period. 3. see **sensitive phase** of behavioral development.

**critical value:** in statistics, the value of the statistic that marks the edge of the region(s) of rejection in hypothesis testing; for example, that value of a $\chi^2$, $z$, $t$, or $F$ statistic that occurs with a relative frequency of alpha or less when a **null hypothesis** is true.

**CRL:** abbreviation for **crown-rump length**.

**Crohn disease:** see **inflammatory bowel disease**.

‡ **Cro-Magnon:** archaeological site found in 1868 in the Vézère Valley near Les Eyzies, Dordogne, France, dated to 30–25 kya (Würm glaciation) that contains artifacts of an 'evolved' **Aurignacian** tool industry as well as ivory pendants and worked antlers and shells. Hominid remains include five to eight deliberate burials with extensive **sexual dimorphism**; all attributed to *Homo sapiens*. One specimen, the 'old man' of Cro-Magnon ('Le vieillard'), has a cranium with a **dolichopentagonal form** and a cranial capacity of >1600 cm³, and was afflicted with **actinomycosis**.

‡ **Cro-Magnons: AMH** peoples that occupied Central Europe 36–10 kya and were contemporary with the Neandertals from 36 to 29 kya (or perhaps even as recent as 24 kya). The Cro-Magnons were slightly more robust than contemporary Europeans, but otherwise identical in morphology. They possessed the **Aurignacian** and subsequent tool traditions; in addition to delicate stone tools, they modified and incised antlers, bone and shells, and were the people responsible for the **cave art** found at **Lascaux** and many other sites.

**Cromerian:** 1. early Pleistocene flake industry that is found in the Cromer Forest region of eastern England. 2. Lower Pleistocene interglacial period between the Günz and Mindel.

**cross:** bring together genetic material from different **genotypes** in order to achieve genetic **recombination**. Aka hybridize; see **hybridization**.

**cross-agglutination test:** 1. technique employed in blood typing in which **erythrocytes** from an unknown donor are mixed with **sera** of known types in order to determine the **blood type** of the unknown sample. 2. any test employing a similar procedure. Aka cross-matching.

**cross-cousin:** a child either of one's mother's brother or of one's father's sister. Cf. **parallel cousin.**

**cross-cutting relationships:** in geology, a series of principles first drawn by Steno concerning the means by which geological strata that have been interrupted by erosion or faulting may be reconstructed; further, that the younger layers may be deduced by examination of such events. See **superposition of strata.**

**cross dating:** relative dating technique whereby an artifact(s) or physical trait(s) found in one cultural context of known age is used to date a second or other cultures that possess the same artifact(s) or trait(s).

**cross infection:** transfer of a pathogen between members of the same species.

**cross-resistance:** acquired immunity against a **pathogen** because of an **infection** by a closely related organism.

**cross striation:** daily increase of enamel during tooth formation.

**crossbite: malocclusion** of teeth so that a mandibular tooth is not making contact with its opposite number in the maxilla.

**crossbreed:** 1. hybrid. 2. to produce a hybrid by the mating of animals or plants of different **breeds** or varieties, hybridize.

‡ **crossing over:** exchange of genetic material by breakage and rejoining between synapsed homologous chromosomes during prophase of meiosis I; in certain **diploid** organisms, events during **meiosis** leading to reciprocal exchange between homologous **linkage groups** (**chromatids**), resulting in **recombination**; structurally, the **synapsis** and **chiasma** of the arms of paired chromatids which have been contributed by a mother and a father; but see **sister chromatid exchange.** In some species only one sex exhibits crossing over (e.g. females in *Drosophila*); in humans, the **recombination rate** is higher in females than in males. Occurs very rarely during **mitosis**, as well.

**crossopterygian:** vernacular for an ancient subclass of Osteichthyes (bony fishes) composed of the predominantly fresh-water lobe-finned fishes. Until recently this group was considered to be the progenitor of the terrestrial tetrapods; that proposal is now disputed both on molecular and morphological grounds. The only living member of this group is the coelacanth, *Latimeria*.

**crossover strand:** one of two homologous chromatid arms that exchange genetic material between chromosomes during **meiosis** when in a state of **synapsis.**

**crossover suppression:** event (or outcome) in which surviving haplotypes tend to be similar because recombinants are eliminated when **crossing over**

occurs an odd number of times (1, 3, 5, . . ., etc.) within the limits of a polymorphic **inversion.**

**Cross River gorilla:** see *Gorilla gorilla.*

**cross-sectional research** (or **study**): measuring different individuals grouped by age and sex, and sometimes other characteristics, i.e. the individual is measured only once, as in a cross-sectional growth study. Cf. **longitudinal research.**

**cross-species genomic comparison(s):** any method that compares gene-based elements among several distantly (usually) related species, e.g. DNA hybridization. Cf. **phylogenetic shadowing.**

**crosstabulation:** in statistics, the methodological display in a tabular chart or data matrix of the value-by-value comparison of two discrete variables, the purpose of which is to suggest nonrandom relationships. Aka crosstab.

*Crouzelia* Ginsburg and Mein, 1980: see *Plesiopliopithecus.*

**crown:** 1. that part of a tooth above the gum line. 2. term sometimes used for the top of the **cranium.**

**crown breadth:** dental measurement pertaining to the transverse diameter of a tooth; maximum buccolingual width. Aka buccolingual breadth or diameter.

**crown group:** all taxa descended from a major cladogenetic event, and characterized by that clade's **synapomorphy.**

**crown height:** dental measurement; distance from the tooth neck to the cusp apex on single-cusped teeth; on multiple-cusped teeth variations in measurement include taking a mid-point between cusps or obtaining a mean for all cusp apices.

**crown index: crown breadth** divided by **crown length** multiplied by 100; $(B/L) \times 100$, where $B =$ crown breadth, $L =$ crown length.

**crown length:** dental measurement; distance between the points of contact with the teeth anterior (mesial) and posterior (distal) to a tooth; maximum mesiodistal length. This measurement is particularly sensitive to dental wear. Aka mesiodistal diameter or length.

**crown module:** dental index; **crown breadth** plus **crown length** divided by two; $(B + L)/2$, where $B =$ crown breadth, $L =$ crown length.

**crown–rump length** (CRL): 1. distance from the **vertex** of the skull to the rump (buttocks) of an **embryo**; the primary estimate of the size of an embryo, used to estimate **fertilization age.** 2. measurement of sitting height (i.e. length) in children between two and three years of age when the child is lying down, on either a recumbent-length board or table, or a **stadiometer;** the measurement is made from the **vertex** of the head to the base of the sacrum.

**crown stream:** in humans, the stream of hair that begins at the crown of the forehead. Cf. **glabellar stream.**

**crowned guenon:** vernacular for *Cercopithecus pogonias*.

**crowned lemur:** vernacular for *Eulemur* (= *Lemur*) *coronatus*.

**C–R–S triangle:** conceptual triad of ecological strategies where extreme adaptations are **C-strategists**, **R-strategists**, and **S-strategists**.

**cruciate:** crosslike in shape.

**crude vital rate:** demographic index expressing the ratio between the number of events (such as births, deaths, or migrations) relative to the entire population sampled at mid-year.

**crural index:** ratio of the length of the lower leg (the **tibia**) divided by the length of the thigh (the **femur**), × 100. The crural index is correlated with body build in modern humans: low index (<80) indicates adaptation to cold climates, whereas a high index (>85) is found among peoples who live in tropical regions. See **Allen's rule**.

**crust:** outermost layer of the earth with a depth of 5–75 km, and occupying less than 1% of the earth's volume. See **continental crust**.

**cryogenic soil modification:** seasonal processes that modify soil in very cold climates (and potentially displace artifacts in archaeological sites); examples include **cryopedogenesis, cryoturbation** (alternation of **freezing** and **thawing**), **frost cracking, solifluction, thermal cracking**, and **patterned ground formation**.

**cryopedogenesis:** in an archaeological site, the sum of all processes occurring in cryogenic soils, including compaction (desiccation), displacement (alignment, rotation, sorting, inclusions), and pore formation. Cryopedogenic processes are slow; decomposition is retarded and organic matter is accumulated. See **cryogenic soil modification**.

**cryopreservation:** maintenance of cells, tissues, embryos or seeds at ultralow temperature, i.e. below −100 °C.

**cryoturbation:** frost churning in an archaeological site; mixing of soil due to **freezing** and **thawing**, and results in the disruption of horizons, displacement of soil material, the incorporation of organic matter into lower horizons, and the orientation of stones in the soil profile. See **cryogenic soil modification**.

**crypsis:** concealment; see **cryptic**.

***Cryptadapis tertius* Godinot, 1984:** adapoid primate from the late Eocene of Europe, belonging to the subfamily **Adapinae; monotypic**. Body mass estimated at 2.5 kg. See Appendix 1 for taxonomy.

**cryptic:** hidden, secretive; sequestered.

**cryptic donor or acceptor:** sequence within an intron that can serve as a splice donor or acceptor if the usual site is disrupted by mutation.

**cryptic ovulation:** see **concealed ovulation**.

**cryptic polymorphism:** genetic variation controlled by a recessive allele such that the genotypes have indistinguishable phenotypes.

**cryptocrystalline siliceous rock** (CCS): sedimentary material composed primarily of silica crystals, formed in tabular bands in geological strata, as fillings in cavities between other rocks (see **breccia**) or as nodules in chalk or **limestone**. Among the most common utilized for making stone tools are **flint, chert**, jasper, agate, and **chalcedony**.

**cryptogenic:** of indeterminate descent; said of a fossil that cannot be related to those in older strata using a current sample.

**cryptohybrid:** hybrid possessing an unexpected phenotype.

**C-strategist:** competitive species, characterized by large body size, rapid growth, long life span, efficient dispersal, and minimal parental investment. See **C–R–S triangle** of ecological strategies.

**C-terminus:** that end of a polypeptide or protein which has a free carboxyl group.

**Cuban monkey:** vernacular for the recently extinct **platyrrhine** species *Paralouatta varonae*.

**cubic centimeter** (cm³, cc): metric unit, the volume of a cube with sides 1 cm long; 1 cm³ of water is a milliliter. One cubic centimeter is a physical volume about the size of a small pea, often used when estimating the volume of an organ, such as the volume of the brain. See **endocranial volume**.

**cubitus, cubital:** pertaining to the elbow; for example, the median cubital vein drains the region of the elbow.

**cuboid:** 1. cube-like. 2. lateral bone in the distal row of **tarsal** bones of the primate hind paw. 3. an alternative name for the triquetral bone of the primate **carpus**.

**cuckoldry:** 1. refers to the mating of the female in a **one-male unit** copulating with an outside male; this type of mating is sometimes referred to as sneaking because it takes place out of the sight of the bonded male. This can potentially lower the fitness of the cuckolded male. 2. investment of a male parent in offspring that are not his own.

**cue:** signal or indicator, such as light cues that indicate changing periods of daylight.

**Cueva Mayor:** see **Atapuerca**.

**cull:** to choose or select, especially something set aside as inferior; to reduce the number of organisms in a population by elimination of selected individuals. See **domestic selection**.

**cultivar:** artificial variety; usually refers to plants maintained by cultivation; aka cultigen.

**cultural animal:** phrase describing the human species, meaning that all humans possess all of the potentials and limitations of any living creature, but also add a cultural layer of dependence on technology, codified social institutions such as kinship and marriage, and ideology.

‡ **cultural anthropology:** area within anthropology that focuses on the origins, history, and development of human culture(s); the study of variations in human cultural behavior(s); includes **archaeology**, linguistics, ethnology and ethnography.

**cultural capacity:** ambiguous term used in some texts in which the quality and/or size of the hominoid brain is implied to be a barrier to understanding, conceptualization, innovation, adaptation, etc.; phrases such as 'the cultural capacity of australopithecines' and 'the cultural capacity of Neandertals' suggest a limitation of abilities compared to **AMHs**. See **brain size**.

**cultural chronology:** process of ordering past material culture into a meaningful temporal sequence.

**cultural construct:** any complex idea formed of simpler elements, especially as applied to similar objects or homologous concepts that exhibit notable variation from one culture to another; nonuniversal ideation. In the context of human evolutionary biology, **race** is a such a construct.

**cultural ecology:** study of the total ways in which human populations adapt to and transform their environments. Founders of this view included J. Steward and L. White. Aka ecological anthropology.

**cultural epoch theory:** synonym for **unilineal evolution**.

**cultural evolution:** the change of a people's language, beliefs, ideas, and materials over times, usually as an adaptation to circumstances.

**cultural evolutionism:** blanket term for all attempts to understand human cultural diversity as the result of a historical process of adaptation stretching from the origins of the human species to the present. There are several varieties of cultural evolutionism, some of which are quite unacceptable to anthropologists. See **unilineal evolution** and **multilineal evolution**.

**cultural inheritance:** historically accumulated knowledge of humankind transmitted between generations by nongenetic methods such as speech, writing, art, music, etc.

**cultural process:** any of the means by which culture is preserved or changed; the primary processes are **invention**, **diffusion** and **migration**.

**cultural reduction:** form of **reductionism** that treats all institutions and systems of meanings as mere expressions of certain basic ideas whose origin is unexplained.

**cultural relativism:** approach to the understanding of other cultures which avoids using one's own culture as a standard against which to measure all others. Cf. **ethnocentrism**.

**cultural system:** means whereby a human society adapts to its physical and social environment; it is made up of many structurally different parts which articulate with one another within the system.

‡ **culture:** system of shared meanings, symbols, customs, beliefs, and practices that are learned either through teaching or by imitation and that are used to cope with the environment, to communicate with others, and to transmit information from one generation to the next; learned rather than instinctive and genetically transmitted behavior. Culture is one of the primary modes of **adaptation** available to humans, and perhaps other animals. Cultural elements are generated through innovation, and may be labels, arbitrary signals, skills (such as tool use), or symbols; only humans display all four kinds of elements, whereas many primates are reported to exhibit the first three kinds; see **primate culture** and **aptitude for culture**.

**culture area:** concept of environmental determinists in the twentieth century that similar human cultures are the result of adaptation to similar environments. See **environmentalism**.

**culture core:** Julian Steward's term for what he considered the central institutional features of all cultures, e.g. subsistence systems, social structure, and political organization. These core features supposedly undergo regular and predictable evolutionary changes in all parts of the world, while the secondary features vary randomly.

**culture history:** description of human cultures that extends back thousands of years into the past, derived from the study of **archaeological sites** and the **artifacts** found within them, and interpreted within the context of time and space.

**culturgen:** see **meme**.

**cuneate:** series of three bones in the proximal **tarsus** given specific names by position: lateral, intermediate, and medial cuneiform. Aka cuneiforme. See **hamate, triquetral**.

**cuneiform:** 1. wedge-like; in anatomy, usually reserved for skeletal elements. 2. name for three of the **tarsal** bones of the primate hind paw.

**curated technology:** artifacts reused and transported such that they are rarely found in their functional contexts.

**cursorial:** pertaining to a fast running gait; cursorial mammals, such as the gazelle, are swift runners. Some workers have referred to the patas monkey (*Erythrocebus* patas) as cursorial.

**curve of Spee:** arc displayed by **occlusal** surfaces of the mandibular teeth on either side.

‡ **cusp:** rounded or pointed projecting surface emanating from the **occlusal surfaces** of premolar and molar teeth.

**cusp pattern:** configuration of the cusps on the **occlusal surface** of a tooth.

**cuspid:** alternative name for a single projection or elevation on a tooth; see **canine**. Cf. **conule**.

**cuspidate:** possessing well-developed **cusps**.

**cuspule:** eminence on the crown of a tooth that is smaller than a **cuspid**; secondary cuspid.

**cut:** 1. to penetrate with a sharp instrument. 2. an incision through both backbones of duplex DNA. Cf. **nicking**.

**cut mark:** scar made on prehistoric material, usually bone, that can be observed by using a scanning electron microscope. Marks in bone made by stone tools tend to be narrow and more V-shaped than marks made by carnivore teeth; stone tool marks also tend to produce multiple striations within a main groove, and to occur in parallel groups at points on a bone where defleshing behavior would have been concentrated. See **bone fracture pattern**.

**cutaneous gland:** exocrine gland located in the skin.

**cutaneous segmentation:** see **dermal segmentation**.

**cute response:** term coined by Lorenz, referring to the recognition of adult vertebrates of the general body form of newborn and young.

‡ **Cuvier, Georges Léopold Chrétien Fréderic Dagobert** (1769–1832): French comparative anatomist and favorite of Napoleon; one of few Royalists to survive the French Revolution. Cuvier publicly rejected **Lamarck**'s transmutation ideas; he cited instead, with Adam Sedgwick, various versions of **catastrophism** ('Noachian deluge') and posited that fresh rounds of Divine Creation renewed life after every catastrophy. Possessed of a complex intellect, Cuvier recognized and named fossils such as the *Mosasaur* and the *Pterodactyl*, and his '**law of correlation**' recognized that an entire animal could be identified and reconstructed from a few fragments. After collapsing **Amerindians** into the Linnaean Asiatic group, Cuvier recognized only three human **races**. Considered the founder of **zoology**, **comparative anatomy**, and **paleontology**.

**CV** or **C/V:** abbreviation for **coefficient of variation**.

**C value:** characteristic amount of DNA found in a species' haploid chromosomes; measured in picograms, daltons, or base pairs of DNA.

**C value paradox:** reference to a lack of correlation between the size of a genome and the traditional graded scaling of organisms as measured by morphological level or evolutionary complexity.

**cybernetics:** study of control systems, feedback loops, and communication systems, in both living and electromechanical systems.

**cycle:** sequence of events that follows a particular pattern and then repeats.

**cyclic AMP:** see **cAMP**.

**cyclic evolution:** perceived pattern of change in a phylum described by an initial phase of rapid radiation and expansion, followed by a long period of stability and a brief episode of degeneration and over-specialization leading to extinction.

**cyclic GMP** (cGMP): cyclic guanosine monophosphate, a molecule that functions normally to open channels on the surfaces of photoreceptors in the dark, thus permitting sodium ions to enter the cells. When the rhodopsin in a cell begins to absorb light, the concentration of cGMP lowers, and the channels close.

**cyclical selection:** sequential reversal of the direction of selection resulting either from cyclical environmental changes such as seasonal changes, or from **frequency-dependent selection**.

**cyclin:** 1. any protein that is part of the control of the **cell cycle**. 2. protein whose concentration rises and falls during the cell cycle. Aka recognition protein.

**cyclopia:** defect found in mammals resulting in a single eye, placed in the center of the forehead; in humans, some cases are genetically controlled.

**cymotrichous:** pertaining to the possession of smooth, wavy hair.

**Cynocephalidae:** only extant family within the mammalian order **Dermoptera**, consisting of the single genus *Cynocephalus*, and two species, *C. volans* and *C. variegatus*; found only on the islands of Southeast Asia. Dental formula: 2.1.2.3/3.1.2.3. These are folivorous, arboreal, gliding mammals, sometimes incorrectly described as volant (flying). See **Flying Primate Hypothesis**.

**cynodont:** literally, 'dog-toothed'; a condition in which the **pulp cavities** of molar teeth are normal, a model condition found in dogs, from which the term is derived. Modern human populations are usually characterized by cynodontism. Cf. **taurodont**.

*Cynodontomys:* see *Microsyops*.

**cynomolgus macaque:** archaic vernacular for *Macaca fascicularis*.

**cynomorphic monkey:** any primate with a protruding snout, such as a **baboon**.

*Cynopithecus niger* Desmarest, 1821: synonym for *Macaca nigra*.

**cyst:** abnormal sac that contains fluid or solid material.

**cysteine** (Cys): an **amino acid**; one of the twenty building blocks of **proteins** and one of the two amino acids with sulfur groups (the other is **methionine**).

**cystic fibrosis** (CF): heritable **ion channel disease** characterized by a chronic increase of **mucus** in many tissues, malfunction of the pancreas and other glands, lung infections, very salty sweat, slow overall growth, and 'failure to thrive'; the ultimate effect is a decreased life expectancy. The respiratory tract is especially affected, owing to an abnormal protein called the **cystic fibrosis transmembrane-conductance regulator** that causes misshapen secretory channels in selected alveolar cells; these trap chloride salts inside cells and thicken exterior secretions. The accumulated mucus provides a medium in which agents of infection thrive. Heterozygote advantage in the presence of past episodes of cholera, typhoid fever, and/or infant diarrhea has been proposed as an explanation for the high frequency of the cystic fibrosis *f* allele in Europe; as many as 1:25 may be carriers. Affected individuals are homozygous (ff); males are sterile. CF affects between 1:500 to 1:3500 live births to American parents of European ancestry. Aka mucovicidosis.

**cystic fibrosis transmembrane-conductance regulator** (CFTR): an enzyme that regulates the transport of fluids across membranes of the lungs, deficient in the disease **cystic fibrosis**; caused by any of several known **mutations** (the most common is a 3-bp deletion, F-508). Because of its high **prevalence** in America, **biotechnology** companies have targeted the gene as a likely candidate for **gene therapy**. Aka cystic fibrosis transport regulator.

**cystinuria**: heritable condition characterized by the accumulation of certain amino acids (cystine, lysine, arginine and ornithine) in the kidneys and excretion of these amino acids in the urine; kidney stones composed of cystine are common.

**cytoarchitectural map**: map of the cerebral cortex that divides the neocortex into different zones based on **cytoarchitecture**. The different zones of this map, originally assigned numbers, have different functions.

**cytoarchitecture**: specific arrangement of cells in tissue, e.g. the arrangement of nerve cells in the cerebral cortex.

**cytobiology**: cell biology.

**cytocatalytic evolution**: change in a lineage, initiated by an abrupt mutation or event, resulting in the appearance of **polyploids** and **aneuploids**.

**cytochrome**: one of a number of complex **porphyrin** pigment molecules (A, B, C, . . .) found in animals; they function as enzymes during **respiration** to transport electrons to and from iron atoms in their heme groups. The C variant is commonly used in comparative and evolutionary studies.

**cytodeme**: local breeding population that differs either numerically or structurally in cytological characters from other such groups in the same taxon.

**cytogenetic disorder**: any condition due to structural or numerical repatterning of a genome. See **major chromosome anomaly**.

**cytogenetic map**: **ideogram** showing the locations of genes on a chromosome.

‡ **cytogenetics**: study of complementary **genetics** and cellular (especially chromosome) mechanics, the influence of genes on cellular events and vice versa, and the **evolution** of such **mechanisms** within cellular systems. Includes the matching of **phenotypes** to a detectable **major chromosome anomaly**.

**cytokine**: any of a number of **hormone**-like molecules that operate during **cell division** and proliferation,

especially certain non-antibody protiens secreted by **T cells** during an **immune response**, such as **interferon** and **interleukin**.

‡ **cytokinesis**: process of **cell division**. Aka cytoplasmic division.

**cytology**: cell biology; the study of cell structures and processes, usually under a light microscope.

**cytomorphology**: study of the configuration of cells.

‡ **cytoplasm**: all the **protoplasm** and **organelles** of a **cell** except the **nucleus** and the outer plasma membrane. Cf. **nucleoplasm**.

**cytoplasmic donation**: the addition of cytoplasm from a younger female's **oocyte** to an older woman's oocyte prior to *in vitro* fertilization.

**cytoplasmic factor**: any genetic factor found in the **cytoplasm**.

**cytoplasmic inheritance**: heritability of characters or traits whose determinants are not located in nuclear **DNA** nor contained in nuclear **chromosomes**; DNA that occurs in certain of the self-duplicating organelles located in the **cytoplasm**. One cluster of such extranuclear DNA in animals is located in the **mitochondrion**. Aka extranuclear inheritance, extrachromosomal inheritance, and **maternal inheritance**. Cf. **nuclear inheritance**.

**cytoplastic androgamy**: apparent fertilization of a male gamete by the cytoplasm of a female gamete.

**cytoplastic gynogamy**: apparent fertilization of a female gamete by the cytoplasm of a male gamete.

‡ **cytosine** (C): one of the two **pyrimidine nucleosides** found in both **DNA** and **RNA**; composed of one carbon–nitrogen ring.

**cytoskeleton**: system of protein membranes, tubules and filaments that provides a structural framework for the **cell** and transport tracks for the **organelles**. The cytoskeleton gives a cell its characteristic shape.

**cytotaxon**: group composed of similar individuals classed according to cell structure, with special reference to chromosome structure.

**cytotaxonomy**: study of the natural relationships of organisms, using data obtained from cellular sources (particularly the **chromosomes**) rather than from anatomical characters or molecular sequences.

**cytotoxic agent**: any chemical compound or agent that can cause cell death.

**cytotoxic T cell**: lymphocyte that attacks nonself cells by agglutinating (binding) them together and releasing chemicals that attack the foreign cells.

**cytotrophoblast**: layer of the cavitated **trophoblast**; part of the mammalian **placenta**. See **trophoectoderm**.

**cytotype**: subspecific variety that has a chromosome complement that differs either numerically or structurally from the species standard.

**D:** abbreviation for (1) **Rhesus factor Rh+**; (2) coefficient of **linkage disequilibrium**.

**$D^2$:** see **Mahalanobis distance**.

**D2700:** see **Homo georgicus** and **Dmanisi**.

**dacryon** (d): **craniometric landmark**; located on the medial wall of the orbit where the frontal, maxillary, and lacrimal sutures articulate.

**dactylion: anthropometric** landmark; most distal point on the third finger excluding the nail.

**dactylolysis spontanea:** spontaneous loss of a digit; thought to be associated with the sickle-cell trait.

**dactyloscopy:** process of making a set of **fingerprints**. See **dermatoglyphics**.

**Daka hominid: calvaria** recovered in 1997 from the **Bouri formation** deposits in the Middle Awash region of Ethiopia, dated to *c.* 1.0 mya. It was described in 2002 and assigned field number BOU-VP-2/66. Characteristics of this specimen include thick and well-defined double-arched **supra-orbital tori**, a slight **sagittal keel**, poorly defined **torus angularis**, angled occipital bone without an occipital torus, and a cranial capacity of 995 cm³; the calvaria showed signs of scraping that was attributed to animal gnawing. No associated artifacts were found, and other human fossils (leg bones) in the same deposit were not closely associated. This calvaria is attributed to **Homo erectus**, and is cited as evidence that this taxon was not exclusively a Far Eastern species and could be the ancestor of subsequent hominid taxa in Africa. The specimen may trigger a reconsideration of Pleistocene hominid taxonomy. Cf. **Homo ergaster**.

**Dali:** archaeological site found in 1978 at Tianshuigou in Dali County, Shaanxi Province, China, dated to 250–128 kya, and that contains over 500 artifacts that consist of cores with small flint and quartzite scrapers. Hominid remains include a 1120–1200 cm³ cranium with massive **supra-orbital tori**, a low vault with **keeling**, and thick parietals; probably male. Attributed to the **archaic Homo sapiens** group. Aka Tianshuigou. See **Ngandong** and **Omo II**.

**Daltonism:** partial color blindness; see **deuteranopia** and **protanopia**.

**D-amino acid: dextrorotatory** stereoisomer of an amino acid; although both D- and **L-amino acids** have been isolated from proteins, all naturally occurring amino acids found in proteins belong to the L stereochemical series, and in the vernacular the D forms are therefore known as the 'dead' form of the amino acid. See **racemization**.

**Danawu:** archaeological site found in 1973 in Yuanmou County, Yunnan Province, China, dating from 1.7 mya to (more probably) 900–500 kya, and that contains chopper-like artifacts. Hominid remains include surface finds of two incisors and a tibial diaphysis; 'Yuanmou Man' is attributed to **Homo erectus**. Aka Shangnabang.

**Dar-es-Soltane II:** archaeological site found in 1959 near Rabat on the coast of Morocco, dating to >100 kya; contains **Aterian** artifacts and hominid remains including fragments from three individuals assigned to **Homo sapiens**.

**dark-handed gibbon:** vernacular for **Hylobates** *agilis*.

**Darling effect:** increase and synchronization in the reproductive state of members of a breeding group owing to the presence of other individuals; aka Orians effect.

‡ **Dart, Raymond A.** (1893–1991): Australian physician, paleontologist; in 1924, Dart discovered and described the **Taung child** (**Australopithecus africanus**), a fossil australopithecine found at a quarry site in what was then Botswana; following criticism by **Keith**, Dart withdrew from the field but, after Robert **Broom** and John T. **Robinson** described further discoveries, he resumed his avocation and produced a steady flow of new fossils and publications through the 1960s. Dart also authored *Adventures with the Missing Link* (1959). Viking Fund medallist (1957).

**darwin:** Haldane's estimate of the rate of change, *e*, in a character per million years; one (1) darwin, $e = (\log_e x_1 - \log_e x_2)/t$, where $t$ = time, $x_1$ = the value of a characteristic at $t_1$, $x_2$ = the value at $t_2$.

**Darwin, Charles Robert** (1809–82): British naturalist; author of *On the Origin of Species* (1859), an early version of **evolution** known as **Darwinism** (or the 'one long argument' contained in the **Darwinian theory of evolution**). His work caused a change in the world view of many contemporary biologists (see the **Darwinian revolution**). Darwin proposed the gradual **transmutation** of species based upon descent with modification and driven by a '**struggle for existence**' and '**survival of the fittest**', i.e. **natural selection**. Darwin's originality was in his recognition of the role of heritable **variation** in nature. He later defined a second force, **sexual selection**, in *The Descent of Man* (1871), and there first suggested the **original hominid homeland** idea and the **tool-feedback hypothesis**. These, and others of his views such as **gradualism**, have been revisited; some have been rejected outright, such as **pangenesis** (cf. **punctuated equilibrium** and **Mendelism**). Many of his most important ideas, however, have been incorporated and expanded into mainline biological theory, especially those portions concerned with **microevolution** (see **neo-Darwinism**). Some of his central ideas have been co-opted and used for other purposes (e.g. **social Darwinism**). Darwin left other biological issues recognized but unsolved, such as the issue of self-sacrifice (**altruism**, cf. the '**second Darwinian**

revolution'). Although frequently incapacitated (see **Chagas' disease**), Darwin was the author of more than 220 publications and thousands of professional letters; these endeavors have resulted in a large body of secondary literature, or Darwiniana.

**Darwinian:** pertaining to Charles **Darwin** or his **paradigm**.

**Darwinian anthropology:** see **behavioral evolution**.

**Darwinian evolution:** see **Darwinism** and **biological evolution**.

‡ **Darwinian fitness:** average relative contribution of an individual **genotype** to the next generation; the **adaptive value** and the reproductive capability of a given genotype compared with the average of other genotypes in the population. Aka **breeding value**, **selective value**. Cf. **inclusive fitness**.

**Darwinian gradualism:** see **phyletic gradualism**.

**Darwinian inheritance:** see **inheritance** (1).

**Darwinian medicine:** search for evolutionary explanations of vulnerabilities to disease. Aka evolutionary medicine.

**Darwinian revolution:** change in the world view of many biologists as the result of the nonteleological nineteenth century argument by Charles **Darwin**, i.e. **Darwinism**, that organisms change through time owing to descent with modification (**transmutation**, now evolution), and that the **mechanisms** include **natural selection** and **sexual selection**. The incorporation of **Mendelism** and the addition of several other mechanisms (**neo-Darwinism**) is sometimes included in an extended view. See **paradigm shift**. Cf. **second Darwinian revolution**.

**Darwinian selection:** see **natural selection**.

‡ **Darwinian theory of evolution:** theory proposed by Charles **Darwin** in 1859 that argues, in brief, that (1) the number of individuals in a species remains more or less constant; (2) many more individuals are born than can ever survive to reproduce; (3) there is high mortality before reproductive age; (4) there is variation in nature, and some of that variation is heritable; (5) those who survive to reproduce are the 'better adapted'; (6) only the 'better adapted' pass on heritable traits to the next generation; (7) this process may be called **natural selection**; (8) over a long period, natural selection gives rise to new forms of life, the **origin of species**.

‡ **Darwinism:** eponym for the theory of **natural selection** of Charles Darwin as proposed in his work *On the Origin of Species* (1859), i.e. descent with modification. The original mechanism of Darwinism — **natural selection** — is still considered valid but has been supplemented by additional data (such as the inheritance system of **Mendelian genetics**) and synthesized as **neo-Darwinism**, which proposes additional mechanisms such as **mutation**, **drift**, **gene flow**, and **assortative mating**. Originally, the term referred to the concepts in Erasmus Darwin's *Zoonomia*.

**Darwinisticism:** term used by historian Morse Peckham since 1959 to define a romantic view of **Darwinism** that is more an evolutionary metaphysic about the nature of reality and the universe, with economic, moral, aesthetic or psychological embellishments, than about a testable scientific theory concerning the origin of extant biological species from pre-existent species. Peckham's concern is with the consumption of derivative novels, plays, and other secondary media from which is formed a mythical view of ideas about evolutionary theory, without having read the primary literature.

**Darwin's finches:** several closely related species of small birds in the subfamily Geospizinae found on the islands of the **Galápagos archipelago**, each characterized by specific morphological adaptations (especially beak size) to food resources unique to each island. Certain ideas attributed to Darwin about **microevolution** in these finches were actually first noticed by him in mockingbirds.

**Darwin's point:** small projection of cartilage found on the inner margin of the **helix**, usually only on long and narrow ears, and interpreted by some earlier anthropologists as an atavistic sign of a flap-eared ancestor. Aka Darwin's tubercle.

**data:** 1. factual information used as a basis for reasoning, discussion, or calculation. 2. plural of datum (1).

**data set:** in statistics, the complete **tabulation** of all **values** collected for all **variables** relevant to a given study.

**date of publication:** date of the description of a taxon, important in establishing the priority of proposed names.

‡ **dating sequence:** outcome of any methods used to establish the chronology of objects in an archaeological field site. Methods used to establish sequences include **relative dating** and **absolute dating** techniques.

**datum:** 1. (plural: data) something given or admitted, especially as a basis for reasoning or inference. 2. (plural: datums) something used as a basis for calculating or reasoning.

**datum point:** zero point used as a fixed reference used to achieve vertical control in an archaeological dig; usually combined with a grid system.

**datums:** things used as a basis for calculating or reasoning (plural of **datum**); cf. **data**.

**Daubenton's angle:** angle formed by the intersection of the planes of the **foramen magnum** and that which bypasses the **opisthion** and the inferior edge of the orbits; created before 1764, it was one of the first comparative **craniometric measurements**.

*Daubentonia* É. Geoffroy St.-Hilaire, 1785: **prosimian** genus to which the aye-aye belongs; one extant species. Found in low densities along the entire eastern coast of Madagascar and a few locations in the north and west. This species was thought to be almost extinct, but new methods of looking for nests in the 1990s revealed that there may be as many as 10 000 individuals, although they remain endangered. Originally placed among the rodents in the genus *Sciurus* because of several rodent-like (and non-primate-like) traits, such as ever-growing incisors, dentin instead of enamel on the posterior surface of the incisors, lack of canines, claws on all digits except the **hallux**, and a bushy tail. They are reported to be very intelligent and have the highest brain-to-body ratio of the prosimians. An unusual feature of this animal is the extremely thin third digit of each fore paw that is used to probe into holes to extract insects under the bark of trees. An adaptation for feeding is the large **pinnae**, which are used to locate insects under the bark of trees. Arboreal. **Nocturnal.** Quadrupedal. Dental formula: 1.0.1.3/1.0.0.3; omnivorous with the diet ranging from insects and grubs to fruit and nuts. This animal is said to fill the woodpecker niche on Madagascar. See Appendix 2 for taxonomy; see **Daubentoniidae.**

**Daubentoniidae:** prosimian family to which the aye-ayes belong. The only **extant** aye-aye is *Daubentonia madagascariensis*, which exists at such low numbers that it is, below its minimum viable population size and, to all intents and purposes, **extinct.** There is evidence that a second species, *D. robustus*, existed in the past. Only postcrania have been recovered from this **subfossil** second species, but the bones suggest it was from two to five times larger than *D. madagascariensis*. Molecular evidence suggests this group has affinities with the indriids.

**Daubentonioidea: prosimian** superfamily used by some authors that includes the living aye-aye and a possible extinct form. See *Daubentonia*

**daughter:** 1. a female offspring; a kinship term that identifies a genealogical or adopted degree of relationship in a **nuclear family** or **extended family.** See **father, mother, brother, sister, son, aunt, uncle, cousin.** 2. In genetic studies the term refers to any offspring of a given generation, and is applicable to both sexes.

**daughter cell:** see **sibling cell.**

**daughter chromosome: chromosome** as it exists after the metaphase of **mitosis** or metaphase II of **meiosis** (after which it is technically a daughter **chromatid**).

**daughter isotope:** product of radioactive decay of an **unstable isotope.** An unstable **isotope** decays into one or more daughter products (that may be either another unstable isotope, or a **stable isotope**) at a constant rate; used in **radiometric dating** techniques such as **radiocarbon dating.**

**Davenport, Charles Benedict** (1866–1944): US zoologist (Ph.D., Harvard, 1902), geneticist. Briefly on the faculties of Harvard and Chicago (1892–1904), first director of the Station for Experimental Evolution at Cold Springs Harbor, NY, after 1904. Founding member of the **Galton Society of New York** (1918), leader of the American eugenics movement, founder of the Eugenics Record Office (*c.* 1910–34). Author of over 400 papers and books, including *Statistical Methods with Special Reference to Biological Variation* (1899), and *Heredity in Relation to Eugenics* (1911).

**Dawkins, Richard** (1941–): Kenya-born British theoretical evolutionary biologist at Oxford; student of ethologist Niko Tinbergen, and one of the foremost popularizers of reductionism and the **adaptationist program.** Dawkins views organisms as survival machines; he developed an 'ethology of the gene', in which the evolution of selfish DNA takes priority over the whole organism. Author of *The Selfish Gene* (1976), *The Blind Watchmaker* (1986), and *The Extended Phenotype* (1992). Dawkins has been awarded numerous literary and scientific prizes. See **replicator** and **selfish DNA.**

**dawn man:** supposed side branch of hominids that arose from an Oligocene pre-cercopithecoid stock, and that also gave rise to the anthropoid apes. Little evidence exists for such an idea today, and the nomen *Eoanthropus dawsonii* has been abandoned.

**Dawson, Charles** (1864–1916): English solicitor and antiquarian; locator of many of the fragments at Piltdown. Dawson has been suggested as both a perpetrator and victim of the subsequently unveiled **Piltdown hoax.** The putative fossil from that site, *Eoanthropus dawsoni*, was named for Dawson.

**day range:** distance a primate or primate group travels in 24 h while going through its normal activities. Day range is generally measured linearly in metric units; it is usually a straightening out of **path length** and is sometimes referred to as daily path length.

**De Brazza's monkey (guenon):** vernacular for *Cercopithecus neglectus*.

**De Ville's tamarin:** vernacular for *Saguinus fuscicollis*.

**De Vries, Hugo Marie** (1848–1935): Dutch cytologist; the first of three to rediscover and cite Gregor **Mendel's** work in 1900. De Vries adopted the term **mutation** for the previous term 'sport', a 'jump' in a lineage arising out of normal parents (1901); he believed that mutations were the cause of speciation, or created variation that could be acted upon by **natural selection.** Author of *Intracelluläre Pangenesis* (1889), *Die Mutationstheorie* (1903) and *Species and Varieties, Their Origin by Mutation* (1906).

**De Vriesianism:** proposal that evolution in general and speciation in particular are the results of drastic and saltatory mutational changes that may be acted upon by **natural selection.** Aka mutationism.

**deafness, neurosensory:** impairment of the sense of hearing, either congenitally or through postnatal loss; the term can refer to either partial or complete deafness. Although over seventy genes are known to cause congenital hearing loss, in the most common mode, hearing loss is due to mutations in the gap junction protein connexin, an autosomal recessive. Hearing loss that is genetic in origin accounts for about half of all cases. Nonsyndromic deafness is a genetic defect in a single gene that causes multiple medical problems, only one of which is deafness, as in **Waardenburg syndrome;** 70% of cases of inherited deafness are nonsyndromic (i.e. 35% of all cases). Syndromic deafness is a genetic defect in a single gene that causes a single medical problem, deafness, as in **Pendred syndrome;** 30% of cases of inherited deafness are nonsyndromic (i.e. 15% of all cases). Aka hereditary hearing loss. See **inherited deafness.**

**deanthropomorphism:** practice of systematic removal, de-endowment, and disenchantment of images that have been attributed by others with human characteristics. Cf. **anthropomorphism.**

**dear enemy phenomenon:** recognition (personalization, in humans) of territorial neighbors as individuals, with the result that aggressive interactions are kept at a minimum; more intense forms of aggression are reserved for 'strangers'. In the extreme forms of depersonalization, strangers become 'enemies'.

**death:** termination of somatic functions, normally the final episode in the complete human **life cycle,** usually following **old age** and **senescence** in latest **adulthood.** Death due to disease or accident may occur at any stage of life, however.

**death assembly:** see **thanatocenosis.**

**death rate:** see **mortality rate.**

**débitage:** waste or debris of the tool-making process, material not intended as a tool; incidental flakes.

**decay:** 1. organic decomposition; putrefaction. 2. in physics, the spontaneous changes that occur in an unstable element, as used in **radiocarbon dating.**

**decay constant:** constant rate by which radioactive elements change spontaneously to lower energy states.

**deceit:** in behavioral biology, a sign that communicates an inaccurate assessment of an individual's condition in order to cheat a potential mate as to the quality of genes it carries. See **honest signal, Machiavellian intelligence.**

**deceleration:** negative **acceleration.**

**deception:** artifice; see **deceit.**

**decibel** (dB): unit that measures the ratio of two powers or intensities such as electric or acoustic power; one tenth of a bel. Ordinary human conversation at a distance of about one meter produces a level of about 60 dB (on a logarithmic scale from 0 to 130).

**deciduous:** pertaining to structures that are shed, such as **deciduous dentition.**

‡ **deciduous dentition (or teeth):** first set of teeth in mammals that are shed as the animal grows. In humans there are 20 deciduous teeth, which are shed between ages five and ten. The deciduous teeth consist of incisors and canines; there is disagreement as to whether the third type of tooth is a premolar (the consensus of most mammalogists) or a molar (commonly held among human anatomists). The deciduous set is replaced by the **adult dentition;** aka milk teeth, primary dentition.

**deciduous forest: forest** consisting of trees that shed their leaves during the autumn of the year when light conditions diminish. Cf. **coniferous** and **evergreen forest.**

**decile:** in statistics, one of the values of a variable after division of the total distribution into ten groups having equal frequencies, and numbered 0–9. Cf. **percentile.**

**decomposition:** breakdown of dead organic material into detritus, primarily by microorganisms; one of the steps of **fossilization.**

**decompression:** 1. transition to an environment of lower pressure, as in diving or a hyperbaric decompression chamber, or from sea level to altitude (hypobaric decompression). 2. increase of niche width owing to relaxation of interspecific competition.

**decussation:** 1. crossing. 2. crossing of nerve fibers from one side of the **central nervous system** to the other; Aka chiasma. 3. interweaving of crystal orientation in dental enamel.

**Dederiyeh Cave:** archaeological site found in 1987 in the Afrin region of northwestern Syria, dating to the Levantine Middle Paleolithic; contains artifacts including **Levallois** type cores and flakes (lower levels) and **Natufian** flakes (upper levels). Hominid remains include the nearly complete skeleton of an immature (2 year old) hominid assigned to *Homo neanderthalensis.* Aka Wadi Dederiyeh.

**dedifferentiation:** process that leads to a cell or cell line that is less specialized that its parent cell, e.g. a cancer cell.

**deduction:** 1. a thing that is deduced; a conclusion. 2. the inference of particulars from known or assumed generalizations, e.g. a syllogism, such as: all *X* are members of *Z*, *Y* is a specific instance of *X*, therefore *Y* is also a member of *Z*. Deduction is the form of logic used in the Popperian **hypothetico-deductive approach** to **hypothesis falsification.** Cf. **induction.**

**deduction theorem:** if the proposition Q can be logically inferred from the proposition P, then 'if P then Q' can be proved as a theorem for most logical systems. Attributed to Charles Dodgson (1832– 98), English mathematician and writer, aka 'Lewis Carroll'.

**deductivism:** proposal that the process of **induction** is logically invalid, and therefore science should dispense with it in favor of **deduction**. Attributed to Austrian philosopher Karl **Popper** (1902–94). Aka falsificationism, **hypothetico-deductive approach.** Cf. **inductivism.**

**deep:** anatomical term of relative position meaning that a structure is more internal than another; for example, the muscles are deep to the skin. Cf. **superficial.**

**deep ecology:** political philosophy in conservation biology that recognizes that all species have value in themselves and that humans have no right to reduce species diversity; because human activities are destroying species richness, human political, economic, and technological practices must be changed, while improving human conditions through environmental quality, esthetics, and religion, rather than through material consumption.

**deep sea core sequence:** see **Emiliani–Shackleton glacial sequence.**

**deep structure:** Chomsky's term for the internal patterns of meaning that reside in the mind of the speaker.

**deep time:** see **absolute geological time.**

**deexoticization:** process or method of overcoming **exotic bias.**

**defecate:** to void or eliminate waste droppings from the anus. Noun: defecation.

**defective ribosomal products** (DRiPs): translation products that misfold and are instantly recycled by **proteasomes**; it has been estimated that about one-third of all translation products are DRiPs. See **prion protein.**

**defended territory:** any area over which an individual or group maintains exclusive control through defense against **conspecifics.**

**deficiency:** 1. lack, incompleteness, or insufficiency. 2. in genetics, a synonym for impaired function of a gene product, usually due to **mutation.** 3. in cytogenetics, synonymous with **deletion.**

**deficiency disease:** **avitaminosis** or other condition produced by an insufficiency of one or more nutritional elements; **malnutrition.** See **nutritional disease.**

**definitive host:** organism in which a parasite resides during its reproductive phase. Cf. **intermediate host.**

**deflecting wrinkle:** central ridge that deviates from the metaconid to the central occlusal pit of a human mandibular **molar.**

**defleshing:** act of removing soft tissue from bones and cartilage, usually with a tool; a behavior thought to be

crucial to adaptation in early hominids who developed tools such as the flesher and end scraper that enhanced this behavior. Cf. **fleshing.**

**deforestation:** permanent removal of forest and undergrowth.

**deformation:** alteration of a developing structure (a) in an **embryo** or **fetus** owing to extrinsic pressure; see **prenatal insult**; (b) in a child or adult owing to binding or mutilation; deformity. See, for example, **cranial deformation.**

**deformity:** any bodily disfigurement. See **deformation.**

**degenerate codons:** said of the **genetic code** because more than one of the 64 possible **triplets** or **codons** specifies one of the 20 common **amino acids**; aka redundancy, degeneracy.

**degeneration:** 1. reversion to a less highly organized or simpler kind. 2. loss of functional activity. 3. see **degradation theory.**

**degenerative:** pertaining to the process of deterioration or the loss of information; lacking in freshness.

**degenerative disease:** change of tissue to a functionally less active state; any **disease** such as **arthritis** or heart disease that is associated with the later years of life and normally considered neither acute nor infectious. Aka degenerative pathologies.

**degradation:** wearing down, breakdown, erosion; see **degeneration** and **habitat degradation.**

**degradation theory:** archaic nineteenth century theological argument that all humans were originally civilized, but that nonliterate peoples had fallen from grace and their cultures became degraded. In a modified view, 'degenerates' were peoples who had adapted to different, 'less favorable' environments after expulsion from Eden.

**degree of genetic determination:** synonym for broad-sense heritability; see **heritability.**

**degree of relatedness** (r): the chance that a gene in one individual will have an exact copy located in a second individual by virtue of direct descent from a common ancestor, as measured by a **coefficient of relatedness.**

**degrees of freedom** (d.f.): in statistics, a value associated with a test statistic that is used in determining the observed significance level; d.f. are calculated from the total number of **observations** minus the number of estimated **parameters.** The more d.f., the more robust the outcome or prediction.

**dehiscence:** 1. splitting apart or bursting open. 2. gap that is the result of the total ossification of the tympanic plate of the temporal bone.

**deimatic behavior:** threatening or intimidating posture by one animal towards another.

**delamination:** 1. separation of cells into layers. 2. process in the development of an embryo in which the **endoderm** separates during **blastogenesis.**

**delayed hypersensitivity:** in a previously sensitized individual, a cell-mediated reaction to an antigen or allergen that occurs about 30 h after the challenge. Cf. **immediate hypersensitivity.**

**delayed mortality:** death that occurs after a recovery period following exposure to an agent. Cf. **concomitant mortality** and **consequential mortality.**

**delayed tanning:** *in vivo*, the second of a two-stage **acclimatization** response resulting in browning or darkening of the living skin known as **tanning**, and caused by exposure to **UV radiation.** Delayed tanning is a durable browning beginning after 24–48 h, maximized 19 days after exposure, and caused primarily by exposure to UV-B (but UV-A and visible light are contributors); it fades in approximately 9–10 months. Cf. **immediate tanning.**

**deleterious:** hurtful, harmful, injurious; describes **mutations** in wild species that lower the **fitness** of their **carriers**, or in domesticated species that impair the **traits** considered desirable by the breeder. In humans, deleterious traits are often thought of as negative and subject to removal; in some cultures this takes the form of repair, but in others, that of removal due either to active intervention or to benign neglect.

‡ **deletion:** 1. in DNA, the removal of one or more base pairs from a sequence. 2. structural change to a **chromosome** that results in loss of a section of that chromosome and loss of genes from a **linkage group.** Sometimes termed a deficiency if it involves the terminal portion of a chromosome.

**deletion hypothesis:** proposal that cancer is due to the loss of one or more cell constituents, probably enzymes or proteins; proposed in 1957 by American biologist Van Rensselaer Potter (1911–).

**deliberate burial:** placement of a dead body in the ground, or in a crypt or urn, or upon some structure; the practice began on present evidence during the **Middle Paleolithic** period (c. 80–35 kya) and became more common during the **Upper Paleolithic.** Decorative items placed on individuals found at archaeological sites are a sign of deliberate burial.

**delimitation:** in taxonomy, a finite list of the character states used to diagnose a taxon.

**delta:** 1. fourth letter of the Greek alphabet, Δ or δ; the fourth member in a set or series. 2. in chemistry, symbol for a double bond between atoms. 3. symbol for change. 4. any triangular space, such as an alluvial deposit at a river's mouth, as in the Nile delta.

**delta globin chain** (δ Hb): one of several globin chains that constitute the family of **hemoglobin** molecules and that form part of **adult hemoglobin.** Aka delta chain.

**delta karyology:** determination of the location of **satellite DNA, nucleolus organizer region**, and 5*S* rRNA loci. An advanced analytical level of **karyology.**

**delta waves:** electrical activity emanating in a general pattern from the cerebral hemispheres, normally detected as rhythmic oscillations of about 1–5 cycles per second. These waves are common in an alert infant and in a sleeping adult; the presence of delta waves in an awake adult indicates brain damage. See **electroencephalogram, brain waves.** Aka delta rhythm.

**deltoid:** muscle that moves the arm. The deltoid originates on the **clavicle, acromion process**, and spine of the **scapula**; it inserts into the **deltoid tuberosity** of the **humerus.** Its action is to extend, **abduct**, and flex the arm.

**deltoid tuberosity:** rough protuberance on the lateral side of the mid-**diaphysis** of the **humerus**; the **deltoid** muscle inserts into this structure.

**demarcation:** in philosophy, and especially that of Karl **Popper**, a theory that attempts to distinguish between science and nonscience; he repudiates **induction** as nonscience, and argues that any notion of pure observation as science is misguided. Science, for Popper, is problem-solving; specifically, the **falsification** of one or more competing hypotheses.

‡ **deme:** local **population** of very similar organisms that interbreed in nature and usually occupy a circumscribed area; hence the largest population unit that can be analyzed by simpler models of **population genetics**; a **panmictic unit.** Often used with a prefix, such as clinodeme, to specify the type of population under consideration. Aka breeding population, local population, Mendelian population.

**demic diffusion:** spread of cultural innovations as the result of small-scale population migrations; one of the principal mechanisms proposed to explain the wave-like behavior of both cultural diffusion and **gene flow.**

**'demi-cranium':** fossil hominid skull, probably a female *Australopithecus* (= *Paranthropus*) *boisei*; see **KNM-ER 732A.**

**Demidoff's bushbaby (or galago):** vernacular for *Galagoides demidoff.*

**demographic profile:** pattern of age distributions making up an overall population.

**demographic shift:** see **demographic transition (model).**

**demographic society:** society that is stable enough through time, usually owing to its being relatively closed to newcomers, for the demographic processes of birth and death to play a significant role in its composition. Cf. **casual group.**

**demographic transition (model):** theory of human population change that proposes that as a population becomes economically developed, there will be a reduction in **mortality** that leads to **population**

growth, sometimes followed by a reduction in **fertility** that leads to growth **equilibrium**. Aka demographic shift.

**demographic transition stage I:** in a model of human population change, describes a population characterized by a high **fertility rate**, an equally high **mortality rate** that results in population growth equilibrium, and (usually) a high infant mortality rate and a modest to high **morbidity rate**. The intrinsic rate of growth in such a population is near zero (0).

**demographic transition stage II:** in a model of human population change, describes a population characterized by a high **fertility rate**, a low **mortality rate** that results in dramatic **population growth**, and (usually) a high infant mortality rate and high **morbidity rate**. The intrinsic rate of growth in such a population is greater than unity (>1).

**demographic transition stage III:** in a model of human population change, describes a population characterized by a low **fertility rate**, an equally low **mortality rate** that results in population growth equilibrium, and (usually) a low infant mortality rate and a modest to high **morbidity rate**. The intrinsic rate of growth in such a population is between zero and unity (0–1).

**demographic transition stage IV:** in a model of human population change, describes a population characterized by a low **fertility rate**, an equally low **mortality rate** that results in population growth equilibrium, and (usually) a low infant mortality rate and a low to modest **morbidity rate**. The intrinsic rate of growth in such a population is near zero (0).

‡ **demography:** statistical study of the **intrinsic rate of increase** and the **age structure** of **populations**, and the processes that determine these properties, such as **survival**, **mortality**, and **reproduction**; also, the spatial distribution of properties that influence populations.

**denaturation:** structural alteration of a protein such that its function is compromised; disassembly of the **quaternary structure** of a protein.

**dendriform:** treelike in form.

**dendrite:** 1. any branching structure. Adjective: dendritic. 2. one of the many branching cytoplasmic processes of a **neuron** that receives impulses from other cells.

**dendritic evolution:** see **cladogenesis** and **reticulate evolution**.

**dendrochronology:** **chronometric dating** method based on the principle that trees in dry climates tend to accumulate one growth ring per year, so the number of rings indicates the age of a tree in years. The width of a ring varies according to climate: as wet years result in broader rings. A specific tree-ring pattern can be compared with a sequential master chart of such rings for a given region, which typically covers the past 10 000 years or so. First applied in 1901. See **cambium**.

**dendroclimatology:** estimation of past climatic conditions, especially drought frequency, using the relative widths of the annual growth rings of trees. See **dendrochronology**.

**dendrogram:** 1. diagram showing evolutionary change in a biological **trait**, including the ordered branching of the trait into different forms owing to the multiplication of the species possessing it. Often, a **cladogram** illustrating the evolution of a specific trait. 2. a **phenogram**. See **cladogenesis**.

**dendrogram, exterior point of:** terminal point on a **dendrogram** where there are no further known descendants of a lineage.

**dendrogram, interior point of:** **node** on a **dendrogram** that has both ancestor(s) and descendant(s).

**dendrogram, root of:** single most ancestral **node** in a **dendrogram** where there are descendants but no known ancestors, within the framework of a certain analysis.

***Dendropithecus macinnesi*** (Le Gros Clark and L. Leakey, 1950): **monotypic** genus of **hominoids** from the early Miocene of East Africa belonging to the **catarrhine** family **Proconsulidae**; previously included in the defunct taxon ***Limnopithecus***; previously included in the family **Hylobatidae** as a gibbon ancestor candidate; it is also suggested by some workers that *Dendropithecus* is closely related to *Pliopithecus* and should be included with the **Pliopithecidae**. Estimated body mass is 10 kg. Dental formula: 2.1.2.3; shearing crests on molars suggestive of **folivorous** and **frugivorous** diet; **sexually dimorphic** canines, but long and sharp in both sexes, suggesting to some that this species was **monogamous** (similar to the gibbons). Postcrania suggest **arboreal quadrupedalism** as mode of locomotion. See Appendix 1 for taxonomy.

***Dendropithecus songhorens***: see ***Kalepithecus songhorensis***.

**Denen Dora Member:** sedimentary Member in the **Hadar Formation**, overlying the fossiliferous **Sidi Hakoma Member**, and underlying the younger **Kada Hadar Member**.

***de novo***: (Latin) new, for the first time. In genetics, arising from an unknown source; not familial.

**dens:** toothlike structure, e.g. the dens of the second **cervical** vertebra.

**dense bone:** see **compact bone**.

**density-independent:** pertaining to a population whose growth is not regulated by the number of individuals in a given area.

**density shift experiment:** laboratory technique in which some bacteria are labeled with heavy radioactive isotopes; centrifugation separates the heavier cells from those that have not incorporated the isotope-laden DNA.

**dental:** of or pertaining to the teeth.

**dental age:** refers to the age of an organism based on the development of its dentition, e.g. the amount of dental calcification present or the stage of dental eruption. See **Tanner stage.**

**dental alveolus:** socket in which a tooth **articulates** with the **mandible** or a **maxillary bone**; this particular type of joint is referred to as a **gomphosis.** Plural: dental alveoli.

**dental anomaly:** structure in a tooth that is unusual.

**dental anthropology:** discipline within physical (biological) anthropology that studies the variation and biology of human dentition.

**Dental Anthropology Association:** organization for people interested in scientific research on dental evolution and variation in the oral health and dental morphology of modern and ancient human populations. It exists to promote the exchange of educational, scientific and scholarly knowledge in the field of **dental anthropology.** Its official publication is *Dental Anthropology.*

**'dental apes':** term applied to certain **Fayum** fossil primates that date to the **Oligocene** and that possessed **molar tooth patterns** similar to those of apes, suggesting that, like the living apes and some **New World monkeys**, these fossil monkeys were **frugivores.** However, they were not apes in the modern sense. See **Y-5 molar pattern.**

‡ **dental arcade:** term most used in human evolutionary biology for the alveolar arch; horseshoe– or U-shaped (parabolic) arch formed by the alveolar process of the **maxillary bones** and the alveolar border of the **mandible.** The dental arcades of other primates are often formed by convergent rows of teeth forming a V or parallel rows forming a hard U. Aka dental arch. See **parabolic dental arcade, parallel dental arcade, convergent dental arcade.**

**dental caries:** common childhood condition in **AMHs**, the result of metabolic activity of *Streptococcus mutans* within dental plaque; untreated lesions in enamel and dentine can cause severe toothache, and lead to loss of the tooth. In **fossil populations**, such infections often became **systemic**, presumably contributing to the eventual death of an affected individual. See **Kabwe.**

**dental comb:** procumbent six lower incisors and two canines that form a scoop in most of the **prosimians**; dental combs are used for grooming and for gouging trees in order to stimulate the flow of sap or gum. The indriids differ from other prosimians in that there are only four teeth in their dental comb. Aka tooth comb.

**dental development:** several stages beginning with calcification, or tooth formation, and eruption (emergence from the gum line) of teeth. Teeth do not grow in the sense that bones do; once they erupt from the gum line they are full size, whether **deciduous dentition** or the adult set (that erupts during childhood). Teeth erupt, for the most part, between birth and age ten. Dental development provides one of the most accurate estimates of age up until adulthood.

**dental disease:** pathological condition of the teeth or gums.

**dental enamel:** see **enamel.**

**dental enamel hypoplasia:** defect in dental enamel, usually the result of environmental stress.

**dental eruption sequence:** order in which the different teeth emerge through the gums. Rapidly developing anthropoid primates such as **macaques, chimpanzees**, and **australopithecines** exhibit an adult eruption sequence of M1 I1 I2 M2 P3 P4 C M3, whereas **AMHs** have the sequence M1 I1 I2 C P3 P4 M2 M3. The later that tooth emergence begins, the earlier the anterior teeth (I1–P4) appear in the sequence. It has been suggested that the shift of M2 to a later position, as well as the overall slowing of the rate of development, greatly enhanced the ability of later hominids to distribute tooth wear over a longer period of the **life cycle**, thus decreasing **mortality** secondary to dental wear and attrition in juveniles and young adults. See **pedomorphosis**, and **dental formula.**

‡ **dental formula:** notation for the number of **incisors** (I), **canines** (C), **premolars** (P), and **molars** (M) in the upper and lower dentition of a species of **heterodont** mammal, I:C:P:M. In humans, the adult dental formula is usually: 2.1.2.3/2.1.2.3. Since mammalian teeth are usually symmetrical, the total number of teeth is equal to the sum of the upper and lower quadrants, times two; in humans, for example, (8 + 8 = 16) × 2 yields a modal number of 32 teeth. The **aye-aye** has a formula of 1.0.1.3/1.0.0.3, illustrating the need for both upper and lower quadrant counts. Its **deciduous** dental formula (dI:dC:dM) is 2.1.2/2.1.2. Both the deciduous and adult dental formulas are identical in all extant **hominoids.**

**dental genetics:** study of the development and growth of both the **deciduous dentition** and the **adult dentition**, as well as the comparison of humans with the nonhuman primates for many homologous variables. Dental genetics includes, but is not limited to, the chronology of tooth growth, dental eruption sequences, variation in tooth size and placement, and the heritability of both normal and exceptional dental structures.

**dental impaction:** condition in which a tooth is so placed in the alveolus as to be incapable of complete eruption. Modes include **vertical dental impaction, low-level dental impaction, high-level dental impaction, mesioangular dental impaction, horizontal dental impaction,** and **distoangular dental impaction.**

**dental inclusion:** tooth enclosed in bone and unable to erupt.

**dental lamina:** thin plate of enamel covering a tooth.

**dental mutilation:** abnormal tooth morphology of cultural rather than natural or pathological conditions; types of mutilation include extraction, pointing, cutting, filing, incrustation and drilling. Dental mutilation is believed to be related to adornment, mourning, initiation, and/or imitation of an animal's dentition.

**dental occlusion:** see **occlusion.**

**dental wear:** thinning of enamel and obliteration of surface features on the occlusal surface of teeth over time owing to normal abrasion.

**dentary:** in mammals, the lower tooth-bearing jaw; in primates (and especially humans) the dentary is normally referred to as the **mandible.** Aka dentary bone.

**dentate:** 1. possessing teeth. 2. possessing toothlike or conical projections. Cf. **edentate.**

**denticulate:** 1. pertaining to any structure that is toothlike. 2. referring to a **tool** with serrated projections along its working edge.

**denticulate assemblage:** middle Paleolithic tool tradition described by Bordes, characterized by delicate flaking techniques.

**dentin:** hard, dense calcareous tissue that makes up the bulk of a tooth that lies under the enamel and encapsulates the pulp cavity; composed mostly of hydroxyapatite and other inorganic matter (70%) and organic molecules such as collagen (30%). Also spelled dentine.

‡ **dentition:** number, type, and arrangement of teeth. See **dental formula.**

**Dent's monkey:** vernacular for *Cercopithecus mona* (= *denti*).

**dentulous:** possessing natural deciduous or permanent teeth, as in a fossil skull that contains the teeth. Cf. **edentulous.**

**denucleated:** deprived of a nucleus.

‡ **deoxyribonucleic acid:** see **DNA.**

**deoxyribose:** pentose (5-carbon) sugar found in **DNA.**

**dependency ratio:** in human demography, a ratio of certain age groups in a population; the numerator is usually the economically productive portion of a population, and the denominator is usually the sum of the two dependent age groups (by convention, those under fifteen and those over sixty-five years).

**dependent:** 1. determined or conditioned by another; contingent. 2. relying for support and maintenance on some other individual, such as in a mother–infant relationship. 3. aged, very young, disabled, or sick organism that must rely on other organisms. Cf. **producer.**

**dependent rank:** rank in a dominance hierarchy that is the result of support from other individuals in their social network.

‡ **dependent trait, character** or **feature:** feature that manifests only if a previous feature is also present. Examples are (1) hair, which is dependent upon the prior presence of skin or other supportive tissue, and (2) the final product of a biochemical pathway, which is dependent upon the successful processing of all prior substrates.

**dependent variable:** in controlled bivariate experimentation, the variable whose values are assumed to be predictable from the values of the **independent variable.** In a bivariate scattergram, the dependent variable is on the *y*-axis.

**Depéret's law:** observation that an increase in size in a lineage is a measure of its evolutionary success. This proposal is considered by many to be an example of anthropomorphic projection; size is more a function of the historical distribution of resources and other variables than a measure of 'success'.

**depigmentation hypothesis:** proposal that organisms that disperse from equatorial latitudes toward either polar region lose pigment, principally **melanin,** in response to the decreasing intensity of **ultraviolet light.** Applies primarily to the long-term genetic adaptation of populations, and to lesser extent to individual **acclimatization.**

**deposit:** accumulation of material such as sediment or **midden** material.

**deposition:** 1. the accumulation of material such as sediment by mechanical settling or remaining after evaporation, etc. 2. in reference to bone, the construction of bony matrix from its chemical constituents by an **osteoblast.**

**depositional process:** transformation of materials from an ecological to an archaeological context, i.e. site formation.

**depression:** 1. area lower than the surrounding surface (e.g. **Fayum depression, Pacchonian depression**); cf. **elevation.** 2. low level of activity. 3. for population genetics, see **inbreeding depression.** 4. with reference to joint movements, the displacement of a part downward or inward, such as drooping the shoulders. 5. dejection and withdrawal; for unipolar depression, see **major affective disorder.**

**deprivation:** absence of a vital nutrient or other factor that leads to impairment of physiological processes, e.g. sleep deprivation.

**deprivation experiment:** experiment in which an animal is socially isolated (deprived of parents, peers, etc.), generally during its infant development period.

The classic study in primatology is the Harlow experiment, in which infant rhesus monkeys were subjected to a number of different treatments. Studies included infants raised without mothers (they were given cloth or wire **surrogates**) or without interaction with peer **cohorts**. The Harlows concluded that abnormal socialization in monkeys is a function of peer deprivation rather than of maternal deprivation.

**depth perception:** see **stereoscopic vision**.

**derived:** received from a common source or origin. Cf. **plesiomorphy**, **ancestral**, and **primitive**. See also **advanced** and **synapomorphy**.

**derived homology:** with respect to a given set of species, a trait or character common to all species within the set of interest, and not present on outgroups, implying that the trait evolved in a species that was the common ancestor of the set of interest. Cf. **ancestral homology**.

‡ **derived trait, character** or **feature:** any specialized morphological (or behavioral) character that departs from the condition found in the ancestors of a species or group of species; i.e. **advanced**, **apomorphic**. The large human brain is considered a derived trait relative to the last **common ancestor** of apes and humans. Cf. **ancestral** and **primitive**.

**dermal bone:** see **intramembranous bone**.

**dermal segmentation:** division of the skin into segments called **dermatomes**, each defined according to the differential nervous innervation of each segment. Aka cutaneous segmentation.

**dermatoglyphics:** study and classification of the highly **heritable** patterns of the ridges and whorls on the skin surfaces of palms, fingers, soles, and toes. The use of fingerprints for identification came as early as 1823 by Purkenje. W. J. Herschel used them to seal documents in 1877. The scientific and **forensic** value of fingerprints was first realized by F. **Galton**.

**dermatology:** branch of medicine concerned with the diagnosis and treatment of diseases of the skin.

**dermatome:** segment of the epidermis with a common source of innervation. See **dermal segmentation**.

**dermatopathology:** study of abnormal development of or trauma to fingerprint and palm ridge development.

**dermestid beetle:** worldwide family (Dermestidae, over 700 species) of coleopteran insects belonging to the superfamily Dermestoidea, commonly called the skin or hide beetles. Adult dermestids are serious agricultural pests, but the larvae consume flesh and tissues. Consequently, dermestid colonies are maintained by vertebrate zoologists, who use the larvae to deflesh zoological specimens in order to collect the skeletons.

**dermis:** thick layer of the skin that is **deep** to the **epidermis**, and that contains blood vessels, nerves, glands, muscles, and hair follicles. Adjective: dermal. Aka **corium**.

**Dermoptera:** 1. mammalian **order** to which the **colugos** belong. Adjective: dermopteran. Consists of one living family, the **Cynocephalidae**. Considered closely related to both the **Chiroptera** and the **Primates**, with which they share a common ancestor in the **Paleocene** or earlier. Some extinct 'primate' families, most notably the **Plesiadapidae**, have been removed from the order Primates and placed within Dermoptera. See Appendix 2, grandorder **Archonta** for the traditional taxonomic relationship to primates. 2. rarely, one of two suborders within the order Primates; the other suborder is **Euprimates**.

**descending colon:** third portion of the **colon** that begins when the **transverse colon** flexes and begins to descend and ends at the **sigmoid colon**.

**descent:** 1. downward inclination, slope or stairway. 2. derivation from an ancestor, as in **matriline** or **patriline** descent. 3. in **Darwinism, descent with modification**.

**descent of the testes:** process in the male fetus that begins after the sixth week, is usually completed during the twenty-eighth week of fetal development, and appears to be mediated by a shortening of the **gubernaculum**. The organs of the **spermatic cord** descend through the abdominal wall and into the scrotal sac.

**descent with modification:** original phrase used by Darwin, as well as **transmutation**, to describe gradual change from an ancestral form to a descendant form over time.

**description:** in taxonomy, a full statement of the character states that are diagnostic of a taxon.

**descriptive statistic:** in statistics, any abstracted value that characterizes a population or sample. Examples of descriptive statistics include the **mean** and **standard deviation** of a distribution, its skewness and kurtosis, etc.

**desert:** arid environment with sparse plant life, with flora and fauna adapted to dry conditions; rainfall averages less than 50 cm per year.

**desert varnish:** polished face of a stone caused by wind-blown sand on the surface oxidation. The amount of polish can be used to estimate the age of the stone.

**desertification:** formation of arid environments through natural climatic changes or due to human alterations.

**desertion:** abandonment of a mate and perhaps offspring in order to maximize fitness, and/or reduce mortality.

**desiccation:** process of removal of water; drying.

**desmocranium:** 1. mesoderm at the cranial end of the embryonic notochord. 2. portion of the adult **cranium** that is derived from the prenatal noncartilaginous cranium, and formed by **intramembranous ossification**. Cf. **chondrocranium**.

**determinate growth:** growth that is limited such that it ceases before the end of the life span of an individual.

**determinism:** 1. theory that certain outcomes are strictly predetermined by definable causes and natural laws, and are therefore entirely predictable. 2. in biology, any form of constraint on the development of an organ, process or behavior; if the constraint is genetic, then some degree of the effect is due to the possession of a particular genotype. Cf. **environmental determinism**.

**deterministic:** in mathematics, referring to a fixed relationship between two or more variables, without taking into account the effect of chance on the outcome of particular cases. Cf. **stochastic**.

**deterministic model:** dynamic mathematical model containing fixed values and relationships such that a given input value always produces the same output value, i.e. probability is not involved in the outcome. Cf. **stochastic model**.

**deterministic process:** any system, pathway or process in which all relationships are fixed so that the beginning event determines the sole outcome exactly. Cf. **stochastic process**.

**deuteranopia:** form of partial color blindness caused by any defect in X-linked recessive genes, resulting in green **color blindness**. While red and blue gene opsins are present in a single dose, the green opsin gene can be present in up to three copies. Aka the green opsin defect. See **protanopia** and **tritanopia**.

**deuterogenesis:** second phase of embryonic development, after **gastrulation**.

**Deutero-Malay:** ethnym for a hypothetical subgroup of **Mongoloids** who migrated from southeast Asia to Malaysia after the initial migration of the **proto-Malays**. See **Malay**.

**Developed Oldowan tradition:** 'expansion' of the **Oldowan tool tradition** that includes some spheroids, pointed choppers (proto-hand-axes), rough bifacial tools, a few very rare hand-axes, and several more evolved scraper tool forms; these tool are usually found in fine-grained sediments (e.g. alkaline lakeside sediments) and removed from sources of fresh water. At **Olduvai Gorge**, this tradition spans the 1.7 to 1.2 mya range.

‡ **development:** process of regulated **differentiation** of **tissues** that results from the interaction of a **genome** with its internal and external **environment**; changes from an undifferentiated or immature state to a highly organized, specialized, or mature state; **hyperplasia**. See **auxology** and **epistasis**. Cf. **growth**.

‡ **developmental acclimation:** see **acclimation**.

‡ **developmental acclimatization:** see **acclimatization**.

**developmental constraint:** any ontogenetic factor, such as an obligatory tissue interaction, that either prevents, limits, or channels a certain evolutionary change; such changes are viewed as modifications of later, rather than earlier, stages in developmental pathways.

**developmental control gene:** any of a large number of genes that function primarily to regulate the timing and course of differentiation during development.

**developmental disease:** any condition that interferes with the normal proliferation of regulative complexity in an organism; state of arrest of the process of differentiation from a simple to a more complex state. Examples are **spina bifida** and **anencephaly**.

**developmental genetics:** study of mutations that alter normal development in order to understand how genes control the developmental process.

**developmental homology:** anatomical similarity in different species owing to derivation from a common embryological source.

**developmental osteology:** study of the formation and growth of bone.

**developmental plasticity:** capacity for variable developmental outcomes in an organism as the result of the influences of environment on the genotype during growth. Cf. **canalization**.

**Devensian glaciation:** fourth major glaciation of the Pleistocene in the British Isles sequence; see **Würm glaciation**.

**Devil's Lair:** archaeological site found in 1978 in southwestern Australia dating to >32 kya (continuously occupied until 12 kya), and containing artifacts including early bone tools and beads. This site provided strong evidence that southwest Australia has been occupied for more than 30 ky.

**Devil's Tower child:** see **Gibraltar**.

**devolution:** retrogression from a derived to a primitive or less differentiated state; the reverse of **evolution**.

‡ **Devonian period:** period of the **Paleozoic era**, lasting from approximately 395 to 345 mya, in which amphibians, the first terrestrial vertebrates, appeared. Fossil teeth from cartilaginous fishes are common from this period. The Devonian was terminated by a major episode of **mass extinction**.

**DeVore, Irven** (1935–): US ethologist and anthropologist at Harvard. DeVore's early work was intended by his dissertation advisor, S. **Washburn**, to provide a model for early hominid behavior and ecology; he began work with studies of **baboons** in East Africa in 1959, and he co-produced several films on baboon behavior and ecology. With Richard **Lee**, he organized the Man the Hunter symposium in 1966 that also resulted in a book with the same title. This symposium recognized the important role of gathering by females and documented the steady caloric input of females to the total diet of bands of hunter–gatherers. DeVore later did fieldwork among human **hunter–gatherers**, and as a result his interests turned to foraging strategies, and eventually to **sociobiology** in which he trained a large number of students. Editor of *Primate Behavior: Field Studies of Monkeys and Apes* (1965).

**dexterity:** skill or adroitness in the use of the hand or body; high flexibility. In human biology this especially refers to the manipulative ability of the hands and fingers.

**dextrality:** state of having the right side of the body or its parts or members different from and usually more efficient than those of the left side. Adjective: dextral. In humans in particular, using and favoring the right hand, as opposed to **sinistrality.**

**dextrorotatory:** turning the plane of polarized light to the right, as with some crystals and solutions. Cf. **levorotatory.** See **D-form.**

**dextrosinistral:** pertaining to a naturally left-handed person who has been taught to use the right hand to write, draw, carve, work, etc.

**d.f.:** see **degrees of freedom.**

**D-form:** dextrorotatory form of a molecule, such as a **D-amino acid.** Cf. **L-form** and **levorotatory.** See **racemic** and **racemization.**

**diabase:** American term for **dolorite.**

**diabase tool:** implement made from **diabase.**

**diabetes insipidus, nephrogenic, type 1:** inherited disease of the kidneys marked by thirst and dehydration that causes copious urination and defective urine concentration by **alcohol dehydrogenase.** The autosomal dominant forms are due to mutations in either a precursor protein gene or the **vasopressin** gene itself. The more common X-linked recessive form (NDI1) is due to mutations in the vasopressin receptor gene. Aka nonsaccharine diabetes, polydipsia.

**diabetes mellitus, type I** (IDDM): juvenile onset, insulin-dependent diabetes mellitus is an inherited autoimmune condition characterized by abnormal sugar metabolism. The *IDDM1* gene is an autosomal recessive. In IDDM, the immune system attacks and kills the pancreatic beta cells that produce **insulin;** this results in chronic **hyperglycemia,** metabolic anomalies, and susceptibility to infections; often leads to a coma. It is treatable by substitution of functional insulin through recurrent injection (**substitutional gene therapy**). IDDM accounts for 10–15% of all cases of diabetes. Aka type I insulin-dependent diabetes mellitus, insulin-dependent diabetes, childhood onset diabetes, juvenile onset diabetes (JOD), ketosis prone diabetes, brittle diabetes.

**diabetes mellitus, type II** (NIDDM): noninsulin dependent diabetes mellitus is an abnormal, partly acquired condition characterized by the lack of an ability to utilize sugar, and by an excess secretion of sugar in the urine. **Insulin** is present at near normal or even above normal concentrations (hyperinsulinemia), but the tissues do not respond optimally (owing to 'insulin resistance'). Adult onset, 2nd–6th decades. Affected individuals are usually noticeably overweight and often have the so-called **metabolic syndrome.** Infrequently, nonobese adolescents acquire NIDDM in the form of maturity-onset diabetes of the young (MODY). Several susceptibility genes have been implicated but **penetrance** is variable and the heritable effect is polygenic. Aka insulin-independent diabetes, adult onset diabetes, noninsulin-dependent diabetes, maturity-onset diabetes (MOD), ketosis-resistant diabetes, stable diabetes. See the **thrifty genotype hypothesis** and **New World syndrome.**

**diachronic:** existing or occurring at a different time than something else; historical, developmental. Cf. **synchronic.**

**diacritica:** elements that distinguish one group from another. Adjective: diacritical.

**diademed sifaka:** vernacular for *Propithecus diadema.*

**diagenesis:** sum of all physical, chemical, and biological changes to which a sediment is subjected after deposition; the alteration of a fossil after deposition; see **permineralization** and **taphonomy.** Aka diagenetic breakage.

**diagnosis:** 1. an answer or solution to a problem. 2. in medicine, determination by examination of the nature and circumstances of a disease. 3. in systematics, a formal set of character states that fully describe a taxon, and that distinguish one taxon from another.

**diagnostic:** describes a distinguishing feature or characteristic, especially as used in taxonomy; a **key trait.** Diagnostic characters may characterize a species, in which case they are autapomorphic, or a group of related species (synapomorphic). See **autapomorphy** and **synapomorphy.**

**diakinesis:** in meiosis, the last of the five stages of prophase, in which the spireme threads break up into shorter and thicker chromosomes, and the nucleolus and nuclear membranes disappear.

**dialect:** local geographic variant of meaningful units of communication, which may include displays, etc. Dialects have been noted among some primate species.

**Diana monkey:** vernacular for *Cercopithecus diana.*

‡ **diaphragm:** see **respiratory diaphragm.**

‡ **diaphysis:** shaft of a **long bone,** located between the two **epiphyses.**

**diaplacental:** passing through the **placenta,** as with certain nutrients.

**diarthrotic joint:** joint that allows free movement. A **saddle joint** would be an example of such an articulation. See **joint**.

**diaspora:** 1. (Greek) term for dispersion. 2. the scattering or dispersion of any population, but especially one formerly united by a common belief system.

**diastem:** gap in the fossil record, often due to erosion or lack of deposition.

‡ **diastema:** space between contiguous teeth in a jaw; in some mammals, there is a diastema that allows space for a large **canine** tooth in the opposing jaw. Plural: diastemata.

**diathesis:** inherited or congenital bodily **predisposition** to a disease or metabolic structural abnormality; susceptibility to certain disorders.

**dicentric:** having two centromeres, as in certain abnormal chromosomes.

**dichopatric:** referring to populations of a species separated by distance or geographic features to the extent that **gene flow** is not possible. Cf. **allopatric**, **parapatric**, and **sympatric**.

**dichorionic placenta:** type of **placenta**, usually associated with twin pregnancies, in which a double **chorion** (one of the placental tissues) surrounds each **twin**.

**dichotomous data:** binary **data**; data that exist in only two states, present (1) or absent (0).

**dichotomous trait, character** or **feature:** trait that exists in only two states, such as presence or absence.

**dichotomy:** any division in an evolutionary line that results in two, and only two, **sister taxa**. Cf. **trichotomy**.

**dichromatic:** involving two colors, e.g. **sexual dichromatism** or **dichromatic vision**.

**dichromatic vision: color vision** made possible by light receptors that are maximally sensitive to two different light wavelengths (and white light) that are combined to form various hues. This type of color vision is found among some of the **prosimians**. Cf. **monochromatic vision**, **trichromatic vision**.

**dictyotene stage:** prolonged **diplotene stage** during meiotic **cell division**, seen during **oogenesis** but not spermatogenesis. Chromosomes have completed crossing over but have not dissociated; chromosomes may remain in this stage of 'suspended animation' for months or, as in humans and other long-lived species, even years. The probability of **nondisjunction** increases in proportion to the length of this stage.

**didymus:** 1. occurring in pairs. 2. synonym for the paired testes.

**Die Kelders Cave** (DK1): archaeological site located on the southwestern coast of South Africa, dated to 70 ± 4 kya, containing **Middle Stone Age** (MSA) and **Late Stone Age** (LSA) artifacts and hominid remains including nine human teeth in the MSA layers, and a child's partial skeleton in the more recent LSA layers,

dated to about 2 kya; all remains are attributed to *Homo sapiens*.

**Diego blood group** (DI): the Diego blood group antibodies, anti-Di(a) and anti-Di(b), are familial or low-incidence **antigens** that can result in **hemolytic disease of the newborn**. The antigens were discovered in a South American family in 1953 and are mutational variants of the *SLC4A1* gene. This so-called 'Mongoloid marker' is useful in population studies as it enables researchers to track the emigration of peoples from the Mammoth Steppe between the Tibetan Plateau and Mongolia to modern destinations in India, New Guinea, Kamchatka, and into the Americas as far south as Chile.

**diencephalon:** posterior region of the forebrain or **prosencephalon**; lies beneath the cerebral hemispheres and includes the **third ventricle, epithalamus, thalamus, hypothalamus,** and **pituitary gland**.

**diet:** 1. in humans, the customary food and drink regularly prepared and consumed by members of a particular culture. 2. substances regularly ingested by members of a species. See **anthropophagy, carnivory, coprophagy, faunivory, folivory, frugivory, geophagy, graminivory, granivory, gummivory, herbivory, insectivory, multivory, nectarivory, omnivory, phthiriophagy, phytophagy, piscivory,** and **zoophagy**.

‡ **dietary hypothesis:** model proposed by John T. Robinson in the 1960s that argues for the existence of two contemporary **hominid** lineages during the **Plio-Pleistocene**, each with contrasting ecological adaptations. One group of hominids is characterized by an adaptation to an **herbivorous** diet, and a second group by an adaptation to a **omnivorous** diet. See the **two-hominid theory**; cf. the **single species hypothesis**.

**dietary plasticity:** ability to switch diets and subsist on a variety of different types of food.

**dietary protein:** see **essential amino acids, complete protein, incomplete protein, partially complete protein,** and **protein quality**.

**dietary reconstruction:** interpretation of the diet of extinct species based on chemical analysis of bone, **coprolites**, evaluation of associated materials from living sites (in the case of humans) such as any disarticulated animal bones and plant material, and physical features of the species in question such as the structure of teeth.

**dietary rickets:** see **hypovitaminosis**.

**differentia:** diagnostic characters, as used by **Linnaeus**.

**differential female mortality:** explanation of increased mortality in females as a function of individual reproductive success. Certain females possess traits that are advantageous in terms of reproduction, but those same traits incur the cost of a lowered probability of ultimate survival. See **sex ratio adjustment**. Cf. **differential male mortality**.

**differential fertility:** tendency for some individuals in a population to produce more offspring than other individuals. See **natural selection**.

**differential fertility by genotype:** one of two fundamental mechanisms of **natural selection** (the other being **differential mortality**), referring to variation in the reproductive success of mature organisms.

**differential heat analysis:** noninvasive or remote sensing technique in which variable heat absorption and dissemination can be used to plot archaeological features.

**differential male mortality:** explanation of increased mortality in males as a function of individual reproductive success. Certain males possess traits that are advantageous in terms of reproduction, but those same traits incur the cost of a lowered probability of ultimate survival. Higher male mortality is common in most species, and is nearly universal in human societies. See **sex ratio adjustment** and **unguarded X chromosome**. Cf. **differential female mortality**.

‡ **differential mortality:** tendency for some individuals in a population to produce more offspring than other individuals who die before reproductive age. See **natural selection**.

**differential mortality by genotype:** 1. one of two fundamental mechanisms of **natural selection** (the other being **differential fertility**), referring to the death of some individuals of a population prior to their reproductive maturation. 2. synonymous phrase for the mechanism of **natural selection**.

‡ **differential net reproductive success:** average number of **offspring** that are produced, **survive**, and are able to reproduce; usually measured as the sum of individuals possessing one **phenotype** when compared with individuals of other phenotypes. Cf. **net reproductive success**.

**differential preservation:** pertaining to the relative abilities of different materials to resist degradation in archaeological and paleontological assemblages over time. An **artifact** made of a softer material such as wood, hair, or tissue is rarely preserved; harder materials such as animal bone, rock, and ashes tend to be found most frequently in older sites. The term is also applied to human bone, as porous bone tends to degrade faster than compact bone, and the bones of children and females faster than those of adult males, which possess a higher calcium content. Awareness of differential preservation is an important factor when one attempts to reconstruct the demographic profile of a paleopopulation.

‡ **differential reproduction:** Darwinian concept that describes the tendency for some individuals in a population to produce more offspring than others.

**differential splicing:** see **alternative splicing**.

**differential success:** see **differential net reproductive success**.

**differentiation:** origin of cellular differences during embryogenesis between the parts of an originally homogeneous cell mass; specialization in structure or function during which cells may lose their ability to divide. Aka **epigenesis**. See **post-mitotic cell**.

**diffuse idiopathic skeletal hyperostosis** (DISH): spontaneous, generalized growth of bony tissue; aka generalized osteohypertrophy.

**diffusion:** 1. the process of becoming widely spread. 2. in anthropology, the transmission of elements of a particular **culture** among synchronic members of a generation, often to another culture, and one of four of Fagan's models used to characterize culture change; cf. **enculturation**. 3. in genetics, the spread of an advantageous **phenotype** through space and time, often leaving as evidence a **cline**. 4. in chemistry, the random movement of molecules from a region of higher to lower molecular concentration.

**diffusionism:** historical approach to anthropology in the midtwentieth century that emphasized the transmission of items from culture from one place to another rather than the temporal development of culture(s). Diffusionists attempted to explain the appearance of pyramids in Egypt, Central America, and southeast Asia as manifestations of a single invention, rather than independent inventions in diverse people. Coined by German geographer Friedrich Ratzel (1844–1904), the term and the approach are no longer considered of major theoretical importance.

**digamety:** having two kinds of gametes, one containing a factor that produces males, and the other, females; aka heterogamety.

**digastric fossa:** groove on the interior, lower side of the mandible and to which the digastric muscles, which help to depress the mandible, are attached. Plural: digastric fossae.

**digenic:** referring to any **trait** explained by the effects a sets of **alleles** at two loci or **genes**. Cf. **monogenic** and **polygenic**.

**DiGeorge syndrome** (DGS): heritable, phenotypically variable condition involving dysmorphologies described by the medical acronym CATCH22: cardiac defects, abnormal facies, thymus defects with loss of T cell function, cleft palate with speech impairment, and hypocalcemia. Death usually occurs before age two. The cause of the condition in type I is a microdeletion of a portion of chromosome 22; the symptomatic variability is directly related to the size of the deletion. Type II is due to a microdeletion in chromosome 10.

**digestion:** process in which food is broken down into smaller chemical components so that it can be absorbed and utilized by the body. Verb: to digest.

**digestive system:** physiological system that receives, breaks down, and absorbs nutrients and eliminates wastes; in primates, that system consists of the **alimentary canal**, liver, and pancreas.

**digging stick:** crude **tool** used by modern people to locate **cryptic** resources such as insects, roots, and tubers. See **termiting** and **Drimolen**.

**digit:** 1. any of the appendages found on vertebrate paws that contain **phalanges**. In primates, the fingers and toes. 2. a number less than ten: 0, 1, 2 ,..., etc. 3. an ancient measure, the breadth of a finger. Adjective: digital.

**digitigrade:** describes a form of **quadrupedal locomotion** in which animals support their body mass on their **phalanges** with the wrist and heel bones held off the ground. Among the primates this condition is found only among some of the African **cercopithecines**, most notably the patas monkey (*Erythrocebus*). Cf. **plantigrade**, **palmigrade**.

**digitize:** to transform into a numerical representation.

**dihybrid cross:** mating between two individuals each of whom is **heterozygous** at two loci of interest.

**dihybrid individual:** individual that is **heterozygous** for each of two pairs of genes of interest. Aka dihybrid. See **dihybrid cross**.

**dihydrotestosterone** (DHT): **hormone** derived from **testosterone** that stimulates the development of male external reproductive structures (including hair growth) and is essential for male sexual function.

**Dillerlemur robinettei:** archaic mammal from the early Eocene of North America belonging to the **Plesiadapiforme** family **Paromomyidae**; consists of one species. Body mass estimated around 40 g. See Appendix 1 for taxonomy.

**dilution effect:** effect that results from a large number of individuals in a group, which decreases the probability that any one individual will be taken by a predator; aka safety in numbers.

**diluvial:** 1. present time in some geological time scales. 2. pertaining to a flood or periods of inundation.

**diluvianism:** eighteenth century idea that certain geological phenomena constitute evidence of the biblical flood; at that time, certain mixed sediments were termed 'diluvial' in the minds of the three chief proponents, William **Buckland**, William Conybeare (1785–1873) and Adam Sedgwick (1787–1857). Diluvianism was replaced by **uniformitarianism** after 1870.

**diluvium:** glacial drift consisting of gravels and, sometimes, the remains of extinct animals; thought by Buckland, Cuvier and other defenders of **catastrophism** to be the result of a deluge.

**dimer:** molecule composed of two identical, simpler molecules (monomers), e.g. **thymine dimer**. Cf. **polymer**.

**dimorphism:** predominance of two forms within a breeding population, usually lacking intermediate forms. See, for example, **sexual dimorphism** and **sexual dichromatism**. Cf. **monomorphism**.

**Dingcun:** archaeological site found in 1953 at Dingcun, Xiangten County, Shanxi Province, China, dated to 210–160 kya, and that contains large points and chopping tools. The hominid remains include an infant parietal and assorted teeth of very reduced size attributed to **archaic *Homo sapiens***. Aka Ting-tsun (Hsiandfenhsien, Shansi), Dingchun, Dingcum, Xiangfen.

***Dinopithecus ingens*** Broom, 1937: species of cercopithecine from the Pleistocene of South Africa; **monotypic**; many workers think that there is not enough difference between this species and ***Papio*** to warrant generic distinction. Known only by skulls from one sample recovered from Swartkrans. Skull and dentition almost identical to that of extant baboons. Large body size, estimated to be around 80 kg. Dental formula: 2.1.2.3. Associated **fauna** usually found with savanna communities; environment and large body size strongly suggestive that this monkey was terrestrial. See Appendix 1 for taxonomy.

***Dionysopithecus*** (= *?Micropithecus*) ***shuangouensis*** Li, 1978: **monotypic** genus of **hominoids** from the early to middle Miocene of China and Pakistan belonging to the catarrhine family **Proconsulidae**. Estimated body mass around 3.5 kg. Dental formula: 2.1.2.3; dentition suggestive of **frugivory**. In many respects *Dionysopithecus* is very similar in appearance to modern gibbons; it is also very similar to *Micropithecus* from East Africa and may eventually be referred to that genus as a species. See Appendix 1 for taxonomy.

**dipheny:** presence in a population of two discontinuous phenotypes without corresponding genetic variability.

**diphyletic taxon:** phylogenetic group that contains members descended from two different groups of ancestors. Cf. **polyphyletic taxon**.

**diphyodont:** describes a mammal that has two sets of teeth during its lifetime. The first set are the **deciduous dentition** and are replaced by the **adult dentition**. **Noun:** diphyodontism. It is the normal state in most mammals and in all primates. Cf. **monophyodont**.

**diploë:** 1. term meaning two or double. 2. **cancellous bone** between the inner and outer layers of compact bone of the cranial bones.

**diplogenesis:** abnormal duplication of a structure or segment, as in **polydactyly**.

**diploic expansion:** see **expanding matrix distortion**.

**diploic veins:** veins that form in the **cancellous bone** between the inner and outer tables of **compact bone**.

‡ **diploid:** having two nearly identical sets of **chromosomes** or **chromatids**. The sets are **homologous**, one of maternal origin and one of paternal origin, and morphologically nearly identical except for the **sex chromosomes** of the **heterogametic sex**, which are homologous but not morphologically identical in most mammals. See **haploid** and **aneuploid**.

**diploid genetic system:** system of sexual reproduction in which both males and females are somatically **diploid**, as in primates.

**diploid life cycle:** describes organisms in which all cells in the multicellular stage of an organism are **diploid**, as in mammals.

‡ **diploid number** (2N): the number of chromatids in a normal somatic cell or in a germ cell prior to meiosis.

**diploidization:** restoration of the diploid chromosome complement, as in a **fertilized ovum**.

**diplopia:** perception of two images of a single object.

**diplotene stage:** during **meiosis**, the fourth of five stages of prophase during which the intimately paired homologous chromosomes begin to separate, forming a characteristic **chiasma** or X appearance; at this stage, blocks of genes are exchanged between **homologous chromosomes**. Aka diplonema.

**diplotype:** combination of two **haplotypes** possessed by an individual.

**direct bilirubin:** bilirubin glucuronide, taken up by the liver and excreted into the bile; Aka excretable **bilirubin**.

**direct calorimetry:** measurement of heat produced in an oxidative reaction. See **bomb calorimeter**. Cf. **indirect calorimetry**.

**direct competition:** exclusion of an individual from resources by aggressive behavior from other individuals or species. See **male–male competition**.

**direct dating:** establishing a range of time within which an artifact was made or deposited in an archaeological context by study of the object or sample itself. Cf. **indirect dating**.

**direct fitness:** portion of a focal individual's **inclusive fitness** that is due to reproduction. Cf. **indirect fitness**.

‡ **direct percussion:** stone tool-making technique in which a flint **core** is held and flakes are detached by striking it with a **hammerstone**; produces a **conchoidal fracture**.

**direct repair:** any mechanism of **DNA repair** involving reversal of damage to **DNA**.

**direct role:** behavior or set of behaviors displayed by a subgroup of a society that benefits other subgroups and therefore society as a whole. Cf. **indirect role**.

**direct value:** worth assigned to biological diversity. Direct value is assigned to those products that are harvested and used by humans. It is divided into consumptive use value, products such as fuelwood and game that are consumed locally, and productive use value, products harvested and sold in commercial markets (this would include **bushmeat**). Also referred to as use value, commodity value. Cf. **indirect value**.

**directed (molecular** or **protein) evolution:** manipulation of proteins *in vitro* by using **recombinant DNA technology** to produce products considered more efficient or useful than their wild type ancestors. See **anthropogenic selection**.

**directed mutation:** controversial 'Lamarckian' hypothesis proposed in 1970 and again in 1988 that bacteria possess genetic programs that alter mutation modes and/or rates under specific environmental conditions. Aka adaptive mutation. See **hypermutability** and **SOS polymerase**.

**directed selection:** control of selection by humans; see **artificial selection**, **directed evolution**, and **anthropogenic selection**.

‡ **directional selection:** selection that operates monotonically against one end of the range of **variation** of a **trait**, and hence over time, tends to shift the entire population **mean** toward an optimum at the opposite end, such as selection for increased body size. Occurs when individual **fitness** tends to increase or decrease with the **selective value** of phenotypic traits. Aka dynamic selection, progressive selection. Cf. **disruptive selection** and **stabilizing selection**.

**disaccharide:** complex sugar formed by the conjugation of two simple sugars (**monosaccharides**); for example, sucrose is formed from glucose and fructose. Cf. **polysaccharide**.

**disaccharide intolerance type I:** fermentation of accumulated sugars by bacteria results in symptomatic abdominal gas and painful, explosive diarrhea due to inability to absorb glucose and fructose after sucrose reduction; the cause is a mutation in the sucrase gene, an autosomal recessive. Aka sucrase deficiency, sucrose intolerance, loss of sucrase–isomaltase activity. One of several types (I, II, etc.); all have in common an inability to process the complex sugars lactose (see type III below), maltose, or sucrose, due respectively to **lactase deficiency**, maltase deficiency, or sucrase deficiency. Cf. **fructose intolerance** and **glucose–galactose malabsorption**.

**disaccharide intolerance type III:** refers to any of a number of autosomal recessive mutations resulting in a deficient enzyme, adult **lactase**; results in an inability to metabolize milk sugar (lactose), causing symptomatic abdominal gas, cramps, and bloating after the ingestion of milk products. Type III is the adult form, in which the enzyme functions only in youth, but is then lost in some populations, producing a persistence/nonpersistence polymorphism. Adult heterozygotes usually experience gas pain after consuming dairy products. This nonpersistence condition is polymorphic and found in high frequency among many human populations that did not domesticate cows or other mammals, and that have not maintained through natural selection a functional allele of the enzyme. Sometimes called adult lactase deficiency, when described in terms of the enzyme itself. Because adult animals lose the ability to digest lactose, and because of the worldwide prevalence of the deficiency in humans, lactose malabsorption and intolerance is considered the normal state for human adults. *Adult lactase persistence*, found in fewer populations, is the rarer, derived form of the polymorphism, and generally characterizes pastoral populations in northern Europe, Arabia, and East Africa. Diversity in the African U-type haplotypes is consistent with the **out of Africa II** model of recent human dispersion.

**disadvantageous mutation:** see **deleterious**.

**disarticulation:** dismemberment; severing a joint between two or more bones.

**disassortative mating:** nonrandom pairing of individuals who differ from each other in one or more traits; **negative assortative mating**.

**disc:** see **disk**

**discard history:** spatial distribution of artifacts, flake debris, animal bones and other remains at a prehistoric living site or camp site.

**disciplinary episode:** event in which one primate, often a dominant male, administers a painful lesson, such as a neck bite, to an offending juvenile or adult female.

**discoid:** tool that is disk-shaped, i.e. flat and circular.

**discontinuous variation:** groups of phenotypes that fall into two or more distinct, nonoverlapping classes; characteristic of simple Mendelian traits; Aka nonmetric variation. Cf. **continuous variation**.

**discordant trait, character,** or **feature:** said of a matched group or pair (such as **twins**) when only one possesses a given character state; discordance. Cf. **concordant trait**.

**discovery:** perception of something extant but that had not previously been observed; a find. Cf. **invention**.

**discrete random variable:** variable that can take on only specific values. For example, sex is sometimes coded as either 'F' or 'M'. Cf. **continuous random variable**.

**discrete signal:** communication that consists of dichotomies (either on or off), such as sexually receptive or not sexually receptive, aggressive or not aggressive, etc.; aka digital signal. Cf. **graded signal**.

‡ **discrete trait, character** or **feature:** 1. a **trait** or **character** with morphs that fall into clear, mutually exclusive categories; e.g. purple versus white flowers in the common garden pea. See **binary trait** and **multistate trait**. 2. **variable** that can take on only specific

values; see **discrete random variable**. Cf. **continuous trait**.

**discrimination learning set** (DLS): measurement of learning in a primate subject as part of an **operant conditioning** study. The subject animal is presented with stimuli with no way of predicting which stimuli will be reinforced but with clues needed to respond correctly in the future. The percentage of correct responses in multiple trials of the same animal is a measurement of learning and forms the DLS.

‡ **disease:** morbid process with a characteristic sequence of symptoms affecting either the whole body of an organism or any of its parts or systems; any illness, sickness or ailment. See **degenerative disease, infectious disease, genetic disease, nutritional disease**. See also **endocrine disorder, metabolic disorder, obstetrical and gynecological disorders, hematologic disorder,** and **cardiovascular disorder**. Cf. **illness** and **disorder**.

**disease reservoir:** alternate **host** of a **pathogen**, usually a passive carrier of an **agent** of disease. Aka reservoir of infection.

**DISH:** see **diffuse idiopathic skeletal hyperostosis**.

**disharmony law:** principle that the **logarithm** of a dimension of any part of an animal is proportional to the logarithm of the body length of an animal. See **allometry**.

**disjunction:** 1. normal separation of homologous **chromosomes** during anaphase I of **meiosis**. 2. the normal separation of **sister chromatids** during anaphase II of **meiosis** and/or anaphase of **mitosis**. Cf. **nondisjunction**.

**disk:** 1. stone implement that is either oval, round, or even square, and that has irregular, sharp edges. 2. short for **intervertebral disk**. 3. short for **embryonic disk**. Also spelled disc.

**disomy:** see **uniparental disomy**.

**disorder:** derangement or abnormality of function; a morbid physical or mental state. Common examples in humans include **affective disorder**, sleep disorder, and vegetative disorder. Cf. **disease** and **illness**.

**dispermy:** fertilization of any haploid egg by two haploid sperm, resulting in a triploid embryo; there is speculation that a theoretical mode of twinning, **uniovular dispermatic twins**, may also occur in this manner. See **polyspermy**.

‡ **dispersal:** 1. permanent emigration of individuals out of a group. Among primates this occurs when members of one sex leave the **natal group** at **puberty** or it may occur when a larger group undergoes permanent **fission** into two or more smaller groups, as has been observed among **chimpanzees**. See **diaspora**. 2. slow, almost imperceptible encroachment or retreat of species into or away from a developing or receding niche; scattering, dispersion. Cf. **migration**.

**dispersal pattern:** biogeographical and temporal scattering of organisms and/or elements in an environment, around barriers, and through **habitats.**

**dispersalist model:** any interpretation of extant biographical distribution of taxa primarily in terms of the **dispersal** (2) of those taxa across or around existing barriers.

**dispersive replication:** old model of DNA replication that proposed that old and newly duplicated fragments of DNA are interspersed among the strands of the duplicated DNA. Cf. **semiconservative replication.**

**displacement:** interaction between two primates in which one approaches the other, who then gives up its place to the approacher.

**displacement activity: conflict behavior** that is seemingly irrelevant and appears to be out of behavioral context; for example, when a primate encounters a member of another group and is conflicted about whether to attack or to flee, but sits and starts scratching with its hind leg. See **redirected behavior, intention movement.**

‡ **display:** 1. behavior pattern that has been modified in the course of **evolution** to convey **information.** A display is a special kind of **signal.** See **distraction display** and **epideictic display.** 2. stage in an immune response when macrophages or other immune cells present fragments of foreign particles they have encountered, on their plasma membranes; this provides a signal to **T cells.**

**disruptive selection:** selection that operates against the middle of the range of variation over time, hence tends to produce a bimodal distribution in a population optimizing the extremes of morphological variation. Occurs when individuals with average phenotypic values of a trait have lower **fitness.** Aka diversifying selection, centrifugal selection. Cf. **directional selection** and **stabilizing selection.**

**dissociation:** 1. separation from. 2. in genetics, the fission of a larger metacentric chromosome into two acrocentric chromosomes, thus splitting the former linkage group into two smaller, independently segregating linkage groups. See **Robertsonian translocation.**

‡ **distal:** 1. anatomical directional term meaning further away from the mid-point of the body or from the attached end of a limb. Cf. **proximal.** 2. in dentition, distal refers to the posterior surface of the back teeth and the lateral surface of the front teeth.

**distal hyperextensibility of the thumb:** ability in some individuals to bend the thumb sharply backward, or dorsally; a human **polymorphism.**

**distal thigh circumference: anthropometric** measurement of distance around the lower thigh as measured with a tape measure placed just superior to the femoral **epicondyles** and passed horizontally around the thigh. Combined with the other thigh circumferences, used for estimations of body density, adiposity, lean body mass, and for various applications in **human engineering.** See **midthigh circumference, proximal thigh circumference.**

**distance:** 1. amount of space between two things, such as points, lines, etc.. 2. remoteness. 3. in taxonomy, refers to the **quantitatively** measured difference between the phenetic appearance of two groups or individuals, such as populations or **species**; aka **phenetic distance.** See **genetic distance.**

**distance curve:** graphic measure of some variable over time, e.g. a person's height at different ages.

**distillization:** mode of fossilization involving the removal of volatile organic compounds, to leave a carbon residue. Cf. **permineralization.**

**distoangular dental impaction:** condition in which a tooth is placed at an angle in the alveolus and in distal contact with either the ramus of the mandible or the tooth behind it as to be incapable of complete eruption. See **dental impaction.**

**distobuccal:** pertaining to the surface or feature of a **premolar** or **molar** that is on both the posterior surface and the cheek surface of the tooth.

**distolingual:** pertaining to the surface or feature of a **premolar** or **molar** that is on both the posterior surface and the tongue surface of the tooth.

**distraction display:** performance by a parent that draws attention of aggressors or **predators** away from its offspring.

**distress call:** loud call made by a startled animal. Aka fright cry, mercy cry, pain cry.

**distribution:** 1. act of arranging or scattering. 2. arrangement or disposition in time and space. 3. frequency of occurrence within a geographical range or landscape. See **clinal distribution, geographical distribution, population distribution.** 4. arrangement of statistical data that exhibits the frequency or the probability of the occurrence of the **values** of a variable; see **normal distribution.**

**disturbance process:** changing the archaeological context of materials within a site; such processes may be either human (construction or farming) or natural (freeze–thaw cycles or erosion).

**disulfide linkage:** chemical bond formed between two sulfur atoms, as occurs between the amino acids cysteine and methionine.

**ditokous:** producing two offspring per brood. See **biparity.**

**ditypic:** having two prominent morphs within a species; see **dimorphism.** Cf. **bitypic.**

‡ **diurnal:** active during daylight. See **nocturnal** and **crepuscular.**

**divergence:** accumulation of dissimilar characters or genetic differences that cause the demes or **species** concerned to become increasingly different.

**divergent evolution:** separation of formerly similar species in different morphological or biochemical directions, and that can produce differences resulting in less resemblance over time. See **allopatry**.

**diversifying selection:** see **disruptive selection**.

**diversity:** used in reference to numbers of taxa, or variations in morphology.

**diversity index:** measure of the number of species in an ecological community, sample, or fossil assemblage; usually a ratio of the number of species to the number of individuals. Examples are the Shannon–Weiner index, richness index, Brillouin index, and Simpson index.

‡ **division of labor:** partitioning of work to subsets within a group of organisms. This may take the specific form of (a) a reproductive division of labor, in which **heterokaryotypes** assume specific roles according to sex (or **ploidy**); or (b) a more general form in which individuals form more or less amorphous behavioral units, ranks, castes, guilds, or vocations, and in which case the criteria for membership may be variable, as in humans.

‡ **dizygotic twins** (DZT): see **twins, dizygotic**.

**dizygous:** 1. pertaining to two zygotes, e.g. fraternal or nonidentical twins; aka dizygotic.

**dizygous twin correlation:** measure of covariation among pairs of fraternal twins for a given trait. If the trait is complex and is heritable, then the correlation for dizygous twin pairs will always be lower than the **monozygous twin correlation**. See **heritability**.

*Djebelemur martinezi* Hartenberger and Marandar, **1992:** poorly known adapoid **prosimian** from the early Eocene of Africa, belonging to the notharctid subfamily **Cercamoniinae; monotypic;** some authors consider this genus to be allied with the anthropoids. Known from mandibular fragment containing cheek teeth; an associated maxilla is referred to *Tabelia*. Small body mass estimated at 100 g. **Bunodont** dental morphology and small body size suggestive of **frugivory**. See Appendix 1 for taxonomy.

**Djurab Desert:** see **Toros-Menalla**. Aka Djourab Desert.

**DK:** Donald's (MacInnes) **Korongo** at **Olduvai Gorge**.

**D : L ratio:** see **amino acid racemization**.

**D-loop:** only significant length of noncoding sequence (about 1 kb) in the 16 kb length of mammalian **mtDNA**. A segment of **mitochondrial DNA** in which one strand contains DNA components and the opposite strand contains the structural components of RNA; the RNA strand is base-paired to the DNA strand, and forms a DNA–RNA hybrid.

**Dmanisi:** archaeological site found in 1936 on the eastern edge of the Black Sea in Georgia, the Caucasus, southern Russia, dated to possibly 1.8–1.6 mya, and that contains both stone artifacts and hominid remains found in 1989 including a fossil mandible (D211) provisionally assigned to *Homo erectus*. The site was reworked in 1999 and yielded choppers, chopping tools and their cores, animal bones of fauna found today only in Africa (giraffe, gazelle, rhinoceros, ostrich), and two partial hominid craniofacial specimens with cranial capacities of 650 cm³ (D2282) and 780 cm³ (D2280) provisionally attributed to *Homo ergaster*; the date was confirmed at 1.75 mya. A third, more complete and even smaller (600 cm³, juvenile?), almost **habiline**-like cranium (D2700, attributed provisionally to *Homo georgicus*) with an associated mandible (D2735) was reported in 2000–02. The smallness of these habiline-like specimens calls into question the idea that tall, large-brained erectines were the first to walk **out of Africa I**.

‡ **DNA:** deoxyribonucleic acid. Usually, a long, unbranched **polynucleotide** of paired **bases** (see the **base pairing rule**) linked by two spiraling **backbones** running in opposite directions (DNA is thus double stranded, forming an **antiparallel double helix**); DNA is the primary hereditary material in all cells. The majority of DNA is located within the **chromosomes**. DNA is the 'genetic blueprint' for an organism. See **ancient DNA, antisense DNA, B-DNA (right-handed DNA), cDNA, dsDNA, duplex DNA, junk DNA (spacer DNA), mitochondrial DNA (mtDNA), nonsense DNA, rDNA, recombinant DNA, repetitive DNA, satellite DNA, selfish DNA (parasite DNA), shared DNA, template DNA, transconformational DNA, vDNA, Y chromosome DNA,** and **Z-DNA (left-handed DNA)**. Cf. **RNA**.

**DNA analysis:** extraction and characterization of **DNA** for any of several reasons of anthropological interest, including for medical diagnosis, **paternity ascertainment, genetic genealogy** and for forensic applications. See **DNA fingerprinting** and **ancient DNA**.

**DNA-binding motif:** certain sequences, also called boxes, that facilitate protein binding to DNA. Such motifs are highly conserved; see, for example, the **SRY box**. Aka DNA-binding domain.

**DNA chip:** see **DNA microarray**.

**DNA cloning:** amplification of a segment of DNA (the clone) after insertion of the **clone** *in vitro* into a suitable DNA **vector** (3), such as a modified virus.

**DNA-cutting enzyme:** see **restriction enzyme**.

**DNA damage and repair theory of aging:** intracellular, stochastic model of aging in which the major premise is that the molecular repair machinery that normally repairs DNA just after **DNA replication** decreases with the age of an organism. DNA repair efficiency is also known to correlate with

**maximum lifespan potential** when viewed across many organisms.

**DNA damage pathway:** biochemical series of events during the 'resting' G1 phase of the cell cycle during which cells with irreparably damaged DNA are tagged for **apoptosis**. The *p53* **tumor suppressor** is at the center of the pathway.

**DNA fingerprint, fingerprinting** or **technique:** use of polymorphic DNA fragments (**STRs** and **VNTRs**) and unique **DNA sequences** to identify specific individuals. Aka DNA typing. See **DNA profile.**

**DNA helix:** see **double helix;** aka Watson–Crick helix.

**DNA hybridization:** process during which one single strand of DNA is bonded to its complementary sequence. With this technique, double-stranded **DNA** is thermally dissociated, creating the potential for single strands from two different **species** to bond *in vitro*, forming a hybrid DNA molecule. Evolutionary relationships can be deduced from the number of mismatched **base pairs** remaining in the hybrid DNA. Aka DNA–DNA hybridization. See **evolutionary conservation.**

‡ **DNA ligase:** repair enzyme capable of rejoining broken strands of DNA.

**DNA-like RNA** (dRNA): RNA molecules that are neither **tRNA** nor **rRNA**. dRNA includes **mRNA, hmRNA,** and **hnRNA.**

**DNA methylation:** addition of **methyl groups** to specific locations on a **DNA** molecule. The absence of methylation is required for **transcription**; methylation causes gene inactivation. Where present, methylation occurs immediately after DNA replication. DNA methylation is important in **genomic imprinting** and **telomeric silencing.**

**DNA microarray:** set of target genes embedded on a glass chip; labeled **cDNAs** bind specifically to these and fluoresce. The technique is use to detect certain **SNPs**, toxic agents, and for other purposes in biotechnology. Aka DNA chip, gene chip, solid phase substrate.

**DNA molecule:** see **DNA.**

**DNA mutation:** see **point mutation.**

‡ **DNA polymerase** (DNAP): any of a class of enzymes that catalyze the formation of a complementary strand of deoxyribonucleotides, using a single strand of DNA as a template during **DNA replication**. Polymerases also repair mismatched base pairs. Cf. **RNA polymerase.**

**DNA probe:** short sequence of labeled DNA that corresponds to a specific gene; when applied to a prepared cell, the probe aligns with the corresponding gene sequence, and the label reveals its exact location in the genome. The label may be either a radioactive isotope or a specific dye-absorbing compound. Aka probe, gene probe, hybridization probe.

**DNA profile:** unique DNA banding pattern profile for an individual, except in the case of **monozygotic twins**, who have the same banding patterns. DNA profiles are used to establish twin type, as well as paternity, by comparing DNA characteristics of cotwins, or fathers and children; also used in **forensic** applications for individual identification. See **DNA fingerprinting.**

**DNA repair:** correction of a **mutation** through mechanisms such as **excision repair** and **direct repair.**

**DNA repair disorders:** class of diseases characterized by deficient DNA replication or repair, including **ataxia telangiectasia, Bloom syndrome,** Fanconi anemia, and **xeroderma pigmentosum.**

**DNA repair mechanisms:** see **direct repair** and **excision repair.**

**DNA replication:** process of DNA synthesis prior to cell division, in which the opened parental strands serve as templates for the construction of sister chromatids. See **semiconservative replication.**

**DNA restriction fragment:** truncated segment of a longer DNA molecule produced by the action of a **restriction enzyme.** See **restriction fragment length polymorphism.**

**DNA sequence:** The linear order of **nucleotides** in **DNA.**

**DNA sequencing:** ascertainment of the linear order of nucleotides in a fragment, gene or longer length of **DNA**, using one of the **DNA sequencing techniques**; once a **DNA sequence** is known, it can be used in clinical or forensic applications, or for solving problems of biological or evolutionary significance.

**DNA sequencing techniques:** analytical procedure that consists of (a) selection of DNA clones; (b) causing base-specific reactions to occur; (c) separation by fragment size on sequencing gels; and (d) automated reading of the banded gels as a sequence of A, T, G, and C bases. There are two common methods: the 'chain termination' method of Sanger and colleagues, and the 'chemical' method of Maxam and Gilbert. Hood and colleagues developed automation devices in the mid-1980s, and this final step made the **Human Genome Project** feasible. Aka **DNA sequence** analysis, nucleotide sequencing.

**DNA structure:** see **DNA** and **double helix.**

**DNA transposition:** change of position of a **transposable genetic element** from one site to another in the genetic material of cells. DNA transposition leaves a copy of the transposable sequence at the original site, and another copy is transposed to the new site. Transposition events can severely alter the integrity of target DNA, potentially causing insertion mutations and changing gene expression. Aka transposition. See **scattered repeat sequences.**

**DNA typing:** see **DNA fingerprint.**

**DNA variation:** deviation from a normal nucleotide sequence within a population. See **SNP.**

**DNAP:** abbreviation for **DNA polymerase.**

**DNH:** see **Drimolen.**

**Dobzhansky, Theodozius Grigorievich** (1900–75): Russian-born US *Drosophila* geneticist and evolutionary biologist; trained initially in Russia (1918–27) with S. **Chetverikov**, then in Brazil; he also worked for a time (1927–33) in **Morgan's** 'fly room' at Columbia, where he studied the mechanism of sex determination in the fruit fly. His work on *Genetics and the Origin of Species* (1937), announced the **modern synthesis.** He applied the principles of genetics and biology to the hominid fossil record, and his discussion of **competitive exclusion principle** was influential. Dobzhansky is also noted for his development of **evolutionary systematics.**

**docosahexanoic acid** (DHA): long-chain polyunsaturated **fatty acid** required for growth of brain structures; the preformed acyl component is found predominately in the marine food chain. Researchers have suggested that DHA and **arachidonic acid** were substances critical to increased **encephalization** in **hominid** lineages. Aka omega-3 fatty acid.

**documented collection:** skeletal collection consisting of known individuals and life data such as sex, age, stature, ethnicity, and cause of death, making them a useful standard with which to compare unknown material.

**dog eye:** vernacular designation among the Chinese for other people without an **epicanthic fold,** i.e. the Caucasoid eye.

**Dolhinow, Phyllis Carol (Jay-Dolhinow)** (1933–): US primatologist at UC Berkeley; Aka Phyllis Jay. A **Washburn** student at the University of Chicago, she studied northern Indian langurs (***Presbytis entellus***) in the field as early as 1958, and focused on mother–infant relations and social development. Dolhinow was one of the first primatologists of the modern era to utilize data from primate field studies. Editor of *Primates: Studies in Adaptation and Variability* (1968); editor of *Primate Patterns* (1972); co-editor (with S. Washburn) of *Perspectives on Human Evolution* (1968).

‡ **dolichocephalic:** pertaining to **dolichocephaly.** Aka dolichocranic.

**dolichocephaly:** having a relatively 'long' or narrow head, with a **cranial index** of 74.99 or less; dolichocranic, dolichocephalic. Applied to skeletal material rather than to living humans. Early humans are considered to have dolichocranic heads, with human heads becoming more **brachycranic** recently. Cf. **brachycephaly, mesocephaly.**

**dolichocranic:** pertaining to **dolichocephaly.** Aka dolichocephalic.

**dolichohieric:** pertaining to a length–breadth sacral index of less than 99.99.

**dolichopentagonal form:** term used by some paleoanthropologists in the past to refer to a five-sided outline of a **cranium** when viewed from behind, in **norma verticalis.** Adjective: pentagonid. See *Homo erectus.*

***Dolichopithecus*** Deperet, 1889: genus of **colobine** monkey known from the Pliocene of Europe and the Far East; two species. Estimated body mass around 20 kg. **Shows sexual dimorphism** in dentition and skull size. **Postcrania** suggestive of a terrestrial habit. It is believed by some workers that *Dolichopithecus* foraged on the forest floor in order to partition resources with the **sympatric** and arboreal *Mesopithecus.* Dental formula: 2.1.2.3; dentition fully adapted for **folivory.** See Appendix 1 for taxonomy.

**dolichouranic:** in reference to the **external palatal index,** with an index of 109.00 or less; such an individual is considered to have a long narrow palate.

**Dollo's law, principle,** or **rule:** statement inferred from the fossil record suggesting that once a complex character has disappeared from a lineage, it would not reappear later in that lineage as exactly the same feature; i.e. that **evolution** is irreversible. Aka irreversibility rule, Arber's law.

**Dolni Vestonice:** archaeological site found in 1985 in Moravia, Czechoslavakia, dated to 27–25 kya, and that contains **Upper Paleolithic** artifacts including three living structures and some of the earliest ceramics consisting of figurines and fired clay. The site also contained fine needles made of bone and possibly evidence of woven textiles. Hominid remains include three adorned **Cro-Magnons** thought to have been buried at the same time.

**dolomite:** type of limestone in which magnesium replaces calcite; sediment containing more than 50% calcium magnesium carbonate.

**dolorite:** medium-grained, dark igneous rock. Aka dolerite.

**domain:** discrete structural unit within either (1) a chromosome, or (2) the amino acid sequence of a protein. Protein domains are modular units characterized by specific molecular sizes, configurations, molecular behaviors or functions. Aka molecular motif. Cf. **CpG island.** See **conserved domain.**

**Domain:** highest taxonomic entity, above the Kingdom; three Domains exist, the **Bacteria,** the **Archaea,** and the **Eukara.**

**domestic selection:** selective **breeding** of plants and animals controlled by humans; the choice of particular individuals for reproduction, based upon the perceived values of inherited characters or **traits.** See **pedigree selection.**

**domestication:** supervised control of plants or animals by human beings.

**dominance effects:** proportion of the **total pheno-typic variance** of a quantitative trait due to genes that create variance effects due simply to segregation; the proportion of total phenotypic variation that is not due to additive or epistatic effects. See **heritability.**

‡ **dominance hierarchy:** system in which an individual's status confers privilege over other members within a community; the physical domination of some members of a group by other members in it is relatively orderly and exhibits long-lasting patterns. Except for the highest- and lowest-ranking individuals, every member dominates one or more of its companions and is, in turn, dominated by one or more of the others. Such a hierarchy is initiated and sustained by **agonistic behavior**, although such hostile behavior is sometimes of a subtle and indirect nature. **Dominance** status is often associated with size and sex.

‡ **dominant:** 1. exerting a ruling or controlling influence. 2. in genetics, capable of expression identical to a dominant homozygote when carried by only one of a pair of homologous chromosomes. An **allele** is dominant if the **phenotype** of a **heterozygote** (e.g. Aa) is the same as the **homozygote** (AA) in an **F1** cross. The other **allele** (a) does not influence the **phenotype** of the heterozygote and is called **recessive.** Noun: dominance.

**dominant hemisphere:** hemisphere of the brain that tends to control the processing of information for a particular task, often used to refer to the hemisphere controlling speech.

**dominant mutation:** change in **DNA** that is expressed when it occurs in a single dose, i.e. in a **heterozygote.**

‡ **dominant pattern of inheritance:** in **Mendelian genetics**, a system of inheritance in which, when one **allele** of any ancestral **homozygote** mutates to form a new heterozygote, the resulting phenotype of that **heterozygote** is distinguishable from the homozygote. In this case the ancestral homozygote is termed the recessive homozygote (aa), the new heterozygote is termed Aa, and the new dominant mutant **allele** is termed A. In many cases the subsequent possible homozygote (AA) is unviable. An example in humans is **achondroplasia.** See **recessive pattern of inheritance, codominant pattern of inheritance,** and **incomplete dominance.**

‡ **Donau glaciation:** earliest of the periods of glaciation or ice ages that define the **Pleistocene epoch** during the past 1.8 million years BP. In the Quaternary sequence of the Alpine region, the Donau had a duration of about 260 ky and reached a maximum extent by about 1.5 mya. Aka pre-Günz glaciation.

**Donghecun:** archaeological site found in 1987 in Luonan county, Shaanxi province, China, dating from 1.15 mya to 700 kya; contains hominid remains including one tooth attributed to *Homo erectus.* Aka Luonan.

**donkey–horse hybrid:** see **horse–donkey hybrid.**

**donor:** 1. one who donates or contributes tissue for transfusion or an organ for transplantation. 2. a substance that donates part of itself to another substance, the **receptor.**

*Donrussellia* Szalay, 1976: adapoid **prosimian** from the early Eocene of Europe, belonging to the notharctid subfamily **Cercamoniinae**; three species; known only from teeth. Originally included among the omomyids, it was subsequently moved to the cercamoniines and may be among the most basal adapoids. Dental formula: 2.1.4.3/2.1.4.3; dentition shows no specializations for herbivory and, combined with small body size, this suggests that this primate was probably **insectivorous** and/or **frugivorous.** Body mass estimated to range from 200 to 700 g. See Appendix 1 for taxonomy.

**dopa:** 3,4-dihydroxyphenylalanine; an amino acid produced by oxidation of tyrosine by monophenol monooxygenase. Dopa is the precursor of **dopamine** and an intermediate product in the biosynthesis of **norepinephrine, epinephrine,** and **melanin.** The naturally occurring form is L-**dopa,** as dopa is **levorotatory.**

**dopamine:** intermediate in the synthesis of **catecholamine** hormones, an intermediate in tyrosine metabolism, and precursor of norepinephrine and epinephrine. Dopamine accounts for 90% of the catecholamines in the body. Dopamine is a key **neurotransmitter** and basal ganglia inhibitor, and is involved in several left-hemisphere skills critical to language and thought. Dopamine also plays a role in counteracting **hyperthermia** during endurance activity by mediating **endorphin** release; in conjunction with **epinephrine** and **phenylethylamine** it can influence emotional perception and behavior.

**dopamine intelligence hypothesis:** proposal that an expansion of dopaminergic systems in early hominid evolution enabled chase-hunting on the savannas of sub-Saharan Africa.

**dopaminergic neurons:** nerve cells responsive to the neurotransmitter dopamine.

**doppel protein** (Dpl): polypeptide containing 179 amino acid residues in humans. The gene on chromosome 20p codes for a native **prion protein** that may interact with the infectious prion protein that has been implicated in the etiology of the **transmissible spongiform encephalopathies.**

**Dordogne:** river and valley in southern France that is rich with late Pleistocene habitation cave sites such as **Combe-Grenal1,2.**

**dormancy:** state of metabolic quiescence and suspended growth; examples include hibernation, estivation, diapause, cryptobiosis, and hypobiosis.

**dormitory:** term used by some **primatologists** in reference to sleeping groups that form during the day among the small Malagasy **prosimians** and the African **bushbabies**; usually all female, although there are male 'visitors'. Dormitories may be either a leaf nest or a hole in a tree. These animals often sleep together in a ball, which helps to conserve body heat (see **thermoregulation**).

‡ **dorsal:** anatomical term of relative position meaning towards or nearest the back or vertebral column; the term **posterior** is more commonly used in human anatomy. Cf. **ventral**.

**dorsal scar:** concave surface on the dorsal surface of a flake where previous flakes had been removed; one of the diagnostic features that archaeologists use to distinguish a stone **tool** from a naturally occurring **geofact**.

**dorsal surface:** back surface of a flake that has been removed from a core, often characterized by an ancient patina that was on the outside of a core when the flake was made; one of the diagnostic features that archaeologists use to distinguish a stone **tool** from a naturally-occurring **geofact**.

**dorsiflexion:** bending, or flexing, the foot upward (dorsally).

**dorsum:** 1. entire rear portion of an animal. 2. upper surface of the tongue.

**dosage compensation:** mechanism that regulates the expression of **sex-linked** gene products. In primates, all but one **X chromosome** is normally inactivated, leaving the genes on only one X chromosome actively expressed in both female (XX) and male (XY) mammals. When stained, the inactive X chromosome appears as a **Barr body**. See **heteropycnosis**.

**dosage sensitivity:** condition related to the number of active loci for a particular trait in a chromosome complement; measured by the phenotypic response elicited by a **duplication** or **deficiency** at that particular genetic **locus**.

**dose:** 1. a standard quantity of something, such as a medicine. 2. the number of times (doses) that a gene is present in a single cell; normally, diploid cells contain two doses of each gene. See **dosage compensation**. 3. in radiation therapy, the total amount delivered to a particular part of the body.

**double-arched supra-orbital torus** (DAST): pertaining to the heavy brow ridge above the orbits in some species of *Homo*. In this case each eye has its own brow ridge that forms an arch, rather than a straight bar. Found among the **Neandertals** and several **archaic *Homo sapiens***. Aka double-arched brow ridges.

**double blind experiment:** research design in which neither the subjects nor experimenters are made aware beforehand of the value(s) of the **independent variable** administered during an experiment.

**double crossing over:** simultaneous recombination at two points in a synapsed pair of homologous chromosomes during meiosis.

**double diffusion test:** see **Ouchterlony technique**.

‡ **double helix:** linear structure of **DNA**; so-called because of its spiral conformation in **quaternary structure**. It consists of a double helix resembling a ladder that has been twisted into a spiral; the sides of the ladder consist of deoxyribose-phosphate units held together by the rung-like pairs of bases joined by hydrogen bonds. Aka DNA helix, twin helix, Watson–Crick helix.

**double-stranded RNA:** families of RNAs that, when cleaved, yield **small RNAs** that can trigger **epigenetic** and **post-transcriptional gene silencing** in the cytoplasm of a genome.

**double trisomy:** simultaneous **trisomy** as in, for example, the very rare occurrence of extra chromosomes 18 and 21 in the same individual.

**double-Y syndrome:** chromosome **aneuploidy** (2N = 47,XYY) in which the extra Y chromosome produces phenotypically tall males prone to acne, who were originally alleged to possess extra copies of male genes (a hormonal dosage effect) that putatively increase aggressive and criminal behavior; this hypothesis is incorrect. The controversial initial studies concerning behavior have never been satisfactorily replicated. Aka Jacob syndrome, supermale, metamale. Affects 1 : 1,000 males. See **primary nondisjunction**.

**doubling dose:** that dose of ionizing radiation required to double the **spontaneous mutation rate** in the organism or species under study.

**doubling time:** see **population doubling time**.

**douc langur:** vernacular for *Pygathrix nemaeus*.

**douroucouli:** vernacular for *Aotus trivirgatus*.

‡ **Down syndrome:** profound phenotype caused by the presence of three copies of all the genes on chromosome 21 (trisomy 21), a true dosage effect. Clinical features include short stature, a characteristically 'pleasant' facies caused by oblique eyelid openings and a pseudoepicanthic fold, palm creases, a wide and flat skull, spots on the iris, a furrowed tongue, and neck and finger webbing. Down syndrome individuals are at an increased risk for **Alzheimer disease**, respiratory **infections**, deafness, and **leukemia**. Few reach the age of 50 years. A **major chromosome anomaly** and an example of aneuploidy due, in the majority of cases, to **nondisjunction** of the maternal 21st chromatids during **meiosis I**, resulting in an ovum with 24 rather than

the normal 23 **chromatids**. When fused with the gamete from the opposite parent (usually a sperm with 23 chromatids), the affected **zygote** begins development with 47 chromatids rather than the normal 46. Both males and females may be affected. An analogue of Down syndrome has been observed in higher primates, where the cause is usually **trisomy 22**. Maternal nondisjunction is responsible for 90% of all cases, with the probability of *de novo* nondisjunction increasing dramatically after maternal age 35; male nondisjunction accounts for 5%. The translocation form causes the other 5%. In populations where **amniocentesis** is not routinely available, Down syndrome affects 1 : 650 live births. Where **genetic counseling** is available, incidence is about 1 : 1000. Incidence increases dramatically as a function of maternal age such that 1 : 16 children born to mothers aged 49 and older have trisomy 21. See **translocation Down syndrome** and **synteny**. Formerly called mongolism; use of this term is now discouraged.

**downstream:** on a chromosome, describes the nucleotide sequences 3′ to the end of the last exon of a gene. See **flanking sequence**. Cf. **upstream**.

***Draconodus** (= **Picrodus**) **apertus***: archaic mammal from the middle Paleocene of the Rocky Mountain region of North America belonging to the **plesiadapiform** family **Picrodontidae**; **monotypic**. Dental formula: probably 2.1.3.3/2.1.2.3; dental morphology suggestive of the **nectarivorous** living bats and has led to speculation that these animals were pollinators

who fed on nectar. Body mass estimated at 200 g. See Appendix 1 for taxonomy.

**Dragon Pool Cave:** see **Longtandong Cave**.

**dragon's bones:** local name for the fossil fauna found at sites near Peking (= Beijing, China), collected for the purpose of distribution by local apothecaries and alleged to have healing powers when ground into a powder and administered in conjunction with certain herbs. See **Zhoukoudian**. Aka 'dragon's teeth bones'.

**drift:** see **genetic drift**.

**drift theory:** eighteenth century proposition advanced by the proponents of **diluvianism** that unconsolidated sediments in Europe and North America were deposited as a result of the biblical flood. The counter-proposal by Charles **Lyell** that the sediments were glacial in origin and compatible with **uniformitarianism** was eventually accepted, but such deposits are still termed drift deposits.

**drill:** vernacular for *Mandrillus leucophaeus*.

**Drimolen:** archaeological site found in 1992 northwest of Johannesburg, South Africa, dated to *c.* 2–1 mya, and that contains artifacts identified as **digging sticks**, made from sharpened bones, and fossil hominids including over 80 specimens of ***Paranthropus** (= **Australopithecus**) **robustus*** and several specimens of another taxon provisionally assigned to the genus ***Homo***. Among the more complete fossils is a pair of crania of a male and female robust form, nicknamed Orpheus (**DNH 8**) and Eurydice. (**DNH 7**); see box below.

---

**Some fossil hominids found at Drimolen**

DNH 7 ('Eurydice'): female specimen of *Paranthropus* (= *Australopithecus*) *robustus* found at the South African site of **Drimolen** in October 1994, dated to 1.5 + mya. The most complete female specimen of that taxon found to that time: comparison with a contemporary male specimen of the same species (DNH 8) will provide estimates of the degree of sexual dimorphism in that species. Eurydice lacks a sagittal crest.

DNH 8 ('Orpheus'): male specimen of *Paranthropus* (= *Australopithecus*) *robustus* found Drimolen. Orpheus has a sagittal crest, a feature lacking in the female specimen, DNH 7.

---

**drive:** term used loosely to describe the tendency of an animal to seek out an object, such as a mate, an item of food, or a nesting site, and to perform an appropriate response toward it.

***Drosophila***: genus of insects known as fruit flies, commonly used in genetic research; Aka vinegar flies.

**drug-dependent genetic disease:** any morbid condition caused by a molecular defect and that can be resolved by the administration of a specific compound.

**drugstore teeth:** see **Ailuropoda-orang fauna**.

**drumstick:** minute, lobelike protrusion from the nucleus of a polymorphonuclear leukocyte, present

in about 2% of individuals who have two X chromosomes, as in normal females (XX) or **Klinefelter syndrome** (XXY).

**drumstick finger:** clubbed digit. Aka Hippocratic finger.

**dry season:** in seasonal **ecozones**, the time of the year when the least moisture is available and resources are scarce. Cf. **wet season**.

**dryas monkey:** vernacular for *Cercopithecus dryas*.

**dryomorph:** vernacular term to describe primitive early and middle Miocene hominoids of East Africa and Eurasia characterized by thin enamel on the molar teeth. See *Dryopithecus*.

**Dryopithecidae:** family of Miocene **hominoids** that historically were placed in a subfamily within the **Pongidae**; family status is not currently widely recognized, but appears to be gaining support.

**Dryopithecinae:** subfamily of Miocene **hominoids** belonging to the family **Pongidae**; in some taxonomic schemes, a subfamily of the **Hominidae**; known from Europe, South Asia, and China depending on which genera are recognized as belonging to this family; dryopithecine. One view is that only *Dryopithecus* should be in this subfamily; number of genera and species in dispute; revisions of the subfamily and the genus *Dryopithecus* are ongoing; it is also common for this group of apes to be included among the pongids without subfamily status. Known mainly from jaws and dentition. Dental formula: 2.1.2.3; the tooth rows are parallel to one another, forming a hard U; relative to the 'ramamorphs', the other major group of large Eurasian Miocene hominoids, there is a thin cap of enamel on the molars and premolars; molar morphology and the thinly enameled molars suggest a nonabrasive diet, such as **frugivory**. Associated with forest habitats. See Appendix 1 for taxonomy.

**dryopithecine dental pattern:** combination of morphological dental features observed in Miocene hominoids that are found in living African apes as well, and that includes a parallel dental arcade, protruding canines, **diastema**, and a **Y-5 molar pattern**.

‡ *Dryopithecus* Lartet, 1856: genus of **hominoids** from the middle Miocene of Europe belonging to the subfamily **Dryopithecinae** (depending on author). This was the first fossil ape described. Historically this genus included many more species and had a more widespread geographic range; revisions in recent years have reduced both the number of species and the geographic range. There have been two major revisions since the 1960s; currently, two to four species recognized. Known principally from jaws, teeth, and several crania. Estimated body mass from 20 to 40 kg. Dental formula: 2.1.2.3; molar morphology and a thin cap of enamel on the cheek teeth suggests a nonabrasive diet such as **frugivory**. Associated with forest habitats. Cf. **Gigantopithecus**, **Rudapithecus**, **Sivapithecus**. See Appendix 1 for taxonomy.

**dsDNA:** double-stranded **DNA**; used in contrast to single-stranded DNA in dissociation experiments, for example.

**dual effector model:** hypothesis for the regulation of cell growth that posits that the role of **human growth hormone** is to cause the differentiation of **fibroblasts** into specific tissue types (such as bone, adipose, muscle, etc.) and that the role of **insulin-like growth factors** is to cause the clonal expansion of the newly differentiated cells.

**dualism:** one version of stratified imagery or being in which **human nature** is divided into a lower (animal, biological) component and a higher (**cultural**, social, spiritual) aspect; these are often seen as conflicting forces battling for control of human affairs. See **limbic system** and **nature–nurture controversy**.

**dubiofossil:** object resembling a known fossil but of unknown or unconfirmed inorganic material; problematic fossil.

**Dubois' coefficient of cephalization** ($k$): an early attempt at allometry in 1897, Dubois' $k$ or proportionality factor was calculated as $k = E/(P^{0.56})$, where $E$ = brain mass, $P$ = total body weight, and 0.56 is an empirical constant for all mammals.

**DuBois formula:** see **Meeh–DuBois formula**.

‡ **Dubois, Marie Eugène Francois Thomas:** (1858–1940) Dutch physician and paleontologist, and pioneer of **brain-size** to **body-size** ratios. Posted to Indonesia in the Dutch Army Medical Service, Dubois was also commissioned by the government to search for **fossils**. Among other extinct mammals, Dubois' team located teeth, a **skullcap**, and a **femur**. The femur approximated a modern human's except for the linear shaft and a pathological **exostosis**, but the estimated **brain size** was intermediate between apes and humans. Dubois named his '**missing link**' *Pithecanthropus erectus* (= *Homo erectus*). Dubois returned to the Netherlands in 1895 with his fossils, which he squirreled away in his house, and died alienated from the scientific establishment.

**Duchenne muscular dystrophy** (DMD): see **muscular dystrophy, Duchenne type**.

**duct:** fully enclosed tubular channel that carries a secretion or other body fluid.

**ductus deferens:** one of two paired reproductive ducts in the male that connects the epididymus of a testis to the urethra; Aka vas deferens.

**Duffy blood group** (FY): the autosomal dominant Duffy antigen is an RBC membrane-bound glycoprotein (GPD) that has two major antigenic determinants defined by their anti-Fy(a) and anti-Fy(b) antibodies. A rare third phenotype defined by the anti-Fy6 antibody is also known. Duffy negativity, Fy(a−b−), seems to confer resistance to malarial infection. Both Fy(a+) and Fy(b+) are apparently an integral part of the *Plasmodium* receptor on RBCs. The Duffy protein functions as a receptor for cytokines and as an attachment site for *Plasmodium vivax* **merozoites**. When certain chemokines (IL-8 and MGSA) are bound to the Duffy antigen site, the malarial agent fails to bind to and enter RBCs. Three major alleles have been identified: FYB (a−b+), FYA(a+b−), and FYO (a−b−); FYB is the suggested ancestral (chimpanzee-like) allele. The polymorphism also gives rise to the possibility of **hemolytic disease of the newborn**.

**duodenum:** first portion of the **small intestine** that leads from the pylorus of the stomach to the jejunum. In humans, the duodenum receives acidic **chyme** from the stomach; here **bile** emulsifies fats and pancreatic secretions help to change the pH to a more alkaline environment. The duodenum is about 25 cm long; its name derives from the fact that Leonardo da Vinci measured the duodenum as twelve finger breadths. See **jejunum** and **ileum**.

**duplex DNA:** double-stranded DNA, as in the Watson–Crick model.

**duplication:** 1. in **DNA**, the addition of one or more base pairs from a sequence. See **DNA replication**. 2. structural change that results in doubling of a portion of a chromosome, i.e. gene duplications within a **linkage group**. Chromosome duplications are sometimes caused by misalignment of homologous pairs during **meiosis**. DNA can occasionally be duplicated in other, nonhomologous chromosomes.

‡ **duplication division:** see **mitosis**.

**duplicative transposition:** see **transposable genetic element**.

**dura mater:** outermost of three **meninges** that cover the **central nervous system**. The dura mater is composed primarily of connective tissue and is in contact with bone.

**durability:** probability that a taxon will be extant during a projected period of time.

**dural venous sinus:** any one of the cavities that form where the dura mater of the brain separates. The dural venous sinuses drain blood from the brain and return it to the internal jugular veins of the neck.

**duration:** measurement in behavioral studies expressed in units of time. It is used in three different ways by different authors. 1. length of time a particular behavior event lasts. 2. total length of time for all occurrences of the behavior over a specified time period. Also referred to as total duration. 3. average length of time for the behavior as it was observed. This is also referred to as mean duration.

**dusky leaf-monkey:** vernacular for *Trachypithecus obscura*.

**dusky titi monkey:** vernacular for *Callicebus moloch*.

**Düsseldorf Neandertal:** Düssel River site; Aka **Feldhofer Grotto**.

**Dutrillaux's hypothesis:** four-part proposal erected to explain both the cytogenetic and molecular data available concerning hominoid evolution: (1) ancestors of the gorilla separated from the human–chimp common ancestor; (2) the human and chimp ancestors separated; (3) repeated hybridizations subsequently occurred between the gorilla and chimp ancestors; (4) reproductive barriers were finally established that precluded hybridization between the gorilla and chimp ancestors.

**dwarf bushbaby:** vernacular for *Galagoides demidoff*.

**dwarf lemur:** vernacular for the two **prosimian** species belonging to the genus *Cheirogaleus*.

**dwarfism, pituitary:** condition of being significantly smaller than average, especially when accompanied by disproportionate growth, and usually caused by low levels of human growth hormone. Aka pituitary dwarfism. There are four modalities of genetic hypopituitary dwarfism, all autosomal recessive; in each case growth dysfunction begins prenatally. Type I is primordial dwarfism, in which only growth hormone (**GH**) is deficient, and the result is a 'mid get' of normal proportions; nanism. Type II is **ateliosis** due to **hGH**-receptor deficiency; this type cannot be treated with exogenous GH. Aka Laron type dwarfism, GH insensitivity. Type III is the panhypopituitarism type of dwarfism, in which all hormones of the anterior **pituitary gland** are deficient. Type IV is Kowarski syndrome dwarfism, in which the receptor is present but GH concentrations are low; unlike type II, exogenous GH induces a significant increase in growth rate. The genetic forms are as a group less common than hypopituitarism caused by a tumor or secondary to an infection. Cf. **achondroplasia** and **nanism**.

**dwarfism, pygmy:** see **hGH-resistant dwarfism**.

**dyad:** 1. in behavior, the formation of a bond between any two individuals; couple, dyadic group. 2. in genetics, a chromosome composed of two **chromatids** united at a centromere; usually refers to a **tetrad**.

**dynamometer:** device used to measure muscular power.

**dynamometric strength:** score obtained by averaging several squeezes of a **dynamometer**.

**dynastic incest:** arrangement of marriages between close relatives in some royal families; consanguinity of a degree prohibited to the common people. See **royal endogamy**.

**dysarthrosis:** malformed joint.

**dyscrasia:** any unidentified disease, malfunction or abnormal condition; used especially in reference to diseases of the blood.

**dysdifferentiation theory of aging:** intracellular, stochastic model of aging in which the major premise is that the mechanisms such as **methylation** that normally suppress or deactivate gene activity, become less efficient over the life of an organism, and that genes become inappropriately activated in stem cell lines where the products are not required, diminishing the efficiency of cells.

*Dyseolemur pacificus* **Stock, 1934:** tarsiiform primate from the late Eocene of North America belonging to the omomyid subfamily **Anaptomorphinae; monotypic.** Estimated body mass around 160 g. Dental formula: 2.1.3.3/2.1.3.3; anterior teeth reminiscent of

*Tarsius*; dental morphology suggestive of **frugivory**. See Appendix 1 for taxonomy.

**dysfunction:** abnormal performance or nonperformance of an anatomical structure.

**dysgenesis:** failure to form or mature.

**dysgenic:** detrimental to the hereditary qualities of a species. Cf. **eugenic.**

**dysharmony:** any unusual or unexpected relationship between the shape of a cranium and the shape of a face. In general, anthropometrists have found that narrow facial features are correlated with **dolichocephaly** and broad faces with **brachycephaly.** Long-headed people with disproportionately broad faces, for example, are considered dysharmonic. Aka disharmony.

**dyslexia** (DYX1): specific reading disability. Thought to be caused by chemical disruption during the **third trimester** (7th month) of gestation. The DYX1 gene is an autosomal dominant; one of nine types of similar effect with a genetic basis. The condition exhibits incomplete penetrance; heritability is about 60%. Dyslexia has a prevalence of about 5–6% in American school-age children.

**dysmorphology:** study of structural abnormalities of human development such as **plagiocephaly**, cleft lip or extra finger. Adjective: dysmorphic.

**dysostosis:** weak or inadequate ossification, especially of fetal cartilage.

**dysploidy:** pertaining to several species grouped into a single genus, and where the diploid chromosome numbers are different and do not relate obviously as a series.

**dysteleology:** 1. purposelessness. 2. the study of organs that seem to have no function and have become **vestigial.**

**DZ, DZT:** abbreviation for dizygous twins. See **twins, dizygotic.**

**3′-end:** end of a DNA chain that is terminated by a hydroxyl group: 'three prime end'.

**5′-end:** end of DNA chain that is terminated by a phosphate group: 'five prime end'.

**e:** base of the natural logarithm, 2.7183. Aka Napierian logarithm. See **logarithm**.

**e²:** abbreviation for the remaining portion of the **total phenotypic variance** not accounted for by h², or, heritability (narrow sense); (1 − *h²*), the nonadditive variance.

**ear:** sense organ that receives auditory stimuli and has structures that are able to detect changes in **equilibrium**; impulses generated in the ear are transmitted to the brain, where they are interpreted.

**eardrum:** see **tympanic membrane**.

**earlier archaic group:** forms of *Homo sapiens* ssp. that postdate *Homo erectus* but antedate **AMHs**; dates for archaics range from about 400 kya to 32 kya. Archaics possessed a nearly human-sized brain but retained certain primitive features of the skull such as a lower cranial height and a **mosaic** of other **primitive** and **derived** features. Candidates for the earlier archaic group include **Arago, Bilzingsleben, Mauer, Petralona** and **Vértesszöllös**; and possibly **Kabwe**. Cf. **later archaic group** and **anteneandertal**.

**earliest AMH site:** see **Klasies River Mouth Cave** site, **Omo I**.

**early *Homo* hypothesis:** argument by Louis **Leakey** and, later, Mary **Leakey** that all nonrobust fossil **hominids** in East Africa (including the earliest then known, such as the **Laetoli** specimens) should be attributed to the genus *Homo*.

**'early man' hypotheses:** group of proposals for locations, sites, tool technologies, etc., for earliest **AMHs** in various geographical regions of the world. See specific regions below.

**early man in Asia hypothesis:** proposal favored in the first quarter of the twentieth century that the origin of **hominids** was in the great plateau of Central Asia, i.e. Turkestan, and that they subsequently spread into the southern hemisphere. See the **origin of man hypotheses**. Cf. the competing **original hominid homeland** hypothesis. Other proposed locations have included northeastern India and southeastern Asia.

**early man in the New World hypotheses:** label that subsumed much research relating to human origins in the Americas, especially that conducted in the 1960s when researchers were polarized into two camps favoring either a conservative (e.g. **Folsom**) time scale or an earlier (e.g., **Monte Verde**) time scale; even earlier entrance dates had been proposed (e.g. **Calico Hills Early Man Site**). Aka early man in America hypotheses.

**early modern human:** see *Homo sapiens* and **AMH**.

**Early Paleolithic:** see **Lower Paleolithic**.

**early weaning:** termination of feeding by lactation earlier than average for a given species; early reduction in **parental investment**.

**earthquake:** movement of the earth's crust due to forces traceable ultimately to **continental drift**.

**ear tuft:** stiff erect hairs in the area of the **pinna** of some primates.

**earwax:** see **cerumen**.

‡ **East African rift system:** geological feature in East Africa, 3,500 miles long and characterized by mountain building, faulting, volcanic activity, and erosion; it stretches all the way from the Red Sea in the north to the southern end of Lake Malawi (bordering Mozambique, Tanzania, and Malawi) in the south. Many hominid fossils have been located in this feature. Aka the Great Rift Valley.

**East African sites:** umbrella term inclusive of prehistoric sites such as **Olduvai Gorge, Omo, Turkana, Shungura, Usno, Koobi Fora, Nachukui, Hadar, Middle Awash, Laetoli, Aramis**, and **Nariokotome**.

**East Rudolf** (ER): east shore of a lake in Kenya; prior to 1974, the **Koobi Fora**, East Turkana, Kenya, region. Expeditions to this area were made as part of the East Rudolf Research Project.

‡ **East Turkana:** see **Koobi Fora**.

**eastern brown mouse lemur:** vernacular for *Microcebus rufus* (= *murinus*).

**eastern chimpanzee:** vernacular for the chimpanzee **subspecies *Pan troglodytes*** *schweinfurthii*.

**eastern greater dwarf lemur:** vernacular for *Cheirogaleus major major*.

**eastern lowland gorilla:** see *Gorilla gorilla*.

**Eastern Negrillos:** traditionally, one of the three geographic divisions of **Negrillo** peoples in Africa. Included in this group are the Efe, Batwa, Bakanga, and Akka; aka Bambutis, as a whole.

**eastern red colobus:** vernacular for *Piliocolobus badius pennanti*.

**eastern woolly lemur:** vernacular for *Avahi laniger*.

**Ebola fever:** infectious hemorrhagic fever of retroviral origin. Several laboratory workers in Germany were killed in 1967 by the Marburg disease, a virus possibly hosted in Ugandan green monkeys. A similar outbreak of the closely related rodlike Ebola virus occurred in the Sudan and Zaire in 1976 and killed 50% and 90% of those infected, respectively (a total of 452 people). Next to HIV, Ebola is considered to be the second most lethal virus in the world. There is no treatment, and death comes much more rapidly than with **AIDS**. In November 1989, 200 cymologous macaques, en route from the Philippines to a research center in Virginia, died from a similar rodlike virus; four humans were eventually infected. This latter virus, although genetically similar to the Ebola virus, did not appear to be as fatal to humans as it was to these monkeys. The Ebola is a river in Zaire. Transmission is **nosocomial**. Aka Ebola–Marburg virus disease.

**Ebola–Marburg virus disease:** see **Ebola fever**.

**eburnation:** condition that results from degenerative joint disease in which articular cartilage is damaged and the underlying bone comes into contact with adjacent bone, producing a highly polished surface on the bones.

**ecad:** any nonheritable change in an organism.

‡ **eccrine sweat gland:** type of sweat gland that is widely distributed throughout the body. Eccrine sweat glands function in **thermoregulation** by removing heat through sweat evaporation. Humans are notable for the large number of these glands, which are sparse in other primates; it is felt by many that eccrine glands helped early hominids adapt to a warm environment on the African savannas and were associated with a decrease in body hair. The glands produce a liquid that consists mainly of water and salt, with a **saline** concentration; see **sweat**. Aka eccrine gland. Cf. **apocrine sweat gland**.

**ecdemic:** not native, foreign. Cf. **endemic**.

**ecochronology:** dating biological events by using paleoecological evidence, e.g. **palynology**.

**ecocline:** grades of variation within a species which correlate with changes in ecozonation along the geographical distribution of a species.

**ecofacts:** nonartifactual remains found in a site, such as pollen, seeds and bone.

**ecogenetics:** branch of genetics concerned with the inheritance of individual differences in response to environmental agents other than drugs. Cf. **pharmacogenetics**.

**ecogeographical divergence:** emergence of two or more species from a common ancestor in which the later species each reside in different geographical areas and occupy dissimilar habitats, to which they become progressively adapted.

**ecogeographical rule:** see **climatic rule**.

‡ **ecological:** of or pertaining to the biological field of **ecology**.

**ecological anthropology:** narrowly, the study of environmental effects on humans and human populations, and vice versa. Each of the subfields of anthropology has its version of ecology, but most acknowledge the sense elaborated by Julian Steward. Broadly, that population mechanisms develop for coping with stressors (especially crises) that originate in the environment, and manifest as enabling or limiting cultural responses to variations in **carrying capacity**. In humans, warfare and religion seem to be two of the more important modalities described in the coping repertoire. Historical or subfield variants include **cultural ecology, paleoecology, primate ecology, physiological anthropology, behavioral ecology**, and ethnoecology (linguistics).

**ecological community:** term that has several levels of meaning in ecology: 1. groups of populations that occur together within a particular geographical location. 2. association of organisms within a particular locality in which one or more species have characteristics that are conspicuous and are said to dominate that area; e.g. a savanna community, tropical rain forest community, etc.; this is also referred to as a biotope. 3. in reference only to those populations that interact within a particular area rather than simply those populations occurring together (the later condition is called an association by some ecologists).

**ecological determinants approach:** research strategy that emphasizes the location of human settlements in response to specific ecological factors.

**ecological equivalents:** unrelated or distantly related species that occupy similar ecological roles in separate geographical regions.

**ecological genetics:** study of evolution through experimental field work and/or laboratory genetics, to relate adaptations to environmental variables.

**ecological hypothesis:** Richard **Leakey's** idea that animals evolved faster at **Lake Rudolf** than at **Omo**, a counter-proposal to Basil Cooke's 1972 assertion that the dating of the **Koobi Fora** sites was too old, based on Cooke's **faunal correlation** of pigs, elephants, and antelopes. Leakey's response was that an ecological barrier had existed between Lake Rudolf and Omo. The original **K–Ar** dates at Koobi Fora were contaminated, however, and Cooke's hypothesis eventually prevailed. See **KBS tuff**.

**ecological isolation:** see **habitat isolation**.

‡ **ecological niche:** role of a species in the ecological community; this term has been defined in several different ways. 1. activity range of each species with every dimension of the physical and biological environment included; this definition sees the niche as a multidimensional space. 2. physical space occupied by an organism. 3. functional role of the organism in the community, e.g. which **trophic level** it occupies.

**ecological pressure:** set of all environmental influences that constitute the agents of natural selection. See **prime movers**.

**ecological pyramid:** in its original form, a proposal that each trophic level in a food chain has fewer members that the level immediately below it; first proposed by British ecologist Charles Elton (1900–91). Recent revisions of the concept have taken into account the amount of energy per unit time in each trophic level, which always forms a pyramid.

**ecological race:** local variant of a species having adaptive characters that are selected for in a given environment or local **habitat**; ecotype. See **geographical race** and **biological race**.

**ecological release:** condition in which an **adaptive radiation** occurs because of species extinctions that make a number of niches available. An example of ecological release is the mammalian adaptive radiation, of which the primates were a part, immediately following the dinosaur extinctions.

**ecological species concept:** defines a species as a set of organisms adapted to a particular niche. Discontinuities are produced outside the biology of the species involved; patchiness in resources, such as the hosts of parasitic species, and interspecific competition, can shape the phenetic distributions of species into discrete clusters.

**ecological zoogeography:** study of the distributions of animal species.

**ecologist:** scientist who studies **ecology**.

‡ **ecology:** 1. scientific study of the relationship between an **organism** and all aspects of its **environment**, including both physical factors and other organisms 2. all aspects of the environment of an organism which affect its way of life. When coined by **Haeckel** in 1869, the term had a more restricted meaning and was used in the sense that an individual organism is the product of **heredity** plus environment.

‡ **econiche:** colloquialism for **ecological niche**.

**ecoparasite:** organism restricted to a specific host or limited group of related taxa.

**ecophene:** range of phenotypes produced from a single **genotype** within the limits of the habitat in which it is found in nature.

**ecophenotype:** any phenotype exhibiting nongenetic adaptations to a local **habitat**.

*Eco*R1: first **restriction enzyme** found in an organism (R1), *Escherichia coli* (*Eco*).

**ecosphere:** see **biosphere**.

‡ **ecosystem:** all of the organisms of a particular habitat, such as a lake or a forest or a campus, together with the physical environment in which they live and interact; aka biotope, biosystem, holocoen, ecological community.

**ecotone:** boundary between **ecozones**.

**ecotope:** 1. smaller habitat within a larger geographical region. 2. the full range of habitat adaptations available to a species.

**eco-tourism:** form of tourism in which visitors come to see environments and organisms and, by so doing, stimulate the local economy; the benefits accrued to local inhabitants make them more willing to preserve the ecosystem.

**ecotype:** population of a widespread species that is adapted and restricted to a particular locality; such populations are still capable of reproducing viable offspring with the **metapopulation**; equivalent to a taxonomic subspecies. See **ecological race, geographical race, biological race**.

**ecozone:** habitat zone or region characterized by a specific mixture of plants and animals adapted to the limiting factors that prevail.

**ectocanthion:** outer corner of the eye; outer epicanthus. Cf. **endocanthion**.

**ectoconchion** (ec): **craniometric landmark**; most lateral point of the orbital lateral wall. See Appendix 7.

**ectocranial:** of or pertaining to the outer surface of the skull.

**ectocranial buttressing feature:** suite of characteristics found in *Homo erectus* and some **archaic H. sapiens** that refer to areas of bony build-up such as ridges, crests, and bars of bone that provide support and sites of muscle attachment for the **cranium**; e.g. **occipital torus, nuchal crest**, etc.

‡ **ectoderm:** outermost of the three primary germ layers of the animal **embryo**. Ectoderm gives rise to most of the integumentary system (the **epidermis** and its derivatives), parts of the special sensory organs, and the nervous system (neural crest). Aka ectoblast. See **epiblast**.

**ectodermal dysplasia, anhidrotic type** (EDA): affected males have hypertrichosis, abnormal or missing teeth, and absence of sweat glands (with hypohidrosis). The *EDA* gene is an X-linked recessive. Heterozygous female carriers show milder symptoms. Affects thermoregulation; the condition tends to cluster, e.g. the 'Whitaker Negroes of Mississippi' or the 'toothless men of Sind' (Hyderabad, India); the latter were mentioned by Darwin in 1875. Aka hypohidrotic type ED.

**ectogenesis:** 1. generation of variation by external agents. 2. development of an **embryo** *in vitro*.

**ectomolare** (ecm): **craniometric landmark**; most lateral point of the **buccal** or outside surface of the **alveolus** containing the second maxillary molar. See Appendix 7.

**ectomorphy:** body type characterized by a lean, elongated build; one of three **somatotypes** proposed by W. H. Sheldon.

**ectoparasite:** any parasite such as a flea or tick that lives on the surface of the host's body. Cf. **endoparasite**.

**ectopic:** 1. event that occurs at an unusual place or in an abnormal manner. 2. displaced.

**ectopic crossing over:** see **unequal crossing over**.

**ectopic gene conversion:** form of nonreciprocal recombination between two **DNA sequences** in which the donor and recipient DNA strands are not alleles at the same locus; see **gene conversion**.

**ectopic pregnancy:** embryo found outside of the uterus, often in the fallopian tube or abdominal cavity.

**ectoplasm:** clear, thin cytoplasm at the periphery of a cell that is more gelled than the rest of the cytoplasm in the cell; its clarity is due to the exclusion of all organelles except filaments.

**ectothermic:** pertaining to an organism that obtains most of its body heat from the environment; see **poikilothermy.**

**ectotympanic bone:** bone that helps support the mammalian tympanic membrane of the ear; in primates a ringlike ectotympanic is found among some lemurs, while a tubular ectotympanic is present among the **anthropoids** and some prosimians. Because a tubular ectotympanic is present among some of the basal primates, it is uncertain which trait is primitive. See **tympanic region of the temporal bone.**

**ectrodactyly:** absence of a digit or digits; among primates, spider monkeys (genus *Ateles*) and colobus monkeys are considered ectrodactyl because of their very reduced thumbs; pottos also fit this condition owing to the reduction of their index fingers, an adaptation for their viselike grips.

**ECV:** see **endocranial volume.**

**edema:** excessive accumulation of fluid in body tissues.

**edentate:** 1. without teeth. 2. member of the order Edentata, a group of South American toothless mammals including anteaters, armadillos and sloths. See **edentulous.**

**edentulous:** refers to a **mandible** or **maxilla** that is missing teeth that were once present. Cf. **edentate.**

**edge effect:** changes seen in the border of a habitat that is an environment that transitions or abruptly changes, containing different species and microclimatic conditions in light, temperature, wind, etc. Although there are natural edges, those created by humans (such as roads) are the most disruptive to a habitat, usually reducing the amount of interior habitat while increasing edge.

**edge species:** species located at the margins of a community.

**edge-to-edge bite:** form of chewing in which the incisors meet during chewing. Many primates masticate in this manner, which leaves a characteristic wear pattern, also seen in those human groups that chew hides to soften them.

**Edward syndrome** (47, 18+): **major chromosome anomaly** and an example of **aneuploidy** in humans due to **trisomy** 18. Three copies of all the genes on chromosome 18 cause, due to a dosage effect, mental impairment, extreme abnormalities in all organ systems, and muscle tonus that twists the head oddly. Aka Trisomy 18.

**Edward's sifaka:** vernacular for the *Propithecus diadema edwardsi.*

**EEG:** abbreviation for electroencephalogram, a graphic record of electrical activity in the brain as recorded from electrodes placed on the scalp, and interpreted as **brain waves.**

**Eemian interglacial:** temperate climatic stage in northern Europe beginning *c.* 125 kya; an interglacial period that preceded the last cold stage in the Quaternary sequence.

**Efe pygmies:** foragers or hunter–gatherers in modern-day Zaire who have survived with a subsistence lifestyle in small-scale societies into the twenty-first century. One of the **Eastern Negrillo** groups.

**effect:** condition resulting from an action, agency, or circumstance.

**effect hypothesis:** assertion that the rate of speciation tends to vary from species to species and that those species with higher rates of speciation are favored over those with lower rates. Proposed by E. S. **Vrba** in 1980.

‡ **effectance motivation:** behavior that does not serve an immediate end, such as curiosity, exploration, investigation, and play activity. A major behavioral trait of mammals.

**effective allele:** any factor in a polygenic system that produces an increase or decrease in a quantitative trait.

‡ **effective breeding population** ($N_e$): 1. the size of the actual population ($N$) that are fecund; in humans, the size of the actual population less children and women after menopause. 2. the number of individuals in an ideal, randomly breeding population with a 1 : 1 sex ratio that would have the same rate of heterozygosity decrease due to **drift** as the real population under consideration. Cf. the **effective population number** or size.

**effective fertility:** pertaining to the average number of offspring produced by individuals affected by a genetic disease and compared with a matched sample of individuals without the condition. The difference between the two values is used to estimate the selective disadvantage (loss of fitness) due to the disease.

**effective lethal phase:** stage of development at which a defective gene causes the death of an organism. See **lethal equivalent (value).**

**effective population number** ($N_e$): 1. population size assumed in theoretical **population genetics** for small populations; a number usually smaller than observed population sizes such as might be measured by an ecologist in nature. Cf. **effective breeding population.** 2. number of individuals in an ideal population that would have the same rate of increase in homozygosity as the empirical population under consideration.

‡ **effective population size** ($N_e$): average number of individuals in a population assumed to contribute genes with equal probability to the next generation. Operationally, its measurement is complex; it increases as a function of the number of breeding individuals, equalization of the sex ratio, and increase in population size of successive generations.

**effector:** muscle or gland that responds to stimulation and reacts, making a change in the body.

**efferent:** transporting or conducting away from; used especially of nerves carrying signals radiating outward from the **central nervous system.**

**efferential ductules:** series of coiled tubules that convey spermatozoa from the **rete testis** to the epididymus.

**e.g.:** see *exempli gratia.*

**egalitarian society:** society in which the number of values, roles, or statuses is about the same as the number of people available to fill them, i.e. there are no sharp divisions of rank, wealth, or status.

**egesta:** portion of consumed resources that is expelled as fecal material or is regurgitated; any food that is not absorbed; part of **rejecta.**

‡ **egg:** colloquial term for (usually) a female **gamete,** an **ovum,** specialized for the storage of both genetic material and nutrients. Eggs have dissimilar forms in nonmammalian species. Although the central component of the mammalian egg is the central haploid reproductive cell, the ovum is actually a complex multicellular structure.

**egg bank:** location where human **eggs** are preserved frozen for future use in artificial insemination. See **germinal choice.**

**ego:** 1. self. 2. term used to designate the point of reference in the working out of any genealogy, pedigree, or descent system; may be either male or female. Only by tracing relations can one know what kind of descent system is being described.

**egocentric:** self-centered; said of traits that enhance the survival of an individual or its components, rather than of a population; as in **selfish DNA.**

**Ehlers–Danlos syndrome:** heritable condition characterized by lax joints and stretchy skin, and caused by mutations in the connective tissue protein **collagen.** There are several variants, each related to a **metabolic block** in collagen synthesis; the genes involved are both X-linked and autosomal.

**Ehringsdorf:** archaeological site found in 1914 in the Kampfe and Fischer quarries near Weimar, Germany, dated to about 225 kya (the last interglacial, 250–102 kya, U series on travertines), and that contains **Mousterian** artifacts that consist of flint scrapers and bifaces, and bits of charcoal. Hominid remains first reported in 1928 include nine individuals (at least one child) attributed to either *Homo neanderthalensis* or to the younger '**anteneandertal**', or **archaic** *Homo sapiens* group. Aka Weimar–Ehringsdorf.

**eidos:** one of the fixed forms that Plato thought lay behind the apparent variability of phenomena. See **Plato's theory of forms.**

**ejaculation:** discharge of semen from the male urethra during climax.

**ejaculatory duct:** tube that transports spermatozoa from the ductus deferens to the prostatic urethra.

***Ekgmouwechashala philotau* MacDonald, 1963:** enigmatic tarsiiform from the early Miocene of North America, belonging to the omomyid subfamily **Ekgmouwechashalinae**; its genus epithet is derived from the Lakota language and means 'little cat man'; **monotypic**; exact relationships within the Omomyidae uncertain; some workers think that this genus is omomyine-derived. Estimated body mass around 2 kg. Dental formula: 2.1.3.3; anterior molar is the largest and the following molars decrease in size, unusual for a primate; all molars are low-crowned; dentition is convergent with the olingo, a member of the raccoon family, and based on this comparison *Ekgmouwechashala* is speculated to be **frugivorous.** See Appendix 1 for taxonomy.

**Ekgmouwechashalinae: monotypic** subfamily containing only the enigmatic primate *Ekgmouwechashala philotau.*

**El Juyo Cave:** archaeological site found in 1978 in Spain, dated to 14 kya, and that contains artifacts that have been interpreted as giving the cave the significance of a religious sanctuary.

**elaboration:** process of evolving complex structures from simpler precursors. Cf. **reduction.**

**Elandsfontein:** archaeological site found in 1951 near Saldanha Bay in South Africa, dated to >300 kya, containing Acheulean artifacts ('Stellenbosch V') and hominid remains including a cranium and an unrelated mandibular ramus assigned to the **archaic** *Homo sapiens* group. Often cited as similar to **Kabwe.** Aka Saldanha, Cutting 10, Hopefield, Elandsfontein farm.

**elastic strain:** reversible phenotypic change in an organism that has been produced by **stress;** see **catch-up growth.**

**Elbe glaciation:** first major glaciation of the Pleistocene in the Poland/German sequence; see **Günz glaciation.**

**elbow breadth: anthropometric** measurement; distance between the medial and lateral **epicondyles** of the humerus with the elbow flexed at 90° as measured with either spreading calipers or sliding calipers. Used for studies of body frame size and skeletal mass.

**elbow joint:** complex joint that includes two articulations between the **humerus** and the bones of the forearm; the humeroulnar and humeroradial joints are enclosed by a single **articular capsule** and together they form a **hinge joint** that permits **flexion** and **extension.**

**elbow–wrist length: anthropometric** measurement; distance between the **olecranon process** of the ulna and the most distal palpable portion of the **styloid** process of the radius; the subject's arm is flexed at the elbow so that the olecranon process and the hand are in the horizontal plane.

**Eldredge, Niles** (1943- ): US paleontologist; curator at the American Museum of Natural History. Since the 1970s, Eldredge has published provocative hypotheses concerning phylogenetic reconstruction; with S. J. **Gould** he was co-author of controversial theoretical works concerning the rate of evolution, which contend that species diverge rapidly and then enter a long period of **stasis**, a process they termed '**punctuated equilibrium**' (1972). Other interests include mass extinctions, biodiversity and human ecology. Co-author (with I. **Tattersall**) of *The Myths of Human Evolution* (1982); author of *The Monkey Business* (1982), *Reinventing Darwin* (1995), *The Pattern of Evolution* (1999) and *The Triumph of Evolution... And the Failure of Creationism* (2000).

**electivity:** nonrandom preference of a food source by a consumer.

**electivity index** ($E_i$): measure of preference for a food source by a given consumer. $E_i = r_i - n_i/r_i + n_i$, where $r_i$ is the percentage of $i$ in a consumer's diet, and $n_i$ is the percentage of $i$ in the environment. Positive values (0–1) indicate relative preference: negative values (−1–0) indicate avoidance.

**electroblotting:** technique following **electrophoresis** that transfers a polynucleotide or protein from a discriminating medium such as a gel onto another such as nitrocellulose. Utilized in processes such as **northern blot analysis, Southern blot analysis,** and **western blot analysis. See blot.**

**electroencephalogram** (EEG): graphic record of the potentials on the skull generated by electrical currents that emanate spontaneously from the nerve cells in the brain. Fluctuations in potentials are seen in the form of waves, which correlate well with different neurologic conditions and can be used as diagnostic criteria.

**electrogram:** graphical record of electrical events in living tissue.

**electrolyte:** substance that dissociates into ions when in an aqueous solution, thus becoming capable of conducting an electric current.

**electromagnetic spectrum:** radiation ranging from cosmic rays of high frequency ($10^{-13}$ m) through light visible to humans (390–750 nm) through infrared waves of low frequency (750 nm–$10^{-4}$ m) to radio waves of low frequency ($10^{-4}$–$10^6$ m). See **UV radiation.**

**electromorph:** any of several allelic forms that can be separated by gel **electrophoresis** in a population or group of samples. Electromorphs migrate varying distances in the gel matrix, and can be identified by the distance migrated relative to standard samples.

**electron:** elementary particle that possesses the unit quantum of negative electric charge. In an electrically neutral atom, the number of electrons in the electron cloud equals the number of protons in the nucleus.

**electron capture:** radioactive decay process in which a proton in the nucleus turns into a neutron, thus decreasing the atomic number by 1, but the mass number remains unchanged; e.g. $^{40}$K to $^{40}$Ar. Exploited by **chronometric dating** techniques.

**electron microscope:** machine with a system of magnification that focuses beams of electrons to permit much greater resolution of objects than is possible with a light microscope.

**electron spin resonance dating:** see **ESR dating.**

**electropherogram:** amplitude plot that indicates the presence of each of the four nucleotides (A, T, G, C) at each position in a DNA sequence.

‡ **electrophoresis:** laboratory method that uses both electric current and variable pore sizes in supporting gels to separate **electromorphs**, permitting **genotypes** to be determined (for whole **proteins**), or **DNA sequences** to be inferred (for **nucleotides**). See **polyacrylamide gel electrophoresis.**

**electroporation:** use of electricity to temporarily increase cell membrane permeability and permit foreign DNA to enter a cell.

**element:** 1. value(s) on which calculations or conclusions are based. 2. an entity that satisfies all the conditions of belonging to a given set. 3. an individual case in a population.

**elementary family:** adult couple with their biological and adopted children. Aka nuclear family. Cf. **family.**

**elevation:** 1. area higher than the surrounding surface; Cf. **depression.** 2. in reference to joint movements, the displacement of a part upward, such as shrugging the shoulders. 3. arousal or heightened activity; for manic activity, see **major affective disorder.**

**ELISA:** abbreviation for enzyme-linked immunosorbent assay, a sensitive immunoassay technique that detects specific **antigens** or **antibodies.**

**elliptocytosis:** hereditary condition in which red blood cells are elliptical instead of circular.

**elongation in translation:** stage of protein synthesis in which the ribosome binds to the mRNA initiation complex and amino acids are joined.

*Elphidotarsius* Gidley, 1923: archaic mammal from the middle Paleocene of North America belonging to the **plesiadapiform** family **Carpolestidae**; composed of four species. Dental formula: 2.1.3.3; small body size, estimates ranging from 25 to 40 g for the four species; dental morphology and body size suggests an **insectivorous** diet; dentition tarsierlike, but it is very unlikely that there is a phylogenetic relationship. Believed to be the ancestor of *Carpodaptes*. See Appendix 1 for taxonomy.

**ELSI:** see **Ethical, Legal, and Social Implications Program.**

**Elsterian glaciation:** second major glaciation of the Pleistocene in the Poland–German sequence; Aka Elster. See **Mindel glaciation.**

**eluviation:** sedimentary process by which coarse soil concentrates on a surface as smaller silt and particles percolate downward through the action of rain water.

*Elwynella oreas* **Rose and Brown, 1982:** archaic mammal from the middle Eocene of North America belonging to the **plesiadapiform** family **Paromomyidae; monotypic.** Body mass estimated at around 180 g. See Appendix 1 for taxonomy.

**emaciation:** condition in which a body has disproportionately low fat content, usually accompanied by muscle atrophy.

**emasculation:** removal of the male reproductive organs; aka gelding. See **eunuch.**

**embrasure:** normal wear space between adjacent teeth. Cf. **diastema.**

‡ **embryo:** the advanced **zygote.** The embryo arises from the **embryonic disk** and is considered to be an embryo after the three **primary germ layers** have developed, and before all the rudimentary organs are present. Prior to that stage it is a **preembryo.** In humans, the embryo exists during the **embryonic stage.** Cf. **fetus.**

**embryo splitting:** method of whole organism cloning in which an 8–16 -cell fertilized embryo is divided by micromanipulation; the separated cells are then implanted into the uteri of foster mothers. Cf. **nuclear transfer.**

**embryoblast:** the apparently undifferentiated inner cell mass that forms within the **blastocyst cavity** of a preimplantation **blastocyst,** and that gives rise to the entire fetus and some of its extra-embryonic membranes. Consists of the **epiblast** and the **hypoblast.** Cf. **trophoblast.**

**embryogenesis:** course of initiation and development of an **embryo.** See **embryonic development.**

**embryology:** study of prenatal development from conception through the eighth week in utero. Sometimes used loosely to describe the entire period of gestation including the **fetal period.** A discipline more often referred to as 'developmental biology' in contemporary biology.

**embryonic development:** canalized process of histogenesis in multicellular organisms whereby the fertilized egg cell duplicates by **mitosis** and undergoes the stages of **cleavage, blastulation,** and **gastrulation;** although presumably endowed with identical genomes, cells are induced to ultimately become specialized tissues of the differentiated body.

**embryonic disk:** area that derives from the inner cell mass of the **zygote** after it has flattened. The **embryo** proper arises from the embryonic disk.

**embryonic hemoglobin:** umbrella term for several forms of **hemoglobin** synthesized in the embryonic yolk sac during the first 12 weeks of human gestation, the most common form of which consists of two **alpha globin chains** and two **epsilon globin chains.** Embryonic hemoglobin has a 30% higher affinity for oxygen than does **adult hemoglobin.** See **fetal hemoglobin.**

**embryonic induction:** interaction of cells during embryonic development as certain cells determine the specific developmental changes of cells nearby.

**embryonic stage (or period):** interval during human gestation following the **preembryonic stage** that extends from the second to the eighth week (14th to the 56th day) after conception (shorter in other primates). The embryonic stage is characterized by rapid structural **development** and differentiation of tissues *in utero:* the **placenta** forms, the main internal organs develop, and the major external body structures develop; only the heart and circulation are functioning, however. Cf. **fetal stage.**

**embryonic stem cell** (ES): any cell from a **preimplantation embryo.** Such cells can be manipulated in **gene targeting.** See **stem cell** and **totipotent** cell.

**embryotrophy:** nutrition of a mammalian egg before implantation.

**emendation:** intentional change in the spelling of a name, as from Neanderthal to **Neandertal.**

**emergenesis:** effect of complex gene combinations on the outcome of unique behavioral and physical traits. See **emergenic trait.**

**emergenic trait, character or feature:** any **trait** that is the result of complex gene combinations that lead to unique behavioral and physical traits. Resemblance in an **emergenic trait** is expected to be high for **identical twins** and low for **fraternal twins.**

**emergent evolution:** appearance of unpredictable and/or novel traits in a lineage, presumably by the rearrangement of existing genetic potential. See **position effect** and **macroevolution.**

**emergent property:** 1. nineteenth century concept referring to any novel characteristic that results from evolution. 2. in any hierarchical organization such as an ecosystem, a property of populations that is not characteristic of individuals, of communities that is not characteristic of populations, etc.

**emergent tree:** any tree in a tropical forest that extends above the relatively continuous canopy.

**emic:** term derived from phonemics that refers to attempts to view the behavior or beliefs of people in terms of the meaningful distinctions they themselves choose to make; parochial. Cf. the **etic** or the outside view of scientists.

**emigration:** movement of an individual or individuals out of one area or population to another area or population. Cf. **immigration.**

**Emiliani–Shackleton glacial sequence:** replacement for the old four-cycle **Alpine glacial sequence;** recently (1955–73) modified and extended using oxygen isotope ratios in deep-sea cores. The new V28-238 deep-sea core sequence contains eight major cycles for the most recent 730 ky (the **Brunhes normal epoch**), or the late and middle Pleistocene; the early Pleistocene (1.6 mya to 730 kya, **Matuyama** reversed **epoch**) contains twenty shorter cycles. Aka world oxygen isotope stage column, marine oxygen isotope chronology. See Appendix 6 for these middle and late Pleistocene cycles.

**eminence:** raised area on the surface of a bone.

**emissary vein:** term that applies to a group of small veins of the skull that pass from the **dura mater** directly to the scalp and down the veins of the neck.

**emotion:** 1. inner feeling such as anger, fear, elation, etc. 2. physiological state that can be measured through heart rate, **electrogram**, skin conductance, etc. Behavioral biologists have been cautious about applying either one of these definitions to nonhuman animals owing to the problem of **anthropomorphism** (see **Morgan's canon**).

**emotional water loss:** nonthermal perspiration characterized by evaporation of water through pores on the forehead, palms and soles, and axillary glands, prompted by emotional stress.

**empathetic learning:** see **observational learning**.

**empathic learning:** see **observational learning**.

**emperor tamarin:** vernacular for *Saguinus imperator*.

**emphysema:** swelling. 1. a pathological accumulation of air in any tissues or organs. 2. pulmonary emphysema; a condition of the lung characterized by increase beyond normal size of the air spaces distal to the terminal bronchioles, alveolar wall destruction and impairment of gas exchange. See **hereditary pulmonary emphysema** and **chronic obstructive pulmonary disease**.

**empiric risk:** in human genetics, the statistical probability that a certain child will have a given genotype, condition or trait.

‡ **empirical:** derived from, or guided by, experimental experience.

**empirical modeling:** mathematical description of a system based solely on experiment and observation; description in the absence of knowledge of biological or physical reasons as to whether relationships could or should exist among variables. Aka correlative modeling.

**empirical taxonomy:** classification based on apparent phenotypic similarity, rather than on genotype and trait homology.

**empiricism:** practice of basing conclusions solely on experience; this implies, in the context of science, that conclusions were drawn from observation and experiment only; *a posteriori* **analysis**, and a general rejection of *a priori* propositions or concepts.

**empiriocriticism:** Austrian version of **positivism** that later also gave rise to **logical positivism;** that science strives for only the most economical of descriptive systems, and on which further predictions are based, eschewing hidden entities or causes. Developed by Ernst Mach (1838–1916) and Richard Avenarius (1843–96).

**enamel:** hard avascular covering on the external surface of a mammalian tooth composed principally of **calcium carbonate** and **keratin**. Enamel is the hardest substance in the primate body. See **tooth**.

**enamel carbon isotope composition:** tooth **enamel** is composed of incorporated dietary isotopes (such as $^{13}C$); hence, the relative proportion of $C_3$ **vegetation** and $C_4$ **vegetation** in an animal's diet can be determined by analyzing its tooth enamel by **mass spectrometry**, with **stable isotopes**.

**enamel–dentin junction** (EDJ): border between the external enamel and inner **dentin** in a **tooth**.

**enamel organ:** epithelial invagination from the dental lamina that covers the dental papilla during fetal growth. The enamel organ provides a mold for the developing tooth and ultimately becomes the enamel of a deciduous tooth.

**enamel pearl:** dental anomaly expressed as secondary growth of enamel on either the crown or root of a tooth, which has the appearance of a pearl.

**enamel prism analysis:** sectioning and etching of teeth in order to observe various classes of enamel prism (and crystallite) pattern arrangement, including the degree of prism **decussation** (interweaving), in order to infer (paleo-)dietary patterns from tooth **enamel thickness** and structure.

**enamel thickness:** relative width of the **dental lamina** in a tooth. See **amelogenin**.

**enamel wrinkling:** See **crenulation**.

**enarthrodial:** of or pertaining to a ball-and-socket joint.

**enarthrosis:** see **ball-and-socket joint**.

**encasement theory:** idea that an individual is contained wholly within either the semen (**animalculism**) or the egg (**ovism**) and that as a **homunculus** it unfolds upon fertilization. Aka **Preformation Doctrine**.

**encephalic:** of or pertaining to structures within the **cranium**, including the brain.

‡ **encephalization:** developmental process by which the cerebral cortex has taken over the functions of subcortical centers. In general, there has been a tendency for classes of animals to evolve larger brains (see **neocortex**) relative to their remaining **body size**, such that there is progressively more encephalization from invertebrates to fish to amphibians to

reptiles and birds to mammals. Within the mammals, **primates** are more **encephalized** than all other groups. The relation of **brain size** to **body size** is expressed as a **ratio**, the **encephalization quotient**. See **thermoregulation** and the **expensive tissue hypothesis.**

**encephalization quotient** (EQ): measure of relative brain size in which the brain mass is compared with that of an 'average' living mammal of equal body mass. EQs less than 1.0 indicate a relatively smaller brain, whereas EQs greater than 1.0 indicate a relatively larger brain. See **allometry.**

**encephalized:** in evolutionary biology, possessing a relatively large brain. See **encephalization.**

**encoding:** modification of stimuli received through the senses; first stage of the memory process.

‡ **enculturation:** 1. adaptation of an individual to a local culture. 2. massive transmission of a particular culture, especially from one generation to the next; **diachronic** learning. Cf. **diffusion.**

**endangered species:** one of the five conservation categories established by the **International Union for the Conservation of Nature.** This category includes those species that are likely to become **extinct** in the near future. Some primate species are in this category. See **extinct species, vulnerable species, rare species, insufficiently known species.**

‡ **endemic:** 1. present or usually prevalent in a population or geographical area at all times; said of a disease or agent, especially when prevalence is at a relatively constant and low rate over time, with low **morbidity.** Cf. **epidemic, pandemic.** 2. restricted or peculiar to a locality or region; **indigenous.**

**endemic center:** geographical area with a very distinctive local **biota** consisting of between five and ten percent **endemic** species. Cf. **center of endemism.**

**endemic syphilis:** see **syphilis.**

**endobasion** (endoba): **craniometric landmark;** most posterior point of the anterior border of the **foramen magnum** that is internal and posterior to the **basion.** See Appendix 7.

**endocanthion:** inner corner or angle of the eye. Aka inner epicanthus, epicanthic fold, plica palpebronasalis. Cf. **outer epicanthus.**

**endocast:** see **endocranial cast.**

**endochondral bone:** bone whose development originates as a cartilaginous model shaped like the adult bone and proceeds by **ossification.** Most bones of the skeleton, especially the bones of the appendicular skeleton, develop in this manner. See **endochondral ossification** and **epiphyseal disk.** Cf. **intramembranous bone.**

**endochondral ossification:** process of formation of **endochondral bone** within a cartilaginous model. Cf. **intramembranous ossification.**

**endocranial:** pertaining to the inner surface of the **cranium.**

‡ **endocranial cast:** mold or impression taken from the inside of a **cranium** that presents surface features of the brain such as blood vessels and convolution patterns. Such casts may be artificially made with latex, plaster, or other material, or they may be produced naturally in the fossilization process. Aka endocast.

**endocranial volume** (ECV): volume of the **cranium,** including that of the brain and meninges. The standard unit of measurement is the **cubic centimeter** (cm$^3$). Some **prosimians** have brains that are about the volume of a walnut (50 cm$^3$), **monkeys** about the volume of a small apple (200 cm$^3$), and **apes** about the volume of a large orange (500 cm$^3$), while **humans** have brains that are about the volume of a cantaloupe melon (1350 cm$^3$). In primates, the endocranial volume is approximately 104% of **brain mass.** See **brain size.**

**endocrine:** secreting internally; denoting a gland whose secretions are discharged into the blood or lymph.

**endocrine action:** secretion of a **hormone** from its tissue of origin and its distribution throughout the body by way of the blood to its **target site.**

**endocrine disorder:** disease or syndrome affecting the pituitary, thyroid, parathyroid, adrenal or pancreatic glands; examples are **acromegaly, gigantism, goiter,** and **diabetes mellitus.**

**endocrine gland:** any ductless gland of the **endocrine system,** such as the adrenal or pituitary glands of vertebrates, that secretes hormones to other parts of the body through the blood or lymph. Other endocrine glands include the pineal gland, thyroid gland, parathyroids, thymus, suprarenal gland, pancreas, ovaries, testes, and certain other structures of the brain. Cf. **exocrine gland.**

**endocrine reflex:** feedback loop, usually negative, by which hormonal secretion is regulated; for example, when circulating levels of dietary glucose are high, beta cells in the pancreas reflexively release **insulin** (facilitated by glucokinase); this stimulates the liver to reduce glucose to glycogen. As the level of circulating glucose drops, the beta cells cease insulin secretion.

**endocrine system:** all the ductless, hormone-secreting glands and tissues in the body, taken as a whole.

**endocrinology:** study of hormones, their origins and actions.

**endodeme:** local interbreeding population; see **deme.**

**endoderm:** innermost primary germ layer of the embryo. Endoderm gives rise to the epithelial linings of the **gastrointestinal tract,** respiratory tract, urinary bladder, and urethra.

‡ **endogamy:** any system of sexual reproduction (such as inbreeding) in which the mating partners are

more closely related than in a random (panmictic) system; endogamous. In a cultural sense, endogamy is a conventionally defined distance defined by a compulsory threshold within which one must mate and beyond which one must not mate. Cf. **exogamy**.

**endogenous:** resulting from internal conditions; occurring or produced within.

**endogenous clock:** any system that displays inherent periodicity.

**endogenous virus:** viroid that has become incorporated into host DNA, and is capable of **vertical transmission** as well as **horizontal transmission**.

**endolymph:** fluid within the membranous labyrinth and cochlear duct of the inner ear that aids in the conduction of vibrations involved in hearing and the maintenance of equilibrium.

**endometrium:** inner lining of the uterus, composed of glandular epithelium.

**endomitosis:** DNA replication within the nucleus of a cell that fails to divide, resulting in **polyploidy**. See **endopolyploidy**.

**endomolare** (enm): **craniometric landmark**; most lateral point on the **lingual** or inside border of the **alveolus** of the second maxillary molar. See Appendix 7.

**endomorphy:** body build characterized by a predominance of visceral development and fat; one of three **somatotypes** proposed by W. H. Sheldon.

**endonuclease:** enzyme that breaks chemical bonds at specific nucleotide sites along strands of **DNA** or **RNA**. Aka nuclease. See **restriction enzyme**.

**endonuclease digestion:** process of digestion of nucleic acids by specific **endonucleases**.

**endoparasite:** parasite that lives within the body of the **host**, such as the various intestinal worms. Cf. **ectoparasite**.

**endophenotypic:** pertaining to phenotypic characters that are presumably not directly adaptive and that may not affect an organism's **fitness**. Cf. **exophenotypic**.

‡ **endoplasmic reticulum** (ER): an **organelle** consisting of a hollow system of cytoplasmic canals, tubes, vesicles, ventricles and caverns, which interlaces the whole cell and that delimits compartmental 'reaction rooms'. One such space is the site(s) of protein synthesis; **polyribosomes** are attached to this type of ER, which is referred to as rough endoplasmic reticulum. Other ER has no ribosomes and is referred to as smooth endoplasmic reticulum.

**endopolyploidy:** 1. **endomitosis**. 2. state of **mosaicism** in which certain of an individual's cells are polyploid while the remainder are diploid.

**endoreduplication:** process of somatic polyploidization by endomitotic reduplication of interphase chromatids. Occurs in both normal plant and animal tissue (e.g. muscle tissue) as well as in tumor cells.

**endorphin:** any of several chemicals secreted by the **pituitary gland**; these serve to mitigate the effects of pain during stress. Endorphins act to modify the **dopamine** pathway to the frontal lobes; they attach to the morphine receptor. High concentrations of dopamine produce a sensation of well-being or euphoria. Endorphin is a contraction of 'endogenous morphine'. Cf. **enkephalin**.

‡ **endoskeleton:** bony skeleton contained within the body of vertebrates. Cf. **exoskeleton**.

**endosteal surface:** internal surface of bone to which the **endosteum** is attached.

**endosteum:** thin layer of epithelial cells that line the **medullary cavity** of a long bone.

**endosymbiosis theory:** hypothesis that eukaryotic organelles such as **mitochondria** and chloroplasts originated when ancient bacteria took up symbiotic residence inside early **eukaryotic cells**, or when plasmids resided in prokaryotes.

**endothelium:** layer of epithelial tissue that forms the thin inner lining of blood vessels and heart chambers.

‡ **endothermy:** state of production of heat within an animal by means of metabolic processes within cells (mainly muscle cells). Birds and mammals are endotherms. Adjective: endothermic. See **homeothermy**.

**endscraper:** stone tool with a sharp edge used for cleaning or softening hides. Aka kratzer, grattoir.

**endurance locomotion:** form of locomotion in which a mammal can continue to move for long periods of time, but usually at slower speeds (some exceptions are found among the artiodactyls, which can move quickly and continue for a long period). Bipedal walking in humans is a form of endurance locomotion.

**energetic cost of brain size:** any measure of metabolism, heat generation, etc., that reflects the proportion of energy required by organisms with different degrees of **encephalization**. On average, **marsupials** dispense only about 2% of resting **metabolism** toward support of brain functions, whereas **chimpanzees** dispense 9%, and humans about 20%.

**energy:** capacity to do work or quantity expended on an activity; available power; exists as heat, light, motion, etc.

**energy budget:** balance between **energy** obtained and energy utilized. Some primatologists have applied this term to the animals themselves, whereas in ecology it is usually applied to the community or ecosystem. Aka energetics.

**energy capture:** in biology, any process during which energy is transferred to an organism; this can take the form of movement into a biosystem (e.g. photosynthesis), transfer from one trophic level to another (predation, parasitism), storage against future use (domestication), etc.

**energy consumption:** amount of energy, both food and fuels, consumed by a human population.

**energy efficiency:** ratio of useful work or energy storage to energy intake. See **energy budget**.

**energy expenditure:** amount of energy used by a population in physical activity.

**energy-maximizing foraging strategy:** technique by which an animal gathers the largest amount of nutrients possible over 24 h. This type of **foraging strategy** is found among many larger mammals or mammals that live in large social units, including primates such as squirrel monkeys (*Saimiri*) and baboons (*Papio*); such animals are called energy maximizers. Cf. **time-minimizing foraging strategy**.

**energy-minimizing foraging strategy:** technique by which the animal conserves energy; such animals (known as energy minimizers) subsist on low-quality diets, which force this **foraging strategy** on them. An example of an energy minimizer is the howler monkey, which consumes low-calorie leaves and conserves energy by spending most of its time resting. It lives in small territories, and delineates these territories by sound (requiring little energy expenditure compared with physically patrolling the boundaries).

**energy production:** amount of **energy** captured by a population.

**engine:** in common usage, any closed system that explains a given set of phenomena; driving force or critical variable(s).

**Engelswies:** archaeological site in southern Germany dating to 17 mya; contains hominoid remains including an upper molar fragment with thick enamel, attributed to Hominoidea *incertae sedis*. This is currently (2003) the oldest **hominoid** found in Europe, and represents a species that arrived with other fauna, including pliopithecoids and *Deinotherium*.

**Engis:** archaeological site found in 1829 in the Meuse River Valley near Liege, Belgium, dated to an Upper **Périgordian Mousterian** horizon, and that contains Upper Paleolithic (**Aurignacian**) artifacts and hominid remains then attributed to *Homo neanderthalensis*, including a two-year-old child's partial cranium; a second partial cranium, since deteriorated; a third skull, dated to only 8 kya, was apparently intrusive. An original 'Ethiopian' attribution has not withstood the test of time. Aka Engis child.

**engram:** see **memory**.

**engraver:** Upper Paleolithic flake knife from which chips have been removed at right angles to the main blade, and that was used to make horn, bone, and ivory implements.

**enhancer:** sequence of **DNA** that regulates the probability of transcription of adjacent sequences.

**enkephalin:** any of a group of substances believed to be neurotransmitters and found in many parts of the brain; enkephalins activate **enkephalin receptor sites** and play a role in pain mediation. Cf. **endorphin**.

**enkephalin mimic:** any substance not normally found in the body and that can activate **enkephalin receptor sites** in the brain. Used in pain mediation. Enkephalin mimics include morphine, codeine and demerol. Mimics are often addictive, because they cannot be degraded enzymatically as rapidly as the enkephalins, and occupy the enkephalin receptor sites for longer periods.

**enkephalin receptor site:** neuroreceptor sites found in the brain that are activated by the **enkephalins** and their mimics, and that play a role in pain mediation. Aka the 'opiate receptor'.

**entelechy:** 1. realization or actuality, as opposed to potential. 2. vital force or life-giving principle alleged to be responsible for **growth and development**. 3. any vital force providing purpose and direction.

**entepicondylar foramen:** distal opening for blood vessels and nerves on the medial surface of the primate **humerus**; used as a diagnostic key and considered primitive. Found in **prosimians** and some **platyrrhines**, among extant primates, and still retained in the extinct **parapithecids**, suggesting they had not reached the catarrhine grade.

**enterobiasis:** benign intestinal infection by a nematode, *Enterobius vermicularis*; worldwide distribution; possibly the most common infection by a parasitic worm. Aka pinworm, seatworm, threadworm, oxyuriasis.

**enteropathy:** any disease of the intestine.

**entoconid:** **cusp** on the distolingual side of the **talonid** that has developed on the lower molars of some primate species.

**entoconulid:** accessory **cuspule** on the **lingual** surface of a lower molar **talonid**.

**entocuneiform:** bone that articulates with the **navicular** bone and **metatarsal** I of the primitive mammalian **tarsus**; referred to as the medial cuneiform in primate and human anatomy.

**entrainment:** synchronization of a biological rhythm to an external time source, as in a lunar frequency.

**entropy:** 1. measure of the amount of energy unavailable for work in a thermodynamic system. 2. measure of the frequency of an event within a closed system; probability of an event in such a system. 3. noise or error in information. 4. degree of sameness or homogeneity; for example, in **population genetics**, the relentless march toward **homozygosity**. Cf. **information**.

‡ **environment:** surroundings of an organism; any external or antecedent conditions that influence or

modify the developmental outcome of a genetic locus, genotype, or organism. Culturally, the complex physical, social, and moral context within which humans live. Adjective: environmental.

‡ **environmental determinism:** variation of cultural evolutionary theory which asserts that the form that any culture takes depends entirely on the type of environment in which it finds itself; thus different cultures, in this view, are results of different environmental influences; much too extreme a position by most anthropological standards.

**environmental estrogen:** any of the chemicals that are **estrogen** mimics, such as those found in pesticides, and that can cause **premature thelarche.**

**environmental grain:** effect of spatial variation (patchiness) relative to the size and behavior of an organism. See **foraging, fine-grained environment, coarse-grained environment,** and **optimal foraging theory.**

**environmental possibilism:** perspective in cultural ecology that views cultures as the product of a series of historical events over time in which cultural factors are the primary causal agents while environmental factors temper the possibilities of any culture. Cf. **environmental determinism.**

**environmental resistance:** limitations put on the reproductive potential of a species or population by unfavorable environmental factors.

**environmental stress:** environment agent to which an organism must adapt to survive; in the absence of **acclimation, acclimatization,** and/or **adaptation,** the agent increases the probability of death of that organism. See **stress** and **strain.**

**environmental variance:** that proportion of the **total phenotypic variance** of a quantitative character explained by all factors to which the members of a population have been exposed; a property of a population, not of individuals or of a particular individual.

**environmentalism:** form of analysis that stresses the role of environmental influences in the development of biological traits or behaviors; also, the point of view that such influences tend to be paramount in behavioral development.

**environmentalist:** in learning theory, a proponent of the hypothesis that all human behavior is learned rather than inherited.

‡ **enzyme:** **protein** produced by living cells that speeds up (or **catalyzes**) a specific chemical reaction; enzymes bind to their **substrates** but are not used up in the reaction. Enzymes are generally given the suffix '-ase' (e.g. phosphatase, dismutase, etc.) and are one of the products of **protein synthesis.**

**enzyme-linked immunosorbent assay:** see **ELISA.**

*Eoanthropus dawsonii:* see **Piltdown hoax.**

‡ **Eocene epoch:** one of the **Tertiary** epochs of the **Cenozoic era,** lasting from about 55.5 to 33.7 mya; the first true **primates (euprimates)** occurred during the Eocene; the first identifiable bats and cats also appeared, while horses and camels were already common. See Appendix 4 for a geological time scale.

**Eocene primates:** earliest **euprimates** that appear in the fossil record of the early **Eocene.** There are two distinct groups, adapoids and omomyoids; in addition, there are primate species that do not conform to either of the established taxa. Revision of Eocene primates may produce additional taxonomic groups.

**eolian:** describes wind-blown geological deposits or sediments, usually sand.

**eolith:** literally, 'dawn stone'; archaic term proposed by de Mortillet in 1883 for the earliest **stone tools;** some may have been of natural origin.

**eon:** largest major subdivision of geologic time; Cf. **era, period,** and **epoch.**

**Eosimiae:** hyporder proposed by Van Valen that includes the extinct parapithecoids and the living ceboids.

*Eosimias* **Beard, Dawson, Wang, and Li, 1994:** putative **anthropoid** from the middle Eocene of China belonging to the family **Eosimiidae;** two species described; known from teeth, cranial fragment, and foot bones. If *Eosimias* is an anthropoid, it would be the earliest one known; some workers think that the affinities of this genus lie with the omomyoids. Small, estimated body mass around 100 g. Dental formula: 2.1.3.3/2.1.3.3. See Appendix 1 for taxonomy.

**Eosimiidae:** early family of putative **anthropoids** from the middle Eocene of China consisting of the genus *Eosimias*.

**eosinophil:** type of white blood cell characterized by the presence of cytoplasmic granules that become stained by acidic eosin dye. Eosinophils normally constitute about 2%–4% of the white blood cell population; they phagocytize antigen–antibody complexes, and allergens, and secrete chemicals that fight infections.

**eotechnic phase:** Mumford's 1934 term for a phase of technological development characterized by the earliest appearance of **prime movers** other than human beings, and the temporal displacement of energy harvesting and its expenditure. See **technology.**

**epactal bone:** alternative name for the Inka (Inca) bone or interparietal bone. See **sutural bone.**

**epiblast:** embryonic cell of the inner cell mass that gives rise to the embryonic **ectoderm** and **primitive streak.** See **paternal X inactivation.**

**epicanthic fold:** fold of skin at the inner corner of the eye, near the base of the nose, that curves down and towards the midline, covering the lacrimal caruncle;

found in some populations of humans including peoples of the Far East, the Khoisan **!Kung** of Africa, Native Americans, and Polynesians. Variation within any population may be obscured by the development of the nose. Common speculation about the fold regards it as an adaptation against glare off bright surfaces such as snow or sand; others have maintained that it is a fetal character state maintained into adulthood in these populations. Aka Mongoloid fold. See **inner epicanthus** and **outer epicanthus**. Cf. **eye folds**.

**epicondyle:** ostelogic landmark; a projection above a **condyle**.

**epicontinental sea:** salt water that covers part of a continental landmass, and that may be exposed during periods of glacial maxima, e.g. the Bering Sea. Cf. **Beringia**.

**epideictic display:** population regulatory mechanism proposed by V. C. Wynne-Edwards that argues that members of a population may perform very intense displays that give an indication of the population density; how intense the display is provides a standard by which members can 'assess' how many matings can take place. See **group selection**.

‡ **epidemic:** 1. affecting or tending to affect many individuals within a population, community, or region at the same time. 2. excessively prevalent. 3. an outbreak of sudden rapid spread, growth, or development; specifically, a natural population suddenly and rapidly enlarged; said of a disease agent, often causing high **morbidity** and/or **mortality**. Cf. **endemic** and **pandemic**.

**epidemiography:** treatise concerning one or more epidemic diseases.

**epidemiologic transition:** change in disease patterns within populations, seen in many developed regions of the world, in which there is a decline in infectious disease and an increase in noninfectious disease, especially **degenerative disease**.

**epidemiological model:** explanation of certain diseases that involve the simultaneous presence of an **agent** of disease, a **vector** of transmission, and the disease **host**.

**epidemiologist:** scientist in the field of **epidemiology**.

‡ **epidemiology:** study of the causes and transmission of **disease**; accumulation and analysis of a variety of statistics about the **etiology** and occurrence of disease.

**epidermis:** outermost nonvascular and nonsensitive layer of the skin; the layer that is composed of flat, usually pigmented cells. Adjective: epidermal. See **melanocyte** and **keratinization**. Cf. **dermis**.

**epidermolysis bullosa** (EB): heritable autosomal dominant genetic disease characterized by blisters and abnormalities of the skin. In the 'simplex' form a mutation results in abnormal keratin; in the 'dystrophic' form a mutation results in abnormal collagen; in the most severe 'junctional' form a mutation results in abnormal laminin, causing a failure of the epidermis and dermis to fuse.

**epididymis:** highly coiled tube located along the posterior border of the **testis**; stores spermatozoa and transports them from the seminiferous tubules of the testis to the **ductus deferens**.

**epigamic:** describes any trait related to courtship and sex other than the essential organs and behavior of copulation.

**epigamic selection:** see **sexual selection**.

**epigastric region:** most **superior** central abdominal region that lies above the umbilical region.

**epigenesis:** theory that new structures and organs develop from an undifferentiated cell mass. Cf. **Preformation Doctrine**.

‡ **epigenetic(s):** 1. pertaining to the sequential interaction of genetic factors and the developmental pathways through which the genotype is expressed, but that may be modified by parallel gene-based elements, or by agents in the environment. 2. the plural form (epigenetics) refers more specifically to the study of the genetic causes of **development**, especially those mechanisms affecting the timing and interaction of gene expression and staged tissue **induction**. See **small RNAs** and **genomic imprinting**. Cf. **'new' epigenetics**.

**epigenetic asymmetry:** developmental dimorphism(s) in phenotypes in a sibship due to **epigenetic** phenomena such as **genomic imprinting** or other **parent-of-origin effects**.

**epigenetic landscape:** C. H. Waddington's term for a model of the multitude of potential developmental pathways faced by each cell in an embryo.

**epigenetic mechanism:** any non-Mendelian mode of genetic expression; see **monoallelic expression**, **uniparental disomy**, and **X inactivation**.

**epigenetic pleiotrophy:** outcome in which widely disparate parts of an overall phenotype are affected by a single developmental event.

**epigenetic reprogramming:** heritable modifications to the genome during **gametogenesis** and early **embryogenesis** by mechanisms such as **DNA methylation**, **histone modification**, and **chromatin remodeling**. Failure of normal reprogramming can result in tissue malformation, mental retardation syndromes, or **cancer**.

**epigenetic sequence:** precise ordination of gene activity that occurs during the development of an organism.

**epigenotype:** global set of potential developmental pathways that may be experienced by an individual genotype during ontogeny, including those perturbations affected by environmental agency; the process of production of a **phenotype**. See **switch gene.**

**epilepsy, progressive myoclonic 2** (EPM2A): a neurological condition characterized by seizures (e.g. grand mal) caused by electrochemical discharges in the brain. One of about 12 recognized gene-based forms. This form is Aka LaFora disease, caused by mutations in the *EPM2A* gene that codes for Laforin, an autosomal recessive protein phosphatase that balances blood sugars in the brain. Highly variable age of onset. There is also a mitochondrial form ('red ragged fibers'). Cf. **essential tremor** and **Parkinson disease.**

**EpiMesolithic:** pertaining to levels reflecting primarily an Old World **Mesolithic** economy but existing during **Neolithic** times, and with a few of the new technologies such as polished axes and pottery.

**epimutation:** mutation not present in the germline DNA but that occurs during early differentiation of stem cells, resulting in a clinical phenotype.

**epinephrine: neurohormone** produced by the **adrenal medulla** of the kidney. It initiates actions similar to those initiated by sympathetic nervous system stimulation (andrenergic stimulation) in the heart, bronchioles, and blood vessels. Aka adrenaline.

**Epipaleolithic era:** pertaining to transitional cultural developments at archaeological levels between the Old World **Upper Paleolithic** era and the **Neolithic** era.

**epiphenomenon:** simultaneous events that have no cause–effect relationship.

**epiphenomenonalist theory of aging:** proposal that aging is caused by environmental insults that can be neither avoided nor prevented, popularized by British writer Alex Comfort (1920–2000) and Canadian physiologist Hans Selye (1907–1982). Aka extrinsic theory.

‡ **epiphyseal disk:** band of cartilage between the **epiphyses** and **diaphysis** that expands, allowing for growth; as cartilage expands it is ossified; zone of growth in an **endochondral bone**. In a vertebra the epiphyseal disks are between the vertebral body and the superior and inferior surfaces. Aka epiphyseal plate, metaphysis, growth plate region.

‡ **epiphysis:** 1. generally, the end of a **long bone**; that part of a long bone that articulates with adjacent bones; in vertebrae the epiphyses are the superior and inferior surfaces of the vertebral body. Plural: epiphyses. Epiphyses (in mammals) are adjacent to an **epiphyseal disk**, which serves as a zone of growth. Epiphyses are composed of a thin layer of **compact bone** surrounding red marrow-filled **cancellous bone**. Cf. **diaphysis.**

**epiphysis cerebri:** see **pineal gland.**

**episematic:** pertaining to an extreme trait that aids in recognition, as in dramatic color marking, e.g. the snout of a male mandrill baboon.

**episome:** DNA that is not incorporated into the genome, but nevertheless is replicated together with the genome.

**epistacy:** production of a larger set of modified characters or of a greater degree of modification in one of two related taxa; aka Eimer's principle. See **paraphyletic group.** Not to be confused with **epistasis.**

**epistasis:** 1. any interaction of nonallelic genes whereby one gene interferes with the phenotypic expression of alleles at another locus; the second level of **gene interaction** parallel to allelic and genotype–environment interactions. Adjective: epistatic. 2. the rise of, or flotation of, insoluble material on the top of a liquid. Cf. **hypostasis.**

**epistatic fitness interaction:** any interaction between the alleles at two or more loci such that the phenotype differs from what would be expected if the loci were expressed independently.

**epistatic gene interaction effect:** proportion of the **total phenotypic variance** of a quantitative trait due to genes that contribute to variance due to other interactions.

**epistropheus:** pivot; axis; term sometimes applied to the second cervical vertebra.

**epiteric bone: sutural bone** that develops at the **pterion** of the cranium.

**epithalamus:** structure in the **forebrain** where **cerebrospinal fluid** is produced and from which the **pineal gland** extends.

**epitheliochorial placenta:** subtype of the **chorionic placenta** in which a separation between the tissues of the **chorion** and the epithelial lining of the uterus is maintained; found in the lemurs and lorises (the strepsirhine primates).

**epithelium:** one of the four basic types of tissue; epithelial tissue is found on free surfaces such as the skin, the respiratory passageways, and **gastrointestinal tract.** Adjective: epithelial.

**epithet:** in taxonomy, the second word of a **binomen,** or the second and third words of a **trinomen.**

*epitheta hybrida*: in taxonomy, specific epithets constructed of conjoined elements from two or more languages.

**epitope:** specific portion of a protein that is recognized by an immune system. Aka antigenic site, antigenic determinant.

**epitreptic:** pertaining to intraspecific attraction; sexually attractive only to a member of the same species. See **recognition species concept.**

**epitriquetrum:** supernumerary bone sometimes found in the **carpus** of humans.

**epitrochlear fossa:** depression located on the posterior region of the medial epicondyle of the humerus that is found in the **parapithecids.** This structure serves as a site of attachment for strong ligaments uniting the humerus and ulna.

‡ **epoch:** subdivision of a **period**; one of the smallest subdivisions of the **Paleozoic**, **Mesozoic**, or **Cenozoic eras**; the epochs of the Cenozoic, for example, are the **Paleocene**, **Eocene**, **Oligocene**, **Miocene**, **Pliocene**, **Pleistocene**, and **Holocene**.

**eponym:** 1. honorific term or phrase derived from a place or surname, e.g. Darwinism, Mendelism, and Bombay blood group. 2. in anatomy, a nondescriptive term applied to an anatomical structure, often in honor of a deceased anatomist. Anatomists agreed in 1960 to revise and rename such terms with names that actually describe the structure, morphology, function, or other characteristic. Aka tombstone name.

**epsilon globin chain** (ε Hb): one of several globin chains that constitute the family of **hemoglobin** molecules and that form part of **embryonic hemoglobin**. Aka epsilon globin.

**epsilon karyology:** determination of distinctive **DNA** loops in lampbrush **chromosomes**. An advanced analytical phase of **karyology**.

**Epstein–Barr virus** (EBV): DNA virus of the herpes group that infects B lymphocytes; transmitted through intimate contact; Aka human herpesvirus type 4. EBV is the cause of infectious mononucleosis, or 'mono', Aka 'kissing disease'. EBV has an integration site on HSA 14. See **Burkitt lymphoma**.

**EQ:** see **encephalization quotient**.

**equal environments assumption:** premise that environmental influences affecting **trait** development are the same for identical and fraternal **twins**; see **twin method** and **cotwin control group**.

**equational division: cell division** during which **centromeres** divide and **sister chromatids** are separated into different daughter cells. Occurs during anaphase of **mitosis** and **anaphase II** of **meiosis**. See **disjunction**.

**equator:** 1. circle separating a sphere into two congruent parts. 2. circle on a sphere or heavenly body whose plane is perpendicular to the axis of rotation, and thus everywhere equidistant from each of the two poles, as in the earth's equator. See **caloric equator**.

**equatorial plate:** see **metaphase plate**.

**equatorial saki:** vernacular for *Pithecia aequatorialis*.

**equatorial zone:** latitudinal zone centering on the **equator**, and ranging about 15° both north and south.

***Equatorius* Ward, Brown, Hill, Kelley and Downs, 1999:** generic name proposed for *c*. 15.58–15.36 mya (Locality BPRP-122) **Miocene** Muruyur fossil hominoid fragments from Kipsaramon in the **Tugen Hills**, Baringo Lake District, Kenya. Remains are attributable to at least five individuals; the ape specimen **KNM-TH 28860** is comparable to a more robust species, *Kenyapithecus wickeri*, but with exaggerated features. The proposal to reassign specimens formerly attributed to another species, *Kenyapithecus africanus*, to the new genus *Equatorius* has met with some resistance. See **Muruyur**.

‡ **equilibrium:** state of rest or balance of forces; **homeostasis**. In **population genetics**, a state achieved either when **balancing selection** against two **genotypes** produces a static population (as in a **balanced polymorphism**), or when no **evolutionary forces** are acting on a population. See **Hardy–Weinberg equilibrium principle**.

**equilibrium density gradient centrifugation:** method of separating macromolecules by means of centrifugal fields and solutions that contain regions of different densities.

**equilibrium, genetic:** see **genetic equilibrium**.

**equilibrium, Hardy–Weinberg:** see **Hardy–Weinberg equilibrium principle**.

**equilibrium model:** 1. any mathematical model in which gross inputs and outputs result in a net change of zero. 2. in genetics, a dynamic model in which **mechanisms of evolution** cause internal changes to a population without a net change in **allele frequencies**, and therefore no evolution. 3. in island biogeography, a state when the rate of immigration of new colonizing species is balanced by the rate of extinction of old species.

**equilibrium population:** any population in which **allele frequencies** have reached a balance between mutation pressure and selection pressure.

**equivalence:** doctrine that all humans have the same biological capacities. Aka biological equivalence.

***Equus:*** generic nomen for a modern horselike mammal, a **Pleistocene**, one-toed browser with its immediate ancestral forms found in Asia. *Equus* dispersed into Africa *c*. 2 **mya**, and thus makes an excellent **index fossil** in Africa, categorically separating sites dating >2 mya from sites <2 mya, in which modern horse bones are present. Brought to the **New World** in historical times as a domesticated animal, many of which immediately became **feral** and repopulated the Great Plains of North America.

**Equus Cave:** archaeological site located near the famous site of **Taung**, South Africa, dated to 103–33 kya, containing **Middle Stone Age** artifacts and hominid remains including gnathic remains from 13 individuals, all attributed to *Homo sapiens*.

**ER:** abbreviation for **East Rudolf**, a lake in Kenya.

**era:** subdivision of a geological **eon**. Cf. **period** and **epoch**.

**erect posture:** see **bipedalism**.

‡ **erectines:** vernacular for that group of extinct fossil **hominids** that were **bipedal**, **encephalized**, and who left cultural traces called the **Acheulean tool tradition**. Erectines first appear in the fossil record

almost 2 **mya**, and apparently survived in certain geographic pockets until fairly recently; their formal **binomial** designation is *Homo erectus*.

**Erer-Gota:** research site located in Ethiopia where long-term field studies of hamadryas baboons (*Papio hamadryas*) have been conducted for decades. The primatologists who have conducted field research at this site include J. J. Abegglen, H. Kummer, and H. Sigg.

**ergonomics:** quantitative study of work, performance, and efficiency. See **optimal foraging theory**.

**ergosterol:** alcohol, $C_{28}H_{43}OH$, which is converted indirectly by **ultraviolet radiation** into vitamin $D_2$, particularly in the skin.

**erosion:** wearing or weathering away, especially the displacement of geological formations into sediment by the agency of water, ice, or wind; loosening and dissolution of the earth's **crust**.

**error:** 1. in statistics, the deviation of an obtained value from an expected value. 2. an unintentional mistake. 3. **bias.** See **Type 1 error**, **Type 2 error**, and **measurement error**.

**error catastrophe theory of aging:** intracellular, stochastic model of aging in which the major premise is that the machinery involved in transcription, editing, and translation becomes less efficient over the life of an organism, and eventually reaches subvital activity levels. The assertion that aging occurs because of accumulated errors during protein synthesis that increase over the life of an organism was first proposed by American biologist Leslie Orgel (1927– ); Aka error theory. As originally proposed, the theory lost influence, but a modern molecular reformulation has revived research interest.

**eruption:** 1. emergence of a tooth as it ascends from the gums. 2. volcanic event characterized by explosions, gas emissions, ash evulsion, and/or the discharge of solid matter into the atmosphere.

**erythema:** 1. severe sunburn 2. reddening of the skin resulting from capillary congestion.

**erythroblast:** nucleated cell from which mature erythrocytes or red blood cells are formed.

**erythroblastic island:** one of two central cells of the bone marrow reticulum; the island is surrounded by immature (nucleated) red blood cells in various stages of development. The cells in the island have two main functions, to digest the ejected nuclei of the normoblasts just prior to their maturity and release as **erythrocytes**, and to digest worn-out red blood cells.

**erythroblastosis:** discharge of nucleated red blood corpuscles from the blood-forming centers into the circulation.

**erythroblastosis fetalis:** disease of the fetus and newborn in which the blood cells of an Rh+ infant are destroyed by maternal **antibodies** produced by an Rh- mother; may also occur in other systems, such as the **ABO blood group**. Aka **hemolytic disease of the newborn** and **hydrops fetalis**. See **Rhesus factor** and **Rhesus isoimmunization**.

***Erythrocebus* Trouessart, 1897:** monotypic catarrhine genus; patas monkey; Aka red hussar, red or military monkey; closely related to ***Chlorocebus*** and the ***Cercopithecus*** species. Broad distribution across sub-Saharan equatorial Africa from Senegal to Ethiopia. Open-country species, usually found in savanna habitats. **Diurnal**. Terrestrial **quadrupeds** that sleep in trees. Patas have long slender limbs and tail, narrow paws with short digits and reduced halluces and polluces (see **hallux, pollux**), adaptations for **cursorial** running. They attain speeds of 55 kph (35 mph). Strong **sexual dimorphism**. Dental formula: 2.1.2.3; mainly **granivorous**. Live in small **one-male units** ranging from 8 to 20 animals with large home ranges; nongroup males form **bachelor herds**. See Appendix 2 for taxonomy and Appendix 3 for species.

**erythrocyte** (Erc): an enucleated cell or corpuscle in mammals that functions to transport oxygen (bound to hemoglobin molecules) from the lungs to the tissues, and to remove a small portion of carbon dioxide that is carried as $HCO_3$ from the tissues to the lungs. In a normal human adult, 2.5 million erythrocytes are formed every second; each erythrocyte has an average life span of about 120 days. Aka red blood cell.

**erythron:** total mass of erythropoietic cells and circulating **erythrocytes**; viewed as a functional, though dispersed, organ.

**erythropoiesis:** see **hematopoiesis**.

**erythropoietin** (EPO): 1. naturally-occurring substance produced by the kidneys that stimulates red blood cell production in bone marrow. 2. a recombinant gene product (see **genetic engineering**).

**ES:** abbreviation for **embryonic stem cell**.

**es-Skhūl:** see **Skhūl**.

**escaper:** see **breakthrough**.

***Escherichia coli:*** gram-negative, rod-like species of enterobacterium constituting the greater part of the intestinal flora of humans and other animals; the genome contains a ring of DNA called a **plasmid**, which is useful in **recombinant DNA** work, or **genetic engineering**. The genome of *E. coli* was sequenced in 1997.

**Eskimo:** see **Arctic Inuit**.

**esophagus:** straight collapsible muscular tube that serves to connect the oral cavity with the stomach and through which the **bolus** and fluids travel.

**ESR dating:** abbreviation for electron spin resonance dating, a **chronometric dating** method based on the accumulated natural radiation damage in crystalline substances such as carbonates and **tooth enamel**.

The method measures the level of radioactive bombardment undergone by tooth enamel by determining the number of electrons that have been knocked out of their energy shells, and subsequently become trapped in crystals of **apatite** found in tooth enamel.

**ESS:** abbreviation for evolutionarily stable strategy; in **game theory**, a **strategy** or set of strategies that cannot be replaced (or beaten) by a new, alternative strategy or invading mutation; used predominantly in animal behavior and behavioral ecology theory. Aka preprogrammed rule. See John **Maynard Smith**.

‡ **essential amino acids:** eight amino acids in adults (nine in infants) that must be obtained by humans from dietary sources: isoleucine, leucine, lysine, methionine, phenylalanine, threonine, tryptophan and valine. Arginine and histidine are considered occasionally essential. The absence of any essential amino acid (**malnutrition**) often results in a clinically recognizable **syndrome**, such as **beriberi** in cultures that consume **maize**, which is deficient in both the amino acid lysine and the vitamin **niacin**.

**essential fatty acid** (EFA): any of a group of **unsaturated fatty acids** termed essential because the growing infant cannot synthesize them fast enough for healthy growth, hence they must be in the normal diet. Sources of EFAs include vegetable oils, animal fats, and organisms in the marine food chain. Principal EFAs include **arachidonic acid** and **linolenic acid.**

**essential nutrient:** substance that cannot be manufactured by the body of an organism from simpler elements and thus must be supplied from the diet; required for normal or optimal body function.

**essential resources:** materials that are absolutely necessary for the survival and maintenance of a population.

**essential tremor** (ETM1): probably the most common hereditary movement disorder; a late-onset (4th–6th decades) manifestation characterized by uncontrollable tremors of the arms, but other muscles may be involved. Affected individuals are reported to live significantly longer than unaffected family members. ETM1 is an autosomal dominant gene. A heterogenous degenerative condition, with similar symptoms is caused by another gene, ETM2. ETM is more common and less acute than **epilepsy** and less debilitating than familial **Parkinson disease.**

**essentialism:** in the history of biology, having the quality of a Platonic essence or type; an inner nature or true substance. Essentialists believed in an ideal type held as a standard against which all others are then compared; variation is considered aberrant, and unimportant. See **typology** and **Plato's theory of Forms.**

**EST:** see **expressed sequence tag.**

**establish:** 1. to found, institute. 2. to gain a foothold, as in colonizing species. 3. in taxonomy, to erect a **taxon**.

**estivation:** adaptation of mammals to hot dry conditions in which they become dormant. Sleeping in the hot season. Verb: to estivate. Found among some of the **Cheirogaleidae**. Cf. **hibernation.**

**estradiol** (E2): one of the three principal forms of the hormone **estrogen**; estradiol is the primary estrogen produced by the ovaries, and is the most potent naturally occurring ovarian and placental estrogen in mammals. With **progesterone**, E2 maintains the structure of female accessory organs and promotes secondary sexual characteristics. It exists in two isomeric forms: the active isomer is estradiol-17β and the inactive is estradiol-17α. Cf. **estriol** and **estrone.**

**estriol** (E3): one of the three principal forms of the hormone **estrogen**; estriol is a weak metabolite of **estradiol** and is found in the female body in large amounts, produced by the placenta during pregnancy, and is detectable in high concentration in the urine, especially human pregnancy urine. Cf. **estrone.**

**estrogen:** generic term for any **estrus**-inducing **steroid** compounds, usually **hormones** secreted from the **ovarian follicle** or the **placenta**. Estrogens have multiple effects on the reproductive tract, breasts, body fat deposition, and bone growth. Examples of estrogens include **estradiol**, **estriol**, and **estrone**. Aka estrogenic hormone, female gonadal hormone. See **environmental estrogens**. Cf. **testosterone.**

**estrogenic hormones:** substances that induce estrus. See **estrogen.**

**estrone** (E1): one of the three principal forms of the hormone **estrogen**; estrone is a weak form and is a metabolite of **estradiol**, and is the most abundant estrogen found in the female body after menopause. Cf. **estriol.**

**estrous cycle:** repeated series of changes in reproductive physiology and behavior that culminates in **estrus**, or time of heat, in most female mammals, and is usually timed to synchronize with the release of eggs. Also spelled oestrous. Cf. **uterine cycle.**

‡ **estrus:** period in the reproductive cycle of all female mammals, with the exception of humans and orangutans, when they are at their maximum sexual receptivity. Adjective: estrous. During estrus the **ova** (eggs) are released in the female. Estrus is distinguished by resorption of the nonpregnant endometrial lining, rather than its expulsion, as in **menstruation**. Also spelled oestrus.

*et alii* (*et al.*) (Latin): and others. Used in a citation when there are more than two authors, in which case the first two names are cited and the remainder are replaced for brevity with *et al.*

*et cetera* (etc.) (Latin): and others, and so forth.

**Ethical, Legal, and Social Implications Program** (ELSI): joint NIH–DOE Working Group on certain issues associated with the **Human Genome Project.**

**Ethiopian:** 1. eighteenth century name for the indigenous peoples of Africa; aka Ethiopids. One of the five often-cited racial varieties recognized by **Blumenbach** in 1790; the others were **Malayan, American, Mongolian,** and **Caucasian.** 2. geographic region comprising Africa south of the Tropic of Cancer, the southern portion of the Arabian peninsula, and Madagascar.

**ethmoid bone:** small bone of the facial skeleton that is anterior to the **sphenoid** and consists of two parts on either side of the nasal cavity and connected by the **cribiform plate.** This bone forms the floor of the braincase under the frontal lobes and the roof of the nasal cavity.

**ethmoidal sinus:** one of two small groups of 8–10 air-filled cavities within the ethmoid bone; in life, they are lined with mucosa and drain into the nasal cavity. See **sinus.**

**ethnic group:** self-defined set of persons who share the same language (often, the same dialect) and certain customs, of behaving in formal situations, of dressing, and perhaps of eating; who sometimes share a common set of myths and beliefs which set them apart from other such groups, and who may also identify with certain recent common origins. See **ethnicity.**

**ethnic profiling:** see **racial profiling.**

‡ **ethnicity:** ethnic quality or affiliation; used to refer to human **variation** that is both cultural and physical. See **ethnic group** and **emic.** Cf. **race.**

**ethnoarchaeology:** 'living archaeology'; the study of the lifeways of living societies to understand and interpret, by ethnographic analogy, the archaeological record. J. Yellin and L. **Binford** are archaeologists who have utilized this method; the former lived among the **!Kung** San in the Kalahari Desert in South Africa and the latter among the Nunamiut caribou hunters of northern Alaska. See **middle range research.**

**ethnobiological classification:** indigenous strategies for separating and joining living elements. See **ethnobiology** (1) and **folk taxonomy.**

**ethnobiological rule:** idea that the cultural importance of botanical taxa is positively related to the lexical differentiation of cultivars.

**ethnobiology:** 1. study of methods of **classification** of plants and animals in different human cultures. See **ethnobiological classification** and **folk taxonomy.** 2. the study of **ethnology** in relation to **physical anthropology.**

**ethnobotany:** study of indigenous peoples' systems of knowledge about plants. See **folk taxonomy** and **ethnobiological classification.**

‡ **ethnocentrism:** tendency to view other cultures from within one's own cultural perspective; this often leads to thinking of other cultures as odd and inferior. In an extreme form, the assertion that one's own culture ('we') is inherently superior to other cultures ('they'), which are often viewed with contempt. Adjective: ethnocentric. See **race** (3) and **folk taxonomy.** Cf. **reverse ethnocentrism.**

**ethnoecology:** area of linguistics that attempts to describe cultures' perspectives from their language.

**ethnoetiology:** folk classifications of diseases and their remedies. See **folk taxonomy.**

**ethnogenesis:** model of biocultural evolution that emphasizes the fluid and interweaving properties of biological groups as they cyclically merge (**fusion**), interbreed, and then separate (**fission**); applies to social and ethnic traits alike.

**ethnographic analogy:** see **ethnoarchaeology.**

‡ **ethnography:** written result of **field study** by a **cultural anthropologist;** the **description** of an individual human society. Cf. **ethnology.**

**ethnological race:** subdivision of a **stock** characterized by a more or less distinctive combination of traits that are transmitted during descent; a cultural construct.

**Ethnological Society of London** (ESL): splinter group of the Aborigines' Protection Society, the ESL was formed in 1843 to study races sympathetically, publishing four volumes of a *Journal* (which ceased publication in 1854) and seven volumes of *Transactions* (1861–). Founded by Thomas Hodgkin (1798–1866), its president from 1847 to 1848 was J. C. **Prichard.** It was from the ESL that the **Anthropological Society of London** was formed.

‡ **ethnology:** comparative study of cultures; the theory of culture. Cf. **ethnography.**

**ethnomedical system:** any body of beliefs and knowledge held in common by both healers and their patients about sickness and health, childbirth, nutrition, dental care, disability, and death. Both healers and patients understand the meaning of certain role behaviors, and the use of conventional methods, implements, and medicines.

**ethnoscience:** 1. non-Western knowledge systems that possess empirical and predictive power. 2. the treatment of culture as if it were a formal code like language; makes use of the **emic–etic** approach for the description and analysis of behavior. Ethnoscience emphasizes the recording of knowledge systems from the **emic** perspective. See, for example, **ethnobotany.**

**ethocline:** geospatial series of different behaviors observed among related species, interpreted to represent stages in an evolutionary trend.

‡ **ethogram:** complete catalog of all the behavioral traits of a species; the behavioral profile of a species.

**ethological:** pertaining to **ethology**.

**ethological barrier:** isolating mechanisms due to behavioral incompatibilities between potential mates.

**ethological isolation:** absence of effective breeding due to behavioral patterns in one population that are not recognized as appropriate by another; see **prezygotic (isolation) mechanism** and **recognition species concept**.

**ethological species concept:** defines a species (**ethospecies**) as distinguished primarily by behavioral traits. See **species concepts**.

‡ **ethology:** study of patterns of animal **behavior** in natural environments, with stress on the analysis of **adaptation** and the **evolution** of those patterns. Adjective: ethological. A European academic tradition, generally in opposition to the philosophy of the American school of **comparative psychology**.

**ethology of the gene:** paraphrase of the **adaptationist program** fostered by the work of W. D. **Hamilton**, G. C. **Williams**, E. O. **Wilson**, Richard **Dawkins**, and others.

**ethonym:** term or label for a specific geographic or **ethnic group**, especially as recognized in the anthropological literature.

**ethospecies:** see **ethological species concept**.

**etic:** adjective derived from phonemics and which refers to the analysis of the behavior or beliefs of people by means of categories and distinctions agreed upon by the 'outside' community of scientific observers; what the people in question personally believe about them is simply not relevant to their truth or falsity. Cf. the **emic** view.

**etiology:** 1. the study of causes. 2. the study of the processes by which a disease is caused and transmitted, including the pathogens involved. Adjectives: etiologic, etiological.

**eubiotics:** science of hygienic living.

**eucaryote:** see **eukaryote**.

**eucatarrhine:** term applied to Old World **anthropoids**, exclusive of the parapithecids, in some systematic schemes in which the two groups are viewed as parallel developments. Cf. **paracatarrhine**.

**euchromatin:** eukaryotic chromosome or region that exhibits normal **chromatid** coiling. These are decondensed regions that are transcriptionally active during cell division (i.e. not **heteropycnotic**), and thus have normal (light) staining properties with Giemsa stain. Cf. **heterochromatin**.

**Euclidean distance:** relative lengths between **OTUs** measured by an extension of the Pythagorean theorem; used in **numerical taxonomy**.

**eugenesis:** Broca's term for the proposal that all species of **Hominidae** living at the same time have been interfertile when they mated.

**eugenic:** pertaining to measures that, in the opinion of some, enhance the genetic endowment of a human population. Cf. **dysgenic**.

**eugenic sterilization:** surgical technique that prevents ova from reaching the uterus or that prevents sperm from reaching the urethral tube.

‡ **eugenics:** controversial study of cultural mechanisms that may improve or impair the hereditary physical or mental qualities of future generations of human populations. One who undertakes such study is known as a eugenist. **Negative eugenics** aims to decrease the frequencies of alleles that produce undesirable **phenotypes**. **Positive eugenics** aims to increase the frequencies of **alleles** that contribute to desirable phenotypes. Term coined by Francis **Galton**. Cf. **euthenics** and **euphenics**.

**euheterosis:** true **hybrid vigor**.

**Eukarya:** **Domain** of life forms that includes animals, plants and fungi, all of which are **eukaryotes**. One of three basic kinds of life; the other two Domains are the **Bacteria** and the **Archaea**.

**eukaryosis:** state of having a true nucleus, as in the higher types of cell. See **eukaryote**.

‡ **eukaryote (cell):** plant or animal that is a member of the superkingdom Eukaryota, characterized by cells that possess **nuclear envelopes** around **chromosomes** that divide by **mitosis** and/or **meiosis**. Also spelled eucaryote.

***Eulemur*** (= *Lemur*) **Simons and Rumpler, 1988:** **prosimian** genus to which the large Malagasy or 'true' lemurs belong. Five species, nine recognized **subspecies**. Found only on Madagascar and the Comoros in forested areas. **Arboreal**. Generally **diurnal**, but active at night as well. **Quadrupedal**. Sexually **dichromatic**. Body mass generally between 2 and 3 kg. Dental formula: 3.1.3.3; diet varies with species but includes **folivory, frugivory**, and **nectarivory**. Males possess **circumanal glands** with which they perform **scent marking**; females scent mark mainly with urine. Synonym: *Petterus* Groves and Eaglen, 1988. The five species of *Eulemur* were included in the genus *Lemur* until 1988. See Appendix 2 for taxonomy, Appendix 3 for living species. Cf. *Lemur catta* and *Varecia variegata*.

**eumelanin:** brown **melanin**.

**eunuch:** castrated male.

***Euoticus*** **Gray, 1863:** **prosimian** genus to which the needle-clawed bushbabies (or galagos) belong; two recognized species. Found in forest habitats of western equatorial Africa and central Africa. Arboreal; **nocturnal**; move by **vertical clinging and leaping**. Small body size, weighs around 250 g. Dental formula: 2.1.3.3; specialized morphology for **gummivory** includes **procumbent dental comb, caniniform** upper anterior premolars, and laterally compressed nails with a raised central keel that function as claws. Social behavior may be **noyau**. See Appendix 2 for taxonomy, Appendix 3 for living species.

**euphallic:** pertaining to an individual possessing the full complement of male reproductive organs and characteristic secondary structures.

**euphenics:** that part of **euthenics** concerned particularly with the engineering of human development; specifically the improvement of **phenotypes** based on the engineering of defective genetic constitutions; see **negative eugenics**.

‡ **euploidy:** literally, the 'good count'; condition of having a normal or full complement of chromosomes or chromatids, i.e. the chromosome number of a cell is an exact multiple of the **haploid** number normal for the species from which it originated. Adjective: euploid. Usually refers to the modal **haploid** or **diploid** number that is characteristic for a given species (N or 2N), but may also refer to other whole multiples as well (3N, 4N,... etc.; see **polyploidy**).

**Euprimates:** one of two suborders within the order **Primates** as proposed by McKenna and Bell in *Classification of Mammals* (1998); the other suborder is **Dermoptera**. Euprimates is a taxon not widely known or accepted by most primatologists, and includes the **prosimians** and **anthropoids** (or **strepsirhines** and **haplorhines**) of traditional primate classifications.

**eupsychics:** educational and psychological engineering as a means of improving individual potential or the potential of the human species. Cf. **eugenics**. See **euthenics**.

*Euranthropus heidelbergensis* Arambourg, 1957: see *Homo heidelbergensis*.

**Eurasia:** see **Laurasia**.

**euroky:** tolerance to a variety of environmental conditions, as in primates.

*Europolemur* Weigelt, 1933: genus of adapoid **prosimian** from the middle to late Eocene of Europe, belonging to the notharctid subfamily **Cercamoniinae**; four species recognized. Known from jaws, teeth, and a badly damaged skull. Estimated body mass ranges from 1400 to 1700 g for the different species. Dental formula: 2.1.4.3/ 2.1.4.3; dental morphology suggestive of a **frugivorous** diet with insect supplements. See Appendix 1 for taxonomy.

**eurycnemic:** pertaining to a **platycnemic index** of more than 70.00.

**Eurydice:** see **DNH 7** at **Drimolen**.

**euryenic:** in reference to the **upper facial index**, having an index between 45.00 and 49.99; such an individual is considered to be broad-faced or euryene.

**eurymeric:** referring to a **platymeric index** between 85.00 and 99.99.

**eurymetopic:** pertaining to a **tranverse fronto-parietal index** of more than 69.00.

**euryon** (eu): **craniometric landmark**; the two points on opposite sides of the cranium that are at the greatest width of the skull; measured by **spreading calipers** and usually at the parietal eminences above the temporal bones. See Appendix 7.

**euryprosopic:** in reference to the **total facial index**, having an index between 80.00 and 84.99; such an individual is considered to be broad-faced.

**eurytropic:** pertaining to highly adaptive organisms; exhibiting phenotypic responses to a wide variety of ecological niches and environmental conditions.

**eusexual:** pertaining to organisms that exhibit a cyclical pattern of **meiosis** and **karyogamy**.

**eustatic:** pertaining to slow, gradual, worldwide fluctuations in sea level, such as would occur at the onset of **glaciation**, or the subsequent melting of glaciers. Aka eustatic movement.

**eutelegenesis:** improvement of domesticated animals by using selected stock and artificial insemination.

**euthenics:** all mechanisms and conditions, both **eugenic** and **euphenic**, that combine to produce better conditions for human populations, but not necessarily tending to produce people who can transmit improvement by hereditary means alone.

‡ **Eutheria:** infraclass of the class Mammalia that is composed of the placental mammals; contains approximately 920 genera, 4000 species. Cf. **marsupial**, **Metatheria**, **Monotremata**.

**EV 9001:** field number for a fossil hominid found at **Quyuanhekou**, Yunxian County, China; one of two of the most complete Middle Pleistocene crania from China. Provisionally dated to about 350 kya. Although a number of mid-facial features are reminiscent of archaic or early modern *Homo sapiens*, the hominid is attributed to *Homo erectus*. Cf. **EV 9002**.

**EV 9002:** field number for a fossil hominid found at **Quyuanhekou**, Yunxian County, China; one of two of the most complete Middle Pleistocene crania from China. Provisionally dated to about 350 kya, EV 9002 is the largest cranium recovered from the region. Although a number of mid–facial features are reminiscent of archaic or early modern *Homo sapiens*, the hominid is attributed to *Homo erectus*. Cf. **EV 9001**.

**evagination:** out-pocketing of an outer membrane. Cf. **invagination**.

**evaporation:** 1. the act of conversion from liquid to vapor, especially the loss of moisture in the form of water vapor. 2. loss of heat in the form of vapor, expressed as calories per unit of surface area.

**'Eve' hypothesis:** see **mitochondrial Eve** and the **out of Africa II** model of human origins.

**event:** change of state with regard to behavior; for example, a sitting lemur suddenly leaping marks an event. Cf. **bout**, **state**.

**evergreen forest: forest** in which the canopy of leaves is intact and green year-round and only a small proportion of the trees lose their leaves at any one time; includes the **coniferous** trees and shrubs. Cf. **deciduous forest**.

**eversion:** outward or **lateral** turning motion of the **plantar** surface of the foot. Cf. **inversion**. See **pronation** and **supination**

**eversporting:** pertaining to a race that does not breed true; originally applied to plants such as **Mendel's** pea plants before the concept of recessive inheritance was generally understood. See **sport**.

**evo-devo:** contraction of **evolution** and **development**; a slang term for studies of the **genetics** of **growth** and phenotypic expression.

‡ **evolution:** change over time. In biology, the process in which organisms are descended with modification from previous organisms; see **biological evolution**.

**evolution, general:** change from heterogeneity to homogeneity; advance or progression, stage by stage. A theme in archaeological and paleontological interpretations of history.

**evolution, human:** see **human genetics** and **human evolution**.

**evolution in little bags:** see 'little bags' theory of evolution.

**evolution, specific:** increasing adaptive specializations that improve the probability of survival of a species, culture, or individuals. An interpretive theme in archaeology and paleontology.

**evolutionary anthropology:** see **behavioral evolution**.

*Evolutionary Anthropology*: publication that presents reviews of large general issues of interest to human evolutionary biologists; publication is by invitation rather than refereed. This journal was first published in 1992 and is written in a manner that makes it accessible to a wide audience.

**evolutionary archeology:** paradigmatic approach in anthropology that originated with American archaeologist Robert C. Dunnell (1942–) that has adopted the premise that **artifacts** are part of the **extended phenotype** of humans, and thus that artifact frequencies through time are explicible by the same processes as those in **evolutionary biology**, i.e. subject to the action of **selection** on phenotypic variation. In this view, supporters argue that artifacts 'reproduce', demonstrate **heritability**, exhibit **variation**, and display differential **fitness**. According to its proponents, artifacts (and certain other cultural traits) 'reproduce' because they are **replicators** (culturgens or **memes**), i.e. they are manifestations of phenotypic behaviors with an underlying genetic component (**DNA**). Aka selectionist archeology. Also spelled evolutionary archaeology. See **sociobiology**.

**evolutionary arms race:** condition in which an adaptation in one species (such as a parasite, or a predator) reduces the fitness of individuals in a second species (such as a host, or a prey), thereby selecting in favor of counter-adaptations in the second species; these counter-adaptations, in turn, select in favor of new adaptations in the first species, and so on.

‡ **evolutionary biology:** collective discipline of biology and ecology that studies the evolutionary process and the characteristics of populations of organisms, as well as their behavior and systematics. When the organism is *Homo sapiens*, cultural processes are also involved, and the collective term becomes **human evolutionary biology**.

**evolutionary classification:** method of practicing taxonomy by applying both **cladistic** and **phenetic** principles of classification.

**evolutionary conservatism:** 1. similarity of an ancestral–descendant set of species due to the retention of a high proportion of **symplesiomorphic** traits. 2. similarity of nucleotide or amino acid sequences in apparently unrelated species, possibly through **parallel evolution** or **convergent evolution**. Aka evolutionary conservation. Cf. **synteny** and **highly conserved sequence**.

**evolutionary constraint:** see **phylogenetic constraint**.

**evolutionary convergence:** evolutionary acquisition of a particular trait or set of traits by two or more species independently, e.g. wings in insects, birds, and bats. A synonym for analogy.

**evolutionary determinism:** proposal by R. A. **Fisher** that **stabilizing selection** or **directional selection** results from deterministic processes.

**evolutionary ecology:** integration of ecology with evolution, genetics, and adaptation; interpretation of organismal structure and function, communities, and ecosystems in the context of evolutionary theory. A criticism of ecology is that it treats systems as static and in unchanging equilibrium; evolutionary ecology addresses this issue.

**evolutionary forces: mechanisms** that can cause changes in **allele frequencies** from one generation to the next. There are almost 20 known evolutionary forces, but the four most commonly cited are: **mutation**, **genetic drift**, **gene flow**, and **natural selection**. Aka the causes or pressures of biological **evolution** and the **mechanisms of evolution**.

**evolutionary grade:** see **grade**.

**evolutionary medicine:** subdiscipline that examines the relationship between a supposed human evolutionary history reconstructed as a foraging way of life with its concomitant patterns of fertility, mortality, and morbidity, and the 'new' diseases of **modernization.**

**evolutionary method:** method of classification of a set of species that also reconstructs their evolutionary history by employing both **cladistic** and **phenetic** methods; Aka synthetic method; **evolutionary systematics.** Cf. **phylogenetic systematics** and **numerical taxonomy.**

**evolutionary novelty:** inherited change in a character state that distinguishes ancestral from descendant species.

**evolutionary psychology:** emerging discipline concerned with the origins and functions of human **behavior,** with a view toward discovering evolved cognitive modules that underly those behavioral **traits** that helped human survival in prehistory; postulates that humans are adaptation executors and optimizers. This differs from central arguments in **sociobiology,** which postulate that humans are fitness maximizers. Cf. **Standard Social Science Model.**

‡ **evolutionary pulse theory:** argument that diversification of **hominids** during the Pliocene and early Pleistocene was linked to periodic episodes of aridity in Africa. There are three spikes of aridity at 2.5, 1.8, and 1.0 **mya,** with some changes in the mammal fauna in at least some parts of Africa.

**evolutionary rate:** speed of evolutionary change within or among lineages.

‡ **evolutionary reversal:** return to an ancestral condition. Complex evolutionary reversals are extremely rare, owing to **evolutionary constraint;** however, simple traits, such as cycles in body size, are observed in the fossil record. See **Dollo's law.**

**evolutionary species concept:** defines a species as any phyletic lineage evolving distinctly from others, possessing a unique evolutionary role and mechanistic tendencies, and with an identifiable set of ancestral–descendant populations; diachronic equivalent to the **biological species concept.** See **species concepts.**

**evolutionary stable strategy:** see **ESS.**

**evolutionary stages:** arbitrarily defined steps or levels, proposed by some nineteenth century anthropological **evolutionists,** through which, it was alleged, people must have passed in the process of evolving; i.e. **savagery, barbarism** and **civilization;** that is from 'lower' to 'higher' stages in that proposed sequence.

**evolutionary synthesis:** 1. modification of the **Darwinism** paradigm that rejects transformational evolution, saltationism, and orthogenesis, while emphasizing natural selection, adaptation, and the study of genetic diversity. E. **Mayr** states that the chief architects of the evolutionary synthesis were **Dobzhansky,** himself, Rensch, G. G. **Simpson,** Stebbins, and Timofeeeff-Ressovsky. 2. The period of this paradigm construction, c. 1940; Aka the modern synthesis, the grand synthesis. Cf. **neo-Darwinism** and **fisherism.**

‡ **evolutionary systematics:** school of biological classification that takes into account both the branching pattern of evolution (**cladogenesis**) as well as the amount of evolutionary change that has occurred along each lineage (**anagenesis**), advocated by Ernst **Mayr.** This 'synthetic' method of classification incorporates aspects of the methodology of both **numerical taxonomy** and **phylogenetic systematics,** the other two main schools of **classification.** Aka evolutionary taxonomy and **evolutionary method.**

**evolutionary theory:** former **hypothesis,** now raised to the level of **theory,** that organisms descend or develop with modification; according to Charles **Darwin** this process (which he called **transmutation**) results in gradual directional change and the formation of new **species.** See **biological evolution.**

**evolutionary tree:** estimate in the form of a treelike diagram of the relationships of ancestry and descent among a group of species; certain trees many be estimates from a fossil record, whereas others may be hypothetical constructs based on the attributes of extant species. See **cladogram, phenogram,** and **phylogram.**

‡ **evolutionary trends in Primates:** pedagogical list of tendencies in species observed across the entire range of the order **Primates** first organized by **Le Gros Clark** and Prue and John **Napier.** This list includes (1) the retention of **pentadactyly;** (2) the possession of **nails** on at least some digits; (3) **prehensile** hands and feet; (4) a tendency toward **erect posture;** (5) the retention of **clavicles;** (6) a **generalized dentition;** (7) a generalized **diet;** (8) a reduction of the **snout** and organs of **olfaction;** (9) an increased emphasis on **vision;** (10) expansion of the **brain** with increasing complexity; (11) more efficient **placentation** and a slowed rate of development (= **neoteny**); (12) greater dependency on flexible, learned behaviors; (13) a tendency for adult males to associate permanently with the **troop.**

**evolutionary unity of species:** theory that **evolution** is itself alone responsible for every kind of organism.

**evolutionism:** 1. theory that the universe and all life within it developed by processes of change and growth, and that individual species arise from extant species. 2. see **cultural evolutionism.**

**evolutionists:** name applied to an early group of anthropologists who proposed a theory of **evolutionary stages** through which they believed all people and cultures must have passed on their way to becoming 'civilized'. See **cultural evolution** and **unilineal evolution**.

**evolvability:** describes a trait that, according to **Dawkins** and some supporters of the **adaptationist program,** can be and has been selected for in the past.

**evolve:** 1. to develop gradually. 2. to change by a process into a more organized state or condition. 3. to undergo gradual directional change. 4. to produce or emit. See **evolution**.

**evulsion:** forcible extraction or tearing out. Aka **avulsion** (1).

**ex *situ* conservation:** preservation of a species that is **extinct** or nearly extinct in its native environment by removing it to another area and managing it; the ultimate goal is to reintroduce the species to its natural environment, but that may not be realized. Examples of *ex situ* conservation of primates include the aye-ayes at Duke University Primate Center or the Golden Lion Tamarin Conservation Program. Also referred to as off-site preservation. Cf. ***in situ* conservation**.

**ex *utero*:** out of the uterus; used principally with reference to testing **blastocysts** for genetic defects before implantation.

**ex *vivo*:** outside of the living body.

**ex *vivo* gene therapy:** genetic modification of cells that have been removed from an individual, followed by the reintroduction of the modified cells into that individual. See **genetic engineering**.

**examination behavior:** curiosity; closely looking at an object; **exploratory behavior**.

**exaptation:** trait that evolved by natural selection for one use, and that is later useful for another; see **preadaptation**.

**excavation:** 1. hole or cavity made by removal of material from an inner part, as by digging, tunneling, probing, or hollowing. 2. exposing or laying bare, as in the unearthing of an archaeological site. Verb: to excavate. Whereas early excavations generally vandalized sites, even in the late nineteenth century archaeologists began to utilize systematic trench sampling, recorded stratigraphic contexts, and improved **artifact** preservation techniques. See **archaeology**.

**excision:** 1. act of removal or resection. 2. prepubertal removal of the clitoris in some human societies.

**excision repair:** mechanism of DNA enzyme-catalyzed repair that cuts thymine dimers and some adjacent nucleotides out of a **DNA** strand, and then repairs the gap by using the other strand as a primer. Cf. **direct repair**.

**excitability:** capacity of a living organism to respond to a stimulus; aka sensitivity, irritability.

**exclusive territory:** area that is inhabited by only a single individual of a species.

**exclusivity:** primate mother's reluctance to allow other members of her group to handle her infant.

**exemplar:** random sample of a **taxon**.

***exempli gratia*** (e.g.): for example.

**exfoliation:** 1. peeling off or weathering , as with granite. 2. desquamation, or shedding of skin. 3. loss of **deciduous teeth**. Verb: to exfoliate.

**exhaustion theory of aging:** proposal that aging occurs when an essential nutrient is depleted or otherwise unavailable.

**exobiology:** discipline that speculates about life beyond the earth; founded by and composed principally of biologists. Exobiologists, at a professional level, focus on microorganisms and simple life forms rather than extraterrestrial civilizations; their work includes the study of life on Earth that lives in extreme conditions, such as Antarctica, as might be encountered in an extraterrestrial environment such as Mars. Completely **Darwinian** in its approach.

**exocrine:** 1. secreting outwardly via a duct. 2. pertaining to such a gland or to a substance secreted externally, such as **sweat** and **mucus**; see **pheromone**. Cf. **autocrine** and **paracrine**.

**exocrine gland:** any gland, such as the salivary gland, that secretes substances to the outside of the body or into the alimentary canal. Exocrine glands are the most common sources of **pheromones**. Aka ectocrine gland. Cf. **endocrine gland**.

‡ **exogamy:** any system of sexual reproduction (such as outbreeding or cross-fertilization) in which the mating partners are less closely related than in a random (**panmictic**) system. Culturally, a conventionally defined threshold beyond which one must mate (or within which one must not mate). Cf. **endogamy**.

**exogenic heredity:** nongenetic **vertical transmission** of information.

**exogenous:** originating outside an organism or system; triggered by factors in the environment.

‡ **exon:** coding portion of **DNA**; the complete nucleotide sequences of some genes in DNA (see **cistron**) consist of stretches that code for amino acids (exons), and some interspersed stretches that are transcribed but not translated, having been edited out of **heterogenous mRNA** (hmRNA); the latter are called **introns**. Cf. **motif** and **domain**.

**exon shuffling:** see **alternative splicing**.

**exon skipping:** mutation that alters the pattern of splicing and results in the splicing out of an **exon**.

**exophenotypic:** pertaining to phenotypic characters that are presumably directly adaptive and that affect an organism's **fitness**. Cf. **endophenotypic**.

‡ **exoskeleton:** hardened outer layer of the invertebrate body that functions both as a protective covering and as a skeletal attachment for muscles. The

exoskeleton may be composed of calcium carbonate, silica, chitin, or other material. Cf. **endoskeleton**.

**exosomatic symbol:** any item of material culture with the potential to transmit encoded messages about an owner's identity, status and/or affinities. They are used to construct identities, alliances and memberships that transcend biological kinship ties.

**exostosis:** bony outgrowth capped by hyaline cartilage; this condition may result from environmental factors or from inheritance.

**exotic:** not indigenous to a region; alien; foreign.

**exotic bias:** preference among anthropologists to conduct fieldwork among peoples in a culture other than the natal culture of the anthropologist; in recent years, **applied anthropologists** have tended to work more frequently in their own societies. See **deexoticization**.

**exotic theory of fossil origins:** eighteenth century proposal that attempted to explain the existence of fossils found in inappropriate contexts, such as fossil tropical plants and animals in western Europe, by asserting that these had been transported after death from their place of origin to their place of burial. Proposed by German philosopher Gottfried Leibniz (1646–1716).

**expanding earth hypothesis:** proposal that the volume of the earth has increased about 20% during the past 200 my; hence, that the crustal surface of the earth has also increased.

**expanding matrix distortion** (EMD): fragmentation of a **fossil** accompanied by infilling of the cracks with geological matrix between the remaining small pieces of varying dimension and geometry, with the result that potential deformation can alter morphology in a nonlinear manner. Aka diploic expansion. See **diagenesis**, **fossilization**, **permineralization**, and **taphonomy**.

**expanding triplet repeat:** class of mutation in which a **cistron** grows larger with each generation.

**expected frequency:** predicted proportion calculated on the basis of an appropriate theory.

**expected value:** prediction of a function equal to a variate under consideration.

**expensive tissue hypothesis:** proposal by L. C. Aiello and P. Wheeler that **gastrointestinal tract size** may constrain **brain mass** because these two ('expensive') tissues are in competition for metabolic resources. See **gut morphology** and **encephalization**.

**experiment:** test, trial or tentative procedure usually designed to find a result or to falsify or validate a supposition or hypothesis. See **hypothesis testing**.

**experimental archaeology:** any attempt to replicate ancient technologies and lifeways under controlled scientific conditions. Most often this consists of mimicking the manufacture and use of ancient tools to accomplish specific tasks such as butchering animals, planting seeds, or clearing forests. Aka experimental archeology.

**experimental error:** inaccuracy in an experiment or sample thought to be due to factors other than the variation accounted for by the hypothesis; observer error, noise.

**experimental group:** see **treatment group**.

**experimenter bias:** preconceived idea, perhaps unconscious, of what the results of an experiment will be and that influences what the observer sees or records; in order to compensate for this problem the researcher can run a **blind experiment** in which the person making measurements is unaware of which treatment a subject has received.

‡ **expiration:** process of expelling air from the lungs; exhalation. Cf. **inspiration**.

**explant:** sample of tissue transferred to an artificial medium to initiate a cell culture.

**'exploded' multimale polygyny:** formation of a large group of individuals seeking mates in a species that breeds on only a few days during the year.

**exploratory behavior:** curiosity; investigation of novelty. Exploratory behavior is prominent in mammals, especially the young; in primates this behavior persists for life. Besides existing as an independent behavior, exploration forms a component of **play behavior**. In the **ethological** literature, some authors separate curiosity as the investigation of novelty, while relegating exploration to the investigation of new spatial conditions; others do not use the term 'curiosity' in association with animals at all because of the implication of consciousness.

**explosive evolution:** rapid splitting of a lineage into several lines, usually because of either a new adaptation or exposure to a new environment to which the lineage shows a **preadaptation**; aka explosive **radiation**.

**exponent:** 1. one who explains. 2. superscript that denotes the power to which a value is to be raised, as in $3^2$, where the exponent two indicates that the value three is to be squared.

‡ **exponential growth:** growth, especially in the number of organisms of a population, that is a simple function of the size of the growing entity; the larger the entity, the faster it grows. Cf. **logistic growth**.

**exponential growth phase:** 1. time of maximum population growth. 2. portion of the **growth curve** that has the steepest gradient. See **logistic growth curve**.

**exponential trend:** data in a time series that takes the form $y = ax^b$. See **allometry**.

**exposure:** 1. the abandonment of corpses to scavengers. 2. killing of an infant by leaving it out in the elements.

**expressed sequence tag** (EST): any short sequence of **cDNA** used by researchers to isolate the location of protein-encoding genes. Identification of the number of ESTs in a genome permits researchers to estimate the number of coding **DNA sequences** in a genome.

**expression:** 1. phrasing. 2. indication of feeling, as in **facial expression.** 3. in mathematics, a symbol or combination of symbols representing a **value** or relationship. 4. conversion or manipulation of information; see **gene expression, expression library,** and **expression vectors.**

**expression library:** collection of peptide molecules in which the amino acid sequences are systematically varied and which are produced by recombinant cells; Aka peptide expression library.

**expression vectors:** sequences of DNA into which **cDNA** fragments have been inserted to encourage cells to transcribe desired cDNA sequences more efficiently.

**expressivity:** range of phenotypes exhibited by a certain specific genotype as a variant from the normal; see **variable expressivity.**

**exsanguine:** with a diluted or weak blood relationship; Cf. **consanguinity.**

‡ **extant:** 1. currently or actually existing; living **taxa** as opposed to **extinct**; usually said of **species** or **varieties.** 2. not lost or destroyed.

**extended burial:** method of placement of a body in a grave during ancient interments in which a body is placed in the ground with the legs extended to their full length, and with the arms either extended or in a semi-flexed or flexed position. See **burial.**

**extended family:** aggregation of close relatives along either the female or the male line, but usually not along both. Cf. **nuclear family.**

**extended phenotype:** controversial concept expounded in a book *The Extended Phenotype* (1992) by Richard **Dawkins** in which he argues that restricting the idea of the **phenotype** to apply only to the phenotypic expression of an organism's own genes is arbitrary, and suggests that a **gene** may have an effect on an organism's environment through that organism's behavior. In exploring the book's subtitle ('the long reach of the gene'), he suggests that not only animal **morphology,** but that ultimately gene-centered animal **behavior,** is part of one's phenotype. Finally, he argues that the phenotype is not advantageous to the animal itself, but rather to the parasitic or **selfish DNA** that created it. See **sociobiology.**

**extension:** movement of a joint to increase the angle between the bones involved. Verb: to extend. See **flexion.**

**extensor:** muscle that works to extend or straighten a limb, or that increases the angle between two bones. See **skeletal muscle.**

**extensor pollicis brevis:** muscle that acts on the hand. The extensor pollicis brevis originates from

the surface of the **radius** and **interosseous** membrane; it inserts into the base of proximal **phalanx I.** Its action is to extend the thumb.

**extensor pollicis longus:** muscle that acts on the hand. The extensor pollicis longus originates from the surface of the **ulna** and **interosseous** membrane; it inserts into the base of distal **phalanx I.** Its action is to extend the thumb.

**extermination:** **extinction** of a species due to **anthropogenic** action.

**extermination theory of fossil origins:** proposal by German theologian Martin Luther (1483–1546) that fossils represent creatures destroyed by the biblical flood. Replaced by the **exotic theory of fossil origins,** this conceptual lineage eventually became popular as **catastrophism;** a second series of concepts represented by Lyell's **uniformitarianism** eventually replaced the biblical explanations.

**external:** anatomical term referring to a structure on or towards the outside of the body or organ or on the side farthest from the body or the **medial line.**

**external auditory meatus:** bony passageway of the **temporal bone** that leads into the ear; the ear canal that leads to the tympanic membrane. Aka external acoustic meatus, external auditory tube. See **internal auditory meatus.**

**external ear:** **auricle** (or **pinna**) and the external auditory meatus. Cf. **inner ear.**

**external genitalia:** reproductive organs: in females, the pudendum and clitoris; in males, the scrotum and penis. See **indifferent genitalia** and **ambiguous genitalia.**

**external naris:** opening into the nasal cavity; commonly referred to as a nostril. Plural: external nares. In terrestrial vertebrates, such as primates, these openings serve as a passageway for air to enter and exit the nasal cavity.

**external occipital protuberance** (EOP): projection of the posterior portion of the **occipital bone.** Cf. **internal occipital protuberance.**

**external palatal index:** numerical relation between palate length and palate width; **external palate breath** divided by **external palate length** multiplied by 100. See **dolichouranic, mesuranic, brachyuranic.**

**external palate breadth** (ecm–ecm): **craniometric measurement;** distance between the left and right **ectomolare** as measured with sliding calipers. See Appendix 7 for an illustration of the landmarks used.

**external palate length** (pr–alv): **craniometric measurement;** maximum distance from the **prosthion** to the **alveolon** as measured with sliding calipers. See Appendix 7 for an illustration of the landmarks used.

‡ **extinct:** no longer existing; said of any **species** in which all members have disappeared. Extinct species

can be identified through their discovery in the **fossil record**, as is the usual case or, rarely, through having become extinct during historical times, as with the dodo. See **pseudoextinction**, **subfossil**, and **fossil**. Cf. **extant**.

**extinct in the wild** (EW): a taxon is EW when a population survives only under cultivation, in captivity, or in maintained, unnatural ranges. See **IUCN Red Data Book**.

**extinct species:** one of the five conservation categories established by the International Union for the Conservation of Nature. This category contains those species that are known to no longer exist in the wild. See **endangered species**, **vulnerable species**, **rare species**, **insufficiently known species**.

**extinct subfossil Malagasy prosimian:** see separate entries under **extinct**, **subfossil**, **Malagasy**, and **prosimian**.

**extinction:** 1. any process of elimination or annihilation. 2. the elimination of a given **species** or **taxon** from a particular **habitat** or geographical feature. See **mass extinction**. 3. reduction or loss of a conditioned response.

**extinction curve:** graph of number of species (Y) plotted against either the **extinction rate** or, more commonly, time (X).

**extinction–impact curve:** see **periodic extinction**.

**extinction rate:** number of species that become **extinct** in a given area per unit of time.

**extinction vortex:** tendency of small populations to be vulnerable to demographic variation, environmental disturbances, and genetic factors such as **genetic drift** and **inbreeding depression**; once a population has entered a vortex, its population size becomes progressively smaller, increasing the negative effects of the vortex and decline toward the species' **local extinction**.

**extracellular:** existing or occurring outside of a cell. Cf. **intracellular**.

**extracellular matrix** (ECM): region outside of the cells of multicellular animal tissues, which includes molecules attached to the plasma membrane and substances adhered to the surface owing to its surface charge. The ECM functions to bind cells together and to buffer them from the environment.

**extraembryonic mesoderm:** embryonic cells that arise from the parietal elements of the **hypoblast**; this tissue supports the epithelium of the **amnion** and **yolk sac**, and the **chorionic villi**.

**extra-male group:** see **bachelor herd**.

**extramolar sulcus:** groove at the junction of the **mandibular body** and ascending **mandibular ramus** present in several species of Plio-Pleistocene hominid.

**extranuclear:** outside the **nuclear envelope** of a eukaryotic cell; describes any **cytoplasmic factor**.

**extrapolation:** projection or estimation of a value beyond the range of known data, using an algorithm obtained from actual data.

**extreme infant helplessness:** state of not being self-sufficient at or shortly after birth; **AMH** infants require from six months to a year to attain the physical competency of a newborn great ape. Humans are considered secondarily **altricial**, whereas primates in general are **precocial**. Aka infant dependency. See **neoteny**.

**extreme sexual dimorphism hypothesis:** phrase sometimes used when alluding to the range of size variation for the fossils attributed by **Johanson** and T. **White** to the taxon *Australopithecus afarensis*. According to their sample, this **hominid** species contains males and females with a greater degree of **sexual dimorphism** than the gorilla, which has the largest of any extant primate.

**extrinsic muscle:** muscle located outside of the area that is acted upon. For example, some of the movements of human fingers are generated by long tendons from muscles that are located in the forearm, rather than in the hand.

**exudate:** substance such as gum, sap, or resin, which flows from any plant or animal vascular system.

**Eyasi:** archaeological site found in 1935 at Njarasa near Lake Eyasi in Tanganyika (now Tanzania), dated to 35 **kya**, (although some suggest the site could be Middle Pleistocene). The site contains hominid remains, including parts of an archaic 1255 cm$^3$ cranium and maxilla, and an occiput and other fragments of a second individual found by Ludwig Kohl-Larsen. These specimens were originally attributed to *Africanthropus njaransensis*, and were often compared both to **Peking Man** and to the **Neandertals**.

**eye:** light receptor organ in animals. Primates have a typical vertebrate eye in which light is gathered and focused by a lens onto a photosensitive layer at the back of the eyeball. See **rod**, **cone**.

**eye color:** pigmentation on the **iris** that ranges continuously from light blue to dark brown including mosaics of light and dark areas. Iris pigmentation is produced by **melanocytes**, but unlike the melanocytes elsewhere in the body, eye melanocytes retain the melanin granules they produce for life. Light eyes lack pigmentation in the superficial layers of the iris; consequently, as light enters these layers blue light is reflected, giving the appearance of a blue iris. The posterior of the iris is also pigmented, but this serves to keep stray light (which would interfere with vision) out of the inner chamber of the eyeball. The inheritance of eye color is not well known except that it is **polygenic**. The adaptive value of different eye color is unknown, but it has been suggested that light eyes may be a response to low light conditions (due to cloud cover and dark conditions in winter) such as those found in Europe.

**eye–ear plane:** plane made by the right and left **tragion** and the left **orbitale** in the same horizontal plane.

**eye fold:** series of accessory eye structures at the anterior eye region that may occur separately or in various combinations in human populations. One fold is the **epicanthic fold** which attaches at the inner corner of the eye. A second type of fold occurs when there is a thick fatty layer in the eyelid; this results in the eyelid (palpebra) puffing forward and sagging on top of the eyelashes. In some populations there are also fatty deposits in the cheeks that accentuate the folds of the eyes, providing the appearance that is stereotypically associated with Far Eastern populations. There is no consensus as to what the function of the eye folds is , but it has been suggested they are associated with cold weather adaptation. However, the eye folds found in the Khoisan **!Kung** have led workers to suggest an adaptation against glare (both in the desert and off of snow).

**eyebrow:** structure that consists of the bony superciliary arches, skin, and hair that are located above the eyes and the base of the nose. Functions of the eyebrows have been stated to include shading of the eyes from strong overhead light, and preventing or slowing down of perspiration flowing into the eyes.

**eyelid:** see **palpebra.**

**eyeshine:** light that enters the eye and is reflected back out by the **tapetum lucidum;** found in some nocturnal primates, as well as other nocturnal mammals. In some instances the color of the eyeshine may be indicative of a particular species or group.

**F, f:** symbol(s) for (1) **coefficient of inbreeding;** (2) **Fahrenheit scale.**

‡ **F1, F2, F3, etc.:** symbols for filial generations after a **cross** or **backcross:** F1 is the first filial generation, F2 is the second generation, etc. Cf. **P1, P2, P3, etc.**

**f$_{ij}$, F$_{ij}$:** symbol(s) for the **coefficient of kinship** between two individuals, *i* and *j*.

**Fabry disease:** X-linked recessive hereditary disease of lipid metabolism characterized by abdominal pain, skin lesions, and kidney failure. The defective **enzyme** is the A form of alpha galactosidase.

**face:** 1. anterior portion of the head that includes the forehead, eyes, nose, cheeks, mouth, and chin. The face contains many organs associated with the special senses of vision, smell, and taste. 2. exposed surface of a structure. 3. look or expression on the facial part of the body; see **facial expression.**

**face form:** measurement of the human face that produces indices of shape; an assessment of the human face made by practitioners of **craniology** and other researchers interested in human variation. Principle forms are **orthognathous** (straight face) and **prognathous** (projecting face). Cf. **head form.**

**face length:** distance between the nasion and the lowest point on the centerline of the maxilla.

**facet:** 1. aspect. 2. small, polished, plane surface. 3. smooth area on a bone covered by hyaline cartilage that articulates with another bone; the vertebral facets are an example.

**facial angle: Camper**'s anthropometric measure of the degree of **prognathism** in a cranium, described as the angular offset of a line tangent to both the forehead and the front of the maxillary dentition on the sagittal plane, relative to an intersecting vertical reference drawn perpendicular to a horizontal plane.

**facial asymmetry:** imbalance of developmental expression that results in differential morphology of the two halves of the face.

**facial expression: mobility** of the features that gives a particular emotional significance to the appearance of the face; behaviors (in certain primates) that imply emotions such as joy, anger, submission, a threat, or invitation to play suggested by facial features more than by body language or vocalization; a form of nonverbal communication. See **alert face (f.), frowning bared-teeth scream f., hoot f., lip smacking f., pout f., relaxed open-mouth f., silent bared-teeth f., staring bared-teeth scream f., staring open-mouth f.,** and **threat f.**

**facial index:** total height of the face × 100, divided by its breadth. Height is measured from **nasion** to **gnathion;** breadth from **zygion** to zygion.

**facial prognathism:** projection of the jaws beyond the upper part of the face; prominence of the snout. Cf. **alveolar prognathism.**

**facial reconstruction:** process of utilizing a skull or cast and applying simulated soft tissues to approximate the appearance of an individual, e.g. what a living member of a fossil species may have looked like, or, in forensic anthropology, as a possible aid in the identification of an individual. Aka facial approximation, facial reproduction (medicine).

**facial skeleton:** fourteen bones that form the shape of the **face,** provide sites for muscle attachments, and articulate with the cranium. These bones include the paired maxillary, palatine, zygomatic, lacrimal, nasal, and inferior nasal conchae bones, and the single vomer and mandible. Aka splanchnocranium, viscerocranium.

**facies:** 1. general appearance of an organism or population. 2. general aspect of a fossil or vertical sedimentary feature. 3. category of vegetation or variation of a **biotope.**

**facilitation:** 1. process of easing forward or helping. 2. helping another organism or system, as in **social facilitation.**

**factor:** 1. any causal **agent.** 2. in genetics, anything responsible for the independent inheritance of a trait, as in a **Mendelian factor.** Aka **gene.** 3. in serology, any identifiable unit, as in a blood group factor; see box below.

**factors of evolution:** see **mechanisms of evolution.**

---

### Blood group factors and deficiencies

At least 13 molecules, called 'factors', are required for normal blood coagulation. Heritable deficiencies are documented for all but one (factor III). Only factors VIII and IX are X-linked. Some of the most common blood group factors and deficiencies are:

factor V Leiden thrombophilia: the factor V Leiden mutation predisposes individuals to venous thrombosis (blood clots in the limbs). Heterozygotes have lowered levels of factor V but do not exhibit abnormal hemorrhaging. The gene is an autosomal recessive.

factor VIII: one of the proteins required for normal blood clotting; the gene for factor VIII (**HEMA**) is located on the X chromosome. A deficiency in this product can cause **hemophilia A**, 'classic' hemophilia. A genetically engineered (recombinant) gene product has been available since the 1980s.

---

**Blood group factors and deficiencies (*cont.*)**

factor IX: one of the proteins required for normal blood clotting; the gene for factor IX (**HEMB**) is located on the X chromosome. A deficiency in this product can cause **hemophilia B**, AKA Christmas disease.

factor XI deficiency: heritable, autosomal recessive condition characterized by excessive bleeding during an injury or surgery, and caused by a mutation in the gene that codes for the protein portion of a plasma glycoprotein, and that when absent interferes with the normal formation of blood clots.

Combinations of deficiencies, such as factor VIII + IX combined deficiency, have also been reported.

---

**factory:** place where manual artifacts such as stone tools are made; manufactory.

**facultative:** referring to an organism that is adapted to a certain environment or niche, but is not restricted to it. Cf. **obligate**.

**faculty of language** (FL): proposal by Chomsky *et al.* that **language** is comprised of several components: a sensory–motor system, a conceptual–intentional system, and the computational mechanisms for recursion; that the FL in the broad sense (FLB) is inclusive of all components, whereas FL in the narrow sense (FLN) includes only recursion, is the only uniquely human component of the FL, and may have evolved for a reason(s) other than language.

**faeces:** see **feces**.

**Fahrenheit scale** (F): gradient of temperature that sets the boiling point of water at 212 ° F and the freezing point at 32 °F under atmospheric pressure at sea level. Cf. **centigrade scale** and **Celsius scale**.

**Fahrenholz's rule:** proposal that the phylogenetic development, modes of speciation, genetic variability, etc., of a host and its parasites are markedly parallel.

**falciform:** sickle-shaped.

**falcula:** curved **claw** that tapers into a sharp point. Plural: falculae.

‡ **Fallopian tube:** see **uterine tube**.

**False pelvis:** see **greater pelvis**.

**false rib:** one of the five inferior **rib** pairs.

**falsifiability:** in **science**, the risk or potential for rejection of an **hypotheses**. See **hypothetico-deductive approach**.

**falsification:** in **science**, the rejection of one or more competing **hypotheses** relative to other competing hypotheses. Verb: to falsify. See **hypothetico-deductive approach**.

**falsificationism:** claim that science should not aim to verify or confirm hypotheses but to falsify them. Associated with the Austrian philosopher Karl **Popper** (1902–94), the method aims specifically to weaken the claims of the verificationists and inductivists. See **hypothetico-deductive approach**. Cf. **inductivism**.

**familial:** affecting several individuals in the same group of related individuals. The term was formerly used to denote disorders caused by a recessive gene. Cf. **hereditary**.

**familial adenomatous polyposis** (FAP): see **adenomatous polyposis of the colon, familial**.

**familial disease:** see **genetic disease**.

**familial fatal insomnia** (FFI): hereditary autosomal dominant disorder characterized by tremors, progressive insomnia and a dream-like state, progressing to coma and death; duration averages 13 months. Like **Creutzfeldt–Jakob disease**, FFI is associated with homozygosity at position 129 (for valine, in this case) and the 'folding' mutation at position 178 in native **prion protein** (PrPc). It is likely that yet another mutation specific to FFI is responsible for its activity, as the FFI form of prion affects a different area of the brain, the thalamus.

**familial Mediterranean fever:** see **Mediterranean fever, familial**.

**familial Down syndrome:** see **translocation Down syndrome**.

**familial hypercholesterolemia:** see **hypercholesterolemia**.

‡ **family:** 1. **parents** and **offspring** (i.e. a **nuclear family**), and possibly 2. other kin who are closely associated with them and related by virtue of common descent (but see **extended family**). 3. **taxonomic rank** below the **order** and above the **genus**; a group of similar, related genera.

**family of orientation:** nuclear family in which the individual of interest is a child.

**family of procreation:** nuclear family in which the individual of interest is a parent or procreator.

‡ **family pedigree (or tree):** any evolutionary tree diagram purporting to show ancestor–descendant relationships among branches of related taxa. See, for example, **cladogram, phenogram, phylogram,** and **phylogeny**.

**family variation:** genetic or phenotypic range of differences existing between nuclear families. Aka between-family variation. Cf. **fraternal variation**.

**Fanconi anemia:** rare inherited autosomal disorder characterized by changes in skin color and malformations in the limbs, kidneys and heart; caused by deficient DNA **excision repair**, a reduction in **erythrocytes**, and the manifestation of chromosome aberrations. Affected individuals are sensitive to ionizing radiation.

**FAP:** abbreviation for **familial adenomatous polyposis**.

**far red light:** solar radiation in the spectral range of 700–800 nm, visible to humans but to few other primates.

**farsightedness:** see **presbyopia**.

**FAS:** see **fetal alcohol syndrome**.

**fascia:** sheet of fibrous connective tissue that encloses and separates muscles.

**fasciculus:** small bundle of muscle or nerve fibers.

**fat:** 1. **adipose tissue**, a yellow-white tissue that forms pads between the organs of the body, and serves as a reserve source of energy. 2. any of the fatty acids, such as oleic acid.

**fat head hypothesis:** proposal that lipids found predominately in the marine food chain, e.g. **docosahexanoic acid** and **arachidonic acid**, were critical to increased **encephalization** in **hominid** lineages.

**fat patterning:** tendency for **fat** to be deposited preferentially in certain regions of the body, resulting in characteristic patterns, e.g. by age, sex, or lifestyle.

**fatal familial insomnia:** see **familial fatal insomnia**.

**fate map:** diagram of an early **embryo** that indicates the pattern of development that various regions will undergo.

**father:** male progenitor; a kinship term that identifies a genealogical or adopted degree of relationship in a **nuclear family** or **extended family**. See **mother, brother, sister, uncle, aunt, cousin**.

**fatty acid:** long hydrocarbon chain with specific terminal molecules through which it can be linked to glycerol to form triacylglycerol. See **essential fatty acid, saturated fatty acid**, and **unsaturated fatty acid**.

**fault:** one or more fractures in rocks large enough to be mapped and along which there is displacement of one side relative to the other.

**fauna:** animals of a given region, time period, or **ecosystem**. Cf. **flora**.

‡ **faunal analysis:** analysis of animal bones found at paleontological or archaeological sites to deduce community structure and environmental features of the site. See **archaeozoology** and **biostratigraphy**.

**faunal assemblage:** entire set of living or fossil animals found in a particular geographic, geological or cultural context.

**faunal break:** sudden change in the character of the fossil **fauna** encountered during excavation of successive layers in a deposit, possibly due to partial **erosion** and subsequent redeposition of later material containing a different fauna, or to faunal **migration**, or to **extinction**.

**faunal correlation:** determination of the relative ages of geological strata by comparing the **fossils** within the various strata and assigning similar ages to strata with similar fossils, using especially horses, pigs, and elephants; a method of **relative dating**. Aka faunal dating. See **A.3 date, index fossil**, and **biostratigraphy**.

**faunal exchange:** reciprocal migration of animals between geographic areas. Such exchanges are usually due to the opening of land bridges between adjacent regions formerly separated by physical or ecological barriers.

**faunal level:** biostratigraphical designation of the age within a particular rock unit. See biostratigraphy.

**faunal region:** location or area supporting a characteristic **fauna**.

**faunal stage:** any **time-stratigraphic unit** that is characterized by a particular **faunal assemblage**.

**faunal succession:** evolution of animals by modification; **anagenesis**, phyletic evolution. See **law of faunal succession**.

**faunivory:** dietary category proposed by Chivers and Hladik to apply to mammals (faunivores) that consume animal matter. Adjective: faunivorous. This term was coined because many prosimians are not exclusively **insectivorous** or **carnivorous**, but consume both invertebrates (not all of which are insects) and tetrapod vertebrates. See also **diet**.

**Fauresmith:** archaeological site found in 1926 in Fauresmith, Orange Free State, Republic of South Africa, dating to 200 **kya**; contains **Fauresmith Industry** artifacts.

**Fauresmith Industry:** Paleolithic stone tool culture found in South Africa; contains artifacts including small, well-finished hand-axes and cleavers made with lydianite, a local mineral; a proposed variant of the South African **Acheulean**. Type site: **Fauresmith**.

**favism:** severe anemia due to abnormally low amounts of the enzyme **glucose-6-phosphate dehydrogenase**, resulting from a recessive **X-linked** allele that causes red blood cells to degrade and fail to function normally; the anemic condition can be provoked in persons **hemizygous** or homozygous for the allele by inhaling pollen of the broad bean (*Vicia faba*), by ingesting the bean raw, or by being sensitive to certain drugs. Breast-fed babies whose mothers had ingested the bean have also developed favism.

‡ **Fayum:** paleontological site found in 1906 southwest of Cairo, Egypt, in the Fayum depression, dated to 37–22 **mya**, and that contains primate remains that include *Aegyptopithecus*, *Parapithecus*, *Propliopithecus*, *Apidium*, and *Oligopithecus*. The fossils were recovered from an **Oligocene** fossil

wood zone (formerly a **gallery forest**) called the **Jebel el Qatrani** formation, now completely desiccated. Aka el Fayum, Fayum Depression.

**fear grin** or **grimace**: facial expression in a lower ranking primate when confronted by a dominant **conspecific** in which the corners of the mouth are drawn back and the teeth show; signalling submission; in **catarrhines** it is used as an **appeasement** greeting. Aka fear face.

**feather-tailed tree shrew**: vernacular for *Ptilocercus lowii.*

**feature**: 1. in biology, a **trait** or character. 2. any nonportable archaeological evidence such as architecture, hearths, garbage pits, soil stains, and artifact clusters.

**feces**: material expelled from the **GI tract** during defecation, composed of food residue, bacteria, and secretions; Aka stool.

**fecundability**: possession of the ability to produce gametes, especially eggs.

**fecundity**: reproductive potential as measured by the quantity of gametes produced, particularly eggs; sometimes used, in human populations, as the number of people capable of having children. Adjective: fecund.

**fecundity ratio**: number of pregnant females expressed as a percentage of the total number of females in a population.

**feedback**: circumstance in which one factor in a dependent system influences, and is influenced by, other factors within the system; positive feedback will amplify a response, whereas negative feedback will reduce or stop it. See **tool-feedback model** and **biocultural feed back model.**

**feedback control**: method used for the regulation of biological activity in an organism based on the flow of information between parts of the organism. An example is negative feedback control in the endocrine system, in which rising concentrations of a hormone in the bloodstream result in a lowering of the level of stimulation of cells that produce that hormone.

**feedback inhibition**: regulation of gene expression at the functional protein level through inhibition by the end product synthesized, of activity of an enzyme required for the first step in a **metabolic pathway.**

**feedback stimulation**: regulation of gene expression at the functional protein level through de-inhibition or stimulation, by the end product synthesized, of activity of an enzyme required for the first step in a **metabolic pathway.**

**feeding association**: group composed of different primate species that exploit food resources together. See **association.**

**feeding party**: see **foraging group.**

**feeding strategy**: pattern of consumption displayed by mobile predators in relation to the abundance of resources in an environment. See **foraging, fine-grained environment, coarse-grained environment**, and **optimal foraging theory.**

‡ **Feldhofer Grotto**: archaeological site found in 1856 at a limestone mine in the Neander gorge, Rhine province near Düsseldorf, Germany, dated to an estimated 100–30 kya; only hominid remains were recovered. A skull cap (1033–1234 cm³, but 1525 cm³ by another estimate) and 13 postcranial bones (the species' **type specimen**) were later assigned by a majority to *Homo neanderthalensis* (although some prefer the trinomen *Homo sapiens neanderthalensis*). The coordinates of the original site were lost almost immediately after the original skeleton was removed. The site was rediscovered in 1997, and more bones were recovered in 1999, including a fragment of the left zygoma that fits the original calotte. Fragments from a second individual in a separate cave (**Feldhofer Kirche**) date to 44 kya. Both **Mousterian** tools dated *c.* 50–40 **kya**, and tools associated with **Cro-Magnon** dated *c.* 30 kya, have been found at the two sites. Aka Hochdal, Neander Valley, the Neandertal site, Neandertal 1, Feldhofen, Düssel River site, Kleine Feldhofer Grotte, Feldhofer Kirche. See Rudolf **Virchow.**

**Feldhofer Kirche**: second cave site interlocked with the original **Feldhofer Grotto,** in which additional hominid remains were found in 1999.

**feldspar**: group of crystalline minerals consisting of silicates of aluminum and smaller amounts of sodium, potassium, barium and/or calcium; decomposition of feldspar produces clays. Stone tools are often made of this material, but feldspar possesses an internal crystal face that produces a preferential cleavage plane and that makes it difficult or impossible to control fracture and to produce a sharp-edged tool. Feldspar is important in the manufacture of porcelain and glazes. Aka felspar, felstone.

**feline night monkey**: vernacular for *Aotus infulatus.*

‡ **female** (♀): 1.in sexually reproducing organisms, an individual of the sex that bears young or that produces female **gametes**, i.e. ova or eggs. 2. (adjective), pertaining to such an individual. Cf. **male.**

**female buffering hypothesis**: hypothesis that females are physiologically buffered from environmental stress during growth and that such buffering affects final adult body size.

**female carrier**: a female who is a heterozygote for an X-linked recessive trait.

**female choice**: see **female mate choice.**

**female cranial capacity** (FCC): the cranial capacity of the cranium of an **AMH** female; estimated by **Pearson's formula**. Cf. **male cranial capacity.**

**female defense polygyny:** situation in which a male has competed for, and won, females; this male attempts to keep 'his' group separated from other males of the social group. For example, a male gorilla acquires a small group of females with whom he will mate, but must be on guard against the band's other males. See **mate guarding.**

**female genomic imprinting:** nonMendelian phenomenon in which the expression of a gene depends on inheritance from the mother of two homologous copies of a gene. Double copies of certain alleles inherited from a female seem to control normal embryogenesis. Aka parental imprinting. Cf. **male genomic imprinting.** See **genomic imprinting** and **Haig hypothesis.**

**female hierarchy:** rank order among females in a social primate group. Movement in this hierarchy often involves **alliances** with high-ranking female relatives, with the support of a male, or, in some instances, mature age (possibly due to social networks); rank appears to be initially inherited from an infant's mother. In those primate societies in which females are the resident sex, the female hierarchy is particularly important.

**female mate choice:** preference by females for some characteristic in males that make them more desired mates; in primates this may be potential parental ability among those species in which the male contributes to offspring rearing (this may be deduced by such things as quality of songs in gibbons), protection (may be based on body size), or territory occupied by the male. It is argued that females are more rigorous in mate choice because they have more invested in the offspring. Cf. **male mate choice.**

**female mosaicism for X:** condition in which different X chromosomes are active in the same individual. Normal human females are **mosaic** for the expressed/inactivated X chromosome, with some lines expressing the mother's, and some cell lines expressing the father's **X-linked** alleles. See **X inactivation.**

**female net reproduction:** number of female deaths less the number of female births in an age cohort; the net production of female offspring. See **net reproductive success.**

**female parental investment** (fPI): allocation of time, energy and resources devoted by a female to her offspring; as females in many species know who their offspring are, social theory predicts that females tend to invest more than males. Cf. **male parental investment.** See **sexual asymmetry.**

**female pseudohermaphroditism:** see **pseudohermaphroditism, female.**

**female reproductive cycle:** see **uterine cycle** and **estrous cycle.**

**female vas deferens:** vestigial tissue found in females, a remnan of undeveloped male sperm ducts (the **vas deferens**), a cluster of tubules located on or near the ovaries. Aka epoophoron. See **Wolffian ducts** and **vestigial trait.**

**feminization:** development of female characteristics by the male.

**femoral condyle:** see **condyle.**

**femoro-condylar angle:** angle between the **diaphysis** of the femur and a plane that runs tangentially to the articular surfaces of the two distal condyles.

**femoro-humeral index:** length of the upper arm × 100, divided by the length of the thigh.

**femoropelvic complex:** characteristics of the **coxal bone** and **femur** that indicate **locomotor patterns** and allow researchers to differentiate between the various species of **hominids** and other **primates.**

‡ **femur:** bone of the upper leg whose head articulates with the **coxal bone**; the distal end helps form the knee joint; largest bone of the human body. Plural: femora. Adjective: femoral. The human femur is characteristically straight, owing to **bipedalism.**

**feracious:** fertile.

**feral:** pertaining to an organism, formerly domesticated or husbanded, that has reverted to a wild state. See **domestication** and **husbandry.**

**feral man (or child):** person raised in complete isolation from other humans, either by animals or under conditions of captive isolation. Aka wild child.

**fermentation:** decomposition of carbohydrates through the action of organisms such as yeast, mold, or bacteria, producing alcohol as a byproduct. Verb: to ferment.

**ferritin:** iron-binding protein; stores iron in the body, mainly in the liver, spleen, intestinal mucosa, and in bone marrow, where it is scavenged from damaged red blood cells. Ferritin is remarkable for its complexity, and consists of products from 20 separate genes.

**fertile:** producing **offspring.** Cf. **fecund.**

**Fertile Crescent:** region consisting of lower Mesopotamia and Egypt and that was the area of early domestication and horticulture.

‡ **fertility:** reproductive potential of an individual or population as measured by the quantity or percentage of developing eggs or fertile matings; usually, the number of births per individual. See **fecundity** and **fecundability.**

**fertility ratio:** all offspring in a populationm, expressed as a percentage of the number of adult females.

‡ **fertilization:** 1. union of female and male gametic nuclei; conception. 2. fecundation or impregnation. Cf. **death.**

**fertilization age:** age, counted from the first day of fertilization, of an embryo, fetus, or delivered baby, usually expressed in weeks. The fertilization age is about two weeks shorter than the **gestational age.**

**fertilization membrane:** sheath that grows outward from the point of contact of a sperm with an egg, and quickly covers the entire surface of the egg.

**fertilized ovum: secondary oöcyte** that a sperm has impregnated; after sperm penetration, the oöcyte becomes a **zygote.**

**fetal:** pertaining to a **fetus** or the post-embryonic stage of **gestation.**

**fetal alcohol syndrome** (FAS): constellation of birth disorders caused by maternal alcohol drinking during pregnancy.

**fetal cell sorting:** test that separates fetal cells from those of maternal origin in a woman's blood.

**fetal growth:** enlargement of cells and tissues during the **fetal period.** Cf. **development.**

**fetal hemoglobin** (HbF): umbrella term for several forms of **hemoglobin** synthesized in the fetal liver after 12 weeks of human gestation, the most common form of which consists of two **alpha globin chains** and two **gamma globin chains.** Fetal hemoglobin is metabolically active in the late embryonic and fetal stages of development and has a higher affinity for oxygen than does **adult hemoglobin.** A small fraction of normal adult hemoglobin also consists of a variant of fetal hemoglobin.

**fetal hemoglobin, hereditary persistence, heterocellular** (HPFH): abnormally high concentrations of circulating **fetal hemoglobin** (HbF) in an adult. Although all normal adults possess a small proportion of HbF, some individuals of African ancestry have higher levels of HbF. The condition has also been found in Greeks carrying either the beta-**thalassemia** or **sickle cell allele,** and is probably an additional mode of adaptation to **malaria,** since individuals with adult **HbS** would be at less risk for a sickling crisis in the presence of HbF. Heterocellular HPFH is an autosomal dominant gene. There is a second form, pancellular HPFH, also an autosomal dominant. See **hydroxyurea.**

**fetal inclusion:** unequal conjoined **twins** in which the less developed one is enclosed within the body of the other. Aka fetus *in fetu.*

**fetal stage (or period):** interval of prenatal growth following the **embryonic stage,** lasting in humans from approximately ten weeks postconception until birth, and characterized by further development and the onset of rapid growth of a **fetus.** See **critical period.** Cf. **neonatal stage.**

**fetal transfusion syndrome:** shared prenatal blood circulation between **identical twins** with a **monochorionic placenta;** morbid condition that can lead to unequal growth, or even death of one or both fetuses, depending on its severity.

**fetal wastage:** loss of embryos or fetuses at a rate estimated to be higher than normal; frequent or chronic spontaneous **abortion.**

**fetalization theory:** proposal by Dutch anatomist Louis Bolk in 1926 that the adult human form is the result of hormonally regulated growth that retains many of the traits of the fetal stage. Aka retardation theory. See **proterogenesis** and **neoteny.**

**fetoscopy:** procedure during which a **fetus** is examined *in utero* with a fiberoptic instrument.

‡ **fetus:** term used to describe the prenatal young of **viviparous** mammals in the latter stages of development, when organs form and body structures become recognizable as characteristic of a species; in humans, the fetus exists from the 8th developmental week until birth. Adjective: fetal. In humans, the fetus exists during the **fetal stage.** Cf. **zygote** and **embryo.**

**fetus** *in fetu*: morbid envelopment of one member of a twin pair within the tissues of another during fetal development. Aka fetal inclusion.

**fever:** elevation of **body temperature** above **normothermia;** pyrexia, usually accompanied by increase in pulse rate, restlessness, delirium, and possibly tissue destruction. The anterior **hypothalamus** is the suspected site of a normal febrile response to either an internal (endogenous) or an external (exogenous) **pyrogen.** A specific hypothalamic **prostaglandin** ($E_2$) initiates the process, which is executed by **hormones** of the **thyroid gland.** See **hyperthermia.**

**FH:** commonly used abbreviation for the craniometric landmark **Frankfort Horizontal.**

**fibrinogen:** blood plasma protein that is required for normal blood clotting, and that is converted to fibrin.

**fibroblast:** one of several kinds of undifferentiated connective tissue cells with cytoplasmic extensions that may differentiate into bone, adipose, or other types of tissue. Fibroblasts secrete collagenous or elastic fibrous proteins such as collagen, and are active in tissue generation and wound repair. See **stem cell.**

**fibroblast growth factor:** family of growth factors, originally identified because of their actions on fibroblasts, but which have much more widespread functions in growth and development.

**fibrocartilage:** type of **cartilage** composed of **chondrocytes** surrounded by a matrix strengthened by collagen fibers; strongest and most durable of the cartilages.

**fibrocyte:** quiescent **fibroblast.**

**fibrous dysplasia:** type of abnormal **bone remodeling** in which bone matrix is incompletely formed or resorbed and replaced by gritty fibrous tissue that contains bony spicules and produces pain. There are two types or stages, one of which is **Albright syndrome.**

**fibrous joint:** articulation stabilized by tough connective tissue containing collagenous fibers. The three types of fibrous joint are **syndesmoses**, **sutures**, and **gomphoses**. See **joint**.

‡ **fibula:** 1. lateral bone of the lower leg that articulates at its proximal end with the **tibia** (but is not part of the knee joint) and with the **tarsus** at its distal end; it is not a weight-bearing bone. In some primates, the fibula and tibia are fused for part of their length. Aka brace bone. 2. the bone in an animal that is ankylosed with the tibia. See **ankylosis**. Adjective: fibular. Plural: fibulae.

**ficon hand-ax:** later variety of tool found in Europe, made from selected materials and worked into shapes that have been interpreted as esthetically pleasing and therefore nonfunctional. These hand-axes may have been ornamental and/or symbolic. Some researchers attribute their manufacture to *Homo heidelbergensis* rather than to *H. erectus*.

**field notes:** record of firsthand observations, written or recorded while on site.

‡ **field study:** 1. **experiment** or **observation** carried out under natural conditions, as opposed to **laboratory studies**; often, the investigation of **behavior**. 2. pertaining to the study of free-ranging primates in their natural habitat; a slight modification of this definition pertains to primates that are free-living, but not in their **endemic** environment, such as the macaques at **Barro Colorado Island**, Panama, or the African green monkeys in the Caribbean.

**field theory:** postulate that the pattern of origin of budding structures at the apex is limited by substances synthesized at that location; applicable in biology to tooth buds and leaf buds. As used to explain dental fields. Aka **repulsion theory**. Cf. **available space theory**.

**'fight or flight' division:** see **sympathetic nervous system**.

**figurine:** small model or carved representation of a human, animal, bird, fish, etc. See **Venus figurine**.

**filament:** fine, threadlike structure consisting of a long chain of proteins; found in flagella, hair, and muscle tissue.

**filial:** of or pertaining to a son (*filius*) or daughter (*filia*).

**filial generation:** any generation of **offspring** that follows the parental **generation**; F1, F2, etc.

**filter bridge:** any geographic or ecological feature that acts as a barrier to some species but not to others, usually a land bridge, mountain pass, or ice-free corridor.

**finalism:** belief in a trend toward a final goal or purpose; see **teleology**.

**findspot:** location at which an artifact or fossil has been located.

**fine-grained environment:** environment in which the resource patches are small and the organism may behave as though the patches did not even exist. Cf. **coarse-grained environment**.

**fine-grained exploitation:** consumption of resources in direct proportion to the environmental abundance of those resources. Cf. **coarse-grained exploitation**.

**fine-grained resource:** consumable harvested by predator species in direct proportion to its abundance in the environment. Cf. **coarse-grained resource**.

**fine-grained species:** coexisting, morphologically similar species that utilize the same resources in different proportions. Species with good internal homeostatic mechanisms and high behavioral plasticity and mobility. Cf. **coarse-grained species**.

**finestra:** aperture for ventilation, especially in the wall of a tomb. Also spelled fenestra.

**finger:** one of four of the five digits of the primate hand or fore paw; **phalanges**. In other vertebrates these digits are usually referred to as toes, whereas in primate anatomy it is generally the phalanges of the hindfoot that are called toes. See **hand**.

**fingernail:** see **nail**.

**fingerprint:** 1. pattern of the ridged skin on the distal **phalanx** of a digit, resulting from the papillary layer of the dermis. 2. method of combining electrophoresis and chromatography to separate the components of a protein. See **DNA fingerprinting**.

**fingerprint ridge count:** total number of lines or ridges across all ten fingers; trait that is genetically influenced to a great degree, but may be modified by prenatal effects, such as an **infection**.

**fingerprinting, DNA:** see **DNA fingerprinting**.

**fire hunting:** practice of burning sections of grassland or forest in order to secure food. See **controlled use of fire**.

**first-arriver principle:** proposal that early colonizers of a region, by way of temporal adaptation, have a selective edge that cannot be decreased by later arrivals. Aka the king-of-the-mountain principle.

**first-degree relative:** see **relative, first-degree**.

‡ **'first family':** collection of 197 specimens, the remains of at least 13 adult, adolescent and infant **hominids** found in the **Afar region** of Ethiopia in 1975, attributed to *Australopithecus afarensis*, and thought to have been a social unit of contemporary individuals, possibly all victims of the same catastrophic event. See **NME AL 333/333W**.

**first polar body:** in females, a small, acytoplasmic cell that is the homologue of the secondary oöcyte, both of which contain 23 chromosomes; the first polar body is discarded from the ovum if pregnancy occurs.

**first premolar:** most anterior of the four premolars in the primitive mammalian dentition. During evolution primates lost this premolar. Some workers, however, refer to the anteriormost premolar as the first premolar; in humans this is actually the third pre-molar from the primitive mammalian set of teeth. See **P1, P2, P3, etc.**

**first trimester:** first of the three **trimesters** of human gestation, consisting of months 1–3, and during which ovulation, fertilization, implantation, placentation, stage 1 of prenatal development, the **critical period**, and very early fetal events all occur. The first trimester starts with the onset of the last menstrual period before pregnancy, and is therefore a clinically, rather than a developmentally, defined interval.

**FISH:** abbreviation for fluorescence *in situ* hybridization, a technique that binds a DNA probe and an attached fluorescent molecule to its complementary sequence on a chromosome.

**fish hook:** device intended to lodge in the gullet or mouth of a fish. The earliest hooks appeared in the **Magdalenian tool tradition**, and were thin pieces of pierced bone sharpened at both ends and attached to a line; if swallowed by a fish, a strong pull would cause the hook to stick in the gullet. Later bone hooks were V-shaped and J-shaped.

**Fisher, Ronald Aylmer** (1890–1962): British statistician and geneticist. In 1930, with **Haldane** and **Wright,** demonstrated that **Mendelism** was compatible with **Darwinism,** a **modern synthesis** that came to be known as **neo-Darwinism.** Fisher was also instrumental in establishing the modern concept of **dominance** and developed the **ANOVA** technique, as well as certain refinements of the *t*-test. He was also interested in the mechanisms of **natural selection** and **sexual selection**; for the latter he proposed the **runaway sexual selection hypothesis.** Winner of the Royal Society's Darwin Medal (1938) and Copley Medal (1955). Author of *The Genetical Theory of Natural Selection* (1930).

**Fisherism:** views held or proposed by R. A. **Fisher** that stressed the importance of selection and emphasized the gene as the unit of selection, the particulate nature of inheritance, and the almost exclusive prevalence of additive inheritance. For Fisher, **evolution** was defined as a change in allele frequencies within a population between generations. Most of Fisher's views are now seen as a subset of **neo-Darwinism,** which then led to the **modern synthesis** of the 1940s.

**Fisher's fundamental theorem of natural selection:** proposed by R. A. **Fisher** in 1930, the formal statement is that the increase in fitness in a population at any given time is directly proportional to the genetic variance in fitness of its members. Cf. **Fisher's secondary theorem of natural selection.**

**Fisher's secondary theorem of natural selection:** proposed by R. A. **Fisher** in 1930, the formal statement is that the rate of change in the mean of an arbitrary character in response to selection is proportional to the additive genetic covariance between character and fitness. Cf. **Fisher's fundamental theorem of natural selection.**

**fission:** 1. cleaving or splitting. 2. division of a cell or organism; see **cell division.** 3. social process of separation of a population into unique and relatively permanent demographic units; budding, splitting of populations; cf. **fusion** (3) and **fission–fusion society.** 4. See **Robertsonian translocation.**

**fission–fusion society** (or **group**): type of social organization in which individuals regularly form small subgroups (**fission**) for foraging but from time to time also join together in larger groups (**fusion**); the variation in grouping usually depends upon the type of food (e.g. the relative scarcity or abundance of a limiting resource).

‡ **fission track dating** (F-T): **absolute** method based on the number of scars or tracks made across glass or volcanic rock as uranium decays into lead, and visible with a microscope; the number of tracks is proportional to elapsed time.

**fissure:** 1. narrow groove or cleft separating sections, such as is found on the **cerebral cortex.** In the **cerebrum,** a fissure that is especially pronounced and deep is called a **sulcus.** 2. in archaeology, fine cracks on the inner surface of a flake radiating from the point of **percussion**; one of the diagnostic features that archaeologists use to distinguish a stone **tool** from a naturally occurring **geofact.**

**fissure of Rolando:** see **central sulcus.**

**fissure of Sylvius:** see **lateral sulcus.**

**fist ax:** see **coup-de-poing.**

‡ **fist walking:** form of **quadrupedal locomotion** found in orangutans (***Pongo***) while they are on the ground in which the fore paws are curled into a fist and the animal uses the outside region of the fist to support the forward body weight.

‡ **fitness:** in **population genetics**, a measure of **reproductive success**; the average number of **progeny** left by a given **genotype** compared with other, dissimilar genotypes. Aka **Darwinian fitness**, adaptive value, selective value. See **inclusive fitness, genetic fitness,** and **overdominance.**

**fitness, Darwinian:** see **Darwinian fitness** and **fitness.**

**fitness, genetic:** see **fitness.**

**fitness, inclusive:** see **inclusive fitness.**

**fitness variance:** differences among individuals within a sex with respect to their reproductive success.

‡ **fixation:** in population genetics, the complete prevalence at a locus of one gene form (allele), and the complete elimination or exclusion of another (or others), such that the frequency of the remaining allele is $p = 1.00$. The allele is then said to have achieved fixation, or to be fixed.

**fixator:** muscle that prevents movement of one or more bones, allowing other muscles attached to the immobilized bone(s) to act from a stable base.

**fixed:** 1. in **population genetics**, said of any allele that has a frequency of 100%. See **fixation** 2. in **creationism**, used to describe immutability of species or the belief that species never change their form and have always appeared as they do now.

**fixed action pattern** (FAP): innate, stereotyped behavior triggered by a well-defined stimulus; any complex behavior that exhibits **heritability**. Once the response is activated it is carried out in its entirety. Human examples include the **yawn** or the **retching response** to rotten carrion. This term is now often replaced by **modal action pattern**. See **instinct**.

**fixed continent theory:** proposal that the continents have always existed in their same geographical locations and sizes; Aka permanent continent theory. For most scientists, this idea has been replaced by the theory of **continental drift** and/or **plate tectonics**.

‡ **fixity of species:** idea that **species** do not change, i.e. they give rise only to others like themselves and do not evolve; the view held by **Linnaeus** and others *c*. 1758.

‡ **flagellum:** long process that is based on the centriole of a cell and extends from the plasma membrane; it performs whiplike motions that propel the cell. **Plural: flagella.** Only sperm possess flagella in primates.

‡ **flake:** stone tool or **débitage** that has been fractured off a stone core. As a tool, flakes may be modified or used unmodified as chipped from the core; in some tool traditions the flakes are prepared on the core before they are detached. Flakes are useful for cutting, especially through hide or flesh. See **Levallois technique**.

**flake-blade:** long, knife-like stone implement found in Africa, Europe and the Middle East *c*. 200–150 **kya**.

**flake scar:** concavity in a **cobble** or **core** representing the negative area from which a **flake** was removed; one of the diagnostic features that archaeologists use to distinguish a stone **tool** from a naturally occurring **geofact**.

**flake tool:** object made from a **flake** that has been removed from a **core**; a **scraper** is an example of a flake tool.

**flanking sequence:** portion of **DNA** located adjacent to a gene of interest, either **upstream** or **downstream**.

**flat bone:** one of the four types of bone classified by their shape; thin **compact bone** covered by **periosteum** with **endosteum**-covered **cancellous bone** inside. Flat bones have broad surfaces (e.g. some of the bones of the skull, ribs, scapulae) and undergo **intramembranous bone** development. Cf. **long bones, short bones,** and **irregular bones**.

**flathead:** see **frontal–occipital deformation**.

**flatworm:** freshwater, parasitic, soft-bodied, flattened animal characterized by bilateral symmetry. The phylum Platyhelminthes contains about 15,000 species and includes the planaria (Turbellaria), flukes (Trematoda) and tapeworms (Cestoda). Flatworms are significant **parasites**, frequently causing death in children (see **schistosomiasis**) and furthermore, absorb substantial quantities of nutrients, resulting in **undernutrition** and/or **malnutrition** of the host.

**flesh:** 1. skin, muscles, and other soft tissue of a body; cf. **fossilized flesh**. 2. animal meat. 3. excess tissue, as in stoutness.

**flesher:** any blunt tool made from stone, bone or flint, and later, metal, used in **fleshing**.

**fleshing:** act of scraping off the **flesh** from the inner side of a skin. Cf. **deflesh**.

‡ **flexed burial:** common method of placing a body in a grave during ancient interments; the arms or legs or both are bent, making the corpse more compact and easier to inter. Several **Neandertals** were found in this position. See **burial** and **grave**.

**flexion:** movement at a joint that decreases the angle between the bones involved. For example, flexion of an extended forearm will bend the arm, producing an angle of less than 180°. Verb: to flex. Cf. **extension**.

**flexor:** muscle that bends a structure, or decreases the angle between two bones. See **flexion**.

**flight distance:** distance to which a primate will flee when confronted by a dominant animal or a predator. Flight distance varies between **conspecifics** and between species.

**flint:** dark variety of **chert** that forms as nodules, usually in chalk; the primary component is silica, and is considered an opaque variety of **chalcedony**. Because of a tendency to form **conchoidal fractures**, flint was often used as a substrate for stone tools, especially in the European **Neolithic**. Flint apparently does not occur in Africa, where a related mineral, **chert**, is frequently utilized. See **cryptocrystalline siliceous rock**.

**flint and pyrite method:** technique used to produce a hot spark in which flint and pyrite are struck together and used to start a fire in dry tinder or, much later, to fire a weapon.

**flint tool:** any implement made from **flint**.

**flint knapping:** process of manufacturing stone tools, using **flint** as a medium.

**FLK:** Frida Leakey's **Korongo** at **Olduvai Gorge**.

**floater:** in **primatology**, an individual primate who is not attached to a social group. See **bachelor herd**.

**floating rib:** one of the two (sometimes three) most inferior of the five **false rib** pairs, so called because they do not articulate anteriorly. See **rib**.

**flooded forest:** see **igapo forest** and **varzea forest**.

**floor:** archaeological horizon usually found below the present land surface and on which there are found undisturbed traces of the activities of prehistoric peoples. See **living floor.**

**floor effects:** results of a behavior test or experiment that is so difficult that the subjects all do poorly and obtain the minimum score, obscuring differences between the subjects. Cf. **ceiling effect.**

**flora:** referring to plants; the plants of a given region, time period, or **ecosystem.** Cf. **fauna.**

**floral assemblage:** group of living or fossil plants found in a particular geographic or geological context. Cf. **faunal assemblage.**

**Florisbad:** archaeological site found in 1932 in the Transvaal, Orange, South Africa, dated to 39–38 **kya** ($^{14}$C), and that contains stone tools of African **Middle Stone Age** culture. Hominid remains include a hyena-gnawed skull and vault fragments assigned to **archaic** *Homo sapiens*, possibly of the **Australoid** variety.

**flow cytometry:** technique whereby cells in suspension are passed through a small tube where analysis is performed.

**flower:** collection of reproductive structures found in flowering plants. See **angiosperm.**

**Flower's index:** standard for the degree of **prognathism; basion–alveolar length** divided by **basion–nasion length** and multiplied by 100. See **orthognathous, mesognathous,** and **prognathous.**

**fluctuating asymmetry** (FA): random deviations from perfect symmetry. In operation, measured in two ways: 1. within a population as intra-individual differences between bilateral traits in symmetrical organisms (left side minus right side: e.g. foot width, ankle and hand width, ear length and width, dental dimensions); there has been considerable speculation that individual asymmetries of this type are due to developmental instability and/or stress. 2. proportion within a population displaying a reversal of normal symmetry, e.g. *situs inversus viscerum.*

**fluke:** type of parasitic flatworm with a sucker-like mouth for attachment to the intestinal lining of its host. Flukes are frequent parasites of humans and other mammals.

**fluorapatite:** mineral that forms when **groundwater** contains free fluorine ions that combine with the **hydroxyapatite** in teeth and bones. See **fluorine dating.** Aka fluoroapatite.

**fluorescence:** emission of visible light by a substance when exposed to light of a shorter wavelength. Ultraviolet light causes fluorescence in many objects. Verb: to fluoresce.

**fluorescence** *in situ* **hybridization:** see **FISH.**

**fluorine** (F): gaseous, highly reactive nonmetallic element that as a fluoride (e.g. sodium fluoride, NaF) is essential to life and health. It easily forms compounds with most other elements, and is found naturally in minerals such as fluorite, cryolite, phosphate rock, etc.

‡ **fluorine dating:** site-specific **relative dating technique** that compares the loss of **nitrogen** to the gain of fluorine (and sometimes uranium) of organic materials such as wood and bone. The more fluorine absorbed and nitrogen lost, the older the sample is expected to be, although no absolute dates can be assigned with the technique. Aka fluorine–uranium–nitrogen dating (F–U–N).

**fluorine test:** assay for the presence of absorbed fluorine in bones that have been buried, and exposed to fluorine-bearing groundwater. Fluorine is combined with bone calcium as **fluorapatite.** The longer a bone has been exposed to this process, the greater the quantity of fluorapatite, hence its use as a **relative dating technique.**

**flush:** explosive increase in population size. Cf. **crash.**

‡ **fluting:** removal of chips of stone from a blade (such as an arrowhead or spearhead) in order to produce a thin neck, which allows for **hafting** to a shaft.

**fluvial:** pertaining to rivers, hydraulic action, and riverine environments; fluviatile.

**fluvialism:** doctrine that geological strata are best interpreted by assuming that their formation was by mechanisms that operate in a uniform mode and rate that were comparable to identical contemporary agencies. See **uniformitarianism** and **Lyell.**

**fluviatile deposits:** deposits produced by river action.

**fluvioglacial:** pertaining to water emanating from a glacier and to the deposits in glacial streams.

**flying lemur:** vernacular for the members of the mammalian order **Dermoptera;** Aka colugo. See *Cynocephalus.*

**'flying primate' hypothesis:** idea proposed by Pettigrew in the 1980s that primates, dermopterans (colugos) and the **Megachiroptera** ('flying foxes') shared a common ancestor in the **Paleocene;** in this scenario, the **Microchiroptera** (insectivorous bats) are considered **convergences** with the larger bats. This relationship was deduced by the nervous pathway from the **retina** to the optic tectum of the mid-brain. Molecular evidence in the 1990s disputed this hypothesis and demonstrated that the Megachiroptera are more closely related to the Microchiroptera than to any other taxonomic group.

**focal sampling:** sampling technique used in primate behavior studies in which one animal is observed exclusively for a determined period while its behavior is recorded; after this time period has elapsed, another animal may be observed for the same period. This technique has the advantage of providing a more detailed sequence of behavior events than an erratic focus on the group as a whole. Aka focal animal sampling. Cf. *ad libitum* sampling, **behavior sampling**, **scan sampling**.

**focus:** 1. point of convergence, attraction, or attention. Plural: foci. 2. to adjust or concentrate. 3. the principal location of a **disease**.

**foetal:** see **fetal**.

**folate:** member of the **vitamin B** complex; required for normal neural tube development, cell growth, and reproduction. It has been suggested that the maintenance of dark skin color (**melanism**) in equatorial latitudes is due, in part, to the maintenance of normal folate levels, which become depleted upon direct exposure to sunlight. Aka folic acid, folacin, PGA, vitamin Bc, vitamin M.

**fold:** 1. doubling of any body part upon itself, as in the **vocal fold**. 2. in geology, strata that have bent.

**foliate:** of or pertaining to something that is shaped like a leaf, e.g. the **Solutrean** willow-leaf or laurel-leaf point.

**folic acid:** see **folate**.

**folivory:** dietary category applied to animals (folivores) that consume predominantly foliage (i.e. leaves, buds, shoots) during the year or during a particular season. Adjective: folivorous. Many primates supplement their **diet** with leaves, but it is only the **colobine** monkeys of Africa and Asia that are specialized folivores consuming mature leaves, while the howlers (*Alouatta*) of the Americas feed on immature leaves. See **frugivory**, **granivory**, and **gummivory**.

**folk:** 1. a group of associated peoples. 2. a primitive, post-tribal organization. 3. lower classes or common people in a region.

‡ **folk taxonomy** (or **classification**): any provincial classification scheme for grouping local plants and animals (including people) into intuitively meaningful categories that are assigned names usually based either on **anthropocentric** utility (e.g., 'things that are poisonous'), function ('things that fly'), or on obvious **phenotypic keys** ('blue birds'). Such **classifications** are most often **phenetic**, utilize perceptions of analogous rather than **homologous** characteristics, and as such seldom reflect true genealogical or evolutionary relationships. When compared to **scientific classification**, folk schemes also lack sufficient collective grouping names (higher taxa), with only four or five levels of general to specific hierarchical depth. These levels are sometimes termed the covert beginner, life form, folk generic, folk specific, and folk varietal; e.g., the terms animal, mammal, dog, wild dog, and dingo could correspond to these levels. Folk schemes also tend to overdifferentiate the local ecosystem (e.g., Arctic peoples discriminate among many varieties of snow) and to under differentiate the unfamiliar. In anthropology, work as early as 1863 by

Durkheim and Mause compared such classifications of plants and animals cross-culturally. See **ethnobiology** and **racial character**.

**follicle:** spherical mass of cells sometimes containing a cavity; a crypt or small body; see **ovarian follicle** and **hair follicle**.

**follicle cell:** one of many nearly transparent cells that surround a developing **oöcyte** and that provide interim nourishment. See **zona pellucida**.

**follicle hormone:** estrogenic substance secreted by the Graafian follicle; aka follicular hormone, **estrone**.

**follicle stimulating hormone** (FSH): one of the gonadotropic **hormones** secreted by the anterior **pituitary gland**; in females it regulates follicular development (Graafian follicles) in the ovary and stimulates the secretion of **estrogen**, and promotes the endometrial changes characteristic of the **proliferative phase** of the mammalian menstrual cycle; in males it stimulates **Sertoli cells** to produce androgen-binding protein, and stimulates **progesterone** secretion and the production of sperm cells.

‡ **Folsom:** archaeological site found in 1926 in New Mexico and dated to *c.* 12 **kya**; the site contained a **Folsom point** embedded in the ribcage of an extinct species of bison.

**Folsom culture:** Paleoindian cultural evidence distributed throughout much of the Great Plains region of North America, dated to about 12–7 **kya**. Aka Folsom complex.

**Folsom point:** thin, leaf-shaped blade made by pressure flaking and the removal of a longitudinal flake near the center of each side. Named for the location of its discovery, at **Folsom**, NM.

**fomite or fomes:** object such as a book or blanket that harbors pathogens, and by which means the organism may be transferred to others.

**fonds de cabane:** literally, foundations of a hut; remains of a prehistoric habitation that was built in the open.

**fontanel:** one of four cartilaginous areas between the cranial bones of a fetus or infant; the fontanels allow some movement of the cranial bones, making the skull compressible and assisting with the passage through the birth canal. All fontanels fuse within 24 months (except in pathologic conditions) and it is during this period that the infant cranium is malleable, which may permit **cranial deformation**. Fontanel size and rate of closure can be used to estimate **skeletal age**. Also spelled fontanelle.

**Fontéchevade cave:** archaeological site found in 1947 in Charente, western France, dating estimated from 200 **kya** (terminal **Riss**?) to as recent as 100 kya, and that contains artifacts that consist of **Tayacian** choppers and large end scrapers. Hominid remains include many fragments of two crania that made reconstruction difficult and debatable. Remains attributed to either **AMH** or *Homo neanderthalensis*.

**food:** any item designated by convention as eligible for consumption by a species; many potentially nutritious resources fail to achieve status as food, and some designated as foods have low nutritional value. In human cultures, 'food' can take on deep symbolic meaning, and sustenance may become secondary.

**food availability:** temporal and spatial distribution of **food**.

**food begging:** behavior observed among **chimpanzees** after an individual or group has killed an animal and is in the process of consuming it; an individual not involved in the hunt, often a female, will extend its hand, apparently asking for some of the meat.

**food-borne disease:** form of **gastrointestinal tract** condition where the **agent** is carried in or on ingested nutrients.

**food chain:** portion of the **food web**, most frequently a simple sequence of prey species and the predators that consume them; a series of producers and consumers that subsists on a resource base.

**food distribution:** location of food in a given area.

**food patch:** clump of a food species within a given area.

**food preference:** type of food that an animal will select most often during a feeding trial; see **preference index**. Aka food choice.

**food pyramid:** triangular graph of the food web in a given ecological community, with producers represented at the lowest trophic levels and consumers at the higher levels. Aka ecological pyramid.

**food quality:** amount of easily digestible, assimilable energy, and variety of nutrients in a food.

**food sharing:** offering of food by one or more individuals to other individuals with no intention of gain by the food giver(s); this is seen in chimpanzees who have obtained meat; the food sharing is usually preceded by **food begging** behavior. See **reciprocal food sharing**.

‡ **food web:** complete set of food links between species in a community; a diagram indicating which ones are the consumers and which are consumed.

**foot:** 1. terminal portion of the lower extremity consisting of the tarsus, metatarsus and digits. 2. paw of a primate; in the higher primates the foot refers to the hind paws, particularly in humans, which have a highly **derived** foot that is specialized for **bipedal locomotion**. Aka pes. 3. unit of measurement equal to 0.3048 m, or one-third of a yard.

**foot arch:** any of three arches (lateral longitudinal, medial longitudinal, and transverse) that help support the human **foot** by providing a springiness that gives when weight is placed on them; these arches are maintained by the interlocking shape of the foot bones, by strong ligaments, and by the pull placed on tendons generated from muscle use. These arches begin to develop in the child's foot at around age eight. Fossil footprints may indicate bipedalism when evidence of these arches are obtained. See **metatarsal** bones.

‡ **footprint tuff:** one of many datable airfall **tuffs** in the **Laetolil Beds**; contains at least 18 tuffs where faunal footprints have been located, and date to between 3.75 and 3.6 **mya**. The famous **hominid** footprints are at **Laetoli Site G.**

‡ **forage:** 1. food or fodder (n.). 2. to seek or search for food or provisions. 3. as applied to humans, to subsist on **hunting**, **gathering**, and/or **marine exploitation**, and to possess no domesticated plants or animals except the dog.

‡ **foragers:** small groups of seminomadic bands that practice a **foraging** subsistence; such bands often organize into 25–50 people for most of the year. See **magic numbers**.

**foraging efficiency:** proportion to which time and energy expenditure allocated to finding and consuming food is offset by amount of energy obtained. See **energy maximizing foraging strategy, time minimizing foraging strategy.**

**foraging group:** social unit which searches for food together; in primates these may be small, temporary, and fluid units that are a subset of the larger social group.

**foraging range:** area over which an individual or population travels in the search for food. Aka feeding range.

**foraging strategy:** technique by which a species obtains its food; it is desirable to use the most optimal strategy, which weighs **costs** and **benefits**. The optimal strategy is the one that obtains the most energy (in terms of pursuit, handling, eating, and digesting) per unit time spent in these activities while exposing the animal to the least amount of danger. See **energy-maximizing foraging strategy, energy-minimizing foraging strategy,** and **time minimizing foraging strategy.**

**foraging theory:** see **optimal foraging theory.**

**foramen:** opening or hole in a tissue, usually bone or membrane, for the passage of a blood vessel or nerve. Plural: foramina.

*foramen ovale basis cranii:* opening in the rear part of the middle portion of the **sphenoid bone** through which nerves and vessels pass into the brain case. Aka oval foramen of sphenoid bone.

‡ **foramen magnum:** large opening in the **occipital bone** through which the **spinal cord** passes. The foramen magnum becomes more centrally located under the skull owing to the need to balance the head

as a result of **bipedalism**; thus, any fossil **hominoid** with such an arrangement is believed to be bipedal and a **hominid**.

**foraminal arc: craniometric** measurement; angle in degrees from the lambda to the foraminal axis.

**Forbes disease:** heritable autosomal recessive condition characterized by diarrhea and due to glycogen storage deficiency and caused by mutations in amylo-1,6-glucosidase. Rare; prevalence is 1 : 100,000. See **glycogen storage diseases.**

**Forbes' Quarry:** see **Gibraltar.**

**forbidden clone hypothesis:** proposal that mutations cause certain cell clones to re-emerge during adult life, leading to autoimmune disease. The source of these forbidden clones is thought to be the primitive self-antibodies in an organism that were created during fetal life and derive from cells that normally undergo **apoptosis.**

**forced copulation:** behavior in which a male inseminates a female against her will; because this is not the male of her choice her fitness is said to be reduced. Some behavioral biologists refer to this behavior as rape in species other than humans.

‡ **forced expiratory volume:** standardized measurement of lung capacity.

**forced vital capacity** (FVC): volume measured during maximum expiration (as fast as possible following maximum inspiration). Cf. **vital capacity.**

**forearm bones:** see **radius** and **ulna.**

**forearm circumference: anthropometric** measurement; distance around the lower arm as measured with a tape measure placed at the position determined to produce the maximum circumference and passed around the arm. Used to help determine body composition in adults.

**forearm–hand index:** hand length × 100, divided by the length of the forearm.

**forearm–hand length: anthropometric** measurement; distance between the **olecranon process** of the ulna and the third (middle) finger of the hand as measured with a **sliding caliper.** The elbow is flexed and the olecranon process and the hand are in the horizontal plane; the palm of the hand faces medially and the fingers are extended. Used in human biomechanics and other areas of **human engineering.**

**forearm length: stylion** height subtracted from the **radiale** height.

**forearm skinfold: anthropometric** measurement; skinfold measured on the posterior surface of the forearm at the location of the maximum circumference. Used for studying individual differences in body fat distribution. See **skinfold thickness.**

**forebrain:** large anterior brain subdivision consisting of the right and left hemispheres of the **cerebrum** and the **diencephalon.** The forebrain is the anterior of three divisions identified by constrictions in a vertebrate embryo. See **prosencephalon.**

**foregut:** anterior alimentary tube in a developing vertebrate embryo; this structure will develop into the pharynx, esophagus, stomach, and anterior small intestine. Cf. **hindgut.**

**foregut fermenter:** mammal that retains high-fiber foods in the stomach, where **symbionts** break down the cellulose component. The most specialized foregut fermenters are the artiodactyl ruminants (such as cattle and deer) that possess compartmentalized stomachs. Other mammals with large stomachs that are divided into sacs include macropods (kangaroos) and sloths; among the primates it is the **folivorous colobine** monkeys that are specialized foregut fermenters. Some workers have reported that woolly lemurs (*Avahi*) possess an incipient **sacculated stomach.** Foregut fermentation appears to be more efficient than **hindgut fermentation.**

**foreign antigen:** any molecule that stimulates a response in an immune system; see **antigen.**

**foremilk:** see **colostrum.**

‡ **forensic anthropology:** 1. the application of anthropological knowledge to questions of civil and criminal law. 2. the occupational field that applies the techniques of anthropology to legal issues and the law. Forensic anthropologists are usually osteologists, archeologists, and/or geneticists. See **forensic archaeology.**

**forensic archaeology:** application of excavation techniques and special archaeological expertise to situations involving subsurface evidence. Examples range from victims of ancient warfare to recent episodes of mass genocide. See **forensic anthropology.**

**forensic science, forensics:** see **forensic anthropology** and **forensic archaeology.**

**foreshaft:** pointed stick, usually of hardwood or bone, mounted on the distal end of an arrow, dart or spear, and sometimes tipped with flaked stone.

**forest:** large area of closely canopied trees. See **bamboo forest, boreal forest, deciduous forest, evergreen forest, gallery forest, igapo forest, lowland evergreen rain forest, Mediterranean scrub forest, monsoon forest, montane forest, primary rain forest, rain forest, secondary rain forest, tropical rainforest, true rain forest, varzea forest,** and **xerophytic forest.**

**forest canopy:** dense upper layer formed by the widest upper branches and broadest leaves in vegetation dominated by trees.

**Forest Negro:** in older terminology, a **Negroid** subgroup found in the western, central, and southern regions of Africa. Aka African Negro.

**fork-crowned dwarf lemur:** vernacular for *Phaner furcifer.*

**fork-marked lemur:** vernacular for *Phaner furcifer*.

**form:** 1. the properties of material composition and arrangement of a feature. 2. one or a population of variant individual(s); often used as a way of avoiding a statement of its rank as a species or subspecies (e.g. a small form of raccoon lives on Cozumel Island). 3. an ambiguous taxonomic level below the **variety**; a morphological variant.

**form analysis:** approach in which behavior patterns are examined, both between and within species, to deduce their evolutionary origins. See **sequence analysis, situation analysis**.

**formation:** in geology, a fundamental rock unit of a stratigraphic section at a given locality.

**formenkreis:** superspecies; any aggregation of species or subspecies, whether living or fossil.

**Formosan rock macaque:** vernacular for *Macaca cyclopis*.

**formula:** 1. a rule or principle usually expressed in algebraic symbols and often containing both **constants** and **variables**. 2. something to be executed after **values** have been assigned to variables.

**formulation:** 1. in taxonomy, the way in which a binomen is formed. 2. in biotechnology, a mixture or prescribed recipe for making a candidate pharmaceutical, or the process of developing such a formulation.

**fornix:** 1. recess around the cervix of the uterus where it protrudes into the vagina. 2. tract within the brain connecting the hippocampus with the mammillary bodies.

**Fort Ternan:** paleontological site found in 1959 near **Koru** in Kenya, dated to *c.* 14 mya (middle **Miocene**), and that contains **hominoid** remains including *Kenyapithecus*, *Proconsul*, and *Ramapithecus*. Superficially explored by L. **Leakey** in 1932.

**Fort Ternan 'tool':** single object made of lava found by Heselon Kukiri among some fractured antelope bones at the **Fort Ternan** site in 1967; as this was the sole lava object at the site, Louis **Leakey** interpreted it as a tool, and attributed its use to *Kenyapithecus wickeri*. This interpretation is questioned by most of the archaeological community.

**forward genetics:** analysis that proceeds from phenotype to genotype by positional cloning or candidate gene analysis. Cf. **reverse genetics**.

**forward mutation** ($\mu$): a **heritable** change of a **wild type** to a mutant condition within the limits of a **gene**; the average rate of forward mutations is about $1 \times 10^{-5}$ gametes per generation. See **allele**. Cf. **back mutation**.

**fossa:** pit or depression in bone or other tissue. Plural: fossae.

**fossa canina:** depression in the outer surface of the **mandible** that serves as a point of attachment for the muscle that lifts the corners of the upper lip and exposes the canine teeth.

**Fossey, Dian** (1932–1985): primatologist who studied primates in their natural habitat. Encouraged by Louis **Leakey**, Fossey habituated the Parc des Virungas **mountain gorillas** at Karisoke in Rwanda, observing and reporting instances of female **troop transfer** and **infanticide** by adult males in **polygynous** family groups. Fossey was murdered, perhaps because of her outspoken criticism of poaching, by a person or persons who have never been identified. See R. A. **Hinde**.

‡ **fossil:** 1. anything removed from the earth (archaic). 2. anything ancient, especially if removed from the ground (e.g. **fossil fuel**). 3. evidence left by a previously living organism, generally dated to older than the **Holocene** epoch, i.e. older than 10 ky; cf. **subfossil**. Fossils are usually removed from consolidated rock, but may be mere impressions or molds between compressed **strata**, or they may be **bone** or **tissue** subjected to **permineralization**, or traces of behavior, e.g. burrowing scars left by **fossorial** organisms or evidence of other motility patterns such as walking or crawling. See **ancient DNA, diagenesis, dubiofossil, endocast, Laetoli footprints, living fossil, microfossil, paleontology, pseudofossil, taphonomy**, and **trace fossil**.

**fossil fuel:** nonrenewable deposits of coal, petroleum, natural gas, etc., that are the remains of ancient organic materials, formed under pressure, and capable of being used as **fuel**. See **fossil**. Cf. **renewable resource**.

‡ **fossil record:** evolutionary history of life or any particular taxon as revealed through the continuum of **fossil** remains.

**fossiliferous:** pertaining to a geological formation that contains fossils.

‡ **fossilization:** process of transformation of a living thing into substances that preserve the form and structure of the original as a **fossil**. Adjective: fossilized. Preservation is enhanced if an organism has been rapidly buried; **weathering** is thus minimized. Some fossils, however, are subject to further postmortem compaction, fragmentation, and other deforming processes such as **expanding matrix distortion**. See **diagenesis, permineralization**, and **taphonomy**.

**fossilized flesh:** desiccated soft tissue, as in mummified tissue. See **mummy**.

**fossorial:** adapted for digging and living in burrows and tunnels underground. Fossorial mammals have short legs and tails, long claws on their forefeet, and small eyes and ears.

**founder analysis:** method for the analysis of nonrecombining **DNA sequence** data (usually **mitochondrial DNA** or **Y chromosome DNA**) with the aim of identifying and dating certain human migrations into new territory. The method picks out founder sequence types in potential source populations and dates lineage clusters derived from them in selected settlement zones.

**founder effect (Mayr's):** observation that small populations that arrive on an island will tend to diverge from the mainland population owing to intense selection pressure and reduced genetic variation. Controversial model proposed in 1954 by Ernst **Mayr**. Not to be confused with the **founder effect** or **principle** of Sewell **Wright**. (see **below**).

‡ **founder effect** or **principle (Wright's):** special case of synchronic genetic drift in which a small population of individuals buds off from a parent population and founds a new colony. The colony may possess only a small proportion of the former total genetic variation present in the parent population. Aka Sewell Wright effect. See **fission** and **Wahlund effect.**

**founder event:** establishment of a new population in a locale, often by a small number of individual organisms.

**founder–flush hypothesis:** proposal that a **founder effect** (**Wright's**) leads to a population increase (the flush) and reduced selection pressure, causing additive genetic variance to be preserved or to increase. Proposed by H. L. Carson to explain variation in populations that move to atolls and coral reefs, especially those in the Hawaiian archipelago.

**founder hypothesis:** proposal that new species are often established when small populations colonize new geographic areas.

**four-cusp molar pattern:** pattern found variably in humans on the **occlusal surface** of **maxillary** molars, in which there are three well-defined cusps and a weakly developed **hypocone**.

**four-hominid hypothesis:** proposal by Richard **Leakey** that four **hominid** species may have lived concurrently in East Africa 3–1 **mya**: one was small-jawed but large-brained (e.g. *Homo*), a second was megadont but small-brained (e.g. *Australopithecus (= Paranthropus) boisei*), a third was a gracile australopithecine (e.g. **KNM-ER 1813**), and a fourth was like **KNM-ER 1482**.

**fourth premolar:** most distal premolar in the primitive mammalian dentition. During evolution, primates have lost anterior premolars; thus the most posterior premolar is actually the fourth premolar, even though no species has four premolars. Humans have only two premolars, but they are premolars three and four from the primitive mammalian set of teeth. See **P1, P2, P3**, etc.

**fourth ventricle:** cavity between the **metencephalon** and **myencephalon** within the hindbrain; the fourth ventricle is filled with **cerebrospinal fluid**.

**fovea:** very small pit or cuplike depression found on bone or other tissue, e.g. **fovea centralis**.

**fovea capitis (of the femur):** pit in the head of the **femur** that marks the site of the ligament that helps attach the femur to the **acetabulum** of the **coxal bone**; Aka facet of head.

**fovea centralis:** depression in the macula lutea of the eye where only cones are located; the area of keenest vision.

*FOXP2*: one member in a family of genes expressed in neural tissue and tied functionally to **communication** in birds and mammals.

**fracture:** 1. the breaking of bone or cartilage, or the result thereof. 2. the process of breaking something, e.g. a mineral.

**fracture interpretation:** analysis aimed at resolving the causal agent for a bone **fracture**; for example, stress fractures may be indicative of excessive physical activity, whereas numerous fractures of the distal ends of the radius and ulna in an individual may indicate frequent falls.

**fragile site:** nonstaining gap in a chromosome at which breaks occur easily, resulting in acentric fragments and deletions. Fragile sites are inherited in a **codominant** Mendelian pattern. Aka fragile chromosome site. See **fragile X syndrome**.

**fragile X syndrome** (FRAX): pervasive developmental disorder that results in profound mental retardation, a consistent facies, and large testicles in males. FRAX is the most common heritable syndrome with symptoms of mental impairment and behavioral change. Transmitted as an **X-linked recessive**, it affects hemizygous males far more frequently than females; females are usually heterozygotes and exhibit milder symptoms, as they possess only one working copy of the gene. The syndrome is caused by a mutation in the fragile X mental retardation protein (FMR1, an X-linked recessive), which amplifies a three nucleotide repeat up to 200 times (see **anticipation**), so that the FMR1 protein is not produced. Normally, the FMR1 protein functions to bind RNA. Female carriers of the disorder have **premutations** that can be identified at the molecular level. **FRAX** is not the same clinical entity as **mental retardation, X-linked nonspecific**.

**frambesia:** see **yaws**.

‡ **frameshift mutation:** mutation that alters the **reading frame** of **mRNA** by the addition or deletion of one or two base pairs of the DNA template; results in a major alteration of the translated amino acid sequence downstream from the event, thus radically altering the properties of the resulting polypeptide.

**Francois' leaf-monkey:** vernacular for *Trachypithecus francoisi*.

**Frankfort Agreement:** consensus reached at Frankfort-am-Main in 1882 with respect to the standardization of 31 anthropometric landmarks, planes, measures, and indices; Aka the Frankfurter Verständigung. Now largely outdated, it also competed with the French system; both were supplanted by the Monaco Agreement of 1906.

**Frankfort Horizontal** (AO or FH): predefined plane of orientation of the skull in side view in which the three horizontal reference points are the bilateral superior margins of the **external auditory meatus** (**porion**) and the inferior margin of the left orbit (**orbitale**). The Horizontal is a standard orientation for comparative purposes. Also spelled Frankfurt horizontal. Aka auriculo-orbitale. See Appendix 7 and **Frankfort Agreement.**

**Franklin, Rosalind Elsie** (1920-1958): English biophysicist; while she was working at Wilkins' lab, Franklin's X-ray diffraction studies on DNA crystals were instrumental in helping **Watson** and **Crick** deduce the chemical structure of **DNA.** Franklin died of cancer before the work was appreciated; some think that she would have been a strong candidate for a Nobel Prize, but Nobel Prizes are not awarded posthumously.

**fraternal polyandry:** case of **polyandry** in which the males involved are brothers. Aka adelphic polyandry.

**fraternal twins:** see **twins, dizygotic.**

**fraternal variation:** genetic or phenotypic range of differences existing within a **nuclear family.** Aka within-family variation. Cf. **family variation.**

**fraternity:** 1. brothers. 2. a society of men. Cf. **sorority.**

**freckle:** area of hyperpigmentation on skin in response to sunlight, and due to the discrete accumulation of **melanin,** and not to an increase in the number of **melanocytes.** Cf. **macula.**

**free oxygen radical:** form of oxygen (a superoxide anion) that is highly reactive, very toxic to cells and causes tissue damage associated with many types of human disease and injury. Free oxygen radicals can be produced by the action of ionizing radiation on water. Aka free radical.

**free radical:** see **free oxygen radical.**

**free radical scavenger:** any molecule with an affinity for a **free oxygen radical.**

**free radical theory of aging:** proposal that animal aging occurs due to the gradual deterioration of body cells caused by the accretion of **free oxygen radical** compounds in body cells and tissues, especially **DNA,** and that the cumulative effect of this process is degeneration and inviability. A controversial theory proposed by American physician Denham Harman (1916–). Limited support has been found in artificial radiation and diet modification experiments. Aka oxidative damage theory of aging.

‡ **free-ranging primates:** primates that live in their natural habitat, unfettered by human constraints.

**free ribosome:** term used to describe a **ribosome** while suspended in cytoplasm; Aka free polysome.

**freemartin:** sterile nonhuman female **fraternal twin,** a result of the **freemartin effect.** Whereas the male twin is normal, the female is usually found, upon dissection, to posses imperfect genitalia of both sexes.

**freemartin effect:** consequence of prenatally shared circulating blood in nonhuman, opposite-sex (and therefore **fraternal twin** pair) mammals, especially cattle; occurs when the blood vessels of a fused placenta become interconnected when chorions fuse, resulting in the masculinization of female members of the pair due to prenatal exposure to male hormones. Opposite-sex **twins** in the higher primates develop in a **bicornuate uterus,** but **partial chimerism** nevertheless occurs in about 10% of human fraternal twin pairs.

**freeze drying:** dehydration of a frozen sample under high vacuum conditions; a method of biological preservation.

**freezing:** in an archaeological site, process precipitated by lowering ambient temperature below 0°C, and associated with an expansion of soil water; the increase in volume with the conversion from water to ice is 9%. Cf. **thawing.** See **cryogenic soil modification.**

**frenulum:** 1. a fold of skin or mucus membrane. 2. fold of skin that immobilizes the upper lip of **prosimians.** 3. membranous fold that attaches the tongue to the floor of the mouth. Aka frenum.

**frequency:** rate of occurrence; regularity per unit of time; complete cycles per unit of time. 1. in population genetics, usually expressed as a **percentage;** e.g. a genotype or **allele frequency** that ranges from 0% to 100%. 2. in behavioral studies, frequency is the number of times a particular behavior occurs during a specified period, i.e. the rate of the behavioral occurrence. Frequency should be expressed in number of occurrences per unit of time, although it is sometimes expressed as the total number of occurrences.

**frequency, allele:** see **allele frequency.**

**frequency-dependent fitness:** referring to changes in the adaptive values of an organism as a function of the frequency of its genotype in a population.

**frequency-dependent selection** (FDS): differential fertility or mortality that occurs when the fitness of a genotype depends on the frequency of the phenotype in a population. See **negative FDS** and **positive FDS.**

**frequency, genotype:** see **genotype frequency.**

**frequency of heterozygotes** ($H$): the proportion of a population ($1-f$) that are not homozygotes ($f$) at a given locus. Aka heterozygosity. Cf. **frequency of homozygotes.**

**frequency of homozygotes** ( $f$ ): the proportion of a population $(1-H)$ that are not heterozygotes ($H$) at a given locus. Cf. **frequency of heterozygotes**.

**Frere, John** (1740–1807): barrister and antiquarian; in 1790 he found several 'shaped flints' that he believed came from antiquity, when people had no knowledge of metal. His 1797 report was ignored until more tools were recovered in 1837 by **Boucher de Perthes**.

**fresco:** method of painting on a wall or ceiling before the plaster has dried, so that colors become incorporated into the plaster.

**friction pad:** dermal ridges on the toetips that aid arboreal mammals in gripping trees. Well developed in primates and a characteristic of all members of the order, not just the arboreal forms. See **tactile pad**.

**frieze:** decorative band or feature, as on a wall.

**fright cry:** any sudden and loud call made by a startled animal; Aka **distress call**, pain cry, mercy cry.

**frontal:** 1. pertaining to the forehead. 2. another name for **frontal bone**. 3. another name for **frontal plane**.

**frontal arc** (n–b): craniometric measurement; distance of the curve from the **nasion** to the **bregma** as measured by a flexible tape measure.

‡ **frontal bone:** anteriormost bone of the **cranium** that forms the forehead; it is superior to the facial skeleton. In **prosimians** the frontal consists of two bones, whereas in **anthropoids** it is fused into one bone.

**frontal chord:** anthropometric measurement; distance between **nasion** and **bregma** as measured with a **spreading caliper**.

**frontal convergence line:** highly variable intersection of the **crown stream** and the **glabellar stream** of hair.

**frontal eminence:** one of two slightly rounded protuberances on the frontal bone, one on either side above the eyes, forming the most prominent portions of the forehead in **AMHs**. Aka tuber frontale.

**frontal index:** an index of facial flatness, internal biorbital **subtense** $\times$ 100/internal biorbital chord. The internal biorbital chord is the distance between the points on the outer edge of the orbits where the frontal and zygomatic bones join. The internal biorbital subtense is the area formed by bisecting an isosceles triangle created by joining the two points of the chord with the **nasion**. See **premaxillary index**, **rhinial index, simotic index**.

**frontal keel:** flat raised area of the **mid-sagittal** portion of the **frontal bone**.

**frontal lobe:** anterior portion of each cerebral hemisphere extending posteriorly to the **central sulcus**. Among the functions of the frontal lobe are voluntary motor control of skeletal muscles, personality, higher-order intellectual processes such as reasoning, planning, decision-making, and verbal communication.

**frontal–occipital deformation:** artificial flattening of the front and rear of the cranium by binding. Several cultures artificially flattened the heads of their children, and were known generically as flatheads.

**frontal plane:** plane or line of anatomical orientation that divides a bilateral organism into front and back halves. Aka **coronal plane**.

**frontal sinus:** one of two cavities in the **frontal bone** over the nasal cavity. In life these sinuses are lined by mucosa. These air spaces are a distinctive feature of **hominids**. See **autapomorphy**.

**frontal trigone:** triangular form of the most lateral portion of the **supraorbital torus**; the apex is defined by a prominent temporal ridge.

**frontal torus:** continuous bar of bone that includes the **supra-orbital tori** and the glabellar torus; fused in anthropoids and in palaeoanthropic fossils.

**frontomalare anterior:** most anterior point of the frontozygomatic **suture**.

**fronto-orbital sulcus:** fissure on the lateral edge of the frontal lobe; one of the best areas of the **brain** for distinguishing human from ape **sulcal patterns**; comparisons can often be made by using fossil **endocasts**.

**frontotemporale** (ft): craniometric **landmark;** most medial point on the curve of the temporal ridge. See Appendix 7.

**frost cracking:** in an archaeological site, transformation of ground surface into polygonal shapes as a result of shrinkage of the ground during cold dry winters. See **cryogenic soil modification**.

**frowning bared-teeth scream face:** facial expression in which the eyes are narrow, and the mouth corners are back, showing the teeth; this expression is associated with **submission**. Found in some anthropoids.

**frozen accident theory:** proposal that the genetic code evolved randomly until the current set of codon assignments became fixed because this set optimizes selective advantages that would have been reduced if the code were changed. Nearly complete correspondence of the code in **eukaryotes** with that of **endogenous** mitochondria and certain **exogenous** species tends to verify this proposition.

**fructose:** yellowish-white sugar found in honey and fruit; aka levulose or fruit sugar. Fructose is a component of **sucrose**.

**fructose intolerance, hereditary, type I:** inability to metabolize **fructose**. Symptoms include hypoglycemia, sweating, nausea, tremors after ingesting fruit sugar, liver and kidney damage, and failure to thrive; fatal if untreated. Defective enzyme is fructose-1-phosphate aldolase (aldolase B, ALDOB, an autosomal recessive). About a dozen allelic mutations are known. Aka ALDOB deficiency. One of two types of fructose intolerance with a genetic basis.

**fructosuria:** autosomal recessive genetic condition characterized by an inability to metabolize **fructose**, which then accumulates in blood and urine. One of the errors of **carbohydrate metabolism.**

‡ **frugivory:** dietary category applied to animals (frugivores) that consume predominantly fruit during the year or during a particular season. Many — perhaps most — primates are frugivorous. See **folivory, granivory,** and **gummivory.** See also **diet.**

**fruit:** in **angiosperms,** the structure that encloses the seeds. In general, fruits evolved after the appearance of flowers. Cf. **nut.**

**FSH:** abbreviation for **follicle-stimulating hormone.**

**$F_{ST}$ analysis:** method of calculating **genetic distance** first suggested by S. **Wright** and applicable to traits that are not normally distributed, and are perhaps even correlated, such as gene frequencies. Cf. **Mahalanobis distance.**

**$F$-test:** in statistics, an algorithm in which two samples are tested for equality of **variance.**

**fuel:** 1. in prehistory, any combustible material used to maintain fire, such as dried moss, plants or wood; see the **controlled use of fire.** 2. in modern times, any substance that provides energy or heat when processed, ranging from coal and oil and other **fossil fuel** to nuclear or chemical sources.

**Fuente Nueva** (FN3): see **Orce Ravine.**

**fugitive species:** inferior competitor in a packed ecosystem that, by virtue of its dispersal ability, persists temporarily in newly disturbed habitats.

**F–U–N:** fluorine–uranium–nitrogen dating; Aka **fluorine dating.**

**function:** 1. proper role, action or activity. 2. in biology, the workings of an organism; physiology. 3. predesigned **formula** or rote **operation;** an **algorithm** or conventional mode of data **transformation,** e.g. the change of a value into its **logarithm.**

‡ **functional adaptation:** short-term adjustments due to physiologic processes or behavior; somatic responses to environmental conditions which offer specific advantages that increase survival in a given environment. Functional adaptations are nongenetic and not inherited (non-Lamarckian). See **acclimation** and **acclimatization.**

**functional anatomy:** perspective in anatomy in which structure is studied in the context of physiology.

**functional constraint:** portion of a molecule that cannot sustain mutations as often as an unconstrained portion; for example, the heme pocket of hemoglobin, which is critical to the molecule, is constrained as compared to the surface or mere scaffolding function of other sections. Unconstrained portions of a genome evolve five to twenty times faster than constrained

portions. Constrained portions are often equivalent to molecular **domains.**

**functional divergence ratio:** fraction of the number of mutations found in functionally constrained domains over the number found in unconstrained domains, using either DNA or amino acid residues, for a given family of homologous sequences; used to measure the **selection pressure** on a protein. See **neutral theory of molecular evolution.**

**functional food:** substances that confer benefits beyond basic nutrition, especially those to which additives yield a product with added value. Examples range from vitamin D that has been added to milk to genetically altered foods.

**functional genomics:** 1. science related to the discovery and definition of the **function,** rather than the mere sequence or description, of genes. 2. the systematic discovery of all gene–gene interactions.

**functional morphology:** relationship between structure (anatomy) and physiology (function).

**functional mosaic:** heterozygous individual that expresses one allele in some tissues and the other allele in other tissues; the **homogametic sex** is always a functional mosaic for the homogametic chromosome, as in female primates, including humans. Cf. **X inactivation.**

**functional response:** change in a rate of predation in response to a change in prey density. See **optimal foraging theory.**

**functional unit of gene action** (fuga): genetic matrix supposed to contain one or more structural, control and regulatory genes, and that acts as a unit to exert a specific regulatory function on the transcriptural activity of other structural genes.

**fundament:** 1. the topography of the earth before the appearance of humans. 2. a habitat that has not yet been affected by anthropogenic modification.

**fundamental niche:** see **niche.**

**fundamental number:** see **nombre fondamental.**

**fundamental theorem of natural selection:** see **Fisher's fundamental theorem of natural selection.**

**funeral mound:** elevation, formed of earth, containing one or more chambers, and that covers a corpse. Cf. **tell.**

**fungus:** simple branching plant-like organism that reproduces either sexually or by forming spores. Fungi can live in animal tissues, causing diseases (mycoses), e.g. tinea pedis (athlete's foot) and **coccidioidomycosis.**

**furrow-carved mammal teeth:** teeth obtained from mammals and carved with a circular furrow or ring, presumably for the purpose of wrapping and suspending them from a sinew cord and for use as personal adornment; found in **Châtelperronian** sites and associated with the presence of Neandertals c. 32–29 **kya.** Cf. **pierced mammal teeth.**

**fusion:** 1.joining or union. 2. union of gametes, cells or organisms; see **cell fusion** and **hybridoma**. 3. social process of joining of formerly unique populations into a larger, relatively permanent demographic unit; cf. **fission** (3) and **fission–fusion society**. 4. See **Robertsonian translocation**.

**fusion–fission social organization:** see **fission–fusion society**.

**fusion gene:** two genes that have fused into one **cistron** after translocation or recombination.

**fusion protein:** product that is the result of one gene moving nearer to another on a chromosome, where both genes transcribe and translate separate products that form a single hybrid molecule. Used to refer to abnormal proteins that form when two nonhomologous chromosomes translocate, bringing genes into abnormal proximity. See **Philadelphia chromosome**.

**fusion society:** see **fission–fusion society**.

**FxJj 50:** archaeological site found in 1968 in **Koobi Fora**, East Turkana, Kenya, dated to 1.6–1.5 **mya** and excavated by a team led by Glynn **Isaac**. The site contained flakes, choppers and scraping tools, possibly **Oldowan**. At least 17 mammal species are represented by over 200 bones, mostly antelope, some of which have also been chewed by other carnivores, but some bones exhibit cut marks, positive evidence of **butchery**, and suggesting **hominid** meat-eating and food transport. Aka Site 50. See **scavenging**.

**G1:** see **gap 1 phase.**

**G-1 Trail:** see **Laetoli Site G** and **footprint tuff.**

**G6P:** see **glucose-6-phosphatase.**

‡ **G6PD deficiency:** see **glucose-6-phosphate dehydrogenase deficiency.**

**ga** or **Ga:** abbreviation for gigayear, term used by geologists and cosmologists for one billion ($10^9$) years ago. Also b.y.a., Byr and (less often) ba; the variant 'by' stands for billion years. Often the abbreviation ga BP is used, meaning $10^9$ years before present.

**gait:** manner of walking or running. See **bipedal gait.**

**galactose:** **monosaccharide** containing six carbons produced by digestion of **lactose** by β-**galactosidase**; galactose is converted into glucose and utilized as energy.

**galactosemia, type I:** inability to digest milk sugar; symptoms in 'classic' galactosemia (type I) include muscle weakness, enlargement of the liver, cataracts, palsy, seizures, and mental impairment; fatal if untreated. The defective enzyme is galactose-1-phosphate uridyl transferase (GALT, an autosomal recessive). GALT catalyzes step 2 of galactose to glucose reduction. About 150 different mutations to the GALT enzyme have been identified worldwide. One of the many known errors of **carbohydrate metabolism**. Aka GALT deficiency.

**galactosemia, type II:** inability to digest milk sugar; symptoms in type II galactosemia are similar to those of type I (see above). The defective enzyme is galactokinase (GALK1, an autosomal recessive). GALK1 catalyzes step 1 of galactose to glucose reduction. Aka GALK deficiency, galactokinase deficiency.

**Galagidae** (= **Galagonidae**): **prosimian** family to which the galagos (bush babies) belong, consisting of four genera and ten species. Vernacular: galagid (galagonid). See Appendix 2 for taxonomy, Appendix 3 for living species.

**galago:** vernacular name for **prosimians** belonging to the **Galagidae.**

*Galago* É. Geoffroy, 1796: **prosimian** genus to which the bushbabies (**galagos**) belong. Two to six species, depending on taxonomic scheme used. Geographic distribution in Africa south of the Sahara, where they occupy varied habitats. Arboreal. Nocturnal. Locomotion modes include **arboreal quadrupedalism** and **vertical clinging and leaping.** Small, most weighing less than 300 g. Dental formula: 2.1.3.3; possess a **dental comb.** Diets include **frugivory, insectivory,** and **gummivory.** Possess mobile **pinnae,** lined with **rugae,** that can move independently, enabling bushbabies to scan for the sound of insects. Foraging pattern tends to be solitary, although some species congregate to form sleeping **dormitories** during the day. Home ranges overlap to form **neighborhoods.** Territories marked

by **urine washing.** Some authors include the species found in *Otolemur, Galagoides,* and *Euoticus* in *Galago.* See **Galagidae;** see Appendix 2 for taxonomy, Appendix 3 for living species.

*Galagoides* (= *Galago*) A. Smith, 1833: prosimian genus to which the dwarf bushbabies (galagos) belong. Four recognized species, which are **sympatric** in East African coastal forests. Occupy closed primary forest or the understory of secondary forest from Senegal through the broad belt of rain forest in eastern Africa and into Zanzibar. Nocturnal. Arboreal quadrupeds, with some leaping. Small, weighing between 60 and 150 g. Dental formula: 2.1.3.3; possess **dental comb.** Predominantly **insectivorous,** with some fruits and plant exudates. **Noyau** social pattern organized into **neighborhoods** of overlapping male and female home ranges; females congregate into sleeping **dormitories** during the day. Some workers include *Galagoides alleni* with *Galago.* See **Galagidae;** see Appendix 2 for taxonomy, Appendix 3 for living species.

**Galagonidae:** see **Galagidae.**

**Galápagos archipelago:** volcanic archipelago of about 14 islands located on the equator in the Pacific Ocean, 500 miles west of Ecuador, that contain several unique species of accidental animal and plant life. Aka Archipelago de Colon. See **Darwin's finches.**

**Galdikas, Birutė** (1946–): Canadian primatologist who investigated the ecology and behavior of orangutans. Galdikas was one of three female primatologists sponsored by Louis S. B. **Leakey** and the National Geographical Society. In recent years, Galdikas has become the major proponent of orangutan conservation; she has taken a role in rescuing and rehabilitating displaced and orphaned orangs which led to the establishment of a captive breeding and release program at the Bohorok Orangutan Rehabilitation Center. Author of *Reflections of Eden* (1995) and (with N. Briggs) *Orangutan Odyssey* (1999).

**Galen, Claudius** (*c.* 130–199): Greek physician in Rome; treated the wounds of gladiators; his animal dissections on pigs and 'apes' provided data for voluminous texts that were influential for twelve centuries; discovered the sympathetic nervous system; described respiration; discovered that arteries contain blood, and not air.

**Galilee:** see **Zuttiyeh.**

**gallery forest: forest** along a river or stream.

**Galley Hill Man:** fossil hominid found in England in 1888, dated roughly to the Late Pleistocene. The remains are attributed to *Homo sapiens,* and consist of a nearly complete male skeleton with a stature of about 5 ft 3 in (1.59 m). Some researchers have speculated that Galley Hill Man was the ancestor of the Mediterranean peoples.

**Galton, Francis** (1822–1911): British statistician and eugenicist, cousin of Charles **Darwin**. Galton was one of the inventors of the **twin method** and believed that behaviors as well as physical traits could be quantified. He also suggested that **fingerprints** could be used to identify individuals; see **dermatoglyphics**. Galton coined the terms **eugenics** and **euthenics**. Author of *Hereditary Genius* (1869). Winner of the Royal Society's Copley Medal (1910). See **regression** and **law of filial regression**.

**Galton Society of New York** (GSNY): organized in 1918 in New York by Charles **Davenport** and Madison Grant (1865–1937), the society was dedicated to the study of 'racial anthropology'. This was a small but politically influential group that also included H. F. **Osborn**, William King Gregory (1876–1970), John C. Merriam (1869–1945), Edward L. Thorndike (1874–1949), Frederick A. Wood (1873–1939), and R. M. **Yerkes**. This group was active during the first two decades of the twentieth century, and influenced Ellis Island policy, culminating in the US Immigration Restriction Act of 1924.

**Galton's law:** principle that in bisexual lineages each individual obtains, on average, one-half of its inherited characters from each parent, one-quarter from each grandparent, one-eighth from each great-grandparent, etc.

**Galton's law of filial regression:** principle that offspring of parents with extreme character values that are **heritable** tend to regress toward the mean of the population; i.e. that parents with both superior and inferior genotypes tend to have offspring that are average for the species.

**game theory:** body of economic behavior theory integrated into biological theory by **Lewontin** and **Maynard Smith** in which individual choices by competitors are seen as economic, optimized, and/or strategic, and determined in part by the behaviors of synchronic players in a common ecological setting. Models are used for situations where an optimum strategy is not fixed and depends upon the outcome most likely to be adopted by opponents. See **tit-for-tat strategy**, **optimal foraging theory**, and **prisoner's dilemma model**.

‡ **gamete:** mature haploid reproductive cell capable of fusing with another haploid cell of similar species origin but from an opposite sex to yield a **zygote**; produced during **gametogenesis**, in which cell division occurs by **meiosis**; the egg or sperm. See **oögenesis** and **spermatogenesis**.

**gamete intrafallopian transfer:** see GIFT.

**gamete pool:** set of all copies of all gamete genotypes in a population that could potentially be contributed by the members of one generation to the members of the next generation.

**gametic gene therapy** (GamGT): alteration, through direct manipulation of a genome (gametes or fertilized zygote), of the alleles that will or will not be passed on from parent to offspring, resulting in human-mediated, instantaneous evolutionary change in a laboratory population or clinical setting. Aka heritable, germline and germ cell gene therapy. See **substitutional gene therapy**, **somatic gene therapy**, **directed evolution**, and **anthropogenic selection**.

**gametic isolation:** in organisms with external fertilization, gametes may not be attracted to each other; in internal fertilizers, gametes may be inviable in the sexual ducts or styles of other species; a premating or prezygotic mechanism.

**gametic number:** synonym for **haploid number**.

**gametic purity:** older synonym for accurate **segregation**.

**gametocyte:** cell from which gametes are produced by division; a spermatocyte or an oöcyte.

**gametogenesis:** specialized process of cell division (**meiosis**) producing male (via **spermatogenesis**) and female (via **oogenesis**) **gametes**.

**gametophyte:** stage in the life cycle of an organism during which **gametes** are produced; a sexually mature organism.

**gamma:** third letter of the Greek alphabet ($\Gamma$, $\gamma$); the third member in a set or series.

**gamma–delta T cell:** T cell type that is important in the interactions between acquired and natural immune responses.

**gamma diversity:** measure of the rate and degree to which additional species serve as replacements within a similar habitat type over distance. Gamma diversity is dependent on both **alpha diversity** and **beta diversity**.

**gamma globulins:** serum proteins consisting of **polypeptides**, some of which possess **antibody** activity. See **globulins**.

**gamma globin chain** ($\gamma$ Hb): one of several globin chains that constitute the family of **hemoglobin** molecules, and that constitute part of **fetal hemoglobin**. Aka gamma globin.

**gamma karyology:** study of the numerical and structural properties of chromosomes by means of Giemsa stain and fluorescent techniques that result in various **chromosome banding patterns**. See **karyology**.

**gamogenesis:** sexual reproduction.

**ganglion:** structure that contains an aggregate of nerve cell bodies, or neurons, and that occurs outside the **central nervous system**. Plural: ganglia.

**Gaolingpo:** archaeological site found between 1988 and 1996 in the **Bose Basin** of the Guangxi Zhuang Autonomous Region of China, dated to 803 **kya** (associated tektites), and that contains many **mode 2**

large cutting tools similar in complexity to those assigned to the **Acheulean tool tradition** at sites located west of **Movius' line**.

**gap 1 phase** (G1): stage of **interphase** when proteins, carbohydrates and lipids are synthesized in preparation for impending cell division. It is also the phase in which DNA replication (which occurred during the **S phase**) is checked and repairs are made.

**gap 2 phase** (G2): stage of **interphase** when additional proteins are synthesized in preparation for impending cell division.

**gaps in the fossil record:** with reference to the **fossil record**, any major hiatus in a supposed continuum. A gap may exist because of erosion of representative strata, or lack of interest in a particular time frame.

**Garden of Eden model:** see **mitochondrial Eve**.

**gargoylism:** congenital condition in which there is abnormal lipid metabolism that is expressed in growth disorders of the skeleton including dwarfism, **kyphosis**, and the two mucopolysaccharide disorders **Hunter syndrome** and **Hurler syndrome**.

**Garn, Stanley M.** (1922–): US applied physical anthropologist at Michigan; a student of E. A. **Hooton**, Garn became a specialist in **growth and development**, malnutrition, bone remodeling, hair growth, pattern–profile analysis, dysmorphogenesis, and osteoporosis. President, **AAPA** (1965–7); author of *Human Races* (1961) and some 900 other publications.

**Garrod, Archibald Edward** (1857–1936): English physician; while studying the rare disease **alkaptonuria** in the children of a marriage between first cousins, Garrod applied **Mendel**'s principles to humans for the first time, concluding that the disease was genetic, and an example of an autosomal recessive. Garrod later showed that **albinism** and other conditions behaved in a similarly predictable manner. Author of 'Inborn errors of metabolism' (1902), in the *Lancet*.

**Garrod, Dorothy Annie Elizabeth** (1892–1968): British archaeologist and paleoanthropologist; studied in France under Breuil and Peyrony. Excavated in Gibraltar, Kurdistan, and at the caves of **Mount Carmel** near Haifa, Israel, in 1929–34; located several important sites, which included Neandertaloid and early modern human fossils. One of the first to view the Levant as the 'gateway' of migration into Europe. First female to become a professor of archaeology at Cambridge. Co-author of *The Stone Age of Mount Carmel* (1937–9, 2 vols.). Daughter of physician Archibald **Garrod**. See **Kebara**, **Tabūn**, and **Skhūl**.

**gas exchange:** during **respiration**, process of osmosis of air-like materials across a **semipermeable membrane**. Takes place predominantly in the alveoli embedded in the mucosa of lung tissues, where $CO_2$ is exchanged with $O_2$; optimal exchange occurs at core body temperature and 100% humidity. Cf. **nasal radiator hypothesis**.

**gastrointestinal** (GI): pertaining to the **gastrointestinal tract**.

**gastrointestinal tract** (GIT): tubular portion of the digestive system that begins at the stomach and ends at the rectum; the GIT is the largest portion of the **alimentary canal**. Ingested **food**, which becomes **chyme**, passes through it and is digested and absorbed. Aka GI tract. Cf. **alimentary canal**.

**gastrointestinal tract size:** any estimation of the size of a compartment of a mammal or primate gastrointestinal tract, or of the entire tract. Measurements commonly used are gut length, surface area, mass, or volume.

**gastrula:** during **gastrulation**, the cells of a **blastocyst** that develop into the three germ layers, the **ectoderm**, **mesoderm**, and **endoderm**.

**gastrulation:** process by which the **blastula** develops into the **gastrula**; cells that will form internal organs migrate from a superficial position to near their definitive positions in the embryo.

**'Gates of Grief':** narrow strait between Africa and Arabia where, according to geneticist Stephen Oppenheimer, early **AMHs** could have waded or rafted **'out of Africa'** 150 **kya** when sea levels were lower during the **Pleistocene epoch**; so named because of the strong currents in the strait. Cf. **Levantine corridor**.

**gatherer–hunters:** see **foragers**.

**gathering:** process of harvesting resources. Usually, preparation for and acquisition of vegetable products, but may also include **scavenging** for animal protein. One of the two primary modes of food acquisition available to subsistence peoples; the other is **hunting**. Verb: to gather.

**gathering hypothesis:** response to the Man the Hunter symposium of 1968 after it was revealed that 60–80% of the food obtained by hunters and gatherers was actually supplied by the gathering women (suggesting these peoples should be referred to as **gatherer–hunters**). The gathering hypothesis was developed by Slocum (nee Linton), Tanner, **Zihlman**, and others; this model brings attention to the fact that most primates gather plant material, as would have the hominid line, and that gathering plays an important role in the divergence of hominids from the other hominoids, suggests that the earliest tools were used for harvesting wild plants rather than for hunting, and asks what females did and their role in human societies. Aka 'woman the gatherer' model.

**Gaucher disease:** heritable lysosomal storage disease with variable symptoms: pain, fatigue, enlarged liver and spleen, nervous system impairment, bone degeneration with fractures, arthritis, skin pigmentation defects; fatal if untreated. Of several modes, type I (GDI) is caused by defective glucocerebrosidase, produced by an autosomal recessive gene that maps to 1q21. Substitutional gene therapy has been available since 1991; the working enzyme is injected intravenously every two weeks, similar to insulin therapy in **diabetes**. Found in high frequency among Ashkenazi Jews (1 : 400). The incidence in the general population is 1 : 100 000.

**Gause's hypothesis or law:** see **competitive exclusion principle**. Aka exclusion principle.

**Gauss normal epoch:** long interval of geologic time (a **chron**) from 3.4 to 2.4 **mya** in which the polarity of the earth's magnetic field was for the most part not reversed compared with that of today. See **normal polarity epoch**, and **paleomagnetism**.

*Gazinius* **Bown, 1979:** genus of tarsiiform primate from the middle Eocene of North America belonging to the **omomyid** subfamily **Anaptomorphinae**; two species. Estimated body size ranges from 600 to 900 g. See Appendix 1 for taxonomy.

**G-banding:** one of the methods of creating identification bands on individual chromosomes after treatment of the metaphase plate with trypsin and **Giemsa stain**. See **chromosome banding technique**.

**GC value:** ratio of the amounts of **guanine** and **cytosine** to the total amounts of all four nucleotides in a certain **DNA sequence**: $(G + C)/(G + C + A + T) \times 100$.

**gelada baboon:** vernacular for *Theropithecus gelada*.

**gemellology:** study of **twins**, twinning, and other multiple births; from the (Latin) root meaning twin, double, coupled.

**gemma:** 1. any budlike structure, such as a tastebud. 2. any outgrowth that becomes a new organism.

**gemmation:** asexual reproduction in which a new organism develops as an outgrowth of the parent; aka budding.

**gemmule:** hypothetical living unit cited by proponents of **pangenesis** as the bearers of hereditary material; aka pangene.

*gen.:* see *genus*.

**Genay:** archaeological site found in 1955 located near the village of Semur-en-Auxoia in Côte-d'Or, Burgundy, France, dating to 65 kya, containing hominid remains from at least two individuals assigned to *Homo neanderthalensis*. Aka Genay man, l'homme de Genay, la Breche de Genay.

**GenBank:** US Federal repository for public **DNA sequences**, and available to all researchers.

**gender:** meanings and roles that a society assigns to sex differences; the cultural use of sexual dimorphism in terms of the characters recognized as important to a society.

**gender identity:** development of strong feelings of masculinity or femininity, from childhood or earlier; possibly independent of genetic, chromosomal, gonadal and phenotypic sex.

**gender theory:** proposal that the majority of the differences between males and females is socially formed and cultivated, i.e. gender is mediated by nurture, rather than nature (genetically mediated sexual dimorphism).

‡ **gene:** basic unit of the **Mendelian inheritance** responsible for a certain physical **character** or biological function, and located in one of the **linkage groups** comprising a **chromatid**. A gene is an ultramicroscopic structure consisting of **DNA**, and capable under certain circumstances of giving rise to a new character; such a change is called a **mutation**. Hereditary traits are controlled by two genes, each at the same position on a homologous pair of **chromosomes**. Organisms may possess thousands of genes. *Homo sapiens* has been estimated to have between 30 000 and 100 000 genes. A gene is a continuous region of DNA consisting of one or more **transcription units**; the particular sequence of nucleotides represents a functional unit of **inheritance**. See **exon**, **intron**, and **cistron**.

**gene amplification:** production of repeated copies of a piece of DNA. See **gene duplication** and **tandem repeats**.

**gene–brain–behavior approach:** method of deducing the relationships of etiologically complex disorders, especially behavioral disorders, by examining a system with a 'bottom up' model, i.e. from a known gene, to its physiological impact, to its behavioral manifestations. See **fragile X syndrome** and **autism**. Cf. **behavior–brain–gene approach**.

**gene chip:** see **DNA microarray**.

‡ **gene cluster:** closely linked genes, often with related functions, grouped in a portion of a chromosome; e.g., the **globin gene** group on human chromosome 11. Sometimes called a **gene family**. Cf. **supergene**.

**gene complex:** group of genes so closely linked they are transmitted as a unit. See **supergene**.

**gene conversion:** 1. result of a rare error during DNA repair in meiotic prophase of a heterozygote that eliminates one of the four **cistrons** present; if a nonsister strand is used as a template, the result is three copies of one allele and only one of the other, instead of the normal count of two each. 2. form of nonreciprocal recombination in which one **DNA sequence** alters another, resulting in the conversion of one allele to another in a polymorphic set; biased conversion favors one allele over another; see **back mutation**. 3. see **ectopic gene conversion**.

**gene–culture coevolution:** model of biocultural evolution proposed by C. J. Lumsden and E. O. **Wilson** in which Wilson's **autocatalysis model** is extended to a complex interaction of both genes and culture, and that these interact and contribute to adaptation in hominids. Compare the **biocultural feedback model**.

**gene dosage:** number of genes present in a diploid cell, in **doses**; on **autosomes**, the atypical presence of three or more copies of a particular chromatid (**trisomy**, such as **Down syndrome** or **trisomy 21**), resulting in 150% of normal gene products. In **sex chromosomes**, constitutions such as XXXX can produce 200% of normal for certain genes. Aka gene dosage effects. See **superfemale**.

**gene duplication:** occurrence of a second copy of any particular sequence of DNA; the duplicate may appear near the original, or be copied elsewhere in the genome; when the duplicated sequence is a gene, the event is called gene duplication.

**gene–environment correlation:** tendency for certain individuals with certain genetic **predispositions** to have, to seek, or to receive particular common experiences.

**gene–environment interaction:** differing effects of environments on individuals with different genetic **predispositions** or backgrounds.

**gene expression:** conversion of genetic information encoded as **DNA** into an active protein during **transcription** and **translation**. Many traits exhibit a consistent pattern of expression; others vary in **penetrance** or **expressivity**.

‡ **gene family:** set of related genes occupying various loci in **DNA**, usually formed by duplication of an ancestral gene, and having a recognizable similar sequence; the **globin family** is an example. Aka gene cluster. See **orthology** and **parology**.

‡ **gene flow:** spread of **alleles** from one breeding **population** to others due to the dispersal of gametes, zygotes, and/or individuals. Gene flow may cause changes in **allele frequency** and is one of the recognized **mechanisms of evolution**.

‡ **gene frequency:** see **allele frequency**.

**gene frequency method:** method of calculating gene frequencies when the number of alleles and the mode of inheritance are known.

**gene interaction:** synergy between alleles or non-allelic genes within a single genotype and that produces a particular phenotype.

**gene library:** any collection of DNA fragments that have been cloned into cosmids, phages, or plasmids.

**gene locus:** position of a gene on a chromosome; location of a gene in the sequence. The term **locus** has come to be preferred.

**gene map:** map of genes in a linkage group with distances expressed as a function of their cross-over frequencies with other genes in the group. Cf. **chromosome map**.

**gene migration:** see **gene flow**.

**gene mimics:** different genetic **loci** that produce similar phenotypic expressions.

‡ **gene mutation:** alteration of a portion of **DNA** that forms a **gene**. See **point mutation**.

‡ **gene pool:** information encoded in the sum total of all the genes in a **deme** existing at a given time. A new generation consists of pairs of gametic combinations drawn from the parental gene pool. See **gamete pool**.

**gene probe:** piece of DNA that binds specifically to a particular gene or part of a gene; see **probe**. Aka probe, DNA probe, hybridization probe.

**gene product:** usually, the polypeptide that was translated from the mRNA that was transcribed from a specific gene. In some cases, the **RNA** is not translated, and the RNA itself is the gene product (as in rRNA, tRNA, and nRNA).

**gene silencing:** inactivation of a gene, a portion of a chromosome, or an entire chromosome by **epigenetic reprogramming**. See **post-transcriptional gene silencing** and **transcriptional gene silencing**.

**gene surgery:** procedure during which a defective gene is excised and removed from an affected cell; a normal gene may be substituted for the defective one.

**gene targeting:** artificial replacement of a gene (the target) by a genetically engineered homologue in a host cell's chromosome, by means of **homologous recombination**.

**gene therapy:** treatment of a **genetic disease** by inserting into cells a normal **gene** or DNA segment that can correct an abnormal cellular function or the disease. See **substitutional gene therapy**, **somatic gene therapy**, and **gametic gene therapy**.

**gene transplantation:** technique during which an entire gene is moved from one organism to another, resulting in a **transgenic** individual.

**gene tree:** estimate of the relationships of ancestry and descent among alleles of a gene or genes in one or more populations or species; ancestors in such a tree may be either known or hypothetical. Mitochondrial DNA trees are typical examples of gene trees.

**genealogical method:** anthropological technique that involves collecting and compiling pedigrees into genealogical tables in order to infer the type of kinship system and the importance of kinship as an institution in a particular society.

**genealogy:** 1. a person's account of his or her own ancestry. 2. the number of significant links separating individuals in a family diagram or tree that indicates the **degree of relatedness** between them. 3. a set of relationships.

**genera:** plural of **genus**.

**generalist:** organism that displays a broad pattern of resource usage. Cf. **specialist.**

‡ **generalized:** in biology, describes any structure adapted to a wide range of conditions and used in numerous ways; the grasping hands of primates (including humans) are generalized structures that permit climbing, food-gathering, tool-making, and many other functions.

**generalized cell:** see **composite cell.**

**generation:** cohort of individuals produced in a single life cycle; in the case of seasonal reproducers, the progeny of one season compared with the parents or progeny of the previous season; for continuous reproducers, those individuals in a successive population equally removed in time from a common ancestor. See **semelparity** and **iteroparity.**

**generation length:** for continuous reproducers, either the mid-point or mean age of a sibship subtracted from the average age of the parents. In hominoids, 15–25 years, with values toward the lower figure in the great apes and early australopithecines, and toward the higher in the later, more $K$-selected hominids. One million years would thus consist of 67 k generations of 15 years each, 50 k generations of 20 years, or 40 k generations of 25 years. Aka generation time.

**generation time hypothesis:** proposal that the evolution of proteins and DNA is faster in species having unusually shorter **generation lengths** than in species with longer generation lengths. A. C. Wilson and others have shown provisionally that this tenet holds true for DNA but not for proteins. Aka generation time effect. See the **relative rate test.**

**generic:** 1. of or pertaining to a **genus.** 2. relating to an entire group. 3. pertaining to the name of a nonproprietary drug.

**generitype:** see **type species** and **generotype.**

**generotype:** type specimen for a **genus**; standard by which members of a genus are compared for classification purposes. Alternate spelling: generitype.

**genesis:** 1. origin, source, creation, beginning (Greek, genesis). 2. first book of the Bible, describing **Special Creation** (Genesis).

**genetic:** refers to variation in traits that is based at least in part on differences in genes; **hereditary.**

‡ **genetic adaptation:** any **diachronic** process of molecular change in members of a species that enhances survival; also, any specific characteristic that affects **fitness** in a positive manner and thus optimizes survival, that is, allows an organism to survive better in its natural environment than if it lacked the feature. Better known as **biological adaptation** or **biological evolution.** See **natural selection.**

**genetic algorithm:** any algorithm employed to determine properties of entities as defined by recursive methods, often based upon an analogy with a biological system or principle.

**genetic assimilation:** Waddington's term for what Simpson called the '**Baldwin effect**', the incorporation of phenotypic traits into a genetic substrate, a Lamarckian process that alleges to penetrate **Weismann's barrier.** See **organic selection theory, teleonomic selection,** and **progressive evolution.**

**genetic bottleneck:** see **population bottleneck.**

‡ **genetic code:** system of transfer of information stored in **DNA** (or **RNA**) which, after **genetic transcription** and **genetic translation,** results in a functional unit called a **polypeptide chain.** Specifically, the systematic relationship of **triplet** combinations to individual **amino acids** or termination instructions. See **codon** and **anticodon.**

**genetic conflict theory:** controversial proposal that attempts to explain **genomic imprinting** in terms of competing evolutionary sex strategies, i.e. because males are uncertain about paternity they have evolved mechanisms to insure large and strong offspring, whereas females attempt to distribute resources over several smaller offspring. Each parent modifies the DNA expression in offspring in a manner that maximizes their **inclusive fitness.** Occurs in marsupials and placental mammals. Aka Haig hypothesis, kinship theory of genetic imprinting, intragenomic conflict theory.

**genetic counseling:** allied medical specialty that provides an understanding of **medical genetics,** including empirical risk of recurrent **inherited disorders** that may or may not be inherent in families or prospective families. Often, the laws of inheritance and **pedigrees,** a complete natural history of a genetic disorder, and the genetics of a chemical disorder are communicated, along with available options for testing and treatment. See **etiology** and **prognosis.**

**genetic death:** preferential elimination by selection of genotypes that are carriers of mutations which reduce their adaptive value or **fitness.**

**genetic discrimination:** any adverse action based on a person's asymptomatic genetic predisposition to, or probability of having, a gene-based disease or medical condition.

**genetic disease:** any condition caused by a malfunctioning gene or cytogenetic error and that affects an organism's capacity for adaptation; an 'inborn error of metabolism' or molecular defect. Excepting lethal defects and sterility, genetic diseases display certain familial modes of inheritance and exhibit morbidity or mortality patterns that may affect direct **fitness.** Aka hereditary disease, familial disease.

**genetic disorder:** disease or syndrome attributed to inherited genetic defects; common examples are **Down syndrome**, **achondroplasia**, **cystic fibrosis**, **hemophilia**, and **rheumatoid arthritis**. See **major chromosomal anomaly**, **autosomal dominant**, **autosomal recessive**, **X-linked**, and **multifactorial** inheritance.

**genetic distance:** 1. an average measure of relatedness between populations based on a number of quantified traits, usually **allele frequencies**; see $F_{ST}$ **analysis**. 2. map distance between loci on chromosomes expressed in **Morgan units**.

**genetic distance map:** diagram that shows the genetic relationships between populations based upon measures of **genetic distance**.

‡ **genetic drift:** change in **allele frequency** that occurs (1) when small groups of individuals are separated from or leave a larger population (**founder effect**), or (2) when offspring differ genetically from the parental population due to **sampling error**. Any differentiation of a small isolated population due to the fact that, by chance alone, its founders contained a set of allele frequencies with values different from those of other populations, and hence have 'drifted' from the other population values; usually referred to in the **diachronic** sense, i.e. between generations. Drift is a possibly **non-adaptive mechanism** of **evolution** and is significant in diploid organisms when the **effective population size** ($N_e$) falls below about 30 sexually mature individuals. Aka the Sewell **Wright** effect.

**genetic engineering:** manipulation of genetic material by any of several technologies such as **recombinant DNA**, **transgenic species**, **gene targeting**, **cloning**, and certain **forensic science** applications.

**genetic epidemiology:** study of genetic elements of disease, and a growing methodology for understanding how those elements interact in complex biological systems.

**genetic equilibrium:** state of random distribution of alleles among genotypes; in the absence of selection, migration, mutation, and other evolutionary **mechanism** or force, a population or deme is said to be in equilibrium if both allele and genotype frequencies are found to be in accordance with the predictions of the **Hardy–Weinberg equilibrium** equation.

**genetic female:** individual with a female **karyotype**; in mammals this normally consists of two X sex chromosomes. Cf. **genetic male**.

**genetic fitness:** measure of relative **reproductive success**; the contribution to the next generation of one **genotype** in a population relative to the contributions of other genotypes. When all genotypes contribute equally to the next generation, then the fitness of the genotypes are all equal to 1.00; when genotypes contribute differentially, however, the contribution of the most frequent genotype is assigned a fitness of 1.00, and the relative proportion(s) of the other genotype(s) are assigned values between 0.00 and 1.00, depending upon their contribution(s). See **fitness**.

**genetic genealogy:** use of genetic techniques to reconstruct the past, including the use of **DNA sequences** to reconstruct likely phylogenetic or genealogical relationships among populations. Aka gene genealogy. Cf. **anthropological genetics**.

**genetic goitrous cretinism:** hereditary autosomal disorder that occurs when a defective enzyme(s) fails to convert the amino acid tyrosine into the hormone thyroxine, resulting in physical and mental abnormalities.

**genetic group:** kinship group based on actual, as opposed to perceived, blood relationships; persons who are all related by some degree of common descent. Relatives by marriage or adoption are excluded from such a group. Cf. **kinship group**.

**genetic heterogeneity:** single phenotype that can be caused by any of several different genes or alleles. Cf. **canalization**.

**genetic homeostasis:** natural self-regulating capacity of populations that enables individuals to adapt to variable conditions and environments. See **homeostasis**.

‡ **genetic introgression:** introduction of new genes, alleles or traits recombined into a population from an outside source. See **gene flow**.

**genetic linkage map:** schematic illustration of the order of genes on chromosomes, determined by the estimation of **recombination frequencies**.

**genetic load** (L): a proportion, the relative decrease in the average **fitness** of a population compared with the fitness it would have if all individuals in the population had the genotype with the maximum fitness. Load is due to the accumulation of **deleterious** forms of genes (**alleles**) in a population, sometimes unexpressed because of recessivity, often arising from recurrent **mutations** and carried by individuals who may possess a **lethal gene**, a **semilethal gene**, or a **sublethal gene**. Load(s) may be viewed as consisting of several components, including **mutational load**, **segregational load** (= balanced load), and **substitutional load**. Cf. **lethal equivalent value**.

**genetic male:** individual with a male **karyotype**; in mammals this normally consists of one X and one Y sex chromosome. Cf. **genetic female**.

**genetic mapping:** process during which the locations of genes are determined on specific chromosomes, and distances between linked genes are measured.

**genetic marker:** 1. any phenotypic trait or character controlled by a gene or genes and used in genetic analysis, usually to detect **recombination** events. 2. piece of **DNA** that contains a detectable **polymorphism** that is closely linked to, and therefore almost always inherited with, a disease-causing **gene**, such as the one that causes **Huntington disease.**

**genetic modification** (GM): intentional change in a genome, artificially introduced by humans. See **biotechnology, genetically modified, genetically modified food, genetically modified organism,** and **transgenic species.**

**genetic nomenclature:** designation of genes by symbols. **Mendel** was the first to use capital letters (e.g. A) to represent dominant factors and small letters (e.g. a) to represent recessive factors in gene systems. See **presence and absence hypothesis.**

‡ **genetic polymorphism:** occurrence of two or more **alleles** at a single locus in a **population**, with the frequency of the second most common allele being greater than 1%. The threshold of 1% is not arbitrary and suggests that a **mechanism** or pressure other than **mutation** alone is operating to maintain the elevated **allele frequencies.** Cf. **monomorphic.** See **polymorphism.**

**genetic potential:** maximum expression of a variable that can be attained by a given **genotype.** Some scientists maintain that this is a popular but incorrect concept.

**genetic program:** information inherent in the **DNA** contained within an organism.

**genetic recombination:** any of several mechanisms that shuffle the order or combinations of genes between generations. Typically, the placement of allele copies into linked genotypes (on chromatids or within gametes) that are different from the linkage combinations they belonged to in a previous generation; most commonly results from **crossing over** during meiosis and sexual reproduction with outcrossing.

**genetic regulation:** overall modulation of the type and rate of cellular and developmental processes by controlling specific reactions.

**genetic revolution:** proposal in the 1950s by E. **Mayr** that the **founder effect** results in a loss of **heterozygosity** and **genetic variance** in a small population that would then result in the relatively sudden appearance of a new **species.** The **punctuated equilibrium** model is considered a generalization of this proposal.

**genetic RNA** (gRNA): ribonucleic acid that is the carrier of genetic information in many **viruses.** Genetic RNA may be either single- or double-stranded, and is transcribed into **DNA** by **reverse transcriptase.**

‡ **genetic screening:** method of identifying individuals in a given population at high risk of having or transmitting a specific genetic disorder.

**genetic sex:** sexual constitution as described by **chromosomal sex** and the individual genes of **sex determination** actually located on the **sex chromosomes.**

**genetic theories of aging:** several intracellular, systemic models of aging in which the major premise of each is that any one of several gene-based processes become less efficient over the life of an organism. See the **altered proteins theory of aging,** the **DNA damage and repair theory of aging,** and the **error catastrophe theory of aging,** for example.

**genetic theory of race:** classification of races on the basis of genetic data rather than on morphology. The genetic theory holds that the nature of human variation is not sufficiently clustered to warrant the use of the taxonomic term **race** in humans.

‡ **genetic transcription:** first step in **polypeptide synthesis;** the process of complementary synthesis of **hmRNA,** catalyzed by **enzymes** (**RNA polymerases** and transcriptases), from the genetic information contained in the **template DNA;** precedes **genetic translation;** occurs in the nucleus of a cell. See **cistron, gene,** and **promoter.**

‡ **genetic translation:** second step in **protein synthesis,** following **genetic transcription,** in the process of the synthesis of **polypeptide chains;** consists of the orderly bonding into a chain of appropriate **amino acids,** catalyzed by **enzymes** and **tRNA,** from genetic information carried in **mRNA;** occurs in the **cytoplasm** at the **ribosomes.**

**genetic transplantation:** technique that moves an entire gene from one organism to another.

**genetic variation** (or **variability**): formation of individuals differing in genotype, or the presence of genotypically different individuals; **mutation** is the ultimate source of all **variation.**

**genetic variance** ($V_g$): that proportion of the **total phenotypic variance** of a quantitative character explained by genetic factors that members of a population have in common; a property of a population, not of individuals or of any particular individual. Genetic variance may be subdivided into several components: **additive genetic variance** ($V_{ga}$); dominance genetic variance ($V_{gd}$); epistatic genetic variance ($V_{ge}$); and interactive genetic variance ($V_{gi}$). Cf. **phenotypic variance.**

**genetical theory of social behavior:** see **altruism, mutual aid,** and **inclusive fitness.**

**genetically modified** (GM): pertaining to **genetic modification.** Such **biotechnology** protocols can insert genes harvested from other genomes (via **recombinant DNA**), delete specific genes (see **knockout mutation**), or suppress or enhance specific natural genes. See **genetically modified food**, **genetically modified organism**, and **transgenic species**.

**genetically modified food** (GMF): any agricultural product whose genome has been **genetically modified**. Some products have been deemed 'substantially equivalent' to the natural or previous food product by government food agencies. An example is a genetically modified pest protected (GMPP) plant known as *bt* corn.

**genetically modified organism** (GMO): any organism whose genome has been **genetically modified**. The first patent for a GMO was issued in 1980, for a bacterium that was enhanced to digest certain components of crude oil.

**geneticism:** any form of thinking or philosophy that proposes that behavior is genetically determined, or that psychological processes are genetically determined either in an individual genotype or at the level of species. Associated with F. **Galton** and his followers, with the **eugenics** movement, and more recently with **sociobiology** and **behavioral ecology**.

‡ **genetics:** science of **heredity**, the patterns of resemblance, trait **inheritance**, and **variation** due to gene structure and action; also, genotype–environment interactions. Term coined by **Bateson**. See **Mendelism** and **heritability**.

**genetics, human:** see **human genetics**.

**genetotrophic:** denoting inherited nutritional factors. The term is usually applied to certain hereditary deficiency disorders.

**genioglossal pit:** area between the **mental spines** of the mandible, which serves as a site of attachment for the **genioglossus** (tongue) muscle.

**genioglossus: extrinsic muscle** of the tongue. The genioglossus originates from the mental spines of the **mandible** and inserts into the **hyoid bone** and the inferior portion of the tongue. Its action is to protrude and depress the tongue; it also is responsible for the groove in the tongue that enables infants to grasp a nipple and channel milk to the pharynx. The attachment to the mandible prevents the tongue from moving posteriorly and obstructing breathing.

**geniohyoid:** one of the suprahyoid group of muscles. The geniohyoid originates from the inner surface of the mandibular symphysis and inserts into the body of the **hyoid bone**. Its action is to elevate and protract the hyoid, resulting in a dilation of the pharynx in preparation for receiving food; it also depresses the mandible when the hyoid is fixed.

**genital:** 1. of or pertaining to reproduction or generation. 2. of or pertaining to the organs of reproduction.

**genital display:** behavior in which the genitals are used to communicate. One form is presenting, in which females and subordinate males may turn their hindquarters towards a dominant animal to solicit **copulation** or as **appeasement** behavior. A second form is the male penile display. This threatening behavior is usually performed with an erect penis; in marmosets it is accompanied by urine marking; in some of the guenons, especially vervets, the display is visually enhanced by a bright red penis and bright blue **scrotum**.

**genital swelling:** enlargement of the sex organs in some groups of primates. In females this involves an engorging of blood in the **sexual skin** when they enter **estrus**, serving as a signal to males. In some species, the testes of males swell in size during the breeding season, presumably a sign of increased sperm production. See **sperm competition**.

**genital tubercle:** external swelling on the mid-line of a developing embryo anterior to the tail that begins about the 6th week of development, and initially consists of sexually indifferent tissues: glans, urethral groove, paired urethral folds, and paired labioscrotal swellings. Dependent upon the absence or presence of an **SRY gene**, these homologous structures develop into female or male genitalia, respectively.

**genitalia:** the organs of reproduction, especially the external organs (external genitalia). Aka genitals.

**genitaloid:** pertaining to primordial sex cells before sexuality is morphologically distinguishable.

‡ **genome:** entire genetic material of an organism. The smallest number of **linkage groups** for a **species**, in which all the **genes** of both sexes in a species are represented; in humans this number would be 22 **autosomes** + 1 **X chromosome** + 1 **Y chromosome**, for a total of 24 possible **chromatids**; hence usually one more chromatid than a species' **haploid** complement. Recently, the term also includes extra-chromosomal DNA (e.g. **mtDNA**). Aka the basic or **monoploid** chromatid set. Cf. **chondriome, proteome**, and **transcriptome**.

**genome mutation:** any change that produces a new individual or species with an increased multiple of the haploid number of chromatids (**polyploidy**), or with fewer or more single chromatids than normal (**aneuploidy**). Aka **major chromosome anomaly**.

**genomic formula:** name for the convention of representing the number of species-specific genomes present in a given cell. A **haploid** cell normally contains (1)N genomes, a **diploid** cell contains 2N, a **triploid** cell has 3N, etc.

**genomic imprinting:** non-Mendelian **epigenetic** phenomenon during gametogenesis in which the expression of a gene or chromosome region depends on whether it is inherited from the mother or the father, the **parent-of-origin effect**. Two modes have been proposed to explain the phenomenon: (a) inheritance of two homologous copies of a gene from one parent (**uniparental disomy**); and (b) **DNA methylation** of the allele contributed by one parent, making an offspring effectively **homozygous** for the other parent's allele. The event would be unique in case (a), but reversible and multigenerational in (b). Aka genetic imprinting, parental imprinting. Cf. **female genomic imprinting** and **male genomic imprinting**. See **Haig hypothesis.**

**genomic library:** collection of modified bacteria that among them contain portions of the entire genome of another species.

**genomics:** science pertaining to the whole **genomes** of any of several species, including humans; refers to the sequencing of **DNA**, the identification of genes, the discovery of normal and abnormal gene functions and **mutations**, and interspecific comparisons; can also include **bioinformatics**, the storage and retrieval of such information in computer databases. See **functional genomics.** Cf. **proteomics.**

**genophagy:** archaic term for the alleged replacement of recessive by dominant genes in an entire population. With the advent of population genetics, this notion was replaced by **genetic equilibrium.**

**genosome:** portion of a **chromosome** that contains the genetic material **DNA.**

‡ **genotype:** 1. the combinatorial pair of **alleles** possessed by an individual at a given genetic **locus**, and the cause of a particular **trait** or **disorder**. 2. the sum total of the genetic information at all loci in an individual organism. Cf. **phenotype.**

**genotype–environment interaction:** level of interaction parallel to **epistatic fitness interactions** and **epistatic gene interactions**, and which takes place between genes and their environment.

‡ **genotype frequency:** proportion of a given genotypic class among the total number of individuals or genotypic classes in a **deme**. Aka the genotypic ratio, genotypic proportion.

**genotypic sex determination:** mode of sexual development in which factors present in the **zygote** determine the outcome, as in mammals, in contrast to some plant and reptile forms where the environment plays a more important role.

**genovariation:** see **point mutation.**

**gens:** 1. a distinct evolutionary lineage. 2. an exogamous, unilinear descent group, usually a **patriline**. Cf. **clan.**

**gentle lemur:** one of the vernaculars for the genus *Hapalemur*.

‡ **genus:** 1. in taxonomy, a group of populations sharing homologies such that they are clearly related **species** yet incapable of interbreeding; aka sister species. 2. a taxonomic rank between **family** and **species**. Plural: genera.

*genus et species nova* (*gen. et sp. nov.*) (Latin): new genus and new species.

*genus novum* (*gen. nov.*) (Latin): new genus.

**genu valgum:** angulation of the femur such that the knees are wider apart than the hip joints, as in the **Pongidae**; individuals with this condition are often described as bow-legged.

**genu varum:** angulation of the femur such that the knees are closer together than the hip joints, a condition normally present in all homind genera such as '**Lucy**' as a consequence of **bipedalism**; aka knock-knee.

**geoarchaeology:** investigation of relationships between archaeological and geological processes.

**geocentric theory of the solar system:** old earth-centered proposal that the earth is at the center of motion in the solar system; that the sun as well as the plants, stars and other celestial bodies revolve around the earth. Aka the Ptolemaic theory of the solar system, geocentricity, geocentrism. Cf. **heliocentric theory of the solar system.**

‡ **geochemistry:** chemistry of the earth and the earth's crust.

**geochronology:** term for dating techniques used in geology; establishment of sequences and time scales of the earth's history.

**geochronometry:** 1. quantitative **geochronology**. 2. the measurement of time, in years.

**geofact:** putative 'artifact' produced by natural geophysical processes rather than by cultural activity. See **Calico Hills Early Man Site.**

**Geoffroy Saint-Hilaire, Étienne** (1772–1844): French natural historian; he was a scientist on Bonaparte's Egyptian campaign that resulted in *Description de L'Egypte par la Commission des Sciences* (1802). Geoffroy commenced comparative anatomical studies the following year and attempted to explain the organic unity he saw throughout the natural world in *Philosophie anatomique* (1818–22). He was convinced that **transformism** was a fact demonstrated by both fossils and living specimens. He attempted experimentally to arrest the development of a chick embryo at the 'fish stage' in order to demonstrate the related concept of recapitulation. He was an early friend but (because of his belief in transformism) later was a rival of Cuvier, and corrected Cuvier's 'crocodile', identifying it as a fossil *Teleosaurus*. Geoffroy was blind after 1840 from cataracts, but with Cuvier's brother was able to produce the monumental *Histoire naturelle des mammifères* (1819–42). Geoffroy was convinced that humans and apes shared a common ancestor, published several papers on the orangutan in support of this thesis, and described several other primate species, e.g. *Galago*.

**Geoffroyism:** environmental induction of appropriate, genetically mediated responses. See **Geoffroy's laws.** Cf. **Lamarckism.**

**Geoffroy's laws:** 1. the law of development, which states that no organ arises or disappears suddenly. 2. the law of compensation, which states that no organ grows disproportionately at the expense of another. 3. the law of relative position, which states that the parts and organs of all animals maintain the same relative anatomical position.

**Geoffroy's black-and-white colobus:** vernacular for *Colobus vellerosus.*

**Geoffroy's tamarin:** vernacular for *Saguinus geoffroyi.*

**geographic barrier:** any terrain that interrupts **gene flow.**

**geographic speciation:** see **allopatric speciation.**

**geographic stratigraphic completeness:** proportion of the whole geographic range as represented by certain rocks that contain a given fossil species.

**geographic vicariance:** replacement of populations in different regions by each other.

**geographical distribution:** frequency of occurrence within a natural geographic range or space where a resource or set of resources occurs. In biology and ecology, this often takes the form of a map of the **distribution** of organism(s) relative to other features in a landscape.

**Geographical Information System** (GIS): analytical software that supports the collection, storage and manipulations of a database of spatially referenced data; a central feature of GIS is its query function and display of results as landscapes.

**geographical isolation:** separation of potential interbreeding populations by vicariance or by geographical barriers. Cf. **isolation by distance.**

**geographical race:** population that is geographically separated from other such populations of the same species with which they could interbreed, and that has evolved to the extent that it might be considered a **subspecies** or **incipient species.** Traditional examples of geographical races in humans include African, American Indian, Asian, Australian, European, Indian, Melanesian–Papuan, Micronesian, and Polynesian. Cf. **local race** and **micro-race.**

**geographical variation:** systematic variation within a taxon that is accounted for by changes in variables that are distributed in space.

‡ **geological time scale:** system that organizes the earth's history (estimated to be 4.6 **by**) into natural **eras,** periods and **epochs.** See **absolute geological time** and Appendix 4.

‡ **geology:** 1. science that studies the physical history of the earth, including its rocks, and the changes it is undergoing and has undergone, and the estimated age of past events. 2. geologic features themselves.

**geomagnetic polarity (reversal) time scale** (GPTS): the magnetic histories of rocks and sediments. See **paleomagnetism.**

**geomagnetism:** See **paleomagnetism.**

**geometric scaling:** see **isometric scaling** and **allometry.**

‡ **geomorphology:** changes in the form of the earth's land features, such as rifting, mountain building, the development of erosional ravines and canyons, etc. Adjective: geomorphic.

**gerontomorphosis:** of or pertaining to a morphological trait found most commonly in a mature member of a species.

**geophagy:** consumption of dirt, soil, gravel and small stones, sand, and/or clay; this is not an exclusive dietary category, but serves as a supplement to the main diet and is not detritivory (consumption of detritus and dirt as practiced by earthworms). An animal that does this is called a geophage. Geophagy is known for a number of primate species, including humans. It is well known for cattle and is believed to supply nutrients (primarily minerals) that the individual is missing. Adjectives: Geophagous, geophagic.

**geophyte:** plant having underground buds.

**geosyncline:** fold or trench of sedimentary rock layers that is convex downwards, usually caused by the accumulation of heavy marine deposits over geological time, and that causes sinking of sediments; aka syncline.

**geotype:** geographic subdivision within a species, with variation restricted to a specific location or region.

**geriatrics:** branch of medicine concerned with old age, aging, agism, and the physiology and diseases of the aging process. See **degenerative disease.**

**germ:** 1. a pathogenic microorganism. 2. any embryonic structure capable of developing into a new organism; aka primordium. See **germ cell.**

**germ cell:** 1. any generative **stem cell** that gives rise through **meiosis** to **gametes** rather than through mitosis to somatic cells. 2. a gamete.

**germ cell gene therapy:** see **gametic gene therapy;** aka germline gene therapy.

**germ layer theory:** proposal that a differentiating embryo has distinct structural layers. Proposed by Christian Pander (1794–1865) and Karl Ernst von **Baer.** In its original form there were many more proposed layers than the three **primary germ layers** still recognized by modern biologists (the endoderm, mesoderm, and ectoderm). See **recapitulation theory.**

**germline:** lineage of germ cells ancestral to gametes and reproductive tissues that, during very early **embryogenesis** (at about six weeks in humans), are set aside on the mid-line of the **endoderm** as distinct from **somatic** tissue; **genitaloid** cells. Aka germ line.

**germline genetic engineering:** see **gametic gene therapy**.

**germline theory of antibody diversity:** any of many theories of immune response that propose that antigens choose a pre-existing, complementary antibody and then amplify that antibody, thus producing a specific immune response. First proposed in 1900 by German bacteriologist Paul Ehrlich (1854–1915). Aka multigene hypothesis.

**germ plasm:** 1. today, a general term for **germ cells** in various stages of development, and for the tissues from which these cells arise. 2. in the nineteenth century, the germ-plasm was thought of as a protean, all-encompassing hereditary agent; see **Weismannism**. Cf. **particulate inheritance**.

**germ plasm theory:** idea that acquired characteristics are not inherited by offspring because, as the German cytologist August **Weismann** demonstrated experimentally in 1892, the **germ cells** of each generation are direct descendants of the germ cells of the previous generation. Aka continuity of the germ-plasm, germ line theory. See **Weismannism**.

**germ theory of disease:** proposal attributed to Italian physician Girolamo Fracastoro (1483–1553) that many diseases are caused by transmissible, self-propagating 'seeds', later known popularly as germs and formally as **agents** (such as bacteria and viruses). The theory was supported by experimental evidence in the nineteenth century.

**germinal:** pertaining to, or influencing, **germ cells**.

**germinal choice:** form of positive **eugenics** advocated by H. J. **Muller** and others in which gametes are donated to germ banks (colloquially, sperm banks and egg banks), and from which individuals can select gametes used in **artificial insemination**.

**germinal mutation:** any **mutation** in **germ cells** that can be passed to a future generation; nonsomatic mutation.

**germinal selection:** 1. choice by farmers and husbandrymen of the seed lines and the animal **germ cells** (as in corn and cattle) to be used when producing future generations of domesticated species. 2. the proposal to select human germ lines in the same manner, beyond simple **assortative mating**. 3. selection during gametogenesis against induced mutations.

**germinal vesicle:** diploid nucleus of a primary oöcyte during oogenesis, usually in a state of arrest (**dictyotene stage**) during meiotic prophase. Cf. **seminal vesicle**.

**germinative cells:** undifferentiated cells, usually sequestered in well-defined regions within tissues, that give rise to differentiated, specialized cells of

mature tissues, organs, and subsystems within the body.

**germline gene therapy:** genetic engineering of gametes or a pre-**morula**, after which certain alterations are perpetuated in all the cell lines of an embryo, and are also transmitted to future generations. Aka gametic gene therapy.

**germline theory of antibody diversity:** any of several theories of immune response holding that antigens complement with a pre-existing antibody and amplify that antibody to produce a specific immune response. Aka multigene hypothesis.

**gerodontology:** study of the dentition of the aged. See **odontology**.

**gerontology:** study of medical and social problems associated with aging and longevity.

**gerontomorphic:** having the characteristics of old age. Cf. **pedomorphic**.

**Gerstmann-Straussler–Scheinker disease**(GSSD): rare 'familial' disease thought in the 1980s to exhibit an autosomal dominant mode of inheritance. Onset is typically in the 4th–5th decades. It was noted in cases such as a 'family of sheepherders' who exhibited ataxia, progressive dementia, and absence of lower limb reflexes. Course of the disease is 2–10 years; amyloid plaques are found on autopsy and GSSD was later reclassified as one of the human **transmissible spongiform encephalopathies** (TSEs) similar to **Kuru** and **nvCJD**. Like these other diseases associated with the **prion protein**, GSSD is characterized by certain predisposing genotypes, in this case a proline to leucine substitutional mutation at position 101, as well as valine at positions 117 and 129. Aka Gerstmann-Straussler syndrome (GSS), subacute spongiform encephalopathy, prion dementia.

**Gervais, Paul François Louis** (1816–79): French zoologist, paleoprimatologist, student of Blainville; Gervais re-evaluated his mentor's description of *Pithecus antiquus*, which he re-classified as *Pliopithecus* (Gervais 1849); he also first described *Oreopithecus* (Gervais 1872) and *Plesiadapis* (Gervais 1877).

**Gesher Benot Ya'aqov** (GBY): archaeological site found in 1937, an open-air, waterlogged site located on the shores of paleo-Lake Hula on the bank of the Jordan River in the Dead Sea Rift, northern Israel, dated to 790 kya (Brunhes-Matuyama chron boundary). The site contains basalt **Acheulean** artifacts (with a Kombewan African affinity), and charred flint, seeds and wood, all of which have been interpreted as indicating the presence of hearths and the **controlled use of fire**. Aka Jisr Banat Yacub.

**gestation:** period lasting from conception to birth in an animal that gives birth to live young; consists of the pre-embryonic, embryonic, and fetal stages.

**gestation length:** typical period lasting from conception to birth in a viviparous animal; the gestation length is species-specific.

**gestational age:** current age, counted from the first day of the mother's last normal menstrual period, of an embryo, fetus or delivered baby, usually expressed in weeks. The gestational age is about two weeks longer than the **fertilization age**, and is the age usually provided by a physician.

**gestural language:** language in which the **symbols** containing meaning are communicated by body movements, i.e. by nonvocal means.

**gesture:** sign conveyed by the body; behavior which in certain primates take the form of begging, tree shaking, and chest beating, suggested more by body language than facial expression or vocalization; a form of nonverbal communication. Aka body language.

**GH:** abbreviation for **growth hormone**.

**ghrelin:** so-called 'hunger hormone'; a 28-amino acid protein secreted cyclically by the stomach that acts as a hormone and is involved in the regulation of appetite and energy expenditure. Ghrelin stimulates the pituitary to secrete **human growth hormone** and seems to have an antagonistic relationship with **leptin** in feeding regulation. Ghrelin concentration also influences blood pressure and blood sugar concentration, insulin metabolism, and cardiac efficiency. The gene for ghrelin maps to HSA 3p26–p25. See **orexin(s)**.

**GI tract:** see **gastrointestinal tract**.

**giant anthropoid:** see *Gigantopithecus*.

**giantism:** growth that is the result of abnormal or excessive hGH effects during normal growth phases; hyperpituitarism. Cf. **acromegaly**. Aka gigantism.

‡ **gibbon:** general vernacular for the small **apes** belonging to the genus *Hylobates*.

**Gibraltar:** archaeological site found in 1848 and reworked in 1926–8 at Forbes' Quarry, Gibraltar, dated to about 50 kya (early **Würm**), and that contains **Levallois–Mousterian** artifacts. Hominid remains included an adult female cranium and the 'Devil's Tower child', with a **perikymata**-estimated age of 3 years, which had a 1400 cm³ brain suggestive of a relatively precocious growth pattern. Attributed to *Homo neanderthalensis*. The significance of the find remained unrecognized until it was discovered in a small local museum in 1864, when it was recognized as a Neandertal. Aka Devil's Tower, Gorham's Cave, Forbes' Quarry, Rock-Gun.

**Giemsa stain:** stain made of two dyes that is used to reveal the pattern of **bands** (2) on chromosomes.

**GIFT:** gamete intrafallopian transfer; treatment for infertility during which oöcytes and sperm are placed artificially into a female's fallopian tube. One of the assisted fertilization techniques. Cf. ZIFT.

**gigantism:** see **giantism**.

*Gigantoanthropus* **Weidenreich, 1945:** defunct genus proposed to include the early specimens of *Gigantopithecus* discovered in 1935; the proposal to hominize these specimens was immediately rejected by most authorities.

*Gigantopithecus* **von Koenigswald, 1935:** genus of **hominoids** from the late Miocene into the middle Pleistocene of Asia belonging to the family **Pongidae** (depending on authority; a minority have suggested **hominid** status for this genus); two to three species recognized. Known almost entirely from a large collection of teeth and several large mandibles; the original specimens (and **holotype**) came from Chinese drug stores during the 1930s. This was the largest primate that ever lived, with body size increasing over time; estimated body mass ranges from 190 kg for the earlier species from India and Pakistan (6–9 **mya**) to 270 kg in the later Chinese and Vietnamese species that lived up until 250 000 years ago. Dental formula: 2.1.2.3; small vertical incisors, reduced canines, enormous cheek teeth characterized by very thick enamel set in **convergent dental arcades** in very robust and deep mandibles. Body size, dentition, and mandibular morphology indicates a diet of hard morsels; it has been suggested that the diet was bamboo, but **phytoliths** recovered from the teeth suggest a more varied diet including fruit. The large body size indicates terrestrial habits. Presumed to be descended from a species of *Sivapithecus*. See Appendix 1 for taxonomy.

**Gigantopithecus Cave:** see **Liucheng** and **Kwangsi**.

*Gigantopithecus giganteus* **von Koenigswald, 1935:** large **hominoid** from the late Miocene of South Asia. May be descended from one of the *Sivapithecus* species. *G. bilaspurensis* was proposed in 1969, but has since been referred to *G. giganteus*. See Appendix 1 for taxonomy.

**Gilbert reversed epoch:** long period of geologic time (a **chron**) from 4.4 to 3.4 mya in which the polarity of the earth's magnetic field was for the most part reversed; see **reversed polarity epoch** and **paleomagnetism**.

**Giles, Eugene** (1933–): US physical anthropologist. Giles is best known for his work on the application of human variation to forensic investigations and for his research on the origin and diversity of Melanesian populations. He was one of the founders of the American Board of Forensic Anthropology. In recent years his interest has been in the history of US physical anthropology during the years when Earnest **Hooton** was a dominant force.

**Gilles de la Tourette syndrome** (GTS): multifactorial neurological condition characterized by motor and vocal tics; other behavioral anomalies are common.

Onset in youth, usually in the second decade. Diagnosed individuals often share co-morbidity with autism, obsessive–compulsive disorder, and/or attention deficit disorder. About 10% of **probands** have a family history of the condition; several genes have been implicated. Aka Tourette syndrome (TS).

**Gilgil:** research site located in Kenya where long-term field studies of olive baboons (*Papio* anubis) have been conducted for decades. Primatologists who have conducted field research at this site include: R. S. Harding, B. B. Smuts, S. C. Strum, and F. B. Berkovitch.

**gingiva:** fleshy covering over the mandible and maxilla through which the teeth protrude within the mouth. Adjective: gingival. Aka gums.

**ginglymoidal joint:** see **hinge joint.**

**GIS:** see **Geographical Information System.**

**glabella:** prominence that is the most anterior point of the **mid sagittal** forehead, slightly superior to the nose.

**glabellare:** variable point on the sagittal arc of the frontal bone, just above the **glabella,** and that marks the junction of the glabellar prominence and the curve of the frontal bone.

**glabellar stream:** in humans, the stream of hair that begins at the bridge of the nose. Cf. **crown stream.**

**glabellar torus:** anterior enlargement of the **glabella** that together with the **supraorbital tori** forms a continuous **frontal torus.**

**glabrous:** describes the condition in which the surface, especially the epidermis, is smooth or hairless.

**glacial drift:** deposits of rocky materials transported by glacial ice and dumped by the melting ice on the land surface; see **moraine.** Aka glacial till, boulder clay.

**glacial maximum:** portion of geologic time in which the total area of the earth's surface covered by glaciers greatly exceeded that of the present; during a glacial maximum up to one-third of the earth was covered by ice and the levels of the earth's oceans was >100 m lower than the present sea level. Plural: glacial maxima. Aka glacial period.

**glacial refugium:** see **refugium.**

**glacial relict:** species that flourished during the Pleistocene, found today in isolated pockets and in vastly reduced numbers; **relict species.**

**glacial theory:** nineteenth century idea that extensive glaciers formerly covered much of the Northern Hemisphere, now generally accepted. See **Agassiz.**

‡ **glaciation:** process of accumulation of ice at higher latitudes and elevations on the earth, the combined mass of which causes the formation of **glaciers.** Adjective: glacial. At times during the earth's history glaciers have covered large parts of the earth and have transformed physical environments. Most flora and much of the earth's fauna are not cold-tolerant.

During the tenure of hominids on earth, major glaciations dominated the northern latitudes during the **Pleistocene** epoch; named for Swiss streams, these were the **Donau glaciation, Günz glaciation, Mindel glaciation, Riss glaciation** and **Würm glaciation.**

**glacier:** stream of ice that flows slowly from higher to lower elevations.

**glacio-eustatic:** referring to the process by which water levels rise and fall as glaciers are formed and then melt.

**Gladysvale:** archaeological site found in 1992 in the Transvaal, South Africa, 13 miles east of Sterkfontein; undated (estimated 2.5 **mya**) but contains hominid remains, including two unerupted teeth assigned to *Australopithecus africanus.*

**gland:** organ that produces a specific substance or secretion. Adjective: glandular.

**glans penis:** cap-shaped expansion of the spongy body at the end of the **penis.** See **baculum.**

**glass:** noncrystalline rock that results from the rapid cooling of **magma,** and highly suitable for making **stone tools.**

**glass bead volumetrics:** method of estimating the cranial capacity of either a fossil or a defleshed specimen. Glass beads about 2–3 mm in diameter are poured into the vacant cranium until full, then emptied into a volumetric container such as a graduated glass beaker or cylinder, from which the volume is read from a scale.

**glaucoma, open-angle type 1:** highly heritable condition (98% in **MZ twins**) caused by progressive damage to the eye and optic nerve; results in blindness if left untreated. The damage is due to obstruction of fluid outflow at the angle of the anterior chamber of the eye. The defective gene is *GLC1A,* an autosomal dominant.

**glenohumeral joint:** shoulder joint; **ball-and-socket joint** formed between the **humerus** and the **scapula.** This is the most freely movable joint of the **hominoid** body, permitting **flexion, extension, adduction,** abduction (see **abductor**), **rotation,** and **circumduction.** It is felt that this joint is a result of pressures for arboreal climbing, although **brachiation** is the most honed expression of this adaptation. Aka humeroscapular joint.

**glenoid cavity:** socket on the head of the **scapula** that articulates with the head of the **humerus** and helps to form the **glenohumeral** (shoulder) **joint.** Aka glenoid fossa (archaic).

**gliding joint:** type of **synovial joint** that allows restricted sliding and twisting movements; an example of this type of joint is the articulations in the **metacarpals** and **phalanges.** Aka arthrodial joint.

**global molecular clock:** hypothesis that the rate of evolutionary change in DNA is constant over long periods of geological time, and that local variation in rate average out over such periods. Cf. **local molecular clock**. See **molecular clock**.

**globin:** simple protein constituent of **hemoglobin**.

**globin families:** any of several sets of genes that code for groups of respiratory proteins, including the mammalian myoglobins, haptoglobins, and hemoglobins. See **gene family**.

**globin gene:** any of the genes that code for portions of the **globin families**.

**globulins:** major group of serum proteins consisting of globular **polypeptides** in blood plasma, soluble in salt solutions, and that include **alpha globulins**, **beta globulins**, and **gamma globulins**; found in both plant and animal tissues.

‡ **Gloger's law or rule:** empirical generalization that among **homeotherms** those varieties living in warm and humid regions are more heavily pigmented than those in cool dry regions; pigments are usually black near the equator (see **eumelanin**), red and yellow in hot and dry regions (see **phaeomelanin**), and reduced or absent in cool areas. Aka pigmentation rule.

**glossopetra:** flint arrowheads, so called because of their resemblance to a human tongue; aka 'axes of the fox'.

**glossopharyngeal nerve:** cranial nerve that arises within the **medulla oblongata** and that innervates the tongue and pharynx. Aka cranial nerve IX.

**glottis:** slitlike opening between the vocal cords in the **larynx**.

**glottochronology:** highly controversial calculation of elapsed time since two related languages diverged from their common ancestral language, using a computational method involving the percentage of shared cognates.

**glucagon:** peptide **hormone** secreted by the alpha cells of the islets of Langerhans in the **pancreas** in response to either hypoglycemia and/or stimulation by **acetylcholine**, by some amino acids, or by **growth hormone**; leads to a rise in plasma glucose by stimulation of glycogenolysis in the liver, and stimulates the release of insulin by the pancreatic islets.

**glucocorticoid:** any of several **steroid** hormones (corticosteroids), e.g. **cortisone**, secreted by the **adrenal cortex** and that exert a primary influence on carbohydrate, lipid, and protein metabolism, especially in the liver and muscles. Glucocorticoids also affect muscle tone and the microcirculation, participate in the maintenance of arterial blood pressure, increase gastric secretion, alter connective tissue response to injury, impede cartilage production, inhibit inflammatory, allergic, and immunologic responses,

invoke shrinkage of lymphatic tissue, reduce the number of circulating lymphocytes, and affect the function of the central nervous system. Aka glucocorticosteroids.

‡ **glucose:** simple **monosaccharide** that is broken down by animal cells to release energy for metabolic processes. It is a component of lactose, is produced during photosynthesis, and is one of the essentials of the human diet. Aka blood sugar.

**glucose 6-phosphatase** (G6P): an enzyme responsible for the hydrolysis of glucose 6-phosphate into glucose and inorganic phosphate; present in many tissues. Mutations in G6P can result in one of the **glycogen storage diseases**.

**glucose-6-phosphate dehydrogenase** (G6PD): an enzyme in the hexose monophosphate pathway, the only NADPH-generation process in mature red blood cells, which lack the citric acid cycle. About 325 allelic variants are known.

‡ **glucose-6-phosphate dehydrogenase deficiency** (G6PDD): deficiency of the red cell enzyme **glucose-6-phosphate dehydrogenase** (G6PD), the basis of **favism** (a defect in the B allele), primaquine sensitivity (a defect in the A allele) and some other drug-sensitive hemolytic anemias, anemia and jaundice in the newborn, and hemolytic anemia. Acute hemolytic anemia is precipitated by certain substances such as fava beans, primaquine, aspirin, sulfas, and some 340 other drugs. The defect is any one of 325 known allelic mutations in DNA specifying a low-activity variant G6PD, coded by an X-linked recessive gene. The precipitating substances deplete reduced glutathione (GSH, a component of RBC membranes), and the low-activity G6PD variants cannot restore GSH, resulting in a rapid loss of RBCs, causing anemia. G6PD deficiency may confer resistance to malaria. G6PD deficiency is the most common human enzyme deficiency.

**glucose–galactose malabsorption** (GGM): a cell membrane transport defect characterized by severe diarrhea and dehydration in early infancy; fatal if lactose and sucrose sugars are not removed from the diet and replaced by a fructose-based formula. The defective gene is an autosomal dominant, solute carrier family 5, member 1 (*SCC5A1*, aka *SGLT1*), that normally transports glucose and galactose from the lumen of the small intestine into the intestinal cells. Mutations in *SGLT1* reverse this process, and the unabsorbed sugars draw water from the intestinal cells, causing diarrhea. The double G–G form is rare, only 200 cases diagnosed annually worldwide, but less severe forms (glucose intolerance) affect 10% of the world's population.

**glutamic acid** (Glu): an **amino acid**; one of the twenty building blocks of **proteins**. Glutamic acid is necessary for ammonia production in the kidney.

**glutamine** (Gln): an **amino acid**; one of the twenty building blocks of **proteins**. Found in free form in blood, it yields **glutamic acid** and ammonia on hydrolysis.

**glutathione** (GSH): tripeptide that is a ubiquitous constituent of all cells; several enzymatic reactions utilize glutathione as a co-enzyme. Can act to oxidize **free radicals** caused by **UV radiation**. Glutathione reductase reduces its oxidized form GSSH to GSH, the reduced form. In human skin cells, exposure to UV radiation thus temporarily lowers GSH levels (GSH → GSSH), so permitting increased activity of tyrosinase, which converts **tyrosine** to **DOPA** to dopaquinone and its eventual derivatives, **eumelanin** and **phaeomelanin**, resulting in **tanning**.

**glutathione reductase:** enzyme that catalyzes **glutathione** (GSH) to its reduced form (GSSH). At least three allelic variants exist in human populations.

**gluteal muscles:** three pairs of muscles in humans that are **prime movers** of the thigh and are instrumental in bipedalism; all three have their **origins** on the **pelvis**. See **gluteus maximus, gluteus medius,** and **gluteus minimus.**

**gluten:** insoluble component of plant proteins found in grains such as wheat, rye, oats and barley and that gives dough a sticky texture; consists mainly of the proteins gliadin and glutenin.

**gluten-sensitive enteropathy** (GSE): condition resulting in malabsorption of food in the **gastrointestinal tract**; can usually be controlled by eliminating **gluten** from the diet. Aka celiac disease (in adults), gluten enteropathy, tropical sprue.

**gluteus maximus:** muscle that moves the thigh. The gluteus maximus originates from the sacrum, coccyx, and posterior surface of the **ilium** and inserts into the gluteal tuberosity of the femur and the iliotibial tract, a thick tendinous region of **fascia** that extends down the thigh. Its action is to extend the thigh forcefully, as when returning it from its flexed position during climbing or running (when the thigh is strongly flexed), but is generally inactive during normal walking; largest muscle of the body, In contrast, it is not as well developed in quadrupeds (including chimpanzees).

**gluteus medius:** muscle that moves the thigh. The gluteus medius originates from between the anterior and posterior gluteal lines of the **ilium** and inserts into the **greater trochanter** of the femur. Its action is to abduct and rotate the thigh medially; it also plays an important role, in concert with the gluteus minimus, in stabilizing the **coxal joint** during bipedal locomotion.

**gluteus minimus:** muscle that moves the thigh. The gluteus minimus originates from between the anterior and posterior gluteal lines of the **ilium** and inserts into the **greater trochanter** of the femur. Its action is to abduct and rotate the thigh medially; it also plays an important role, in concert with the gluteus medius, in stabilizing the **coxal joint** during bipedal locomotion. This is the smallest and deepest of the **gluteal muscles**.

**glycine** (Gly): an **amino acid**; one of the twenty building blocks of **proteins**. Found in sugar cane; a neurotransmitter. Aka aminoacetic acid.

**glycogen:** high-molecular-mass, complex polysaccharide composed of subunits of glucose; the form in which carbohydrate is stored in the body, especially in the liver and muscles.

**glycogen storage diseases** (GSDs): group of recessive familial lysosomal storage diseases characterized by abnormal glycogen metabolism. Symptoms involve the liver and muscles. About 10 heritable forms are known (0–IX), e.g. Andersen (IV), Antopol–Danon (IIb), Forbes–Cori (III), Hers (VI), McArdle (V), Pompe (II), Tarui (VII), and Von Gierke (I) disease. Various enzymes in the **glycolysis** pathway are affected. Individually, each is rare; cumulatively, their incidence is roughly 1 : 20 000. See **carbohydrate metabolism**.

**glycogenesis:** glycogen synthesis from carbohydrates.

**glycogenolysis:** breakdown of **glycogen** to **glucose**.

**glycolysis:** multistep process in which sugar is broken down into lactic acid, especially in muscles; the last step occurs anaerobically and is thus aka anaerobic glycolysis. See **carbohydrate metabolism**.

‡ **glycoprotein:** any membrane-bound protein bonded to saccharide (sugar) molecules; conjugated protein. The sugars usually constitute less than 4% of the molecule. Glycoproteins function in cell recognition systems such as those of the human **blood groups** and **immune system** response(s). Examples are the mucins and chondroproteins.

**glyph:** character or figure that is incised or carved in relief.

**GM food:** abbreviation for **genetically modified food**.

**GMO:** abbreviation for **genetically modified organism**.

**gnathic index:** endobasion–prosthion distance divided by endobasion–nasion distance, × 100.

**gnathion** (gn): **craniometric landmark**; most anterior and inferior point of the medial plane of the mandible; also referred to as the menton. See Appendix 7.

**GnRH:** abbreviation for **gonadotropin-releasing hormone**.

**Gobineau, Count Arthur de** (1816–82): French diplomat, historian and orientalist who expanded on the earlier work of Niebuhr on national character; for Gobineau, 'the racial question overshadows all other questions of history, … it holds the key to them all, and … the inequality of the races from whose fusion a people is formed is enough to explain the whole course of its destiny', found in *The Inequality of Human Races* (1853). Gobineau thought that most races were not capable of civilization. The first influential writer concerned with social selection.

**Goeldi's marmoset:** vernacular for *Callimico goeldii*.

‡ **goiter:** abnormal enlargement of the thyroid glands due to a goitrogen. Some soils are iodine-poor but iodine is generally plentiful in many ecosystems. In iodine-poor environments, people often trade for sea salt; iodine is plentiful in the sea and thus abundant in many seafoods and sea salt. Goiterogenic thiocarbamides (thiocyanate compounds) can be produced by digesting vegetables from the cabbage group (cabbage, broccoli, Brussels sprouts, kohlrabi, kale) and, because they inhibit iodine metabolism, can induce the formation of goiter; these compounds cannot be detected by **PTC** nontasters. Iodine is critical to the synthesis of a molecule which provides a negative feedback shunt to the hypothalamus; in its absence, the hypothalamus–pituitary–thyroid pathway remains open, resulting in thyroid hyperplasia. Aka goitre.

**goitrogen:** any substance or product such as soy, millet, or alkaloidal plants such as the cruciferous vegetables (cabbage, broccoli, Brussels sprouts, turnips, and kale) that may cause thyroid enlargement and/or formation of a **goiter**. Specific agents include goitrin, thiouracil, thiocyanate, and isothiocyanate. These chemicals inhibit the formation of **thyroid hormones** and specifically interfere with **iodine** metabolism, causing the **thyroid gland** to enlarge in an effort to produce more of these **hormones**.

**gold-and-black (lion) tamarin:** vernacular for the geographic race *Leontideus rosalia chrysomelas*.

**gold standard:** in biology, any goal where both the quantity and quality of the work have been acknowledged by consensus as sufficient to achieve veracity and to withstand future scrutiny; for example, the gold standard for the **human genome project** was achieved in February 2001 (see Appendix 8) because a minimum of 99% of the human genome was sequenced at least ten times over.

**golden and black-headed lion tamarin:** vernacular for the geographic race *Leontideus rosalia chrysomelas*.

**golden-backed squirrel monkey:** vernacular for *Saimiri ustus*.

**golden (bamboo) lemur:** vernacular for *Hapalemur aureus*.

**golden-cheeked gibbon:** vernacular for *Hylobates gabriellae*.

**golden-headed lion tamarin:** vernacular for the subspecies *Leontideus rosalia chrysomelas*.

**golden langur:** vernacular for *Trachypithecus geei*.

**golden lion tamarin:** vernacular for both the species and subspecies *Leontideus rosalia rosalia*.

**golden marmoset:** vernacular for the subspecies *Callithrix humeralifer chrysoleuca*.

**golden potto:** vernacular for *Arctocebus calabarensis*.

**golden-rumped lion tamarin:** vernacular for the lion tamarin subspecies *Leontideus rosalia chrysopygus*.

**golden snub-nosed langur:** vernacular for *Rhinopithecus roxellanae*.

**golden-white tassel-eared marmoset:** vernacular for *Callithrix chrysoleuca*.

**Goldschmidt, Richard B.** (1878–1958): German evolutionary biologist; working with butterflies in Germany and later at UC Berkeley, Goldschmidt propounded two major theories, both of which were viciously criticized during his lifetime: (a) that **chromosomes**, not genes, are the fundamental units of heredity (now largely discredited); and (b) in *The Material Basis of Evolution* (1940) that **systemic macromutations** produce 'hopeful monsters' that are the basis of at least some new species (an idea resurrected by S. J. **Gould**, and now supported by recent work on **homeotic mutations**). See **saltation**.

**Golgi apparatus:** cytoplasmic organelle consisting of a series of organized, folded membranes and vesicles in the cell that coordinate and store secretory products. Sugars, proteins and lipids are complexed to form starches, glycoproteins and glycolipids. Proteins are folded into their quaternary structures prior to transport. Aka Golgi body or complex.

**Golgi body:** see **Golgi apparatus**.

**Gombe National Park:** research site located in Tanzania where long-term field studies of olive baboons (*Papio anubis*) have been conducted for decades. Primatologists who have conducted field research at this site include C. Packet, L. T. Nash, and T. Ransom.

**Gombe Stream Chimpanzee Reserve:** location in Tanzania on Lake Tanganyika where a field research site was established by Jane **Goodall** in 1960; inhabited by common chimpanzees (*Pan troglodytes*) and red colobus monkeys (*Piliocolobus badius*), the site has been a fertile research center utilized by several generations of field primatologists, including Goodall, T. H. Clutton-Brock, G. Teleki, P. W. Marler, L. T. Nash, B. B. Smuts, J. B. Silk, R. W. Wrangham, C. B. Stanford, R. Jurmain, L. Kilgore, M. E. Morbeck, K. Morris, and D. Riss.

**Gomboré II:** see **Melka Kuntur**.

**gomphosis:** type of fibrous articulation in which a peglike structure is connected to a bony socket; teeth are joined to the jaws by this type of joint, fastened to bone by a periodontal ligament. Plural: gomphoses

**Gona River:** see **Kada Gona**.

**gonad:** organ that produces sex cells; ordinarily, either an **ovary** (female gonad) or **testis** (male gonad).

**gonadal dysgenesis:** see **Turner syndrome**.

**gonadal ridge:** one of a pair of masses that form from the mesonephros in the posterior gut of a developing embryo, and which eventually become the **gonads**.

**gonadal sex:** appearance of maleness or femaleness by examination of the **gonads**. See **anatomical sex**.

**gonadarche:** maturation of the **gonads** (testes or ovaries), resulting in the secretion of **pituitary gonadotropic hormones** (**androgens** or **estrogens**).

**gonadotropic hormones:** see **pituitary gonadotropic hormones**.

**gonadotropin:** any substance having an effect on the gonads; see **pituitary gonadotropic hormones**. Also spelled gonadotrophin.

**gonadotropin-releasing hormone** (GnRH): any **neurohormone** secreted by the **hypothalamus** that regulates the secretion of both **luteinizing hormone** and **follicle stimulating hormone** by the anterior **pituitary gland**. Aka luteinizing-hormone releasing hormone.

‡ **Gondwanaland hypothesis:** proposal that the southern continents broke off from the supercontinent **Pangaea**. Gondwana included present-day South America, Africa, Antarctica, Australia and India; named for a province in India. Cf. **Laurasia**.

**Gongwangling Hill (Lantian 2):** archaeological site found in 1964 in the Chinling Mountains, Lantian County, Shaanxi Province, China, dated to 1.15 mya – 730 kya, and that contains chopping tools, cores and flakes. Hominid remains include a partial primitive cranium of about 780 cm³ attributed to *Sinanthropus lantianensis* (= *Homo erectus*). This is the oldest **erectine** found in China as of 1998. Aka Kungwangling, Lantian 2.

**gonial angle:** see **mandibular angle**.

**gonial cell:** cell in the ovary or testis that divides by mitosis and gives rise to daughter cells destined to undergo meiosis.

**goniocraniometry:** measurement of the angles of the cranium, using **craniometric landmarks** as references.

**goniometer:** **anthropometric** instrument used to measure angles. Its uses vary from measuring angles of the mandible to measuring the range of motion of a joint. Aka arthrometer.

**gonion:** 1. primary sex cell such as an ova or sperm. 2. a craniometric landmark, the point most inferior, posterior, and lateral on the external angle on the mandible.

**gonochorism:** possession in an individual of the gonads of only one sex, in breeding populations composed of both males and females. Adjective: gonochoristic.

**gonosomatic index** (GSI): ratio of total gonad mass to total body mass, expressed as a percentage. The GSI can refer either to an individual or to a population.

**'good genes' hypothesis:** see **handicap principle or theory**. Cf. **runaway selection**.

‡ **Goodall, Jane** (1934–): English-born primatologist and conservationist: After working as an assistant to Louis **Leakey**, Goodall began to **habituate** the chimpanzees at **Gombe Stream Chimpanzee Reserve**, and since 1960 her observations and publications have placed her among the world authorities on chimpanzee **behavior**. Goodall was among the first to document **termiting** behavior and to describe cases of **infanticide** in **pongids**. Author of *In the Shadow of Man* (1971), and *The Chimpanzees of Gombe: Patterns of Behavior* (1986). Awarded the Hubbard Medal in 1955. See R. A. **Hinde**.

**Goodman, Morris** (1925–): US molecular systematist at Wayne State. Since 1960 Goodman has devised means of comparing primate and mammalian **antisera**, using **immunodiffusion**, **electrophoresis**, and then both **amino acid sequence** and **DNA sequence** techniques. From this body of work has emerged a broad picture of phylogenetic relationships, resulting in the shift of primate **systematics** from an emphasis on adaptation to an emphasis on genealogical interpretations, and resulting in a narrowing of the measured genetic distance between humans and apes. An early critic of the **molecular clock**, Goodman was later convinced of the clock's utility by Λ. C. **Wilson's** use of the **relative rate test**.

**goodness-of-fit test:** see **chi-square test**.

**gorget:** perforated artifact made of bone, shell or stone, usually suspended and worn as personal adornment.

*Gorgopithecus major* Broom and Robinson, 1949: **cercopithecine** known from the Pleistocene of South Africa; **monotypic**. Known only from one distorted male cranium and a female maxilla recovered at **Kromdraai**; part of the male specimen remains embedded in matrix. A notable characteristic is lack of **sexual dimorphism**. Estimated body mass around 40 kg. Dental formula: 2.1.2.3/2.1.2.3. See Appendix 1 for taxonomy.

**Gorham's Cave:** see **Gibraltar**.

‡ **gorilla:** vernacular for *Gorilla gorilla*; nomen derived from the Greek term probably borrowed from western Africa meaning gorillas or hairy humans.

*Gorilla* (I. Geoffroy, 1852): currently, a **monotypic hominoid** genus to which the largest living primate, the gorilla, belongs. See *Gorilla gorilla*.

*Gorilla beringei* Matschie, 1903: see *Gorilla gorilla*.

*Gorilla gorilla* (Savage and Wyman, 1847): gorilla; three subspecies currently recognized. **Hominoid** that prefers dense primary and secondary forest and lowland swamp in a discontinuous distribution in western and central Africa. **Sexually dimorphic** in canines, **sagittal crest**, and body mass with females weighing between 70 and 100 kg and males 150–200 kg. Terrestrial; diurnal; shows specialized quadrupedal locomotion called **knuckle-walking**. Dental formula: 2.1.2.3; diet predominantly **frugivory**. Live in small **polygynous** bands containing a mature **silverback** male, several younger males, and several adult females with offspring; males are the resident sex. The three subspecies of this taxon are *Gorilla gorilla gorilla*, the **western lowland gorilla**, *Gorilla gorilla graueri*, the **eastern lowland gorilla**, and *Gorilla gorilla beringei*, the **mountain gorilla**. This taxon is in flux: if *Gorilla beringei* Matschie, 1903 re-emerges as a valid species (as proposed by the IUCN/SSC Primate Specialist Group in 2000), then the two eastern subspecies that would be referred to that taxon would be *Gorilla beringei beringei*, the Virunga and Bwindi mountain gorillas, and *Gorilla beringei graueri*, the eastern lowland or Grauer's gorilla. In the IUCN/ SSC scheme the remaining western subspecies, *Gorilla gorilla gorilla*, would be split into two taxa: *Gorilla gorilla gorilla*, the western lowland gorilla proper, and *Gorilla gorilla diehli*, the **Cross River gorilla**. See Appendix 2 for taxonomy, Appendix 3 for living species. See also box below.

---

**Possible subspecies of the genus *Gorilla***

**Bwindi mountain gorilla:** vernacular for *Gorilla gorilla beringei* (or *Gorilla beringei beringei*). See mountain gorilla.

**Cross River gorilla:** vernacular for (taxon pending) *Gorilla gorilla diehli*. Population census size: *c.* 200 gorillas found in five small populations in Nigeria.

**eastern lowland gorilla:** vernacular for *Gorilla gorilla graueri* (or *Gorilla beringei graueri*). Population census size: *c.* 17,000 gorillas found only in the Democratic Republic of Congo (formerly Zaire). Aka Grauer's gorilla.

**mountain gorilla:** vernacular for *Gorilla gorilla beringei* (or *Gorilla beringei beringei*). Population census size: *c.* 600 gorillas found in two populations: (1) the Virunga Volcanos of Rwanda, Uganda, and the Democratic Republic of Congo, and (2) the Bwindi Impenetrable National Park, Uganda. There is a possibility that the Virunga and Bwindi populations might be distinguished at the subspecific level in the future.

**Virunga mountain gorilla:** vernacular for *Gorilla gorilla beringei* (or *Gorilla beringei beringei*). See **mountain gorilla**.

**western lowland gorilla:** vernacular for *Gorilla gorilla gorilla*. Population census size: *c.* 110,000 gorillas found in Gabon, the Democratic Republic of Congo, Congo, Cameroon, Equatorial Guinea, and Central African Republic.

---

**Gorillina:** nomen for a subtribe of the tribe **Hominini** used in some taxonomic schemes; this subtribe consists of *Gorilla gorilla* and its subspecies.

**Gorillinae:** subfamily of either the **Pongidae** or **Hominidae**, depending on author; this is an alternative classification used by some and consists of *Gorilla gorilla* and its subspecies and, as used by some authors, *Pan* and its species and subspecies.

**Gorillini:** nomen for a tribe of the subfamily Homininae used in some taxonomic schemes; this tribe consists of *Gorilla gorilla* and its subspecies.

**Gorontalo macaque:** vernacular for *Macaca nigra* (= *nigrescens*).

**Göttweiger interstadial:** period between the glacial episodes known as Würm I and Würm II; aka Göttweig.

‡ **Gould, Stephen Jay** (1941–2002): US zoologist, paleontologist, historian and writer at Harvard; controversial but heuristic author of works that discussed **recapitulation theory** (*Ontogeny and Phylogeny*, 1977), **mass extinction** *vs.* **natural selection** (*Wonderful Life*, 1990), and **punctuated equilibrium**. His speculative columns in *Natural History* have been reprinted under several titles. Among his most lasting works is *The Mismeasure of Man* (1981) in which he criticized racial **craniometry** and **psychometry**. His final work was *The Structure of Evolutionary Theory* (2002).

**gout:** X-linked recessive genetic condition characterized by inflamed and arthritic pain caused by deposits of sandy uric acid in the joints and kidneys. First described about 400 BCE; the etiology (excess uric acid) was identified in 1848.

**Graafian follicle:** round, fluid-filled vesicle in the mammalian ovary; each follicle contains an **oöcyte**. Aka primordial follicle.

**graben:** in geology, a fault trough.

**gracile:** relatively small-boned, slender or delicately built. Used in reference to the smaller of the **australopithecine** species or to any small individual. Cf. **robust**.

‡ **gracile australopithecine:** hominid with small back teeth, face and body, as compared with the larger, more **robust australopithecine** species (see ***Paranthropus***). Gracile australopithecines lived in Africa between about 4 and 2 million years ago. Like the robust forms, the gracile forms were not highly **encephalized**, possessing an average cranial capacity of about 450 cm³ and relatively small body masses of 34–45 kg (75–100 lb).

**grade:** 1. a unit of biological improvement from an evolutionary point of view comprising a group of individuals, populations, or species similar in their level of organization, but not necessarily a clade. Primates are usually graded, for example, into prosimians, tarsiers, monkeys, apes, and humans. 2. an evolutionary level of development in a particular structure, physiological process, or behavior occupied by a species or group of species.

**graded signal:** display that is variable with intermediate levels and can vary in intensity, frequency, or both. For example, in rhesus monkeys a stare is a low-intensity aggressive display, which may be increased with an open-mouth threat, ground slapping, growls, head bobs, etc. Aka analog signal. Cf. **discrete signal**.

**gradient:** 1. rate of change of a variable in space. 2. a character gradient, i.e. directions that are perpendicular to (iso-)**clines**; path of maximum change in space.

**grades:** see **anatomical grade scale**.

**gradistic classification:** classification in which organisms are grouped according to **grade** or level of organization rather than according to ancestry or phylogeny; carnivores (lions, hunting dogs, and some primates), for example, could be lumped into the same grade.

**gradual speciation:** splitting of demes into reproductively isolated populations for a time sufficient to establish a reproductive barrier; generally synonymous with **phyletic gradualism**.

‡ **gradualism:** see **phyletic gradualism**.

***Graecopithecus freybergi* von Koenigswald, 1972:** **monotypic** genus of **hominoids** from the late Miocene (12–8 **mya**) of Greece, belonging to the subfamily **Pongidae**; known from teeth, jaws, and a facial skeleton. Estimated body mass around 70 kg. Dental formula: 2.1.2.3; small vertical incisors, reduced canines, thick cap of enamel on the cheek teeth. Dentition suggests a diet of hard gritty morsels. It appears to have inhabited open woodland and grassland environments. This species was originally referred to ***Sivapithecus meteai***; recently some workers have suggested that it is allied with the African apes and hominids. See Appendix 1 for taxonomy.

**graft:** transfer of a part of an organism to another location, or to another organism.

**graft-versus-host disease:** serious condition that sometimes develops when cells in transplanted bone marrow attacks the recipient's body.

‡ **gram calorie** (cal, c): the amount of energy required to heat one gram (cubic millimeter) of water by one degree Celsius, from 14.5° to 15.5 °C, at one atmosphere. Aka small calorie. Cf. **kilocalorie**.

**graminivory:** dietary category reflecting a specialization on the plant subfamily Gramineae, i.e. grasses. Sometimes occurs with **granivory**. Among primates, baboons (***Papio***) are considered graminivores, as are gentle lemurs (***Hapalemur***), who eat bamboo, a type of tropical grass. 'Gramnivore' is a term often incorrectly used to describe an animal that eats grasses or seeds. Cf. **granivory**. See also **diet**.

**Gran Dolina:** archaeological cave site in the Sierra de Atapuerca, Burgos, Spain, found in the nineteenth century by railroad construction workers. Recent excavations begun in 1976 date the site to perhaps 780 **kya**; it contains pre-Acheulean pebble and chopper tools and the remains of at least four archaic individuals assigned to either *Homo heidelbergensis* or *Homo antecessor*. These individuals, especially a child, are described as having the faces of **AMHs** but the brows of **Neandertals**. One incomplete skull has a 'possible' cranial capacity >1000 cm³. The majority of the remains are from the so-called Aurora Stratum, aka TD6. Aka **Atapuerca, Trinchera del Ferrocarril sites**, Trinchera Dolina (TD), 'Big Sinkhole'. See **Sima de los Huesos**.

**Grande Coupure:** massive extinction and/or replacement event during the late **Eocene epoch** (*c*. 38 mya) during an episode of global cooling and sea level regression, at which time opportunites for intercontinental migration resulted in the replacement of European **fauna** with fauna from North America and Southeast Asia. The catarrhine **primates** adapted to the new conditions and radiated into several new lineages; several prosimian species became extinct.

**Grand Design:** see **argument from design** and **Paley's watchmaker argument**.

**Grande Grotte:** archaeological cave site found in 1999, in **Arcy-sur-Cure**, Burgundy, France, dated to 28 **kya**, and that contains red-ochre-based painting of mammoths. Aka Arcy-sur-Cure.

**grandmother hypothesis:** proposal by K. Hawkes that grandparental investment reduces **parent-offspring conflict** (and reproductive competition) and makes a significant contribution to longevity and long-term survival by nurturing not only one's own offspring but grandchildren as well. Specifically, researchers have argued that human females experience **menopause** to be free from their own childbearing to care for grandchildren, and that nurturing behavior and human longevity evolved together. Other researchers, using fossil data, have suggested that increased human longevity occured about 32 kya. Aka stopping-early hypothesis, grandmothering. See **inclusive fitness.**

**grandorder:** taxonomic level above the **order** that consists of several orders of animals presumed to be closely related. The grandorder relevant to the study of primate and human evolution is the grandorder **Archonta,** which includes the orders **Dermoptera, Chiroptera, Scandentia,** and **Primates.** Aka **cohort** by some workers.

**granivory:** dietary category applied to animals (known as granivores) that predominantly consume seeds during the year or during a particular season. Among the primates, patas monkeys (**Erythrocebus**) and black colobus monkeys (**Colobus** *satanus*) are considered granivores. See **diet.**

**granulocyte:** one of three types of **leukocyte** that contain a multilobed nucleus and distinct cytoplasmic granules that stain to particular dyes; granulocytes constitute about 70% of all leukocytes. Aka granular leukocyte, polymorph, polymorphonuclear leukocyte. See **basophil, eosinophil, neutrophil.**

**grasp climbing and leaping:** see **grasp leaping** and **quadrumanual locomotion.**

**grasp leaping:** hypothesized form of locomotion of the ancestral prosimians in which the animal jumped from branch to branch, anchoring itself with its hindfoot. This behavior was selected for and led to the superior grasping abilities in the primate line. Aka grasp climbing and leaping: see **quadrumanual locomotion.**

**grasp-leaping hypothesis:** model of **primate origins** proposed by Szalay *et al.* in which grasping and leaping modes of locomotion evolved simultaneously in early primates.

**grassland:** see **savanna.**

**grattoir:** flaked planing tool or endscraper; plane. Variations include grattoir à bec, a beaked scraper, and grattoir caréné, an oblong keeled endscraper found at **Aurignacian** sites.

**Grauer's gorilla:** see *Gorilla gorilla.*

**grave:** site at which a deceased person is placed. They vary greatly in shape, depth and the position of the bodies within the site. See **burial.**

**grave goods:** weapons, food, adornments, or other materials buried with a deceased person. Grave goods are usually interpreted as indicative of social status.

**graver:** stone tool with a protruding edge used for fine cutting or shaving, similar in function to a modern chisel.

**gravette point:** small blade with either a square or pointed tip, and with a blunted back nearly parallel to the sharp edge. Aka gravette.

‡ **Gravettian tool tradition: Upper Paleolithic** stone tool assemblage in Europe, dated to around 27 kya.

**gravid:** pregnant; swollen by fertilized eggs or young; from the (Latin) prefix meaning 1. weight, heavy, serious. 2. pregnancy.

**Gray, Asa** (1810–88): US botanist, Professor at Harvard, 1842–72. First met **Darwin** on visit to Kew Gardens in the 1850s, and later became a friend and supporter of a soft version of Darwin's ideas, i.e. Gray accepted natural selection as a mundane principle secondary to Design. Gray was the only individual known to have received correspondence detailing Darwin's ideas prior to 1858, in the famous letter of September 1857. Author of *Manual of Botany* (1848) and *Darwiniana* (1876).

**gray-backed sportive lemur:** vernacular for *Lepilemur dorsalis.*

**gray-cheeked mangabey:** vernacular for *Lophocebus albigena.*

**gray lemur:** vernacular for *Hapalemur griseus.*

**gray matter:** outermost layer of the **cerebral cortex** of the **cerebrum** of the brain; nonmyelinated nerve tissue.

*Gray's Anatomy:* name by which *Anatomy, descriptive and surgical* by Henry Gray is best known. First published in 1858, it is frequently updated, still in print and is a standard reference work in gross human anatomy for physicians, anatomists, and physical anthropologists. It contains over 200 original illustrations.

**Gray's Inn:** construction site in London where in 1690 workmen found early artifacts including a **coup-de-poing,** believed at that time to be a tool of Roman origin.

**grazers:** animals such as antelopes, horses, cows. etc., that ingest food primarily by grazing. Owing to their predominantly $C_4$ **vegetation** consumption, grazers have an increased $\delta^{13}C$ ratio ($^{13}C : {}^{12}C$) ratio. Aka $C_4$ **consumers.** See **carbon isotope analysis.**

**great apes:** general vernacular for the large-bodied ape genera, *Pongo, Gorilla,* and *Pan.*

**Great Chain of Being:** Aristotelian to sixteenth century view of the world as consisting of a graded hierarchy of entities with lowest living forms at the bottom, animals at the next higher scale, humans in the middle, various angels at the second highest level, and with a Supreme Being at the top. See *Scala Naturae.*

**Great Ice Age:** see **Pleistocene epoch.**

**Great Rift Valley:** see **Rift Valley system.**

**greater bamboo lemur:** vernacular for *Hapalemur simus*.

**greater multangular (carpal bone):** see **trapezium**.

**greater palatine foramen:** opening in the posterior portion of the **palatine bone** through which the palatine blood vessels and nerves pass.

**greater pelvis:** broad portion of the **pelvis** that is superior to the **pelvic inlet**. This part of the pelvis helps to support the abdominal organs. Aka false pelvis.

**greater sciatic notch:** deep indentation in the posterior **ilium** of the **coxal bone** inferior to the **posterior inferior iliac spine** through which several nerves, including the thick sciatic nerve, and blood vessels pass to enter the upper leg.

**greater trochanter:** larger of the two large processes on the proximal **femur**; the greater trochanter is on the lateral side and is superior to the **lesser trochanter**; serves as a site for the attachment of the **gluteus maximus** and **gluteus medius** muscles.

**greater tubercle (of the humerus):** process on the lateral side of the proximal portion of the **humerus**; the muscles that help move the upper limb insert into this structure.

**greenbeard effect (or alleles):** argument by W. D. **Hamilton** that individuals are able to recognize kin because of the presence of **alleles** that serve for recognition among closely related animals. These alleles express themselves in the **phenotype** and enable possessors to recognize others who also bear these alleles; this elicits altruistic behavior towards recognized kin members. This term was coined by Richard **Dawkins**. Many workers consider this phenomenon to be unlikely, but see the **Haig hypothesis**.

**green fluorescent protein gene** (GFP): gene that produces a glowing product. A GFP gene obtained from a jellyfish was inserted into the sperm that fathered the first transgenic primate, ANDi, late in 2000. Similar genes have been obtained from other sources, such as fireflies; see **luciferase**.

**green monkey:** vernacular for *Chlorocebus aethiops sabaeus*.

**greenhouse effect:** trapping of excess heat in the earth's atmosphere by carbon dioxide, which serves as a reflector, re-radiating heat back toward the surface. Aka greenhouse model.

**greeting:** primate behavior that occurs when animals meet after an absence and acknowledge one another's presence; greetings vary from species to species, but may include an eyebrow raise, an aggressive display, and other postures and gestures. In chimpanzees it may end with hand-holding.

**gregarious:** describes animals that regularly live and interact in social groups. Used in reference to primate species that are social, i.e. the **anthropoids**, but

applied to only a limited number of **prosimian** species. Contrasts with solitary behavior, or **noyau**.

**Gregory, William King** (1876-1970): US anatomist and paleontologist at the American Museum of Natural History. An early supporter of the idea that humans are closely related to the African apes, based on comparative dental evidence; was one of the first to support **Dart's** interpretation of the **Taung child** but also supported G.E. Lewis' interpretation of *Ramapithecus* as a hominid. Author of *Man's Place Among the Anthropoids* (1934); president of the **AAPA** (1941–3); 4th Viking Fund medallist (1949).

**Greig cephalospondyly syndrome** (GCPS): heritable, autosomal dominant condition characterized by polydactyly, fused toes and fingers, large thumbs, a broad nose and large head, abnormalities of the liver, skin, and heart, and developmental delays.

**Greulich–Pyle method:** one of several techniques for the estimation of **skeletal age** that utilizes radiographs of various growth centers such as the ossification centers of the wrist, the epiphyses of long bones, and sutures of the cranium. Cf. **Tanner–Whitehouse method**.

**grid system:** two-dimensional intersecting network superimposed on a site, defining the squares in which archaeologists dig, usually laid out with strings, stakes and a transit.

**grimace:** see **fear grin**.

**Grimaldi:** archaeological site found in 1872 near the French frontier in Grimaldi-Menton, Italy, undated, and that contains Upper Paleolithic artifacts (Aurignacian or Gravettian) and hominid remains including two deliberate burials, the use of red ochre, and attendant shell beads, ornaments, and other artifacts. The features of the flexed skeletons — a young male and an old female — have been regarded as negroid. Aka Grotte des Enfants, Baoussé Roussé Cave, Grimaldi Man and Mentone Man. One of seven caves found at this location. See **Venus figurines**.

**grinding stone:** lithic tool for processing plant foods, and made by abrasion with a harder material. Grinding tools were developed in the latest Paleolithic times.

**grip:** see **precision grip, power grip**.

***Griphopithecus* Abel, 1902:** poorly known genus of **hominoid** from the middle Miocene of Austria and Turkey, belonging to the subfamily **Dryopithecinae**; three species described. Estimated body mass between 25 and 50 kg. Dental formula: 2.1.2.3; thick cap of enamel on cheek teeth suggests a diet of hard fruit and nuts. See Appendix 1 for taxonomy.

**grivet:** one of the vernaculars for *Chlorocebus aethiops*.

**grizzled:** describes **pelage** colors that, when closely examined, are formed by admixtures of different colored hairs.

**gRNA:** abbreviation for **genetic RNA**.

‡ **grooming:** cleaning of the body surface by licking, biting, picking with fingers or claws, or other kinds of tactile manipulation. Among **primates**, grooming serves as a form of **communication** that soothes and provides reassurance. See **allogrooming** and **phthiriophagy**.

**grooming claw:** claw present on the second digit of the hind foot of **prosimians**; in tarsiers both the second and third digits house grooming claws. The claw is used for scratching; Aka toilet claw.

**gross anatomy:** anatomy of structures visible without instrumentation.

‡ **gross ecological efficiency:** percentage of energy transfer from one trophic level to the next higher level.

**gross primary production** (GPP): 1. the total amount of energy captured by green plants; AKA gross primary productivity. 2. amount of organic material produced by autotrophs (or producers) over a given period in a specific area.

‡ **gross productivity:** rate at which organic material is assimilated by an individual, population, or trophic level over a given period in a specific area; aka gross production.

**Grotte de Coupe Gorge:** see **Montmaurin**.

**Grotte des Contrabandiers:** see **Smuggler's Cave**, Témara.

**Grotte des Enfants:** see **Grimaldi**.

**Grotte du Lazaret:** see **Lazaret**.

**ground-penetrating radar:** remote sensing technique that detects buried discontinuities by interpreting the echo from a radar pulse.

**groundwater:** water contained in the void space within rocks, and usually taken to mean rainwater or other surface sources (meteoric water), water formed in **magma** (juvenile water), or old water trapped during original **sedimentation** (connate water). Groundwater may contain elements in **solution** (1, 2) with the potential to contribute to **permineralization** and **diagenesis**.

**group:** 1. any set of organisms belonging to the same species that remain together for a time while interactive with one another to a distinctly greater degree than with other conspecific organisms. See **foraging group pattern**. 2. in behavior, a number of animals that associate and interact with one another, remaining together separate from other such **conspecific** units or remaining together within a larger unit (technically as a subgroup); the composition of a group is known. See **party**.

**group cohesion:** stable association of adult animals and their offspring in a social unit. Cohesion is usually maintained by certain behaviors such as vocalizations, appeasement behavior, and a set of rules that strengthen the bond between group members and restrain disruptive behavior and aggression.

**group effect:** referring to the benefits of communal living such as added defense against predators (more eyes and teeth), reproductive synchronization and proximity to potential mates, collective foraging, etc.

**group effect signal:** alteration of behavior or physiology within a species brought about by signals that are directed in either space or time. An example would be social facilitation, in which there is an increase of activity due merely to the sight or sound coming from other individuals engaged in the same activity. Aka **group effect**.

**group predation:** hunting and retrieving of living prey by **groups** of cooperating animals.

**group selection:** mode of differential reproduction or mortality in which features are selected for the benefit of the **group** rather than for that of the individual. Cf. **kin selection**, **group selection**, and **group selection fallacy**.

**group selection fallacy:** proposal that natural selection acts at the level of groups, such as species; usually associated with the works of V. C. Wynne-Edwards. Most biologists accept that selection acts on variation among individuals.

**group selection theory:** differential reproduction of groups; any process — such as **competition**, the effects of **disease**, or the ability to reproduce — that operates on two or more members of a lineage group as a unit, and that results in one group of individuals leaving more descendants than another group; broadly, group selection includes aspects of both **kin selection** and **interdemic selection**. Not widely accepted.

**group size:** number of individuals that comprise a social unit.

**group transfer:** see **intergroup transfer**.

‡ **growth:** process of increasing the size of cells (**hypertrophy**) during **ontogeny**; any quantitative increase in size or mass. Cf. **development**.

**growth allometry:** relationship between size and shape during the growth (**ontogeny**) of an individual organism. See **allometry**.

**growth analogy:** mode of evolutionary thought that likens the evolution of cultures to the birth–growth–maturity–death cycle of organisms; very pervasive in Western thought; unacceptable to anthropologists because cultures are not organisms and because culture change does not have an inherent direction.

**growth and development:** see **growth and development**; also, a subdivision within any academic discipline that studies either or both of these phenomena.

**growth arrest lines:** see **Harris lines**.

**growth curve:** line that describes changes over time in a growing tissue, organ, individual, or population. See **logistic growth curve**.

**growth diet:** high-quality food that provides enough nutrients to sustain the individual plus energy that can be converted into offspring.

**growth disease:** any condition that interferes with the normal increase in size of an organism; state of arrest or enhancement of the process of growth. See **dwarfism, giantism, acromegaly,** and **endocrine disorder**.

**growth factor:** any of many naturally occuring, complex protein-based **hormones** and other substances that promote growth of specific types of cell; such factors may be generated in a wide variety of tissues and achieve growth effects both independently and interactively with similar factors. Stimulants of mitosis and cellular differentiation. See **growth hormone** and **insulin-like growth factor**. Abnormalities in growth factors may be involved in benign and malignant **neoplasia**.

**growth hormone:** 1. any of several related **hormones** secreted episodically by the **adenohypophysis** that regulate mitotic activity and growth of body cells, and that also affect protein, carbohydrate, and lipid metabolism and control the rate of skeletal and visceral growth; an example is **human growth hormone**. Their secretion is controlled in part by the **hypothalamus**. Aka somatotropin, somatotrophin, somatotropic hormone, somatotrophic hormone. 2. any substance that stimulates growth, such as a growth factor, e.g. **insulin-like growth factor**.

**growth hormone inhibiting factor** (GHIF): polypeptide secreted by the hypothalamus and which inhibits the release of **human growth hormone** (hGH). **Somatostatin** modulates the effects of GHIF. **hGH** is stimulated by the **growth hormone releasing hormone**.

**growth hormone releasing hormone** (GHRH): hormone produced by the hypothalamus that stimulates the secretion of **human growth hormone** (hGH); aka somatocrinin. hGH is inhibited by **growth hormone inhibiting factor**.

**growth plate region:** site of formation of bone tissue in a growing long bone. The growth plate consists of highly ordered rows of cartilage cells; the row farthest removed from the bony shaft is a **germinative cell** layer, and is responsible for cell replication and cartilage growth at the bone shaft. Over time the **cartilage** will be reformed into true **bone** tissue. Cf. **epiphyseal disk**.

**growth rate:** generic term for the speed or velocity at which a particular organ or feature increases in size. There is no single growth rate, but growth rates for specific organs or regions of the body. See **adolescent growth spurt**.

**growth standard or reference:** well established set of data that is used as a reference for evaluating growth.

**growth suppression model:** hypothesis that human children are small-for-age compared with other primates. In this model, human children are regarded as growth-suppressed, and the **adolescent growth spurt** in **AMHs** represents a period of **catch-up growth**. This pattern of growth has been interpreted as having two advantages over other primates: (1) as channeling energy into other metabolic and behavioral activities (such as brain growth and learning); and (2) as eliciting parental care (rather than competition) from adults, thus prolonging childhood without altering the timing of subsequent life stages. The tall stature of the **Nariokotome** youth (*Homo erectus*) has been interpreted as possible evidence that the distinctly human pattern of suppression–spurt had not yet evolved.

**Grundstock:** hypothetical non-Mendelian form of inheritance of anatomical structures, located either in the cytoplasm or throughout the cell, described as supramutational and requiring macroevolutionary forces to implement.

‡ **guanine** (G): one of the two **purine nucleosides** found in **DNA** and **RNA**, composed of two carbon–nitrogen rings.

**guardhair:** see **awn**.

**guarding behavior:** protection of individuals in a **group**; this may be evident in a situation where an adult picks up an infant in a threatening situation. See **mate guarding**.

**Guatemalan howler:** vernacular for *Alouatta pigra*.

**Guattari Cave:** archaeological site found in 1939 on the Tyhhrenian coast of western Italy, dated to 76–44 **kya**, and that contains **Mousterian** (Pontinian) artifacts. Fragmentary hominid remains were assigned to *Homo neanderthalensis*, and were reportedly found in a circle of stones, but some suggest that this is more likely a hyena collection site. Grotta Guattari is located in the **Monte Circeo** cave complex.

**gubernaculum:** primordial structure in the developing fetus that, in males, shortens and pulls the **spermatic cord** during the **descent of the testes**.

**guenon:** general vernacular for African **cercopithecine** monkeys of the genera *Cercopithecus*, *Allenopithecus*, *Miopithecus*, *Chlorocebus*, and *Erythrocebus*.

**guereza:** specific vernacular for *Colobus guereza*. Guereza is sometimes used to refer to a group of three colobine monkeys that also includes *C. polykomos* and *C. angolensis*.

**guevedoces:** Spanish slang for **pseudohermaphroditism, male.**

**Guianan saki:** vernacular for *Pithecia pithecia*.

**guide species:** see **index species.**

**guild:** set of species with similar requirements and foraging strategies.

**Guinea baboon:** vernacular for *Papio papio*.

**gum:** 1. a plant exudate. 2. see **gingiva.**

**gummivory:** dietary category applied to animals (gummivores) that consume predominantly plant exudates (gums) during the year or during a particular season. Alternative spellings in the literature include gumivory, gumnivory, and guminivory. Primates that are gummivores, at least part of the year, include bushbabies (*Galago, Galagoides, Otolemur*) and marmosets (*Callithrix*). See **diet.**

**Günz glacial maximum:** first major glacial episode (= earliest) in the **Alpine glacial sequence,** which lasted from more than 700+ **kya** until about 450 kya; often divided into two peaks, Günz I and Günz II. See **Mindel, Riss** and **Würm** glacial maxima, and **Günz–Mindel** (Cromerian), **Mindel–Riss** (Holstein), and **Riss–Würm** interglacials (or interstadials).

‡ **Günz glaciation:** one of the four traditional periods of glaciation or ice ages that define the Pleistocene epoch during the past 1.8 million years. The first stage in the Quaternary sequence of the Alpine region, the Günz had a duration of about 100 ky and reached a maximum about 1.0 mya.

**Günz–Mindel interglacial:** first major interglacial episode (= earliest) in the **Alpine glacial sequence** of the Pleistocene, which lasted from more than 450+ kya until about 800 kya. See **Günz, Mindel, Riss** and **Würm** glacial maxima, and **Mindel–Riss** (Holstein) and **Riss–Würm** interglacials (or interstadials). Aka Cromerian, Aftonian.

**gut:** gastrointestinal tract or a portion thereof; generally used in reference to the embryonic digestive tube, consisting of the foregut, mid-gut, and hindgut. Cf. **large gut** and **hindgut fermenter.**

**gut morphology:** shape of the digestive tract; see **mouth, pharynx, esophagus, stomach, intestine,** and **anus.**

**GVHD:** see **graft-versus-host disease.**

**gymnogenous:** naked at birth; from the (Greek) prefix meaning naked, bare, exposed.

**gymnosperm:** vernacular for any plant having its seeds exposed (seeds not enclosed in an ovary) and that does not flower (conifers, cycads, ginkgos, etc.). These primitive plants have a fossil record that dates to the **Carboniferous period.** See **coniferous.** Cf. **angiosperm.**

**gynandrism:** congenital defect marked by overdevelopment of the **clitoris** and fusion of the **labia majora,** and having the appearance of a **penis** and **scrotum.**

**gynandromorph:** individual with both female and male characteristics; gynandromorphous person.

**gynandromorphic component:** extent to which a body resembles a person of the opposite sex, rated on a seven-point scale according to **Sheldon.**

**gynecomastia:** excessive development of the male breast.

**gynetype:** in taxonomy, a **type specimen** that is a female. Cf. **androtype.**

**gynocentric:** female-centered; viewed from the perspective of the female sex. Cf. **androcentric.**

**gynocentric models of evolution:** female-centered models in paleoanthropology, which include 'woman the gatherer' model. Cf. **androcentric models of evolution.**

**gyrus:** convoluted elevation or ridge; from gyr(o)-, the Greek prefix meaning ring or circle.

**H:** abbreviation for (1) **heterozygosity**; (2) **Holzinger's *H***; (3) heritability (broad sense).

**H$_0$:** abbreviation for **null hypothesis**.

**$h^2$:** abbreviation for heritability (narrow sense). Cf. *e$^2$.*

**H$_A$:** abbreviation for **alternative hypothesis**.

**ha:** see **hectare**.

‡ **habiline:** vernacular for certain **encephalized, bipedal fossil hominids** that first appeared in Africa about 2 **mya**. Although they lived at the same time as several species of **australopithecine** and have many characteristics in common, habilines are distinguished as relatively larger-brained, with an intermediate average **cranial capacity** of 630 cm$^3$, about one-third larger than australopithecines and almost half that of **AMHs**. See *Homo habilis*.

**habitable spaces:** environments that are suitable for colonization or habitation. Such spaces are occupied and sometimes shaped by organisms; humans often use **tools** to reshape, build, and manipulate unsuitable environments, thus creating habitable spaces, dwellings, communities, etc.

‡ **habitat:** natural place within a **biotope** inhabited by a particular population, **species**, or group of species; habitation. See **habitable spaces**.

**habitat degradation:** loss of biological diversity within a **habitat**.

**habitat fragmentation:** process in which a large continuous area of **habitat** is reduced in size and divided into two or more sections separated by a gap that is environmentally different. For example, an airfield built in a tropical rain forest divides that forest and makes it difficult for some species to traverse the expanse between forest edges.

**habitat hypothesis:** proposal that the principal mode of **evolution** is the adaptational response of species to climate change; a recent incarnation in hominids has been proposed by E. S. **Vrba**.

**habitat islands:** approach in which biological reserves are treated as islands surrounded by a 'sea' of unsuitable **habitat**. The **island biogeography model** is often applied to these areas.

**habitat isolation:** separation of populations that prevents mating; the populations concerned occur in different habitats in the same general region; a premating or **prezygotic mechanism** of **isolation**. Aka ecological isolation.

**habitat selection:** capacity of a dispersing individual or population to choose an appropriate, species-specific **habitat**.

**habitat types:** different grades or types of environments; one simple scheme with standardized names and symbols is: A = arid; EG = evergreen; GF = gallery forest; M = montane; OW = open woodland; SD = semideciduous; SG = savanna grassland; SR = secondary riverine; V = very moist.

‡ **habitual bipedalism:** refers to the usual mode of locomotion of a **bipedal** organism, i.e. walking on two limbs. See **striding gait**. Cf. **bent-knee gait**.

**habituation:** 1. condition in which an animal becomes unafraid of an object or individual in its environment to the point that it can be ignored. For example, a human observer nearby may initially elicit fear in a primate, but over repeated occurrences, the animal loses its fear and ignores the observer. 2. in adaptation physiology, the gradual reduction of perception of and/or responses to repeated stimulation. Verb: to habituate.

**habitus:** 1. morphology or genetic constitution of an organism that represents its immediate adaptation to its environment, in contrast to those ancestral traits that were adapted for previous environments. 2. body build, especially as used within a system of constitutional types, such as that of W. H. **Sheldon**.

‡ **Hadar:** fossiliferous area found in 1972 in the **Afar Triangle** region of northeastern Ethiopia (Africa), with localities that date in the 3.9–3.0 **mya** range. The remains of at least 35, and perhaps as many as 65, **hominid** individuals have been excavated from the region. It was once a lakeside with bushlands and patchy forests, and some 6,000 faunal specimens have also been excavated, providing a good picture of its **Pliocene** ecosystem. Hominids from Afar are identified by the prefix 'AL' (**Afar Locality**), such as **NME AL 288-1**. Many tools have been found in the region, although none are associated with hominid-bearing sites; the tools are grouped into five categories ranging from chopper/chopping to very recent lithic industries. In 1976, **Oldowan**-type tools dated at 2.6 mya were found at Hadar.

**Hadar Formation:** Plio-Pleistocene sedimentary unit consisting of four named members, each with discrete subunits; the main Members are the **Basal Member, Sidi Hakoma Member, Denen Dora Member,** and **Kada Hadar Member**. Hominids have been recovered principally from about 40 m above and below a basalt unit in the Sidi Hakoma Member. The sediments of interest contain indications of a paleoenvironment that was primarily lacustrine, with fauna typically found at lake margins.

*Hadropithecus* **Lorenz von Liburnau, 1899:** monotypic genus of extinct **subfossil Malagasy prosimian** belonging to the **Archaeolemuridae**; *H. stenognathus* is the sole species. Recovered from sites located in central, southwest, and southern Madagascar dating between 2000 and 1000 BP. Terrestrial; diurnal; quadrupedal. Dental formula: 2.1.3.3/1.1.3.3; canines and incisors reduced in size, lower back premolar molarized, and the other cheek teeth quickly worn flat in life; dentition suggestive of **graminivory**. See Appendix 2 for taxonomy, Appendix 3 for living species.

**Hadza:** foragers or hunter–gatherers in modern-day Tanzania who have survived with a subsistence lifestyle in small-scale societies into the twenty-first century.

**Haeckel, Ernst Heinrich** (1834–1919): German anatomist, physician and Professor at Jena after 1865. Known for his **biogenetic law** that ontogeny recapitulates phylogeny, Haeckel was a strong supporter of Darwin's ideas and promoted them in the German literature, even strategizing in correspondence with **Darwin** as to how best to promote **natural selection** and to discourage its detractors. Haeckel first linked humans to apes in a tree-like diagram in *General Morphology* (1866), coined the name *Pithecanthropus alalus* and both the term for and the concept of **ecology**. In his *History of Creation* (1868) Haeckel proposed that there were 36 human races. Unfortunately, Haeckel was also among those who linked natural selection to cultural evolution in the German-speaking world; see **social Darwinism.**

**Haeckel's law of recapitulation:** see **biogenetic law.**

**haemo-:** see entries beginning with **hemo-.**

**hafting:** process of fastening an axe, spearpoint, or arrowhead onto a handle or shaft.

**Haig hypothesis:** see **genetic conflict theory.**

**hair:** filament-like outgrowth of the epidermis, consisting of cornified epidermal cells. True hair is present only in mammals. Hair functions as insulation in most mammals, as well as serving as camouflage and providing social cues. In humans, hair now has a predominantly social function.

**hair cell:** 1. any specialized receptor nerve ending for detecting sensations, such as in the spinal organ. 2. sensory cell in the inner ear that lies between the **basilar membrane** and the tectorial membrane of the cochlea, semicircular canals, utricle, and saccule; hair cells receive their name from the fringe of specialized surface **cilia** at their tips. These stereocilia respond to the motion of the gelatinous tectorial membrane that triggers action potentials in fibers of the auditory nerve.

**hair follicle:** tubular epithelial structure in the skin of mammals that invades the dermis; the **hair** develops in the follicle. The hair follicle is also associated with a papillary muscle (responsible for the erection of hair such as during displays or, in humans, shivering) and a **sebaceous gland.**

**hair form:** one of the traits that, because of its variation in humans, has a long history of use in racial taxonomy. For example, **Topinard** classified humans into three races: straight-haired, wavy/frizzy-haired, and woolly-haired.

**hairiness:** measure of the amount of **hair** on the human body, including the beard; used by some anthropologists as a variable to define human groups.

**hairy-eared dwarf lemur:** vernacular for *Allocebus trichotis.*

**hairy pinnae:** genetic trait that causes growth of **hair** along the rim of the ear; possible **holandric inheritance.**

**hairy-faced tamarin section:** division of the genus *Saguinus* based on face fur, or lack of face fur, and other **pelage** patterns; not a subgenus distinction. The hairy-faced tamarins are distinguished by long hairs on the forehead, temple, and crowns. They are divided into two groups. The *S. nigricollis* group does not develop a moustache, although it has short white hairs surrounding the mouth, and consists of *S. nigricollis* and *S. fuscicollis*. The *S. mystax* group has a moustache, although the degree of development varies; short white hairs around the mouth are also present in this group. This group includes *S. mystax, S. labiatus,* and *S. imperator*. The *S. midas* group consists of only this species and lacks both the moustache and the white hairs around the mouth.

**Haldane, John Burton Sanderson** (1892–1964): British physiologist, geneticist, Marxist. With **Fisher** and **Wright**, promoted the theory of **neo-Darwinism** (1932). Haldane demonstrated that enzymes obey the laws of thermodynamics (1924), demonstrated **linkage** between **hemophilia** and **color blindness** (1936), and was among those who anticipated **Hamilton** regarding **altruism** and **cost–benefit analysis** ('I'd lay down my life for two brothers or eight cousins'). Another conundrum regarding **genetic load** led to **Haldane's dilemma** (1957), which was later broached by **Kimura.** See **Haldane's law.**

**Haldane's dilemma(s):** two famous, casually constructed conundrums offered by J.B.S. **Haldane,** concerning: (1) **altruism,** and (2) **genetic load.**

**Haldane's law** or **rule:** observation, in certain hybrid crosses in which only one gender of the offspring is inviable or infertile while the other develops normally, that the **heterogametic sex** usually has reduced viability or fertility. See J.B.S. **Haldane.**

‡ **half-life:** 1. amount of time required for one-half of an element to decay into a daughter element; see **radiometric dating.** 2. amount of time for half of a biochemical substance (hormone, enzyme, etc.) or drug to be cleared from the blood by the liver or kidneys.

**half-sibling:** one of two or more children having only one parent in common. Aka half-sib. See **second degree relative.**

**Hall, Kenneth Ronald Lambert** (1917–65): British psychologist, primatologist, ornithologist. During five years at the University of Capetown (1955–9), Hall studied chacma baboons, vervets and patas monkeys, describing their behavior and ecology; he emphasized quantification of behaviors in field studies. Aka Lambert Hall.

**hallux:** most medial digit of the mammal hind paw; digit I; the great toe in humans. The hallux in humans is highly derived and plays a vital role in **bipedalism** by pushing off from the substrate. Sometimes spelled hallus. Plural: halluces. Adjective: hallucal. Cf. **pollex**.

**hamadryas baboon:** vernacular for *Papio hamadryas*.

**hamate:** 1. hook-shaped. 2. most medial bone in the distal row of **carpals**, articulating with the **capitate**, **triquetral**, and **metacarpals** IV and V. A hooklike projection (the hamulus) has a lateral groove that makes up part of the carpal tunnel. Aka unciforme, cuneiforme.

**Hamilton, William Donald** (1936–2000): British biologist; Hamilton developed the concept of **inclusive fitness** and **kin selection** and was able to demonstrate, at least mathematically, how it could be possible to model altruistic behaviors in terms of neo-Darwinist principles. These two seminal papers led to the elaboration of **sociobiology**: 'The evolution of altruistic behavior' (1963), and 'The genetical evolution of social behavior' (1964). Hamilton's collected papers appear in two volumes called *The Narrow Roads of Geneland*. Volume 1: *Evolution of Social Behavior* (1996), and Volume 2: *Evolution of Sex* (2002). Winner of the Royal Society's Darwin Medal (1988). See **altruism** and **second Darwinian revolution**. Cf. G. C. **Williams**.

**Hamilton–Zuk hypothesis:** proposal that parasite load decreases viability (in the competing sex), and that the other sex (the choosing sex) will prefer showy individuals, i.e. conditional traits (e.g. sexual displays) are expressed only in high-quality individuals.

**Hamilton's genetical theory of social behavior:** proposed mechanism to explain the possible evolution of **altruism** by extending **Darwin's** concepts of direct fitness to **inclusive fitness** and natural selection to **kin selection**.

**Hamilton's Rule:** precept that presents the conditions under which an **altruistic** act will occur. For an altruistic **allele** to increase in frequency, the altruist must be related to the recipient(s) in such a way that the genetic **benefit** to the recipients outweighs the genetic **cost** to the altruist. This has often been expressed as genetically worthwhile to the altruist if it saved the lives of two siblings (who share half the alleles of the altruist), four nieces or nephews (who share one-fourth of the altruist's alleles), or eight cousins (who share one-eighth of the altruist's alleles); i.e. $Br - C > 0$, where $B$ is the benefit to the recipient, $C$ is the cost to the actor, and $r$ is the **coefficient of relatedness** between the two individuals. Proposed by British biologist W. D. **Hamilton**.

**Hamlyn's monkey:** vernacular for *Cercopithecus hamlyni*.

**hammerstone:** stone temporarily used as an instrument to modify something into an intended **tool**. When struck directly against another stone, a **bulb of percussion** will remain both on the **core** and on the removed **flake**. In advanced tool-making **industries**, a hammerstone is tapped against an intermediate tool such as an antler that is positioned to absorb the blow so that delicate flaking can be achieved. A hammerstone can also be used in conjunction with an **anvil** to crush long bones.

**hamulus:** any hooklike process. See **hamate**(2).

**Hamy, Jules Ernest Théodore** (1842–1908): French physician, physical anthropologist, student of Broca; Hamy translated Lyell's *The Geological Evidences of the Antiquity of Man* into French. After 1872, Hamy worked as assistant to **Quatrefages**, and succeeded his mentor at the Muséum National d'Histoire Naturelle de Paris. Author with A. de Quatrefages of *Crania Ethnica* (1882).

**hand:** 1. terminal portion of the upper extremity, consisting of the carpus, metacarpus, and digits. 2. dexterous fore paw in primates. Among the lower primates and the monkeys the fore paw serves a dual purpose of hand and foot; it is only among the apes and, especially, the humans that a true hand is found. The term is generally not used for other mammals. See **metacarpal** bones.

‡ **hand axe:** see **hand-ax** and **coup-de-poing**.

**hand breadth:** linear measure based upon the breadth of the human hand, and that varies from 8 to 13 cm.

**hand dominance:** see **hand preference** and **handedness**.

**hand–eye coordination:** nervous connection between the visual areas of the brain and the motor area that helps to synchronize hand movements with vision; **stereoscopic vision**, a primate characteristic, is the basis for this coordination.

**hand index:** hand breadth $\times$ 100, divided by its length.

**hand length:** **anthropometric** measurement; distance from the **styloid** process of the radius to the tip of the third (middle) finger; the subject's forearm breaks the horizontal plane and the hand is palm up with the fingers extended.

‡ **hand-ax:** large, **bifacially** worked core tool that normally is ovoid or pear-shaped; typical tool of the **Acheulean** tradition. Aka **coup-de-poing**, hand-ax, fist ax.

**handedness:** tendency to display left- or right-hand task preference. Left-handedness is referred to as **sinistrality**, right-hand preference is called **dextrality**. There is some evidence that handedness has a genetic component. Tools found at **Koobi Fora**, **Zhoukoudian**, and Ambrona, and humeral asymmetry in Neandertals, indicate that the right hand was preferred by early hominids whenever tasks requiring some power were performed. Aka hand preference. See **brain lateralization** and the **learning rule**.

**handicap principle** or **theory:** proposal that the possession of an exceptional variant in a sexual dimorphic trait such as a large chromatic tail evolved only because exceptionally strong individuals could survive with such a handicap. Proposed in 1975 by A. Zahavi, it is a specific application of **Darwin's** principle of **sexual selection**; in this instance, female choice of such a male would ensure that the trait appears in her offspring. The model has remained controversial, and several critiques have diminished its general application. Aka the 'good genes' hypothesis.

**H antigen:** found in varying quantities on the red blood cells of most people, most commonly and in the greatest quantity of people with blood type O in the **ABO blood group**. Consists of the four sugars that are precursors to the A and B antigens, and is identical to the O null allele. Aka **H substance**.

**Hanuman langur:** vernacular for *Semnopithecus entellus*. Hanuman is a Hindu word for a monkey god.

*Hapalemur* **I. Geoffroy, 1851:** lemurid genus to which the gentle, or bamboo, lemurs belong; three species; all three species are **sympatric** over parts of their range. Prefer bamboo forests and found predominantly in the eastern rain forests, with small pockets in the west and north, of Madagascar. Arboreal; **crepuscular** (they sleep at the base of bamboo trunks during the day); locomotion includes **arboreal quadrupedalism** and **vertical clinging and leaping**. Body mass ranges from 700 to 3000 g. Dental formula: 2.1.3.3; diet is specialized **graminivory** (bamboo) with leaf and flower supplements; species are able to coexist because they partition resources by consuming different parts of bamboo. Mark home ranges with scent. Live in small groups, presumed to be family units. See Appendix 2 for taxonomy, Appendix 3 for living species.

**Hapalidae:** former family name of the **Callitrichidae**.

**haplodiploid hypothesis:** proposal that an individual can increase its fitness and that of close relatives by taking risks that enhance the fitness of close relatives, a net result measured as **inclusive fitness**. Attributed to W. D. **Hamilton** as an extension of **kin selection**, and applied to the Hymenoptera where males are haploid and females are diploid, Hamilton pointed out that a female shares three-quarters of her genes with her mother, and would therefore enhance her own inclusive fitness by helping her mother care for the sisters in her sibship.

**haplodiploidy:** mode of **sex determination** in which males are derived entirely from unfertilized **haploid** eggs and females from **diploid**, usually fertilized,

eggs. Common in certain insects such as the Hymenoptera (four-winged wasps, bees, ants, etc.). Such systems are of interest to scientists who entertain hypotheses that attempt to relate certain social behaviors and systems to **degree of relatedness**. See **sociobiology** and **haplodiploid hypothesis**.

‡ **haploid:** half set; having the gametic number of **chromatids**, or half the number of somatic cells. Said of certain cells with a complete single set of a **diploid** genome or chromosome set. The human haploid complement consists of 23 chromatids out of a total pool of 24, the 23rd or 24th being either an X or a Y **sex chromatid**. Normally, only **gametes** are haploid in mammals.

‡ **haploid number** (*n*): the normal number of **chromatids** in a germ cell or **gamete** after the completion of **meiosis**. Aka gametic number.

**haplorhine:** primate belonging to the suborder **Haplorhini**.

‡ **Haplorhini:** in cladistic classification, one of two suborders of primates (the other being **Strepsirhini**) suggested to replace the older prosimian/anthropoid classification dichotomy. Vernaculor: **haplorhine**. Haplorhines are primates without a moist rhinarium, nostrils surrounded by hairy skin, advanced placentation, etc., and includes the tarsiers, monkeys, apes, and humans.

**haplotype:** static combination or set of genetic factors at more than one locus; it is the multi-locus analog of an **allele**; like alleles, haplotypes have **haplotype frequencies** in populations. Because **mitochondria** are haploid and all loci are linked, haplotype analysis is especially relevant in the case of mtDNA studies.

**haplotype frequency:** proportion of individuals in a populations who possess a given **haplotype**.

**haplotype X:** one of five **mitochondrial DNA** haplotypes found in high frequency in Native Americans, and the only one that can be traced back to Europe as opposed to the Far East.

**HapMap:** projected map of variation in human DNA **haplotypes**.

**hapten:** substance that can bind to an **epitope** without provoking an immune response, but only when conjugated with a molecular carrier; aka incomplete antigen, haptene.

‡ **haptoglobin:** protein found in the **serum** of blood, the function of which is the capture of free **hemoglobin** and its transportation to sites of protein breakdown or synthesis. See **alpha globulins**.

**hard-hammer percussion:** see **percussion flaking technique**.

**hard inheritance:** hypothesis that genetic material is constant and unaffected by lifestyle or environment; therefore, that none of the phenotypic changes experienced by an organism during its lifetime can be passed on to offspring. Aka the **central dogma**. Cf. **soft inheritance**.

**hard palate:** bony separation between the oral and nasal cavities, formed by the maxillae and palatine bones and lined by mucous membrane. It forms part of the roof of the mouth. Cf. **soft palate**.

**hard release:** abrupt release of captive animals that are being reintroduced to an environment. These animals receive no special care or assistance after release. Cf. **soft release**.

**hard selection: natural selection** in the absence of cultural mechanisms that might otherwise buffer the intensity of selection. Cf. **soft selection** and **relaxed selection**.

**hard tissues:** term applied loosely to those elements such as bones and especially teeth that are degraded late in the decay process, and may be preserved during the fossilization and/or **permineralization** process. Cf. **soft tissues**.

**hard-wired:** in reference to behavior that is strongly genetically determined; instinctual. Cf. **soft-wired**. See **program**.

**Hardy, Godfrey Harold** (1877–1947): English mathematician. A number theorist, Hardy independently demonstrated in 1908 that **Mendelian 'factors'** segregate under certain conditions according to outcomes predicted by the **binomial theorem** and its variants, an application later known as the (Castle–) **Hardy–Weinberg equilibrium principle**. Winner of the Royal Society's Copley Medal (1947). See **Weinberg** and **Castle**.

‡ **Hardy–Weinberg equilibrium principle or theorem:** mathematical relationship that expresses, under theoretical conditions, the expected distribution of **alleles** among diploid **genotypes** in a population when **allele frequencies** do *not* change between generations; the central theorem of **population genetics**. The formula in a two allele case is: $p^2 + 2pq + q^2 = 1$. Given certain **allele frequencies**, the relationship predicts **genotype frequencies** when a gene pool is static. Aka Castle–Hardy–Weinberg law. See **equilibrium**.

**harelipped tamarin:** one of the vernaculars for *Saguinus fuscicollis*; synonym: *S. lagonotus*.

**harem:** see **one-male unit**.

**Harris lines:** radio-opaque striations that sometimes occur in the **epiphyseal disk** regions of long bones. Interpreted as a **stress indicator** resulting from arrested metabolic growth, they result from a concomitant deposition of **calcium**, which appears as intense lines under X-ray examination.

**Haua Fteah:** archaeological cave site found in 1951 near the coast on the north side of the Gebel el Akhdar in northeastern Libya, dating to 90 kya in the lower levels; contains a **Levallois**-dominated **Mousterian** assemblage with marine exploitation and hominid remains including late **archaic** *Homo sapiens*.

**Haversian canal:** see **central canal**.

**Haversian system:** see **osteon**.

**Hawaiian radiation:** specific instance of **adaptive radiation** proposed by H. L. Carson and others to explain the current diversity of the Hawaiian flora and fauna, and used as a general model of **founder effect** and **speciation**.

**Hawthorne effect:** behavioral change in an animal because of the presence of an observer.

**Hayflick limit:** maximum number of cell divisions of a species' cultured **fibroblasts** dividing mitotically *in vitro* before cells enter a degenerative state called **cell senescence**. The Hayflick limit is correlated with the **maximum lifespan potential** of that species, its brain mass, and other variables, even when interrupted by cryogenic suspension of **cell division** activity. Named after Leonard Hayflick, who observed that the number of cell divisions is distinct for each species.

**Hb:** abbreviation for **hemoglobin**.

**HbA:** abbreviation for **hemoglobin A**.

**HbA2:** abbreviation for **hemoglobin A2**.

**HbC:** abbreviation for **hemoglobin C**.

**HbO$_2$:** abbreviation for **oxyhemoglobin**.

**HbS:** abbreviation for **hemoglobin S**.

**hCG:** abbreviation for human **chorionic gonadotropin**.

**hCS:** abbreviation for human **chorionic somatomammotropin**.

**H chain:** larger peptide in antibody molecules; specifies the class to which the immunoglobulins belong; Aka **heavy chain**.

**HDLs:** high-density lipoproteins, a group of plasma proteins of relatively high molecular mass that contain proportionally less protein and more **cholesterol** and triglycerides. Aka 'good' cholesterol. See **alpha globulins**. Cf. **LDLs**.

**HDN:** see **hemolytic disease of the newborn**.

**head:** 1. rounded eminence on bone or other tissue; e.g. head of the femur, mandible, or epididymis. In the past, the Latin term *capitus* was used predominantly. 2. region of the vertebrate body where the skull, sense organs, brain, mouth, and other associated structures are found.

**head circumference: cephalometric** measurement; distance around the head as measured with a tape measure placed just superior to the eyebrows and passed tightly around the **head**. Used principally in studies of infant brain size.

**head form:** shape of the head. Craniologists and cephalometrists believed that head form was the product of inheritance and assigned types based on measurements of populations. Head form has since been demonstrated to have an environmental component. See **brachycephalic, brachycranic, mesocephalic,**

mesocranic, **dolichocephalic, dolichocranic,** and **face form.**

**head height: cephalometric** measurement; distance from **vertex** to the auditory opening.

**'headhunter' hypothesis:** see **'killer ape' hypothesis.**

**head length:** distance from the **glabella** to the **opisthocranion** measured with a spreading caliper.

**head spanner: craniometric** instrument used for measuring height along the midsagittal plane using the **porion** as a reference point into which the tips of movable arms are placed.

‡ **health:** condition of optimal physical, mental and social well-being, and not merely the absence of disease or infirmity; healthy.

**hearing range:** range of sound frequencies that can be detected by a species. See **sound spectrogram.**

**heart:** hollow muscular organ that pumps blood through the **circulatory system;** positioned in the thoracic cavity, usually slightly to the left of mid-line (Cf. **situs inversus viscerum**). In mammals, birds and Crocodilia, the heart has four chambers and pumps blood to two circuits, the pulmonary circuit (to and from the lungs) and the systematic circuit (to the rest of the body). The four-chambered heart is more efficient at delivering highly oxygenated blood to the tissues than is the three-chambered heart.

**heart-weight rule:** empirical observation that the ratio of **body mass** to heart mass ('weight') increases in animals living in colder regions compared to those found in warmer regions; attributed to a need to maintain a greater temperature differential between the body and the environment in cold regions. Aka Hesse's rule.

‡ **hearth:** floor of a fireplace or fire pit.

**heat:** 1. energy in transit from a body of higher temperature to a body of lower temperature. 2. state of elevated temperature. 3. **estrus.**

**heat exhaustion:** condition caused by prolonged exposure to hot temperatures, marked by prostration and muscle weakness, plasma volume depletion secondary to sweating and extreme dilation of blood vessels in the skin; thermoregulatory centers remain functional.

**heat stroke:** condition caused by prolonged exposure to hot temperatures, marked by high fever, cramps, cessation of sweating that results in dry skin, vertigo, and coma in severe cases; heat stroke is more severe than **heat exhaustion** in that the thermoregulatory system becomes overloaded to the point of failure during exposure to heat stress.

**heavy chain:** one of the two longer polypeptide chains that comprise the constant portion of an antibody. Aka **H chain.** Cf. **light chain.**

**heavy-duty tool:** stone tool made of a **cobble** or chunk of rock from which large flakes have been struck by a **hammerstone;** e.g. a **chopper.**

**HEB:** Heberer's gully at **Olduvai Gorge.**

**Heck's macaque:** vernacular for *Macaca maura.* (Many workers place this monkey in *Macaca nigra*)

**hectare** (ha): an area of 10,000 square meters, or 2.471 acres.

**heel:** 1. **distal** end of a structure. 2. often understood to be the posterior area of the **calcaneus bone** of the foot; aka heel bone.

**Heidelberg Man:** see **Mauer.**

**height:** vertical linear dimension of an anatomical structure. Cf. **stature.**

**HeLa cells:** aneuploid human established cell line obtained from cervical cancer cells harvested in 1951 from *Henrietta Lacks,* and commonly used in tissue culture research.

**helicase:** enzyme capable of unwinding and dissociating the complementary strands of a **DNA** double helix during normal replication.

**heliocentric theory of the solar system:** now accepted proposal that the sun is at the center of the motion in the solar system; that the planets, including the earth, revolve around the sun. First proposed in the 3$^{rd}$ century BCE, and most revived by **Copernicus.** Aka the Copernican theory of the solar system, heliocentrism heliocentricity. Cf. **geocentric theory of the solar system.**

*Heliopithecus* **Andrews and Martin, 1987:** genus **nomen** for a maxilla recovered in Saudi Arabia. Most workers refer it to *Afropithecus.*

**helix:** 1. a spiral structure, a coil. See **double helix.** 2. the incurved rim of the inner ear. See **tuberculare.**

**Hellin's law:** approximation of the number of multiple births in a population, given as $1/n$ for the fraction of births that are **twins,** $1/n^2$ for triplets, and $1/n^3$ for quadruplets, where $n$ is usually given as 80. Aka Hellin's rule of multiple births.

**helminthic disease:** infection by parasitic worms, either directly or by **vector.** Helminthic diseases include **trichinosis, enterobiasis,** and **schistosomiasis.**

**helminths:** worms or parasites that resemble worms, including **flatworms** and nematode **roundworms,** some of which cause (e.g. **trichinosis**) infestations in humans. Such infestations are known as filariasis.

**helper:** individual who assists in the raising of young; in general, helpers tend to increase the probability of survival of young. See **alloparenting.**

‡ **helper T cell:** lymphocyte that recognizes foreign antigens on macrophages, activates B cells and cytotoxic T cells, and secrete **cytokines.**

**HEMA:** gene for blood clotting **factor VIII** that, when mutated, causes **hemophilia A.**

**hemagglutination:** clumping of red blood cells.

**hemagglutinin:** protein present in blood serum and some viruses that causes the clumping of red blood cells.

**hemangioma:** birthmark; patch of discolored skin caused by benign tumors of the dermal blood vessels.

**hematite:** reddish material often used for body paint and pictographs; iron ore mixed with grease. Hematite was used by many native peoples as protection against the cold, and such people have been erroneously identified as 'redskins'.

**hematocrit** (Hct): percentage of whole blood volume occupied by erythrocytes; hematocrit exhibits **sexual dimorphism** as normal females exhibit about 40–45%, and normal males exhibit about 45–50%. Aka packed cell volume.

**hematologic disorder:** disease or syndrome affecting the blood; common examples are **anemia, sickle cell anemia, thalassemia, polycythemia, hemophilia** and **von Willebrand disease.**

**hematopoiesis:** process in which the formed elements of blood (**erythrocytes, leukocytes, thrombocytes** {platelets}) are produced; aka hemopoiesis.

**hematopoietic tissue:** embryonic tissue from which white blood cells arise.

**HEMB:** gene for blood clotting **factor IX** that, when mutated, causes **hemophilia B.**

**heme:** complex nonprotein, iron-containing pigment molecule found in animals; a **porphyrin**, heme is bound to each of the four polypeptide chains of **hemoglobin** and **cytochrome**, where it is the oxygen-binding element of these molecules. Aka ferroprotoporphyrin. Formerly called hematin.

‡ **heme group:** portion of a hemoglobin molecule that contains an iron atom that readily binds with oxygen; each hemoglobin molecule contains four heme groups.

*Hemiacodon gracilis* Marsh, 1872: tarsiiform primate from the middle Eocene of North America, belonging to the omomyid subfamily **Omomyinae; monotypic.** Estimated body mass around 1 kg. Dental formula: 2.1.3.3/2.1.3.3; dental morphology suggestive of **frugivory.** Some **postcrania** are known; these fragments indicate quadrupedalism and leaping capabilities. See Appendix 1 for taxonomy.

**hemibun:** slight bun on the occipital region of the skull; cf. **occipital bun.**

**hemikaryon:** cell nucleus containing the **haploid** number of chromatids.

**hemimandible:** half of the mandible (i.e. the right or left side).

**hemisphere:** half of a sphere or spherelike object, e.g. **cerebral hemisphere.**

**hemisphere dominance of the brain:** see **brain lateralization** and **dominant hemisphere.**

**hemisphericity:** tendency for one cerebral hemisphere to be dominant independent of the task at hand; aka hemisphere dominance of the brain. See **brain lateralization** and **dominant hemisphere.**

‡ **hemizygosity:** state of having or being characterized by one or more genes that have no allelic counterparts. Said of genes that are present in only one **dose** in a **diploid** genome. Found normally in **haploids** (e.g. certain insects) and in non-homologous portions of the **sex chromosomes.** Found abnormally in diploid cells as the result of either **aneuploidy** or **deletion** of chromatid segments. Normally, the **heterogametic sex** (males in mammals) is hemizygous for genes on both the X and the Y **sex chromosomes.** See **sex-linked inheritance.**

**hemochorial placenta:** subtype of the **chorionic placenta** in which the cell walls of the maternal blood vessels break down and invade the **chorion** so that the chorion and the fetal circulation are bathed directly by maternal blood; found in tarsiers, New World monkeys, Old World monkeys, apes and humans (the haplorhine primates).

**hemochromatosis, hereditary** (HH, HFE1): an autosomal recessive condition characterized by defective iron metabolism that overloads iron storage sites such as the liver, and that can progress to liver cancer. Symptoms include chronic fatigue, infections, hair loss, skin pigmentation, infertility, muscle pain, liver damage, diabetes, and the perception of feeling cold. Fatal if left untreated. According to the CDC, hemochromatosis is the most common serious genetic disorder in humans. Current treatment includes therapeutic phlebotomy and ferritin monitoring; females often have less severe symptoms owing to menstruation. There is a **parent-of-origin effect.** Of four common forms, the classic (HH, HFE1) and the more severe juvenile onset forms (JH, HFE2) are the most prevalent. The affected locus (C282Y in the *HFE1* gene) can be detected by a simple clinical test.

**hemocyte:** any cell formed in the blood; a blood corpuscle such as a blood cell. Aka hematocyte.

‡ **hemoglobin** (Hb): protein molecule critical to metabolism, and the component in **red blood cells** (RBC) that binds reversibly and transports **oxygen** to tissues and **carbon dioxide** back to the lungs during **respiration.** Hb binds less reversibly to carbon monoxide (hence CO poisoning). Hb is found in the blood of most chordates and in the roots of some legumes. See **adult hemoglobin, carboxyhemoglobin, oxyhemoglobin, hemoglobin alleles,** and **coloration.**

‡ **hemoglobin alleles:** genetic adaptations to **malaria** in humans and other primates seem to be allelic variants of normal **adult hemoglobin**, which consists of two alpha (α) and two beta (β) polypeptide chains, each characterized by a specific normal sequence of amino acids. Common **alleles** of hemoglobin (see box below)

are usually found in regions where malaria is (or was) endemic, and often confer a fitness advantage to the heterozygotes. Mutations and deletions of Hb chains are also responsible for other **hemoglobinopathies**. See **fetal hemoglobin, hereditary persistence**. Cf. **thalassemia**.

---

**Notable hemoglobin allelic variants**

hemoglobin A (HbA): so-called normal human adult hemoglobin, a protein composed of two alpha and two beta chains, and possessing glutamic acid at beta chain position six.

hemoglobin A2 (HbA2): one of two so-called normal human **adult hemoglobins**, a protein composed of two alpha and two **delta globin chains**; aka the minor component of adult hemoglobin.

hemoglobin C (HbC): variant of HbA caused by a lysine for glutamic acid **point mutation** at position 6 in the beta chain.

hemoglobin D Bushman (HbD): variant of HbA caused by a glycine to arginine substitution at beta 16.

hemoglobin D Ibadan (HbD): variant of HbA caused by a threonine to lysine substitution at beta 87.

hemoglobin D Punjab (HbD): variant of HbA caused by a glutamic acid to glutamine substitution at beta 121.

hemoglobin E (HbE): variant of HbA caused by a glutamic acid to lysine substitution at beta 26.

hemoglobin S (HbS): variant of HbA, a so-called abnormal adult human hemoglobin; responsible for **sickle cell disease**. A protein composed of two alpha and two beta chains, and possessing a valine substitution for glutamic acid at position 6 in the beta chain; the AS gentotype has a relatively high fitness in a malarial environment.

---

**hemoglobinopathy:** any of several disorders of **hemoglobin** synthesis and function, such as **sickle cell anemia** and **thalassemia**.

**hemolysis:** bursting apart (lysis) of a red blood cell, releasing its constituents into the blood plasma. Adjective:hemolytic.

**hemolytic anemia:** form of anemia that develops owing to the shortened survival *in vivo*, and subsequent destruction, of red blood cells. Aka chronic hemolytic anemia.

**hemolytic disease of the newborn** (HDN): any condition resulting in the abnormal destruction of fetal blood products, but commonly refers to Rh incompatibility between a mother and fetus. In the **Rh incompatibility** type of hemolytic disease of the newborn, some infants who can break down red blood cells coated with maternal **antibody** into **hemoglobin** and then into **indirect bilirubin** may lack the final enzyme necessary to convert the latter into harmless, excretable bilirubin; **bilirubin** thus accumulates in toxic amounts in brain tissues, causing **kernicterus** and **jaundice** (see **Rhesus isoimmunization**; aka **erythroblastosis fetalis**). The ABO form of HDN also results in destruction of the erythrocytes of a fetus, a condition roughly twice as common as the Rh-incompatibility form of HDN, but is almost always clinically milder in its manifestation, and is caused by some of the smaller anti-A or anti-B antibodies in a mother's immune system that can permeate the placental membranes, causing jaundice, **anemia**, and an enlarged liver and spleen. HDN can also be a clinical feature of the **Diego, Duffy**, Kell-Cellano, and Gerbich blood groups.

**hemophilia:** any one of several inherited blood disorders caused by failure of one component of the normal blood-clotting system, characterized by bleeding and very slow or absent clotting of blood following an injury. The best-known form (the 'royal hemophilia') is due to a mutant gene on the X chromosome. See **hemophilia A**.

**hemophilia A** (HEMA): one of several inherited blood disorders caused by failure of one component of the normal blood-clotting system (**factor VIII**, an X-linked recessive). HEMA is characterized by spontaneous, unchecked bleeding into large joints and muscles, easy bruising, poor blood clotting, hematomas and chronic arthritis; fatal if untreated. HEMA is the best-known form of hemophilia (the 'royal hemophilia'), accounting for 80% of all coagulation disorders. Cf. **hemophilia B**.

**hemophilia B** (HEMB): rare, abnormal X-linked recessive condition in which clotting **factor IX** is deficient, which causes poor blood clotting (aka 'Christmas disease'). Found in high frequency among several human populations; the prohibition against circumcision may be related to the high frequency of this condition in some groups. Cf. **hemophilia A**.

**hemophiliac:** person who has **hemophilia**.

**Hendee's yellow-tailed woolly monkey:** vernacular for *Lagothrix flavicaudata*.

**Hengshandao:** archaeological site found between 1988 and 1996, in the **Bose Basin** of the Guangxi Zhuang Autonomous Region of China, and dated to 803 **kya** (associated tektites). Contains many **mode 2** large cutting tools similar in complexity to those assigned to the **Acheulean tool tradition** at sites located west of **Movius'** line.

**Hennig, Emil (Willi)** (1913–76): dipteran systematist; while attempting to classify insects, Hennig formalized a unique method based upon the use of shared, derived characters to identify sister groups; author of *Phylogenetic systematics* (1966) and *Insect Phylogeny* (1981). Hennig was a strong proponent of **cladistic** methods of classification in the mid-twentieth century.

**Hennigian taxonomy:** see **phylogenetic systematics** and E. **Hennig.**

**Hennig's deviation rule:** proposal by Willi **Hennig** that one of two daughter species will diverge more rapidly from the ancestral state than the other following a **speciation** event.

*Heoanthropus* Sergi, 1909: synonym for *Homo.*

**Hepalidae:** archaic nomen for the **Callitrichidae.**

**heparin:** mucopolysaccharidic acid found naturally in the liver and lung tissue that has the ability to prevent blood from clotting by binding to antithrombin III. In commercial preparations, heparin is an anticlotting agent.

**hepatobiliary disorder:** disease or syndrome affecting the liver or gallbladder; common examples are hepatitis and cirrhosis.

**herbivory:** 1. dietary category applied to animals that consume plant matter; that is, **primary consumers**; see **phytophagy.** 2. more specific dietary category applied to animals (herbivores) that consume predominantly the nonreproductive parts of plants during the year or during a particular season. Adjective: herbivorous. Herbivory in this sense includes **graminivory, folivory,** and **gummivory,** but does not include **frugivory** or **granivory.** See **diet.**

**herding:** behavior in **polygynous** male hamadryas baboons (*Papio hamadryas*) in which one-male unit females are prevented from wandering far away from the male. He does this by aggressively chasing any females that have strayed away and biting them on the neck; many believe this behavior is strongly genetic.

**hereditarianism:** idea that all human traits are caused or determined solely by one's genotype, ignoring the contributions of the environment.

**hereditary:** genetically transmitted from parent to offspring. Cf. **heritable.**

**hereditary disease** or **disorder:** see **genetic disease.**

**hereditary emphysema:** inherited type of **emphysema** caused by defective **alpha-1 antitrypsin.** See **emphysema, congenital.**

**hereditary factor:** any hereditary character; now usually called a **gene.**

**hereditary fructose intolerance, type I:** see **fructose intolerance, hereditary.**

**hereditary nonpolyposis colon cancer, familial** (HNPCC): see **colon cancer.**

**hereditary predisposition theory:** proposal that certain pathological conditions, such as schizophrenia, seem to involve an inherited **predisposition** that becomes manifest in the appropriate environmental context. Attributed to the French naturalist **Lamarck.** Cf. **anlage.**

**hereditary pulmonary emphysema:** type of **emphysema** that is caused by or predisposes individuals who carry any of three known alleles implicated in **alpha-1 antitrypsin deficiency.** Depending on the alleles and the degree of **penetrance,** also called familial emphysema and/or congenital (lobar) emphysema, although these may be different entities.

‡ **heredity:** capacity for continuity between generations of living organisms; the mechanism of transmission of genetic **traits** from parents to offspring.

**heredodegeneration:** genetic retrogressive change in cells and tissues. See **apoptosis.**

**heritability:** proportion of total **variance** in a certain trait attributable to genetic variation; additive variance. The value of the heritability estimate is a function of genetic factors, environmental factors, and the interaction of genetic with environmental factors. There are several standard methods of measurement: (1) **Holzinger's** *H*; (2) broad-sense heritability (*H*), the proportion of total population variance in a phenotypic character due to individual differences in genotypes; and (3) narrow-sense heritability ($h^2$), the proportion of total population variance in a phenotypic character due to individual differences in genotypes that will be inherited in offspring. Only narrow-sense heritability is the proportion of the genetic variance that is additive. Cf. $e^2$.

**heritable:** pertaining to traits passed down from parent to progeny cells; any trait that is identical owing to descent.

**heritage:** those traits indicative of a previous mode of ancestral adaptation differing from the current adaptation of an organism.

**Hermansky–Pudlak syndrome** (HPS): a form of **albinism** similar to OCA1 and OCA2 with the additional complications of fibrosis and colitis; these can be severe and lead to death, owing to mutations in the autosomal recessive HPS gene.

**hermaphrodite:** 1. animal or plant that has both female and male sex organs in the same individual; the condition is described as hermaphroditism. 2. in botany, describes a species with both male and female structures in the same flower. 3. in humans, true hermaphrodites are **mosaic** for the sex chromosomes, i.e. some cells in the body are XX, others XY or XXY. Such individuals possess both ovarian and testicular tissue, present either in separate gonads or together in a single **gonad**. Aka **ambiguous genitalia**, intersexuality. True hermaphrodites are very rare, about 1:100,000 worldwide, but see the more common **pseudohermaphroditism**.

**Herodotus** (c. 484–c. 410 BCE): Greek historian, geographer; one of the first scholars to recognize variation in humans, and to describe peoples according to physical characteristics (*Historiae*, Book IX: 191). Observed that land is shaped by water that may have once covered the earth; postulated that Europe, Asia and Africa are separate continents. In some cases he was a fabulist and recorded hearsay, myths, and traditions. Bachofen and other anthropologists used the material compiled by Herodotus.

**herpes simplex virus** (HSV): virus that causes cold sores (type 1) and genital lesions (type 2). HSV is active among individuals with cellular immune deficiency states; one of the DNA viruses in the family Herpesviridae (human herpesvirus type 7).

**Hershkovitz, Philip** (1909–1997): US mammalogist at the field Museum of Natural History, noted for work on neotropical mammals, especial faunal origins, metachromism, evolution, taxonomy, and the systematics of **New World primates**. It was his work with rodents and primates that led to the **rafting hypothesis**, that these groups originated in Africa rather than North America as had been earlier supposed. He described 75 mammalian taxa including many primates and was instrumental in the rigorous revision of neotropical primate taxonomy. His work with field mice helped end an epidemic of hemorrhagic fever and he was credited with saving hundreds of lives in Bolivia. He was the ASP Distinguished Primatologist in 1991. Author of *Living New World Monkeys (Platyrrhini, Vol. I)* (1977). Volume II was never completed.

**Hershkovitz's owl monkey**: vernacular for *Aotus hershkovitzi*.

**Herto hominids**: several calvaria recovered in 1997 from the Herto member of the **Bouri formation** deposits in the Middle Awash, Afar rift region of Ethiopia, radioisotopically dated to *c.* 160–154 kya ($^{40}$Ar/$^{39}$Ar). They were described in 2003; the holotype was assigned field number **BOU-VP-16/1**. Characteristics of this specimen include a long and high vault and a strongly flexed occiput with a massive occipital protuberance. A presumed male, the mastoid processes are large and projecting; the zygomatic bone is orbitally robust. Alveolar prognathism is moderate. The glabellar region is prominent with rugose and well defined double-arched **supra-orbital tori**; the estimated cranial capacity is 1450 cm³. The calvaria show signs of slight post-mortem distortion; the left frontal bone was lost before discovery. Linear measurements are within or near the limits of *Homo*

*sapiens*, and do not suggest an affinity with Neandertals. This calvaria is attributed to *Homo sapiens idaltu* subsp. nov. Three other specimens were also found: a partial calvaria from a second major specimen, an even larger adult, BOU-VP-16/2; a left parietal fragment, BOU-VP-16/43 (calotte?); and a nearly complete immature cranium, BOU-VP-16/5. BOU-VP-16/1, -16/2 and -16/5 each exhibit defleshing cutmarks. Associated archaeological assemblages contain elements of both **Acheulean** and **Middle Stone Age** industries, and additional evidence of systematic butchery of hippopotamus carcases.

*Hesperolemur actius* Gunnell, 1995: recently described adapoid prosimian from the middle Eocene of North America, belonging to the notharctid subfamily **Notharctinae**; **monotypic**; known from a single compressed and deformed skull. Dental formula: 2.1.4.3/2.1.4.3. Body mass estimated at 4 kg. See Appendix 1 for taxonomy.

*Hesperopithecus haroldcooki* Osborn, 1907: mistaken example of **early man in the New world**, a fossilized fragment found in Nebraska that turned out to be an extinct species of pig.

**Hesse's rule**: see the **heart-weight rule**.

**heterauxesis**: growth rate of some part of an organism compared with the growth rate of the whole. See **allometry**.

**heterobathmy of traits, characters** or **features**: presence of a mosaic of relatively primitive and relatively derived features in a set of related taxa.

**heterochromatin**: 1. densely staining chromatin that appears as nodules in or along extended chromatids. 2. during cell division, densely staining portions of condensed chromosomes. These regions are positively **heteropycnotic** and thus have different staining (e.g. dark with Giemsa stain) properties than **euchromatin**, and have relatively few active genes. Adjective: heterochromatic. Thought to consist of highly repetitive DNA and some protein-coding genes.

**heterochromia**: difference in color of a part or parts that are normally alike in color, as in heterochromia iridis, in which eyes are of different colors (usually, one eye is brown and the other is blue).

**heterochromosome**: differentiated chromosome involved in sex determination.

**heterochronic mutation**: mutation that changes the relative timing of developmental events.

**heterochrony**: 1. differential rates of development for two or more properties due to evolved changes in developmental timing; used to distinguish between the effects of differential rates of sexual and somatic maturation. Term coined by **Haeckel**. See **neoteny**. 2. change in the order of appearance of traits when an ancestral and descendant species are compared.

**heterodisomy:** unusual inheritance of two copies of a gene from one parent, and none from the other. One of the forms of **non-Mendelian inheritance.** Heterodisomy describes the case where the alleles are different owing to nondisjunction during the first meiotic division. Cf. **isodisomy.**

‡ **heterodont:** describes teeth that vary in shape and function; a trait of **mammals.** Primates have four different types of tooth in their heterodont dentition. See **incisor, canine, premolar, molar.** Cf. **homodont.**

**heteroduplex:** double-stranded molecule derived from two similar, but not identical **DNA** or **RNA** sources.

**heterogamete: gamete** that contains the different kinds of sex chromatids; in humans, males produce the heterogametes that contain both X and Y sperm.

**heterogametic sex:** the sex that during **meiosis** gives rise to **gametes** that contain either a male (Y) or female (X) **chromatid.** The other sex, usually with homologous sex chromosomes, is the **homogametic sex.** In mammals and fruit flies, the male is heterogametic; in some birds, the female is the heterogametic sex.

**heterogamy:** 1. having sex cells of different types with respect to the sex chromosomes, as in human males. Adjective: heterogametic. Cf. **homogamy.** 2. union of two gametes of different size, structure, and function. 3. alternation of two kinds of generation, one that reproduces bisexually and another in which the female reproduces asexually without fecundation by the male, as in some aphids; parthenogenesis. Cf. **isogamy.**

**heterogeneity:** quality of certain genetic disorders that consist of two or more fundamentally distinct entities formerly thought to represent single entities. Adjective: heterogenetic.

**heterogenous mRNA** (hmRNA): see **pre-mRNA;** primary transcript.

**heterogenous nuclear RNA** (hnRNA): 1. a specific **nuclear RNA** molecule edited such that a specific portion leaves the nucleus to function in translation in the cytoplasm. Aka pre-RNA. Cf. **hmRNA.** 2. hnRNA can also refer to the pool of nuclear RNAs (nRNAs), dRNA, and discarded intron transcripts.

**heterokaryon:** cell with two or more genetically different nuclei that share a common cytoplasm, usually the result of cell fusion. Cf. **homokaryon.**

**heterokaryotype** (HKT): **karyotype** from an individual who is heterozygous for a **chromosome mutation** or familial anomaly, in contrast to a normal or **standard karyotype** or **homokaryotype.** Adjective: heterokaryotypic.

**heterologous species:** 1. in immunological taxonomy, those species whose similarity to a **homologous species** have been assayed by way of reaction to an **antiserum** specific to the homologous species. 2. in molecular taxonomy, **DNA sequences** of species compared to the sequence of a homologous species.

**heteromorphism:** possession of homologous chromosomes that differ in size and/or shape. Adjective: heteromorphic. Examples are primates in which the X chromosome is larger than the Y.

**heteromorphosis:** formation of an organ or appendage that is in an inappropriate location. Aka homeosis. See **hopeful monster.**

**heterophenogamy:** mating between persons that have a lesser degree of somatic resemblance than would be expected under random mating; **negative assortative mating.** Cf. **isophenogamy.**

**heterophthalmia:** difference in the appearance of the two eyes, as in the differential coloration of the eyes; see **heterochromia.** Aka heterophthalmus.

**heteroplasmy:** occurrence of two or more populations of genetically distinct **mitochondrial DNAs** in a single cell. In mammals, heteroplasmy usually consists of **single nucleotide polymorphisms** that arise as the result of **mutation.**

**heteroploidy:** state of a cell or individual with a chromosome number other than the normal diploid number; aka aneuploidy.

**heteropycnosis:** state of variable density or condensation of different chromosomes or between segments of the same chromosome. Conventionally used to specify eukaryotic chromosomes or regions thereof that are out of phase with respect to coiling cycle and exhibit differential staining properties, generally consistent with regions of **inactivation,** or negative heteropycnosis; in this latter sense, an example is the **sex chromatin** in an inactivated X chromosome, which stains as the **Barr body.**

**heterosexual:** person (or animal) who engages in sexual relations with another of the opposite sex in a species. Anthropologists have noted that cross-cultural attitudes toward this behavior range from mandatory to taboo. Cf. **homosexual.**

**heterosexuality:** one of several modes or roles available in many cultures by which individuals adopt roles that symbolize and express gender identification; in this case individuals assume roles that are by convention aligned with their 'anatomical sex'. Cf. **homosexuality.**

**heterosis:** superiority of a heterozygous genotype(s) with respect to one or more characters without an increase in fitness, compared to the homozygotes for the same genetic locus or loci; produced by matings of homozygotes from different geographic regions. Results in greater genetic variability in the **F1** offspring. In humans, heterosis can also result in greater cultural variability in these offspring. Aka hybrid vigor, and luxuriance. Cf. **heterozygote superiority** and **overdominance.**

**heterosome:** sex chromosome. Cf. **autosome.**

**heterotrisomy:** condition in which an individual with **trisomy** received different alleles from each of three grandparents.

‡ **heterotroph:** any organism that must consume other organisms to supply its metabolic needs; hence, a consumer. Cf. **autotroph.**

**heterozygosis:** inheritance of a different allele from each parent at a locus.

**heterozygosity** (H): the proportion of a population $(1-f)$ that are not homozygotes $(f)$ at a given locus. Aka frequency of heterozygotes.

**heterozygosity in the F1, Mendelian principle of:** see **Mendelian principle of heterozygosity in the F1.**

‡ **heterozygote:** diploid organism possessing different **alleles** at a single locus on **homologous chromatids.** Adjective: heterozygous. An organism may be heterozygous with respect to one locus and yet **homozygous** with respect to another. May also refer to certain chromosomes or **chromosomal aberrations.**

**heterozygote advantage:** situation where the fitness of a heterozygote is higher than the fitness of either homozygote; **overdominance.**

**heterozygote superiority:** see **heterosis.**

**heuristic:** pertaining to a mechanism that facilitates learning in a person, especially sole exploratory learning behavior.

**hexadactyly:** possessing six toes or fingers, a form of **polydactyly.**

**Hexian:** see **Longtandong Cave.**

**hexosaminidase:** enzyme involved in ganglioside metabolism, and consisting of subunits of HSA 5 and 15. Mutations in these subunits result in **Tay–Sachs disease** and **Sandhof disease.**

**hGH:** abbreviation for **human growth hormone.**

**hGHr:** abbreviation for recombinant **human growth hormone.**

**hGH-resistant dwarfism:** syndrome that gives rise to members of a breeding population who are characterized by universally short stature (pygmies). Such populations consist entirely of individuals that are homozygous recessives for a hepatic growth hormone (or hormone receptor) normally stimulated by hGH, such as **insulin-like growth factor** I. Such populations are found in Africa, Australasia, Ecuador, and on the Andaman Islands in the Indian Ocean. See **dwarfism,** type II. Aka somatomedin C deficiency, insulin-like growth factor I deficiency, Laron dwarfism.

**HGP:** abbreviation for **Human Genome Project.**

**hiatus:** gap.

**hibernation:** condition of dormancy, often seasonal, as in *Cheirogaleus.*

**hide:** see **blind** (3).

**hierarchical classification:** system or organization of entities in which the lowest elements are progressively combined into larger and larger inclusive sets.

**hierarchical promiscuity:** any mating system in which preferential sexual access to a female or females depends on the social status of the males.

**hierarchy:** in general, a system of two or more levels of units, the higher levels controlling at least to some extent the activities of the lower levels in order to integrate the group as a whole. In dominance systems within societies, a hierarchy is the sequence of dominant and dominated individuals. See **dominance hierarchy** and **Linnaean hierarchy.**

**high altitude:** in adaptation physiology, any altitude over 3,000 meters above sea level, a threshold requiring substantial **acclimation** and/or **acclimatization** by humans who exceed this altitude.

**high altitude studies:** in adaptation physiology, the study of the adaptations of indigenous peoples to the stress of high altitude on their growth and development.

**high-density lipoproteins:** see **HDLs.**

**high-level dental impaction:** condition in which a tooth is placed at an angle high in the alveolus and in contact with an adjacent tooth so as to be incapable of complete eruption. See **dental impaction.**

**high-quality diet:** food source that is easily digestible and contains rich quantities of calories and other nutrients. Cf. **low-quality diet.** See **growth diet.**

**high-resolution chromosome band:** product of an enhanced technique that stains chromosomes that have been suspended early in **mitosis** and that reveals, after staining, many more **bands** on each **chromosome** than can be demonstrated by standard techniques. See **chromosome banding technique.**

**high-throughput screening:** fast screening for compounds by using automated assays to search through large numbers of substances for desired activity, resulting in less costly and faster systematic processes.

**higher category:** taxon of a rank higher than the species, e.g. **genus.**

**higher order multiples:** individuals born as part of a set of **triplets, quadruplets,** or more; aka supertwins.

**higher primate:** see **anthropoid.**

**highly conserved (sequence):** said of nucleotide sequences that have been preserved through **natural selection** across many species, usually because the gene product is critical to a basic cellular housekeeping function, such as **ubiquitin.** Cf. **homeobox gene.**

**hilum:** depression or opening in an organ through which structures such as nerves, blood vessels, or ducts enter; aka hilus.

**hindbrain:** see **rhombencephalon.**

**Hinde, Robert A.** (1923–): British biologist and psychologist at Cambridge and the MRC; studied at

Cambridge, then took a D.Phil. at Oxford (1950). Hinde was influenced in his early studies of bird behavior by David Lack and Niko Tinbergen. At the suggestion of John Bowlby, Hinde studied mother–infant relationships in rhesus monkeys, and particularly the effects of mother–infant separation. This led to the supervision of students who worked on non-human **primates** and elephants in Africa and the Caribbean, including the work of Jane **Goodall** on chimpanzees and Dian **Fossey** on gorillas. Hinde next studied the relationships of human four-year-olds with their mothers and peers. Hinde has also written on the biological bases of religions and of moral codes. Hinde is the recipient of several medals, has been awarded many honorary degrees, and is a Commander of the British Empire. In addition to over 300 journal articles and book chapters, Hinde has co-edited 15 books, and is author of *Ethology* (1982) and *Why Good is Good: Sources of Morality* (2002).

**hindfoot:** back paw of a quadrupedal animal.

**hindgut:** end of the digestive tract; cf. **foregut.**

**hindgut fermenter:** mammal or bird that retains high-fiber food in the hindgut (usually the **cecum**), where **symbionts** break down the cellulose component. Cf. **foregut fermenter.**

**hindlimb:** posterior appendage that includes the **pelvic girdle**, thigh (femur), leg (tibia and fibula in primates, varies in other mammals), **tarsals**, and hindfoot; the hindlimb corresponds to the lower limb of humans.

**hinge joint:** type of **synovial joint** in which the convex surface of one bone fits into the concave surface of another bone; this type of joint allows for movement in one plane only. An example is the joint formed between the humerus and ulna at the elbow. Aka ginglymoidal joint.

**hinny:** 1. the cross between a female donkey or ass and a male horse or stallion; cf. **mule** and **horse–donkey hybrid.**

**hip breadth: anthropometric** measurement; now subsumed under **biiliac breadth** and bitrochanteric breadth.

**hip circumference: anthropometric** measurement; distance around the buttocks as measured with a tape measure placed at the level of the maximum extension of the buttocks and passed horizontally around the body. Used for various body indices pertaining to adipose distribution and for various applications in **human engineering.** Aka buttocks circumference.

**hippocampal formation:** complex portion of the brain involved with memory formation that utilizes input from multiple senses; a part of the **limbic system.**

**hippocampus:** curved structure located in the medial part of the floor of the lateral ventricle, a submerged gyrus forming part of the olfactory cerebral cortex, and a part of the limbic system associated with learning, memory, language, and emotions. Aka Ammon's horn.

**Hirschsprung disease:** heritable, autosomal recessive condition characterized by severe constipation, autism, and mental retardation, and caused by missing nerves in the rectum, colon, and **CNS.**

**hirsute:** 1. covered with long, stiff hairs. 2. shaggy.

**Hispaniolan monkey:** vernacular for the recently extinct **platyrrhine** species *Antillothrix bernersis.*

**histamine:** inflammatory neurotransmitter found in all animal and plant tissue; its release within the human body results in constriction of the bronchioles, dilation of arterioles, an increase in gastric secretions, and lowered blood pressure.

**histidine** (His): an essential **amino acid**; one of the twenty building blocks of **proteins.** Aka propionic acid.

**histocompatibility antigen:** see **cell-surface antigen** and **HLA complex.**

**histogram:** representation of frequency distribution by means of rectangles whose widths represent class intervals and whose heights represent the corresponding frequencies. A histogram can, for example, represent the **variation** among individuals in a sample, with each interval bar representing the **frequency** of each **value** or range of values; often used to compare a variable's distribution to a **normal distribution.**

**histoincompatibility gene:** see **MHC.**

**histology:** study of the function and microscopic structure of tissues.

**histone code:** regulation of **DNA** expression by **chromatin modification** and other **epigenetic** phenomena, achieved by combinatorial **histone modification**, and that greatly extends the information potential of the original **genetic code.**

**histone genes:** genes that code for **histone** proteins. Most histone genes lack introns. See **nucleosome.**

**histone modification:** acetylation, phosphorylation, methylation, and/or ubiquitylation of **histones.** The primary components of modification include DNA cytocine methyltransferases, methyl-CpG-binding proteins, histone-modification enzymes, and ATP-dependent remodeling complexes.

**histones:** class of heavy proteins associated with **DNA** that modulate chromosome microarchitecture and events such as DNA coiling and uncoiling during **nucleosome** formation and other cellular processes. Histones seem to coat inactive DNA. Common stains such as **Giemsa stain** bind to such proteins, not to DNA, and it is the histone-bound stains that are seen on examination of **chromosome structure.** Cf. **nonhistone protein.**

**historical archaeology:** study of human behavior when written history affects the interpretation of material remains.

**historical racial groups:** outcome of a typological exercise, not accepted as valid by many biological anthropologists, in which humans are clustered into a few infraspecific categories or **varieties** (see **Linnaeus**) or **races** (see **Blumenbach**). Anthropologists today speak of such categories as archaic, and instead refer to people in terms of adaptation to local climates, migration history, and microevolutionary genetic variation. Aka standard racial groups.

**historicity:** one of the three bases of modern biology (the others being **natural selection** and **mechanism**); the component that recognizes that evolution is historical in that it is a sequence of stages following one after another. Two important concepts relating to historicity are **contingency** and **evolutionary constraint.**

**history:** that portion of human existence during which written documents and archives have existed, about the past 5 ky. Cf. **prehistory.**

**hitchhiking:** coincidental increase or decrease in the frequency of a trait that occurs because of changes occurring at another, unlinked locus.

‡ **HIV:** Human Immunodeficiency Virus, a type D **retrovirus** (Retroviridae), one of a number of molecularly related retroviral genomes that utilize mammalian hosts. There are two common forms of the virus that cause **AIDS** in humans: HIV-1 and HIV-2 (a third form, HIV-O, is very rare). Since the late 1970s, the HIV-1 form has been introduced from Africa into Europe, Asia, and the Americas, and has mutated into several new variant **alleles.** HIV-2 was until recently still confined to Africa, but it too has begun to appear in HIV variant surveys on other continents. The original source of HIV-1 is chimpanzees, and of HIV-2 is sooty mangabeys. The 'outbreak' of an **agent** such as HIV from an animal host into humans in a disturbed environment is a scenario familiar to epidemiologists; in this case researchers suspect it was due to the use of primates as **bushmeat.** The retrovirus contains none of the machinery required for reproduction, so replication and assembly of new viroids occurs by using the host's molecular machinery. Infection occurs when the virus enters a host's **circulatory system** and selectively attaches to the **CD4 co-receptors** on **T cells,** which it then invades. An encapsulated reverse transcriptase transcribes the viral **RNA to DNA,** which is inserted into host DNA by a viral integrase. Eventually, viral mRNA copies are produced by the molecular machinery of the host cell, which are then shuttled (along with host mRNAs) into the **cytoplasm** where all the **polypeptide chains** required for the complete assembly of new virions are mechanically produced by the host cell. Finally, the assembled virions erupt from the host cell; eruption lyses host CD4+ (T4 helper) cells, an event that eventually

compromises the host's **immune system.** HIV was formerly known as **HTLV**-III.

**HIV disease:** see **AIDS.**

**Hiwegi Hill:** paleontological site found in 1926 on **Rusinga Island** in Lake Victoria, Kenya, dated to *c.* 20–18 **mya** (middle **Miocene**), and that contains fossil hominoids that are attributed to *Proconsul and Nyanzapithecus,* and fossil monkeys attributed to *Victoriapithecus.* See **Kiahera Hill** and **Kathwanga Point.**

**HKT:** abbreviation for **heterokaryotype.**

‡ **HLA complex** (HLA): human leukocyte antigen complex; six highly polymorphic loci with over 90 alleles, located on human autosome 6p; the loci are closely linked such that persons have a **haplotype** for cell surface proteins that are important in immune system response (see **linkage disequilibrium**). These genes are in **synteny** with other species and molecularly **highly conserved;** the homologue in other species is called the **major histocompatibility complex** (MHC). The MHC/HLA complex controls cell surface identification determinants and mediates cell surface recognition. The HLA system is thus critical to matching donors and recipients of transplanted tissues, who are said to be 'tissue-typed' when an HLA **haplotype** is characterized.

**HLA disease associations:** nonrandom correlation of human immune-response antigens of the HLA complex with certain diseases, either causal or coincidental. The HLA B7 antigen, for example, is associated with malignant **melanoma;** B27 with **ankylosing spondylitis;** and B47 with **congenital adrenal hyperplasia.** The **HLA DR3** antigen is associated with several diseases.

**HLA DR3:** human immune-response, D-related **antigen** on lymphoid cells, encoded by the D locus of the **HLA complex.** Humans with **haplotypes** containing the DR3 antigen are associated with or strongly predisposed to **adrenoleukodystrophy, celiac disease,** Grave's disease, dermatitis herpetiformis, early-age onset myasthenia gravis, **systemic lupus erythematosus, rheumatoid arthritis,** juvenile diabetes (see **diabetes mellitus, type I**), and opportunistic infections in **AIDS.**

*H* **locus:** genetic locus in humans that codes for the enzyme fucosyl transferase and that, when mutated, causes the **Bombay phenotype.**

**hmRNA:** see **heterogenous mRNA.**

**hnRNA:** see **heterogenous nuclear RNA.**

*Hoanghonius stehlini* **Zdhansky, 1930:** prosimian known from the Eocene of China; **monotypic;** phylogenetic relationship unknown and assigned to a family *incertae sedis;* some workers consider this species an adapoid but others believe its affinities lie with the omomyids. Estimated body mass around

700 g. Dental formula unknown; molars suggest **insectivory**. See Appendix 1 for taxonomy.

**Hochdal:** see **feldhofer grotto**.

**Hodgkin, Thomas** (1798–1866): British physician, anthropologist, philanthropist, Quaker; described **Hodgkin's disease** in 1832. Concerned with the maltreatment of native peoples under colonial rule, he founded the Aborigines' Protection Society in 1837 and, later, the **Ethnological Society of London**. Hodgkin was a **monogenist**, holding that racial differences are superficial, and due to climatic adaptation.

**Hodgkin's disease:** neoplastic condition of unknown etiology characterized by a painless but progressive enlargement of lymphoid tissues as the result of morbid cell proliferation, especially a characteristic class of giant cells. Aka Hodgkin's lymphoma, cancer of the lymph nodes. Cf. **Burkitt lymphoma**.

**holandric gene:** see **Y-linked gene**.

**holandric inheritance:** see **sex-linked inheritance**.

**holandry:** mode of **Y chromosome**-linked inheritance; see holandric **trait**. Cf. **hologyny** and **maternal inheritance**.

**holarctic:** distributed throughout the higher latitudes of the northern hemisphere.

**Holarctica:** land mass(es) consisting of Asia, North America, Europe, and North Africa.

**holding behavior:** putting the arms around another individual; this behavior is one of the primary modalities of tactile communication in primates and serves to strengthen social bonds. See **huddling**.

‡ **holistic:** emphasizing the organic or functional relation between parts and wholes. Noun: holism. Refers to the viewpoint that all aspects of existence are interrelated and therefore important in understanding **human variation** and **evolution**. In **anthropology**, holistic refers to an integrated approach to understanding history, which views **culture** and **biology** as interacting intimately. Cf. **dualism** and **Arcadianism**.

**holistic explanation:** explanation claimed to be especially required when explanations cannot be given in terms of single factors, but only in terms of systems of variables or factors that are interrelated in complex ways.

**Holliday model:** model for genetic crossing over in eukaryotes that requires an intermediate molecule that facilitates the genetic exchange between homologous chromatids. Proposed in 1964 by Robin Holliday.

**Holloway, Ralph H.** (1936–): US physical anthropologist and primate paleoneurologist at Columbia University. Holloway has published comparative descriptions of primate cranial anatomy, and speculated on the origins of speech and tool use. He also publishes on neural biological variability, **sexual dimorphism** in the human **corpus callosum**, and **allometry**. Co-author of *The Human Fossil Record*, *Brain Endocasts: The Paleoneurological Evidence*, Volume 3 (2004).

‡ **Holocene epoch:** one of the **Quaternary Epochs** of the **Cenozoic Era**, beginning about 8 kya and continuing to the present. During the Holocene epoch, the first **civilizations**, each with a unique local set of domesticated **flora** and **fauna**, appeared independently in several locations around the world. Aka Recent. See Appendix 4 for a geological time scale.

**holocrine:** pertaining to a gland that is wholly secretory, e.g. a **sebaceous gland**. Such glands secrete not only accumulated fluids, but disintegrated cells from the gland itself.

**hologenism:** 1. doctrine that human life originated globally, in thousands of places, wherever climatic and biochemical conditions permitted. Cf. **polygenism** and **monogenism**. 2. proposal that different parts of an organism respond at different rates to the process of evolution, a meaning now largely subsumed by the concept of **mosaic evolution**.

**hologyny:** mode of **maternal inheritance**; genes present only in females and passed from mothers to their daughters Adjective: hologynic. Cf. **holandry** and **paternal inheritance**.

**holophyletic group:** taxonomic group of organisms that has a single common ancestor, and that includes all descendants of that ancestor.

**holotype:** specimen that serves as the standard, or type, for a particular taxon; see **type specimen**.

**holozoic nutrition:** pertaining to organisms that require a diet of complex organic foods.

**Holstein:** interglacial period in northern Germany and Poland that dates from 300 to 265 kya. Contemporaneous with the **Mindel-Riss** interglacial of the Alpine region.

**Holzinger's H** (*H*): a measure or estimate of **heritability** in populations that uses variances and/or correlations obtained from **twin studies**.

‡ **home base:** among some human **bands**, any stable campsite where individuals store and/or utilize resources they have collected through gathering, hunting, or other harvesting activity, and that are often shared. See **core area**.

‡ **home range:** area occupied on a regular basis by an individual, pair (with offspring), or group. Unlike a **territory**, a home range is not defended against **conspecifics**. Among some prosimians there is a set of female home ranges overlapped by male home ranges, but in a way such that no two home ranges of the same sex overlap. Home range is a term applied almost exclusively to mammals among terrestrial vertebrates.

‡ **homeobox gene** (*hox*): any one of a group of regulatory genes that consist in part of a sequence of 180

base pairs, and that encode a chain of 60 amino acids (a protein **motif**) that functions to regulate embryonic development. Homeobox genes subdivide a developing embryo from head to tail into different regions, including redundant body segments. They are structurally similar in many organisms, such as insects, mice, and humans, i.e. they are **highly conserved sequences**. Aka homeodomain. See *HOX* gene.

**homeodomain:** synonym for **homeobox gene**.

**homeorhesis:** equilibrium property characteristic of developmental pathways that ensures that the combined genetic activities of many loci delimit the range of possible outcomes; aka **canalization, homeostasis**.

**homeorhetic:** referring to a growth pattern seen in malnourished children in which the child has normal weight for height but is unusually short in stature.

‡ **homeostasis:** 1. tendency of a system to maintain a dynamic equilibrium and in the case of environmental disturbance to restore that **equilibrium** by means of its own regulatory mechanisms; applied especially to higher animals that readily adjust to conditions that are optimal for survival. 2. stability of extracellular fluids.

**homeostatic system:** any system, such as a physiologic system, that is capable of maintaining internal stability or equilibrium.

‡ **homeotherm:** any organism capable of self-regulation and maintenance of a constant core body temperature in the face of fluctuating ambient temperatures. Adjective: homeotherm, homeothermic. Cf. **poikilothermy**. Sometimes spelled homoiotherm.

**homeotic mutation:** mutations to **homeobox genes** that cause **macromutations** such as the addition of body segments, or the growth of duplicate or misplaced organs. An organism with such a mutation is called a homeotic mutant. See **heteromorphosis**.

‡ **hominid:** member of, or pertaining to, the zoological family **Hominidae**; derived from the Latin term meaning man (genitive *hominis*).

‡ **hominid evolution:** history of **AMHs** and their immediate ancestors, conventionally taken to mean any species grouped in the genus *Homo* as well as those hominid species in the genera *Paranthropus*, *Australopithecus* and *Ardipithecus*, that evolved during roughly the past 6 my. See **human evolution**.

‡ **Hominidae Gray, 1825:** mammalian family that includes all genera of **bipedal** primates, including all living and extinct species of the genera *Australopithecus*, *Paranthropus*, and *Homo*; hominids.

**Hominina:** nomen for a subtribe of the tribe **Hominini**, subfamily **Homininae**, that is used in some classificatory schemes; this subtribe consists of the genus *Homo* and its species and subspecies.

**Homininae (Wilder *c*. 1926):** subfamily of the family

**Hominidae**; many authors do not recognize this level of taxonomy; consists of the genus *Homo* and its species and subspecies. Despite not being widely used, this subfamily is justified by the reference to the genera *Australopithecus* and *Paranthropus* as **australopithecines**.

**Hominini:** nomen for a tribe of the subfamily **Homininae**, family **Hominidae**, used in some classificatory schemes; this tribe consists of *Homo*, *Pan*, and *Gorilla* among the living apes.

‡ **hominization:** process of evolving into one of the **hominid** lineages, as opposed to becoming an ape. When the case under consideration is modern humans, the process includes, as a minimum, changes in mode of locomotion to **bipedality, thermoregulation, progenesis**, and, for some lineages, **encephalization**. A consequence of encephalization is an increase in the capacity to carry **culture**.

‡ **hominoid:** member of or pertaining to the superfamily **Hominoidea**.

‡ **Hominoidea Gray, 1825:** primate **superfamily** that includes the living apes (families **Pongidae** and **Hylobatidae**), humans (family **Hominidae**), and their extinct ancestors; see **hominoid**. Members of this taxon are generally large (except gibbons) and tailless, have a shoulder structure adapted for climbing and hanging, and have the highest ratio of **brain size** to **body size** among the **primates**.

‡ *Homo* Linnaeus, 1758: nomen for the **primate** genus that includes one **extant** species, **AMHs**, as well as at least six closely related extinct **species**. Literally, 'man', or 'earthly one'. Characterized by 'upright posture, with its shift to a terrestrial mode of living and the freeing of the forelimbs for new functions, which, in turn, may have stimulated brain development' (Mayr). Other traits include a centrally situated **foramen magnum**, a range in brain size from 550 to 2000 cm$^3$, reduced lingual cusp on the third premolar, relative size reduction of the third molar, and a nasal sill. Criteria for inclusion in this genus by fossil species has not been consistent, but for the most part is based on derived feature separating these species from *Australopithecus* and *Paranthropus*: larger brain size (over 680 cm$^3$.), thicker cranial vault, decreased postorbital constriction, smaller molars and premolars, smaller face, and, according to some authorities, the increased cranial vault thickness, reduced postorbital constriction, increased contribution of the occipital bone to cranial sagittal arc length, increased cranial vault height, reduced lower facial prognathism, narrower tooth crowns (especially in the lower premolars) and reduction in length of the molar tooth row. This genus first appears *c*. 2.3 **mya**. See individual species in the box below and also Appendix 2 for taxonomy, Appendix 3 for living species.

## Proposed species and subspecies in the genus *Homo*

*Homo afer* Linnaeus, 1758: species of humanity as defined by **Linnaeus** in the tenth edition of his *Systema Naturae* (1758); Africans.

*Homo africanus* Robinson, 1972: see *Australopithecus africanus*.

*Homo africanus aethiopicus* Olson, 1985: see *Australopithecus afarensis*.

*Homo americanus* Linnaeus, 1758: species of humanity as defined by **Linnaeus** in the tenth edition of his *Systema Naturae* (1758); Native Americans.

*Homo antecessor (cf. heidelbergensis)* Bermudez de Castro, Arsuaga, Carbonell, Rosas, Martinez, Mosquera, 1997: putative **hominid** species based on material recovered from northeastern Spain; dated between 780 and 625 **kya**. This species shows a mix of both primitive and derived human features; it possesses several primitive traits in comparison to *H. heidelbergensis*. The discoverers propose that *H. antecessor* is ancestral to both *H. heidelbergensis* and *H. neanderthalensis*, while most workers think that these materials should be assigned to *H. heidelbergensis*. See Appendix 1 for taxonomy.

*Homo antiquus*: 1. binomen applied by Adloff, 1908 to material now referred to *Homo neanderthalensis*. 2. binomen applied by Ferguson, 1984 to material recognized as *Australopithecus afarensis* by almost all authorities.

*Homo asiaticus* Linnaeus, 1758: species of humanity as defined by **Linnaeus** in the tenth edition of his *Systema Naturae* (1758); Asians.

*Homo cepranensis* Mallegni, Carneiri, Bisconti, Tartarelli, Ricci, Biddittu and Segre, 2003: proposed hominid species with distinctive frontal bone characteristics comparable to **Bouri** and *H. rhodesiensis*. The type specimen is the calvaria from **Ceprano**, Italy.

‡ *Homo erectus* (Dubois, 1894) : species of *Homo* that lived from *c.* 1.2 mya (many say 1.6 mya) to perhaps 27 **kya** in an isolated pocket of Southeast Asia. There is a growing trend among paleoanthropologists to treat *H. erectus* as a Far Eastern species only and to refer to African contemporaries as *H. ergaster*. The anatomical features that epitomize this group include a unique **taurodont** molar structure, retention of three roots on the upper third premolar, molars with **cingula** and basal **tubercles**, shovel-shaped incisors, a narrow but rounded **dental arcade**, a thick and chinless mandible with large **bicondylar** breadth and in many cases multiple **mental foramina**, a **prognathous** face with a large **interorbital breadth** and broad nasal bones, a low and long cranial vault with flattened frontal and parietal bones (**platycephaly**), an angled **occiput**, a strongly marked and continuous **supra-orbital torus**, a small **mastoid process** with a marked **supramastoid crest** and a **torus angularis** on the **parietal bone**; the vault also shows a frontal and parietal **keel** with **parasagittal** flattening, a 'tent-shaped' coronal section, and a low maximum skull breadth between the supramastoid crests as well as a low triangular **squamosal** portion of the **temporal bone**. The **vault** bones are thick, there is pronounced **postorbital constriction**, and the **inion** and **opisthocranion** coincide. The **cranial capacity** is between 700 and 1225 cm$^3$. The femora are unusual in the great thickness of the cortical bone and are **platymeric**, have a low narrow point and a prominent convexity of the medial border of the shaft; the pelvis has a large acetabulum, a stout acetabulocristal buttress, and laterally rotated ischial tuberosities. See **out of Africa I model**. There have been no fossil materials of *H. erectus* recovered from Europe; in the past archeological remains were attributed to *H. erectus*, but that is now questioned and they may be attributed to another species such as *H. heidelbergensis*. A mandible dated to 1 mya was recovered in the Eurasian country of Georgia and is currently referred to *H. erectus*; this may be revised. *H. erectus* was associated with Acheulean tools (see **Acheulean tool tradition**) and appears to have been a hunter–gatherer or scavenger–gatherer. They are associated with fire, but it does not appear that they knew how to make it. See Appendix 1 for taxonomy.

*Homo erectus bilzinglebensis* Vlcek, 1978: see *Homo heidelbergensis*.

*Homo erectus erectus* Dobzhansky, 1944: subspecies designation applied to the Indonesian (Java) material belonging to *Homo erectus*.

*Homo erectus javensis* Weidenreich, 1940: subspecies designation applied to the Trinil Indonesian (Java) material belonging to *Homo erectus*. Most authorities include these specimens in *H. e. erectus*.

*Homo erectus modjokertensis* (von Koenigswald, 1973): subspecies designation applied to some of the **Sangiran** specimens of Indonesian *Homo erectus*. Most authorities include these specimens in *H. e. erectus*.

*Homo erectus ngandongensis* (Sartono, 1982): subspecies designation applied to several **Sangiran** specimens of Indonesian *Homo erectus*. Most authorities include these specimens in *H. e. erectus*.

*Homo (erectus seu sapiens) paleohungaricus* Thoma, 1966: designation for a recovered occipital bone from Hungary; Vertezollos man. Now generally referred to *Homo heidelbergensis*.

## Proposed species and subspecies in the genus *Homo* (cont.)

*Homo erectus pekinensis* Weidenreich, 1940: subspecies designation applied to the Chinese material belonging to *Homo erectus*; aka Peking man, Choukoutien man, Zhoukoudian man.

*Homo erectus petraloniensis* Murrill, 1983: taxonomic designation for a recovered cranium from Petralona, Greece; considered neandertaloid by many. Now generally referred to *Homo heidelbergensis*.

*Homo erectus yuanmouensis*: see Danawu.

‡ *Homo ergaster* Groves and Mazák, 1975: species of *Homo* that first appears in the fossil record *c.* 1.8 mya; known from East Africa. **Sympatric** and contemporaneous with *Paranthropus boisei*, *Homo habilis*, and *H. rudolfensis*. This species became increasingly accepted during the 1990s, replacing and incorporating those specimens formerly assigned to *H. erectus* in Africa; many authorities now consider *H. erectus* to be solely a Far Eastern species. The main differences between *H. ergaster* and its predecessors are a reduction in dentition size and increased cranial capacity; it differs from *H. erectus* in cranial thickness. Associated with **Acheulean** tools. It has been proposed as the ancestor to later humans. See **out of Africa I** and **out of Africa II** models. The name means 'working man'. See Appendix 1 for taxonomy.

*Homo europaeus* Linnaeus, 1758: species of humanity as defined by **Linnaeus** in the tenth edition of his *Systema Naturae* (1758); Europeans.

*Homo faber*: archaic name sometimes applied to **Neandertals**, meaning 'man the smith'.

*Homo ferus* Linnaeus, 1758: species of humanity as defined by **Linnaeus** in the tenth edition of his *Systema Naturae* (1758); savages.

*Homo floresiensis* Brown, Sutikna, Morwood, Soejono, Jatmiko, Saptomo and Due, 2004: fossil/subfossil species of dwarf **hominin** found in 2003 at **Liang Bua**, a limestone rockshelter on the island of Flores, eastern Indonesia. The remains of up to seven individuals were initially recovered. The majority of the remains were associated with pebble tools and an extinct pygmy elephant (*Stegodon*), dated to 38–18 kya, and thus overlapped temporally with **AMH** occupation in the region. A radius was recovered from an earlier level (95–74 kya). Adult stature of the most complete individual (LB1), possibly a female, is estimated at 106 cm; body mass is estimated at 16–29 kg, and adult cranial capacity at 380 cm³. Researchers contend that the EQ of LB1 approximates that of *Homo habilis*, although the overall morphology of LB1 resembles a megadont *Homo erectus* (e.g. **Sangiran 2**). Insular dwarfism has been invoked as an explanation for the small size of the dwarf hominins.

*Homo florisbadensis helmei* Drennan, 1935: trinomen for a partial cranial specimen (the Florisbad skull) recovered in South Africa during the 1930s. Absolute dating of the strata in which this specimen was found suggests an antiquity greater than 100 kya. Most workers recognize this **hominid** as an archaic *Homo sapiens*.

*Homo georgicus* Gabunia, M.-A. de Lumley, Vekua, Lordkipanidze and H. de Lumley, 2002: name of a habiline-like species of fossil hominid found at **Dmanisi**. The holotype is D2700 (and possibly D2735, an associated mandible). D2700 consists of a nearly complete cranium with a cranial capacity of about 600 cm³; stature is estimated to be approximately 1.5 m (4ft 11in). Cf. **KNM-ER 1813**.

‡ *Homo habilis* Leakey, Tobias and Napier, 1964: earliest fossil species of *Homo* that first appears around 2.3 mya and persists until around 1.6 mya. **Sympatric** and partly contemporaneous with *Paranthropus boisei*, *Homo rudolfensis*, and *Homo ergaster* in East Africa. *H. habilis* has traits intermediate between the **gracile** *Australopithecus* species and later early humans; the teeth are reduced in size, canine eruption is later than in *Australopithecus*, the foot is similar to the modern human foot, but the forearms are longer than in modern humans, suggesting retention of arboreal capabilities. The species is characterized by incipient **encephalization** (cranial capacities of 509–775 cm³). Over 100 specimens have been referred to this taxon; **habilines** are thought by many paleoanthropologists to be the earliest members of the genus *Homo*; others place these specimens in *Australopithecus habilis*. Sites that yield *H. habilis* contain **Oldowan tools** as well as collections of animal bones; the species type specimen is **OH 7**. Many of these sites also yield *Paranthropus* remains and its hand anatomy suggests this genus too was also capable of making and using tools; thus, it is uncertain which genus, perhaps both, were responsible for the tool collections. It is also uncertain whether the animal remains are the result of hominid activity, hunting, scavenging, or natural accumulations. See Appendix 1 for taxonomy.

‡ *Homo heidelbergensis* Schoetensack, 1908: taxonomic designation for the specimens that were previously referred to as 'transitionals' or 'archaic' *Homo sapiens*; most of these specimens are European. *H. heidelbergensis* is a species in flux with additional specimens being referred to it and with a call by

## Proposed species and subspecies in the genus *Homo* (*cont.*)

some to split it into more species. These humans occupied Europe (and Africa, according to some workers) from approximately 700 kya to about 130 kya. *H. heidelbergensis* follows the trend in human evolution for smaller teeth through time; it has a broad mandibular ramus and deep mandibular body, massive paired superciliary arches, and a vertical nasal aperture. Postcrania for this species are rare, but size estimations from skull measurements suggest they were large humans, perhaps weighing as much as 100 kg. *H. heidelbergensis* is associated with Acheulean tools, crude structures, and fire use. They were hunter–gatherers or scavenger–gatherers who, in at least one site, had a seasonal migration pattern in which they returned to the same area each year.

*Homo helmei* Dreyer, 1935: proposed species of transitional humans that would be considered the immediate predecessors to modern humans; this is an African group based on the Florisbad remains; some think that any specimens attributable to this species should be included in *Homo heidelbergensis*. See *Homo florisbadensis helmei* and *Homo sapiens*.

*Homo kanamensis* Leakey, 1933: putative fossil species of 'early-Pleistocene' hominid proposed by Louis Leakey on the basis of the type specimen, a mandible found at Kanam in Kenya. See Kanjera.

*Homo leakeyi* Heberer, 1963: provisional name for OH 9; aka *Homo erectus leakeyi*. See *Homo ergaster*.

*Homo marstoni* (Paterson, 1940): synonym for the Swanscombe specimens now usually included in *Homo heidelbergensis*.

*Homo modjokertensis* (von Koenigswald, 1950): see *Homo erectus*.

*Homo monstrous* Linnaeus, 1758: species of humanity as defined by Linnaeus in the tenth edition of his *Systema Naturae* (1758); abnormal individuals.

*Homo mousteriensis*: archaic nomen sometimes assigned to Neandertals because of the close association of that taxon with implements of the Mousterian tool tradition.

‡ *Homo neanderthalensis* King, 1864: species of hominid that lived between 250 and 28 kya; known from sites in Europe and the Middle East. Neandertals were sympatric with AMHs c 36–28 kya (see last of the Neandertals). The type specimen (from Feldhofer Grotto) and other finds were initially discovered in the first half of the nineteenth century but were not recognized as ancient humans until after the publication of Darwin's *Origin of Species* in 1859. Generally recognized morphological characteristics of the cranium include: inflated skull form with maximum transverse diameter at mid-parietal; a low frontal bone; a suprainiac fossa as well as an occipitomastoid crest; an elongation of the occipital region referred to as a bun; extensively pneumatized bones of the cranium; the face is large with voluminous orbits and nasal cavities; the mid-face exhibits prognathism and the supra-orbital torus is divided centrally; known specimens have a large average cranial capacity (mean 1450 cm$^3$; range 1200–1750 cm$^3$); there is no chin on the mandible, which has a sloping mandibular ramus; there is usually a retromolar space; and the teeth are frequently taurodont. Postcranially, the distal limb segments are short; the scapula has a dorsal axillary groove; the superior pubic ramus is flat and elongate. Body mass estimated at 75 kg; height around 160 cm in females and 170 cm in males. Other characteristics include an extra pair of nasal conchae, which may have been an adaptation to cold, dry air. In general the skeleton suggests thick-set, muscular individuals with large hands and feet, and a body form not unlike that of cold-adapted modern humans. These people were hunters and gatherers, controlled fire, built shelters, and had a Mousterian material culture that has been preserved; these were the first humans to bury their dead, including placing funerary objects with the deceased, and some of these behaviors have been interpreted as consistent with religious beliefs. The presence of older and disabled individuals has been cited as evidence of care by other members of their societies. Neandertals occupied temperate and boreal, even periglacial environments. Neandertals have been previously classified by some researchers as a subspecies (*Homo sapiens neanderthalensis*), particularly by US physical anthropologists, but recent research on the ancient DNA of multiple specimens indicates no close relationship with modern humans; a last common ancestor has been estimated at 600 kya. Neandertal antecedents may include *Homo heidelbergensis* and/or *Homo antecessor*. Neandertal sites include La Chapelle-aux-Saints and Saint Césaire. Cf. Châtelperronian and Lagar Velho 1. See Appendix 1 for taxonomy.

*Homo neanderthalensis* var. *krapensis* (Skerlj, 1953): revised taxonomic designation for the hominid materials recovered from Krapina, Croatia, from 1899 to 1905. Originally given the nomen *Homo primigenius krapinensis*. See *Homo neanderthalensis*.

*Homo neanderthalensis soloensis* von Koenigswald, 1934: original taxonomic designation of the hominid materials recovered in Java, Indonesia, by ter Haar and von Koenigswald; aka Solo man, Ngandong man. Now referred to *Homo erectus*.

## Proposed species and subspecies in the genus *Homo* (*cont.*)

*Homo paleojavanicus modjokertensis* Sartono, 1981: Solo man, Ngandong man; see *Homo erectus*.

*Homo paleojavanicus robustus* Sartono, 1982: Solo man, Ngandong man; see *Homo erectus*.

*Homo paleojavanicus sangiranensis* Sartono, 1981: Solo man, Ngandong man; see *Homo erectus*.

*Homo primigenius asiaticus* Weidenreich, 1933: Solo man, Ngandong man; see *Homo erectus*.

*Homo primigenius* var. *krapensis* Gorjanovic-Kramberger, 1906: original nomen for the hominid materials recovered from Krapina, Croatia, from 1899 to 1905. Later referred to *Homo neanderthalensis*.

*Homo rhodesiensis* (cf. *heidelbergensis*) Woodward, 1921: Rhodesian man, Broken Hill man, Kabwe man, Zambian human; neandertaloid species of *Homo* often referred to as transitional between *Homo erectus* and moderns. Dates are poorly known, but it appears this species was present in Africa more than 130 kya. Species characterized by low receding forehead, massive paired superciliary arches, slight sagittal keel, and angled occipital region with an occipital torus. Cranial capacity around 1100 cm$^3$.

*Homo rudolfensis* (Alexeev, 1986): early species of *Homo* that first appeared around 2 mya and persisted until around 1.6 mya. Sympatric and partly contemporaneous with *Paranthropus boisei*, *Homo habilis*, and *Homo ergaster* in East Africa. This species has some traits reminiscent of *Paranthropus*, such as a flat face and projecting maxilla. The molars and premolars are large and thickly enameled; the cranial capacity of 800 cm$^3$ is larger than that of *H. habilis*; known postcrania suggest that the hindlimbs were longer than the forelimbs, a trait more like modern humans and different from *H. habilis*. The species lectotype is KNM-ER 1470.

‡ *Homo sapiens* Linnaeus, 1758: binomen for AMHs; there is only one living subspecies, but many workers recognize extinct races of *H. sapiens*; type locality, Uppsala, Sweden. Worldwide distribution. Terrestrial; diurnal; completely bipedal with highly derived foot. Great variation in body mass, but, in populations of western European descent, averages around 70 kg for males, 50 kg for females; slight sexual dimorphism in body size, also secondary sexual characteristics are present. Spoken language, and anatomical and physiological adaptations that accompany it, is a characteristic of this organism; large brain. Appears relatively hairless (although has same number of hair follicles as *Pan*) and has large concentration of sweat glands, mostly used for thermoregulation. Dental formula: 2.1.2.3; reduced canines, third molars not always present; reduction in tooth size has led to recession of anterior mandible with a mental protuberance (chin) present, unlike previous humans; omnivorous. Possesses technology which permits occupation of ecozones that would be unavailable otherwise; transgenerational culture. Social organization extremely variable. See *Homo*, archaic *Homo sapiens*, and Hominidae.

*Homo sapiens afer* Wells, 1969: completely modern fossil subspecies of *Homo sapiens* based on material recovered from Border Cave, South Africa. Dating of the materials from the site indicates a range from 90 to 115 kya. This material supports the out of Africa II model.

*Homo sapiens daliensis* Wu, 1981: Dali man; skull from China that represents a transitional stage between Chinese *Homo erectus* and *Homo sapiens*. Cited as evidence for the multiregional continuity model. Synonym: *H. s. mapaensis*.

*Homo sapiens idaltu* White, Asfaw, DeGusta, Gilbert, Richards, Suwa, and Howell, 2003: see BOU-VP-16/1 and the Herto hominids.

*Homo sapiens neanderthalensis* Campbell, 1964: see *Homo neanderthalensis*.

*Homo sapiens protosapiens* Montandon, 1943: see *Homo heidelbergensis*.

*Homo sapiens rhodesiensis* Campbell, 1964: Rhodesian man, Broken Hill man, Kabwe man, Zambian human; see *Homo rhodesiensis*.

‡ *Homo sapiens sapiens* Linnaeus, 1758: trinomen for AMHs; there is only one extant subspecies.

*Homo sapiens shanidarensis* Senyaruk, 1957: Shanidar Neandertals; see *Homo neanderthalensis*, Neandertals.

*Homo sapiens steinheimensis* Campbell, 1964: Steinheim woman; see *Homo heidelbergensis*.

*Homo soloensis* Oppenoorth, 1932: Solo man, Ngandong man; see *Homo erectus*.

*Homo steinheimensis* Berckhemer, 1936: Steinheim woman; see *Homo heidelbergensis*.

*Homo swanscombensis* Kennard, 1942: Swanscombe man; see *Homo heidelbergensis*.

*Homo sylvestris* Linnaeus, 1758: species of humanity as defined by Linnaeus in the tenth edition of his *Systema Naturae* (1758); the orangutan.

*Homo transvaalensis* Mayr, 1950: see *Australopithecus africanus*.

*Homo troglodytes* Linnaeus, 1758: putative ape-like creature listed in the eighteenth century dissertation of Hopius, a student of Linnaeus. See anthropomorpha.

*Homo wadjakensis*: see Wajak.

**Homo moyen:** Quetelet's archaic conception of an individual who is an average specimen from a larger group, especially with respect to various racial characteristics. See **typology**.

**homocystinuria:** inherited, autosomal recessive condition characterized by blood clots, thin bones, mental retardation, muscle weakness, and seizures. Caused by an inability to metabolize the amino acid methionine owing to a deficient enzyme, serine dehydratase.

‡ **homodont:** describes dentition that is characterized by teeth that are the same shape, although they may differ in size. This type of dentition is found in vertebrates such as fishes, amphibians, and reptiles, but is not usual in mammals, with a few exceptions such as toothed whales. Nouns: homodonty, homodontism. Cf. **heterodont**.

**homogametic sex:** that one of two normal karyotypes which during **meiosis** gives rise to only one type of haploid gamete. In mammals, the female is the homogametic sex, possessing an X chromosome in cell gametes; in many birds, it is the male. Cf. **heterogametic sex**.

**homogamy:** synonym for **positive assortative mating**; isophenogamy.

**homokaryon:** cell with two or more genetically identical nuclei that share a common cytoplasm, usually the result of cell fusion. Cf. **heterokaryon**.

**homokaryotypic:** pertaining to an individual with two copies of a chromosomal aberration. Cf. **heterokaryotypic**.

**homolog:** 1. a character that defines a clade. 2. characters that are similar in different species due to descent from a common ancestor. 3. one of a pair of **homologous chromosomes**. Cf. **homologue**.

‡ **homologous:** pertaining to similarity of structure but not necessarily of function. Identical in otherwise dissimilar organisms due to common descent, e.g. **homologues**, specific **genes**, transcription elements, **domains**, or physiological or anatomical structures. Also said of **chromatid** pairs, as in 'homologous chromatids'.

**homologous antigen:** see **alloantigen**.

‡ **homologous chromosomes:** in **diploid** species, pairs of **chromosomes** that consist of identical **linkage groups** of genes, or that contain parallel sequences of genetic **loci**. One of the homologues is normally maternal and the other paternal in origin. Aka homologous pair.

**homologous genes: genes** with similar structures and functions.

**homologous proteins:** group of proteins with commonality due to a single evolutionary origin, which are thus structurally and functionally similar.

**homologous recombination:** normal exchange of DNA among chromosome pairs during **meiosis**; aka crossing over.

**homologous species:** in immunological taxonomy, the species that was the source of the material against which an **antiserum** was produced that is specific to the homologous species, but that also reacts weakly with other closely related **heterologous species** in proportion to the degree of the relationship.

‡ **homologous structures:** structures that are similar in the same or different organisms due to similar hereditary and developmental origin, such as the similarity between the bones in the arm of a primate and those in the wing of a bat.

‡ **homologue:** 1. one of a pair (or set) of homologous structures that are similar due to common ancestry. 2. in genetics, one of a pair of **chromatids**, having the same overall sequence of genes (exact **synteny**). Cf. **homolog**.

‡ **homology:** similarity of a structure due to common heredity or to shared descent from a **common ancestor**, and which, by inference, was also present in that common ancestor. In zoology and biology, the definition is strict; however, among some geneticists and molecular biologists, homology can refer to similarity of **convergent** nucleotide sequences, or even to differing sequences that perform similar molecular functions. See **synapomorphy**. Cf. **analogy**.

**homomorphic:** similar in size and shape but not necessarily similar in function.

‡ **homoplasy:** E. R. Lankester's (1847–1929) term for any resemblance not due to direct inheritance from a common ancestor; similarity due to **adaptation**, **analogy**, **parallelism**, **convergence**, or **mimicry**.

**homosequential:** pertaining to closely related species that possess similar chromosome banding patterns, and hence whose underlying gene sequences are suspected of being identical. See **synteny**.

**homosequential species:** pertaining to species that possess identical **karyotypes**, such as in the **baboons** and **macaques**.

**homosexual:** person (or animal) who engages in sexual relations with another of the same sex in a species. Cf. **heterosexual**.

**homosexuality:** in humans, one of several modes or roles available in many cultures by which individuals adopt roles that symbolize and express gender identification; in this case individuals assume roles that are by convention the opposite to their **anatomical sex**. Anthropologists have noted that cross-cultural attitudes toward this behavior range from mandatory participation to tolerance to taboo. Cf. **heterosexuality**.

**homotype:** specimen that is compared to the **holotype** of another taxon and determined to be conspecific. Alternative spellings: homeotype, homoeotype.

**homozygosis:** inheritance of identical alleles from each parent at a locus.

**homozygosity** (*f*): the proportion of a population (1−*H*) that does not consist of heterozygotes (*H*) at a given locus. Aka frequency of homozygotes.

‡ **homozygote:** in a **diploid** organism, individual possessing exactly identical **alleles** at a locus on **homologous chromatids**. Adjective: homozygous. An organism may be homozygous with respect to one locus and **heterozygous** with respect to another. May also refer to certain chromosomes or **chromosomal aberrations**.

**homunculus:** fully formed, miniature human body believed, according to some medical theories of the sixteenth and seventeeth centuries, to be contained in the spermatozoon. See **Preformation Doctrine** and **encasement theory**.

**honest signal:** in behavioral biology, a sign that communicates an accurate assessment of an individual's condition and the quality of genes it carries. See **deceit**.

**honing:** 1. sharpening by abrasion of an edge, as with a tool. 2. tooth sharpening; **thegosis**. See **canine – third c premolar honing complex**.

**honing facet:** smooth articular surface on a **sectorial premolar** in primates that contacts the upper canine and sharpens it. See **sectorial premolar**.

**Hoolock gibbon:** vernacular for *Hylobates hoolock*.

**hoot face:** primate facial expression in which the mouth takes on a pout, in the way in which a human plays a trumpet; used in long-distance calling. Particularly marked in gibbons and howler monkeys.

**Hooton, Earnest Albert** (1887–1954): US anthropologist and teacher; at Harvard, Hooton was mentor to many of America's second and third generations of physical anthropologists; President, AAPA (1936–8); second Viking Fund Medalist (1947). In *Up from the Ape* (1931), Hooton strongly opposed the **arboreal theory of primate evolution**, and also proposed that human races branched as early as the basal **Pleistocene**, a form of **polygenism**.

**Hopefield:** see **Elandsfontein**.

**'hopeful monsters':** vernacular coined by R.B. **Goldschmidt** to popularize his belief that **macromutations**, such as **chromosomal mutations**, accumulate in populations until a threshold is breached, propelling a species across 'an unbridgeable gap' to a new **species**. Most carriers of such macromutations (his 'monsters') would fail to survive, but a rare few could have a high **fitness** ('hopeful monsters'). Most modern geneticists reject this theory. See **saltational speciation** and **mutant**. Cf. **gradualism**.

**Hopkin's bioclimatic law:** observation that in temperate North America the life history events of organisms tend to occur with an average delay of four days for each degree of latitude northward, or 5° of longitude eastward, or 122 m of altitude in early spring; there is a corresponding occurrence of anticipation in the autumn.

**horizon:** 1. in geology, thin layer found in a stratified sequence characterized with features that render it unique relative to other layers above and below. 2. in archaeology, an identifiable habitation layer or sterile break in a column.

**horizontal dental impaction:** condition in which a tooth is placed at a perpendicular angle in the alveolus and with its crown in contact with an adjacent tooth so as to be incapable of complete eruption. See **dental impaction**.

**horizontal evolution:** 1. the simultaneous and parallel evolution of many molecular sequences in the gene complement of a species, resulting in geographic variation. 2. **allopatric speciation**.

**horizontal ramus:** see **mandibular body**.

**horizontal transmission:** infection of one organism by another contemporary organism. Cf. **vertical transmission**.

‡ **hormone:** any chemical substance produced in the body by an **organ**, by cells of an organ, or by scattered cells, and which has a specific regulatory effect on the activity of a certain organ or of certain cell types. Originally applied to substances secreted by various **endocrine glands** and transported in the bloodstream to distant target organs on which the effects of the hormone were produced, the term is now also applied to various substances not produced by special glands but having similar action, both locally and anatomically remote. Hormones can also influence the nervous system and thus the **behavior** of an organism. Examples of principal hormones by organ of origination include: adrenal gland (cortex: aldosterone, cortisone; medulla: epinephrine, noreipnephrine); gonads (ovary: estrogens {**estrone, estradiol, estriol**}, **progesterone, relaxin**; testis: **testosterone, dihydrotestosterone**); hypothalamus (**gonadotropin-releasing hormone, oxytocin, prolactin-inhibiting hormone, prolactin-releasing hormone, thyrotropin-releasing hormone, vasopressin**); liver (**insulin-like growth factor**); pancreas (**glucagon, insulin**); placenta (**chorionic gonadotropin, chorionic somatomammotropin, placental lactogen, progesterone**); pineal gland (**melatonin**); pituitary gland (adenohypophysis: **adenocorticotropic hormone, follicle-stimulating hormone, growth hormone**/ somatotropin, **luteinizing hormone, prolactin, thyrotropin**; intermediate lobe: **menalocyte-stimulating hormone**; neurohypophysis: **oxytocin** storage, **vasopressin** storage); thymus gland (**thymosin**); thyroid gland (**calcitonin, thyroxine**). See **target site**. Cf. **pheromone**.

**Horn principle:** rule that posits that when food resources are patchy in space and time it is not optimal for an individual or pair to defend these areas, but rather move towards a communal society and forage in groups. This principle was devised for birds, but it has been applied in an attempt to explain why open-country **cercopithecines** live in larger groups than closely related forest species.

**Horner's law:** nineteenth century observation that the most common form of **color blindness** (red–green) in humans is transmitted from male to male through unaffected females. See **X-linked trait**.

**horotely: Simpson's** term for an average rate of evolution.

**horse–donkey hybrid:** cross between a horse and a donkey (ass) that produces either a **mule** (female is a horse) or a **hinny** (female is a donkey). Since horses have a **diploid number** of 2N = 64 chromosomes while donkeys have 2N = 62, the union of their **haploid** gametes (32 + 31) produces an **aneuploid** F1 hybrid with 2N = 63; an odd number of chromosomes generally produces viable but eventually sterile individuals owing to meiotic difficulties. In this specific cross, the hybrids uniformly possess the **mitochondrial DNA** of the maternal species. Phenotypic differences are **epigenetic**, owing to **parent-of-origin effects** during differentiation and development.

**Horsfield's tarsier:** vernacular for *Tarsius bancanus*.

**horticulture:** 1. cultivation of flowers, fruits, and ornamental plants. 2. in subsistence farming, a method in which only simple hand tools are used for tillage and small-scale gardening, most frequently utilizing a **digging stick**.

**Hortus:** archaeological site found in 1972 in southern France dating to *c.* 45 kya and containing artifacts including a disputed 'Shaman's cape' made of leopard skin. Hominid remains include fragments from at least twenty individuals assigned to *Homo neanderthalensis*. Some of these are reported to show evidence of **defleshing**, and their remains were cached in a 'fissure'. Other fauna were also found at the site, which has also been interpreted as a hyena den. Aka La Grotte de L'Hortus.

**host:** 1. any organism that harbors and provides nourishment for another organism, a **parasite** or **symbiont**. 2. the recipient of a transplant or transfusion.

**host cell:** in biotechnology, the cell in which **recombinant DNA** is inserted so that it may be cloned as the cell divides, so that the recombinant DNA it codes for can be produced in commercial quantities.

**Hottentot: ethonym** for one of the **autochthonous** peoples of the Kalahari in sub-Saharan Africa; the **ethonym** itself is a corruption of an identified language family, Hottentot–Bushman, made up of both Hottentot and **Bushman** dialects. Aka **Khoisan**, Bushman, Nama.

**Hottentot apron:** enlargement of the **labia minora** found among Hottentot and Bushman women, owing either to a genetic trait or to an intentional deformation.

**housekeeping gene:** gene actively expressed in all cells of the body and therefore associated with some fundamental activity present in all cells, e.g. **cell division** or **glycolysis**.

**Howell, Francis Clark** (1925–): US paleoanthropologist; academic positions at Washington University (St. Louis), Chicago, and Berkeley. Among his major excavations were the **Torralba** and **Ambrona** sites in Spain, where an *in situ* mastodon kill with associated **Acheulean** tools was unearthed. He also worked in Ethiopia, where he was codirector of the Omo Research Expedition in 1966, and his research there helped to push back the age of the earliest hominids by 2 my. Co-author (with Y. **Coppens**) of 'Inventory of remains of Hominidae from Plio-Pleistocene formations of the lower Omo basin, Ethiopia (1967–1972)', *Am. J. Phys. Anth.* (1974), 40(1): 1–16.

**Howells, William White** (1908–): US physical anthropologist at Harvard University; conducted fieldwork in Oceania. Known for his development of multivariate statistics and its applications to human populations. His cranial database of 17 reference populations from around the world is one of the most extensive ever collected. Editor of the *AJPA* (1949–54); Viking Fund medalist (1954). Editor of *Ideas on Evolution* (1962); author of *Mankind in the Making* (1967), *The Pacific Islanders* (1973), *Cranial Variation in Man* (1978), and *Who's Who in Skulls* (1995).

**Howieson's Poort:** archaeological site found in 1925 near Grahamstown in South Africa, possibly dated to 70–50 **kya** (others contend the oldest reliable date is 19.6 kya); contains a blade-dominated assemblage with microliths (Upper Paleolithic = **Howieson's Poort industry**).

**Howieson's Poort industry:** a distinctive South African artifact assemblage that contains tools specifically designed for hafting of **composite tools** as previous flakes wear out.

**howler monkey:** general vernacular for the six **platyrrhine** species belonging to the genus *Alouatta*.

*Hox* **gene:** 1. one of the class of **homeodomain** protein transcription factors that regulate patterns of gene expression in most organisms. 2. **homeobox genes** that encode transcription factors, i.e. proteins that initiate and regulate the synthesis of **mRNA**.

**Hoxne:** archaeological site found in 1790 in Suffolk, England, containing prehistoric stone artifacts that caused John Frere to state that 'The situation in which these weapons were found may tempt us to refer them to a very remote period indeed...and to a people who had not the use of metal' (1800).

**Hrdlička, Aleš** (1869–1943): Bohemian-born US physical anthropologist, physician; founder and first president of the **American Association of Physical Anthropologists** (AAPA) in 1930, and first editor of the *American Journal of Physical Anthropology* (AJPA) in 1918. An early supporter of the view that Native Americans originated in Asia (**Hrdlička's thesis**) and that there had never been Neandertals in the Americas. Correct in his dismissal of **Piltdown** as an anomaly and in his critique of the hominid status of *Ramapithecus*, but he incorrectly dismissed the **Taung child** as a great ape. Author of *Ancient Man in North America* (1907).

**Hrdlička fauna:** cercopithecid-rich fauna located at the **Taung** australopithecine site, dated to about 2.6–2.4 **mya**, and younger than either the **Thabaseek deposits** or the hominid-bearing breccia.

**Hrdlička's thesis:** proposal by **Hrdlička** as early as 1917 for the peopling of the Americas in which Mongolian immigrants of northeast Asiatic origin arrived in the New World in successive waves by way of the ice-bound Bering Strait during the last (Wisconsin) glacial maximum. This model has proven to be the most durable of the several **early man in the New World** hypotheses.

**Hrdy, Sarah (Blaffer-)** (1946–): US primatologist, recently at UC Davis and Harvard. Best known work was done at Abu, India, where a long-term study of **langur** monkey troops resulted in observations of **infanticide** and sororal **polygynous** social groups interspersed with **bachelor herds** of roving young males engaged in strategies of delayed **troop transfer** and **male–male competition.** Author of *The Langurs of Abu* (1977), *The Woman that Never Evolved* (1981), *Infanticide* (1984), and *Mother Nature* (1999).

**HSA:** abbreviation in the cytogenetic literature that stands for H*omo* s*apiens*, and used to denote specific chromosomes, e.g. HSA 1.

**H substance:** polysaccharide precursor to the A and B antigens in the **ABO blood group**, and identical to the O null allele. The addition of a single (different) terminal sugar to the H chain yields the A and B antigens. See **H antigen**.

**HSV:** see **herpes simplex virus**.

**HTLV:** abbreviation for **human T-cell lymphotrophic virus**.

**Huangshanxi:** archaeological site found in 1952 in Ziyang County, Sichuan Province, China, dated to 39 **kya**; contains hominid remains, including a partial cranium attributed to *Homo sapiens*. Aka Tzeyang Man (Huangshanshi, Szechuan).

**Huanglong:** see **Xujiafenshan**.

**huddling:** close proximity of **conspecifics** in which their bodies are in contact. There are different rea-sons for huddling among primates. Among snow monkeys this can be for conservation of body heat with as much body surface touching other animals as possible, as is the case with dwarf lemur sleeping balls. In other primates it may be the result of stress and an effort to find comfort.

**Huerzeleris quercyi (Stehlin, 1916):** adapoid **prosimian** believed to have lived in the late Eocene and belonging to the notharctid subfamily **Cercamoniinae; monotypic;** known from a single maxillary fragment containing several cheek teeth. Some workers think that *H. quercyi* should be included in *Archomomys*. Estimated body mass 190 g. Dental formula uncertain; dental morphology suggests either **insectivory, gummivory,** or both. See Appendix 1 for taxonomy.

**HUGO:** abbreviation for Human Genome Organization. See **Human Genome Project.**

**Hulse, Frederick Seymour** (1906–90): US physical anthropologist who specialized in anthropological genetics and forensic anthropology. Hulse was trained in the traditional race-centered physical anthropology of his mentor, Earnest **Hooton**. He altered his views as he conducted genetic research with many different peoples and recognized the effects of culture on the gene pool of human populations; nevertheless, he also found cases in which there were genetic effects independent of environment. Hulse was editor of the *American Journal of Physical Anthropology* from 1964 to 1969 and president of the **American Association of Physical Anthropologists** from 1967 to 1969.

**Huludong Cave:** see **Tangshan Hill.**

‡ **human:** vernacular for any member of the family **Hominidae.** This includes members of *Australopithecus*, *Paranthropus*, and any species of *Homo*.

*Human Biology*: academic journal devoted to the study of human population biology and genetics. The journal was founded in 1929 and is published by Wayne State University Press. It was formerly the official journal of the Human Biology Council. See **Human Biology Association.**

**human biology:** study of humans from the point of view of their biological adaptations, and as zoological beings.

**Human Biology Association (or Council):** North American academic society devoted primarily to the study of human biology. Its members include individuals from physical anthropology, medicine, dentistry, public health, genetics, nutrition, and other areas of human biology. The Human Biology Council was established in 1940 and incorporated in 1974. Its organ was *Human Biology* from 1940 to 1988 and from 1988 to the present its journal has been the *American Journal of*

*Human Biology*. Currently it has approximately 600 members. It holds its annual meetings concurrently with the **American Association of Physical Anthropologists.**

**human calorimeter:** chamber that is used to measure heat output of the human body during different levels of physical exertion. This chamber has enclosed air circulation and a series of pipes containing water whose temperature is measured, providing a caloric number. A type of **indirect calorimetry.** Cf. **bomb calorimeter.**

**human chorionic gonadotropin** (hCG): a recombinant (genetically engineered) gene product; see **chorionic gonadotropin.**

**human ecology:** field within human biology that studies the relationship of individual humans and of human populations to both the biotic and abiotic environments. The term human ecology has also been adopted by some academic home economics departments, as at Cornell University.

**human engineering:** 1. use of **anthropometry** to design human products ranging from clothing to working space. 2. theoretical manipulation of the human genome for particular phenotype results.

**human ethology:** relatively recent (1970s) branch of behavioral biology that focuses on the biological bases for human behavior. Human ethology focuses on the human species, rather than on the individual as would be the case in psychology, has a comparative approach (to both other species, such as primates, and to different human populations), and investigates the development of behavior in infants. Although it developed from zoology and other areas of biology, it has strong overlaps with **anthropology.**

‡ **human evolution:** process of **adaptation** among **AMHs** and their immediate ancestors, conventionally taken to mean any species grouped in the genus *Homo*, that evolved during approximately the past 2 my. See **hominid evolution.**

**human evolutionary biology:** study of **AMHs** and their ancestors (**hominids** and other nonhuman **primates**), of their **biologic** and **genetic** adaptive systems, of their capacity to invent and transmit **culture**, and of the **evolution** of those **hominids** and systems. Aka physical anthropology.

**human genetics:** scientific study of human characteristics with a genetic component.

‡ **Human Genome Project** (HGP): project initiated in 1989 and funded by the US government; has the initial goal of locating and identifying all of the coding genes in the human **genome** by the year 2005; a secondary goal, to sequence all the **DNA** in the entire genome, will take somewhat longer. Currently, the HGP is substantially ahead of schedule. One of the major findings of the Human Genome Rough Draft published in February, 2001, is that the number of genes may be closer to 30,000 than to the previously estimated 100,000, and that the enormous library of human proteins is produced by fewer **cistrons** and **differential splicing;** yet other species have a gene : protein ratio that is closer to 1 : 1. The American HGP has recently combined with the international Human Genome Organization (HUGO) to make the project global in scope. See **gold standard.**

**Human Genome Rough Draft:** two versions of the sequence of the human genome were published in February, 2001. Each sequence unveiled almost 2.7 billion bp of an estimated 3.2 billion bp in the entire human genome; more than 95% of the **euchromatic** regions had been sequenced. One public version of the complete sequence is mirrored at several sites on the internet. Principals in the sequencing effort, which included work by over 500 scientists who co-authored the two papers, included Francis Collins of the US NIH, Eric S. Lander of the Whitehead Institute, and J. Craig Venter of Celera Genomics. The Consortium paper is: Lander *et al.* (2001), *Nature* (15 February 2001), **409**(6822): 860. The Celera paper is: Venter *et al.* (2001), *Science* (16 February 2001), **291**(5507): 1304.

**human growth hormone** (hGH): 1. substance secreted in humans by the anterior **pituitary gland** that functions like **growth hormone** in many other species; uninterrupted sleep is important during growing periods because pulsating release of hGH occurs primarily during deep sleep. Aka somatotropin. 2. hGHr, a preparation manufactured by **recombinant** (genetically engineered) technology and used to treat **dwarfism** in children with congenital deficiency of growth hormone.

**human growth hormone gene family:** humans, like all other primates, possess five endoreduplicated growth hormone genes. In humans, these genes map to HSA 17q21; the 5′–3′ order of the genes is *GH1-CSHP1-CHS1-GH2-CSH2*. *GH1* codes for pituitary hGH; *GH2* is a **pseudogene**, and the others are expressed in the placenta. *GSH1* and *GSH2* code for hCS; *CSHP1* codes for an hCS variant. All are structurally similar.

**human hairless gene** (*HR*): gene located on HSA 8p12 that when mutated can cause inherited **congenital atrichia.**

‡ **human immunodeficiency virus:** see **HIV.**

‡ **human leukocyte antigen complex** (HLA): human homologue of the **major histocompatibility complex;** see **HLA complex.**

**human milk:** see **breast milk.**

**human nature:** in the broadest sense, according to E. O. **Wilson**, the full set of innate behavioral predispositions that characterize the human species; and in the narrower sense, according to Wilson, those **predispositions** that affect social behavior. Any philosophy that holds that there is a natural character, just as plants and animals have natural forms.

**human odontology:** see **odontology**.

**human origins models:** models of human origins fall generally into three clusters: (1) the **polycentric models**, (2) the **monocentric models**, and (3) the **hybrid models of human origins**. Each cluster has many variants; some of the variants have multiple synonyms.

‡ **human osteology:** see **osteology**.

**human physiology:** study of the mechanisms by which the human body functions.

**human polygenic traits, characters** or **features:** any phenotypic trait that is controlled by a set of integrated genes to produce a complex outcome but with appreciable **heritability**, such as **stature** or **skin color**.

**human T-cell lymphotrophic virus** (HTLV): virus that is similar to **HIV** and that was simultaneously researched; two common types exist, HTLV-I and HTLV-II (formerly called type C oncoviruses); an RNA virus (Retroviridae).

**human universals:** cultural traits that seem to be present in all human groups, such as religion and an **incest taboo**.

‡ **human variation:** physical and cultural differences among **AMHs**. Cultural variation includes differences in language, religious belief, clothing, and so forth. Physical variation includes differences in **skin color**, body shape, and **blood groups**, etc. **Anthropologists** believe that such variations, whether cultural or physical, have helped local groups of humans to adapt uniquely to a wide variety of environmental conditions.

**Humboldt's woolly monkey:** vernacular for *Lagothrix lagothricha*.

**humerofemoral index:** ratio of the length of the upper arm to the thigh; **humerus** length divided by the length of the **femur** and multiplied by 100.

‡ **humerus: long bone** that makes up the upper arm. The proximal portion helps form the **glenohumeral joint** between the **scapula** and the upper arm. Plural: humeri.

**humidity:** measure of moisture in the air; an important variable in the measurement of stress in warm environments because heat conductance is directly proportional to humidity at any given temperature; in conditions of high humidity there is less heat dissipation and greater thermal stress.

**humoral:** pertaining to body fluids or substances within them.

**humoral action, concept of:** theory that every gland and tissue releases products that can have effects on other glands and tissues. Although proposed long before the isolation of specific hormones and specifically critical of the *elan vital* and other mystical

products, the 1742 model of Théophile de Bordeau (1722–76) nevertheless used the term 'humors' for these proposed products.

‡ **humoral immune response:** immune response that is mediated by **antibody** molecules; **B cells** that secrete antibodies into the bloodstream; the primary protection against bacteria and viruses in extracellular fluid. Aka antibody-mediated immunity, humoral immunity. See **immunoglobulin**. Cf. **cellular immune esponse**.

‡ **hunter–gatherer:** see **foragers**.

**Hunter syndrome:** see **mucopolysaccharidosis, type II**.

**hunting:** 1. in humans, the preparation for, pursuit of and potential acquisition of animal protein and byproducts; one of the two primary modes of food acquisition available to subsistence peoples; the other is **gathering**. 2. competitive animal behavior during which a member of one species, known as the hunter or predator, captures a member of another species, the prey. See **optimal foraging theory** and **foraging**.

**hunting dog:** vernacular for the African canid *Lycaon pictus*; this dog has been used as an ecological model (diurnal hunter) for early hominids.

**hunting response:** see **cold-induced vasodilation**.

**Huntington disease** (HD): inherited condition characterized by progressive degeneration of the nervous system and premature death; onset generally occurs at middle age, but age of onset decreases with each generation. HD is caused by a mutation in an autosomal dominant gene (*HD*) that codes for the huntingtin protein (HTT). The defect consists of up to 85 expansion repeats or 'stutters' of the nucleotide sequence CAG in the first exon. The resulting mutant protein, mHTT, apparently folds differently than native HTT, is cleaved, and then migrates abnormally into the cell nucleus. Five per cent of the population of the villagers of Maracaibo, Venezuela, have HD due to **founder effect** and **genetic drift**. HD exhibits evidence for **anticipation** of a trinucleotide repeat, for **genomic imprinting**, and for a **parent-of-origin effect**; the symptoms appear in adolescence and are more severe if inherited from the father, less severe and occur in middle age if inherited from the mother. Aka 'chorea St. Vitus', Huntington's chorea, Woody Guthrie disease.

**Hurler syndrome:** see **mucopolysaccharidosis, type I**.

**husbandry:** maintenance of nondomesticated animals; these animals may be tame, but they are not genetically altered through artificial selection (i.e. **domestication**).

**Hutton, James** (1726–97): Scottish natural historian and geologist. Author of *Theory of the Earth* (1785), in which he argued for a lengthy geological history and formulated **uniformitarianism**, an early view of geological change, a position further developed by Charles **Lyell**. Hutton's views were criticized by religious fundamentalists.

**Huxley, Julian S.** (1887-1975): British biologist whose studies of human **variation** resulted in his coinage of the term **cline** (1939); this led to a 'non-race' statement in the **UNESCO Statement on Race**, an institution of which he was the first general director. Huxley later founded the World Wildlife Fund (now the World Wide Fund for Nature).

**Huxley, Thomas Henry** (1825–95): anthropologist, comparative zoologist, physiologist, and 'Darwin's bulldog'; surgeon on HMS *Rattlesnake* in New Guinea and Australia (1847–50). When he heard them, Huxley immediately supported Darwin's ideas. 'How extremely stupid not to have thought of that', he said on reading the *Origin of Species*. Huxley's review of the book in *The* [London] *Times* was one of the factors in the book's success. Huxley is also remembered for an 1860 debate with anti-evolutionist Archbishop 'Soapy Sam' Wilberforce, for Huxley's works on primate comparative anatomy in 1863, for his proposal of the **arboreal theory of primate evolution**, and for a letter to **Darwin** asking him to remove or de-emphasize his dependence on **gradualism**. Huxley also coined the term 'agnosticism'. Author of *Evidence as to Man's Place in Nature* (1863). President of the Royal Society (1883–5), winner of the Royal Society's Darwin Medal (1893).

**hyaline cartilage:** tissue with a homogenous matrix, the most common type of **cartilage**. Hyaline cartilage occurs at the articular ends of bones, in the trachea, and in the nose. Most of the bones in the body are formed from hyaline cartilage during embryogenesis.

**H-Y antigen:** any of several minor histocompatibility **epitopes** (or inducers) that map to HSA Yq; candidate genes are *SMCY*, *DFFRY* and *UTY*. One or more of the antigen(s) are reportedly identical to the **Mullerian-inhibiting hormone**. Homogametic individuals (males, in humans) produce the antigen; heterogametic individuals (females) have a homologous antagonistic locus (H-Y regulator, *SMCX/DFFRX/ UTX*) on the portion of their Xp22.3 chromosomes that does not undergo **heteropycnosis**. An autosomal H-Y structural gene has been reported, and maps to the MHC on 6p. *SMCY* is highly conserved and has been located on the **Y chromosome** of most mammalian species for 120 **my**. Because males experience more germ cell divisions per generation than females, it is possible that the Y chromosome evolves faster than the X chromosome; *SMCY* evolves 1.8 times faster than *SMCX* and has accumulated three times more mutations in the most recent 28,000 year period.

‡ **hybrid:** 1. a **heterozygote**. 2. any offspring of a cross between two genetically dissimilar individuals. The term is often used to describe unlikely offspring between phenotypically very different parents, who may sometimes even be members of different **species**, such as the **mule**. Aka intergrade.

**hybrid breakdown:** situation when **F2** (or backcross) hybrids have reduced **viability** or **fertility**; a **postzygotic isolating mechanism**.

**hybrid cell:** cell formed by fusion of two somatic cells from different sources, as in human–mouse cell hybridization.

**hybrid inviability:** situation when **F1** hybrid zygotes have reduced viability or are inviable; a **postzygotic isolating mechanism**.

**hybrid models of human origins:** models that posit hybridization after multiple origins for hominids and/or humans; among these are the **assimilation model of human origins**, the **hybridization and replacement model**, and the **out of Africa again and again model**. See **human origins**.

**hybrid sterility:** partial or complete sterility of **F1** or later generation hybrids between genetically different populations; a **postzygotic isolating mechanism**. F1 hybrids of one sex (or both sexes) fail to produce functional gametes.

**hybrid vigor:** see **heterosis**.

**hybrid zone:** geographic zone in which two populations, formerly separated by **geographical isolation**, hybridize after the breakdown of the geographic barrier. Aka allopatric hybridization zone.

**hybridization:** 1. any crossing of genetically dissimilar individuals that leads to hybrid progeny after secondary contact. 2. *in vitro* fusion of somatic cells from two different species; **somatic cell hybridization**. 3. normal complementary base pairing of DNA:DNA, DNA:RNA, or RNA:RNA.

**hybridization and replacement model:** complex version of the **human origins** hypothesis of **AMHs** that proposes Africa as the center of a recent radiation, yet allows for gene flow between new and 'replaced' demes; its primary supporter is Günter **Bräuer**. Cf. the **out of Africa II** hypothesis and the **multiregional continuity model**.

**hybridization probe:** small piece of **DNA** used to identify by hybridization the corresponding sequence in a DNA sample. Aka probe, DNA probe, gene probe.

**hybridoma:** cell culture composed of fused cells of different kinds, cloned for the purpose of producing antibody of a single specificity. The fusion usually involves an antibody-producing tumor cell (myeloma) and a normal, antigenically stimulated plasma cell. The antibody produced is called a **monoclonal antibody**, and is directed against the antigen **epitope** of the tumor cell.

**hydric:** 1. applied to conditions that are extremely wet. 2. adapted to wet conditions. Cf. **mesic** and **xeric**.

**hydrocephalus:** mode of mental deficiency as the result of excess cerebrospinal fluid in the ventricles of the brain. An affected individual's head is extremely large and physical condition is poor. Hydrocephalus is caused by an X-linked recessive allele.

**hydrogen** (H): colorless, odorless, combustible gas that combines with **oxygen** to form **water**, a substance critical to life for most organisms, including **primates.**

**hydrogen bond:** weak chemical attractive force that holds many kinds of molecules together. Such bonds are important in holding polynucleotide chains together as **DNA** and in determining the arrangement of polypeptide and carbohydrate chains in proteins and cellulose, and are also an important force in adhesion.

‡ **hydrolysis:** process of decomposition or breakdown of a chemical into two portions on the addition of the elements of water; a hydrogen ion (-H) is added to one portion and a hydroxyl group (-OH) to the other. Aka hydrolytic reaction.

**hydrops fetalis:** see **thalassemia.**

**hydroxyapatite:** crystalline calcium phosphate that binds to duplex DNA, and is the transportable form of **apatite.** Found in the matrix of true bone, and one of the components of teeth. This substance is found only in vertebrates.

**hydroxyurea:** pharmaceutical compound that inhibits **semiconservative replication** of **DNA**, induces **fetal hemoglobin** (HbF) production, and increases biodeformability of HbS-containing erythrocytes. See **sickle cell disease.**

**hyena:** general vernacular for a nocturnal terrestrial carnivore belonging to the family Hyaenidae and species of *Proteles*, *Crocuta*, or *Hyaena*; inhabits savannas and deserts of Africa and southwest Asia. Hyenas are both hunters and scavengers; they are often considered the agents responsible for some of the bone accumulations in paleontological sites.

*Hylobates* **Illiger, 1811: hominoid** genus to which the gibbons (and, for most workers, the **siamang**) belong; six to eleven species, depending on author. Some workers recognize three subgenera: *Nomascus*, *Symphalangus*, and *Hylobates*. If the siamang is considered to be a separate species, then all *Hylobates* species are **allopatric.** Distributed in the forests of Southeast Asia. Arboreal; diurnal; locomotion is **brachiation**, but they can walk **bipedally** on the rare occasions when they are on the ground; elongated forelimbs with long slender fingers on the fore paws, which curve and enable the animal to grasp and release branches quickly. These are the smallest apes, weighing between 5 and 11 kg; lack **sexual dimorphism.** Dental formula: 2.1.2.3; predominantly **frugivorous**, but some species also have a certain degree of **folivory**; said to practice **terminal branch feeding. Monogamous** families are the rule, with both males and females defending their territory; territories

delineated by sound. See Appendix 2 for taxonomy, Appendix 3 for living species.

**Hylobatidae:** monotypic **hominoid** family to which the gibbons and siamangs belong, consisting of the genus *Hylobates*, four subgenera, and eleven species. Vernacular: hylobatid. See Appendix 2 for taxonomy, Appendix 3 for living species.

**Hylobatinae:** nomen for a subfamily of the family **Hominidae** used in some taxonomic schemes; this subfamily consists of the genus *Hylobates*; not widely recognized.

**hyoid:** bone inferior to the mandible which serves as an attachment for the muscles of the tongue; the hyoid is the only bone that does not articulate with any other bone. The hyoid of **Neandertals** is similar in size and shape to modern humans and some workers interpret this as evidence for sophisticated spoken language among Neandertals; others dispute this.

**Hyopsodontidae:** archaic mammals from the **Paleogene system** that contains fossil members that have been mistaken for early primates.

**hyper IgM syndrome:** X-linked recessive condition in which antibody protection cannot switch from IgM to IgA and IgG, and characterized by large tonsils and disorganized lymphoid tissue; the immune system destroys blood cells.

**hyperacute rejection reaction:** rapid destruction of a **xenograft** due to the global differences in tissue antigens.

**hyperbilirubinemia:** toxic accumulation of **bilirubin** in tissues. Cf. **jaundice** and **kernicterus.**

**hyperbrachycephalic:** in reference to the **cephalic index**, having an index of 85.00 of greater; such an individual is considered to be very broad-headed. Cf. **hyperbrachycranic.**

**hyperbrachycranic:** in reference to the **cranial index**, having an index of 85.00 or greater; such an individual is considered to be very broad-headed. Cf. **hyperbrachycephalic.**

**hyperbrachyskelic:** pertaining to a **stem-leg length index** of less than 74.99. see **brachyskelia.**

**hypercalcemia:** 1. a dominant genetic trait in humans that causes an elevated concentration of calcium in the blood. 2. any increase in plasma calcium.

**hyperchamaerrhinic:** in reference to the **nasal index**, having an index of 58.00 or greater; such an individual is considered to have a broad **nasal aperture.**

**hypercholesterolemia, familial** (FH or FHC): one of the genetic forms of coronary heart disease that manifests in the fourth or fifth decade of life. Genetically deficient low-density lipoprotein protein receptors (LDLRs) in the liver cause LDL cholesterol to accumulate in the blood, resulting in high blood cholesterol, atherosclerosis and heart disease. Most mutations in the *FHC* gene prevent the synthesis of LDLR;

others prevent its removal from the endoplasmic reticulum; still other mutations interfere with LDL binding. Affected individuals are often **compound heterozygotes**. The condition is a rare example of **incomplete dominance** in humans. Aka inherited hypercholesterolemia.

**hyperdisease extinction hypothesis:** aka the hyperdisease theory of mammoth extinction; see **Pleistocene extinction hypotheses**.

**hyperdolichocranic:** pertaining to a **cranial index** of between 65.00 and 69.99.

**hyperdontia:** hereditary condition characterized by the presence of one or more extra teeth. Cf. **hypodontia**, **adontia**.

**hypereuryenic:** in reference to the **upper facial index**, having an index of 44.99 or less; such an individual is considered to be very broad-faced. Cf. **hypereuryprosopic**.

**hypereuryprosopic:** in reference to the **total facial index**, having an index of 79.99 or less; such an individual is considered to be very broad-faced. Cf. **hypereuryenic**.

**hyperextension:** stretching beyond the normal limits of a joint; extreme extension.

**hyperflexion:** **flexion** of a structure beyond the normal limits.

**hypergamy:** female practice of acquiring a mate of equal or higher social rank. Cf. **hypogamy**.

**hyperglycemia:** abnormally high concentration of glucose in the blood.

**hyperleptenic:** in reference to the **upper facial index**, having an index of 60.00 or greater; such an individual is considered to be very narrow-faced. Cf. **hyperleptoprosopic**.

**hyperleptoprosopic:** in reference to the **total facial index**, having an index of 95.00 or greater; such an individual is considered to be very narrow-faced. Cf. **hyperleptenic**.

**hyperlipoproteinemia:** heritable condition with symptoms that include abdominal pain, **xanthomas** (in some types), and concentrations of LDL and plasma triglycerides in the blood; additional symptoms are secondary to **obesity** and/or cardiovascular disease. Type 1 is one of five major types and subtypes, all inherited. The defective enzyme is lipoprotein lipase (PLP, an autosomal recessive), but lipoprotein receptor-related protein 5 (LRP5) variants have also been implicated. PLP lines the walls of capillaries, and is activated by **HDLs** (high-density lipoproteins) such that it metabolizes **LDLs** (low-density lipoproteins, the so called 'bad' cholesterol). The enzyme also regulates cell size; certain PLP alleles are expected to contribute to high concentrations of triglycerides and/or increased cell size (hypertrophy). Simple clinical tests are available to detect elevated HDL, LDL and triglycerides. Clinical severity is associated with apolipoptotein genotype. Aka Frederickson's hyperlipoproteinemia, lipase D deficiency, leptin deficiency. Another variant (hyperlipoproteinemia, Type I(b), an autosomal recessive) causes hypoproteinemia due to apolipoprotein C-II deficiency, Type I. PLP, LRP5, and apoE variants are also implicated in **type II diabetes**.

**hypermacroskelic:** pertaining to a **stem-leg length index** of more than 100.00.

**hypermorph:** 1. in some archaic classifications, the proposal that a group or groups represent a more developed form compared with another group. The term was often invoked by those seeking to rationalize a hierarchy of human races. Cf. **hypomorph**. 2. in genetics, a **mutant** allele whose effect is higher or more pronounced than that of the **wild type** allele.

**hypermorphosis:** category of **heterochrony** that extends one or more stages of development and growth of a descendant species beyond that of an ancestral species.

**hypermutability:** genetic trait that leads to high rate of mutation during DNA replication; characteristic of some neoplastic cells.

**hyperostosis:** excessive increase of bone tissue; bone **hypertrophy**. See **exostosis**.

**hyperparathyroidism:** excessive secretion of **parathyroid hormone** that manifests as high serum calcium and low serum phosphate. The abnormal levels are often secondary to an adenoma or carcinoma, or to chronic renal disease.

**hyperpigmentation:** deposition of excess pigment in a tissue or organ.

**hyperpituitarism:** see **acromegaly** and **giantism**.

‡ **hyperplasia:** 1. increase in the number of cells by cell division, either during development, or in a tissue or culture. 2. abnormally large organ or structure.

**hyperplatymeric:** pertaining to a **platymeric index** of less than 74.99.

**hyperrobust:** in paleoanthropology, pertaining to those hominids larger than the **robust** forms, i.e. *Paranthropus boisei* and *P. aethiopicus*.

**hypersensitivity:** response with clinical symptoms to amounts of allergens that are innocuous to most people; see **allergy**.

**hypertension:** unstable, chronically elevated or excessively high arterial blood pressure; in an adult human, greater than 140/90 mmHg; aka high blood pressure. Hypertension is multifactorial, but with a recognized genetic component.

**hyperthermia:** any increase in **body temperature**, regardless of cause. In adult humans, the hyperthermia threshold is $\geq 37.2\,°C$ (oral). See **fever**. Cf. **hypothermia**. See **normothermia**.

**hypertrichosis:** 1. a rare genetic disease; see **hypertrichosis, congenital generalized.** 2. growth of hair along the rim and on the auricle of the ear, or on the elbows.

**hypertrichosis, congenital generalized** (CGH, HTC2): rare congenital condition characterized by an increase in the number of hair follicles in locations such as the face and upper body, resulting in profound hirsutism; has been called an **atavism** (a 'reactivated' ancestral **DNA sequence**). The mutation is in an X-linked dominant gene, *HTC2*. Aka the 'wolf man' syndrome. Related conditions include hypertrichosis universalis, and congenital generalized hypertrichosis with gingival hyperplasia.

‡ **hypertrophy:** 1. an increase in the size (volume) of individual cells (but not in the number of cells) during normal growth and development of an organism, due to an increase in protein relative to DNA. Hypertrophy increases the surface area of a cell. Cell edema is not hypertrophy. 2. excessive growth or enlargement of an organ or tissue, rather than increased cell number.

**hypertrophy, behavioral:** enlargement; according to E. O. **Wilson** and others, most kinds of human social behavior are hypertrophic variants of original, simpler responses that were of more direct adaptive advantage in hunter–gatherer and primitive agricultural societies.

**hypertrophic, trait, character or feature:** preexisting trait that is extremely developed. The enlargement of the elephant's tusk, for example, occurred because of the enlargement and change in shape of a tooth that originally (in the fossil record) had an ordinary form; the molarization of premolars in the **megadont** robust australopithecines, and the crenulation of their grinding surfaces, may be another example.

**hypervariable region** or **site** (hv): site containing amino acids located within the variable region of an **immunoglobulin** heavy or light chain. Such sites exhibit great variation. After folding the antibody into its **quaternary structure**, these sites are found in the antigen-binding region, or **paratope**, of the molecule.

‡ **hyperventilation:** condition marked by fast and deep breathing that tends to remove increasing amounts of carbon dioxide from the body and to lower the partial pressure of the gas; ventilation without an increase in oxygen consumption or carbon dioxide production; results in buzzing in the ears, tingling in extremities, and fainting. Aka overventilation.

**hypervitaminosis:** condition resulting from ingestion of an excess of one or more vitamins.

**hypervitaminosis A:** metabolic excess of vitamin A, which is found in high concentrations in animal liver, honey, and insect larvae, and can cause hyperpigmentation, loss of hair, and changes in horny tissues; can also cause pathological changes in **fossil** hominids if ingested in large doses. The Koobi Fora hominid **KNM-ER 1808**, a *Homo erectus* with the most complete postcranial skeleton until **Nariokotome** was found, appears to have several centimeters of deposition on the surface of many bones; this abnormal deposition has been suggested as a case of hypervitaminosis A.

**hypoblast:** differentiated cells that line the inner surface of the **blastocyst** cavity; gives rise to the parietal endoderm elements of the extra-embryonic membranes such as the primary **yolk sac**. Aka primitive endoderm.

**hypocalcification:** low level of calcium deposition in hard tissues.

**hypochondriac region:** area of the abdomen that borders the **epigastric region** on either side and lies above the lumbar regions.

**hypocone: cusp** that is distal to the **protocone** on the buccal side that has developed in some anthropoid molars. The addition of a hypercone makes **bilophodont** dentition possible.

**hypoconid: cusp** on the distobuccal side of the **talonid** that has developed on the lower molars of some primate species.

**hypoconulid: cuspule** on the distal heel of the **talonid** between the **hypoconid** and **entoconid** that has developed on the lower molars of some primate species.

**hypocretin(s):** see **orexin(s).**

**hypodigm:** entire sample of known material attributed to a given **species**, and available to a taxonomist for study.

**hypodontia:** hereditary condition characterized by the absence of certain teeth. Cf. **hyperdontia, adontia.**

**hypogamy:** female practice of acquiring a mate of lower social rank. Cf. **hypergamy.**

**hypoglossal canal:** opening in the **occipital** bone through which the **hypoglossal nerve** passes. This nerve can be deduced to be large in human species, beginning with **erectines**, based on the size of the hypoglossal canal. The size of this canal contrasts with the narrow chimpanzee-like condition in the **australopithecines** and **habilines**. This is interpreted by some to mean that a complex spoken language began at the erectine stage of **hominid evolution.**

**hypoglossal nerve:** large **motor nerve** in modern humans that **innervates** the muscles of the tongue for speaking, chewing, and swallowing; cranial nerve XII. See **hypoglossal canal.**

**hypogonadism:** inadequate development of the gonads (ovaries or testes), resulting in inadequate sexual development and function during growth. Etiology variable.

**hypomorph:** 1. in some archaic classifications, the proposal that a group or groups represent a less developed form of another group. The term was often invoked by those seeking to rationalize a hierarchy of human races. Cf. **hypermorph.** 2. in genetics, an allele that is not fully expressed, such as a party active enzyme; aka leaky allele.

**hypophosphatasia, familial:** heritable autosomal dominant condition characterized by early tooth loss in adults, and vitamin D-resistant rickets; causes a type of bow-leggedness that cannot be cured by the administration of **vitamin D.** Onset during the first year of life. A cell membrane transport defect due to a mutated gene that codes for alkaline phosphatase, an X-linked dominant, which results in abnormal reabsorption of phosphate in the kidneys, thus producing abnormally low concentrations of phosphorus in the blood. Deficient calcium absorption in the intestines results in softened bones. Aka X-linked hypophosphatemia.

**hypophysis:** see **pituitary gland.**

**hypopituitary dwarfism:** see **dwarfism, pituitary.**

**hypoplasia:** 1. deficiency in the number of cells or structural elements. 2. arrest or incomplete development of an organ or part.

**hyporder:** taxon that is below an **infraorder.** In the primates, the hyporders **Eosimiae** and **Simiae** have been proposed as taxa within the infraorder **Anthropoidea.**

**hypostasis:** 1. settlement of insoluble material to the bottom of a liquid; see **sediment.** Cf. **epistasis.** 2. an interaction of nonallelic genes in which one (the hypostatic gene) is masked by another at a separate locus.

**hypotension:** low blood pressure.

**hypothalamus:** evolutionarily ancient structure in the **forebrain** that lies below the **thalamus,** where it provides a connection between the **nervous system** and the **endocrine system.** It functions as an autonomic center and regulates the **pituitary gland,** a part of the **limbic system.** The hypothalamus regulates cardiovascular activity, body temperature, water and electrolyte balance, hunger and control of gastrointestinal activity, sleeping and wakefulness, sexual response, emotions, and control of endocrine functions. See **diencephalon.**

**hypothermia:** any decrease in **body temperature,** regardless of cause. In adult humans, the mild hypothermia threshold is $\leq 36$ °C (oral); the severe hypothermia threshold is $\leq 33$ °C, below which **shivering thermogenesis** ceases. Cf. **hyperthermia.**

**hypotheses:** for examples, see the **Camin–Sokal hypothesis,** the **evolutionary hypothesis,** the **maximum homology hypothesis,** the **uniform convergence hypothesis,** and the **uniform rate hypothesis.**

‡ **hypothesis:** proposed explanation for certain observed facts. In science, a hypothesis must be testable, and possibly falsifiable (see **falsification**). Although many **hypotheses** can be, and routinely are, disproved, technically, a given hypothesis can never be proved with finality. However, some hypotheses have been so thoroughly tested that they have come to be accepted as fact; in other words, they are currently not capable of falsification. Cf. **theory.**

‡ **hypothesis testing:** formal presentation of an argument leading to prediction(s) that can be compared to results obtained through experimentation, observation, modeling, or other methods. See **hypothetico-deductive approach.**

**hypothetico-deductive approach:** 1. approach to science popularized by Austrian philosopher Karl **Popper** that utilizes a method of pairwise **hypothesis testing** and is currently a standard approach to any **research design** that employs statistical methods. 2. an approach to knowledge about the world derived from **logical positivism.**

**hypothyroidism, congenital:** heritable, autosomal recessive deficiency characterized by mental retardation, slow growth, and hearing loss. The cause is defective thyroid hormone.

‡ **hypovitaminosis:** condition due to a deficiency of one or more essential **vitamins.**

‡ **hypoxia:** absence of sufficient **oxygen** in body tissues; a state brought about by exercise, thin atmosphere at high altitude, or certain clinical conditions; aka oxygen starvation.

**hypsicephalic:** referring to high-headedness; a **basion–bregma height** that is at least 75% of the maximum length of the **cranium.**

**hypsiconchic:** in reference to the **orbital index,** having an index of 85.00 or greater; such an individual is considered to have narrow orbits.

**hypsicranic:** in reference to the **cranial length-height index,** having an index of 75.00 or greater; such an individual is considered to have a high skull.

**hypsiloid:** pertaining to an arch or curve that is u-shaped, after the (Greek) letter upsilon.

**hypsodont:** describes 1. teeth that have high crowns, but short roots that continue to grow as the crown is worn down. Characteristic of nonprimate herbivores. Cf. **brachydont.** 2. as used by some primatologists, teeth with high molar cusps, interpreted as a specialization for eating more foliage than fruit, and more common in monkeys than apes. Cf. **bunodont.**

**I:** abbreviation for **incisor**; see **I1**.

**I1, I2, I3,** etc.: notation that makes reference to incisor teeth in which the most medial tooth is the lowest number and the lateral tooth is the highest number. The notation is either lower case (indicating a mandibular tooth) or upper case (indicating a maxillary tooth). There are two ways in which this is used: 1. in reference to retention or absence of a tooth from the primitive **eutherian** mammalian set of teeth, the dental formula of which is: 3.1.4.3/3.1.4.3. Incisors have been lost, in which case the existing teeth may have incisors designated by a number larger than the number of actual teeth; primates with incisal reduction are considered to have lost I3, so this is not an issue when referring to this order. 2. in reference to the teeth that are present in an existing species. The medialmost incisor is I1, regardless of the ancestral condition.

**iatrogenesis:** 1. causation by a healer; used of an illness unwittingly induced in a patient by attitude, treatment, or comments. Adjective: iatrogenic. 2. transmission of a condition in a clinical environment. Cf. **nosocomial**.

**'Iberia not Siberia' hypothesis:** see the **Solutrean/Clovis similarity hypothesis**.

**Ibero-Maurusian:** stone tool tradition following the **Aterian** in the **Epipaleolithicera** of Maghreb in North Africa.

**Ice Age:** vernacular for the **Pleistocene epoch**, aka the Age of Glaciers and the Great Ice Age.

**ice core:** bored sample of a polar glacier in which annual depositional layers are defined by variation in $^{18}O/^{16}O$ (see **oxygen isotope analysis**), acidity, and (volcanic) dust content. Up to 14,000 layers have been counted in some long cores.

**'Iceman':** 'Ôtzi', a 5.3 kya intact human preserved in a glacier in the Similaun Pass of the Italian Ôtzil Alps. Found in 1991. Geneticists from Oxford University were able to extract **ancient DNA** from the cryo-mummified remains. International teams have analyzed the mummy's Bronze Age tools, clothing, stomach contents, and general condition of health. See **mummification**.

**ichthyosis congenita:** rare, severe X-linked recessive condition characterized by deeply fissured, rough, scaly skin on the scalp, ears, neck, abdomen, and legs.

**ICPMS:** see **inductively coupled plasma-mass emission spectrometry**.

**ICZN:** see **International Commission on Zoological Nomenclature**.

**-idae:** in zoological taxonomy, the suffix of a **family**. See **Linnaean hierarchy**.

**IDDM:** see **insulin-dependent diabetes mellitus**.

**-idea:** in zoological taxonomy, the suffix of a **super-family**. See **Linnaean hierarchy**.

**identical by descent:** describes alleles, within a single individual or different individuals, that have been inherited from the same ancestral copy of the gene. Cf. **alike in state**.

**identical twin half-sibling family:** family formed by the marriages and children of **identical twins**; that is, when two male and two female identical twin pairs have offspring; the resulting children are genetically **half-siblings** as well as first cousins.

**identical twins:** see **twins, monozygotic**.

**ideogram:** (i) schematic molecular and cytogenetic diagram of a **chromosome** that shows stained bands and locations of known **genes**; see **karyotype**. Also spelled idiogram.

**ideotechnic:** describes the properties of an artifact that reflect the cognitive component of culture.

**idiographic:** pertaining to any study whose purpose is to establish specific factual statements or propositions.

**idiokinesis:** process of change in a person's hereditary characteristics.

**idiopathic disease:** condition arising from sources or agents within an organism.

**idiotype:** specific part of an antibody binding site that binds to a particular foreign antigen; paratope.

**-iformes:** in zoological taxonomy, the suffix of an **infraorder**. See **Linnaean hierarchy**.

**$I$ fraction:** ratio between the time in which air is inhaled ($I$) and the duration of the entire respiratory cycle. This ranges from 0.04 to 0.45 during ordinary breathing, and is about 0.16 during speech.

**Ig:** abbreviation for **immunoglobulin**. Similarly, for **IgA** see **immunoglobulin A**; for **IgD** see **immunoglobulin D**, etc.

**igapó forest:** term used in Brazil for Amazonian forest that is seasonally flooded by **blackwater** for long periods during the year. Cf. **varzea forest**. See also **forest**.

*Ignacius* **Matthew and Granger, 1921:** archaic mammal known from the middle Paleocene to late Eocene of North America belonging to the **plesiadapiform** family **Paromomyidae**; four species; may be descended from *Paromomys*. Known from dentition, jaws, and cranial fragments. Dental formula: 2.1.3.3/2.1.2.3; diet possibly fruit, perhaps with insect supplements. Body size of the species between 50 and 150 g. See Appendix 1 for taxonomy.

**igneous rock:** molten material that flows up as magma from the deeper part of the earth's crust (asthenosphere); one of the main groups of rock that make up the earth's crust (lithosphere). Some igneous rocks that have cooled quickly are suitable for tools, and include **lavas**, **ignimbrites** and **obsidian**.

**ignimbrite:** rock produced by the settling of volcanic ash, usually originating from hot clouds that have been ejected from an erupting volcano. Ash particles can become fused by the intense heat. Some forms can be used to make stone tools. Aka welded tuff.

**ileum:** region of the **small intestine** between the **jejunum** and the **cecum** of the large intestine. There is no distinct separation between the jejunum and ileum except that the ileum tends to have a smaller diameter. Functionally, absorption of nutrients occurs in the jejunum.

**iliac crest:** superior crest of the **ilium** of the **coxal bone;** the iliac crest extends from the **anterior superior iliac spine** to the **posterior superior iliac spine.**

**iliac pillar:** thickening of the bone on the **ilium** of hominids that runs from the **iliac crest** to the **acetabulum;** this structure serves as a site of attachment for some of the **gluteal muscles** and helps resist forces generated by pelvic abductor muscles during **bipedal** walking; strongly developed in *Homo.*

**iliofemoral ligament:** ligament that proceeds from the anterior inferior spine of the **ilium** to the proximal **femur;** the iliofemoral ligament supports the **coxal joint** from the anterior side. When standing, this ligament helps pull the head of the femur tightly into the **acetabulum.**

‡ **ilium:** one of a pair of bones (that fuse in the human adult) that constitutes the largest and most superior portion of the **coxal bone.** The **gluteal muscles,** important in **bipedalism,** have their origin on this bone.

**illegitimate signal:** deceptive sign given to a **conspecific;** for example, a female langur in the early stages of pregnancy may feign **estrus** if there is a change in the hareming male to deceive the **usurper** that any offspring born to the female are his.

**illegitimate recombination:** recombination with a nonhomologous segment of **DNA;** see **translocation.**

**Illinoian glaciation:** third of the fourth major glaciations of the Pleistocene in the North American sequence; see **Riss glaciation.**

**illness:** any culturally structured and personal experience that entails the perception of suffering. Cf. **disease** and **disorder.**

**Imanishi, Kinji** (1902–92): Japanese ecologist and zoologist at Kyoto University. Known as the 'founder of Japanese primatology', Imanishi and his colleagues provided detailed naturalistic studies of free-ranging Japanese macaques from the late 1940s through the 1960s. Imanishi was also a pioneer evolutionary theorist in his country. He founded the journal *Primates* in 1957, and was instrumental in establishing the Primate Research Group (1952), the Japanese Monkey Centre (1956), and the Kyoto University Africa Primatology Expedition (1958). Author of numerous scholarly publications and coeditor (with S. **Altmann**) of *Japanese Monkeys* (1965).

**immature:** 1. unripe. 2. not fully developed. Cf. **mature.**

**immediate hypersensitivity:** in a previously sensitized individual, a humoral immune reaction to an antigen or allergen that occurs within minutes of the challenge. Cf. **delayed hypersensitivity.**

**immediate tanning:** *in vivo,* the first of a two-stage **acclimatization** response of the living skin known as **tanning,** and caused by exposure to **UV radiation.** Immediate tanning is a transient browning maximized after 1-2 h, caused by exposure to UV-A and visible light, and that fades within 24 h. Cf. **delayed tanning.**

**immigration:** movement of individuals into a region or habitat to which they are not native, usually for the purpose of permanent occupancy. Cf. **emigration.**

**immune:** describes 1. a person (or animal) that has been sensitized by an **antigen,** or 2. something associated with the reaction to that antigen.

**immune antibody:** antibody produced in response to a blood group **antigen** present on red blood cells after exposure.

**immune decoy proteins:** **epitope**-like molecules on the cellular surfaces of some parasites (e.g. *Plasmodium* sporozoites and merozoites) that can be sloughed off when conjugated by a host **antibody,** and later renewed.

**immune deficiency syndrome:** group of indications indicating impairment of one or more of the major functions of the immune system.

**immune disorder:** disease or syndrome attributed to dysfunction of the **immune system** or one of its components; common examples are **allergy, autoimmunity,** and immunodeficiency.

**immune reaction:** binding of an antigen and an antibody. Cf. **immune response.**

‡ **immune response:** reaction of an individual after stimulation (challenge) by a foreign substance, an antigen. See **cellular immune response, humoral immune response,** and **phagocytosis.**

‡ **immune system:** one of the systems in the body that helps an organism to **adapt** and to survive; the immune system identifies challenging organisms and chemicals, and attempts to isolate and destroy them; consists of a **cellular immune response** and a **humoral immune response.**

**immune tolerance:** condition of nonreactivity towards certain molecules or cells that might normally be expected to produce an immune response. Aka immunotolerance.

‡ **immunity:** 1. state that enables a body to recognize materials as foreign to itself and to neutralize and eliminate them. 2. any inherited, acquired, or induced conditioning to a specific pathogen. See **acquired immunity, active immunity,** and **passive immunity.**

**immunization:** see **inoculation**.

**immunocompetence:** possessing the ability to develop an immunological response, especially **cell-mediated immunity**, when exposed to an **antigen**.

**immunocyte:** lymphoid cell capable of producing an **antibody** in response to an **antigen**.

**immunodiffusion:** precipitin test in which the reactants form a visible immune precipitate in a gel medium (usually agar) into which one or both reactants have diffused. Aka gel diffusion reaction.

**immunogen:** substance that causes an immune response; see **antigen**, and **epitope**.

**immunogenetics:** study of **antigens**, gene-controlled synthesis of **antibodies**, and the **organelles** and molecular structures that facilitate their interreactions.

**immunogenicity:** degree to which an antigen is capable of eliciting an immune response.

**immunoglobulin** (Ig): one of several electrophoretically disguisable classes of proteins found in the **serum** of blood that are involved in the destruction and neutralization of pathogenic materials; protein with known **antibody** activity. Sometimes aka antibody. See box below.

---

### Immunoglobulin classes

**immunoglobulin A** (IgA): Ig found in milk, saliva, urine, tears, and both the respiratory and digestive systems; IgA molecules are small enough to pass through the placental membrane, and provide passive immunity to a fetus. It provides protection against microorganisms at points of entry into body cavities. Aka alpha antibodies.

**immunoglobulin D** (IgD): Ig found on B cells in blood, and secreted by the lining of the gastrointestinal, respiratory, and urinary tracts. It stimulates B cells to make other **antibodies**, especially in infants. Aka delta antibodies.

**immunoglobulin E** (IgE): Ig that mediates immediate **hypersensitivity** (allergy) and resistance to parasites. IgE is found in body secretions along with **IgA** and in mast cells in tissues, where it triggers the release of **histamine**. It acts as a receptor for antigens that cause mast cells to secrete allergy mediators. Aka epsilon antibodies.

**Immunoglobulin F** (IgF): see **insulin-like growth factor**.

**immunoglobulin G** (IgG): the most abundaut Ig, found in blood plasma and tissue fluid. IgG molecules are small enough to pass through the placental membrane to a fetus. It protects against bacteria, viruses and toxins, especially during the **secondary immune response**. Aka gamma globulin; gamma antibodies.

**immunoglobulin M** (IgM): Ig found in blood plasma. It combats bacteria during the **primary immune response**. The IgMs are large molecules, and include the anti-A and anti-B **antibodies**.

---

**immunoglobulin class:** group of antibodies having a specific type of heavy chain constant region. The classes IgA, IgD, IgE, IgG, and IgM have $\alpha$, $\beta$, $\epsilon$, $\gamma$, and $\mu$ heavy chains, respectively.

**immunological diffusion test:** test for genealogical affinity in which **antisera** from one species reacts to **antigens** from another species on an immunodiffusion plate *in vitro*, and the amount of resulting precipitate is scored visually, exploiting the empirical observation that closely related individuals produce less precipitate. M. **Goodman** applied this test to many animals beginning in 1962, and was thus one of the first to produce a molecular phylogeny of mammals, including the primates.

**immunological distance:** quantitative difference between two antigens measured immunologically. See **microcomplement fixation**.

**immunological memory:** capacity of the immune system to mount a rapid and vigorous response to a second challenge by an **antigen**.

**immunological suppression:** inherited or induced condition in which an organism's ability to respond to an immune challenge is impaired.

**immunological surveillance theory:** proposal that **cell-mediated immunity** arose and evolved to detect and modulate cancer cells or cells containing foreign pathogens.

**immunological theory of aging:** intercellular, systemic model of aging in which the major premise is that cell recognition mechanisms begin to fail as an organism ages, resulting in failure of feedback mechanisms, or even, in some cases, autoimmunity, as originally proposed in 1969 by American pathologist Roy Walford (1924-2004). Certain haplotypes of the **HLA complex** seem to be associated with rates of aging, and are also factors in degenerative diseases, such as **rheumatoid arthritis**.

**immunology:** study of the mechanisms regulating the response of an individual to foreign **antigens**, and immunity to **disease** by either natural or artificial means. Aka immunogenetics, immunobiology.

**immunotherapeutic:** therapeutic approach to the treatment of diseases by stimulating or enhancing the immune response against the disease.

**immutability:** quality or state of being unchangeable. Linnaeus, for example, held that **species** were immutable. See **fixity of species**.

‡ **implantation:** attachment of the **blastocyst** to the intrauterine lining six to ten days after **ovulation** and **fertilization**.

**implement:** 1. to perform or carry out. 2. equipment, furniture or clothing; see **tool**. 3. to provide with tools or implements.

**imprinting:** form of learning in which a bird or mammal at an early stage of development is exposed to key stimuli to which it forms a bond. Well known in birds, which imprint on a parent or parent-surrogate (including species other than their own); also seen in primates and demonstrated in **deprivation experiments** with rhesus monkeys in which cloth dolls were substituted for mothers. Imprinting also occurs at other stages of development, such as learning the calls of adults. Aka imprinting behavior.

**imprinting, genomic:** see **genomic imprinting**.

**improving invention:** secondary concept and its application to a **basic invention** in material or cognitive culture.

*in silico*: computer algorithm, model, or simulation; an estimate or model obtained by computation. Cf. *in vivo* and *in vitro*.

‡ *in situ*: describes something that remains where it was found; in place.

*in situ* **conservation:** preservation of primates and ecosystems in their native place; aka on-site preservation. Cf. *ex situ* **conservation**.

*in situ* **gene therapy:** manipulation of genes by directly accessing body parts.

*in utero*: occurring within the uterus; in reference to a conception, occurring naturally in the uterus.

‡ *in vitro*: in glass; outside a living organism (e.g. in test tubes).

*in vitro* **fertilization:** see **IVF**.

*in vitro* **senescence:** common observation among cell culture biologists that cell lines are mortal, that they exhibit a limited capacity to divide, and that this capacity diminishes with time. The number of cell divisions seems to be described by the **Hayflick limit**, and has influenced theories of aging.

‡ *in vivo*: in life; within a living organism.

*in vivo* **fertilization:** natural fertilization; cf. *in vitro* **fertilization**.

*in vivo* **gene therapy:** direct genetic manipulation of cells in the living body.

**-ina:** in zoological taxonomy, the suffix that designates a **subtribe**, e.g. **Hominina**.

**inactivation:** chemical silencing of a gene or portion of a chromosome. Inactivation can occur either for purposes of sex chromosome dosage compensation, as in **X inactivation**, or in autosomal locations, where it is called **genomic imprinting**. See the **Haig hypothesis**.

**-inae:** in zoological taxonomy, the suffix of a **subfamily**. See **Linnaean hierarchy**.

**inborn:** ambiguous term generally meaning gene-caused; cf. **congenital**.

**inborn error of metabolism:** 1. concept suggested by Archibald Garrod that many inherited anomalies are due to alterations in biochemical pathways. 2. any genetically determined biochemical **disorder** in which a specific **protein** defect produces a **metabolic block**; most are **autosomal recessive** disorders (e.g. **Tay-Sachs disease**), but some are **autosomal dominant** (e.g. **achondroplasia**), or **sex-linked** defects (e.g. **hemophilia**).

**inbred line:** theoretically **homozygous** population derived from a formerly wild population by repeated, often artificial **inbreeding**. Certain strains of mice have been consistently inbred for research purposes. Almost all domesticated species are inbred to some degree, and have experienced a loss of **genetic variation**. Small populations that experience **isolation** are characterized by **inbreeding depression**.

**inbred mouse strain:** any of several lines of mice that have been produced for many generations by brother–sister matings or other close intrafamilial breeding. After about twenty generations, the surviving mice are genetically identical to every other mouse in the strain. The first such strain (DBA) was started by C. C. Little in 1909, but many of the common laboratory lines were not developed until after 1942.

‡ **inbreeding:** mating and conception of offspring among kin or 'blood relatives', the degree of which is measured by the proportion of genes that are identical owing to common descent. Aka **endogamy** and **consanguinity**. See **inbreeding coefficient**. Cf. **outbreeding**.

**inbreeding coefficient** (*F*): measure of genetic identity; the probability that two **alleles** at one locus on a pair of chromosomes are identical by virtue of common descent.

**inbreeding depression:** reduced fitness in individuals or populations resulting from kin matings, often due to increased homozygosity, sometimes because homozygotes for deleterious alleles have become more common. Cf. **heterosis**.

**Inca bone:** see **sutural bone**.

*incertae sedis* (*inc. sed.*) (Latin): of uncertain affinity; used to indicate a specimen of uncertain taxonomic position. In use, *incertae sedis* usually follows a broader taxon name, such as Plesiadapiformes, family *incertae sedis*, *Purgatorius*. See **species indeterminata**.

**incest:** 1. sexual relationships or matings between parents with their offspring, and often, of siblings or cousins with each other; sex among first or second degree relatives; close **endogamy**. See **incest taboo**. 2. production of offspring by parents who share genes by way of a common ancestor of a specified but culturally variable degree; a form of **inbreeding**. Cf. **inbreeding coefficient** (*F*), **dynastic incest**, and **royal endogamy**.

‡ **incest taboo:** prohibition against sexual relationships and marriage of parents with their offspring, and often, of siblings or cousins with each other. Apparently nearly all human societies have such rules, but they apply to different degrees of relationships in different groups. Aka kapu, tabu, incest prohibition.

**inchworm theory:** model of mRNA translation in which the messenger model is likened to that of an inchworm creeping along a stem, creating mechanical kinks that facilitate peptide release from tRNA and the formation of peptide bonds.

**incidence:** number of new cases of a disease over a given period. Cf. **prevalence**.

**incidental effect:** behavioral or morphological trait that exists in its form because of the interaction of some other feature that was selected for.

**incipient species:** any population in the process of evolving into a distinct, separate species.

**incisiform:** pertaining to a tooth that resembles an incisor tooth; incisorlike. When present in primates, such a tooth is usually a canine or, sometimes, a premolar that resembles an incisor.

**incision** (inc): **craniometric landmark**; point on a central maxillary incisor that is at the **labial** margin. See Appendix 7.

**incisive foramen:** opening in the anterior portion of the hard palate through which the nasopalatine nerves and the vomeronasal organ pass. The portion that opens into the nasal cavity is sometimes referred to as the nasal incisive foramen, while the portion that opens into the oral cavity is called the oral incisive foramen; Aka incisive canal.

‡ **incisor** (I): one of four types of tooth found in **heterodont** mammals. Incisors are flat, spatulate, single-rooted teeth, usually in the front and center of the mouth and that serve for cutting, gnawing and scraping. See also **canines, premolars,** and **molars**. See also **shovel-shaped incisor** and **barrel-shaped incisor**.

‡ **inclusive (genetic) fitness:** total contribution of an individual **genotype** to the next generation both directly through offspring produced (**direct fitness**) and collaterally through its weighted effects on its

relatives' fitness (**indirect fitness**); hence, the total effect of **kin selection** with reference to an individual. Cf. **Darwinian fitness**.

**incomplete antibody:** agglutinin that reacts with its specific antibody, causing agglutination of red blood cells in a protein medium (usually **serum albumin**).

**incomplete dominance:** failure of a dominant allele to be fully expressed in the heterozygous condition; such heterozygotes have a discontinuous phenotype that is intermediate between those of the homozygous forms. Cf. **codominant**.

**incomplete protein:** food source whose protein component does not contain all of the **essential amino acids** needed to maintain human body tissues and to promote normal growth and development. See **complete protein** and **partially complete protein**.

**incomplete sex linkage:** state of a gene having loci on homologous segments of both the X and Y sex chromosomes, as in the **H-Y antigen**. See **pseudoautosomal region**.

**incompletely penetrant:** describes a trait in which alleles do not display the same phenotypic manifestation in every individual. Aka incomplete penetrance. See **penetrance**.

**incompletely sex-linked genes:** homologous genes located on the portions of the X and Y chromosomes that pair during the **synapsis** phases of **meiosis**.

‡ **independent assortment:** random rearrangement of maternal and paternal chromosome pairs at the metaphase plate during **metaphase I** of meiosis and that results in a mixture of maternal and paternal chromosomes after **anaphase I**. See **Mendelian principle of independent assortment**.

**independent events:** in statistics, condition in which the occurrence of one event has no influence on the occurrence of another event.

**independent rank:** rank in a **dominance hierarchy** that is the result of the individual's ability to dominate others in the group.

**independent variable:** the causal variable that is manipulated in an experimental situation and the values of which influence or display a relationship with the values of the **dependent variable**.

**index:** 1. a detailed, sequential listing of elements, as of topics in a text. 2. a pointer, as in **index fossil**. 3. standard used for comparison; often a numerical ratio or quotient. 4. in anthropometry, the ratio of two measurements (such as width over length), often multiplied by 100 to remove decimals; e.g. the **cranial index**. Plural: indices.

**index fossil:** fossil specimen or species that is presumed to have had an extensive geographic range (is highly **vagile**), and is found in several geographically distant regions. Index fossils are used to correlate the geological strata in which they are found, from site to site, even if discontinuous, a process known as **biostratigraphy.**

**index of dextrality:** measure of hand preference during a prescribed series of activities.

**index of dispersion:** measure of population deviation from a mean in a biological population, calculated as the ratio of the variance to its mean. A value of 1 suggests a pattern of randomness, more than 1 suggests an aggregated population, and less than 1 suggests a uniform population. Cf. **coefficient of variation.**

**index species:** any species that is characteristic of a particular habitat; aka characteristic species, guide species, indicator species.

**indicator species:** see **index species.**

**indifferent genitalia:** reproductive organs of the **embryo** prior to the establishment of definitive **sex** at about the end of the **first trimester**; see **external genitalia** and **ambiguous genitalia.**

**indigenous:** pertaining to a species or a people that occurs naturally in a region; native, **autochthonous.**

**indigenous science:** any non-Western knowledge system with the properties of empiricism and predictive power; **ethnoscience.**

**indigenous theory of fossil origins:** eighteenth century proposal that fossils are typical of the region in which they are found. Cf. **exotic theory of fossil origins.**

**indirect bilirubin:** nonexcretable **bilirubin**; see **Rh incompatibility** and **hemolytic disease of the newborn.**

**indirect calorimetry:** estimation of heat produced as determined from oxygen consumption or carbon dioxide produced. See **human calorimeter, calorimetry.** Cf. direct calorimetry.

**indirect dating:** establishing a range of time within which an artifact was made or deposited in an archaeological context by establishment of an association with another object or sample that is amenable to **direct dating.**

**indirect fitness:** portion of a focal individual's **inclusive fitness** that is due to increased reproduction by collateral relatives and that is made possible by the focal individual's actions. Cf. **direct fitness.**

**indirect measurement:** see **projective dimension.**

**indirect role:** behavior or set of behaviors that benefits only the subgroups that display it and that is neutral or even destructive to other subgroups of the society. See **direct role.**

**indirect value:** worth assigned to those components of biological diversity that are not harvested and destroyed by humans, but provide benefits. Indirect values can be applied to such features as water quality, protection from soil erosion and flooding, ecotourism, scientific research, maintenance of normal climate patterns, etc. An examples is nonconsumptive use value, an attempt to place a monetary value on certain types of biodiversity such as the number of crops pollinated by insects or dispersed by wild primates. Cf. **direct value.**

**individual differential sterility:** differences among individuals in the number of offspring produced; aka reproductive variance.

**individual distance:** minimal distance to which an animal will tolerate the approach of a **conspecific**; encroachment beyond this boundary leads to either an altercation or a withdrawal. Individual distance varies depending on kin relationship, rank of approaching individual, sex, or age. In some cases individual distance is removed completely, such as in mating circumstances.

**individual recognition:** 1. ability to recognize **conspecific** individuals; among the vertebrates this is most evolved in birds and mammals and is especially well developed in primates. Individual recognition is a requirement for social groups and the **hierarchies** contained within; it is important for **kin recognition**, restriction of **altruism** to relatives, and **inbreeding** avoidance. Individual recognition in primates occurs through visual characteristics, vocalizations, and olfactory cues (especially in prosimians). 2. ability of primatologists to recognize individual animals that they work with. This is done by various means, including individual characteristics of the animal or extraneous markers placed on the animal by the observer. See **marking.**

**individual selection:** selection in the **Darwinian** sense that natural selection favors an individual and its direct descendants. See **selection.**

**individualization:** in physical anthropology, the gradual process of phenotypic modification as the result of individual dietary habits, exercise and activity patterns, **occupational stress trauma**, and the subsequent bone and tissue remodeling that reflects one's lifeway.

**individualized group:** animal group in which the individual members can recognize one another. Primate social units are such groups. See **individual recognition.**

**Indonesian:** ethonym for the **autochthonous** peoples of southeast Asia and Malaysia. Aka Malays, attenuated Mongoloids, proto-Malays, deutero-Malays.

**Indonesian-Malay:** ethonym for an **autochthonous** people of southeast Asia, considered one of the earliest immigrant groups to that area, followed by the so-called **Malays**, a more **Mongoloid** subgroup. Aka proto-Malay.

**Indonesian Mongol:** ethonym for a widely distributed Mongoloid subgroup with some **Ainu** and perhaps Mediterranean features.

*Indraloris himalayensis* (Pilgrim, 1932): adapoid **prosimian** from the late Miocene of South Asia, belonging to the family **Sivaladapidae; monotypic;** known from fragmentary teeth and jaws. Body mass estimated at 2.5 kg. Dental morphology suggestive of **folivory.** See Appendix 1 for taxonomy.

*Indri* É. Geoffroy & G. Cuvier, 1796: monotypic **prosimian** genus to which the indris belongs; aka short-tailed indris, dog-faced lemur, endrina, or babakoto. Inhabits rain forest of east-central Madagascar. Arboreal; diurnal; **vertical clinging and leaping** locomotion. Tail is a short stub. Largest of the living **prosimians**, body mass ranging from 7 to 11 kg. Dental formula in dispute, either 2.1.2.3/2.0.2.3 or 2.1.2.3/1.1.2.3. Proponents of both formulae agree there are 30 teeth and that there are only four teeth in the **dental comb. Folivorous,** but chooses young leaves and shoots; adaptations to leafy diet include enlarged salivary glands. Live in **monogamous** family groups; territories are delineated by sound. See Appendix 2 for taxonomy, Appendix 3 for living species.

**Indriidae: prosimian** family to which woolly lemurs, indris, and sifakas belong; consists of three genera and six species. Vernacular: indriid. See Appendix 2 for taxonomy, Appendix 3 for living species.

**indris:** one of the vernaculars for *Indri indri.*

**induced abortion:** see **abortion.**

**induction:** 1. development of laws, principles, or generalizations from specific observations; **synthesis.** In science, the perception of patterns in data that leads to the formation of **hypotheses.** Cf. **deduction.** 2. initiation of development of a structure, organ or process *in vitro*; see **embryonic induction.**

**induction, method of:** mathematical technique for proving an ordered set of statements; the statements are numbered from the 1st (through $k$th) to the $n$th; if the first statement can be proven, then if the $k$th statement is also proven true, then the $(k + 1)$th statement is also true. The technique is used in **maximum parsimony problems** and other complex genetic and taxonomic applications.

**inductively coupled plasma–mass emission spectrometry** (ICPMS): method of quantitative and chemical isotopic analysis that combines atomic emission spectrometry with mass spectrometry. In this technique, a digested sample in solution is introduced to an argon plasma, and the mass spectrum of a sample is measured (instead of the atomic emission in similar techniques) and compared with standard solutions of known concentrations. Isotope ratios can be determined.

**inductivism:** claim that inferences made in accordance with the method of induction are at least rationally legitimate, even if not proven logically valid. See **induction, method of.**

‡ **industrial melanism:** in regions where habitats have been blackened by pollution and a pigment polymorphism exists in certain indigenous species, **natural selection** tends to favor those darker morphs that were less conspicuous in the altered environment. The best-known case involves *Biston betularia*, the peppered moth, first studied by R. B. Goldschmidt (1921) and later by Kettlewell (1956) in England.

**industry:** set of tools characterized by uniformity of material (e.g. stone) and design, and defined by a limited region and/or time span. Industries are often associated with certain peoples, as is the **Mousterian tool tradition.**

‡ **infancy:** stage in the postnatal period of the human **life cycle** that ranges from the end of the first four weeks after birth to one year. This period is marked by rapid growth, eruption of **deciduous dentition,** coordination of the nervous and muscular systems, and the beginnings of language acquisition; follows the **neonatal stage.** See **infant.** Cf. **childhood.**

**infant:** child in the human **life cycle.** See **infancy.** Cf. **neonate** and **child.**

**infant care:** see **parental care** and **paternal investment.**

**infant mortality:** number of deaths per one thousand infants between birth and one year of age.

**infant–mother bond:** social tie between a female and her offspring; prominent in mammals and especially well developed in primates. The physical closeness that occurs between a primate mother and her infant during suckling and carrying allows for the development of the infant–mother bond. This close association facilitates the transmission of knowledge (such as which plants are safe to eat). See **clinging infant.**

**infant parking:** behavior exhibited by females of some prosimian taxa in which they place their infants on a safe branch or stem while the mother forages.

‡ **infanticide:** killing of infants, usually by adults. In primates and other mammals this is usually associated with **one-male units** in which the male has been displaced, followed by the destruction of his unweaned offspring by the **usurper.** The explanation is that lactating females do not come into **estrus** until their offspring cease suckling; by killing unweaned offspring, the usurper male enables the females to come into estrus earlier, and is able to father more offspring and reproduce his **alleles.** In primates, infanticide has been documented in langurs and other species with **polygynous** mating systems.

**infantile amaurotic idiocy:** severe genetic condition characterized by the accumulation of fatlike substances or **lipids** in the brain cells and retina, and that progresses to severe mental abnormalities and blindness in early infancy.

**infantilization:** arrest of development of an organism at an infantile stage.

**infection:** invasion and multiplication of microorganisms on or in body tissue of another organism (including humans) that produce signs and symptoms, as well as an immune response in higher organisms.

‡ **infectious disease:** 1. any condition caused by the introduction of an organic foreign substance such as a **virus, bacterium,** or **parasite** into the body. 2. a disruption of normal homeostasis caused by a living organism (**pathogen**). Infectious disease was the main limiting factor of human longevity from the advent of agriculture until well into the 20th century. Cf. **communicable disease.** Examples are **AIDS, malaria, typhus, coccidioidomycosis,** and **schistosomiasis.** See also **disease** and **disorder.**

**inferential statistics:** any method that results in a conclusion(s) about an entire population based upon a sample(s) from that population.

**inferior:** anatomical term of relative position meaning that a structure is below another structure; towards the feet. **Caudal** is a synonym.

**inferior colliculus:** structure within the mid-brain or **mesencephalon** that functions to control auditory reflexes and coordination. Cf. superior colliculus.

**inferior transverse torus:** see **simian shelf** and **mandibular torus.**

**infertility:** in humans, the inability to conceive after a year of unprotected **intercourse.**

**infinite site model:** presumption in theoretical population genetics that each new mutation occurs at a site that has not previously mutated. Only when mutation rates at all sites are relatively low does this model approach reality; several alleles have already been shown to be the result of two or more 'hits' at the same site. See **back mutation.**

**inflammation:** process by which the immune system reacts to a localized surface infection, characterized by swelling, heat, and redness.

**inflammatory bowel disease I** (IBD1): one of a group of chronic autoimmune disorders that cause ulceration in the intestines. In type 1 (which includes Crohn disease) the inflammation extends deep into the intestinal wall. Onset is generally between 15 and 35 years of age, with a second peak in decades 5–7. About 1 in 5 cases of IBD1 are familial; prevalence is greater than 1 : 1,000. Several autosomal recessive genes appear to be involved in the inflammatory response (including the *NOD*$_2$ gene on chromosome 16q12), but the condition is generally regarded as heterogenous. A less severe form of IBD, type 2, is usually called ulcerative colitis. Females appear to be at an slightly increased risk for IBD.

**influenza:** common infectious RNA viral disease characterized by fever and chills, and often accompanied by intestinal symptoms. Some strains can be fatal. Hosted by pigs and waterfowl (the **disease reservoir**); becomes newly virulent every twenty years or so, not by primary mutation of its genome but by **genetic recombination** of its internal and surface H and N glycoproteins. It is thus called a perpetually emerging **virus**; this mode of phenotypic change is called **antigenic drift.** It can be transmitted by several means, but the most common mode is via airborne droplets. The 1918–19 influenza epidemic killed 50 million people worldwide; most of these deaths were due to pneumonia (secondary to influenza) and death occurred with 48h of the initial symptoms. Recent serial **pandemics** of influenza have been called 'Asian flu', 'Swine flu', and 'Hong Kong flu'. New forms of influenza usually break out in areas where pig manure is used as a fertilizer for fish aquaculture ponds, or where pigs, ducks, and farmers are in close contact (e.g. in southeast Asia). There are three common variants, A, B, and C, one of which can also cause a version of the **common cold.** Aka flu.

**informatics:** see **bioinformatics.**

**information:** 1. knowledge, especially that on which choices might be made. 2. coded data. 3. efficiency or maximization of energy; cf. **entropy.**

**information theory:** body of hypotheses that attempt to explain the codification of information and its transmission through channels of limited capacity, taking into account the **entropy** within a given system, which is a measure of error or noise.

**informative mating:** mating in which one partner is **heterozygous** such that the polymorphic marker and alleles can be distinguished from those contributed by the **homozygous** partner to offspring; used in genetic linkage analysis.

**informativeness:** likelihood of informative mating for a particular genetic polymorphism.

**infraclass:** in taxonomy, that rank within a **Linnaean hierarchy** below the **class** and above the **order** or **superorder.**

**infradentale** (idi): **craniometric landmark;** most anterior and superior point of the septum (i.e. the lowest alveolar point) between the two central mandibular incisors. See Appendix 7.

**infradian rhythm:** cycle that occurs in a period longer than 24 h, but less than a year. Cf. **ultradian rhythm, periodic behavior.** See **circadian rhythm, rhythmic behavior.**

**infraorbital foramen:** opening inferior to the **orbit** in the **maxillary bone** through which the infraorbital blood vessels and nerves pass.

**infraorder:** in taxonomy, that rank within a **Linnaean hierarchy** below the **order** and above the **family** or **superfamily.**

**infrared radiation:** invisible portion of the spectrum of electromagnetic radiation with wavelengths longer than those of visible light (about 0.77 μm, or 7700 Å, i.e. below the red end, and thus too long to be seen by the human eye).

**ingestion:** process of taking food into the oral cavity.

**ingroup:** in **phylogenetic systematics**, any set of taxa thought to be more closely related to each other than these are to an **outgroup**.

‡ **inheritance:** 1. in **genetics**, said of the process whereby any **trait** or **character** is passed from one generation to the next and results in a resemblance of offspring to parents that is not the result of learning (see **heritability**). Aka Darwinian inheritance. 2. non-genetic transfer of objects and/or knowledge from one organism or group to another organism or group, often following lines of descent; aka **cultural inheritance**.

‡ **inheritance of acquired characteristics:** see **acquired characteristics**.

**inherited deafness:** deafness that is genetic in origin, which is about half of all cases. Two major forms of inherited deafness are recognized: **syndromic deafness** and **nonsyndromic deafness**.

**inhibin:** either of two **glycoproteins** secreted by the **gonads** and present in seminal plasma and follicular fluid and that inhibit pituitary production of **FHS**. Inhibins also contribute to the control of **gametogenesis**, embryonic and fetal development, and **hematopoiesis**.

**inhibiting hormone:** a **hormone** elaborated by one structure that inhibits release of hormones from another structure (the **target site**). The term is applied to substances of established clinical identity, whereas substances of unknown chemical structure are called inhibiting factors.

**inhumation:** burial of the dead.

**inhumist:** pertaining to a group or society that buries its dead.

**-ini:** in zoological taxonomy, the suffix that designates the **tribe**, a taxon just below the **subfamily** and above the **genus**, e.g. Hominini.

**inion** (i): **craniometric landmark**; point where the medial sagittal plane and the superior nuchal line intersect at the base of the external occipital protuberance. See Appendix 7.

**initiation:** 1. beginning, commencement. 2. ceremonies attendant at an event marking transition; the ceremonies often assume the form of ordeals and rites, and mark the passage from one state or status to another.

**initiation codon: nucleotide** triplet, usually AUG, the codon for methionine, that marks the beginning of a transcription sequence; aka initiator codon.

**initiation complex:** aggregation of all the components required as **mRNA** is either transcribed or translated into a polypeptide.

**initiation sites:** regions in chromosomes where **DNA** replication begins.

**Inka** or **Inca bone:** see **sutural bone**.

**innate:** describes a structure or aptitude that is inborn or inherited, as opposed to acquired or learned during the lifetime of an individual organism; the same as **genetic**.

**innate defense:** generalized immune response.

**innateness hypothesis:** innate knowledge of a structure that is genetically available to a child, proposed by American linguist Avram Noam Chomsky (1928– ). Chomsky and others suggest that an innate knowledge of linguistic universals explains the ease of first acquisition of language.

**inner cell mass:** see **embryoblast**.

**inner ear:** portion of the ear that is contained within the ear cavity and that consists of a bony labyrinth and a membranous labyrinth. Its functions include both **hearing** and **balance**. Aka internal ear, labyrinth. Cf. **external ear**.

**inner epicanthus:** fold of skin that extends from the root of the nose to the inner termination of the eyebrow and covers the **endocanthion** (inner angle) of the eye. Aka epicanthal fold, plica palpebronasalis. Cf. **outer epicanthus**.

**innervation:** distribution of nerves to a particular region or organ; nerve pattern that innervates. Historically, innervation has been used in comparative anatomy to deduce evolutionary relationships.

‡ **innominate:** see **coxal bone**.

**inoculation:** 1. purposeful injection of a dead or attenuated pathogen into a subject in order to confer **active immunity** to a disease-causing organism; aka **vaccination**. 2. purposeful introduction of microbes into an individual for beneficial purposes, such as when an herbivorous female mammal inoculates her offspring with fecal matter that contains symbionts that help break down food.

‡ **inorganic:** describes any molecule not containing carbon; aka inorganic compound. Cf. **organic**.

**insectivory:** dietary category applied to animals (insectivores) that consume predominantly insects (although other invertebrates such as mollusks are often included in the diet) during the year or during a particular season. Adjective: insectivorous. Many **prosimians** are insectivores, and insects constitute a significant portion of the **diet** of many callitrichids.

**insensible perspiration:** secretion of sweat when there is no need for temperature regulation. See **insensible water loss**.

‡ **insensible water loss:** nonthermal perspiration characterized by constant evaporation of water from human tissues unless relative humidity is 100%. Diffusion occurs through the pores of the skin and lungs. In humans, about 900 ml per day is lost through the skin, and 400 ml per day through the lungs. Most other species have much lower rates of water loss. See **sweat**.

**insertion:** 1. area where a muscle attaches to a structure (usually bone, but may be other connective tissue) and produces movement during muscle contraction; the **origin** and insertion of a particular muscle may not be the same for different actions of the muscle. 2. addition of one or more base pairs into an existing **DNA sequence**.

**insertion mutation:** addition of exogenous **DNA** into an existing sequence in a genome. Insertions are commonly foreign DNA from a virus or **transposon**, but can also be the result of unequal crossing over. Insertions that occur within a functional **exon** usually inactivate or diminish the function of a working gene.

**insertional mutagenesis:** mutation caused by exogenous **DNA** inserted into a genome.

‡ **inspiration:** process of filling the lungs with air; inhalation. Cf. **expiration**.

**instantaneous sampling:** type of **time sampling** in which a behavior recording session is divided into a series of short sample intervals. The observer records whether or not the behavior pattern being studied occurred at the moment (or instant) that there was a signal from a timekeeping device. Cf. **one–zero sampling**.

**instantaneous speciation:** see **saltational speciation**.

**instinct:** behavior that is highly stereotyped, more complex than the simplest reflexes, and usually directed at a particular object in the environment. Learning may or may not be involved in the development of instinctive behavior; the important point is that the behavior develops toward a narrow, predictable end product.

**Institute for Primate Research:** facility established as the **Tigoni Primate Research Centre** near Nairobi, Kenya, in 1958 by Louis **Leakey** for studying the behaviors of captive monkeys; renamed as the Institute for Primate Research in 1974.

**Institutional Review Board** (IRB): an in-house committee that reviews research proposals for compliance with federal regulations before submission to a federal agency for funding.

**insufficiently known species:** one of the five conservation categories established by the **International Union for the Conservation of Nature**. This category contains those species for which there is not enough information to place them in one of the other categories. Many primate species are in this group. See **extinct species, endangered species, vulnerable species** and **rare species**.

**insula:** one of the five major lobes in each of the cerebral hemispheres of the brain, lying deep to the lateral sulcus and covered by portions of the frontal, parietal, and temporal lobes. Among its little-understood functions are memory and the integration of other cerebral activities.

**insulative adaptation:** adaptation to cold stress that is accomplished by heat conservation in the form of larger body size, body form, body composition (i.e. additional fat), and regulation of blood form. Cf. **metabolic adaptation**.

**insulin:** 1. natural protein **hormone** secreted in the kidney by beta cells in the **pancreatic islets** into the blood, where it regulates **carbohydrate** metabolism by controlling blood glucose concentrations. The gene for human insulin has been mapped to chromosome 11p. 2. a nonhuman therapeutic product since 1922, homologous porcine or bovine insulin was used as a substitute product in cases of **diabetes mellitus**. 3. since 1983, a **recombinant** product of **genetic engineering**, historically the first such production by the **recombination** of a human gene into the E. coli plasmid.

**insulin-dependent diabetes mellitus** (IDDM): see **diabetes mellitus, type I**.

**insulin-like growth factor** (IGF): one of a group of peptides secreted by the liver and that circulate in the blood. Formerly called somatomedins, they have growth-promoting, insulin-like, and mitogenic effects. The *igf* genes (*igf1, igf2*) control the production of IGF-I, IGF-II, etc. IGF-I (formerly somatomedin C) is an important **growth hormone**-dependent mediator of cell growth and replication in young adults, and has been implicated in **hGH-resistant dwarfism**. IGF-II (formerly somatomedin A) is a determinant of the size of the **placenta**, appears to be essential for normal embryonic development, and may play special roles in the **central nervous system**; it exhibits evidence of **genomic imprinting**. Both are similar in sequence and structure to both mammalian **proinsulin** and human **relaxin**. See **genetic conflict theory** and **dual effector model**.

**insulin-like growth factor I** (IGF-I): one of a group of peptides that mediates the mitosis-stimulating effect of **growth hormone** on **bone**; aka somatostatin C. See **insulin-like growth factor**.

**integrase:** enzyme that causes recombination between exogenous and endogenous **DNA**. Integrases are active elements of viral genomes, and necessary for integration into the host genome. An excisionase is required for disintegration.

**integument:** skin; the largest organ of the body.

**integumentary system:** skin and its derived accessory organs (hair, nails/claws, various skin glands).

‡ **intelligence:** ability of an organism to learn and respond from previous experience or to solve problems from insight. See **cognition, problem solving.**

**intelligence quotient:** see **IQ.**

**intelligent design** (ID): modified **scientific creationism** argument that life was created by a transcendent mind, a supreme being who shepherds the purposeful unfolding of life and who has provided critical structures of sufficient complexity that they cannot be explained by a Darwinian evolutionary process. Supporters are self-styled as Intelligent Designers (IDs). Aka intelligent design creationism (IDC). See **argument from design** and **Paley's watchmaker argument.**

**intensity:** measurement in behavioral studies; intensity is the amplitude of the behavior; i.e. it is the strength of the behavior observed. For example, a baboon drinking water is the behavior, but how much water it drinks is the intensity.

**intensity of selection:** the measure of **natural selection,** calculated as the **coefficient of selection.**

**intention movement:** motion made in preparation for a response, but where the animal does not follow through to the complete behavior; e.g. a snarl before a bite. Intention movements can communicate to **conspecifics** an animal's motivational state and what it is likely to do next.

**intentionality:** planning or performing an action that has goals. Behavioral biologists have avoided attributing intentionality to animals, especially because it may only represent **anthropomorphism** (see **Morgan's canon**), but recently the development of **cognitive ethology** has led to a re-evaluation of this subject. For example, work with vervet monkeys sounding alarm calls for particular predators has asked the question of whether these animals intend to warn **conspecifics.**

**interaction:** in behavioral biology, an encounter between individuals in which each responds to the other. Interaction includes signal exchange in which both animals are not present, such as scent or physical signals such as scratchings on a tree. This may result in one individual withdrawing; interaction may be across species as well as **interspecific.** Examples are **greetings, parental care, submission, courtship, agonistic behavior, displays,** etc.

**interaction, genotype–environment:** see **genotype–environment interaction.**

**interbirth interval:** average time differential between births for a population or species.

**intercalate:** 1. the addition or subtraction of some interval to a particular calendar in order to make it coincide with external, usually solar, cycles. 2. to insert between adjacent structures; interpolate.

**intercalating agent:** any molecule that inserts itself between the base pairs in a **DNA** molecule, but is not a part of normal DNA metabolism; some intercalating agents disrupt the alignment and pairing of bases in DNA, resulting in mistakes during replication.

**intercellular:** occurring between cells.

**intercellular substance:** matrix or material between cells that largely determines tissue types. See **major histocompatibility complex.**

**intercept** ($c_o$): see **proportionality coefficient.**

**intercompensation:** effect caused by the domination of some density-dependent factors over others in population control. If the leading factor, say food shortage, is eliminated, a second factor, such as disease, takes over. This compensation follows a sequence peculiar to each species.

**intercondylar:** between **condyles.**

**intercondylar tubercle:** in reference to either the medial or lateral tubercles that are articular surfaces located on the proximal end of the **tibia.**

**incontinentia pigmenti:** X-linked recessive condition characterized by swirls of skin color, hair loss, seizures, and abnormal teeth in females. The condition is usually fatal to males *in utero*. There are indications of a **paternal age effect.**

**interconvertibility:** refers to the ability of humans to satisfy energy needs by means of carbohydrates, fats, or amino acids; allows survival under stressful conditions as well as permitting dietary diversity.

**intercourse:** sex act; **copulation.**

**intercuneiform:** supernumerary bone sometimes found between the navicular and medial **cuneiforms** on the **plantar** portion of the foot.

**interdemic selection:** selection of entire breeding populations as the basic unit. One of the extreme forms of **group selection,** and contrasted with **kin selection.** The dispersion of similar genotypes with high adaptive value from their population of origin.

**interdigitation:** interlocking, as in the joining of the fingers of two hands.

**interferon** (IFN): glycoprotein produced by the body that stimulates the immune system, especially against viral infections, and interferes with cancer cell growth; see **cytokines.** There are two varieties, known as types 1 and 2.

**interfluvial:** living between rivers.

**interglacial period:** warm period of significant glacial ice retreat between two peaks of glacial advance, or Ice Ages. Cf. **interstadial.**

**intergrade:** **hybrid** individual, usually found in a zone between two clearly defined morphological groups. Intergrades arise through frequent admixture.

**intergroup transfer:** migration from one social unit to another. This is common in **anthropoid** groups. Among many non-one-male-unit cercopithecines the females tend to be the **resident sex** and males migrate to other groups as they reach puberty; among the African apes, the males tend to be the resident sex and the females migrate.

**interkinesis:** that part of the eukaryotic cell cycle during which the **chromatids** are decompacted.

**interlaminar:** between layers.

**interleukin: cytokine** used by cells of the immune system to control lymphocyte differentiation and growth. See **immune response.**

**intermediate host:** organism in which a parasite resides during its larval or asexual phase. Cf. **definitive host.**

**intermembral index** (IM): ratio of the length of the forelimb to the hindlimb; **humerus** + **radius** length divided by the combined length of the **femur** and **tibia** and multiplied by 100.

**intermembrane:** area between membranes. Adjective: intermembranous.

**intermetarsaeum:** area between the metatarsal bones.

**intermixture:** allele exchange between members of different populations. Earlier term for genetic **migration.**

**internal auditory meatus:** the passage through which the facial, intermediate, and vestibulocochlear nerves and the labyrinthine artery pass. Cf. **external auditory meatus.**

**internal balance:** balanced **epistatic** interaction of many genetic loci within an organism or population.

**internal carotid (artery):** main division of the common carotid artery that enters the cranium through the carotid canal of the **temporal bone.** The internal carotid artery distributes blood to the orbits and about 80% of the **cerebrum.** After entering the cranium each internal carotid gives rise to three branches: the ophthalmic, anterior cerebral, and middle cerebral arteries.

**internal marginality:** pertaining to any group of people with a subsistence-level culture who are surrounded by agrarian or industrial peoples.

**internal occipital protuberance** (IOP): point where ridges cross that help form the lateral and sagittal sinuses of the posterior cranial fossa. Cf. **external occipital protuberance.**

**International Biological Programme** (IBP): in 1964, the IBP was chartered to 'study ecological factors that influence human productivity and welfare'. The convenor was J. S. **Weiner.** Among its participants was J. M. **Tanner.** The IBP was responsible for internationalizing studies on growth and development, **population biology,** and human adaptation.

**International Code of Zoological Nomenclature** (ICZN): regulations that govern the use of names applied to animal **taxa** at all levels of taxonomic hierarchy. See **International Commission on Zoological Nomenclature.**

**International Commission on Zoological Nomenclature** (ICZN): the governing body that oversees and regulates the International Code of Zoological Nomenclature; this commission makes judgments on questions of validity and priority of taxonomic designations. Rules are slightly different for paleontological species in that a paleontological taxon becomes valid if it is used and accepted by continual use in the literature.

*International Journal of Primatology:* journal produced by the **International Society of Primatologists,** dealing with all aspects of primate biology, but papers primarily relate to behavior and ecology. Published by Plenum Press in New York and London.

**International Society of Primatologists:** organization of primatologists whose members are worldwide. This society's organ is the *International Journal of Primatology.*

**International Union for the Conservation of Nature** (IUCN): organization of conservation biologists dedicated to the preservation of biodiversity. They have established five main conservation categories that have proved helpful by directing attention toward species of special concern. See **extinct species, endangered species, vulnerable species, rare species,** and **insufficiently known species.**

**interobserver reliability:** check of the consistency between several different observers' measurements of the same behavior on the same occasion. Cf. **intraobserver reliability.**

**interorbital breadth** (mf–mf): **craniometric** measurement; distance between the left and right **maxillofrontale** as measured with sliding calipers.

**interorbital distance:** distance between the orbits measured at their medial margins.

**interorbital pillar:** region located between the medial edge of the orbits that is composed of the nasal bones, the frontal process of the frontal bone, and portions of the maxillae, ethmoids, and lacrimals.

**interosseous:** between bones; for example, an interosseous ligament binds two bones together.

**interparietal bone:** alternative name for the Inka (Inca) bone or epactal bone. See **sutural bone.**

‡ **interphase:** 1. first phase during **mitosis,** when the replication of chromatids takes place. In **meiosis,** two interphase stages occur, **interphase I** and **interphase II.** 2. that part of the eukaryotic cell cycle during which the **chromatids** are decompacted and enclosed in a **nuclear envelope;** many genes are transcriptionally active. See **Gap 1 phase, S phase** and **Gap 2 phase.**

‡ **interphase I:** first phase during **meiosis I**, when the replication of chromatids takes place. See **interphase II**.

‡ **interphase II:** intermediate phase during **meiosis**, when the chromosomes uncoil slightly during a brief pause. See **interphase I**.

**interpluvial:** dry phase between two rainy periods. See **pluvial**.

**interpretation:** an explanation, elucidation or explication; conceptual judgement as to meaning. See **scientific method** and **statistics**.

**interproximal:** of or pertaining to the space between adjacent surfaces.

**intersex individual:** individual exhibiting secondary sexual characteristics of both sexes; such individuals are often sterile. See **hermaphrodite**.

**intersexual selection:** differential mating success among individuals of one sex due to interactions with members of the other sex; typically, variance in mating success is higher in males than in females, usually said to be owing to female choice. See **sexual selection** and **mate choice**.

**intersexuality:** blending of feminine and masculine in a single individual, usually as the result of incomplete manifestation of primary and secondary sexual characteristics. See **pseudohermaphroditism**.

‡ **interspecific:** between species.

**interspecific allometry:** relationship between size and shape among a range of different species; comparison, for example, between species of mouse and elephant. See **allometry**.

‡ **interspecific variation:** variation between species.

‡ **interstadial:** irregular but well-defined episode of somewhat milder climatic conditions occurring during a glacial period; not as extensive as an **interglacial period**.

**interstitial:** 1. forming an intervening space. 2. pertaining to the area between adjacent teeth; aka interdental, interproximal. 3. situated in the body of a chromosome, rather than near the **telomere**.

**interstitial cells:** cells in the fetal testes that secrete testosterone, causing the development of male internal reproductive structures. Aka Leydig cells.

**interstitial cell-stimulating hormone** (ICSH): see **luteinizing hormone**.

‡ **interstitial wear:** wear between adjacent teeth; aka interdental or interproximal wear.

**intertrabecular:** of or pertaining to the space between **trabeculae**.

**intertrochanteric:** of or pertaining to the area between the **greater** and **lesser trochanters** of the **femur**.

**intertubercular:** of or pertaining to the area between **tubercles**.

**intervertebral disk:** layer of fibrocartilage that separates individual **vertebrae** and provides resilience and cushioning to the **vertebral column**.

**intestine:** tubular portion of the **gastrointestinal tract** that includes the small intestine, cecum, and colon. See **small intestine, large intestine**.

**intimidation display:** behavior suggesting the possibility of physical danger; intimidation among **primates** is usually expressed by visual or vocal signals such as body posture, facial expressions (such as open mouth threats), or loud vocalizations, particularly by a dominant animal to a subordinate.

**intracellular:** occurring within a cell.

**intracytoplasmic sperm injection:** insertion of a sperm nucleus into an **oocyte**, used when male sperm motility is low.

**intrademic selection:** emergence of selectively favored genotypes within a population and their increasing frequency as a result of superior adaptive capacity.

**intragenomic conflict theory:** see **genetic conflict theory**.

**intramembranous bone:** bone whose developmental origin is in layers of connective tissue and the development of which proceeds by **ossification**; **flat bones** of the skeleton develop in this manner. Cf. **endochondral bone**.

**intramembranous ossification:** developmental process by which **flat bones** are formed; results in **intramembranous bone**. Cf. **endochondral ossification**.

**intraobserver reliability:** check of the consistency of a single observer's measurements of the same behavior on several different occasions. Aka observer consistency, self-reliability. Cf. **interobserver reliability**.

**intraparietal sulci, bilateral:** region of the brain involved in estimations and calculating approximate mathematical solutions that are dependent on visuo-spatial representations of numbers. These regions are also part of the circuitry controlling finger movements, and it has been suggested that they are likely to be crucial to finger counting.

**intrapopulation variation:** variability within a population.

**intrasexual competition: competition** between the members of the same sex within a species, i.e. male–male competition or female–female competition.

**intrasexual selection:** competition between members of the same sex for access to members of the opposite sex, considered to be a scarce resource; the first stage of **sexual selection**. See **mate choice**.

‡ **intraspecific:** occurring or observed within a species. Cf. **interspecific**.

**intraspecific allometry:** relationship between size and shape among members of the same species. See **allometry** and **growth allometry**.

‡ **intraspecific variation:** variation within a species.

**intrinsic (muscle):** muscle located completely in the area on which it acts; i.e. its **origin** and **insertion** are both in this region. For example, some of the movements of the human fingers are generated by muscles between the **metacarpals.**

**intrinsic rate of increase** (*r*): the fraction by which a population grows in each unit of time. Aka maximum intrinsic rate of increase.

**intrinsic value:** tenet in conservation biology that each species has value in its own right, regardless of the value placed on it by humans. See **deep ecology.**

‡ **introgression:** see **genetic introgression.**

‡ **introgressive hybridization: gene flow** among unlike groups. According to theory, if fertile hybrids are produced they tend to backcross with the more abundant group, and the result is a population of individuals who most resemble the more abundant parents but who also possess some characters of the less abundant group.

**intromission:** behavior in which one structure is inserted into another; normally understood to be the insertion of the penis into the vagina. Adjective: intromittent.

**intromittent organ:** male copulatory organ that implants sperm within a female.

‡ **intron:** intervening sequence, a noncoding portion of **DNA**; the part of a **cistron** or length of DNA that is transcribed into **hmRNA** (pre-mRNA) and consists of stretches that are excised before edited mRNA is translated. Cf. **exon.**

**intrusion:** presence of a younger **artifact** into an older **assemblage** or stratigraphic layer; such anomalies are usually the result of human or animal activity such as a deliberate, intrusive **burial** of human remains and grave goods into a pit that has been dug for that purpose, or animal burrowing activity, which allows younger artifacts to settle into older sediments or depositional layers.

**intrusive:** thrusting, invasive; as a burial that is intrusive within a deeper cultural stratum; intrusive object.

**intussusception:** 1. growth of an organism by conversion of nutrients into protoplasm, and the incorporation of this into an existing framework. 2. morbid condition involving intestinal telescoping.

**Inuit:** see **Arctic Inuit.**

**inustus tamarin:** vernacular for *Saguinus inustus.*

**invagination:** inpocketing; folding inward of a membrane or sheet of cells.

**invention:** change or adjustment to an object, concept or practice in material or cognitive culture. See **basic invention, improving invention.** Cf. **discovery.**

**inventory:** in conservation biology, a census of individuals in a population of a species. By repeating the inventory several times it can be determined whether a population is stable, decreasing, or increasing in size.

‡ **inversion:** 1. inward, or **medial**, turning of the **plantar** surface of the foot. Verb: to invert. Cf. **eversion.** See **pronation** and **supination.** 2. event, or the product of such an event, that results in a reversed order of a segment of a **chromosome** and also the order of the genes in its **linkage group.** Inversions are often detectable by examining the **banding** patterns of chromosomes, and are one of the most common modes of **chromosome evolution** in mammals. See **pericentric inversion** and **paracentric inversion.**

**inversion heterozygote:** diploid individual **heterokaryotypic** for an **inversion** (2). If the number of crossovers that occur between the inverted region and its normal homologue is an odd number, reproductive problems may occur due to **recombination**, resulting in **duplications** and **deletions** of genes in the **gametes** of the individual. Inversions normally do not change the **diploid number.**

**inversion loop:** loop formed due to gene-to-gene pairing during **synapsis** in a chromosome carrying an **inversion** (2) not carried by its homologue.

**inversion polymorphism:** polymorphism for one or more chromosome inversions maintained in a population. Inversion polymorphisms are rare except in species that have evolved specific mechanisms (such as meiotic 'crossover absence' in one or both sexes, as in *Drosophila*) because of the cost of zygote wastage whenever an odd number of crossovers occurs within the limits of an inversion heterozygote, resulting in duplications and deletions. Inversions thus 'suppress' crossovers and result in greater functional (not physical) linkage among loci within the inversion.

‡ **invertebrate:** animal lacking an internal vertebral column, e.g. protozoans, insects, starfish.

**invisible biotic baggage:** referring to the pathogens that accompany humans and the animals they domesticate, and jump from species to species as humans migrate from one region to another.

**involuntary:** independent of choice or free will; reflexive, **autonomic.**

**involuntary muscle:** muscle tissue whose contraction is not controlled by conscious thought; cardiac muscle and smooth muscle tissue are involuntary muscle. Cf. **voluntary muscle.**

**iodine:** nonmetallic, micronutritional element; in its protein-bound form it is found in serum and thyroid hormone. One of the essential nutrients of the human diet. It can also be used as an antiseptic. See **thyroxine** and **goiter.**

**ion:** any atom or small molecule that has an unequal number of electrons and protons; ions with an excess of electrons are termed cations and carry a net negative charge, while those with an excess of protons are termed anions and are positively charged. Ions are the source of electrical signals in the brain.

**ion channel diseases** (ICDs): set of diseases caused by faults in the proteins that conduct **ions** of sodium, potassium and chloride across cell membranes. ICDs include hyperkalemic periodic paralysis, **long-QT syndrome** and **cystic fibrosis.**

**ion channel:** membrane protein that conducts **ions** across cell membranes. See **ion channel diseases.**

**ionizing radiation:** electromagnetic or corpuscular radiation that is capable of producing **ions** during interaction with other matter, including biological molecules.

**Iowan glaciation:** first of two major episodes of the fourth major glaciation of the Pleistocene in the North American sequence; see **Würm glaciation.**

**ipsilateral:** positioned on or affecting the same side. Cf. **contralateral.**

**Ipswichian interglacial:** third major interglacial of the glacial sequence in the British Isles; also a pseudosynonym for the **pre-Abbevillian tool tradition.**

**IQ:** intelligence quotient, a score derived from standardized tests that is calculated by dividing the individual's mental age, as determined by the test, by her or his chronological age, $\times$ 100. A tested mental age of 10 for a child aged ten would thus yield an IQ of 100, of average or normal intelligence.

**iridium:** rare earth element found at the K/T boundary rocks at Gubbio (Italy), suggesting that the mass extinction may have been caused by the collision of an asteroid, about 10 km in diameter, with the earth. See **Cretaceous-Tertiary boundary.**

**iridium anomaly:** presence of a high concentration of the element **iridium** in certain geological strata.

**iris:** circular portion of the vascular tunic of the eye that contains pigment in **melanocytes** that influences **eye color,** and that surrounds the **pupil,** which increases and decreases in diameter as the iris expands and contracts to regulate light input to the retina.

**iron:** metallic micronutritional trace element and one of the essential nutrients of the human diet. Iron is found in **hemoglobin, myoglobin, cytochrome, catalase,** and peroxidase, and is involved predominately with respiration. It is stored in the liver and pancreas. Iron deficiency can result in **anemia;** the iron storage disorders include **hemochromatosis.**

**iron storage disease:** see **hemochromatosis.**

**irregular bones:** one of the four types of bone as classified by their shape. Irregular bones have no single shape as a group, but a diversity of complex forms; in most cases these bones consist of **cancellous bone** surrounded by a thin layer of **compact bone.** This group includes vertebrae, coxal bones,

and many facial bones. Cf. **long bones, short bones,** and **flat bones.**

**irreversibility rule:** see **Dollo's law.**

**irritability:** ability to react to a stimulus, an ability basic to living organisms.

**Isaac, Glynn** (1937–85): South African-born Berkeley and Harvard archaeologist; prolific publisher and tireless field director; excavated at **Olduvai Gorge** and **Olorgesailie** with the Leakeys; later, co-director of the Koobi Fora Research Project in Kenya. Isaac excavated several other East African sites, including **Peninj,** and provided ongoing commentaries regarding hominid foraging strategies and tool use until his untimely death. Author of *Olorgesailie* (1977).

**isauxesis:** growth in which a part or organ of interest grows at the same rate as the organism as a whole. See **heterauxesis** and **allometry.**

**ischemic phase:** fourth phase of the human **uterine cycle,** encompassing days 27–28, and characterized by relatively low concentrations of the hormones **LH** and **FSH** and lowering of **estrogens** and **progesterone.** The blood supply is diminished and the influence of hormones is minimized, causing a marked shrinking of the **endometrium,** followed by ischemic necrosis of the superficial tissues, which eventually detach and pass into the uterine cavity.

‡ **ischial callosity:** pad of calloused skin that overlies the ischial tuberosity (a part of the pelvic bone) that serves as a sitting pad in cercopithecines and **gibbons.**

**ischial tuberosity:** roughened area on the human **ischium** that provides attachments for ligaments and leg muscles. In most other primates these structures are at the caudal end of the **coxal bone** and may be covered by an ischial callosity.

**ischiofemoral ligament:** ligament that supports the **coxal joint** from the posterior side. When standing, this ligament helps pull the head of the **femur** tightly into the **acetabulum.**

‡ **ischium:** one of a pair of bones (which fuse in the human adult) that forms the lower portion of the **coxal bone.** Ligaments and several muscles that move the leg have their origin on this bone. In most other primates the ischium is elongated and ends **caudally** in **ischial tuberosities;** these structures may be covered with callused skin. See **ischial callosity.**

**ischium–pubis index:** pubic length $\times$ 100, divided by the length of the **ischium.**

**island biogeography model:** theory developed by MacArthur and E. O. **Wilson** to explain the distribution of biological diversity. The major tenet of this model is the **species–area relationship.** Although devised from studies of island communities, island biogeography is now used in conservation biology for biological reserves and fragmented habitats.

**islets of Langerhans:** see **pancreatic islets**.

**isoagglutinogen:** any antigen that occurs normally in an individual, i.e. without an artificial challenge to the immune system. Aka agglutinogen.

**isoallele:** normal allelic gene that can be distinguished from other normal ones only by the differences in the expression of a dominant trait when paired with another allele in a heterozygous person.

**isoantibodies:** naturally occurring antibodies in an individual; antibodies not generated by artificial immunization.

**isocaloric:** having similar food energy value.

**isochromosome: major chromosome anomaly** produced when the **centromere** splits abnormally along the transverse plane, resulting in a **chromatid** with identical arms.

**isocline:** portion of a **cline** in which values of a variable remain constant, as opposed to its **gradient**.

**isocortex:** see **neocortex**; aka neopallium.

**isodisomy:** unusual inheritance of two copies of a gene from one parent, and none from the other. One of the forms of **non-Mendelian inheritance**. Isodisomy describes the case where the alleles are identical owing to nondisjunction during mitosis or the second meiotic division. Cf. **heterodisomy**.

**isoform:** alternative gene product constructed by **alternative splicing**.

**isogamy:** condition in which the male and female gametes are of the same size (isogametes). Cf. **anisogamy**.

**isogenic:** genetically alike; aka isogeneic.

**isograft:** transplant in which the donor and recipient are identical **twins**. Cf. **allograft, xenograft**.

**isolate:** 1. to set apart, detach, or segregate. 2. a population or **deme** that is separated from other breeding populations in a species, and within which **inbreeding** subsequently occurs. See **isolating mechanism**.

**isolating mechanism:** barrier to reproductive exchange or **gene flow** between **populations**. Can be geographical, behavioral, or physiological. Any **prezygotic mechanism** or **postzygotic mechanism** that results in **reproductive isolation**.

**isolation:** 1. restriction of **gene flow** between demes; see **reproductive isolation, spatial isolation, geographical isolation, environmental isolation, ecological isolation** (habitat isolation), **mechanical isolation, ethological isolation, seasonal isolation**, and **gametic isolation**. See also **isolating mechanism**. 2. setting apart of an individual from a group of which she/he is a nominal member.

**isolation by distance:** separation of potential interbreeding populations by linear space, even though contiguous breeding populations may bridge the space between the isolated populations. This type of isolation, introduced by S. **Wright**, limits the degree of **gene flow, admixture**, and genetic affinity to proximate populations, and is a function of **migration** and time. See **genetic distance**. Cf. **geographical isolation**.

**isolation species concept:** see **allopatric speciation**.

**isoleucine** (Ileu): an essential **amino acid**; one of the twenty building blocks of **proteins**.

**isologous:** marked by an identical genotype. Aka isoplastic.

**isomers:** compounds with the same chemical formula that differ in shape. See **racemization**.

**isometric:** 1. of or pertaining to equal dimensions. 2. see **isauxesis**.

**isometric scaling:** in studies of body size, a one-to-one increase in units between two variables producing a regression slope or mass exponent of 1.0.

**isometric strength:** estimation of muscle strength by having a subject push or pull against a stationary object and measuring static muscle contractions.

**isonymy:** having the same surname.

**isonymous mating:** mating or cohabitation between people with the same surname.

**isophenogamy:** mating between people who have a greater degree of somatic resemblance than would be expected under random mating; **positive assortative mating**. Cf. heterophenogamy.

**isostasy:** process by which the earth's crust gradually lifts after the weight of a melted glacier has been removed.

**isotope:** one of any pair of atoms that have the same number of protons but a different number of neutrons and hence differ in atomic mass. Some isotopes are unstable and decay spontaneously at fixed rates; other isotopes are stable. See **carbon 14**.

**Isotype:** set of antigenic molecules shared by all immunocompetent members of a species, but missing in members of other species.

**isozymes:** different molecular forms of an **enzyme** within an individual that catalyze the same reaction(s). Isozymes are products of two or more nonallelic loci that evolved by gene duplication. Examples of isozymes include the carbonic anhydrases and the lactate dehydrogenases. Cf. **allozyme**.

**iterative evolution:** repeated origin of morphologically similar evolutionary stocks, as has been proposed by the supporters of the **multiregional continuity model**.

**iteroparity:** condition of a species or population in which individuals normally experience more than one episode of reproduction over the course of a lifetime, as in humans. Adjective: iteroparous. Cf. **multiparity, semelparity**. See **parity**.

**IUCN:** see **International Union for the Conservation of Nature.**

**IUCN Red Data Book:** see **red data book.**

**IVF:** *in vitro* fertilization, the joining of oöcytes and sperm in a laboratory dish with appropriate nutrients such that fertilization and **cleavage** occurs; after a few cell divisions (at the **morula** stage) the **preimplantation embryo** is transferred to a woman's uterus, or frozen for future use.

**J-shaped growth curve:** see **exponential growth curve.**

**Jacob–Monod model:** proposal that protein synthesis of a structural gene in prokaryotes is regulated by an upstream operator gene and a regulator gene located elsewhere in the genome. The three genes together are termed an **operon.** Cf. **Britten–Davidson model** for eukaryotes.

**Jacob syndrome:** see **double-Y syndrome.**

**Jacobsen's organ:** see **vomeronasal organ.**

**Jacovec Cavern:** chamber explored in 1995 at the **Sterkfontein** hominid site, filled by fossiliferous orange **breccia** provisionally dated to 4.02–3.76 mya (**cosmogenic radionuclide dating**). The breccia produced cranial remains (StW 578), isolated teeth, and postcranial remains that include vertebrae, humeri, femora, and clavicles, all provisionally assigned to *Australopithecus* sp. Cf. 'Little Foot'.

**Jamaican monkey:** vernacular for the recently extinct **platyrrhine** species *Xenothrix mcgregori.*

**Japanese macaque:** vernacular for *Macaca fuscata.*

**japonicum:** **zygomatic bone** in which there is incomplete fusion between the two primary growth centers, resulting in two supplementary sutures (bipartite malars) in the adult. This condition was previously believed to occur in high frequencies among the Japanese. Aka *os japonicum.*

**Jarmin–Bell principle:** rule relating body size of mammals to the nutritional quality of the foods they eat; small mammals eat high-quality (high-energy), quickly digested foods such as insects; larger mammals require relatively fewer **calories** per unit of **body mass**, and can subsist on low-quality (low-energy) but harder-to-digest foods processed in bulk, such as leaves.

**jaundice:** yellowing aspect to the skin caused by **hyperbilirubinemia** and the abnormal deposition of bile pigment in the skin and mucous membranes; among other factors, can be due to **hemolytic disease of the newborn.**

**Java man:** vernacular for fossil hominids found in Southeast Asia at the end of the nineteenth century. See **Ngandong** and **Trinil.**

*Javanthropus soloensis* Oppenoorth, 1932: aka Solo man, Ngandong man; see *Homo erectus.*

**jaw:** two sets of bones that contain the teeth in mammals; evolutionarily they are derived from the second and third gill arches of ancestral fishes. The upper jaw is called the **maxillary bone,** the lower jaw, a single bone in **anthropoids,** is called the **mandible.** In other mammals the jaws are referred to as the **dentary** bones.

**Jay-Dolhinow, Phyllis C.:** see **P. C. Dolhinow.**

**Jebel el Qatrani: Oligocene** geological formation of the **Fayum,** dated to 37–22 mya, consisting of lower, middle and upper fossil wood zones, capped by basalt dated at 22 mya. Several early primate fossils have been found in the formation. See *Aegyptopithecus.*

**Jebel Irhoud:** archaeological site excavated in 1961–8 near Safi, Morocco, dated to 150 kya (190–87, by **ESR dating; Middle Pleistocene**), and that contains **Middle Paleolithic** ('Aterian') artifacts (see **Levalloiso-Mousterian**). Hominid remains of at least five individuals are now attributed to late **archaic *Homo sapiens.*** One of the skulls has a cranial capacity of 1305 cm³, one of 1480 cm³. Often compared to **Saccopastore, Amud,** and **Skhul 5.** An original proposal for a Neandertal attribution has had little recent support. Aka Djebel Ibhoud, Ighoud.

**Jebel Zelten:** early Miocene paleontological site in Libya, dated to about 19 mya, and that contains fossils of *Prohylobates.*

**jejunum:** region of the **small intestine** between the **duodenum** and the **ileum.** There is no distinct separation between the jejunum and ileum except that the jejunum tends to have a greater diameter. Functionally, absorption of nutrients occurs in the jejunum.

*Jemezius szalayi* Beard, 1987: tarsiiform primate from the early Eocene of North America, belonging to the subfamily **Omomyinae.** Estimated body mass around 150 g. See Appendix 1 for taxonomy.

**Jingniushan Cave:** archaeological site found in 1984 in Yingkou County, Liaoning Province, China, dated to 280–200 kya; contains hominid remains, including a 1300 cm³ cranium with broad cheek bones and an **occipital bun** associated with some postcranial material, and assigned to the **archaic *Homo sapiens*** group. Aka Jinniushan Man, Jinniu Shan, Jingchuan, Yingkou.

**JK:** Juma's (Gitau) **Korongo** at **Olduvai Gorge Bed III.**

**jog trot bipedalism:** relatively inefficient form of early **bipedal locomotion** suggested by Napier as characteristic of **australopithecines,** due to the latter's relatively long **ischium,** which precluded a fully **striding gait** as in modern humans.

‡ **Johanson, Donald Carl** (1943– ): US paleontologist known for his excavations (*c.* 1973) of early **australopithecine** sites in East Africa ('**Lucy**' and the '**first family**'). Johanson is a prolific campaigner and promoter of paleoanthropology. In 1981 he founded the Institute of Human Origins, which is currently affiliated with Arizona State University. Johanson is co-author of *Lucy: Beginnings of Humankind* (1981) and other works.

**John's langur:** vernacular for *Presbytis johnii.*

**Johnston, Francis E.** (1931– ): US physical anthropologist; specialist in childhood development and growth physiology, especially with respect to nutritional effects. Editor of the *AJPA* (1977–83), *Human Biology* (1987–8), and the *American Journal of Human Biology* (1988–90); president, **AAPA** (1983–5); was instrumental in founding the Human Biology Association. Co-editor (with D. H. O'Rourke and G. M. Peterson) of *Genetics, Evolution, and Disease* (1983).

**joint:** point where two or more bones form an **articulation**. Joints are classified either by tissue type (see **fibrous joint, cartilaginous joint, synovial joint**) or by degree of motion (see **amphiarthrotic joint, diarthrotic joint, synarthrotic joint**).

**joint cavity:** area in a **synovial joint** that is contained within and bordered by the **synovial membrane** and **articular cartilage;** this cavity is filled with **synovial fluid.**

**Jones, Frederick Wood** (1879–1954): functional anatomist at the Royal College of Surgeons; appointments in Egypt, Australia and Hawaii gave Jones ample opportunity to study mammals in the field; published several anatomical treatments with an evolutionary emphasis; supported the **arboreal** theory of primate **evolution** proposed by T. H. **Huxley;** remembered for an unorthodox view that hominids split from the apes as early as the **Eocene epoc;** also expounded a personal view of **Lamarckism.**

**Jordan's rule:** axiom that the ranges of closely related species or subspecies are usually adjacent and separated by an ecological barrier.

**joule:** unit of energy equal to work when a force of 1 newton is applied to for a distance of 1 meter in the direction of the force; equal to 0.2388 calories.

**jugum:** any ridge connecting two structures. Plural: juga.

**jumping genes:** vernacular for genetic elements proposed by **McClintock** in 1931 for **genes** that can move from one **chromosome** to another. Such transpositions change the genetic programming of a cell. See **transposons.**

**'jungle fever':** see **malaria.**

**junk DNA:** stretches of **DNA** that do not code for genes under the current paradigm; Aka **selfish DNA,** parasitic DNA. Most of the human genome consists of this noncoding DNA.

**junior synonym:** in taxonomy, any of two or more synonyms other than the first published. Aka later synonym, younger synonym. Cf. **senior synonym.**

‡ **Jurassic period:** period of the **Mesozoic era,** lasting from approximately 190 to 136 mya; dinosaurs flourished; shallow seas in western North America retreated as mountains began to form. Ammonite fossils are very common; fossil fish resembling modern bony fish appear; large reptiles, both terrestrial and aquatic, become dominant animal forms, as reflected in the fossil record.

**juvenile:** subadult animal that has not yet reached puberty. See **juvenile growth stage.** Cf. **child** and **adolescent.**

**juvenile growth stage** (or **period**): interval in the development of many higher primates, defined as the interval prior to sexual maturation when an individual is no longer dependent on adults for survival. See **juvenile.** Cf. **adolescent stage.**

**juxtamastoid eminence:** bony crest on the mastoid process posterior to the **styloid** process of the cranial base; lateral to the **occipitomastoid crest;** one of the origins for the digastric muscle.

*K*: symbol for the **carrying capacity** of an environment. Cf. I.

**K or k blood group:** see **Kell blood group**.

‡ **Kabuh Formation:** stratigraphic unit in central Java, dated to the Early/Middle Pleistocene, and that contains **Trinil fauna** with Sino-Malayan affinities. The base of the unit is marked by a 1–2 m thick layer called the Grenzbank sands, dated to approximately 900 kya, a visually distinct marker sediment important because the sediments immediately above and below it (see the **Pucangan Formation**) are fossiliferous. The Kabuh Formation is up to 59 m thick. Aka Kabuh Beds. See **Bapang Formation**.

**Kabwe:** archaeological site found in 1921 at the Broken Hill Mine near Lusaka in Zambia (formerly Rhodesia), dated to 200–125 kya, and that contains artifacts of African **Middle Stone Age**. Hominid remains found in a limestone cave shaft include postcranial material and an 1100–1280 cm³ cranium with extensive ante-mortem dental **sepsis**. Assigned to the **archaic *Homo sapiens*** group. Some postcranial material may not belong to the cranium; it appears that 3–4 individuals are represented. Aka Broken Hill Mine, Rhodesian Man, Zambian human.

**Kada Gona:** region with multiple Pliocene-age archaeological sites in East Gona (EG10, EG12) found in 1992 in the Afar triangle, Hadar, Ethiopia, dated to 2.6–2.52 mya (**single crystal laser fusion**, ⁴⁰Ar/³⁹Ar, and magnetostratigraphy). The surface sites contain thousands of pebble tool artifacts (cf. the **Oldowan tool tradition**) that are younger than nearby hominid remains; the Gona artifacts are at this time (2004) considered the oldest in the world. Aka East Gona, Gona River, Kada Hadar. Cf. **Bouri Formation**, **Hadar, Omo Valley, Lokalalei 2C**.

**Kada Hadar Member:** youngest sedimentary Member in the **Hadar Formation**, overlying the **Denen Dora Member**.

**Kalambo Falls:** archaeological site found in 1953 near the southeast end of Lake Tanganyika in Zambia by J. Desmond **Clark**, dated to as old as 180 kya (U series). It contains Acheulean artifacts (cleaver) and with a continuous occupation sequence 60 ky long through the later Iron Age.

***Kalepithecus songhorensis* Harrison, 1988:** **monotypic** genus of **hominoids** from the early Miocene of East Africa; previously included within ***Dendropithecus***. Estimated body mass around 5 kg. Dental formula: 2.1.2.3; dentition suggests **frugivory**. See Appendix 1 for taxonomy.

**Kalibeng Formation:** stratigraphic unit in central Java, dated to the Middle (3 mya, K/A) and Late Pliocene, and that contains a marine fauna; the thickness of the unit exceeds 125 m, and represents a gradually shallowing marine basin. Aka Kalibeng Beds.

**Kalodirr Riverbed:** archaeological site found in 1985 by Richard and Maeve **Leakey**, located at West Lake Turkana, Kenya, dated to 18–16 mya (early **Miocene**), containing **hominoid** remains including *Afropithecus* and *Turkanapithecus*.

**Kamarora tarsier:** vernacular for *Tarsius dianae*.

***Kamoyapithecus hamiltoni* Leakey, Ungar, and Walker, 1995:** poorly known **monotypic** genus of **hominoids** from the late Oligocene – early Miocene of East Africa; systematics uncertain. Dental formula: 2.1.2.3; key features of the dentition links this species to the Oligocene **Propliopithecidae**; it also has some traits that show affinities with *Afropithecus*. See Appendix 1 for taxonomy.

**Kanam:** archaeological site found in 1932, located at Kendu Bay, Lake Victoria in Kenya, dated to the 'early **Pleistocene**' (>500 kya), and that contains **hominid** remains including a mandibular fragment originally attributed to *Homo kanamensis*. The validity of Louis **Leakey's** claims for great antiquity were strongly challenged by the geologist Boswell; the ultimate attribution of the fossil is still in doubt. See **Kanjera**.

**Kanam beds:** geological strata dated to between 6 mya and 200 kya, located near Lake Victoria in Kenya.

**Kanam Man:** fossil species of 'early **Pleistocene**' **hominid** proposed by Louis **Leakey** on the basis of the type specimen, a mandible found at **Kanam** in Kenya. This specimen, attributed to *Homo kanamensis*, was influential in establishing Africa as the 'cradle of mankind'. See **Kanjera**.

‡ **Kanapoi** (KP): archaeological surface site found by Bryan Patterson southwest of Lake Turkana, Kenya, in 1965, dated to 4.2–3.4 mya, and that contains nine fragments of hominid remains, including a left distal humerus (**KNM-KP 271**) attributed to *Australopithecus anamensis*, found near an ancient lake bed called Lake (anam) Lonyumun. See **Allia Bay**.

**Kangatukuseo III:** archaeological site found in 1985 near west Lake Turkana, Kenya, dated to 2.45 ± 0.05 mya, and that contains hominid remains, including a hyper-robust mandible (**KNM-ER 16005**) attributed to *Australopithecus* (= *Paranthropus*) *aethiopicus*.

**Kanjera:** archaeological site found in 1932, located at Kendu Bay on Lake Victoria in Kenya, alleged to date to the 'middle **Pleistocene**', containing **hominid** remains including a partial cranium (No. 3) originally attributed to an ancient species of *Homo*. Found by Louis **Leakey**, this site was subsequently dated to less than 10 kya, relegating the Kanjera specimen to the same fate as Reck's **Olduvai Man**. See **Kanam**.

**Kansan glaciation:** second of the four major glaciations of the **Pleistocene epoch** in the North American sequence; see **Mindel glaciation**.

**Kapcheberek:** see **Rondinin**.

**Kaposi's sarcoma:** soft tissue cancer characterized by purple skin lesions, and often seen as the proximal cause of death, often secondary to **HIV** infection in **AIDS** patients.

**Kapsomin:** see **Rondinin**.

**Kapthurin:** archaeological site located in the Lake **Baringo** region of Kenya, dated to 870–230 kya. Hominid remains include upper limb bones and two mandibles (**KNM-BK 63** and **KNM-BK 8518**), both attributed to *Homo* **Cf.** *erectus*.

**Kapthurin Formation:** sedimentary unit in the Lake **Baringo** region of Kenya, dated to 870–230 kya.

**K/Ar dating:** abbreviation for **potassium–argon dating**.

**Karari Escarpment** (or **Ridge**): archaeological site found in 1972 near **Koobi Fora**, East Lake Turkana, Kenya, dated to 1.9–1.88 mya (**KBS tuff**, Gregory Rift), and that contains hominid remains including **KNM-ER 1470** and several other hominid specimens. Aka Karari Ridge.

**Karari tool industry:** tool variant of the Oldowan toolmaking tradition, characterized by the presence of large core-scrapers; first found at **Karari Escarpment**, Koobi Fora, Lake Turkana, Kenya, dated by K/Ar to 1.3–1.2 mya.

**Karari tuff:** Pleistocene volcanic deposit at Koobi Fora, Lake Turkana, Kenya, dated by K/Ar to 1.3–1.2 mya.

**Kariandusi:** archaeological site found in 1929 near Lake Naivasha, Kenya, by John Solomon, dated to 500 kya, and that contains **Acheulean** artifacts; this was the first site in Africa to yield an Acheulean assemblage.

**Karisoke National Park:** research site located on the Virunga volcanoes, Rwanda, where long-term field studies of mountain gorillas (*Gorilla gorilla* beringei) have been conducted for decades. Primatologists who have conducted field research at this site include: D. **Fossey**, A. Harcourt, K. Stewart, A. Veddar, D. Watts, D. Cheney, and R. Seyfarth.

**karst:** limestone region characterized geologically by sinks, abrupt ridges, protruding rocks, and underground streams and caverns.

**karstic caves:** caves formed in a limestone by the action of water; several of the fossil-bearing South African caves are karstic in origin.

**karyogamy:** second step in **syngamy**: fusion of the nuclei of two cells during cell conjugation. See **plasmogamy**.

**karyology:** cytology subspecialty dealing with nuclear structures, especially **chromosomes**; see **alpha karyology, beta karyology, gamma karyology, delta karyology**, and **epsilon karyology**.

**karyopycnosis:** shrinkage of cell nuclei and condensation of the chromatin that is a normal part of the aging process.

**karyosome:** one of the spherical masses of chromatin resembling a knot in the chromatin network of a resting nucleus during **mitosis**. Aka net knot, chromatin, false nucleolus.

‡ **karyotype:** graphic arrangement of an individual's **chromosomes** in order of decreasing size and position of **centromere**, usually compared to a **standard karyotype**. Technique (karyotyping) used clinically to identify any grossly visible **chromosome mutation** such as **trisomy**.

*Kasi* Reichenbach, 1862: subgenus within *Trachypithecus*; this subgenus consists of two species, *T. johnii* and *T. vetulus*.

**Kaspar Hauser syndrome:** see **psychosocial dwarfism**.

**Kataboi Member:** Pleistocene sedimentary deposit at Lake Turkana, Kenya, located below the **Tulu Bor Tuff** and above the **Lokochot Tuff**, and with an estimated age of 3.5 my.

**Katanda:** archaeological site found in 1985 in Kivu Province, Zaire, and dated to >89 kya. The site contains Middle Stone Age artifacts, a shellfish midden, and carved barbed bone fishing points.

**Kathwanga Point:** paleontological site found in 1926 on **Rusinga Island** in Lake Victoria, Kenya, dated to *ca.* 20–18 mya (middle **Miocene**), and that contains fossil hominoids that are attributed to *Proconsul* and *Nyanzapithecus*, and fossil monkeys attributed to *Victoriapithecus*. In 1948, Mary Leakey excavated the nearly complete skull of *Proconsul* (**KNM-RU 2036**). See **Kiahera Hill** and **Hiwegi Hill**.

**Kay's threshold:** the body mass, about 500 g, that is roughly the upper size limit of predominately insectivorous primates, and the lower size limit of predominately folivorous primates.

**kb(p):** see **kilobase** (pairs).

**KB 5223:** unassigned hominid from **Kromdraai** in the Transvaal, South Africa, which dates from 1.7 mya (or earlier) to about 1.0 mya. Hominid remains consist of isolated juvenile teeth.

**KBS industry:** Olduvai-like choppers and flake tools found embedded in a volcanic tuff found by Kay **Behrensmeyer** at **Koobi Fora**, Kenya, in 1969.

**KBS tuff: Pleistocene** volcanic **tuff** found by Kay **Behrensmeyer** in 1969 at **Koobi Fora**, Kenya, originally misdated by **K/Ar dating** in 1972 at 2.6 mya, and later revised downward in 1975 by Garniss Curtis to 1.88–1.64 mya (the original sample was contaminated by erosional mix from an older tuff). KBS = Kay Behrensmeyer Site. This tuff may be the same as Tuff H2 in the **Shungura Formation**.

**KBS tuff site:** archaeological site found in 1969 and surveyed in 1970 by Glynn **Isaac** and Richard **Leakey**, a **Pleistocene** volcanic deposit at **Koobi Fora**, Kenya, dated by **K/Ar dating** to 1.88–1.64 mya.

**Kebara** (**Cave**): archaeological site found in 1927, a limestone cave in Mount Carmel, near Haifa, Palestine (now Israel), with early horizons, dated to 64–45 kya (TL, ESR), and that contains **Mousterian** artifacts. Hominid remains from the earliest horizons include an infant (Kebara 1), and a nearly complete postcranial adult male skeleton (Kebara 2) and hyoid bone possibly representing a burial; the pelvis has been the focus of special attention. Associated remains are attributed to *Homo neanderthalensis*. Upper deposits include elements of sequentially more recent traditions, including the **Aurignacian**, a Kebaran variant of the Upper Paleolithic, the **Natufian**, and deposits from the historic period, as well. The Aurignacian level yielded fragmentary remains of nine **AMHs**, eighteen charred individuals from the Kebaran, and fifteen from the Natufian. Aka Wadi el-Mughara, Mugharet el-Kebara.

**Kedung Brubus:** archaeological site found in 1890 on the Solo River in Central Java, dated to 750–500 kya (lower Kabuh Beds). Hominid remains include one juvenile mandible, the very first located by Eugene **Dubois**, the **Trinil** 2 calotte (cranial capacity estimates range from 850 to 940 cm³), and the controversial Trinil 3 femur. All remains attributed to *Pithecanthropus (= Homo) erectus*. Aka Kedungbrubus, Trinil.

**Kedung Brubus 1:** designation for the single juvenile mandible, the first located by Eugene **Dubois** and attributed to *Pithecanthropus (= Homo) erectus*. The find was actually at Kedung Lumbu.

**keel:** in certain fossil hominids, especially *Homo erectus*, a ridged, rather smooth and round **sagittal suture** formed by the parietal bones meeting at an angle. Also found, especially in the frontal region, in the crania of some living robust *Homo sapiens* males.

**Keilor:** archaeological site found in 1940 on the Maribyrnong River near Melbourne in southeastern Australia, dated to 12.0 kya; contains hominid remains including a skull with a cranial capacity of 1590 cm³, and that is attributed to *Homo sapiens*. Often compared to **Wajak**.

‡ **Keith, Arthur** (1866–1955): British anatomist and teacher, conservator at the Hunterian Museum. Remembered for his errors concerning the **Piltdown** fragments, Keith was nevertheless a capable mentor to a generation of British anatomists and a popularizer of human antiquities. Postulated a '**cerebral Rubicon**' of 750 cm³ below which no hominid would fall. With American T. D. **McCown**, proposed the **preneandertal hypothesis** of human origins, lumping the Levantine specimens into a heterogenous 'Neandertalian' group. Author of *A New Theory of Human Evolution* (1948).

**Kell blood group:** red blood cell antigens specified by the K gene, antibodies to the K antigen (anti-K). Kell is the cause of one of the forms of hemolytic disease of the newborn and was named after a Mrs Kell, in whose blood those antibodies were discovered. Aka Kell–Gallano blood group, K blood group.

**Kennewick:** archaeological site found in 1996 on the Columbia River, Washington, dated to 9.3 kya, and that contains a skeleton from one male Paleoindian individual, initially thought to have caucasoid cranial affinities and attributed to **AMH**, and according to some anatomists morphologically 'not like Native Americans'. Aka Kennewick Man and K man.

**Kent's Cavern:** archaeological site found in 1825 near Torquay, Devon, England, dated to 30 kya, and that contains artifacts and hominid remains including *Homo sapiens*. Excavated by Fr. John MacEnery and William Pengelly; report left unpublished in ms. form until 1859.

*Kenyanthropus platyops* M. G. Leakey, Spoor, Brown, Gathogo, Kiarie, L. N. Leakey, and McDougall, 2001: *gen. et sp. nov.* Fossil hominid found in 1999 at Lomekwi in the Turkana district of Northern Kenya; the type locality is **LO-6N**. The holotype is **KNM-WT 40000** and was situated between the upper bound Tulu Bor Tuff and the lower bound Lokochot Tuff, providing an estimated date of 3.5 mya; it consists of a fragmentary cranium. The paratype, **KNM-WT 38350**, was situated above the Tulu Bor Tuff, and has an estimated age of 3.3 mya. According to the authors the cranium is similar to **KMN-ER 1470**. The composite specimen has a derived flat lower face with a tall malar region, moderate subnasal prognathism, roof of palate thin, molars small with thick enamel, small acoustic opening; the **occipital–marginal venous system** is absent. The derivation of the species name means 'flat-faced' (Greek). See Appendix 1 for taxonomy.

*Kenyapithecus* Leakey, 1962: genus of **hominoids** from the middle to late Miocene of Kenya; two species recognized; phylogenetic relationships uncertain, but this genus is sometimes included with the **Proconsulidae**; it has also been suggested as the earliest **hominid** representative. Estimated body mass between 25 and 45 kg. Dental formula: 2.1.2.3; thick enamel on cheek teeth. Postcrania suggests adaptation to terrestrial locomotion. It appears this genus inhabited a dry woodland environment. See Appendix 1 for taxonomy.

*Kenyapithecus africanus* (Le Gros Clark and Leakey, 1950): **hominoid** from the middle Miocene of East Africa. See *Kenyapithecus*.

*Kenyapithecus wickeri* Leakey, 1962: **hominoid** from the middle and late Miocene of East Africa. See *Kenyapithecus*.

**keratinization:** conversion of stratified squamous epithelium into tough proteinaceous structures such as the **corneum** of epidermis or any epidermal derivatives such as hair, nails, claws, or horns; aka cornification.

‡ **keratins:** group of cystine-rich insoluble **proteins,** a major constituent of the outer layers of skin, claws, feathers, horn, antlers, hoofs, nails, and insect silk. In humans, there are more than 20 keratins that are synthesized by epithelial cells. Different forms of keratin may be soft (e.g. hair) or hard (e.g.) nails.

**kernicterus:** condition associated with high concentration of **bilirubin** in the blood, in which abnormally high concentrations of bile pigments penetrate neural tissues, causing widespread destructive changes and severe neural symptoms; can be caused by neonatal **hyperbilirubinemia** secondary to **Rhesus incompatibility;** one of the symptoms of **hemolytic disease of the newborn.**

**Kettlewell, Henry B. D.** (1907–79): English ecologist, lepidopterist and geneticist. After field studies in South Africa (1949–52), Kettlewell was a genetics researcher at Oxford; remembered for his explanation of **industrial melanism** in the peppered moth (*Biston betularia*), Kettlewell documented one of the first clear instances of **natural selection** in the wild.

*K*-**extinction:** regular extinction of populations when they are at or near the **carrying capacity** of the environment. Cf. *r*-**extinction.**

**key innovation:** any new phenotype with a strongly associated genotype with potential for further evolutionary change.

**key resource:** essential resource that is rare or difficult to obtain.

**key trait, character** or **feature:** any diagnostic attribute that is used to identify organisms at various taxonomic levels. A key character is usually a dichotomous **autoapomorphy,** and can be used with a suite of other such keys to identify an unknown organism through a process of elimination.

**keystone resource:** in conservation biology, a resource that is of vital importance to the preservation of an **ecosystem.** For example, elevation gradients in the tropics are viewed as a keystone resource because they allow **frugivorous** primates to move in elevations where there are different species of tree that provide nutritional diversity as well as different fruiting seasons. Loss of keystone resources can mean loss of animal diversity (for example, cutting down trees in the tropics leaves primate species without a habitat).

**keystone species:** species important in determining the persistence of biological diversity within its **ecological community.** First described in a study of the Pacific Northwest tidal community where it was observed that removal of starfish led to overpopula-

tion of mussels (starfish prey), which in turn led to a decrease in diversity as mussels crowded out other animal species and overconsumed plant species. Primates have been suggested as keystone species in some ecosystems because of their role as seed dispersers and pollinators.

**kg.:** kilogram, an **SI unit** used to describe the mass (or 'weight') of something. A kilogram is about 2.2 pounds, so someone who weighed 155 lb would weigh about 70 kg.

**KGA 10-525:** field number for a fossil hominid found in 1993 at **Konso-Gardula** in Ethiopia, dated to about 1.4 mya. The specimen consists of the major portion of a cranium with mandible, with an estimated cranial capacity of 545 cm³. Morphologically, the specimen is comparable to *Australopithecus (= Paranthropus) boisei,* but if included in that species would greatly extend the range of species variation.

**Khoisan:** ethnonym for an indigenous people of the Kalahari Desert of Africa. Aka Bushman, Hottentot, Khoin; Khoisanid.

**Kiahera Hill:** paleontological site found in 1926 on **Rusinga Island** in Lake Victoria, Kenya, dated to *c.* 20–18 mya (middle **Miocene**), and that contains fossil hominoids that are attributed to *Proconsul* and *Nyanzapithecus,* and fossil monkeys attributed to *Victoriapithecus.* See **Hiwegi Hill** and **Kathwanga Point.**

**Kibale Forest:** research site located in Uganda where long-term field studies of red colobus monkeys (*Piliocolobus badius*) and black-and-white colobus monkeys (*Colobus* sp.) have been conducted for decades. Primatologists who have conducted field research at this site include: T. H. Clutton-Brock, T. T. Struhsaker, J. F. Oates, R. W. Wrangham, and D. L. Gebo.

**Kibish Formation:** recent sedimentary unit found in the Lower **Omo Valley** of East Africa, dated 130 kya to 3.1 kya.

**Kidd blood group:** human blood group defined by antigens coded by the *Jk* gene mapped to HSA 1p.

**Kiik-Koba:** archaeological site found in 1924–6 near Simferopol in the Crimea (Ukraine) in the valley of the River Zuya, undated; contained two **Mousterian** occupation levels and hominid remains including an adult male and an infant (possible burials) assigned to *Homo neanderthalensis.* Aka wild cave.

**kill site:** location where animals were slain, and where primary disarticulation took place.

**'killer ape' hypothesis:** largely outdated idea that the earliest humans were carnivorous apes who were selected for because they adopted a **social organization** based on a hunting lifestyle where males provided meat for mates and offspring; these 'killer apes' were as likely to murder and eat one another as they were to butcher other species. This proposal was most associated with playwright and popular writer Robert **Ardrey** and a series of books he wrote beginning in the early 1960s. Ardrey actually heard these speculations, based on evidence from **Makapansgat**, from Raymond **Dart**, whom he visited in the 1950s; see **osteodontokeratic culture**. Aka the headhunter hypothesis. Others who subscribed to this hypothesis included Sherwood **Washburn** and Konrad Lorenz. An implication of the hypothesis was that humans were aggressive and warlike by nature; this part of the 'killer ape' proposal struck a negative chord with many scientists. By the end of the 1960s this proposal was largely discredited and supplanted by taphonomic testing and the **scavenging hypothesis**. Sometimes compared to **sociobiology**, which is also Darwinian in nature, the 'killer ape' hypothesis has a selective mechanism. See *African Genesis* and **man the hunter hypothesis**. Cf. **gathering**.

‡ **killer cell** (K): specialized white blood cell that originates in bone marrow and is able to kill invading microorganisms only after activation by other cells of the immune system by becoming charged with antibodies. Cf. **natural killer cell**.

**killer T cell:** see **cytotoxic T cell**.

**kilobase** (kb): one thousand nucleotides, used to characterize sizes of genes, or of **RNA** and **DNA** segments during analysis. Cf. **megabase**.

‡ **kilocalorie** (Cal, C, kcal): calorie used in metabolic and nutritional studies as a measure of energy-producing value of various foods. In **SI unit**s, 4.184 joules; the amount of energy required to raise one kilogram of water from 14.5 to 15.5 °C at a pressure of one atmosphere. Aka large calorie, Calorie. Cf. **gram calorie**.

**kilogram:** see **kg**.

**Kimeu, (Bwana) Kimoya** (1938–): Kenyan (Kamba tribe) hunter and field researcher in West Africa; joined the Leakeys at **Olduvai Gorge** in 1959, and ever since has been a central member of paleontological expeditions. Kimeu is remembered for having personally located several significant East African hominids, such as **Peninj, KNM-ER 1808, KNM-ER 1813, KNM-WT 15000, Omo I**, and critical specimens of *Australopithecus anamensis*. Awarded the John Oliver La Gorce Medal by the **National Geographic Society** (1985) and the Morris F. Skinner Prize (2001); in 2000 Kimeu was inducted into the Order of the Grand Warrior of Kenya, the highest civilian honor awarded by Kenya to its citizens.

**Kimura, Motoo** (1924–): Japanese biologist; in 1968, Kimura argued that **polymorphism** in natural populations was too great to be maintained by **natural selection** acting alone (see **Haldane's dilemma**), and

that many mutations were 'neutral' with respect to natural selection, that is, the environment plays no role in their fixation or loss. Now seen as a significant contribution to evolutionary theory, **neutral drift** has been shown to operate in some cases not explained by natural selection, and led directly to the application of **molecular clocks**. Winner of the Royal Society's Darwin Medal (1992).

**kin:** blood relations; kinship ties are not always genealogical, and are culturally conditioned.

**kin recognition:** ability to discern the degree of one's genetic relatedness to other individuals.

‡ **kin selection theory:** process by which genes are contributed to successive generations through collateral relatives as well as one's own, thus contributing to total, or **inclusive fitness**. One of the extreme forms of **group selection**. Commonly used by **sociobiologists** to explain altruistic behaviors that could be selected for if they increase the probability of survival of close relatives. See **kinship selection, Hamilton's rule, interdemic selection**, and **second Darwinian revolution**.

**Kinda baboon:** vernacular for the subspecies *Papio cynocephalus kindae*.

**kindred:** bilateral descent group related by marriage or ancestry; people with either a common relative or a common ancestor.

**kinesics:** study of the use of the body in human and primate communication; nonvocal communication.

**kinesiology:** study of body movement.

**king colobus:** one of the vernaculars for *Colobus polykomos*.

**king-of-the-mountain principle:** see **first-arriver principle**.

**kingdom:** in taxonomy, the highest-level hierarchical category, just above the **phylum**. **Animalia**, for example, is the kingdom that contains all animals.

**King, Mary-Claire** (1946–): clinical and forensic geneticist at UC Berkeley and the University of Washington, human rights activist; PhD Berkeley, worked with Allan **Wilson**. Their 1975 paper reported that human and chimpanzee DNAs are 98.4% identical. King later was the first to find that **breast cancer** is inherited in about 5% of families. She also does research on inherited deafness and systemic lupus erythematosis. She has worked with the Argentinian Commission on the Disappearance of Persons and the United Nations War Crimes Tribunal, and has published 200 scientific papers, including 'Evolution at two levels in humans and chimpanzees' (1975), with A. Wilson (*Science*, **188:** 107).

**kinship:** 1. social recognition and expression of genealogical relationships. 2. social organization of reproductive activity. 3. possession of a **common ancestor** in the not too distant past; in genetics, kinship is measured precisely by the **coefficient of kinship** and the **coefficient of relatedness**.

**kinship, coefficient of:** see **coefficient of kinship**.

**kinship group:** any group formed on the basis of perceived kinship ties, or **kin recognition**. Aka kin group. Cf. **genetic group**.

**kinship rules:** in human culture, conventional sets of rules governing marriage, residence, and right(s) to succession, material inheritance, and descent; such rules position individuals and groups in definite, mutually understood relationships to each other within a society.

**kinship selection:** choice of trait(s) because they increase the probability of survival in close relatives. See **kin selection theory**.

**kinship term:** label(s) to identify genealogical or fictive (adoptive) degree of relationship in a **nuclear family** or **extended family**; see **father, mother, brother, sister, uncle, aunt, cousin**. Variants used as prefixes, such as 'grand-', 'great-', and 'old' may be further attached to some terms.

**kinship theory:** explanation of social behavior in which behavioral events are interpreted in terms of **costs** and **benefits** to an actor and recipient, weighted by the degree of genetic relatedness, *r*.

**kinship theory of genetic imprinting:** see **genetic conflict theory**.

**Kipsaramon:** see **Muruyur** and *Equatorius*.

**Kirk's colobus:** vernacular for *Piliocolobus kirki*.

**kitchen midden:** heap consisting primarily of shellfish remains mixed among unidentifiable organic matter, an indication that a shore-dwelling people used to live in the area. Such **middens** are found from the **Mesolithic** and later periods.

‡ **Klasies River Mouth Cave(s)** (KRM): archaeological site(s) composed of five (the 'main site') or more caves found in 1967 near the mouth of the Klasies River on the Tsitsikama coast in South Africa, dated to 130–70 kya (94–88 kya by **ESR dating**), and containing **Middle Stone Age** and **Howieson's Poort** artifacts, and hominid remains that include fragments from several MSA I individuals assigned to *Homo sapiens* (**AMHs**). The degree of marine resource exploitation at the site is remarkable. Cf. **Herto hominids**.

**Kleiber's rule (or law):** empirically derived biological rule that basal metabolic rate (**BMR**) plotted onto body mass will produce a regression slope of 0.75 instead of 0.67. According to theory, based on the square–cube law of mathematics, as an object increases in size its surface area squares, while volume cubes, so because BMR is based on surface relationships it should scale at the 0.67 power. There is no fully accepted explanation for the observed relationship, but it has become tacitly accepted that a regression slope of 0.75 indicates a metabolic relationship between the variables.

Kleiber's rule has been demonstrated in a number of **allometric** studies with variables other than BMR.

‡ **Klinefelter syndrome:** symptoms of this **aneuploid** condition (47, XXY) appear at puberty: affected males are tall with long limbs, experience a precocious puberty but lack secondary sexual characters, have hypogonadism (small penis and prostate gland), breast swelling (gynecomastia), a protruding stomach, **taurodont** dentition, and irreversible sterility caused by primary testicular failure. **Osteoporosis** is common in later adulthood. Cause is due to the dosage effect of a supernumerary X chromosome, and one **Barr body** is present. Androgen therapy and subcutaneous mastectomy restores a male phenotype in milder cases. A tendency toward learning disabilities increases in proportion to the number of supernumerary X chromosomes. Affects 1 : 500 males; up to 1% of clinically institutionalized males are Klinefelter patients. See **XX male syndrome** and **primary nondisjunction**.

**Kloss's gibbon:** vernacular for *Hylobates klossii*.

**km²:** abbreviation for square kilometer(s). See **ha** (hectares).

**knap:** to strike or hammer sharply; to chip, as a flint or stone. See **flint knapping** and **stone-knapper**.

**knapper:** an individual who produces a stone tool by flaking a core.

**knee:** region where the **femur** and **tibia** articulate.

**knee breadth: anthropometric** measurement; distance between the medial and lateral **epicondyles** of the **femur** with the subject sitting and the leg flexed as measured with either **spreading calipers** or **sliding calipers**. Used for studies of body frame size, skeletal mass, or **somatology**.

**kneecap:** see **patella**.

**knee joint:** largest and most complex **synovial joint** of the human body. Two joints are present: the tibiofemoral joint is a modified **hinge joint** that permits flexion, extension, and slight rotation, and the femoropatellar, joint is a **gliding joint** that permits slight movement.

**knife:** cutting tool with a long edged blade. The earliest knives were made of stone.

**KNM:** abbreviation for National Museums of Kenya (Kenya National Museum). KNM followed by -ER refers to a specimen found at East Rudolf; the letters are followed by a field identification number for the specimen, such as **KNM-ER 1470**, or **KNM WT-15000**, and so forth. See box overleaf.

**knock-knee:** condition in which the feet remain apart while the knees touch when standing.

**knockout (mutation):** informal designation for a null allele in a mutant organism, e.g. knockout mouse, introduced in order to study the phenotypic manifestations of the nonfunctional allele.

## Some specimens in the National Museums of Kenya

**KNM-BC 1:** fossil hominid found in 1967 at the Lake **Baringo** basin, near Lake Turkana, Kenya, initially dated to 2.5–1.5 mya (**K/Ar**, Chemeron formation, recently confirmed at 2.4 mya), and assigned to *Australopithecus* cf. *boisei*; consists of a temporal fragment. Aka the **Chemeron** temporal fragment. Later, some workers referred this specimen to *Homo habilis*.

**KNM-BC 1745:** fossil hominid found in 1983 at the Lake **Baringo** basin near Lake Turkana, Kenya, dated to 5.1–1.4 mya (**K/Ar**, Chemeron formation), and assigned to *sp. indet.*; consists of a humerus. Aka the **Chemeron** humeral fragment and **Mabaget**.

**KNM-BK 63:** fossil hominid found in 1969 at the Lake **Baringo** basin near Lake Turkana, Kenya, dated to 870–230 kya (**K/Ar**, Kapthurin formation), and assigned to *Homo erectus*; consists of limb bones and a mandible. Aka the **Kapthurin** mandibles.

**KNM-BL 8518:** fossil hominid found in 1983 at the Lake **Baringo** basin near Lake Turkana, Kenya, dated to 870-230 mya (**K/Ar**, Kapthurin formations), and assigned to *Homo erectus*; consists of a 'second' mandible (see KNM-BL 63). Aka the **Kapthurin** mandibles.

**KNM-BN 1378:** fossil hominid found in 1970 at the Lake **Baringo** basin near Lake Turkana, Kenya, dated to 12–9 mya (**K/Ar**, Ngorora formation), and assigned to *sp. indet.*, family Hominidae; consists of the crown of an upper left molar. Aka the **Ngorora** tooth.

**KNM-CH 1:** fossil hominid found in 1971 at the Lake **Baringo** basin near Lake Turkana, Kenya, dated to >1.34 mya (**K/Ar**, Chesowanja formation), and assigned to *Australopithecus* cf. *boisei*; consists of skull fragments. Aka the **Chesowanja** australopithecine.

**KNM-CH 302:** fossil hominid found in 1971 at the Lake **Baringo** basin near Lake Turkana, Kenya, dated to >1.34 mya (**K/Ar**, Chesowanja formation), and assigned to *Australopithecus* cf. *boisei*; consists of upper molar teeth. Aka the **Chesowanja** australopithecine.

**KNM-CH 304:** fossil hominid found in 1981 at the Lake **Baringo** basin near Lake Turkana, Kenya, dated to 1.25 mya (**K/Ar**, Chemiogut formation), and assigned to *Australopithecus* cf. *boisei*; consists of a fragmentary cranium. Aka the **Chemiogut** australopithecine.

**KNM-ER 406:** fossil hominid found by Richard **Leakey** in 1969 near Ileret at East Rudolf/Lake Turkana, Kenya, dated to >1.64 mya (**K/Ar**, **Koobi Fora** Formation, area 10) and assigned to *Australopithecus* cf. *boisei*; consists of a virtually complete, heavily built skull with a small neurocranium (cranial capacity estimated at 525 cm³), pronounced postorbital constriction, and broad zygomatic arches; possesses sagittal, occipital and **supramastoid crests**. Cf. *Zinjanthropus boisei* from **Olduvai Gorge**.

**KNM-ER 407:** fossil hominid found in 1969 near Ileret at East Lake Rudolf (now Lake Turkana), Kenya, dated to 1.6 mya (**K/Ar**), and assigned to *Australopithecus* cf. *boisei*; consists of a nearly complete cranium with an estimated cranial capacity of 508 cm³. Cf. *Paranthropus*.

**KNM-ER 732:** hominid fossil found in 1970 at Koobi Fora, Lake Turkana, Kenya, dated to >1.5 mya (**K/Ar**), and assigned to *Australopithecus boisei*; consists of a partial skull, the 'demi-cranium' as a possible female with a cranial capacity of 500 cm³. Many researchers believe that this specimen is similar to **OH 5**, and that the differences are due to **sexual dimorphism**. Cf. *Paranthropus*.

**KNM-ER 732A:** fossil hominid found in 1970 at East Rudolf/Koobi Fora, Lake Turkana, Kenya, dated to >1.6 mya (**K/Ar**, below Okote tuff), and assigned to *Australopithecus* sp.; consists of a gracile partial cranium (cranial capacity estimated at 500 cm³) with right maxilla; thin vault bones, prominent supramastoid crest; temporal lines do not form a crest; partial dentition. Aka 'demi-cranium'.

**KNM-ER 1470:** fossil hominid found in 1972 by Bernard Ngeneo at **Koobi Fora**, Lake Turkana, Kenya, dated to 1.9 mya (**K/Ar** below the **KBS tuff**, Gregory Rift), and attributed to either *Homo rudolfensis* or *Homo habilis*. Remains consist of a partial distorted adult **cranium** and facial fragments; the cranial capacity has been estimated at 780 cm³. The fossil has moderate postorbital constriction, thin vault bones, broad face, a supra-orbital torus that is not pronounced, and little or no subnasal prognathism. Thought to be a male. Reconstructed by Meave **Leakey**.

**KNM-ER 1481:** fossil hominid found in 1972 at East Rudolf/**Koobi Fora**, Lake Turkana, Kenya (and within a few kilometers of **KNM-ER 1470**), dated to 1.9 mya (**K/Ar**, below **KBS tuff**), and attributed to *Homo* cf. *habilis*; consists of a well-preserved femur and associated left tibia and partial fibula.

**KNM-ER 1482:** fossil hominid found in 1972 at **Koobi Fora**, East Rudolf/Lake Turkana, Kenya, and dated at 1.9 mya (**K/Ar**, Upper Burgi tuff); fragment of a mandible comparable to certain fossils from the Omo Valley in Ethiopia, **Omo 1967-18**; 1482 is attributed to *incertae sedis*. Richard **Leakey** has suggested

**Some specimens in the National Museum of Kenya** (*cont.*)

that these fossils may represent a fourth contemporary hominid species in East Africa. Others attribute the specimen to *Homo rudolfensis*.

KNM-ER 1500: fossil hominid found in 1972 at East Rudolf/Koobi Fora, Lake Turkana, Kenya, dated to 1.9 mya (K/Ar, below KBS tuff), and assigned to *Australopithecus* sp., cf. *boisei*. Consists of associated skeletal elements from a small individual; has pronounced anteroposterior compression of the femoral neck.

KNM-ER 1590: fossil hominid found in 1972 at East Rudolf/Koobi Fora, Lake Turkana, Kenya, dated to 1.9 mya (K/Ar, below KBS tuff), and assigned to *Homo ergaster* or *Homo habilis*; consists of a partial cranium with juvenile dentition. Has thin vault bones; parietals suggest a large cranial capacity.

KNM-ER 1802: fossil hominid found in 1973 at East Rudolf/Koobi Fora, Lake Turkana, Kenya, dated to 1.9 mya (K/Ar, below KBS tuff), attributed to cf. *Homo rudolfensis* or *Homo habilis*; consists of a mandible and tooth fragments; second molars are larger than the first molars; no significant **curve of Spee**.

KNM-ER 1805: fossil hominid found by Paul Abell in 1973 at East Rudolf/Koobi Fora, Lake Turkana, Kenya, dated to 1.85 mya (K/Ar, below Okote tuff); attributed to *incertae sedis*, but cf. *Homo habilis* or *Homo ergaster*; consists of a nearly complete cranium (estimated cranial capacity 582 cm³), including a mandible with dentition; has a heavily built vault with a sagittal crest and marked left supramastoid crest. The cranial **endocast** has been interpreted by some researchers as having an indication of a **fronto-orbital sulcus** that is ape-like, but others consider it human-like. This fossil has remained enigmatic since its discovery because of the combination of the sagittal crest, indicating robusticity, in conjunction with small teeth, expected only in species such as *H. habilis*. Aka the 'mystery skull'.

KNM-ER 1808: fossil hominid found in 1973 by Kimoya **Kimeu** at East Rudolf/Koobi Fora, Lake Turkana, Kenya, dated to >1.6 mya (K/Ar, below Okote tuff), and attributed to a female *Homo* cf. *erectus*; consists of associated skeletal and cranial elements, with very thickened cortical bones; the skeletal pathology has been attributed to **hypervitaminosis** A due to an excessive intake of carnivore liver.

KNM-ER 1813: fossil hominid found by Kimoya **Kimeu** in 1973 at East Rudolf/Koobi Fora, Lake Turkana, Kenya, dated to 1.9 mya (K/Ar, upper member, Koobi Fora formation, Gregory Rift), and attributed by some to *Australopithecus* sp., but by others to *Homo habilis* or *Homo ergaster*; consists of a small, lightly built cranium with small molars; cranial capacity estimated at 510 cm³; modest supra-orbital ridges; no cranial cresting; face exhibits a small degree of nasal prominence; thought to be a female. Often compared to OH 24.

KNM-ER 3228: hominid fossil found in 1975 at Koobi Fora, Lake Turkana, Kenya, dated to 1.95 mya (K/Ar), and assigned provisionally to the genus *Homo*; consists of a partial pelvis (= **innominate** bone). This fragment suggests the narrowing found in later *Homo ergaster* specimens such as KNM-WT 15000.

KNM-ER 3732: hominid remains found by Kimoya **Kimeu** and recovered in 1975 from Koobi Fora, Kenya, dated to 1.9 mya; remains include a partial cranium said to be a 'dead ringer' for KNM-ER 1470; attributed to *Homo habilis* or *Homo rudolfensis*.

KNM-ER 3733: fossil hominid found in 1975 by Bernard Ngeneo at East Rudolf/Koobi Fora, Lake Turkana, Kenya, dated to >1.64 mya (K/Ar, below Okote tuff) and assigned to *Homo erectus*; consists of a remarkably preserved cranium with partial dentition and a cranial capacity of 848 cm³; many striking similarities to the **Zhoukoudian** skulls leaves its *Homo erectus* status undoubted. As this skull is contemporary with KNM-ER 406, a robust australopithecine, the 'single species hypothesis' of hominid evolution seems convincingly refuted.

KNM-ER 3883: fossil hominid found in 1976 at East Rudolf/Koobi Fora, Lake Turkana, Kenya, dated to <1.64 mya (K/Ar, above Okote tuff) and assigned to *Homo erectus*, although some researchers now prefer *Homo ergaster* as an attribution; consists of a cranium with partial dentition; the cranial capacity has been estimated at 804 cm³.

KNM-ER 16005: field number for hominid remains found at Kangatuguseo, dated to 2.45 ± 0.05 mya, consisting of a hyperrobust mandible attributed to *Australopithecus* (= *Paranthropus*) *aethiopicus*.

KNM-KP 271: Kanapoi left distal humeral fragment, dated to about 4 mya and attributed to *Australopithecus anamensis*.

KNM-KP 29281: Kanapoi mandible with dentition found in 1994, dated to about 4 mya and attributed to *Australopithecus anamensis*. (cont. overleaf)

## Some specimens in the National Museum of Kenya (*cont.*)

KNM-KP 29285: Kanapoi tibial fragment found in 1994, dated to about 4.1 mya and attributed to *Australopithecus anamensis*. Currently, this is the oldest known evidence for bipedalism in hominids.

KNM-LU 335: fossil hominid found in 1975 at the Lake **Baringo** basin near Lake Turkana, Kenya, dated to 6.5 mya (K/Ar, Lukeino formation), and assigned by some to *sp. indet.*, family Hominidae, but by others to the Pongidae; consists of a lower left molar crown. Aka the **Lukeino** tooth.

KNM-OL 4550: set of cranial fragments discovered in 2003 at **Olorgesailie**, Kenya, dated to 970–900 kya (Ar/Ar, Members 5–8), stratigraphically associated with handaxes of the **Acheulean tool tradition**. The reconstructed **hominid** cranium consists of 11 fragments, with substantial portions of frontal and temporal bones present, and is reported to be from a very small adult or near-adult with a cranial capacity less than 800 cm$^3$; assigned to *Homo erectus* by its discoverers, although others have suggested that it may belong to *Homo ergaster*.

KNM-RU 2036: fossil ape from **Rusinga Island**, Kenya, dated 24–18 mya; a female with postcranial material reconstructed by Mary **Leakey**, Alan Walker and Martin Pickford, and attributed to *Proconsul africanus*.

KNM-SH 8531: holotype of *Samburupithecus kiptalami*.

KNM-TH 28860: type specimen for *c.* 15–14 mya Miocene fossil hominoid fragments from the **Tugen Hills**, Kenya, tentatively attributed to a new ape genus, *Equatorius*.

KNM-WT 15000: the 'Turkana boy'; see *Homo erectus* and *Homo ergaster*.

KNM-WT 17000: the **black skull**, *Paranthropus aethiopicus*, found at Lomekwi 1 (**LO-1**).

KNM-WT 38350: fossil hominid found at locality LO-5 in 1998. This specimen consists of a partial left maxilla and is a **paratype** for *Kenyanthropus platyops*. The specimen consists of the maxillary fragment with two partial premolars and a partial first molar. The measurable molars in both this specimen and in KNM-WT 40000 are notably small; both have relatively thick enamel. See **Lomekwi localities**.

KNM-WT 40000: fossil hominid found at Lomekwi locality LO-6N in 1999. This specimen consists of a partial cranium and is the **holotype** for *Kenyanthropus platyops*. The cranium consists of two main parts, a distorted neurocranium and a face that is missing only some anterior teeth; the specimen has a derived flat lower face with a tall malar region, moderate subnasal prognathism, roof of palate thin, molars small with thick enamel, small acoustic opening; the **occipital–marginal venous system** is absent. See KNM-WT 38350.

KNM-WT 40001: partial right temporal bone attributed to *Kenyanthropus platyops*, found at Lomekwi 6N (LO-6N). See **Lomekwi localities**.

**knuckle:** dorsal region around a joint of a finger, especially the metacarpophalangeal joints of fingers when flexed.

‡ **knuckle-walking:** form of **quadrupedal** locomotion found in gorillas, bonobos, and chimpanzees, in which the dorsal surfaces of flexed fingers contact the substrate and support the anterior weight of the animal. The hind feet are **plantigrade**.

**koala lemur:** vernacular for all species in the **extinct subfossil Malagasy prosimian** genus *Megaladapis*.

**Koenigswald, Gustav Heinrich Ralph von** (1902–82): German-born Dutch paleontologist; with the Dutch Geological Survey in the 1930s he excavated many sites in Java (**Ngandong, Perning, Sangiran**), where he located several skullcaps of early *Homo erectus*, then known as *Pithecanthropus*, and later the remains of two additional taxa he had created, *Meganthropus paleojavanicus* and *Gigantopithecus*. He published extensively on the fauna of Southeast Asia, and recovered fossils of *Sivapithecus* and *Ramapithecus* from the **Siwalik Hills**.

*Kohatius coppensi* **Russell and Gingerich, 1980:** tarsiiform primate from the early to middle Eocene of Pakistan and assigned to an omomyoid family *incertae sedis*. Estimated body mass around 200 g. See Appendix 1 for taxonomy.

**koilorachic:** pertaining to a **vertical lumbar index** of greater than 102.00.

*Komba* **Simpson, 1967:** genus of fossil **prosimian** known from the early to middle Miocene of Africa and belonging to the family **Galagidae**; three species. Very similar to extant galagos, although it cannot be determined to which genera it gave rise. Body mass between 300 and 1000 g. Dental formula: 2.1.3.3/2.1.3.3; shearing crests on molars; diet in the smaller species probably **insectivory**. Large orbits indicative of nocturnality. Postcrania similar to those of extant galagos, except that the tarsal bones are not as long. See Appendix 1 for taxonomy.

**Konso-Gardula:** archaeological site found near Lake **Baringo**, Kenya, dated to 1.4 mya, and that contains Acheulean artifacts and cut marks on animal bones; hominid remains include fragments of 11 individuals.

A mandibular fragment shows indications of 'tooth pick' use; this is currently the 'earliest' site where the Acheulean appears 'abruptly' at 1.4 mya in Africa. See **KGA 10-525.**

‡ **Koobi Fora:** fossiliferous region first identified in 1967–8 near East **Lake Turkana**, Kenya, where many archaeological sites were found from 1968 through 1990. These sites date from 4.3 mya to 600 kya (**K/Ar**, see specific tuffs: **Lonyumun, Moiti, Lokochot, Tulu Bor, Burgi,** KBS, Okote, Chari and **Karari**) and contain **Oldowan** tools and >200 hominid fragments, primarily from the **KBS, Okote** and **Chari tuffs.** The notable hominid remains include **KNM-ER 1470.** Other remains include a partial pathological skeleton (**KNM-ER 1808**), two nearly complete crania (**KNM-ER 3733** and **KNM-ER 3883**), parts of three other crania, nine partial mandibles, and many limb bones, all attributed to *Homo erectus.* Contemporary **australopithecines** (e.g. **KNM-ER 406**) have also been recovered. The paleoenvironment was probably a lake and floodplain with braided streams. Before 1975 known as the **East Rudolf Research Project,** now called **East Turkana.**

**Koobi Fora Research Project:** interdisciplinary project started in 1967 by Glynn **Isaac** and Richard **Leakey** and that included Kay **Behrensmeyer,** Bernard **Wood,** and many others, organized to explore the fossil sites in the **Lake Turkana** (formerly East Lake Rudolph, ER) region of Kenya and Ethiopia.

**Koro Toro** (KT): see **Yayo.**

**korongo:** Swahili for 'gully'. The drainages at **Olduvai Gorge** were named affectionately for family and friends of the Leakeys, thus **FLK** was an abbreviation for Frida Leakey's Korongo.

**Koru:** paleontological site found in 1927, located in Kenya, East Africa, dated to *c.* 20 mya (early **Miocene**), and that contains hominoid remains including *Proconsul* and *Rangwapithecus*; the **type site.**

**Koshima Islet:** research site located on a small island off Japan where long-term field studies of Japanese macaques (*Macaca fuscata*) have been conducted for decades. Primatologists who have conducted field research at this site include: K. **Imanishi,** J. Itani, S. Kawamura, and K. Watanabe.

**Kostenki–Borshevo (site cluster):** archaeological sites found in 1879 near Voronezh, Russia, on the Don River, dated variously to 34.7, 24.1 and 19.9 kya, etc.; contain **Upper Paleolithic** artifacts, including mammoth-bone living structures with storage pits, shouldered projectile points, and **Venus figurines.** Voluminous faunal remains were found at several locations. The cluster contains 24 open-air sites.

**Kow Swamp** (KS): an archaeological site found in 1967 in southeastern Australia, dated to 13.0–9.5 kya, and that contains quartz artifacts. Hominid remains, including a facial skeleton with some archaic traits (KS-15) were found in about 40 graves, thought to be burials. Some of the remains show signs of cremation. The remains were originally assigned to *Homo erectus* but later attributed to *Homo sapiens* and are now considered within the range of variation seen in modern Australian aboriginals.

**KP:** see **Kanapoi,** Kenya.

**Krapina:** archaeological site found 1895–1905, near Zagreb, Croatia, Yugoslavia, dated to 125–85 kya (late Eemian), and that contains mainly **Mousterian** points and scrapers, although **Acheulean** and 'pre-Aurignacian' tools have been mentioned. Hominid remains comprise about 70 individuals assigned to *Homo neanderthalensis* or to the older **anteneandertal** group, or to the **archaic *Homo sapiens*** group. Krapina is possibly a deliberate burial site. Evidence for **cannibalism** at the site is controversial.

**Krebs cycle:** see **citric acid cycle.**

**Krogman, Wilton Marion** (1903–87): US osteologist, pathologist, and growth and development specialist; University of Pennsylvania; president, **AAPA** (1945-9), fifth Viking Fund medallist (1950). Known for his many contributions to population biology and biometry, and author of two classic compilations, *Growth of Man; Tabulae Biologicae Vol. XX* (1941) and *Child Growth* (1972). Krogman was one of five physical anthropologists who participated in the identification of American war dead at Oahu, Hawaii, after World War II.

‡ **Kromdraai** (TM, KB): an archaeological site found in 1938 by R. **Broom** in the Transvaal, South Africa, dating from 1.7 mya or even earlier to about 1.0 mya, and that contains one questionable flake tool. Hominid remains include the craniofacial fragment of one robust individual with an estimated cranial capacity of 650 cm³ assigned to *Australopithecus (=Paranthropus) robustus* (**TM 1517a and b**), some postcranial bones (**TM 1517c–g**), a juvenile mandible (**TM 1536**), and some isolated juvenile teeth (**KB 5223**). Site actively excavated through 1980. See *Paranthropus.*

**Ksar 'Akil:** archaeological site found in Lebanon and dating to 37 ± 10 kya. It contains **Aurignacian** artifacts (high-speed, low-mass projectile points) and hominid remains including a child's skull ('Egbert') attributed to *Homo sapiens.*

**K-selected species:** species (such as humans) produced by stable environments that live near the **carrying capacity** of the environment, grow up slowly, have few **altricial** offspring but invest more in each, and exhibit a relatively late development of the reproductive system, in terms of metabolic energy expended toward systems such as the brain and body. *K*-selected species gain advantage by increasing competitive ability. Cf. *r*-selected species. See *K* selection.

‡ *K* selection: McArthur and E. O. Wilson's mode of selection favoring superiority in stable, predictable environments in which rapid population growth is unimportant. Cf. *r* selection. The parameter *K* is taken from carrying capacity. See *K*-selected species.

K/T: abbreviation for Cretaceous–Tertiary boundary. Aka K–T boundary.

KT 12: see Bahr el Ghazal.

KT12/H1: see *Australopithecus bahrelghazali*.

Kudaro–Tsona (cave sites): archaeological site(s) found in the 1970s on the slopes of the Greater Caucasus in Southern Ossetsia, Georgia, dating to 360 kya for the levels that contain Acheulean artifacts, and 44 kya for the Levallois–Mousterian levels. Faunal remains are dominated by the cave bear. Includes nearby Tsona Cave.

Kulna: archaeological site found in 1965 in Czechoslovakia, dated to 47–38 kya, and that contains Mousterian artifacts. Hominid remains include fragments from one or more adults attributed to *Homo neanderthalensis*.

!Kung: ethonym for foragers or hunter–gatherers of Botswana who have survived with a subsistence lifestyle in small-scale societies into the twenty-first century. Aka Koisan !Kung San.

Kurgan: ethonym for ancient Indo-Iranian peoples, a group of linguistically related tribes who invaded present-day India *c*. 1.8–1.5 kya. Aka Aryans. This label later came to mean Indo-Europeans in general, and still later was transformed and associated with Aryanism.

kurtorachic: pertaining to a vertical lumbar index ranging up to 97.00.

Kuru: disease characterized by ataxia and progressive dementia accompanied by bouts of inappropriate laughter. Discovered in 1957, Kuru was at first thought to be a form of viral encephalitis transmitted only by the ritual ingestion of the nervous tissue of an infected individual during funerary processing involving cannibalism. Found only among the Fore people of Highland New Guinea, it was also thought to be a sex-limited disease because of its high prevalence in females and children. Carlton Gajdusek won the Nobel prize after he showed that he could transfect chimpanzees with what turned out to be not a slow virus but a prion, an autosomal recessive. Diseases like Kuru that appear to be inherited, but turn out to be environmentally precipitated, are known as phenocopies. As in the other prion diseases nvCJD, fatal familial insomnia and Gerstmann-Straussler–Scheinker disease, Kuru-affected individuals were found on autopsy to possess a predisposing genotype, in this case a characteristic mutation at position 178, and were invariably methionine homozygotes (MM) at position 129 of the prion protein. Rare; no new cases reported since funerary practices were changed. May be identical to nvCJD.

Kwangsi: paleontological site(s) found in 1956 in Kwangsi Province, China, dated to the middle Pleistocene. This Provincial name refers to several sites, including a cave in Tahsin County and another cave on Luntsai Mountain in Liucheng County. The fossil hominoids recovered include a mandible from Luntsai and three teeth from Tahsin, all assigned to *Gigantopithecus*. The same expedition also recovered 47 teeth of this species from Chinese apothecaries in the same Province. Aka Hsinshechung village. Also spelled Kwangxi, Guangsi, Guangxi.

kwashiorkor: extreme form of malnutrition resulting from a severe deficiency in proteins but not in calories, characterized by failure to grow, wasting of muscles, loss of appetite, irritability, anemia, and changes in the hair and skin (desquamation); one of the most obvious symptoms is a striated or ribbon-like quality of hair color, the result of periodical melanin and keratin production. A nutritional disease common among grain-eating peoples who sometimes feed children a gruel made from grains, which is plentiful but deficient in protein. Aka marasmic kwashiorkor; 'golden boy'. See marasmus.

‡kya: thousands of years ago; abbreviation used by some human evolutionary biologists. Also k.y.a. and Kyr. Informally and in the SI system of units, the letter k means 1,000; more technically it equals 1,024, or $2^{10}$.

kyphoscoliosis: condition that is a combination of kyphosis and scoliosis affecting the vertebral column.

kyphosis: abnormal curvature of the vertebral column, characterized by hyperflexion; commonly referred to as hump-back. Cf. scoliosis and kyphoscoliosis.

**l:** 1. abbreviation for **length**. 2. commonly used abbreviation for the craniometric landmark **lambda**.

**L-form:** **levorotatory** form of a molecule such as an **L-amino acid**. Cf. **D-form** and **dextrorotatory**. See also **racemic** and **racemization**.

**L gene blood group:** see **MNS blood group**.

**labia majora:** portion of the external genitalia of a female consisting of two longitudinal folds of skin extending downward and backward from the **mons pubis**.

**labia minora:** two small folds of skin, devoid of hair and sweat glands, lying between the **labia majora** of the external genitalia of a female.

**labial:** 1. pertaining to the lips. 2. on anterior dentition, the surface of a tooth facing the lips.

**labium:** lip or liplike structure. Plural: labia.

**labor:** 1. productive activity, as in working or tilling soil. 2. working class. 3. the stage in childbirth in which the fetus and placenta are expelled. It begins with uterine contractions and culminates in the actual birth.

**laboratory study:** research done in a laboratory setting rather than under natural conditions; an advantage of laboratory studies is that controlled experiments can be set up that are difficult to perform in the field. Cf. **field study**.

**labyrinth:** any system of intercommunicating cavities, vessels, or canals, such as that of the inner ear or the placental layer closest to the fetus. See **endolymph**.

*Laccopithecus robustus* **(Li, 1978):** primitive **hominoid** from the late Miocene of Asia belonging to the family **Propliopithecidae**; known from jaws, teeth, and an incomplete skull. Estimated body mass around 12 kg. Dental formula: 2.1.2.3; **sexually dimorphic** canines. This species has been suggested as an ancestor of the modern gibbons; its primitive hominoid features and geography are points that make the case for this primate over other known Miocene pliopithecids. See Appendix 1 for taxonomy.

**lacerate foramina:** term used in mammalian anatomy and paleontology for three separate apertures that can be seen from an inferior view of the cranium and transmit nerves and blood vessels. In human anatomy the posterior lacerate foramen is called the superior orbital fissure, the middle one is the foramen lacerum, and the posterior one is called the jugular foramen. The relative size of the middle lacerate foramen is related to brain size.

**La Chaise:** archaeological site found in 1850 in southwestern France consisting of a complex of caves, dated to 151–71 **kya** (U series as early as 151 ± 15 kya), and that contains **Middle Paleolithic** artifacts. Hominid remains from 3–4 individuals, including a possible female, are attributed to *Homo neanderthalensis*. Aka Suard, Abri Bourgeois-Delaunay.

‡ **La Chapelle-aux-Saints:** archaeological site found in 1908 in a grotto near Brive, Corrèze, France, dated to about 56–47 kya (**ESR dating**; Würm), and that contains evolved **Mousterian** (**Quina**) artifacts and hominid remains that include a deliberately buried male with a cranial capacity of 1625 cm³, which has been assigned to *Homo neanderthalensis*. The remains of this male were the first Neandertal postcranial material ever discovered, and represent a robust, pathological old man with extensive **antemortem** tooth loss, osteoarthritis, and long bone curvature. He was buried with a bison leg and food offerings. Aka the 'Old Man' of La Chapelle.

**La Cotte de Saint-Brelade:** archaeological site found in 1910 on Jersey, Channel Islands, UK, dated to about 250–238 kya (sequence continues for almost 200,000 years), and that contains Middle Paleolithic artifacts associated with a large mammoth and wooly rhinoceros, and hominid remains including 13 teeth attributed to *Homo neanderthalensis*, found near a hearth. Believed to contain evidence of hunting episodes where herds of rhino and mammoth were stampeded over a cliff and butchered.

**lacrimal bone:** one of a pair of small thin bones located on the medial wall of each **orbit**. This bone contains a groove that provides a passageway for tears to the nasal cavity. Its angle and size is indicative of total nose size in fossil hominids.

**lacrimal canaliculus:** drainage duct for tears located at the medial corner of an eyelid; conveys the tears medially into the lacrimal sac, part of the system that drains tears into the nasal cavity. Aka lacrimal canal.

**lacrimal foramen:** opening in the **lacrimal bone** through which the tear (nasolacrimal) duct passes into the nasal cavity. Plural: lacrimal foramina.

**lacrimal fossa:** depression in the **lacrimal bone** that is the seat of the lacrimal gland in life; superior portion of the inferior **nasal concha** that articulates with the lacrimal bone. Plural: lacrimal fossae.

**lacrimal gland:** tear-secreting gland located on the superior lateral portion of the eyeball and underneath the upper eyelid.

**lacrimal process:** portion of the **ethmoid bone** that articulates with the **lacrimal bone**.

**lacrimale** (la): **craniometric landmark**; point where the posterior lacrimal crest intersects with the fronto-lacrimal suture. See Appendix 7.

‡ **lactase:** liver and intestinal enzyme that catalyzes the conversion of **lactose** (milk sugar) into glucose and galactose. See **disaccharide intolerance type III**.

**lactase deficiency:** now called adult lactase persistence; see **disaccharide intolerance type III**.

‡ **lactation:** production of **milk** in mammals, expressed through the **mammary glands**.

**lactational amenhorrhea:** postpartum cessation of ovulation due to the effects of **lactogenic hormone.** Aka lactation suppression. Also spelled lactational amenorrhoea.

**lactic acid:** syrupy, colorless substance formed as the end product of the breakdown of **lactose** in muscles and red blood cells; probably responsible for the sensation of muscle fatigue.

**lactogenic hormone:** see **prolactin**

**lactoglobulin:** any of the globulins that occur in the **colostrum** and milk of mammals. See **immunoglobulin A.**

‡ **lactose:** sugar formed by the **mammary glands,** a **disaccharide** consisting of glucose and galactose. Human milk contains 7% lactose; other mammalian milks contain about 4%. Aka milk sugar.

‡ **lactose intolerance, adult:** now called adult lactase persistence; see **disaccharide intolerance type III.**

**lacuna:** hollow cavity, especially in reference to cartilage and bone. Plural: lacunae.

**lacustrine:** 1. of or pertaining to a lake. 2. formed at the bottom or along the shore of lakes; lacustrine geological deposits are laid down in relatively still water.

**lacustrine silt:** fine particles of argillaceous (clay-like) matter suspended in lake water or deposited in layers after water has evaporated.

**ladder of nature:** ordination scheme used by **Aristotle** and his students to classify objects from inanimate matter at the bottom rung of the ladder to plants, lower animals, and higher animals, with humans on the top rung. Later much elaborated as the **Great Chain of Being.** Aka échelle des êtres.

**Ladino:** 1. archaic term for the inhabitants of the Americas whose ancestry is from both the Iberian Peninsula and the indigenous peoples of the Americas. Ladinos were considered a sub-race or a full race, depending on the author. 2. living Central American who is urban-born, speaks Spanish, and is non-American-Indian. 3. semi-sacred language of the Sephardic Jews.

**Ladinoization:** process in Central America experienced by people moving from an American Indian culture to the **Ladino** culture.

**Ladogan:** **ethnym** for a hypothetical Upper Paleolithic element supposed to persist in present-day European populations, and derived from a hypothetical **Caucasoid** subgroup that occupied the East Baltic region.

‡ **Laetoli:** archaeological site found in 1935 in the drainage of the Gadjingero River south of **Olduvai Gorge** in Tanzania. The site contained no **artifacts.** The first **hominid** remains recovered included a maxilla found by Ludwig Kohl-Larsen, originally attributed to *Meganthropus africanus,* but later reclassified as *Australopithecus afarensis.* The site was reworked after 1974 by **Mary Leakey** and dated to 5–3.35 mya

(**K/Ar**). She found **footprints** imbedded in a fossil ash layer (**Laetoli Site G**) that suggest some form of **bipedalism.** Other hominid remains include at least 24 individuals assigned to *Australopithecus cf. afarensis* (although some prefer *A. africanus*). The type specimen is **LH-4.** The paleoenvironment is thought to have been grassland with patchy forests. Aka Garusi. See **footprint tuff** and **Eyasi.**

**Laetoli footprints:** see **Laetoli Site G** and **footprint tuff.**

**Laetoli hominids:** see entries beginning with **LH.**

**Laetoli Site G:** archaeological site found by Paul Abell and Mary **Leakey** in 1976; contains more than 50 **hominid** footprints made by three individuals, a small individual on the left, a large one on the right, and a third, medium-sized set superimposed on those of the larger individual on the right; the biomechanics are remarkably similar to those of the modern human. The footprints were made in Tuff 7 of the **Laetolil Beds,** an airfall tuff dated 3.75–3.6 mya. Aka the **footprint tuff,** the G-1 Trail and the G-2/3 Trail.

**Laetolil beds:** fossiliferous beds at Laetoli named Laetolil Beds in 1935; dated by **K/Ar** at 3.75–3.35 mya; the **footprint tuff** (Tuff 7) is one of several datable airfall tuffs recognized in the Beds. Aka Garusi, Vogel River series.

**La Ferrassie assemblage:** Middle Paleolithic tool tradition as defined by **Bordes,** characterized by high percentages (14–30%) of **Levallois technique** use; associated with **Neandertals;** aka Charentian Mousterian. Cf. **La Quina assemblage.**

**La Ferrassie rockshelter:** archaeological site excavated in 1909–12 and reworked in 1920–1 and 1973 near Bugue, Dordogne, France, dated to 38–28 kya (Würm II), and that contains artifacts (see **La Ferrassie assemblage**). **Hominid** remains are from the intentional burials of at least two adults and six children and **neonates** (aka the 'family cemetery') assigned to *Homo neanderthalensis.* The adult male has a cranial capacity of 1640–1681 cm$^3$.

**Lagar Velho 1:** field number assigned to fossil hominid remains comprising the nearly complete skeleton of a child that is attributed to either *Homo sapiens* or *Homo sapiens neanderthalensis.* The ochre-stained four-year-old child, probably a male, is reported to have Neandertal limb proportions but modern craniofacial features, including a prominent chin. Aka the Lapedo Valley 'kid' site. See **Abrigo do Lagar Velho rockshelter.**

*Lagothrix* É. Geoffroy, 1812: **platyrrhine** genus to which the woolly monkeys belong; two species recognized. Geographic range in the Amazon basin of South America; occupy tropical and montane forests. Arboreal; diurnal; **arboreal quadrupedal** locomotion with some **brachiation** and use of **prehensile tail. Sexually dimorphic** in canine length and body size, adult females weighing from 3.5 to 6.5 kg and adult males from 3.6 to 10 kg. Clitoris of female is long and often causes confusion in identifying the sexes. Dental formula: 2.1.3.3; **frugivorous**. Social organization dependant on species. See Appendix 2 for taxonomy, Appendix 3 for living species.

**lag phase: see growth curve** and **logistic growth curve.**

**Laishui:** archaeological site found in 1988 in Hebei Province, China, dated to 28 kya; contains hominid remains, including a cranium and skeleton attributed to *Homo sapiens*.

**Lake Mungo:** Pleistocene lake in Australia, now dry; see **Mungo**.

**Lake Natron:** salt flat and saline lake in Northern Tanzania. See **Peninj**.

**Lake Ndutu:** archaeological site in Tanzania, dated to 400–200 kya, containing **Developed Oldowan** artifacts and hominid remains including a (female?) cranium with high but thick parietals and a mosaic of other features, and assigned to the **archaic** *Homo sapiens* group.

**Lake Rudolf:** see **Lake Turkana**.

**Lake Turkana:** lake in northern Kenya, reaching just into Ethiopia near the Sudan border. Formerly Lake Rudolf, the name was officially changed to Lake Turkana in 1974. The western portion of the lake is now referred to as simply Turkana. Lake Turkana and the sediments in its basin are divided into three regions from north to south: these are (in order) **Ileret**, **Koobi Fora**, and **Allia Bay**. The term 'Koobi Fora' refers to a region and also to a geological formation in that region, and is also synonymous with East Turkana. The region has several Plio-Pleistocene sites that date to 5–1 mya, and has produced several important fossil hominids; see, for example, **Kanapoi** and **Nariokotome**. The Plio-Pleistocene environment was probably a lakeside forest enclosed by an arid region. Aka (formerly) Lake Rudolf.

**La Madeleine:** archaeological site found in 1863 in the Vérèze Valley in southern France, dated to 17.5–13 kya, and that contains **Magdalenian** artifacts including lance points, polishers, engravers (burins) and an engraved mammoth bone, needles, harpoons, spear throwers and hominid remains, including two skeletons attributed to *Homo sapiens* (Cf. **Cro-Magnon**). Type site for the **Magdalenian tool tradition**.

‡ **Lamarck, Jean-Baptiste Pierre Antoine Monet de** (1744–1829): French naturalist whose book *Philosophie zoologique* (1809) proposed a theory of evolution with a mechanism called **acquired characters**; his theory has since been rejected as generally invalid. He was also known for exploring other environmental effects that led to his **hereditary predisposition theory**. See **Lamarckian inheritance**.

**Lamarckian evolution:** see **acquired characteristics** and **Lamarckism**.

‡ **Lamarckian inheritance:** evolution brought about by volition or by environmental induction; theory of **Lamarck** that included a **mechanism** of **acquired characters** proposed in his *Philosophie zoologique* (1809), in which **traits** enhanced through the exercise of 'memory' during an animal's lifetime, were said to be passed directly to offspring in their enhanced form. Used today to refer to any such proposition, other than **mutation**, by which an organism is said to have modified its genome by acquisition or design. Cf. **natural selection**.

‡ **Lamarckism:** eponym for **Lamarckian inheritance**; an historically misleading synonym for **inheritance of acquired characters** and a belief in **spontaneous generation**.

**lambda:** 1. the 11th letter of the Greek alphabet, ($\Lambda$, $\lambda$). 2. **craniometric landmark**; point where the **sagittal suture** and **lambdoidal suture** intersect medially.

**lambdoid:** resembling the Greek letter **lambda**.

**lambdoidal bone:** **sutural bone** that develops near the area of the **lambdoidal suture** and **sagittal suture** of the cranium.

‡ **lambdoidal suture:** cranial articulation between the **occipital bone** and the two **parietal bones**.

**lamella:** concentric ring of matrix surrounding the **central canal** in an osteon of mature bone tissue. Plural: lamellae: adjective lamellar.

**lamellated corpuscle:** sensory receptor for pressure; found in tendons, around joints, and in several visceral organs. Aka Pacinian corpuscle.

**lamina:** thin layer or sheet of tissue.

**L-amino acid: levorotatory** stereoisomer of an amino acid; although both L- and **D-amino acids** have been isolated from proteins, all naturally occurring amino acids found in proteins belong to the L stereochemical series, and in the vernacular are therefore also known as the 'living' form of the amino acid. See **racemization**.

**La Naulette cave:** archaeological site found in 1865 near Dinant, Belgium, dated to the late Pleistocene, consisting of hominid remains including an **edentulous** mandible attributed to *Homo neanderthalensis*, found in direct association with the bones of extinct mammals. Located by Edouard Dupont, this is the first specimen of a Neandertal mandible ever recovered. Aka Troue da la Naulette.

**lanceolate:** pertaining to something that is narrow and tapers to a point at its peak.

**land bridge:** floor of a shallow sea between continents that is exposed when sea levels fall, typically during periods of glacial maxima, e.g. **Beringia**, **Sahul shelf** and **Sunda shelf**; these have provided dispersal routes for the great **faunal exchanges** of the past.

**land mammal age** (LMA): any of the stages of regional and world **stratigraphic columns** that are defined by a characteristic suite of fauna; LMAs can usually be correlated with stages of the **geomagnetic polarity time scale** and a corresponding **oxygen isotope stage**, as well.

**landmark:** in anatomy, an anthropometric point from which measurements are made. Those on the cranium are called **craniometric landmarks** or points.

**Landsteiner, Karl** (1868–1943): Austrian–American immunologist, Nobel laureate; discoverer of the **ABO blood group** system in 1900–02; discoverer of the **MNS blood group** and **P blood group** in 1927; co-discoverer of the **Rhesus factor** in 1940; discoverer of the polio virus; developed a clinical test for **syphilis**; co-developed techniques for **paternity exclusion**. Landsteiner's work helped to establish the science of **immunology.**

**langerhansian hormones:** substances secreted by the islets in the pancreas, i.e. **insulin** and **glucagon.**

**language:** 1. a systematic means of communicating information, ideas, or feelings by the use of signs, sounds, gestures, or marks that have understood meanings. 2. a set of signs, sounds, gestures, or marks used to communicate information, ideas, or feelings. 3. the specific set of words and/or symbols used by a particular subset of the human population. See **faculty of language.** Cf. **speech.**

**language acquisition:** process by which an individual gains language skills including spoken words, grammar, and nonverbal forms of communication. In humans this is a natural process and the particular language learned is based on the language(s) of individuals around the infant; however, the capacity to learn human language is a biological characteristic of our species, although there has been little research demonstrating what factors (endocrine, nervous pathway, etc.) are involved. We do know that first language acquisition is reduced after puberty begins in the sense that individuals who do not have a language can learn words, but have difficulty learning grammar. A number of studies have demonstrated that apes have the ability to learn a limited amount of language in a laboratory setting; thus the biological potential for language may have been present in a common ancestor. See **faculty of language.**

**language and race:** tendency to think of a people collectively in terms of the languages spoken by various groups; thus, speakers of the Bantu family of languages include Swahili, Xhosa, and Zulu, although there is arguably little genetic differentiation among these groups. See **folk taxonomy.**

**language faculty:** see **faculty of language.**

**langur:** general vernacular for the Asiatic monkeys belonging to the subfamily **Colobinae.**

**Lantian:** county in Shaanxi Province, China, with archaeological sites found in 1963–4. Faunal remains from these sites include the giant panda and primitive elephants. See **Gongwangling Hill** (Kungwangling Hill) for the Lantian 2 cranium, and **Chenjiawo** for the Lantian 1 mandible.

**lanugo:** short, silky fetal hair that may be present for a short time on a premature infant. It is present on every human fetus during the sixth to eighth fetal months.

**Lapedo Valley 'kid' site:** see **Abrigo do Lagar Velho rockshelter** and **Lagar Velho 1.**

**Lapps:** see **Sami.**

**La Quina:** archaeological site found in 1908–10 in Charente, France, dated to 35–28 kya, and that contains artifacts of the **La Quina** type. Hominid remains from at least three individuals, including a partial cranium with a cranial capacity of 1350 cm³, were attributed to *Homo neanderthalensis*. See **La Quina assemblage.**

**La Quina assemblage:** Middle Paleolithic tool tradition as defined by **Bordes**, characterized by a low percentage (<10%) of **Levallois technique** use; associated with Neandertals. Cf. **La Ferrassie assemblage.**

**large calorie:** see **kilocalorie.**

**large cutting tool** (LCT): any of the large Pleistocene-age tools classified in the **Oldowan, Developed Oldowan,** and **Acheulean** tool traditions.

**large-eared greater bushbaby:** vernacular for *Otolemur crassicaudatus.*

**large gut:** term descriptive of the typically triangular aspect of the torso of many **hominoids**, with a wide girth at the waist rising to a rib cage that decreases in size at an apex near the sternum and collarbones (the 'inverted funnel'). The interpretation of some functional anatomists is that this shape is an adaptation for the consumption of large amounts of vegetable matter, as, for example, in gorillas and some early **hominids** such as **'Lucy'**; the narrow rib cage indicates little control over shallow breathing and argues against a sophisticated use of **language.**

**large intestine:** inferior portion of the **gastrointestinal tract** consisting of the **cecum** and **colon.**

**Lartet, Édouard Armand Isidore Hippolyte** (1801–71): French solicitor and prehistorian who systematically excavated the cave floor at **Aurignac** in 1860, finding isolated human remains associated with the bones of extinct animals. Lartet also discovered several sites in the Périgord region, including Les Eyzies, La Madeleine, and **Le Moustier**. With Henry Christy, proposed a cultural sequence for the region (1861). In his early career he worked in Miocene sediments, and described early examples of both *Pliopithecus* (1837) and *Dryopithecus* (1856).

**laryngeal sac:** inflatable air sac that communicates with the ventricles of the **larynx**, found in certain apes.

**laryngopharynx:** lowermost portion of the **pharynx** near the opening of the **larynx.**

‡ **larynx:** region of the throat near the trachea (windpipe) and the **pharynx;** the vocal cords are contained in the larynx, and this is the region in which the sounds of the human voice are produced. Aka voice box. Unlike other mammals, in humans the larynx descends into the neck, altering breathing, swallowing, and vocalization patterns. Adjective: laryngeal.

**Lascaux (Cave):** archaeological site found in 1940 near Montignac in the Dordogne, France, dated to 17–15 kya, and that contains Perigordian-age artifacts, 600 elaborate pieces of **cave art,** and 1500 engravings. For site conservation reasons, the cave is now closed to the public, but replicas of the main galleries have been recreated nearby.

**Lasker, Gabriel Ward** (1912–2002): US physical anthropologist and human biologist. A specialist in adaptive physiology, Lasker helped to dismantle the typological concept of race with the paper 'Human biological adaptability', published in *Science* (1969, **166**: 1480); this paper emphasized human **plasticity** and provided evidence, based on previous work, that the adult human body is influenced by environmental factors as well as by genes. Lasker was editor of *Human Biology* (1953–87), and the first editor of the *Yearbook of Physical Anthropology*. He was also a co-founder of the Cambridge University Press monograph series *Cambridge Studies in Biological Anthropology,*[1] which he initiated with volume 1 as *Surnames and Genetic Structure* (1965).

**last common ancestor** (LCA): most recent identifiable **common ancestor** to a set of taxa.

**last of the Neandertals:** see **Saint Césaire, Vindija, Mezmaiskaya Cave, Zafarraya,** and **Abrigo do Lagar Velho rockshelter.**

**Late Paleolithic:** see **Upper Paleolithic.**

**Late Pleistocene:** subdivision of the **Pleistocene epoch** from 127 to 10 kya; aka the Upper Pleistocene.

**late-replicating X chromosome:** after **X inactivation,** that X chromosome which has entered **heteropycnosis** last and completes replication later than other sex chromosomes and the autosomes.

**Late Stone Age** (LSA): the **Upper Paleolithic** of southern Africa that generally postdates about 40 kya; characterized by a predominance of blade tools, microliths and tiny geometrically shaped blades often set into handles made of bone or wood.

**latency:** measurement in behavioral studies; latency is the period of time from when a specified event begins (such as observation) until the behavior first occurs. Latency is expressed in units of time.

**latent:** present, but not visible or obvious.

**later archaic group:** forms of *Homo sapiens* ssp. or late *Homo* sp. that postdate *Homo erectus* but generally antedate **AMHs;** dates for archaics range from about 400 kya to 32 kya; archaics possessed a nearly human-sized brain but retained certain primitive features of the skull such as a lower cranial height and a mosaic of other **primitive** and **derived** features. Includes **Dali, Ngandong,** and **Omo II.** Aka younger archaic group. Cf. **anteneandertal.** See **earlier archaic group.**

**lateral:** anatomical term of relative position meaning towards the sides.

**lateral gene transfer:** natural movement of genetic elements across species.

**lateral geniculate nucleus** (LGN): portion of the **thalamus** that relays signals from the eye to the visual cortex, and vice versa.

**lateral incisor:** incisor that is farthest from the midsagittal line of the incisors in a set.

**lateral pterygoid:** muscle of chewing. The lateral pterygoid originates from the lateral pterygoid plate of the **sphenoid bone;** it inserts into the medial surface of the **mandible.** Its action is to depress and protrude the mandible and move it from side to side when performing grinding movements.

**lateral sulcus:** fissure on the brain on the lateral side of each **cerebral hemisphere** that separates the temporal lobe from the frontal and parietal lobes; aka sylvian sulcus, fissure of Sylvius.

**lateral ventricle:** central cavity within each of the two **cerebral hemispheres** of the **cerebrum;** these are lined with special cells and filled with **cerebrospinal fluid.** Aka first and second ventricles.

**laterality quotient:** measure of **hand preference** constructed by subtracting the number of tasks in which the left hand is dominant from those in which the right is dominant, dividing by the total number of tasks, and multiplying by 100. A score of 100 indicates complete **dextrality;** a score of −100 indicates complete **sinistrality.** About 85% of all people are dextral (right-handed).

**lateralization:** see **brain lateralization.**

**laterocone:** **cuspule** present laterally on the side of incisors in some **plesiadapiforms.**

**Laugerie:** archaeological site found in 1872 in the Vérèze Valley in southern France, dated to 18–12 kya, and that contains **Magdalenian** artifacts and hominid remains, including the skeleton of an adult male attributed to *Homo sapiens* Cf. **Cro-Magnon.** The skeleton has been interpreted as resembling a modern Eskimo. Aka Laugerie-Basse (lower) and Laugerie-Haute (higher).

---

[1] Now the *Cambridge Studies in Biological and Evolutionary Anthropology.*

**Laughlin, William S.** (1919–): US physical anthropologist, biobehavioral scientist, student of E. A. **Hooton;** became an acknowledged authority on the population biology and prehistory of Native Americans. His theory of the origins of Native Americans postulated one migration out of Asia approximately 17 kya. From this ancestral population, according to Laughlin, branched the Aleuts and Eskimos while, on the southern margin of **Beringia;** the remaining populations migrated southward down the ice-free corridor to colonize the rest of the New World. His work is summarized in *The First Americans: Origins, Affinities, and Adaptations* (1979).

‡ **Laurasia:** northernmost mass of **continents** that were once part of the supercontinent **Pangaea;** included North America, Europe, and Asia. See **Gondwanaland hypothesis.**

**laurel leaf point:** very thin, long point of oval, tanged, or triangular shape, and with delicate pressure flaking over its entire surface. The laurel leaf point is one of the keys to the **Solutrean tool tradition.**

**lava:** rocks formed by molten magma flows and that include andesites, basalts, phonolites, rhyolites and trachytes. Lavas tend to be gray or black in color, and many types are suitable for making stone **tools.**

**law:** empirical generalization that appears to be without exception at the time proposed, and consolidated and verified by repeated testing. There are few, if any, law-like statements in the history of biology that have withstood the test of time; biology today is rather thought of as a discipline of probabilities and approximations, unlike certain other natural sciences such as physics. Cf. **rule.** See box below.

---

### Some proposed 'laws' in the biological sciences

law of chance: in the nineteenth century, a vernacular phrase that implied that certain events occurred with a predictable frequency, rather than being due to some ultimate cause or **Grand Design.**

law of compensation: see Geoffroy's laws.

law of constant extinction: empirical law stating that for any group of related organisms sharing a common ecology there is a constant probability of extinction of any single taxon per unit of time. Aka Van Valen's law.

law of correlation: **Cuvier's** principle that a complete animal can be reconstructed from a partial skeleton, or even a single bone.

law of development: see Geoffroy's laws.

law of evolutionary potential: law stating that the group that possesses the more generalized adaptation has a greater potential for change than groups with more specialized adaptation.

law of faunal assemblages: empirical law stating that similar groups of fossils indicate similar geological stages for the formations in which they occur. See **faunal correlation.**

law of faunal succession: proposal that phyla succeed one another in the fossil record in a definite and recognizable sequence; that geological strata are characterized by assemblages different from those located above and below; that the ordering of phyla is from least to most complex.

law of filial regression: Galton's principle that **regression toward the mean** of traits will occur between members of filial generations; for example, for traits with high **heritability** such as stature, and when considering large populations, individual offspring will tend to be larger than their mid-parental value, but smaller than the population average.

law of independent assortment: see Mendelian principle of independent assortment.

law of mutual aid: assertion that mutual assistance among members of the same species is more beneficial than competition; that societies that have prospered are those characterized by voluntary support rather than by competition. Proposed by Russian anarchist Pëter Alekseevich Kropotkin (1842–1921) and used to criticize **Darwin's** evolutionary theory and especially **natural selection** at the beginning of the twentieth century.

law of original horizontality: proposal that fine sediments are usually deposited nearly horizontally; hence, tilting of strata can be estimated by geologists as the declination from horizontal. Proposed by Danish naturalist Nicolas Steno (1638–86).

‡ law of segregation: see Mendelian principle of segregation.

law of substitution: empirical law stating that any extrinsic factor may be substituted for another as long as its effect on an organism is the same.

law of superposition: see superposition of strata.

---

---

**Some proposed 'laws' in the biological sciences (*Cont.*)**

**law of the minimum:** empirical principle that the minimal requirement with respect to any given variable is the ultimate determinate in controlling the distribution or survival of a species. Aka Liebig's law.

**law of tolerance:** principle that an organism's distribution is determined by its tolerance of a single environmental factor. For some cercopithecoid populations in Africa this factor is the presence of water.

---

**Lazaret:** an archaeological site (rockshelter) located on the Cote d'Azur near Nice, France, dating to between 200 and 130 kya (U/T series), containing Acheulean or Mousterian (transitional) artifacts, rock and bone supports, fire hearths, 'bedding', and evidence of a framework of poles for a large structure, a hut that held up to 10 people. Hominid remains include partial remains of 6–12 children and adults that appear to have been processed with tools; assigned to *Homo neanderthalensis* or *H. heidelbergensis* by various workers. Aka La Lazaret Cave, Grotte du Lazaret.

**LB1:** see *Homo floresiensis*.

**L chain:** smaller or light polypeptide in **antibody** molecules. Cf. **H chain**.

**LDLs:** low-density lipoproteins, a group of plasma proteins of relatively low molecular mass that contain proportionately more protein and less **cholesterol** and triglycerides; LDLs carry plasma cholesterol to cells. Cf. **HDLs**.

**L-dopa:** see **dopa**.

**Le Gros Clark, Wilfred Edward:** see **Clark, Wilfred Edward Le Gros**.

‡ **Le Moustier:** archaeological site found in 1908–14 near Peyzac, Dordogne, France, dated to 56–39 kya, and that contains **Mousterian** artifacts (the **type site**); **hominid** remains from several individuals included one adolescent male skeleton assigned to *Homo neanderthalensis* (or *Homo sapiens neanderthalensis*). Of two adults (Moustier 1 and 2), one has been 're-excavated' several times for the amusement of visiting dignitaries.

**Le Vieillard:** see **Cro-Magnon**.

**leadership:** 1. the quality of being able to lead; capacity to lead. 2. the office or position of a leader or leaders.

**leaf-eating monkey:** generally in reference to members of the catarrhine subfamily **Colobinae, folivorous** monkeys with specialized dental apparatus and gut adaptations for a leafy diet.

**leaf monkey:** term generally applied to the Asiatic members of subfamily **colobinae**. The members of the genus *Presbytis* are specifically referred to as leaf monkeys.

**leaf-sponge:** term used for leaves that are crumpled and used to sop up water for drinking by chimpanzees; a **tool** made by chimpanzees.

**leaky genetic control:** control of gene action that is not complete, thus allowing a small amount of a gene product to be produced.

‡ **Leakey, Louis Seymour Bazett** (1903–72): Kenyan anthropologist and paleontologist, 'father of Kenyan archaeology'. At a time when **human origins** were considered to lie in Asia (1931), Leakey excavated at **Olduvai Gorge** in support of **Darwin's** proposal that Africa was the cradle of mankind. Leakey and his wife **Mary Leakey** eventually described fossil specimens of *Kenyapithecus* (found at **Fort Ternan** and **Rusinga Island**); *Zinjanthropus* (= *Paranthropus boisei*); *Homo habilis*, associated with **Oldowan tools**; and *Homo erectus*, associated with **Acheulean tools**. The Leakeys also described many possible **scavenging** or **butchering sites**. Awarded the Hubbard Medal in 1962.

‡ **Leakey, Mary Douglas Nicol** (1913–96): Kenyan archaeologist; discovered fossil remains of *Proconsul* on **Rusinga Island** (1948), *Zinjanthropus* (1959), the **habiline** specimen known as 'George', and in the 1970s and 80s, the **Laetoli footprints** and other **hominids**; described the complete sequence of **tools** at **Olduvai Gorge**. Author of *Olduvai Gorge*, Vol. 3 (1971) and *Olduvai Gorge: My Search for Early Man* (1979). Awarded the Hubbard Medal in 1962, the Gold Medal from the American Society of Women Geographers in 1975, and the Golden Linnaean Medal in 1978.

‡ **Leakey, Meave G. Epps** (1942–): Kenyan paleoanthropologist; with husband **Richard Leakey**, reconstructed **KNM-ER 1470** in the 1970s, and, with Alan **Walker**, both **KNM-WT 15000** and **KNM-WT 17000**; in 1995, located and described the 4.12 mya old fossil *Australopithecus anamensis*, an early bipedal **hominid** but with ape-like **dentition**. Also described *Kenyanthropus platyops*. Head of the paleontology department at the **National Museums of Kenya** after 1985. Co-editor of *Koobi Fora Research Project*, Vol. 1: *Fossil Hominids and an Introduction to Their Context 1968–74* (1978).

‡ **Leakey, Richard Erskine F.** (1944–): Kenyan paleoanthropologist and environmental activist; son of **Louis Leakey** and **Mary Leakey**. Codirector of the **Koobi Fora Research Project**; Leakey and his team found the significant fossil remains called **KNM-WT 17000** (*Paranthropus aethiopicus*), **KNM-ER 406** (*Paranthropus boisei*), **KNM-ER 1470** (*Homo rudolfensis*), and **KNM-WT 15000** (a *Homo erectus* or *H. ergaster* boy found near **Nariokotome**). Director of Kenya's Department of Wildlife Conservation and

Management (1989–94). Awarded the Hubbard Medal in 1993.

**lean body mass:** body mass minus body fat.

**learn:** 1. to gain knowledge or understanding of or skill in by study, instruction, or experience. 2. to memorize. 3. to gain the ability. 4. to come to realize. 5. to come to know.

**learned:** past tense of learn. In anthropology, describes anything acquired during the life cycle of an organism and placed in its memory and which cannot be passed on to descendants by a known genetic mechanism. Many physical **traits** have at least some component of variance that is due to such environmental modification. The memory of an organism's immune system is so acquired. Many — if not all — appropriate behaviors, values, and knowledge of cultural norms are so acquired. Contrast **innate, inborn, inheritance.**

**learning:** process in which experience and conditioning affects behavior; learning requires the capacity to store memories for future reference, a capacity found in mammals and especially primates. Learning is associated with **soft-wired** animals. See **learned, learning capacity,** and **learning disposition.**

**learning capacity:** range and limitation of an animal's ability to learn; this refers to what an animal can learn, how it learns, and its ability to store experiences for future use. Learning capacity assumes a genetic basis for the range of learning possible, which interacts with the environment in the species in question. See **learning disposition.**

**learning disposition:** genetic constraints on **learning capacity** within a species. Those things that an animal is predisposed to learn quickly are of vital importance, such as types of predators in the environment, whereas less important things are learned more slowly. See **learning capacity.**

**learning rule:** **predisposition** to learn one alternative behavior as opposed to another, even when both are taught with equal intensity; **handedness,** for example, is learned only with difficulty if a person predisposed to be right-handed is trained to be left-handed and vice-versa.

**learning set:** concept in primate laboratory behavioral studies pertaining to the transfer of information from one learning trial to the next. See **discrimination learning set.**

**learning theory:** proposal that **learning** is an evolved trait and that, because all animals learn in the same way, principles of learning in one species can be generalized to others. Associated especially with behaviorist Burrhus Frederic Skinner (1904–90). Aka universal law of learning.

**least squares regression:** asymmetrical linear regression model in which it is assumed that error variance is confined to $Y$, the dependent variable. The model generates a **regression** equation that minimizes the sum of the squared differences between the observed values and their respective expected values represented by a **best fit line.** Aka Model I regression technique.

**Leber hereditary optic neuropathy** (LHON): one of the maternally inherited **mitochondrial myopathies** characterized by sudden loss of central vision at about the third decade, owing to optic nerve degeneration. The defective gene in mtDNA codes for a respiratory enzyme. Aka Leber optic atrophy.

**lectotype:** in the absence of a **holotype,** the **type specimen** chosen from the **syntype** series by someone other than the original author of a **taxon.**

**Lee, Richard Borshay** (1937–): Canadian anthropologist at the University of Toronto; has worked since 1963 among the Dobe Ju/'hoansi-!**Kung,** hunter-gatherers in the Kalahari. His ecological studies provide quantitative data regarding **nutrition** among foraging peoples. Publication interests include ecology, history, African studies, indigenous peoples, AIDS, political economy, and the politics of culture. Co-editor (with I. **DeVore**) of *Man the Hunter* (1968), which contained Lee's classic paper 'What scavengers do for a living, or how to make out on scarce resources'. Coeditor (with I. DeVore) of *Kalahari Hunter-Gatherers: Studies of the !Kung San and Their Neighbors* (1976); coeditor (with R. H. Daly) of *The Cambridge Encyclopedia of Hunters and Gatherers* (1999). Author of *The Dobe !Kung* (1984) and among others a popular article 'Eating Christmas in the Kalahari' (1969), *Natural History*, 78(10): 336.

**left cerebral hemisphere:** left lateral portion of the **cerebrum.** In most people, the left hemisphere controls analytical and verbal skills such as reading, writing, and arithmetic. The left hemisphere is separated from the **right cerebral hemisphere** by the **longitudinal cerebral fissure,** but portions of the two hemispheres are connected internally by the **corpus callosum.** Each cerebral hemisphere contains a central cavity called the **lateral ventricle.**

**left-handed DNA:** see **DNA.** Cf. **right-handed DNA.**

**left-handedness:** see **sinistrality, handedness,** and **hand preference.**

**left inferior frontal lobe:** region of the **brain** involved in calculating exact mathematical solutions.

**left-occipital–right-frontal petalia pattern:** combination of left-occipital and right-frontal cortical **asymmetry.** Pongid brains are often asymmetrical in the anteroposterior plane, but those of modern humans are asymmetrical in both the anteroposterior and lateral planes. This latter pattern of **brain** asymmetry is thought to be related to **hand dominance.**

**leg:** 1. appendage used for locomotion and support; especially the **hindlimb**, as in humans. 2. in anatomy, the segment of the lower limb between the knee above and the ankle below. Cf. **thigh**.

**leg length:** distance between the tibiale and the lowest point of the medial malleolus on the ankle.

**legal medicine:** see **medical jurisprudence**.

**leiotrichous:** pertaining to the possession of straight hair.

**Leishmaniasis:** infection caused by a flagellate protozoan (*Leishmania braziliensis*). Endemic in Central and South America, where it is vectored by sand fly females, genus *Phlebotomus*; reservoirs include rodents and domestic dogs. Causes ulceration of the mucous membranes of the nose and throat; similar forms occur in Asia, Africa and the Mediterranean, where it is caused by *Leishmania tropica*. Aka kala-azar, forest yaws, bouba braziliana, espundia, and uta; Cf. **Bartonellosis**.

**lek:** area regularly used for courtship displays and copulation in **polygynous** species during the mating season. Leks are divided into small male territories that have no vital resources, but the females visit these sites to find mates. The term lek generally relates to birds, although some mammals, such as bats and kob, are said to use leks. This term has not been applied to primate mating systems, but is often encountered in the sociobiology literature.

**Le Mas d'Azil:** see **Mas d'Azil**.

**lemur:** 1. primate belonging to the **prosimian** family **Lemuridae**. 2. any of the prosimians of Madagascar. This term does not apply to living non-Malagasy prosimians.

***Lemur*** Linnaeus, 1758: monotypic **prosimian** genus to which the ring-tailed lemur belongs. Five species were removed from *Lemur* in 1988 and reassigned to *Eulemur*. *Varecia variegata* has also been included in *Lemur* in the past. See *Lemur catta*.

***Lemur catta*** Linnaeus, 1758: ring-tailed lemur; **monotypic** species. Located in southern and southwestern Madagascar. Inhabits variable environment, ranging from dry deciduous forest to scrub forest. Semiterrestrial (spends about 30% of time on the ground); diurnal; quadrupedal. Gray **pelage** with black-and-white ringed tail; slight **sexual dimorphism** in body size. Body mass ranges from 1.5 to 3 kg. Possess **carpal glands**; in the male these are overlaid by horny spurs, with which they scent-mark areas. Dental formula: 3.1.3.3; diet varies according to habitat, but shows some degree of **frugivory** or **folivory**. Social organization is mixed-sex **troops** of 20–30 individuals; females dominant. See Appendix 2 for taxonomy, Appendix 3 for living species. See also *Eulemur* and *Varecia*.

***Lemur laniger*** Gmelin, 1788: synonym for *Avahi occidentalis*.

***Lemur olivaceous*** I. Geoffroy, 1851: synonym for *Hapalemur griseus*.

***Lemur psilodactylus*** Shaw, 1800: synonym for *Daubentonia madagascariensis*.

**Lemuria:** continental **land bridge** thought to have connected South Africa, Madagascar, and India. This land mass is thought to have existed at least through the **Cretaceous** period.

**Lemuridae:** **prosimian** family to which the lemurs, ring-tailed lemurs, and ruffed lemurs belong, consisting of four genera and eight species. Vernacular: lemurid. See Appendix 2 for taxonomy, Appendix 3 for living species.

**Lemuriformes:** infraorder of the suborder **Prosimii**; lemurlike primates. Vernacular: lemuriform. Includes the superfamilies **Lemuroidea** and **Lorisoidea**. Some authors remove the lorisoids and give them equal rank in the infraorder Lorisiformes. See Appendix 2 for taxonomy, Appendix 3 for living species.

**Lemurinae:** subfamily of the **prosimian** family **Lemuridae**. The lemurines consist of the genera *Lemur*, *Eulemur*, *Varecia*, and the recently extinct *Pachylemur*. See Appendix 2 for taxonomy, Appendix 3 for living species.

**lemurine night monkey:** vernacular for *Aotus lemurinus*.

‡ **Lemuroidea:** superfamily of the **prosimian** infraorder **Lemuriformes** that includes all of the families of the Malagasy primates. See Appendix 2 for taxonomy, Appendix 3 for living species.

**lemurophile hypothesis:** hypothesis of primate phylogeny that considers the **plesiadapiforms** to be the sister group of the omomyids and **tarsiers** (all three groups comprising the Plesatarsiiformes), and the lemurs, lorises, and adapids to form a sister group of the **anthropoids** (together comprising the Simiolemuriformes). See **omomyophile hypothesis** and **tarsiphile hypothesis**

**length:** linear extent of an object; a measurement from end to end.

**length–breadth sacral index:** anterior sacral breadth × 100, divided by anterior sacral length.

**length of the foramen magnum** (ba–o): **craniometric** measurement; distance between the **basion** and the **opisthion**. Aka foraminal length.

**lentiform:** see **pisiform**.

***Leontideus*** Cabrera, 1956: synonym for *Leontopithecus*, the replacement epithet considered the proper designation for this genus.

***Leontocebus*** Wagner, 1840: synonym for the genus *Saguinus* that was used until recently.

***Leontopithecus*** (= ***Leontideus***) Lesson, 1840: **platyrrhine** genus to which the lion or golden tamarins belong; consists of from one to four **allopatric** species, depending on authority. Found only in primary forest of southeastern Brazil. Arboreal; diurnal; **arboreal quadrupeds**. Largest of the callitrichids, ranging in body mass from 450 to 700 g. Dental formula: 2.1.3.2; **frugivorous** with insect supplements. Possesses modified nails that have been laterally compressed to form 'claws' on all digits except the **hallux**. Long slender fingers are used to reach into crevices and hollows of trees to snare insects. Lives in family groups, but may combine with other units to form temporary associations that number up to 20 animals. All species highly endangered. See Appendix 2 for taxonomy, Appendix 3 for living species.

**leopard hill hypothesis:** proposal by C. K. **Brain** that hominids were deposited at **Swartkrans** as the result of predation by leopards rather than as primary deposits.

*Lepilemur* I. Geoffroy, 1851: **prosimian** genus to which the sportive (or weasel) lemurs belong; confusion regarding taxonomy; some authors recognize one species with many subspecies that have different numbers of chromosomes, yet breed and produce reproductively viable hybrids with an intermediate number of chromosomes; more commonly in recent years workers recognize up to seven separate species. Formerly placed within the **Lemuridae**, but molecular evidence indicates it belongs to a separate family (**Lepilemuridae** or **Megaladapidae** depending on the source). Occupies variable types of forest throughout the peripheries of Madagascar. Arboreal; nocturnal; **vertical clinging and leaping** locomotion. Body mass ranges from 500 to 1000 g. The upper incisors are lost in the adult, but are present in the **deciduous dentition**. Adult dental formula: 0.1.3.3/2.1.3.3 = 32; **folivorous**. Noyau; territorial; these animals are referred to as sportive lemurs because they take a boxer's pose when conspecifics encroach on their territory; territories delineated by sound. See Appendix 2 for taxonomy, Appendix 3 for living species.

**Lepilemuridae:** synonym for the lemuroid family **Megaladapidae**.

**Lepilemurinae:** depending on taxonomic scheme used, subfamily of the **prosimian** family **Lemuridae** when the sportive lemurs are included with the lemurs; or, one of two subfamilies within the family **Megaladapidae** that contains the genus *Lepilemur* (sportive lemurs). See Appendix 2 for taxonomy, Appendix 3 for living species.

*Leptadapis* Gervais, 1876: adapoid prosimian from the late Eocene to early Oligocene of Europe, belonging to the adapid subfamily **Adapinae**; five species; formerly included within *Adapis*, which it antedates. Body mass ranges between 1.5 and 4 kg. Smaller size of orbits suggest **diurnal** activity. Dental formula: 2.1.4.3/2.1.4.3; dental morphology

and cranial-chewing apparatus suggestive of **folivory**. According to Gingerich, *Leptadapis* shows evidence of sexual dimorphism cranially and in canine tooth size; this is the first appearance of sexual dimorphism among primates and suggests, based on living mammals, that *Leptadapis* lived in **polygynous** groups. **Postcrania** have been interpreted as providing for slow methodical climbing. See Appendix 1 for taxonomy.

**leptenic:** in reference to the **upper facial index**, having an index between 55.00 and 59.99; such an individual is considered to have a slender face.

**Lepticidae:** family of archaic mammals from the Cretaceous that are probably insectivoran precursors and are suggested as candidates for the primate root. Vernacular: lepticid.

**leptin:** the so-called 'obesity protein'. Acts as a hormone that carries signals from **adipocytes** and the **hypothalamus** and is involved in the regulation of appetite, energy expenditure, and bone mass. See **ghrelin** and **orexin(s)**.

**leptoprosopic:** in reference to the **total facial index**, having an index between 90.00 and 94.99; such an individual is considered to have a slender or narrow nose.

**leptorrhine:** see **leptorrhinic, nasal morphology**, and **Topinard**.

**leptorrhinic:** in reference to the **nasal index**, having an index of 46.99 or less; such an individual is considered to have a slender **nasal aperture**. See **nasal morphology** and **Topinard**.

**leptostaphyline:** in reference to the **palatal index**, having an index of 79.99 or less; such an individual is considered to have a narrow palate.

**leptotene stage:** in **meiosis**, the first of the five stages of **prophase**, in which the chromosomes appear as individual, slender threads, well separated from each other. Aka leptonema.

**Lesch–Nyhan syndrome:** heritable X-linked recessive condition characterized by spastic cerebral palsy, and severe mental retardation coupled with aggressive and self-destructive behaviors; death before puberty. A metabolic disease affecting hypoxanthine–guanine–phosphoribosyl transferase (HGPRT)-mediated guanine conversion, resulting in failure to recycle nucleic acids, converting them instead to uric acid, which manifests as urinary stones (seen as an orange 'sand' in diapers). Fibroblasts of female carriers exhibit about 50% HGPRT activity due to the random effects of **X inactivation**.

**lesser apes:** vernacular for the small-bodied apes belonging to the **hominoid** family **Hylobatidae**, represented by the genus *Hylobates*.

**lesser bushbaby:** vernacular for *Galago senegalensis*.

**lesser multangular (of the carpus):** see **trapezoid**.

**lesser palatine foramen:** smaller opening in the posterior portion of the **palatine bone** posterior to the **greater palatine foramen.**

**lesser pelvis:** narrower portion of the **pelvis** that begins at the **pelvic inlet** and continues inferiorly, forming a deep bowl that contains the pelvic organs. The pelvic inlet and outlet form a passageway through which the infant must pass during **parturition**; the dimensions of the lesser pelvis' inlet and outlet are critical to an uncomplicated birth. Aka true pelvis.

**lesser sciatic notch:** indentation in the posterior **ischium** of the **coxal bone** inferior to the **ischial spine** and superior to the **ischial tuberosity** through which several nerves and blood vessels pass to the anogenital area. Cf. **greater sciatic notch.**

**lesser slow loris:** vernacular for *Nycticebus pygmaeus.*

**lesser spot-nosed guenon:** vernacular for *Cercopithecus petaurista.*

**lesser trochanter:** smaller of the two large processes on the proximal **femur**; the lesser trochanter is medial and inferior to the **greater trochanter**, and serves as a site for the attachment of the iliopsoas muscle.

**lesser tubercle (of the humerus):** process on the anterior side of the proximal portion of the **humerus**; the subscapularis muscle that helps move the upper limb inserts into this structure.

**lesser white-nosed guenon:** vernacular for *Cercopithecus petaurista.*

**lethal:** capable of causing death by direct action.

**lethal allele:** see **lethal gene.**

**lethal equivalent (value):** average number of **deleterious** alleles carried in a population, multiplied by the probability that each will cause a death when in the homozygous state. see **effective lethal phase.** Cf. **genetic load.**

**lethal gene:** mutant allele that is incompatible with life and that causes the death of an organism at some time between conception and maturity. Lethals are usually effective only in the homozygous state (or **hemizygous**, if X-linked). In reference to humans, initial expression of the gene before the age of one year is also stipulated by some researchers. See **genetic load.** Cf. **sublethal gene, semilethal gene.**

**lethal trait, character or feature:** inherited attribute that causes the death of an organism prior to reproduction.

**leucine** (Leu): an essential **amino acid**; one of the twenty building blocks of **proteins.** Found especially in the pancreas and spleen.

**leucoderm:** light-colored skin; Von Eickstedt's name for **Caucasoid.**

**leukemia:** a progressive, malignant disease of the blood-forming organs, characterized by distorted proliferation and development of **leukocytes** and their precursors in the blood and bone marrow. Its various manifestations are classified according to degree of cell differentiation as acute or chronic (terms that in leukemia do not refer to duration of disease); and according to the predominant type of cell involved, such as myelogenous or lymphocytic. Examples include **acute promyelocytic leukemia** and **chronic myeloid leukemia.**

**leukocyte:** white blood cell; nucleated amoeboid cell of the **circulatory system**, although it interacts with the immune system; leukocytes may have a granular cytoplasm that stains with certain dyes, or they may have a non-granular cytoplasm. Aka white corpuscle, leukocyte. See **granulocyte.**

**leukoderma:** complete or partial absence of skin pigment; literally, white (depigmented) skin.

**Levallois core:** extensively preshaped stone artifact that remains after the production of one or more blades.

**Levallois flake:** type of flake that succeeded the **coup-de-poing** in Europe. See **Levallois technique.**

‡ **Levallois technique:** complex technique for the manufacture of **tools** by striking **flakes** from a flat **flint** nodule, and requiring coordinated preparatory steps after which it was possible to produce the desired flake tool with one final blow to the **core.** See **Levalloiso-Mousterian industry.**

**Levalloisian:** Paleolithic flake tool culture produced by striking serviceable flakes from a prepared core; recognized in Europe, Asia and Africa. Type site: Levallois-Perret.

**Levalloiso-Mousterian industry:** rich **Upper Paleolithic** industry containing denticulate tools, scrapers, **Levalloisian** points, backed knives and burins. Found associated with both **neandertaloid** (**Amud** and **Tabūn**) and anatomically modern human (**AMH**) remains (**Qafzeh**) in the **Levantine corridor** sites.

**Levant:** lands bordering the eastern shores of the East Mediterranean and Aegean Seas, especially those in present-day southern Turkey, Syria, Lebanon, Israel, Palestine, Jordan, and northern Egypt. Many sites of archaeological significance, dating from over 790 kya to the present, have been found in the region. See **Gesher Benot Ya'aqor, Qafzeh, Skhūl,** and **Tabūn.**

**Levantine (corridor):** pertaining to the **Levant.** The term 'corridor' refers to a possible migration route **out of Africa.** Cf. **'Gates of Grief'.**

**Levantine Aurignacian tool tradition:** pertaining to the **Aurignacian tool tradition** when found in the **Levant.** Cf. **Sebilian.**

**level of confidence:** in statistics, the width of an interval that reflects a certain probability that a certain parameter will be contained within it. A 95% confidence interval, for instance, would contain the parameter in 95% of instances.

**levels of integration:** plateaus of complexity at which

new properties emerge that apparently are not predicted by an assessment of individual components.

**levorotatory:** turning the plane of polarized light to the left, as with some crystals and solutions. Cf. **dextrorotatory**. See **L-form.**

**Lewis blood group** (Le): antigens of red blood cells, epithelial cells, saliva, and other body fluids, specified by the *Le* gene, that react with the antibodies designated anti-*Le*ᵃ and anti-*Le*ᵇ; named after a Mrs Lewis, in whose white blood cells the antibodies were discovered. The gene codes for the enzyme fucosyltransferase, and adds a fucose sugar molecule to the **ABO blood group** precursor. Type O individuals with the Lewis antigen are susceptible to gastric ulcers because the bacterium responsible, *Helicobacter pylori*, attaches to the gastric mucosa by binding to receptors that contain exposed fucose. The *Le* gene maps to HSA 19.

**Lewontin, Richard D.** (1929–): US evolutionary biologist at Harvard; he was among the early converts to Kimura's theory of **neutral evolution**, and almost immediately published corroborating evidence (with Hubby, 1966) on extensive polymorphisms in wild populations. Lewontin espoused the 'dialectical' approach to any problem, and thus he seemed to object to almost every popular biological concept; see, for example, his classic paper (with S. J. **Gould**) on the 'panglossian paradigm' (1979). Another important paper on human diversity was 'The apportionment of human diversity', in *Evolutionary Biology* (1972), **6**: 381–98. Author of many other scholarly articles and books, including *Evolution and the Theory of Games* (1961), *The Genetic Basis of Evolutionary Change* (1974), *Human Diversity* (1995), and *Triple Helix: Gene, Organism and Environment* (2000).

**lexicostatistics:** method whereby differences between related **languages** are quantified and used to estimate the amount of time the languages have been separated; also used as a way of mapping and writing the history of human **migrations** when no written records exist.

‡ **lexigram: glyph** on a computer board containing keys with symbols representing meaningful parts of words (morphemes) or perhaps even smaller units of discrimination (phonemes) in a 'language'.

‡ **LH:** 1. abbreviation for **Laetoli** Hominid. See box below. 2. See **luteinizing hormone.** 3. a recombinant (genetically engineered) gene product with the same name as in (2).

**L/H material:** Laetoli/Hadar fossils, tools and faunal assemblages.

---

### Some hominids found at Laetoli

**LH-2:** Laetoli Hominid 2; a juvenile mandible with both deciduous and adult dentition, found in 1974 at locality 3 in the Laetolil Beds near Tuff 7 and dated to 3.6 mya; assigned to *Australopithecus afarensis*.

**LH-3:** Laetoli Hominid 3; partial upper and lower dentition found in 1974–5 at locality 7, Laetolil Beds, between Tuffs 7 and 8, dated to 3.6 mya, and assigned to *Australopithecus afarensis*.

**LH-4:** Laetoli Hominid 4; the **type specimen** of *Australopithecus afarensis*, a partial adult mandible and dentition found in 1974 at locality 7, Laetolil Beds beneath Tuff 7, dated to 3.75–3.6 mya. One researcher has suggested that this specimen might be a dryopithecine.

**LH-6:** Laetoli Hominid 6; partial upper and lower dentition found in 1974–5 at locality 7, Laetolil Beds near Tuff 7, dated to 3.6 mya and assigned to *Australopithecus afarensis*.

**LH-18:** Laetoli Hominid 18; a cranium with a capacity of over 1200 cm³ found in 1976 at locality 2S, Upper **Ngaloba** Beds, dated to 120 ± 30 kya; assigned to **archaic** *Homo sapiens*; a mosaic of features including double-arched supra-orbital torus with a recessed forehead, keeled frontal, rounded occiput with small mastoid process, and a prominent occipitomastoid crest. Currently one of the oldest examples of *Homo sapiens* known.

**LH-21:** Laetoli Hominid 21; a partial immature skeleton found in 1976 at locality 12E, Laetolil Beds, between Tuffs 6 and 7, and dated to 3.6 mya; assigned to *Australopithecus afarensis*. Aka 'Timothy' (after Tim **White**).

---

**L'Hoest's monkey:** vernacular for the **guenon** species *Cercopithecus l'hoesti*.

**Liang Bua:** (LB) limestone rockshelter excavated in 2003, located on the island of Flores, eastern Indonesia. Hominin remains include cranial and postcranial fragments from up to seven individuals dated to 38–18 kya (¹⁴C, luminescence, U-series, ESR, AMS) assigned to a new species, *Homo floresiensis*.

The hominins were also associated with **pebble tools** and fauna remains, including *Stegodon*, an extinct pygmy elephant.

**Li-Fraumeni syndrome:** familial cancer due to mutations in the *p53* **tumor suppressor** gene. The germline mutation must be followed by secondary somatic mutations that cause problems in various tissues.

**Libby, Willard Frank** (1908–80): US nuclear chemist,

Nobel laureate; in 1946–8 devised the chronometric technique for determining the age of organic or fossilized specimens called **radiocarbon dating**. A member of the Manhattan Project, he noted that a certain isotope, **carbon-14**, should theoretically decay at a rate steady enough to permit dating, and with much fanfare later successfully dated Egyptian and other artifacts of known calendrical age.

**library:** in **recombinant DNA**, a collection of clones that contains all the genetic information in an individual; Aka genetic bank.

*Libyapithecus markgrafi* **Stromer, 1913:** colobine known from the late Miocene of North Africa; **monotypic;** known only from a single skull and isolated lower molar. Estimated body mass around 8 kg. Face is longer relative to **extant** colobines. Dental formula: 2.1.2.3/2.1.2.3; molars possess shearing crests adapted to a **folivorous** diet. See Appendix 1 for taxonomy.

*Lichanotus laniger* **Illiger, 1811:** synonym for *Avahi occidentalis*.

*Lichanotus mitratus* **W. Peters, 1872:** synonym for *Indri indri*.

**life:** state or quality manifested by growth through active metabolism, reproduction, and the power of adaptation to environment. An obscure quality whereby organized **organic** beings are peculiarly endowed with certain powers and functions not associated with inorganic matter. Adjective: living. Aka vitality.

**life cycle:** 1. the entire span of the existence of an organism (or of a society) from the moment it originates to the time that it reproduces and dies; in higher organisms, the period from conception to death. Cf. **life span**. 2. schedule of stages and roles a human (or other organism) should pass through during a normal human career. See **stages of the human life cycle**.

**life–dinner principle:** hypothesis that attempts to explain why prey are a step ahead of predators in **evolutionary arms races**; essentially the prey must be one step ahead because their lives depend on it, whereas for the predator only a meal is at stake. If prey are killed, they do not reproduce; if dinner is missed the predator may still reproduce, even if it eventually starves.

**life expectancy:** average period that an organism can expect to live after a specific age, given a constant level of mortality.

**life expectancy at birth** (LEB): a measure of the average length of life for a newborn child; LEB is population-specific. See **reproduction**.

‡ **life history:** 1. the chronological progression of changes through which an organism passes in its development from the primary stage to its death. 2. the chronological progression of an individual's development in his or her social environment. 3. the

biographical study of a people. 4. pattern of allocation of time and energy, throughout life, to fundamental components of an animal's **development** and **physiology**, including **body size**, relative **brain size**, **metabolism**, rate of **maturation**, lifestyle variables, and reproductive parameters.

**life history artifact:** evidence of life without the presence of a causal organism, such as a fossilized bird's nest, bee hive, or **coprolite**.

**life history parameters (traits):** see **life history variable**.

**life history strategy:** any of various adaptations by biological lineages that involve the lineage-specific timing of events such as reproduction (many vs. few offspring), maturation (fast vs. slow), longevity (short vs. long), etc.

**life history theory:** proposal that life cycle outcomes are complex but predictable functions of energy allocation, based on a general principle of thermodynamics: that energy allocated for one purpose cannot be retrieved or used for another, and therefore rates of energy harvest impinge on outcomes.

**life history variable:** characteristic of the **growth and development** of an organism such as the length of **gestation**, degree of dependency at birth, timing of the **tooth eruption sequence** (in dentates), timing of **sexual maturity**, length of reproductive period, and **maximum lifespan potential**, among others. In current models of hominid **life history** reconstruction, one (or more) of these variables is a candidate(s) for the cause of hominid behavioral adaptations. Cf. the **'man the hunter' hypothesis**. Aka life history parameter.

**life span:** duration of the life of an organism (or of a society) from the moment it originates to the time that it dies. Cf. **life cycle**; see also **maximum lifespan potential**.

**life table:** table for a population that provides an estimate of the probability of an individual dying by any given age. Life table analysis is used to estimate life expectancy.

**life zone:** altitudinal and latitudinal belt that contains characteristic flora and fauna.

‡ **ligament:** flexible cord or sheet of dense fibrous connective tissue binding two or more bones at a **joint**.

**ligamentum nuchae:** **ligament** that helps support the neck and extends from the seventh cervical vertebra to the **external occipital protuberance** of the skull.

**ligand:** molecule of a compound that is capable of binding to a **receptor**.

**ligase:** enzyme that catalyzes the formation of covalent bonds in the sugar–phosphate backbone of **DNA**, thus facilitating repairs. Aka DNA ligase.

**ligase chain reaction** (LCR): technique that screens for mutations in **DNA**, using thermal cycling; failure of DNA amplification means that a strand of test DNA contains one or more variant nucleotides relative to a standard of comparison.

**light chain:** one of the two shorter polypeptide chains that contains the **variable region** of an **antibody**. Aka L chain. Cf. **heavy chain.**

**light-duty tool:** stone **tool** made of a small **cobble** or chunk of rock from which small flakes have been struck by a hammerstone; for example, a light scraper, awl, or burin.

**Lightfoot, John, Dr** (1602–75): Hebraist, chronologist. Master of St. Catharine's college and vice-chancellor of Cambridge University. Pinpointed the Creation of Genesis by the Holy Trinity at nine o'clock in the morning of 23 October, 4004 BC, (23 October was the beginning of the university term at Cambridge). From 1701 this date began to be printed in the Authorized Version of the bible. Cf. **Ussher.**

**limande:** French for flounder, and the vernacular for an **Acheulean** stone tool known as the **coup-de-poing** that is shaped roughly like the fish.

**limb index:** ratio between the length of comparable bones, or of the total length, of the forelimb and hindlimb.

**limb proportions:** comparison between the length of the hindlimb and forelimb; this varies greatly in primates. See **limb index.**

**limbic:** 1. pertaining to the **limbic system** of the brain. 2. relating to any border or cusp.

**limbic forebrain:** consists of the prefrontal cortex and the **orbitofrontal cortex;** a part of the **limbic system** involved with planning and reaction. Aka prefrontal cortex, the 'executive region'.

**limbic midbrain:** structure connected to the **hypothalamus,** the **pons,** and the **medulla oblongata;** mediates emotional facial responses, and cardiovascular and respiratory function. See **limbic system.**

**limbic system:** group of structures in the **brain** that function as a unit to mediate the responses associated with emotional autonomic activity as well as the internalization of conditioned responses; all of the structures involved are located below the **cerebral cortex.** The principal components are the **hypothalamus, rhinencephalon** (nosebrain), **hippocampus, cingulate cortex,** and **orbitofrontal cortex.** Chemicals released into the limbic system can sometimes override reasoning systems found in the cerebral cortex. Primate **vocalizations,** attention, **motivation,** arousal, and certain emotions and behaviors (pain, **affection, submission,** rage, alarm, ecstasy, **attachment behavior,** and surprise) seem to be controlled by these centers. Aka emotional brain.

**limestone:** sedimentary rock formed of more than 50%

calcium carbonate (**calcite**); some limestones have been used as material for the manufacture of **stone tools.**

**limestone tool:** any implement made from **limestone.**

**limited resource:** a particular consumable or factor in a particular environment the shortage of which prevents an organism from reaching its full potential.

**limiting factor:** element of the environment that limits the amount of life that can be supported in that environment.

***Limnopithecus* Hopwood, 1933:** genus of small **hominoids** from the early Miocene of East Africa, belonging to the catarrhine family **Proconsulidae;** two species recognized; both taxonomy and systematics in flux. Originally, *Limnopithecus* was considered to be the ancestor of the gibbons and was included among the **Hylobatidae;** revision in the 1970s removed several species from the genus (including the **holotype**), removing the validity of the genus. See ***Dendropithecus*** and ***Proconsul africanus.***

**limonite:** one of the **ochres;** limonites range in color from yellow to orange. See **red ochre.**

**line:** 1. an element that is very long but narrow. 2. a continuous, identifiable **lineage** of reproductive individuals.

**LINE:** see **long interspersed nucleotide element.**

**line breeding:** method of **breeding** designed to perpetuate the desirable traits of an animal by crossbreeding its descendants. See **inbreeding.**

**LINE sequence:** see **long interspersed nucleotide element;** a sequence type of repeated DNA, concentrated in noncoding regions. LINE-1 elements are especially prolific on the mammalian X chromosome, where they are thought to play a role in **X inactivation.** See **selfish DNA.**

**linea aspera (of the femur):** roughened area on the posterior side of the femoral **diaphysis** that is a continuation of the **lesser trochanter.** It serves as a site of attachment for a number of muscles of the leg.

‡ **lineage:** 1. descent in a line from a common progenitor. 2. a group of individuals tracing its descent from a common ancestor regarded as its founder; cf. **clan.** 3. ancestor–descendant sequence of **populations, cells,** or **genes.**

**lineage group:** group of species allied by common descent. Also said of populations, cells, or genes.

**lineal evolution:** idea that cultural evolution in all societies is parallel to that of all other societies. Cf. **unilineal evolution.**

**linear enamel hypoplasia:** poor development of tooth enamel during growth as a result of environmental stresses.

**linear relation:** in statistics, a relationship between two variables $X$ and $Y$ of the form $Y = AX + B$, where

*A* and *B* are constants. The graph of a linear relation is a straight line. Aka linear **regression**.

**lingual:** pertaining to the tongue.

**lingual cingulum:** ridge that surrounds the tongue-side base of a lower tooth crown, always above the **enamel–dentin junction**. See **cingulum**.

**lingual phase:** second sequence of the **power stroke** of the **masticatory cycle** in which the **mandibular** teeth continue in medial movement but are pushed down by the cusps of the **maxillary** teeth.

‡ **linguistic anthropology:** area within anthropology that studies the origins and cultural perceptions and uses of **language**, the relationship(s) of language to **culture**, and the languages of peoples without a tradition of writing.

‡ **linguistics:** 1. the study of human speech, including the units, nature, structure, and modification of **language**. 2. patterns of **learned** sounds, **signs** and **symbols** that allow **communication** to occur within a human group. The original use of linguistic studies with regard to **human variation** studies was the deduction of migration patterns and the relationships between 'races'. See L. L. **Cavalli-Sforza**, who has continued this application.

‡ **linkage:** state of nonrandom association of different **genes** or loci when present physically close on the same **chromosome** so that they are often transmitted together and do not undergo **recombination**; loci that are members of the same **linkage group**.

**linkage disequilibrium:** condition in which **haplotype** frequencies in a population differ from the values they should have if the genes at each locus have recombined randomly; linkage is implied, but is not a requirement; can arise because of nonrandom mating, random sampling, and natural selection. See **coefficient of linkage disequilibrium**.

**linkage disequilibrium positional cloning:** method of mapping candidate genes that exploits the nonrandom association of genes with markers (typically, **SNPs** of known location) on the same chromosome.

**linkage equilibrium:** condition in which the recombination fractions of alleles at different loci in a population equal the values they should have if the genes at each locus recombined randomly.

**linkage group:** set of genes clustered together on a **chromatid** such that they are seldom rearranged by **recombination**, i.e. a set of loci whose pairwise **recombination fraction** is less than one-half. Each linkage group corresponds to a specific chromatid or chromosome; humans thus have 25 linkage groups in the **genome**, including the **mitochondrial chromosome**.

**linkage map:** see **genetic linkage map**.

**linkage study:** method of identifying individuals who possess a certain unexpressed gene by locating a marker sequence that is very close to the gene in question, i.e. that is linked to the gene. A linkage study is useful for identifying individuals who carry genes with delayed **penetrance**, as in the case of **Huntington disease**.

‡ **linked trait, character or feature:** see **dependent trait**.

**Linnaean hierarchy** or **classification:** system of hierarchical ranking and **classification** of organisms devised by Carolus **Linnaeus** in the eighteenth century. Organisms are placed in a hierarchy in which each higher taxon or category includes a set of one or more lower categories; see **kingdom** and **binomial nomenclature**.

**Linnaean species:** concept that idealizes the species as possessing an essence, thus distinguishing it permanently from all other species. Aka Linnaean concept of species. See **morphic resonance**.

‡ **Linnaeus, Carolus (Carl von Linné)** (1707–78): Swedish botanist who instituted the system of **binomial nomenclature** still used by scientists today, e.g. *Homo sapiens*. By 1758 (*Systema Naturae*, tenth edition), Linnaeus and his students had described over 14,000 species of **flora** and **fauna**, which were arranged in a **taxonomy** to which were also ascribed various attributes such as **immutability** (**fixity of species**), the lack of successful **hybridization**, and the impossibility of **extinction** or later **special creation** of species. Linnaeus himself questioned some of these ideas later in his life, but his popular scheme had already become irreparably institutionalized. Linnaeus 'quartered' humanity into **varieties** (*varietas*), each associated with specific physical characters, and attributed one of the four Galenic behavioral 'humors' to each type: *Homo sapiens europaeus* was sanguine, *Homo sapiens afer* was bilious, *Homo sapiens asiaticus* was melancholic, and *Homo sapiens americanus* was choleric. See **Great Chain of Being**.

**linoleic acid:** one of the **essential fatty acids**, found in vegetable oils, mammalian lipids, soybeans, corn, and egg yolks.

**linolenic acid:** one of the **essential fatty acids**, found in vegetable oils.

**lion-tailed macaque:** vernacular for *Macaca silenus*.

**lip:** anatomical term for the margin of a groove, crest or line. see also **lips**.

**lip eversion:** outer epithelial surface of the **lips**, which varies in width between and within human populations; aka red margin.

**lip smacking face:** primate facial expression in which there are sucking jaw movements and the tongue protrudes, akin to suckling. This behavior is found among some **anthropoids** such as baboons and capuchins and is used for greeting, grooming, or mating.

**lipid:** any fat, oil or wax, or metabolic derivative of these substances that is insoluble in water.

**lipid metabolism:** process during which fatty molecules are either broken down or synthesized in the cells of the body.

**lipocyte:** fat cell.

**lipoprotein:** conjugated protein coat containing fat as the nonprotein substance. See **high-density lipoprotein** and **low-density lipoprotein**. Aka plasma lipoprotein.

**liposome:** fatty bubble (lipids) with an aqueous interior that can enclose and transport **DNA** into cells; liposomes have been explored as vectors to deliver **recombinant DNA** into other cell compartments or organisms.

**lips:** in human morphology, the two mobile and fleshy structures that surround the opening of the mouth. They contain sensory receptors that are able to judge the properties of food that is brought to the mouth.

**Lissapol:** hardening agent used by archaeologists to remove fragile bones and artifacts.

**lissencephaly:** inherited, autosomal recessive condition characterized by profound mental retardation, seizures, and other neurological problems. One of the features at autopsy is a smooth **cerebrum**, a structure which is normally very convoluted.

**lissoir:** spatulate polishing or rubbing **tool**, probably used for burnishing.

**Lister's tubercle:** tubercle located on the dorsal surface of the **radius**.

‡ **lithic:** pertaining to stone, as in **Paleolithic**, **Mesolithic**, etc. From the (Greek) prefix meaning stone, calculus.

**lithic materials:** varieties of stone from which **stone tools** are constructed; typical lithic materials include granite, **quartz**, **flint**, **chert**, **chalcedony**, siliceous **tuff**, and rhyolites.

**lithopedion:** rare (1/20,000) pathological condition involving the abnormal calcification of a fetus or fetal membranes. Often the result of an abdominal pregnancy. At least two such cases have been identified in the archaeological record. Aka 'stone children'.

**lithosphere:** top layer of the earth including the oceanic and continental crusts, about 70 km (40 miles) thick.

**lithostratigraphy:** system of organization and classification of rock **strata** utilizing their lithic characteristics.

**litter:** 1. set of several siblings born during one birth event; multiple births (including twins) are rare among anthropoid primates. See **polyembryony**, **parity**, and **multiparity**. 2. detritus of fallen leaves and bark that accumulates on **forest** floors.

**'Little Foot':** **australopithecine** found between 1994 and 1997 near the Silberberg Grotto at **Sterkfontein** in South Africa, which has several depositional Members dating from 3.3 mya. The lowest and earliest fossiliferous layer, Member 2, contained the foot bones of 'Little Foot', **Stw 573**. The rest of this individual, almost a complete skeleton, was recovered after 1997. Provisional dates range from 3.6 to 3.01 mya (**paleomagnetism**, **faunal correlation**, and sedimentation rates) or perhaps from 4.72 to 3.78 mya (**cosmogenic radionuclide dating**). Cf. **Jacovec Cavern**.

**littoral:** describes area or habitat adjacent to a shore, and often a preferred habitat of early **AMHs**.

**Liucheng:** paleontological site found in 1956 in a cave on Luntsai Mountain near Hsinshechung village, Liucheng County, Kwangsi Province, China, dated to *c.* 500 kya, and that contains primate remains including a mandible attributed to *Gigantopithecus*. The same expedition recovered other remains; see **Kwangsi**. Aka Gigantopithecus Cave.

**Liujiang:** see **Tongtianyan**.

‡ **live-born offspring:** see **viviparity**.

**living dead: extant** species whose numbers have fallen below the critical threshold needed to maintain genetic viability. See **Minimum Viable Population**. Cf. **moribund**.

‡ **living floor:** in archaeology, a surface characterized by a significant accumulation of **artifacts** associated with human occupation; these may include **tools**, hearths, burials, remains of prey, and other materials, e.g. **FLK-NN**. Aka living surface.

**living fossil:** term used almost exclusively by lay persons to indicate: 1. a living species with a morphology similar to that of fossils of great age; indicative of a successful adaptation to an ancient **niche**, and the maintenance via **natural selection** of conservative traits that permit the species to flourish in that environment. 2. any species thought to be extinct, but subsequently found to be extant. Cf. **subfossil**, **fossil**.

**living site, the:** see site **DK** at **Olduvai Gorge**.

**living surface:** applied to a perceived level of occupation within an archaeological site; see **living floor**.

**Livingstone, Frank B.** (1928–): US biological anthropologist; argued that standard or **historical racial groups** are arbitrary and that the taxonomic category **race** should not apply to **AMHs**, and that **human variation** is better explained by employment of the **cline** concept; by 1962 he was also able to show that the reconstruction of phylogenies was possible using **neontological** data exclusive of the fossil record (**paleontological** data).

**livres de beurre:** common name for the ubiquitous flint cores found in the soil of French farmers; literally, 'pounds of butter'.

**LLK:** abbreviation for Louis Leakey's **Korongo** at **Olduvai Gorge.**

**LO:** abbreviation for **Lomekwi locality.**

**load:** 1. quantity borne or sustained by an organism or part, e.g. **parasite load.** 2. deviation from normal of any body contents (water, salt, etc.): positive load is more than normal and negative load is less than normal. 3. the introduction of a defined quantity for some test purpose or to achieve a desired level. 4. see **genetic load.**

**lobe:** rounded projection or division of a body structure.

**local extinction:** condition in which a species that inhabited a particular area is no longer found there, although it still exists elsewhere.

**local hormone:** substance with hormone-like properties produced by body fluids at the location where it is required, and usually with a very short **half-life**(2).

**local mate competition:** condition in which brothers compete with each other for mates. Under these circumstances it is advantageous for a female to produce largely female offspring and only a few male offspring in order to maximize her genetic fitness. Cf. **local resource competition.**

**local molecular clocks:** observation that the rate of molecular change per unit of time appears to vary among classes of proteins and the genes that code for them, hence specific clock rates may exist within such classes, but that there is little support for a **global molecular clock.** See **molecular clock.**

**local optimum:** local fitness peak in an adaptive topography, but usually not the highest in the landscape being considered.

**local population:** synonym for **deme** and Mendelian population.

**local race:** population that is a member of a larger **geographical race** or group, but that has adapted to local conditions such that they can be distinguished from neighboring groups. Traditional examples of local races include the **Bushmen** of Sub-Saharan Africa, the Apache, **Arctic Inuit**, and other clusters within the Americas, and the Basques, **Alpines** and Southern Mediterraneans of Europe. Aka varieties. Cf. **geographical race** and **micro-race.**

**local rate:** behavioral index of **intensity**; the number of times a particular **behavior** is performed over a given period.

**local resource competition:** condition in which a mother and daughter(s) compete for resources in the mother's home range. This has been described for galagos, in which the daughters do not disperse far from their **natal** range. Thus, it is advantageous for a female to produce more male offspring than females (who will compete with her). Cf. **local mate competition.**

**local resource enhancement:** response to **intraspeci-**fic resource competition by increasing the population and retaining offspring in the **natal** group so they can help contribute to resource defense.

**locality:** geographical position; in the context of anthropology, a **site** occupied, or formerly occupied by people or primates, e.g. **Locality 1.**

**Locality 1 or 4 or 15:** see Zhoukoudian.

**loci:** plural of **locus.**

‡ **locomotion:** 1. movement from one place to another. 2. any of several means by which an organism navigates through a landscape. Common locomotor behaviors among **primates** include **bipedalism, knuckle-walking, quadrupedalism, brachiation grasp leaping**, and **vertical clinging and leaping.** See **striding gait.**

**locomotor behavior:** see **locomotion** (2).

**locomotor reconstruction:** extrapolation of the way an extinct species may have moved around in its environment. This is done through anatomical comparison with living species and through experimentation when there is no living counterpart to the anatomy of the species in question.

‡ **locus:** 1. in genetics, the physical location of a particular **gene** or **DNA sequence** on a **chromatid**; gene locus. 2. predicted archaeological site **locality.** Plural: loci.

**LOD score:** statistical measure of the likelihood that two or more genes are located together on the same chromosome. LOD stands for logarithm of the odds.

**loess:** fine windblown deposits of glacial dust, produced by the grinding of boulders carried along within glacial ice against bedrock; aka löss.

**log:** see **logarithm** and **logarithmic transformation.**

**logarithm:** exponent of the power to which a base number must be raised to equal a given number. There are two common bases used in biology: 10 and $e\,(=2.718282)$, called the common logarithm and the natural (or Naperian) logarithm, respectively. The common logarithm of the number 100 to the base 10 is 2 $(100 = 10^2)$; the natural logarithm of the number 100 to the base $e$ is 4.605 $(100 = 2.718282^{4.605})$. Aka log. Logarithms are used in biology to describe aspects of growth (**logistic growth**) or for **logarithmic transformation.**

**logarithm of the odds:** see **LOD score.**

**logarithmic transformation:** procedure in which arithmetic data is converted into **logarithms**, e.g. for the purpose of reducing skewness. See **transformation.**

**logical positivism:** twentieth century extension of **positivism** that originated with the membership of the Vienna circle, and whose central tenet is the **verifiability principle.**

**logistic growth:** growth, especially in the numbers of organisms constituting a population, that slows steadily as the entity reaches its maximum size. Cf. **exponential growth**.

**logistic growth curve:** growth in a population that follows a sigmoid, or S-shaped, **growth curve** in which growth is initially slow (the lag phase) followed by a period of rapid growth (an **exponential growth phase**) and then levels off (the stationary growth phase) when the population reaches the **carrying capacity** of the environment. The logistic growth curve assumes that there is a limit to the maximum size of a population.

**Lokalalei 1:** archaeological site found in 1991 in West **Lake Turkana**, Kenya, dated to 2.34 mya (Nachukui formation), and that contains choppers and animal remains.

**Lokalalei 2C:** archaeological site found in 1997 in West **Lake Turkana**, Kenya, dated to 2.34 mya (Nachukui formation), and that contains choppers and animal remains. Some 3000 individual specimens made possible the refitting of some 60 sets of stone artifacts. According to researchers, the **core** reduction sequences could be reconstructed, which led to the conclusion that the early **hominids** responsible had a greater cognitive capacity and motor skill than previously assumed.

**Lokochot tuff:** Pleistocene volcanic deposit at Koobi Fora, **Lake Turkana**, dated by **K/Ar** to >3.3 mya.

**Lombardy leprosy:** see **pellagra**.

**Lombroso, Cesare** (1836–1909): Italian criminologist at Turin; founder of the continental 'criminal anthropology' movement of the late nineteenth century, now discredited, according to which criminals were either situational criminals (forced by poverty, and so forth), or 'born criminals'. This latter group, alleged Lombroso, could be identified by certain stigmata, atavistic anomalies (see **atavism**) usually found in 'primitive men and inferior animals' but could be 'reproduced in our times' in born criminals. Lombroso is important to the history of physical anthropology because of his extreme typological thinking.

**Lomekwi localities:** archaeological sites found *c.* 1982 in the Lomekwi drainage near West **Lake Turkana**, Kenya, dated to the middle **Pliocene** epoch (3.5–2.5 mya), containing hominid remains including a skull of *Paranthropus aethiopicus*

(**KNM-WT 17000**) and *Kenyanthropus platyops* (**KMN-WT 40000**). Other mammalian fossils found in association suggest that the region consisted of a mosaic of grassland and wooded habitats. As of 2003, fragments of more than ten hominids had been excavated. See box below.

**long bone:** one of the four types of bones as classified by their shape: a bone longer than it is wide with a shaft (**diaphysis**) and two ends (**epiphyses**), composed principally of **compact bone** covered with **periosteum**, but with **cancellous bone** and **red marrow** inside the epiphyses. Many of the bones of the **appendicular skeleton** are long bones, such as the femur, humerus, and phalanges. Long bones undergo **endochondral ossification**. Cf. **flat bone**, **short bone**, and **irregular bone**.

**long childhood:** vernacular phrase that refers to the extended developmental period of **hominids** relative to that of other primates. See **neoteny**.

**long-haired spider monkey:** vernacular for *Ateles belzebuth*.

**long interspersed nucleotide element** (LINE): one of the nonviral type **retroposons** found dispersed throughout eukaryotic genomes, such as Kpn I in primates; see **LINE sequence**. Cf. **short interspersed nucleotide element**.

**long journey hypothesis:** argument to explain the one million year fossil gap between the **Dmanisi** *Homo ergaster* population living in the Republic of Georgia from 1.7 mya and later humans in Spain at 780 kya. The long journey posits that humans left Africa around 2 mya, but were prevented from entering western Europe due to climate; consequently, they traveled east, reaching China by 1.9 mya and Indonesia by 1.8 mya. Subsequent migrations from Africa turned north and west when climate permitted.

**long-range restriction map:** map of cutting sites of **restriction enzymes** over a large region of **DNA**.

**long-term memory:** see **memory**.

**longevity:** refers to the achievement of long life and to the average **life span** characteristic of the individuals in a population or species under specific environmental constraints. Much evidence suggests that some portion of the variance of life span is inherited. Studies of adoptees, twin studies, and research with other mammals all suggest that complex organisms,

---

**Lomekwi localities**

LO-1: site where Alan **Walker** found the black skull, *Paranthropus aethiopicus*, in 1985.

LO-5: site where the specimen **KNM-WT 38350**, the paratype of *Kenyanthropus platyops*, was found in 1998.

LO-6N: type locality for fossil hominids found during 1982–99. The specimens include a fragmentary cranium, **KNM-WT 40000**, which was situated between the upper bound Tulu Bor and the lower bound Lokochot Tuffs, providing an estimated date of 3.5 mya. The fossil specimens have been attributed to *Kenyanthropus platyops*.

including humans, inherit a tendency for a species-wide fixed longevity. There has been recent interest by gerontologists in certain maternally transmitted genes, especially the *TERC* locus (telomerase RNA component). There apparently are no long-lived human groups, i.e. populations with a notably high proportion of centenarians. Three candidate populations — the Abkhazians and Ossetian people of Russian Georgia, the people of Vilcabamba in southern Ecuador, and the Hunza of Pakistan — have all been accounted for by age exaggeration, record alteration, or unusual demographic phenomena. See **progeria**.

**Longgupo:** archaeological site found in 1995 near Wanxian in Wushan County, Sichuan Province, China, dated to 1.9–1.8 mya, and that contains both chopper-like artifacts and hominid remains from one individual (fragment of a left mandible) attributed to the genus *Homo*, and compared to *H. ergaster* and *H. habilis* from Africa. Aka 'Dragon Hill', Wanzian, Wushan.

**Longgushan Cave:** archaeological site in Yunxian County, Hubei Province, China, dating to *c.* 550 kya and containing hominid remains including five assorted teeth attributed to *Homo erectus*. Aka Yunxian.

**longitudinal cerebral fissure:** separation between the two **cerebral hemispheres** of the **cerebrum**. See **corpus callosum**.

**longitudinal research (or study):** measurements on one individual repeated at regular intervals throughout his or her life, as in a longitudinal growth study. Cf. **cross-sectional research**.

**long-QT syndrome** (LQT): congenital, heritable condition predisposing affected individuals to heart arrhythmia, fainting, and sudden cardiac arrest in the presence of loud sounds or during exercise. Defective potassium channels result in the accumulation of potassium in the heart and inner ears, resulting in heart defects and deafness. The mutant autosomal dominant gene in LQT is *KCNQ1*. One of the **ion channel diseases**. Exhibits evidence for **genomic imprinting**. LQT has also been investigated in some **SIDS** cases. Aka Romano–Ward syndrome; includes a variant known as the Jervell and Lange-Nielson syndrome.

**long-sightedness:** see **presbyopia** (2).

**Longtandong Cave:** archaeological site found in 1980 in Wangjiashan Hill, Hexian County, Anhui Province, China, dated to 412 ± 25 kya (oxygen isotope stages 12-11), and that contains worked bones and horns. Hominid remains include a 1025 cm³ cranium and other remains of at least four individuals attributed to *Homo erectus*. The dentition is large compared to **Zhoukoudian** Locality 1, skull V. AKA Dragon Pool Cave, Lontandong, Hexian (Ho-hsien), Anhui.

**Lonnberg's tamarin:** one of the vernaculars for *Saguinus mystax*.

**Lonyumun tuff:** Pleistocene volcanic deposit at Koobi Fora, Lake Turkana, dated by **K/Ar** to 4.4–4.1 **mya**.

**lookup table:** $4 \times 4 \times 4$ schematic representing the **genetic code** by which mRNA **codons** are translated into the corresponding **amino acids**. Generally, the code for nuclear DNA is universal, and the table used by mitochondria differs slightly.

**loop:** principal **dermatoglyphic** pattern in which the ridges of fingerprints swirl around one head and toward the margin. See **ulnar loop** and **radial loop**.

**loph:** pair of cusps on upper cheek teeth joined by a crest or ridge. Cf. **lophid**.

**lophid:** pair of cusps on lower teeth joined by a crest or ridge. Cf. **loph**.

*Lophocebus* ( = *Cercocebus*) Palmer, 1908: cercopithecine genus to which the black mangabeys belong; two species, five subspecies. Found in the band of tropical rain forest that goes across equatorial Africa. Highly arboreal; diurnal; arboreal quadrupeds. Body mass ranges from 6 to 10 kg; slight **sexual dimorphism**. Dental formula: 2.1.2.3; **frugivorous**; possesses **cheek pouches** for storing food. A **throat sac** is present (larger in males than in females) that serves as a resonator for calls. **One-male units** appear to be the main social organization. Previously the species in this genus were included with *Cercocebus*. See Appendix 2 for taxonomy, Appendix 3 for living species.

**lordosis:** ventrally convex curvature of the back, usually in the lumbar region.

**Loridae:** see **Lorisidae**.

**Loriformes:** see **Lorisiformes**.

**loris:** general vernacular for nocturnal **prosimians** belonging to the genera *Loris* and *Nycticebus*; these primates are found in Asia.

*Loris tardigradus* (Linnaeus, 1758): slender loris; six **subspecies** recognized; currently a monotypic genus, it has been suggested that more than one species may actually be included in *L. tardigradus*. This **prosimian** is found in understory of woodlands and the canopy of forests in southern India and most of Sri Lanka. Arboreal; nocturnal; slow methodical climbers; tail is a short stump. The second digit is reduced and possesses a grooming claw, and the **pollex** is 180° from digit 3, providing for a powerful vice-like grip that can be held for long periods; circulatory adaptations in the paws provide an ample oxygen supply that prevents lactic acid build-up in the muscles. Body mass from 250 to 300 g. Dental formula: 2.1.3.3; lower incisors and canines form a **dental comb**; upper anterior dentition is peg-like and short; **insectivorous**. Scent marks through **urine washing**. Probably **noyau**, but male–female pairs have been observed (although these may be temporary mating bonds). Aka *Loris gracilis*. See Appendix 2 for taxonomy, Appendix 3 for living species.

**Lorisidae (= Loridae): prosimian** family to which the lorises and pottos belong, consisting of four genera and five species. Vernacular: lorisid (lorid). See Appendix 2 for taxonomy, Appendix 3 for living species.

**Lorisiformes (= Loriformes):** infraorder of the suborder **Prosimii**; no longer widely recognized; includes the African and Asian prosimians. Vernacular: lorisiform (loriform). See Appendix 2 for taxonomy, Appendix 3 for living species.

‡ **Lorisoidea (= Loroidea):** superfamily of the **prosimian** infraorder **Lemuriformes (= Loriformes)** that consists of the families **Lorisidae (= Loridae)** and **Galagidae (= Galagonidae)**. Vernacular: lorisoid (loroid). See Appendix 2 for taxonomy, Appendix 3 for living species.

**Loroidea:** see **Lorisoidea.**

**Los Cedros Biological Reserve:** cloud forest in western Ecuador established by conservation biologists from the Rainforest Information Center in the 1990s. Three primate species are present: ***Cebus*** *capuchinus*, ***Ateles*** *belzebuth*, and ***Alouatta*** *palliata*.

**loss-of-function mutation:** any mutation that incapacitates a gene so that no functional product is produced; a **knockout** or nullifying mutation. In the strictest sense, a **missense mutation** or **nonsense mutation** only, but some use the term **forward mutation**, $\mu$, synonymously.

**loss of heterozygosity** (LOH): 1. the loss of one of a pair of homologous **chromatids**, resulting in aneuploidy ($2N = 45$) and hemizygosity for the chromatid. 2. the spontaneous, apparent **conversion** of all of the loci on an entire chromatid to the identity of the opposite homologous allele, resulting in homozygosity at every locus; this is thought to be due to **trisomy** followed by the loss of the uniparental isochromatid (see **disomy**). 3. the apparent conversion of a single locus or small region of a chromatid by methylation and **parental imprinting**. Loss of heterozygosity is a feature of several forms of **cancer.**

**'lost twin' syndrome:** see **vanishing twin phenomenon.**

‡ **Lothagam:** archaeological site found in 1967 by Bryan Patterson south of Lake Rudolf in Kenya, dated to 5.6–5.5 mya, and that contains hominid remains, including a single hemimandibular fragment (KNM-LT/ER 329) the attribution of which is *incertae sedis*, but possibly *Australopithecus* cf. *afarensis*; others have assigned hominoid status to this specimen.

**lottery hypothesis:** proposal to explain why sexual reproduction and the diversity of **genotypes** it produces is advantageous; this is similar to a lottery in that it is advantageous to select a diverse series of numbers rather than a great quantity of the same number. According to this hypothesis the environment serves as a lottery because it changes and favors diversity over homogeneity.

***Loveina*** **Simpson, 1940:** genus of tarsiiform primate from the early Eocene of North America, belonging to the omomyid subfamily **Anaptomorphinae**; three species. Estimated body mass between 100 and 175 g. Dental formula: 2.1.3.3/2.1.3.3; incisors and canines small; dental morphology suggestive of **frugivory** with insect supplements. See Appendix 1 for taxonomy.

**Lovejoy, C. Owen:** functional anatomist at Kent State University, Director of the Matthew Ferrini Institute for Human Evolutionary Research. Best known for his work regarding australopithecine locomotion; also published in forensic anthropology and paleontology. Author of a well-known article 'The origin of man' (*Science*, 211: 341, 1981); see the '**provisioning monogamist' hypothesis.**

**low birth weight:** mass at birth of 2500 g (5.5 lb) or less for a neonate of normal gestation length (38 weeks).

**low-crowned molar: molar** in which the crown of the tooth is close to the gum line.

**low-density lipoproteins:** see **LDLs.**

**low-level dental impaction:** condition in which a tooth is placed at an angle low in the alveolus and in contact with an adjacent tooth as to be incapable of complete eruption. See **dental impaction.**

**low-quality diet:** food source that is difficult to digest and contains few calories and other nutrients for the energetic expense of digesting it; low-quality diets often have high insoluble fiber content. Cf. **high-quality diet.**

**Lower Acheulean:** cultural substage of the **Acheulean tool tradition** in which lithic implements termed **proto-handaxes**, picks, and cleavers are found, primarily in African sites.

**lower arm length:** dimension of the body obtained while a subject is in a standing position, arm hanging naturally and with the palm facing the body: the distance from the stylion to the radiale.

**lower critical temperature:** ambient temperature threshold at which an animal must increase heat production if normal **body temperature** is to be maintained. Cf. **normal human body temperature.**

**lower leg bones:** see **tibia** and **fibula.**

**lower leg length:** dimension of the body obtained while a subject is in a standing position: the sphyrion height subtracted from the tibiale height.

**lower leg–foot index:** length of the foot × 100, divided by the length of the lower **leg.**

**lower limb:** term in human and ape anatomy for the inferior appendage, i.e. the **pelvic girdle**, thigh, **leg**, and tarsals, metatarsals, and phalanges; the lower limb corresponds to the hindleg of quadrupeds. See **hindlimb**.

**Lower Omo Valley:** see **Omo Valley, Omo Kibish**.

**Lower Paleolithic** (LP): Lower **Old Stone Age**; general term used to refer collectively to the stone tool technologies of **habilines** and **erectines**; existed roughly 2.5 mya to 70 kya. See **Abbevillian, Oldowan, Developed Oldowan**, and **Acheulean**.

‡ **Lower Pleistocene:** subdivision of the **Pleistocene epoch** from 1.6 mya to 900 kya.

**lower primate:** lemurs, lorises and tarsiers; members of the **Prosimii**.

**lowland evergreen rain forest:** tropical rain **forest** below 1000 m elevation and characterized by trees that reach heights of 35–50 m. These forests receive at least 140 cm of rain a year, but there are usually wet and dry seasons (less rain) and considerable biological diversity. This is a major **biome** for primates.

**luciferase:** enzyme that catalyzes the conversion of luciferin to oxyluciferin, a reaction that produces bioluminescence in the firefly. Used extensively in **biotechnology** as a reporter assay to confirm **recombination**. See **green fluorescent protein gene**.

‡ **'Lucy':** sobriquet for **NME AL-288-1**, a female *Australopithecus afarensis* skeleton recovered from the **Afar triangle** of Ethiopia in 1974. Forty percent of 'Lucy' was recovered, including the lower limbs, which indicated some form of **bipedalism**. Her stature was estimated at 117 cm (3'10"), mass 28 kg (62 lb). At the time of discovery, this specimen radically changed the current view of **hominid evolution**. Combined with the new molecular data, the discovery decreased the estimate of time elapsed since the African ape/hominid split, previously thought to have occurred around 15 mya; 'Lucy' now dates from around 3.6 to 2.9 mya, yet shows a number of **primitive traits**, particularly in the wrist, rib cage, **skull**, and **dentition**. Cf. the *Ramapithecus-as-first-hominid* debate.

**'Lucy's Child':** sobriquet applied to specimen **OH 62** by supporters of the perspective that *Australopithecus afarensis* is the ancestor of *Homo habilis* and, thus, of all later humans. According to this argument, **OH 62** is *H. habilis* when the skull is analyzed, but the postcrania show strong evidence of a link to *A. afarensis* (the species to which **Lucy** is attributed).

*ludus naturae:* Latin for 'joke of nature', and often applied to early art in which a stone that had a perceived resemblance to some object, was touched up to enhance the resemblance. Cf. *lusus naturae*.

**Ludwig's theorem:** proposal that new genotypes will survive in a population if they can occupy a new sub-niche by utilizing new components in the environment, even when they have a lowered fitness in the original niche.

*Lufengpithecus lufengensis* Wu, 1987: monotypic genus of **hominoid** from the late Miocene of China, belonging to the subfamily **Dryopithecinae**. Known from dentition and several skulls. Estimated body mass around 50 kg with extreme **sexual dimorphism** (greater than in any **extant** ape). Dental formula: 2.1.2.3; thin enamel cap on cheek teeth links it with *Dryopithecus* and suggests a **frugivorous** diet. Synonyms: *Sivapithecus yunnanesis, Ramapithecus lufengensis*. See Appendix 1 for taxonomy.

**Lukeino:** archaeological site found in 1975 in the Lake **Baringo** region of Kenya, dated to 6.5 mya; the Lukeino tooth (KNM-LU 335) is attributed to the family **Hominidae**. One of the few specimens from the gap in the hominid fossil record.

**Lukeino Formation:** sedimentary unit in the Lake **Baringo** region of Kenya, dated to 6.5–5.5 mya. Paleoenvironment suggests a large freshwater lake.

‡ **lumbar:** pertaining to the loin; the region of the back between the thorax and the pelvis.

**lumbar curvature:** convex anterior (secondary) curvature of the vertebral column corresponding to the region of the **lumbar vertebrae**; one of the four curvatures of the **vertebral column** that helps distribute the body's weight over the center of gravity and provides resiliency.

**lumbar vertebra:** any one of the five vertebrae of the lower back that are larger and support more weight than the superior vertebrae in humans; the vertebrae of the loin.

**lumper:** one who combines things into simple, highly variable categories; in taxonomy, one who creates taxa that include variable morphs that might, to a **splitter**, be better allotted to several taxa.

**lunar:** pertaining to any structure that has a crescent or moonlike shape.

**lunate:** bone of the **carpus** located in the proximal row of carpals, articulating with the **radius** to help form the wrist joint and with the **scaphoid, triquetral, capitate**, and **hamate**; aka semilunar, os lunatum.

**lunate sulcus:** crescent-shaped groove that approximates the anterior boundary of the **visual cortex** in **anthropoids**. The lunate sulcus is located farther back in human than in nonhuman primate brains, presumably because of the expansion of the parietal **association cortex** in front of the lunate **sulcus**.

*Lushius qinlinensis* Chow, 1961: adapoid **prosimian** from the late Eocene of China; **monotypic**; phylogenetic relationship uncertain and placed in a family *incertae sedis*; known only from a maxillary fragment containing two teeth. Estimated body mass around 3 kg. Dental formula unknown. See Appendix 1 for taxonomy.

*lusus naturae*: Latin for 'sport of nature'; said of any suddenly appearing (**saltational**) variant in nature (see **monster**); the term '**sport**' was also applied to any saltational variant well into the twentieth century. Aka freak of nature. Cf. *ludus naturae*.

**luteal hormone**: substance secreted by the **corpus luteum**; see **progesterone**.

**luteinizing hormone** (LH): 1. glycoprotein gonadotropic substance secreted by the anterior **pituitary gland**; acts with **follicle-stimulating hormone** to promote ovulation as well as secretion of **androgens** and **progesterone**. LH instigates and maintains the **secretory phase** of the mammalian estrus and menstrual cycles. In females, it is concerned with formation of the **corpus luteum** and in males, it stimulates the development and functional activity of testicular Leydig cells to secrete **testosterone** and stimulates the interstitial cells of the testis, resulting in **spermatogenesis**. Aka Aschheim-Zondek hormone, interstitial cell-stimulating hormone (ICSH), luteotropin, lactogenic hormone. See **gonadotropin-releasing hormone**. 2. a recombinant (genetically engineered) gene product of the same name.

**luteotropic hormone**: see **prolactin**.

**Lutheran blood group**: antigens coded for by the **Lutheran gene** on HSA 19.

**Lutheran gene**: locus that determines the presence or absence of the Lutheran antigen on red blood cells; a human polymorphism. Aka *Lu* gene.

**Lutong leaf monkey**: vernacular for *Trachypithecus auratus*.

‡ **Lyell, Charles** (1797–1875): English barrister and geologist, and author of *The Principles of Geology* (1830–3), which Henslow advised **Darwin** to read during his *Beagle* voyage 'but on no account to believe' because of Lyell's caution over the possibility of **evolution**. Among the principles redefined by Lyell was **uniformitarianism**, a form of geological **gradualism**. Lyell was later a close friend and supporter of **Darwin**, finally conceding the possibility of **human evolution** in his book *Geological Evidence of the Antiquity of Man* (1863).

**Lyellian curves**: plots of percentages of fossil fauna that are still extant.

**Lyme disease**: infection caused by a **spirochete** (*Borrelia burgdorferi*) and **vectored** by a minute tick (*Ixodes dammini* or *I. pacificus*); endemic in North America and possibly Europe. Adult ticks feed on deer, but nymph forms feed on deer mice (*Peromyscus maniculatus*), which are the immediate cause of transmission to humans. Three progressive stages: 'bull's eye' rash (*erythema chronicum migrans*, or ECM), facial palsy, and migrating arthritis. Aka Lyme borreliosis.

**lymph**: clear or slightly yellow, plasmalike fluid that flows through lymphatic vessels and is derived from tissue fluids. Lymph is occasionally of a light rose color from the presence of red blood corpuscles and is often opalescent from particles of fat (chyle). Another primary constituent of lymph is white blood cells, especially **lymphocytes**. Lymph is collected from all parts of the body and returned to the blood via the **lymphatic drainage** system.

**lymph node**: aggregation of soft lymphatic tissue surrounded by a fibrous capsule; nodes are located throughout the body along the course of the **lymphatic drainage** network, with some concentrations such as in the **axillary** region. Lymph nodes produce immune cells and filter the noxious elements collected in **lymph** while resident **lymphocytes** and **macrophages** respond to filtered foreign particles. When bacteria are recognized in the lymph fluid, the lymph nodes enlarge as they produce additional white blood cells to help fight infection. Aka lymph gland.

**lymphatic drainage**: special subsystem of the **lymphatic system** that transports lymph and certain fats; the lymphatics communicate with the venous system at the juncture of the jugular and subclavian veins.

**lymphatic system**: a network of organs, lymph vessels, lymph nodes, and lymph ducts that produce and transport **lymph** from tissues to the bloodstream. The **lymphatic drainage** subsystem is a major component of the body's **immune system**. The organs within the lymphatic system are the **spleen, tonsils**, and **thymus**. See **peripheral lymphoid organs**.

‡ **lymphocytes**: diverse group of agranular white blood cells that are active components of the immune system, e.g. **B cells** and **T cells**. Such cells function to either identify or eliminate foreign antigenic substances, thus providing immunity. Constitute 20–30% of all leukocytes and are a principal component of **lymph**.

‡ **lymphokine**: any of a class of glycoproteins that function as chemical signals, allowing communication between cells of the immune system. Lymphokines play a role in **cell-mediated immunity** and the inflammation response.

**lymphoma**: cancer of the lymph nodes; see **Hodgkin disease**.

‡ **lymphotoxin**: general term for any of the substances secreted by **cytotoxic T cells**; more commonly referred to as **cytokines** or **lymphokines**. See **interleukin**.

**Lyon hypothesis**: 1960 proposal by Mary Lyon that **dosage compensation** in female mammals is accomplished by the random inactivation of all but one of the **X chromosomes**. In a normal XX female, one X chromosome would thus be inactivated. See female mosaicism for **X**, **X inactivation**, and **Barr body.** Aka Lyonization.

**lyse:** dissolve or disrupt, as in the decomposition of a cell, or the loosening of an organ from adhesions. Noun: lysis.

**Lysenkoism:** application of the political Marxist doctrine of individual improvement through training and environment to plant breeding by Russian geneticist Trofim D. Lysenko (1898–1976), who believed that characteristics acquired during life could be passed on to offspring. Lysenkoism was the antithesis of the gene concept and **Mendelism;** the consistent failure of the Russian wheat program and the success of the American program led to the eventual abandonment of what was essentially a form of neo-Lamarckism. See **neo-Lamarckian inheritance** and **Baldwin effect.**

**lysine** (Lys): an essential **amino acid;** one of the twenty building blocks of **proteins.** Produced by the hydrolysis of casein (milk protein).

**lysosomal storage disease:** any clinical disorder due to absence of activity of a specific lysosomal enzyme, leading to a build-up of proteins and/or carbohydrates in **lysosomes.** See, for example, **Tay–Sachs disease, glycogen storage diseases**, and **Gaucher disease.**

**lysosome:** spherical cellular membranous organelle that contains digestive enzymes; found in eukaryotic cells.

‡ **lysozyme:** antibacterial enzyme naturally present in human tear fluid, sweat, saliva, and nasal secretions; lysozymes digest mucopolysaccharides and have a bacteriolytic action. Aka mucopeptide glucohydrolase.

**+ 3 molar pattern**, etc.: See **plus 3 molar pattern**, etc.

**μ**: in statistics, the parametric **mean** of a population.

**M.** or **M**: abbreviation for 1. medicine. 2. maxillary **molar.**, as in **M1**. 3. Monday. 4. mountain. 5. The primate genus *Macaca*.

**m.** or **m**: abbreviation for 1. the SI unit, meter. 2. mass. 3. mile. 4. minute (also ″). 4. male or masculine. 5. mandibular **molar**, as in m1 (see **M1**). 6. mill-, milli- (million), as in **mya**. 7. medium or middle.

**M1, M2, M3**, etc.: notation that makes reference to **molar** teeth in which the most anterior tooth is the lowest number and the most posterior tooth is the highest number. The notation is either lower case (indicating a **mandibular** tooth; m1, m2, m3) or upper case (indicating a **maxillary** tooth; M1, M2, M3). There are two ways this system of numbering is used. 1. in reference to retention or absence of a tooth from the primitive **eutherian** set of teeth, the **dental formula** of which is: 3.1.4.3/3.1.4.3. Molars may have been lost, in which case the existing teeth may have molars designated by a number larger than the actual number of teeth if the first molar has been lost; thus the molars would be designated as M2 and M3; the primate trend has been not to lose molars with the exception of the **callitrichids** (Family **Callitrichidae**), which have lost the third molar. 2. in reference to the teeth that are present in an existing species. The anterior molar is numbered M1, regardless of the ancestral condition.

**M3 distal accessory cusp**: extension of enamel on the posterior surface of the back molar present in *Australopithecus africanus*, *Paranthropus*, and early species of *Homo*.

**ma**: see **mya**.

**Maba**: archaeological site found in 1958 near Maba village in Qujiang County, Guangdong Province, China, dated to about 140–120 kya; contains hominid remains, including the **calotte** with modest keel of a middle-aged male, attributed to **archaic *Homo sapiens*** 'of mongoloid type'. Aka Mapa (Shaoquan, Kwangtung), Shiziyan Hill.

**Mabaget**: archaeological site found in 1965 near west Lake **Baringo** in the **Tugen Hills**, Kenya, dated to 5.1–4.0 mya, and that contains **hominoid** remains, including one subadult humeral fragment (KNM-BC 1745), genus and *sp. indet.*, but referred to **Hominidae** Cf. *Australopithecus afarensis*. Aka Chemeron formation.

**Maboko Island**: paleontological site found in 1933 in Kenya, dated to 16–15 mya (middle **Miocene**), and that contains primate remains, including *Victoriapithecus*, *Proconsul*, *Dendropithecus* and *Kenyapithecus*.

*Mabokopithecus clarki* **von Koenigswald, 1969**: poorly known **hominoid** from the middle **Miocene** of East Africa; known only from teeth and a mandible. This primate was described as an oreopithecid, but it has been questioned whether the type specimen is even a primate. Estimated body mass 10 kg. Dental formula: 2.1.2.3. See Appendix 1 for taxonomy.

*Macaca* (= *Cynopithecus*) **Lacepede, 1799**: catarrhine genus to which the macaques belong. Contains 12–19 species depending on source; sometimes separated into four species groups (see box below) based on reproductive morphology. Most geographically widespread primate group except for humans; mainly Asian, but with one species in North Africa. Occupy a wide variety of habitats ranging from semi-desert to temperate montane forest. All species are arboreal and terrestrial, although they differ in the amount of time they spend in either environment; diurnal; quadrupedal. Range in body size from 2.5 to 15 kg; **sexually dimorphic** in body and canine size. Dental formula: 2.1.2.3; **frugivorous**; possess **cheek pouches** for food storage. **Ischial callosities** well developed. Live in mixed-sex troops, which undergo **fission** into smaller foraging units during the day; females are the **resident sex** and there are two to four more females than males in groups. The troop can be as small as 8 or number over 700 individuals. See Appendix 2 for taxonomy, Appendix 3 for living species.

---

### Species groups within the genus *Macaca*

*Macaca arctoides* group: one of the four clusters of *Macaca* species that are grouped according to the anatomy of male and female genitalia; presumably the members of each group share a derived condition and common ancestry; *M. arctoides* is the only member of this group.

*Macaca fascicularis* group: consists of four species, *M. fascicularis, M. mulatta, M. cyclopis*, and *M. fuscata*.

*Macaca sinica* group: consists of four species, *M. sinica, M. assamensis, M. radiata*, and *M. thibetana*.

*Macaca sylvanus* group: consists of seven species, *M. sylvanus, M. silenus, M. nemestrina, M. brunnescens, M. ochreata, M. nigra*, and *M. tonkeana*. (*M. brunnescens, M. ochreata*, and *M. tonkeana* are included within *M. nigra* by many workers).

‡ **macaque:** cercopithecine monkey belonging to the genus *Macaca;* most widespread and successful (at least 16 species) group of monkeys.

**macaroni style:** motif of cave decoration found at Pech Merle in France and Spain during the Mesolithic and Neolithic in which figures are represented schematically by lines that look like pieces of macaroni.

**Machiavellian hypothesis:** any testable proposal that suggests that proximate, apparently cooperative or altruistic acts are ultimately selfish.

**Machiavellian intelligence:** in primate behavior, the apparent strategy of tactical deception in order to advance the fitness of the deceiver. See **deceit**.

**macrocephaly:** possession of an abnormally large head, without the bulging or other distortion characteristic of hydrocephaly.

**macrocheilia:** having large, fleshy and everted lips.

**macrocormic:** in reference to the **cormic index**, having an index of 53.00 or greater; such an individual has long limbs in relation to trunk size. The most macrocormic human populations are found in Africa. See **metriocormic, brachycormic**.

**macrocranium, macrocrania:** pathological condition characterized by enlargement of the bones surrounding the brain case presenting a relatively small face, as in **hydrocephalus**.

**macrocyte:** **erythrocyte** with diameter at least 2 μm larger than normal, commonly found in individuals diagnosed with anemia.

**macrodiacritic:** pertaining to a condition where 90% or more of the members of a taxon are recognizable as such; usually applied to variation below the species level. Cf. **pandiacritic, microdiacritic, mesodiacritic**.

**macrodont:** see **megadont**.

**macrodontia:** see **megadontism**.

‡ **macroevolution:** 1. genetic change sufficient to form new species. 2. evolution on a scale above the species level. 3. a large amount of change or a significant number of evolutionary steps, which may, however, consist of only minor alterations in **allele frequencies, chromosome structure**, or **chromosome numbers**, but with large phenotypic effects. 4. (of proteins) process of major, rapid evolutionary change in which new adaptive functions are brought about by intense selective pressure. Aka one-step speciation, **saltation**. Cf. **microevolution**.

**macrogenesis:** proposal that new types of organisms originate by the sudden origin of a single new individual, which then becomes the progenitor of a new line of organisms.

**macrognathia:** pathological condition in which the jaw is elongated.

*Macromerus typicus* **(Smith, 1833):** synonym for *Propithecus* diadema.

**macromolecule:** any molecule composed of several simpler units; examples of macromolecules include proteins, nucleic acids, polysaccharides, glycoproteins, and glycolipids.

**macromutation:** mutation associated with extensive phenotypic changes, such that which produces **Down syndrome**. Most often a **chromosome mutation**, although recently certain **point mutations** that cause multiple phenotypic changes have been addressed as macromutations, i.e. **homeotic mutations**.

**macronucleus:** 1. nucleus that occupies a large area of the cell. 2. larger, nonreproductive nucleus in ciliated protozoa.

**macronutrient:** nutrient that can be used for energy production. Carbohydrate is the primary macronutrient; lipids and protein are secondary macronutrients that can enter the **citric acid cycle** when insufficient carbohydrates are available. Cf. **micronutrient**.

**macroparasite:** parasite that is relatively large, with a generation time longer than that of **microparasites**, and does not reproduce within the host.

**macropathology:** disease process or trauma that is detectable by simple visual examination. Bruises and broken bones are examples of macropathology. Cf. **micropathology**.

‡ **macrophage:** 1. large phagocytic cell derived from a monocytic blood cell; part of the reticuloendothelial system; not a **leukocyte**. Wandering macrophages function in removing debris and another important function is the breakdown of aging red blood cells; see **cellular immune response**. 2. another name for **macrocyte**.

**macroscopic:** pertaining to an object that is large enough to be seen with the unaided eye; gross.

**macroskelia:** in reference to **Manouvrier's index**, having an index of 90.00 or greater; such an individual has long limbs in relation to trunk size. See **mesatyskelia, brachyskelia**. Cf. **macrocormic**.

**macrosomatic animal:** mammal with a well developed sense of smell. Among the primates this applies to the **prosimians**.

**macrospecies:** large, polymorphic species; Linnaean species.

**macrosplanchnic type:** body type characterized by extreme **obesity**; one of the biotype variables of Viola, an Italian Classical biotypologist. Aka megalosplanchnic type.

*Macrotarsius* **Clark, 1941:** genus of tarsiiform primate from the late Eocene and early Oligocene of North America, belonging to the subfamily **Omomyinae**; five species. Estimated body mass between 1.5 and 2.5 kg; largest member of the subfamily. Dental formula: 2.1.3.3/2.1.3.3; molars notable for shearing crests and similarity to the molars of *Alouatta,* suggesting a **folivorous** diet. See Appendix 1 for taxonomy.

**macrotaxonomy:** term used by E. **Mayr** to denote the subfield of **taxonomy** whose subject is the methodology and principles of classifying organisms into categories (**taxa**) higher than the species level. Cf. **microtaxonomy.**

**macula:** designation for a stain or spot, especially on the retina or skin; see **Mongolian spot.**

**macula lutea:** concentration of **cones** that forms a yellow depression in the **retina** of the eye. It contains the fovea retinalis, the area of maximum visual acuity. Aka macular area, macula retinae, macula lutea retinae.

**mad cow disease:** see **bovine spongiform encephalitis.**

**'Madame X':** see **haplotype X.**

**Madelung deformity:** congenital condition in which there is disproportionate growth between the **radius** and the **ulna.**

‡ **Magdalenian tool tradition:** final stage of the **Upper Paleolithic** stone tool **assemblage** series dating from around 18–12 kya; named for the **La Madeleine** rockshelter on the Vézère River, France. It is characterized by the use of long and thin blades, delicate ivory carving, composite instruments such as the harpoon and atlatl, polychrome paintings, and engraving with both geometric and representational motifs. Aka Reindeer Age. See **Chancelade.**

**'magic numbers':** so-called equilibrium numbers proposed by J. B. **Birdsell** and others that foraging bands of hunter-gatherers average about 25 individuals, and the 'dialectic tribe' about 500.

**magma:** 1. molten rock. 2. a paste or salve.

**magnetic field:** force surrounding a magnet or other polarized body, such as the earth, which has a field approximately aligned with its axis of rotation that has reversed several times during the earth's history. Cf. **paleomagnetic reversals.** See **paleomagnetism.**

**magnetic resonance imaging** (MRI): technique used for discerning internal structures of a living individual. MRI is accomplished through the use of a chamber lined with magnets and possessing a radio antenna. The subject receives an injection of a dye (which provides for contrast between the different tissue structures); this is followed by placing the subject in the MRI chamber and generating a magnetic field. This action causes hydrogen atoms to release weak radio waves, received and amplified by the antenna, and computer software processes the data and provides an image of the brain. Aka functional magnetic resonance imaging (fMRI).

**magnetic reversals:** see **paleomagnetic reversals** and **paleomagnetism.**

**magnetostratigraphy:** arrangement of geological strata based upon their residual magnetism compared to the **world geomagnetic polarity column.** See **paleomagnetism.**

**magnum (of the carpus):** see **capitate.**

**Magosian:** Mesolithic tool tradition of East Africa.

**Mahalanobis distance** ($D^2$): a form of **Euclidean distance** during which normally distributed data are standardized by scaling elements in terms of standard deviations, and adjustments are made for the intercorrelations between the variables. See **genetic distance**; Cf. $F_{ST}$ **analysis.**

**Mahale Chimpanzee Research Site:** field station in Tanzania established by Japanese researchers in 1965; long-term research on chimpanzees at this site has been continuous since that time. Primatologists who have conducted field research at the site include T. Nishida, S. Uehara, C. Boesch, and H. Boesch.

***Mahgarita stevensi* Wilson and Szalay, 1976:** adapoid **prosimian** from the late Eocene of North America and the only North American member of the notharctid subfamily **Cercamoniinae; monotypic;** known from **crania** and teeth. Estimated body mass around 700 g. Dental formula: 2.1.3.3/2.1.3.3; tall crests on the molars interpreted by some workers as indicating a dietary regime of either **insectivory** or **folivory;** fused **mandibular symphysis.** See Appendix 1 for taxonomy.

**maidism:** see **pellagra.**

**maintenance selection:** see **stabilizing selection.**

**maize:** *Zea mays,* one of the four most important food crops in the world, a domesticated plant food item that originated in both Central and South America. Maize is thought to be an end product of the domestication of **teosinte,** a wild weedy crop (*Zea mexicana*); maize (corn) is low in certain necesary nutrients such as **niacin,** and is classified in the $C_4$ **vegetation** group. See **pellagra.**

**major affective disorder (1)** (MAFD1): a suite of behaviors characterized by radical mood swings, from euphoria to depression. Two major, distinct modes are recognized: bipolar affective disorder (BPAD, aka manic depressive illness), and unipolar affective disorder (depression without mania). Onset in the first case is usually the second decade, and in the third decade for the latter. Affected individuals with a family history apparently respond better to lithium than do sporadic cases. MZ:DZ twin concordance rates of 57%:14% (see **twins** and **concordant trait**) , and studies of adoptees correlated with biological parents, suggest some contribution of genetic factors, but with incomplete penetrance. MAFD is an ambiguous multifactorial disorder. Families with affected individuals tend to show co-morbidity with schizoaffective disorder, alcoholism, and/or anorexia nervosa. The possibility of genetic **anticipation** as an additional mechanism has been proposed. Early linkage studies reporting genes on chromosomes 11 and X (MADF2) have been retracted; other current factors map to 18p.1.

**major chromosome anomaly** (MCA): a clinically detectable mutation involving chromosomes. Common MCAs include **polyploidy, trisomy, inversion, translocation, duplication,** and **deletion.** MCAs often affect an individual's **phenotype.** MCAs are a significant component in human **infertility** as well as one of the major modes of **chromosome evolution.** Cf. **point mutation.** See **MCA.**

**major gene:** in a complex trait, any gene that has a primary effect on its phenotypic distribution; additional variation is explained by both minor gene effects and the influence of the environment. Aka oligogene.

‡ **major histocompatibility complex:** see **MHC.**

**Maka:** archaeological site found in 1981 in the Afar Basin along the **Middle Awash** River region of Ethiopia, dated to about 4–3.4 mya, and that contains **hominid** remains, including a proximal femoral fragment (MAK-VP-1/1), an adult mandible (MAK-VP-1/12), and other remains from both large and small individuals, all attributed to *Australopithecus afarensis* and comparable to similar fossils from **Hadar** and **Laetoli.**

**Makalian:** so-called wet period in the geological strata of east Africa, considered intermediate between today's drier period and the earlier **pluvial** interval.

‡ **Makapansgat** (MLD): an archaeological site found in 1947 by **Tobias** in South Africa, dating from 3.32 to about 2.9 mya (possibly >3.06 mya), and that contains artifacts, including **Dart's** alleged '**osteodontokeratic**' tools and now-discounted evidence of fire. **Hominid** remains include fragments of 12–30 individuals attributed to *Australopithecus prometheus* (= *A. africanus*). Among the most important fragments are two juvenile ilia (**MLD 7** and MLD 25) and an incomplete cranium (**MLD 37/38**). Actively excavated through 1983. Aka Makapansgat Limeworks Cave and the Cave of the Hearths.

*Maki mococo* **Muirhead, 1817:** synonym for *Lemur catta.*

*Maki nigrifrons* **É. Geoffroy, 1812:** synonym for *Eulemur mongoz.*

*Maki vari* **Muirhead, 1817:** synonym for *Varecia variegata.*

**MAK-VP-1/1:** see **Maka.**

**maladaptive:** describes any trait that reduces the **fitness** of individuals possessing it, compared with others without it. Cf. **adaptive.**

**malar:** see **zygomatic bone.**

**malar bone:** see **zygomatic bone.**

‡ **malaria:** 'bad air'; infectious disease of the liver and **red blood cells** in humans (the **host**) caused by any of four **protozoan** species of the genus *Plasmodium* (the

agent), and transmitted primarily by several species of mosquito of the genus *Anopheles* (the **vector**). Often known locally as 'black water fever' because of the presence of black urine in severely affected individuals as the **hemoglobin** molecules are parasitized for globin and the heme portion is filtered by the kidneys; often fatal, about 2–4 million deaths per year worldwide. Roughly one billion people carry the parasite, and 300 million are symptomatic. Erythrocytes of infected individuals rupture, releasing *Plasmodium* **merozoites,** toxins, and cell debris; toxins and loss of erythrocytes produce complications, and death is usually ascribed to cardiovascular problems. At least three *Plasmodium* species also infect primates. Old World origin. Aka paludism and 'jungle fever'. See **sickle cell anemia** and **epidemiology.**

**malarial crescent:** gametocyte of the malarial parasite *Plasmodium falciparum,* which is crescent-shaped. Aka sickle form.

**Malay** or **Malayan: 1. ethnym** for an indigenous people of Southeast Asia, a more **Mongoloid** subgroup that migrated to Indonesia after an initial **Indonesian-Malay** group. Aka Deutero-Malay, Malaysians, Malays. **2.** one of the five often cited racial varieties recognized by **Blumenbach** (1790); the others were **Ethiopian, American, Mongolian,** and **Caucasian.**

‡ **male** (♂): in sexually reproducing organisms, that individual of the sex that produces male gametes, i.e. **spermatozoa** or pollen. Also, (adjective): pertaining to such an individual. Cf. **female.**

**male care:** parental care administered by males; in marmosets this is considerable, the **male** taking on substantial duties outside of suckling. In other social primates male care consists principally of group defense, grooming, and periodic holding and carrying of young.

**male cranial capacity** (MCC): the capacity of the cranium of an **AMH** male; estimated by **Pearson's formula.** Cf. **female cranial capacity.**

**male genomic imprinting:** nonMendelian phenomenon in which the expression of a gene depends on inheritance from the father of two homologous copies of a gene. Double copies of certain alleles inherited from a male seem to control normal placental development. Aka parental imprinting. Cf. **female genomic imprinting.** See **genomic imprinting** and **Haig hypothesis.**

**male–male aggression:** intrasexual **competition** between males exists for the benefit of all members of a species; see the **group selection fallacy.**

**male–male competition:** see **male–male mate competition.**

**male–male cooperation:** behavior in which two or more males act together to improve their chances of reproducing. Often these males are kin, but not always. An example is two langur bachelor males forming an **alliance** in order to oust a **harem** male; olive baboon males may assist one another by diverting the attention of a consort male while one sneaks in to copulate, an act considered to be a case of **reciprocal altruism** because it is unlikely these individuals are related.

**male–male mate competition:** any behavior(s) that lessens another male's access to ovulating females and, hence, reproductive success; this may come in the form of fighting or an alternate strategy such as gaining access to females when competitors are otherwise occupied.

**male mate choice:** concept that males prefer to mate with females whom they assess as being fecund and will reject copulations with those females who may not be ovulating; despite the idea that sperm is cheap, some proponents of this concept think that unfruitful copulations deplete a male's supply of sperm and decrease the likelihood of producing more offspring. Cf. **female mate choice.**

**male mutation rates:** mutation rates in human males have been shown to be greater (1.7×) to considerably greater (5.1×) than in human females. These same studies also suggest a **paternal age effect,** presumably due to the lack of somatic protection of gonadal **DNA** compared to that of females. See **ratio of male to female mutation rates.**

**male net reproduction:** number of male deaths less the number of male births in an age cohort; the net production of male offspring. See **net reproductive success.**

**male parental investment** (mPI): allocation of time, energy and resources devoted by a male to its offspring; as males in many species tend not to know who their offspring are, social theory predicts that males tend to invest less. Cf. **female parental investment.** See **sexual asymmetry.**

**male pattern baldness:** autosomal dominant genetic condition characterized by the gradual loss of hair from the top of the scalp, a condition augmented by the presence of testosterone. Females very rarely have this condition and the allele is dominant in males but recessive in females. Human populations vary with respect to the proportions of individuals who exhibit this trait.

**male pseudohermaphroditism:** see **pseudohermaphroditism, male.**

**male-specific region of the Y chromosome** (MSY): major portion including the **centromere** of the human **Y chromosome,** which, although it contains segments that are homologous, is characterized by at least five **inversions** relative to the human **X chromosome** and is thus prevented from **recombination**

with it. The older name for this region, the nonrecombining region of the human Y chromosome (NRY), was discarded when researchers found that the region is recombinogenic, i.e. recombination occurs between arms of nine large MSY **palindromes,** resulting in **gene conversion.** Cf. **pseudoautosomal region.**

**male uterus:** vestigial tissue found in males, a remnant of undeveloped female reproductive organs; located on or near the male prostate gland. See **Müllerian ducts** and **vestigial trait.**

**malformation:** 1. a type of anomaly; 2. a morphologic defect of an organ or larger region of the body that results from an intrinsically abnormal developmental process.

**malignant:** threatening to life; virulent. See **malignant tumor.** Cf. **benign.**

**malignant tumor: tumor** that grows and infiltrates other tissue, either directly or through **metastasis.** Cf. **benign.**

**malleolus:** knoblike projection at the **distal** end of either the **tibia** or the **fibula.** Plural: malleoli. The tibial malleolus is medial and forms the inner bulge of the ankle; the fibular malleolus is lateral, forms the outer bulge of the ankle, and articulates with the **talus.**

‡ **malnutrition:** any disorder of **nutrition.** In practice, often taken to mean unbalanced nutrition, i.e. the absence or diminution of one or more specific **nutrients,** as opposed to **undernutrition.**

**malocclusion:** deviation from the normal contact between the dentition of the upper and lower jaws.

‡ **Malthus, Thomas Robert** (1766–1834): English clergyman, political economist, and professor at East India Company College (1805–34). Malthus quantified the relationship between growth in **populations** and food supplies (see **subsistence**) in his *Essay on the Principles of Population* (1798), in which he stated that limited (arithmetic) growth in food supplies provides natural 'checks to increase' on the geometric growth characteristics of human populations. Malthus was widely read, and his writings directly influenced both Charles **Darwin** and A. R. **Wallace.**

**Malthusian doctrine:** eponymous model of population growth toward a limit, especially the pedagogical use of the 1798 model of **Malthus** as first encountered by **Darwin** and **Wallace.**

**Malthusian parameter** (*r*): see **intrinsic rate of increase.**

**Malthusian population theory:** economic model that the British population would increase at a geometric rate while food supply would increase at an lower arithmetic rate (**ratio of increase**), leading to poverty and starvation that would eventually bring about famine, high infant mortality, disease, war, or moral restraint. Proposed by Thomas **Malthus** in 1798, the theory has been modernized in the assertion that virtually any species' reproduction exceeds the **carrying capacity** of its environment, and that balance is restored through mechanisms such as predation.

**mamma, mammae:** see **mammary gland.**

‡ **Mammalia:** class of animals (mammals) within the subphylum **Vertebrata,** phylum **Chordata;** contains 18–35 orders (varies by authority) including **Primates.** Major characteristics, with a few exceptions, include **mammary glands, viviparity, heterodonty,** three **auditory ossicles, epiphyseal disk** growth of long bones, **endothermy/homeothermy,** a muscular **respiratory diaphragm,** a four-chambered heart, enucleated red blood cells, and the skin being more or less covered by **hair.** Three subclasses: **Monotremata, Metatheria,** and **Eutheria.**

**mammary areola:** pigmented circular area that surrounds the nipple of the breast; aka areola mammae, areola papillaris.

**mammary gland:** modified sebaceous or sweat gland that produces milk in female mammals; in most mammals the mammary glands are found on the ventral surface and vary in the number of pairs. Among **anthropoids** only a single pectoral pair is present; there are often one or more additional abdominal pairs in **prosimians.** Mammary glands are unique to mammals and give the name to the class **Mammalia.** Aka breast.

**mammelon:** rounded eminence normally associated with newly erupted **incisor** teeth that wears down with age; also spelled mamelon.

**mammoth hunters:** late **Pleistocene** Ice Age peoples (= **AMHs**) who ranged across open steppe–tundra plains of northern Europe, Asia, and Siberia from roughly 35 to 15 kya, establishing elaborate base camps from which they ranged outward in search of **big game;** since the plains were treeless, dwellings were constructed from mammoth bones and turf (sod). See **Mezhirich.**

**man:** 1. **male** human being; usually, an adult. 2. formerly, an individual fossil, especially a representative specimen, e.g., 'Rhodesian Man'. 3. formerly, generic term for humans, as in 'man the hunter'. Cf. **woman.**

**'man the hunter' hypothesis:** argument by **Washburn, DeVore** and others that **hunting** was a behavior central to **Plio-Pleistocene** hominid evolution, that hunting required **intelligence** and that greater intelligence was thus achieved through natural selection and reflected in the fossil record as increased **encephalization.** In this scenario, life-history parameters are considered **dependent variables,** and hunting behavior is the **independent variable.**

‡ **mandible:** tooth-bearing bone that comprises the lower jaw; in **anthropoids** the mandible is a single fused bone, but in **prosimians** it consists of two separate bones joined by a **mental** symphysis. In other mammals this bone is referred to as the **dentary.** It is the only moving bone in the **skull.** Cf. **maxilla.**

**mandibular:** of or pertaining to the lower jaw, the **mandible.**

**mandibular angle:** posterior portion of the **mandibular body,** the lower rear corner that turns upward.

**mandibular body:** horizontal, tooth-bearing portion of the **mandible** that ends at the **ramus;** in the past this portion of the mandible was referred to as the horizontal ramus; the word ramus is now understood to be that part of the mandible that projects upward (i.e. the vertical ramus). See **mandibular ramus.**

**mandibular body breadth: craniometric** measurement: maximum thickness of the **mandibular bone** at the location of the second molar, measured with sliding calipers held parallel to the body of the mandible.

**mandibular body height: craniometric** measurement: perpendicular distance from the base of the **mandibular body** to the alveolar line on the buccal surface between the first and second molars as measured with sliding calipers. Aka mandibular corpus height.

**mandibular body length** (gn–go): **craniometric** measurement: distance from the **gnathion** to the **gonion** as measured with a **mandibulometer;** aka mandibular corpus length.

**mandibular condyle:** rounded process at the most posterior and superior projection of the ascending or **mandibular ramus.** Each process consists of two portions: a neck, and the articular condyle that it supports. The condyle is an oval surface that articulates with the articular disk of the temporomandibular joint of the **temporal bone.** Aka condylar process, processus condylaris mandibulae.

**mandibular diastema:** condition in which there is a gap between the canine and the first premolar on the mandible. See **canine diastema.**

**mandibular foramen:** opening in the mesial surface of the body of the **mandibular ramus** through which vessels and nerves pass. There is variation in the form of this foramen that can be used to classify populations: modes are the common form and the horizontal-oval form.

**mandibular fossa:** depression on the **temporal bone** that forms an articulation with the **mandibular condyle** of the **mandible;** aka glenoid fossa of the mandible, articular fossa, *fossa mandibularis.*

**mandibular groove:** slot that extends down from the lower rim of the **mandibular foramen** (or just below it).

**mandibular ramus:** vertical projection that rises from the **mandibular body**. The ramus is divided into an anterior **coronoid process** (that serves as a site for chewing muscle attachments) and a posterior **mandibular condyle** (that articulates with the **temporal bone**). In the past this structure was referred to as the vertical ramus (the mandibular body was referred to as the horizontal ramus).

**mandibular symphysis:** joint between the right and left halves of the **mandible**. In humans and other higher primates, this joint is fused.

**mandibular symphysis height** (gn–idi): **craniometric** measurement; distance from the **gnathion** to the **infradentale** measured with spreading calipers. See Appendix 7 for an illustration of the landmarks used.

**mandibular torus:** one of two shelf-like thickenings of bone (plural: mandibulares tori) that bridge the two sides of the mandible to the posterior of the mandibular symphysis. There are two such bony supports, or bars, which are faint in humans: the **superior transverse torus**, located just superior to the genial tubercles, and the **inferior transverse torus**, just superior to the digastric fossae, which is prominent in apes and is referred to as the **simian shelf**.

**mandibular trigone:** raised triangular pattern at the base of the **mandibular symphysis**. Aka mental trigone.

**mandibulometer:** **anthropometric** instrument consisting of two hinged boards and a protractor. The **gonial angle**, length of the **mandibular body**, and the height of the ascending ramus (see **mandibular ramus**) can be measured with this tool.

**mandrill:** vernacular for *Mandrillus* (= *Papio*) *sphinx.*

*Mandrillus* Ritgen, 1824: catarrhine genus to which the forest-dwelling baboons belong; two species. Found in rain forests of western equatorial Africa. Terrestrial; arboreal; quadrupedal; relatively short tail; **ischial callosities** present. **Sexually dimorphic** in body size, canine size, and, in the mandrill, coloration. Body mass for males ranges from 20 to 26 kg, females 7 to 15 kg. Dental formula: 2.1.2.3, with large canines and lower **sectorial premolars** that hone the upper canines; **frugivorous**; possess **cheek pouches**. Elongated muzzle. Social organization variable, **one-male units**, mixed-sex groups of 30–60 animals, and large **troops** of 250 individuals have been reported; high ratio of females to males in social units; solitary males common. Some workers include these species in *Papio.* See Appendix 2 for taxonomy, Appendix 3 for living species.

**mangabey:** general vernacular for the species of monkey belonging to the genus *Cercocebus.* Those of the closely related genus *Lophocebus* (formerly in Cercocebus) are referred to as the black mangabeys.

**mangrove:** coastal community along mudflats that are regularly inundated by sea water; this community is characterized by mangrove trees (family Rhizophoraceae) that are adapted to the salinity of the water and have wide-spreading roots that obtain oxygen from the air rather than from the waterlogged soil. Several species of primate visit these forests on a regular basis, most notably the proboscis monkey (*Nasalis larvatus*).

**manifesting heterozygote:** female carrier of a **sex-linked** recessive gene who expresses a dominant phenotype equivalent to that of the hemizygous male because the **wild type** allele is activated in some affected tissues. See **hemizygosify**.

**manipulation:** 1. alteration of the environment in some way by an animal. This includes nest making, nut cracking, tool making, etc. 2. act of maneuvering another individual into performing behavior that benefits the individual initiating the behavior. Not all behavioral biologists accept that such intentional behavior is present in nonhuman animals. See **intentionality**.

**Manouvrier, Léonce-Pierre** (1850–1927): French anthropometrician, physiologist, student of Paul Broca; it was Manouvrier who entertained Aleö **Hrdlicka** in 1896 during his visit to Paris (Hrdlicka had been a student there, and they had remained friends). Director of the Laboratoire d'Anthropologie at the École (1903–1927); his views were very different from Broca's: Manouvrier was a functional anatomist who recognized a large environmental influence on appearance, and avoided association with Broca's scientific racism, which was used to justify French colonial enterprises. In 1885, Manouvrier calculated a relative brain mass after dividing the brain into two parts, one for intelligence and a second for innervation of the body; his formulae were not accepted. He was one of the first to argue that the absolute differences in the brain mass of women and men were due to body size alone, and thus that women should be accorded more rights. Inventor of the **platycnemic index** and the **platymeric index**.

**Manouvrier's skelic index (of body build):** ratio between the lengths of the **torso** and the lower limbs; **standing height** minus **sitting height** divided by sitting height and multiplied by 100. Aka indice skelique, stem– leg length index. See **brachyskelia, mesatyskelia, macroskelia**. Cf. **cormic index**.

**mantle:** portion of the earth that lies between the **crust** and the core.

**mantled howler:** vernacular for *Alouatta palliata.*

**manubrium:** superior bone of the **sternum** that articulates with the **clavicle** and the first two ribs. This bone generally fuses with the body of the sternum in middle age.

**manufactory:** place where manual artifacts such as stone **tools** are made; factory.

‡ **manuport:** unaltered object carried some distance before use as a **tool** or for some other function.

**manus:** hand; the mammalian fore paw.

**map unit:** see **Morgan unit**.

**maple syrup urine disease** (MSUD): heritable condition characterized by syrupy-smelling urine, lethargy, breathing and swallowing problems, mental impairment, coma, and inevitably, death. A genetic disease of faulty amino acid metabolism. The defective protein is branched chain keto-acid dehydrogenase, an autosomal recessive, and it results in an inability to metabolize leucine, isoleucine and valine. Aka branched chain ketoaciduria.

**marasmus:** extreme form of protein-calorie **undernutrition** resulting from severe deficiencies in both proteins and calories/energy; in an advanced state in children there is a ravenous appetite, chronic diarrhea, failure to thrive (especially, a failure of both **hyperplasia** and **hypertrophy** of brain tissue), apathy, loss of muscle tonus resulting in edema with a marked swollen appearance, and finally death. Aka marasmic **kwashiorkor**.

**Marburg disease:** see **Ebola fever**.

**Marfan syndrome** (MFS1): degenerative disease of connective tissue caused by a defect in fibrillin (FBN1), an elastic tissue protein found in the eyes, aorta, and limb, finger, and rib bones. Affected individuals present as tall and loose-jointed with 'spindly fingers' and long and slender limbs, hands, and feet. A concave chest deformity is also a feature, as are a curved spine, displaced lenses, and cardiovascular problems. Manifests in the third decade of life. It is usually rupture and dissection of the aorta that causes death. MFS is an example of **pleiotrophy**, in which a single gene affects many target tissues in a body. MFS is an autosomal dominant. Indications of a **paternal age effect**.

**marginal:** pertaining to an edge, cusp, or periphery.

**marginal ridge:** elevated ledge on the vertical edge of the inner surface of an incisor.

**marginal sinus:** see **marginal venous sinus**.

**marginal value theorem:** assertion that a predator will continue to utilize a high-return resource until the level of depletion equals that of adjacent areas, at which point—known as the marginal value—the predator will move on in an attempt to locate a new **patch** of high return. Proposed in 1976 by Eric L. Charnov. See **optimal foraging theory**.

**marginal venous sinus:** one of two large bilateral venous sinuses found in the **dura mater** of the nuchal region inferior to the occipital sinus and that functions to drain blood from the brain. Found in the Hadar hominids and australopithecines, this structure is part of the **occipital-marginal venous system**. Replaced by or modified as the **transverse sinus** in anatomically modern humans.

***Marikina bicolor:*** synonym for ***Saguinus*** *bicolor*.

***Marikina leucopus*** **Hershkovitz, 1949:** synonym for ***Saguinus*** *leucopus*.

***Marikina martinsi:*** synonym for ***Saguinus*** *martinsi* (Martin's tamarin); now included within *S. bicolor*.

**marine archaeology:** underwater archaeology; literally, in salt water. Marine archaeology is important not only for the information revealed by shipwrecks, but also because many occupation coastal sites were inundated at the Pleistocene–Holocene boundary. Now aka freshwater archaeology.

**marine exploitation:** utilization of marine resources; the exploitation of the narrow coastal zone is one of the characteristic cultural features of early **AMHs**. According to some archaeologists, exploitation of the marine biome may have provided the consistent resources that permitted AMHs to disperse **out of Africa** and to arrive eventually in Asia and Australia. See **Klasies River Mouth**.

**marine isotope stage** (MIS): see **oxygen isotope stage**.

**marine oxygen isotope chronology:** see **Emiliani–Shackleton glacial sequence**.

**marine oxygen isotope stage:** see **oxygen isotope stage**.

**marital fertility:** number of children given as a function of the number of wives in a given population.

**marker:** 1. characteristic or factor by which a cell, molecule or disease can be identified. 2. general term for any trait that helps to throw light on the genetic nature of a disorder, such as a defect of structure or a deviant enzyme. 3. an **autapomorphy**.

**marking:** 1. leaving a cue in the environment that indicates the presence of the marker. Marking may signify ownership of an object or a larger entity, such as a territory, that the object is in. Marking among primates is generally by scent. See **scent marking, scent gland**. 2. **marking (of subjects):** placing some identifier on an animal so that an observer can make a reliable recognition of the subject in the field. Markers for primates differ from those used for other mammals (such as ear tags) because of the primate ability to remove them; they include collars, hair dye, patterns cut into the fur, and radio transmitters.

**Markov process: stochastic process** in which future events are determined completely by the present state and are independent of development prior to the present state.

**marmoset:** general vernacular for the seven species of monkey belonging to the genus ***Callithrix***.

**maroon leaf-monkey:** vernacular for ***Presbytis*** *rubicunda*.

**Maroteaux–Lamy syndrome:** see **mucopolysaccharidoses**.

**marriage:** socially recognized bonding of males and females. Most marriages are **monogamous**, even within societies that recognize other forms of marriage (Cf. **polygamy**). Marriage allows for legitimized reproduction and development of a nuclear household, and often solidifies alliances and support between families that are not closely related.

**marrow:** see **red marrow**, **yellow marrow**.

**marrow cavity:** see **medullary cavity**.

**Marsh, Othniel Charles** (1831–99): taught paleontology at Yale. During several fossil-hunting expeditions to the western US, Marsh found many example of early horses; these fossils were used to support evolutionary hypotheses. Competed with E. D. **Cope** to find and name fossils. Colleague of the Social Darwinist W. G. Sumner.

‡ **marsupial:** animal belonging to the subclass **Metatheria**; the only extant order of metatherians is *Marsupalia*. Most marsupials have a pouch (the **marsupium**) that contains milk glands and shelters the developing young; well-known examples are opossums and kangaroos. Many, but not all, living marsupials are found in Australia.

**marsupium:** pouch in the abdomen of a female **marsupial**.

**Martin, Rudolf** (1864–1925): Swiss philosopher, anthropologist at Zurich and Munich; Martin was concerned with growth and development deficits in children, and his practical concerns with anthropometry and somatology led to many editions of the classic *Lehrbuch der Anthropologie* (1914).

**Martin's tamarin:** vernacular for *Saguinus martinsi*. Most workers include this callitrichid in *S. bicolor*.

**Mas d'Azil:** archaeological site found in 1887 in the northern Pyrenees in southwestern France, a large natural grotto with materials dated to 11–9 kya, containing Azilian artifacts including striped and spotted pebbles, scrapers, stone points, and engraved stones and bone. Partial remains of at least one **hominid** attributed to *Homo sapiens* were also recovered. Type site for the **Azilian culture**. **Magdalenian** tools were found in the lowest levels. Aka Le Mas d'Azil.

**Ma's night monkey:** vernacular for *Aotus nancymaae*.

**Masek Bed:** fossil-bearing sedimentary layer in **Olduvai Gorge**, Tanzania, dating to 600–400 kya (**K/Ar**) and yielding hominid fossils including *Homo erectus* (**OH 23**). Tools, which include many quartzite scrapers but no cleavers, represent an **Acheulean** phase. Fauna is similar to that of **Olduvai Bed IV**.

**masked titi:** vernacular for *Callicebus personatus*.

**mass:** 1. characteristic of matter which gives it inertia. 2. a body of coherent material, as a cell mass.

‡ **mass exponent:** assessment of body size that controls for proportionality in the form of body or organ mass to a fractional power between 0.5 and 1.0.

**mass extinction:** event in which many species become extinct at the same time; most geological boundaries between time stratigraphic units are characterized by mass extinction events. Cf. **background extinction**.

**mass recruitment:** behavior that brings a large number of members of a social unit to a resource; For example, vocalizations by primates that have found a fruiting tree will bring other individuals to the tree.

**mass spectrometry:** 1. technique used during gene sequencing assays that can detect **SNPs** at a very low error rate. 2. see **stable isotope analysis**.

**masseter** (**muscle**): muscle of mastication. The masseter originates from the lower border of the **zygomatic arch** and inserts into the **mandibular angle** and **mandibular ramus**. Its action is to elevate the mandible. This muscle is particularly large and well developed in the genus *Paranthropus*.

**mast cell:** cells found in connective tissues, the spleen and bone marrow, and lymph nodes. Mast cells are characterized by the presence of **IgE** receptors and are important in the production of allergy symptoms.

**mastication:** act of chewing by which food is physically broken apart by the teeth. Verb: to masticate.

**masticatory cycle:** series of events that occur during chewing. It consists of three distinct sequences: **closing stroke**, **power stroke**, and **opening stroke**.

**mastoid:** breastlike or nipplelike, e.g. the **mastoid process** of the temporal bone.

**mastoid length** (po–ms): **craniometric** measurement; distance from the **porion** to the **mastoidale** measured with sliding calipers.

‡ **mastoid process:** prominence on the inferior portion of the **temporal bone** where it provides a site of attachment for some of the neck muscles; more prominent in *Homo sapiens*, especially males.

**mastoidale** (ms): **craniometric landmark:** most inferior point of the **mastoid process**.

**mate choice:** second stage of **sexual selection**.

**mate guarding:** in primate **one-male units**, the prevention of **bachelor** males from approaching and copulating with one-male unit females. See **guarding behavior**.

**mate recognition species concept:** see **recognition species concept**.

‡ **material culture:** physical remains of human cultural activity; elements of the physical environment modified during human cultural practices.

**maternal:** relating to or derived from the mother.

**maternal age effect:** any event in a newborn which increases or decreases in frequency or **incidence** as a function of the age of the mother. Both **Down syndrome** and **dizygotic twin**s increase in frequency with advanced maternal age.

**maternal disomy:** form of **uniparental disomy** in which two chromosomes (or regions) are both inherited from the mother of a recipient. One of the forms of **non-Mendelian inheritance.**

**maternal effect:** 1. immediate but nonlasting effects of a mother's cytoplasmic material on the phenotype of offspring. 2. variation among individuals due to variation in nongenetic maternal influences, such as habitual feeding behavior, in which large mothers might produce larger offspring, which in turn might produce larger offspring.

**maternal inheritance:** process by which **DNA** or **organelles** are inherited from the mother but not from the father; all children are thus **hemizygous** for **mtDNA** and certain cytoplasmic organelles; males are further **hemizygous** for a single **X chromosome**, which is maternal in origin. Cf. **paternal inheritance.**

**maternal PKU:** see **PKU, maternal.**

**maternal rejection:** negative behavior of a mother toward its infant during the period of weaning. See **termination of parental investment.**

**maternity ascertainment:** method(s) of assessment that a given female is the mother of a certain offspring. Although a female 'always' knows her offspring because she was present at birth, events such as adoption (in primates, as well as humans), hospital misidentification, and **surrogate mothers** have made maternity ascertainment as necessary as **paternity ascertainment** in some cases.

**mating:** conjugation and/or union of genetic material from different individuals (as opposed to selfing); in **eukaryotes**, the production of **zygotes** after the pairwise union of **unisexual** individuals for the purpose of **sexual reproduction.**

**mating behavior:** see **mating system.**

**mating frequencies:** proportions of matings between given genotypes.

**mating pair:** see **consortship.**

**mating season:** annual period when females come into **estrus**, copulate, and conceive offspring. This results in a **birth season.**

**mating system:** pattern of matings between individuals in a population with respect to **mate choice**, the degree of **inbreeding**, pair-bonding, and the number of simultaneous mates; of major importance in determining the demographic structure and evolutionary potential of **populations**, which may or may not be consistent within a species. See **assortative mating** and **random mating; monogamy** and **polygamy.**

**matrices:** Plural of **matrix.**

**matrifocal:** pertaining to a society in which most of the activities and personal relationships are centered on the mother.

**matrifocal unit:** group consisting of a mother and her offspring.

‡ **matriline:** pertaining to the lineal descent of anything passed from a mother to her offspring such as access to territory or other resource, social status within a dominance system, or specific genes that display a pattern of **maternal inheritance** such as those contained in **mitochondrial DNA;** matrilineal. Aka uterine descent, matrilinear inheritance. See **hologyny.** Cf. **patriline** and **holandry.**

**matrilocal:** describes a settlement pattern in which females remain within their natal community while males transfer to marry or mate in another community.

**matrix:** 1. in biology, the nonliving ground substance between connective tissue cells; this includes the fluid portion of blood. 2. in mathematics, a rectangular array of $m$ rows each containing numbers or **elements** arranged in $n$ columns; a two-dimensional array; an $m \times n$ matrix; trellis diagram.

**Matschie's needle-clawed bushbaby:** vernacular for *Euoticus inustus.*

**maturation:** 1. stage or process of becoming developed or physically **mature.** 2. **reduction division.** 3. the automatic development of a behavior pattern, which becomes increasing complex and precise as the animal matures. Unlike learning, maturation does not require experience to occur; **predisposition** (3).

**maturation division:** see **meiosis.**

**mature:** 1. ripen, ripe. 2. to come to maturity. 3. fully developed. Cf. **immature.**

**maturity:** 1. the threshold and duration of maturation for a given trait, behavior or property; e.g. sexual maturity. 2. in the human **life cycle**, the interval following **transition to full maturity** during the 5th and 6th decades, and characterized by peaking of social roles but continued decline of multiple tissue and body systems. Cf. **old age.**

**maturity-onset diabetes of the young** (MODY): see **diabetes mellitus, type II.**

**Matuyama reversed epoch:** long interval of geologic time (a **chron**) from 2.4 mya to 780 kya in which the polarity of the earth's magnetic field was for the most part reversed. Cf. **normal polarity epoch.** See **Olduvai event** and **paleomagnetism.**

**Mauer:** archaeological site found in 1907 in a sand quarry near Heidelberg, Germany, dated to about 700–400 kya (Günz–Mindel interglacial, **Pleistocene** fauna), and that contains **hominid** remains, including a robust mandible with a complete dentition, the **type specimen** for *Homo heidelbergensis*, which possesses a **mosaic** of features such as no chin but relatively small teeth. The mandible has been attributed by others to the **earlier archaic cf.** *Homo erectus* group. The mandible was found in association with horse and rhinoceros remains. Aka Mauer Jaw, Heidelberg Man and Rösch sandpit.

***Maueranthropus heidelbergensis* Montandon, 1943:** see *Homo heidelbergensis*.

**Maues marmoset:** vernacular for *Callithrix mauesi*.

**Maupertuis, Pierre Louis Moreau de** (1698–1759): French mathematician, astronomer, naturalist; in 1736 he traveled to Lapland to measure the curvature of the earth. *Venus physique* (1746), partly on the origin of skin color, foreshadowed the concepts of **epigenetics**, **mutation**, and **particulate inheritance**; analyzed pedigrees of families to show that the trait **polydactyly** was not inherited solely through males, thus potentially falsifying the **Preformation Doctrine** (in *Systeme de la Nature*, 1751). His principle of 'least action' (1744) stated that nature chooses the most economical path for moving bodies; also anticipated **natural selection** in *Essai de Cosmologie* (1750). Virtually all of his works were ignored for a hundred years, primarily because of **Rousseau's** negative influence.

**maxilla, maxillary:** see **maxillary bone**.

‡ **maxillary bone:** either one of a symmetrical pair of tooth-bearing bones of the face that forms the upper jaw. The upper jaw is often referred to as the maxilla, which includes both maxillary bones. Cf. **mandible**.

**maxillary notch:** distinct angle between the base of the cheek and the outer wall of the palate.

**maxillary sinus:** one of a pair of air-filled cavities lined with mucous membrane and located inside the **maxillary bone**, lateral to the nasal cavity. These sinuses help resonate the voice, as well as to reduce the weight of the skull.

**maxillary torus:** protuberance usually found at the maxillary **suture**.

**maxillo-alveolar breadth:** see **external palate breadth**.

**maxillo-alveolar index:** see **external palatal index**.

**maxillo-alveolar length:** see **external palate length**.

**maxillofrontale** (mf): **craniometric landmark:** point where the anterior lacrimal crest (on the medial border of the orbit) and frontolacrimal suture intersect. See Appendix 7.

**maximum bizygomatic breadth:** maximum breadth separating the two **zygomatic arches**.

**maximum cranial breadth** (eu–eu): a cranial measurement, one of the few taken imprecisely and with no definite landmarks, that measures the maximum width of the brain case between the **euryons**. In modern humans, it is almost always taken high up and towards the rear of the skull near the region of parietal bossing, but in other hominids (such as **australopithecines**) it is measured much lower down on the cranium, and in some species even below the level of the ear. It is usually measured with a **head spanner**. Cf.

**biparietal breadth.** See Appendix 7 for an illustration of the landmarks used.

**maximum cranial length** (g–op): **craniometric** measurement: the length of the cranium along the midsagittal line from the **glabella** (g) to the **opisthocranion** (op); normally measured by using **spreading calipers**.

**maximum facial breadth:** distance from **zygion** to zygion.

**maximum foot length:** measured while in the standing position, the distance from the most posterior point of the heel to the most anterior point of the longest toe.

**maximum head breadth:** maximum transverse diameter on the head, usually over each parietal bone.

**maximum head length:** distance from the **glabella** to the farthest point on the back of the head.

**maximum homology hypothesis:** optimum reconstruction of a phylogenetic tree that maximizes identity due to common ancestry. Aka red king hypothesis.

**maximum lifespan potential** (MLP): the greatest longevity ever recorded for an individual of a species. Considered a parameter of a species' **life history**.

**maximum likelihood method:** in genetics, a method that compares probabilities that observed combinations of traits in parents and children would arise under alternate hypotheses of either linkage or no linkage.

**maximum parsimony hypothesis:** idea that the best reconstruction of ancestral character states is that which requires the fewest mutations in the proposed evolutionary tree to account for character states observed in living species. Aka **maximum homology** hypothesis.

**maximum parsimony problem:** unsolved portion of the **maximum parsimony hypothesis** having to do with ancestor reconstruction without prior knowledge of the probable branching arrangement.

**maximum physiognomic nasal breadth:** greatest transverse distance between the most lateral points on the wings of the nose.

**maximum projective mandibular length** (gn–idi): **craniometric** measurement: distance from the most anterior point on the chin to the most posterior point on the mandibular condyle when the **mandible** is placed on an osteometric board or a mandibulometer. See Appendix 7 for an illustration of the landmarks used.

**Maynard Smith, John** (1920–2004): worked with J. B. S. **Haldane** as a theoretical behavioral ecologist at University College London (1952–65); dean of Life Sciences at Sussex (1965-85). Trained as an engineer, Maynard Smith applied mathematics to problems in biology, and contributed the concept of the evolutionarily stable strategy (**ESS**) to the evolution of the **sex**

**ratio** and to **game theory.** Author of *Mathematical Ideas in Biology* (1968), *The Evolution of Sex* (1978), *Evolution and the Theory of Games* (1983), *Evolutionary Genetics* (1989), *Did Darwin Get It Right? Essays on Games, Sex and Evolution* (1989), and (with E. Szathmary) *The Major Transitions in Evolution* (1995), among others. Winner of the Royal Society's Darwin Medal (1986), Royal Medal (1997), Copley Medal (1999), Crafoord Prize (1999) and the Kyoto Prize (2001). See **second Darwinian revolution.**

**Mayr, Ernst Walter** (1904–2005): German-born US evolutionary biologist, ornithologist, historian of biology; early fieldwork in the Solomons and New Guinea led him to support the **neo-Darwinian** view of evolution then developing; known especially for a 1950 paper on fossil taxonomy in which he lumped, rather than split, taxa; appointed professor of Zoology at Harvard; author of many subsequent books on **systematics** and 'the species question' (especially **allopatric speciation** and **evolutionary systematics**), on **evolutionary theory**, and on **Darwinism.**

**Mb:** abbrev. for **megabase.**

**Mbuti pygmies:** foragers or hunter–gatherers in modern-day Zaire who have survived with a subsistence lifestyle in small-scale societies into the twenty-first century.

**MCA:** major chromosome anomaly, a clinically detectable mutation involving abnormal chromosomes. Common MCAs include **22q11 deletion syndrome, cri-du-chat syndrome, deletion, dicentric Y syndrome, Down syndrome, duplication, double Y syndrome, Edward syndrome, isochromosome, Klinefelter syndrome, monosomy 21, mosaicism, paracentric inversion, Patau syndrome, pericentric inversion, Philadelphia chromosome, polyploidy, reciprocal translocation, Robertsonian translocation, triploidy, triplo-X syndrome,** and **trisomy 22.** MCAs often affect an individual's **phenotype.** MCAs are a significant component in human **infertility** as well as one of the major modes of **chromosome evolution.** Cf. **point mutation.**

**McArdle disease:** see **glycogen storage disease (V).**

**McClintock, Barbara** (1902–92): US geneticist; winner of the Nobel Prize (1983) for identifying **transposons** in corn ( **maize,** *Zea mays*), although she was also among the first to demonstrate cytological proof of **crossing over** (1931).

**McCown, Theodore D.** (1908–69): US physical anthropologist who collaborated with Arthur **Keith** in the examination of the **Skhūl** and **Tabūn** fossil remains. He co-edited *Climbing Man's Family Tree; A Collection of Major Writings on Human Phylogeny, 1699 to 1971*, with Kenneth A. R. Kennedy.

**M chromosome:** human **mitochondrial chromosome.**

**Meadowcroft Rockshelter:** Paleoindian archaeological site found in 1970 near Avella, Pennsylvania, dated to 19–14 kya (controversial radiocarbon dates obtained in 1973–8), and that contains stone artifacts including unfluted points and 'woven materials'. As currently dated, the site antedates most others in North America by 8 ky. Cf. **Cactus Hill** and **Topper.**

‡ **mean** ($\bar{x}$): the numerical average; usually a quantity equal to the sum of the **observations** divided by the number of them, denoted by $\bar{x}$ as a **sample** statistic and by μ as a **population parameter.**

**mean age of tooth eruption:** average age for a given species at which a certain tooth erupts. The age of eruption of the lower first molar ($M_1$) is highly correlated with **brain** mass and other **life history variables** in primates. Such parameters can thus be used in the **life history** reconstruction of fossil species such as the **australopithecines** and **habilines.**

**mean basion height index:** expression of the ratio of height to width of a skull; **cranial height** divided by **maximum cranial length** + **maximum cranial breadth** divided by 2 and multiplied by 100. An index of 78.99 or less is considered low, 79.00 to 85.99 is considered medium, and 86.00 and greater is considered to be high. Cf. **mean porion height index.**

**mean body temperature:** sum of the products of the heat capacity and temperature of all the tissues of the body divided by the total heat capacity of the organism.

**mean fitness** (*W*): average **survivability,** considering all members of a breeding population.

**mean height index:** older name for **mean basion height index.**

**mean intrapair variance:** average difference between members of twin pairs.

**mean life expectancy:** average age to which the members of a **cohort** live; in practice (for humans) the median life expectancy is used, i.e. the age to which half of a cohort live.

**mean porion height index:** comparison of skull height to the length and width; **porion–bregma height** divided by **maximum cranial length** + **maximum cranial breadth** divided by 2 and multiplied by 100. An index of 66.99 or less is considered low, 67.00 to 71.99 is considered medium, and 72.00 and greater is considered high. Cf. **mean basion height index.**

**mean square** (MS): in statistics, a synonym for **variance.**

**meaning:** in reference to what a message sent by one individual conveys to those who receive it; in animal communication this is studied through message-meaning analysis.

**meaningful mutation:** see **missense mutation** and **nonsense mutation.**

**measles:** acute, highly infectious and **communicable disease** first described *c.* 900 CE; an Old World **zoonotic**; the viral agent was identified in 1914 (an RNA virus, Rubeola, family Paramyxoviridae); an effective prophylactic vaccine was created in 1963. The virus usually enters other hosts upon contact with respiratory droplets; bluish spots are followed by the eruption of a characteristic rash; mortality ranges from 1 to 10%, most often in infants and older adults. Related animal diseases include canine distemper and bovine rinderpest.

‡ **measurement:** 1. the **quantification** of an object, pattern, behavior, or idea, represented by a number or set of numbers that can be compared to other such numbers obtained in the same manner. 2. a number resulting from such a process. Measurement is one of the fundamental ways in which **physical anthropology** differs from some other, but not all, types of **anthropology**. See **statistics**.

**measurement error:** degree to which data values do not truly measure the characteristic represented by the variable.

**meat eater hypothesis:** model of human evolution which proposes that adaptations for feeding on protein-rich items such as muscle, bone marrow, intestine, and brain provided the **selection pressures** for the evolution of later **hominid** biological characteristics. Cf. **large gut** and **seed-eating hypothesis**.

**meat head hypothesis:** hypothesis that the larger **brain size** of **Neandertals** is explained by more robust **body size**; larger bodies and consequently individual body segments tend to be a response of mammals, generally, to cold climates; term coined by **Holloway**.

**meatus:** external opening or passageway or channel into the body.

**mechanical function:** physical features of a trait included within an animal without reference to the environment in which the organism lives.

**mechanical isolation:** physical noncorrespondence of the genitalia of animals or flower parts that prevents copulation or pollen transfer; a premating or **prezygotic mechanism** of isolation.

**mechanism:** agency or means by which an effect is produced or a result is obtained.

**mechanisms of culture change:** explanation proposed by B. Fagan, in which four descriptive models are used to characterize culture change: inevitable variation (individual differences in learning behaviors), invention (innovation, the evolution of a new idea), diffusion (the spread of ideas), and migration (movements of entire societies, including their technology).

**mechanisms of evolution:** major factors that cause changes in populations between generations. These include **annidation**, **artificial selection**, **assortative mating**, **chromosome mutation**, **domestic selection**, **extinction**, **gene flow** (migration), **hitchhiking**, **isolation**, **meiotic drive**, **natural selection**, **genomic imprinting** (parental imprinting), **'point' mutations** (**DNA**), **relaxed selection**, and **sexual selection**. Aka pressures or forces of evolution.

**mechanistic model:** any description, usually mathematical, of a relationship(s) among variables and that stresses chemical, physical, and biological principles.

**mechanistic theory:** proposal that natural processes can be fully explained by laws such as those of physics and chemistry.

**mechanoreceptor:** sensory receptor that responds to a mechanical stimulus.

**Mechta-el-Arbi:** see **Afalou-bou-Rhommel**.

**Meckel–Serres law:** putative law that states that there are parallels between the stages of ontogeny and a phylogenetic series. See **biogenetic law**.

**meconium:** mucoid substance present in the intestines of a newborn that is normally eliminated in the first defecation.

**medial:** anatomical term of relative position, meaning toward or near the mid-line of the body.

**medial calf skinfold: anthropometric** measurement: skinfold measured on the medial surface of the calf at the area of greatest circumference. Used in combination with other **skinfold measurements** to estimate body composition. See **skinfold thickness**.

**medial epicondyle:** see **medial** and **epicondyle**. Many bones of the skeleton have medial epicondyles. Cf. **condylion**.

**medial line or plane:** line that bisects the body or an organ into equal left and right halves; aka **midsagittal** plane, **mid-line**, or median line or plane.

**medial projection:** bony intrusion from the lateral wall of the nasal aperture, a feature unique to the **Neandertal** nasal region.

**medial pterygoid:** muscle of mastication. The medial pterygoid originates from the surface of the lateral pterygoid plate of the **sphenoid, palatine,** and **maxillary bones**; it inserts into the medial surface of the **mandible**. Its action is to elevate the mandible and move it from side to side when performing grinding movements.

**median:** in statistics, the middle number in a given sequence of numbers. If the number of values is even, the two numbers closest to the middle are averaged.

**medical anthropology:** subdiscipline that studies human health problems in the context of overarching social and cultural systems. Within the subdiscipline itself there are those who differ in approaches, the most common of which are the ethnomedical, biomedical, ecological, critical, and applied approaches.

**medical genetics:** pertaining to medicine and the treatment of diseases and conditions that have a **genetic etiology,** in whole or in part; the study of **genetic disease.**

**medical jurisprudence:** application of medical knowledge to legal questions. Aka forensic medicine, legal medicine.

**medicine:** 1. any substance with the capacity to change the condition of a living organism; a drug or remedy. 2. the art or science of healing diseases.

**mediocone: cuspule** anteriorly placed on the incisors of some **plesiadapiforms.**

**Mediterranean anemia:** see **thalassemia.**

**Mediterranean crisis:** refers to the desiccation or drying up of the Mediterranean Sea about 5.3 mya; aka the **Messinian salinity crisis.**

**Mediterranean fever, familial** (FMF or MEF): rheumatic condition characterized by recurrent episodes of fever and inflammation of the abdomen. The candidate gene, pyrin (*MEFV*, autosomal recessive; maps to 16p13), functions normally in granulocytes to suppress the immune response; several known mutations disable pyrin, and permit an inflammatory reaction. Affects 1:200 individuals in non-Ashkenazi Jewish, Armenian, Arabian, and Turkish populations; 1:5 may be carriers.

**Mediterranean scrub forest:** region found in temperate zones bordering a sea and further delimited by a mountain range that produces a rain shadow desert on the inland side. A Mediterranean scrub forest is hot and dry during the summers, and rainy and mild during the winters. See **forest.**

**medulla:** pertaining to the inner or central section of a structure, e.g. the renal medulla; in the case of hair, the central canal (see **medulla of hair**). For **medulla of bone:** see **medullary cavity.**

**medulla oblongata:** structure within the hindbrain or **rhombencephalon** that functions as a relay center and as the visceral autonomic center that controls respiration, heart rate, and vasoconstriction. See **myelencephalon.**

**medulla of hair:** innermost core of a hair that consists of loosely arranged cells and air spaces. Populations of the Far East and the Americas have the largest medullas, whereas the different populations of pygmies are said to have the smallest or none at all.

**medullary:** of or pertaining to the inside of an organ.

**medullary cavity:** cavity within the **diaphysis** of long bones; this cavity is filled with **yellow marrow** in life. Aka marrow cavity.

**Meeh–DuBois formula:** specification for determination of body surface area in humans from the height and mass of an individual, given as $A = W^{0.425} \times H^{0.725} \times 71.84$, where $A$ is surface area in cm$^2$, $W$ is mass in kg, and $H$ is height in cm. Aka **DuBois formula.**

**megabase** (Mb): one million **base pairs,** a unit of measurement of **DNA** length. Cf. **kilobase.**

**Megachiroptera: monotypic** suborder of the mammalian order Chiroptera (bats) consisting of the family Pteropodidae with approximately 42 genera and 169 species; flying foxes, also referred to as fruit bats; confined to the Old World and the islands of the Pacific. These bats are larger than the smaller microchiropterans. Flying foxes are of interest to paleoprimatologists for several reasons. First, there appears to be a strong phylogenetic relationship between all bats and primates; Paleocene chiropterans have been mistaken for basal primates, indicating the close evolutionary relationship. Second, it has been proposed that the Megachiroptera may be **convergent** with microchiropterans and that flying foxes are descended from an early group of primates. See **Flying Primate Hypothesis.**

*Megadelphus lundeliusi:* archaic mammal of the early Eocene of the Rocky Mountain region of North America belonging to the **plesiadapiform** family **Microsyopidae; monotypic.** Estimated body mass around 2.5 kg. See Appendix 1 for taxonomy.

**megadontia:** condition of having an enlarged tooth relative to body size; Aka megadontism, macrodontism. Cf. **microdontia.**

**megadontia quotient** (MQ): McHenry's measure of the size of the rear teeth, given by the postcanine tooth area divided by ($12.15 \times$ body mass$^{0.86}$). The MQ is large in *Paranthropus*, progressively smaller in the gracile **australopithecines** and *Homo*.

‡ **megaevolution:** 1. evolution of higher **taxa.** 2. rapid evolutionary events, punctuated evolution, or **macroevolution.**

**megafauna:** in reference to the large animals of the **Pleistocene.** Many of these mammals and birds became extinct at the end of this geological period, about 10 kya. There is ample evidence that humans hunted many of these animals.

**megakaryocyte:** large cell of the **red marrow** of bone; blood **platelets (thrombocytes)** bud off from the surface and are active during blood clotting.

**Megaladapidae Forsythe Major, 1894:** family to which the genera *Lepilemur* (sportive lemurs) and *Megaladapis* (recently extinct koala lemurs) belong; eight species. Megaladapidae has replaced the former nomen Lepilemuridae. See Appendix 1 for taxonomy.

*Megaladapis* **Forsyth Major, 1894:** genus of **subfossil Malagasy prosimians** called the koala lemurs; three species known. All materials relating to this genus were recovered from sites in the north of Madagascar, with radiocarbon dates ranging from 3000 to 600 years ago. The closest affinities of these lemurs is with the sportive lemurs, with whom they are included in the family **Megaladapidae.** Arboreal;

limb structure and proportions unlike any other primate; presumed to have been clingers and climbers similar to the koala of Australia; may have made short leaps in the trees; forelimbs long relative to hindlimbs; very large paws. Large lemur, body mass estimates range from 40 to 80 kg. Unusual cranial features: elongated flattened cranium and **foramen magnum** at most posterior portion of occipital bone; fused **mandibular symphysis** (unusual in recent prosimians). Adult dental formula: 0.1.3.3/2.1.3.3; upper incisors lost in the adult and presumed replaced by a horny pad, similar to the condition found in the **artiodactyls**; very high and large molars; **folivorous**. See Appendix 2 for taxonomy, Appendix 3 for living species.

**megalith:** any large stone structure, especially of the Middle Neolithic period.

*Meganthropus africanus* **Weinert, 1950:** see *Australopithecus afarensis*.

*Meganthropus modjokertensis*: See *Pithecanthropus modjokertensis* and *Homo erectus modjokertensis*.

*Meganthropus paleojavanicus* **Weidenreich, 1945:** binomen given to material found at **Sangiran**, Indonesia. The taxonomic relationship of these specimens is unclear and it has been suggested they represent **paranthropines** or their equivalents in Southeast Asia; others think that this material should all be assigned to *Homo erectus*. Aka ancient Java ape-man.

‡ **meiosis:** reduction division; process of **cell division** that leads to the formation of sex cells (**gametes**); aka meiotic cycle. A diploid **stem cell** divides twice but the **chromatids** have only replicated once, so that the four end products are **haploid** (i.e. have only a single complement of chromatids each). Aka maturation division, **gametogenesis**.

‡ **meiosis I:** initial series of stages in gamete production characterized by **synapsis** of homologous chromosomes, the appearance of **sister chromatids**, **crossing over**, and the movement of homologues to the opposite poles of a cell.

‡ **meiosis II:** second series of stages in gamete production during which the centromere of each chromosome splits and the two **sister chromatids** of each chromosome separate and are pulled to opposite poles.

**meiotic:** pertaining to **meiosis**.

**meiotic drive:** any meiotic mechanism that results in the asymmetrical recovery or expression of the two types of gametes produced by a heterozygote. See **epigenetics** and **genomic imprinting**.

**meiotic spindle:** gelatinous, bipolar, ellipsoidal bundle of fibers (**microtubules**) visible during cellular division, responsible for the accurate **segregation** of **chromosomes** or **chromatids** into daughter cells

during both anaphase I and anaphase II of **meiosis**.

**meiotic spindle:** see **spindle**.

**Meissner's corpuscles:** encapsulated organs in the skin, serving touch. Present in all primates.

**Melanesian: ethonym** for the peoples that inhabit the Oceanian islands of New Guinea, New Britain, New Ireland, the Admiralties, the Solomons, New Hebrides, New Caledonia, Fiji, and the Santa Cruz Islands.

‡ **melanin:** yellow, reddish, or dark brown **pigment** that is one of the components of **coloration** in plants and animals (along with **collagen**, **hemoglobin**, **carotene**, and other factors). In animals, melanin is one of the primary pigments responsible for **skin color**. Melanin is produced by specialized epidermal cells called **melanocytes**. In animals, melanin is found in skin, hair, and the iris of the eye. A major function of melanin in the skin is to absorb ultraviolet radiation and protect the deeper tissues; in the eye, melanin helps keep the inner chamber of the eyeball completely dark. This type of brown melanin is also referred to as eumelanin. See **pelage**. Cf. **phaeomelanin**.

**melanin-stimulating hormone** (MSH): see **melanocyte-stimulating harmone**.

**melanism:** any increase in the average amount of dark **pigment** in an organism or group of organisms. See **tanning**; Cf. **industrial melanism**.

**melanoblast:** immature **melanocyte**.

**Melanocroi:** any **Caucasoid** with dark hair and a pale complexion. Aka melanchroi. Cf. **Xanthochroi**.

**Melanocroid:** one of T. H. **Huxley's** five major racial groups. Melanocroids consisted of southern Europeans, Arabs, Afghans, and Hindus. Also spelled melanochroid.

**melanochrous:** referring to dark skin; term used by northern Europeans when referring to people south of the Alps.

**melanocortin-1 receptor** (MC1R): binding site for **melanocyte-stimulating hormone**; MC1R is located in the membrane of **melanocytes**. In mammals and birds, single amino acid substitutions caused by mutations in the *Mc1r* gene are correlated with darkened or melanic coloration.

‡ **melanocyte:** specialized cell that produces the pigment **melanin**, which is then distributed to surrounding epidermal cells; the melanocytes of the eye are an exception in that they retain their melanin granules (see **eye color**). Melanocytes of the skin and the hair are located in the basal layer of the epidermis.

**melanocyte-stimulating hormone** (MSH): peptide **hormone** secreted by the intermediate lobe of the **pituitary gland**; it stimulates the production of pigmentation (**melanin**) within the **melanocytes** of the skin of birds and mammals, and can produce a rapid change in skin coloration in some nonhuman species. See **melanocortin-1 receptor**. Aka intermedin, melanotropin.

**melanoderm:** 1. pertaining to dark skin. 2. Von Eickstedt's term for **Negroid**.

**melanoderma:** region of skin that is darkened by excessive deposition of melanin.

**melanoma, malignant** (MM): an aggressive form of skin **cancer** that affects predominantly lightly melanized populations, especially Europeans. First signs are a mole or patch of rapidly growing skin, which metastasizes via the bloodstream. One of the predisposing genes is *CDKN2*, which codes for an autosomal dominant protein named p16, a checkpoint regulator of cell division. MM is also associated with the HLA-B7 haplotype (aka skin cancer, cutaneous malignant melanoma, CMM). Highest incidences of MM are in equatorial countries where lightly melanized individuals reside, e.g. New Zealand. Lowest rates (often nil) are found in highly melanized populations (e.g. Maori in New Zealand, Australian aboriginals).

**melanophore:** skin cell containing diffusible black pigment, **eumelanin**.

**melanosome:** intracellular organelle that contains **tyrosinase**, found in **melanocytes**.

**MELAS:** see **mitochondrial encephalopathy lactic acidosis syndrome**.

**melatonin:** hormone synthesized by the **pineal gland** in many species of animal; its secretion increases during exposure to light. In adult amphibians, melatonin produces lightening of the dermal pigmentation by promoting aggregation of **melanosomes**. In mammals, it influences hormone production, and in many species it regulates seasonal changes such as reproductive pattern and fur color. In humans, it is implicated in the regulation of mood, sleep, puberty, and ovarian cycles.

**Melka Kuntur:** archaeological site excavated in the 1960s in Ethiopia, dating to as old as 1.5 mya; contains **Oldowan, Developed Oldowan**, and **Acheulean** artifacts and hominid remains attributed to *Homo erectus*. A full publication of the site has not appeared. Aka Melka Kunturé, Melka konturé, Gomboré II.

**Member:** in geology, a rock unit that is a subdivision of a formation.

**meme:** hypothetical unit of cultural transmission; controversial term coined by **Dawkins** to serve as an analogy to a gene, the unit of genetic transmission. Theoretically, memes are reproduced from one generation to the next, are subject to natural **selection** and prone to **mutation**, can migrate and **drift**, and can experience **extinction**. Despite this analogy with **evolutionary biology**, many biologists believe that memes represent **Lamarckian inheritance** rather

than examples of Darwinian evolution. Aka culturgen. See **adaptationist program**.

**memetic evolution:** change in the content or meaning of a **meme** over time. Aka cultural evolution.

**memory:** information stored in the **central nervous system** that is retrievable by the individual. It has been theorized that memory is stored in a structure called an engram, which is a series of neurons and/or synapses that become physically changed and form an association with one another; not all researchers accept this concept. In humans short-term memory lasts for a few seconds to a few minutes; long-term memory lasts considerably longer and can last the life of the person.

‡ **memory cell:** descendants of activated B and/or T cells which participate in a **secondary immune response**.

‡ **menarche:** first menstrual discharge in the female; in humans, usually occurring sometime between the ages of 11 and 16. In many cultures this event denotes the transition between childhood and adulthood in females. Cf. **menopause**.

‡ **Mendel, Gregor Johann (Fr)** (1822–84): Austrian Moravian monk who conducted classic experiments with the garden pea, defining basic genetic principles such as the **recessive pattern of inheritance**. Mendel demonstrated that what he called 'factors' (today's **genes**) are discrete units inherited in predictable patterns (see **segregation**). Two papers (1866, 1869) and a few letters are all that remain of his scientific work, which was misunderstood and infrequently cited during his lifetime. When Mendel's work was rediscovered in 1900, it became the foundation for modern **genetics**. Adjective: Mendelian.

**Mendelian 'factor':** any one of the segregating forms identified by Gregor **Mendel** during his study of inheritance in the garden pea, and after the rediscovery of his work, renamed as a **gene**.

**Mendelian genetics:** branch of genetics concerned with patterns and processes of **particulate inheritance**; named after Gregor **Mendel**, who was among the first scientists to demonstrate many of the important principles, such as **segregation** and **recessive** factors.

**Mendelian inheritance:** mode of **particulate inheritance** of nuclear or chromosomal **genes**. See **non-Mendelian inheritance**.

**Mendelian principle of heterozygosity in the F1:** in a monohybrid cross of a P1 dominant homozygote with a P1 recessive homozygote, the phenotypically similar F1 offspring will all be heterozygotes. **Mendel's** third principle.

‡ **Mendelian principle of independent assortment:** in a **dihybrid cross**, the random distribution of **alleles** into **gametes** results from the random

distribution of **chromosomes** and **chromatids** during **meiosis. Mendel's** second principle.

‡ **Mendelian principle of segregation:** in sexually reproducing organisms, the two members of an **allele** pair or of **homologous chromatids** are separated at **meiosis** during **gametogenesis**, with each gamete receiving only one member of the pair; these then recombine when gametes fuse during **fertilization. Mendel's** first principle.

**Mendelian ratios:**

**1:2:1:** expected number of each of four segregating genotypes in a monohybrid cross when a trait system contains one locus with two alleles. One of the fundamental Mendelian ratios. See below, **3:1** and **9:3:3:1**.

**3:1:** expected number in the F2 generation of each of two segregating phenotypes in a monohybrid cross when a recessive trait system contains one locus and two alleles. One of the fundamental Mendelian ratios. See above, **1:2:1**, and below, **9:3:3:1**.

**9:3:3:1:** expected number of each of four segregating phenotype pairs in a dihybrid cross when each of two unlinked loci has two alleles. One of the fundamental Mendelian ratios. See above, **3:1** and **1:2:1**.

‡ **Mendelian trait, character** or **feature:** any genetically defined **discrete trait** or attribute of an organism ascribable to a discrete **genotype** and expressed according to the principles of **Mendelian inheritance**; controlled by **genes** located on nuclear **chromosomes**.

**Mendelism:** eponym for the recollected ideas of Gregor **Mendel** concerning **particulate inheritance** of 'factors' (nuclear **genes**) according to the **chromosomal theory of inheritance**.

**mendelize:** segregate according to **Mendel's principles** or **laws**.

**Mendel's principles** or **laws:** principles of **heredity** described by Gregor **Mendel** in the nineteenth century; see the **Mendelian principle of segregation**, the **Mendelian principle of independent assortment**, and the **Mendelian principle of heterozygosity in the F1**.

**meningeal arteries:** vessels that supply blood to the meningeal covering of the brain.

**meninges:** three-layered connective tissue membranes that surround and protect the spinal cord and brain; the pia mater lies closest to the nervous tissue, and above it the arachnoid mater and **dura mater**; the pia mater also envelops the **cerebrospinal fluid**. Singular: meninx.

**meniscocyte:** sickled red blood cell.

**meniscus:** fibrocartilaginous disk found in some **synovial joints** that separates the articulating surfaces of the bones. Plural: menisci.

**Menkes syndrome:** heritable disorder characterized by cerebral degeneration and atrophy, microscopically kinky gray hairs, abnormal facial features, and bone damage; death in early childhood. The cause is abnormal copper transport; the defective gene is for ATPase (*ATP7A*, an X-linked recessive); aka 'steely hair disease'. Other diseases such as Ehlers–Danlos syndrome (occiput horn syndrome) may be allelic variants of this gene.

‡ **menopause:** cessation of the menstrual cycle in females, identified in retrospect after 12 months of **amenorrhea**, and signaling the cessation of ovulation and fertility. One of the **life history variables**; in humans, a universal parameter that usually occurs between the ages of 46 and 50, and marks a period of increasing bone loss and changing serum lipid profiles. Aka climacteric. Cf. **menarche**.

**menorrhea:** normal discharge of the menses. Cf. **amenorhea**.

**menstrual cycle:** see **uterine cycle** and **estrous cycle**.

**menstrual phase:** first phase of the human **uterine cycle**, encompassing days 1–5, and characterized by relatively low concentrations of the hormones **LH**, **estrogen**, and **progesterone**, but higher concentrations of **FSH. Menstruation** occurs as the uterine wall is sloughed off and is discarded through the vagina; the eroded endometrium is thin.

**menstrual synchrony:** condition in which the **menstrual cycle** of several human females occurs at the same time; this situation occurs when women are living in close proximity to one another. See **reproductive synchrony**.

**menstruation:** loss of blood and tissue from the uterine lining at the end of the female reproductive cycle. It has been proposed that menstruation is an evolutionary adaptation of humans to year-round sexual receptivity; because the male penis is a source of bacteria and viruses, it is advantageous to release the superficial layer of the **endometrium**, which removes potential sources of infection. Aka menses, menstrual period. See **menstrual cycle**.

*menta:* pertaining to the brain and thought processes; *menti*.

**mental:** 1. of or pertaining to the chin; aka gonial. 2. of or pertaining to the mind.

**mental defective:** person with intelligence measured below the normal level, usually below an arbitrary threshold of 50. Cf. **mental retardation** and **mental deficiency**.

**mental deficiency:** intelligence measured below the normal level, usually below an arbitrary threshold of 70. Cf. **mental retardation** and **mental defective**.

**mental foramen:** opening in the **mandible** inferior to the anterior **premolar** tooth through which the **mental** (1) blood vessels and nerves pass.

**mental protuberance:** chin; projection of bone on the mid-line of the **mandible** in modern humans; the chin is one of the landmarks that currently distinguishes **AMH**s from other, closely related hominids. Aka mental eminence, chin eminence.

**mental retardation:** intelligence measured below the normal level, usually between the arbitrary thresholds of 50 and 70. Cf. **mental deficiency** and **mental defective**.

**mental retardation, X-linked nonspecific** (MRX): heritable condition characterized by mental impairment; large testes, ears and jaw; high-pitched voice, and jocular speech. Defective gene also has a fragile site (aka Martin–Bell syndrome). One of tens of sites, many X-linked, that cause mental impairment; the defective gene is an X-linked recessive, *MRX*. MRX is not the same entity as FRAX, **fragile X syndrome**.

**mental spine:** two pairs of small processes on the lingual surface of the **mandible** (i.e. on the surface opposite the chin). These structures serve as sites for the attachment of the **geniohyoid** and **genioglossus** muscles of the tongue complex.

**mental template:** prescribed, highly standardized way of producing **artifact** forms, with a clear idea in the mind of the tool maker of what the end product should be; term associated with James Deetz.

**Mentawai Island leaf-monkey:** vernacular for *Presbytis* potenziani.

**mentifact:** term created by certain anthropologists to contrast with an **artifact**; calls attention to any cultural phenomenon that is organized but does not have direct physical manifestations.

**mercy call:** vocalization made by a frightened animal.

**mericlinal chimera:** organ or organism consisting or two genetically different individuals, one of which partly or wholly engulfs the other. See **vanishing twin phenomenon**.

**meristic variation:** varying with respect to number, especially segmental parts, as in **polyploidy**.

**merozoite:** stage in the life cycle of the *Plasmodium* parasite when it invades red blood cells, where it requires seven weeks to replicate before lysing the cell. The merozoite can produce **immune decoy proteins**. See **sporozoite**.

**mesaticephalic:** see **mesocephaly**.

**mesatyskelia:** having a **stem–leg length index** of between 85.00 and 89.99.

**mesencephalon:** mid-brain, that structure in the **brain** composed of the **superior colliculi**, the **inferior colliculi**, and the **cerebral peduncles**.

**mesenchyme:** cells which may derive from the neural crest and that underlie the **epithelium** and often interact with it during the development of an organ or structure. The mesenchyme is active in the formation of blood, muscle, and connective tissue.

**mesenic:** having an **upper facial index** of between 50.00 and 54.99.

**mesenteric patches:** clusters of lymph nodes on the walls of the small intestine. Aka Peyer's patches.

**mesial:** term of dental orientation; for the back teeth mesial refers to the anterior surface, for the anterior teeth mesial refers to the medial surface; the Latin root *mes* means middle; toward the center.

**mesic:** 1. describes conditions that are neither extremely wet nor extremely dry. 2. adapted to such conditions. Cf. **hydric** and **xeric**.

**mesioangular dental impaction:** condition in which a tooth is placed at an angle in the alveolus and in mesial contact with an adjacent tooth so as to be incapable of complete eruption. See **dental impaction**.

**mesiobuccal:** pertaining to the surface or feature of a **premolar** or **molar** that is on both on the anterior surface and the cheek surface of the tooth.

**mesiodistal:** running along the length of a cheek tooth, i.e. from the **mesial** (or anterior) surface to the **distal** surface.

**mesiolingual:** pertaining to the surface or feature of a **premolar** or **molar** that is on both the anterior surface and the tongue surface of the tooth. Aka mesiolabial.

**mesoblast:** see **mesoderm**.

**mesocephalic:** pertaining to **mesocephaly**. Aka mesocranic.

**mesocephaly:** condition of having a **cephalic index** of between 75.00 and 79.99; such an individual is considered to have a head shape that is intermediate between narrow-headed (**dolichocephaly**) and round headed (**brachycephaly**). See **mesocranic**.

*Mesochoerus olduvaiensis:* species of extinct fossil pig found in East African sediments that date to *c.* 2 mya; an important species in **faunal correlation**.

**mesoconchic:** in reference to the **orbital index**, having an index between 76.00 and 84.99; such an individual is considered to have medium-sized orbits.

**mesochouranic:** pertaining to a an **external palatal index** of between 110.00 and 114.99.

**mesocnemic:** pertaining to a **platycnemic index** of between 63.00 and 69.99.

**mesocranic:** pertaining to **mesocephaly**. Aka mesocephalic, mesaticephalic, middleheaded.

**mesoderm:** middle layer of the three primary germ layers of the embryo. Mesoderm gives rise to all types of muscle, to the skeletal system, connective tissue (including blood), kidneys, internal reproductive organs, and the epithelial membranes of the body cavities (coelom). Aka mesoblastoma, mesoblast.

**mesodiacritic:** pertaining to a condition where between 30% and 80% of taxon members are recognizable as such; usually applied to variation below the species level. Cf. **pandiacritic**, **microdiacritic**, and **macrodiacritic**.

**mesognathous:** in reference to the **Flower's index**, with an index between 98.00 and 102.99; such an individual is considered to have medium projection of the jaws.

‡ **Mesolithic:** of or relating to the **Middle Stone Age** of Europe. Mesolithic **tool** technologies were in use during the period of transition from **hunting** and **gathering** to **agriculture** among populations of *Homo sapiens*, roughly 14–6 kya. The Mesolithic contained the **Azilian**, **Tardenoisian**, Maglemosian, **Campignian**, and **Capsian** periods.

**mesomelic shortening:** condition in which the forearm and lower leg are abnormally short. Cf. **acromelic shortening**, **rhizomelic shortening**.

**mesomorphy:** condition of having a stocky body build emphasizing bone and muscle; one of the three **somatotypes** of W. H. Sheldon. Adjective: mesomorphic.

**mesopallium:** portion of the cerebral cortex identified with the cortex of the cingulate gyrus. It is intermediate in form between the **archepallium** and the **neopallium** and has four or five distinct layers; now often called the juxtallocortex. One of G. Elliot **Smith's** tripartite divisions of the **pallium**.

*Mesopithecus* Wagner, 1839: genus of colobine monkeys known from the late Miocene through the Pliocene of Europe and western Asia; two species; most primitive of the colobines. Estimated body mass ranges from 5 to 8 kg; **sexually dimorphic**. Dental formula: 2.1.2.3/2.1.2.3; dentition similar to that of living colobines, indicating a **folivorous** diet. The robust **postcrania** of the older species, *M. pentelici*, differ from the modern species, suggesting it was at least **semiterrestrial**; the younger species, *M. monspessulanus*, possessed more derived limbs and was probably fully arboreal. It was also **sympatric** in part of its range with *Dolichopithecus* and some workers think that the latter species foraged on the ground, avoiding competition with the more arboreal *Mesopithecus*. See Appendix 1 for taxonomy.

*Mesopropithecus* Standing, 1905: genus of **extinct subfossil Malagasy prosimians** belonging to the Palaeopropithecidae; this family is called sloth lemurs. Three known species, *M. globiceps*, *M. pithecoides*, and *M. dolichobrachion*; in form, appears very similar to *Propithecus*, but slightly larger. Materials relating to this genus were recovered in the south and far north of Madagascar. Arboreal; diurnal; limb structure suggests arboreal quadrupedalism with suspension as mode of locomotion. Smallest of the subfossil prosimians, weighing around 10 kg. Dental formula: 2.1.2.3/1.1.2.3 or 2.1.2.3/2.0.2.3; dentition suggests **folivory**. See Appendix 2 for taxonomy, Appendix 3 for living species.

**mesoprosopic:** in reference to the **total facial index**, with an index between 85.00 and 89.99; such an individual is considered to have a medium width face.

**mesorrhine:** see **mesorrhinic**, **nasal morphology**, and **Topinard**.

**mesorrhinic:** in reference to the **nasal index**, with an index between 47.00 and 50.00; such an individual is considered to have a medium **nasal aperture**; aka mesorrhine. See **Topinard** and **nasal morphology**.

**mesostaphyline:** in reference to the **palatal index**, with an index between 80.00 and 84.99; such an individual is considered to have a medium-sized palate.

**mesosternale chest girth:** circumference of the chest as measured across the middle of the **sternum**; an average of readings taken during **inspiration** and **expiration**.

‡ **Mesozoic era:** second geologic era of the **Phanerozoic eon**, dating roughly between 245 and 65 mya, also known as the Age of Reptiles. The first primitive **mammals** and the birds appeared during this era.

**Messel primate:** reference to one of the middle Eocene adapoid primate specimens recovered from deposits in Messel, Germany; notable for **postcranial** remains.

‡ **messenger RNA:** see **mRNA**.

**Messinian salinity crisis:** dropping of sea levels worldwide about 5.3 mya, which caused the temporary desiccation of the Mediterranean Sea. Aka the **Mediterranean crisis**.

**mestizo:** 1. person of mixed blood, usually European and Native American. 2. originally, in the sixteenth century, the offspring of a Spanish male and Native American female.

**mesuranic:** in reference to the **external palatal index**, with an index between 110.00 and 114.99; such an individual is considered to have a medium-sized palate.

**metabolic adaptation:** adaptation to cold stress that is accomplished through increases in basal metabolism and metabolic heat production from muscles. Cf. **insulative adaptation**.

**metabolic block:** truncation in a metabolic pathway that prevents the completion of a process or product. See **inborn error of metabolism**.

**metabolic disorder:** disease or syndrome that affects normal **metabolism**; common examples are **galactosemia**, **glycogen storage disease**, **fructose intolerance**, **lactose intolerance**, **phenylketonuria**, and **porphyria variegata**. Aka metabolic disease. See **nutritional disorder**.

**metabolic pathway:** any sequence of enzyme-mediated chemical reactions in which intermediates are synthesized and/or broken down in cells.

**metabolic scaling:** proportionality of a trait such as body mass to whole-animal metabolic rate. See **Kleiber's law**.

**metabolic syndrome:** set of noninfectious diseases: **type II diabetes**, insulin resistance, **hypertension**, and hypertriglyceridemia. Cf. **New World syndrome**.

**metabolic theory of aging:** intracellular, systemic model of aging in which the major premise is that longevity is inversely proportional to metabolic rate across many species, and that it thus affects aging by some unknown mechanism. In its original form, many exceptions to the general thesis were found, but it has been reformulated as the **free radical theory of aging**.

‡ **metabolism:** aggregate of the biochemical reactions within a cell that support life. Verb: to metabolize. Cf. **anabolism**, **catabolism**, and **basal metabolism**.

**metabolite:** substance produced by **metabolism**.

**metabotropic glutamate receptor** (mGluR5): receptor for the neurotransmitter glutamate.

**metacarpal:** of or pertaining to the region between the wrist and the fingers of the hand or fore paw.

**metacarpus:** five bones of the hand or fore paw between the **carpus** and **phalanges**. The metacarpals are numbered I–V, beginning with the thumb metacarpal. The lateral metacarpus I is the most movable and permits the thumb to oppose the other digits, a major anatomical adaptation of humans.

‡ **metacentric chromosome:** chromosome in which the **centromere** is very near the middle of the **chromatids** such that the **p arm** and **q arm** are about the same length.

**metacommunication:** communication about communication; metacommunicative signals provide information about the context of forthcoming signals. A play-invitation signal, for example, indicates that subsequent threat displays should be taken as play and not as serious hostility.

**metacone:** cusp on the distobuccal surface of an upper molar; it helps form the buccal portion of the **trigon**. Cf. **metaconid**.

**metaconid:** main **cusp** on the distobuccal surface of a lower molar; it helps form the buccal portion of the **trigonid**. Cf. **metacone**.

**metaconule:** cuspule on the distal heel of the **trigon** between the **metacone** and **protocone** that has developed on the upper molars of some primate species.

**metacrista:** ridge of enamel that courses from the **metacone** of an upper molar in some archaic mammals and early primates.

**metafemale:** human female with a normal complement of 44 autosomes, but with three X chromosomes rather than the normal XX. The condition is marked by a certain degree of **obesity** and some females with the condition are slightly retarded. Aka superfemale, trisomy X, triplo-X. See **poly-X female**.

**metamale:** human male with a normal complement of 44 autosomes and one X chromosome, but with two Y chromosomes rather than the normal single Y. The condition is marked by a certain degree of tallness and leanness; there are controversial reports of increased aggressive behavior. Aka supermale, XYY syndrome, Jacob syndrome, poly-Y male.

‡ **metamere:** see **somite**.

**metamorphic rock:** sedimentary or igneous rock that has been transformed through heat and/or pressure into another kind of rock such as **quartzite**.

‡ **metaphase:** stage in **mitosis** during which the chromosomes are arranged along the equatorial plane of the cell.

‡ **metaphase I:** stage during **meiosis I** when homologous chromosome pairs align at the equator of a diploid cell.

‡ **metaphase II:** stage during **meiosis II** when unpaired chromosomes align at the equator of a dividing cell.

**metaphase arrest:** artificial termination of cell division by treatment of a cell culture with colchicine or other spindle poison. Used to obtain chromosome spreads that are made into a **karyotype**.

**metaphase plate:** cluster of chromosomes aligned at the equator of the cell during **mitosis**.

**metaphysis:** see **epiphyseal disk**.

**metapopulation:** set of populations or **demes** existing simultaneously, belonging to the same **species**, and, by definition, occupying different geographic ranges.

**metastasis:** spread of diseased cells (including cancer cells) from a site of origin to distant parts of an individual's body. Verb: to metastasize; adjective: metastatic.

**metatarsal:** of or pertaining to the region between the ankle and the toes of the foot or hind paw. The metatarsal bones are numbered I–V beginning with the medial metatarsal. Each metatarsal **bone** is bound by ligaments to form the **foot arches**. See **metatarsus**.

**metatarsal I seldom:** supernumerary bone on the **plantar** surface of the foot near the first **metatarsal** bone.

**metatarsus:** portion of the foot or hind paw between the **tarsus** and **phalanges**; its skeleton consists of the **metatarsal** bones. Aka the instep.

‡ **Metatheria:** taxon containing nearly all the pouched mammals, such as the kangaroo and opossum. Most give birth to immature offspring that must further mature inside the mother's **marsupium** (pouch) before they are capable of independent survival; the marsupial mammals, or metatherians.

‡ **metazoan:** applied with reference to any **multicellular** animal, excepting the sponges; any member of the taxon Metazoa.

**metencephalon:** that region of the superior hindbrain or **rhombencephalon** composed of the **cerebellum** and the **pons**.

**methallothionein:** any protein that binds metallic ions.

**methionine** (Met): an essential **amino acid**; one of the twenty building blocks of **proteins**. Present in nature in egg albumin and other proteins. Along with **cysteine**, one of two amino acids with sulfur groups. Methionine is usually the leading amino acid in proteins, but is often removed by an enzyme before final assembly.

**methionine homozygosity:** genotype of individuals susceptible to acquiring new variant **Creutzfeldt–Jakob disease**. The individuals are homozygous for **methionine** at amino acid position 129 of the **prion protein**, as well as another mutation at position 178.

**method of contradiction and induction:** mathematical technique for proving the nonfalsifiability of a collection of statements, operationally proved by assuming that one is false, but that the negation of the statement leads to a contradiction. See **hypothesis testing**.

**methodology:** 1. a system of methods, principles or rules that govern a given discipline, as scientific methodology. 2. the study of scientific inquiry. 3. in pedagogy, the study of teaching practices.

**methyl group** (-CH$_3$): in genetics, usually refers to the addition of a methyl radical to DNA. See **DNA methylation**.

**methylation:** addition of methyl groups to cytosine bases (usually at CpG dinucleotides). See **CpG island**.

**metmyoglobin** (metMb): brownish-red pigment resulting from the oxidation of **myoglobin**.

**metopian:** mid-point of that line which connects the two **frontal eminences**.

**metopic suture:** place of articulation between the two **frontal bones**, as found in **prosimians**. In **anthropoids** the metopic suture completely ossifies, producing a single frontal bone.

**metopism:** persistence of the frontal or **metopic suture**; the **obliteration** of this suture usually occurs by about the sixth post-natal year in humans.

**metric trait, character** or **feature:** see **continuous trait**.

**metriocormic:** in reference to the **cormic index**, with an index of 53.00 or greater; such an individual has limbs that are intermediate in length relative to trunk size, compared with **brachycormic** or **macrocormic** individuals. The most metriocormic human populations are Europeans and western and south Asians. Cf. **mesatyskelia**.

**metriocranic:** in reference to the **cranial breadth-height index**, with an index between 92.00 and 97.99; such an individual is considered to have a medium skull.

**metriometopic:** pertaining to a **transverse fronto-parietal index** of between 66.00 and 68.99.

**Mexican black howler:** vernacular for *Alouatta pigra* (= *villosa*).

**Mezhirich:** an archaeological site found in 1965 on the Dnepr River near Kiev in the Ukraine, dating to 18–15 kya (late Pleistocene), containing Upper Paleolithic **Gravettian** artifacts. Known as the mammoth camp, a large dome-shaped house had been constructed using the bones of at least 95 mammoths, and roofed with hides and sod. One mammoth skull (the 'drum') had been decorated. Other implements such as a bone needle were also reported.

**Mezmaiskaya Cave:** archaeological site found in the Hrvatsko Zagorje region, Croatia, in the northern Caucasus, dated to 29–28 kya (AMS radiocarbon), and that contains **Mousterian** artifacts. The hominid remains include fragments from at least eight individuals, of which one is the fragmentary skeleton of an infant attributed to *Homo neanderthalensis*. Some of the hominid fragments are burned and display cut marks that have been cited as evidence of **cannibalism**. Aka Mezmaskaya Cave. Mitochondrial DNA was extracted from the ribs of the fossil neonate in 2000 and compared to mtDNA extracted in 1997 from the **Feldhofer Grotto** Neandertal. Both the Mezmaiskaya infant's and the Feldhofer adult's DNA were found to be equally distant from all modern human populations, but similar to each other. This result has been interpreted by some as indicating little if any gene flow between Neandertals and contemporary **AMHs**, and thus supportive of the **out of Africa** model. See **last of the Neandertals** and **Vindija Cave**. Cf. **Abrigo do Lagar Velho rockshelter**.

**Mfwangani (Island):** paleontological site on an island in Lake Victoria, Kenya, East Africa, dated to the early Miocene, and that contains primate remains including fragments attributed to *Proconsul nyanzae*. Cf. **Rusinga Island**.

‡ **MHC:** major histocompatibility complex, a group of genes in mammals that code for **antigens** that are important in tissue immune function. An older term applied to humans for this complex is the **human leukocyte antigen complex**.

**Miaohoushan (Locality A):** archaeological site found in 1985 at Miaohoushan, Benxi County, Liaoning Province, China, dated to 290–130 kya; contains **hominid** remains including a femoral shaft and teeth attributed to **archaic *Homo sapiens***.

**Micoquian:** variant assemblage of a Middle Paleolithic variety, but with the reappearance of handaxe-like implements, named for a French site (La Micoque);

also referred to as **Mousterian of Acheulean Tradition** (MAT).

**microabrasion:** 1. evidence of friction or use that is microscopic in extent. 2. subtle patterns of edge damage on a **tool** (microscopic polish, flakes, scars) that provides evidence as to the tool's previous usage. Near-synonyms include microflakes, micropolish, and microscars. See **microwear.**

*Microadapis sciureus* **Szalay, 1974:** adapoid prosimian from the middle Eocene of Europe belonging to the family **Adapidae; monotypic.** Estimated body mass around 600 g. Dental formula: 2.1.4.3/2.1.4.3; noted for well-developed canines; cheek teeth suggestive of **frugivory** with perhaps insect supplements. See Appendix 1 for taxonomy.

**microanatomy:** study of structures that cannot be seen with the unaided eye. Microanatomy includes histology and cell and structural biology.

**microarray:** see **DNA microarray.**

**microblade:** long, narrow flake, about 30 mm × 7 mm.

*Microcebus* **Geoffroy, 1834:** prosimian genus to which the mouse lemurs belong; three to four species depending on authority. Found in lowland regions of Madagascar. Arboreal; nocturnal; quadrupeds that employ some leaping. Very small, three of the species weighing between 60 and 70 g. Dental formula: 3.1.3.3; **dental comb** present; diet **faunivory** and **frugivory. Grooming claw** on second digit of hind paw. **Noyau;** build nests and often sleep together in ' **dormitories';** females have home ranges that are overlapped by the male home ranges; territories scent marked with urine and feces. Normal litter size is two. *M. coquereli* is separated into the genus *Mirza* by many workers. See Appendix 2 for taxonomy, Appendix 3 for living species.

**microcephaly:** abnormal condition in which there is an unusually small cranium and brain; the head is characterized by **oxycephaly** and the chin and forehead are markedly recessed.

**Microchiroptera:** suborder of the mammalian order **Chiroptera** comprised of approximately 17 families, 150 genera, and 810 species of bat. Microchiropterans are small (body mass 2–170 g, with most under 50 g) and over 70% of species are **insectivorous;** they conserve energy by **estivation.** They use echolocation for obstacle avoidance in darkened caves and for locating prey during nocturnal foraging; 40% of the brain is devoted to the auditory regions. Although they are more derived than their sister taxon **Megachiroptera,** microchiropterans appear earlier in the fossil record (*c.* 50 mya) and some **Paleocene** fossil 'bats' have been mistaken for basal primates. Because bats are closely related to the **Dermoptera,** and both are related to the **Primates,** all three orders are grouped in the grandorder **Archonta.** Aka insectivorous bat, microbat.

**Microchoeridae:** family of **omomyoids** known from the middle Eocene to the early Oligocene of Europe; four genera and twenty species; well known from many specimens. This group may be descended from an early member of the **Anaptomorphinae.** Orbits are large, suggesting nocturnality; postorbital wall only partly closed; short snout. Great variation in body mass between the genera, ranging from 50 g to 2 kg. Dental formula variable, although maxillary dentition is 2.1.3.3/2.1.3.3; dental morphology suggests diversity of diet among the different genera. **Postcrania** indicate leaping abilities. See Appendix 1 for taxonomy.

**Microchoerinae:** subfamily of omomyoid primates belonging to the family **Omomyidae** under some classificatory schemes. Vernacular: microchorine.

*Microchoerus* **Wood, 1846:** genus of tarsiiform primate from the late Eocene and early Oligocene of Europe belonging to the omomyoid family **Microchoeridae;** five species. Short snout; body mass for these species ranges from 500 g to 1.5 kg. Dental formula: 2.1.3.3/2.1.2.3; well-developed shearing crests have been interpreted as adaptation for **folivory.** See Appendix 1 for taxonomy.

**microclactonian:** lower Paleolithic flint industry of Europe characterized by small flakes or **microliths.** See **Clactonian.**

**microclimate:** environment of a small local area.

*Microcolobus turgensis* **Benefit and Pickford, 1986:** colobine from the late Miocene of Africa; **monotypic.** Very small for a colobine, estimated body mass around 4 kg. Dental formula: 2.1.2.3/2.1.2.3; one of the geologically older colobines, reflected in the poorly developed shearing crests on the molars; it is felt by some workers that this monkey was only partly **folivorous.** See Appendix 1 for taxonomy.

**microcomplement fixation:** 1. process of binding serological **complement** (2) during an antigen-antibody interaction. 2. measurement of the quantity of complement that participates in an individual antigen-antibody binding event. When immunological reactions between different taxa are measured, the amount of complement fixed (bound) during the reaction serves as an estimate of taxonomic distance, since complement fixation is proportional to **genetic distance.** See **immunological distance.**

**microcythemia:** condition characterized by abnormally small red blood cells.

**microdiacritic:** pertaining to a condition where less than 30% of the members of a taxon are recognizable as such; usually applied to variation below the species level. Cf. **pandiacritic** and **mesodiacritic.**

**microdifferentiation:** accumulation of minor genetic differences in populations isolated from each other, with a resultant divergence in their genetic composition.

**microdontia:** possessing small teeth; aka microdontism.

**microenvironment:** small volumetric space with a set of physical features (e.g. climate, topography, etc.) that may be more conducive to particular organisms than is the surrounding habitat; aka microhabitat.

‡ **microevolution:** 1. changes of **allele frequencies** in a **population** between generations. 2. a small amount of change or a limited number of evolutionary steps that consists of minor alterations in **allele** frequencies, **chromosome** structure, or chromosome numbers. 3. local evolution within **populations** and **species.** 4. (of proteins) process of minor, slow evolutionary changes that occur in proteins after specific adaptive functions have stabilized; optimization of function by trial-and-error substitution of one amino acid at a time. Cf. **macroevolution.** See **evolution.**

**microfilament:** strand of protein that forms part of a cell's cytoskeleton.

**microfossil:** fossil remnant that is too small to be visible to the unaided eye and therefore best seen with the aid of an instrument such as a microscope.

**microgeographic race:** small population that also occupies a finite region and that is characterized by small genetic differences from other such populations.

**microhabitat:** see **microenvironment.**

**microinjection:** process of introducing small quantities of material into a single intact cell by using a microscopic needle that penetrates the cell membrane.

‡ **microlith:** small, carefully manufactured stone blade chipped from prepared wedge-shaped, conical cores and designed to be mounted in antler, bone, or wooden hafts; served as spear barbs, arrow points, and as small knives and scraper blades; first appear in China about 30 kya, and were eventually used almost worldwide.

**Micromomyidae:** family of archaic fossil mammals belonging to the order **Plesiadapiformes;** known from the late Paleocene to the early Eocene of North America; four genera. Vernacular: micromomyid. These are the smallest plesiadapiforms, ranging in size from 10 to 30 g. Dental formula appears to be 2.1.2.3/2.1.2.3; procumbent incisors, enlarged upper and lower fourth premolars; teeth and small body size suggest that these forms practised **insectivory.** See Appendix 1 for taxonomy.

**Micromomys Szalay, 1973:** archaic mammal known from the late Paleocene and early Eocene of North America belonging to the order **Plesiadapiformes,**

family **Micromomyidae;** four species. Dental formula probably 2.1.2.3/2.1.3.3; small body size strongly suggestive of **insectivory.** Body size of the species very small and estimated to be between 10 and 15 g. See Appendix 1 for taxonomy.

**micromutation:** any **mutation** with a small phenotypic effect; **point mutation.**

**micron:** metric unit of measurement equal to one ten-thousandth of a centimeter (0.0001 cm). Aka micrometer.

**Micronesia:** region in Oceania consisting of the Caroline, Gilbert, and Marshall Islands, and of Guam and Truk. All of the islands are inhabited by humans.

**micronucleus:** 1. smallest of the nuclei in a multinuclear cell. 2. smaller (reproductive) of the two nuclei in certain cell lines, organelles, and organisms that divide mitotically, the larger being the vegetative nucleus.

**micronutrient:** any organic or inorganic molecule required for nutritional function; micronutrients are vitamins and minerals needed as components of coenzymes.

**microorganism:** any living entity too small to be seen by the human eye; any form of microscopic life. Common microorganisms include bacteria, blue-green algae, some fungi, protistans, viroids, and viruses.

**micropaleontology:** study of **microfossils** as an adjunct to the understanding of sites containing artifacts and bones.

**microparasite:** small organism that infects and reproduces inside a host; these organisms typically have short generation times. Cf. **macroparasite.**

**micropathology:** disease process or trauma that is not detectable by simple visual examination, but that requires the use of a tool such as a microscope. Cf. **macropathology.**

**Micropithecus clarki (Fleagle and Simons, 1978):** **monotypic** genus of **hominoid** from the early Miocene of East Africa belonging to the catarrhine family **Proconsulidae.** One of the Miocene apes that has been suggested as an ancestor to living gibbons; an endocast from this species reveals a very gibbon-like brain surface pattern. *Dionysopithecus* from Asia is very similar and some workers think that it should be included in *Micropithecus.* Smallest verified ape, with an estimated body mass ranging between 3 and 4 kg. Dental formula: 2.1.2.3; large incisors and small cheek teeth, similar to those of living gibbons and suggestive of **frugivory.** See *Simiolus* and Appendix 1 for taxonomy.

**micro-race:** isolated population that is not a member of a larger **geographical race** or group, and that had adapted to isolation and local conditions such that they can be easily distinguished from other groups.

Traditional examples of micro-races include the **Ainu** of Japan, the **Andamanese**, the **Mbuti pygmies**, and the **Sami** of Scandinavia. Cf. **geographical race** and **local race**.

**microsatellite DNA:** sequential tandem repeats in DNA; di-, tri-, tetra-, or pentanucleotide repeats found in the **centromere** and scattered throughout some genomes. Aka short tandem repeats.

**microscopic:** of or pertaining to something that cannot be seen by the unaided eye.

**microsomatic animal:** mammal with a poorly developed sense of smell; in fact, this term applies mainly to primates. Among the primates this applies to most of the **anthropoids**.

**micro-spectrophotometry:** ablation of a specimen using an electron microscope; the electrons that are focused on a specimen create emissions that can be used to identify the specimen.

**microsplanchnic type:** in Viola's body build typology, the extremely thin.

**microstratigraphic acuity:** amount of geologic time represented in a given sediment sample.

**Microsysopidae:** family of archaic fossil mammals belonging to the order **Plesiadapiformes**. Vernacular microsysopid. Known from the late Paleocene to late Eocene of North America and Europe; nine genera of forms ranging from 20 g to almost 3 kg. Considered to be closely related to the **Palaechthonidae** and some authors include that family within the Microsyopidae. Dental formula, maxilla: 2.1.3.3; mandibular dental formula variable; family characterized by a caniniform upper incisor and lanceolate lower central incisors. The dentition resembles that of other plesiadapiforms and the cranial arterial system resembles that of extant primates, but the structure of the ear (e.g. nonpetrosal **auditory bulla**) is insectivore-like and some authors think that this group should be included in order Insectivora. Diverse group in which diet ranged from insectivory to plant material. See Appendix 1 for taxonomy.

*Microsysops* Leidy, 1872: archaic mammal of the Eocene of the Rocky Mountain region of North America belonging to the plesiadapiform family **Microsyopidae**; consists of six to eight species, depending on authority. This genus has a cranial arterial pattern similar to that of living primates, but the **auditory bulla** does not emanate from the petrosal bone and this, along with other traits, has led some workers to assign this genus to the order Insectivora. Dental formula: 2.1.3.3/1.0.3.3. Estimated body masses for the different species range from 400 g to 2 kg. See Appendix 1 for taxonomy.

**microtaxonomy:** term used by E. **Mayr** to denote the subfield of **taxonomy** whose subject is the

methodology and principles used to determine species. Cf. **macrotaxonomy**.

**microtektites:** tiny glass particles created when minerals are melted by the heat generated by an impacting asteroid or meteor; typically found in a large, concentric circle and used to pinpoint an impact site. See **Chicxulub structure**.

**microtubule:** one of the filamentous, tubular structures in eukaryotic cells ultimately responsible for cell polarization and that consist primarily of tubulin and other proteins. Microtubules organize both stable structures such as **centrioles** and transient structures such as the **spindle**.

**microtubule organizing center** (MTOC): bundles of protein tubes found at the base of a eukaryote flagellum such as that of a sperm cell; in animals these also function to construct the arrays of **microtubules** that cause normal disjunction of chromosomes.

‡ **microwear:** 1. patterns of **tooth enamel** abrasion or damage on fossil teeth, signatures of foods consumed by an animal before its death. 2. microscopic polishing, flaking, or scarring on a tool; see **microabrasion**.

**micturition:** process of voiding urine; Aka urination.

**midas tamarin:** vernacular for *Saguinus midas*.

**mid-Atlantic ridge:** **mid-ocean ridge** located on the bottom of the Atlantic Ocean, and stretching from Iceland nearly to Antarctica.

**mid-axillary skinfold: anthropometric** measurement: skinfold measured at the height of the xiphoid–sternal junction in the mid-axillary line. Used to complement other **skinfold measurements** of adiposity of the torso. See **skinfold thickness**.

**midbrain:** the **mesencephalon**, the mid-portion of the embryonic brain. See **limbic midbrain**.

**midden:** refuse deposited as the result of human activities, consisting of soil, food remains (animal bones and shells), and discarded artifacts. The word is derived from the Danish *mödden*, meaning muck heap. Cf. **kitchen midden**.

**mid-digital hair:** see **mid-phalangeal hair**.

**middle age:** stage of the human **life cycle** that is variably defined, but characterized by decreasing physiological vigor; a substage of **adulthood**. Some authorities suggest that it commences with the onset of **presbyopia** and commences with **maturity**. Cf. **transition to full maturity**.

**Middle Awash:** region found in 1968 located in the **Afar triangle**, Ethiopia, rich in archaeological sites, dated to much of the past 6 my, and that contains artifacts of many industries including **Oldowan, Acheulean, Middle Stone Age** and **Late Stone Age**. Abundant hominid remains include more than 100 fossil **hominids** recovered since 1990; excavated by the International Afar Research Expedition in 1974–78 and then by J. Desmond Clark and Tim White from 1981 on. Aka **Hadar**. See **Maka, Belohdelie**.

‡ **Middle Paleolithic** (MP): the Middle **Old Stone Age**; a general term used to refer collectively to the stone tool technologies of **archaic** *Homo sapiens*, including but not limited to a decrease in the use of **handaxes** and an increase in the use of artifacts produced by the **Levallois technique**; this Age may have commenced as early as 200 kya (70 kya is more commonly cited), and lasted until about 50–32 kya.

**Middle Pleistocene**: subdivision of the **Pleistocene epoch** from about 900 to 127 kya.

**middle range research**: investigation aimed at linking static archaeological data with the dynamic processes that formed it.

**Middle Stone Age** (MSA): in Africa, a stone tool tradition generally dated from about 100 to 40 kya; characterized by the carefully prepared stone cores used for the production of flake tools. The African MSA was also a time when regional variation in technologies became greater than in the past. In some sites, researchers think they see African antecedents to the **Sebilian** and **Aurignacian** tool traditions found later and further north. In Europe, cultures that flourished about 150–35 kya; the best-known tradition among these is the **Mousterian** culture carried by the **Neandertals**. Aka **Mesolithic**.

**mid-facial length**: prosthion–endobasion distance when measured in the median sagittal plane.

**midget**: exceptionally small adult human but with normal body proportions. The famous Tiny Tim was a midget. See **pituitary dwarfism**.

**mid-growth spurt**: relatively small increase in the rate of growth in height that occurs in many children between the ages of six and eight years.

‡ **mid-line**: hypothetical line that divides the body or a structure into left and right halves; medial line. See **mid-sagittal**.

**mid-ocean ridge**: any elongated rise on the ocean floor where **basalt** erupts periodically, and forming new oceanic **crust**; similar to a continental **rift zone**. See **mid-Atlantic ridge**.

**mid-offspring value**: mean phenotypic value of all the offspring (the **sibship**) within a family.

**mid-parent value**: mean phenotypic value of an individual's (or a sibship's) parents.

**mid-phalangeal**: pertaining to the middle section of a finger or toe.

**mid-phalangeal hair**: autosomal dominant condition characterized by dorsal hair on the top of the third (middle) segment of the fingers; aka mid-digital hair. Occurs with high frequency among the Dunkers in Pennsylvania.

**mid-sagittal**: describes a plane or line of anatomical orientation that runs medially through a bilateral organism and divides it into equal right and left halves; also describes a structure on this plane. Aka mid-sagittal plane. Cf. **sagittal**. See **sagittal crest**.

**mid-tarsal**: describes the area between the two rows of tarsal bones.

**mid-thigh circumference**: **anthropometric** measurement: distance around the middle of the thigh as measured with a tape measure placed mid-way between the inguinal crease (skinfold between groin and thigh) and the proximal border of the **patella** and passed horizontally around the body. Combined with the other thigh circumferences, used for estimations of body density, adiposity, lean body mass and for various applications in **human engineering**. See **distal thigh circumference** and **proximal thigh circumference**.

**migrant selection**: selection based on the different abilities of individuals of different genetic constitutions to migrate; for example, if new populations are founded more consistently by individuals with gene *A* as opposed to those bearing gene *a*, gene *A* is said to be favored by migrant selection.

‡ **migration**: 1. movement of individuals and cultural materials from one population to another, or from one location to another; one of Fagan's four models used to characterize culture change. Migration may be either short- or long-term. 2. in genetics, the transfer of genetic information by the movement of individuals from one population to another, which movement may change **allele frequencies** in both **populations**; **introgression**. See **dispersion** and **gene flow**. 3. movement of cells within the body.

**migration coefficient**: factor, $M$, that represents the proportion of a gene pool represented by migrant genes, expressed per generation. See **gene flow**.

**migration effect**: differences observed between migrants and their descendants. Common migration effects include height, head form, and body form.

**migration inhibition factor**: lymphokine that inhibits the migration of macrophages.

**Milankovich, Milutin** (1879–1958): Serbian mathematician and clinatologist; proposed that variations in the earth's climate are in part due to systematic variation in the pattern of solar radiation, which came to be known as the **Milankovich orbital forcing hypothesis**. Author of *Canon of Insolation of the Earth and Its Application to the Problem of Ice Ages* (1941).

**Milankovich orbital forcing hypothesis**: proposal that solar radiation is a function of the interaction of the changing orbits of the earth and the sun; the fundamental variables include eliptical precession, tilt, and eccentricity of the earth. Proposed in 1920 by M. **Milankovich**, the hypothesis states that glacial–interglacial cycles are driven by periodic changes in July insolation at 65 °N, and are caused by predictable variations in the earth's orbit. Aka Milankovich orbital cycles, Milankovich mechanism, wave hypothesis, orbital forcing theory.

**military monkey:** vernacular for *Erythrocebus patas*.

‡ **milk:** 1. white or yellowish secretion of the mammary glands of female mammals, primarily for the nourishment of offspring; milk contains protein, sugar, lipids, and certain antibodies that provide **passive immunity**; see **breast milk**. The proportion of nutrients in milk is unique to each species. 2. any milklike liquid.

**milk line:** one of two bilateral lines connecting the paired nipples or teats of mammals. In humans a similar line exists in certain rare conditions such as **polymastia**.

**milk molar:** in the **deciduous** dentition of **anthropoid** primates, the two rearmost teeth in each quadrant are assumed to be molars (dM) by most researchers.

**milk teeth:** baby teeth; see **deciduous** dentition.

**milking:** expression of breast milk; usually refers to the obtaining of milk from domesticated animals. The process is thought to have originated in southwest Asia, probably with the goat. Cattle, sheep, mares, and reindeer have been milked.

**'Millennium Man':** see **Rondinin**.

**Milne-Edwards' sportive lemur:** vernacular for *Lepilemur edwardsi*.

**Milton, Katherine** (1941–): US primatologist and anthropologist at UC Berkeley who investigates the energetics, digestive physiology, and dietary ecology of primates. Her work on howler monkey energetics moved the study of primate foraging behavior in new directions. In recent years she has expanded her study to include the nutritional ecology of humans in Amazonia and Papua New Guinea. Author of *The Foraging Strategy of Howler Monkeys* (1980).

**mimicry:** case in which one species resembles another, unrelated species. See **Batesian mimicry** and **Müllerian mimicry**.

**Mindel glacial maximum:** second major glacial episode in the **Alpine glacial sequence** of the Pleistocene, which lasted from more than 420+ kya until about 270 kya. See **Günz**, **Riss**, and **Würm** glacial maxima, and **Günz–Mindel** (Cromerian), **Mindel–Riss** (Holstein), and **Riss–Würm** interglacials (or interstadials).

‡ **Mindel glaciation:** one of the four traditional periods of glaciation or ice ages that define the Pleistocene epoch during the past 1.8 million years BP. The second stage in the Quaternary sequence of the Alpine region, the Mindel had a duration of about 90 ky and terminated between 350 and 300 kya.

**Mindel–Riss interglacial:** second major interglacial episode in the **Alpine glacial sequence** of the Pleistocene, which lasted from more than 300+ kya until about 270 kya. See **Günz, Mindel, Riss**, and **Würm** glacial maxima, and **Günz–Mindel** and **Riss–Würm** interglacials (or interstadials). Aka Great Interglacial Period, Hoxnian, Holsteinian, Yarmouthian.

**mineral:** any naturally occurring, homogenous, inorganic substance, i.e. without carbon. Minerals important in human metabolism include calcium, phosphorous, potassium, sulfur, sodium, chloride, and magnesium. Outside the body minerals assume a characteristic crystalline structure.

**mineral replacement:** fossilization process during which organic material is displaced by minerals such as calcium carbonate; see **permineralization**.

**minimal neck circumference:** anthropometric measurement: distance around the neck as measured with a tape measure placed just inferior to the laryngeal prominence (Adam's apple) and passed around the neck. Used in studies of growth, athletic performance, body fat content, and **human engineering**.

**minimum breadth of the mandibular ramus:** craniometric measurement: minimum distance between the anterior and posterior borders of the **mandibular ramus** as measured with sliding calipers; there are no established craniometric landmarks for this measurement.

**minimum dynamic area** (MDA): in conservation biology, the smallest land area required for maintaining the **minimum viable population**. See **population viability analysis**.

**minimum frontal breadth** (ft–ft): craniometric measurement; width between the left and right **frontotemporale** as measured with sliding calipers. See Appendix 7 for an illustration of the landmarks used.

**minimum frontal cranial breadth:** minimum breadth between the temporal crests of the frontal bone.

**minimum mutation distance:** in molecular taxonomy, the quantitative difference in the sequences of two homologous proteins, measured as the minimum number of mutations required to transform one into the other; operationally, counted as the number of changes at the nucleotide level.

**minimum number of individuals** (MNI): the number of animals necessary to account for all the skeletal remains of a particular species found in a faunal assemblage; applies to hominids, as well.

**minimum viable population** (MVP): lowest number of individuals in a population necessary to provide the genetic **diversity** needed for that population's survival over a specified time period. See **biodiversity**.

**minisatellite DNA:** DNA consisting of a variable number of repeats of a characteristic short sequence of 30–60 base pairs; minisatellites are possible examples of **selfish DNA**. Minisatellites have **mutation**

**rates** as high as $10^{-2}$ per generation as they arise in high frequency, possibly by unequal crossing over, in eukaryotic genomes.

‡ **Miocene epoch:** one of the **Tertiary** epochs of the **Cenozoic era**, lasting from about 23.8 to 5.3 mya. The first **apes** evolved and flourished during the Miocene; mastodons, weasels, raccoons, and early deer and antelopes also appear in the fossil record from this epoch. See Appendix 4 for a geological time scale.

*Mioeuoticus* **Leakey, 1962:** genus of fossil prosimians known from the early Miocene of Africa belonging to the family **Lorisidae**; two species; known from two **crania**. Body mass estimated around 300 g. Dental formula: 2.1.3.3/2.1.3.3; dental morphology suggestive of **frugivory** and **insectivory**. See Appendix 1 for taxonomy.

*Miopithecus* **I. Geoffroy, 1862:** monotypic genus to which the talapoin monkey belongs. Distribution in forests of western equatorial Africa. Smallest catarrhine: body mass ranges from 750 to 1400 g. Arboreal; diurnal; quadrupedal; reported to be good swimmers. Dental formula: 2.1.2.3; **frugivorous**; possess **cheek pouches**. Live in large troops of up to 150 individuals; although the troops are mixed-sex, the males and females segregate into subgroups until breeding season. See Appendix 2 for taxonomy, Appendix 3 for living species.

**miosis:** contraction of the pupil of the eye. Not to be confused with **meiosis**.

*Mioxicebus griseus* **Lesson, 1840:** synonym for *Cheirogaleus major*.

**mir-:** in taxonomy, a prefix used for the taxon below super- or grand-. Thus, a **mirorder** is below a superorder or grandorder. See **Primatomorpha**.

**mirorder:** in taxonomy, rarely used superordinal **taxon** that consists of a group of orders that, itself, is contained within a higher taxon, the **grandorder**.

**mirror-imaging:** reversals of physical features observed in some identical twin pairs; e.g. **hand preference**, hair whorls, and **fingerprint ridge count**. Only a few traits are affected.

*Mirza* **Gray, 1870: monotypic prosimian** genus to which Coquerel's dwarf (mouse) lemur belongs. Discontinuous range along the coast of western Madagascar where it occupies dry deciduous forest. Arboreal; nocturnal; locomotion quadrupedal with leaping. Body mass ranges from 270 to 330 g. Dental formula: 3.1.3.3; **omnivorous** with diet including animal prey, fruit, nectar, gums, and insect secretions. **Noyau**, with overlapping male and female home ranges; sleep in leaf nests, sometimes with other individuals. This species is sometimes included in **Microcebus**, but is three times the size of those species and has different dental characteristics. See

Appendix 2 for taxonomy and Appendix 3 for species.

**miscarriage:** 1. failure to attain a result. 2. expulsion of an inviable human **fetus**, usually between the third and the seventh month of **gestation**. See **abortion**. Cf. **stillbirth**.

**miscegenation:** marriage or cohabitation between a man and a woman of different **races**, especially in the USA between a black person and a white person, a legacy from the antebellum slavery period.

**mismatch repair:** proofreading DNA for misalignment segments of **microsatellite DNA**, which are normally the same size in an individual.

‡ **missense mutation:** base substitution in DNA that is transcribed into **mRNA**, and by translation leads to a simple amino acid substitution in the polypeptide produced which, because of the properties of the new amino acid, substantially alters the function of the gene product; may be either a **transition** or a **transversion**.

**missing link:** vernacular for any hypothetical intermediate form between two known **species** in the **Great Chain of Being**. Around 1900, for example, the fossil 'missing link' between humans and apes was expected by **Keith** to have a large **brain** but ape-like **teeth** and **locomotion**, an expectation that was reversed by the actual **australopithecine** fossil evidence. See **Piltdown**.

**mitis monkey:** one of the vernaculars for *Cercopithecus mitis*.

**mitochondria:** plural of **mitochondrion**.

**mitochondrial chromosome:** ring of extranuclear DNA found in a **mitochondrion**. Aka M chromosome.

‡ **mitochondrial DNA** (mtDNA): circular **DNA** organized as a **nucleoid**, found in the mitochondrial organelle located in the extra-nuclear **cytoplasm** of **eukaryotes**, and transmitted by **maternal inheritance**. Researchers have found 199 mtDNA variants in African populations, 98 in European populations, and 73 in Asian populations, prompting some researchers to propose that the oldest variants are among the African populations. See **chondriome**.

**mitochondrial encephalopathy lactic acidosis syndrome** (MELAS): heritable adult-onset muscular degenerative condition that manifests in the fourth decade. Symptoms include hearing and speech impairment, difficulty walking, memory loss, diabetes, seizures, and dementia; fatal. Caused by a mutation in a mitochondrial gene that codes for a tRNA. Aka mitochondrial encephalopathy, lactic acidosis, and stroke-like episodes syndrome.

**mitochondrial 'Eve':** hypothetical female ancestor to all **AMHs**. Since **mtDNA** is passed down in a continuous **matriline**, in the 1980s Berkeley geneticists suggested that the **common ancestor** of all living humans was a single female and that she lived about 290–140 kya, according to still controversial estimates. Aka 'Garden of Eden' model, **'out of Africa II' model**, 'African Eve', recent replacement model.

**mitochondrial genome:** usually circular but occasionally linear genome of **mitochondria** consisting of **mitochondrial DNA**. In mammals, the mtDNA ring contains some 16,569 **bp** and codes for 13 plasmagenic **proteins**, 22 **tRNAs** and two **rRNAs**. All mitochondrial genomes employ UGA as a tryptophan **codon** rather than as a **stop codon**. mtDNA evolves rapidly and is useful for tracking short term evolutionary events. mtDNA contains little noncoding information between genes, and no **introns**. There is only one significant noncoding sequence, the **D-loop**.

**mitochondrial inheritance:** children (both males and females) inherit mtDNA from their mothers only; the father's mtDNA was located in the sperm mid-piece (the mitochondrial sheath) which was lost at fertilization. Current evidence suggests that **ubiquitin** molecules tag the foreign male mtDNA for degradation. All children in a sibship are **hemizygous** for mtDNA and thus identical to each other and to their mother; cytoplasmic mtDNA does not undergo meiosis, hence there is no opportunity for introgression of the father's mtDNA since there is no **recombination**. Aka **maternal inheritance**.

**mitochondrial myopathies:** group of inherited disorders that cause profound muscle weakness and that are inherited strictly from the mother (**maternal inheritance**). The mitochondrial myopathic disorders include KSS (Kearns–Sayre syndrome), LHON (**Leber hereditary optic neuropathy**), infantile bilateral striatal necrosis, NARP (neuropathy, ataxia, and retinitis pigmentosa), MILS (maternally inherited Leigh syndrome), MELAS (**mitochondrial encephalopathy lacticacidosis syndrome**), PEO (progressive external ophthalmoplagia), and MERRF (myoclonic epilepsy with red ragged fibers: see **epilepsy**).

‡ **mitochondrion:** membrane-bound **organelle**, hundreds of which are present in the **cytoplasm** of all cells of higher organisms; mitochondria are sites of energy production within cells (**respiration**) via ATP synthesis. Both because of this high-energy respiratory environment in which **mutagens** are abundant (see **free oxygen radicals**), and because they lack the sophisticated repair molecules available to nuclear DNA, **mutations** occur at a high and seemingly constant rate, and these can be used as a **molecular clock**. Mitochondria are semiautonomous and able to replicate themselves independently of nuclear mitosis or meiosis. Although their ribosome structure and translation mechanism is unique, they

rely on many mRNAs that are imported from the nucleus. Aka chondriosome. See **mitochondrial inheritance**, the **endosymbiosis theory**, and **cellular respiration**.

**mitogen:** substance, hormone, or growth factor that stimulates cell mitosis and lymphocyte transformation. Adjective: mitogenic.

‡ **mitosis:** duplication division; process of somatic **cell division** in which a body cell replicates, forming two identical daughter cells or genetic copies of the parent cell, each with an identical **diploid** set of **chromatids**. Adjective: mitotic. In mitosis, five main stages occur: **interphase, prophase, metaphase, anaphase**, and **telophase**; in **meiosis** (cf.), additional stages occur. Aka karyokinesis.

**mitotic index:** proportion of cells within a given tissue that are undergoing **mitosis** at a given moment.

**mitotic spindle:** bipolar, ellipsoidal bundle of fibers (**microtubules**) visible during cellular division and responsible for the accurate **segregation** of **chromatids** into daughter cells during anaphase of **mitosis**.

**Mivart, St. George Jackson** (1827–1900): barrister, biologist; Lecturer at St. Mary's Roman Catholic College, Kensington. Author of *On the Genesis of Species* (1871) in which he strongly criticized Darwin's *On the Origin of Species* and *The Descent of Man*, providing the Catholic point of view that relied principally on Darwin's inability to explain self-sacrifice. Mivart also provided a reclassification of the order **Primates**. See **altruism**.

**mixed fauna:** 1. fauna found in association after death that lived in different niches during life, and brought together after deposition; see **taphonomy**. 2. a transitional fauna, e.g. both cold- and warm-tolerant fauna that appear together in a region during a period of temperature change such as the Pleistocene–Holocene transition.

**mixed motivation:** condition in which there are several behavioral tendencies that are present in an action or pattern.

**mixed-sex group:** primate social unit with several adult males and several adult females and their offspring. These societies typically have a well defined **dominance hierarchy** among both the males and the females, although **rank reversals** may occur. Examples of mixed-sex groups can be found among baboons, macaques, and ring-tailed lemurs. Aka multimale group, multimale/multifemale group.

**mixed signal:** signal composed of two or more simpler signals, which separately convey opposing messages; perfume, for example.

**mixed species group:** see **polyspecific association**.

*Mixocebus microdon* **Peters, 1874:** synonym for *Lepilemur mustelinus* (= *microdon*).

**mixoploidy:** 1. state of having cells with different chromosome complements or numbers within the same tissue, owing to **mosaicism**, cancer, etc. 2. loss of more than one chromosome in a cell.

**mixovariation:** intermediate form; see **hybrid**.

**Mladeč Cave:** archaeological site found in 1881 in Moravia, Czech Rebublic, dated to 33–30 kya, and that contains **Aurignacian** artifacts. Hominid remains comprise at least seven robust, prognathic individuals; however, they are attributed to *Homo*

*sapiens*. Average cranial capacity estimated at 1557 cm³. Some material destroyed during World War II. See **Predmosti**. Aka Lautsch, Bocek's Cave.

**MLD:** field abbreviation for **Makapansgat**, South Africa. Fossil hominid fragments found at the site have been attributed to *Australopithecus prometheus* (*=africanus*).

**MN blood group:** codominant genetic locus with two major alleles, M and N, and with some minor alleles. See **MNS blood group**.

---

### Some fossil specimens from Makapansgat

**MLD 2:** a juvenile mandible. See **MLD**.

**MLD 7:** an almost complete male ilium. See **MLD**.

**MLD 8:** an almost complete female ilium. See **MLD**.

**MLD 37/38:** a partial cranium with an estimated capacity of 435 cm³ and an estimated date of $< 2.8$ mya. This specimen compares favorably with **Sts 5** from **Sterkfontein**. See **MLD**.

**MLD 40:** Portion of a mandible. See **MLD**.

---

**MNK:** Mary Nicol's **Korongo** at **Olduvai Gorge**.

‡ **MNS blood group** (MNS): a human **polymorphism** of RBC **antigens** based on the presence or absence of M, N, and/or S antigens on cell membranes of **erythrocytes** and other cells. The M, N, and S alleles are **codominant**, and ten different **genotypes** are possible.

**mob call:** one type of vocalization emitted that signals that a predator or intruder is present; mob calls signal the group to harass the intruder by assembling around it. This has been observed in a number of primate species including sifakas, ruffed lemurs, and squirrel monkeys. See **mobbing**.

**mobbing:** combined, cooperative assault on a predator too formidable to be handled by a single individual, in an attempt to frustrate it, disable it, or at least drive it from the vicinity. This behavior is well described in the bird literature, in which a large number of **conspecifics** assemble around a predator and harass it. This type of behavior has also been described for primates, but it differs in that the harassed individual(s) are not necessarily predators, but rather competitors; for example, smaller squirrel monkeys will mob larger cebid monkeys and force them to leave a fruiting tree. Female primates may also mob a male that they perceive as dangerous to an infant.

**modal action pattern** (MAP): smallest behavioral unit that is observable as a repeated pattern, although variation in the behavior is recognized; formerly referred to as a **fixed action pattern**.

**modality:** in reference to stimuli that are detected by specific sensory receptors leading to sensations and perceptions that are similar to one another, but different from other sensations and perceptions.

**mode:** 1. any of various processes or mechanisms employed by taxa during their evolution. The term was brought into popular usage by G. G. **Simpson** during discussions of **tempo** and mode of evolution. 2. in statistics, the value of the variate at which a relative or absolute maximum occurs in a frequency distribution; in a discrete sample, the most common value. Aka modal number. 3. any of the large Pleistocene-age **large cutting tools**: see **mode 1** and **mode 2**.

**mode 1:** any of the large Pleistocene-age **large cutting tools** classified in the **Oldowan** or **Developed Oldowan**, such as those found in Beds I and II at **Olduvai Gorge**.

**mode 2:** any of the large Pleistocene-age **large cutting tools** classified in the **Acheulean** or **Bose Basin LCTs**, such as those found in Bed IV at **Olduvai Gorge**, **Olorgesailie**, and (possibly) the Bose Basin sites in China.

**mode of inheritance:** see **pattern of inheritance**.

**model:** representation that displays the pattern, mode of structure, or formation of an object, organism, or process; an idealized representation of nature used as a tool by scientists. Models can take many forms and may be structural, such as Crick and Watson's metal and wire representation of the DNA molecule, theoretical, or mathematical.

**Model Law:** prototypical legislation written in 1914 by Harry Laughlin, Director of the Eugenics Record Office, and that was provided to many state legislatures, some of which passed legislation permitting involuntary sterilization of the feeble-minded and other 'defectives'. This document was used by the Nazi Party in Germany to create the infamous 1933 'Law for the Prevention of Defective Progeny'.

**model organism:** species that is preferred for use in experiments. This may be because it is easy to care for in a laboratory or has been well characterized, permitting subsequent comparison. In many cases model organisms have some trait that serves as a useful analogy with humans; among primates, rhesus macaques have been one of the principal model organisms in medical and laboratory behavioral research.

**modern synthesis:** school of evolutionary biology that argues that the larger evolutionary process can be best understood by understanding variation within natural populations and, by extension, that species arise because of extant variation within populations, and that natural selection is the primary mechanism of evolution. See **neo-Darwinism.**

**modernization:** process by which previously isolated human groups gain modern technology and the know-how to become industrialized and become part of the world community, as well as the consequences of that process.

**modesty hypotheses:** opposing proposals (1) that modesty accounts for the origin of clothing, and (2) that modesty is a result of wearing clothing.

**modifier:** any gene that changes the expression of another gene at a different locus.

**modifying gene:** any factor that influences the expression of a nonallelic factor.

**Modjokerto:** see **Perning.**

**MODY:** see **diabetes mellitus, type II.**

***Moeripithecus markgrafi* Schlosser, 1910:** synonym for ***Propliopithecus*** *markgrafi.*

**Moghara:** early Miocene paleontological site in Egypt, dated to about 19 mya, and that has produced examples of ***Prohylobates.***

**Moiti tuff:** Pleistocene volcanic deposit at Koobi Fora, **Lake Turkana,** dated by **K/Ar** to about 4.1–3.8 mya.

‡ **molar** (M): one of four types of tooth found in **heterodont** mammals. Molars are low, flat teeth, usually in the rear of the mouth, that are used for crushing and grinding if low-cusped and for puncturing if high-cusped. There are normally three molars per quadrant in the human jaw. Cf. **incisor, canine,** and **premolar.**

**molar cusp swelling:** pertaining to one or more inflated cusps on the **molar** teeth.

**molar tooth pattern:** see **cusp pattern.**

**molariform:** pertaining to a tooth that resembles a **molar** tooth; molar-like. In primates, such a tooth is usually a premolar.

**molarization:** tendency to evolve more complex grinding surfaces on the cheek teeth, often used in connection with the appearance of more complicated (crenulated) occlusal surfaces on premolars.

**molecular:** pertaining to, or composed of, molecules.

**molecular anthropology:** study of the evolution of informational macromolecules such as proteins and polynucleotides; provides comparative taxonomic data regarding the relationship of humans to the other primates.

**molecular archaeology:** see **anthropological genetics.**

**molecular biology:** subfield within biology that studies molecular phenomena as an explanation, in whole or part, for biological phenomena.

‡ **molecular clock:** hypothetical tool or system of estimated dates for a **common ancestor** based upon the premise that many molecular differences (either DNA or proteins) among taxa are **neutral mutations** that accumulate at a relatively constant rate when averaged over geologic time, thus allowing statistical estimates of **cladistic** events. Aka DNA clock, protein clock.

**molecular diagnostic testing:** identification of specific nucleic acid sequences for medical diagnosis.

**molecular drive:** proposal that gene families are the result of a combination of gene conversion, unequal crossing over, and duplicative transposition.

**molecular evolution:** change in **protein sequences** and **DNA sequences** over time. See **molecular clock** and **neutral theory of molecular evolution.**

**molecular evolutionary clock:** see **molecular clock.**

**molecular genetics:** 1. study of genetic systems at the molecular level. 2. control of metabolic processes by genetic material, including regulatory processes in genetic material. See **genomics** and **proteomics.**

**molecular medicine:** practice of healing that utilizes recent molecular knowledge of abnormal cellular processes, as well as more traditional techniques.

**molecular phylogenetics:** estimation of **phylogenetic trees** after comparing molecular sequences between organisms or species.

**molecular sex determination:** 1. estimation of biological sex by utilizing sex-specific molecular factors such as **X chromosome** genes or gene fragments. Molecular sex determination is useful in forensic applications, as well as for probing bone and fecal material obtained from archaeological sites, primate field sites, and for testing hypotheses of evolutionary interest. 2. specific sexing of skeletal material can be attempted by utilizing an assay for the **amelogenin** gene, aka the X/Y specific amelogenin test. Cf. **skeletal sexing.**

**molecular systematics:** approach to evolutionary reconstruction based on molecular sequence data.

‡ **molecule:** chemical combination of two or more atoms that form a specific chemical substance, e.g. water or an **amino acid.**

**Mollison's tincture:** liquid hardening agent used in archaeological field work.

**moloch gibbon:** vernacular for ***Hylobates*** *moloch.*

**mona monkey:** vernacular for ***Cercopithecus*** *mona.*

**Monaco Agreement:** consensus reached at Monaco in 1906 with respect to the standardization of anthropometric landmarks, planes, measures, and indices. It largely replaced both the French system and the

German system established at the **Frankfort Agreement** of 1882.

**monandry:** marriage or mating of one female to one male; **monogamy.** Cf. **polyandry.**

**Monge's disease:** condition in which an individual acclimatized to high altitude abruptly loses that acclimatization.

**Mongol:** ethnym for the **autochthonous** peoples of Central Asia, Northern China, and Mongolia. Aka Classic Mongol, **Mongoloid.**

**Mongolian:** eighteenth century **ethnym** for the indigenous peoples of Asia. One of the five often-cited racial varieties recognized by **Blumenbach** in 1790; the others were **Ethiopian, Malayan, American** and **Caucasian.** See **Mongoloid.**

**Mongolian spot:** see **congenital dermal melanocytosis;** aka Mongoloid birthmark.

**mongolism:** archaic term for **Down syndrome;** aka Mongolian idiocy, now discouraged.

**Mongoloid:** ethnym for **autochthonous** peoples of East Asia, latitudinally from western Chinese to Japanese in the east, longitudinally from Chuckchi in the north to Malaysia in the south, and consisting of all the groups within these boundaries. Aka Classic Mongol.

**Mongoloid eye or fold:** see **epicanthic fold, eye folds.**

**mongoose lemur:** vernacular for *Eulemur mongoz.*

‡ **mongrelization:** rarely used term in modern studies referring to racial admixture.

**monk saki:** vernacular for *Pithecia monachus.*

‡ **monkey:** any of the **anthropoid** primates that are members of the Infraorder **Platyrrhini** or the family **Cercopithecidae** of the Infraorder **Catarrhini;** any one of the large number of species within the anthropoid **primates,** which are found almost worldwide, possess **tails,** usually use all four limbs during **locomotion,** and are **arboreal** at least part of the time. Monkeys are usually gregarious. In terms of primate **grades,** monkeys are smaller and developmentally simpler than **hominoids,** but are structurally and behaviorally more **complex** than **prosimians.**

**'monkey law'** and **'monkey trial':** see **Scopes trial.**

**monoallelic expression:** genotype in which only one of two alleles is expressed in a heterozygote, owing to **genomic imprinting** or other **epigenetic mechanism;** asymmetrical, non-Mendelian expression. Cf. **biallelic expression.**

**monoamine:** any one of a group of neurotransmitters containing one amine group but by convention excluding all peptides and amino acids.

**monoamine oxidase A deficiency:** lack of MAOA, an enzyme found in the outer membranes of **mitochondria** and that normally catalyzes reactions that metabolize the neurotransmitters **dopamine, serotonin,** and **noradrenaline.** Owing to one of several mutations, affected individuals process chemicals in wine, cheese, and certain Chinese foods differently, increasing the risk of heart attacks. MAOA deficiency is an X-linked recessive. This controversial syndrome has also been described as 'borderline mental impairment and abnormal behavior', with familial aggregations of exhibitionism, voyeurism, and arson. Panic disorder has also been linked to the *MAOA* polymorphism (aka Brunner syndrome). A second form of the enzyme, MAOB, also exists.

**monocausal:** describes any hypothesis or theory that explains or attempts to explain an observed phenomenon as the result of the action of a single cause. Cf. **multicausal.**

**monocentric model:** 1. name for any single-origin hypothesis. 2. hypothesis that humans originated recently, in Africa; see **human origins.**

**monochorionic placenta:** type of placenta, usually associated with **twin** pregnancies, in which a single **chorion** (one of the placental tissues) is shared by both **twins.**

**monochromatic light:** light that is composed of a single wavelength or frequency.

**monochromatic vision:** vision in which the light receptors are sensitive to only one light wavelength and white light. This results in what is commonly referred to as black-and-white vision. Monochromatic vision is found among some nocturnal **prosimians.** See **color vision.** Cf. **dichromatic vision, trichromatic vision.**

**monoclonal:** derived from a single clone of cells.

**monoclonal antibody** (mAb): antibody produced by a single clone of **hybridoma** cells; an immunoglobulin that is homogenous rather than normally heterogenous.

**monocyte:** type of **white blood cell** (WBC) normally constituting about 3–8% of the WBC count; can leave the bloodstream and be transformed into a **macrophage,** active in **phagocytosis.**

**monoestrus:** with only one mating period in a breeding season.

**monogamous:** Pertaining to the practice of **monogamy.**

**monogamous family group:** social unit consisting of a mated pair and their offspring.

**monogamous pair bonding:** mated pair and their resulting offspring.

**monogamy:** mating system in which one male is paired up with one female during the breeding season, often longer. Monogamy is almost always associated with parental care by both parents. It exists among titi monkeys (*Callicebus*) and the hylobatids. It has long been described for many callitrichids, but some workers now question whether this is true in all cases. Aka monandry. Cf. **polygamy.**

**monogenesis:** 1. hypothetical development of all life from a single cell; monogeny. Cf. **polygenesis**. 2. early view that all of humankind descended from one pair of progenitors, a view held by **Linnaeus, Buffon, Blumenbach** and **Prichard**; a monogenist is anyone who held or holds such a view.

**monogenic:** referring to any **trait** explained by the effects of a set of **alleles** at a single locus or **gene**. The human **ABO blood group** locus is monogenic. Cf. **polygenic trait, oligogenic trait.**

**monogenism:** development of all life from a single cell; or, of all human beings from a single pair; see **monogenesis**. Cf. **polygenism.**

**monoglacialism:** doctrine that there was only one glacial period during the Pleistocene epoch. Cf. **polyglacialism.**

**monogynopaedium:** female parent and her progeny.

**monogyny:** condition in which each male mates with only one female; **monogamy**. Cf. **polygyny.**

**monohybrid cross:** cross between parents that differ in one character.

**monohybrid individual:** 1. offspring from parents that differ in one character. 2. individual heterozygous for the pair of alleles of a single gene of interest.

**monokine:** protein secreted by monocytes and macrophages to send instructions to other cells in the immune system; e.g. **interferon.**

**monomer:** a simple molecule that can be linked to other identical molecules to form a **dimer** or **polymer.**

**monomorphic:** relating to a population where the allele frequency of the most common allele is greater than 95%. Cf. **polymorphism.**

**monomorphism:** 1. a trait that is always expressed in the same way. Adjective: **monomorphic**. 2. one structural characteristic; often refers to a lack of **sexual dimorphism**. Cf. **dimorphism** and **polymorphism.**

**monophyletic:** 1. characterized by one phylum or lineage. 2. pertaining to a taxon descended from a **common ancestor**; monophyly.

**monophyletic assemblage:** cluster of nodes and **dendrogram exterior points** due to their common descent from a recent ancestor. Cf. **polyphyletic assemblage.**

**monophyletic group:** taxonomic group of organisms that has a single **common ancestor**; a set of species in which the descendants all resemble their ancestors.

**monophyletic hypothesis of racial origins:** see the **mitochondrial 'Eve'** model, aka the **'out of Africa' II** model of modern human origins.

**monophyly:** state in which organisms or taxa are derived from the same ancestral taxon and share that **common ancestor**. Adjective: monophyletic.

**monophyodont:** condition in which a vertebrate has only one set of teeth during a lifetime; this is rare among mammals, occurring only among the toothed whales and a few others. Cf. **diphyodont.**

**monoploid:** of cells or individuals with one basic set of chromatids (or **chromosomes**); haploid.

**monosaccharide:** single sugar molecule; simple sugar not further broken down by hydrolysis. Cf. **polysaccharide, disaccharide.**

**monosome:** in genetics, a single **ribosome** composed of two subunits, each of which contains **ribosomal RNA** and proteins.

‡ **monosomy:** rare abnormal condition in which only one chromosome, rather than a normal homologous pair, is present in body cells. An example in humans is **Turner syndrome**: monosomic individuals have $2N-1 = 45$ chromosomes, rather than the normal **diploid number** of $2N = 46$. See **aneuploidy.**

**monosomy 21:** rare **major chromosome anomaly** characterized by mental and physical retardation and malformations of the skull, jaw and face.

**monothely:** see **polyandry.**

**monothetic key:** 1. a dichotomous feature $(+/-$, binary). 2. one of a set of necessary and sufficient features to qualify for membership in a **monothetic taxon.**

**monothetic taxon:** group of organisms that have in common a set of **monothetic keys** that are both necessary and sufficient for membership.

**Monotremata:** see **monotreme.**

‡ **monotreme:** member of the order Monotremata belonging to the mammalian monotypic subclass **Prototheria**; the most primitive living mammal, characterized by reptile-like limb placement and **oviparity**. The egg-laying mammals include the duck-billed platypus and the spiny anteater or echidna of Australia.

**monotypic:** 1. pertaining to a taxon in which there is only a single subordinate taxon or, in the case of a species, in which there are no subspecies. 2. a species lacking geographical races.

**monotypic species concept:** idea that a species is a highly dispersed, morphologically coherent metapopulation that is adapted to local environments; unlike the **polytypic species concept**, gene flow supersedes geographical replacement.

**monotypical evolution:** evolutionary event that is unique to a given lineage, i.e. that happened only once to a given species (e.g. the speciation event leading to *Homo sapiens* happened only once). See **monophyletic.**

**monounsaturated fatty acid:** long carbohydrate chain that contains triglycerides and more than one double bond and with only one 'missing' hydrogen atom. Sources include avocados and olives. See **unsaturated fatty acid.**

‡ **monozygotic twins** (MZT): see **twins, monozygotic**.

**monozygous:** referring to one zygote.

**monozygous twin correlation:** measure of covariation among pairs of identical **twins** for a given trait. If the trait is complex and is heritable, then the correlation for monozygous twin pairs will always be higher than the **dizygous twin correlation**. See **heritability**.

**mons pubis:** rounded, fleshy prominence located over the **pubic symphysis**.

**monsoon forest:** seasonal tropical **forest** that has very defined wet seasons and dry seasons. On its borders monsoon forest grades into **tropical rain forest**. Deeper into its area monsoon forest contains a large percentage of **deciduous** trees and areas that are prone to drought as well as higher elevations than found in the evergreen tropical rain forests. Referred to as upland forest by some authors.

**monster:** 1. fabled animal composed of parts of several animals, e.g. a **troglodyte**, centaur, or griffin. 2. any grotesque or abnormal creature; an unnatural entity. 3. a grossly malformed organism, with extra or missing features as the result of abnormal development.

**Montagu, M. F. Ashley** (1905–99): English-born US physical anthropologist; studied under G. E. **Smith** and **Boas**, influenced by **Keith**. Successful freelance anthropologist, writer, and lecturer; known for his stance against racial taxonomy and for biosocial issues such as **gender** awareness; central contributor to the *UNESCO Statement on Race;* a proponent of the Boasian **American Historical School**.

**Montandon's thesis:** proposal by G. Montandon in 1933 that the Americas were initially populated by boatloads of people from the islands of Polynesia, specifically embarking from Easter Island (Rapanui), island-hopping, and making a final landfall on the Chilean coast of South America; he also proposed that an Australoid element arrived simultaneously in the form of slaves of the Polynesians.

**montane:** of or pertaining to the mountain (alpine) biome; the area below the altitude of the tree line that is dominated by evergreen trees.

**montane forest:** forest community at higher elevations. In the tropics these forests are characterized by shorter trees with very short roots, and steep cliffs.

**Monte Bamboli:** paleontological site found in 1872 in Tuscany, Italy, dated to the late **Miocene**, and that contains hominoid remains including mandibular fragments, teeth, and some postcranial bones attributed to *Oreopithecus bambolii*.

**Monte Circeo:** see **Circeo Cave complex**.

**Monte Verde:** Paleoindian archaeological site found in 1977, 50 km inland on Chinchihuapa Creek in southern Chile, dated by $^{14}$C to 12.5 kya (some allege the site to be >33 kya) containing cobble artifacts, hearths, remains of 12 wood dwellings, bolas, the imprint of a human foot in clay, and abundant plant remains of local species such as a variety of potato.

**Montmaurin:** archaeological site found in 1949 in the Grotte du Coupe Gorge, in the cave system of Montmaurin, Haute-Garonne, France, dated to approximately 200 kya; contains hominid remains of several individuals including a mandible assigned to the younger, 'anteneandertal', or **archaic** *Homo sapiens* group.

**mood disorder:** group of behavior disorders associated with manic and/or depressive syndromes; see **affective disorders**.

**Moor macaque:** vernacular for *Macaca maura*.

**moraine:** ridge of glacial drift built up from the material riding on the ice; moraines delineate the melting zones along the margins and bottoms of **glaciers**, and therefore mark the maximum advance of glaciers in the past. Aka ground moraine.

**morbidity:** condition of being infected or diseased. Adjective: morbid. Cf. **mortality**.

**morbidity rate:** ratio of the cases of a given condition to the total population size.

**Morgan, Lewis Henry** (1818–81): US lawyer and ethnologist. Morgan elaborated a school of cultural change called **unilinear evolution**. As for Tylor, culture was for Morgan considered progressive and unilineal, with stages from **savagery** to **barbarism** to **civilization**. He compiled and compared data on over 200 societies, beginning with the Iroquois. Author of *Ancient Society* (1877), in which he synthesized the social histories of aboriginal Oceania, Native America, and ancient Greece and Rome.

**Morgan, Thomas Hunt** (1866–1945): US *Drosophila* geneticist; Nobel laureate (1933) and strong critic of Darwin's 'gradualist' requirement for **natural selection**. Morgan produced a number of brilliant students, e.g. A. H. Sturtevant, H. J. **Müller**, and C. B. Bridges, who all worked in the 'fly room' at Columbia University.

**morgan unit:** unit for mapping the distance between loci on a chromosome; one **centimorgan** indicates one percent of **recombination**. Aka map unit.

**Morgan's canon:** 1. axiom postulated by British psychologist C. Lloyd Morgan (1852–1936) that the best theory is the simplest one that also accounts for all the known facts. Morgan's canon was a restatement of **Occam's razor**. 2. principle from the late nineteenth century that animal behavior should not be attributed to intention and forethought; animal behavior should be interpreted as the simplest action unless there is ample reason to consider otherwise. This was Lloyd Morgan's reaction to the **anthropomorphism** of this time.

**morning sickness:** nausea alleged to occur in the early part of the day during weeks 6–14 of pregnancy;

actually occurs both day and night. The symptoms are rare in vegetarian societies; see the **Profet hypothesis.**

**Moro reflex:** startle reaction, exhibited by newborns to loud noise, in which they abduct and extend their extremities followed by abduction and **flexion** that is sometimes referred to as an embrance.

*Morotopithecus bishopi* **Gebo, MacLatchy, Kitio, Kingston, and Pilbeam, 1997: hominoid** from the early Miocene of Uganda; known from maxillary remains and several postcrania. The type specimen was originally referred to *Proconsul,* and the dental remains are almost identical to *Afropithecus;* owing to the lack of postcrania from the latter, it is not possible to compare any overlap. This species may eventually be referred to *Afropithecus.* Estimated body mass around 40 kg. Dental formula: 2.1.2.3. The postcrania known from *Morotopithecus* is derived and clearly allied to the apes. See Appendix 1 for taxonomy.

**morph:** form or shape; may refer to any structural, behavioral, or physiological **phenotype,** or to an allele, **DNA sequence,** or chromosome.

**morphic resonance:** contemporary application of aspects of (1) the **Linnaean species** concept that incorporates, literally, the idea that species have essences, called morphic fields, and (2) the Lamarckian concept that acquired traits can be passed on. Proponents insist that such resonant fields also broadcast their resonance across space and time, i.e. provide a form of species telepathy. Such ideas have found little support in the established scientific community.

**morphism:** see **polymorphism.**

**morphocline:** abstract arrangement of the morphological variation of a homologous character into a continuum from primitive to derived states. Aka morphological transformation series.

**morphocline polarity:** ordering of a homologous character into its primitive and derived states through time. See **morphocline.**

**morphogen:** any substance, hormone, or growth factor that induces **morphogenesis.**

**morphogenesis:** 1. change of a structure from an undifferentiated to a differentiated state. 2. development and growth of structures. Adjective: morphogenetic.

**morphological dating:** see **R.4,** the **relative dating** context with the lowest level of confidence.

**morphological distance:** perceived (or measured) phenetic divergence between two similar taxa.

**morphological facial height:** gnathion–nasion distance.

**morphological index:** height divided by body mass. Aka Naccarati's index. Largely replaced by measures such as the **body mass index.**

**morphological species concept:** see **phenetic species concept.**

**morphological support:** structures that have evolved in conjunction with display behavior; in primates, an examples is the brightly colored swollen **sexual skin** on receptive female cercopithecines.

**morphological transformation series:** see **morphocline.**

**morphological type:** 1. descriptive and abstract grouping of individuals or artifacts where the focus is on overall similarity rather than specific form or function. 2. in humans, one of usually three classes of individuals grouped on the basis of physique; these have been called the slender type, the medium type and the broad type. Identified or created by the classical **somatologists** or **biotypologists,** such categorical classifications have given way to recent hypotheses that appreciate more fully the continuous nature of **human variation.**

**morphological variation:** variation among members of a group provided by differences in size, shape, color, and other features.

‡ **morphology:** study of the shape of anatomical **structures** or **phenotypes;** also, the study of structural forms.

**morphometric:** pertaining to the measurement of the external form of an organ, organism, or other structure. See **anthropometry.**

**morphoplasy:** plasticity; range of potential variation for a developing organ or organism.

**morphospecies:** populations designated as separate species and defined by morphological differences.

**morphostratigraphy:** system of organization and classification of rock **strata** based on their landform morphology.

**morphotype:** list of the known character states likely to be diagnostic of the ancestor of a species.

**Morquio syndrome:** see **mucopolysaccharidoses.**

**mortality:** death. With **fertility** and **migration,** mortality is one of the three primary variables that describe population size and structure. See **demography.**

**mortality rate:** 1. frequency of individuals dying from all causes in a population over a given period of time. 2. frequency of individuals dying from a particular disease in a population over a given period of time.

**Mortillet, Gabriel de** (1821–98): French geologist, prehistorian; revised Lartet's chronology, and in the 1860s proposed his own early scheme of Pleistocene chronology based on the prevalence of artifact types, stimulated by the publication of Darwin's *Origin* in 1859. He coined the terms 'eolith' (*Eolithique*) and *Anthropopithecus,* and founded the journal *Matériaux pour l'histoire naturelle et primitive de l'homme.* He was an anthropologist at Broca's École d'Anthropologie after 1875. Politically active, he proposed massive social reforms.

**Morton, Samuel George** (1799–1851): US physician, anatomist and craniometrician; in his *Crania Americana* (1839), Morton created the first American racial typology, changing **Blumenbach's** five human **varieties** into fully distinct, categorical 'primeval' **races**; supported the **polygenism** of Lord Kames (Henry Home). Morton's scheme was used to justify slavery in the US South as elaborated by the Americans Josiah Knott and George Gliddon. Morton's methodology was later expanded by the French anthropologist Paul **Broca**.

**morula:** solid, compact ball of 12 or more **blastomeres** that form as the cells of a preimplantation **zygote** reduce in size and change shape during **compaction**. The morula stage usually occurs as the zygote leaves the fallopian tubes and enters the uterus, 3–4 days after fertilization.

**morulation:** formation of the **morula** by mitotic **cell division**.

**mosaic:** 1. a pattern made of numerous small pieces fitted together. 2. in genetics, an individual or cell culture that has two or more cell lines that are genotypically or karyotypically distinct but derived from a single zygote; cf. **chimera**. 3. in **human evolutionary biology**, commonly used to refer to specimens such as the **archaic** hominids that possess features of more than one species.. Cf. **mosaic evolution**.

‡ **mosaic evolution:** concept that major evolutionary changes tend to take place in independent stages or trait clusters, not all at once. The **fossil record** for **hominid evolution**, for example, shows a mosaic pattern in the fact that smaller **canine** teeth, **bipedal locomotion**, larger **brains**, and **tool use** apparently did not all evolve at the same time. Mosaic evolution is thought to be the rule rather than the exception. Aka **hologenism** (2).

**mosaic tissue:** organized mass of cells consisting of cells of two or more types.

**mosaicism, chromosomal:** 1. most commonly refers to a somatic mutation during development, so that an individual is a **mosaic**, e.g. Down syndrome in only some cell lines. 2. normal females are mosaics for the expressed/inactivated X chromosome, with some cell lines expressing the mother's and some the father's X-linked alleles. 3. another (very rare) form of mosaicism occurs when two embryos fuse very early in development and express, in one organism, the genotypes of two individuals.

**most surviving offspring:** selection to maximize the number of surviving offspring; used to describe the Darwinian version of **fitness**; combines both differential fertility and differential mortality. Cf. **inclusive fitness**.

**mother:** one's female progenitor; a kinship term that identifies a genealogical or adopted degree of relationship in a **nuclear family** or **extended family**. See **father**, **brother**, **sister**, **uncle**, **aunt**, **cousin**.

**mother-centered subunit:** see **matrifocal unit**.

**mother–infant attachment:** see **infant–mother bond**.

**mother-surrogate:** see **surrogate mother** and **surrogate**.

**motif:** partial **DNA sequence** common to several different genes, and sometimes among many organisms, often an entire **exon**. Aka molecular motif. See **domain**.

**motility:** in reference to an organism's capacity for motion; this includes locomotion, postural changes, movement of body parts, and movement through internal organs such as the intestine.

**motivation:** internal state that encompasses a large range of factors (such as fear, appeasement, aggression, etc.) of an individual that precedes any action taken; many behavioral biologists caution use of this term in reference to animals because of the danger of **anthropomorphism** (see **Morgan's canon**).

**motor area:** region of the cerebral cortex from which motor impulses to muscles or glands originate. Aka motor region, motor strip.

**motor control area:** portion of the frontal lobe of the cerebral cortex that controls voluntary movement of the torso and limbs.

‡ **motor cortex:** region of the frontal lobe of the cerebral cortex from which motor impulses to muscles and glands originate. In humans, the movements of the mouth, larynx and tongue required for language production all originate in this area of the brain. Aka motor area, motor control area, motor region, motor strip. See **motor speech area**.

**motor nerve:** nerve that carries an impulse away from the **central nervous system** and towards an effector (e.g. a **muscle** or **gland**). Motor nerves form the ventral roots of the spinal nerves. Aka motor neuron, efferent nerve.

**motor skills:** in reference to the degree of facility in the performance of actions requiring muscular responses.

‡ **motor speech area:** region of the **brain** located in the left inferior frontal **gyrus** of the **frontal lobe**. One of the motor areas responsible for the production of speech or utterances following rules of grammar; controls the muscles of the mouth, tongue, and larynx. Aka area subcallosa, Broca's area.

**mottled-faced tamarin section:** division of the genus *Saguinus* based on face fur, or lack of face fur, and other **pelage** patterns; not a subgeneric distinction. The mottled-faced tamarin group consists of only one species, *S. inustus*. The distinctive feature of this species is a thickly furred crown, but naked cheeks and sides of the face. See *Saguinus*.

**mottle-faced tamarin:** vernacular for *Saguinus inustus*.

**Moula-Guercy Cave:** archaeological site found in 1991 near Ardèche on the Rhone River in southeastern France, dated to 120–100 kya, containing Mousterian scrapers and Levallois **débitage**, and fossil hominids that included at least six cannibalized individuals attributed to *Homo neanderthalensis*. Aka Baume ('cave') Moula-Guercy.

**mount:** term used in primatology for the act of a male approaching a female in **estrus** from the rear, grasping her back, and copulating; Aka **mounting.**

**Mount Carmel:** eroded limestone feature 20 km long above the Wadi el Mughara, located 3.5 km from the Mediterranean shore on the western side of the Kishon Valley in the **Levant**, and that contains several significant archaeological sites; see **Kebara, Tabūn** and **Skhūl.**

**mountain gorilla:** see *Gorilla gorilla*

**mounting:** behavior of a male primate that approaches a female from behind, stands on the hindlegs, and grasps the flanks of the female in order to copulate. This behavior can also have meaning in the social hierarchy, as when a high-ranking individual mounts another individual of either sex.

**mouse lemur:** vernacular for those species belonging to the genus *Microcebus.*

**moustached guenon:** vernacular for *Cercopithecus cephus.*

**Mousterian assemblage of Acheulean tradition:** (MAT) Bordes' Middle Paleolithic tool tradition characterized by two groupings: assemblages with handaxes (MAT A), and those without handaxes (MAT B). Bordes thought that MAT B might have given rise to the **Châtelperronian**. See **Micoquian.**

**Mousterian Man:** Neandertals; see **Le Moustier.**

**Mousterian point:** pointed, almond-shaped tool made from a flake, usually with a faceted butt and step flaking. Associated with the **Mousterian tool tradition.**

‡ **Mousterian tool tradition: Middle Paleolithic** stone tool technology usually associated with **Neandertals** and perhaps some early modern *Homo sapiens* groups, characterized by the pre-preparation of stone **cores** from which finished **flakes** could be removed as needed. The Mousterian **tool kit** also included side **scrapers** and spear points, the latter being early examples of **composite tools**; represented in Europe, North Africa and Western Asia. Named after the **type site** of **Le Moustier** in southwestern France. See **Levallois** and **Levalloiso-Mousterian**. Cf. the **Upper Paleolithic** traditions such as the **Châtelperronian.**

**Moustier:** see **Le Moustier.**

**mouth:** oral cavity and its associated structures. The mouth is situated at the anterior end of the alimentary canal and is the structure through which nutrients are ingested. See **gut morphology.**

**mouth transport:** movement of infants from one place to another by the mother carrying them in her mouth. A behavior associated with many nonprimate mammals, but mouth transport is also present among galagos; the young being carried adopts a posture in which it contracts its body and holds still while being carried by a dorsal fold of skin.

**Movius' line:** demarcation between what H. Movius considered in 1944 to be more advanced **Acheulean** hand-ax cultures of Europe and Asia and the alleged 'sub-standard' chopper–chopping tools of southeast Asia; the original line extended in a northwesterly direction, roughly dividing the Indian subcontinent (Acheulean) from the east Asian plateau (chopper–chopping).

**MRI:** see **magnetic resonance imaging.**

‡ **mRNA:** messenger ribonucleic acid; the complementary strand of **RNA** transcribed from **DNA** and **translated** by **tRNA** at the **ribosomes** into peptides or **polypeptides** (proteins). Heterogenous mRNA (**hmRNA**) consists of a complementary copy of the DNA **cistron**, and contains both **exons** and **introns**, which are then edited. Aka template RNA, complementary RNA.

**MSY:** see **male-specific region of the Y chromosome.**

**mtDNA:** see **mitochondrial DNA.**

**mu:** 1. the twelfth letter of the Greek alphabet, (M, $\mu$); see **mutation.** 2. a micron ($\mu$). 3. in statistics, the parametric **mean** ($\mu$) of a population. 4. abbreviation for the SI prefix micro-, as in $\mu$g (microgram, $10^{-6}$ g).

**mucin:** molecule found in **mucus**; consists of a peptide covered with a large number of sugar molecules, which makes it very viscous. The addition of sugars is frequently disregulated in cancers, which may give rise to some cancer antigens.

**mucopolysaccharidoses:** group of eight similar major genetic diseases (I–VIII, with at least five subtypes), characterized by defective metabolism of mucopolysaccharides, each due to a mutant enzyme. Types III–VI include Sanfilippo syndrome (III), Morquio syndrome (IV), Scheie's syndrome (V), and Maroteaux–Lamy syndrome (VI). See **mucopolysaccharidosis, type I** and **mucopolysaccharidosis, type II.**

**mucopolysaccharidosis, type I** (MPS1): heritable condition characterized by mental impairment, enlarged liver and spleen, heart disease, bone defects, hearing loss, large tongue, corneal clouding, and coarse facial features; fatal. A lysosomal storage disease in which the defective enzyme is an autosomal recessive enzyme, α-l-iduronidase. Aka Hurler syndrome.

**mucopolysaccharidosis, type II** (MPS2): heritable defect of carbohydrate metabolism characterized by severely deformed face, dwarfism, joint stiffness, deafness, mental impairment, heart defects, and enlarged liver and spleen; fatal in adolescence. Diagnostic heparitin sulfate is excreted in urine. Defective gene is an X-linked recessive, coding for iduronate sulphate sulfatase. Aka Hunter syndrome.

**mucosa:** epithelial tissue that overlies a layer of loose connective tissue; this type of membrane lines body cavities and tubes that open to the external environment. Specialized goblet cells scattered within the tissue secrete **mucus**. Aka mucous membrane.

**mucus:** viscous slimy substance composed primarily of the protein **mucin**; secreted by **mucosa**.

**Mueller's gibbon:** vernacular for *Hylobates muelleri*.

**Mugharet es-Skhūl:** see **Skhūl**.

**Mugharet et-Tabūn:** see **Tabūn**.

**mulatto:** person of mixed ancestry, with one parent from the Caucasian group and one from the Negroid group.

**mule:** 1. the cross between a male donkey or ass and a female horse; Cf. **hinny** and **horse–donkey hybrid**. 2. generally (but usually archaic), any **hybrid** as in roses, pigeons, sheep, especially as used before the twentieth century. Cf. **sport**.

**muliebrity:** state of being a female; any quality characteristic of females; the change in character of a female at puberty.

**muller:** stone used for pounding or grinding; aka mano.

**Muller, Hermann J.** (1890–1967): US geneticist, eugenicist, Nobel laureate; an ardent **selectionist**, Müller conducted fundamental research in error copying, **genetic load**, and mutability, using X-rays to induce **mutations** in laboratory populations of *Drosophila*; his **eugenic** views made him a *persona non grata* in several countries.

**Müllerian ducts:** unspecialized tissue in an early embryo that can develop into a female reproductive tract; the Müllerian ducts normally degenerate in male embryos owing to the action of **Müllerian-inhibiting hormone**. Cf. **Wolffian ducts**.

**Müllerian-inhibiting hormone** (MIH): a hormone produced by the fetal **sustentacular cells** in the developing testis, which causes the breakdown and resorption of the **Müllerian ducts** in a male embryo. Aka anti-Müllerian hormone.

**Müllerian mimicry:** a kind of mimicry in which two or more poisonous species evolve to look like one another. Cf. **Batesian mimicry**.

**Muller's ratchet:** proposal by H. J. **Muller** in 1964 that the **genetic load** in populations and hence in species increases inevitably as deleterious mutations are not removed from a population or species owing to **overdominance** and other phenomena, and that load thus increases to a theoretical limit known as the **lethal equivalent**. The name 'Muller's ratchet' was applied by J. Felsenstein in 1974. Aka the **cost of selection**.

**multangular:** see **trapezoid, trapezium bones**.

**multicausal:** describes any kind of theory that explains or attempts to explain an observed phenomenon as the result of the interaction of a variety of causes. Aka multifactorial. see **multivariate**. Cf. **monocausal**.

**multicellular:** describes any organ, tissue, or organism consisting of many cells; usually refers to **metazoans**.

**multidimensional species concept:** defines a species as a set of morphologically distinct populations, possible without clinal gradation, that are dispersed geographically yet that form a network and are capable of replacing each other. Since the individual populations may be regarded by other researchers as **morphospecies**, the multidimensional species concept is an extreme form of **lumping**. Cf. **nondimensional species concept**, the **phenetic species concept**, and **typology**.

**multidisciplinary:** of interest to several sceintific disciplines or subdisciplines. Aging, for example, is often referred to as a multidisciplinary phenomenon.

**multi-exon gene:** any genetic transcription unit (**cistron**) that consists of two or more **exons** separated by one or more **introns**. About 75% of known human genes are of this type.

**multifactorial:** see multicausal.

**multifactorial inheritance:** situation in which more than one factor is responsible for the development of a trait. In unqualified usage, both genetic and environmental factors are implied.

**multifactorial trait, character** or **feature:** any trait that results from the interaction of one or more environmental factors and two or more genes.

**multifetal pregnancy reduction:** elimination of one or more embryos in **higher-order multiple** pregnancies in order to improve the chances of survival of others.

**multigene family:** set of genes generated by duplication and modified by selection on mutations to produce dissimilar but often related functions, and with striking sequence homology. Such genes may be scattered throughout a genome, or linked on a single chromosome, especially if produced by sequential **endoreduplication**. Examples of such families include the genes that code for the collagens, hemoglobins, histocompatibility antigens, histones, immunoglobulins, and keratins.

**multilinear evolution:** evolution along multiple tracks; a mode of cultural evolutionary thought associated with Julian Steward; argument that cultures throughout the world differ greatly but their cultural core follows a similar evolutionary sequence insofar as the environment permits; sometimes termed multilineal evolution. Cf. **unilineal evolution.**

**multi-male/female group:** group of animals in which several adult males and several adult females are reproductively active, together with their immature offspring. See **mixed sex group.**

**multi-male/multi-female group:** see **mixed sex group.**

**multimale polygyny:** see **polygyny.**

**multimammae:** more than one pair of mammary glands; condition found among many of the **prosimians.**

**multinuclear:** having more than one nucleus; aka polynuclear.

**multiparity:** 1. condition in which a female has produced more than one previous **litter** or brood. Adjective: multiparous. 2. the production of two or more offspring in a single litter or brood. Among primates this condition exists in many prosimian species and among the callitrichids. Cf. **primiparity.** see **parity.**

**multiple alleles:** set of two or more **alleles,** any one of which may occupy the same locus on a chromatid.

‡ **multiple births:** polyembryony in humans is considered to be a clinically exceptional, teratogenic event, the production of multiple embryos from a single fertilized egg, such as monozygous **twins.** Most **higher-order multiples** (three or more births) are mixed sets of identical and fraternal twins. The predicted number of natural births (not induced by hormone therapy) of each kind is the subject of **Hellin's law** of multiple births. The so-called 'vanishing twin' phenomenon has recently led to a renewed interest in the twin events. Multiple births occur approximately once in every 73 births (incidence is .02725); of these, the majority are twins (94.4%), 5% are triplets, 0.5% are quadruplets, and 0.1% are quintuplets or higher.

**multiple neurofibromatosis:** hereditary condition characterized by abnormal growth of benign tumors on nerve endings in the skin.

**multiple-peaked fitness surface:** a graph of average **fitness** in a population in relation to the fitness of the **genotypes** within it; the **adaptive landscape** of Sewall **Wright.** Random **genetic drift** could supplement **natural selection** by enabling populations to explore the valley bottoms of adaptive topographies.

**multiple regression:** in statistics, regression model with two or more independent variables.

**multiplex PCR:** simultaneous amplification of multiple **DNA sequences** in a single reaction by using multiple sets of primers. See **PCR.**

**multiplier effect:** amplification of the effects of evolutionary change in behavior when the behavior is incorporated into the mechanisms of social organization.

‡ **multiregional continuity model:** hypothesis that modern humans evolved throughout the Old World as a single species after the first dispersal of Homo erectus out of Africa roughly 2–1 mya. According to this view, the transition from *Homo erectus* to *Homo sapiens* occurred in separate and parallel lines in the three major geographic regions of Africa, Europe and Asia, with the assumption that **gene flow** maintained some genetic homogeneity; essentially, the major racial stocks (as seen by those who hold this view) have deep regional roots. This argument for multiple centers of **human origins** is a restatement of the **Neandertal phase of man hypothesis** and of the even earlier concept of **polygenism.** Aka regional development hypothesis, multiregional evolution, the multiregional development model, and the **polyphyletic hypothesis of racial origins.** Cf. **monophyletic hypothesis of racial origins, out of Africa model.**

**multistate trait, character** or **feature:** any feature having more than two states or manifestations in a population or other taxon; more complex than a **binary trait.**

**multituberculate:** vernacular for a member of the Multituberculata, a very successful group of primitive herbivorous mammals that flourished during the Mesozoic.

‡ **multivariate analysis (or method):** any of several statistical techniques such as **factor analysis** or **cluster analysis,** all of which provide **summary statistics** after the simultaneous or sequential manipulation of several variables or traits. Other such techniques include: canonical correlation analysis, correspondence analysis, discriminant function analysis, linear probability modeling, multidimensional scaling, multiple discriminant analysis, multivariate analysis of covariance (MANCOVA), multivariate analysis of variance (MANOVA), path analysis, and principal component(s) analysis. Cf. **univariate analysis, bivariate analysis.**

**multivory:** dietary category that is more refined than **omnivory;** it refers to the consumption of many different food items such as fruit, insects, gums, leaves, etc. It reflects the fact that most primates have a varied diet.

**Mumba Rockshelter:** archaeological site located in Tanzania dated to 65–26.9 kya (U series, possibly as old as 131 kya); contains **Middle Stone Age** artifacts and hominid remains assigned to early *Homo sapiens.*

**mummification:** process of preservation of bodies of the dead, resulting in a **mummy**. Mummification may occur by chance (e.g. freeze-drying as in the European 'Iceman' or the desiccated mummies of the Chilean coast; cryomummification) or intentionally (such as the mummies of ancient Egypt and many other cultures). Intentional mummification is a practice intended to enhance preservation of a body.

**mummy:** body that has been subjected to either chance or intentional **mummification.**

**mummy bundle:** seated or flexed mummified cadaver, often wrapped in textiles and offerings to form a large bundle; found in Andean South America.

**Muna-Butung macaque:** vernacular for *Macaca brunnescens.*

**Mungo** (WLH): archaeological site found in 1968 near Muldura in New South Wales, southeastern Australia, and thought to date to 40 ± 2 kya (**OSL**, 2003; other $^{14}$C dates of 24.7 and 31.1 kya have also been obtained, and in 1999, OSL, **ESL** and **U-series** dating yielded controversial dates of 82, 78, and 62 kya). The site was a Pleistocene lake thought to have last been full around 15 kya; fish, shell and bird remains are common. Contains undated artifacts of the Australian core-tool and scraper tradition from the Mungo B trench. Hominid remains have since been repatriated, and included fragments of three individuals with some archaic traits (Mungo I–III) that were attributed to *Homo sapiens*. Aka Lake Mungo, WLH I, II and III. Cf. **Willandra Lakes.**

**Munsell Color Chart:** standardized color chips mounted in a loose-leaf notebook, each graded along scales of value, hue, and color; a standard means of matching and describing color gradations, and used in several disciplines.

**muriqui:** vernacular for *Brachyteles arachnoides.*

**Mursi Formation:** Pliocene sedimentary deposit found in the Lower **Omo Valley** of East Africa, dated to 4.1 mya.

**Muruyur:** an archaeological site found at Kipsaramon in the Murumur Beds of the **Tugen Hills**, Kenya (Africa), dated to >13 mya (middle Miocene) that contains disputed hominoid remains including fragments assigned to *Equatorius*. Aka Kipsaramon.

‡ **muscle:** contractile tissue; as it shortens and thickens it produces a pull on an attached structure, thereby producing movement. Muscle cells are referred to as muscle fibers; muscle tissue and supporting connective and nervous tissue constitute a muscle organ. There are three types of muscle tissue, **cardiac, skeletal,** and **smooth muscle.**

**muscle contraction:** shortening of **muscle** fibers that results in a pull on a structure attached to the muscle.

**muscle recruitment:** increase in the number of motor units involved in muscular action as stimulation increases.

**muscle strength:** 1. force that can be provided by a **muscle** based on its cross-sectional area. 2. absolute maximum force exerted against a resistance in an isolated movement of a single muscle group.

**muscular diaphragm:** see **respiratory diaphragm.**

**muscular dystrophy, Duchenne type:** DMD is caused by a X-linked recessive mutation in dystrophin, an essential structural muscle protein, and which results in collapsed muscle cells and produces chronic, progressive muscle weakness. Deterioration of muscle cells causes a secondary immune reaction. Different mutations in the *DMD* gene lead to several types of null mutations that each have characteristic ages of onset. The *DMD* gene is the largest known gene in humans. The Becker type of muscular dystrophy (BMD) differs in that it features reduced amounts of dystrophin.

**musculoskeletal disorder:** disease or syndrome attributed to abnormal formation of bones, muscles, ligaments, tendons, and/or other connective tissue; common examples are **muscular dystrophy, osteoarthritis,** and **osteoporosis.**

**musculoskeletal system:** muscular and skeletal systems considered as a functional whole rather than individual systems.

‡ **mutagen:** any substance or agent capable of inducing mutations in germinal or gonadal DNA; typically, radiation or a chemical. Aka mutagenic agent. Cf. **carcinogen** and **teratogen.**

**mutant:** 1. any phenotypic variant of a strain, individual, cell or gene that results from a genetic **mutation** from the **wild type** condition. 2. any **transgenic** organism.

**mutant selection:** anthropogenic manipulation of a toxic growth medium so that only toxin-resistant cells survive.

‡ **mutation:** any discontinuous change in the genetic constitution of an organism. Mutations can occur in **DNA** (see **point mutation**) or in **chromosome structure.** Mutation is the ultimate source of all **genetic variation.** Mutations must occur in **germ cells** before evolutionary change can occur, but **somatic mutations** can cause, for example, **cancer** and **teratomas.** Several classes of mutation have been defined, including **synonymous mutation, silent mutation, neutral mutation, missense mutation,** and **nonsense mutation;** each of the above may in addition be either a **transition** or a **transversion.** See also **micromutation, macromutation,** and **major chromosome anomaly.**

**mutation pressure:** evolution caused solely by varying **mutation rates** at several loci.

**mutation rate:** rate at which an unrepaired **mutation** accumulates in a gene.

**mutation rate, average:** rate(s) at which unrepaired mutations accumulate in the DNA of organisms. The rate in **nuclear DNA** is about 1 in 10,000 gametes per generation, but is 5–10 times higher in **mtDNA**, and about 100 times higher in the unrepaired DNA found in organisms such as viruses (vDNA, vRNA). The **vDNA** rate is probably that experienced by many terrestrial life forms, but many higher organisms possess enzymes that can repair mutations under certain conditions.

**mutation–selection balance:** equilibrium in the frequency of an allele because new copies of an allele are introduced by **mutation** at exactly the same rate that old copies are eliminated by **natural selection.**

**mutation theory:** proposal in 1903 that new forms or even species arise by **mutations** that occur randomly in a population and are then acted upon by **natural selection.** In the form proposed by Dutch botanist Hugo **De Vries** (1848–1935), these mutations were **saltational**, a theme supported for a time by certain others (see **hopeful monsters**) but that gave way gradually to **neo-Darwinism** as the roles of **segregation** and **crossing over** became better understood.

**mutational load:** reduction of the mean fitness of a population owing to the accumulation of deleterious alleles resulting from recurrent **mutation.** see **genetic load.**

**mutationism:** see De Vriesianism and hopeful monsters.

**muton:** smallest element in a DNA molecule that, when altered, gives rise to a mutant form of an organism; usually, a nucleotide.

**mutual aid:** nineteenth century term for behaviors later ascribed to **altruism.** See **law of mutual aid.**

**mutualism:** type of **symbiosis** involving interaction between two or more individuals from different species in which all individuals benefit; mutualism is often a relationship of complete dependence by those involved.

**muzzle:** long snout of a mammal; the muzzle is often made up of a **premaxilla** and is prominent in some primates, notably baboons.

**my:** million years; abbreviation used by some human evolutionary biologists. Also m.y. and Myr.

‡ **mya:** millions of years ago; abbreviation used by some human evolutionary biologists. Also m.y.a., Myr and (less often) ma.

**mycosis:** any disease caused by a fungus, e.g. **coccidioidomycosis.**

‡ **myelin:** white lipoprotein material that forms a sheathlike covering around nerve fibers; insulation that aids in the transmission of electrical impulses.

**myelocyte:** 1. an immature cell of the **granulocyte** variety, which occurs in red bone marrow. 2. nerve cell found in **gray matter.**

**myeloma:** tumor originating from an antibody-producing cell; a myeloma originating in a mouse is the most universal partner of fusion for the formation of **hybridomas.**

**myelencephalon:** posterior region of the hindbrain or **rhombencephalon** composed of the **medulla oblongata**; it connects to the **spinal cord** and contains nuclei for certain cranial nerves and other nuclei that control cardiac, vasomotor, and respiratory functions.

**mylohyoid groove:** furrow on the internal surface of the mandible that travels inferiorly and medially from the **mental foramen.**

**myoblast transfer therapy:** form of somatic gene therapy in which modified immature voluntary skeletal muscle cells (myoblasts) are transferred to affected muscles where they replace dystrophin that is abnormal or absent; used to treat muscular dystrophy.

**myoglobin:** analog of **hemoglobin** found solely in muscle tissue and that transports oxygen. The human myoglobin gene maps to HSA 22q12.3, and is remarkable in that 95% of its **cistron** consists of three introns.

**myopia:** visual defect in which objects may be seen distinctly only when very close to the eyes. Aka shortsightedness, nearsightedness, low or high myopia. Cf. **presbyopia** and **myopia 2.**

**myopia 2 (MYP2):** hereditary nearsightedness of severe degree; aka extreme myopia (EM). Myopia is classified as low, high, and extreme. Myopia is multifactorial and is measured as a metric character, with a heritability of 0.58. In urban populations there is an apparent high correlation between severity of myopia and high performance on certain aptitude tests. MYP is considered a case pf pleiotrophy, with a suspected autosomal recessive major gene that has been located. In general, the categories of low and high myopia are positively correlated with the prevalence of extreme myopia (EM). Prevalence rates of EM are: (a) *low* (<0.5%) in Americans, Australian aboriginals, Eskimos, European Australians, Fijians, Finns, French Canadians, Greenland Eskimos, Labradorans, most Native Americans, natives of New Guinea, Yupik Eskimo males; (b) *medium* (0.5–2%) in Chinese, subcontinental Indians, Israelis; and (c) *high* (>2%) in Alaska Native Americans, Icelanders, Danes, Malays, Nigerians, Sioux Native Americans, and Yupik Eskimo females.

**myosin:** protein found in most eukaryotic cells; two classes exist. Myosin I (cytoplasmic myosin) is involved in **development** and cell locomotion. Myosin II (muscle myosin) acts as both a structural protein and an enzyme, and is involved in muscle contraction by interacting with actin (forming acto-myosin) to convert energy stored in **ATP**. Numerous isoforms of myosin are known to exist, and are coded for by at least ten genes; many of the isoforms are generated by **alternative splicing**. One of these **isoform** variants (**myosin heavy chain 16**) is inactivated in humans, but active in other primates and a variety of vertebrates.

**myosin heavy chain 16:** protein component of skeletal muscle sarcomeres found in jaw muscles; this protein is active in primates and other vertebrates but not in humans. It has been proposed that the gene for this protein, *MYH16*, became inactivated in certain hominids 2.4 mya, reduced the size of jaw muscles in that lineage, and removed a constraint preventing expansion and remodeling of the cranial vault.

**myositis ossificans:** ossification of muscle and tendon tissue; the femur of the first *Homo erectus* specimen discovered by DuBois has been cited as a possible case of this pathology.

**myotonic dystrophy** (DM): heritable autosomal dominant disease characterized by difficulty relaxing contracted muscles; causes muscle wasting, cataracts, balding; other defects in gonads and heart; mental impairment. Onset in young adulthood. The defective protein is a muscle kinase; the trait exhibits evidence for a progressive **trinucleotide repeat mutation** that makes symptoms more severe in successive generations, a phenomenon known as **anticipation**, and for **genomic imprinting**. Aka Kennedy disease, dystonia myotonica (DM).

*Myrmekomomys* **Robinson, 1994:** archaic mammal known from the late Paleocene and early Eocene of North America belonging to the **Plesiadapiformes** family **Micromomyidae**, consisting of only one species. Small body size strongly suggestive of **insectivory**. Body size very small, estimated between 10 and 15 g. See Appendix 1 for taxonomy.

**MZ, MZT:** abbreviation for monozygous twins. See **twins, monozygotic**.

**N (or n):** abbreviation for number. 1. in mathematics, an indefinite, constant whole number. 2. the sample size. 3. in biology, usually either a census population size or the **haploid** chromatid complement (but see *Ne*, the **effective breeding population**).

**N, 2N, 3N, etc.:** in **genetics**, nomenclature for expressing the number of complete sets of **chromosomes** or **chromatids** in a cell. N is usually the **haploid** number, 2N is the **diploid** number, 3N the **triploid** number, etc.

**N_e:** abbreviation for **effective breeding population**.

**Nachola (Formation):** an archaeological site (or region) found in 1982 in the Samburu district near the Baragoi River south of Lake Turkana, Northern Kenya, K/Ar dated to 15.4–12.8 mya (middle **Miocene**). Hominoid remains from the Nachola formation and the Aka Aiteputh formation include skeletal fragments attributed to *Kenyapithecus* and/or *Nacholapithecus*. Cf. **Samburu Hills**.

**Nacholapithecus kerioi:** species of **hominoid** from the Nachola formation in the Samburu district, Northern Kenya, dated to *c.* 12 mya (middle **Miocene**). There is currently some confusion concerning the taxonomy of the remains, which are similar to those assigned to *Kenyapithecus* and/or *Equatorius*.

**Nachukui Formation:** geological unit found in 1985 in the west Lake Turkana region, Kenya, dated to 2.5 mya, and that contains hominid remains, including **KNM-WT 17000** – the '**black skull**' of *Australopithecus ( = Paranthropus) aethiopicus* – and the young boy of **Nariokotome**.

**Nägeli, Karl Wilhelm von** (1817–1891): Swiss microscopist, botanist at Zurich; correctly described cell division, identified chromosomes ('transitory cytoblasts'), and protoplasm. He is infamously remembered as the scientist who failed to understand Mendel's work, even after an extended correspondence (*c.* 1860). Following Lord Kelvin's inaccurate underestimation of the age of the earth, Nägeli (and others) suggested that evolution must occur by 'jumps' (**saltations**), a notion that was later to take form as **De Vries**' mutation theory. Nägeli was recognized by **Charles Darwin** in the Introduction to the third edition of the *Origin of Species* as a 'precursor'.

**NAGPRA:** see **Native American Graves Protection and Repatriation Act**.

**nail:** hard keratinous structure that covers the dorsal aspect of terminal phalanges in primates (rather than **claws**). In anthropoids, with the exception of the callitrichids, each digit has a nail; all primates have a nail on at least one digit. Nails are also found, usually on the first digit only, among some arboreal mammals such as opossums. It has been suggested that nails evolved in primates to support the **tactile pads** on the ventral aspect of the terminal **phalanges**.

**nail–patella syndrome** (NP): hereditary condition characterized by oddly shaped nails and peculiar, small, or missing kneecaps (patellas). Closely linked to the ABO blood group locus on chromosome 9q.

**Naisiusiu (Olduvai Bed V):** uppermost sedimentary layer in **Olduvai Gorge** dated to 22–15 kya, yielding hominid fossils identical to living **AMHs**. Formerly known as Bed V.

**Naivasha rockshelter:** archaeological site near Lake Naivasha north of Nairobi, Kenya, an African **Late Stone Age** site excavated by Mary Leakey in 1939; contained thousands of artifacts and one **AMH** burial.

**nanism:** arrested or stunted growth, resulting in individuals that are small-bodied for age but whose heads are of normal size; aka dwarfism. Cf. **ateliosis**.

**Nannodectes Gingerich, 1974:** archaic mammal of the late Paleocene of the Rocky Mountain region of North America belonging to the family **Plesiadapidae**; consists of four species. Appears to have been derived from the earlier *Pronothodectes*. Dental formula: 2.1.3.3/1.1.3.3 except in the youngest species, *N. gidleyi*, which lacks the lower canine. Dentition suggests a diet of plant material. See Appendix 1 for taxonomy.

**Nannopithex Stehlin, 1916:** genus of tarsiiform primate from the middle Eocene of Europe belonging to the omomyoid family **Microchoeridae**; approximately eight species; earliest and most primitive microchoerid; some workers argue that this genus is ancestral to **Necrolemur**. Short snout; nocturnal; body mass for the species ranges between 125 and 200 g. Dental formula: 2.1.3.3/2.1.2.3; dental morphology suggestive of **insectivory**. See Appendix 1 for taxonomy.

**Nannopithex fold:** see **postprotocingulum**.

**nanoknives:** tools (i.e. enzymes) capable of cutting chromosomes.

**nanometer** (nm): unit of length equal to $1 \times 10^{-9}$ m the equivalent of 10 **Ångström units**; AKA millimicron. The nanometer is the unit of measurement of for example, the wavelength of **UV radiation**.

**Napak:** an archaeological site found in 1999, located on volcanic Mount Napak (Akisim) in northeastern Uganda near the Kenya border in East Africa, provisionally dated to *c.* 17 mya (early **Miocene**). The site contains more than 1,000 fossils; hominoid remains include *Proconsul major*. Aka Napak 1.

**nape:** back of the neck.

**Napier, John Russell** (1917–87): British primatologist, functional anatomist; trained as an orthopaedic surgeon, Napier made significant contributions to the understanding of bipedalism, brachiation, knuckle-walking, and other subjects. Napier was also involved in the description of several major hominoid taxa such as *Proconsul africanus* and *Homo* *habilis* (1964). Co-author (with Prue H. Napier) of *A Handbook of Living Primates* (1967); author of *The Roots of Mankind* (1970).

**nariale: craniometric landmark:** lowest point on the inferior border of the **nasal aperture.**

‡ **Nariokotome III:** archaeological site found by Kamoya **Kimeu** in 1984 on the Nariokotome River west of **Lake Turkana,** Kenya, dated to 1.6 mya (above the 1.65 mya component of the **Okote tuff**), and that contains hominid remains of one male juvenile (see 'Turkana boy', **KNM-WT 15000**), assigned variously to *Homo erectus* or *Homo ergaster.*

**naris, nares:** see **external nares.**

**nasal:** of or pertaining to the nose.

**nasal aperture:** triangular opening into the nasal cavity of the skull; aka pyriform aperture.

**nasal bone:** one of a pair of bones of the facial skeleton that join at the mid-line to form the bridge of the nose. In the genus *Homo* these bones project out, whereas in the **australopithecines** these bones are flat against the face producing a flattened nose that contributes to the 'dish' face of that group of humans.

**nasal breadth** (al–al): **craniometric** measurement; maximum width between the left and right **nasions** of the **nasal aperture** as measured with sliding calipers. See Appendix 7 an illustration of the landmarks used.

**nasal bridge index:** see **simotic index.**

**nasal cavity:** one of the two cavities contained within the nose and separated by the **nasal septum.** During inspiration the air is filtered, warmed, and humidified in this chamber. See **nasal concha.**

**nasal complex:** functional anatomical unit consisting of the nose, nasal aperture, and tissues and structures of the upper respiratory tract: the **paranasal sinuses,** nares, throat and upper trachea.

**nasal concha:** one of six curled bones (plural: conchae) that extend medially from the lateral walls of the nasal cavity; in life they are covered with **mucosa** that help filter, warm, and humidify the inspired air. Recent research suggests that Neandertals had larger conchae than moderns, perhaps as an adaptation to their cold environment. Aka turbinate bone, especially in skeletal specimens.

**nasal height** (n–ns): **craniometric** measurement: height of the nose measured with sliding calipers from the **nasion** to the **nasospinale.** See Appendix 7 for an illustration of the landmarks used.

**nasal incisive foramen:** see **incisive foramen.**

**nasal index:** ratio of nasal width to nasal height: **nasal breadth** divided by **nasal height** multiplied by 100. See **leptorrhinic, mesorrhinic, chamaerrhinic, hyperchamaerrhinic.**

**nasal length:** distance from **subnasale** to **nasion.**

**nasal morphology:** nose shape and size; one of the traits that, because of its variation in humans, has a long history of use in racial taxonomy; **Topinard,** for example, classified humans into three major racial groups: white **leptorrhine,** yellow **mesorrhine,** and black **platyrrhine.**

**nasal pillar:** type of facial buttressing found among some **hominoids** including *Australopithecus* and *Paranthropus;* bony strut on either side of the nasal aperture that provides reinforcement to the face for stresses placed on it from vigorous chewing. This structure disappears from the *Homo* line.

**nasal radiator hypothesis:** proposal by **Carlton Coon** that the large apertures and surface areas of the noses of European **Neandertals** functioned to warm and moisten the cold, dry air of the European **Pleistocene** glacial times. See **nasal concha.**

**nasal septum:** wall that runs vertically through the medial line of the nose and separates the two nasal cavities. This wall is composed of cartilage and bone and joins the **vomer** anteriorly. In life the nasal septum is covered with **mucosa** that helps trap particles from the inspired air.

*Nasalis* É. Geoffroy, 1812: monotypic catarrhine genus to which the proboscis monkey belongs. Occupy mangrove forests on Borneo and two northeastern coastal islands. Arboreal; diurnal; quadrupedal with leaping. Reported to dive from trees into rivers, where they swim. Highly **sexually dimorphic** in body size, males weighing about 20 kg, females around 10 kg; males have large pendulous nose, females with smaller upturned nose. Dental formula: 2.1.2.3; **folivorous.** Live in mixed-sex bands of about 20 individuals; known to form **associations** with macaques and leaf monkeys. See Appendix 2 for taxonomy and Appendix 3 for species.

**nasion** (n): **craniometric landmark:** point where the internasal and nasofrontal sutures intersect. See Appendix 7.

**nasoalveolar clivus:** sloping portion of the maxilla extending from the nasal to the **alveolar process.**

**nasofrontal suture:** line of union of the frontal bone and the two nasal bones.

**nasospinale** (ns): **craniometric landmark:** medial point of a line drawn between the two inferior margins of the nasal apertures. The nasospinale lies on the mid-sagittal plane. See Appendix 7.

**natal:** 1. pertaining to one's birth. 2. describing one's place of birth. 3. referring to customs and beliefs learned at or near one's place of origin, especially when compared with knowledge obtained elsewhere.

**natal coat:** newborn's **pelage** that is different from the adult pelage; for example, infant colobus monkeys are born with a white coat, in contrast to the black-and-white pelage of the adults. It has been hypothesized that this difference advertises the infant as an individual that needs assistance. See **cute response**.

‡ **natal group:** group of individuals into which an infant is born. See **philopatric**.

**natality:** increase of young into a population via births over a particular period of time. Physiologically, natality is the maximum number of births possible under ideal environmental conditions; realized natality is the actual number of offspring produced under existing conditions. See **fecundity** and **fertility**.

**National Geographic Society** (NGS): founded in 1888, the NGS promotes and funds exploration, education, and conservation around the world. Also dating from 1888, its printed organ, the *National Geographic Magazine*, often includes fold-out maps that have become international icons. The NGS continues to fund projects germane to human biology and evolution. Sponsor of the prestigious Hubbard Medal award; past recipients include Louis **Leakey** and Mary **Leakey** (1962), Richard **Leakey** (1994), and Jane **Goodall** (1995).

**National Museum of Ethiopia** (NME): founded in 1944, the museum in Addis Ababa is the repository for all fossils recovered in Ethiopia.

**National Museums of Kenya** (KNM): nationalized upon independence in 1964, the former Coryndon Natural History Museum in Nairobi is the repository for all fossils recovered in Kenya; some of the collections from Tanzania have also been retained.

**native:** 1. indigenous or natural to a given region. 2. a consistent member of a certain habitat.

**Native American:** ethnym for an **autochthonous** peoples of the Americas; **American Indian**. For US census purposes the term Native American also includes Hawaiians, Aleuts, and Inuit, peoples not traditionally included among American Indians. The ethnym Native American is employed by many non-Indians (especially academics), but many American Indians do not favor the use of that label, preferring individual tribal names instead.

**Native American Graves Protection and Repatriation Act** (NAGPRA): a Federal law passed in 1990 that provides a process for museums and Federal agencies to return certain Native American human remains, funerary objects, sacred objects, and other objects of cultural patrimony to lineal descendants, culturally affiliated Indian tribes, and Native Hawaiian organizations. National NAGPRA is a program of the National Park Service's National Center for Cultural Resources, and develops regulations and guidelines for implementing NAGPRA. It provides support for the Native American Graves Protection and Repatriation Review Committee whose responsibility is to assist Indian tribes, Native Alaskan villages and corporations, Native Hawaiian organizations, museums, and Federal agencies with the NAGPRA process.

**natron:** salt obtained from **Lake Natron** and similar lakes in Egypt, an important ingredient in the Old World mummification process.

**Natufian culture:** late **Mesolithic** culture found in the **Levant** about 12.8–10.5 kya. Natufians display both nomadic and sedentary lifeways, hunting and gathering during some seasons and exploiting harvested cereals during others. Among the earliest users of sickles and pounding tools. Type site is Wadi el-Natuf.

**Natufian hypothesis:** proposal by V. Gordon Childe that the first instance of the **Neolithic Revolution** occurred within the **Natufian culture**.

*natura non facit saltum* (Latin): 'nature does not make jumps', a phrase coined by Leibniz and affirmed by **Linnaeus** and **Darwin**; cf. **gradualism**.

**natural antibody:** 1. antibody to a natural substance. 2. see **natural immunity**.

**natural cranial deformation:** change in the size and/or shape of the cranium owing to pathological conditions such as microcephaly, macrocephaly, acrocephaly, etc.

**natural history:** descriptive science that was the precursor to many of the modern disciplines such as anthropology, biology, botany, geology, zoology, and, especially, ecology. Naturalists recorded and attempted to explain events observed in nature, but rarely made deductions through experimentation. When the ecological concept first developed in the 1880s, it was referred to as the New Natural History.

**natural immunity:** defunct idea that some 'naturally occurring antibodies' are inherited, and require exposure to foreign antigens. This was thought to be the case for antibodies to the A and B antigens in the **ABO blood group**. Current hypotheses require exposure before an antibody can be generated.

**natural increase:** change in population size expected due to effects of fertility and mortality, but not migration; the number of births minus the number of deaths.

**natural killer cell** (NK): specialized white blood cell that originates in bone marrow and is able to kill invading microorganisms without activation by other cells of the immune system. Cf. **killer cell**.

**natural philosophy:** 1. study or knowledge of objects or processes observable in nature, as in biology, physics, etc. 2. the study, in former times, of supposed symmetries between science and religion such that the manifestation of a **Grand Design** was apparent in creatures great and small, as well as in the unbroken hierarchy of formed creatures known as the **Great Chain of Being**, with humans positioned between the monkeys and the angels.

**natural remnant magnetism:** primary magnetism aligned parallel to the existing magnetic field of the earth found in iron-bearing rocks and sediments, and used as a fossil compass in **paleomagnetic dating**.

‡ **natural selection:** nonrandom process by which some individuals in a species who possess adaptive phenotypic traits have a higher **net reproductive success** than individuals without those traits. This can occur only for those adaptive traits that possess **heritability**, i.e. **genotypes** that contribute underlying adaptive **genes** disproportionately to successive **generations** as the result of differential fecundity, or, differential **mortality** or **fertility** by genotype. In a simpler form, this was the first **mechanism** proposed (by Charles **Darwin**, 1859) to account for **evolution**, in which forces in the environment select which individuals will leave the most offspring; still generally regarded as the principle nonteleological force in evolution. It is supported by the findings of modern genetics. See **transmutation**.

**natural theology:** theology based upon reason and knowledge of the natural world, as opposed to revelation; knowledge of creation and **intelligent design** as revealed in nature.

**nature–nurture controversy:** in the context of behavior, the opposing points of view that much of **behavior**, including humans and nonhuman primate behavior, is **hereditary** ('nature'), vs. the view that all or most behaviors are learned ('nurture') and strictly **cultural**.

**Naturphilosophie:** eighteenth- and nineteenth-century romantic movement in central Europe that attempted to unify all natural phenomena and processes through transcendental beliefs.

**nausea:** sickness when referred to the region of the stomach or epigastric area; feeling of the need to vomit.

*Navajovius* **Matthew and Granger, 1921:** archaic mammal of the late Paleocene and early Eocene of the Rocky Mountain region of North America belonging to the plesiadapiform family **Microsyopidae**; consists of one or two species depending on author; taxonomy equivocal, this genus has even been assigned to Eocene primate families. Dental formula: ?.1.3.3/1.1.3.3 or 2.1.2.3; enlarged central incisors. Estimated body mass around 30 g. Small body size and dentition suggests **insectivory**. See Appendix 1 for taxonomy.

**navicular:** 1. pertaining to a structure that has a boat-like shape. 2. medial **tarsal** bone that articulates with the **talus** and **calcaneus** posteriorly, the **cuboid** laterally, and the three **cuneiforms** anteriorly; formerly called the scaphoid (of the foot). 3. bone of the human hand, now aka **scaphoid** in order to avoid confusion with the tarsal bone of the same name.

**nDNA:** nuclear DNA; DNA located in the **nucleus** of a cell, as opposed to extranuclear DNA.

**Ndutu:** see **Lake Ndutu** and **Ndutu Bed**.

**Ndutu Bed:** fossil-bearing sedimentary layer in **Olduvai Gorge** dated 400–32 kya (**K/Ar**), yielding hominid fossils such as *Homo* sp. (OH 11); tools are found in the Upper Ndutu only, and are Middle Stone Age tools made by a **Levallois** technique. Fauna is identical to living African species, except for a giant form of baboon, *Theropithecus*.

**Neander Valley:** see **Feldhofer Grotto**.

‡ **Neandertal:** 1. modern spelling of the archaic Neanderthal. Technically, the original binomen *Homo neanderthalensis* was spelled (in 1856) with the 'thal' suffix (meaning valley), and by the rules of nomenclature the original spelling must be carried forward whenever the binomen is used. As this leads to much confusion, both versions are still common in the professional literature. 2. Any member of a regional population of **archaic *Homo*** sp. found in Europe and the Middle East, dating from approximately 200–135 to 29 kya. Neandertals are characterized culturally by their **Mousterian** (and **Châtelperronian**) **tool kit**, and physically by their large and especially wide and flat braincases, double-arched **tori** over each eye, **prognathous** faces with large noses, special **occipital** features, and certain dental specializations. Their geographic distribution was limited to Europe and the Middle and Near East. See *Homo neanderthalensis*, *Homo sapiens neanderthalensis* and **preneandertal hypothesis**.

‡ **Neanderthal:** see **Neandertal**.

**Neandertal phase of man hypothesis:** model attempting to explain the position of the **Neandertals** and proposed by G. Schwalbe, who argued that the Neandertals arose from a Middle **Pleistocene** predecessor by unilinear and gradual evolution and passed through a Neandertal phase to become **AMHs**. A. **Hrdlicka**, C. L. **Brace**, M. L. **Wolpoff**, A. **Thorne**, F. H. **Smith**, G. Pope, E. **Trinkaus** and others have also embraced and/or refined this view. See the **multiregional continuity model**. Compare the **preneandertal hypothesis**, the **presapiens hypothesis**, the **monophyletic hypothesis**, and the **polyphyletic hypothesis**.

**'Neandertal problem', the:** during the late nineteenth and early twentieth centuries, the absence of a hominid **fossil record** anywhere else but Europe and Asia led researchers to focus on the relationship of the **Neandertals** to both **AMHs** and to the then next-lowest taxon, the **pithecanthropines**, leading to a historiographic emphasis on this taxon.

**'Neandertal question':** perennial problem in paleoanthropology concerning the source and, especially, the fate of the **Neandertals**, and the potential for their relationship to succeeding modern European populations. See the **preneandertal hypothesis**, the **Neandertal phase of man hypothesis**, and the **Neandertal retreat hypothesis**.

**Neandertal retreat hypothesis:** proposal that the Neandertals were forced to retreat into small pockets owing to the advance of **AMHs** between 36–30 kya. After 30 kya, Neandertals with **Mousterian** culture are found only on the Iberian peninsula (possibly **Abrigo do Lagar Velho rockshelter**) and the Crimea; Neandertals with **Châtelperronian** and other **Upper Paleolithic** industries are found only in Yugoslavia (**Mezmaiskaya Cave** and **Vindija**) and the southern tip of Great Britain. After 30 kya, **Aurignacian**-bearing AMHs occupied the rest of habitable Europe.

‡ **Neandertal site:** see **Feldhofer Grotto**.

**neandertaloid:** grade of human evolution representing the **hominids** that lived during the middle **Pleistocene** and are characterized by large cranial capacity, robust build, heavy brow ridges and **postorbital constriction**, and that lack a chin. In addition to the Neandertals of Europe and western Asia, humans that are considered neandertaloid are found in Africa and the Far East.

**neanthropic:** pertaining to recent man, AMHs; *Homo sapiens*. Cf. **paleoanthropic**, **protoanthropic**.

**Near Eastern fossil group(s):** grouping of sites, mostly in the **Levant** region, containing artifacts that exhibit a mixed **Levalloiso-Mousterian** culture, and hominid fossils that are either predominantly modern in physical appearance (the Near Eastern modern group; see **AMHs**, **Skhūl** and **Qafzeh**), or are predominantly **neandertaloid** in physical appearance (the Near Eastern Neandertal group; see **Amud**, **Tabūn**, **Shanidar** and **Zuttiyeh**.

**near-human:** pertaining to the fossil populations of the Old World; recent antecedents of **AMHs**.

**Nearctica:** New World portion of **Holarctica**.

**Nebraskan glaciation:** first of the fourth major glaciation of the Pleistocene in the North American sequence; see **Günz glaciation**.

**neck:** 1. constricted or narrower area; often referred to as a cervix; e.g. neck of the femur, humerus, etc. 2. cervical region of the body between the head and thorax; see **cervical vertebra**. 3. in dental anatomy, the constricted portion of a tooth, surrounded by the gingivae (gums) that joins the crown to the root; aka cemento-enamel junction. 4. portion of a bone that connects an **epiphysis** to the **diaphysis**.

*Necrolemur* Filhol, 1873: genus of tarsiiform primate from the late Eocene of Europe belonging to the omomyoid family **Microchoeridae**; two species; some workers think that this is the direct descendant of the earlier *Nannopithex*. Short snout; nocturnal;

body mass around 300 g. Dental formula: 2.1.3.3/2.1.2.3; procumbent incisor that appears to have been used for gouging (as used by a **gummivore**) as well as for grooming; overall dental morphology suggestive of frugivory with gum supplements. Known **postcrania** indicate some leaping capabilities. See Appendix 1 for taxonomy.

**necrosis:** cell or tissue death due to disease or trauma. Cf. **apoptosis**.

**nectar feeding hypothesis:** model of **primate origins** that attempts to explain basic arboreal adaptations in primates as the result of feeding on small food items located on terminal branches of trees and bushes; a recent variant of the **visual predation model**.

**nectarivory:** feeding category for animals (nectarivores) that primarily consume the sugary fluid, or nectar, from the flowers of plants; nectarivores serve as pollinators for the plants that attract them. Adjective: nectarivorous. see also **diet**.

**needle:** bone implement, varying greatly in size, found in some **Magdalenian**-age sites, and with eyes probably made with an **awl**.

**needle-clawed galago (bushbaby):** vernacular for the two **prosimian** species in the genus *Euoticus*.

**Neel, James Van Gundia** (1915–2000): US physician and human geneticist at Ann Arbor; MD and PhD from the University of Rochester (NY); he was a student of geneticist Curt Stern. Neel was acting Director of Field Studies for the Atomic Bomb Casualty Commission (ABCC, 1947–8); radiation effects were a focus of much of his career. He later worked for several years among the Xavante of Brazil and the Yanomamö of Venezuela. Among his colleagues in Venezuela was Napoleon **Chagnon**. Neel was the author of a much-cited (and debated) **thrifty genotype hypothesis** concerning **diabetes** among the Pima. Neel served on the editorial board of 15 journals, was a member of 12 professional societies, and was the recipient of numerous career achievement awards. He published over 400 articles and wrote or participated in a dozen books. Co-author (with W. J. Schull) of *The Effect of Exposure to the Atomic Bomb on Pregnancy Termination in Hiroshima and Nagasaki* (1956, Washington, DC); author of *Physician to the Gene Pool* (1994).

**negative allometry:** allometric relationship in which the slope of the line comparing two variables is less than zero; as one variable increases (say, body size) the second variable decreases (say, relative head size), producing a negative slope. Cf. **positive allometry**.

‡ **negative assortative mating** (NAM): less common type of **nonrandom mating** in which individuals of differing **phenotypes** mate more often than expected when compared with a theoretical standard

called **random mating**. NAM results in an increase in the proportion of **heterozygotes** in a **population**. Aka dissortative mating, heterophenogamy. Cf. **positive assortative mating**.

**negative bulb:** hollow on a cobble or core that matches the positive **bulb of percussion** of a flake that has been removed during the tool-making process; one of the diagnostic features that archaeologists use to distinguish a stone **tool** from a naturally occurring **geofact**.

**negative correlation:** in statistics, the situation that exists when high values of one variable tend to be associated with low values of another, and vice-versa. Cf. **positive correlation**.

**negative eugenics:** policy of interference with or prevention of the reproduction of individuals considered genetically inferior; the removal of **deleterious alleles** from a population. Aka preventative **eugenics**. Cf. **positive eugenics**.

**negative FDS: frequency-dependent selection** that occurs when the fitness of a genotype is inversely proportional to the frequency of that genotype in a population; thus, a higher fitness when rare and a lower fitness when common. This is the more typical case of FDS, and can maintain a **balanced polymorphism** in a population. See **positive FDS**.

**negative result:** situation in which the **null hypothesis** has not been rejected.

**negative sanction:** social disapproval of certain individual behaviors. Negative sanctions are in general more definitively outlined than are positive sanctions. See **sanction**.

**negative selection:** natural selection against deleterious **mutations**.

**Negrillo:** ethnym for the many **autochthonous** peoples of Africa with short stature, generally found in the forests of the Congo region. Negrillos have a **tripartite** geographic distribution: Eastern, Central, and Western groups. Partially synonymous with **pygmy**, but see **Negrito**. Aka African pygmy.

**Negrito:** 1. T. H. **Huxley**'s 1870 **ethnym** for the inhabitants of the island of Tasmania, which he considered to be distinct from the **Australoids** of mainland Australia. 2. a term subsequently applied to the pygmoid peoples of southeast Asia, especially when found in the Philippines and the coastal forests of Australia. 3. in more recent usage, any **pygmoid** people. Cf. **Negrillo**.

**Negrito hypothesis:** older proposal based on the idea that the worldwide distribution of **pygmoid** peoples is explained by an ancient pan-equatorial Old World distribution; that portions of Africa, India, southeast Asia, and Australasia were once inhabited by **Negritos**, and that these populations were subsequently marginalized by invading populations of

taller humans. In this view, surviving populations subsist in refuge areas; the **Andamanese** peoples of southeast Asia have been a focus of research concerning this hypothesis.

**negro:** synonym for **Negroid** as well as an archaic colloquial term for a dark-skinned person, particularly one whose ancestry is from sub-Saharan Africa, Australasia, or certain regions of Oceania.

**negro tamarin:** vernacular for *Saguinus tamarin*.

**Negroid:** archaic **ethnym** for many **autochthonous** peoples of Africa, Australasia, and the Pacific, derived from the Spanish term for black or dark. Negroid peoples are characterized by moderate to deep melanization, slight body hair, small ears, black head hair that may range from a light curl to woolly or frizzy, a nose with a low bridge, a narrow to medium broad face, and everted lips; height extremely variable. This group includes the **Forest Negro**, the **Nilotic Negro**, and the **Oceanic Negro**. Historically, one of the major races of humans. Over time, this definition has changed, and included the sub-Saharan peoples of Africa and sometimes peoples of the South Pacific, but it usually excluded the Khoisan. See **Capoid, Congoid**.

**neighborhood:** term used for Malagasy and African **prosimians** in reference to localized groups which consist of overlapping home ranges of males and females. Common pattern among **mouse lemurs** and **bushbabies**.

**Neoanthropidae:** putative **hominoid** family proposed by Louis **Leakey** in 1934 to include a lineage that gave rise to modern humans; this family included the fossils then known as **Piltdown** and *Homo kanamensis*. Cf. **Paleoanthropidae**.

**Neoasiatic:** older scholarly subdivision of the so-called **Mongoloid** stock, a central-eastern Asian peoples with an extreme development of the internal **epicanthic fold**.

**neoblastic:** referring to the origin of new tissue.

‡ **neocortex:** nonolfactory, phylogenetically younger part of the cerebral cortex; so-called because its cellular and fibrous layers are distributed in a uniform pattern. Region of the mammalian brain associated with 'higher' level motor and sensory activities and the integration of those activities into complex patterns of behavior. It is 3–6 times larger in humans than in the great apes. See **neopallium**.

**neocortex hypothesis:** proposal to explain selective pressures on primate group size. This argument suggests that **neocortex** size in a species is a determinant of group size because there is a finite number of individuals with which a primate can socially interact, owing to nervous development.

**neo-Darwinism:** explanation of biological **evolution** by two primary mechanisms: **point mutations** and natural selection; historical term used to refer to the synthesis of **Weismannism**, **Darwinism** and **Mendelism** in the period from 1900 to 1930, principally by **Chetverikov, Haldane, Fisher,** and **Wright**. This term can exclude the period *c.* 1930, which is often called **Fisherism**, and the next decade is then the **Modern Synthesis**. Sometimes the works of **Dobzhansky, Simpson,** and others around 1940 are also associated. Aka the neo-Darwinian revolution. Cf. **second Darwinian revolution**.

**Neogene system:** in geology, the time-stratigraphic unit composed of the **Tertiary** sub-period, and that contains the Miocene and Pliocene epochs of the **Cenozoic era**. See **Paleogene system** and **Quaternary**.

**neo-Lamarckian inheritance:** term for any one of many recurrent proposals (and subsequent falsifications) of any hypothesis which suggests that some character or process acquired during an individual's lifetime is transmitted directly to its offspring.

‡ **Neolithic:** of or relating to the **New Stone Age**. Neolithic **stone tool** technologies are associated with plant **domestication** and self-sufficient **agriculture** and characterized by the presence of polishing and/or **grinding stones** and the origin of fired ceramics, commencing about 6–4 kya.

**Neolithic Revolution (hypothesis):** proposed by V. Gordon Childe to explain the origins of agriculture but now regarded by many as too simplistic, the model supposed that in response to post-Pleistocene climate changes humans changed from food collecting to haphazard and then systematic food growing, animal husbandry, and living in permanent housing, and developed methods of storing inventoried crops. Now supplanted by more complex models such as the risk management models and the ecological models.

**Neolithicum:** archaic term for the study and contemplation of newer, polished, stone implements. Cf. **Paleolithicum**.

**neo-Mongoloid:** see **Sinodont**.

**neomorph:** biological feature that is the result of independent development; a new feature (e.g. the entotympanic ossification of eutherian mammals).

**neomorphic allele:** mutant allele that produces an entirely new phenotypic effect not just a variation of the wild-type allele.

**neonatal (stage or period):** 1. of or pertaining to a newborn. 2. in humans, that interval of postnatal development of the **life cycle** that lasts from **birth** to 28 d after birth; follows the **fetal stage**. See **neonate**. Cf. **stage**.

**neonatal body size:** mass or dimension of an organism at birth.

**neonatal body weight:** average mass of the bodies of newborns within a species.

**neonatal brain size** (NBS): average size of the brains of newborns in a species, expressed in cm³ (or cc). Monkeys such as **macaques** have NBS about two thirds of adult size at birth, and great apes about half, whereas the human NBS is only about one fourth of its eventual adult size. Unlike mammals, which exhibit the fastest rate of brain growth *in utero*, humans sustain high rates of growth, including brain size **hypertrophy,** for nearly a year after birth.

**neonatal brain weight:** average mass of the brains of newborns within a species, expressed in grams. See **neonatal brain size**.

**neonatal coat:** see **natal coat**.

**neonatal line:** permanently visible striation in a cross-section of dentin and enamel observable in some mammals (including humans), the result of the interruption of tissue formation at birth. See **perikymata**.

‡ **neonate:** human at the stage of postnatal development lasting from birth to 28 days after birth. The neonate exists during the **neonatal stage**. Cf. **fetus** and **infant**.

**neonatology:** study of the newborn.

**neontology:** study of **extant** species by scientists who utilize the **scientific method** and (often) an evolutionary **paradigm** for their interpretation. Adjective: neontological. Cf. **paleontology**.

‡ **neopallium:** one of G. Elliot **Smith's** three divisions of the pallium of the cerebral hemispheres; that portion characterized by stratification and a certain organization indicative of the most highly evolved kind; now called the **neocortex**. Cf. **archepallium** and **mesopallium**.

**neoplasm:** clone of cells released from the normal controls of growth, and that no longer retains its former physiological function; a neoplastic tumor.

**neoplastic disorder:** disease or syndrome attributed to cell transformation that is characterized by loss of control of the cell cycle, usually resulting in a tumorous growth; common examples are lung cancer, **breast cancer, leukemia,** and **retinoblastoma**.

**neo-saltationism:** reference made by some authors to the **punctuated equilibrium** model of Gould and Eldredge. See **saltationism**.

**neotechnic phase:** Mumford's 1934 term for a phase of technological development characterized by the application of science and its methodology to technology. See **technology**.

**neotene ape:** synonym for humans. See the **fetalization theory**.

**neoteny:** 1. the attainment of sexual maturity in the larval state. 2. retention of the features of an infantile or juvenile animal of one species in the adult form of a different species; **pedomorphosis** achieved when sexual maturation take place while the individual is still in a pre-adult stage of phenotypic development by prolonging the rate of somatic maturation. Certain features of late development, such as delayed tooth eruption in humans, when compared with similar stages in chimpanzees, are examples of neoteny in humans. Cf. **progenesis**. See **proterogenesis**.

**neotropics:** tropical regions of North America, Central America, and South America. Adjective: neotropical.

**Neozoic:** synonym for **Cenozoic era.**

**nepotism:** favoring relatives; in **sociobiology**, nepotism is expressed in the form of **kin selection** and **altruism.**

**neptunism:** eighteenth century theory that the rocks of the earth had crystallized from a primordial sea that included all the necessary materials; crystallization was followed by erosion and sedimentation, and internal heat caused volcanoes, i.e. basalts were deposited from aqueous solutions. Cf. **vulcanism.**

‡ **nerve:** conductive organ of the **peripheral nervous system**. Nerves are a collection of **axons** wrapped by **neuroglia**. See entries following **neuro-**. Cf. **tract.**

**nerve fiber:** see **axon.**

**nervous system:** subsystem of the body specialized for perceiving and responding to events in the external and internal environments; it consists of the **central nervous system** and the **peripheral nervous system.**

**nest:** construct built by an animal from vegetation or other material to serve as a place for birthing, raising young, and/or sleeping. Used mainly by **prosimians** among primates, but both orangutans and chimpanzees build **sleeping platforms,** which are abandoned on a daily basis and are not used for birthing or rearing young.

**net primary productivity:** amount of energy captured by plants minus the amount they consume in respiration.

**net (or nett) production:** total accumulation of organic material minus catabolic processes by an individual, population, or trophic level per unit time per unit area; aka net productivity.

‡ **net reproductive success** ($R_0$): the average number of offspring produced by each individual during its entire lifetime. Aka net reproductive rate. See **female net reproduction** and **male net reproduction.** Cf. **differential net reproductive success.**

**neural crest:** opposing edges that emerge during the invagination phase of neural tube formation.

**neural crest cells:** cells that are released from the **neural crest,** that migrate especially into the potential head region and that are involved with the **epithelium** in organ and structure formation.

**neural tube:** **primordium** of the **central nervous system,** the earliest discernible portion of the brain and spinal chord. The neural tube is formed by fusion of the neural folds, ridges of tissue on either side of the **primitive streak.**

**neural tube defect** (NTD): failure of the **neural tube** to close normally at day 28, resulting in symptomatic **alpha fetoprotein** in the mother's blood stream. The risk of NTD is about 0.1% (1/1000) but increases greatly (to >10%) if there is a previously affected sibling, suggesting a partial genetic etiology. However, taking the vitamin **folic acid** during pregnancy lowers the risk of an NTD pregnancy by 70%. NTDs can manifest as **spina bifida** or **anencephaly.** A **multifactorial** condition.

**neuroanthropology:** intersectional subdiscipline of anthropology and neuroanatomy that attempts to understand the evolution of the primate brain, neuroanatomical variation among modern humans, and cross-cultural cognitive neuropsychiatry.

**neurobiology:** scientific study of the anatomy (neuroanatomy) and physiology (neurophysiology) of the nervous system.

**neuroblast:** embryonic cell that will develop into a nerve cell.

**neuroblastoma:** malignant tumor found primarily in infants and children, characterized by abnormal growth in immature cells.

**neurocranium:** portion of the cranium that forms the braincase and is composed of the **frontal, parietal,** and squamous portions of both the **temporal** and **occipital bones.** The bones of the neurocranium, which also form the calvaria, develop by **intramembranous ossification.** These bones have markings on the interior surfaces and can be used to reconstruct the surface of a fossil skull. See **cranium.**

**neuroendocrine theory of aging:** intercellular, systemic model of aging in which the major premise is that the failure of certain cells with normal integrative functions increases with the age of an organism, resulting in the decreased homeostatic efficiency of an organism, leading to senescence and death. This mechanism seems plausible in the case of female reproductive aging, but is less clear in others.

**neurofibrillary tangle:** deposits of **tau amyloid** protein found in the brain tissue of people affected with **Alzheimer disease.**

**neurofibromatosis type I** (NF1): relatively benign inherited disease characterized by mild tumors of muscular, skeletal, and nervous system tissues, especially on nerve endings in the skin, often accompanied by café-au-lait spots and soft tumors. The usual cause is one of several autosomal dominant defects in a cytoplasmic protein, neurofibromin (NF1), which normally suppresses the activity of a second gene (p21, the *Ras* oncogene) that causes tumor formation; the result is uncontrolled cell proliferation. A **paternal age effect** is suspected. Aka von Recklinghausen disease, peripheral neurofibromatosis. Cf. **Proteus syndrome**.

**neurofibromatosis type II** (NF2): heritable condition characterized by tumors of cranial nerves, and deafness. The NF2 gene, *merlin*, normally functions to link cell membranes to cytoskeletal structures. Many mutations in the NF2 gene have been documented. Aka central neurofibromatosis.

**neuroglium**: connective cell that supports the nervous system. Plural: neuroglia. There are five classes of neuroglia, including cells that provide myelin for axons, and microglia that function as immune cells in the nervous system.

**neurohormone**: a hormone secreted by a specialized neuron into the bloodstream, the cerebrospinal fluid, or the intercellular spaces of the nervous system; examples include neuropeptides and other types of neuromodulators, e.g. **norepinephrine**.

**neurohypophysis**: posterior lobe of the **pituitary gland**, the neural portion of the gland. It consists of the neural stalk (infundibulum), which is continuous with the **hypothalamus**, and the neural lobe, which is the main body of the neurohypophysis. Aka posterior pituitary, posterior lobe of hypophysis, posterior lobe of pituitary gland, lobus posterior hypophysis. Cf. **adenohypophysis**.

**neurological disorder**: disease or syndrome that affects the **central nervous system**, peripheral nervous system, or autonomic nervous system; examples are **epilepsy, Huntington disease, Parkinson disease, amyotrophic lateral sclerosis** and **Tay-Sachs disease**.

**neuromelanin**: pigment found in the brain that is an end product of a biochemical pathway that converts **tyrosine** to **DOPA** to **dopamine** to neuromelanin in cells found in the brain stem; the final product is catalyzed by the neurotransmitters **adrenaline** and **noradrenaline**. This is a different process from, and should not be confused with, the pathway in skin cells that produces **eumelanin** and **phaeomelanin**. Neuromelanin contributes to the inactivation of **free radicals** in neural tissues.

**neuromuscular junction**: area where axons of a **motor nerve** form a synapse with the muscle that it innervates.

**neuromuscular system**: aggregate of the sensory and motor nervous systems and the muscles, ligaments, and tendons, which controls all movement and activity.

‡ **neuron**: cell, that is the basic structural unit of the nervous system. A neuron consists of a cell body, one or more branching **dendrites** that carry nerve impulses towards the cell body, and one **axon** that carries nerve impulses away from the cell body. There

are approximately 100 billion neurons in the human brain. Aka nerve cell, neurone.

**neuronic**: pertaining to a **neuron**; neuronal.

**neurophysiology**: scientific study of the nervous system, especially the physiological processes by which it functions. See **neurobiology**.

**neuroscience**: 1. study of the mind and nervous system. 2. discipline combining psychology, medicine, and zoology that seeks to understand the relationship of chemicals found in the nervous system to mood, emotion, and behavior. Cf. **evolutionary psychology**.

**neurotransmitter**: any chemical messenger that assists in impulse transmission either between two nerve cells or between a nerve and an effector such as a muscle; an example is acetylcholine.

**neurula**: name sometimes given to an **embryo** during the fourth week of gestation when the formation of the **neural tube** (neurulation) occurs.

**neutral drift**: older synonym of **genetic drift**; more recently applied to **neutral drift theory**.

**neutral drift theory** (NDT): in molecular evolution, a body of propositions by **Kimura** and others which argued that the **genetic load** on populations is too great, and that the degree of polymorphism maintained would be too small, to be explained by **natural selection** acting alone. Neutral mutations, Kimura argued, would be invisible to selection as they would possess selection coefficients of 0 (or nearly so), and therefore explain the observed high degree of **transient polymorphism** without imposing impossibly high genetic loads, as they **drift** toward fixation or loss.

‡ **neutral mutation**: base substitution in DNA that is transcribed into mRNA, and by translation leads to a simple amino acid substitution in the polypeptide produced; because the new amino acid has the same functional properties as the original amino acid, however, the final gene product is functionally equivalent to the original product.

**neutral theory of molecular evolution**: proposal that genetic change at any level (during replication, transcription, translation, and phenotypic expression) produces changes in fitness that are sufficiently small that chance rather than natural selection is the greater force in determining evolutionary outcomes. According to this view, **molecular evolution** is due mainly to **neutral drift**; the mutations that have been substituted during evolution are selectively neutral with respect to the alleles that they replaced; proposed by **Kimura** in 1983. See **neutral drift theory, genetic load**, and **neutral mutation**.

**neutralism**: symbiotic association between two or more species in which the presence of the others has no effect on any of the species; aka neutral association.

**neutron:** elementary subatomic particle that is electrically neutral and has approximately the same mass as a **proton**.

**neutrophil:** large **granulocyte** with a multilobed nucleus whose function is to phagocytize invading microbes. Neutrophils normally constitute 60–70% of the white blood cell count, and are usually the first cells of the body's internal defense to arrive at the site of an infection.

**new archaeology:** see **processual archaeology**.

**New Cave:** recently discovered archaeological site at **Zhoukoudian** near Beijing, China, dated to 175–135 kya; contains hominid remains that include an upper P3 tooth attributed to **archaic Homo sapiens**. Aka Xindong Cave, Locality 4.

**'new' epigenetics:** study of the causes of **development**, timing, and interaction of gene expression and staged tissue **induction**, the processes that reprogram or reverse those causes between generations during or after **meiosis** (i.e. nuclear inheritance that is not based on DNA sequence differences), and the mitotic inheritance of given patterns of gene expression. Examples are **X inactivation**, centromere inactivation, position effect varigation, **DNA methylation**, and **genomic imprinting**. Cf. **epigenetics**.

**'new genetics':** recent re-evaluation of old syndromes in the light of recently proposed molecular mechanisms, especially involving **epigenetic** modes of **non-Mendelian inheritance**.

**New Natural History:** see **natural history**.

**New Stone Age:** see **Neolithic**.

**New World:** Eurocentric term descriptive of the Americas; Cf. **Old World**.

**New World monkey:** **anthropoid** primate that belongs to the suborder **Platyrrhini**; found only in Central and South America (i.e. the **New World**).

**New World syndrome:** controversial set of noninfectious diseases alleged to appear in elevated frequencies in individuals with Native American ancestry: **hypertension**, **obesity**, hyperlipidemia, and **diabetes mellitus, type II** (hyperinsulinemia). Aka syndrome X. Cf. **metabolic syndrome**.

**Ngaloba:** archaeological site found in 1976 near Laetoli in Tanzania, dated to 130–120 kya (K/Ar), and that contains early African **Middle Stone Age** artifacts. Hominid remains include an unusual cranium (**LH-18**) with a 1350 cm³ capacity, attributed to the late **archaic Homo sapiens** group, but remiscent of **Neandertals** in some features.

**Ngandong:** archaeological site found in 1931 on the Solo River in central Java, originally dated to 1.4–1.0 mya (but a recent reassessment proposed dates as recent as 100–27 kya), and that contains only a very few **Developed Oldowan** cores and flakes of chalcedony. Hominid remains collected in 1931–3 and attributed to **Homo erectus** include Ngandong 1 (cranial capacity 1172 cm³, aka Solo I), Ngandong 6 (1251 cm³, aka Solo V), Ngandong 7 (1013 cm³, aka Solo VI), Ngandong 11 (1231 cm³, aka Solo X), and Ngandong 12 (1090 cm³, aka Solo XI). Older material was attributed to **Pithecanthropus** (= **Homo erectus**) **soloensis**. Cf. **Homo wadjakensis**. The original fossils were shipped as 'tiger skulls' to von Koenigswald. The reassessment of both the later date and the morphology of this site has resulted in the proposal that this material now be classified in the **archaic Homo sapiens** group. Aka Solo River, Solo Man. See **Sambungmacan**.

**Ngorora:** archaeological site found in 1970 in the Lake **Baringo** region of Kenya, dated to 12–9 mya. The Ngorora tooth (**KNM-BN 1378**) may be the oldest **hominid** fragment from anywhere in the world, although others think that it resembles the **Nachola Formation** fragments of **Kenyapithecus**.

**Ngorora Formation:** sedimentary unit on the Lake **Baringo** region of Kenya, dated to 13–9 mya. Paleoenvironment suggests a freshwater lake with oscillating levels.

**niacin:** see **nicotinic acid**.

‡ **niche:** 1. a multidimensional space that supplies the factors necessary for the existence of an organism or **species**; a microhabitat. 2. the ecologic role of an organism in a community, especially in regard to food consumption; see **ecological niche**. Variables defining a habitat include the **ambient temperature**, **humidity**, **food**, and other environmental requisites necessary for a species to exist and to reproduce. The fundamental niche for any species is the set of resources a species is capable of utilizing, the preferred niche is the one in which the species performs best, and the realized niche is the one in which it actually exists, in a particular **environment**.

**niche construction:** term that refers to the choices, activities, and metabolic processes of organisms, through which they define, choose, modify, and partly create their own niches. Aka ecosystem engineering.

**niche divergence:** diversification in traits (such as structure or behavior) of two similar species competing for the same resources, thus reducing competition. Aka character displacement, niche diversification.

**niche partitioning:** see **resource partitioning**.

**nicking:** 1. constriction of a blood vessel in the retina. 2. cutting and fragmentation of DNA at sites specifically recognized by **restriction enzymes**.

**nicotinic acid:** water-soluble **vitamin**, part of the B-complex; one of the essential nutrients of the human diet, but can also be synthesized from tryptophan in microorganisms. In humans, lack of dietary nicotinic acid (aka niacin) can result in **pellagra**.

**NIDDM:** see **diabetes mellitus, type II.**

**nidus:** ecological **niche** or geographic focus of a known or potential **zoonotic** disease.

**nightblindness:** state of **malnutrition** caused by a reversible deficiency (**avitaminosis**) of **vitamin A.** The symptoms include poor growth, inability to adapt to dim light, keratinization of the skin, compromise of the reproductive and immune system, and eventual eye atrophy (**xerophthalmia**) and blindness. The primary cause is a deficiency of vitamin A, which interferes with the production of **rhodopsin.** Aka nyctalopia.

**night monkey:** vernacular for the species belonging to the genus *Aotus*.

**Nigritian:** African culture thought by some Africanists to be a relic of an older culture with both Egyptian and Indian elements. This older, hypothetical culture is sometimes called Old Sudanese, and is thought to be constituted by people with variable genetic attributes generally labeled as **Negroid,** and that occupied a common culture area from the upper Nile to the sources of the Niger River.

**Nilgiri langur:** vernacular for *Trachypithecus johnii.*

**Nilote: ethonym** for any of several **autochthonous** peoples that inhabit the Sudan and Ethiopia, and who speak Hamitic languages.

**Nilotic:** pertaining to the Nile River or any of the inhabitants of the Nile region.

**Nilotic hypothesis:** early proposition that extant **Nilotes** are an African culture that is a blend of Hamites and **Forest Negroes,** and that the resulting hybrids migrated south during the seventeenth century.

**Nilotic Negro:** in older terminology, a **Negroid** subgroup found in the eastern Sudan and the region of the upper Nile.

**nipple:** see **areola** (2).

*Niptomomys* **McKenna, 1960:** archaic mammal of the early Eocene of the Rocky Mountain region belonging to the plesiadapiform family **Microsyopidae;** consists of two species; some authorities assign this genus to the order Insectivora. Maxillary dental formula unknown; mandibular formula = 1.1.3.3. Estimated body mass around 30 g. Small body size and dentition suggests **insectivory.** See Appendix 1 for taxonomy.

**nitrogen** (N): colorless, odorless gas that constitutes about 80% of the earth's atmosphere; the stable isotope is $^{14}$N. Nitrogen is critical to life for most organisms, including **primates.** Cf. **oxygen.**

**nitrogen isotope analysis:** method of differentiating between plant consumers that utilizes the differential uptake of the **nitrogen** isotopes $^{15}$N and $^{14}$N. The method can distinguish among animals that have a legume vs. nonlegume diet, as well as aquatic vs. terrestrial diets.

**nitrogen test:** one of the means to measure how long a bone has been involved in the process of **fossilization,** based upon the amount of **nitrogen** remaining in it, which decreases over time; Cf. **fluorine test.**

**nitrogenous base:** any **purine** or **pyrimidine** that is a component of **nucleotides.**

**Nkalabong Formation:** Pliocene sedimentary deposit found in the Lower **Omo Valley** of East Africa, dated to 3.95 mya.

**nm:** see **nanometer.**

**NME:** abbreviation for the **National Museum of Ethiopia.** See box below.

---

**Some fossils in the National Museum of Ethiopia**

NME AL 129-1: field number for Afar Locality 129; fossil hominid no. 1 found in 1973 in the **Hadar** region (Afar triangle) of Ethiopia, Africa, dated to 3.4 mya; hominid remains include an associated partial skeleton consisting of both legs with a complete knee, assigned to *Australopithecus afarensis*. Probably a small adult.

NME AL 162-28: field number for a fossil partial cranium found in the **Hadar** region of Ethiopia, dated to >3 mya and attributed to *Australopithecus afarensis*, and with an estimated brain size of 375–400 cm³. A cranial **endocast** has been interpreted variously as chimp-like and also as possessing some degree of reorganization. See **lunate sulcus.**

NME AL 200a and b: field numbers for Afar Locality 200 a and b, found in 1972 in the **Hadar** region (Afar triangle) of Ethiopia, dated to 3.9–3.0 mya; hominid remains include a broken palate with full dentition assigned to *Australopithecus afarensis*. Tooth rows are sub-parallel; spatulate central incisors, marked diastemata between the canines and lateral incisors; pronounced alveolar prognathism. Possibly a male.

NME AL 288-1: field number for Afar Locality 288; fossil hominid no. 1. see 'Lucy'.

NME AL 333-45: field number for a fossil hominid found in 1975–6 in the **Hadar** region of Ethiopia, dating from 3.2–2.9 mya. Remains include a partial cranium exhibiting some postmortem distortion but which has an estimated capacity of 485–493 cm³ and which is attributed to *Australopithecus afarensis*. One of the 'first family' fossils.

---

**Some fossils in the National Museum of Ethiopia (*cont.*)**

**NME AL 333-105:** field number for a fossil hominid found in 1975–6 in the **Hadar** region of Ethiopia, dating from 3.2–2.9 mya. Remains include a partial cranium with an estimated capacity of 320–343 cm³ and attributed to *Australopithecus afarensis*. One of the 'first family'.

**NME AL 333/333W:** Afar Locality 333; field numbers for fossil hominids found in 1975 in the **Hadar** region, Afar triangle, Ethiopia, dating from 3.2–2.9 mya. Remains include 197 fragments from a minimum of 13 individuals (9 adult, 4 immature). None shows carnivore damage; thus the grouping is considered an assemblage of individuals who died in a catastrophic event. All assigned to *Australopithecus afarensis*. Aka the 'first family'.

**NME AL 444-2:** field number for a fossil partial cranium found in 1991 in the **Hadar** region of Ethiopia, dated to about 3 mya and attributed to *Australopithecus afarensis*, and with an estimated brain size of 540 cm³. Currently, this is the most complete adult *afarensis* skull known.

**NME AL 666-1:** field number of a partial maxilla from Afar Locality 666, dated to 2.4–2.3 mya and associated with stone tools; the mandible is comparable to **OH 16**.

---

**Noah's Ark model:** see the **single origin hypothesis,** aka the **mitochondrial Eve** model and the **out of Africa** model of modern **human origins**.

‡ **nocturnal:** active during the night. Cf. **diurnal** and **crepuscular**.

**node:** 1. any knot-like protuberance. 2. point on any evolutionary tree at which a branch splits into two or more daughter branches. See **cladistics** and **dendrogram, interior point**. 3. anterior tip of the **primitive streak**.

**noise:** 1. nonharmonious, discordant, unpatterned sound. 2. variation in a variable due to unmeasurable or unaccountable effects, i.e. **experimental error**.

**noisy owl monkey:** vernacular for *Aotus vociferans*.

**nomad:** organism that moves continuously in search of resources. Adjective: nomadic.

**nomadic pastoralism:** lifestyle practiced by herders that move from place to place in order to find feed for their animals; this type of economy is dependent on other food producers to meet all of their needs via trade. Cf. **pastoralism**. Aka pastoral nomadism, husbandry.

**nomadism:** movement of a social group from place to place to find resources. For example, hunter-gatherer peoples' wanderings over a particular range may be described as nomadism.

*Nomascus* **Miller, 1933:** subgenus of *Hylobates*.

**nombre fondamental:** the sum total of chromosome arms representing a species, discounting the p-arms of small acrocentric chromosomes. Aka fundamental number. See **chromosome number**.

*nomen:* (*nom., n.*) (Latin): formal name used in taxonomy. plural *nomina*.

**nomenclature:** system of name application to organisms. See **binomial nomenclature**.

*nomina:* plural of *nomen*.

**nominalistic race concept:** idea that race is a cultural abstraction formulated as a convenient means of referring to groups of individuals, without necessarily implying any real existence in nature; can be applied to other taxonomic levels, as well. Cf. **typological race concept**.

**nominalistic species concept:** defines a species as the arbitrary inclusion or bracketing of a set of individuals under a species name.

**nonadaptive radiation:** several related but morphologically divergent forms evolving without evident ecological diversification.

**nonadaptive trait, character** or **feature:** any feature that is neither beneficial nor detrimental to the fitness of an individual.

**nonDarwinian:** term that is misleadingly applied to describe certain mechanisms of evolution other than **natural selection,** especially those nondirectional factors such as **genetic drift** and **neutral mutations**.

**nondimensional species concept:** defines a species as a set of sympatric and morphologically similar but noninterbreeding populations; lacking a statement of dimension in space and/or time. Cf. **multidimensional species concept**.

**nondirectiveness:** in genetic counseling, respect for a patient's choice. A counselor does not force a professional opinion on a patient or otherwise influence the patient after presentation of background material and the patient's options.

‡ **nondisjunction:** abnormal, unequal division of **chromosomes** or **chromatids** into daughter cells during either **mitosis** or **meiosis** and resulting in an **aneuploid** cell. See **primary nondisjunction** and the **sister chromatid cohesion protein**. Cf. **disjunction**.

**nondominant hemisphere:** brain hemisphere not dominant for speech. Cf. **dominant hemisphere**.

**nonhistone protein:** array of proteins other than **histones** that are complexed with DNA in chromosomes.

**non-insulin-dependent diabetes mellitus:** see **diabetes mellitus, type II**.

**nonlithic model:** hypothetical account of the amorphous nature of Pleistocene Southeast Asian

Paleolithic assemblages, advanced to explain the absence of Acheulean assemblages in the Far East. The exploitation of lightweight but strong materials such as **bamboo**, wood, rattan, and liana is central to the model. Aka lignic model.

**nonMendelian (inheritance):** pertaining to any mechanism that distorts chromosome segregation ratios, or concerns an extrachromosomal hereditary factor.

**nonMendelian mechanisms:** any of a number of inherited patterns of gene or DNA transmission which do not follow the classical patterns of inheritance (dominance, codominance, recessive, etc.); examples of non-Mendelian mechanisms include **genomic imprinting, position effect, slippage,** and **unequal crossing over.**

**nonmetric trait, character** or **feature:** see **discrete trait.**

**nonparametric test:** any statistical method that does not involve population parameters, or that is only concerned with the form of a population frequency distribution. Such procedures are useful for testing hypotheses involving one or more variables measured on a nominal or ordinal scale, or using interval or ratio data when assumptions associated with parametric procedures are not met. Examples are the **chi-square test** and contingency table analysis. Aka distribution-free procedure, nonparametric procedure.

**nonpaternity:** finding that the stated father is not the biological father of a child. Cf. **paternity.**

**nonrandom event:** any event where the *a priori* probability of occurrence is either zero or unity (0,1).

‡ **nonrandom mating:** any pattern of **mate choice** other than complete **random mating** that influences the distribution of **phenotype** and **genotype frequencies;** nonrandom mating influences **allele frequencies** in some, but not all, cases. Aka **assortative mating.**

**nonrecombinant chromatid:** chromatid that after meiosis retains an allelic linkage sequence identical to that of the parents, owing to an absence of crossing over. Cf. **recombinant chromatid.**

**nonrecombinant gametes:** those **gametes** that carry linked alleles on a particular pair of homologous chromosomes that have not undergone **recombination.**

**nonrecombining region of the human Y chromosome** (NRY): see **male-specific region of the Y chromosome.**

**nonrenewable resources:** natural resources that cannot be replenished.

**nonsecretor:** person whose body secretions do not contain antigens of the **ABO blood group.**

**nonsense DNA:** any **DNA sequence** that has no coding function, such as an **intron.**

‡ **nonsense mutation:** deleterious base substitution in DNA that is transcribed into mRNA, resulting in the creation of a new termination codon somewhere in mRNA, thus allowing only a fragment of the necessary mRNA to be translated; may be either a **transition** or a **transversion.**

**nonshared environments:** unique experiences that family members experience apart from one another and that contribute to differences in behaviors or other trait outcomes.

**nonshivering thermogenesis:** adaptation found in a number of mammals and a few birds, in which brown fat, a specialized adipose tissue, stores and releases the hormone norepinephrine, which increases heat production.

**nonsite archaeology:** recovery and analysis of unclustered physical remains formerly collected from a site produced by human activities.

**nonsyndromic deafness:** genetic defect in a single gene that causes multiple medical problems, including **deafness,** e.g. **Waardenburg syndrome.** About 70% of cases of **inherited deafness** are non-syndromic, i.e. 35% of all cases. See **syndromic deafness.**

**nontaster:** person who perceives a neutral flavor when **PTC** is placed on the tongue; Cf. **taster.** See **PTC taster/nontaster polymorphism.**

**nonthermal sweat:** see **insensible water loss** and **emotional water loss.** Cf. **thermal sweat.**

**nonvenereal syphilis:** see **syphilis.**

**nonvenereal treponematoses:** see **bejel.** Aka endemic **syphilis** (1), **pinta,** and **yaws.**

**nonviable:** incapable of development, growth, and life; dead. Cf. **viable.**

**NOR staining:** method of staining the **nucleolus organizer region** of acrocentric chromosomes.

**noradrenaline:** hormone and **neurotransmitter** released from the adrenal **medulla** and also found at sympathetic nerve endings; a precursor for **adrenaline.** Noradrenaline constricts small arteries and assists in muscle contraction, primarily in response to hypotension. Aka norepinephrine.

**Nordic:** historically, one of the races (or subraces) of Europe; Nordics occupied northwestern Europe and were characterized as tall, narrow-nosed, and blond. Few workers adhere to this term today as either a race or a narrowly defined typology.

**Nordic fold:** extra fold of skin on the upper eyelid that masks the outer epicanthus, found in some Europeans.

**norepinephrine:** one of the naturally occurring catecholamines, a **neurohormone** released from the **adrenal medulla** and also found at sympathetic nerve endings; a precursor for **adrenaline.** It constricts small arteries (vasopression) and assists in muscle contraction, primarily in response to hypotension. Aka noradrenaline.

**norm of reaction:** limits of the environmental conditions to which an individual organism can adapt and survive.

**norma:** any line established to define one of the aspects of the **skull** while oriented to the **Frankfort horizontal**.

**norma basilaris:** one of the standard orientations of the skull while in the **Frankfort horizontal**. Norma *basilaris* refers to the view of the skull from below. Aka norma inferior, norma ventralis.

**norma frontalis:** one of the standard orientations of the skull while in the **Frankfort horizontal**. Norma frontalis refers to the view of the skull from the front. Aka norma anterior, norma facialis.

**norma lateralis:** one of the standard orientations of the skull while in the **Frankfort Horizontal**. Norma lateralis refers to the profile of the skull from either the left or the right side. Aka norma temporalis.

**norma occipitalis:** one of the standard positions from which the skull can be observed while in the **Frankfort horizontal**. Norma occipitalis refers to the view of the skull from behind. Aka norma posterior.

**norma verticalis:** one of the standard positions from which the skull can be observed while in the **Frankfort horizontal**. Norma verticalis refers to the view of the skull from above. Aka in norma verticalis, norma superior.

**normal:** conforming to a standard or common; natural or regular; not exceptional or abnormal. Noun: normalcy.

**normal distribution:** theoretical frequency distribution of data points that, when arranged from smallest to largest, have the most common values in the middle of the range near the mean; i.e. a symmetrical unimodal (bell-shaped) distribution. Many statistical tests (see **parametric tests**) are based on the assumption of a bell-shaped curve even though such distributions are not the norm in nature. Aka Gaussian distribution.

**normal human body temperature:** the **body temperature** of a normal adult human at rest, usually about 98.6°F or 37°C, taken orally. See **hyperthermia, hypothermia**, and **normothermia**.

**normal polarity epoch:** period of geological time in which the earth's magnetic field pointed north, as it does at present; compare with **reversed polarity epoch**. See **Gauss normal epoch, Brunhes normal epoch**, and **paleomagnetisn**.

**normal science:** working out details of predictions, or problem-solving, given the existence of an accepted larger body of theory (a **paradigm**); work based firmly upon replicable research and scientific achievement that some particular scientific community acknowledges (at least for a time) as supplying the foundation for its further practice. In the Kuhnian sense, normal science is what happens between **paradigm shifts**; attempts to force nature into the inflexible box supplied by the paradigm.

**normalizing selection:** see **stabilizing selection**.

**normative:** view of human culture stressing shared culture.

**normosplanchnic type:** person of medium body build; one of the biotype variables of Viola, an Italian Classical biotypologist.

**normothermia:** 1. normal state of temperature, especially **body temperature**. 2. normal **ambient temperature**; that which causes neither elevation nor depression of body cell **metabolism**. Cf. **hyperthermia, hypothermia**.

**northern blot analysis:** method of identification of RNA fragments separated by **electrophoresis**, electroblotted onto a suitable membrane, and hybridized with labeled **cDNA**. Aka northern blotting. See **blot**.

**northern night monkey:** vernacular for *Aotus trivirgatus*.

**northern sportive lemur:** vernacular for *Lepilemur septentrionalis*.

**nose:** structure of the upper respiratory tract that includes the two nasal cavities and the two nostrils (external **nares**). Air is inhaled through the nose where it is warmed and humidified by **mucus** on the **nasal conchae**. The nose is also associated with the sense of smell (**olfaction**).

**nose-spotted monkey:** vernacular for *Cercopithecus erythrotis*.

**nosocomial:** pertaining to a hospital or infirmary; often used in epidemiology in reference to transmission of a disease through contact with infected blood, semen, secretions, or organs. Cf. **iatrogenic**.

**nosology:** branch of medicine that classifies diseases; **pathology**.

*Notanthropus* **Sergi, 1909:** synonym for *Homo*.

**notch:** 1. an indentation or depression in tissue. In bone, useful landmarks include the acetabular notch, the **asterionic notch**, the **maxillary notch**, the **parietal notch of the temporal bone**, the greater and lesser **sciatic notches**, and the **trochlear notch** 2. a trimmed indentation in one or both sides of a **blade**, and characteristic of middle **Aurignacian** industries.

**Notharctidae:** family of adapoid **prosimians** belonging to the lemuriforms. Known from the early Eocene to the early Oligocene; members known from Europe, North America, Asia, and Africa; consists of two subfamilies. Previously included within the family Adapidae. See **Notharctinae, Cercamoniinae**, and Appendix 1 for taxonomy.

**Notharctinae:** subfamily of prosimians belonging to the adapoid family **Notharctidae**; known from the early through middle Eocene; predominantly a North American taxon with a few early representatives in

Europe; six genera of medium-sized forms ranging from 1 to 7 kg. Dental formula: 2.1.4.3/2.1.4.3; dietary adaptations suggest **frugivory** that shifts to **folivory** over time. Fused **mandibular symphysis** over time (i.e. not present in the two earliest genera). Known **postcrania** indicate leaping abilities. Small size of orbits suggests diurnality. Notharctines comprised a sizable portion of the western North American fauna. See Appendix 1 for taxonomy.

*Notharctus* Leidy, 1870: adapoid prosimian from the middle Eocene of North America, belonging to the notharctid subfamily **Notharctinae**; four species. Descended from the earlier *Cantius*. Dental formula: 2.1.4.3/2.1.4.3; dental morphology suggests **folivory**; sexually dimorphic in canine size. Unlike that of living prosimians, the mandible is fused. Body mass estimated to range between 4 and 7 kg. Cranial morphology similar to the living **Lemur**, **postcrania** reminiscent of both *Propithecus* and *Lepilemur*, although *Notharctus* is more heavily built; *Lepilemur* is frequently used as a model for this genus. Locomotion appears to be leaping in the trees and quadrupedalism when on the ground. See Appendix 1 for taxonomy.

**nothocline:** graded series produced by hybridization.

‡ **notochord:** flexible internal rod of nervous tissue that runs along the back of an embryonic animal; animals that possess a notochord at some stage of their development are known as chordates. A notochord is retained in the adult stage only by certain aquatic forms which do not develop a backbone.

**Notopuro Formation:** stratigraphic unit in central Java, dated to the Late Pleistocene, and that contains Ngandong fauna. The base of the formation is marked by the Upper Lahar, which dates to <500 kya. The thickness of the Notopuro Formation ranges up to 47 m. Aka Notopuro Beds.

*nova species* (*nov. sp., n. sp.*) (Latin): new species.

*novus* (*nov., n.*) (Latin): new.

**noyau:** type of social organization in which adult individuals have separate home ranges; ranges of individuals do not overlap with those of other individuals of the same sex, but they do overlap with ranges of individuals of the opposite sex.

**NP:** see **nail–patella syndrome**.

**nRNA:** see **nuclear RNA**.

**NRY:** see **male-specific region of the Y chromosome**.

**N-terminus:** end of a polypeptide or protein that has a free amino group.

**nu:** 1. thirteenth letter of the Greek alphabet (N, v). 2. abbreviation for **back mutation** or reverse mutation (v).

**nubile:** pertaining to a female ready for marriage or mating. Noun: nubility.

‡ **nuchal:** of or pertaining to the nape of the neck; usually refers to an area on the **occipital bone** where muscles attach.

‡ **nuchal crest:** bony ridge on the **occipital bone** for the attachment of powerful neck muscles including the trapezius, splenius capitis, semispinalis capitis, and spinalis capitis muscles.

**nuchal line:** one of two faint ridges of bone to which the neck and some of the back muscles attach in modern humans. The inferior and superior nuchal lines are the remnants of the more robust **nuchal crests** of other primates and earlier humans. The superior nuchal line marks the upper limit of the neck.

**nuchal muscles:** muscles at the back of the neck that attach to the nuchal line in modern humans. These muscles extend the head backwards and are the major force that hold the hominid head upright, and include the trapezius, splenius capitis, semispinalis capitis, longissimus capitis, and spinalis capitis.

‡ **nuchal torus:** projecting transverse bar of bone on the **occipital bone** that is characteristic of *Homo erectus*; this bar of bone begins where the sharp angle of the *H. erectus* occipital ends superiorly and divides the occipital bone into upper and lower parts. Heavy neck musculature attached just below the nuchal torus. Aka occipital torus. See **torus**.

**nuclear:** of or pertaining to a nucleus.

**nuclear chromosomes:** chromosomes, chromatids, or **chromatin** found in or derived from the nucleus of a eukaryotic cell and that contain nuclear DNA (**nDNA**). Cf. **mitochondrial chromosome** and **mtDNA**.

**nuclear DNA:** see **nDNA**.

‡ **nuclear envelope:** bi-layered, porous interface surrounding the eukaryotic **nucleus**, and that regulates the traffic of materials between the nucleus and the **cytoplasm**; aka nuclear membrane.

**nuclear family:** social unit consisting of a mated pair and their immediate offspring. Aka elementary family. Cf. **family**.

‡ **nuclear inheritance:** inheritance of traits determined by the **genes** on **DNA** located in the **nucleus** of a cell; the prevalent and most important kind of inheritance. Cf. **cytoplasmic inheritance**.

**nuclear membrane:** outer limits of a **nucleus**. Aka **nuclear envelope**.

**nuclear RNA** (nRNA): RNA molecules found in the cell nucleus, either associated with a chromosome or in the **nucleoplasm**.

**nuclear transfer** (NT): method of whole-organism cloning in which the nucleus is removed with a special pipette from an unfertilized egg cell; the enucleated egg is then fused with a **totipotent** cell taken from a 16–32 cell embryo. The fused cells are transplanted into the uterus of a foster mother. Cf. **embryo splitting**.

‡ **nucleic acid:** large chemical polymer that stores genetic information and mediates its transfer during **protein synthesis; DNA** and **RNA** are nucleic acids.

**nucleoid:** aggregation of **DNA** that resembles a **nucleus** but lacks **histones** and a **nuclear envelope;** found in **prokaryotes** and in the **mitochondria** and chloroplasts of **eukaryotes.**

**nucleolus:** dense body in the nuclear region that functions in the synthesis of **ribosomal RNA** and proteins, and the site of the assembly of **ribosomes.** It is associated with the **nucleolus organizer region.**

**nucleolus organizer region** (NOR): any site on an acrocentric chromosome containing rRNA, and associated with the **nucleolus.** see **secondary constriction.**

**nucleoplasm:** protoplasmic contents of the nucleus of a cell. Cf. **cytoplasm.**

**nucleoprotein:** organic compounds constituted of both nucleic acids and protein.

**nucleoside:** any **purine** or **pyrimidine** nitrogenous base attached to a ribose or deoxyribose sugar.

**nucleosome:** knob-like structure composed of eight **histones,** two copies of each of the core histones wrapped by 146 bp of **DNA.** Nucleosomes are separated from each other by strands of DNA about 50 bp in length; together the multiplexed structure resembles a string of beads. Aka nu body ($\upsilon$).

‡ **nucleotide** (nt): a building block of **DNA,** consisting of a **nucleoside** (a phosphate ester of **adenine, thymine, uracil, guanine,** or **cytosine**) and a pentose (5-carbon) sugar.

**nucleotide divergence:** degree of differences in **DNA** sequences as the result of nucleotide substitutions.

**nucleotide excision repair:** mass replacement of up to 30 nucleotides to repair damage to DNA.

‡ **nucleotide pair:** see **complementarity.**

**nucleotide sequence:** 1. the linear order of nucleotides in a **cistron.** 2. the linear order of nucleotides in **messenger RNA.**

**nucleotide substitution:** **mutation** that involve the substitutions, insertions or deletions of one or more nucleotides in a DNA molecule; Aka **point mutation.**

‡ **nucleus:** spherical central **organelle** of the eukaryotic cell, containing most of the hereditary material of the organism; separated from the **cytoplasm** by the bi-layered membrane of the **nuclear envelope.** See **genes, chromosomes** and **chromatids.**

**nucleus accumbens:** portion of the **basal ganglion** that regulates motor activities and that is the 'seat' of reward or punishment situations; a part of the **limbic system.**

**null allele:** gene that produces no product and therefore behaves like a recessive, e.g. the O null allele in the **ABO blood group.**

**null hypothesis** ($H_o$): predicted outcome, under the simplest possible assumptions, of an experiment or observation. In a typical experiment, the null **hypothesis** usually posits that two outcomes will not be different, or that small differences are due to chance. See **hypothetico-deductive approach.** Cf. **alternative hypothesis.**

**null model:** simple and explicit assumptions that allow a researcher to state a **null hypothesis.**

**null mutation** ($\mu$): any mutation that incapacitates a gene so that no functional product is produced; also called a loss-of-function or **knockout mutation;** strictly, a **missense mutation** or **nonsense mutation,** but some use the term **forward mutation** synonymously.

**nulliparity:** said of females who have never given birth. Adjective: nulliparous. see **parity.**

**nullosomic:** lacking both members of a single pair of chromosomes.

**numerical hybrid:** interspecific hybrid derived from parents with different chromosome numbers, e.g. a **horse–donkey hybrid.**

**numerical mutation:** evolutionary change in the number of chromosomes in an evolutionary lineage, due to mechanisms such as **aneuploidy, polyploidy,** and **Robertsonian translocation.**

**numerical phenetics:** see **numerical taxonomy.**

**numerical taxonomy:** any method of **classification** that emphasizes numerical methods; in particular, the term refers to phenetic classification using combinations of comparable linear measurements (**quantitative traits**) that are **unweighted traits.** One of the three main schools of classification; cf. **phylogenetic systematics** and **evolutionary systematics.**

**numerical trait, character** or **feature:** see **quantitative trait.**

**nurse cell:** see **sustentacular cell.**

**nut:** dry **fruit** with a single meaty kernel enclosed in a woody or leathery shell, often edible.

**nut-cracking:** behavior in which a primate opens a hard-shelled **nut** by cracking it against a substrate or using a stone (the anvil) to crack open the nut. Some paleontologists believe that nut-cracking behavior was characteristic of early hominids, and may have spurred a connection between the available tool and the later cutting task.

‡ **nutrient:** any element, compound or substance necessary for the growth, health and survival of an organism; nutrients may be inorganic (air, water) as well as organic (food).

**nutrient cycling:** processes by which **nutrients** are transferred from one to another organism. See **food web** and **food pyramid.**

**nutrient foramen:** opening in bone for the entry of blood vessels which supply nutrients for bone tissue. plural: nutrient foramina.

‡ **nutrition:** 1. the sum of the process involved in taking in nutrients and assimilating and utilizing them. 2. **food** or nutrient. 3. study of the sources and interactions of the foods consumed by an organism.

**nutritional disease** (or **disorder**): pathological condition due to the absence or deficiency of **proteins**, **carbohydrates**, **fats**, and/or **vitamins** and **minerals**. See **undernutrition**, **malnutrition**, and **avitaminosis**.

**nvCJD:** abbreviation for new variant **Creutzfeldt–Jakob disease.**

*Nyanzapithecus* **Harrison, 1986:** genus of **hominoid** from the early to middle Miocene of East Africa belonging to the family **Oreopithecidae**; one or two species, depending on author; known primarily from dentition. Estimated body mass from 8 to 10 kg. Dental formula: 2.1.2.3; dentition suggests **folivorous** diet. Some workers believe this genus is descended from *Rangwapithecus* and that *Nyanzapithecus* itself is the ancestor of *Oreopithecus*. See Appendix 1 for taxonomy.

*Nycticeboides simpsoni* **(MacPhee and Jacobs, 1986):** fossil prosimian known from the late Miocene of South Asia belonging to the family **Lorisidae**; monotypic; earliest known lorisid from Asia. Body mass estimated at 500 g. Dental formula: 2.1.3.3/ 2.1.3.3. See Appendix 1 for taxonomy.

*Nycticebus* **É. Geoffroy, 1812:** one of the two **prosimian** genera to which the lorises belong; *Nycticebus* contains the two slow loris species. Found in Southeast Asia; natural history poorly known. Arboreal; nocturnal; slow methodical climbers; tail is short stump. The second digit is reduced and possesses a **grooming claw**, and the **pollex** is 180 degrees from digit 3, providing for a powerful vice-like grip that can be held for long periods of time; circulatory adaptations in the paws provide an ample oxygen supply that prevents lactic acid build-up in the muscles. Body mass ranges from 300 to 900 g. Dental formula: 2.1.3.3; lower incisors and canines form a **dental comb**; believed to be **frugivorous**. *Nycticebus* has been reported to have poisonous **axillary** glands; poison is applied to the teeth and an attacker is bitten. It has been theorized that this is a form of **Batesian mimicry** that deters an 'educated' predator from future loris attacks. Social organization unknown. See Appendix 2 for taxonomy, Appendix 3 for living species.

**Oakley, Kenneth Page** (1911–81): British geologist at the BMNH (London); Oakley is best-remembered for the part he played (with **Le Gros Clark** and J. S. **Weiner**) in showing that the jaw and cranium of the **Piltdown** specimen(s) were from different individuals, using the **fluorine test**. Author of *Man the Tool-Maker* (1949) and *The Fluorine-dating Method* (1951).

**obelion** (ob): **craniometric landmark**; point on the mid-sagittal plane between the two parietal emissary foramina. Adjective: obelionic.

**Oberkassel:** archaeological site found in 1914 near Bonn, on the Rhine River, Germany, dated to 18–12 kya, and that contains **Magdalenian** implements and remains of fossil hominids, including two nearly complete skeletons attributed to *Homo sapiens* cf. **Cro-Magnon**. The skeletons had been treated with red ochre.

**obesity:** condition characterized by chronic weight gain and retention, the result of excessive caloric intake and inadequate energy expenditure. The WHO–CDC criteria for obesity is at the 95th **percentile** of BMI for sex and age (roughly ≥30), and overweight at the 85th percentile (roughly ≥25). Obesity is a complex condition in humans, and genetic factors play only a part. Cf. **leptin, ghrelin, adiposity, overnutrition.**

**obiculare:** see pisiform.

**objective:** 1. goal or target. 2. lens. 3. free from personal feelings; unbiased, factual. 4. that which can be known; reality. Cf. **subjective.**

**object manipulation:** modification of something in the environment, usually involving greater behavioral and organizational complexity than simple reshaping or building, and involving a learning component that contributes to individual variation. See **tool.**

**obligate:** in biology, restricted to a particular condition or mode of life. Cf. **facultative.**

‡ **obligate bipedalism:** refers to the fact than a bipedal organism cannot use any other form of **locomotion** without difficulty.

**obliteration:** terms used to describe the disappearance of a feature during normal development and growth, e.g. the gradual obliteration of the cranial **sutures.**

**observation:** 1. act or instance of viewing or noting a fact or occurrence for some scientific purpose. 2. the information or record secured by such an act.

**observational learning:** 1. communication in mammals by which information is passed to young (or 'naive') individuals by observing their mothers or other adults repeatedly. Through observational learning the young primate learns lessons vital to survival such as the choice and handling of food items, social rules, and its place in the social hierarchy. 2. unrewarded learning; aka empathic learning.

**observed:** actual (or real) datum as opposed to an **expected value.**

**observer effect:** change in the behavior of an animal being studied due to the presence of the observer or to a stimulus, such as odor, from the observer.

**observer error:** contribution to the total variance of a sample due to random error introduced by inconsistent observer measurement, observation, sampling technique, etc. Cf. **bias.**

**obsidian:** volcanic glass produced as a result of the rapid cooling of a molten magma flow, often used as raw material for the manufacture of **stone tools**; quarried and prized for the fine conchoidal fracture that produces sharp-edged **flakes.**

**obsidian hydration dating:** technique of dating obsidian artifacts by measuring the microscopic amount of water absorbed on fresh surfaces.

**obsidian tool:** any implement made from **obsidian.**

**obstetrical and gynecological disorders:** any of the diseases or syndromes affecting female genitalia, reproduction, and pregnancy; common examples or topics include **precocious puberty, menopause,** female **infertility, amenorrhea,** and **ectopic pregnancy.**

'**obstetrical dilemma' hypothesis:** proposal by **Washburn** that in greatly **encephalized hominids,** bipedal adaptatations in the **pelvis** combined eventually with large-brained infants and constrained infants to be born at a more **altricial** state after a shorter **gestation.**

**obturator:** in reference to any structure that blocks or closes an opening.

**obturator foramen:** largest opening in the skeleton, located between the **pubis** and the **ischium.** In life this foramen is covered by the obturator membrane, which closes most of the opening; the small area left open transmits several blood vessels and nerves. This foramen is triangular in human females, oval in males, and is a criterion for sexing skeletons.

**Occam's razor:** see **principle of parsimony.**

**occipital:** of or pertaining to the inferior and posterior region of the **cranium.**

**occipital arc** (l–o): **craniometric** measurement: distance of the curve from **lambda** to **opisthion** as measured with a flexible tape measure.

‡ **occipital bone:** bone that forms the posterior portion and base of the **cranium.** The nuchal portion of this bone is formed by **endochondral ossification,** but the superior portion grows through **intramembranous ossification.**

‡ **occipital bun:** elongation or protrusion of the occipital bone that is characteristic of *Homo neanderthalensis.* This feature was first described during the Victorian Age and received its name from the

hair fashion of that time when women wore their hair in buns; aka chignon.

**occipital chord: anthropometric** measurement: distance between **lambda** and **opisthion** as measured with spreading calipers.

‡ **occipital condyle:** one of two rounded tubercles on the inferior portion of the **occipital bone** that is lateral to the **foramen magnum**. In life these structures articulate with the first cervical vertebra.

**occipital crest:** bony crest running horizontally across the occiput on some apes and hominids.

**occipital lobe:** posterior portion of each cerebral hemisphere of the brain; the occipital lobes are the site of the visual cortex. Functions include the integration of eye movements and focusing; correlation of current visual images with visual memory and other visual stimuli; conscious perception of vision.

**occipital–marginal venous system** (O/M): one of several pathways for venous return of blood from the brain in which blood from the **sagittal sinus** flows into the **occipital venous sinus** and from there into the **marginal venous sinus** in the vicinity of the **foramen magnum**. An 'enlarged' state is characteristic of *Australopithecus afarensis* and *Paranthropus*. Modified as the **transverse sinus** in **AMHs**. Aka the marginal and the occipital venous system.

**occipital pole:** most posterior point of the brain on the surface of the **occipital lobe**; there are two poles, one on each lobe.

**occipital protuberance:** prominence on the **occipital bone** to which the **nuchal** ligament attaches.

**occipital torus:** see **nuchal torus**.

**occipital venous sinus:** in Hadar hominids and australopithecines, a large blood vessel that helps drain blood from the brain; located in the **dura mater**, the occipital venous sinus is a posterior and inferior extension of the **sagittal sinus** that has been modified as the **transverse sinus** in later hominids of the genus *Homo*.

**occipitomastoid crest:** small ridge of bone on the mastoid process posterior to the **styloid** process of the cranial base and medial to the groove for the occipital artery; this is the lateral border for attachment of the superior oblique muscle. In modern humans this structure is greatly reduced in comparison to earlier humans such as **Neandertals**.

‡ **occiput:** abbreviated usage for **occipital bone**.

**occlusal area:** dental measurement: length of chewing surface multiplied by the width of the chewing surface.

**occlusal harmony:** condition when opposing sets of teeth fit one another without any gaps in the **occlusal plane**.

**occlusal index:** dental index; length of chewing surface multiplied by 100 and divided by width; $L(100)/B$,

where $L$ = occlusal length $B$ = occlusal width (or breadth).

**occlusal plane:** level at which opposing teeth make contact with material that is masticated; chewing level. The occlusal plane is often used as a reference for erupting teeth.

**occlusal surface:** pertaining to the chewing surface of a tooth or, in the case of incisors, the surface that makes contact with its upper or lower counterpart.

**occlusal wear:** abrasion that occurs over time between the chewing surface of upper and lower teeth in opposition.

‡ **occlusion:** 1. relationship between upper and lower teeth. 2. a closing off, such as when a blood vessel becomes blocked.

**occupational stress trauma:** injuries resulting from an individual's profession. Currently, there is concern about repetitive motion injuries occurring among individuals who use computer keyboards; however, such injuries are known from ancient times, as evidenced on the arm bones of hunters that used **atlatls** or squatting facets on the **tibiae** of Egyptian scribes. Aka occupational mark.

**oceanic crust:** portion of the earth's **crust** formed at the **mid-ocean ridges**.

**oceanic island:** land mass surrounded by water and assumed to have risen from the sea, and not a part of any continent; Hawaii is an example. Cf. **continental island**.

**Oceanic Negrito: ethonym** for **pygmoid** peoples found in the Andaman Islands, the Philippines, New Guinea, and the coastal forest regions of Australia. Cf. **Oceanic Negro**.

**Oceanic Negro:** on older terminology, a **Negroid** subgroup found in New Guinea and nearby islands. Traditionally, this subgroup is divided into two varieties, the Melanesian and the Papuan.

**ochre:** iron ore compound generally mixed with earth, clay, blood, urine or grease, most often to be used as paint, and that varies in color from yellow to chocolate; iron oxide; hematite. Aka red ochre, ocher.

**ochre macaque:** vernacular for *Macaca ochreata*.

**Ockham's razor:** see **principle of parsimony**; also spelled 'Occam'.

**octoroon:** person whose ancestry is 1/8 from a minority variety and 7/8 from a majority variety.

**ocular dominance:** tendency of nerve cell clusters of the visual system to respond predominately to one eye.

**oculocutaneous albinism:** see **albinism**.

**odd-nosed monkeys:** term used for the Asian colobine monkeys that belong to the genera *Nasalis*, *Simias*, *Pygathrix*, and *Rhinopithecus*. These monkeys' noses range from a snub-nose in which the **nares** are deeply recessed, to a small upturned nose, to a large pendulous nose (in the male **proboscis**

**monkey).** *Pygathrix* and *Rhinopithecus* are also referred to as **snub-nosed monkeys.**

**oddity learning** or **problem:** laboratory experimental method in which a primate is presented with a series of objects, one of which does not belong with the others. In order to receive a reward the primate needs to identify the odd object.

**odontic:** of or pertaining to the teeth. Synonym: **dental.**

**odontoblast:** specialized cell that produces **dentin** in a developing tooth.

**odontoclast:** specialized cell that resorbs the roots of the **deciduous dentition.**

**odontogenesis:** process of **dental** development; odontogeny.

**odontology:** study of dentition. Comparative odontology is the study of dentition across species and higher taxa; human odontology generally limits study to variation within the human species.

**odontoma:** secondary growth of enamel on a tooth. See **enamel pearl.**

**odontome:** dental anomaly expressed as development of a tooth or dental cyst in a location in the oral cavity other than in the **dental alveoli.**

**odontometrics:** measurements of the dimensions and qualities of the teeth.

**oedema:** see **edema.**

**oestrogen:** see **estrogen.**

**oestrus:** see **estrus.**

‡ **offspring:** newly hatched, erupted, or born young of a particular **progenitor;** a **sibship** of brothers and sisters; the next generation of a former **generation.**

**Ofnet Cave:** archaeological site found in 1907–08 near Hohlheim, Bavaria, dated to the **Mesolithic,** and that contains the crania of 33 individuals assumed to be buried after decapitation, as the mandibles were removed and arranged in symmetrical concentric circles. No postcranial remains were recovered. The remains were attributed to *Homo sapiens.*

‡ **OH:** abbreviation for Olduvai Hominid; any fossil **hominid** recovered from **Olduvai Gorge,** Tanzania. See box below.

**Ohno's conjecture:** that the chromosome complement of amphibians differs from antecedent genomes by a factor of about two, probably as the result of a single polyploidy event followed by partial degeneration about 350 mya.

---

### Some fossil specimens recovered from Olduvai Gorge

**OH 1:** field number for Olduvai Hominid 1; an intrusive burial recovered from Bed II at site RK (Reck's **Korongo**), found by Hans Reck in 1931. The first hominid recovered from **Olduvai Gorge,** Aka Oldoway Man, **Olduvai Man.** See *Homo sapiens,* **AMHs.**

**OH 2:** Olduvai Hominid 2; two thick fragments of a skull from **MNK,** lower Bed IV; nothing more was ever found of this hominid; later attributed to *Homo erectus.*

**OH 4:** field number for a mandibular fragment found at **Olduvai Gorge** site MK I, and attributed to *Homo habilis.* This specimen was among the paratypes of *Homo habilis.*

**OH 5:** field number for Olduvai Hominid 5, 'nutcracker man'; a robust **hominid** cranium with maxillary teeth intact but missing the mandible, and, dated to 1.8 mya. Cranial capacity estimated at 530 cm$^3$. Probably male. The cranium has a sagittal crest, postorbital waisting, flaring zygomatic arches, and a prominent supraorbital torus. Over 3,000 fossil specimens, 2,500 **Oldowan** stone implements, and 2,200 flakes were collected from the **living floor** at site FLK. There was no evidence of fire at the site. See *Zinjanthropus (= Paranthropus) boisei* and **Olduvai Bed I.** In the following season a tibia and fibula (OH 35) were recovered from the same living floor; analysis suggested that this second individual was bipedal, but these lower leg fragments, as well as some additional skull fragments and tooth, were later reassigned to *Homo habilis.*

**OH 6:** field number for several teeth and cranial fragments found in **Olduvai Gorge** site FLK I (the '*Zinj* site'); some limb bones found at the site may also belong to this individual, attributed to *Homo habilis.* This specimen was among the paratypes for this species.

**OH 7:** field number for Olduvai Hominid 7, 'Jonny's child', recovered in 1960 from **Olduvai Gorge** Bed I, site FLK-NN. Hominid material includes fragments from a juvenile including a mandible, parietals, and wrist bones found by Jonathan Leakey, dated to about 1.8 mya; cranial capacity estimated at 687 cm$^3$. OH 7 became the **type specimen** for the taxon *Homo habilis.* A hole and fracture lines in one of the **parietals** was at first interpreted as the result of a blow to the head; scientists later ascribed this to erosion. See **Olduvai Bed I.**

**OH 8:** field number for Olduvai Hominid 8, recovered from **Olduvai Bed I** site FLK-NN, dated to 1.8 mya. A partial ?adult foot with a nonopposable metatarsal that has most of the specializations associated with the **plantigrade** propulsive feet of man. Attributed to *Homo habilis,* but this attribution has been questioned; some researchers now think that this is an adolescent foot belonging to **OH 7.** This specimen was among the paratypes for *Homo habilis.*

**Some fossil specimens recovered from Olduvai Gorge (*cont.*)**

**OH 9:** field number for Olduvai Hominid 9, 'Chellean Man'; recovered in 1960 from upper **Olduvai Bed II**, site **LLK II**, dated to 1.4–1.3 mya. A thick **calvaria** with a prominent nuchal crest and large and flaring brow ridges. Cranial capacity estimated at 1067 cm$^3$. Attributed to *Homo erectus*.

**OH 12:** field number for Olduvai Hominid 12, 'Pinhead'; a small partial cranium, dated to 800–600 kya, with an estimated cranial capacity of 750 cm$^3$, and attributed to *Homo erectus*; see **Olduvai Bed IV** site VEK IV.

**OH 13:** field number for Olduvai Hominid 13, 'Cinderella'; a partial cranium, mandible and palate found in 1963 by Ndibo Mbuika at site MNK in Lower Middle Bed II of **Olduvai Gorge**, dated to >1.6 mya. Cranial capacity estimated at 655 cm$^3$. Found associated with **Oldowan** tools. Attributed by some to *Homo habilis*, by others to *H. ergaster*, and by others to a gracile *Australopithecus* sp. For some, it was this fossil that confirmed the presence of a second hominid taxon in the gorge, contemporaneous with the australopithecines. This specimen was among the original paratypes for *Homo habilis*.

**OH 16:** field number for Olduvai Hominid 16, 'George'; hominid fragments found in 1963 at **Olduvai Bed II**, site **FLK**, Maiko Gully, dated to 1.7–1.6 mya. Includes 1,500 skull fragments and upper and lower dentition; the fossil had been trampled by Masai cattle. The estimated cranial capacity of this reconstructed hominid is about 640 cm$^3$. Inferred **Oldowan** tools. Attributed to *Homo habilis*, possibly *H. ergaster*.

**OH 24:** field number for Olduvai Hominid 24, 'Twiggy'; hominid fragments found in 1968 in lower Bed I (site **DK East**), dated to 1.85 mya. Remains included a partial skull and face with seven teeth, crushed and embedded in a limestone matrix; after partial reconstruction, cranial capacity estimated variously at 590 to 650 cm$^3$. Attributed to *Homo habilis*, but some researchers suggest that the specimen may be a pre-habiline form of early *Homo*, or a gracile australopithecine. Often compared to **KNM-ER 1813**.

**OH 28:** field number for Olduvai Hominid 28; hominid remains found in 1970 in **Olduvai Gorge Bed IV** at site **WK**, dated at 1.0 mya to 500 kya; consists of a fragmentary innominate and femoral shaft associated directly *in situ* with **Acheulean** tools; fossil bones attributed to *Homo erectus*.

**OH 62:** field number for Olduvai Hominid 62, the 'Dik-dik' hominid; the first major **hominid** in the **Olduvai Gorge** series not discovered by the Leakeys, found by T. **White** and D. **Johanson** in 1986; a partial cranium with palate, mandible and 300 postcranial fragments from Bed I, dated at 1.8 mya and attributed to *Homo habilis*, but with limb proportions that are 'remarkably ape-like', such that some refer to it as a gracile **australopithecine**; body mass estimate > 30 kg. See **Olduvai Bed I**. OH 62 was the first habiline found with both cranial and postcranial portions represented. Because of the direct association of limb bones with the cranium in a single individual, the find is considered especially significant; the small size of the body (104 cm or 3'5") and the long arm length relative to leg length suggest that this individual differed dramatically from later, more modern hominids. Probably a female. Aka **Lucy's child**.

**OH 65:** field number for Olduvai Hominid 65, a nearly complete maxilla recovered from 'Trench 57' in the **western Olduvai Gorge** in 1995, dated to 1.84–1.79 mya (Ar/Ar). The specimen is comparable in many respects to **KMN-ER 1470** (*Homo rudolfensisv*) but also shares a broad anterior dimension and postincisive shelf with OH 7, the *type specimen* of *Homo habilis*, and this, for some researchers, questions the validity of *H. rudolfensis* as a taxon. The OH 65 specimen was subsequently assigned to *H. habilis*.

---

**Ohno's hypotheses:** that the **X chromosome** is highly conserved among mammals owing to the **dosage compensation** mechanism; translocations between the X chromosome and any autosome would disturb this mechanism and be selected against. Thus, any gene found on the human X is also likely to be found on nearly all mammalian X chromosomes. Aka Ohno's law, law of conservation of the X chromosome.

**-oidea:** in zoological taxonomy, the suffix of a **superfamily**. See **Linnaean hierarchy**.

**OIS:** see **oxygen isotope stage**.

**Okote tuff:** Pleistocene volcanic deposit at Koobi Fora, **Lake Turkana,** dated by **K/Ar** to 1.64–1.39 mya.

**old age:** stage in the human **life cycle** that commences variably after the child-bearing years, but which may not occur (according to some sources) until after **middle age** and/or another period of **transition to full maturity**. Old age is characterized by a noticeable decline in the function of many body tissues or systems in late **adulthood**, and a shift or transition in community roles. Cf. **senescence**.

‡ **'Old Man' of Cro-Magnon:** see **Cro-Magnon**.

‡ **'Old Man' of La Chapelle:** see **La Chapelle-aux-Saints**.

**Old Stone Age:** see **Paleolithic**.

**Old World:** Eurocentric term descriptive of the known world exclusive of the Americas; cf. **New World**.

‡ **Old World monkey:** any anthropoid and catarrhine primate belonging to the superfamily **Cercopithecoidea**.

**older archaic group:** see **earlier archaic group**.

‡ **Oldowan tool tradition: Early Paleolithic** stone tool culture; a method of manufacturing crude tools used by certain **hominids** in Africa between 2.6 and 1.5 mya that was practiced by *Homo habilis* and possibly one or more of the **australopithecine** species. Oldowan tools are simple **chopper** tools made by removing several **flakes** from an unquarried local stone, by striking with a **hammer stone**. The **cores** were used as choppers and the flakes were used as **cutting tools**. Type site: **Olduvai Gorge**; named by Louis **Leakey** in 1936. Mary **Leakey** has identified more than twenty distinct implements considered part of the **habiline** tool kit, but the earliest levels (Bed I) contain six implement types, whereas later Bed II sites contain ten. Aka Oldowan Culture and Oldowan Industry. See **Kada Gona**. Cf. **Developed Oldowan tradition**.

**Oldoway:** original term for the **Oldowan tool tradition**.

**Oldoway Gorge:** see **Olduvai Gorge**.

**Oldoway Man:** see **Olduvai man**.

**Olduvai Bed(s):** sedimentary layers found at **Olduvai Gorge**. See box below.

---

### Principal fossil-bearing beds at Olduvai Gorge

**Olduvai Bed I:** sedimentary layer dated to 1.85–1.7 mya (K/Ar) and yielding hominid fossils such as *Zinjanthropus (= Paranthropus) boisei* (OH 5), *Homo habilis* (OH 7 and OH 24), and many Oldowan tools. Fauna is identical to Lower Bed II. **Lava** is the most common rock type used for stone artifacts. See **paleo-Lake Olduvai**.

**Olduvai Bed II:** sedimentary layer dated to 1.7–1.2 mya (K/Ar) and yielding hominid fossils such as *Homo erectus* (OH 9) and tools of the **Chellean, Developed Oldowan**, and **Acheulean** traditions. Lower Bed II geologically belongs with Bed I; fauna includes elephants, pigs, bovids, giraffids, carnivores, primates, equids, and rodents. Upper Bed II also includes hippopotami and rhinoceroses. **Quartz** is the most common rock type used for stone artifacts.

**Olduvai Bed III:** sedimentary layer dated 1.15 mya–800 kya (K/Ar), yielding tools such as hand-axes. Fauna include rabbits, rodents, carnivores, Perissodactyla and Proboscidea. This bed is easily identified by its bright red coloring, but known for its paucity of hominid fossils and tools, probably due to a lack of water and vegetation during Bed III times; only site **JK** has produced tools.

**Olduvai Bed IV:** sedimentary layer dated to 800–600 kya (K/Ar) and yielding hominid fossils such as *Homo erectus* (OH 22). Tool industries include a derivative of the Bed II **Developed Oldowan**, as well as an **Acheulean** variant. Fauna is similar to that of Bed III, with the addition of crocodiles and catfish.

**Olduvai Bed V:** see **Naisiusiu**.

---

**Olduvai event:** paleomagnetic reversal event, a **subchron** within the **Matuyama reversed epoch**, at 1.6 mya that defines the current Neogene/Quaternary boundary. Aka anomaly 2, Olduvai subchron. See **paleomagnetism**.

‡ **Olduvai Gorge:** archaeological site(s) found in 1911 located on the Serengeti plain in northern Tanzania, Africa, containing deep sedimentary deposits dating from 1.8 mya (early **Pleistocene**) to as recent as the Holocene. More than 37,000 artifacts of the **Oldowan** and **Acheulean** and more recent tool traditions, and about sixty hominids including **australopithecines** (*Zinjanthropus* (= *Paranthropus*) *boisei*), **habilines** (*Homo habilis*), **erectines** (*Homo erectus*), and **AMH** (*H. sapiens*) have been found at the main gorge. The site was once a perennial salt lake and floodplain bordered by dry woodlands and savanna. The main gorge cuts through the paleolake margin zone at the southeastern shore of **paleo-Lake Olduvai**. In the early twentieth century it was known as **Oldoway Gorge**, a Masai place name. The most prominent archaeologists to have worked there are members of the **Leakey** family. Cf. **western Olduvai Gorge**. See box below for some of the most important sites.

---

### Major sites located in Olduvai Gorge

**BK:** (Peter) Bell's Korongo at **Olduvai Gorge**; site excavated 1951–5, nicknamed the 'slaughterhouse', a possible **living floor** or a **butchering site** containing hundreds of tools and skeletons of extinct species of buffalos and pigs at the base of bed II; the Leakeys labeled the tools as **Chellean** Stage I. The butchering site hypothesis has recently been challenged by **taphonomists**. Aka BK II.

---

---

**Major sites located in Olduvai Gorge (*cont.*)**

**DK East:** archaeological site found in 1968 at **Olduvai Gorge**, dated to *c.* 1.85 kya (lower Bed I), and containing fossil hominids that included the nearly complete but crushed skull of 'Twiggy' (**OH 24**), attributed to *Homo habilis*.

**DK I:** Donald's (MacInnes) **Korongo**; a paleontological site at **Olduvai Gorge** in Tanzania. It was in this gully in 1961 that Philip Leakey found a site at the base of Bed I, later called the 'stone circle', a possible habitation site, dated to nearly 2 mya. Although the site has been interpreted as a 14-foot diameter circle of **manuports**, which may have anchored the base of a primitive shelter, others have ascribed the stones to a natural agency, such as tree root displacement. Crocodile and flamingo bones were also found at the site.

**FLK I:** archaeological site found in 1959 at **Olduvai Gorge**: dated to 1.75 mya, and that contains **Oldowan** artifacts, some broken animal bones (both in direct association), and the hominid remains of **OH 5**, '*Zinjanthropus boisei*' (= *Paranthropus boisei*) found by Mary **Leakey**. AKA 'Zinj site', Oldovai Man site, FLK *Zinjanthropus*, FLK 22. Cf. *Paranthropus.*

**FLK II:** Frida Leakey's Korongo (named before 1959), later an archaeological site found in 1962 at Maiko Gully, **Olduvai Gorge**, dated to *c.* 1.6 mya and that contained **Oldowan** tools and fossil hominids including a trampled but reconstructed skull that is attributed to *Homo habilis*; aka 'George'; see **OH 16**. See FLK 22, the 'Zinj site'.

**FLK-NN I:** archaeological site found in 1960 at **Olduvai Gorge**, dated to 1.8 mya (Bed I), and that contains hominid remains including the *Homo habilis* **type specimen** (**OH 7**): parietals, mandible, and wrist bones of an immature 'child' found by Jonathan Leakey, and a nearly complete foot (**OH 8**) found by Mary Leakey. Aka living floor, 'Jonny's child', 'Jonny's site', FLKNN I.

**FLK-North:** archaeological site found in 1960 in **Olduvai Gorge**, dated to 1.8–1.6 mya, the 'elephant kill site' containing the remains of *Deinotherium giganteum*, but remains of horse/zebra, deer, pig and buffalo are also present; containing **Oldowan** choppers, **anvils**, **manuports** and flaking debris. A hominid great toe was also found.

**HEB:** Heberer's gully; an archaeological site found in 1971 in **Bed IV** at **Olduvai Gorge**, dated to 700–200 kya, and that contains five artifact-bearing levels of **Acheulean** tools made primarily of **phonolite**, a hand-ax of elephant bone, and a mortar made from an elephant pelvis.

**JK:** Juma's (Gitau) **Korongo**; an archaeological site discovered in 1962 in **Bed III** at **Olduvai Gorge**, dated to about 1 mya, containing only a few **Acheulean** tools but more than a dozen foot-deep 'siltstone pits' found during further excavations (1972); these enigmatic pits were 'connected' by small channels and seemed formed by fingerlike scrapings, according to Mary **Leakey**, their discoverer. There has been speculation that these were used for **salt** extraction.

**LLK II:** archaeological site found in 1960 at **Olduvai Gorge**, dated to 1.4–1.2 mya (Bed II). Contains no directly associated artifacts, but hominid remains recovered include *Homo erectus* (**OH 9**), a massive individual cranium with a 1065 cm$^3$ capacity. Other erectine fragments from Olduvai include the OH 12 cranial fragments, the OH 22, OH 23, OH 51 mandibular fragments, and the OH 28 hip bone and femoral shaft found in direct association with **Acheulean tools**.

**MNK II:** archaeological site found in 1963 at **Olduvai Gorge**, dated to 1.7 mya (lower Bed II), and that contains a mandible, portions of a maxilla, and many skull fragments of 'Cinderella' (**OH 13**), a fossil hominid attributed to *Homo habilis*. MNK stands for Mary Nicol's **Korongo**. Some larger hominid teeth were also retrieved from the site.

**SHK:** Sam Howard's **Korongo**; a possible living site at **Olduvai Gorge**.

**VEK IV:** archaeological site found in 1962 at **Olduvai Gorge**, dated to 800–500 kya; contains hominid remains including a partial cranium (**OH 12**) attributed to *Homo erectus*.

**WK:** Wayland's **Korongo** at **Olduvai Gorge**.

---

‡ **Olduvai hominids:** see **OH** on pp. 374–5.

**Olduvai Lake:** see **paleo-Lake Olduvai.**

**Olduvai Man:** **AMH** skeleton found at **Olduvai Gorge** (then Oldoway) in 1913 by Hans Reck, who incorrectly put its age at 500 kya, proposing that this bent-knee burial in Bed II was not intrusive. For the next 15 years, it influenced discussions of the antiquity of modern humans in Africa, but **radiocarbon dating** subsequently gave an age of only 17 kya. Aka Oldoway Man, **OH 1**.

**olecranon fossa:** depression on the posterior surface of the distal **humerus** that receives the **olecranon process** of the **ulna** when the arm straightens at the elbow.

**olecranon process: process** on the proximal end of the **ulna** that fits into the **olecranon fossa** of the **humerus** when the arm straightens at the elbow. The triceps brachii muscle inserts into this structure and extends the forearm. Aka 'funny bone'.

**olfaction:** sense of smell, which is detected through **chemoreceptors** in the nose and interpreted in the temporal lobes of the brain. Adjective: olfactory.

**olfactory bulb:** region located in the lower front of the brain that processes odors collected by **chemoreceptors** in the membranes of the snout of primates and other mammals; notably diminished in size in the anthropoid primates compared with the prosimians; aka **rhinencephalon.**

**olfactory cell:** neuron that senses odorant molecules (esters), located in the upper part of the nose, and that consists of terminal hairlike cilia and an axon that passes to the olfactory bulb.

**olfactory center:** part of the brain associated with the reception and interpretation of odors. The olfactory center is located deep within the temporal lobes at the base(s) of the frontal lobes, and anterior to the **hypothalamus.** Aka olfactory cortex. See **olfactory bulb.**

**olfactory communication:** portion of a complex signaling system in animals, including all primates, in which scents are exchanged that contain information about personal identification, location, territory, reproductive status, and level of arousal. Scents may contain **hormones** and **pheromones**, as well as waste products (urine, feces). See **scent** marking and **urine washing.**

**olfactory lobe:** portion of the inferior frontal lobe where the olfactory nerves terminate; includes the **olfactory tract, olfactory bulb**, and trigone. The olfactory lobe is associated with the sense of smell; it is well developed in most vertebrates, but noticeably reduced in anthropoids, and especially in humans.

**olfactory receptor:** one of a family of membrane-bound receptors located in the sensory neuroepithelium of the nose, and capable of binding volatile odorants (esters). The binding process initiates an electrical signal to the **olfactory bulb.**

**olfactory sensitivity:** the ability to smell musk-like sexual odors; the ability is **polymorphic** in human populations. See **anosmia.**

**olfactory system:** sensory cells in the nose, plus the region of the brain to which they are connected; organs of the sense of smell.

**olfactory tract:** olfactory sensory tract of axons that conveys impulses from the **olfactory bulb** to the olfactory portion of the cerebral cortex.

‡ **Oligocene epoch:** one of the **Tertiary** epochs of the **Cenozoic era**, lasting from about 33.7 to 23.8 mya.

Ancestral dogs and pigs appeared in the fossil record, as well as early elephants and monkeys; see *Aegyptopithecus*. See Appendix 4 for a geological time scale.

**oligogenic trait, character** or **feature:** any feature whose outcome is determined by relatively few genetic factors. Cf. **polygenic trait.**

**oligonucleotide:** short sequence of DNA or RNA formed by the union of a small number of nucleotide bases, generally fewer than 20.

**Oligopithecidae:** family of **anthropoids** known from the late Eocene of North Africa and the Arabian peninsula. Two genera and three species; owing to lack of materials, this family was not established until fairly recently. This family contains a mixture of **prosimian** and anthropoid traits and may lie at the origins of the higher primates. Dental formula: 2.1.2.3/2.1.2.3. See Appendix 1 for taxonomy.

*Oligopithecus* **Simons, 1962:** poorly known **anthropoid** genus from the late Eocene of North Africa and the Arabian Peninsula; two species recognized. Body mass ranges between 1 and 1.5 kg. Dental formula: 2.1.2.3/2.1.2.3; dental morphology is a mix of adapid and anthropoid traits and leads to confusion regarding the phylogenetic relationship of this genus. See Appendix 1 for taxonomy.

**oligospermia:** abnormally low concentration of sperm in the semen.

**olivaceous:** greenish brown color usually produced by a mixture of black and yellowish or fulvous (yellow-gray-brown) hairs, or hairs individually banded with those colors.

**olive baboon:** vernacular for *Papio anubis.*

**olive colobus:** vernacular for *Procolobus verus.*

**Olorgesailie:** famous archaeological site found in 1918 near Nairobi, in Kenya's **Rift Valley system**, dated from 1.4 mya to 200 kya, and that contains both **Developed Oldowan** and **Acheulean** artifacts (handaxes, cleavers and '**bolas' stones**). Thought in 1943 to consist of a **home base** site with several living floors on the shore of a **Pleistocene** lake, **taphonomists** later demonstrated that the tools had accumulated in ancient stream channels. Excavated principally by Mary **Leakey;** her application of a technique that exposed artifacts *in situ*, horizon by horizon, was perhaps the first excavation of a **Paleolithic** site using such advanced techniques. Few hominid remains have been recovered; see **KNM-OL 4550.** The site is now an open-air museum containing hundreds of undisturbed artifacts.

*Omanodon minor* **Gheerbrandt, Thomas, Sen, and Al-Sulaimani, 1993:** adapoid prosimian from the early Oligocene of Arabia and belonging to the notharctid subfamily **Cercamoniinae; monotypic;** known only from dentition. Small, estimated body mass at 100 g. See Appendix 1 for taxonomy.

**omega:** 1. the twenty-fourth and last letter of the Greek alphabet, (Ω, ω). 2. symbol for the goal or endpoint in **progressive evolution** according to **Teilhard de Chardin;** Omega.

**omega fatty acids:** see **arachidonic acid** and **docosahexanoic acid.**

**omental fat:** visceral fat.

**OMIM:** acronym for Online Mendelian Inheritance in Man; developed by geneticist V. McKusick, this database of virtually all conceivable genetic manifestations in humans went online in 1995. Each condition is assigned an OMIM number (formerly McKusick's number). OMIM is now the standard reference database of morbid conditions in human genetics.

**omnifarious:** of all forms, varieties or kinds; see **totipotent.**

**omnivorous:** pertaining to **omnivory.**

**omnivory:** dietary category applied to animals that do not have a specialized **diet** and will eat what is available to them; opportunistic feeding. One of the hallmarks of human adaptation. Aka euryphagy.

**Omo hominids:** see entries beginning with **Omo** in box below.

**Omo Valley:** archaeological region north of **Lake Turkana** in East Africa; the Omo deposits had been discovered by Compte de Boaz in 1902. **Arambourg** had worked the area in 1934, but it then lay fallow until 1959, when Clark **Howell** surveyed the region. Intense surveys began after 1966. Aka Lower Omo Valley. See box below.

---

### Some hominid fossils from Omo, Ethiopia

**Omo 1967-18:** field number for hominid remains recovered in 1967, dated to 2.6 mya; remains include a partial mandible attributed to *Paraustralopithecus aethiopicus*.

**Omo 323:** field number for hominid remains recovered in 1976 from Member G of the Shungura Formation, lower Omo Basin, dated to 2.1 mya. Hominid remains include a partial cranium with a sagittal crest, heavily worn teeth with a large canine. This male is attributed to *Australopithecus (= Paranthropus) boisei*, and was the oldest known cranium of that species in 2002.

**Omo I:** archaeological site and fossil found in 1967 in Omo Kibish, dated to <130 kya (U series), and that contains a few flake tools. Hominid remains include a partial skeleton with an incomplete vault assigned to **archaic** *Homo sapiens*, found by Kimoya **Kimeu** and R. **Leakey**. Aka 'Joseph', the 'pathfinder', Omo Kibish I; Omo Valley I, site KHS.

**Omo II:** archaeological site and fossil found in 1967 in the **Omo Valley**, Ethiopia, dated to about 130 ± 50 kya (U series, disputed). Hominid remains include an almost intact black-tinted cranial vault attributed to *Homo* cf. *erectus*. Aka 'Joseph's relative', Omo Kibish II; Omo Valley II, site PHS.

**Omo III:** archaeological site and fossil found in 1967 dated to <130 kya (U series). Hominid remains include cranial fragments, *sp. indet*. Aka Omo Kibish III; Omo Valley III.

**Omo Kibish I:** see Omo I.

**Omo L7A-125:** field number for a hominid fossil found in the Lower **Omo Valley**, dated to 3.0 mya (K/Ar), and that contains hominid remains, including the body of a robust mandible assigned to *Australopithecus aff. africanus*. Flake tools were also found at the same location.

**Omo L40-19:** field number for a hominid fossil found in the Lower **Omo Valley**, dated to 3.0 mya (K/Ar), and that contains hominid remains, including a right ulna assigned to *Australopithecus aff. africanus*. Flake tools were also found at the same location. This ulna has been reported to be similar to KNM-BK 66.

**Omo L894-1:** field number for hominid remains recovered from the **Omo Valley**, dated to 1.9 mya; remains include a partial cranium attributed to *Homo habilis*.

---

**Omo Valley geology:** five formations have been recognized in the Omo Valley: **Mursi, Nkalabong,** Usno, Shungura and Kibish fluvial deposits. The dates of the four older deposits range from 4.1 to 1.34 mya. Hominids have been recovered from the **Usno, Shungura,** and **Kibish formations.**

‡ **Omomyidae:** family of tarsiiform primates belonging to the superfamily **Omomyoidea.** Consists of two or three subfamilies, depending on authority, and from 35 to 39 genera and 71 to 91 species; composition in flux. Very large group with a great diversity of forms; however this family may be **polyphyletic** and is often referred to as a **'wastebasket taxon';** revision may remove many species. Dental formula variable. See **Anaptomorphinae, Omomyinae,** and **Microchoerinae,** and Appendix 1 for taxonomy.

**Omomyiformes:** infraorder used in some classificatory schemes to which the majority of Eocene **haplorhines** are assigned.

**Omomyinae:** subfamily of the tarsiiform family **Omomyidae** known from the early Eocene to perhaps the late Oligocene; predominantly a North American group, but some members known from China; approximately 16 genera and 24 species; appears to be descended from an **anaptomorphine** whom they replaced in the mid-Eocene. Body mass ranges from 100 g to 2 kg. Variable dentition and dietary niches. See Appendix 1 for taxonomy.

**Omomyoidea:** extinct superfamily of the infraorder **Tarsiiformes** containing the families **Omomyidae** and **Microchoeridae** and an *incertae sedis* family containing genera whose precise relationship is uncertain. See Appendix 1 for taxonomy.

**omomyophile hypothesis:** hypothesis of primate phylogeny that considers the omomyids to be the sister group of the **tarsiers**. See **lemurophile hypothesis** and **tarsiphile hypothesis.**

*Omomys* **Leidy, 1869:** genus of tarsiiform primate from the early to middle Eocene of North America belonging to the omomyid subfamily **Omomyinae;** two species. Estimated body mass between 200 and 300 g. Mandibular dental formula: 2.1.3.3; dental morphology suggestive of **faunivory.** One of the few omomyines for which the **postcrania** are known; postcrania suggestive of quadrupedalism with leaping capabilities. See Appendix 1 for taxonomy.

*Omopithecus:* subgenus of fossil *Theropithecus* that consist of two species from the Plio-Pleistocene of Africa.

**OMU:** abbreviation for **one-male unit.**

**oncogene:** any of a class of dominant **housekeeping genes** found in animals, plants and some viruses that promote and control cell division through signal transduction, but that can be involved in the processes leading to cancer when mutated. See **proto-oncogene.**

**oncogene hypothesis:** proposal that all species prone to cancer had viral genomes that became integrated into their DNA; such genes have been transmitted with the rest of the genome ever since, and that **carcinogens** transform these **proto-oncogenes** into cancer-causing agents, or **oncogenes.** Suggested in 1969 by American biochemists Robert Joseph Huebner (1923– ) and George Joseph Todaro (1937– ); aka the virogene-oncogene hypothesis. See **cancer (theories of),** the **provirus hypothesis,** and the **protovirus hypothesis.** It is now suspected that the process occurs in the reverse direction: that cellular oncogenes are the progenitors of the viral genomes.

**oncology:** branch of medicine that studies **cancer.**

**oncolytic:** describes any agent capable of destroying cancer cells.

**one gene–many polypeptides hypothesis:** refinement of the **one gene–one polypeptide hypothesis** made necessary by discovery by the **HGP** that most proteins are composed of subunits (**exons**) encoded by different genes and assembled by **alternative splicing.** Cf. **central dogma.**

**one gene – one enzyme hypothesis:** central dogma of molecular genetics in the 1960s and 1970s. See **one gene – one polypeptide hypothesis.**

**one gene – one polypeptide hypothesis:** refinement of the **central dogma** and the **one gene – one enzyme hypothesis** made necessary by the discovery that many proteins are composed of subunits (**exons**) encoded by several different genes.

**one-male unit** (OMU): social group consisting of one male, several females, and their nonpubescent offspring; OMUs are found habitually among some primates such as hamadryas baboons, for whom there may be a genetic component to this behavior, but OMUs may be the result of environmental conditions in other primate species such as howlers. The older term **harem** in the ethological literature also referred to this type of social organization; however, OMU is now preferred, especially in reference to primates, owing to **anthropomorphic** connotations associated with the older term. Aka one-male group.

**one–zero sampling:** type of **time sampling** in which the recording session is divided into sample intervals. The observer records whether or not the behavior pattern being studied occurred during the preceding time interval. This recording occurs at regular intervals, usually regulated by a signal from a timekeeping device. Aka Hansen frequencies. Cf. **instantaneous sampling.**

**Online Mendelian Inheritance in Man:** see **OMIM.**

**onset of sexual maturity:** chronological age at the onset of puberty; one of the intervals known in biology as a **life history variable.**

**ontogenesis:** history of the process of development and growth in the early life of an organism. Adjective: ontogenetic. Aka **ontogeny.** Cf. **phylogenesis.**

**ontogenetic allometry:** see **growth allometry.**

**ontogeny:** somatic **development** and **growth** of an organism throughout its lifetime, from conception to adulthood, a span known as the **life history** Cf. **phylogeny.** Term coined by **Haeckel.**

**'ontogeny recapitulates phylogeny':** see Haeckel's **biogenetic law.**

**O null allele:** lack of antigenic specificity that characterizes the O in the **ABO blood group.** It consists of four precursor sugars attached to glycoproteins of the cell membrane, aka **H substance;** it is missing a fifth terminal sugar that would he attached by an enzyme, but the 'enzyme' is nonfunctional. This null product differs from its homologues that attaches the A- and B-specific sugar by a critical frame shift substitution that makes it a null product. See **A antigen** and **B antigen**.

**oöblast:** cell from which the **ovum** develops.

**oöcyesis:** ovarian pregnancy, a type of **ectopic pregnancy**.

‡ **oöcyte:** maternal cell that divides to form the egg or **ovum** and that will contain one-half of a mother's **chromatids**, if fertilized. See **primary oöcyte**.

‡ **oögenesis:** female **gametogenesis**; the formation, development, growth and maturation of a female gamete (**ovum**); takes place in the **gonad** (**ovary**). Female mammals differ from males in that **premeiotic phenomena** take place in the female **fetus** during the late **first trimester** of **gestation**, whereas in males these events are postponed until **puberty**.

**oögonium:** primitive germ cell; proliferates by mitotic division. Plural: oögonia. All oögonia develop into primary **oöcytes** prior to birth; no oögonia are present after birth.

**oökinesia:** movement of the egg during maturation and fertilization.

**oölemma:** cell membrane of the ovum.

**oöphoron:** ovary.

**oöplasm:** cytoplasm of an **ovum**.

**oötheca:** ovary.

**oötid:** archaic term for **oöcyte**, an immature haploid cell that will develop into an **ovum** if **fertilization** occurs.

**opal:** transparent or translucent noncrystalline mineral composed primarily of silica (as are the related minerals **chalcedony**, **chert**, and **flint**); opal has a waxy, iridescent luster that make it valued as a medium for decoration rather than for **stone tools**.

**open-field test:** laboratory experiment procedure in which an animal subject is placed in a space (the open field) with which it is completely unfamiliar; the open space is square or rectangular, contained within walls, and the floor is divided into grids. Behavior such as locomotion or exploration is measured by the number of grids entered or some other criterion that the researcher selects. Small rodents are the most frequently used subjects for this type of study, but some primate researchers have also used this method.

**open find:** archaeological context in which a particular horizon is found to have been disturbed, from which it is inferred that the objects located there were deposited at different times. Open sites are the result of intrusion, the burrowing of animals, displacement and redeposition due to erosion, etc.

**open mouth threat:** see **staring open mouth face**.

**open population:** deme that is exposed to **gene flow**. Cf. **closed population**.

**open reading frame** (ORF): region of **cDNA** sequence starting with an AUG codon that initiates protein synthesis and that includes a region which encodes protein, ending at a stop codon. The number of open reading frames in an organism's genome yields an estimate of the number of genes present.

**opening stroke:** third sequence of the **masticatory cycle** in which the jaws open and the teeth are raised above their opposites.

**openness:** in communication, refers to systems of communication that have basic elements that are capable of combination and recombination to create new meanings; e.g. human language. Cf. **closed system**.

**operant conditioning:** conditioning in which an experimenter waits for the targeted response (for example, head scratching) to be emitted, immediately after which the test subject is given a reinforcing reward. After the procedure is repeated many times, the frequency of the targeted response will have increased significantly over its pre-excitement base rate. Cf. **classical conditioning**.

**operation:** 1. manner of functioning. 2. procedure or activity. 3. in medicine, surgery. 4. mathematical process such as addition, subtraction, etc.

**operational definition:** working definition that is consistent with the application of empirical standards that are consistent and rigorous, that are linked to objective reality, and that lead to concepts of greater validity; aka operatism, operationism.

**operational hypothesis:** hypothesis actually being tested in a **research design**, as opposed to the **null hypothesis**. Rejection of a null hypothesis supports its operational hypothesis, whereas failure to reject may weaken or falsify the operational hypothesis. Aka **alternative hypothesis**.

**operational sex ratio:** (OSR) ratio of sexually receptive females to potentially sexually active males in a population at any one time.

**operational taxonomic unit:** see **OTU**.

**operational thought:** Piagetian concept in which an individual is able to categorize the world, recognize variation, and understand temporal series; demonstrated in **anthropoids**.

**operationalism:** statement that scientific concepts must be defined in terms of the operations by which they are measured or applied, developed by American physicist Percy Williams Bridgman (1882–1961). Bridgman's application applies to concepts rather than to sentences or propositions, and is a specification of the **verifiability principle**, the central tenet of **logical positivism**.

**operationism:** see **operational definition**.

**operator:** region of **DNA** that is part of an **operon** to which a specific **repressor protein** can become attached; attachment blocks the operator thus preventing the initiation of **genetic transcription**.

**operator site:** in bacteria, a segment of DNA that controls the expression of a structural gene.

**operon:** long transcription unit in prokaryotes following a single **promoter** site. Cf. **cistron**.

**operon model:** see **Jacob–Monod model**.

**ophyron:** point in the center of the forehead where the temporal lines converge most closely.

**'opiate receptor':** see **enkephalin receptor site**.

**Opismiolithic:** pertaining to a culture during **Neolithic** times that preserves a **Mesolithic** economy (hunting, fishing, gathering), but that may also show a few Neolithic traits such as pottery or polished axes.

**opisthion** (o): **craniometric landmark**; medial point of the posterior margin of the **foramen magnum**. See Appendix 7.

**opisthocranion** (op): **craniometric landmark**; most posterior point of the skull in the mid-sagittal plane. See Appendix 7.

**opponens pollicis:** **intrinsic muscle** of the hand. The opponens pollicis originates from the **trapezium** and inserts into **metacarpal** I. Its action is to oppose the thumb; one of the thenar group of muscles.

**opportunism:** proposal that all potential modes of existence will be tried by some organism and that all ecological niches will be occupied, although not necessarily all at the same time.

**opportunistic infection:** any infection caused by an agent already present in the living organism and that is normally kept under control by the immune system; examples are Kaposi's sarcoma or thrush.

**opportunistic species:** species specialized to exploit newly opened habitats; such species are usually able to disperse over long distances and to reproduce rapidly, i.e. they are *r*-selected.

**opportunistic tools:** simple, unaltered objects used as tools.

**opposable:** in human biology, describes a digit with the ability to touch, or oppose, another digit. Most primates have an opposable **thumb** and an opposable or partly opposable great toe (**hallux**). These digits are capable of rotating to bring their tips into contact with one or more of the other four digits.

‡ **opposable digit(s):** 1. some primates, but not humans, have a great toe (**hallux**) that can rotate to bring its tip into contact, or opposition, with the other digits of the foot. 2. an opposable thumb, a highly mobile **pollex** that is capable of rotating to the other **digits**, which allows the grasping of objects and is necessary for a **precision grip**. A characteristic of primates, and especially well developed in humans.

**opposition:** see **opposable**.

**opsins:** class of poplypeptides coded for by genes on the X chromosome (red and green) or on chromosome 7 (blue). Opsins bind to visual pigments (retinene) in cone cells in the retina; the conjugated molecule (rhodopsin) is sensitive to light of a given wavelength, and the absence of a particular opsin results in **color blindness** in that wavelength range.

**optic chiasma:** X-shaped structure on the inferior aspect of the brain, the point at which the nerves transmitting visual stimuli from the retina of the eye cross over to enter the contralateral side of the brain; in humans and some other species, the crossover is not complete. Some forms of albinism dramatically disrupt this pathway. Aka optic chiasm.

**optic disc:** small region of the retina where the fibers of the ganglion neurons exit from the eyeball to form the optic nerve; aka blind spot.

**optic nerve:** cranial nerve that arises in the **visual cortex** located in the occipital lobe of the brain and conducts impulses from the **photoreceptors** on the retinal surface of the eye. Aka cranial nerve II.

**optic tectum:** area that forms the roof of the midbrain (**mesencephalon**); it contains nuclei important for both the visual and the auditory systems.

**optical dating:** see **optically stimulated luminescence**.

**optical convergence:** see **orbital convergence**.

**optical isomers:** two different chemical substances, e.g. **amino acids**, that have the same chemical formula even though they have different structures. See **racemization**.

**optically stimulated luminescence** (OSL): a variant of **TL dating** that measures emitted light rather than heat. OSL can be used on unheated sediments exposed to sunlight prior to deposition. Aka optical dating, optical age.

**optimal foraging theory** (OFT): a body of hypotheses dealing with the **ergonomics** of **subsistence** strategies, the central premise of which is that **foragers** will switch from one **prey** or food type to another if the new type is denser, easier to handle or catch, higher in nutritional value, etc. 'Prey' may consist of many objects, both organic and inorganic. Many **primate** species, including humans, have been shown to conform to the rules of OFT. See **marginal value theorem** and **patch**.

**optimal yield:** highest rate of increase that a population can sustain in a given environment. This yield is realized at a lower population size than the **carrying capacity**.

**optimization:** process of correction that makes something more effective, useful, or perfect; making the best of in certain circumstances. Optimization often refers to a self-regulating system that makes necessary adjustments as the need arises.

**optimization theory:** body of mathematical models concerned with the simultaneous derivation of minimum and maximum functions for several variables subject to constraints, and whether unique, optimal solutions can be subsequently derived and characterized, when the system of interest is complex. Portions of this body of theory have been incorporated in **optimal foraging theory** and **sociobiology**, for example.

**optimum genotype:** any genetic combination in a species best able to achieve **reproductive success** in a given environment.

**option value:** potential economic value of a species at some point in the future; a type of **indirect value**.

**OPV–HIV hypothesis:** proposal that the **HIV** allegedly jumped to humans from contaminated oral polio vaccines (OPVs) distributed and administered in Africa during the 1950s.

**oral:** of or pertaining to the mouth.

**oral incisive foramen:** see **incisive foramen**.

**orale** (ol): **craniometric landmark**; mid-point on the hard palate of a line drawn from the lateral borders of the two central maxillary incisors. See Appendix 7.

‡ **orangutan:** vernacular for *Pongo pygmaeus*.

**orbicularis oculi:** muscle of facial expression. The orbicularis oculi originates from the **maxillary** and **frontal bones**; it inserts in the skin around the eye. Its action is to close the eye, as in blinking.

**orbicularis oris:** muscle of facial expression. The orbicularis oris originates from muscles surrounding the mouth and inserts in the skin of the central lip. Its action is to close the lips, as when kissing.

**orbit:** cavity in the anterior of the face, superior to the nasal cavity and interior to the forehead, that protects and contains the eyes and its associated musculature and nerves. Adjective: orbital. In **anthropoids** the orbits are a composite of six different cranial and facial bones: **lacrimal, ethmoid, frontal, sphenoid, zygomatic**, and **maxillary bones**; aka eye socket.

**orbital breadth:** (mf–mf) **craniometric** measurement; width from the **maxillofrontale** to the **ectoconchion** as measured with sliding calipers. See Appendix 7 for an illustration of the landmarks used.

**orbital convergence:** realignment of the visual axes of the **orbits** during primate evolution from laterally facing to anteriorly facing lines of sight.

**orbital height: craniometric** measurement; maximum height from upper to lower borders of the **orbit** perpendicular to the horizontal axis of the orbit as measured with sliding calipers. See Appendix 7 for an illustration of the landmarks used.

**orbital index:** ratio of orbital height to orbital width; **orbital height** divided by **orbital breadth** multiplied by 100. See **chamaeconchic, mesoconchic, hypsiconchic**.

**orbitale** (or): **craniometric landmark**; most inferior point on the margin of the **orbit**. See Appendix 7.

**orbitofrontal cortex:** part of the **limbic system** involved with planning and reaction.

**orbitosphenoid bone:** portion of the sphenoid bone that forms part of the posterior wall of the **orbit**.

**Orce Ravine:** an archaeological locale found *c.* 1982 in the Guadix-Baza Basin near Orce, Granada, south central Spain, dating to 1.07–0.78 mya (Baza Formation, **paleomagnetism**; probably older than 1.07 mya) that contains artifacts (cores and flake debris) mixed with mammoth and other mammal bones at two sites (Barranco León and Fuente Nueva 3). A third site, Venta Micena, produced contentious hominid remains including a 'child's' cranial fragment (VM-0, 'Orce Man') assigned to *sp. indet.*

**orchidic hormone:** any substance secreted by the **testis**, e.g. **testosterone**.

**orchidometer:** any of several devices used to measure or estimate testicle size and/or mass.

‡ **order:** in taxonomy, the hierarchical category below the **class** and above the **family**; a group of similar, related families. The order **Primates**, for example, includes monkeys, apes and humans, amongst others.

**order effects:** repeated testing of the same subject that changes its behavior over time. For example, a ball is rolled toward an infant rhesus may initially elicit fear and backing away; after this treatment has occurred several more times the subject may become curious and lose its fear.

**Ordos:** see **Salawusu**.

‡ **Ordovician period:** period of the **Paleozoic era**, lasting from approximately 500 to 430 mya; characterized by massive inundation of North America with shallow inland seas. Trilobites are a common fossil from the period. Cephalopods appear near the end of the period.

**Oreopithecidae:** family of **hominoids** belonging to the infraorder **Catarrhini**; known from the Miocene of Africa and Europe; up to three genera may be included, but some authors only include the enigmatic genus *Oreopithecus*. **Diurnal** apes ranging in size from 10 to 30 kg. Dental formula: 2.1.2.3; members of this family appeared to be **folivorous**. Locomotion is extrapolated from only one genus, whose postcranial elements suggest suspensory abilities similar to the modern orangutan. See Appendix 1 for taxonomy.

*Oreopithecus bambolii* Gervais, 1872: enigmatic catarrhine from the late Miocene of Europe belonging to the family **Oreopithecidae**; monotypic genus. Known from jaws, teeth, and almost complete, but badly crushed, skeleton. The phylogenetic relationship of this genus has been a source of debate for over a century; it has an odd mix of primitive, derived, and completely unique traits. It has been aligned with both the **cercopithecines** and the **hominoids**;

most current research suggest an ape affinity for this primate; it has been suggested as ancestral to both the hylobatids and the **hominids**; one researcher proposed that *Oreopithecus* is descended from the middle Miocene East African genus **Nyanzapithecus**. Estimated body mass of this genus is 30 kg. Dental formula: 2.1.2.3; dentition suggests **folivorous** diet. This species has a broad thorax and long forearms; this has been interpreted as indicating either **brachiation** or **suspensory locomotion**. See Appendix 1 for taxonomy.

**orexin(s):** so-called 'sleep hormone'; either of a pair of neuropeptides (A and B) secreted by orexin neurons in the lateral **hypothalamus** that interact both with feeding centers in the hypothalamus, and with arousal and sleep-wakefulness centres in the **brainstem**, sympathetic and parasympathetic nuclei, and the **limbic system**. Orexin neurons are regulated by metabolic cues, including **leptin, glucose**, and **ghrelin**. Activation of the orexin neurons apparently contributes to wakefulness, whereas their inactivation permits **sleep**; mutations or other contributors to inactivation have been linked to narcolepsy. Aka hypocretin(s).

‡ **organ:** structure that is composed of two or more tissues performing a specialized function.

‡ **organelle:** any of several membrane-bound living structures within a **cell** and associated with specific functions; these include the **nucleus, mitochondria, plasmids, Golgi apparatus, lysosomes**, etc.

‡ **organic:** loosely, any carbon-based compound, but often meant to refer to molecules contained in living or **extinct** organisms. Cf. **inorganic**.

**organic evolution:** see **biological evolution**.

**organic selection theory:** idea that behavioral changes can precede and precipitate changes in biological structures and the underlying genetic substrate; purposive and directed change (**teleonomic selection**) resulting in the progressive emergence of complex, hierarchically organized systems. See **progressive evolution** and the **Baldwin effect**. Not universally accepted by evolutionary biologists.

‡ **organism:** any individual living creature.

**organizer:** 1. group of cells on the dorsal lip of the blastopore that stimulates the differentiation of cells in the embryo. 2. any group of cells having such an ability.

‡ **organogenesis:** 1. formation of body organs and systems during the **first trimester** of prenatal life. 2. dissociated cells that exhibit organization into a structure and that exhibit normal organ function or form, or both.

**Oriental Region: Old World** tropics from India east to South China and south to **Wallace's line**. Cf. **Palearctic Region**.

**orientation:** 1. awareness of self in place, time, etc. 2. to find one's bearings. 3. relative position. 4. placement of an object in line with a cardinal direction, as a grave offering or architectural structure.

**orifice:** opening or hole; mouthlike structure.

**origin:** 1. genesis; beginning or start. 2. area of muscle attachment that remains fixed during muscle contraction; the origin and **insertion** of a particular muscle may not be the same for different actions of the muscle.

**Origin and Evolution of Man Conference:** symposium held at Cold Spring Harbor (New York) in June, 1950, and attended by 129 influential anthropologists and biologists. The *Proceedings* (1951) contained state-of-the-art knowledge concerning all aspects of physical anthropology to that date.

**origin of man hypotheses:** two long-standing hypotheses have competed to demonstrate the locational origin of man: the first, proposed by Charles **Darwin**, viewed the **original hominid homeland** as Africa; the second, known as **early man in Asia**, championed the great plateaus of Central Asia as the cradle of **hominid** evolution. Both ideas have current supporters.

*Origin of Species:* abridged title of work, *On the Origin of Species by Means of Natural Selection, or the Preservation of Favoured Races in the Struggle for Life*, by Charles **Darwin** in 1859. The book appeared in six editions and 35 printings during Darwin's lifetime.

**original hominid homeland:** proposal by Charles **Darwin** that Africa, since it was the homeland of the African apes, could also be the continent in which early man evolved.

**original horizontality, law of:** see **law of original horizontality**.

**ornament:** device used to decorate the body, including objects, paints, tattoos, scarification, and mutilation.

**ornithine carbamoyl transcarbamylase deficiency:** X-linked recessive genetic defect characterized by progressive mental deterioration and caused by an accumulation of ammonia in the blood due to a specific enzyme deficiency in the nitrogen cycle. Aka transcarbamylase deficiency.

**ornithosis:** disease of humans where the **agent** is found in any of several animal **disease reservoirs** such as sheep, goats, and especially avian species; an influenza-like systemic infection when transferred to humans. Symptoms include pneumonia and 'fever of unknown origin'. The infection is caused by gram-negative *Chlamydia psittaci*. Ornithosis was a significant killer of humans in 1929–30; transmitted to humans by inhalation of the dust of dry fecal droppings. Aka psittacosis, chlamydiosis, and **parrot fever**.

**orogeny:** mountain-building, especially through the folding of the earth's crust.

**Orpheus:** see DNH 8 at **Drimolen.**

*Orrorin tugenensis* **Senut, Pickford, Gommery, Main, Cheboi, and Coppens, 2001** (*gen. et sp. nov.*): binomen for a composite fossil specimen found in October 2000 near the village of **Rondinin** in the **Tugen Hills,** Kenya, dated to about 5.88–5.72 mya (Lukeino Formation at Kapcheberek), containing hominoid remains including cranial and postcranial fragments from at least five individuals from which a composite was constructed. *Orrorin* means 'original man' in the local dialect. Three partial femora suggest **bipedalism** while on the ground, but a humerus and phalanx suggest arboreal adaptations. Central incisors are large, the canine is large for a hominid, and the lower fourth premolar is ape-like. The molars are relatively small, with thick enamel. Aka Lukeino hominid, 'Millennium Man', and 'Millennium Ancestor'.

**orthal:** pertaining to the movements of the lower jaw in a straight up-and-down direction.

**ortho-cousin:** see **parallel cousin.**

**orthocranic:** in reference to the **cranial length–height index,** with an index between 70.00 and 74.99; such an individual is considered to have a medium skull.

**orthogenesis:** largely discredited idea that **evolution** would continue in a given direction because of some vaguely defined physical force internal to a species. Aka progressive evolution, rectilinear evolution, aristogenesis, entelechy.

**orthogenetic evolution:** see **orthogenesis.**

**orthognathism:** condition of having a vertical, less protruding jaw; a characteristic of **AMH.** Aka straight-faced, orthognathic; see **orthognathous.** Cf. **prognathism.**

**orthognathous:** in reference to the **Flower's index,** with an index of 97.99 or less; such an individual is considered to have a flat face.

**orthograde posture:** upright or vertical walking; bipedal walking.

**orthologous homology:** any homologous structure, whether morphological or molecular, in which two taxa are identical, and therefore are also identical to the common ancestor shared by them. Cf. **paralogous homology.**

**orthology:** homologous variants of a single genetic locus in different species, i.e. a **DNA sequence** that has not been duplicated. See **synteny.** Cf. **parology** and **xenology.**

**orthorachic:** pertaining to a **vertical lumbar index** of between 98 and 100.9.

**orthoselection:** continuous selection by the same agents on the same traits in an evolutionary lineage, producing **directional selection;** in retrospect, such lineages may be perceived by some workers to possess 'inertia' or 'evolutionary momentum'. See **progressive evolution.** Cf. **opportunism.**

**orthostatic:** pertaining to upright posture.

**orthotolidine solution:** chemical liquid that can be used to test for the presence of blood in a stain or other specimen.

**oryctology:** study of fossils and other remains recovered from the earth, with the exception of cultural material that is recovered by archaeologists; includes **paleontology,** geology, petrology, mineralogy, and **taphonomy.**

**os** (Latin): bone. Previously, the term *os* was a standard prefix for all bones, e.g. *os centrale,* but with recent terminology reformation in anatomy this practice has fallen into disfavor.

**os ainoicum: zygomatic bone** with two supplementary sutures (bipartite malars) formerly believed to occur at high frequencies among the **Ainu** people of Japan.

**os clitoris:** see **clitoris.**

**os coxa, coxae,** and **os innominatum:** see **coxal bone.**

**os penis:** see **baculum.**

**Osborn, Henry Fairfield** (1857–1935): US paleontologist (Sc. D., Princeton, 1881); studied briefly with T. H. **Huxley** in England. Osborn rose through the ranks to become president of the American Museum of Natural History (1908–33). He was a neo-Lamarckian and orthogeneticist, and supported the concept of an ancient evolutionary link between apes and humans, yet did not believe that the extant European fossil hominids (**Heidelberg, Piltdown, Cro-Magnon**) were predecessors of modern humans. Rather, Osborn held that each of these were extinct lineages. Osborn was also highly political and, with C. R. **Davenport,** was a founding member of the **Galton Society of New York** (1918), a group that sought to apply **eugenic** principles to US immigration policies. He was nevertheless opposed to the fundamentalism of W. J. **Bryan,** and developed a polygenetic view of human evolution that resulted in *Men of the Old Stone Age* (1915), a work with limited long-term influence. He was also the author of *Fifty-two Years of Research, Observation, and Publication* (1930).

**OSL:** see **optically stimulated luminescence.**

**osseous:** bony; composed or partly composed of **bone.**

‡ **osseous breccia:** sedimentary concretion that also contains bones. See **breccia.**

**ossification:** process by which cartilage cells are broken down and replaced by bone cells; **osteoblast** formation in skeletal tissue; to ossify. Ossification begins during the fetal stage and continues after birth. See **osteogenesis, endochondral ossification** and **intramembranous ossification.**

**ossuary:** place of deposit for the bones of the dead, often pertaining to the bones of several persons.

**osteoarthritis** (OA): a degenerative disease of joints characterized by swelling, deformation, and pain. Some forms of OA are heritable, and have an autosomal dominant mode of inheritance caused by mutations in the connective tissue gene(s) that make collagen.

**osteoblast:** specialized cell fibroblast that forms bone tissue by **deposition** of protein matrix. Cf. **osteoclast**.

**osteochondritis:** inflammation of bone and its related cartilages.

**osteoclast:** specialized multinucleated **macrophage** that erodes bone tissue by resorption of matrix with digestive enzymes. See **osteoporosis**. Cf. **osteoblast**.

**osteoclastogenesis:** formation and differentiation of new **osteoclasts** and that contributes to **bone remodeling**.

**osteocranium:** fetal **cranium** following ossification of the membranous cranium.

**osteocyte:** mature bone cell that is encased in a non-cellular matrix.

**osteodentin:** form of dentin that is rapidly formed, trapping **odontoblasts**, and that superficially resembles bone.

‡ **osteodontokeratic culture:** pertaining to an **assemblage** of putative **tools** alleged to be made from bone (osteo-), tooth (-donto-) and horn (-keratic); misguided proposal by R. **Dart** and based on fragmentary animal remains in the South African **hominid** cave site of **Makapansgat**. Not accepted by most paleontologists; see the '**killer ape' hypothesis**.

**osteogenesis:** formation of new bone tissue. Adjective: osteogenic.

**osteogenesis imperfecta:** heritable prenatal developmental disease that results in skeletal fragility, osteoporosis, brittle and easily broken bones, blue **sclera**, poor teeth, and hearing loss. The embryonic (congenital) form is usually fatal; a late-appearing (delayed) form is characterized by recurring fractures of the extremities after the first year of life. Caused by a defect in one of the **procollagen** genes that affects embryonic collagen formation. More than one gene is required to assemble **collagen**; the various defective genes behave as dominants and recessives. Aka brittle bones.

**osteogenic layer:** inner layer of the **periosteum** that is involved in bone formation and **bone remodeling**.

**osteoid:** 1. bonelike or resembling bone. 2. organic matrix of bone that is filled with calcium salts.

‡ **osteology:** study of bone structure and function. Human osteology focuses on the interpretation of the skeletal remains of past populations.

**osteomalacia:** softened bone; caused by deficiency of **vitamin D**, **calcium**, and/or phosphorus, or by a failure of **collagen** to mineralize in newly formed bone; a similar condition in children is called **rickets**.

**osteomere:** any of a series of bony structures, e.g. a vertebra.

**osteometric board: anthropometric** instrument that consists of a flat board with two ends, one of which is movable and travels along a routed track; this is the preferred instrument for measuring long bones. The object to be measured is placed between the two end pieces and the movable end brought up to the object, where the measurement scale can be read.

**osteometric measurements:** standard measures of the postcranial skeleton; some 531 or more measures have been defined, and at least 256 indices have been created. Cf. **craniometric measurements**.

‡ **osteometry:** field of study that measures the skeleton and its components, and analyzes the data obtained. Adjective: osteometric.

**osteomyelitis:** form of bone and joint tissue infection caused by a fever-causing organism, and characterized by hardening, spindling and/or fibrous thickening of bone. There are several commonly recognized forms.

**osteon:** cylindrical structure that contains bone cells surrounding an **osteonic canal**; aka Haversian system.

**osteonia:** tumor composed of bony tissue.

**osteonic canal:** microscopic channel in bone tissue through which a blood vessel passes; aka Haversian canal.

**osteopathology:** 1. any bone disease. 2. field of medicine that views the body as an integrated whole that, when functioning properly, is capable of curing itself against infectious agents and other stresses; aka osteopathy.

**osteopenia:** reduced bone mass or density; bone rarefaction.

**osteophyte:** small abnormal bony outgrowth that develops on bone surface.

**osteoporosis:** multifactorial metabolic bone disorder, a degenerative condition in which there is abnormal loss of bone mass (but not size); results from an imbalance between factors that destroy and resorb old bone (**osteoclasts**) and those that deposit new bone in its place (**osteoblasts**); inappropriate bone resorption. Bones affected by this disease become porous, brittle, and vulnerable to fracture. Primary osteoporosis is more apparent in females after menopause (aka senile osteoporosis, postmenopausal osteoporosis), although osteoporosis may be secondary to an underlying disease. Some forms of osteoporosis have a genetic component due to defects in **collagen**; the autosomal location of a susceptibility gene is on HSA 17p.

***Otavipithecus namibiensis* Conroy, Senut, Gommery, Pickford and Mein, 1992:** monotypic genus of **hominoids** from the middle Miocene (*c.* 13 mya) of southern Africa (Namibia); phylogenetic relationships uncertain, but the recovered material shows affinities with **Dryopithecus**; the cheek teeth are thinly enameled. The holotype consists only of a right mandible bearing four teeth; a phalanx is also known. Estimated body mass between 14 and 20 kg. Dental formula: 2.1.2.3; dentition suggests either **frugivory** or **folivory**. The phalanx suggests arboreal quadrupedalism. See Appendix 1 for taxonomy.

**otic:** of or pertaining to the ear. Cf. **auditory**.

**otic capsule:** cartilaginous structure of embryological development that surrounds the auditory sac that encloses the internal ear; it later fuses with the sphenoid and occipital cartilages.

**otobasion inferius:** point at which the lower lobe of the external ear attaches to the head.

**Otolemur (= Galago) Coquerel, 1859:** prosimian genus to which the greater bushbabies (galagos) belong; two subspecies recognized. Distribution in southern Africa moving from the Atlantic coast east until the Indian Ocean coastline is reached; occupies open **woodland** and **savanna**. Arboreal; **nocturnal**; locomotion is arboreal quadrupedalism and a form of **saltation** when on the ground. Largest of the galago genera, weighing from 700 to 1200 g. Dental formula: 2.1.2.3; diet varies depending on the season, but is principally **frugivory** and **gummivory**. Generally give birth to **twins**, which are carried in the mouth; female builds nest. Social pattern is **noyau**. See Appendix 2 for taxonomy, Appendix 3 for living species.

**OTU:** operational taxonomic unit; in **numerical taxonomy**, any one item, individual, or taxon in a larger set used during an analysis.

**Ouchterlony technique:** precipitin test that visualizes the degree of identity between two species, commonly used in phylogenetic studies. Aka double diffusion technique.

**Ouranopithecus macedoniensis de Bonis and Melentis, 1977:** large **hominoid** from Greece; this taxon is known from more material, but **Graecopithecus freybergi** has precedence and this species has been referred to the latter by many authorities.

**Ourayia Gazin, 1958:** genus of tarsiiform primate from the middle to late Eocene of North America, belonging to the subfamily **Omomyinae**; two species. Some workers think that this genus may be descended from **Omomys** or an unknown genus close to it; others have suggested that *Ourayia* is ancestral to **Macrotarsius**. Estimated body mass between 1 and 2 kg. Dental formula: 2.1.3.3/2.1.3.3; dental morphology reminiscent of that of modern **Callicebus** and suggestive of **frugivory** with insect supplements. See Appendix 1 for taxonomy.

‡ **out of Africa I model:** model of early **human origins**, which holds that the transition from early *Homo* (the **habilines**) to *Homo erectus* was restricted to Africa, after which dispersion out into the rest of the Old World occurred, earlier than 1.5 mya.

‡ **out of Africa II model:** model of modern **human origins**, which holds that the biocultural transition from late **archaic Homo sapiens** to early **AMHs** was restricted to Africa, after which dispersion *c.* 200 kya into the rest of the **Old World** occurred; considers that modern humanity has shallow temporal roots compared with the results of alternative hypotheses, such as the **multiregional continuity model**. Aka **mitochondrial Eve**, ROA. See **monophyletic hypothesis** and **polyphyletic hypothesis**.

**out of Africa again and again model:** model of early **human origins**, which holds that the original migration of *Homo erectus* out of Africa (see the **out of Africa I model**) about 1.7 mya was followed by a second expansion out of Africa between 840 and 420 kya, followed by a third expansion 150–80 kya (see the **out of Africa II model**), all followed by a much more recent introgression of genes from Asia back into Africa as proposed by the **out of Asia II** model. Developed by geneticist A. R. Templeton, the again and again model argues that there were at least two major radiations of humanity from Africa into Eurasia subsequent to the original **out of Africa I** model, and that the global replacement predicted by the **mitochondrial Eve** model is better explained by interbreeding (**gene flow**).

**out of Africa corridor:** debated route of exit of early **AMHs** from northern Africa into Eurasia: one set of researchers have proposed the **Levant**; a second set favor a coastal route along the Arabian Peninsula. This second suggestion is a very recent proposal, and little supporting evidence has been accumulated to date. See 'Gates of Grief'.

**out of Asia I:** model proposed to explain the presence of certain DNA patterns among catarrhine primates. In this model DNA variation suggests an influx of Asian primate DNA into Africa about 10 mya. Cf. **out of Africa**.

**out of Asia II:** model proposed to explain the presence of an HSA Y-specific Alu insets (TAP +) found in certain human Y chromosomes. In this model, Y chromosome variation suggests an influx of Asian chromosomes into Africa during the past few thousand years. Cf. **out of Africa model(s)**.

**outbreeding:** pairing of unrelated individuals for the purpose of mating. Aka outcrossing and **exogamy**.

**outcome:** the result of an experimental trial.

**outcrop:** bedrock exposed by weathering, and that contains materials such as **lava** or **quartz** that can be gathered and used for the manufacture of **stone tools**.

**outer epicanthus:** most lateral point of the eye, where the lower and upper eyelids meet furthest from the nose, the lateral canthus (outer angle) of the eye. Cf. **inner epicanthus**.

**outgroup:** in **phylogenetic systematics**, any taxon thought to be less closely related to the others comprising an **ingroup**; any taxon used to resolve the polarity of characters.

**outgroup comparison:** process that contrasts the traits of a particular set of taxa with those of another in an attempt to determine evolutionary relationships.

**outlier:** any observation that has a substantial difference between the actual value for a dependent variable and the predicted value; a value more than 3 standard deviations from a mean, a regression line, a centroid, etc.

**outwash:** sloping heap of fragments deposited in caves near the mouth where it has washed in from the exterior surface; often contains the bones of animals. See **talus** (2).

**ovarian follicle:** small sac in the **ovary** where the primordial **ova** are produced; the follicle grows as an egg matures, secreting female sex hormones prior to **ovulation**.

**ova:** plural of **ovum**.

**ovarian hormone:** any substance secreted by the **ovary**, e.g. **relaxin**.

**ovarian ligament:** cordlike connective tissue that attaches the ovary to the uterus.

**ovary:** the female **gonad**, one of the two sexual glands in which the ova are formed. The ovary is a flat oval body along the lateral wall of the pelvic cavity, attached to the posterior surface of the broad ligament. It consists of stroma and ovarian follicles in various stages of maturation and is covered by a modified peritoneum. It is also the source of certain **estrogens**.

**ovate:** egg-shaped.

**overbite:** condition in which the upper incisor teeth overlap the lower incisors during **occlusion**. Aka vertical overbite. Cf. **overjet**.

**overdominance:** common instance when the **fitness** of a **heterozygote** is greater than that of both **homozygotes** in a case of **Mendelian inheritance**; overdominance of fitness can lead to a **balanced polymorphism**, as in **sickle cell anemia**. Cf. **heterosis** and **underdominance**.

**overjet:** projection of either the **incisors** and/or the **molars** beyond their opposite teeth during occlusion. Aka horizontal **overbite**, overjut, horizontal overlap.

**overlap area:** space that is part of several **conspecific** home ranges. Overlap areas may contain a valuable resource; nevertheless, members of different groups attempt to avoid one another in these areas.

**overlap promiscuity:** mating system in which the separate home ranges of males and females overlap, and the sexes mingle occasionally in the **overlap area**.

**overnutrition:** form of **malnutrition** in which excess caloric intake is lacking key nutrients and the end result is one form of obesity.

‡ **oviduct:** see **uterine tube**.

‡ **oviparity:** egg laying; producing eggs that develop, are laid, and hatch externally. Adjective: oviparous. Aka ovipary. Cf. **viviparity**. See **parity**.

**ovism:** form of the **Preformation Doctrine** in which it was believed that a complete organism was dormant in the ovary of the female, and that growth was started by fertilization. Aka **encasement theory**. Cf. **animalculism**.

**ovist:** proponent of **ovism**.

**ovisorption:** resorption of oocytes. In humans some two million oocytes begin to develop while a female is still *in utero* but only about 100,000 remain at puberty. Of these, fewer than 500 will be ovulated.

**ovulation:** release of a mature **oöcyte** (an **ovum** or egg) from a mature **ovarian follicle** into the reproductive tract of a female, where in the **fallopian tube** it has an opportunity to undergo **fertilization** and to develop into a **zygote, embryo**, and **fetus**.

‡ **ovum:** unfertilized egg cell; a female **gamete**, the product of **oögenesis** known as a **secondary oöcyte**. Plural: ova. See **polar body**.

**Owen, Richard** (1804–92): leading comparative anatomist and influential administrator at the British Museum (1856–83); developed Linnaean distinction between homology and analogy; coined the term 'dinosaur'. Owen described the Beagle fossil mammal specimens, but later became one of the best known and most vicious detractors of **Darwinism**, and strove to prove an unbridgeable gap between man and the apes.

**owl-faced monkey:** vernacular for *Cercopithecus hamlyni*.

**owl monkey:** vernacular for species of the genus *Aotus*.

**oxidation:** 1. combining, or causing to combine, with oxygen; the removal of hydrogen. 2. the opposite of **reduction**.

**oxycephaly:** possession of a cone-shaped head. Adjective: oxycephalic. See **microcephaly**.

**oxygen** (O): colorless, odorless gas that constitutes about 20% of the earth's atmosphere; the stable isotope is $^{16}$O. Oxygen is critical to life for all aerobic organisms, including **primates**, for which oxygen deprivation results in **hypoxia**. See **oxygen isotope analysis**. Cf. **nitrogen**.

**oxygen isotope analysis:** measurement of various oxygen isotope ratios found in the calcareous shells of deep-sea marine organisms obtained from deep-sea cores; the ratios can be calibrated with known chronological periods and used to estimate both past ice volumes and past oceanic temperatures.

**oxygen isotope ratio:** ratio of the stable isotopes $^{16}$O : $^{18}$O found in calcareous fossils, and that yields information about the temperature of environments in the past; especially informative concerning the advance and retreat of glacial ice.

**oxygen isotope stage** (OIS): any one of the stages in the **world oxygen isotope stage column**. Any OIS can usually be reconciled with a corresponding stage of the **geomagnetic polarity time scale** and a stage of the **land mammal ages**. Aka marine oxygen isotope stages, oxygen isotope ratios. See **Emiliani–Shackleton glacial sequence** and Appendix 6.

**oxygen radical theory of aging:** see **free radical theory of aging**.

**oxygen uptake:** rate at which oxygen is removed by the blood from **alveolar** gas; Aka oxygen intake.

**oxyhemoglobin** (HbO$_2$): bright red hemoglobin combined with oxygen that is present in arterial blood. Aka oxygenated hemoglobin. Cf. **carboxyhemoglobin**.

‡ **oxytocin:** one of two similar **hormones** produced in the **hypothalamus** but stored and secreted by the **pituitary gland**; it stimulates muscle contractions in the uterine wall and also in muscle cells in the mammary glands, resulting in milk ejection. Oxytocin variation has also been implicated in behavior modification in mammals, and has been proposed as a genetic mediator of attachment behavior in females. Cf. **vasopressin**.

**p:** symbol for the frequency of the first, often dominant, **allele** in a series of alleles in a **Hardy–Weinberg** population. See **q,r.**

**(p+q) = 1:** basic principle that summation of any two **allele frequencies** (p, q) in a one-locus, two-allele genetic system will equal unity (= 1); see $p^2+2pq +q^2=1$.

**(p+q)$^2$=1:** see $p^2+2pq+q^2=1$.

$p^2+2pq+q^2=1$: fundamental principle in biology that summation of any two **allele frequencies** in a one-locus, two-allele genetic system will equal unity {(p+q)=1}; further, that when both sides of such an equation are squared, the resulting binomial expansion results in three terms ($p^2$, $2pq$, $q^2$) that represent three expected **genotype frequencies** when the values of the two allele frequencies (p, q) remain constant. See **Hardy–Weinberg equilibrium.**

**P:** abbreviation for **premolar;** see **P1** (2).

**P1 phage vector:** cloning vector derived from a P1 **bacteriophage** that can accommodate large inserts of foreign DNA.

‡ **P1, P2, P3, etc.:** 1. Mendelian nomenclature for the first parental generation (P1, the parents), the second parental generation (P2, the grandparents), and so forth. Cf. **F1, F2, F3, etc.** 2. notation that makes reference to **premolar** teeth in which the most anterior tooth is the lowest number and the most posterior tooth is the highest number. The number is either lower case (indicating a mandibular tooth) or upper case (indicating a maxillary tooth). There are two ways this is used: (a) in reference to retention or absence of a tooth from the primitive **eutherian** mammalian set of teeth, the dental formula of which is: 3.1.4.3/3.1.4.3. Premolars may have been lost in which case the existing teeth may have premolars designated by a number larger than the number of actual teeth; this is the case among the catarrhines, which have two premolars, P3 and P4, P1 and P2 having been lost through time. (b) in reference to the teeth that are present in an existing species. The anterior most molar would be P1 regardless of the ancestral condition. Cf. **M1, M2, M3, etc.**

**p53 tumor suppressor (protein)** (TP53): a protein with a molecular mass of 53 kilodaltons; normally restrains the proliferation of cells, and is involved in 60% of all cancer types, but especially cervical and colon cancers. 'Wild type p53' normally functions as a tumor suppressor or 'cancer killer', by proliferating rapidly in the presence of a nascent tumor. p53 normally activates cell growth inhibitors, resulting in **apoptosis**; it suppresses DNA transcription until polymerase enzymes can repair DNA damaged by carcinogens. Mutations in p53 can cause cessation of these functions, leading to familial cancers. Most p53 mutations are new (de novo) somatic mutations. About 35 allelic mutations have been described, each associated with a specific cancer or variant. The unmutated p53 tumor suppressor is a candidate for **gene therapy.** The p53R2 gene may mediate the effects of the p53 tumor suppressor gene. Cf. **ras oncogene.**

**Pääbo, Svante** (1955– ): Swedish molecular biologist, Director of the Max-Planck-Institute for Evolutionary Biology in Leipzig; one of the first technicians to consistently extract **ancient DNA** from a variety of fossil specimens. Using the **PCR** technique, Pääbo and his colleagues have extracted DNA from Egyptian mummy tissue, Paleoindian bone, and the bones of **Neandertals.** In the latter case, he has suggested that Neandertals may not be closely related (i.e. ancestral) to **AMHs.** He has published extensively, including 'Neandertal DNA sequences and the origin of modern humans', Cell 90(1): 19–30 (1997).

**Pacchonian depression:** any one of several small pits found on the internal surface of the parietal and posterior frontal along the sagittal suture. In life these pits are occupied by arachnoid granulations and associated tissues.

**Pachylemur Lamberton, 1948: monotypic** genus of **subfossil Malagasy prosimian** with an affinity to the **extant** lemurid species **Varecia variegata;** known from several sites in north, central, and south Madagascar. The skull and dentition are very similar to those of Varecia and suggest **frugivory.** However, the appendicular skeleton is much more robust and has led some workers to propose that this lemur was terrestrial or semi-terrestrial. The one accepted species is P. insignis and this species appears to have become **extinct** between 2–1 kya. See Appendix 2 for taxonomy, Appendix 3 for living species.

**pachyostosis:** benign increase in bone thickness.

**pachytene stage:** in **meiosis**, stage of prophase in which each paired chromosome separates into its two component sister chromatids so that each homologous chromosome pair becomes a set of four intertwined chromatids called a **bivalent.** Aka pachynema.

**Pacinian corpuscle:** see **lamellated corpuscle.**

**paedomorphosis:** see **pedomorphosis** and **neoteny.**

**Pagai langur:** vernacular for **Simias** concolor.

**PAGE:** polyacrylamide gel electrophoresis, a method that separates DNA fragments based upon their size and net molecular charge, which combine to determine the speed of migration of individual fragments through a porous gel in the presence of an electrical field.

**pair:** any two similar, identical, or associated things.

**pair bond:** behavioral association between a male and a female that form a transient **consortship**, as opposed to a mating pair that end their relationship following copulation. The relationship may be of short duration, lasting only until the end of the **breeding season**, or it may last a lifetime. In animals, pair bonding often facilitates the cooperative rearing of offspring. See **monogamy**. Cf. **pairmates**.

**pairing:** attachment of two homologous chromosomes in a sideward direction, prior to their exchange of genetic material (**crossing over**) during **meiosis**.

**pairmates:** unit consisting of a male and a female, but not an exclusive mating pair. Cf. **pair bond**.

*Palaeanthropus* **Bonarell, 1909:** synonym for *Homo*.

*Palaechthon* **Gidley, 1923:** archaic mammal known from the middle to late Paleocene of North America belonging to the **Plesiadapiformes** family **Palaechthonidae**; three or four species. Dental formula: 2.1.2.3/2.1.2.3; reduced canines; may have been **omnivorous**. Body mass of the species ranges between 60 and 150 g. Large **infraorbital foramen** indicates possession of **vibrissae**; features of the cranium reveal laterally placed eyes and poorly developed stereoscopic vision, if at all. See Appendix 1 for taxonomy.

**Palaechthonidae:** family of archaic fossil mammals belonging to the order **Plesiadapiformes**. Known from the middle to late Paleocene of North America; six genera of forms ranging from 50 to 600 g. Considered to be closely related to the microsyopids, and some authors include the palaechthonids with the **Microsyopidae**. Dental formula: 2.1.3.3/2.1.3.3; dentition and body size of smaller forms suggest **insectivory**, larger forms consuming plant matter with insect supplements. Cranial features indicate these animals had poor, if any, stereoscopic vision, and a large infraorbital foramen attests to **vibrissae**; it has been suggested that these animals were **fossorial**. See Appendix 1 for taxonomy.

**Palaeopropithecidae:** subfossil Malagasy prosimian family to which the sloth lemurs belong. There are four genera and five species. Affinities appear to be with the **Indriidae**. All members of this family have experienced a recent extinction, possibly due to human intervention. See *Mesopithecus*, *Babakotia*, *Palaeopropithecus*, and *Archaeoindris*.

*Palaeopropithecus* **Grandidier, 1899:** monotypic genus of extinct **subfossil Malagasy prosimians** belonging to the **Palaeopropithecidae**. One recognized species, *P. ingens*, with a second species proposed. Known from central, southwest, and south Madagascar. Curved **phalanges** and forelimbs that are longer than hindlimbs suggest extreme arboreal suspensory mode of locomotion; diurnal. Body mass estimates between 40 and 60 kg. Dental formula: 2.1.2.3/1.1.2.3 or 2.1.2.3/2.0.2.3; dentition suggests **folivory**. See Appendix 2 for taxonomy, Appendix 3 for living species.

**palatal breadth** (ecm–ecm): distance between the left and right **endomolare** measured with sliding calipers or a **palatometer**. See Appendix 7 for an illustration of the landmarks used.

**palatal index:** ratio of palatal width to palatal length; **palatal breadth** divided by **palatal length** multiplied by 100. See **leptostaphyline, mesostaphyline, brachystaphyline**.

**palatal length** (pr–alv): **craniometric** measurement; distance from prosthion to alveolon measured with sliding calipers or a palatometer. See Appendix 7 for an illustration of the landmarks used.

**palate:** roof of the mouth. A mammalian characteristic that separates the buccal cavity from the nasal cavity; it allows breathing to continue while food is masticated. Adjective: palatal, palatine. See **palatine bone, hard palate,** and **soft palate**.

**palatine bone:** one of a pair of L-shaped bones situated posterior to a **maxillary bone**. These bones help construct the **hard palate** and portions of the floor and sides of the **nasal cavity**.

**palatine process:** portion of the **maxillary bone** that projects horizontally and medially; this structure helps to form the **hard palate**.

**palatometer: anthropometric** instrument designed to obtain measurements of palate depth and width; a type of caliper.

**pale-faced saki:** vernacular for *Pithecia pithecia*.

**Palearctic Region:** Europe, North Africa, and all of Asia exclusive of the **Oriental Region**.

*Palenochtha* **(Simpson, 1937):** archaic mammal known from the middle to late Paleocene of North America, belonging to the **Plesiadapiformes** family **Palaechthonidae**; monotypic. Body mass estimated to average 20 g. Dental formula: 2.1.2.3; enlarged incisors, reduced canines; sharp cusps on molars. Diet probably **insectivory**. See Appendix 1 for taxonomy.

**paleoanthropic:** referring to any actual fossil specimen or to a hypothetical construct of early humans, especially when applied to intermediate forms such as **Neandertals**. Cf. **neanthropic, protoanthropic**.

**Paleoanthropidae:** putative **hominoid** family proposed by Louis **Leakey** in 1934 to include a presapiens clade that he suggested had branched off from the line that later gave rise to modern humans (see **Neoanthropidae**); the older family included the **Neandertals**, Broken Hill (**Kabwe**), **Mauer**, and the Asian hominids *Pithecanthropus* and *Sinanthropus*, according to Leakey.

‡ **paleoanthropology:** a subdiscipline within **physical anthropology** that studies older material evidence for **hominid evolution**. Paleoanthropology is a multidisciplinary science encompassing **paleontology**, the earth sciences, **prehistoric archaeology**, behavioral science, **paleopalynology**, vertebrate

and invertebrate **paleontology, taphonomy, functional morphology**, biomechanics, **systematics, evolutionary theory**, and **molecular biology**.

***Paleoanthropus heidelbergensis* Bonarelli, 1909:** Mauer mandible; see ***Homo heidelbergensis*.**

***Paleoanthropus palestinensis* McCown and Keith, 1939:** binomen applied to the material recovered in the 1920s from the **Tabūn** and **Skhūl** caves at Mt. Carmel in modern Israel. It is now recognized that the Tabūn material belongs to ***Homo neanderthalensis*** whereas the Skhūl material is referred to ***Homo sapiens*.**

**Paleoarctica:** Old World portion of **Holarctica**.

**paleoautopsy:** technical analysis of a human burial by a trained physical anthropologist specializing in paleopathology.

**paleobotany:** study of prehistoric **flora**.

‡ **Paleocene epoch:** one of the **Tertiary** epochs of the **Cenozoic era**, lasting from about 65 to 55.5 mya, in which the horses, hares, whales, and many rodents (rats, mice, squirrels) first appeared in the fossil record. See Appendix 4 for a geological time scale.

**paleoclimatology:** study of prehistoric climates.

**paleocommunity:** all preserved taxa comprising a fossil **faunal assemblage**.

**paleodemography:** study of populations that existed in the past; paleodemography differs from **demography** in that estimates of population size, rates of **migration, fertility**, and **mortality** are subject to the vagaries of differential fossil bone preservation and other uncontrollable factors that all contribute to a wide latitude in possible estimated values.

**paleodontology:** study of fossil teeth that provides ecological information about an animal, such as type of diet, perhaps information on the role of the organism in the environment, the size of the animal, and systematic relationships to other species.

**paleoecological reconstruction:** extrapolation of an ancient environment based on physical evidence such as fossilized plant material (that helps to indicate climate, pH, etc.) and fossilized animal remains (certain types of animal are found in certain ecozones).

‡ **paleoecology:** study of extinct communities and ancient environments, e.g. types of food eaten by fossil forms, or their requirements for reproduction.

**paleoethnobotany:** analysis and interpretation of interrelationships between people and plants from evidence in the archaeological record; sometimes called archaeobotany.

**paleoethnography:** study of extinct human lifeways.

**paleofeces:** see **coprolite**.

**Paleogene system:** in geology, the time-stratigraphic unit composed of the **Tertiary** sub-period containing the Paleocene, Eocene and Oligocene epochs of the **Cenozoic era**. See **Neogene system** and **Quaternary**.

**paleogeography:** study of spatial conditions in ancient times such as the physical location of land masses and bodies of water, and the habitats of the organisms that later were uncovered as fossils.

**paleoindian:** 1. earliest well-defined archaeological phase in the Americas, dating from the oldest sites to about 12 kya. 2. a **Native American**. See **Clovis**.

**paleo-Lake Olduvai:** depressed area of water collection that formed initially 3.6 mya when the eruption of the Sadiman volcano just west of the Ngorongoro crater covered the area with a thick layer of ash that was compressed and stabilized by rain (the same eruption that captured the footprints at **Laetoli**). The Ngorongoro volcano then erupted at 2.5 mya, depositing another layer of volcanic ash. Finally, at 1.89 mya, the Olmoti volcano, north of Ngorongoro, erupted and covered the whole area with a thick, nonporous black **basalt**. This layer formed the bottom of the gorge, just beneath **Olduvai Bed I**, and formed the basin of a brackish permanent lake in which Plio-Pleistocene sediments collected for the next 400 ky. Paleo-lake Olduvai was a semi-arid, enclosed basin in which seasonal rainfall patterns controlled sediment deposition at the lake margin: waxy clays deposited during wet periods and earthy sediments characteristic of dry periods. The perennial (minimum) diameter of the lake was about 5–10 km, but episodically the maximum expansion was to about 15–20 km. Finally, owing to tectonic faulting and uplifting about 1.5 mya, the paleolake drained, although a stream remained that eventually cut today's **Olduvai Gorge**. See **western Olduvai Gorge**.

**paleolith:** archaic term for any Pleistocene stone implement. Cf. **eolith**.

‡ **Paleolithic Age:** of or relating to the **Old Stone Age** and consisting of lower, middle and upper **stages**. The paleolithic assemblages emcompass the range roughly 2.4 mya to 14 kya.

**Paleolithic edge-to-mass ratios:** ratio indicating the length of cutting edge per mass unit of material; cutting edge-to-mass ratios in Paleolithic tools increased dramatically as **knapping techniques** improved: **Oldowan** (2 : 1), **Abbevillean** (3 : 1), **Acheulean** (8 : 1), **Mousterian** (40 : 1), **Magdalenean** (250 : 1).

**Paleolithicum:** archaic term for the study of any older chipped stone implement. Cf. **paleolith**.

**paleomagnetic column:** magnetographic profile of a region. See **paleomagnetism**.

**paleomagnetic dating:** method of dating sites based on the fact that the earth's magnetic poles have shifted polarity at irregular intervals during the earth's history; a **relative dating technique**. See **paleomagnetism**.

**paleomagnetic reversal:** reversal of the magnetic polarity of the earth that occurs irregularly, e.g. **Olduvai event**. See **paleomagnetism**.

‡ **paleomagnetism:** study of the residual magnetism of rocks that were formed in earlier time periods, usually deposited as the result of volcanic action. The study of changes in the earth's magnetic fields during geologic time has resulted in the observation that the earth's current **polarity** (3) (a **normal polarity epoch**) has often been reversed in the past (a **reversed polarity epoch**). The (paleo)magnetic time scale of the earth is now well known, so that **magnetostratigraphy** and **paleomagnetic dating** are now common. Aka archaeomagnetism, geomagnetism.

**paleoneurology:** study of the nervous system, particularly the anatomy of the brain, in fossils, using information derived primarily from **endocasts**. See **cranial capacity**.

**paleo-Olduvai Lake:** see **paleo-Lake Olduvai**.

‡ **paleontology:** study of **fossils** by scientists (paleontologists) who utilize the **scientific method** and (usually) an evolutionary **paradigm** for their interpretation. Adjective: paleontological. Cf. **neontology**.

**paleonutrition:** reconstruction of prehistoric diets and their nutritional value from archaeological remains; chemical analysis of both food waste and skeletal remains at archaeological sites, as well as types and frequency of harvesting implements are used to estimate the nutritional state of prehistoric populations. See **carbon isotope analysis** and **paleopathology**.

**paleopalynology:** see **palynology**.

‡ **paleopathology:** study of **disease** in prehistoric populations based upon the analysis of **mummies**, remains of **skeletons**, and other archaeological evidence. The term was first applied to the study of diseases in early animals, but has come to be increasingly applied to human populations as well.

**Paleopathology Association:** organization composed of researchers, scientists and students from many fields, including physical anthropology, medicine, archaeology, and egyptology from around the world. The Association meets annually in North America, and biennially in Europe. It sponsors *The Paleopathology Newsletter*, a quarterly publication.

**paleosol:** sedimentary rock formed from an ancient or fossil soil; a stratigraphic marker for interglaciation.

‡ **paleospecies: fossil** organisms that are assigned to the same species. Because of the time spans involved, paleospecies often exhibit more **variation** than living **species**. In the **hominid** lineage, for example, the paleospecies nomen *Homo erectus* has been applied to fossils that span over a million years.

**paleotechnic phase:** Mumford's 1934 term for a phase of technological development characterized by the increasing use of **prime movers** such as coal and iron, and that culminated as the industrial revolution. See **technology**.

‡ **Paleozoic era:** first geologic era of the **Phanerozoic eon**, dating roughly between 545 and 245 mya. The first vertebrates (see **Vertebrata**) appeared during this era, including the reptiles and mammal-like reptiles.

**paleozoogeography:** study of the geographical distributions of animals and their habitats during past geological **epochs**. Cf. **zoogeography, phytogeography**.

**Paley, William** (1743–1805): Anglican clergyman and theologian; author of *Natural Theology* (1802) and inventor of one of the better-known statements on the 'Grand Design'. See **Paley's watchmaker argument**.

**Paley's watchmaker argument:** famous anti-evolution 'watchmaker' argument by **William Paley** for the existence of God. 'The marks of design are too strong to be gotten over. Design must have had a designer. That designer must have been a person. That person is God.' Paley argued specifically that the eye is too complex to have evolved. Cf. **argument from design**.

**palindrome:** word, phrase or sentence that reads the same in both directions; applied to a sequence of base pairs in DNA that reads the same in the 5′ to 3′ direction on complementary strands of DNA. Many recognition sites for **restriction enzymes** are palindromic sequences.

**palingenesis:** 1. the development of individuals already preformed within an egg. 2. recapitulation of past phylogenetic stages manifested in the ontogeny of a descendent; term coined by **Haeckel**. Adjective: palingenetic.

**pallium:** gray matter covering the cerebral hemispheres. G. Elliot **Smith** distinguished three constituents, the **archepallium, mesopallium**, and **neopallium**. Aka *cortex cerebri*.

**palmar:** regional term for the inferior surface of the hand; i.e. the palm. Cf. **Plantar**.

**palmaris muscle:** muscle that acts on the hand. The palmaris longus originates from the medial epicondyle of the humerus and inserts into the fascia of the palm. Its action is to flex the hand at the wrist and is useful during hanging and climbing. This muscle is missing in 11% of modern **AMHs**. See **vestigial trait**.

**palmigrade:** type of quadrupedal locomotion in which the mass of the upper body is placed on the palms of the fore paws rather than on the digits or knuckles. Cf. **digitigrade, plantigrade, knuckle-walking, fist walking**.

**palmprint:** dermatoglyphic grooves of the skin in the palmar region. They are unique to each individual, making them equivalent to **fingerprints** as a potential means of identification. However, their larger size makes them more difficult to obtain than fingerprints.

**palpebra:** eyelid; movable protective section of skin that covers and uncovers the eyeball of most terrestrial vertebrates. In humans the palpebra may have a thick fat layer or almost no fat at all, influencing the appearance of the eye. See **eye fold**.

**paludism:** French term for **malaria**.

‡ **palynology:** study of fossil pollen that allows prehistoric plant species to be identified, and paleoclimates to be reconstructed based upon the ecology of those species. Aka pollen analysis.

*Pan* **Oken, 1816: hominoid** genus that includes the chimpanzees and bonobos; two species. Found in variable environment of western and central equatorial Africa. Terrestrial and arboreal; diurnal; locomotion is a specialized form of quadrupedalism referred to as **knuckle-walking**; lacks tail. **Sexually dimorphic** in body size; body mass, males 45–80 kg, females 33–68 kg. Dental formula: 2.1.2.3; primarily **frugivorous**; diet also includes **faunivory** with small vertebrates and social insects consumed. Live in mixed-sex groups, which undergo **fission** into foraging parties during the day; males are the **resident sex**. See Appendix 2 for taxonomy, Appendix 3 for living species. See *Pan paniscus* and *Pan troglodytes*.

*Pan gorilla* **Tuttle, 1967:** synonym for *Gorilla gorilla*.

‡ *Pan paniscus* **Schwarz, 1929:** bonobo; aka lesser or pygmy chimpanzee; **monotypic** species. Has restricted distribution in the tropical forests of Zaire, south of the Zaire River (and south of the distribution for *P. troglodytes*). Slight **sexual dimorphism** in body size; body mass for males about 45 kg, females 33 kg. Principally **frugivorous**, but also consumes small vertebrates. Social organization similar to that of *P. troglodytes*, but more interaction between males and females. Some researchers think that bonobos are more appropriate models for human evolution than common chimpanzees are; they share several behavioral traits with humans, particularly in the bonding between females and males. Bonobos were not accepted as a valid taxon by the majority of workers until fairly recently; the vernaculars lesser and pygmy chimpanzee are now not in favor. See *Pan* and *Pan troglodytes*.

‡ *Pan troglodytes* **(Blumenbach, 1775):** chimpanzee; three subspecies recognized. Occupies variable habitats ranging from savanna to tropical rain forest throughout western and central equatorial Africa. **Sexual dimorphism** in both body and canine size; males weigh 56–80 kg, females 45–68 kg. Since the 1960s chimps have been studied extensively; they are considered an important model for early human evolution. Among the findings relating to human evolution are that chimps make and use tools, that they are capable of learning language in a laboratory situation, and that males hunt small mammals; food sharing occurs through 'begging'. Molecular evidence shows that chimp DNA is 98.4% identical to human DNA. The word 'chimpanzee' itself comes from a Congolese dialect and means 'mock man'. See *Pan*.

**pancreas:** mixed **exocrine/endocrine** organ located in the abdominal cavity near the stomach that secretes gastric juice into the **gastrointestinal tract** as well as **insulin**, somatostatin and glucagon into the bloodstream.

**pancreatic islets:** clusters of hormone-secreting cells in the vertebrate **pancreas**; alpha cells secrete glucagon, and beta cells secrete **insulin**. Aka islets of Langerhans.

‡ **pandemic:** extensive outbreak of **disease** that affects large numbers of people or animals over a wide geographic region. See **endemic** and **epidemic**.

*Pandemonium dis* **Van Valen, 1994:** recently recognized species from the early Paleocene of the Rocky Mountain region of North America belonging to the archaic mammal family **Plesiadapidae**. Considered by some to be a link between *Purgatorius* and the basal plesiadapid *Pronothodectes*; it shares traits with both. Complete dental formula unknown. See Appendix 1 for taxonomy.

**pandiacritic:** pertaining to the condition in which every member of a race or breed is recognizable as such. Cf. **typology**, **microdiacritic**, and **mesodiacritic**.

**panecumenical:** referring to an organism found in all kinds of environments.

**panethnic:** of or pertaining to a belief, behavior, feature, trait, or disease that is found in two or more ethnic groups.

‡ **Pangaea:** literally, 'all lands'; the supercontinent that included all of the present-day continents; during the early **Mesozoic**, Pangaea began to break up into **Gondwana** and **Laurasia**. Also spelled Pangea.

**pangenesis:** obsolete theory of development that claimed that pangenes or gemmules from different parts of a body collected in the reproductive cells and were transmitted to offspring. The idea originated with Hippocrates, was implicit in the work of **Lamarck**, and explicit in Charles **Darwin's** theory of reproduction (but not evolution or natural selection). Discarded in 1892 in favor of the **germ-plasm theory** and the proposal of **Weismann's barrier**, which specifically countered the proposed action of granular pangenes or gemmules.

**Panina:** nomen for a subtribe of the tribe **Hominini** used in some classificatory schemes; this subtribe consists of the genus *Pan* and its species and subspecies.

**panmictic unit:** any population in which there is **random mating**; a **deme**.

**panmixia:** complete promiscuity, a synonym for **random mating**; panmixis. The opposite of **assortative mating** and **sexual selection**.

**panmixis:** see **random mating**.

**pan-neutralism:** strong form of the **neutral drift theory** (NDT) that denies the existence of **natural selection**. The weak form of NDT allows for some cases of selection.

**Panninae:** subfamily of the family **Pongidae**, **Pannidae**, or **Hominidae** depending on the classificatory scheme used; this subfamily consists of *Pan*, its species and subspecies, and may include *Gorilla* and its species and subspecies.

**Panobius afridi Russell and Gingerich, 1987:** adapoid prosimian from the middle Eocene of Africa belonging to the notharctid subfamily **Cercamoniinae**; **monotypic**. Body mass estimated at 130 g. See Appendix 1 for taxonomy.

**papillae:** small nipplelike projections; e.g. the papillae of the primate tongue. Singular: papilla.

**papillary pattern:** feature of the ridges on the fingers and palms. See **dermatoglyphics**.

**papilloma:** benign **neoplasm** of the skin, commonly known as a wart.

**Papio Erxleben, 1777:** cercopithecine genus to which the baboons belong; taxonomy in dispute; there is a great deal of hybridization on the boundaries of the species. Most authorities recognize five **allopatric** species; however, some workers include the two *Mandrillus* species as a **subgenus** within *Papio*; another view treats all five species as **subspecies** of *P. hamadryas*, which is regarded as a superspecies. Found throughout Sub-Saharan Africa in open areas and in southwestern Arabia. Terrestrial; diurnal; quadrupedal. **Sexually dimorphic** in body size and dental proportions. Largest of the cercopithecines, with body mass 10–50 kg, with females about half the male body mass. Dental formula: 2.1.2.3 with large canines and lower **sectorial premolars** that hone the upper canines; **omnivorous**; possess **cheek pouches**. Elongated muzzle. Social organization varies. Baboons, occupying environments similar to that of early hominids, have been used as ecological models for human evolution. See *Mandrillus*. See Appendix 2 for taxonomy, Appendix 3 for living species.

**parabolic dental arcade: alveolar arch** that is horseshoe- or soft-U shaped; characteristic of the genus *Homo*. Cf. **parallel dental arcade**, **convergent dental arcade**.

**paracatarrhine:** term applied to the Oligocene parapithecids in some systematic schemes in which the parapithecids and catarrhines are viewed as parallel developments. Cf. **eucatarrhine**. See **Parapithecidae**, **catarrhine**.

**paracentric inversion:** major chromosome anomaly in which a portion of a chromosome that does not include the **centromere** is inverted compared with the normal **linkage** sequence for a species. See **inversion**.

**Paracolobus R. Leakey, 1969:** genus of colobine monkeys known from the Pliocene and Pleistocene of eastern Africa; two species. The type specimen is a remarkable recovery of an almost complete articulated male skeleton. Several features of the **postcranial** skeletal appear to be adaptations for terrestrial quadrupedalism; *Paracolobus* was probably **semiterrestrial**. Estimated body mass around 35 kg, making it the largest colobine currently described. Dental formula: 2.1.2.3/2.1.2.3; dentition similar to that of **extant** colobines and indicates a **folivorous** diet. See Appendix 1 for taxonomy.

**paracone: cusp** on the mesiobuccal **occlusal surface** of an upper molar; it helps form the **buccal** portion of the **trigon**. Cf. **paraconid**.

**paraconid: cusp** on the mesiobuccal **occlusal surface** of a lower molar; it helps form the **buccal** portion of the **trigonid**. Cf. **paracone**.

**paraconule: cuspid** on the mesiolingual **occlusal surface** of some mammalian and primate upper molars, adjacent to the **paracone**.

**paracrine:** denoting a type of **hormone** function in which a hormone that is synthesized in and released from endocrine cells binds to its receptor in nearby target cells of a different type and affects their function. Cf. **autocrine** and **exocrine**.

**paracrista:** ridge of enamel that courses from the **paracone** of an upper molar in some archaic mammals and early primates.

‡ **paradigm:** 1. model of the world or a part of the world nested within a cosmology. 2. a fixed arrangement or pattern, often seen as a set of elements. 3. term often synonymous with **normal science**.

**paradigm shift:** in science, a change in meaning ascribed to a pattern of data; reinterpretation, as in the shift from **geocentrism** to **heliocentrism** during the **Copernican revolution**.

**Paradolichopithecus Necrasav, Samson and Radulesco, 1961:** genus of **cercopithecines** known from the Pliocene of Europe; two species recognized; this genus is very similar to the Asian *Procynocephalus* and may eventually be included within that genus. It has a mosaic of macaque and baboon traits;

the cranium is macaque-like, the teeth and **postcrania** are baboon-like; limb structure suggests this was a terrestrial monkey. Estimated body mass ranges between 20 and 35 kg. Dental formula: 2.1.3.3; dental morphology suggests a **graminivorous** diet with tuber and fruit supplements. See Appendix 1 for taxonomy.

**paradoxical sleep:** resting state in which an **elecroencephalogram** depicts **brain waves** that resemble the arousal state, yet it is during this state that the sleeper is most difficult to awaken. During paradoxical sleep the eyes move rapidly under the eyelids, dreams occur, and males experience penile erection although muscles are inhibited. Aka REM sleep. See **sleeping behavior.**

**paragene:** any extrachromosomal replicating unit or hereditary determinant such as a **plasmid** or **mitochondrion.**

**paragenetic:** of or pertaining to an effect on the expression of a gene that is not due to a structural change in the gene itself, but to a chromosomal repatterning that introduces a **position effect** or **spreading position effect.**

**parahippocampal gyrus:** connection pathway for several regions of the brain, including the **cerebral cortex** and the **hippocampal formation**; a part of the **limbic system.**

**parallel cousin:** a child either of one's mother's sister or of one's father's brother. Aka ortho-cousin. Cf. **cross-cousin.**

**parallel dental arcade: alveolar** row in which the molars and premolars are parallel to their opposite tooth and the anterior teeth are perpendicular to the cheek teeth, forming a hard-U shape; characteristic of the great apes and many other primates. Cf. **parabolic dental arcade, convergent dental arcade.**

‡ **parallel evolution:** 1. changes that continue along similar lines in related taxa that have become separated but that remain exposed to similar selective pressures; for example, **New World monkeys** and **Old World monkeys** have been separated for at least 26 my, yet have both evolved clearly as monkeys; see **parallelism.** 2. as used by some workers, independent evolution of similar morphological features in separate lineages due to a similarity of selection pressures; **convergence.**

**parallelism:** evolution of similar characters from ancestral traits in two different taxa that have a recent common ancestry, but are isolated from one another. Aka **parallel evolution.**

**paralogous homology:** pseudo-homologous structures that have arisen independently in two taxa, and not shared by their remote most common ancestor. In molecular taxonomy, such convergences arise through **gene duplication.** Cf. **orthologous homology.**

*Paralouatta* **Rivero and Arredondo, 1991:** Cuban monkey; **monotypic** platyrrhine genus. *P. varonae* is the sole species; presumed recently extinct (no dates yet available, but some workers think that this species survived until around 5 kya, although others think that it is not a recent primate). Known from a small amount of material, including a well-preserved skull, recovered in western Cuba in the late 1980s and early 1990s. Similar in size to *Alouatta*, but the cusp pattern on the molars is quite different, suggesting a very different diet. See Appendix 2 for taxonomy, Appendix 3 for living species.

**paralysis:** loss of voluntary control of muscles owing to some impairment of the nervous system.

**parameter:** quantity that can be held constant in a model while other quantities are being varied to study their relationships, but which may be changed in other particular versions of the same model; also used loosely to designate any variable property that exerts an effect upon a system. See **population parameter.**

**parametric statistics:** statistics obtained for a sample assumed to have been drawn from a population with a **normal distribution**, and to which estimations of **population parameters** can be made (mean, mode, standard deviation, etc.). Cf. **nonparametric test.**

**parametric tests:** in statistics, any test in which the **null hypothesis** is stated in terms of population parameters.

**paramolar:** supernumerary tooth located near the mesiobuccal margin of a molar.

**paramorphic homology:** presence in two distinct species of fixed polypeptide variants whose ancestral forms were polymorphic alleles in the single common ancestral species. Aka polymorphism-dependent homology.

**paranasal:** pertaining to the area running parallel to the nasal cavity.

**paranasal sinuses:** four pairs of air-filled cavities that occur within the maxillary, frontal, ethmoid, and sphenoid bones. In life these sinuses are lined by mucous membranes that are continuous with the lining of the nasal cavity. As these sinuses develop during growth, along with the mastoid air cells, they reduce the density of the head and serve as resonation chambers for the human voice. Energetics physiologists also attribute energy conservation to the sinuses because muscle size can be smaller with a less dense head. These sinuses are expanded in **Neandertals.** See **sinus.**

**Paranthropinae Broom, 1950:** defunct subfamily erected by R. **Broom** to include specimens from **Kromdraai** and **Swartkrans** then attributed to the species *Paranthropus robustus* and *Paranthropus crassidens*, respectively.

‡ **paranthropine:** referring generally to any species in the more pongid-like genus *Paranthropus*. In the formal sense, a member of the subfamily **Paranthropinae** of the family **Hominidae**. See *Paranthropus* and *Australopithecus*.

‡ *Paranthropus* **Broom, 1938:** generic nomen assigned to a group of robust South African fossil **hominids**; literally, 'beside or equal-to-man', 'next-to-man'. **Paranthropines** are distinguished by relatively smaller incisors and canines, relatively larger premolars and molars, a shorter snout and flatter face, more robust **zygomatics** and presence of a **sagittal crest** (both sexes), and a flatter forehead with 'dished' face that is hafted high on the **neurocranium**. There is no trace of a chin; the strongly developed root systems are set in massive bone; the areas of support and the channels of dissipation of the forces generated by chewing are well developed.

The total lack of a true forehead and the relatively great **postorbital constriction** make the brow ridges seem massive and projecting, although in fact they are not especially strongly developed. The paranthropines have an **encephalization quotient** equivalent to that of a modern ape. The craniofacial specialization, along with increased tooth wear, led **Robinson** to conclude that *Paranthropus* was a plant eater, and the presence of grit in the diet suggested the consumption of roots and bulbs. Aka robust australopithecines. See box below for species.

**paranucleus:** accessory nucleus or small chromatin body resembling a nucleus, sometimes seen in the cell protoplasm lying just outside of the cell nucleus. Adjective: paranuclear.

*Parapapio* **Jones, 1937:** genus of cercopithecines known from the late Miocene through the early Pleistocene of sub-Saharan Africa; five species

---

### Species within the genus *Paranthropus*

*Paranthropus aethiopicus* (Walker, Leakey, Harris and Brown, 1986): hominid species from the Pliocene of East Africa, dating from 2.8 to 2.2 mya. So far, the earliest member of the robust line of australopithecines, but with even more rugged features associated with **mastication**, which were probably an adaptation to tough, gritty and fibrous vegetable foods. The first **fossil** found representing this species was this so-called **black skull**; Aka *Australopithecus aethiopicus*. See **Lomekwi localities**.

*Paranthropus africanus* Olson, 1981: see *Australopithecus africanus*.

*Paranthropus boisei* (Robinson, 1960): hyper-robust, highly **derived** East African **hominid**, dating from *c*. 2–1 mya. **OH 5** is the type specimen. The **skull** is highly adapted for chewing tough, hard morsels. The cheek teeth are the largest and most enameled of any known hominid species. The canine is reduced above the tooth row; incisors are small. The mandible is thick and heavily buttressed in the symphyseal region. The **mandibular ramus** is vertical and tall. This species possesses an anteriorly oriented **sagittal crest** and a well-developed **nuchal crest**. The face is **orthognathous**, presenting a dish-shaped appearance. Mean **cranial capacity** about 520 cm$^3$. Skull heavily **pneumatized**. Body mass estimated at 50 kg; height 135–170 cm. Some researchers consider this form to be a **subspecies** (*P. robustus boisei*) of the South African robust form. *P. boisei* differs from *P. robustus* in a number of features, including greater maxillary depth, more flared **zygomatics**, and a generally more heavily built skeleton. The highly derived nature of *P. boisei* excludes it as the ancestor of later humans. See *Paranthropus robustus*.

*Paranthropus crassidens* Broom, 1949: 'large-toothed robust equal of man'; species binomen proposed from material recovered at **Swartkrans**. This material is now subsumed under *Paranthropus robustus*.

*Paranthropus paleojavanicus* Robinson, 1954: binomen applied to material found at **Sangiran**, Indonesia; this material was included within *Paranthropus* because certain features led researchers to think that this was either an extension of the range of this genus or an equivalent grade of hominid in Southeast Asia.

*Paranthropus* (= *Australopitnecus*) *robustus*: see *Australopithecus robustus* and *Paranthropus robustus*.

*Paranthropus robustus* (Broom, 1938): robust **hominid** that lived between 2.2 and 1 mya; found in South Africa only. Type specimen from **Kromdraai**. Skull highly adapted for chewing tough, hard morsels. Cheek teeth are large and heavily enameled; canines reduced; incisors small. Mandible is thick and heavily buttressed in the symphyseal region; the **mandibular ramus** is vertical and tall. This species possesses an anteriorly oriented **sagittal crest** and a well-developed **nuchal crest**. Face is **orthognathous**, presenting a dish-shaped appearance. Pronounced **supra-orbital torus**. Mean **cranial capacity** about 530 cm$^3$. Heavily **pneumatized** skull. Estimated body mass 32–40 kg; height 110–132 cm. The derived nature of *P. robustus* excludes it as the ancestor of later humans. See *Paranthropus boisei*.

recognized; known from **crania** only. It has a mosaic of baboon and mangabey traits. Very little **sexual dimorphism**. Estimated body mass ranges from 17 to 30 kg. Dental formula: 2.1.2.3/2.1.2.3. Presumed to be terrestrial. See Appendix 1 for taxonomy.

**parapatric speciation:** speciation in which the new species forms from a population contiguous with the ancestral species' range. Aka peripatric speciation, peripheralistic speciation. See **centrifugal speciation**.

**parapatry:** living in contiguous ranges or zones of habitation. Adjective: parapatric. Cf. **sympatry, allopatry**.

**paraphyletic:** pertaining to a taxon that does not include all descendant species; for example, the Class Reptilia does not include birds, which are nevertheless believed to be descended from Jurassic reptiles.

**paraphyletic classification:** classification in which a taxonomic group contains some, but not all, of the members of a clade.

**paraphyletic group:** set of species containing an ancestral species together with some, but not all, of its descendants; the species included in the group are those that have continued to resemble the ancestor; the excluded species have evolved rapidly and no longer resemble their ancestor. See **bushy lineage**.

**paraphyly:** see **paraphyletic group**.

**Parapithecidae:** family of **anthropoids** known from the late Eocene to Oligocene of North Africa. Contains five genera and nine species. Most primitive anthropoids; dental formula: 2.1.3.3/2.1.3.3; these are the only Old World higher primates with three premolars. See Appendix 1 for taxonomy.

**Parapithecoidea:** 1. superfamily of fossil **anthropoids** consisting of the family **Parapithecidae** and genera whose precise phylogenetic relationships are unknown. 2. infraorder of **Anthropoidea**; not widely recognized.

*Parapithecus* Schlosser, 1910: catarrhine genus from the early Oligocene of North Africa belonging to the **anthropoid** family **Parapithecidae**; most workers recognize two species; known from only a few jaws; relationship to later primates uncertain. Dental formula equivocal; formerly thought to be 2.1.3.3/ 2.1.3.3, but now it is uncertain whether this species had adult incisors; rounded cusps on molars suggestive of **frugivory**. Estimated body mass around 1.7 kg. See Appendix 1 for taxonomy.

**parasagittal:** parallel to the sagittal suture.

**parasagittal depression:** 1. one of the slight depressions along both sides of the **sagittal suture** of the two parietal bones. 2. small **fossa** that extends along the side of the mid-sagittal keel in some *Homo erectus* specimens.

**parasagittal plane:** any of the plane(s) that run parallel to the **mid-sagittal** plane (that divides the body into left and right halves); the number of these planes is considered infinite.

‡ **parasite:** organism or agent that lives on or within another organism, the **host**, from the body of which it obtains nutrient or other advantage without compensation.

**parasite detection:** study of the taxonomy of parasites found on mammals in order to determine the contact relationships among those mammals. Parasite taxonomy mirrors host taxonomy.

**parasite load:** types and numbers of parasites that can be tolerated by a host organism.

**parasitic DNA:** see **junk DNA** and **selfish DNA**.

**parasitism:** 1. a parasitic mode of life. 2. relationship between organisms, at least one of which is a parasite. 3. diseased condition caused by parasites.

**parasitology:** field of biology that studies symbioses between parasites and hosts.

**parastyle:** most anterior **cuspule** on the **stylar shelf**.

**parasympathetic division:** one of the two divisions of the **autonomic nervous system**. The parasympathetic division arises from the brain and the sacral region of the spinal cord and consists of those nerve fibers that are involved with involuntary functions and in basic maintenance of the organism; colloquially referred to as the 'rest and repair' division. The parasympathetic division **innervates** the same effectors as the **sympathetic division,** but the effects are generally antagonistic. Cf. **sympathetic nervous system**.

**Para-Tethyan theory:** argument used by biogeographers to explain dispersal of animals from the **Tethyan region** and the land masses and islands that surround it. Adapted to primate evolution it is used to suggest that the origins and diversifications of anthropoids should focus on this Para-Tethyan area, i.e. Africa, Arabia, and southern Europe, rather than looking at one continent as the center of evolution for anthropoids. Cf. **pretarsioid hypothesis**.

**parathyroid gland:** one of the small, usually paired, endocrine glands that are attached to the posterior region of the **thyroid gland**. Secretes **parathyroid hormone**; involved in blood calcium and phosphate ion regulation.

**parathyroid hormone:** polypeptide **hormone** secreted by the **parathyroid glands**. It promotes release of **calcium** from bone to extracellular fluid by activating **osteoclasts** and inhibiting **osteoblasts**, indirectly promotes increased intestinal absorption of calcium, promotes renal tubular resorption of calcium and increased renal excretion of phosphates, and is a major regulator of bone metabolism. Secretion of parathyroid hormone increases when the level of calcium in the extracellular fluid is low. Cf. **calcitonin**.

**paratope:** antigen-binding site of an antibody, the active portion of an **immunoglobulin** molecule that specifically interacts with an **epitope**.

**paratype:** specimen(s) resembling the **type specimen** remaining in a collection of a new taxon after the **holotype** has been designated.

*Paraustralopithecus aethiopicus* **(Arambourg and Coppens, 1967):** binomen for a poorly known species based on materials from **Omo** and **Koobi Fora**; dated at around 1.9 mya. Many authorities consider this some form of *Homo*.

**parent:** 1. mother or father (usually biological); one that produces or generates another. 2. ancestor, precursor, or **progenitor**. 3. source, origin.

**parent–infant conflict theory:** see **parent–offspring conflict**.

**parent isotope:** unstable **isotope** that decays into one or more daughter products (which may be either stable or unstable isotopes) at a constant rate; used in **radiometric dating** techniques such as **radiocarbon dating**.

**parent-of-origin effect:** change of phenotype due to a factor(s) transmitted from only one parent to off-spring, such as a mitochondrial gene (see **maternal inheritance**), or an **epigenetic** effect due to, for example, **parental imprinting**.

**parent–offspring conflict:** concept that parental fitness is increased by ceasing investment in an off-spring that is capable of surviving so that the parent can reproduce sooner; this time may not be the optimal time for the young. Primate females do not ovulate until they stop lactating; consequently, weaning an infant as soon as possible is advantageous for the mother's (and potential male mates') reproductive success.

**parent–offspring (P/O) correlation:** measure of the degree of covariation among members of a parental generation with members of their F1 generation. A high P/O correlation can indicate a high **heritability** for a trait, whereas the opposite is true for low correlations.

**parental care:** protection, nourishment, and nurturing of offspring. In most primate species this behavior is performed by the mother; however, in some groups, including humans, males also participate.

**parental imprinting:** see **genomic imprinting**.

‡ **parental investment** (PI): 1. allocation of resources towards offspring that requires some **cost** to the parent(s). 2. in sociobiology, care by a parent or parents towards an existing offspring that increases the chance that particular offspring will reproduce, but at the expense of producing potential offspring in the future. Aka differential investment. See **period of parental investment** and **sexual asymmetry**.

**parental manipulation:** concept from the socio-biological literature that suggests **altruism** arose because parents were selected for who were capable of manipulating their offspring into being altruistic towards one another, ensuring higher survival rates, and, consequently, enhancing the parents' fitness.

**parental selection:** see **preadoption**.

**parents:** in sexually reproducing organisms such as primates, that pair of individuals who are the biological progenitors of an **offspring**; a father and mother.

**parietal:** 1. wall or side. 2. of or pertaining to the side and top of the skull, especially the **parietal bone**.

**parietal arc** (b–l): **craniometric** measurement; distance of the curve from **bregma** to **lambda** as measured with a flexible tape measure. Similar to the **cephalometric** measurement **parietal chord**.

**parietal art:** art executed on cave walls (pariétal), especially in France. See **cave art**.

‡ **parietal bone:** one of the two **flat bones** that form the lateral walls and roof on each side of the **cranium**.

**parietal chord:** **cephalometric** measurement: distance between the **bregma** and **lambda** as measured with spreading calipers. Similar to the **craniometric** measurement **parietal arc**.

**parietal foramina:** pair of small apertures in the **parietal bones** near the mid-line that transmit blood vessels from the meninges to the scalp. Variable manifestation; not always present in all **Hominidae**.

**parietal lobe:** portion of each cerebral hemisphere that lies beneath the parietal bone; bounded posteriorly by the **occipital lobe**, anteriorly by the **frontal lobe**, and inferiorly by the **temporal lobe**. Among the functions of the parietal lobes are the understanding of speech and formulation of words to express thoughts and emotions, and the interpretation of textures and shapes.

**parietal notch of the temporal bone:** angle in the posterior **temporal bone** just superior to the petrous portion along the suture shared with the **parietal bone**. Aka parietal notch bone.

**parietal thinning:** condition in which the **cancellous bone** of the **parietal bone** decreases in size, resulting in a decreased thickness of this bone and the development of pits on the exterior surface of the bone. This process is a normal function of age.

**parieto-occipital fissure:** major cleft inferior and posterior to the parietal lobe that is tangential to the occipital lobe for a portion of its anterior region.

**parity:** 1. number of pregnancies a woman has completed, or the number of times a given female brings a **litter** to term. 2. number of individuals produced during a **parity event**. See **uniparity, biparity, iteroparity, multiparity, nulliparity, primiparity, semelparity, uniparity**.

**parity event:** completion of **gestation**, either by normal **birth** or by a premature termination such as **abortion**.

**parking:** see **infant parking**.

**Parkinson disease, familial** (PD1): heritable, autosomal dominant neurodegenerative condition characterized by tremors, muscular stiffness, and walking and balance difficulties; Lewy bodies are inclusional in many regions of the brain. Mutations in alpha synuclein (SNCA) cause fragmentation; SNCA fragments are characteristic of some forms of both PD1 and **Alzheimer disease**. Not all forms of PD are inherited.

**p arm:** shorter of the two arms of a chromosome or **chromatid**. Arms are defined by the position of the **centromere**. See **q arm**.

**parology:** homologous variants of multiple genetic loci in different species, i.e. a **DNA sequence** that has been duplicated to form a **gene cluster** or **gene family**. See **synteny**. Cf. **orthology** and **xenology**.

**Paromomyidae:** family of archaic fossil mammals belonging to the order **Plesiadapiformes**. Known from the middle Paleocene to the late Eocene; predominantly a North American taxon, but very widely distributed with some members even above the Arctic Circle and several genera known from Europe; eight genera of forms ranging from 50 g to 600 g. Number of teeth variable across genera; procumbent incisors, tall sharp premolars; this combination of teeth has led to disagreement on diet, some workers think that this family was **insectivorous**, some workers think it was **gummivorous**, and yet others see it as consuming plant matter in general. See Appendix 1 for taxonomy.

*Paromomys* Gidley, 1923: archaic mammal known from the middle Paleocene of North America belonging to the **Plesiadapiformes** family **Paromomyidae**; two species; most primitive of the paromomyids; postulated to share a common ancestor with *Palaechthon* and *Plesiolestes*; appears to be the ancestor of *Ignacius* and *Phenacolemur*. Known only from dentition and mandibular remains. Dental formula of mandible: 2.1.3.3; diet probably fruit. Body mass of the species between 100g and 300 g. See Appendix 1 for taxonomy.

**parotid gland:** salivary gland located between the skin and the **masseter muscle** of the posterior portion of the lower jaw just anterior to the ear, and connected to the oral cavity by the parotid ducts. The parotid gland secretes a clear watery serous **saliva** that is rich in the carbohydrate-splitting enzyme **amylase**.

**parous female:** female that is reproducing or has reproduced.

**parrot fever:** see **ornithosis**.

‡ **parsimony:** see **principle of parsimony**.

**parsimony analysis:** statistical method that identifies a subset that contains the most probably correct evolutionary tree generated by using certain data.

**parthenogenesis:** production of an organism from an unfertilized egg. Term increasingly applied to certain aspects of whole-organism **cloning** and **assisted reproductive techniques**.

**partial chimeras:** see **chimeric twins** and **freemartin effect**.

**partial color blindness:** hereditary inability to distinguish certain colors in one's environment; see **deuteranopia** and **protanopia**. Cf. **complete color blindness**.

**partial penetrance:** failure of a dominant allele to always produce a consistent phenotype, or failure of homozygous recessives individuals to manifest a common, expected phenotype in every individual. Cf. incomplete **penetrance**.

**partial pressure:** that portion of total gas pressure that is due to molecules of one gas species; a measure of the concentration of a gas in a mixture containing multiple gases.

**partially complete protein:** food source whose protein component includes all of the **essential amino acids**, the concentrations of some of which are not high enough to promote human growth, although there is enough to maintain life. See **complete protein, incomplete protein**.

**partially sex-linked gene:** see **incompletely sex-linked gene**.

**particle bombardment:** physical insertion of DNA fragments into target cells by using a gun-like device, one of the techniques used in **biotechnology** to transfect cells.

**particulate inheritance:** in inheritance, the possession of genetic information in the form of nonblending particles that retain their character even when reassorted through the reproductive process; **hard inheritance**. **Mendel's** model was particulate, and replaced the earlier idea of a protean, all-encompassing hereditary agent, often called the **germ-plasm**. Cf. **pangenesis**.

**partitional calorimetry:** analysis of heat exchange between a body and its environment in order to establish the relationship of evaporation, convection and radiation and their roles in heat exchange and metabolism. See **thermoregulation**.

**parturition:** process of giving **birth**.

**parturition fossa:** pit on the inner surface of a pubis of a female who has given birth. The presence of these fossae provides information that can be used to help identify a recovered skeleton.

**party:** social unit that consists of a temporary aggregation of members. See **group**.

**pasimology:** communication by the use of sign language.

**passage:** 1. act of passing. 2. channel through which something passes. 3. bowel movement. 4. in cell culture, the number of times cells have been subcultured.

**passive:** 1. not reactive; nonparticipatory, inert or quiescent. 2. influenced, acted upon, or affected by some external agency; receiving. Cf. **active**.

**passive immunity:** immunity due to receipt of maternal antibody or injection of antibody.

**pastoralism:** subsistence pattern in which much of the food resources is from the herding of domesticated mammals. This type of life can be relatively sedentary (cf. **nomadic pastoralism**) if there is pasture for the animals nearby and land available for supplementary crops and/or a trading network. Aka husbandry.

**pastoralist:** human whose subsistence involves the herding of domestic animals. See **pastoralism**.

**patas monkey:** vernacular for *Erythrocebus patas*.

**Patau syndrome:** chromosomal defect (**aneuploidy**, $2N = 47,13+$) due to three copies of all the genes on chromosome 13. The syndrome features mental impairment, a large triangular nose, cleft lip and other facial deformities, systemic organ defects, and polydactyly. Aka Trisomy 13.

**Pataud:** see **Abri Pataud**.

**patch:** area or object (the **prey**) in an environment in which a resource return is seen as greater than for the environment as a whole, and therefore worthy of pursuit by an organism (the **predator**). The patch concept is integral to the **marginal value theorem** and **optimal foraging theory**.

**patella:** flat triangular **sesamoid** bone embedded in the **quadriceps femoris group** muscle tendon that passes anteriorly over the **knee joint**. Adjective: patellar. It develops in its tendons as a child begins to walk. The patella protects the knee and serves as a lever for the muscles acting across the knee joint. It forms the patellofemoral joint with the **patellar ligament** and **femur**. Aka kneecap, knee pan or pan.

**patellar groove:** depression in the anterior border of the lateral femoral condyle. This feature is deeper in humans than it is in apes and is therefore considered to be an important characteristic of bipedalism.

**patellar ligament:** ligament that is a continuation of a tendon of the **quadriceps femoris group**, forming a flat band that extends from the **patella** and inserts into the **tibia** to help secure the knee joint. It is the patellar ligament that is tapped when testing the knee-jerk reflex.

**paternal:** relating to or derived from the father.

**paternal age effect:** any event in a newborn that increases or decreases in frequency or **incidence** as a function of the age of the father; **achondroplasia**, for example, increases in frequency with advanced paternal age. See **male mutation rates**.

**paternal care:** parental care that is at least partly provided by the father. This is not the norm among primates, but does exist among some groups, notably the callitrichids, hylobatids, and **humans**.

**paternal certainty:** 1. knowledge of which male is the father of a primate offspring. See **paternity ascertainment** for the term used by geneticists. 2. in sociobiology, knowledge by a male that an offspring is his. See **paternity uncertainty**.

**paternal disomy:** form of **uniparental disomy** in which two chromosomes (or regions) are both inherited from the mother of a recipient. One of the forms of **non-Mendelian inheritance**.

**paternal inheritance:** **DNA** or **organelles** that are inherited from the father but not from the mother; males are **hemizygous** for a single **Y chromosome**, for example, which is paternal in origin. Cf. **maternal inheritance**.

**paternal X inactivation:** nonrandom dosage compensation found in marsupials, in which it is always the paternal X chromosome that is inactivated in females. **X inactivation** in eutherians is a two-stage process: (1) preferential inactivation by **genomic imprinting** of the paternal X chromosome prior to fertilization via *XIST* (and which remains inactivated in **blastocyst** cells destined to become placental tissues, i.e, the **trophoblast**); but then (2) the imprinted paternal X chromosome is reactivated in cells within the inner cell mass (**epiblast**), and in these subsequent **random X inactivation** occurs.

**paternity:** 1. state of being a father or progenitor. 2. pertaining to a legal dispute in which a mother accuses a male of being the father of her offspring. Cf. **paternity exclusion** and **paternity ascertainment**.

**paternity ascertainment:** method(s) of estimation of a probability that a given male is the father of a certain offspring. Methods range from trust, to likelihood estimates based upon phenotypic similarity, blood type analysis, or **DNA fingerprinting**. Cf. maternity ascertainment.

**paternity exclusion:** finding, after testing, that the alleged father is not the biological father of a child; aka nonpaternity. Cf. **paternity** and **paternity ascertainment**.

**paternity uncertainty:** questionable relatedness of a male to his putative **offspring**; paternity uncertainty has been associated with some males' reduced investment in some children, relative to females, as they actually give birth. See **maternity ascertainment** and **parental investment**.

**path analysis:** in genetics, a graphical mode of analysis used to determine an **inbreeding coefficient**, sometimes called path coefficient analysis, developed by Sewell **Wright**.

**path length:** linear distance a primate or primate group moves in 24 h, including distance from back-tracking, moving in circles, etc. See **day range**.

'pathfinder': see **Omo I**.

‡ **pathogen:** any disease-causing **agent**.

**pathogenesis:** course or development of a disease.

**pathogenic mutation:** any **mutation** responsible for a genetic disorder.

**pathogenicity:** measure of an organism's ability to cause disease; pathogenic.

**pathology:** branch of medicine which studies the essential nature of disease; **nosology**.

**pathway:** channel or set of nerve connections through which information can travel from one region to another.

**patient autonomy:** in medical or genetic counseling, the right of a patient to make decisions without influence by a health care provider. In counseling, influence extends only to patient education, and not to an actual decision.

**patina:** film or incrustation on weathered rock. Patination varies in thickness depending upon local conditions and time of exposure to the elements. Aka incrustation, oxidation.

**Patjitan:** chopper tool culture phase found in Java, probably contemporary with *Homo erectus*. Aka **Developed Oldowan**.

**patriline:** pattern of inheritance in which a trait is passed from a male to his offspring; aka patrilineal. Cf. **matriline** and **holandry**.

**patrilocal:** describes a settlement pattern in which males remain within their natal community, while females move to mate or marry in another community.

**patristic:** referring to the condition in a taxon in which there is a combination of both **primitive** and **derived** **traits**.

**patristic affinity:** degree of similarity due to common ancestry; cf. **cladistic affinity**.

**patristic trait, character or feature:** any feature that has been inherited by all the taxa derived from a recent common ancestor; a feature present in all members of a **monophyletic group**.

**pattern baldness:** see **male pattern baldness**.

**patterned ground formation:** in an archaeological site, a process that results in special features on the ground surface such as circles of stones, nets, polygons, steps, or stripes. See **cryogenic soil modification**.

**patterns of inheritance:** there are five distinct systems or patterns of simple genetic inheritance, the **recessive pattern of inheritance, codominant pattern of inheritance, dominant pattern of inheritance, X-linked pattern of inheritance**, and **Y-linked pattern of inheritance**. Cf. **polygenic inheritance**.

**PAUP:** phylogenetic analysis using parsimony, a computer algorithm (program) used for phylogenetic analysis and tree estimation, authored by D. L. Swofford.

**Paviland Cave:** archaeological site found in 1822–3 in Glamorgan, South Wales, dated to 18.5 kya, and that contains numerous mammoth-ivory artifacts and **hominid** remains including the skeleton of a young male covered with red ochre (the 'Red Lady' of Paviland) and contemporary with the mammoth; the first discovered human fossil known to modern science. The site was first excavated by the Rev. William Buckland, an Oxfordian geologist, who interpreted the skeleton as that of a young Roman-era Welsh girl whose kin made artifacts from the ivory found in the cave. Aka 'Goat's Hole', Glamorgan, Kent's Hole.

**Pavlovian conditioning:** see **classical conditioning**.

**paw:** fore- or hindfoot of a terrestrial mammal.

**P blood group:** glycolipid antigen that specifies a dominant gene product, denoted P. The recessive form is a null allele, P-. Since the P antigen binds to *E. coli*, individuals with the P-P- genotype are less susceptible to infection by that organism.

‡ **PCR:** polymerase chain reaction, an *in vitro* technique used to amplify a specific region of **DNA** in order to produce many copies; **dsDNA** is thermally denatured and a complementary strand is elongated by a **polymerase**, a process known as a cycle; each cycle doubles the number of copies of the DNA region of interest. This Nobel prize-winning technique is utilized extensively in research, and is especially useful when DNA samples are minute, as in certain **forensic** applications.

**peak growth velocity:** maximum rate of growth in height, weight, etc., achieved during the **adolescent growth spurt**.

‡ **peak height velocity:** maximum growth rate observed in an individual.

**Pearl, Raymond** (1879–1940): US biometrician, population biologist at Johns Hopkins; an early student of K. **Pearson**, Pearl later became an outspoken opponent of the eugenics movement, and even his colleagues admitted that his science was sometimes propagandistic. His professional work centered on the phenomena of human longevity, mortality, and disease. Pearl was among the first to conduct epidemiological studies of popular substances, and he concluded in 1938 that tobacco caused cancer but that small quantities of alcohol were not harmful. Pearl was fascinated with curve-fitting, and extolled the explanatory robustness of the logistic curve. He was a friend of feminist Margaret Sanger (1883–1966) and a member of H. L. Mencken's inner circle. If not the originator of the term **human biology**, Pearl is reputed to have codified it. Pearl founded the journals *Quarterly Review of Biology* (1926) and *Human Biology* (1929), and much of his work appeared in those vehicles.

**Pearson, Karl** (1857–1936): English statistician, eugenicist; extended Galton's regression and correlation techniques', and coined the term **biometry** to describe measurements of living phenomena (1901). One of the founders of *Biometrika*, the journal of the **biometricians**. Developed the **chi-square test** in 1900.

**Pearson's formula:** method of estimating **cranial capacity** (cc) by using the external dimensions of a human skull. For females (F), FCC = (0.000375 × length × breadth × height) + 296.4; for males (M), MCC = (0.000365 × length × breadth × height) − 359.34.

**peasant's perspective:** C. L. **Brace's** term for the point-of-view of the parochial individual; one who sees the world from the perspective of self, from one's own region or geographic location, etc. See **race** (3) and **folk taxonomy.**

**peat bog:** wet, spongy ground that contains highly organic soil found in marshy or damp regions, often combustible and used for fuel. Bogs often preserve organisms deposited in them (see **bog person**), and often possess a microstratigraphy entrapping trace elements, such as mercury, which can be used to reconstruct paleoclimate profiles for the most recent 20–10 ky.

**pebble:** in various classification systems, a particle of sediment about 35 ± 30 mm in diameter, smaller than either a **stone** or a **cobble.** Cf. **rock.**

‡ **pebble tool:** tool resulting from a **pebble** being split; see **Oldowan tool tradition.**

**Pech de l'Azé:** archaeological site found in 1815 in France, dated to 103–54 kya, and that contains **Mousterian** artifacts in the upper occupation levels, and associated hominid remains later attributed to *Homo neanderthalensis.* The lower levels contain **Acheulean** artifacts, dated to 162–130 kya.

**pecked stone:** rock that has been abraded rather than chipped.

**pecking order:** dominance order in birds; loosely, any ordered sequence. See **rank order** and **dominance hierarchy.**

**pectineal line:** bony marking that courses from the pubic crest to the iliopubic eminence of the **pubic bone.**

**pectoral:** of or pertaining to the chest area.

**pectoral girdle:** that part of the **appendicular skeleton** that consists of the **scapula** and **clavicle** and provides support, site of muscle attachment, and connection for the bones of the upper arm or foreleg to the **axial skeleton**; aka shoulder girdle.

**pectoral mammae:** mammary glands located on the chest area of a mammal; this is the condition in primates, although some of the prosimians also possess abdominal mammae. At one time this was one of the criteria for inclusion in the order Primates.

**pectoral skinfold: anthropometric** measurement; skinfold measured at the area of the anterior axillary fold. Used in combination with other **skinfold measurements** to estimate total body density. Aka chest skinfold. See **skinfold thickness.**

**pedigree:** written record, often accompanied by a **pedigree chart,** that lists various individuals that are related by blood; a tool of **transmission genetics.**

**pedigree analysis:** study of the patterns of heredity of certain traits as passed down in a group of related individuals, by using a **pedigree chart.**

‡ **pedigree chart:** diagram with symbols that represent the members and ancestral relationships in a family and that indicates paths of inherited traits, used in the study of **heredity.**

**pedigree selection:** artificial or anthropogenic selection of an individual for the purpose of mating, based on attributes of relatives in addition to those of the individual. Used extensively in **domestic selection,** and covertly in human **assortative mating.**

**pedocephaly:** having an intermediate **cephalic index** of between 78 and 82. Adjective: pedocephalic. See **mesocephaly.**

**pedogenesis:** Von Baer's 1828 term for mature germ cells that develop in a larval body.

**pedomorphism:** possession of features like those of a child in a reproductively mature individual. Pedomorphism results in only the appearance of childlike features, which are in fact unlike the childlike condition in actual form and function. Adjective: pedomorphic. Can be achieved through either **progenesis** or **neoteny.** Cf. **pedomorphosis.**

**pedomorphosis:** change from a rugged to a more graceful morphology in some of the traits used to describe fossils. Aka paedomorphosis. Cf. **pedomorphism.**

**peer group:** individuals of a comparable rank within a primate group.

**Pei Wenzhong** (1904–1982): Chinese geologist; excavated first **calvaria** from **Zhoukoudian** in 1929 (*Sinanthropus pekinensis* III), dated at almost 600 kya and associated with tool assemblages. In 1930, he undertook an extensive study of the artifacts recovered at Localities 1, 13 and 15. Pei was a leading figure in Chinese prehistory both before and after the founding of the People's Republic in 1949, and later directed the exploration of many sites, including the *Gigantopithecus* horizon at **Kwangsi.** Aka Pei Wenchung.

**Peking Man (site):** see Zhoukoudian.

**pelage:** fur coat of a mammal; hair.

**paleobiology:** study of fossils by biologists using the scientific method, and usually also using an evolutionary paradigm for interpretation.

**Pelican Rapids Woman:** vernacular for a fossil from an archaeological site found in 1931 near Pelican Rapids, Minnesota, and dated to *c.* 7.9 kya, containing one fossil hominid, a '**paleoindian**' female aged about fifteen years and assigned to **AMH**, but who possessed 2 cm canines, well outside the modern range; the burial may have been intrusive. This specimen was repatriated and reburied in 1999 under **NAGPRA** guidelines. Aka Minnesota Man.

‡ **pellagra:** rough skin; a state of **malnutrition** caused by a reversible deficiency (**avitaminosis**) of the vitamin **niacin**. The symptoms include apathy, followed by dermatitis (skin lesions), diarrhea, dementia, and death. Niacin is required (with coenzymes) for the reduction of sugars. Classic pellagrins are also deficient in **thiamine, riboflavin**, and **folic acid**. Pellagra is common where maize (which is deficient in **niacin**) is a dietary staple, and also among alcoholics. Aka Lombardy leprosy and maidism.

**pelvic breadth: anthropometric** measurement; distance between the most lateral portions of the left and right **iliac crests** as measured with an **anthropometer** behind the subject's back. Used for body frame indices and for measures of pelvis size. See **bicristal breadth**.

**pelvic breadth–height index:** maximum pelvic height × 100, divided by maximum pelvic breadth.

**pelvic curvature:** concave anterior (primary) curvature of the vertebral column corresponding to the region of the **sacrum** and **coccyx**; one of the four curvatures of the **vertebral column** that help distribute the body's weight over the center of gravity and provides resiliency.

**pelvic dimorphism:** condition found in humans in which the male and female pelves are substantially different to the point that they can be used to determine the sex of a skeleton. This sexual dimorphism does not occur until puberty, during which time the female pelvis changes. The reason for the differences involve evolutionary compromises with bipedalism and large-brained neonates. See **sexing, skeletal**.

**pelvic girdle:** that part of the skeleton that provides support and place of attachment for the hindlegs; aka hip girdle; consists of the two **coxal bones**. In humans the body's weight is transmitted through the pelvic girdle onto the lower limbs.

**pelvic inlet:** superior portion of the central opening of the pelvis and superior border of the **true pelvis**; the pelvic brim is the bony border surrounding this aperture. The dimensions of this opening, in combination with that of the pelvic outlet, is critical to uncomplicated childbirth. It is round or oval in female humans, heart-shaped in males.

**pelvic inlet index:** sagittal diameter of the **pelvic inlet** × 100 and then divided by the transverse diameter of the pelvic inlet.

**pelvic outlet:** inferior portion of the central opening of the pelvis and inferior border of the **true pelvis**. The dimensions of this opening, in combination with that of the **pelvic inlet**, is critical to uncomplicated childbirth.

**pelvicephalometry:** measurement of a mother's **pelvic outlet** diameter relative to the size of the fetal head.

**pelvimeter:** calipers designed for the measurement of pelvic diameters.

**pelvis:** basin-shaped set of bones in humans that supports the **axial skeleton**; includes the **coxal bones, sacrum**, and **coccyx**. In other primates the pelvis is long and bladelike.

*Pelycodus (= Cantius)* **Cope, 1875:** prosimian from the early Eocene of North America belonging to the subfamily **Notharctinae**; two species; primitive adapoid. Previously grouped with *Cantius*, which some authorities still consider to be a valid grouping; one of the distinctions between *Pelycodus* and *Cantius* is geographical location; *Pelycodus* is found primarily in the southwestern region of the USA. Some authors think that *Pelycodus* is derived from *Cantius*; *Pelycodus* may be the ancestor of *Notharctus* (although most workers think that *Cantius* gave rise to that genus). Dental formula: 2.1.4.3/2.1.4.3; dental morphology suggests both **insectivory** and **frugivory**. Body mass estimated to range from 5 to 6 kg. One of the three adapoids with an unfused **mandibular symphysis**, a condition found in the living prosimians. See Appendix 1 for taxonomy.

**Pendred syndrome** (PDS): inherited autosomal recessive condition characterized by thyroid goiter and deafness. The mutant gene is PDS; normally this gene makes pendrin, a protein found in the thyroid that is involved in sulfate transport. Common, accounts for 10% of all cases of deafness. Aka 'goiter-deafness syndrome'.

**penecontemporary:** living at or almost at the same time, as **Neandertals** and **AMHs**.

**penetrance:** frequency of expression of a certain **phenotype**; some alleles, even when present, are expressed less than 100% of the time, and thus are said to have a lowered penetrance.

**penile display:** see **genital display**.

**Peninj:** archaeological site and hominid fossil found in 1964 on the Peninj River near Lake Natron, Tanzania, dated to 1.5–1.2 mya, and that contains hominid remains including a complete **megadont** mandible located by Kimoya **Kimeu** and excavated by Glynn

Isaac and Richard **Leakey**. Attributed to *Australop-ithecus (= Paranthropus) boisei*. Although the mandible is several hundred thousand years younger, it articulates well with the cranium of **OH 5**. Aka Lake Natron.

**penis:** male organ of copulation, used to introduce spermatozoa into the female vagina and through which urine passes during urination. See **baculum**.

‡ **pentadactyly:** condition in which the **paw** has five digits. In primates this is the case always, although some primates have a reduced digit that is merely a stub. In other orders of mammals there may be fewer than five digits, and a difference between the number of digits on the fore paw and the hind paw (e.g. in rodents). Cf. **polydactyly**.

**pentagonal contour of the cranium:** diagnostic feature of Asian varieties of *Homo erectus* in which the cranial plates are relatively thick and flat so that a skull, when viewed from the rear, appears to have two converging walls rising above a floor, and two 'roof' portions which meet in a peak or keel, not unlike the five-faced shape of a canvas tent. Aka pentagonid.

**pentose sugar:** five-carbon sugar molecule found in nucleic acids.

**pentosuria:** relatively benign recessive genetic disorder of sugar metabolism characterized by the accumulation of xylulose in the blood and urine. See **carbohydrate metabolism**.

**penultimate glaciation:** next to last (i.e. third) glaciation of the Pleistocene; see **Riss glaciation**.

**peppercorn hair:** very tightly curled hair that rolls up into a ball of knots with adjacent hairs; hair structure found among the Khoisan **!Kung** of southern Africa. Aka spiral tuft hair form.

**peppered moth:** *Biston betularia*; see **industrial melanism**.

**pepsin:** family of several protein-digesting enzymes synthesized in the stomach; these break down complex proteins into peptide fragments (peptones and proteases).

**peptide:** short chain of linked **amino acids**.

‡ **peptide bond:** chemical link between the carboxyl group of one amino acid and the amino group of another **amino acid**.

**percentage:** rate or proportion per hundred.

**percentage decrease (or increase):** fraction of change, calculated as: %change = $(N/O) - 1$, where $N$ = new value and $O$ = old value.

**percentile:** in statistics, one of the **values** of a variable that divides the distribution of the variable into 100 groups having equal **frequencies** numbered 0–99. Cf. **decile**.

**percentile of growth:** method of ranking growth status for height, weight, or other variable, of an individual relative to other members of a sample or population; for example, a child at the 65th percentile for height is taller than 65% of the other children in the comparison group.

**perception:** understanding and conscious awareness of sensory stimulation by events in the external world. Cf. **sensation**.

**perceptual world:** sensory reality of a species; this may be quite different from the perceptual world of the human observer. For example, many prosimians emit vocalizations that are at frequencies that cannot be detected by humans without technological assistance.

**percussion:** striking of one object against another with force; impact.

‡ **percussion flaking technique:** stone tool-making technique in which a flint core is held and flakes are detached by striking it with a hammerstone. Aka hard-hammer percussion. See **direct percussion**.

**perdurance:** phenotypic condition that remains changed long after the responsible gene has ceased expression, owing either to the long half-life of its molecular product, or to the permanence of its effects in tissues such as bone.

**pericentric inversion:** major chromosome anomaly in which a portion of a chromosome that includes the **centromere** is inverted compared with the normal **linkage** sequence for a species. See **inversion**.

*Periconodon* Stehlin, 1916: poorly known adapoid prosimian from the middle Eocene of Europe; exact affinities in dispute; this genus has been included among the omomyids, adapids, and, most recently, with the newly created notharctid subfamily **Cercamoniinae**; five species generally recognized, but in dispute. Body mass estimated to range from 250 g to 1 kg. Dental formula unknown. See Appendix 1 for taxonomy.

**periglacial zone:** region peripheral to Pleistocene ice sheets, which suffered rigorous climate, frost action, and similar effects.

**Perigord:** region in France almost identical to the department of Dordogne, and which contains hundreds of Middle and Upper **Paleolithic** sites *c.* 130–10 kya.

**Perigordian:** Upper **Paleolithic** stone tool tradition in southwestern France and in Spain dating *c.* 33–18 kya.

**perikaryon:** cell body of a neuron.

**perikymata:** enamel ridges visible on teeth that represent 6–11 day microscopic increments of enamel laid down as teeth are formed; see **stria of Retzius**. Comparative studies have shown that **australop-ithecines** developed nearly twice as fast as modern humans, or about the same rate as that seen in apes, and that *Homo neanderthalensis* developed at about the same rate as *Homo heidelbergensis*; these species would have taken only about 15 years to reach adulthood, if rates of dental development reflect overall growth velocities.

**perimortem:** around death; refers to injuries, pathologies, or any other phenomenon on a fossil or skeleton that occurred at about the time that the individual died. Cf. **antemortem** and **postmortem.**

**perinatal:** referring to the period immediately before, during, and after birth; technically, the perinatal period in humans begins at 20 weeks of gestation and terminates 28 days after birth.

**perineal skin:** area of skin that surrounds the anus, vagina, and urethra.

‡ **perineum:** 1. floor of the pelvis and associated structures. 2. external body region between the scrotum and anus in the male, and the vulva and anus in the female.

**period:** 1. any specific, especially large, time interval. 2. time of the month during which menstruation occurs. 3. in geology, the abstract geological time unit that corresponds to a geological system; a subdivision of an **era.** See **epoch.**

**period of parental investment:** period during which a parent invests energy and resources in an offspring and during which benefits outweigh costs, as measured in terms of reproductive success. See **termination of parental investment.**

**periodic behavior:** behavior that occurs in a cycle of equal intervals. Cf. **rhythmic behavior.**

**periodic extinction:** proposal by Raup and Sepkowski that **mass extinctions** occurred on a 27 my cycle during the **Mesozoic** and **Cenozoic eras**, and that this periodicity is explained by regular extraterrestrial impacts; the hypothesis remains controversial.

**periodicity:** rhythmic repetition of some event; a cycle. See **circadian rhythm, circannual rhythm, infradian rhythm, rhythmic behavior.**

**periodontal disease:** any pathology of the teeth and/or gums.

**periodontal ligament:** fibrous membrane that surrounds a tooth and anchors it to **dental alveolus**; the ligament also supplies blood vessels and nerves to the **pulp cavity.** Aka periodontal membrane.

**periodontitis:** inflammation of the tissues surrounding a tooth; often caused by a response to bacterial plaque buildup on the adjacent teeth. Periodontitis can result in destruction of alveolar bone and the eventual loss of the tooth.

‡ **periodontium:** tissues surrounding the teeth. Adjective: periodontal.

**periodontosis:** pathology in which the attachment level of the **periodontal ligaments** is lowered; periodontosis may result from either periodontal disease or general aging.

‡ **periosteum:** fibrous connective tissue that covers and is attached to compact bone. Adjective: periosteal.

**peripatric speciation:** synonym for **peripheral isolate speciation;** a form of **allopatric speciation** in which a new species is formed at the edge of the ancestral population's range; characteristic of less **vagile** organisms such as the rooted plants.

**peripheral:** of or pertaining to locations found toward the extremities or outside of structures.

**peripheral isolate speciation:** form of **allopatric speciation** in which the new species is formed from a small population isolated at the edge of the ancestral population's range. Aka parapatric speciation. See **centrifugal speciation.**

**peripheral lymphoid organ:** lymph node, spleen, tonsil, or lymphocyte accumulation in gastrointestinal, respiratory, urinary, or reproductive tracts.

**peripheral male:** male primate associated with a social group, but usually found on the edges of the unit; often these males are not integrated into the group, in other cases they are low ranking members. See **bachelor herd.**

**peripheral nervous system** (PNS): structures of the **nervous system** that lie outside of the **brain** and **spinal cord;** the major structures are nerves and ganglia. One of the two encompassing branches of the nervous system; cf. **central nervous system.**

**peripheral thermoreceptor:** temperature receptor in skin of certain mucous membranes. If overstimulated, they become pain receptors.

‡ **Perissodactyla:** order of ungulates; perissodactyls are mammals with an odd number of toes in their hooves, such as a tapir or rhinoceros. Cf. **Artiodactyla.**

**peristalith:** circle of stones or **manuports,** often surrounding a mound or dolmen.

**peritoneum:** 1. strong, colorless membrane that surrounds several structures in vertebrates. 2. membrane lining the walls of the diaphragm, abdomen and pelvis (the parietal peritoneum) and that defines the peritoneal cavities. 3. membrane that infuses the viscera (the visceral peritoneum). 4. the pericranium.

**permafrost:** pemanently frozen ground.

**permanent teeth:** see **adult dentition.**

**permeability:** openness or porosity; the degree of openness of a society to new members.

**permeable:** describes the property of membranes that allows the passage of substances such as molecules or ions.

‡ **Permian period:** most recent period of the **Paleozoic era,** lasting from approximately 280 to 225 mya, during which the Appalachian mountains formed; the climate was cooler and drier, and **glaciers** formed in the southern hemisphere on the **Antarctic** land mass. Fossil reptiles first appeared during this period.

‡ **permineralization:** one of several processes that cause the replacement of organic with inorganic compounds such that the form and sometimes even structural details of an organism are preserved as a **fossil**; typical replacement materials include silicates, carbonates, and travertines, usually transported by **groundwater**. Some of the original biological tissue may remain intact, depending upon conditions, so that hard materials (containing **calcium,** such as **tooth enamel**) may preserve organic molecules with varying integrity even in very old fossils. In other cases, materials may be replaced through **recrystallization**. Aka petrifaction, **petrified**, mineralized. See **taphonomy, fossilization, collagen, diagenesis,** and **ancient DNA.** Cf. **recrystallization, solution,** and **carbonization**.

**permissive:** describes a female that allows other individuals in her social group to handle and care for her infant(s). Cf. **exclusivity**.

**Perning:** archaeological site found in 1936 in central Java, dated to possibly as old as 1.9–1.6 mya (Pucangan or **Kabuh Formation**), containing hominid remains including a child's 650 cm³ braincase (Perning 1) attributed to *Pithecanthropus* (= *Homo erectus*) *modjokertensis.* Aka Modjokerto, Mojokerto.

*Perodicticus* Bennett, 1831: monotypic **prosimian** genus to which the (Bosman's) potto belongs. Distribution from western equatorial Africa into central Africa; occupies the canopy level of tropical rain forests; **sympatric** with *Arctocebus* in western range, but **resource partitioning** prevents competition. Arboreal; nocturnal; slow methodical climbers; moderate tail. Digit 2 is reduced and possesses a grooming claw; **pollex** is 180° from digit 3, providing for a powerful vice-like grip that can be held for long periods of time; circulatory adaptations in the paws provide an ample oxygen supply that prevents lactic acid buildup in the muscles. Body mass from 850 to 1600 g. Dental formula: 2.1.3.3.; **dental comb** present; upper anterior dentition is peg-like and short; **frugivorous** with insect supplements in western range; in the eastern part of their range they are reported to be **gummivorous** with fruit supplements. Possesses a defensive cervical shield formed by thick skin, the processes of cervical vertebrae and associated musculature, and equipped with **guard** (tactile) **hairs** that helps the animal detect danger. **Noyau** with overlapping home ranges that form a 'neighborhood'. See Appendix 2 for taxonomy and Appendix 3 for species.

**peroneal:** pertaining to the fibula.

**peroneal tubercle (of metatarsal I):** bony eminence extending from the **plantar** surface of **metatarsal** I (of the **hallux**) that serves as a site for insertion of a tendon.

**peroxisome:** membrane-bound cytoplasmic organelle with a double membrane that contains enzymes that break down lipids, synthesize bile compounds, and detoxify compounds containing free radicals such as hydrogen peroxide. Peroxisomes are abundant in liver and kidney cells.

**peroxisome proliferator-activated receptor-gamma** (PPAR-γ): a protein that governs the maturation and function of fat cells. Humans are **polymorphic** for PPAR-γ; one allele has alanine but a second and more common allele has proline at a specific amino acid sequence site. The proline-encoding PPAR-γ has been linked to an increased susceptibility to **non-insulin-dependent diabetes mellitus**.

**personal adornment:** ornaments such as shell beads and modified animal teeth that were suspended from or attached to clothing or to the body itself. See **ochre, furrow-carved mammal teeth,** and **pierced mammal teeth**.

**personal communication** (pers. comm.): a form of professional citation in which an author's source of information is direct, via an oral or written medium, as in 'Benedictus Umpti, pers. comm'.

**pes: foot** (1,2).

**Peschel's law:** postulate that there is an inverse relationship between the amount of clothing worn and the degree of skin pigmentation. Globally, there is little evidence for this suggestion.

**Pestera cu Oase:** archaeological site found in 2002 located in a cave in the Carpathian Mountains of Romania, tentatively dated to *c.* 35 kya (radiocarbon, mandible) that contains remains of cave bears and hominid remains that include a mandible, a partial skull containing the face from an immature male, and other cranial fragments. Although the bones have been provisionally attributed to *Homo sapiens* (**AMH**), researchers report that the bones possess a mix of modern and archaic traits, including large, crenulated third molars. Cf. **Lagar Velho 1**.

**PET imaging:** positron emission tomography imaging, a technology that utilizes radioactive isotopes that naturally emit positrons that enable biochemical activities to be detected in a specific body region. Used extensively in medicine, PET imaging of brains is also used by neurobiologists to monitor activity while a subject performs certain actions.

**petalia:** see **left-occipital–right-frontal petalia pattern**.

**Petralona Cave:** archaeological site found in 1959 near Thessalonika, Khalkidhiki, Greece, dated to earlier than 350 kya (disputed dates range from 620 to 160 kya), and that contains Crenian (= early **Mousterian**) artifacts. Hominid remains found embedded in a **stalactite** include a mosaic 1220 cm³ cranium, possibly male, with a sharply angled occiput, transverse torus, very thick bones, double-arched supra-orbital torus, and pneumatization. Attributed to the **earlier archaic *Homo sapiens*** group, although a few refer to it as a Neandertal. AKA Petralona I.

**petrified:** state of a fossil changed by **permineralization** to the extent that it has 'turned to stone'. As the fossil decayed, the organic material was slowly replaced by minerals, leaving behind a stone mould or cast.

**petroglyph:** technically, any picture or design peckedor incised on a rock or other natural surface. Often confused with **pictograph**. See **cave art**.

**petrological analysis:** study of the origin, mineralogy, texture and structure of rocks and rock formations.

**petrosal bone:** division of the **temporal bone** that develops from cartilage instead of membrane; the petrous portion of the temporal helps form the primate **auditory bulla**. Aka petrous bone.

**petrous:** 1. in hardness, like stone. 2. pertaining to the hard, dense portion of the temporal bone.

***Petterus* Grove and Eaglen, 1988:** alternative genus proposed for five species of *Lemur*. The synonym *Eulemur* appears to be favored by primatologists and is used in this dictionary.

**pH:** logarithmic scale of the degree of acidity or alkalinity in an aqueous solution; a pH of 7.0 is neutral, a value below 7.0 is acidic, and above 7.0 is alkaline.

**Ph[1]:** abbreviation for **Philadelphia chromosome**.

**phaeomelanin:** form of melanin found in humans that has a yellow or reddish hue. Present in some red and black hair. Phaeomelanin is found predominately in climates that are hot and dry. Cf. **eumelanin**.

‡ **phagocyte:** any cell with the ability to surround and engulf viruses and microorganisms, i.e. of phagocytosis. Adjective: phagocytic.

**phagocytosis:** process by which a specialized cell ingests a substance by engulfing it using extensions of its protoplasm in a process called endocytosis. Following uptake, the substance is enclosed in a cytoplasmic vesicle where it is digested. Phagocytosis functions in both a nutritive and a defensive role.

**phagocytosis theory of aging:** intracellular, systemic model of aging in which the major premise is that senescent cells accumulate certain membrane proteins that identify them as candidates for destruction by other cells, such as **macrophages**.

**phalange:** finger or toe bone; see **phalanx**.

**Phalanges:** plural of **phalanx**.

**phalangeroid:** type of marsupial that includes the Australian possums and cuscus; these mammals are considered to occupy niches similar to those of some primates (both past and present) and are used as models for primate evolution by some workers.

**phalanx:** any of the bones that make up the fingers or toes; there are three bones per finger or toe, two per **hallux** or **pollex**.

***Phaner furcifer* (Blainville, 1839):** fork-marked (-crowned) dwarf lemur; aka fork-tailed mouse lemur. Four recognized **subspecies**. Found in a discontinuous distribution around the peripheries of Madagascar with the exception of the east coast. Arboreal; nocturnal; locomotion is quadrupedalism with leaping. Body mass ranges from 350 to 500 g. Dental formula: 3.1.3.3; gummivorous. Specialized morphology for **gummivory** includes **procumbent dental comb**, **caniniform** upper anterior premolars, long and narrow tongue, large cecum for **hindgut fermentation**, and laterally compressed nails with a raised central keel that function as claws. Conflicting reports about social behavior, but appears to have the typical cheirogalid pattern of **noyau** with overlapping male and female home ranges that produce a **neighborhood**; known to sleep in nests abandoned by *Mirza*. Vocalizations are very important in this species and appear to be used to maintain contact between males and females. See Appendix 2 for taxonomy, Appendix 3 for living species.

**Phanerozoic eon:** past 545 million years of the earth's history, during which complex (= multicellular) forms of life evolved.

**pharmacogenetics:** branch of genetics and pharmacology that is concerned with the inheritance of individual differences in response to drugs. Cf. **ecogenetics**.

**pharmacogenomics:** branch of **biotechnology** that identifies DNA that codes for certain enzymes, receptors and other immune system components, and that can be used to model and predict people's responses to drug candidates.

**pharynx:** muscular tube of the alimentary canal between the region extending posterior from the nasal cavities to the esophagus where respiratory and digestive passages cross; aka throat. Adjective: pharyngeal.

**phase:** 1. any perceived aspect, mode or condition of something; point of view; construct. 2. any stage in a process, especially a developmental sequence; state. 3. zone or subdivision of a system. 4. archaeological construct possessing traits sufficient to distinguish it from other such units; usually further delimited in both space and time.

**phase specificity:** period in development in which environmental influences have a lasting effect on behavioral development; the effects depend on the specific age phase and are called **sensitive phases** or periods.

**Phayre's leaf-monkey:** vernacular for *Trachypithecus phayrei*.

***Phenacolemur* Matthew, 1915:** archaic mammal known from the late Paleocene to middle or late Eocene of North America and Europe belonging to the **Plesiadapiformes** family **Paromomyidae**; four species; may be descended from *Paromomys*. Known from dentition, jaws, and cranial fragments. Dental formula: 2.1.3.3/1.0.1.3; **procumbent** incisors more pronounced than in other paromomyids; lower anterior molars reduced in height; diet uncertain, but possibly fruit, perhaps with insect supplements. Body mass of the species ranges between 50 and 400 g. Known appendicular skeleton has been interpreted as adapted for gliding and as showing a very close relationship to the **Dermoptera**; others dispute this and think that the limb bones are more robust than is found in any living glider. See Appendix 1 for taxonomy.

**phene:** phenotypic character that is controlled by a gene or genes.

‡ **phenetic:** pertaining to overall similarity; comparison without regard to source of character states, i.e. whether because of **patristic affinity** or through **parallelism** or **convergence**. See **folk taxonomy**.

**phenetic classification:** practice of taxonomy where species are grouped with others based solely on the **phenetic principle**.

**phenetic distance:** measure of the distance between any two points in a phylogenetic tree that has been constructed using phenotypic traits.

**phenetic fossil species concept** (PFSC): fossil species described in terms of no more metrical variation than is present in living species.

**phenetic principle:** method of **classification** in which a taxon is grouped together with other **taxa** that it most closely resembles by **phenotype**. One of the two main organizing principles of **taxonomy**. Cf. **phylogenetic principle**.

**phenetic species concept:** defines a species as a set of organisms that are sufficiently phenetically similar to one another that individuals choose to mate with each other.

**phenetic taxonomy:** school of **classification** that stresses the overall physical similarities among organisms when forming a biological classification; Aka **numerical taxonomy**.

**phenetics:** see **numerical taxonomy**.

‡ **phenocopy:** variation that mimics the effects of a known gene mutation but that is environmentally produced. The thalidomide babies of the 1950s were teratogen-induced phenocopies of **phocomelia**.

**phenogram:** tree diagram relating similar things according to **phenotype**; no genealogy is assumed.

**phenology:** study of the influence of climate on annual behavior or phenomena such as migration, plant flowering, desiccation, etc.

**phenon:** one or more individuals representing a morphologically rather uniform sample of a population or a species.

‡ **phenotype:** 1. observable physical or behavioral properties of an organism that are produced by the interaction of **genotype** and **environment** during growth and development; appearance. 2. a group of organisms that share a particular phenotype. Adjective: phenotypic.

**phenotype matching:** kin recognition in which the behavior of individuals is based on some phenotypic similarity such as appearance, smell, or other characteristic that is detectable to the individuals involved. See **greenbeard effect**.

**phenotypic key:** any obvious trait, usually characterized by a distinctive shape or color, used to classify organisms or objects into categories, species, etc. Such keys are often **anthropocentric** and reflect **phenetic** rather than evolutionary relationships. See **folk taxonomy** and **racial character**.

‡ **phenotypic ratio:** ratio of various classes of possible phenotypes produced by allelic combinations at the locus or loci producing a phenotypic trait. See 9:3:3:1.

**phenotypic sex:** appearance of maleness or femaleness; apparent sex. Normal development of internal and external reproductive structures in the fetus, and compatible continuation of that development as **secondary sexual characters** at **puberty**. See **guevedoces**.

**phenotypic variance: total phenotypic variance** of a character in a population; explained by all developmental factors to which the members of a population have been exposed; a property of a population, not of individuals, or any particular individual.

**phenylalanine** (Phe): an essential **amino acid**; one of the twenty building blocks of **proteins**.

**phenylethylamine** (PEA): natural trace neurotransmitter with psychoactive antidepressant activity that is alleged to act as a **sympathomimetic**; also found in natural chocolate, almonds, and citrus. Aka 2- or beta-phenylethylamine. See **dopamine**.

‡ **phenylketonuria:** see **PKU**.

**phenylthiocarbamide:** see **PTC taster/nontaster polymorphism**.

**pheromone:** chemical substance, usually a glandular secretion, that is used in communication between members of a species (see **conspecific**). One individual releases the substance as a **signal** and another or others respond after tasting or smelling it. Because of the historical separation of humans from other animals, the human literature tends to ignore or deny that there are human pheromones. The term is also not usually applied to **primates**, although it is clear that many (especially **prosimians** and **callitrichids**) secrete pheromone-like substances. See **primer pheromone** and **releaser pheromone**. Cf. **hormone**.

**Philadelphia chromosome** (Ph¹): a **major chromosome anomaly** caused by the balanced translocation of a portion of chromosome 9 to 22 (t9;22, 9q34 and 22q11.21) that results in a new 'tiny' chromosome, Ph¹. The clinical outcome is a condition characterized by abnormal proliferation of bone marrow cell lines, and **chronic myeloid leukemia** (CML), produced when the Abelson **oncogene** (ABL) and the breakpoint cluster regions (BCR) demonstrate a synergistic **position effect**, and produce an abnormal **fusion protein** that causes **cancer**. Patients live about four years until immature WBCs overtake other cells, resulting in death. The breakage on chromosome 22 occurs in the BCR. Cf. **Burkitt lymphoma**.

**Philippine tarsier:** vernacular for *Tarsius syrichta*.

**philopatry:** remaining in the **natal group** or home range as an adult. Adjective: philopatric. In primates, only one sex, usually females in monkeys and males among the African apes, tends to be philopatric.

**philtrum:** 1. vertical cleft in the **rhinarium** of **prosimians**. 2. shallow vertical groove located mid-sagittally and inferior to the apex (tip) of the nose and superior to the upper lip in humans. Note that this is not considered to be **homologous** with the prosimian philtrum.

**phocomelia:** failure of the limbs to develop properly, resulting in small limb buds and other dysplasias. The most usual manifestation is the absence of the most proximal bone of a limb, e.g. the humerus or femur. Three forms occur, all autosomal recessive. Very rarely seen in a full-term fetus. The 'thalidomide baby syndrome' is a **phenocopy**. Aka Roberts syndrome.

**phonation:** production of sound by using the **vocal folds**.

**phonolite:** fine-grained green lava that was a preferred material for later tools at **Olduvai Gorge** in Tanzania, because it held an especially sharp edge; its source was located by geologist Richard Hay near a small volcano, 12 miles distant.

**phosphate:** ion used in the construction of nucleic acids; $PO_4$.

**phosphate determination:** measurement of **phosphate** content in the soil of an archaeological site in order to determine the most densely inhabited portion. Settlement rubbish deposits a high phosphate content in the soil that can be measured centuries after habitation.

**phosphodiester bond:** covalent bond between a sugar and a phosphate in DNA or RNA.

**phospholipid bilayer:** paired structure within a cell membrane formed by parallel sheets of aligned fatty acid molecules.

**photobiology:** study of the effects of radiant energy on organisms, especially in the electromagnetic range between 380 and 760 nm.

**photodermatitis:** 1. any inflammation of the skin after exposure to light. 2. development of skin lesions after exposure to light in individuals who have developed allergic reactions to certain drugs such as tetracycline.

**photodynamic:** pertaining to the energy-producing effects of light.

**photogene:** any gene that increases the rate of transcription upon exposure to illumination.

**photogrammetry:** stereophotographic method used in topographic surveying and medicine, that plots the contours of a surface with great precision. Adjective: photogrammetric.

**photolysases:** enzymes that absorb energy from visible light and use that energy to bind to pyrimidine **dimers**, then break the covalent bonds that created the dimers.

**photolysis:** destruction of chemical compounds by light, usually in the **ultraviolet** range.

**photometry:** measurement of the intensity of light.

**photoperiodism:** regulation of the biological activities of plants and animals by daily, lunar and solar cycles, the photoperiods.

**photoprotection:** any barrier to or within the **integument** that prevents light from penetrating deeply into the epidermis. Photoprotection in the case of humans is provided by **melanin**, clothing, sunscreening agents, and shelters. Protection is necessary to prevent both **mutations** and photolysis of vitamins such as **folate**.

**photoreactivation:** mode of DNA repair during which pyrimidine **dimers** formed after exposure to **UV radiation** are cleared by exposure to a specific form of white light.

**photoreactivation enzyme:** enzyme that removes **thymine dimers** induced by **ultraviolet light** from DNA molecules.

**photoreceptive:** pertaining to the ability to be stimulated by light waves. See **photoreceptor**.

**photoreceptor:** specialized receptor cell or group of cells that contains photopigments that are sensitive to light energy; in primates they are only found in the eyes and are of two types, **rod cells** and **cone cells**.

**photosensitization:** affective reaction of skin upon exposure to light or **ultraviolet radiation**, often caused by ingestion of plants or drugs. Aka photoallergy.

**photosynthesis:** conversion of water and carbon dioxide into carbohydrates by green plant cells, utilizing solar radiation as an energy source, and chlorophyll as a catalyst. The bonds in the carbohydrates contain energy that can be released during cellular metabolism.

**phragmite:** peat formed from reeds and other shallow water plants.

**phratry:** 1. a division of a tribe or other breeding isolate. 2. in taxonomy, a subtribe or clan.

**phrenology:** archaic eighteeth century analytical method founded on the belief that mental faculties are manifested in the physical configuration of the **cranium**.

**phthalates:** chemicals that are **estrogen** mimics, such as those found in plastics, lubricants, and certain solvents found in colognes, and possibly that can cause **premature thelarche**.

**phthiriophagy:** eating of lice, a common behavior of humans and other primates during **grooming**.

**phyla:** lineages, each usually characterized by a specific body plan; plural of **phylum**.

**phylad:** small phylogenetic stock, used generally to describe a small and isolated cluster of species that are closely related.

**phyletic:** pertaining to a lineage of descent, a group of species with a common ancestor.

**phyletic change:** evolution of a new **species** through the gradual change of an existing species; phyletic change does not add new species so there is no increase in species diversity.

**phyletic classification:** any classification in which taxonomic groupings correspond to **monophyletic groups**.

**phyletic evolution:** term used to mean either **phyletic gradualism** or **anagenesis**.

‡ **phyletic gradualism:** model of **evolution** in which change takes place slowly, in small steps, within a population. **Darwin** strongly held this view, denying even the existence of what would today be called **point mutations**, which he viewed as **saltations**. Cf. **punctuated equilibrium**.

**phyletic group:** group of species related to one another by common descent.

**phyletic lineage:** any ancestor–descendant pair of nodes in a **phylogenetic tree**; see **chronospecies**.

**phyletic speciation:** successional speciation; aka **anagenetic speciation**.

**PHYLIP:** phylogeny inference package, a computer program for the analysis of data which estimates phylogenetic trees, authored by J. Felsenstein.

**phylogenesis:** evolutionary development of a species or lineage; phylogenetic. Aka **phylogeny**. Cf. **ontogeny** and **anagenesis**.

**phylogenetic analysis using parsimony:** see **PAUP**.

**phylogenetic constraint:** trait that developed in the history of a taxon that lead that group in a direction from which it cannot then change; e.g. after the loss of a particular structure. For example, panda ancestors lost the **cecum**, which in other animals is used for the fermentation of fibrous foods. Their descendants today need to process large amounts of fiber, but do not have the morphological structures to digest it efficiently, and consequently are constrained to consume an extraordinarily large amount of bamboo in order to survive only off the soluble components. A factor of **historicity**. See **contingency**.

**phylogenetic density:** in reference to the topology of a **dendrogram**, a dense tree would be one in which a region of the tree contained many closely related species as represented by short branch lengths; a sparse tree would contain few and distantly related species with long branch lengths.

**phylogenetic footprinting:** a method of **cross-species genomic comparison** that compares anciently conserved gene-based elements (= genetic **symplesiomorphies**) among several distantly related species. Cf. **phylogenetic shadowing**.

**phylogenetic inertia:** basic genetic mechanisms and prior adaptations which are maintained by a species or a group of species that make certain changes more likely or less likely. See **prime mover**.

**phylogenetic inference:** construction of phylogenies in the form of testable hypotheses. See **phylogenetic reconstruction**.

**phylogenetic noise:** presence of **character states** due to **convergent evolution**, and that confound an evolutionary analysis.

**phylogenetic principle:** method of **classification** in which taxa are grouped together with other taxa according to how recently they shared a **common ancestor**. Aka **cladistic** method. One of the two main organizing principles in biological **taxonomy**. Cf. **phenetic principle**.

**phylogenetic reconstruction:** process of deducing evolutionary relationships over time and between living species. There are many different methods and perspectives as to how phylogenetic reconstruction should be done, in many cases reflecting the strengths and limitations of disciplines (e.g. paleontology compared with neontology).

**phylogenetic relationship:** affinity due to recency of common ancestry; an evolutionary or genealogical relationship.

**phylogenetic shadowing:** a method of **cross-species genomic comparison** that compares anciently conserved gene-based elements (= genetic **symplesiomorphies**) among several closely related species, accounting as well for the phylogenetic set of species analyzed. Cf. **phylogenetic footprinting**.

**phylogenetic species concept** (PSC): idea of a **species** based on morphology rather than reproductive behavior; in this concept the species is the smallest cluster of individuals who can be diagnosed as having common ancestry and descent. PSC and its emphasis on morphology is popular with paleontologists.

‡ **phylogenetic systematics:** 1. method of **classification** based upon the presence or absence of large

numbers of traits or **character states**; sister groups are formed on the basis of sets of shared derived characters (**synapomorphies**), and species on the basis of unique derived characters (**autapomorphies**); size is ignored. 2. school of **classification** that employs phylogenetic **hypotheses** and uses recency of common ancestry as the sole criterion for grouping taxa. Aka **cladistics**; see **clade** and **Hennig**. One of the three main schools of biological classification; Cf. the **evolutionary systematics** of **Ernst Mayr** and others, and the **numerical taxonomy** of Sokal and Sneath.

‡ **phylogenetic tree:** see **phylogram**.

‡ **phylogeny:** 1. evolutionary history and/or genealogical relationships of a group of organisms. 2. the family tree that indicates which **species** gave rise to others and which species share recent **common ancestors**. Term coined by **Haeckel**. Cf. ontogeny; see also **cladogram**.

**phylogeny inference package:** see **PHYLIP**.

**phylogeography:** study of the geographical distribution of genealogical lineages. The tools of the phylogeographer are protein and **DNA sequence** variation.

‡ **phylogram:** 1. a genealogical tree in which branching patterns have been derived by using cladistic methods, and arm lengths have been derived using phenetic methods. 2. a branching diagram for a set of descendant species that shows their ancestral relationships; the vertical axis usually represents time and the horizontal axis usually demonstrates some perceived degree of divergence. Aka a phylogenetic tree.

‡ **phylum:** in taxonomy, a high-level category just beneath the **kingdom** and above the **class**. **Chordata**, for example, is the phylum that contains all vertebrates, and other forms with a chordate nervous system. Plural: phyla. Term coined by **Haeckel**.

‡ **physical anthropology:** subfield within **anthropology** that focuses on the study of physical human **variation** and the forces that generated that variation; physical anthropologist. This generally means the study of **evolution** as it applies to **paleoanthropology**, but can also include **biology, primatology, embryology, auxology, genetics, osteology, forensics**, and **medical anthropology**.

**physical development:** 1. umbrella term for the assessment of all phenotypic traits reflecting the state of **development** and **growth** during **ontogeny**. 2. (pd) a measure for grouping developing children that sums an individual's height, weight, and vital capacity **deciles**, and divides this total by 3.

**physiognomic breadth:** distance between the **subaurale** and the **superaurale**.

**physiognomic ear breadth:** distance between the **postaurale** and the preaurale.

**physiognomic facial length:** distance from **gnathion** to the **trichion**.

**physiognomy:** physical appearance, especially of the face, used in estimating an individual's character; aka anthroposcopy.

**physiological age:** degree of development of tissues of the nervous system, muscles, glands, and genitals relative to chronological norms. Cf. **dental age** and **skeletal age**.

**physiological anthropology:** study of human adaptability; the **acclimation, acclimatization**, and somatic adaptation (i.e. noncultural and nongenetic adaptation) of humans to various, especially extreme, environments.

**physiological race:** local population characterized by unique physiological properties; a physiological variant. Differing in **chromosome structure** (cytotypes) or **chromosome number** (polyplotypes); several primate species contain polyplotypic variants.

‡ **physiology:** scientific study of the functions of organisms and of the individual organs, tissues, and cells of which they are composed.

**physiometry:** measurement of any of the physiological functions of the body.

**phytogeography:** study of the geographical distributions of plants and their habitats. Cf. **zoogeography**.

**phytohemagglutinin:** active ingredient of red kidney bean extract that is used to stimulate cells to replicate DNA and undergo **mitosis**.

‡ **phytoliths:** tiny silica particles contained in plants; if recoverable from archaeological sites they can provide evidence of the existence of certain flora long after the plants have decayed.

**phytophagy:** dietary category pertaining to an animal that consumes plants. Adjective: herbivorous, phytophagous. See **frugivory, folivory, graminivory, granivory, gummivory, nectarivory**. Cf. **zoophagy**.

**pi:** 1. sixteenth letter of the Greek alphabet ($\Pi$, $\pi$). 2. symbol for the ratio of the circumference of a circle to its diameter, $3.141592+$.

**Piagetian:** pertaining to the works or paradigm of the genetic epistemologist Jean Piaget (1896–1980), who held that mental development in children could be characterized by universal stages; Piaget's world view has been criticized by many anthropologists engaged in cross-cultural research.

**Picrodontidae:** family of archaic fossil mammals belonging to the order **Plesiadapiformes**. Known from the middle to late Paleocene of North America; three genera, although some workers think that all forms should be collapsed into one genus. With the exception of one crushed cranium, this family is known only from jaw fragments and teeth. In the past these forms were mistaken for bats. Dental formula: 2.1.3.3/2.1.2.3. Incisors are enlarged, but the molars differ from any other plesiadapiform, the lower molars most resembling extant bats. For this reason it has been suggested that they were **nectarivorous**. Estimated body mass of genera ranges from 40 to 200 g. See Appendix 1 for taxonomy.

*Picrodus silberlingi* **Douglass, 1908:** archaic mammal of the middle and late Paleocene of the Rocky Mountain region of North America belonging to the **plesiadapiform** family **Picrodontidae**; most workers recognize one species, but some authorities collapse the other two picrodontid genera into *Picrodus* and recognize three species. Dental formula: 2.1.3.3/2.1.2.3; first molars enlarged, basins are present in the other molars, along with crenulated enamel; this is suggestive of the extant **nectarivorous** bats and has led to speculation that these animals were pollinators who fed on nectar. Estimated body mass around 40 g. See Appendix 1 for taxonomy.

**pictograph:** technically, any picture or design painted on a rock or other natural surface; often confused with a **petroglyph**. See **cave art**.

**pied tamarin:** vernacular for *Saguinus bicolor*.

**pierced mammal teeth:** teeth obtained from mammals and pierced, presumably for the purpose of suspending it from a sinew cord and for use as personal adornment; found in **Aurignacian sites** and associated with the presence of **AMHs** *c.* 36–29 kya. Cf. **furrow-carved mammal teeth**.

*Pierolapithecus catalaunicus* **Moyà-Solà, Köhler, Alba, Casanovas-Vilar and Galindo, 2004:** partial fossil **hominoid** found in 2002 at the locality of **Barranc de Can Vila** near the village of Els Hostalets de Pierola near Barcelona in Catalonia, Spain, dated to 13–12.5 mya (lowermost MN 7/8 biostratigraphic unit = Middle **Miocene**). The hominoid material consists of well-preserved craniofacial, dental and postcranial specimens (83 bones) from a single adult male individual (IPS-21350). No caudal vertebrae were found. Based on characters such as diminished muzzle size with a posteriorly situated **glabella**, proportions and lack of a **cingulum** on upper postcanine teeth, a wide and shallow rib cage, chimp-like **clavicle** indicative of dorsal scapulae, and flexible wrists (but with small hands and straight fingers indicating a lack of **suspensory locomotion**), the authors suggest that the new fossil differs from all extant Miocene specimens of fossil great apes, including *Griphopithecus*, *Kenyapithecus*, *Morotopithecus*, *Equatorius*, and *Nacholapithecus*.

**pig-tailed langur:** vernacular for *Simias concolor*.

**pig-tailed macaque:** vernacular for *Macaca nemestrina*.

**pigment:** substance whose presence in the tissues of plants or animals adds color to them. Pigments absorb or block sunlight, and are important in sexual displays. Aka **biochrome**. See **chromoprotein** and **porphyrin**.

**pigmentation:** coloration of the body and its organs due to a type of compound called a biochrome (which includes such pigments as melanin, heme, and carotene) present in certain cells and tissues.

**pigmentation rule:** see **Gloger's rule**.

**pilaster:** bracing ridge on the back of the shaft of the femur.

**pilastric index:** cross-sectional index of the **femur** established at the middle of the shaft.

**Pilbeam, David R.** (1940– ): British/US paleoanthropologist at Yale and Harvard. With his mentor Elwyn **Simons**, revised Miocene hominoid taxonomy in the 1960s and, in so doing, greatly collapsed the number of primate genera and species. Pilbeam was an advocate of *Ramapithecus* (later included in *Sivapithecus*) as the earliest hominid ancestor with the divergence of humans and the other African apes placed around 15 mya. After political upheaval forced him to leave the paleontological sites he was working in South Asia, he relocated to Africa and became director of the Baringo Research Project in Kenya. Author of *The Ascent of Man* (1972).

**pileated gibbon:** vernacular for *Hylobates pileatus*.

**Pilgrim, Guy Ellock** (1875–1943): British geologist, vertebrate paleontologist; Pilgrim conducted surveys at several Cenozoic deposits in the Persian Gulf and northwestern India. He revised the stratigraphy of the Siwalik Hills, and published on the vertebrates in each of the three major fossiliferous strata. In 1915, Pilgrim described two Miocene hominoids, *Dryopithecus punjabicus* and *Sivapithecus indicus*.

*Piliocolobus* **Rochebrune, 1887:** 1. catarrhine genus to which the red colobus monkeys belong; 3–5 species. Distribution discontinuous in equatorial Africa and on Zanzibar; variable habitats. Body mass ranges from 7 to 13 kg. Dental formula: 2.1.2.3; strongly **folivorous**. Live in troops of up to 100 individuals. See Appendix 2 for taxonomy, Appendix 3 for living species. 2. subgenus of *Colobus* when the red colobus monkeys are included within that genus.

**piloerection:** erection of a hair follicle when the arrector pili muscle contracts. This action generates heat from the muscle contraction and the hairs provide insulation. Another function of piloerection is a bristling of the hair in displays among nonhuman primates.

**pilosity:** referring to the degree of hairiness on a body. Adjective: pilous. Cf. **hirsute**.

**pilot study:** preliminary test of a research design that considers the feasibility of the plan and allows the researcher to work out any problems that are encountered.

‡ **Piltdown:** archaeological site found in 1908–15 at the Piltdown gravels, Sussex, England, dated as 'Pleistocene gravels', and that contains '**hominid**'

remains that included the intentionally modified mandible of a juvenile **orangutan** and portions of the skull of an **AMH**, first recognized as such by **Boule** in 1921. But at the time (*c*. 1915), these fragments were considered to belong to the same individual, and named *Eoanthropus dawsonii*. The fragments had been cleverly modified and placed at the site; see **Piltdown hoax**.

**Piltdown hoax:** fraudulent presentation of material from **Piltdown** as having belonged to a single hominid individual; in fact, a fossil **chimera**. In 1953, Le Gros **Clark**, Kenneth **Oakley** and Joseph Weiner applied the **fluorine test** (aka **F-U-N**) to the skull fragments and jaw, and demonstrated that these could not have been buried for the same length of time, and therefore came from different individuals; later analysis showed that they were from a 500 year-old human and a juvenile orangutan, respectively. The perpetrators of the hoax have not been conclusively identified.

**pinche:** vernacular for *Saguinus oedipus*.

**pineal gland:** neuroendocrine gland extending from the **epithalamus** in the **forebrain**. The pineal gland is stimulated by light and is involved with **circadian rhythms**; it secretes the hormone **melatonin**. Aka pineal body, epiphysis cerebri, corpus pineale.

**Pinjor:** fossil-bearing geological formation in the Siwalik Hills of India, laid down during the first of four Himalayan glaciations, and thus Lower Pleistocene in age.

**pinna:** outer region of the external ear of mammals that forms a trumpet-like structure; referred to as the auricle in humans. Plural: pinnae.

**pinta:** nonvenereal infection involving only the skin, characterized by white or coffee-colored spotting (Spanish, 'painted'); caused by a spirochete (*Treponema carateum*). New World origin, where it is still endemic;

transmitted by person-to-person contact. Aka mal de pinto, carate, azul, boussarole, tina, lota, empeines, spotted sickness. See **nonvenereal treponematoses**.

**pioneer:** first species of a given trophic level to become established in a region. In oceanic island ecosystems such as the **Galapagos archipelago**, for example, each accidental species that survived was a pioneer.

**piscivory:** dietary category applied to animals (piscivores) that consume predominantly fish during the year or during a particular season. Adjective: piscivorous. The majority of mammalian piscivores are marine mammals. Several nonhuman primates consume fish opportunistically, but none are truly piscivores. See **diet**.

**pisiform:** smallest bone of the **carpus** located in the proximal row of carpals on the medial side, articulating only with the **triquetral**. The pisiform is a **sesamoid** bone that develops within a tendon and changes the direction in which its muscle pulls. Aka subrotundum, obiculare, lentiform.

**pit:** depression, small hole, or pocket.

**pit of bones:** see **Sima de los Huesos**.

**Pitcairn Island:** island in Polynesia, a natural laboratory for the **founder effect** in humans. In 1789 the crew of the HMAV *Bounty* mutinied, and the mutineers together with some Tahitians colonized the island. Pitcairn Island is of interest to human biologists because of the founder effect that resulted from this documented event. There were 61 people living on the island in 1991.

**pithecanthropine:** any member of, or pertaining to, the genus *Pithecanthropus*; any colloquial reference to the *Homo erectus* group of fossils, most especially those found in Southeast Asia.

‡ *Pithecanthropus*: genus proposed by E. **Haeckel** in 1866 for the 'ape-man' he expected would be

---

**Species within the genus *Pithecanthropus***

*Pithecanthropus alalus*: mythical 'missing link' between humans and apes proclaimed by Ernst **Haeckel** in 1866. This is not a legitimate human species, but Haeckel gave it a Linnaean **binomen** and exhorted his students to mount expeditions to find it; Haeckel believed it would be found in Java or Borneo. Ironically, his medical student Eugene **Dubois** followed Haeckel's instructions and found a fossil **calotte** that he named *Pithecanthropus erectus*, later referred to *Homo*.

*Pithecanthropus capensis* (Simonetta, 1957): see *Telanthropus capensis*.

*Pithecanthropus dubius* (Koenigswald, 1949): binomen for the **Sangiran 5** specimen recovered in Indonesia. It consists of a mandible and two lower molars. Now usually referred to *Homo erectus*.

*Pithecanthropus erectus* Dubois, 1894: see *Homo erectus*.

*Pithecanthropus modjokertensis* von Koenigswald, 1950: see *Homo erectus*.

*Pithecanthropus paleojavanicus* Piveteau, 1957: see *Homo erectus*.

*Pithecanthropus pekinensis* Boule and Vallois, 1946: see *Homo erectus pekinensis*.

*Pithecanthropus robustus* Weidenreich, 1944: binomen for some of the material recovered from Sangiran, Indonesia; now generally referred to *Homo erectus*.

*Pithecanthropus sinensis* Piveteau, 1957: see *Homo erectus pekinensis*.

*Pithecanthropus soloensis* Jacob, 1973: see *Homo erectus*.

descended from *Dryopithecus*, a Miocene ape. The nomen was adopted by Dubois in 1894, but most specimens with this name have subsequently been referred to **Homo erectus**.

**Pithecanthropus Dubois, 1894:** literally, 'ape-man'; second genus erected by Eugene **Dubois** to replace the original *Anthropopithecus erectus* (1891); the **holotype** is **Trinil 2**; included the fossil **hominids** found in Southeast Asia (**Trinil, Solo, Ngandong**, among others); nomen later dropped in favor of *Homo erectus*. See box below for species.

**Pithecanthropus IX:** field number for a hominid found at **Sangiran** in 1993, the same locality that yielded similar hominids in 1937; 'Pith 9' is a recently discovered 856 cm³ skull tentatively dated to 1.6 mya; others think that the specimen is more recent, *c.* 700–500 kya.

**Pithecia Desmarest, 1804:** platyrrhine genus to which the sakis belong; five recognized species. Wide distribution in the tropical rain forest of the Amazon basin. Arboreal; diurnal; locomotion is quadrupedalism with leaping. Body mass ranges from 700 to 2800 g. Natural history poorly known. Dental formula: 2.1.3.3; **frugivorous** with insect, leaves, and seed supplements; also consume small birds and mammals; have been observed to go into tree hollows to capture bats, which they tear apart before eating. Reported to live in **monogamous** groups that undergo **fission** with a larger aggregation of such groups. See Appendix 2 for taxonomy, Appendix 3 for living species.

**Pitheciinae:** subfamily of the platyrrhine family **Cebidae**, consisting of the genera *Pithecia*, *Chiropotes*, and *Cacajao*. See Appendix 2 for taxonomy, Appendix 3 for living species.

**pithecoid:** pertaining to the higher apes.

**Pitjitanian:** Middle Pleistocene tool tradition found in Java characterized by coarse flakes in the shape of cleavers.

**pituitary dwarfism:** see **dwarfism, pituitary**.

‡ **pituitary gland:** hypophysis; small, pea-sized **endocrine gland** situated in a bony socket (the sella turcica) in the **mid-brain** below the **hypothalamus**; consists of anterior (**adenohypophysis**) and posterior (**neurohypophysis**) lobes of differing embryonic origin that function to regulate other **endocrine glands**. It is attached to the hypothalamus by the infundibulum, and is highly vascularized to promote rapid diffusion of **hormones** (see **pituitary gonadotropic hormones** and **human growth hormone**). Aka cerebral hypophysis, glandula pituitaria, hypophysis, hypophysis cerebri, pituitary body.

**pituitary gonadotropic hormones:** any of the substances secreted by the anterior **pituitary gland** (**adenohypophysis**) that have an influence on the **gonads**, i.e. **follicle stimulating hormone**, **luteinizing hormone**, and **lactogenic hormone**.

**pituitary growth hormone:** see **human growth hormone**.

**pituitary point** (pp): **craniometric landmark:** midpoint of the tuberculum sella of the **sphenoid bone**.

**pivot joint:** type of **synovial joint** in which a projection from one bone rotates within a ring of bone and connective tissue of a second bone; movement is restricted to rotation around the central axis; an example is the atlantoaxial joint formed by the first two cervical vertebrae. Aka trochoidal joint.

‡ **PKU:** abbreviation for phenylketonuria, a heritable autosomal recessive condition characterized by an inability to metabolize dietary phenylalanine; the subsequent toxic accumulation of this amino acid can cause mental defects. Symptoms begin to appear at about 4 months of age, and include irritability, depigmented and dry skin with a musty odor, and abnormal EEG patterns with seizures; phenotypic symptoms are variable. There are five types; in classic or type I PKU the defective enzyme is hepatic phenylalanine hydroxylase, PAH, which results in failure to convert phenylalanine to tyrosine; this causes abnormal myelin formation. PKU can be managed by a phenylalanine-deficient diet but early detection is difficult; after six months the neuronal damage is irreparable. Recent mass screenings for carriers and dietary management of PKU has resulted in longer lives for many PKU-affected babies; one consequence was an overall increase in the frequency of the abnormal allele, as well as a clinically new condition known as **maternal PKU** (see below). Aka Følling disease.

**PKU, maternal:** for symptoms, see **PKU** (phenylketonuria), above. Adult females diagnosed with PKU as infants and who received prophylactic dietary intervention therapy and survived the critical developmental postnatal period without experiencing damage to their nervous systems frequently abandoned the dietary constraints in later life; the serum phenylalanine concentrations in these individuals increased dramatically but with no direct ill effects to themselves. However, these females subsequently produced a new generation of PKU-affected individuals. When pregnant, their second-generation fetuses (irrespective of genotype) were subject to the same cumulative effects of PKU on their developing nervous systems, even though the source was their mother's serum. When such mothers are untreated during pregnancy, 95% of the resulting offspring are microcephalic and/or mentally retarded. Maternal PKU occurs only in societies where PKU has been treated by dietary management.

**placebo:** treatment that is supposed to have no physical effect on the outcome of an experiment; a null treatment administered to a control group. Literally, 'I will please' (Latin).

‡ **placenta:** temporary vascular organ found in most mammals, a wall of tissue formed by the fusion of membranes generated by both the **fetus** and its mother during pregnancy; the placenta functions to provide fetal **nutrition**, and to permit the exchange of respiratory gases and other materials, including the elimination of wastes, between the mutually exclusive **circulatory systems** of the mother and the fetus. See **chorioallantoic placenta, chorionic placenta, choriovitelline placenta, dichorionic placenta, epitheliochorial placenta, hemochorial placenta, monochorionic placenta.**

**placental barrier:** semipermeable membrane presented by the placental wall. Certain molecules are too large to cross the membrane, whereas other, smaller substances are free to cross.

**placental hormone:** any substance secreted by the **placenta** during pregnancy, including **chorionic gonadotropin** and certain other substances that have estrogenic, progestational, or adrenocorticoid activity.

**placental lactogen:** polypeptide **hormone** secreted by the **placenta** that enters the maternal circulation and disappears from the circulation immediately after delivery. Placental lactogen has growth-promoting activity, is immunologically similar to **growth hormone**, and inhibits maternal **insulin** activity during pregnancy. By inhibiting glucose oxidation, it can increase the **glucose** supply to a **fetus** developing in a malnourished mother. Aka choriomammotropin, chorionic somatommatropin, placental growth hormone.

‡ **placental mammal:** mammal with a true **placenta**, i.e. a member of the **Eutheria**. Cf. **Metatheria** and **Prototheria**.

**Placental membrane:** see **placenta.**

‡ **placentation:** formation of the **placenta** and fusion to the wall of the uterus.

**plagiaulacoid dentition:** cheek teeth that form an upper shearing blade that cuts against a lower tooth in which there are two rows of parallel cusps providing a valley into which the upper blade occludes. Characteristic of the living pygmy possum, certain **plesiadapiforms** and the **multituberculate** mammals. Aka butcher-block dentition.

**plagiocephaly:** asymmetrical, twisted shape of the infant skull due to irregular closure of the cranial sutures, a condition that may be due to intrauterine crowding, postnatal positioning (invariant sleeping position resulting in **torticollis**), **synostosis**, or deliberate binding and/or molding of the **cranium**. See **higher-order multiples** (births) and **cranial deformation.**

**plague:** an acute infection caused by a bacillus, *Yersinia pestis* (formerly *Pasturella pestis*). The most common form is **bubonic plague.** Other forms include septicemic plague, a severe, systemic form with rapid progression, and pneumonic plague, which can be secondary to the other forms. Mortality is about 60% in bubonic plague, and approaches 100% in the septicemic and pneumonic forms. Until recently plague was restricted to specific habitats in Asia. Sylvatic (wild rodent) plague is now **endemic** in rodent populations in many of the mountainous regions of the world. The bacillus is **vectored** by fleas (*Xenophylla cheopis*), and is occasionally transmitted to humans by the bite of this flea. Plague is thought to have been indigenous to Africa, as the clinical symptoms had been accurately described there in ancient times.

**Plan of Nature:** philosophy that nature is organized according to a plan and usually that everything has meaning. The idea was influential in the early history of **classification**, and is related to **essentialism.** See **Grand Design.**

**planimeter:** device for measuring the area of a flat figure by running a tracer over the boundary; often used by physical anthropologists.

**planooccipitaly:** deformation of the back of the head, often artificial and associated with the use of a cradle board or similar device.

**plant defensive chemical:** see **allochemical.**

**plant macrofossils:** preserved or carbonized plant parts in an archaeological site.

**plantar:** regional term for the inferior surface of the foot, i.e. the sole of the foot. Cf. **palmar.**

**plantarflexion:** bending, or flexing, the foot downward.

**plantaris muscle:** muscle in the lower limbs that functions to assist nonhuman primates in grasping with their feet. This muscle is highly atrophied in all **AMHs**, and is completely absent in 9%. See **vestigial trait.**

**plantigrade:** type of locomotion in which the mass of the body is placed on the **plantar** (sole) and **palmar** surfaces of the paws; technically, humans are plantigrade because we stand on the plantar surfaces of our feet. Cf. **digitigrade, palmigrade.**

‡ **plasma** (P): yellowish extracellular fluid portion of whole blood; plasma contains nutrients, proteins (such as **globulins**) and the **white blood cells.**

‡ **plasma cell:** type of **B cell** cloned by a sensitized B cell; plasma cells secrete antibodies. See **antibody-mediated immunity.**

**plasma membrane:** outer boundary of a cell, composed of a bilayer of phospholipids embedded with proteins; the plasma membrane is selectively **permeable.** Aka cell membrane, plasmalemma.

**plasma proteins:** albumins, **globulins**, fibrinogen, and other proteins present in blood plasma. These molecules function to retain fluids in blood vessels by osmosis, as well as performing other specific functions.

**plasma thromboplastin component** (PTC): component of the blood-clotting process; PTC is defective in individuals with **hemophilia B**.

**plasmagene:** self-replicating gene located within an organelle or symbiont of a eukaryotic cell; for example, **mitochondrial DNA** in eukaryotes, or a **plasmid** in bacteria.

**plasmid:** small circular loop of DNA found in prokaryotes that can exist in a cell separate from the cell's main DNA as an **episome**. Plasmids are used extensively in biotechnology as a **vector**. See **plasmagene**.

‡*Plasmodium*: protozoan blood parasite (family Plasmodidae) that is the agent of **malaria** (blackwater fever) in humans. Over 25 species are known to infect mammals; at least four are specific to humans, i.e. *P. falciparum*, *P. malariae*. *P. ovale* and *P. vivax*. At least seven species are found in nonhuman **anthropoid primates**.

**plasmogamy:** first step in **syngamy**: fusion of the cytoplasm of two cells. See **karyogamy**.

**plasmon:** umbrella term for all extrachromosomal entities that are heritable. See **chondriome**.

**plastic method:** any technique utilized to display a specimen that uses plaster, gelatin cast, glycerin cast, skull reconstruction, etc.

‡ **plasticity:** 1. the ability of an individual to change in response to the environment within the constraints of its genetic endowment; such variations produce many of the differences in growth observed between individuals or groups of people. 2. the ability of the brain to recover functions lost through damage, by reorganization. 3. ability of neural tissue to change its responsiveness to stimulation because of its past history of activation.

**plate:** rigid part of the earth's **crust** that moves with or without portions of the **mantle** during **tectonic activity**.

‡ **plate tectonics:** of or pertaining to continental **plates**, their creation, erosion, modification, and relative positions, due to their interaction with the molten rock in the earth's interior; the cause of **continental drift**.

**platelet:** small fragment of specific bone marrow cells that functions in blood coagulation; aka **thrombocyte**.

**Plato's theory of Forms:** proposal that things contain transcendent Forms, otherwise known as Platonic essences, universals and paradigms. Forms are nonmaterial, abstract (nonmental), eternal, changeless, real, and independent of the objects themselves. Proposed by Plato (*c.* 427- *c.* 347 BCE), who himself criticized this early thinking in his later works ('Parmenides'); nevertheless, his argument either influenced, or reflected, human tendencies toward typological thinking.

**platybasia:** state of having a cranium with a flat base.

‡ **platycephaly:** in reference to the superior surface of a cranium that is low in profile; this term is usually applied to the low and flatter cranium characteristic of *Homo erectus*. Adjectives: platycephalic, -ous.

*Platychaerops* Charlesworth, 1854: archaic mammal belonging to the family **Plesiadapidae** from the early Eocene of Europe consisting of two species; first plesiadapid described (although not recognized as a primate at the time). Derived from *Plesiadapis*. Dental formula: 1.1.3.3/1.0.2.3; body size (estimated at 2 kg) and crenulated upper molars suggest diet of **folivory** supplemented with fruit. See Appendix 1 for taxonomy.

**platycnemic:** pertaining to a tibia compressed from side to side; having a **platycnemic index** of between 55 and 62.9; exhibiting platycnemia.

**platycnemic index:** cross-sectional index of the **tibia** established at the middle of the shaft.

**platycrania:** artificial flattening of the cranium.

**platymeric:** 1. pertaining to a **platymeric index** value of between 75 and 84.9; platymeria. 2. in reference to a femur **diaphysis** that has an anterior–posterior flattening; platymeria is a characteristic of *Homo erectus*.

**platymeric index:** anterior–posterior platymer diameter × 100, then divided by the medio-lateral diameter.

**platyhieric:** having a wide sacrum; having a sacral index that exceeds 100.

**platypellic:** pertaining to a wide pelvis; having a pelvic index less than 90.

**platypelloid:** in reference to a **pelvic inlet** that is wide from left to right, but narrow from front to back; this is the condition in the '**Lucy**' (*Australopithecus afarensis*) pelvic remains. A very small percentage of modern humans have this condition.

‡ **platyrrhine:** 1. monkey belonging to the **anthropoid** infraorder **Platyrrhini**; New World monkey. 2. pertaining to a nose breadth on a cranium that is more than 52% of the nose length, or, on a living subject, a breadth that is 84% of its length.

**Platyrrhini:** primate **infraorder** containing all the New World monkeys. Platyrrhines have broad noses and a greater number of premolar teeth; some species have prehensile tails. Cf. **Catarrhini**.

**platytopic:** marked by platytopia, a broad face.

**play behavior:** activity engaged in by young animals, although among primates adults sometimes participate; play is a hallmark of mammals and is particularly well developed in primates. It is understood by the participants that this behavior is not serious, as when play fights occur. The precise function of play is unknown, but it appears to enable the young individual to gain confidence and learn skills for surviving as an adult, including social skills.

**play signal:** in primates a facial expression called the play face, which signals commencement of play. The play signal declares the nonserious intention of the behavior in order to avoid any misunderstanding. See **metacommunication**.

**play theory:** body of hypotheses that propose in general that young animals and children engage in play behavior because it reinforces specific motor patterns, introduces novel stimuli, and builds socialization skills. Play theory has been criticized by the animal behaviorists.

**pleiomorphic:** pertaining to phenotypic variation in a group of genetically uniform organisms, such as an **inbred mouse strain** or set of cloned organisms.

‡ **pleiotropy:** control of more than one phenotypic characteristic by the same gene or set of genes; usually one primary effect and several secondary effects. Adjective: pleiotropic. **Eye color** in humans, for example, is thought to share at least one (of two) loci with **pigments** affecting hair color and **skin color**. Aka genetic pleiotropy, pleiotropism.

**pleiotropic gene:** any locus that has more than one phenotypic effect. see **pleiotropy**.

**Pleistocene climate:** climate during the **Pleistocene epoch** (1.8 mya to 10 kya) continued to become cooler, and the earth entered a period of constantly fluctuating climate known as the **Great Ice Age**; the fluctuations were minor until about 800 kya, when periods of intense cold occurred about every 90 ky, with minor oscillations about 20 ky and 40 ky apart; about one third of the earth's surface was covered during glacial maxima; sea levels fell at least 100 m (some report up to 250 m) as sea water became permanently locked up in glacial ice sheets.

‡ **Pleistocene epoch:** one of the **Quaternary** epochs of the **Cenozoic era**, lasting from about 1.8 mya to 8 kya (0.01 mya); the **Age of Glaciers**, during which the genus *Homo* radiated into several species and adapted culturally as well as physically to several new habitats. Large Ice-Age mammals or **megafauna** appeared but became extinct by the end of the epoch (e.g. the mastodon, an elephant-like mammal, and saber-toothed cats). See Appendix 4 for a geological time scale.

**Pleistocene extinction hypotheses:** 135 species of New World **megafauna** became extinct within four centuries *c.* 12 kya. There have been three major competing explanations for these events. 1. the *Pleistocene climate change hypothesis* invokes concurrent climatic changes that accompanied the retreat of the major ice pack from North America. 2. the *Pleistocene disease hypothesis* proposed by Ross D. E. McPhee in 1997 invokes pathogens that jumped from the Native Americans or their domesticates who had recently arrived from Asia via **Beringia**;

Aka the hyperdisease extinction hypothesis, or hyperdisease theory of mammoth extinction. 3. the *Pleistocene overkill hypothesis* proposed by Paul S. Martin in 1967 invokes overhunting by Native Americans; Aka the prehistoric overkill hypothesis. Similar hypotheses exist to explain similar rates of extinction in Australia, cf. the '**blitzkrieg' human-induced extinction model**.

**Pleistocene glaciation:** see **Quaternary Ice Age**.

**Pleistocene soil modification:** see **cryogenic soil modification**.

**pleomorphism:** 1. the assumption of two or more forms by a single organism during its life cycle. 2. occurrence of various shapes in the same species.

**Plesiadapidae:** most abundant family of archaic fossil mammals belonging to the order **Plesiadapiformes**. Plesiadapids are known from the Paleocene and early Eocene of North America and Europe; six genera with large range in body size, 100 g to 3 kg. Lower incisors are **procumbent** and the dental formula is variable between genera and through time; molars and premolars are primate-like with low bulbous cusps, suggesting diets comprised of plant material. See Appendix 1 for taxonomy.

**plesiadapiform:** archaic mammal belonging to the order **Plesiadapiformes**, formerly included within the order **Primates**.

**Plesiadapiformes:** problematic fossil taxon known mainly from dentition and jaws that historically was included as either an infraorder or suborder among the primates by some and, more recently, placed outside the order Primates by others. As an order it contains ten families. This group is considered a **wastebasket taxon** by most researchers and contains more taxonomic diversity than that found among the living primates. Nevertheless, this group is considered by many workers to contain the best candidates for the primate progenitor, although it may also contain the ancestors of bats, tree shrews, and colugos. Plesiadapiforms were the most common mammals in many of the known Paleocene faunas, especially in North America. The primitive dental formula is 3.1.3.3, but later members show reduced dentition and many members developed specialized dentition. The primitive dental formula precludes the plesiadapiforms as ancestors of the earliest prosimians, which have four premolars; another unprimate-like characteristic is that the **auditory bulla** does not appear to be derived from the petrosal region of the temporal bone. See Appendix 1 for taxonomy.

***Plesiadapis* Gervais, 1877:** best known mammal of the family **Plesiadapidae** from the late Paleocene and early Eocene of Europe and the Rocky Mountain region of North America; contains from 13 to 15 species. This animal, previously considered if not a basal primate then closely related to whatever gave rise to the primate line, provides a model for what primate evolutionary biologists believe the niche of the earliest primates would have been; it may have evolved from the earlier **Pronothodectes**. *Plesiadapis* species were arboreal quadrupeds with short, but stout, legs, long claws, and a bushy tail (the impression of which was preserved in limestone). Dental formula uncertain: 2.0.3.3 or 1.0.2–3.3; the number of lower premolars reduced over time; some species (e.g. *P. anceps*) may have retained canines; the dentition is suggestive of adaptations for plant eating; the dental formula precludes any *Plesiadapis* species as an ancestor for any of the earliest known primates of the Eocene. Another unprimate trait is the development of the **auditory bulla** from entotympanic bone rather than from petrosal bone. Estimated body mass for the *Plesiadapis* species ranged between 300 and 1750 g. See Appendix 1 for taxonomy.

**Plesianthropus transvaalensis** Broom, 1937: see **Australopithecus transvaalensis**.

**Plesiolestes** (= **Palaechthon**) Jepsen, 1930: archaic mammal known from the middle to late Paleocene of North America belonging to the **Plesiadapiformes** family **Palaechthonidae**; two to four species depending on authority. Known only from dentition and mandibular remains. Dental formula probably 2.1.3.3/2.1.3.3; enlarged anterior dentition, enlarged third molars, low-crowned molars all suggestive of herbivorous diet, probably **frugivory**. Mandible unfused, as in modern **prosimians**. Body mass of the species ranges between 150 and 600 g. Some authors include **Talpohenach** and **Torrejonia** in this genus. See Appendix 1 for taxonomy.

**plesiomorph:** character of common inheritance found in an evolving lineage but not useful in distinguishing diverging taxa.

**plesiomorphy:** possession of primitive or ancestral character states. Adjective: plesiomorphic. Cf. **apomorph**.

**plesion:** proposed rank in a taxonomic hierarchy reserved exclusively for extinct fossil taxa.

**Plesiopliopithecus** (= *Pliopithecus*) Zapfe, 1961: poorly known primitive **hominoid** from the middle Miocene of Europe belonging to the family **Pliopithecidae**; approximately three species; many authors retain these species within *Pliopithecus*. Estimated body mass at 5 kg. Dental formula: 2.1.2.3. Another synonym is *Crouzelia*. See Appendix 1 for taxonomy.

**plesiotype:** specimen identified by a later researcher as a member of a particular species.

**plesitarsiiform:** member of the taxon Plesitarsiiformes; see **lemurophile hypothesis**.

**pleural:** of or pertaining to the pleural cavity and its associated structures, the serous membranes associated with the lungs.

**plica palpebronasalis:** see **inner epicanthus**.

**plication:** folding; process of making fissures by folding.

**Plinian eruption:** large volcanic eruption, as defined by measures on the Dust Veil Index and the Volcanic Explosivity Index, e.g. the eruption of Mt. Vesuvius in AD 79. Such eruptions are thought to reduce the amount of solar radiation that reaches the earth by more than 10% annually, and to have a cooling effect on the earth's climate. Smaller eruptions are termed Hawaiian, Strombolian, and Vulcanian. See **ultra-Plinian eruption**.

**Pliocene climate:** climate during the **Pliocene epoch** (5.3 – 1.8 mya) continued to become cooler and drier; at the beginning of the Pliocene a massive 'desiccation event' (the Messinian) occurred when the remaining water in the Tethys Sea (Mediterranean) dried up, about 5.3 mya; large ice sheets began to form on the northern continents about 3.2 mya, and intensified about 2.5 mya.

‡ **Pliocene epoch:** one of the **Tertiary** epochs of the **Cenozoic era**, lasting from about 5.3 to 1.8 mya. The **hominids** first appeared and radiated into several species during this time. Some modern plants first appeared in the fossil record; some species of mammals declined. See Appendix 4 for a geological time scale.

‡ **Pliocene–Pleistocene boundary:** see **Tertiary–Quaternary boundary**.

**pliomorph:** vernacular term used to describe early and middle **Miocene** hominoids of Eurasia that share many primitive features diagnostic of the **Catarrhini**.

**Pliopithecidae:** family of **hominoids** belonging to the infraorder **Catarrhini**. Known from the middle to late **Miocene** of Europe and Asia. Some authors include these genera within the **Propliopithecidae**; the number of recognized genera is disputed, but consists of about four genera and ten species. Small, primitive, **diurnal** apes that range in size from 5 to 15 kg. Dental formula is 2.1.2.3; the family included both **frugivorous** and **folivorous** members. Locomotion was probably arboreal quadrupedalism with limited suspensory ability. See Appendix 1 for taxonomy.

**Pliopithecinae:** subfamily of the hominoid family **Hylobatidae**. These small, primitive apes were believed to be the ancestors of the gibbons, but most authorities now question this ancestral relationship and place this subfamily within its own family, the **Pliopithecidae**.

**Pliopithecus** Gervais, 1849: genus of primitive **hominoid** from the middle and late Miocene of Europe and Asia belonging to the family **Pliopithecidae**; up to five species recognized. Estimated body mass from 7 to 15 kg. Dental formula: 2.1.2.3; **sexually dimorphic** canines; this genus appears to include both **frugivorous** and **folivorous** species. Contains a mixture of primitive and derived catarrhine traits. This genus resembles modern gibbons cranially and, consequently, was considered to be the gibbon ancestor; however, reevaluation, particularly of many features that would require parallel evolution with other apes, has led researchers to consider questioning the phylogenetic relationship of *Pliopithecus* to any living hominoid. See Appendix 1 for taxonomy.

**Plio-Pleistocene:** subset of geologic time used to describe the period during which early **hominid** fossils are found, dating to roughly 5–1 mya.

**-ploid:** combining form used in cytogenetics to indicate the number of chromosomal genomes, e.g. **haploid, diploid, triploid, polyploid,** etc.

**ploidy:** degree of repetition of the basic number of chromosomes. Refers to the standard number of **chromosome** or **chromatid** sets per cell. See **euploidy**.

**pluricausal:** 1. having two or more causes. 2. describes a disease that develops in the presence of two or more causative factors.

**pluripotent:** pertaining to unspecialized **stem cells** not yet committed to becoming specific types of derived cells; pluripotency is the retention of the potential to develop into several (but not all) kinds of **specialized cells**. Aka multipotentiality. See **restriction**. Cf. **totipotent**.

**plus 3 (+ 3) molar pattern:** 1. pattern found variably in humans on the **occlusal surface** of **mandibular** molars in which there are only three cusps, two **mesial** and one **distal**. 2. pattern found on the **maxillary** molars in which the **hypocone** is absent.

**plus 4 (+ 4) molar pattern: occlusal surface** pattern on some human mandibular molars in which there are four well defined cusps with the fissures separating the cusps forming a T pattern. Cf. **Y-4 molar pattern**. See **bilophodont** and **quadritubercular** teeth.

**plus 5 (+ 5) molar pattern:** pattern found variably in humans on the **occlusal surface** of **mandibular** molars in which the fissure separating the cusps does not form the Y valley present in the **Y-5 molar pattern**.

**plus 6 (+ 6) molar pattern:** pattern found variably in humans on the **occlusal surface** of **mandibular** molars in which an additional cusp, an **entoconulid**, is added to the **Y-6 molar pattern**.

‡ **pluvial:** rainy interval, especially during the Pleistocene. In Africa such periods are believed to have corresponded more or less to intervals of **glaciation** in northerly regions.

**pluvial hypothesis:** proposition advanced by geologist E. J. Wayland in the 1920s to explain lake level fluctuations in East Africa; according to this view, water levels were tied to the European glaciation cycles; largely discredited by the 1950s. Aka the pluvial/interpluvial hypothesis.

**pluvial periods:** periods during the **Quaternary** characterized by tropical and subtropical rainfall much greater than today, and the consequent formation of great lakes in those regions.

**PM:** older abbreviation for **premolar**; the abbreviation **P** is more common.

**pneumatization:** presence of air-filled cavities that help reduce the mass of the bone (relative to surface area) that make up the skull. Adjective: pneumatized. See **sinus**. Examples of pneumatized bones are the **mastoid process, frontal sinus,** and **maxillary sinus**.

**PNP deficiency:** heritable autosomal recessive disorder caused by a deficiency in the enzyme **purine nucleoside phosphorylase**.

**PNS:** abbreviation for **peripheral nervous system**.

**pogonion** (pg): **craniometric landmark**; most anterior point of the chin mid-sagittally. See Appendix 7.

**Pohjajar Formation:** revised name proposed for the **Notopuro Formation** in central Java, a member of the Kendeng Group.

**poikilothermy:** condition found in an organism with absence of or poorly developed **thermoregulation**, generally associated with **ectothermic** animals; poikilothermic. The temperature of poikilotherms fluctuates with the temperature of the environment. Aka heterothermy. Cf. **homeothermy**.

**poinçon:** punch, usually made from a pointed bone.

**point:** implement that served as the tip of a dart, lance, spear, or other device used in hunting. Among the many types of point are: Châtelperron, Clovis, Folsom, Gravette, laurel leaf, Mousterian, shouldered, side-notched, willow leaf, and Yuman.

‡ **point mutation** (μ): rare, unpredictable, and permanent change that results in a small, localized alteration to the chemical structure of DNA, especially a **gene**; usually the change in the quantity or quality of a **nucleotide sequence** in **DNA**. One of the **mechanisms** or forces of **evolution**, and the ultimate source of all new **genetic variation**. Aka micromutation.

**pointe à cran: Solutrean** triangular, laurel-leaf point that had a tang made by chipping a hollow at the base on one edge.

**pointe à soie: Gravettian** point that had a tang made by chipping a hollow at the base on both edges.

**pointe de lance: Solutrean** spear point that had one of several bases: concave, stemmed, or straight.

‡ **polar body:** cell produced in the first (**anaphase I**) or second division (**anaphase II**) in female **meiosis** (**oögenesis**) that owing to unequal division contains very little **cytoplasm** and thus cannot usually function as a gamete.

**polar body biopsy:** genetic testing of a polar body to infer the genotype of the attached oöcyte.

**polarity:** 1. the direction or trend of features in a system. 2. the direction of a morphocline from **primitive** to **derived**, i.e. in **phylogenetic systematics**, the plesiomorphic or apomorphic status of a trait. 3. the direction of magnetism with respect to the poles, considered normal if it matches the earth's current magnetic field, and reversed if in the opposite direction. See **paleomagnetism**.

**polarity epoch:** extended interval during which the earth's geomagnetic field has predominantly one polarity. Cf. **chron** and **subchron**. See also **paleomagnetism**.

**polarity event:** short-lived geomagnetic polarity reversal occurring within a polarity epoch, e.g. **Olduvai event**. See **paleomagnetism**.

**polisher:** wedge-shaped device made of antler and used for dressing skins, usually associated with the Lower **Aurignacian**.

**pollen:** plant spore containing the male gamete in **angiosperms**.

**pollen influx:** estimation of the number of pollen grains incorporated into a fixed volume of sediments over a particular time.

**pollen profile:** tabulation of percentages of pollen grain species taken from a vertical sample series; aka pollen diagram.

**pollen spectrum:** report of the percentage of pollen grains of different species taken from a single sample. See **palynology**.

**pollex:** most medial digit in the fore paw; digit I; in humans, the thumb, which is the most lateral digit when viewed from the **anatomical position**. The pollex consists of two **phalanges** and in humans is **opposable**. Also spelled pollix.

**pollinator:** any organism that carries **pollen** from one seed plant to another, thereby unwittingly aiding plant reproduction.

**pollinator hypothesis:** argument that the earliest primates were nectarivorous (see **nectarivory**) and served as pollinators. Part of their adaptation was color vision by which they could identify the flowers of plants that they pollinated; binocular vision equipped them with depth perception for close work with flowers; grasping hands enabled them to manipulate flowers while inserting their tongues. Aka angiosperm radiation hypothesis, pollinator hypothesis of primate origins. Cf. **arboreal theory of primate evolution** and **visual predation model**.

**pollutant:** substance that contaminates, especially air, water or food; used to express the degree to which the substance impairs the quality or diminishes the life-supporting capacity of an environment.

**polyacrylamide gel electrophoresis:** see PAGE.

‡ **polyandry:** rare type of polygamous **mating system** in which there are two or more reproductively active mates (usually related males) acquired by a single reproductively active female during the **breeding season**; the males may or may not cooperate with the female in raising offspring. In humans, polyandry is found in certain Nepalese demes. In primates, polyandry is found among some of the callitrichids. Aka monothely. Cf. **monandry** and **polygyny**.

**polycentric models of human origins:** models that posit multiple origins for hominids and/or humans; these include the **trellis model** and its many derivative versions and synonyms, such as the **multiregional continuity model**.

**polycentrism:** model of **human origins** proposed by Franz **Weidenreich** that featured multiple centers of human evolution connected by a network of genic exchanges.

**polychronism:** independent origination of a species on more than one occasion. See the **multiregional continuity model** and **polyphyletic model of racial origins**.

**polycistron:** length of DNA that includes several genes, usually serial members of a **biochemical pathway**, and are transcribed and translated simultaneously.

**polycyclic aromatic hydrocarbons:** carcinogens that cause specific mutations in the *p53 tumor suppressor* gene; these hydrocarbons are byproducts of coke ovens and foundries, and so iron and steel workers exhibit high rates of certain resultant cancers.

**polycystic kidney disease, adult** (PKD1): autosomal dominant genetic disease featuring fluid-filled cysts in the kidneys, and one of the major causes of renal failure in adults; manifests in the fourth decade of life. The defective gene is polycystin, which functions normally in cellular signal transduction.

**polycythemia:** increase (from *c.* 43% to over 50%) in the proportion of blood accounted for by red blood cells. Aka erythrocythemia.

**polydactyly:** congenital genetic anomaly in which extra fingers or toes, sometimes not completely developed, are present in an individual. There are two common forms of hexadactyly (6-digit polydactyly). In the autosomal dominant *postaxial* form, a single full or partial extra digit is located distal to the little finger. The GLI3 gene has been implicated. In the autosomal dominant *preaxial* form, a single full or partial extra digit is found proximal to the thumb. Both forms manifest during prenatal development. There are nine other less common forms, some with more than six digits; these latter are all very rare; aka polydactylism.

**polyembryony:** formation of multiple embryos from a single **zygote**, i.e. twins or **higher-order multiples** that are identical.

**polygamy:** any mating system other than monogamy; in polygamous systems, each sex may mate with multiple partners during the **breeding season.** Polygamy is common among primates and occurs in species in which males offer little or no **parental care.** Variations in polygamy include **polyandry** and **polygyny.** In addition, polygamy may be characterized by **promiscuous** mating in which the partners break off association, or by mating that has a longer lasting relationship.

**polygene:** one of a group of genes that, acting together, control a quantitative character, such as human stature.

**polygenesis:** 1. hypothesis of the development of life forms from multiple and independent origins. Cf. **monogenesis.** 2. See **polygenism.**

**polygenic inheritance:** familial resemblance of a complex trait caused by several independent genes and where the similarities among relatives are due to positive **heritability.**

‡ **polygenic trait, character** or **feature:** an attribute that is affected by two or more genetic loci; in humans, complex (quantitative) traits such as **skin color** and **stature** are polygenic, and often have a significant environmental component as well.

‡ **polygenism** (or **polygeny**): theory that living humans are descended from two or more pairs of humans, each of which led eventually to one of the different human **races.** Polygenism is usually associated with nineteenth century polygenist thinkers such as Samuel **Morton** and L. **Agassiz,** for example, proposed nine independent centers of Genesis; other polygenists have proposed as few as three. Aka polygenesis. Cf. **monogenism.**

**polyglacialism:** doctrine that there were several glacial periods during the Pleistocene epoch. Cf. **monoglacialism.**

**polygraph:** device that simultaneously charts respiration, **galvanic skin response,** and other bodily functions. Theoretically, when a person knowingly makes false statements, involuntary changes in these functions occur that can be detected by experts; hence the vernacular, lie detector.

‡ **polygyny:** common type of primate **mating system** in which there are two or more reproductively active mates (usually females) acquired by a single reproductively active male during the **breeding season;** a form of **polygamy;** polygynous. In humans, the females usually cooperate in the raising of offspring. See **one-male unit.** Cf. **polyandry.**

**polygyny threshold model:** argument that female reproductive success improves if, in a system where there is little male **parental care,** habitat quality improves by mating with a male who has other female mates. See the **sexy son hypothesis.**

**polymastia:** supernumerary breasts; in humans, a rare **atavism** in which one or more nipples or breasts appear, usually on the **milk line.**

**polymer:** chain of similar molecular units linked together in a specific sequence, as in the chains of amino acids making up proteins; a functional molecule constructed from elements originating from two or more loci. Cf. **monomer.**

**polymerase:** enzyme required for the process of bonding together two or more similar molecules to form a **polymer.** See **DNA polymerase** and **RNA polymerase.**

‡ **polymerase chain reaction:** see **PCR.**

**polymerization:** construction of a **polymer** utilizing nucleic acids, amino acids, or sugars.

**polymorphic:** occurring in many morphological forms; aka polymorphous. Cf. **monomorphic.**

‡ **polymorphism:** 1. any trait that varies in a population or set. 2. any discrete genetic **trait,** such as a blood group, in which there are at least two **alleles** at a locus each having frequencies greater than 1%, aka **genetic polymorphism;** Cf. **monomorphic.** 3. the co-occurrence of several different forms of a trait, such as a **chromosomal polymorphism** or **transient polymorphism.** See **balanced polymorphism.**

**polynuclear:** see **multinuclear.**

**polynucleotide:** linear sequence of **nucleotides** in **DNA** or **RNA.**

**polyovular follicle:** ovarian follicle that contains more than one ovum. See **dizygotic twins.**

**polyp:** any growth attached to the substrate by a small stalk; commonly found in the nose, rectum, and uterus, and frequently neoplastic. See **neoplasm.**

‡ **polypeptide:** long chain of linked amino acids. Aka peptide, protein, polypeptide chain.

‡ **polypeptide synthesis:** process of constructing a **gene product** in the cytoplasm of a cell from the **template DNA** located in its nucleus; a two-stage process, beginning with **genetic transcription** and ending with **genetic translation.**

**polyphyletic:** concerning, or derived from, several ancestral forms; refers to a taxon that has more than one ancestral line, e.g. the order Insectivora among the mammals, which may include a number of species that are not actually closely related.

**polyphyletic assemblage:** taxonomic assemblage consisting of many terminal branches originating from many different sources, with the kinship of at least one of the branches closer to another branch outside of the assemblage than to those with which it is being compared. Cf. **monophyletic assemblage.**

**polyphyletic group:** set of species descended from more than one common ancestor, owing to **convergence;** the ultimate **common ancestor** is not a member of the polyphyletic group.

**polyphyletic hypothesis (of racial origins):** see the **multiregional continuity model.**

**polyploid:** individual containing more than two, usually complete, sets of genes and chromosomes. If the **common ancestor** of a polyploid species was **diploid** (2N), subsequently derived species may be **tetraploid** (4N), and so forth. Polyploidy is a mode of **chromosome evolution,** not uncommon in plants and rare but significant in animals.

**polyploidy:** wholesale duplication of a genome, usually followed by the loss of certain critical chromosomes.

**polyposis of colon, familial:** see **adenomatous polyposis of the colon, familial.**

**polyribosome:** structure in the cytoplasmic or extranuclear part of the cell which form the site of **polypeptide synthesis;** sometimes also called a **ribosome,** but more correctly a **polysome.**

**polysaccharide:** long carbohydrate molecule formed by linking **monosaccharides** together. Cf. **disaccharide.**

**polysome:** complex formed by the conjugation of an mRNA molecule with several ribosomes; aka polyribosome.

**polysomy:** condition of having one or more, but not all, chromosomes in the polyploid state; see **aneuploidy.**

**polyspecific association:** affiliation of two or more species. These units may be traveling and/or feeding groups. Polyspecific associations may aid the participating species involved in finding food or detecting predators; for example, different South American cebid species are often found in association with each another, and baboons may associate with gazelles or other grazing mammals at waterholes.

**polyspermy:** entry of more than one sperm into an ovum during fertilization. See **uniovular dispermatic twins.**

**polythetic taxon:** group specified by a large number of characters or keys, of which none is uniquely diagnostic. Cf. **monothetic taxon.**

**polytopic:** referring to taxa, especially subspecies, that reside in geographically discontinuous regions.

‡ **polytypic:** literally, 'many types'; pertaining to any taxon comprised of several distinct taxa in the next lower category, e.g. below species, geographical and/or morphological variants, often called regional populations. Proponents of the **multiregional continuity model** maintain that *Homo sapiens* is a polytypic species, rather than one characterized by continuous and **clinal variation.** Cf. **monotypic.**

**polytypic species concept:** idea that a species can be a multi-population system composed of several morphospecies and without phenotypic intermediates; this concept considers phenotypically disjunct metapopulations as dispersed members of a single species network in which morphological variants replace each other geographically. Aka multidimensional species concept; polytypism. See **Rassenkreis.** Cf. **monotypic species.**

**polytypical evolution:** evolutionary event that is common to several lineages, i.e. that happened more than once to a given species. For example, that the speciation event leading to *Homo sapiens* happened several times. See **polyphyletic.**

**polyunsaturated fatty acid:** long carbohydrate chain that contains triglycerides and more than one double bond, and with two or more 'missing' hydrogen atoms. Examples include fish oils and vegetable oils (e.g. safflower and sunflower). Humans cannot produce polyunsaturated fatty acids; hence these essential fatty acids are acquired from dietary sources. **Essential fatty acids** include **linoleic acid, arachidonic acid,** and **linolenic acid.** See **unsaturated fatty acid.**

**poly-X female:** see **triplo-X syndrome** and **metafemale.**

**poly-Y male:** see **XYY syndrome** and **metamale.**

**Pompe disease:** autosomal recessive genetic disease in which heart failure is brought on by the accumulation of glycogen in muscle and liver cells, and caused by abnormal lysosomal storage. See **glycogen storage disease (II).**

*Pondaungia cotteri* **Pilgrim, 1927:** enigmatic primate from the middle to late Eocene of Myanmar (Burma); one species; known from jaws and molars; phylogenetic relationships unknown, but *Pondaugia* was suggested as an **anthropoid** ancestor from the time of its discovery based on low-crowned cusps and the large basin on the teeth; other workers think that it has either adapid or omomyid affinities. Estimated body mass around 7 kg. Dental formula unknown; preserved dentition suggestive of **frugivory.** See Appendix 1 for taxonomy.

**ponderal index:** quantitative assessment used in human growth studies in which height is divided by the cube root of mass.

**ponderosity:** measure of mass that takes height into account. See **body mass index.**

‡ **pongid:** pertaining to any **anthropoid ape** other than a gibbon or a siamang; i.e. the living great apes (**chimpanzee, gorilla, orangutan**) and their fossil ancestors.

‡ **Pongidae:** hominoid family which includes the living great apes (**orangutan, gorilla,** and **chimpanzee**) and their fossil ancestors, i.e. **pongids.** Some researchers make these **anthropoid apes** a subfamily (**Ponginae**) of the family **Hominidae.**

**Ponginae:** subfamily of the family **Hominidae** used in some classificatory schemes; this subfamily only contains *Pongo pygmaeus* and its subspecies among the living primates.

**Pongini:** nomen for a tribe of the subfamily **Homininae** used in some classificatory schemes; this tribe consists only of the genus *Pongo* and its species and subspecies.

***Pongo* Lacepede, 1799: hominoid** genus to which the orangutan belongs. See *Pongo pygmaeus*.

***Pongo pygmaeus* (Linnaeus, 1760):** orangutan (meaning 'forest man' in a Malay language); two **subspecies** recognized, although there is some movement to consider these separate species. Inhabits tropical rain forests of Borneo and Sumatra. Primarily arboreal, but do descend to ground, particularly the males; diurnal; **quadrumanual** climbers; on ground, locomotion is a form of quadrupedalism referred to as 'fist walking'. **Sexually dimorphic** in body size and several morphological features including canine size, skull anatomy, and the presence of large **cheek flanges** on the side of the face, and **throat sacs** used in loud vocalizations in the adult males; these last two features develop about five years after puberty. Body mass ranges from 35 to 50 kg in females, 60 to 90 kg in males. Dental formula: 2.1.2.3; primarily **frugivorous** with leafy supplements; some data suggests differences in diet between males and females. **Noyau** social behavior. See Appendix 2 for taxonomy, Appendix 3 for living species.

**pons:** rounded structure within the hindbrain or **rhombencephalon** that functions as a relay center; contains the pontine nuclei that are associated with several cranial nerves, as well as two respiratory centers. See **medulla oblongata** and **metencephalon**.

**Pontnewydd Cave:** archaeological site found in 1874 and reworked in 1980/85 in the lower Elwy Valley of North Wales, dated to 225–200 kya (TL), and that contains **Acheulean** artifacts manufactured from crude rhyolites and volcanic tuffs. Hominid remains include dental, mandibular and vertebral fragments assigned to the younger, archaic, **anteneandertal**, or **archaic *Homo sp. indet.*** group; the molar teeth are markedly **taurodont**.

**popliteal:** regional term for the concave area behind the knee; the popliteal ligaments help secure the joint of the knee.

**Popper, Karl Raimund** (1902–94): Austrian philosopher of science; member of the 'Vienna Circle' (*Der Wiener Kreis*) of philosophers who originated **logical positivism**, although from the beginning Popper was critical of their central tenet, the **verifiability principle**. Popper substituted **falsifiability** in place of verifiability; this became the centerpiece of his theory of **demarcation**, of distinguishing between science and nonscience. Author of *The Logic of Scientific Discovery* (1959) and *Objective Knowledge* (1972). See **verisimilitude**.

‡ **population:** 1. the universe of cases; see **sample**. 2. any group of interbreeding individuals. See **deme** and **metapopulation**.

**population, biological:** see **biological population**.

**population biology:** study of the spatial and temporal distribution of organisms; see **demography**. Among anthropologists, human population biology also refers to the **acclimation** and **acclimatization** of populations to various environments.

**population bottleneck:** severe reduction in a population followed by an increase. The result is sometimes the growth of a population with **allele frequencies** differing from those prevalent before the event occurred; may also result in a severe reduction in **genetic variability** through the loss of **alleles**. See **genetic drift**.

**population census size** (N): the actual number of individuals of all developmental stages within a species that occupy a finite area; colloquially, population size. Cf. **effective breeding population**.

**population crash:** sudden reduction in the number of individuals of a species, generally following a period of population increase sufficient to exceed the carrying capacity of the habitat.

**population, cultural:** specific society, such as the Shoshone or the Yanomamö.

**population density:** 1. the number of individuals of a species or type found within a given region. 2. number of any entity per unit area or volume, such as cells in a culture vessel.

**population distribution:** in statistics, the frequency distribution for a variable of interest that utilizes every member of the population.

**population doubling time:** interval required for a group of organisms to increase twofold in census number. e.g. to increase from 1,000 to 2,000 organisms. The doubling time for humans in the 1990s was approximately 37 years.

**population equilibrium:** condition where the local or global **birth rate** is equal to the **death rate**. See **zero population growth** and **demographic transition model**.

‡ **population genetics:** study of **allele frequencies** in different **populations**; the mathematical description of the consequences of **Mendelian genetics**.

**population growth:** condition where the local or global **birth rate** is greater than the **death rate**. See **zero population growth, population equilibrium**, and the **demographic transition model**.

**population parameter:** in statistics, characteristic abstracted from a population; common population parameters are the **mean** ($\mu$) and **variance** ($\sigma^2$).

**population pyramid:** graphic illustration of the age–sex structure of a population.

**population regulation:** control of population size and density by factors that influence **fecundity** and **mortality**.

**population sex ratio:** variation in **sex ratio** due either to chance or to an attrition strategy.

**population size** (N): see **population census size.**

**population structure:** manner in which a population is distributed regionally, the census numbers and **effective population size** of the constituent **demes,** and the relative isolation that either permits or inhibits **gene flow.**

**population study:** contrast of disease incidence among several groups.

**population thinking:** perspective within biology that **species** should be understood as a reproducing population of individuals who themselves display individual **variation;** population thinking has, according to Ernst **Mayr,** replaced typological thinking. See **essentialism** and **Plato's theory of forms.**

**population viability analysis** (PVA): demographic analysis used in conservation biology which examines the prospect that a species has the ability to persist in its environment. One of the most thorough PVAs has been conducted for the Tana River mangabey in eastern Kenya. See **minimum viable population, minimum dynamic area.**

**pore:** any opening into or through a tissue or structure.

**porion** (po): **craniometric landmark;** most lateral superior point on the margin of the **external acoustic meatus.** See Appendix 7.

**porion–bregma height: craniometric** measurement; height from the **porion** to the **bregma** measured with a head spanner. Similar to **auricular height,** but does not require preservation of the facial skeleton (for **Frankfort horizontal** orientation); consequently, often used when the base of the skull is damaged or missing. See Appendix 7 for an illustration of the landmarks used.

**porosis:** porous condition.

**porotic hyperostosis:** condition resulting from iron-deficiency **anemia** which manifests as a thinning of the outer table of bone, exposing the porotic bone underneath; evidence of paleonutritional **stress** in prehistoric skeletons. See **paleonutrition** and **crista orbitalia.**

**porphyria variegata:** less common form of several types of inherited porphyria, the variegate form is characterized by a failure to metabolize the porphyrin ring in **hemoglobin** and results in obvious red urine; other clinical symptoms include photosensitivity, abdominal pain, constipation, weak limbs, rapid heartbeat, hoarseness, and mental confusion with periodic stupor. Manifests in the fifth decade of life. Porphyria variegata is an autosomal dominant, pleiotropic disease that, like hemophilia, segregated in the royal families of Europe. The symptoms can manifest in various forms, giving the appearance of several

diseases; there is also a recessive mode. Although the variegata form is the most celebrated, porphyria cutanea tarda is the most common form; each involves a different gene in the porphyrin pathway.

**porphyrins:** complex pigment molecules found widely distributed in plants and animals; in humans, examples are **bile, cytochrome,** and the heme portion of **hemoglobin.**

**position effect:** change in the phenotypic effect of a gene owing solely to a change of its linkage position in a **chromosome.** See **paragenetic** and **spreading position effect.**

**positional cloning:** means of cloning a gene based on its location in the genome.

**positive allometry:** allometric relationship in which the slope of a line representing the correlation of two variables is greater than unity (>1.0), producing a positive slope. Cf. **negative allometry.**

‡ **positive assortative mating** (PAM): common type of **nonrandom mating** in which individuals of similar **phenotypes** mate more often than expected when compared with a theoretical standard, **random mating.** PAM results in an increase in the proportion of **homozygotes** in a **population.** Aka homogamy, isophenogamy.

**positive correlation:** in statistics, the situation that exists when high values of one variable tend to be associated with high values of another, and vice versa. Cf. **negative correlation.**

**positive eugenics:** policy of providing incentives for individuals considered genetically superior to reproduce; the enhancement or addition of certain **alleles** — or guarding against their decrease — in a **population.** Aka progressive **eugenics.** Cf. **negative eugenics.**

**positive FDS:** positive **frequency-dependent selection;** occurs when the fitness of a genotype is proportional to the frequency of the phenotype in a population; thus, a lower fitness when rare and a higher fitness when common, resulting in probable fixation of a common allele and loss of the other allele; not the typical case. See **negative FDS.**

**positive sanction:** social approval of certain individual behaviors. See **sanction.**

**positivism:** nineteenth-century philosophy pioneered by the French philosopher Auguste Comte (1798–1857) who made a scientific approach to the world a priority; viewed the approach to knowledge as an evolved hierarchy that involved three stages: religious, metaphysical, and scientific. Positivism later evolved into **empiriocriticism** and **logical positivism;** in psychology, **operationalism** is a related approach.

**positron emission tomography imaging:** see **PET imaging.**

**post mold:** tubular discoloration of the earth that indicates that a wooden post existed in an archaeological site; typically, rotting wood stains encroaching soil differently from the surrounding soil. Aka post mould.

**postadaptation:** adaptation in the strict sense; evolution in some trait that occurred in response to a specific selection pressure from the environment, and did not precede it by chance, as in a **preadaptation**.

**postaurale:** rearmost point on the **helix** of the ear. Cf. **preaurale**.

**postcanine teeth:** in reference to the teeth that are posterior to the **canines**, i.e. the **premolar** and **molar** teeth; cheek teeth.

**postcentral gyrus:** major convolution of the parietal lobe that is defined anteriorly by the **central sulcus** and thus tangent to the **precentral gyrus** of the **frontal lobe**. The postcentral gyrus is the location of those sensory areas involved with cutaneous and other senses.

**postcrania:** alternative term for **postcranial skeleton**.

**postcranial:** situated posterior (or inferior) to the **cranium**.

‡ **postcranial skeleton:** that part of the skeleton that does not include the **skull** or **hyoid** bone; the skeletal parts of the torso and the appendages; aka postcranium.

**posterior:** anatomical term of relative position meaning behind. In humans, posterior is often used synonymously with **dorsal**.

**posterior inferior iliac spine:** protrusion of the posterior **ilium** of the **coxal bone** superior to the greater sciatic notch; serves as the site of attachment for the pear-shaped piriformis muscle in the lower back.

**posterior pituitary hormones:** substances secreted by the posterior lobe of the **pituitary gland**, which are formed in the neuronal cells of the hypothalamic nuclei and stored in nerve cell endings in the **neurohypophysis**. The principle ones are **vasopressin** and **oxytocin**.

**posterior root ganglion:** cluster of cell bodies of sensory neurons located along the posterior root of a spinal nerve; aka sensory ganglion.

**posterior superior iliac spine:** protrusion of the **ilium** located where the **iliac crest** terminates posteriorly; on the living body it is marked by a dimple in the **sacral** area. Serves as a site for part of the origin of the **gluteus maximus** muscle.

**posterocone:** **cuspule** located on the **lingual** surface of the incisors, found in some **plesiadapiforms**.

**posterolingual:** pertaining to the surface or feature of a **premolar** or **molar** that is on both the distal surface and the tongue surface of the tooth. Frequently referred to as distolingual.

**postglacial:** period since the last ice age, a synonym for the **Holocene epoch** or **Recent epoch**.

**posthumous trepanation or trephination:** either **trepanation** or **trephination** performed on a corpse before burial.

**post-mitotic cell (**or **tissue):** cell that is programmed to stop dividing by **mitosis** after a certain stage of development has been reached. Such cells are non-proliferative, i.e. capable of only limited repair and regeneration. Examples of post-mitotic cells and tissues are the neurons in the brain and spinal column, and cells in certain muscles (such as skeletal muscles and the heart).

**postmortem:** pertaining to an event that occurred after death of the individual.

**postmortem dismemberment:** separation of body parts after death. This may occur owing to scavenger activity. It may also be the result of intentional dismemberment by someone utilizing saws or other instruments. In most forensic cases such dismemberment takes place in parts of the limbs rather than at the joints.

**postnatal:** referring to the portion of an animal's life from birth until death.

**postnatal growth:** pertaining to enlargement of cells and tissues during any period after the birth of an organism; after the natal period.

**postnatal stage (**or **period): 1.** referring to the portion of an animal's life from birth until death. 2. period in the human **life cycle** that commences with birth. Cf. **prenatal stage**.

**postorbital:** pertaining to the area behind the eyes; e.g. postorbital plate, **postorbital constriction**. Also referred to as circumorbital.

‡ **postorbital bar:** ring of bone that encloses the eye sockets in the primate cranium.

‡ **postorbital closure:** condition in which the posterior portion of the **orbit** is closed off by a wall of bone called the postorbital plate; this gives the orbit a cup-like appearance. This condition, unusual among other mammals, is found among the primate **anthropoids** and **tarsier**; its function is unknown. Also referred to as closed orbits.

‡ **postorbital constriction:** narrowing of the skull behind the orbits when the cranium is viewed superiorly.

‡ **postorbital plate:** plate of bone at the back of the eye orbit in primates.

**postprotocingulum:** structure occurring on the upper **molars** of some early primates in which a ridge of enamel runs from the distal lingual corner of the **protocone** to the **cingulum**; aka the Nannopithex fold (after the Eocene omomyid *Nannopithex*).

**postreplication repair:** mechanism of **DNA repair**

that utilizes the template strand to repair defects in DNA **replication.**

**postreproductive:** pertaining to the stage of life after the final **parity event.**

**postsynaptic potential:** local potential that arises in a postsynaptic neuron in response to activation of synapses upon it.

**posttranscriptional gene silencing** (PTGS): inactivation of a gene, portion of a chromosome, or an entire chromosome by **epigenetic reprogramming,** after **transcription.** Aka RNAi, **RNA interference.** See **gene silencing** and **transcriptional gene silencing.**

**post-transcriptional processing:** modifications to pre-RNA molecules within the nucleus, in which pre-mRNA is transcribed from the DNA **cistron,** the methyl cap and poly-A tail are added, introns are removed, and within the **spliceosome,** the exons are spliced together to form the post-processing mRNA product that will leave the nucleus. Aka nuclear processing, RNA processing.

**post-translational processing:** modifications to polypeptide chains after they leave the ribosome, during which occurs acetylation, hydroxylation, phosphorylation, attachment of sugars and prosthetic groups, oxidation of cysteines (to form disulfide bonds), cleavage of specific regions (that convert proenzymes to enzymes), prenylation to lipids, etc. Aka protein folding.

**post-translational theory of aging:** intercellular, stochastic model of aging in which the major premise is that modifications to the structural matrix of macromolecules increases with the age of an organism. Such time-dependent modifications as increased cross-linkage of proteins such as collagen impair normal molecular function and reduces the overall vitality of an organism.

**postural reflex:** reflex that maintains or restores upright, stable posture.

**postzygotic (isolating) mechanism:** any mechanism that, after gametic fusion, results in a zygote that cannot itself reproduce. See **hybrid inviability, hybrid sterility, hybrid breakdown.** Cf. **prezygotic (isolating) mechanism.**

**pot lid:** rounded flake split from flint through the action of frost. A pot lid shows no **bulb of percussion.**

‡ **potassium–argon dating** (K/Ar): chronometric (absolute) dating technique that exploits the decay of an isotope of potassium ($^{40}$K) into calcium ($^{40}$Ca) plus an inert gas, argon ($^{40}$Ar); especially useful when volcanic eruptions occur, as the argon present in the lava at that time is given up as a gas; thus a 'zero' event occurs where new basalt (lava) contains almost no argon; eventually 89% of the potassium atoms will become Ca and 11% Ar, with a half-life of 1.25 billion years, making the technique useful for dating strata deposited from 100 kya to the very oldest rocks known.

**potato-washing behavior:** activity observed among **Japanese macaques** in which animals learned to wash sand off of sweet potatoes provisioned by researchers; it is also theorized that these monkeys like the taste of the salt water on these potatoes. A juvenile female first learned this behavior and it spread among the other young macaques up to adult females; adult males did not learn the behavior. An example of **cognition** and **culturally transmitted behavior** among primates. See **rice-washing behavior** and **tool use in primates.**

**potentiation:** state in which presence of one agent enhances a response to a second agent, such that a final response is greater than the sum of the two individual responses.

**pottery:** fired earthenware or stoneware; ceramics.

**potto:** vernacular for *Perodicticus potto.*

**potto gibbon:** vernacular for *Perodicticus potto.*

**pout face:** primate facial expression in which the eyes are wide and the mouth corners forward, producing an O-shaped mouth that is present during contact calls and infant begging.

**power:** in statistics, the probability of identifying a treatment effect when it actually exists in a sample, defined as $(1-\alpha)$ or **beta,** the complement to **alpha.**

**power formula or curve:** relationship of size between two variables (such as body parts of an organism) $y$ and $x$ that can be expressed by the formula $y = bx^a$, where $b$ and $a$ are parameters, the **intercept** and the **slope,** respectively. See **allometry.**

‡ **power grip:** grasping of objects between the palm and one or more of the digits with the thumb acting as a buttress, as when grasping a pole-like object. In chimpanzees the thumb is aligned with the other digits. In humans there are three variations of the power grip: squeeze grip, disc grip, and spherical grip.

**power stroke:** 1. second sequence of the **masticatory cycle** in which food is crushed and ground by the **occlusal surfaces** of the teeth. It consists of two phases: **buccal phase** and **lingual phase.** See **closing stroke, opening stroke.** 2. part of the contraction cycle in a muscle sarcomere in which the crossbridge flexes, pulling the actin filaments towards the A band.

*p,q,r,* . . . : letters designating **allele frequencies** in a **polymorphism;** $p$ is often the frequency of the most common allele, $q$ of the second most common, etc. Cf. *P, Q, R.*

*P,Q,R,* . . . : letters designating **genotype frequencies** in a **polymorphism;** $P$ is often the frequency of the homozygote of the most common allele, $Q$ of the first heterozygote, etc. Cf. *p, q, r.*

**Prader–Willi syndrome** (PWS): neurogenetic condition characterized by mental impairment, obesity, small hands and feet, and lack of sexual maturity. Exhibits evidence for **genomic imprinting**; PWS is an autosomal dominant, caused by a small deletion on chromosome 15, and is transmitted paternally. See **Angelman syndrome**.

**pre-Abbevillian tool tradition:** all European tool traditions that antedated the **Abbevillian**. Aka Ispwichian.

‡ **preadaptation:** any previously existing gene, anatomical structure, physiological process, or behavior pattern that makes new forms of evolutionary adaptation more likely. Any trait that confers an eventual advantage before the conditions that will make it adaptive prevail; see **exaptation**. Bipedalism, for example, is a preadaption for **encephalization**. Cf. **postadaptation**.

**preadoption:** eugenic idea that some parent(s) could choose to utilize germ cells from other, supposedly superior individuals, rather than their own. See **sperm bank** and **artificial insemination**.

**preaurale:** anteriormost point of the external ear where the free portion of the **auricle** meets the skull. Cf. **postaurale**.

**pre-Aurignacian industry:** see **Mousterian** and **Châtelperronian**.

**Preboreal period:** stage of the **Blytt–Sernander classification**, dated to about 10–9 kya, characterized by pine and birch vegetation and by conditions relatively wetter and colder than the **Boreal period**.

**precentral gyrus:** major convolution of the frontal lobe that is defined posteriorly by the **central sulcus** and thus tangent to the **precentral gyrus** of the **parietal lobe**. The precentral gyrus is the location of those motor areas involved with the control of voluntary muscles.

**pre-Chellean:** older term pertaining to early flint artifacts from the earliest Pleistocene gravels found in western Europe.

**precious substance:** substance valued for its rarity, texture and color; such evaluations are cultural, associated with the genus **Homo** and usually restricted to **AMHs**. The earliest archaeological examples were **shell**, ivory, amber, jade, gold, lapis lazuli, turquoise and **chalcedony**.

‡ **precision:** refers to the closeness of repeated measurements of the same quantity; measurement error.

‡ **precision grip:** grasping of objects between the **palmar** pads of an **opposable thumb** and one or more of the other digits, such as when writing with a pencil.

**precocial:** pertaining to species characterized by larger litters, short gestation, and rapid development, that have a short or absent period of dependency upon parents, and that are able to move about independently at a very early age. Said of offspring of

**r-selected species.** The order **Primates** is generally considered a relatively precocial order, except for the **anthropoids**. Cf. **altricial**.

**precursor:** substance that is in a pathway that leads to another substance; for example, L-tryptophan is a precursor of serotonin.

**predation, group:** see **group predation**.

**predation pressure hypotheses:** proposals to explain selective pressures on primate group size. There are two hypotheses: 1. primates live in larger groups when there is high predation pressure; this provides for greater protection and with more individuals being vigilant predators are more likely to be detected. 2. predator pressure leads to smaller groups that evade predators through **crypsis**.

**predator:** any organism that kills and eats other organisms; both **carnivores** and **herbivores** are predators.

**predator pressure:** selective pressure on prey species by their predators. See **evolutionary arms races**.

**prediction:** in science, the act of foretelling or extrapolating toward a certain outcome, within the limits of a range of error, from among other mutually exclusive outcomes. Cf. **retrodiction**.

**predictive testing:** evaluation, usually after a blood test, that provides a probability that a healthy person will eventually develop a disease.

**predisposition:** 1. state of being predisposed or susceptible to a disease; any special tendency or inclination toward a disease; **anlage**. 2. susceptible to the action of any stressor, substance, or agent. 3. possession of innate factors, such as genes, that preclude alternative outcomes.

**Predmosti:** archaeological site found in 1880 in Czechoslovakia, dated to 26 kya, and that contains artifacts including examples of some of the earliest ceramics, use of red ochre, and hominid remains including 25 complete male and female skulls of **AMHs**, *Homo sapiens*. The entire collection was lost in an arson attack during WWII.

**Pre-Dravidians:** ethonym for a hypothetical **autochthonous** people of south Asia. Aka Veddoids.

‡ **preembryo:** fertilized **zygote**; the preembryo arises from the union of complementary **gametes** and is considered to be an **embryo** only after the three **primary germ layers** have developed. See **embryonic development**.

**preembryonic stage** (or **period**): interval during development that lasts in humans from **fertilization** through the second week of pregnancy. See **preimplantation embryo**. See **preimplantation stage**. Cf. **embryonic stage**.

**preference index:** measurement of food choice by a species. It compares the relative occurrence of food items consumed by the organism to the relative occurrence of these resources within the environment.

**preferential mating:** rules approving the marriage of individuals that have a specific kinship relationship, such as first cousin matings.

**Preformation Doctrine:** outdated idea, predating microscopic studies, that organisms exist in a small, preformed state in the germ, and **growth** (in the absence of **development** or differentiation) consists of the unfolding of a pre-existing form sometimes called a **homunculus**. Associated with Italian physiologist Marcello Malpighi (1628–94) and others, replaced historically by **blending inheritance** and later by **Mendelian inheritance**. There were two forms of preformation: **ovism** and **animalculism**. Aka preformation theory, preformationism.

**prefrontal:** pertaining to the anteriormost region of the frontal lobe of the cerebral cortex.

**prefrontal cortex:** see **limbic forebrain**.

**pregnancy:** condition in which a female is carrying a developing offspring within the body.

**pregnancy urine hormone** (PUh): see **estriol** and **chorionic gonadotropin**.

**pregravid:** before pregnancy.

**prehallux:** term applied to a small sesamoid bone that is occasionally present on the dorsal surface of the tarsometatarsal articulation of phalanx I (i.e. the **hallux**). See **tibale externum**.

‡ **prehensile:** pertaining to a capability for grasping; e.g. a **prehensile tail** or the flexible digits of the human hand. Noun: prehension.

‡ **prehensile tail:** muscular tail that can wrap around and grasp objects tightly to support the weight of the body. Such a tail usually has a naked gripping surface near its tip. An adaptation of arboreal animals, e.g. some platyrrhine monkeys.

**prehistoric archaeology:** study of cultures that did not leave written records; usual usage refers to **Mesolithic** and **Neolithic** deposits. Cf. **protohistoric archaeology**.

**prehistoric overkill hypothesis:** see **Pleistocene extinction hypotheses**.

**prehistory:** that portion of human history that extends back some 2.5 my before the time of written documents and archives. See **world prehistory**.

**prehominid:** defunct term used by **Weidenreich** to describe the fossil hominids found at Java, Peking, and Eyassi.

**preimplantation embryo:** prenatal **zygote**; in humans, an embryo so-called during the first two weeks following **fertilization**, and before **implantation** in the intrauterine lining. See **preimplantation stage**.

**preimplantation genetic diagnosis:** procedure in which *in vitro* **fertilization** is performed and one of the eight cells of the preembryo is removed and genetically analyzed in order to detect any defective genes. If none are found the seven-cell ball is implanted in the mother's intrauterine lining. Aka preimplantation genotyping. Cf. **chorionic villus sampling** and **amniocentesis**.

**preimplantation stage** (or period): interval between **fertilization** and **implantation** of a **blastocyst**; in humans this is usually about six days, but may be as long as ten days. See **preembryonic stage**. Cf. **embryonic stage**.

**prelogical mentality:** older concept that ascribed emotional rather than logical thought to **primitive** peoples, by some early anthropologists such as Lévy-Bruhl.

**Premack principle:** proposal that the initiation of a highly probable behavior will reinforce the initiation of a less probable behavior, if associated hierarchically. Suggested in 1959 by American psychologist David Premack (1935–).

**preman:** human of the fossil era; **hominid**.

**premature birth:** any human birth that occurs prior to 37 weeks of **gestation**.

**premature puberty:** early onset of sexual development. In human females, the early development (*c.* 9 years) of **secondary sexual characters** has been tied to both childhood obesity and to an enzyme that breaks down **testosterone** faster in some family lines than in others.

**premature thelarche:** early breast development in females, before puberty. Premature breast development is thought to be due in some cases to **environmental estrogens** and in other cases to **phthalates**.

**premaxilla:** anterior portion of the mammalian upper jaw that holds the **incisor** teeth; it consists of the two premaxillary bones. The premaxilla varies in length among primates and is most prominent in some of the **Cercopithecinae**. In humans it exists only during the **embryonic stage**.

**premaxillary index:** an index of facial flatness; face breadth multiplied by 100 and divided by the facial chord. Face breadth is the chord between at the lowest points on the zygomatic-maxillary suture in reference to the eye–ear plane. The subtense extends down to the **prosthion**. See **frontal index, rhinial index, simotic index**.

**premeiotic phenomena:** during **oögenesis**, female mammals differ from males in that premeiotic phenomena take place in the late **first trimester** of a female **fetus**, whereas in males these events are postponed until **puberty**. These consist of the initial stages of **meiosis** through late **prophase**/early **metaphase**, such that the **chromatids** are **synapsed** and are **chiasmate**, at which point meiosis is suspended and not resumed until **ovulation**. This profoundly influences the probability of **nondisjunction** in females of advanced age; see **maternal age effect**.

**Premnoides:** archaic mammal known only from the middle Paleocene of North America, belonging to the **Plesiadapiformes** family **Palaechthonidae; monotypic.** Dental formula: 2.1.3.3/2.1.3.3. Body mass estimated at 200 g. See Appendix 1 for taxonomy.

‡ **premolar** (P, PM): one of four types of **teeth** found in **heterodont** mammals. Premolars are double-cusped teeth, located behind the canines, that are used for shearing and grinding. According to some researchers these are the two most distal teeth in the human **deciduous dentition;** others think that the deciduous dentition contains molars rather than premolars. Because they have two cusps, premolars are referred to in dentistry as bicuspid teeth. Upper premolars tend to have two roots, although these two roots may fuse to appear as one with a groove down the center; lower premolars have one root. See **incisor, canine,** and **molar.**

**premolar cone:** protuberance in the center of an upper **premolar,** and sometimes found in the teeth of certain Asiatic peoples.

**premolariform:** in reference to a tooth that resembles a **premolar** tooth; premolar-like. In primates, such a tooth is usually a **molar** that resembles a premolar.

**premortem:** in reference to an event that occurred to an individual before death.

**pre-mRNA:** pre-messenger ribonucleic acid; an original transcript from a **cistron** that is converted to **mRNA** after splicing, i.e. the removal of certain sequences and the addition of others; aka primary transcript, nascent RNA, **heterogenous mRNA.** See **intron** and **exon.**

**premutation:** sequence variation that predisposes to **mutation;** usually moderate expansion of a **trinucleotide repeat mutation** that leads to further expansion, such as in **fragile X syndrome.**

**prenatal:** referring to the portion of life from conception until birth in higher animals. Cf. **postnatal.**

**prenatal adoption:** see **preadoption.**

**prenatal diagnosis:** diagnosis of a medical problem in an embryo or fetus.

**prenatal insult:** event that may adversely affect fetal development, such as intrauterine crowding, insufficient nutrition, and maternal infections. Cf. **teratogen.**

**prenatal stage (or period):** referring to the portion of life from conception until birth in higher animals. Cf. **postnatal stage.**

**preneandertal hypothesis:** model that attempts to explain the position of the **Neandertals** proposed by S. Sergi, who argued that the Neandertals arose from a 'preneandertal' stock that became progressively specialized for resisting cold and underwent severe natural selection and restricted gene flow that led to 'classic' **Neandertal** isolates exemplified by **La**

**Chapelle, La Ferrassie, Neander Valley,** and others. Supporters of this view have included **Keith** and **McCown, Howell, Le Gros Clark, Howells, Stringer,** and **Trinkaus.** Cf. the **Neandertal phase of man hypothesis,** the **presapiens hypothesis,** the **monophyletic hypothesis,** and the **polyphyletic hypothesis.**

**pre-Nebraskan glaciation:** early major glaciation of the Pleistocene in the North American sequence; see **Donau glaciation.**

‡ **prepared core:** rock that serves as the source for flakes that are fractured off of this stone.

**prepuberty:** phase of life immediately before **puberty.**

**presacral:** of or pertaining to the area superior to the **sacrum.**

**presapiens hypothesis:** model attempting to explain the position of the **Neandertals** proposed by Marcellin **Boule** and Henri **Vallois,** who argued that, compared with moderns, Neandertals were an old relict species with unshared, derived traits, and which suggested that they were a **congeneric** species; a modern European sapient lineage, as exemplified by **Swanscombe** and **Steinheim,** existed quite separately from the Neandertals and ultimately gave rise to modern Europeans, and Neandertals became extinct at the end of the Würm glaciation. Proposed *c.* 1915 and supported by **Keith,** but now largely out of favor. Cf. the **Neandertal phase of man hypothesis,** the **preneandertal hypothesis,** the **monophyletic hypothesis,** and the **polyphyletic hypothesis.**

**presbyopia:** 1. decline or loss of visual accommodation. 2. normal long- or farsightedness due to advancing years, often at age 42 ± 3 years; hyperopia due to loss of elasticity in the crystalline lens that removes the nearest point of distinct vision farther from the eye.

*Presbytis* **Eschscholtz, 1821:** 1. catarrhine genus to which the leaf monkeys belong; eight species recognized by most workers, some authorities list more. Before recent revision, this genus was often subdivided into subgenera or into species groups. Located in the tropical forests of the islands of Southeast Asia. Arboreal; diurnal; locomotion is quadrupedal with leaping. Body masses range from 5 to 8 kg. Dental formula: 2.1.2.3; primarily **frugivorous** with secondary **folivory;** retain dietary adaptations for a high-fiber diet, such as an enlarged **sacculated stomach** and large **salivary glands.** Social organization variable depending on environment and species; may be **one-male units** and **bachelor** herds, or mixed-sex troops (from 5 to 125 individuals). See Appendix 2 for taxonomy, Appendix 3 for living species. 2. **subgenus** used in schemes that lump the leaf monkeys in the genus *Presbytis;* the most current approach is to split these monkeys into several genera. This subgenus consists

---

### Species groups within the genus *Presbytis*

The traditional genus *Presbytis* (a lumping of leaf monkeys and langurs) contains as many as 24 different species. However, many researchers think that some of these species may actually be part of other species (as subspecies) and include them with the other species in four species groups.

*Presbytis cristata* group: consists of *P. cristata*, *P. francoisi*, *P. geei*, *P. obscura*, *P. phayrei*, and *P. pileata*. In an alternative taxonomic scheme, some workers include these species in the subgenus *Trachypithecus*. Most workers currently recognize these species as belonging to the genus *Trachypithecus*.

*Presbytis entellus* group: consists of only *P. entellus*. In an alternative taxonomic scheme, some workers include *P. entellus* the subgenus in *Semnopithecus*. Recent revision has raised this subgenus to a full genus.

*Presbytis melalophos* group: consists of *P. melalophos*, *P. comata* (= *argula*), *P. frontata*, *P. hosei*, *P. potenziani*, *P. rubicunda*, and *P. thomasi*. In an alternative taxonomic scheme, some workers include these species in the subgenus *Presbytis*.

*Presbytis vetulus* group: consists of *P. vetulus* (= *senex*) and *P. johnii*. In the alternative taxonomic scheme in which langur species are included in a subgenus, these two species are included in *Semnopithecus*. However, recent revision has placed both of these species in the genus *Trachypithecus*.

---

of the species from the islands of Southeast Asia, *P. (P.) melalophos*, *P. (P.) aygula*, *P. (P.) rubicunda*, *P. (P.) thomasi*, *P. (P.) potenziani*, *P. (P.) frontata*, and *P. (P.) hosei*. The langurs are also divided into species groups by some workers as an alternative to subgenera. See box below.

**presence and absence hypothesis:** incorrect proposal by William **Bateson** that a recessive trait is merely the absence of a dominant allele. Bateson proposed the use of upper- and lower-case letters to represent the dominant and recessive alleles, respectively, a convention still in use today. Recessive alleles are, however, recognized today as genetic entities in their own right, albeit often mutational variants of dominant alleles. See **genetic nomenclature**.

**presentation:** 1. position of a fetus in the birth canal during labor. 2. introduction of an individual, or the act of **presenting** in primates. 3. exhibition or delivery, as with visual or oral material.

‡ **presenting:** behavior in nonhuman primates in which a subordinate individual positions itself so that its rear is towards a dominant individual, and raises its hind quarters. This has been compared to the position that the female takes while being mounted. See **genital display**.

‡ **pressure flaking technique:** use of a blunt tool to press off small flint chips; this technique produces tools with a higher resolution than is produced by percussion techniques.

**pretarsioid hypothesis:** argument that **anthropoid** origins are to be found on the continent of Africa, but that the actual anthropoid stem is unknown.

**pre-Upper Paleolithic Age** (PUP): blade-based **stone tool** industries that appear and disappear regionally in the Middle East, Africa, and (possibly) Europe, *c.* 50–40 kya.

**Preuss' monkey:** vernacular for *Cercopithecus preussi*.

**prevalence:** total number of individuals carrying a disease within a period of time. Prevalence is almost always higher than **incidence** because a majority of affected patients will carry their disease for several years before being cured or dying.

**prey:** organism that is considered to be the food of another. While this generally applies to animals, plants are the prey of herbivorous animals and have developed **predator**-defense mechanisms such as poisonous chemicals and physical structures such as thorns.

**prezygotic (isolating) mechanism:** any mechanism that prevents members of different demes or species from achieving gametic fusion. See **ecological isolation**, **habitat isolation**, **seasonal isolation**, **temporal isolation**, **sexual isolation**, **ethological isolation**, **recognition failure**, **mechanical isolation**, and **gametic isolation**. Cf. **postzygotic (isolating) mechanism**.

**prezygotic isolation:** reproductive isolation in which two species never reach the stage of successful mating, and thus no zygote is ever formed. Examples are closely related species with different breeding seasons or courtships displays (recognition failure), or species that mate but experience zygote wastage because of chromosomal or genetic differences.

**Prichard, James Cowles** (1786–1848): British physician; one of the first to appreciate that human variation is not typological, and to recognize that population pressure culls varieties. He proposed that the first humans may have been black, and other varieties were produced sequentially; this was later modified to include the influence of environment on human variation. Prichard was a monogenist who came very close to recognizing the full implications of both **domestic selection** and **natural selection** in *Researches into the Physical History of Man* (1813). Prichard's *Natural history* *of Man* (1843) synthesized data on the races of humans to that time and had a great influence on the development of anthropology in England.

**pricker:** rounded or flat slip of bone, pointed at one end, and found typically in the Lower **Aurignacian** tool kit.

**primaquine sensitivity:** see **G6PD deficiency.**

**primary burial:** initial burial during which the flesh of a deceased person decomposes, followed by a **secondary burial.**

**primary constriction:** unspiralized, lighly staining region in a metaphase **chromosome** determined by and associated with the **centromere.** Cf. **secondary constriction.**

**primary consumers:** organisms that eat only plants and are the heterotrophs at the first trophic level.

**primary dentition:** see **deciduous dentition.**

**primary germ layers:** three distinct layers of cells from which the structures of the developing embryo will arise. The three layers are individually called the **ectoderm, mesoderm,** and **endoderm.**

**primary host:** organism in which the mature **parasite** resides when it has two or more stages of existence in different organisms.

**primary immune response:** immune system response to the first encounter with a challenging **foreign antigen;** compare with **secondary immune response.** See **memory cells.**

**primary intergradation:** occurrence of hybrids in a contact zone formed through mating between phenotypically dissimilar populations; the three morphs sometimes present as a **step cline.**

**primary nondisjunction:** in organisms with an XX, XY system of chromosomal sex (such as humans), abnormal nondisjunction of the sex chromosomes that results in aneuploid gametes. In the homogametic sex (females) gametes are produced with two X chromosomes (24,XX), or none (22,0). In the heterogametic sex (males), primary nondisjunction during meiosis I produces gametes with no sex chromosome (22,0), or with both (24,XY); primary nondisjunction during meiosis II produces gametes with either (22,0) and (24,XX) or (22,0) and (24,XY). Primary nondisjunction is the supposed mechanism by which all sex aneuploids first arise. Once it exists in a family, it can be maintained by **secondary nondisjunction.** See **sex chromosome aneuploid.**

**primary oöcyte:** diploid cell in the ovary that undergoes **meiosis I** to product two **secondary oöcytes.**

**primary production:** total mass of organic matter produced by autotrophs of an ecosystem over a specified period of time. Cf. **primary productivity,** and **net primary productivity.**

**primary productivity:** rate at which organic matter is produced by the autotrophs of an ecosystem. Cf. **primary production.**

**primary race:** one of the major divisions of human beings in older schemes, such as that of **Blumenbach;** aka 'primeval' race, great race.

**primary rain forest: rain forest** characterized by the later stages of the vegetational succession cycle. See **forest.**

**primary sex cord:** stringlike masses that form within the **gonadal ridge** in a developing embryo.

**primary sex ratio:** see **sex ratio.**

**primary sexual trait, character** or **feature:** sexual character that is directly related to the production of gametes. Cf. **secondary sexual trait, character** or **feature.**

**primary speciation:** splitting of one species into two. See **speciation modes.**

**primary spermatocyte:** diploid cell in the **testis** which undergoes **meiosis I,** and produces two **secondary spermatocytes.** See **spermatogenesis.**

**primary structure:** the linear amino acid sequence in a polypeptide chain; see **protein structure.**

**primary succession:** sequence of **ecological communities** that develop in newly created or disturbed environments. Cf. **secondary succession.**

**primary type:** see **type species;** Cf. **collateral type.**

**primary visual cortex:** initial portion of the visual cortex activated by stimulation of visual pathways via the **LGN.** Aka the striate cortex. See **visual cortex.**

**primase:** enzyme active at the initiation of DNA replication that constructs a short RNA primer. See **PCR.**

‡ **primate:** any member of the mammalian Order **Primates:** prosimians, monkeys, apes, and humans. Primates are characterized by a set of **traits** related to an initial **adaptation** to life in the trees. See **arboreal theory of primate evolution** and **evolutionary trends in primates.**

**primate behavior:** area within **primatology** that studies the behavior of the members of the Order **Primates.** There are three basic approaches: 1. study of behavior (and in recent times, ecology) of a species for its own sake. This approach is conducted in the field and is usually done by zoologists and anthropologists. 2. studying a **model organism,** usually in a laboratory, to deduce the evolution of human behavior; this type of study is usually done by psychologists. 3. studying free-ranging primates as models for early hominid behavior; this approach is often strongly tied to ecology and is done primarily by anthropologists.

**primate culture:** socially transmitted behavior in non-human primates. A behavior is most likely to be **cultural** if it is not displayed by every individual in all environments, i.e. if it is customary or habitual in many groups, and absent in others. Criteria suggested by Krober in 1928 for cultural acts in nonhuman species include: innovation, dissemination, standardization, durability, diffusion, and tradition; nonsubsistence and naturalness are additional criteria sometimes appended to Krober's list. Recent intraspecific studies have nominated 24–39 qualifying behavioral traits in **pongids**. Cf. **protoculture** and **culture**.

**primate ecology:** research area within primatology in which the relationships of primate species with one another, other organisms (including microorganisms), and their physical environment are examined. Topics include, but are not limited to, **behavioral ecology**, nutritional ecology, population ecology, and predator-prey relationships. See **ecology**.

'**primate origins' hypotheses:** see the **arboreal theory of primate evolution**, the **angiosperm radiation hypothesis**, the **nectar feeding hypothesis**, the **visual predation model**, the **grasp-leaping hypothesis**, and the **arboreal grasper hypothesis**.

*Primates:* first journal established as a venue for behavioral primatology, published in Japanese during the first year (1957), but in English as well after 1958. Its first editor was K. **Imanishi**.

‡ **Primates Linnaeus, 1758:** mammalian **order** to which the lemurs, bushbabies, lorises, tarsiers, monkeys, apes, and humans belong. There is no one characteristic that defines the order; rather, a suite of characters (sometimes listed as **evolutionary trends**) that include possession of nails, grasping paws with opposable thumb and great toe, binocular vision, and a relatively large brain. The order contains more than 200 extant **species**. Undoubted members of the order first appear in the fossil record during the **Eocene**. See **Prosimii**, **Strepsirhini**, **Anthropoidea**, **Haplorhini**, and **Tarsioidea**. See also **classification**.

‡ **primatologist:** scientist who studies the behavior and biology of primates, including their evolution. See **primatology**.

‡ **primatology:** a **taxonomically related discipline** that studies the biology of the mammalian order **Primates**. Although the subject matter is zoological, the membership of humans in the primates has led to this discipline being subsumed under anthropology in many universities and nations. Practitioners (primatologists) are found in biologically related disciplines such as anatomy, systematics, ecology, genetics, behavioral biology, physiology, and paleontology. Anthropologists originally became interested in primates for use as models of early human behavior, whereas psychologists sought to understand human behaviors through behavior present in our closest relatives.

**Primatomorpha: mirorder** proposed in 1993 as part of the grandorder **Archonta**; the Primatomorpha consists of the order Primates, **Dermoptera**, and a problematic order *incertae sedis*; supraordinal taxon consisting of some nonprimate mammals that are considered to be closely related to the stem of the primate line.

**prime mover:** 1. muscle most responsible for a particular body movement. Cf. **antagonist**. 2. energy source utilized by humans to accomplish work. During the **Eotechnic phase** the prime movers were wood, wind, and water; in the **Paleotechnic phase** these also included coal. 3. according to E. O. **Wilson**, one of the two ultimate factors that determine the direction and velocity of evolutionary change: **phylogenetic inertia** and **ecological pressure**.

**primer pheromone:** substance that acts to alter the physiology of the receiving organism that eventually causes that organism to respond. Cf. **releaser pheromone**. See **pheromone**.

**primeval:** appellation used by early naturalists to describe any unfamiliar, **primitive**, and/or impenetrable environment or culture. Aka primaeval.

**primigenius:** pertaining to early hominids that had a large supra-orbital torus and a low, platycephalic cranial vault, i.e. *Homo erectus* and the **Neandertals**.

**priming stimulus:** in behavioral research, a stimulus that prepares the animal for a response to a second stimulus.

**primiparity:** stage in the life history of a female at which the first **litter** or brood is produced; condition in which a female has given birth only once. Adjective: primiparous. Cf. **uniparity**, **multiparity**. See **parity**.

‡ **primitive:** 1. primary or embryonic. 2. not **derived**, i.e. occurring earlier in a series. 3. ancestral or **plesiomorphic**, when used to describe character states. 4. simple. 5. old term for any **autochthonous** people, especially those without a written history, but now considered pejorative.

**primitive band:** most fundamental social group beyond the individual family in a human foraging system; the type of social organization found where hunting and gathering form the basis for subsistence; said by some to average about 25 individuals.

**primitive endoderm:** see **hypoblast**.

**primitive promiscuity:** 1. Victorian belief that the 'savages' did not have the institution of marriage and therefore lacked the family concept and were thus amoral. 2. any unfocused sexuality.

**primitive streak:** identifiable structure along the posterior portion of an early embryo that eventually develops into the nervous system, and that serves as an axis around which other structures arise; the embryonic **mesoderm** and **endoderm** are derived from it.

‡ **primitive trait, character** or **feature:** any behavioral or morphological **trait** that is characteristic of a species and many of its fossil ancestors. Some opine that primitive features are often (but not always) less complex than more advanced ones. Aka **symplesiomorphy.**

**primitivism:** older term describing the glorification of any earlier 'noble savage' stage of human cultural or physical development, lost paradise, etc. See **Rousseau.**

**primordial:** pertaining to an embryonic group of cells that develop into a structure. 2. formed during an early stage.

**primordial dwarfism:** see **pituitary dwarfism.**

**primordial germ cells:** cells in a **gonad** that will eventually give rise to eggs or sperm.

**primordium:** 1. earliest cells that form an organ in an embryo. 2. **anlage.**

**principle:** tenet; see **rule** and **law.**

**principle of association:** central rule in archaeology, which states that an **artifact** is contemporary with the other objects found in the same archeological level in which it is located.

**principle of complementarity:** see **base-pairing rule.**

‡ **principle of parsimony:** rule stating that, in the presence of two competing and otherwise equal explanations, the simpler of the two should be considered the most likely; accounting for all the known facts with the fewest assumptions. Aka 'Occam's razor' (or 'Ockham's razor'). See **Morgan's canon.**

‡ **principle of segregation:** see **Mendelian principle of segregation.**

**principle of veracity:** 1. truthfulness. 2. habitual accuracy. 3. in science, capable of verification, such as by repeated measurement.

**prion:** 'proteinaceous infectious particle(s)', proposed by Stanley Prusiner *c.* 1982 as the infectious agent of the **transmissible spongiform encephalopathies,** and central to his **protein-only hypothesis.**

‡ **prion protein** (PRNP or PrPc): protein identified *c.* 1996, when a new variant of **Creutzfeldt–Jakob disease** in Great Britain was linked to exposure through the consumption of beef and dairy cattle infected with bovine spongiform encephalopathy (BSE, aka 'mad cow disease'). New variant CJD is one of the **transmissible spongiform encephalopathies.** Native prion protein exists in the human CNS, and increases in those tissues with age.

**prion conversion mechanism:** in humans, the modification of the native cellular **prion protein** (PrPc) to the infectious form appears to require two events: 1. a genotypic predisposition to conversion (see **methionine homozygosity**); 2. exposure to the infectious form of the prion protein (PrPSc) derived ultimately from sheep (but infected beef can be an intermediate vector). In addition to the requirement of MM (or VV) homozygosity at codon 129, a second mutation in native PrPc at codon 178 (aspartic acid to asparagine) is also required. The normal 3D topology is somehow disturbed by this second mutation, causing templated refolding, and the final result is PrPSc, a mutant isoform of PrPc. A second prion-like particle (see **Doppel protein**), also seems to participate in this process. It is assumed that the conversion process cascades in brain tissue, producing symptomatic ameloid-filled spongiform abscesses and progressive muscular and cognitive impairment. See **transmissible spongiform encephalopathies** and **defective ribosomal products.**

**prion protein polymorphism:** population variation in the **prion protein.** At certain amino acid positions, sheep, cows, humans, and other animals share apparently homologous clinical variants. At position 129 of the PRNP gene on HSA 20p, for example, humans can have either valine or methionine; this results in three possible genotypes: VV, VM, and MM. The MM genotype predisposes individuals to both new variant **Creutzfeldt–Jakob disease** and **Kuru.** People with the VV genotype seem to be genotypically predisposed to another condition, **fatal familial insomnia.** The VM heterozygote appears to have a higher fitness than either of the homozygotes, VV or MM.

**priority of access:** privilege that comes with higher rank in a primate hierarchy.

**prism analysis:** see **enamel prism analysis.**

**prisoner's dilemma model:** model within **game theory** that works to explain the evolution of cooperation. It weighs the costs and benefits to individuals within an **evolutionarily stable strategy** and whether it is advantageous, in a given situation, to cooperate or to be selfish.

**probability:** chance that a given event will occur; probability is expressed as values between 0 and 1.0 or as percentages between 0 and 100; the probability of an impossible event is 0, while the probability of an inevitable event is 1.0. Probability is used heavily in statistical significance tests.

**probability of survival:** 1. chance of remaining alive in a given situation. 2. a likelihood of enduring to a further time given an elapsed time; for example, the chances of living decrease with increasing longevity.

**probable mutation effect:** Brace's hypothetical explanation for structural reduction in tooth size among Plio-Pleistocene hominids.

**proband:** original person who presents with a disorder and whose case stimulates further inquiry into a **pedigree;** index case. See **propositus.**

**probe:** 1. single-stranded molecule of DNA or RNA with a sequence that is complementary to target DNA or RNA. Aka DNA probe, gene probe, hybridization probe. 2. see **probe-using behavior**.

**probe-using behavior:** any behavior that involves the use of a stick or similar instrument, usually to obtain food. See **termite stick** and **ant-dipping**.

**problem:** the central focus of a research design; often the **testing** of hypotheses; a statement requiring a **solution**.

**problem solving:** primate behavior research that assesses animal intelligence; in problem solving studies an animal is presented with a new situation which it must analyze and adapt to. A classic example is an orangutan that used a rope to reach the key to its cage; when the keepers tied knots in the rope to make it too short to reach the key, the ape untied the knots. Primates, among animals, excel at problem solving; some researchers refer to this as reasoning, but see **Morgan's canon**. In natural conditions such abilities led to tool use among our ancestors.

**proboscis monkey:** vernacular for *Nasalis larvatus*.

**procallus:** granulated tissue and fibrocartilage that forms at the site of a bone fracture, uniting the break. The procallus is the antecedent to the bony **callus**.

**procaryote:** see **prokaryote**.

**proceptive behavior:** behavior by a female primate in **estrus** to solicit copulation by presenting herself to a male; aka proceptivity.

**process:** 1. projection from a bone or other anatomical structure. 2. a series of actions, usually purposeful.

**processual archaeology:** approach to archaeology following the lead of Kent Flannery (1967) that emphasized culture process rather than culture history. The latter utilized the construction of historical narratives (e.g. those of Childe and Willey), whereas Flannery sought laws and mechanisms that made culture possible in a given region. Following Flannery, many American and some European archaeologists utilized quantitative methods and especially spatial analysis (see GIS) to deduce culture patterns; David Clarke and Lewis Binford represented British and American interests in this approach. A splintered reaction to this approach *c.* 1990 has been labelled post-processual archaeology. Aka new archaeology, scientific archaeology.

**procollagen:** assemblage of three polypeptide chains before a final cleavage step at each end that forms collagen.

***Procolobus* Rocheburne, 1887:** monotypic catarrhine genus to which the olive colobus belongs; aka magic monkey; van Beneden's monkey. Found in far western equatorial Africa. Occupies varied habitats; primarily utilizes the understory. Arboreal; diurnal; arboreal quadruped. Body mass ranges from 3 to 5 kg. Dental formula: 2.1.2.3; **folivorous**. **Cryptic** species that is camouflaged by its **pelage** color. Natural history poorly known. Social unit appears to be small mixed-sex groups. See Appendix 2 for taxonomy, Appendix 3 for living species.

**‡*Proconsul* Hopwood, 1933:** genus of extinct fossil ape (**Hominoidea**) found in early Miocene deposits (22–12 mya) in eastern Africa. *Proconsul* was a quadrupedal, tailless, monkey-sized 'ape' thought to have been adapted to a diet that included soft fruits. An almost complete skull was found by Mary **Leakey** on **Rusinga Island**. 'Consul' was a well-known chimpanzee at the London Zoo. Type site: **Koru**, Kenya. Distinguishing anatomical features include a mosaic of primitive, derived, and autapomorphic features. (see **autapomorphy**). *Proconsul* was the most primitive of the early **hominoids**, and was previously considered a direct ancestor of the modern gorilla and chimpanzee, the African apes. The clade may have originated 31–22 mya. See **Napak, Songhor, Koru,** and **Mfwangano**.

**Proconsulidae:** family of **hominoids** belonging to the infraorder **Catarrhini** known from the late Oligocene to the middle Miocene of Africa and the Far East; approximately ten genera and fifteen species. Great diversity resulting from a spectacular **adaptive radiation** that appears to have been centered in eastern Africa; the members of this family occupied diverse habitats ranging from tropical rain forest to open woodlands. Body size ranged from small species of 3.5 kg to large species weighing 50 kg or more. Dental formula: 2.1.3.3; large **sexually dimorphic** canines that were honed by anterior **sectorial premolars**; family included both **frugivorous** and **folivorous** members. Postcranial remains suggest a great diversity in locomotion. It is unknown what the phylogenetic relationship of the proconsulids is to any of the living apes; some features, such as the extreme development of a **superior transverse torus** and lack of an **inferior transverse torus** at the mandibular symphysis, appear to be unique. See Appendix 1 for taxonomy.

**‡ procumbent:** projecting or protruding forward; e.g. procumbent incisors.

***Procynocephalus* Schlosser, 1924:** genus of cercopithecines known from the Pliocene of China and India; two species. The European genus ***Paradolichopithecus*** is very similar and may eventually be included within *Procynocephalus*. *P. subhimalayensis* was the first fossil monkey whose description was published, as well as the first fossil recognized as a primate. This monkey has skull morphology resembling that of the macaques, but dentition and **postcrania** reminiscent of baboons. Estimated body mass around 22 kg. Dental formula: 2.1.2.3/2.1.2.3; dental morphology suggestive of a diet of tubers, fruit, and grasses that would be part of a terrestrial habit; limb bones also reflect a terrestrial adaptation. See Appendix 1 for taxonomy.

**producer:** 1. an organism that brings energy into an ecosystem from inorganic sources, such as plants. 2. in demography, a productive member of a population, as opposed to a **dependent.**

**product:** any specific entity that results from a process; in genetics, a specific compound that is the result of enzyme action; in biochemical pathways, a compound can serve as the product of one reaction and the substrate of the next reaction.

**product rule:** chance of the occurrence of two simultaneous events in the same individual; the crossproduct of the probability of each separate event.

**Profet hypothesis:** proposal that **morning sickness** is an inherited aversion that protects a fetus from natural toxins, and is a likely evolutionary adaptation. Cross-cultural data suggest that meat and animal products are the primary symptomatic trigger, but spices and other foods containing secondary compounds are implicated as well.

**profile:** 1. section or exposure of excavated wall showing primary depositional or developmental strata within a buried archaeological site. 2. see **DNA profile.** 3. see **racial profiling.**

**profundal:** referring to **deep** structures, particularly nerves and blood vessels.

*Progalago* **MacInnes, 1943:** genus of fossil prosimian known from the early Miocene of Africa belonging to the family **Galagidae;** two species. Very similar to extant galagos, although it cannot be determined which genera it gave rise to. Body mass between 800 and 1200 g. Dental formula: 2.1.3.3/2.1.3.3; dental morphology suggestive of a combination of **insectivory** and **frugivory;** incisor roots suggestive of a **dental comb.** Smaller orbits indicative of nocturnality. **Postcrania** similar to extant galagos except tarsal bones not as long. See Appendix 1 for taxonomy.

**progenesis: pedomorphosis** achieved by accelerating the rate of sexual maturation and thus suspending an individual in a physically juvenile state.

**progenitor:** 1. any biological or nonbiological ancestor. Cf. **parent.** 2. one who originates or models.

**progeny:** offspring resulting from a particular mating.

**progeria:** any one of a small set of accelerated aging disorders. Progerias include **Werner syndrome** and Hutchinson–Gilford H–G syndrome (the latter is aka progeria proper). In H–G progeria, children usually die of a heart attack before the age of twelve. There

are indications of a paternal age effect. Cells from affected individuals display a reduced number of replicative passages and a reduced ability to repair DNA. Recent evidence also suggests an autosomal recessive mode of inheritance.

**progesterone:** principal progestational steroid **hormone** of the body, liberated by the **corpus luteum** and **placenta** and in minute amounts by the **adrenal cortex.** Progesterone prepares the **uterus** for the reception and development of the **blastocyst** by transforming the **endometrium** from the proliferative to the **secretory stage** and maintains an optimal intrauterine environment for sustaining pregnancy; influences metabolism in the **mammae.** Progesterone of placental origin has the same functions. Aka progestational hormone.

‡ **prognathism:** 1. forward projection of the jaws, or prominence of the snout. Adjectives: **prognathous,** prognathic. 2. in modern humans, a heritable condition in which the **mandible** extends well forward of the **maxilla,** nose and forehead; aka Hapsburg jaw. 3. in general zoology, having a head that is horizontal with the mouth located anteriorly.

**prognathous:** in reference to the **Flower's index,** with an index of 103.00 or greater; such an individual is considered to have projecting jaws.

**prognosis:** prediction of an outcome, especially of a disease.

**program:** term that has entered behavioral biology via analogy with computers. Some behavior is genetically determined and is referred to as **hard-wired** (corresponding to computer hardware), other behavior is the result of experience and it is referred to as **soft-wired** (corresponding to computer software). In any species there is a mix of hard- and soft- wired behavior; however, some species have predominantly one or the other and are referred to as hard-wired species (such as primitive vertebrates) or soft-wired species (such as mammals).

**programmed aging:** idea that aging is orchestrated by material inherited by an organism, rather than random wear-and-tear events that an organism encounters in its environment. First proposed in 1881 by August **Weismann,** the idea has had many incarnations as knowledge of cell mechanics has progressed. Aka pacemaker theory of aging, aging clock theory, biological death clock. See **aging.**

**programmed cell death:** see **apoptosis.**

**progressionism:** idea that progress is a natural process that is intrinsic to the character of the natural and social sciences.

**progressive:** 1. forward-looking; advanced. 2. in paleontology, describes any specimen with traits similar to the **type specimen** of a species, yet with traits present in later species or specimens, as well.

**progressive evolution:** putative model of **evolution** that occurs in a straight line, presumably toward some preordained goal, an idea not commonly supported by modern evolutionary biologists; evolution toward increased independence from and control over the environment. Aka orthogenesis, rectilinear evolution. See **Omega**, **synergism hypothesis**, and **organic selection theory**. Cf. **sympodial**.

*Prohylobates* **Fortau, 1918:** genus of **cercopithecoids** from the early Miocene of Africa; two species recognized; known only from tooth-bearing mandibular fragments. Originally believed to have features in common with living gibbons for whom it was postulated to be an ancestor. Estimated body mass: *P. tandyi*, 7 kg: *P. simonsi*, 25 kg. Dental formula: 2.1.2.3/2.1.2.3; poorly developed **bilophodont** molars; diet is presumed to be **frugivory**. *P. simonsi* has a thick mandible, suggesting that it was subjected to strong chewing stresses; for this reason, it has suggested that this species was also eating leaves for part of the year. See Appendix 1 for taxonomy.

**proinsulin:** homologue to human **insulin** in mammalian species that contains an additional set (C) of amino acids that is an excised **intron** in the functional human form, which consists of two exons, A and B.

**projectile point:** chipped stone artifact used to tip a spear, an arrow, or an atlatl dart.

**projection:** 1. a prominence. 2. used with reference to sensations from any of the sense organs to the source of a stimulus. 3. reference of one's own attributes upon another. 4. the application of direction to light or other wave or ray.

**projective dimension:** pertaining to an anthropometric dimension obtained by measurement of perpendiculars between a fixed plane and landmarks in soft tissue, used when direct measurement is difficult. Aka derived measurement, indirect measurement, subtractive measurement.

‡ **prokaryote (cell):** cellular organism that has no membrane-enclosed nucleus that divides by mitosis and meiosis, no spindle mechanisms, and no chromosome condensation. Examples are the archebacteria and eubacteria. Aka procaryote. See **eukaryote**.

**prolactin** (hPRL): gonadotropic polypeptide **hormone** secreted by the anterior **pituitary gland** that stimulates and sustains **lactation** in postpartum mammals, the mammary glands having been prepared by other hormones. It also stimulates formation of crop milk substance in the crop sac of birds such as doves and pigeons, is luteotropic in certain mammals, and has many other effects, including essential roles in the maintenance of immune-system functions. Aka galactopoietic hormone, lactogenic hormone, lacta-tion hormone, lactogen, luteotropic hormone, lactotropin, luteotropin, mammotropin. The structure of hPRL shows some sequence identity with **human growth hormone** (hGH).

**prolactin-inhibiting factor** (PIH): dopamine-like **hormone** secreted by the **hypothalamus** that inhibits the secretion of **prolactin** by the anterior **pituitary gland**. Aka prolactin release-inhibiting hormone, prolactin-inhibiting hormone, prolactostatin.

**prolactin-releasing hormone** (PRH): one or more hypothalamic **hormones** that stimulate **prolactin** release from the anterior **pituitary gland**.

*Prolemur simus* **(Gray, 1870):** synonym for *Hapalemur simus*.

**proliferation:** 1. growth by spreading. 2. in cells, **development** through **mitosis**.

**proliferative phase:** second phase of the human **uterine cycle**, encompassing days 5–14, and characterized by relatively low concentrations of the hormone **progesterone**, and peak concentrations of **LH**, **FSH**, and **estrogens**. Estrogen peaks around day 11; FSH and LH surges occur around days 12–13, and ovulation occurs 24–36 h later, in the **secretory phase**. There is growth in the ovarian follicles, and the water content of the endometrium increases during its repair as glands increase in number. Aka estrogenic phase.

**proline** (Pro): an **amino acid**; one of the twenty building blocks of **proteins**. Found naturally in collagen and other proteins.

**prometaphase:** stage of **mitosis** between prophase and metaphase marked by the disintegration of the nuclear membrane and formation of the spindle.

**promiscuity:** 1. indiscriminate sexual intercourse. Cf. **primitive promiscuity**. 2. mating system in which sexual partners only form a bond during copulation, then separate, with the females mating with other males and the males attempting to mate with other females; found in a number of primate species. Characteristics of promiscuous societies include no **paternal care** and marked **sexual dimorphism**. This later feature has led some to suggest that the highly sexually dimorphic *Australopithecus afarensis* was promiscuous.

**promontory:** projection from a bone or other anatomical structure; process.

**promontory artery:** artery that supplies the middle ear cavity of living primates; in humans this is a branch of the ascending pharyngeal artery, which in turn is a branch of the internal carotid artery. See **stapedial artery**.

**Promoter** (site) (P): upstream **DNA sequence** that directs **RNA polymerase** to initiate **genetic transcription**.

**promutagen:** nonmutagenic compound that is a metabolic precursor to a **mutagen**.

**pronasale:** anthropometric point at the tip of the nose.

**pronation:** medial rotation of the forearm, which results in the palms of the hands facing posteriorly (in reference to **anatomical position**). Cf. **supination**. See **eversion** and **inversion**.

**pronograde:** walking with the spine or long axis of the body parallel to the ground. Aka quadrupedal.

*Pronothodectes* **Gidley, 1923:** archaic mammal and earliest member of the family **Plesiadapidae** from the middle Paleocene of North America; consists of three species. It has been suggested that *Pronothodectes* is the ancestor of *Plesiadapis* and *Nannodectes*. Known from jaws and teeth. Dental formula: 2.1.3.3. Estimated body mass around 300 g. See Appendix 1 for taxonomy.

**pronucleus:** one of two packages of DNA in a fertilized **ovum**. One pronucleus came from the oöcyte, the other from the spermatid. Plural: prounclei.

*Pronycticebus* **Grandidier, 1904:** adapoid prosimian from the middle and late Eocene of Europe, belonging to the notharctid family **Cercamoniinae**; two species recognized; one of the species represents one of the most complete skeletons of a cercamoniine. Estimated body mass between 800 and 1100 g. **Postcrania** suggestive of arboreal quadrupedalism, some leaping, and climbing. Dental formula: 2.1.4.3/ 2.1.4.3; dental morphology suggestive of **faunivory**. See Appendix 1 for taxonomy.

**propalingual:** pertaining to the **retraction** and **protraction** of the mandible during **mastication**.

‡ **prophase:** stage in **cell division** in which the **centriole** divides and cell polarity is established; the chromosomes become visible under a light microscope and split longitudinally except at the centromere.

**prophase I:** stage of **meiosis I** during which the chromosomes become visible, the homologous chromosomes pair and the sister chromatids become discrete, and recombination occurs.

**prophase II:** stage of **meiosis II** during which the chromosomes recoil.

*Propithecus* **Bennett, 1832:** prosimian genus to which the sifakas belong; two or three species, depending on authority. Found only on Madagascar in either evergreen or **deciduous forest**. Arboreal; diurnal; **vertical clinging and leaping** locomotion; hinds limbs longer than forelimbs; on the ground employ bipedal **saltation**; on terminal tree branches these animals use a variety of suspensory postures. Body masses range from 4 to 7 kg. Dental formula equivocal: number and type of teeth have been interpreted as 2.1.2.3/2.0.2.3 by some and 2.1.2.3/1.1.2.3 by others; possess **dental comb** consisting of four teeth; **frugivorous**. Live in mixed sex groups of between 3 and 12 individuals. See Appendix 2 for taxonomy, Appendix 3 for living species.

**Propliopithecidae:** catarrhine family known from the early Oligocene of North Africa. Consists of two genera and five species; best known of the Oligocene primates. See Appendix 1 for taxonomy.

**Propliopithecoidea:** superfamily of the infraorder **Catarrhini** that existed during the late Eocene to early Oligocene of North Africa. Not all authorities recognize this taxon. Some workers consider the families in this superfamily to be ancestral hominoids and, consequently, place them in the **Hominoidea**. See Appendix 1 for taxonomy.

*Propliopithecus* **Schlosser, 1910:** genus of catarrhines from the early Oligocene of North Africa belonging to the family **Propliopithecidae**; three to four species, depending on authority; phylogenetic relationships uncertain, but the members of this genus are often referred to as apes; known from jaws and teeth plus a few **postcrania**. Estimated body mass ranges from 4 to 6 kg. Dental formula: 2.1.2.3/2.1.2.3; dental morphology resembles that of extant **hominoids**, but may represent the primitive condition for catarrhines; large **sexually dimorphic** canines; dentition suggestive of **frugivory**. Postcranial remains suggest arboreal quadrupedalism. See Appendix 1 for taxonomy.

**proportionality coefficient** ($c_o$): in statistics, value on the $Y$ axis (criterion variable axis) where the line defined by the regression equation $Y = c_o + b_o X_o$ crosses the axis, and is described by the constant term $c_o$ in the regression equation. Aka intercept.

**propositus, proposita:** in clinical genetics, the individual which brought a pedigree or family to the attention of the genetic researcher; a male is a **propositus**, a female is a **proposita**. See **proband**.

**Proprimates:** proposed order of archaic mammals that includes the plesiadapiforms along with other mammals considered to be archaic primates. It was suggested that the tupaiids (order **Scandentia**) might also be included among the proprimates. This order has not gained much acceptance and the mirorder **Primatomorpha** and order **Plesiadapiformes** appear to be preferred among primatologists.

**prosencephalon:** that structure in the brain made up of an anterior portion, the **telencephalon**, and a posterior portion, the **diencephalon**. Aka forebrain.

‡ **prosimian:** primate that is a member of the suborder **Prosimii**. Prosimians include the various lemurs, bushbabies, and the lorises. If the suborder **Prosimii** is used (instead of **Strepsirhini**), according to most workers, then the **tarsiers** are also included among the prosimians. See **Lemuroidea**.

‡ **Prosimii:** suborder of order **Primates** that includes the lemurs, pottos, lorises, and galagos. Prosimians retain many ancestral traits including a **postorbital bar**, no fusion of the mandible or the frontal bones, a

**grooming claw** on the second digit of the hind foot, and other traits suggestive of the primates of the **Eocene**; in addition prosimians have a **bicornuate uterus**, two pairs of mammary glands, and usually the production of more than one infant. This suborder is considered a **grade** and many, if not most, primatologists now subscribe to the placing the members of this group into the alternative suborder **Strepsirhini** (excluding the tarsiers that historically have been included in the prosimians). Many paleontologists found this latter group to be unacceptable because the defining features are soft tissue structures that are not discernible in fossils. See Appendix 2 for taxonomy, Appendix 3 for living species. Cf. **Anthropoidea**.

**prospective potency:** Dreisch's term for what might possibly be achieved in embryonic development; cf. **prospective value**.

**prospective study:** in science, any experiment designed to produce a result that can be extrapolated into the future; predictive study. Cf. **retrospective study**.

**prospective value:** Dreisch's term for that which is actually achieved in embryonic development; cf. **prospective potency**.

**prostaglandin** (PG): any one of a large group of hormone-like acidic compounds occurring in nearly all tissues and that are derived from polyunsaturated fatty acids; prostaglandins function as **paracrine** or **autocrine** hormones.

**prostate gland:** walnut-shaped gland surrounding the male urethra just below the urinary bladder that secretes an additive to seminal fluid during ejaculation.

**prostate-specific antigen** (PSA): a molecule synthesized by cells of the **prostate gland**, whether cancerous or normal.

**prosthion** (pr): craniometric landmark; most anterior mid-sagittal point of the maxillary alveolar process; aka prealveolar point. See Appendix 7.

**protanopia:** form of partial **color blindness** caused by any defect in an X-linked recessive gene, resulting in red color blindness. Aka the red opsin defect. See **deuteranopia** and **tritanopia**.

*Protanthropus steinheimensis* Berckhemer, 1937: see *Homo heidelbergensis*.

**protease:** any of the enzymes that catalyse the digestion of proteins.

**proteasome:** tube-shaped cellular structure that digests proteins that have been tagged for recycling.

**protection hypothesis:** 1. proposal that clothing originated as a means of protection from animals and the elements. 2. proposal to explain why male **cercopithecines** grab an infant during a fight, in this case to protect the infant by removing it from danger.

There are two possible reasons for the male's behavior: the infant may be his offspring or other relative and he is protecting his genetic investment, or he may be attempting to show the female that he is protective of her offspring and would make a good mate. See **agonistic buffering**.

‡ **protein:** any one of the large, complex **molecules** composed of **amino acids** that control most biological reactions in the body and receive and transmit most of the chemical signals within and between cells. Most proteins are constructed of smaller fragments called **polypeptides** that are folded or knotted into 3-dimensional functional shapes (see **quaternary structure**). Functions of proteins include catalysis (**enzymes**), regulation (**hormones**), protection (**antibodies**), structure, and storage (**lipoproteins**). Proteins are produced by **protein synthesis**.

**protein–calorie malnutrition** (PCM): a group of **nutritional diseases** resulting from an inadequate amount of proteins and/or calories in a diet; PCM is a severe problem today in regions of economic development. See **marasmus**.

**protein changes theory of aging:** see **altered proteins theory of aging**.

**protein clock:** see **molecular clock**.

**protein folding:** refers to the conjugation of multiple protein chains (if necessary), the formations of secondary structure bonds, and the manipulations of the polypeptides into the **tertiary structure** and, finally, the **quaternary structure** characteristic of the protein in question. Aka post-translational processing.

**protein misfolding disorder:** any of several heritable or induced conditions caused by or leading to predisposition to misfolded proteins. Some of these conditions lead to the accumulation of misfolded or fibrillized proteins in the brain, called amyloid. Examples are **Alzheimer disease**, **amyloidosis**, and the infectious **PrPSc** form of the **prion protein**.

**protein-only hypothesis:** proposal by Stanley Prusiner in the 1980s that proteins could be transmitted interspecifically, and that proteins could reproduce without a DNA template. Received with initial skepticism, the protein-only hypothesis has gained currency as a probable explanation of the **transmissible spongiform encephalopathies**. Prusiner called the fragments proteinaceous infectious particles, or prions. See **prion protein**.

**protein phylogeny: cladogram** or **phenogram** based on information from **DNA hybridization, microcomplement fixation, immunodiffusion, amino acid sequence** data, or other related molecular method.

**protein polymorphism:** existence within a population of different **polypeptide** products generated from alleles at the same locus. See **polymorphism**.

**protein profiling:** detection of various states of a **protein,** from primary sequence to quaternary physiological structure, as well as states and modifications achieved during stages of physiological function, through final disassembly and degradation. See **proteomics.**

**protein quality:** in reference to the inclusiveness of the **essential amino acids** needed by humans in a protein source. See **complete protein, incomplete protein, partially complete protein.**

**protein sequence:** linear order of amino acids in a polypeptide chain; the order that determines the composition and structure of the protein.

**protein sequencer:** instrument that sequentially removes amino acids from the parent protein chain in order to determine the composition and structure of the protein.

**protein structure:** conceptual hierarchy of polypeptide function involving four progressive stages. See **primary, secondary, tertiary,** and **quaternary structure.**

‡ **protein synthesis:** see **polypeptide synthesis.**

**protein variation:** deviation from a normal amino acid sequence within a population.

**proteinaceous:** said of anything composed mostly of protein.

**proteome:** entire complement of proteins produced by a particular **genome.** Cf. **genome** and **transcriptome.**

**proteomics:** 1. the study of gene expression and function at the protein level, by means of high-throughput techniques. 2. the systematic characterization and cataloguing of the entire set of protein–protein interactions in a **genome,** both *in vivo* and in artificial and virtual systems, as used in **biotechnology,** and known as the Human Proteomics Project.

**proterogenesis:** early attempt by Schindewolf (1950) to describe **fetalization theory** and **neoteny.**

**Proteus syndrome:** heritable condition characterized by highly variable and asymmetrical growths, swelling, limb or digit gigantism, and multiple hyperostoses of the calvaria, facial bones, and mandible. Asymmetries extend to the postcranial tissues in rare cases. An autosomal dominant lethal allele that survives in tissues of chimeric or mosaic individuals has been suggested; hence the rarity. This syndrome has been proposed as likely in the case of John Merrick, the 'elephant man', rather than **neurofibromatosis.** Aka elattoproteus syndrome.

*Protoadapis* Lemoine, 1878: adapoid **prosimian** from the early and middle Eocene, belonging to the notharctid subfamily **Cercamoniinae;** ten to twelve species, depending on authority. *Protoadapis* may be the ancestor to both *Protonycticebus* and *Europolemur.* Dental formula: 2.1.4.3/2.1.4.3; dental morphology suggests

adaptations for herbivory, ranging from **frugivory** to a more fibrous and course diet. Body mass of the species belonging to this genus estimated to range from 700 g to 3 kg. See Appendix 1 for taxonomy.

**protoanthropic:** in some older systems of terminology (e.g. S. Sergi), pertaining to the earliest of three grades of humans, e.g. *Homo erectus.* Cf. **paleoanthropic, neanthropic.**

**protocone: cusp** on the mesiolingual occlusal surface of an upper molar; it forms the lingual portion of the **trigon.** Cf. **protoconid.**

**protoconid: cusp** on the mesiolingual occlusal surface of a lower molar; it forms the lingual portion of the **trigonid.** Cf. **protocone.**

**protocooperation:** form of **symbiosis** in which both symbionts benefit, but the relationship is not obligatory. Cf. **mutualism.**

**proto-Cro-Magnon:** term applied to *Homo sapiens* populations that are more robust than moderns, but not **neandertaloid,** and are associated with **Mousterian** technology. This term has been applied to Middle Eastern populations, dated to between 30,000 and 80,000 BP, depending on dating technique used and author.

**protoculture:** anticipatory or fragmentary culture, as among some anthropoids. See **primate culture.**

**proto-hand-ax:** simple or pre-ax characteristic of the **Lower Acheulean** of Africa, lacking the complete bifacial, uniformly sized flaking of true hand-axes of the **Acheulean tool tradition.**

**protohistoric archaeology:** study of cultures that date from the time of the earliest tools and up to the time of **prehistoric archaeology.**

‡ **protohominid:** colloquial term for a hypothetical human ancestor that is not yet bipedal or in possession of any of the traits associated with the **hominids.**

**proton:** elementary subatomic particle of positive electric charge exactly equal in magnitude to the negative charge of an **electron,** and that has approximately the same mass as a **neutron.**

**Proto-Malay:** ethonym for a hypothetical **Mongoloid** subgroup from southeast Asia that migrated to the East Indies and the Philippines. Aka Indonesian-Malay. See **Malay.**

**proto-Neolithic: Campignian** and other contemporary cultures in some classifications of the Early/Lower Neolithic.

**proto-oncogene:** any of a class of **housekeeping genes** that control the normal cell cycle. If overexpressed, it functions as an **oncogene,** and causes cancer.

**protoplasm:** essential substance of which all living cells are made. A heterogenous assemblage of ions, molecules and fluid. See **cytoplasm.**

**protoplast fusion:** removal of the natural walls of plant cells and the subsequent hybridization of two or more genomes to produce **genetically modified food** products.

‡ **Prototheria:** subclass of class **Mammalia** consisting of the order Monotremata and the families Tachyglossidae (spiny anteater or echidna) and Ornithorhynchidae (duck-billed platypus). This taxon is the most primitive of the mammals featuring traits unusual among mammals such as **oviparity**, very undeveloped young, mammae without nipples, skull features that are birdlike, and a reptilian positioning of the fore limbs (although the hind limbs are therian-like). These animals lack teeth as adults. Cf. **Theria**.

**prototroph:** wild-type organism found in the greatest numbers in nature and which, under laboratory conditions, is able to grow on minimal medium.

**prototype:** primitive or ancestral species; species from which others develop that possessed or possesses **plesiomorphic** traits.

**protovirus hypothesis:** proposal that retroviruses emerged when portions of RNA became reverse-transcribed into DNA products that became integral parts of the genomes of host cells. In time, such retroviral fragments became capable of emerging as independent and infectious viral particles, and after millions of years of evolution, homologous particles are found deposited randomly in the DNA of many animals. First proposed in 1970–71 by American molecular biologist Howard. M. Temin (1934–94). See **provirus hypothesis**. Cf. **oncogene hypothesis** (which it replaced).

**protozoan:** one of the parasitic single-celled organisms in the phylum Protozoa that include flagellates, amoebae, sporozoa, and ciliates. See **Chagas' disease** and **malaria**.

**protraction:** anterior movement of an anatomical structure; only a very few structures, such as the **mandible**, are capable of this movement. Cf. **retraction**.

**provenance:** origin or source of fossils or artifacts; the exact geographic and geologic location in which they were found. Aka provenience.

**provirus:** **cDNA** copy of a retroviral RNA genome. Proviruses have been inserted into chromosomal DNA and can be transmitted from one host cell generation to another without causing lysis of the host cell. See **protovirus hypothesis**.

**provirus hypothesis:** idea that some cancers are caused by RNA viruses that are reverse-transcribed into the DNA of a host cell where they act as a **proto-oncogene**. First proposed in 1960-64 by American molecular biologist H. M. Temin (1934–94), this idea that information could reside in RNA and could be copied in reverse and inserted as DNA (the provirus) into a host genome conflicted with the then **central dogma** of molecular biology. The eventual isolation of **reverse transcriptase** independently by Temin and David Baltimore provided support for Temin's hypothesis. See **protovirus hypothesis**.

‡ **provisioning:** 1. act of providing food to the young, a hallmark of both mammals and birds. 2. providing food to a primate group that is being studied and observed, whether in a captive situation or free-ranging primates.

**'provisioning monogamist' hypothesis:** argument by **Isaac**, **Lovejoy** and others that early **hominids** improved **reproductive success** by increasing both **survivorship** and **birth rate**, and that this was possible through the development (or evolution) of intense parenting, a sexual division of labor, monogamy, and the sequestration of ovulation; these elements led to male provisioning of females and their offspring. The hypothesis has met with intense resistance and criticized as an unrealistic androcentric model.

**proxemics:** study of the nature, degree, and effects of the spatial separation that individuals maintain, and of the variation of spatial separation owing to environmental and cultural factors; a form of nonverbal communication. Perception of one's personal space or 'body bubble'.

‡ **proximal:** anatomical term of relative position, meaning closer to the mid-line or origin (if a muscle or appendage). Cf. **distal**.

**proximal consequence:** see **proximate effect**.

**proximal shoulder angle:** measurement reflecting the shape of the base on a projectile point; angle formed by the hafting notch and the axis of the shaft.

**proximal thigh circumference: anthropometric** measurement; distance around the upper thigh as measured with a tape measure placed immediately below the gluteal furrow and passed horizontally around the body. Combined with the other thigh circumferences, used for estimations of body density, adiposity, lean body mass, and for various applications in **human engineering**. See **distal thigh circumference, mid-thigh circumference**.

**proximate:** next to; nearest; immediate; close by.

**proximate causation:** conditions of the environment or internal physiology that trigger the immediate responses of an organism. They are to be distinguished from the environmental forces, referred to as the **ultimate causation**, that led to the evolution of the response in the first place.

**proximate effect:** immediate effect of conditions brought about by the change in a variable or variables. Medicine, for example, often has the proximate effect of lowering mortality rates. See **ultimate effect**.

**proximity:** spatial distance that one individual is to another individual or an object.

**PrP (PrPc, and PrPSc):** see **prion protein**. Also abbreviated PrPc for the cellular form, in contrast to PrPSc, the infectious form that is transmitted ultimately from sheep (hence the 'S').

**psaliodont:** of the incisor teeth, projecting forward in both jaws.

**PSC:** acronym for **phylogenetic species concept**.

*Pseudhomo heidelbergensis* **Ameghino, 1909:** Mauer mandible; see *Homo heidelbergensis*.

**pseudoallele:** gene that behaves as an allele but which occupies a different, closely linked position on a chromosome; it can be separated by crossing over.

**pseudoarchaeology:** unsolved mysteries of the past which appeal to a taste for adventure, escapism, and science fiction, all of which have in common epic journeys or voyages based on illusory data. Among those who have authored works in this genre are E. von Daniken, T. Heyerdahl, A. C. Clark, and J. Auel.

**pseudoautosomal inheritance:** pattern of **inheritance** for any homologous gene located on both the X and Y chromosomes. In the absence of other information, such genes appear to be inherited in an autosomal fashion. See **autosomal inheritance**.

**pseudoautosomal region** (PAR): gene-containing sections on the tips of the human **Y chromosome** that have homologous portions on the **X chromosome**, and that synapse with the X during **meiosis** in male mammals. The PAR is gene-dense, but comprises only about 5% of the Y chromosome. Cf. **male-specific region of the Y chromosome**.

**pseudocopulation:** copulation whose purpose is not fertilization. This may occur between male and female or between two males. In some instances it consists of an immature male **mounting** a female; when it involves two males it may be a demonstration of higher status, with the dominant animal mounting the subordinate one.

**pseudodiploid:** describes a karyotype with a diploid chromosome count that is characteristic of the species, but in which structural rearrangements have occurred and linkage relationships have been disrupted.

**pseudoevolutionary argument:** argument that refers to the idea that all of the cultures of the world pass through a similar set of **evolutionary stages** in their 'progress' from **savagery** to **barbarism** to **civilization**; the argument uses evolutionary terms but is entirely antievolutionary because it insists that the direction of human history is predetermined; that is, it is a 'teleological' theory. See **unilineal evolution**.

**pseudoextinction:** apparent extinction of a taxon owing to its evolution into a new taxon; i.e. the extinct group no longer exists but has direct descendants.

**pseudofossil:** structure of inorganic origin that may be mistaken for an actual fossil form that it resembles.

‡ **pseudogene:** segment of DNA that resembles a functional gene but that carries one or more mutations that render it functionless. Pseudogenes are thought to originate as tandem repeats that, because of their redundancy, accumulate mutations that are not selected against; they evolve 5–10 times faster than their functional counterparts and some researchers target these sequences as ideal candidates for **molecular clocks**.

*Pseudogorilla* **Eliot, 1913:** synonym for *Pan*.

**pseudohermaphroditism, female, with skeletal anomalies:** autosomal recessive condition in chromosomally XX females; virilizing clinical signs include ambiguous genitalia, bony abnormalities of the face and long bones, an enlarged clitoris, and fused labioscrotal folds. Cf. **androgen insensitivity syndrome**.

**pseudohermaphroditism, male:** ('with gynecomastia and hirsutism') group of several similar conditions characterized by an XY chromosomal genotype with an **SRY gene** present on the Y, and (sometimes) internal male reproductive organs (male gonadal sex), but with a female phenotype. Germline mutations that interfere with the production of **testosterone** and/or DHT are the cause of the conditions. In some cases, masculinization can take place at puberty. The most common agents of male pseudohermaphroditism — **gynecomastia** at puberty coupled with hirsutism — can be caused by 17-β hydroxysteroid dehydrogenase deficiency (HSD17B3 deficiency), 17-ketosteroid reductase deficiency (17-KSR deficiency), or 5-α reductase-2 deficiency (PPSH, the '**guevedoces**' mutation), all phenotypically indistinguishable without a serum assay. See **androgen insensitivity syndrome**.

**pseudohypertrophic muscular dystrophy (Duchenne type):** see **muscular dystrophy**.

**pseudohypocone:** type of tooth cusp that develops through cleavage of the **protocone**, unlike the true **hypocone**, which arises from the **cingulum**; found in Eocene notharctines.

*Pseudoloris* **Stehlin, 1916:** genus of tarsiiform primate from the middle and late Eocene of Europe, belonging to the omomyoid family **Microchoeridae**; five species. Short snout; nocturnal; body mass estimated to range between 50 and 120 g. Dental formula: 2.1.3.3/2.1.2.3; shearing crests on cheek teeth; dental morphology suggestive of **insectivory**. See Appendix 1 for taxonomy.

**pseudo-Mongoloid fold:** incomplete **epicanthic fold** often found in very young or in very old persons. See **Down syndrome**.

**pseudomosaic:** chromosomally abnormal cell line found in cultured prenatal cells that is believed to have arisen during the culture process.

**pseudoscience:** any collection of ideas that have been tested scientifically and shown to be false, but nevertheless remain tenable to dissenters, and who take them on faith to be true. Examples are **scientific creationism** and **intelligent design**.

*Pseudotetonius* (= *Tetonius*) *ambiguus* Bown, 1974: tarsiiform primate from the early Eocene of North America belonging to the omomyid subfamily **Anaptomorphinae**; **monotypic**; some workers include this genus within *Tetonius*. Estimated body mass around 170 g. Dental formula: 2.1.3.3/2.1.3.3. See Appendix 1 for taxonomy.

**P site:** section of a **ribosome** that holds a growing polypeptide chain. Cf. **A site**.

**psychiatric disorder:** mental disorder; any clinically significant behavior or pattern associated with mental distress or disability or with significantly greater risk of suffering, death, pain, disability, or an important loss of freedom. Common examples are **schizophrenia** and **mood disorders**.

**psychic unity of mankind:** belief that the minds of human beings are basically similar no matter in which culture or environment they are found; and that, given the proper conditions, people have the capacity to develop similarly.

**psychometry:** measurement, usually by a psychologist (psychometrician), of mental processes, traits or aptitudes, often in a quantifiable manner. The results are often taken as part of the **extended phenotype** of an individual. See **IQ**.

**psychosocial dwarfism:** growth retardation thought to be caused by maternal deprivation, emotionally induced pituitary deficiency, nutritional deprivation, and/or sleep deprivation. Aka Kaspar Hauser syndrome.

**psychosocial sex:** individual's sexual identity or **gender** as determined by their self-perceptions, and influenced by other's attitudes.

**PTC:** abbreviation for (1) **phenylthiocarbamide**; (2) **plasma thromboplastin component**.

‡ **PTC taster/nontaster polymorphism:** benign autosomal polymorphism characterized by an ability to taste or not taste phenylthiocarbamide, a stereolog of many **goitrogens**, all of which have a bitter taste to tasters. The taster ability is polymorphic in humans. PTC is in fact a more **complex trait** than a simple autosomal recessive as generally presented; it is likely a two-locus trait with incomplete **penetrance** at one locus that maps to chromosome 5. In 2003, a major gene in the system was mapped by positional cloning to a location in the bitter taste receptor gene family on human chromosome 7q, and

was subsequently renamed *PTC*. This classic pedagogical polymorphism has been tested in hundreds of populations; in general, urban populations tend to have higher frequencies of the nontaster allele than populations recently removed from a gathering/hunting mode of subsistence. Aka taste blindness.

**pterion** (pt): **craniometric landmark**; region where the superior portion of the greater wing of the **sphenoid** articulates with the **frontal**, **parietal**, and **temporal** bones. See Appendix 7.

**pterygoid muscles:** see **lateral pterygoid**, **medial pterygoid**.

**pterygoid plate:** one of a pair of bony projections on the interior surface of the **sphenoid bone** that serves as the site of origin for the lateral and medial pterygoid muscles, two of the muscles of mastication.

*Ptilocercus* Gray, 1848: **monotypic** genus in **Scandentia** to which the pen-tailed (aka feathertailed) tree shrew belongs; *P. lowii* is the single species. Distributed throughout the islands of Southeast Asia. Small: body mass ranges from 25 to 60 g. See **Tupaiidae**.

**Ptolemaic cosmogony:** proposal that the planets and other celestial bodies orbited the earth; the complexity of the system was cumbersome, as planets were required to orbit in epicycles, deferents, etc.; proposed by Claudius Ptolemy (90–168). Aka **geocentrism**, it was replaced by the **heliocentrism** of Galileo and Copernicus.

**puberty:** period of development during which the reproductive organs become functional. In common terms, refers to the 3–5 years of sexual development that culminate in sexual maturity and the appearance of **secondary sexual characteristics**.

**pubescence:** onset of sexual maturity; the earliest stages of **puberty**. Adjective: pubescent.

**pubic arch:** angle formed by the two pubic bones below the **pubic symphysis**. The size of this angle is greater in adult human females than in males and is one of the criteria used to determine the sex of a skeleton.

**pubic bone:** see **pubis**.

**pubic length:** **osteometric** measurement; distance between the most superior point of the pubic symphysis to the junction between the ischium and pubis in the acetabulum, measured with a spreading caliper.

**pubic ramus:** either of the two bony branches that connect the **pubic bone** to the other bones of the **coxal bone**; the superior pubic ramus joins with the **ilium** and **ischium** at the **acetabulum**, whereas the inferior pubic ramus joins with the ramus of the ischium. Both pubic rami help enclose the **obturator foramen**. This structure was especially long in Neandertals.

**pubic symphysis:** cartilaginous joint formed at the articulation of the two **pubic bones** at the anterior portion of the pelvis; it permits slight movement.

‡ **pubis:** one of a pair of bones that forms the anterior portion of the **coxal bone**. The two bones articulate at the pelvic mid-line to form the **pubic symphysis**. Ligaments and several muscles that move the leg have their origin on this bone.

**Pucangan Formation:** stratigraphic unit in central Java, dated to the Early Pleistocene (2 mya, K/A, Lower Lahar mud flow), and that contains Jetis (Djetis) fauna with Siva-Malayan affinities. The unit is up to 46 m thick. Mammal-bearing levels occur in this unit, and become increasingly common toward the top of the section. Aka Pucangan Beds.

**pulmonary gas:** air containing carbon dioxide that is exhaled from the lungs during breathing.

**pulmonary ventilation:** volume of air moved into or out of the lungs per unit of time; calculated as the product of breathing frequency and tidal volume.

**pulp:** connective tissue that fills the central **pulp cavity** of a tooth.

**pulp cavity:** cavity within a tooth that is formed by the **dentin**. The pulp cavity contains the **pulp chamber** and the **root canal**. Aka central cavity.

**pulp chamber:** chamber within the tooth that contains pulp, blood and lymphatic vessels, and nerves.

**pulse pressure:** difference between systolic blood pressure and diastolic arterial blood pressure.

**pulsed-field gel electrophoresis:** method for separating DNA fragments of large size.

*Pulverflumen:* archaic mammal from the early Eocene of Europe belonging to the family **Paromomyidae**; **monotypic**. Body mass estimated at around 600 g. See Appendix 1 for taxonomy.

‡ **punctuated equilibrium:** model of evolution in which species are viewed as being relatively stable and long-lived, with little change reflected in the fossil record until a relatively abrupt change results in a new, eventually stable, daughter species, and a new episode of **stasis**. Cf. **phyletic gradualism**. See **macroevolution**.

**punctuated evolution:** see **punctuated equilibrium**.

**punctuation:** supposed large-scale morphological change in a lineage that occurs rapidly relative to geological time.

**punctuationalism:** adherence to a mode of growth, change, or **evolution** in which changes are concentrated into brief periods; cf. **phyletic gradualism**. Aka punctuationism, speciational evolution.

‡ **Punnett square:** graphic logical device consisting, in the simplest case, of a square subdivided into four (2 × 2) quadrants, each containing the genotypic outcome of a simple **monohybrid cross** such as Aa × Aa.

**pupil:** opening through the **iris** that permits light to enter the vitreous chamber of the eyeball and be refracted by the lens.

**pure-breeding line:** strain of individual identically homozygous for all the genes under consideration. A pure line of all descendants of a single homozygous parent produced by close inbreeding.

**Purgatoriidae:** family of Paleocene mammals consisting of the genus *Purgatorius* and belonging to an *incertae sedis* order of mammals placed in the mirorder **Primatomorpha** by some authors. See Appendix 1 for taxonomy.

*Purgatorius* **Van Valen and Sloan, 1965:** genus of archaic mammal from the early Paleocene of North America consisting of three species. Dental formula: 3.1.4.3. This genus is problematic and has moved in and out of several primate families; currently, most workers recognize it as *incertae sedis* and it has been moved out of the primates belonging to either the order **Proprimates** or **Plesiadapiformes**, depending on author. It is only known from a single tooth for one species (*P. ceratops*) and jaws and teeth for the other species (*P. uncio, P. titusi*). Body size is estimated to range between 60 and 90 g. Although its affinities are uncertain, there is nothing that precludes it as a primate ancestor. See Appendix 1 for taxonomy.

*Purgatorius ceratops* **(Clemens, 1974):** see *Purgatorius*.

‡ **purines:** class of organic molecules with a double carbon–nitrogen ring structure; includes the nitrogenous bases **adenine** and **guanine**. Other purines include caffeine and theobromine. Cf. **pyrimidines**.

**purine metabolism:** oxidation of purines to produce uric acid and other metabolites.

**purine nucleoside phosphorylase** (PNP): an enzyme that is involved in the purine salvage pathway, and is essential to the production of T cells in the immune system. Cf. **adenosine deaminase**.

**purple-faced langur:** vernacular for *Trachypithecus vetulus* (= *senex*).

**push plane: scraper** made of flint, probably from the Aurignacian.

**putty-nosed guenon:** vernacular for *Cercopithecus nictitans*.

*p* **value:** see **significance**.

**pycnosis:** constriction of a nucleus into a small, densely staining mass, indicative of cell death. Cf. **heteropycnosis**.

*Pygathrix* É. Geoffroy, 1812: colobine genus to which the douc langur and snub-nosed monkeys belong; four species, but some authorities place the snub-nosed monkeys in the genus *Rhinopithecus*, leaving only the douc langur in *Pygathrix*. See Appendix 2, Appendix 3, and *Rhinopithecus*.

*Pygmaeus edwardii* **Hopius:** putative ape-like creature listed in the nineteenth century dissertation of Hopius, a student of **Linnaeus**. See **anthropomorpha**.

**pygmoid:** see **pygmy**.

**pygmy:** member of a population characterized by being markedly below the average height of other human populations. Pygmoid populations average under 1.5 m in stature, and are usually highly melanized and have woolly hair. Synonymous with **Negrillo** and **Negrito**. Among the pygmoid populations of the world are included the Bushmen of South Africa, the Efe and other groups in the Congo Basin, the Andamanese of India, the Semang on the Malay Peninsula, the Aeta in the Philippines, and the Tapiro and Aiome in New Guinea. Small body size is thought to be a very efficient adaptation to hot and humid tropical environments. See the **Negrito hypothesis** and **nanism**.

**pygmy chimpanzee:** vernacular for *Pan paniscus*. Aka **bonobo**.

**pygmy marmoset:** vernacular for *Cebuella* pygmae.

**pygmy slow loris:** vernacular for *Nycticebus* pygmaeus.

**pygmy tarsier:** vernacular for *Tarsius* pumilus.

**pyramidalis muscle:** triangular, pouchlike muscle that attaches to the pubic bone. It is thought to be a relic from a **marsupial** stage, and is in only 80% of **AMHs**. See **vestigial trait**.

**pyriform:** pear-shaped.

**pyrimidale (of the carpus):** see **trapezoid**.

‡ **pyrimidines:** class of organic molecules with a single carbon–nitrogen ring structure, including the nitrogenous bases **cytosine**, **thymine**, and **uracil**. Cf. **purines**.

**pyroclastic rock:** volcanic rock that has been blown into the atmosphere.

**pyrogen:** any substance that causes a **fever**.

**pyrotechnology:** branch of knowledge that investigates the effects of fire and heat. In anthropology, the study of the effects of the controlled use of fire on human adaptation, including fired clay and ceramic products. See **Venus figurines** and **controlled use of fire**.

**pyruvic acid:** organic molecule intermediate in the glycolytic pathway that either forms lactic acid (in the absence of oxygen) or enters the Krebs cycle (in the presence of oxygen).

*q*: symbol for the frequency of the second, often **recessive**, **allele** in a series of alleles in a **Hardy – Weinberg** population. See *p* and *r*.

**Qafzeh:** archaeological site found in 1933 near Nazareth in northern Israel, dated to 120 – 40 kya (at least 92 kya by **TL**, 120 by **ESR**), and that contains a **Levalloiso-Mousterian** artifact assemblage. Hominid remains comprise at least 20 individuals. The restored Qafzeh 6 cranium has a 1570 cm³ capacity and is attributed to *Homo sapiens*. Some of the remains were deliberate burials. Aka Jebel Qafzeh Cave. Cf. **Skhūl** and **Cro-Magnon**.

**q arm:** longer arm of a chromosome or chromatid. Arms are defined by the position of the **centromere**. See **p arm**.

*Qatrania* **(Simons and Kay, 1983): anthropoid** from the late Eocene and early Oligocene of North Africa belonging to the catarrhine family **Parapithecidae;** two species recognized. Known from mandibles and teeth. Dental formula: 2.1.3.3/2.1.3.3; low rounded cusps on molars suggest **frugivory** and perhaps **gummivory**. Estimated body mass around 300 g. See Appendix 1 for taxonomy.

**Q-banding:** one of the methods of creating identification **bands** on individual chromosomes after treatment of the metaphase plate with colchicine and staining with **quinicrine**.

**Qizianshan:** archaeological site found in 1988 in Yiyuan County, Shandong Province, China, dated to about 440 kya; contains hominid remains including cranial fragments and teeth attributed to *Homo erectus*. Compares favorably with **Zhoukoudian**. Aka Yiyuan Man.

**quadrant:** 1. referring to a division of four. 2. in reference to mammalian dentition, the four tooth-bearing bones, i.e. left and right **maxillary** bones and left and right **dentary** bones.

**quadrate tooth:** cheek tooth (premolar or molar) that has a square outline when the **occlusal surface** is viewed; human cheek teeth are such teeth.

**quadriceps femoris group:** large fleshy muscle group that is located on the anterior and lateral sides of the thigh. It is a powerful extensor of the knee, especially in climbing, jumping, running, pumping (as in bicycle riding) and rising from a seated position; it consists of four separate muscle heads.

**quadritubercular:** condition in which there are four **cusps** on a mammalian **molar** tooth. There is an added cusp from the primitive mammalian condition of three cusps; this condition is common among primates. Cf. **tritubercular**.

**quadrivalent:** abnormal synapsis of interchanged chromosomes and their normal homologues during **meiosis,** forming a characteristic cross-shaped configuration of the four chromatids involved in the translocation.

**quadroon:** person whose ancestry is 1/4 from a minority variety and 3/4 from a majority variety.

‡ **quadrumanualism:** type of locomotion in which the four paws are used in a grasping manner, i.e. all paws are used as hands. Adjectives: quadrumanual, quadrumanous. This type of locomotion is associated with climbing in primates. Aka quadrumanous climbing or clambering, quadrumanual locomotion.

‡ **quadrupedalism:** form of locomotion that utilizes all four legs on a substrate. Aka quadrupedal locomotion. See **arboreal quadrupedalism** and **terrestrial quadrupedalism**.

‡ **qualitative:** relating to a state of representing a concept or relationship in words, pictures, or other subjective form; describes the process or approach of ranking one **element** in a series of objects, behaviors, or concepts. Cf. **quantitative**.

**qualitative inheritance:** positive heritability in any character that displays discrete variation, and that is **monogenic**. Cf. **quantitative inheritance**.

**qualitative trait, character** or **feature:** see **discrete trait**.

‡ **quantitative:** describes a concept or relationship that is expressed (quantified) in numerical, rather than verbal or other **qualitative**, subjective form, or the process or approach of making a numerical mirror of an object, behavior, or concept. See **reduction**. Cf. **qualitative**.

**quantitative genetics:** discipline concerned with **traits** controlled by many genes; considers the changes in phenotypic and genotypic frequency distributions between generations, rather than following the fate of individual genes.

‡ **quantitative inheritance:** positive heritability in any character that displays continuous variation, and that is **polygenic**. Cf. **qualitative inheritance**.

**quantitative method:** any means of describing a phenomenon by measurement; an estimate of quantity. In general terms, any method or analytical procedure, especially in science, that utilizes numerical representation.

**quantitative trait, character** or **feature:** any trait exhibiting **continuous variation** within a population; **stature** in humans is such a character. A quantitative trait can be either homologous or analogous, and which is quantified by linear measurement.

**quantitative trait loci:** alleles that contribute to the phenotype of polygenic traits.

**quantity concept:** neural capacity to understand numerical properties; for example, a subject being presented with two or more sets of elements in which it must select either the numerically smallest or largest set. This has been demonstrated for anthropoids and supports the supposition that human quantitative abilities are a product of primate evolution.

**quantum evolution: Simpson's** term for the idea that relatively rapid and exceptional change can occur in a lineage, providing the population is small. See **population bottleneck**; Cf. **genetic revolution** and **punctuated equilibrium**.

**quantum speciation:** see **saltation speciation**.

**quartz:** transparent or translucent mineral composed primarily of silica (as are the related minerals **chalcedony**, **chert**, and **flint**); a tendency to fracture conchoidally (producing a shell-like fracture) makes it valued as a medium for **stone tools**. See **cryptocrystalline siliceous rock**.

**quartzite:** a siliceous metamorphic rock consisting of quartz grains or minute quartz crystals set in a quartz cement, often used as a material in the manufacture of **stone tools**. See **metamorphic rock**.

**quartzite tool:** implement made from **quartzite**.

**quasidominance:** direct transmission, from generation to generation, of a recessive trait occurring in inbreeding populations; it results from the mating of a homozygous affected person with a heterozygous carrier of the same recessing gene, and results in a **pedigree** pattern that superficially resembles that of a dominant trait, hence the name.

**quaternary:** fourth in a series, or a set of four elements.

‡ **Quaternary (period):** most recent **period** of the **Cenozoic era**, lasting from approximately 1.6 mya to the present, and consisting of the **Pleistocene** and **Holocene** epochs. The fourth period of an older classification (1921) that also included the Primary (= **Paleozoic**), Secondary (= **Mesozoic**) and **Tertiary period**. Aka Anthropogene. See **Tertiary-Quaternary boundary**.

**Quaternary Ice Age:** see **Pleistocene epoch**.

**quaternary structure** (4°): the structure formed by the interaction of two or more polypeptide chains in a protein. See **protein structure**.

**Quatrefages de Breau, Jean Louis Armand de** (1810–92): French physician, draftsman, anti-Darwinist; Quatrefages' anthropological work dates to after his appointment as anthropologist to the Muséum National d'Histoire Naturelle. Although a committed monogenist (*Unité de l'espèce humaine*, 1861), Quatrefages held humans separate from the apes, and never acknowledged an ape–human ancestry. His denial of evolution did not conflict with his belief in a great antiquity for humanity, however, and he published extensively on what he saw as the anticipation of racial characteristics in the European hominid fossil record. With Théodore Hamy, he co-authored *Crania ethnica* (1882) in which they styled the then-known Neandertal remains (Neander, La Naulette, Cannstatt, and Gibraltar) collectively as a racial variant of modern Europeans. Quatrefages also wrote one of the earliest studies of pygmies, in 1871.

**Quételet, Lambert Adolphe Jacques:** (1796–1874): French astronomer, mathematician. Student of Laplace, director of the Royal Observatory at Brussels, 1828–74. Applied statistical methods to measurements of humans in 1856, using inductees and census data, obtaining 'bell-shaped' curves, and noted the random distribution of values around central tendencies. Also wrote an encapsulation of the ideas of **Malthus**, which was read by C. **Darwin**, among others.

**Quetelet's index:** see **body mass index**.

**quiescence:** state in which all but the most basic functions of a cell or group of cells has ceased, often in response to stress. Some cell lines may lie dormant until the agent of stress has been removed.

**quinicrine:** fluorescent stain, used to identify specific chromosomes and structural rearrangements. It is expecially useful for distinguishing the **Y chromosome** and various polymorphisms involving **satellites** and **centromeres** of specific chromosomes. Aka quinicrine mustard dihydrochloride. Cf. **Giemsa stain**.

**quinine:** white crystalline powder, the principal **alkaloid** of **cinchona bark**, used in the treatment of **malaria**. It acts by destroying the malarial parasite, *Plasmodium*. Quinine is a protoplasmic poison; it diminishes metabolism by retardation of **enzyme** action.

**Quyuanhekou:** archaeological site found in 1976 in Yunxian County, Hubei Province, China, dated to 350 kya (some estimate up to 800 kya), and that contains hominid remains including two relatively complete crania (EV 9001, EV 9002) with mid-facial features of **archaic** *Homo sapiens*, but assigned by many to *H. erectus*. Facial features dissimilar to **Petralona**, **Arago**, **Atapuerca**, **Bodo** and **Kabwe**. Aka Yunxian, Quyuan River Mouth.

**1 : 2 : 1, 3 : 1** and **9 : 3 : 3 : 1 ratios:** see **Mendelian ratios.**

***r*:** 1. symbol for the frequency of the third **allele** in a series of alleles in a **Hardy–Weinberg** population. See ***p*** and ***q*.** 2. in demography, the symbol for the **intrinsic rate of increase.** 3. symbol for the coefficient of relatedness. 4. symbol for the **correlation coefficient.** 5. alternate symbol for the **recombination fraction.**

**$R_o$:** abbreviation for **net reproductive success.**

**R.*n* dates:** see Oakley's dating series in box below. Cf. **A.*n* dates.**

---

### Oakley's relative dating series

**R.1 date:** highest of Oakley's hierarchical levels of relative dating, the age relation between a specimen and its containing deposit or associated fossils. It was R.1 dating that unmasked the Piltdown fraud.

**R.2 date:** one of Oakley's hierarchical levels of relative dating, the stage in the local or regional stratigraphic sequence to which a fossil-bearing horizon can be inferred.

**R.3 date:** one of Oakley's hierarchical levels of relative dating, the inferred position of a stage in terms of wide scale, or world, stratigraphy.

**R.4 date:** lowest of Oakley's hierarchical levels of relative dating, the geological age of a specimen inferred from the morphology; AKA morphological dating.

---

**Rabat:** archaeological site found in 1959 near Temara, Morocco, dated to 200 kya, containing **Acheulean** and associated **Aterian** artifacts and hominid remains including a partial cranial vault with an occiput lacking a transverse torus, and a mandible with a bony chin; 'essentially modern'. Aka Témara. Cf. **Salé** and **Sidi Abderrahman.**

**RAC:** abbreviation for **Recombinant DNA Advisory Committee.**

‡ **race:** 1. in nonhuman biology, a group of intraspecific **populations**, often geographically isolated, sharing certain conspicuous traits that make them perceptively distinct from other groups or sub-populations within a **species**; a taxonomic rank considered equivalent to or just below the **subspecies**. The biological concept of race is very difficult to apply to observed patterns of **human variation**; rather, human varieties can be considered **cultural constructs** that are contingent facts of history. See **biological race, ecological race, geographic races**, and **physiological race.** 2. In law, any group of persons related by common descent, blood, or heredity; a known stock; any group distinguished by self-identification or commonly known to others by a group name; a population so identified in the literature of the legal profession. 3. colloquially, any commonly recognized nation, strain, tribe, or ethnic stock of humans distinguished by physical traits as well as by codes of behavior and moral conduct that are different from, and usually perceived as less correct than one's own; aka the peasant's perspective. See **folk taxonomy.**

‡ **race concepts:** see **typological race concept** and **nominalistic race concept.**

**race consciousness:** cultural knowledge that one belongs to a certain racial group, usually accompanied by feelings of race interest and race superiority.

**race, ecological:** see **ecological race.**

**race, geographic:** see **geographical race.**

**race marker:** any **discrete trait** that exists in high frequency in a **geographical race.**

**racemic:** 1. consisting of clustered parts, as with glands. 2. pertaining to a compound that is a mixture of **dextrorotatory** and **levorotatory** molecules.

**race mixture:** interbreeding between races; **miscegenation.** Race differences are relative, not absolute; any race is able to breed freely with any other race of the same species. Racial admixture is sometimes measured by the proportion of a **discrete trait**, sometimes called a **race marker**, that has been introduced by **gene flow** from one to another population.

**race, physiological:** see **physiological race.**

**race psychology:** older term descriptive of studies made under the assumption that human races could have different interests, intelligence, reaction times, aptitudes, sense acuity, etc. Such studies peaked at the time of the Torres Straits Expedition in 1898.

**racemization:** 1. chemical conversion of an optically active substance into another that is relatively inactive. 2. see **amino acid racemization.** 3. process that is useful for dating individual tissues in a living organism. Amino acids in tooth enamel, for example, racemize linearly and can be used to estimate the chronological age of an individual. The technique is very accurate if the individual is living, as the tissues have been maintained at a relatively constant temperature.

**races, classification of human:** see **racial classification.**

**racial affinity:** ethnicity of a recovered body or skeleton based on a series of features and formulae. It should be noted that most anthropologists discount the race concept and prefer the term ethnicity; however, many, if not most, osteologists and forensic anthropologists think that there are racial features that can be discerned on skeletal material.

**racial amalgamation:** blending of a group by interbreeding with another such group.

**racial antipathy:** invidious differentiation of two or more different individuals or groups due to the consciousness of presumed factors of race.

**racial character or characteristic:** any of the conspicuous **traits** humans employ to group humanity into a relatively few groups termed **races**. The most common traits utilized include **skin color**, body shape, hair color and **hair form**, and facial features. The importance of such features is strictly arbitrary, and favoring these over other adaptive traits (such as blood groups) distinguishes peasant or **folk taxonomy** from formal scientific **classification**.

**racial classification:** typological exercise, not accepted as valid by many biological anthropologists, in which humans are clustered into a few infraspecific **types**, termed **races**. Various schemes devised to group humans into taxa have been published during the past several centuries; there is little agreement among them. See **folk taxonomy**.

**racial determinism:** belief, now totally discredited in anthropology, that cultural differences can be explained by racial characteristics.

**racial groups, historical:** see **historical racial groups**.

**racial hygiene:** see **Rassenhygiene**.

**racial profiling:** form of stereotyping in which members of an ethnic group are considered more likely to be involved in criminal activity.

**racial type:** see **racial classification**.

‡ **racialism:** 1. belief in racism. 2. belief in the practice of **racism**.

**raciation:** differentiation into racial groups within a species.

**raciology:** study of the races of humankind.

‡ **racism:** 1. belief in the natural category **race**; that human races have distinctive characteristics. 2. the belief that one's own culture is superior to that of other peoples because others are genetically inferior.

**racloir:** Mousterian side **scraper**.

**radiale: anthropometric** landmark; most proximal point that can be felt on the head of the **radius** in the elbow region.

**radial loop: dermatoglyphic** pattern in which the ridges of fingerprints swirl around one head and toward the margin and open toward the inside of the hands. See **loop** and **ulnar loop**.

**radial unit model of cortical evolution:** hypothesis that the cortical surface of the **brain** expands as a result of changes proliferating radial arrays of postmitotic **neurons**; the larger the number of columns, the larger the cortical surface.

**radiation:** 1. the process by which energy travels through space or a medium such as air. 2. emission of heat radiant energy from the surface of an object in the form of electromagnetic waves. 3. see **adaptive radiation**.

**radiation constant:** heat flux per degree of temperature difference between mean body surface temperature and the ambient temperature of the surrounding air, expressed in calories (or joules) per person or per square meter per hour.

**radiator hypothesis (of human brain growth):** proposal by Dean Falk that the pattern of cranial blood drainage in the gracile **australopithecines** and *Homo* lines was selected for in order to provide more efficient cooling of the heat-sensitive brain; with more efficient temperature regulation, the brain was free to enlarge.

**radiator theory (Coon's):** see **nasal radiator hypothesis**.

**radio collar** or **transmitter:** collar with a battery-powered transmitter, placed around the neck of a mammal for the purpose of tracking the animal's movement and/or monitoring several physiological variables. Because primates have greater dexterity than other mammals and can remove such collars, these types of **biotelemetry** devices have had to be modified; one modification is a radio backpack, although a second monkey can help remove the pack from the tracked animal.

**radioactive decay curve:** plot of the remaining quantity of an unstable isotope on the *Y*-axis, against time (usually in **half-life** increments) on the *X*-axis. Such a plot is identical for all unstable isotopes, such as radiocarbon. It is the half-life that varies among elements.

**radioactivity:** emission of ionizing radiation from an unstable source; radioactive. See **half-life**.

**radiocalcium dating:** method for dating bone directly that has a useful range of about 300 ky. As in **radiocarbon dating**, radiocalcium ($^{41}$Ca) is taken up by organisms during their lifetimes in small quantities along with stable calcium ($^{40}$Ca); $^{41}$Ca has a half-life of 100 ky. The technique is highly dependent upon local $^{41}$Ca : $^{40}$Ca ratios, and burial of bone in a thick overburden that shields it from further transformation by cosmic rays.

**radiocarbon dating:** system of **chronometric dating** that exploits the rate of decay of **carbon 14**, which has an empirical **half-life** of 5,568 years, into **nitrogen** 14. By measuring the ratio of carbon 14 to carbon 12 or of carbon 14 to nitrogen 14, the absolute age of organic objects such as wood, bone, leather and charcoal can be determined. The useful range of the conventional technique of radiocarbon dating is from the very recent to about 60 kya. See **accelerator mass spectrometry, carbon**, and **nitrogen**.

**radiocarbon years:** since older radiocarbon dates nonsystematically deviate from solar (calendar) years due to inconsistencies in the $CO_2$ reservoir, uncalibrated radiocarbon dates are usually reported as radiocarbon years before present (rybp). Dates subsequently calibrated with solar years (with a method such as CALIB 4.1) are reported as calibrated years before present (cal yr or cal age) or as **BP**.

**radiocarpal joint: condyloid joint** between the **radius** and the distal **carpals** that permits flexion, extension, adduction, abduction, and circumduction.

**radiogenic:** pertaining to any **unstable isotope** that produces **radioactivity**.

**radiographic analysis:** examination of an object such as a painting or bone for which an X-ray image has been made.

**radiometric dating:** any of a number of techniques that exploit the properties of **unstable isotopes**, all of which change stochastically into a lower energy state by emission of radioactivity. Because radioactive elements decay into daughter products at known and stable rates, measurement of the accumulated decay can be extrapolated to yield the age of many fossils and fossil-bearing rocks. See, for example, **radiocarbon dating**.

**radiotelemetry:** see **biotelemetry**.

**radius:** lateral bone of the forearm when the skeleton is viewed from **anatomical position**. Its proximal end helps form the elbow, and its distal end articulates with the **carpals**. The radius crosses over the **ulna** when the hand is rotated so that the palms face posteriorly.

**Raffle's tarsier:** vernacular for *Tarsius bancanus*.

**rafting:** dispersal of **biota** on chunks of land that have broken away from a larger landmass or other floating materials. Rafting is an explanation for dispersal of some primate groups. See **rafting hypothesis**.

**rafting hypothesis:** suggestion that New World monkeys originated in Africa and migrated to South America during the Oligocene as unintended passengers on natural rafts. Although this hypothesis is most closely associated with New World monkeys, rafting hypotheses have also been proposed for the movement of primates from European Laurasia to Africa and from Africa to Madagascar. See **rafting**.

**rain dance:** term coined by Jane **Goodall** for a display that occurs among the male chimpanzees at **Gombe Stream Chimpanzee Reserve** during a rain storm, in which they swing on low branches, tear up vegetation, and make loud vocalizations.

**rain forest:** tropical rain **forest** with an annual rainfall of at least 100 in (250 cm) per year.

**ramamorph:** vernacular applied to middle Miocene **hominoids** inhabiting Europe and East Africa; the main characteristic of this group is thick enamel on the molars. The term does not have taxonomic status and is derived from the genus *Ramapithecus* (and its

subfamily Ramapithecinae), which has subsequently been subsumed into *Sivapithecus*.

***Ramapithecus* Lewis, 1934:** genus now referred to *Sivapithecus*, but previously touted as the earliest **hominid** ancestor. The type specimen was a mandible found in the Siwalik Hills of India; in the 1960s it was noted that a maxilla of another genus, *Bramapithecus*, matched perfectly with the *Ramapithecus* mandible; thus *Bramapithecus* was referred to *Ramapithecus*. During a period of revision in the 1980s it was suggested and accepted by most workers that *Ramapithecus* was the female of a sexually dimorphic genus, *Sivapithecus*. Consequently, the species contained within *Ramapithecus* have been referred to other taxa.

***Ramapithecus*-as-first-hominid debate:** proposal by Lewis that the juxtaposed mandibular portions of *Ramapithecus* with a maxilla of *Bramapithecus* suggested that this Miocene hominoid was in fact the first **hominid**. This idea found support among authorities such as W. K. **Gregory** and, later, E. L. **Simons**. Subsequent fossil evidence has not supported the original interpretation of the tooth row as parabolic in shape, and *Ramapithecus* has been sunk into the hominoid taxon *Sivapithecus*.

**ramus:** 1. any branch of a bone, artery, or nerve that is at an angle to the main body. 2. see **mandibular ramus**.

**random:** of or characterizing a process of selection in which each item of a set has an equal **probability** of being chosen; haphazard, having no recognizable pattern.

‡ **random assortment:** chance distribution of whole **chromatids** to daughter cells during cell division; see **assortment**. In practice, also refers to the **segregation** of alleles during the same processes. See **independent assortment**.

**random dispersion:** in ecology, pattern of spatial distribution of individual members of a species within its geographic range. In a random dispersion the distribution of any one individual is not influenced by where another individual is. This is not the case in primates; social primates are in a clumped dispersion whereas **noyau** primates are in either ranges or territories and generally avoid contact with other individuals. See **clumped dispersion, uniform dispersion**.

**random drift:** synonym of **genetic drift**.

**random event:** any event where the *a priori* probability of occurrence is neither zero nor unity (0,1), i.e. is greater than 0 but less than 1.

**random evolutionary hits** (REHs): estimate of the actual countable plus superimposed fixed nucleotide changes that separate any two nucleic acid sequences.

‡ **random mating:** complete **panmixia**; a theoretical **mating system** in which the selection of partners is governed entirely by chance.

**random sample:** 1. in statistics, a smaller set of values selected from a population when every member of the larger population has an equal chance of being selected. 2. in genetics, any sample that has the same gene frequencies as the larger population from which it is drawn.

**random walk:** 1. any irregular movement. 2. any random process that can be modeled as a sequence of random variables with discrete steps of uniform periodicity such that the differences between successive pairs forms a sequence of independent, identically distributed random variables. Random walks are exhibited by processes involving molecules as well as the behavior of whole organisms.

**random-X inactivation:** kind of **X inactivation** seen in **Eutheria**, but not marsupials. In the Eutheria (including humans), the process of inactivation is random in the cells of a female fetus; however, all of her extraembryonic membranes (the **amnion, placenta**, and **umbilical cord**) have the father's X chromosome nonrandomly inactivated. See **paternal-X inactivation**.

**range:** 1. limits of geographic distribution; see **home range**. 2. A measure of variation, being the difference between the maximum and minimum values of a distribution.

**range of motion** (ROM): type(s) of movement that a **synovial joint** allows; these may be nonaxial motion (slipping movements only), uniaxial motion (movement in one plane), biaxial motion (movement in two planes), or multiaxial motion (movement in or around all three planes of space and axes). ROM is dependent on such factors as structure and articular surfaces of bones, action of muscles, and strength and tautness of ligaments, tendons, and the **articular capsule**. ROM varies not only between joints, but between different individuals at the same joints.

*Rangwapithecus* (**Andrews, 1974**): genus of **hominoids** from the early Miocene of East Africa belonging to the catarrhine family **Proconsulidae**; one or two species, depending on author. Estimated body mass ranges from 9 to 15 kg. Dental formula: 2.1.2.3; shearing crests on molars suggest a **folivorous** diet. Appears to have inhabited tropical rain forest **ecozones**. See Appendix 1 for taxonomy.

**rank:** 1. (behavior) position an individual holds within a social hierarchy. See **basic rank, dependent rank**. 2. (taxonomy) position of a taxon in classification hierarchy. 3. in statistics, a class in any scale of comparison; relative position or standing in an inclusive hierarchical series.

**rank mimicry:** imitation of the behavior of higher-ranking individuals by lower-ranking individuals; found in **polygynous** societies in which this behavior may help attract mates. It also appears to play a role in **dependent rank**.

**rank order:** see **hierarchy**.

**rank reversal:** change in the social status, or rank, of one or more individuals in a primate group's social hierarchy, usually because of a challenge from subordinate individuals.

**ranked society:** society in which there is unequal access to high-status categories; many people who may be qualified for such roles are unable to realize them.

**Rapaport's rule:** biological dictum that species inhabiting equatorial areas have smaller geographic ranges than those found further from the equator.

**rape:** see **forced copulation**.

**rapid eye movement** (REM): see **paradoxical sleep**.

**rare species:** one of the five conservation categories established by the **International Union for the Conservation of Nature**. This category includes those species that have small total population sizes. These species are not in immediate danger, but are candidates for endangered status due to their small numbers. See **extinct species, endangered species, vulnerable species, insufficiently known species**.

*ras* **oncogene** (KRAS): oncogene that functions normally as a switch, relaying signals from hormones, e.g. at cell surface receptors, into the interior of the cell, causing cell growth. In cases where *ras* is mutated, this switch can be permanently 'on', and cell growth occurs even in the absence of receptor activation. The various autosomal dominant forms of *ras* proteins (KRAS, HRAS, and NRAS) are involved in about 30% of all cases of **tumorigenesis**. About ten alleles have been well characterized in terms of specific varieties of cancer. Aka *ras* p21 protein activator. Cf. *p53* **tumor suppressor protein**.

**Rassenhygiene:** literally, 'racial cleansing', a concept associated with the Nazi Party in Germany after 1933, when an official (and legal) policy of both **positive eugenics** and **negative eugenics** was adopted as policy by the German government.

**Rassenkreis:** German term for a group of closely related subgroups within a species that are distributed according to a geographical replacement pattern; see **ring species** and **polytypic species concept**.

**Rassenkunde:** literally, 'ethnology', but in Nazi Germany this term had the meaning 'racial science'.

**ratchet:** see **Muller's ratchet**.

**rate(s) of development:** relative timing of **life history** events. In primates, although the sequences of homologous events are similar, monkeys such as **macaques** develop about twice as fast as **apes**, who in turn develop about twice as fast as **AMHs**. Much research has focused on the possible rates of development of intermediate fossil forms such as the **australopithecines**, which seem to resemble apes more than humans in this regard. See **neoteny** and **pedomorphism**.

**rate of living theory:** proposal based upon observations that the total energy burned per gram of body mass is about the same for all mammalian species, and therefore that the lifespan of a mammal is inversely proportional to its rate of metabolism. Proposed in 1908 by German physiologist Max Rubner (1854–1932); aka heartbeat theory because of the finite and approximately equivalent number of heartbeats seemingly available to all mammalian species.

**ratio:** comparison of any two items of information; in arithmetic form, by simple division. Cf. **sex ratio**.

**ratio of increase:** see **Malthusian population theory**.

**ratio of investment:** with reference to the sexes, the total work invested in the raising of males divided by the total invested in raising females.

**ratio of male to female mutation rates** ($\alpha_m$): fraction of mutation rates for specific loci in human males over that of human females. Studies have shown $\alpha_m$ to range from 1.7× to 5.1×. See **male mutation rates**.

**rationality:** in anthropology, a supposed motive force in **cultural evolution**; its essence is assumed to be logical and self-conscious thought and the planned control of environment and society; ethnocentric theories often hold incorrectly that Western cultures are more evolved than others because Westerners are more rational. Cf. **cultural relativism**.

**Ray, John** (1627–1705): English clergyman, naturalist. His classification greatly aided **Linnaeus**. Helped by patron and collaborator Francis Willoughby. Influenced by Nils Steensen, a Danish anatomist and geologist. His published work in botany became a standard reference text. It was Ray who in 1686 introduced the idea of reproductive isolation into the concept of a species.

**R-banding:** one of the methods of creating identification bands on individual chromosomes after treatment of the metaphase plate with heat in a phosphate buffer and **Giemsa stain**. R-bands are the reverse of **G-banding** patterns. See **chromosome banding technique**.

**RBC:** see **erythrocyte**.

**rDNA:** ribosomal **DNA**; many copies of a repeat containing the genes for 5$S$, 8$S$, 18$S$ and 25$S$ **ribosomal RNA**.

**reading frame:** register in which the **genetic translation** apparatus associated with the ribosome senses the information encoded within an **mRNA codon**; the reading frame is dictated by the position of the **initiation codon**.

**realized niche:** see **niche**.

**recapitulation theory:** see **biogenetic law**.

**recDNA:** abbreviation for **recombinant DNA**.

**receding forehead:** frontal bone that slopes posteriorly; characteristic of most **hominids** including archaic *Homo sapiens*; in some cases there actually is no forehead.

**recent African origin model** (RAO): see the **out of Africa II model** and **mitochondrial 'Eve'**. Aka African monogenism.

**Recent epoch:** see **Holocene epoch**.

**receptor:** 1. cell or nerve ending at the tip of a sensory neuron that is specialized to respond to a particular type of stimulus. Examples are the free nerve endings of sensory nerve fibers associated with touch, gustatory cells in the taste buds of the tongue, and photoreceptors embedded in the retina of the eye. 2. structure, usually a protein, embedded in the **plasma membrane** of a cell that binds with a specific substance. Receptors have numerous functions, including opening channels in the membrane for substances to pass through and beginning a cascade of metabolic effects within the cell.

‡ **recessive:** referring to a genetic **allele**, the expression of which is suppressed when it occurs in combination with a **dominant** allele. Recessive alleles are expressed phenotypically only in the **homozygous** condition; thus a trait that is unexpressed in the **F1** generation of a monohybrid cross may be re-expressed in some members of the F2 generation.

**recessive mutation:** change in **DNA** that is fully expressed only when it occurs in a double dose, i.e. in a recessive **homozygote**.

‡ **recessive pattern of inheritance:** in Mendelian **genetics**, a system of **inheritance** in which, when one allele of any ancestral **homozygote** mutates to form a new heterozygote, the phenotype of that **heterozygote** is not distinguishable from that of the ancestral homozygote. In this circumstance, the ancestral homozygote is termed the dominant homozygote (AA), and the *de novo* heterozygote is termed Aa, with the lower-case 'a' used to symbolize the new recessive mutant. In a recessive system, the heterozygote is often called the **carrier** of the trait, whereas the recessive homozygote (aa) often exhibits subvital phenotypic changes and reduced **fitness**. An example is pea shape in common garden peas. See **dominant pattern of inheritance**, **codominant pattern of inheritance**, and **incomplete dominance**.

‡ **reciprocal altruism:** trading of altruistic acts by individuals at different times; for example, one person saves a drowning person in exchange for the promise (or reasonable expectation) that the altruistic act will be repaid if circumstances are ever reversed. See **sociobiology** and **altruism**.

**reciprocal cross:** simultaneous or successive crosses of the form A × B and B × A (female first, male second, in each case). Such crosses, when they do not yield identical results in the hybrids, suggest that the inequality is due to **sex linkage** or **maternal inheritance**.

**reciprocal food sharing:** distribution of nutrient resources among the members of a group regardless of the amount of food contributed by each individual with the expectation that food will be equally shared over time. Condition found among human hunters and gatherers.

**reciprocal translocation: any major chromosomal anomaly** that results in the exchange of chromosome segments between nonhomologous chromosomes. A reciprocal translocation alters the sequence of genes on the affected chromosomes, but not the total number of genes, thus preserving genetic balance. Aka illegitimate crossover. See **Philadelphia chromosome.**

**reciprocity:** 1. the return of objects or favors to others, usually among nonkin. 2. the concept that social relations develop through a set of reciprocated duties and privileges, proposed by Malinowski. 3. **reciprocal altruism.**

**recognition failure:** a weak or absent mutual attraction between the sexes of different species; a premating or **prezygotic mechanism.**

**recognition species concept:** defines a species as a set of organisms with a shared specific mate recognition system. Different members of the species recognize one another by an evolved method of communication as potential mates.

**recombinant:** 1. any organism, chromosome, or DNA fragment that has resulted from the introduction of genetic material from an outside source. 2. pertaining to **recombination.**

**recombinant chromatid:** chromatid resulting from the process of **crossing over** that consists of a mixture of genetic information due to the exchange of some genes between **homologous chromosomes.** Cf. **nonrecombinant chromatid.**

**recombinant DNA** (recDNA): any DNA molecule consisting of strands originating from two or more distinct sources. recDNA may be found in nature as during meiosis or fertilization, or may be produced anthropogenically, as with human genes inserted into bacteria with the use of restriction enzymes.

**Recombinant DNA Advisory Committee** (RAC): United States Senate Committee commissioned to oversee recombinant DNA and **genetic engineering** activity.

**recombinant DNA technology** (recDNA): hybrid DNA produced in a test tube by joining segments of DNA from natural or synthetic sources; these segments can then be inserted into the genetic material of an organism to introduce a novel function. In biotech applications, individual human genes are often isolated and combined with a vector or DNA transporter such as a plasmid, and this recombinant plasmid is inserted into host cells so that it can be cloned.

**recombinant fraction** (RF): proportion or percentage of **recombinant** cells or individuals. Aka recombination fraction, proportion or rate ($r$).

‡ **recombination:** 1. any of several processes giving rise to **recombinants;** usually, where the **linkage groups** of parental organisms are 'reshuffled' in **progeny,** thus giving rise to new combinations of **genotypes** or **haplotypes** while maintaining the **alleles** that were present in the parents; in eukaryotes the two most common mechanisms of recombination are whole **chromatid segregation,** and **crossing over** (recombination within **linkage groups**). In meiotic crossing over, DNA is normally exchanged between either homologous or sister chromatids. Recombination tends, in the absence of other factors, to make the alleles of different loci appear in random (or independent) proportions in haplotypes. An allele A1 at one locus will then be found with alleles B1 and B2 at another locus in the same proportions as B1 and B2 as a whole; this condition is called **linkage equilibrium.** Cf. **linkage disequilibrium.** 2. In **biotechnology,** the synthetic production of **recombinant DNA** by **genetic engineering.**

**recon:** 1. in genetics, the smallest unit of a single DNA fragment capable of **recombination.** 2. abbreviation for a reconstituted cell.

**reconciliation:** re-establishment of normal social behavior after individuals have been in conflict; this differs between primate species, but in many instances involves touching.

**reconstruction:** re-creation of an individual or situation, based on collected evidence and, often, extrapolation. Reconstruction is often applied to fossil materials and is used in **forensic anthropology** to identify an unknown individual (often from skeletal material) as to age, race, sex, and stature. Sometimes called restoration.

**recruitment:** 1. a form of gathering by which some members of a society are directed toward some place where work is required; see **mass recruitment.** 2. activation of additional cells in response to an increased stimulus strength. 3. see **muscle recruitment.**

**recrystallization:** change in the internal physical structure of a **fossil** such as a bone or shell during **permineralization** as a result of **solution** and/or reprecipitation. See **diagenesis.**

**rectilinear:** describes growth or movement that proceeds in a straight line.

**rectilinear series:** set of fossils in a phyletic series perceived to be related in a linear and progressive manner.

**rectum:** inferior portion of the **alimentary canal** that follows the **sigmoid colon** and precedes the **anus.**

**recumbent length:** measurement of height (i.e. length) in children between two and three years of age in which the child is lying down, on either an osteometric board or a **stadiometer.**

**recurrence risk:** probability that any trait will occur again in a family, given that one relative already has the trait. Usually calculated for genetic diseases or birth defects.

**red-backed saki:** vernacular for *Chiropotes* *satanas*.

**red-backed squirrel monkey:** vernacular for *Saimiri* *oerstedii*.

**red-bellied lemur:** vernacular for *Eulemur rubiventer*.

**red-bellied monkey:** vernacular for *Cercopithecus* *erythrogaster*.

**red blood cell** (RBC): see **erythrocyte.**

**red blood cell mosaic:** individual possessing two or more kinds of red blood cells with respect to their antigens; see **freemartin.**

**redcapped tamarin:** one of the vernaculars for *Saguinus* *mystax*.

**red-chested tamarin:** vernacular for *Saguinus* *labiatus*.

**red colobus:** vernacular for *Piliocolobus badius*.

**Red Data Book:** publication of the World Conservation Monitoring Centre of the **International Union for the Conservation of Nature** that lists extinct, endangered and threatened wildlife species, including primates.

**red-eared monkey:** vernacular for *Cercopithecus* *erythrotis*.

**red-fronted brown lemur:** vernacular for the **subspecies** *E. fulvus rufus*; found in both southern east and west Madagascar.

**red graph:** technique for analyzing wrist X-rays that evaluates carpal bones of varying maturation rates and enables an investigator to estimate the **skeletal age** of a subject.

**red–green color blindness:** most common form of colorblindness due to a recessive allele(s) located on the X chromosome causing defective **opsins** in the retina of the eye. About 8% of the US male population is affected. See **X-linked.**

**red-handed howler:** vernacular for *Alouatta belzebul*.

**red-handed tamarin:** vernacular for *Saguinus* *midas*.

**red howler:** vernacular for *Alouatta seniculus*.

**red Hussar:** vernacular for *Erythrocebus patas*.

**Red King effect:** proposal that in mutualism evolution the slower evolving species is likely to gain a disproportionate share of the benefits; in coevolution, the slowest runner sometimes wins the evolutionary race. Aka red king hypothesis or model. See **ESS.** Cf. **Red Queen hypothesis or model.**

**red king hypothesis:** see **maximum homology hypothesis.**

**red-mantled tamarin:** one of the vernaculars for *Saguinus fuscicollis*.

**red marrow:** connective tissue that occupies the cavities of **cancellous bone** in ribs, coxals, and, particularly, the **epiphyses** of long bones. Involved in **hematopoiesis.**

**red (muscle) fiber:** type of muscle fiber having a high oxidative capacity and a large amount of myoglobin; found in slow contracting postural muscles.

**red ochre:** see **ochre.**

**Red Queen hypothesis or model:** 1. proposal that speciation is driven by competition among populations that share the same habitat; hence that as some species evolve others will be forced to adapt via countermeasures to the environment that has changed as the result of the others' evolution. Aka evolutionary arms race, lag load, zero sum game. 2. sexual **recombination** is an adaptation which augments a population's capacity to evolve quickly. A metaphor derived from a Lewis Carroll novel. Cf. **Red King effect.**

**red-ruffed lemur:** vernacular for the subspecies *Varecia variegata rubra*.

**red-tail monkey:** vernacular for *Cercopithecus* *ascanius*.

**red-tailed sportive lemur:** vernacular for *Lepilemur ruficaudatus*.

**red uakari:** vernacular for *Cacajao rubicundus*.

**redirected activity or behavior:** behavior, such as an act of aggression, that is directed away from the primary target and toward another, less appropriate object or subject. See **conflict behavior, displacement activity**, and **intention movement.**

**reduction:** 1. mirroring on a smaller scale. 2. diminishment. 3. representation of a complex or large phenomenon by a symbol. 4. the addition of hydrogen or electrons; cf. **oxidation.**

**reduction division:** see **meiosis.**

**reductionism:** 1. any general attempt to explain one range of phenomena in terms of the operations of another range of phenomena, allegedly leaving no room for causal interactions between them, e.g. **cultural reduction** and **biological reduction.** 2. philosophy that complex systems behave according to principles that can be reduced without residue to the laws of the physical sciences, and thence to its smallest components.

**redundancy of the genetic code:** see **degenerate codons.**

**redundant trait, character** or **feature:** any feature that does not contribute new or specific information to a taxonomic analysis.

**reference genome:** gene sequence of a composite organism for a given species, i.e. the sum of several individual genomes with private SNPs eliminated to show the most common gene sequences in a population or species.

**reference laboratory:** laboratory carrying out specialized clinical tests on samples referred by private clinics or hospital physicians.

**reference time datum** (RTD): geological time horizon used as a starting point for a study of taxonomic survivorship, proceeding from the RTD either forward (up) or backward (down) in time.

**referential model (of hominid evolution):** any of the behavioral models that utilize the social system of a particular nonhuman primate species to model early hominid behavioral evolution; see, for example, Jolly's **'seed-eating' hypothesis.**

**referred specimen:** any example or fossil subsequently attributed to a taxon after its designation based upon the description of a **type specimen** has been completed.

**reflectance:** ratio of reflected to incident radiation above a reflecting surface. See **albedo.**

**reflex:** rapid involuntary response to a stimulus; biological control system mediated by a **reflex arc.**

**reflex arc:** basic conduction pathway through the nervous system, consisting of a sensory neuron, an association neuron, and a motor neuron.

**refuge:** location relatively free from environmental stress, such as predator pressure. See **home range.**

**refugium:** smaller area not as affected as broader regions where flora and fauna have changed radically owing to changes in climate, especially due to **glaciation.** Refugia are usually centers for **relict species** and postglacial dispersal.

**regional continuity:** appearance of similar traits within a geographic region over time. See **multiregional continuity model** of modern **human origins.**

**regional development hypothesis:** see **multiregional continuity model, polyphyletic hypothesis,** and **polygenism.**

**regression:** 1. reversal, as in the direction of evolution or the abatement of the symptoms of a disease. 2. return to a more primitive pattern; see **atavistic regression.** 3. retreat of the sea from a land area. 4. in statistics, the estimation of a relationship between a dependent variable and one or more independent variables, by expressing one as a function of the other(s).

**regression coefficient** ($b_n$): 1. in statistics, the numerical value of any parameter estimate directly associated with the independent variable(s). In the model $Y = c_1 + b_1 X_1$, e.g., the value $b_1$ is the regression coefficient for the variable $X_1$. Aka **slope,** scaling coefficient. 2. When the regression is a parent–offspring correlation, the regression coefficient, $b_n$, is an estimate of the **heritability** of the trait being measured. Cf. **intercept.**

**regression toward the mean:** in any polygenic system, the tendency of the offspring of parents with extreme phenotypic differences to exhibit a phenotype that is the average of the two parental phenotypes. Cf. **heterosis.**

**regressive evolution:** simplification of a trait over time.

**regressive trait, character** or **feature:** trait or feature that exhibits a loss of differentiation. The loss may be either ontogenetic, as in the process of aging, or phylogenetic.

**regulation:** 1. more, rule or law designed to control procedures or behavior. 2. maintenance of homeostasis. 3. process(es) by which an embryo maintains a normal pattern of development when stressed. 4. **genetic regulation.** 5. **population regulation.**

**regulative development:** open embryonic development, in which the fate of each element is not necessarily decided before fertilization; all processes are dependent upon the outcome of previous processes such that a perturbation in one affects all subsequent others. Cf. **canalization.**

‡ **regulatory gene:** 1. gene that encodes for the regulation of biological processes such as growth and development, usually by the production of a repressor protein; aka regulator gene. 2. any gene that controls the expression or activity of other genes, e.g. **homeobox genes.** Cf. **structural gene.**

**rehabilitation:** conservation technique in which captive members of endangered species are trained to survive in their native environment (with skills such as recognizing predators and food) with the goal of releasing them into their endemic area. See **soft release, hard release.**

**Reifenstein's syndrome:** familial **male pseudohermaphroditism** associated with hypospadias, small testes, sterility, absence of beard, short stature, and often **gynecomastia;** inherited as an X-linked recessive or an autosomal dominant male-limited trait. Aka hereditary familial hypogonadism.

**reification:** process of reducing or collapsing a complex set of phenomena into a single vector, component, or number. **IQ** test scores are an example. See **reduction.**

**Reindeer Age:** last stage of the **Upper Paleolithic** when reindeer became increasingly abundant as the climate became drier *c.* 18–12 kya; see **Magdalenian tool tradition.** Aka reindeer period.

**reinforcement:** increase in reproductive isolation between incipient species by natural selection. Natural selection can directly favor only an increase in prezygotic isolation; reinforcement therefore amounts to selection for assortative mating between the incipient speciating forms.

**reinforcement schedule:** distribution of rewards to an animal in a learning experiment. On a continuous schedule the animal is rewarded each time it makes a correct response; on a fixed-interval schedule the animal is rewarded after a set period of time after each correct response; on a variable-interval schedule the animal is rewarded at random periods; on a fixed-ratio schedule the animal is rewarded after it has made a fixed number of correct responses; on a variable-ratio schedule the animal is rewarded after it has made a random number of correct responses.

**reinforcing selection:** operation of selection pressures on two or more levels of organization such as the individual, kin group and deme, such that certain alleles are favored at all levels and their spread through the population is accelerated. Cf. **counteracting selection**.

**reintroduction:** act of returning rehabilitated or wild-caught animals to an area that was included within their historic range where they are no longer present. See **soft release, hard release**.

**reject:** worked stone apparently intended as a tool but discarded without use.

**rejecta** (FU): in ecological genetics, the proportion of total consumption (C) not utilized for production (P) and/or respiration (R); rejecta are lost as **egesta** or excreta. See **consumption**.

**rejection:** 1. a negative immune response, as with an organ rejection. 2. something rejected, as with a proposed taxonomic name or scholarly work.

**relaxed open-mouth face:** anthropoid primate expression in which the mouth is wide with the corners up; present during play.

**relatedness:** 1. in taxonomy, a property attached to clades that share a recent common ancestor and more traits between them than they do with any other clade. 2. in genetics, the **degree of relatedness**.

**relation:** position of one object when considered in association with another.

**relationship:** association; kinship.

**relative:** 1. describes the measure of a trait or character with reference to some other, possibly comparative, scale of measurement. 2. an individual to whom one is related; see **relatives**.

**relative attractiveness:** physical trait or traits that increase the **reproductive success** of an individual.

**relative brain weight:** simple measure first established by **Cuvier** for comparing the proportion of the nervous system among classes of animals; initially, calculated as a simple proportion such that lion = 1/546, human = 1/46, mouse = 1/49, etc. Cf. **encephalization quotient**.

‡ **relative dating** (**technique**): determination of the age, in subjective terms, of two or more events or specimens relative to each other, on the basis of stratigraphy or relative proportions of chemicals (such as **F–U–N**), in contrast to absolute dating. See the hierarchy **R.1, R.2, R.3**, and **R.4**.

**relative, first-degree:** family member that shares 50% of her/his genes with a **proband** owing to direct common descent; includes parents, siblings, and offspring. Aka 1° relative.

**relative of interest:** in genetic counseling, anyone who seeks counsel about recurrence of a disease in a family. Cf. **proband** and **consultand**.

**relative parental investment:** ratio of parental investment by sex of parent; in most species males invest far less in offspring than females. See **sexual asymmetry, female parental investment**.

**relative rate test:** device proposed by A. C. **Wilson** *et al.* that tests for **generation length** effects in both protein and nucleotide sequences of widely divergent species that have evolved since last sharing a common ancestor. The test involves checking for asymmetry of branch lengths in an **unrooted cladogram**.

**relative risk:** probability that an individual will develop a certain condition, usually given as a function of risk in the general population, e.g. 1 : 100.

**relative, second-degree:** family member that shares 25% of her/his genes with a **proband** owing to direct common descent; includes grandparents, aunts and uncles, nieces and nephews, half-siblings, etc. Aka 2° relative.

**relative, third-degree:** family member that shares 12.5% of her/his genes with a **proband** owing to direct common descent; includes great-grandparents, first cousins, etc. Aka 3° relative.

**relatives:** two or more members that have a specifically acknowledged relationship within a larger group. Anthropologists define many more types than simple relatives that have a biological relationship, known as genetic or consanguineal relatives. See **relative, first-degree, relative, second-degree**, and **relative, third-degree**.

**relativism:** philosophical position that 1. all beliefs are true for those who hold them; and/or 2. since there are many radically different ways of looking at the world, none is ultimately more or less correct than another; aka perspectivism.

**relaxed maternal selection:** hypothesis proposed to account for the increased incidence of aneuploid children with advanced maternal age; maternal selection, according to the hypothesis, results in the spontaneous **abortion** of chromosomally abnormal embryos, but as women age this alleged process becomes less effective, allowing abnormal embryos to implant and develop.

‡ **relaxed selection:** term generally applied to any event that results in the cultural buffering of **natural**

selection; any cultural solution to a biological dilemma as, for example, the innovation of cooking with controlled fire by hominids, which relaxed selection for robust gnathic chewing architecture via cultural premastication, and resulted eventually in smaller chewing muscles, jaws, and teeth. The removal of species from the wild to protected environments is also a form of relaxed selection. Aka iatrogenic selection, **anthropogenic selection.**

**relaxin:** a polypeptide **hormone** secreted by the **corpus luteum** of many mammals during pregnancy. Relaxin facilitates the birth process by causing a softening and lengthening of the pubic symphysis and cervix; it also inhibits contraction of the **uterus** and may play a role in timing of **parturition.** In humans, however, relaxin is at its highest concentration in early pregnancy, leading researchers to believe that it is involved in the implantation of the **blastocyst.** Animal extracts of relaxin can be used to induce labor. Aka cervilaxin, ovarian hormone, releasin. Cf. **insulin-like growth factor.**

**releaser:** sign stimulus used in communication; loosely, any sign stimulus.

**releaser pheromone:** substance that is quickly perceived and causes a more or less immediate response. Cf. **primer pheromone.** See **pheromone.**

**relict:** surviving beyond others of a kind; a **vestige.**

**relict organ:** organ that has lost its original function. Aka vestigial organ.

**relict species:** persistent remnants of formerly widespread flora or fauna that survive in isolated habitats. Aka relic.

**rem:** amount of **radiation** that has the same biological effect as one rad of X-rays; the Roentgen Equivalent Man.

**REM sleep:** see **paradoxical sleep.**

*Rencunius zhoui* Gingerich, Holroyd, and Ciochon, 1994: adapoid **prosimian** from the middle Eocene of China; phylogenetic relationship uncertain and assigned to a family *incertae sedis*; monotypic. Estimated body mass around 700 g. Dental formula uncertain. See Appendix 1 for taxonomy.

**rendzina:** unusually dark Italian limestone-derived soil.

**renewable resource:** natural source of supply for human consumption that can be restored. Cf. **fossil fuel.**

**Rensch's desert rule:** generalization that fat stored in the bodies of desert animals will tend to be in lumps. Cf. **steatopygia.**

**Rensch's first law:** observation that in cold climates mammals have larger litters and birds larger clutches of eggs than varieties of the same species that reside in warmer climates.

**Rensch's second law:** observation that mammals have shorter fur and birds have shorter wings in warmer climates than in cold regions. Aka the wing rule, Rensch's hair rule.

**Renzidong:** archaeological site found in 1997, in Anhui Province, eastern China, and dated to 2.25 mya (faunal dating), containing about 50 stone tools or flakes in association with stacked bones from a mastodon and tapir. Aka Renzi Cave.

**repatriation:** return of objects or remains; in the context of anthropology, the return of formerly curated items to the rightful state or group from which they were originally obtained. Alternatively, the permission granted by a state or group to a curating institution to maintain curated items or collections at such an institution. See **NAGPRA.**

**repeat:** see **duplication.**

**repeat frequency:** frequency with which mothers who have experienced a certain event subsequently have the same experience; used to estimate the probability that a mother will have a second set of **twins** given a first set, a second child with Down syndrome, etc.

**repertoire:** all of the behavior that it is believed that a species is capable of performing. See **catalog of behavior, ethogram.**

**repetitive DNA:** sequences of DNA with iterative repeats. Repetitive DNA is classified as being either tandem repeat sequences or scattered repeat sequences. Tandem repeats, in turn, are distinguished by the size and number of the repeats, as being **microsatellite DNA, minisatellite DNA,** or **satellite DNA.** Much of the human genome consists of repetitive DNA.

**replacement dentition (or teeth):** adult teeth that replace the **deciduous dentition.**

**replacement level:** for any population, the number of births required so that the number of adults of reproductive age remains constant, given the local **mortality rate.**

**replacement model:** see **out of Africa** I and II and **mitochondrial 'Eve'** model.

**replicated chromosome:** 'X'-shaped chromosome; two sister **chromatids** attached at the centromere after DNA replication has occurred. Conventionally, a **chromosome.**

‡ **replication:** 1. duplication from a preexisting template; used in the process of **DNA** reproduction at the beginning of **mitosis** and **meiosis.** 2. the duplication or readministration of an experiment or test, especially to expose or reduce **error,** or to validate the results obtained in a previous sample.

**replication fork:** region of a duplicating DNA molecule that is temporarily separated into single-stranded DNA.

**replicator:** hypothetical minimal unit of evolution according to **Dawkins** and other supporters of the **adaptationist program.** Cf. **meme.**

**repressor protein:** substance manufactured by a cell during the action of a gene that regulates the rate of polypeptide product synthesis by other genes; the repressor is bound with the **operator** until released by binding with another compound such as lactose; the operator is then no longer blocked and thus transcription occurs.

‡ **reproduction:** propagation; the process by which living organisms give rise to offspring. See **sexual reproduction** and **asexual reproduction**.

**reproductive barrier:** see **reproductive isolation**.

**reproductive behavior:** behavior related to reproduction including courtship, copulation, mating system, etc.

**reproductive biology:** pattern of events and behaviors specific to a species that results in reproduction. Aka breeding biology.

**reproductive character displacement:** reproductive isolation of two closely related species that cohabit the same geographic region.

**reproductive compensation:** parity event(s) that occurs after the loss of offspring in order to maintain a particular number of offspring, the target family size.

**reproductive effort:** effort required to reproduce, measured in terms of the decrease in the ability of the organism to reproduce at later times.

**reproductive fitness:** capacity of an individual to produce offspring who will survive to adulthood and also reproduce; see **fitness**.

**reproductive isolation:** genetic isolation of a population(s) that can eventually render them incapable of producing fertile offspring with members of the main population; isolation may be anatomical, physiological, behavioral, or geographic.

**reproductive potential:** potential number of offspring an individual or population might produce under optimum circumstances.

**reproductive seasonality:** see **breeding season**.

**reproductive species concept:** pluralistic amalgamation of the biological plus recognition concepts, and a typical practical definition of species; adult individuals who recognize and choose to mate with another individual of the opposite sex, and who produce viable and fertile offspring, are valid members of the same species. Interbreeding between species is prevented by **isolating mechanisms**.

‡ **reproductive strategy:** organism's complex of behavioral and physiological features concerned with reproduction. Males and females within a species sometimes exhibit **asymmetrical reproductive strategies**. See **r-selection** and **K-selection**.

‡ **reproductive success** (RS): measure of the contribution of an individual to the gene pool of the next generation; the relative number of surviving offspring; sometimes includes the number of surviving collateral offspring. See **fitness** and **inclusive fitness**.

**reproductive synchrony:** condition in which all the females of a population ovulate at the same time. In modern urban humans the number of women ovulating is smaller than the entire breeding population, but there is a limited amount of synchrony among women in close contact; see **menstrual synchrony**.

**reproductive value** ($v_x$): the potential remaining reproductive output of an individual ($v$) of age $x$.

**repulsion linkage:** in a dihybrid cross, the presence of one dominant and one recessive allele on each chromosome, e.g. Ab/aB. Cf. **coupling linkage**.

**repulsion theory:** see **field theory**.

**research:** diligent and systematic inquiry or investigation into a subject in order to discover or revise facts, theories, applications, etc.

**research design:** any systematic plan formulated in advance to coordinate **research**: to ensure the efficient use of resources, to guide the choice and interrelationships of a set of experimental variables, and to determine the selection and assignment of participants to experimental and control conditions. Includes specifications, schedule, and budget. See **scientific method**, **prospective study**, and **retrospective study**.

**research hypothesis:** in statistics, an indication that two or more variables may be related and that leads to a research design and experimental test.

**reservoir host:** animal that serves as a host to species of **parasites** that are also parasitic for humans and by which humans may be infested, either directly through ingestion or indirectly through a carrier or **vector**.

**reservoir of infection:** see **disease reservoir**.

**resharpen:** to trim the edge of a worn stone tool.

**resident sex:** in primatology, that sex which tends to remain within a group as the individual members become sexually mature; in general, females are the resident sex (as in baboons) but more rarely it is the males, as in common chimpanzee.

**residential group:** concentration of people at the domestic, subsistence, or community level.

**resorption:** physiological process in which the bony matrix is broken down into its chemical constituents by **osteoclasts**. Verb: to resorb.

**resorting:** disturbance to soil in an archaeological site that confounds the original stratification.

**resource:** any element in an environment utilized by an organism.

**resource-defense polygyny:** form of **polygyny** in which males defend resources that attract females. A primate example exists among orangutans, in which males defend feeding areas that bring females into their territories; the richer the area the longer the female remains, and the better the chance that she will enter **estrus** while there.

**resource-holding potential** (RHP): competitive ability of a male to acquire and hold a harem (**one-male unit**) or a valuable resource for the purpose of attracting females. Predictive factors for a successful male include size, strength, and **rank**.

**resource partitioning:** division of resources by populations of coexisting species which have become specialized on a particular part of the resources; for example, three **sympatric** species of **Hapalemur** are all bamboo specialists, but can coexist because they have further specialized on different parts of the plant.

**respiration:** 1. the act of ventilation (inhalation or breathing in and exhalation or breathing out) and gas exchange (principally oxygen and carbon dioxide) across the respiratory membrane of the lungs; external respiration. 2. gas exchange between the blood and the cells of the body; internal respiration. 3. use of cellular oxygen in the degradation of food molecules into energy; cellular respiration. See **citric acid cycle.**

‡ **respiratory diaphragm:** sheetlike skeletal muscle that separates the thoracic cavity from the lower abdominal cavity. When this muscle contracts it creates negative pressure, resulting in a flow of air into the respiratory passages. This structure is only found among mammals, although some workers report a membranous respiratory diaphragm in birds. Aka muscular diaphragm.

**respiratory distress syndrome:** disease of premature infants in whom surfactant cells do not function adequately.

**respiratory heat loss:** dissipation of body heat associated with pulmonary ventilation.

**respiratory quotient** (RQ): ratio of carbon dioxide produced to oxygen consumed during metabolism.

**respiratory rate:** number of breaths per minute.

**respiratory system:** structures involved in gas exchange between blood and the external environment, i.e. lungs, tubes leading to the lungs, and the chest structures responsible for **breathing**.

**response:** action from an organism or cell, resulting from a **stimulus**.

'**rest and repair' division:** see **parasympathetic division**.

**resting behavior:** in reference to an animal that is awake, but not moving or expending more energy than is needed for physiological maintenance.

**resting cell:** apparently quiescent (not dividing) cell nucleus. Many other cell activities are being carried out during this time, including all of the transcrip-

tional activities of genes characteristic of the specialized cell.

**restless leg syndrome** (RLS): condition characterized by feelings of creeping and crawling, aching, and tingling in the lower limbs; affected individuals experience delayed onset of sleep and multiple awakenings. A susceptibility gene has been mapped to HSA 12q. About 1 in 20 humans experience RLS. A similar gene, *timeless*, may have been found in the fruit fly.

**restriction:** 1. regulation or conditional limitation. 2. limitation to a certain set of circumstances, e.g. obligate parasitism. 3. ability of a phage to infect only certain strains of bacteria.

**restriction enzyme:** any enzyme capable of nicking or breaking down DNA molecules at specific points. Restriction enzymes are used in biotechnology as molecular scissors to cut DNA at specific points so that DNA from different organisms can be recombined. The first restriction enzymes were isolated from bacteria. The nick point is a sequence of 4–12 bps that is not recognized by any endogenous enzyme. The original and natural function of such enzymes is to restrict the growth of certain invading phages within bacteria by cleavage and inactivation of the phage. Aka restriction endonuclease.

**restriction fragment:** one of several pieces of DNA of variable lengths produced by the action of a **restriction enzyme** on a target sample.

‡ **restriction fragment length polymorphism:** see **RFLP.**

**restriction site:** set of bases in DNA (or RNA) recognized exactly by a **restriction enzyme**. It is the variation in the physical locations of such sites that gives rise to **restriction fragment length polymorphisms**.

**restriction site mapping:** description of the nucleotide sequence of a DNA segment that is cut from the larger DNA macromolecule by a restriction enzyme.

**restriction site polymorphism** (RSP): see **restriction fragment length polymorphism**.

**retaliation:** action taken towards an individual that fails to reciprocate; for example, if a female grooms a male and he does not return the action, the female may retaliate by withholding future grooming. In the case of individuals of equal size and social rank, failure to reciprocate may lead to physical attacks.

**retardation:** 1. slowing. 2. depression of mental and physical processes. 3. decrease in velocity. 4. decrease in the rate of ontogenetic development; see **neoteny**.

**retardation theory:** see **fetalization theory**.

**retching response:** involuntary gagging reflex in response to some well-defined stimulus such as rotten carrion; see **fixed action pattern**.

*rete mirabile*: literally, 'miraculous network'. Meshwork of interlaced veins and arteries that functions as a thermal circulatory exchange mechanism in such animals as bluefin tuna, wading birds, and some cervids. A similar meshwork is found in the limbs of **lorisids**, presumably as an adaptation for supplying oxygen to the muscles of the lower limbs, which allows lorisids to grip branches for long periods of time. The latter case is more accurately termed collateral vascularization, however, as it does not function in temperature regulation.

**rete testis**: network of ducts in the center of the **testis** site.

**reticular activating system** (RAS): function seated in the **reticular formation** of the **hindbrain** that serves to rouse the **cerebellum**; the **sleep response** is thought to occur because of decreased RAS activity, and a coma is associated with profound inactivity of the RAS.

**reticular formation**: structural network within the **hindbrain** that functions as the **reticular activating system** to integrate information from other regions of the **central nervous system**.

**reticulate evolution**: netlike pattern of cladogenesis and hybridization among a set of related species. See **trichotomy**.

**reticulate speciation**: formation of a new species by the hybridization of two closely related species; aka secondary speciation.

**reticulocyte**: immature **erythrocyte** with fiber-filled cytoplasm, and in the state of hemoglobin synthesis. Aka reticular cell.

**reticuloendothelial system** (RES): **macrophage** component of the immune system; aka reticular system, hematopoietic system.

**retina**: photoreceptive layer on the inner surface of the eye wall that contains light-sensitive cells, nerves, and blood vessels. See **rod cell** and **cone cell**.

**retinal**: 1. form of **vitamin** A that forms the chromophore component of photopigment; the aldehyde of **retinol**. 2. pertaining to the retina.

**retinal cone**: see **cone**.

**retinal fovea**: see **fovea**.

**retinol**: see **vitamin**.

**retinitis pigmentosa** (RP): autosomal recessive condition caused by degeneration of photoreceptor cells called **rod cells**, and characterized by constriction of the visual field, night blindness, and clumps of pigment in the eye. Caused by a **point mutation** on chromosome 3q.

**retinoblastoma** (RB1): rare form of eye cancer in infants characterized by bilateral tumors in the retina of the eye, and a predisposition to bone cancer. An inherited autosomal germline mutation plus a new somatic mutation are both required in the hereditary form. The affected gene is *Rb1*, portions of which are abnormally deleted from chromosome 13 in the cells of an immature retina. The normal function of *Rb1* in other body cells is to act as a tumor suppressor by preventing certain regulatory proteins from initiating DNA replication (Cf. the *p53* **tumor suppressor**). Retinoblastoma exhibits evidence for **genomic imprinting**; there are also indications of a **paternal age effect**. Other mutations to the *Rb1* gene cause cancers in other types of cells. Sporadic, nonhereditary, unilateral forms of retinoblastoma also exist, in which two simultaneous somatic mutations are required.

**retouch**: 1. site of removal of additional small **flakes** from a **tool** after each use as the edges of a stone implement had become dull and crushed, where its edge was refreshed. Aka retouche. 2. the process of such retouching or refreshing.

**retraction**: posterior movement of an anatomical structure; only a very few structures, such as the **mandible**, are capable of this movement. Cf. **protraction**.

**retreat of the Neandertals**: see **Neandertal retreat hypothesis**.

**retrodiction**: prediction of undiscovered events that occurred in the past; one of the main activities of archaeologists, paleontologists, and evolutionary biologists. Cf. **prediction**. See **retrospective study**.

**retroflex**: to bend or flex backwards.

**retrograde**: moving backward; retracing an original course.

**retrograde evolution**: proposal that current viruses evolved from portions of the genomes of intracellular parasitic microorganisms and that, with time, the protoviruses lost various independent metabolic functions and become more dependent upon host cells for functions such as reproduction.

**retrogression**: 1. return to an earlier, more primitive condition; dedifferentiation, reversal. 2. degeneration, used especially of tissues.

**retromolar space** or **gap**: space behind the third molar; a characteristic of **Neandertals**.

**retroposon**: dispersed **DNA sequences** generated by reverse transcription from RNA intermediates, of either viral or nonviral origin. Examples of retroposons include **SINEs** and **LINEs**. Cf. **transposon**.

**retrospective diagnosis**: clinical analysis of an event or object in or from the past, with the aid of modern diagnostic tools; e.g. an autopsy of a mummy. See **paleopathology**.

**retrospective study**: in science, any experiment designed to produce a result that can be extrapolated into the past; aka retrodictive study. In **paleoanthropology**, many studies are retrodictive in nature. Cf. **prospective study**. See **retrodiction**.

**Retroviridae:** family of icosahedral capsids, enveloped RNA viruses transcribed by viral reverse transcriptase into DNA proviruses capable of integration into the host cellular genome, which cause sarcomas and various other clinical manifestations in humans and many other animals, including immunodeficiency and/or leukemia. There are three subfamilies: spumaviruses ('foamy' agents found in cats, cattle and monkeys), oncornoviruses (oncogenic and leukemia-causing group), and lentiviruses (all with long latent periods, the agents of **AIDS** and some cancers).

**retrovirus:** any of a family of small viruses whose genetic material is RNA, and that invade a host cell where **reverse transcriptase** transcribes DNA that is subsequently integrated into the host genome from which it can reproduce using the host's molecular machinery.

**Rett syndrome** (RTT): heritable, **X-linked** dominant, progressive neurodevelopmental arrest disorder characterized by mental retardation, neuronal impairment, reduced muscle tone, hand wringing, autistic-like behaviors, and seizures. RTT is lethal in **hemizygous** males, so clinical cases are always females; the responsible gene is thought to be defective in half the cells of a female's body because of **female mosaicism for X.** Onset usually between 5th and 18th year. Defective molecule is methyl-CP6-binding protein 2 (MECP2). Evidence of **genomic imprinting.**

**Retzius, Anders Adolph** (1796–1860): Swedish physician, anatomist, anthropologist. Professor of Anatomy, Karolinska Institute, Stockholm. Devised a ratio of skull width to length ($\times$ 100), which he called the **cranial index.** A CI of < 80 was termed dolichocephalae (**dolichocephaly,** 'long-headed'); > 80 was termed brachycephalae (**brachycephaly,** 'short-headed'). Retzius developed the **Aryan migration hypothesis** in an attempt to temper the growing tendency to see Indo-Europeans as direct and pure descendants of an Aryan ancestor. He also named several cavities, fibers, ligaments, spaces, and veins.

**reversal learning:** behavior research in which a primate is conditioned to respond to a particular stimulus for which it is rewarded; a second stimulus is not rewarded. The second part of the study involves rewarding the previously incorrect response, and failing to reward the previously correct response. Of interest is how long it takes the subject to adapt to the reversal.

**reverse ethnocentrism:** practice of using other cultures as a means of criticizing the value of one's own culture, e.g. when Westerners romanticize the life of hunters and gatherers in order to negatively emphasize the complexities of industrial society. Also spelled reverse ethnocentrism.

**reverse genetics:** analysis that proceeds from genotype to phenotype by gene manipulation techniques. Such techniques include the **knockout** of a gene's function, or homologous recombination in a stem cell.

**reverse mutation** (v): see **back mutation.**

**reverse paternity DNA:** identification of a person's blood by comparison of the **DNA profiles** of individuals believed to be a person's parents.

‡ **reverse transcriptase** (RT): a **DNA polymerase** common in specific retroviral families and found in limited use in certain mammalian processes; copies RNA into DNA, normally inside a host cell. See **provirus hypothesis.**

**reverse transcription:** process of producing DNA from an RNA template; the reverse of **transcription.**

**reversed polarity epoch:** period of geologic time in which the magnetic field points to the south, rather than to the north, as it does now, e.g. **Gilbert reversed epoch, Matuyama reversed epoch.** Cf. **normal polarity epoch.** See **paleomagnetism.**

**revolution:** in science, any idea that causes people to look at the world differently, e.g. the **Copernican revolution** or the **Darwinian revolution.** See **paradigm shift.**

**r-extinction:** extinction of entire populations shortly after colonization and while they are at an early stage of growth and expansion. Cf. **K-extinction.**

‡ **RFLP:** restriction fragment length polymorphism; fragments of **DNA** produced by **enzymes** (**endonucleases**) found in certain single-celled organisms (e.g. *Eco1*; see *Eco***R1**); when introduced *in vitro* into a sample of human DNA, for example, the enzyme cuts the **DNA** at specific **restriction sites** into fragments of variable numbers and lengths, depending upon the **DNA sequence** possessed by the individual from which the sample was obtained. The resulting sample, when compared by **electrophoresis** with other variants, becomes data that are part of the RFLP (pronounced 'rif lip').

**R group:** term used to indicate the position of an unspecified group in a chemical reaction; a radical.

**Rh:** abbreviation for Rhesus; see **Rhesus blood group locus, Rhesus factor,** and **Rhesus incompatibility.**

**Rh blood group or system:** see **Rhesus blood group locus.**

*Rhenanthropus:* genus **nomen** that did not gain acceptance applied to the Mauer mandible; see *Homo heidelbergensis.*

‡ **Rhesus blood group locus** (Rh): autosomal locus found on chromosome 1p; a complex **blood group** with at least six **antigen**-producing alleles at up to three **polymorphic** loci; the clinically significant **alleles** are D, d. **Antibodies** in most **blood groups,** such as those responding to the **Rhesus factor** (anti-D), are manufactured in response to specific

antigenic challenges from an individual's environment. Other major polypeptides in the Rh blood group include the Cc/Ee antigens (autosomal recessives), but there are over 40 other antigens in this series as well. For clinical purposes, Rh phenotypes are reported as Rh+ (DD, Dd) or Rh− (dd), but denoting haplotypes for the three major alleles (e.g. cde, cDe) is common. The antibodies of the Rh system are **IgG** class **immunoglobulins**, and small enough to permeate the **placental membrane**, creating potentially significant problems in certain pregnancies. See **Rhesus incompatibility** and **hemolytic disease of the newborn**. Aka Rh system.

**Rhesus factor** (D): one of the **alleles** at the **Rhesus blood group locus**; in practice usually referring to the presence of either one or two **dominant** D alleles in an individual **genotype**, and that produces the Rh+ **phenotype**. This group of red blood cell antigens was discovered when it was found that some humans have red blood cells that react with antibodies formed against **Rhesus macaque** cells. Aka Rh Factor.

‡ **Rhesus incompatibility:** condition in which an Rh− woman (genotype dd) is pregnant, carrying an Rh+ fetus (Dd) because the father is Rh+ (either DD or Dd). The result is a potential for the mother to manufacture anti-D antibodies if fetal blood is introduced to her immune system; **hemolytic disease of the newborn** is then a potential problem in her second and subsequent children. Aka Rh incompatibility. See **Rhesus blood group locus, rhesus isoimmunization.**

**Rhesus isoimmunization:** coincidental condition characterized by loss of fetal **RBCs** owing to the agglutination *in utero* by maternal anti-D antibodies, causing jaundice, anemia, hypoxia with CNS damage, and an enlarged liver and spleen in the affected fetus. Isoimmunization also occurs in several other blood groups, including the ABO, **Diego, Duffy,** Kell− Cellano and Gerbich blood groups, but Rh incompatibility accounts for more than 90% of cases. See **hemolytic disease of the newborn.**

**rhesus macaque:** vernacular for *Macaca mulatta.*

**rheumatoid arthritis:** multifactorial condition characterized by inflammation and severe deformation of distal joints. Generally late onset; females are affected three times more than males. One of the autoimmune disorders: antibodies are produced against cells lining the joints (see **rheumatoid factor**), probably in response to a particular antigen or allergen. Certain HLA haplotypes are associated with specific diseases; both ankylosing spondylitis and rheumatoid arthritis are diseases of joint surfaces, and there are significant risks for persons who carry the HLA DR3 and DR4 haplotypes, respectively. The **CCR5 co-receptor** also attenuates the severity of rheumatoid arthritis.

**rheumatoid factor:** specific gamma globulin present in the serum of individuals diagnosed with **rheumatoid arthritis.** There is conjecture that the antibodies are abnormal or altered, and that the immune system responds by making additional antibodies against these antibodies that are identified as nonself.

‡ **rhinarium:** moist, hairless pad at the end of the nose in most mammalian species.

**rhinencephalon:** 1. in humans, the portion of the brain homologous with similar olfactory portions of the brains of lower animals, comprising the structures medial to the rhinal sulcus in the inferior part of the cerebral hemisphere. 2. one of the portions of the **telencephalon** in the early embryo.

**rhinial index:** index of facial flatness, mid-orbital **subtense** multiplied by 100 and divided by the midorbital chord. The midorbital chord is the distance between the points on the lower border of the orbit where the zygomatic and maxilla bones join. The midorbital subtense is the lower tip of the suture between the nasal bones. See **frontal index, premaxillary index, simotic index.**

**rhinion:** point superior to the nasal aperture; most inferior and anterior point on the internasal suture between the two nasal bones.

*Rhinocolobus turkanensis* M. Leakey, 1982: colobine known from the late Pliocene and early Pleistocene of East Africa; **monotypic.** Estimated body mass around 20 kg. Distinctive feature is an elongated snout, unusual among colobines. Dental formula: 2.1.2.3/2.1.2.3; dental morphology consistent with **folivory.** Known **postcrania** indicates arboreal quadrupedalism. See Appendix 1 for taxonomy.

*Rhinopithecus* (= *Pygathrix*) Milne-Edwards, 1872: colobine genus to which the snub-nosed or golden monkeys belong; four species. Many workers include these species in the genus *Pygathrix*. Arboreal; diurnal; arboreal quadrupeds. **Sexually dimorphic** in body size and several surface features. Among the largest of the colobines, female body mass around 10 kg, males about 15 kg. These animals have an up-turned nose, a bluish face, and a shaggy **pelage.** Dental formula: 2.1.2.3; **folivorous.** Appear to live in mixed-sex groups. See Appendix 2 for taxonomy, Appendix 3 for living species.

**rhizome:** elongated, specialized stem, usually grown horizontally, from which leaves and roots arise.

**rhizomelic:** 1. pertaining to the hip joint and shoulder joint. 2. the portions of the limbs nearest these joints, e.g., rhizomelic shortening. Cf., **acromelic shortening, mesomelic shortening.**

**rhizosecretion:** technique used in **biotechnology** in which recombinant proteins are secreted by a plant's roots into a hydroponic (liquid) medium.

**Rhodesian man:** see **Kabwe**.

**rhodopsin** (RHO): light-sensitive pigment found in the membrane of the rod-shaped photoreceptor cells of the retina; composed of a derivative of vitamin A (11-*cis*-**retinal**) and **opsin**, the protein group. When rhodopsin absorbs a photon of light, its shape changes and it releases an electrical signal. Aka visual purple.

**RhoGAM:** in serology, the trade name for an anti-Rh (D) gamma globulin used in the prevention of Rh **hemolytic disease of the newborn**.

**rhombencephalon:** that structure in the brain made up of the **metencephalon** and the **myelencephalon**. Aka hindbrain.

**rhomboides (carpal bone):** see **trapezium**.

**rhythmic behavior:** behavior that repeats over time in a regular pattern. Cf. **periodic behavior**.

**rib:** in humans, one of approximately 12 paired, long curved bones attached to the thoracic vertebrae and that form the bony wall of the **thorax**. Collectively, the upper seven pairs attached to the **sternum** are true vertebrosternal or sternal ribs (costae verae), while the lower five pairs are the false ribs (costae spuriae), of which the lowest two, which have no ventral attachment, are the floating ribs. Aka (collectively) costae, rib cage, **thoracic cage**. The range of variation in most primates is 11–14 pairs of ribs; African apes average 13 pairs.

**riboflavin:** see **vitamin**.

‡ **ribonucleic acid:** see **RNA**.

**ribonucleoprotein:** small, protein portion of the RNA – protein complex that edits introns from transcribed mRNA (**pre-mRNA**) during **RNA processing**.

**ribonucleotide:** unit of an **RNA** strand composed of a ribose (a five-carbon sugar), a phosphate group, and a **purine** or **pyrimidine** base.

**ribose:** pentose (5-carbon) sugar found in RNA.

‡ **ribosomal RNA:** see **rRNA**.

‡ **ribosome:** one of many small granular complexes of protein and **ribosomal RNA** found primarily in the cytoplasm and associated with the **endoplasmic reticulum**. An organelle principally involved with **polypeptide synthesis**. Aka polysome.

**ribosomes of organelles:** ribosomes normally present in cytoplasmic structures such as mitochondria.

**ribozyme:** RNA molecule that has the ability to catalyze a chemical reaction; typically responsible for intron removal and exon splicing during **RNA processing**.

**rice-washing behavior:** behavior observed among **Japanese macaques**. Japanese researchers provisioned these animals (in order to keep them in the area) with sweet potatoes and finally, rice, which required laborious sorting from sand particles. The same juvenile female who started the **potato-washing behavior** grabbed a handful of rice and sand, threw it in the water, and the rice was separated from the sand because it floated. Others learned the same behavior. An example of primate **cognition** and **culturally transmitted behavior**. See **tool use in primates**.

‡ **rickets:** state of malnutrition caused by a reversible deficiency (**avitaminosis**) of **vitamin** D. Often observed in children between the ages of 1 and 2. The symptoms include restlessness, profuse night sweats, lack of muscle tone, retardation of motor development, and most prominently retardation of bone growth, resulting in grotesquely bowed legs (enlargement of the epiphyses), and malformations of the skull and knobs on the ribs (rickettsial rosary). The deficiency in adults is called **osteomalacia**, and results in softened bones; it is common among Muslim women. The primary cause is a deficiency of vitamin D; conversion of ergosterol, 7-dehydrocholesterol, and other sterols leads to the synthesis of vitamin D in animal skin upon exposure to ultraviolet light. Considerable vitamin D is required during the adolescent growth spurt; it has been a standard supplement in milk since the 1940s. Rickets was first described in 1650.

**rickettsiae:** very small gram-negative, bacteria-like parasites that cause **disease** when introduced into the cells that line small blood vessels; like viruses (and unlike true bacteria), rickettsiae require a host cell for replication; transmitted to humans by **vector**s such as fleas, ticks or louse bites, and a significant cause of **disease** (e.g. **typhus**) and the opportunity for **natural selection**. Three genera have been recognized: *Rickettsia*, *Coxiella*, and *Rochalimaea*.

**ridge:** elevated line of bone or enamel; **crest**.

**ridge characteristic:** in fingerprint identification, those characteristics including ridge endings, enclosures, bifurcations, and ridge details, that must be matched in order to establish a common origin.

‡ **Rift Valley Province:** one of the Provinces within Kenya; some of its districts containing archaeological sites include **Baringo**, **Turkana**, and **Samburu Hills**.

‡ **Rift Valley system:** see **East African Rift system**.

**rift zone:** large trough-like structure formed on continents by normal faulting and crustal extensions, similar to that formed by a **mid-ocean ridge**.

**right acromiale height:** on a standing subject, distance from the floor to the furthermost lateral projection of the outer border of the acromion of the scapula.

**right cerebral hemisphere:** right lateral portion of the **cerebrum**. In most people, the right hemisphere controls spatial and artistic skills. The right hemisphere is separated from the **left**

cerebral hemisphere by the **longitudinal cerebral fissure**, but portions of the two are connected internally by the **corpus callosum**. Each cerebral hemisphere contains a central cavity called the **lateral ventricle**.

**right dactylon height:** on a standing subject, distance from the floor to the tip of the extended middle finger, palm inward.

**right-handed DNA:** see **DNA**. Cf. **left-handed DNA**.

**right-handedness:** see **dextrality, handedness,** and **hand preference.**

**right iliocristale height:** on a standing subject, distance from the floor to the point on the crest of the right ilium that projects most laterally.

**right iliospinale height:** on a standing subject, the distance from the floor to the right anterior–superior iliac spine.

**right lymphatic duct:** major vessel of the **lymphatic drainage** network that evacuates lymph from the upper right portion of the body into the right subclavian vein.

**right radiale height:** on a standing subject, the distance from the floor to the highest point of the head of the radius.

**right sphyrion height:** on a standing subject, the distance from the floor to the inner surface of the medial malleolus.

**right stylion height:** on a standing subject, the distance from the floor to the distolateral end of the styloid process of the radius.

**right tibiale height:** on a standing subject, the distance from the floor to the upper surface of the medial condyle of the tibia.

**right trochanter height:** on a standing subject, the distance from the floor to the upper surface of the greater trochanter of the femur.

**rigidity:** stiffness, immobility; hypertonia with normal muscle reflexes.

**rigor mortis:** stiffness of the body due to ATP loss resulting in coagulation of muscle plasma; occurs one to seven hours after death.

**ring species:** situation in which two reproductively isolated populations, living in the same region, are connected by a geographic ring of populations that can interbreed, but where the populations curve back and the terminal links overlap, the populations are noninterbreeding species. See **reproductive isolation**. Aka circular overlap, Rassenkreis.

**ring-tailed lemur:** vernacular for *Lemur catta*.

**Rio Maues marmoset:** vernacular for *Callithrix mauesi*.

**Rio Napo tamarin:** vernacular for *Saguinus nigricollis* (= *graellsi*).

**riparian:** pertaining to the edges of streams or rivers.

**ripple marks:** undulations on the inner surface of a flake that radiate in a series of progressively larger arcs from the point of percussion, reminiscent of the ripples in the shell of a conch; one of the diagnostic features that archaeologists use to distinguish a stone **tool** from a naturally occurring **geofact**.

**risk:** see **empiric risk** and **relative risk**.

**risk factor:** any feature that alters the probability that a person is likely to be more susceptible to a particular illness than another member drawn randomly from the same population, and who does not have the feature.

**Riss glacial maximum:** third major glacial episode in the **Alpine glacial sequence** of the Pleistocene, which lasted for more than 270 kya until about 125 kya. See **Günz, Mindel** and **Würm** glacial maxima, and **Günz–Mindel** (Cromerian), **Mindel–Riss** (Holstein), and **Riss–Würm** interglacials (or interstadials). Aka penultimate glaciation.

‡ **Riss glaciation:** one of the four traditional periods of glaciation or ice ages that define the Pleistocene epoch during the past 1.8 million years BP. The third stage in the Quaternary sequence of the Alpine region, the Riss had a duration of about 100 ky and terminated about 125 kya.

**Riss–Würm interglacial:** third major interglacial episode in the **Alpine glacial sequence** of the Pleistocene, which lasted from more than 125 + kya until about 75 kya. See **Günz, Mindel, Riss** and **Würm** glacial maxima, and **Günz–Mindel** (Cromerian) and **Mindel–Riss** (Holstein) interglacials (or interstadials). Aka Ipswichian, Eemian, Sangamonian.

**rite:** sequence of acts, often involving religion or magic, established by tradition, and stemming from the daily life of a people. Adjective: ritual. Often associated with observance of events and times of solemnity and importance, e.g. birth, fertility, increase, initiation, medicine, puberty, purification, and transition.

**rites of passage:** first used in 1909 to classify the specifically emotional ceremonies that facilitate bridging the gap between the old and the new. Traditionally there are three types: those that separate a person from previous associations, those that prepare for a marginal period, and those rites of aggregation that prepare one for incorporation into a new existence.

**ritual:** in animal behavior, nondisplay behavior that is transformed over evolutionary time into repetitive **display** behavior with specific meaning; see **ritualization**. Aka rite.

**ritualization:** evolutionary modification of a behavior pattern such that it turns into a signal used in communication or at least improves its efficiency as a signal.

‡ **ritualized behavior:** act that is removed from its original context.

**river terrace:** relatively level plain consisting of sediments deposited by the action of a river, and often consisting of episodic depositions of gravels running parallel with the river.

**Rivet's hypothesis:** proposal in the 1940s that Native Americans evolved from four racial **types**, and that several migrations occurred both across the Bering strait and across the Pacific Ocean by way of outrigger canoes, utilizing knowledge of ocean currents and trade winds. This hypothesis continues to find supporters among researchers interested in the question of **early man in the New World.**

‡ **RNA:** ribonucleic acid; a cellular polynucleotide chemically related to **DNA** except that RNA is single-stranded, contains **uracil** rather than its counterpart **thymine**, and has ribose sugars in the backbone; some forms of RNA also contain the genetic information necessary for **protein synthesis (mRNA)**, whereas other forms are structural (**rRNA**) or catalytic (**tRNA**). Aka nongenetic RNA. See **antisense RNA, charged tRNA, double-stranded RNA, DNA-like RNA, genetic RNA (gRNA), heterogenous messenger RNA (hmRNA), heterogenous nuclear RNA (hnRNA), pre-mRNA, sense RNA, small RNAs, soluble RNA (s RNA), suppressor tRNA,** and **template RNA.**

**RNA editing:** addition and/or deletion of uridine (uracil attached to ribose) molecules at precise sites in an mRNA molecule after **RNA processing.** See **small RNAs.**

**RNA interference** (RNAi): technique that shuts down the function of a gene in a research organism, similar to the physical gene **knockout mutation** technique, but that only neutralizes specific RNAs, thus aborting the expression of the gene, and effectively shutting down the function of the gene that generated them. See **posttranscriptional gene silencing.**

**RNA ligase:** enzyme that splices exons together after introns are removed.

‡ **RNA polymerase** (RNAP): enzyme that catalyzes the formation of an RNA polynucleotide chain from a template DNA strand and ribonucleotides. RNAP also synthesizes short pieces of RNA that initiate DNA replication. See **polymerase.**

**RNA primer:** short sequence of RNA that initiates DNA replication.

**RNA processing:** enzymatic removal of a intron sequence(s) from newly transcribed RNA. Aka posttranscriptional processing, RNA editing. See **small RNAs.**

**RNA splicing:** process of excising **introns** and joining **exons** at the **spliceosome;** aka **RNA processing.**

**RNA virus:** infectious agent consisting of a single-stranded genome. Because the RNA must revert to a double-stranded DNA form before it can be replicated, many RNA viruses, such as the Rous Sarcoma Virus or the **Human Immunodeficiency Virus**, are known as **retroviruses** and contain other proteins such as **reverse transcriptase.**

**Robertsonian translocation:** either 1. **fusion** of two small nonhomologous chromosomes into one large chromosome with conjoined but preserved linkage groups, or 2. **fission** of one large chromosome into two small nonhomologous chromosomes. Either case is considered a clinical aberration within a species (see **MCA**), but also a potential mode of normal **speciation.** A special case is centric fusion in which two acrocentric chromosomes join at their centromeres to form a metacentric chromosome, thus preserving all former genes and annealing them into one large linkage group. Human chromosome number two (HSA 2) is thought to have arisen by such a centric fusion event in some remote common ancestor, as the great apes have two pairs of small nonhomologous chromosomes with extensive genetic **synteny** to the larger HSA 2. Aka Robertsonian fusion, Robertsonian fission.

**Robinson, John Talbot** (1923– ): South African zoologist; after 1947, assistant (later Assistant Director) to Robert **Broom** at the Transvaal Museum in South Africa, where he assisted in excavations at **Sterkfontein, Swartkrans,** and **Kromdraai;** authored major papers on **hominid** anatomy and taxonomy. During 1963–85 he was a teacher at the University of Wisconsin. Author of *Early Hominid Posture and Locomotion* (1972).

**robust:** stocky, large, bulky; muscular. In primates, said of relatively larger species, such as the **robust australopithecines.** Cf. gracile.

‡ **robust australopithecine:** member of any of several species of **australopithecine** with large back teeth, cheekbones, and faces, all of which are anatomic **adaptations** to heavy chewing. **Microwear** analysis suggests that their diet included tough, gritty foods that left pits and scratches on their teeth. The robust forms lived in Africa between 2.5 and 1.0 mya and include *Paranthropus robustus, P. boisei,* and *P. aethiopicus.* The group is characterized by an average **cranial capacity** of about 520 cm$^3$. Aka *Australopithecus* spp. See **megadont** hominids.

**robust tool-user hypothesis:** proposal that the **robust australopithecines** may have been the first tool users, based on the argument that these forms are more numerous in critical sites, they are capable of approximately the same **power grip** as early members of the genus *Homo*, and finally that the robust forms were relatively more **encephalized** than earlier hominids.

**robusticity index:** measure obtained by expressing the thickness of a bone in terms of its length.

**Roc de Combe:** archaeological site found in the Dordogne district, France, dating to 39 kya in the upper layers, which contain **Châtelperronian** artifacts alternating with **Aurignacian**; lower layers are Mousterian. The site is often cited as providing conclusive evidence that **Neandertals** and **AMHs** coexisted in Europe.

**rock:** 1. aggregate of either consolidated or unconsolidated minerals and/or organic matter assembled in nature by the action of heat or water. 2. a particular kind of such matter, e.g. **igneous rock**. 3. loosely, a stone of any size. Cf. **cobble, pebble,** and **stone.**

**rock art:** vernacular term that refers to both **pictographs** and **petroglyphs.** Cf. **cave art.**

**rock-levering:** behavior used by chimpanzees and hominids to locate food under rocks; using a stick as a lever.

**rockshelter:** protection from weathering elements afforded by a natural geological outcrop that has been suberoded such that a room or cave exists. In anthropology, usually applied to a habitation site in which artifacts and other human debris can be found, constituting evidence of former occupation. In French, the term *abris* is applied to the location of a particular open site or rock shelter, yielding names such as **Abri Pataud,** and so forth. See **shelter.** Cf. **covolo.**

**rock unit:** body of distinct rock types that are distinguishable to a field worker (a group, **formation, bed, member,** and so forth).

**rod cell:** photoreceptor in the retina of the eye that is specialized for colorless, dim-light vision and that contains **rhodopsin**; one of two photic receptor types. See **cone cell.**

**roentgen** (R, r): the amount of ionizing radiation that produces $2.083 \times 10^9$ ion pairs in one cubic centimeter of air.

**roentgenogram:** see **X-ray.**

**rogue:** 1. a usually inferior organism, differing markedly from the normal, i.e. a **monster,** mutant, or **sport** (noun). 2. to destroy organisms or genetic variants (rogues) that do not conform to a desired standard (verb). See **domestic selection.**

**role:** pattern of behavior displayed by certain members of a society that has an effect on other members.

**rolling:** mechanical weathering of bone or other artifact due to the action of stream or beach water. See **taphonomy.**

**roloway:** vernacular for *Cercopithecus diana.*

**rondelle:** round object, especially a disk of bone removed from the cranium. See **trephination.**

**Rondinin:** name for several archaeological sites found in October 2000 near the village of Rondinin in the **Tugen Hills,** Kenya, dated to about 5.88–5.72 mya (Lukeino Formation at Kapcheberek), containing hominoid remains including cranial and postcranial fragments from at least five individuals attributed to *Orrorin tugenensis.* Three partial femora suggest bipedalism. A composite specimen was nicknamed 'Millennium Man'. Aka Kapsomin, Kapcheberek, Aragai, 'Millennium Ancestor'.

*Rooneyia viejaensis* **Wilson, 1966:** enigmatic tarsiiform primate from the early Oligocene of North America, assigned to an omomyoid family *incertae sedis*; phylogenetic relationships unknown; many features of this species are unusual for an omomyoid and it is sometimes placed in the Omomyidae, the Microchoeridae, or its own family. Known from a skull; short snout, **postorbital closure** with smaller orbits suggesting diurnality. Estimated body mass around 1.5 kg. Dental formula: 2.1.2.3/2.1.2.3; dental morphology suggests **frugivory.** See Appendix 1 for taxonomy.

**root:** 1. portion of a tooth that is anchored by the **periodontal ligament** to a **dental alveolus** in the jaws; the root is enclosed by a thin bonelike material called **cementum.** 2. part of a plant that typically grows down into the soil.

**root canal:** canal within the root of a tooth. The root canal contains pulp, blood and lymphatic vessels, and nerves.

**rooted cladogram: cladogram** in which genealogy is assumed; the root **node** is determined by comparison with an **outgroup.**

**rooting reflex:** reaction in newborns that orients the head in preparation for finding the nipple to begin nursing.

**rostrocarinate:** pertaining to an eagle beak core, the hypothetical Pliocene predecessor of the **coup-de-poing.** Aka beak and keel core.

**rostrum:** beak-shaped structure.

**rotation:** movement in which a bone is turned around its longitudinal axis.

**rough endoplasmic reticulum:** see **endoplasmic reticulum.**

**round scraper:** small circular flake tool sharpened all around its circumference. Aka thumb scraper. See **scraper.**

**roundworm:** any of about 80,000 species in the phylum Nematoda. Roundworms include potentially parasitic forms such as hookworms, pinworms, *Ascaris,* and *Trichinella.* See **trichinosis.**

**Rousseau, Jean-Jacques** (1712–78): Swiss-born French philosopher and author; Rousseau was among the earliest speculators on the social life of early humans, to whom he applied the term 'noble savage'.

He elaborated the idea that the social nature of humans is inherent (*Social Contract*, 1762), that morality degenerates with the progress of civilization (*Discours sur les arts et scïences,* 1750), and that education is sociocultural; these were all ideas that greatly influenced nineteenth-century evolutionist thought. Rousseau believed that apes and humans were members of the same species. He held that humanity graded from apes through Europeans, and also therefore in the inequality of races, i.e. he was a polygenist. Rousseau failed to realize fully the implications of his musings on natural selection, not least of which was the proposal that early humans must have been dark-skinned, and that light-skinned Europeans were a recent oddity. Although he never saw an orangutan, his speculations on the 'noble savage' concept was based upon hearsay descriptions of African apes.

**royal endogamy:** sibling marriage in royal families; see **dynastic incest.**

**royal hemophilia:** see **hemophilia.**

‡ **rRNA:** ribosomal RNA; **RNA** that combines with proteins to form the **ribosomes** that attract **mRNA.**

*r*-**selected species:** species (such as rats) produced by unstable environments that are opportunistic, grow up quickly, have large numbers of **precocial** offspring and invest less in each, and exhibit a relatively earlier development of the reproductive system in terms of metabolic energy expended toward organs such as the brain and body. Such *r*-selected species gain advantage through their ability to reproduce rapidly. Cf. *K*-**selected species.** See *r* **selection.**

‡ *r* **selection:** MacArthur and E. O. **Wilson**'s polarized selection favoring rapid rates of population increase, especially prominent in species that specialize in colonizing short-lived environments or undergo large fluctuations in population size. Cf. *K* **selection.** The parameter *r* was taken from maximum **intrinsic rate of increase.**

*R*-**strategist:** ruderal species, characterized by small body size, rapid growth, short life span, efficient dispersal, and relatively large parental investment. Aka *r*-**selected species.** See **C–R–S triangle** of ecological strategies.

**Rubicon:** irrevocable commitment, threshold; see **cerebral Rubicon.**

***Rudapithecus hungaricus* Kretzoi, 1969:** binomen for fossil materials recovered in Hungary. Later referred to ***Dryopithecus brancoi.***

**rudimentary:** 1. incompletely developed. 2. retained in an undeveloped state or ancestral condition.

**ruffed lemur:** vernacular for the genus ***Varecia.***

**ruga:** crease in a structure that results in a corrugated appearance. Plural: rugae. Rugae serve various functions. In the human (and many other primate) stomach, they stretch to expand the surface area of a full stomach. In some primate **pinnae,** they may help direct sound waves into the **external auditory meatus.**

**rules:** important general principles in human evolutionary biology. Among these are: **Allen's rule, Bergmann's rule, Cope's rule, Gloger's rule, Haldane's rule, Hamilton's rule,** and the **superposition of strata.**

**runaway sexual selection hypothesis:** proposal of **sexual selection** that is an alternative to the **handicap principle.** It posits that females in an ancestral population preferred a particular elaborate trait in males and that the resulting female offspring inherited genes for the preference of males with these elaborate traits. Because these genes are inherited together there is a positive feedback loop that amplifies the presence of these alleles in the population. Aka runaway selection. See R. A. **Fisher.**

**Rusinga Island:** paleontological site found in 1926, an island in Lake Victoria, Kenya, East Africa, and dated to *c.* 20–16 mya (early **Miocene**), containing primate remains of over 500 individual apes including ***Proconsul, Nyanzapithecus, Victoriapithecus*** and ***Dendropithecus.*** Most of the Rusinga fossils are the result of a single catastrophic eruption of Kisingiri, a mainland volcano, which deposited heavy ashfalls in the region, killing and preserving many of the plants and animals. See **Kiahera Hill, Hiwegi Hill,** and **Kathwanga Point.**

**rut:** synchronized episode of male sexual arousal in certain mammalian species; corresponds to heat or **estrus** in females.

**rybp:** see **radiocarbon years.**

**1966 skull:** see **skull V**

$s_i$: symbol for the **coefficient of selection** against alleles in a **Hardy–Weinberg** population; the **fitness** of the $i$ th genotype is given as **1 - $s_i$**.

**Saale:** second continental icecap in Northern Europe, corresponding to the **Riss glacial maximum.**

**Saccopastore:** archaeological site found in 1920 in Italy and worked through 1935, dated to about 125 kya; contains hominid remains from at least two individuals (Saccopastore I, a female cranium found in 1929, and Saccopastore II, a partial male cranium found in 1935), both attributed to *Homo neanderthalensis*, but possessing relatively small brain capacities.

**sacculated stomach:** type of stomach found only in the folivorous primates, particularly in the colobines; it is greatly enlarged and has several chambers, which help to digest the large amounts of leaves these animals consume.

**sacral:** of or pertaining to the five fused vertebrae that make up the **sacrum** and help make up the pelvis.

**sacral canal:** passageway formed by the five fused vertebrae of the **sacrum** through which the spinal cord passes.

**sacral spot:** see **congenital dermal melanocytosis.**

**sacral vertebra:** in humans, any one of the five vertebrae that fuse (between ages 18 and 30) to form the **sacrum.**

**sacred baboon:** vernacular for *Papio hamadryas.*

**sacroiliac joint:** one of the fibrocartilage articulations between the **sacrum** and the two **coxal bones** of the pelvis.

**sacrum:** triangular structure composed of five vertebrae that fuse in the adult human; the sacrum is bounded by the **lumbar vertebrae** superiorly, the **coccyx** inferiorly, and the two **coxal bones** laterally. The sacrum is part of the vertebral column and part of the pelvis.

**saddle-back tamarin:** vernacular for *Saguinus fuscicollis.*

**saddle joint:** type of **synovial joint** in which two bones with both concave and convex surfaces (forming a saddle shape) form a joint at the complementary surfaces. This type of joint allows a variety of movements; an example is the **carpometacarpal joint.** Aka sellar joint.

**safari: chimpanzee** consortship formed by a lower ranking male and an **estrus** female (see **female mate choice**) who wander to the edges of their territory in order to avoid harassment by the more dominant males.

**sagittal:** referring to a line that bisects an organism into right and left sides.

‡ **sagittal crest:** bony, ridge-like feature, more prominent than a sagittal ridge, that runs anteroposteriorly on the top of the **cranium** at the attachment of the **temporalis muscles** and that is caused by the stresses exerted by the action of those muscles. Present in many primates, including the hominid *Paranthropus.* See **neurocranium.** Cf. **sagittal ridge.**

‡ **sagittal keel:** flat area running mid-sagittally along the top of the **cranium;** predominant among *Homo erectus* populations and also known for some modern populations such as the **Inuit** peoples of the Arctic.

**sagittal plane:** plane or line of anatomical orientation that divides a bilateral organism into right and left halves; these halves are not necessarily equal in size. Aka sagittal section, sagittal axis. Cf. **mid-sagittal.**

‡ **sagittal ridge:** bony, ridge-like feature, not as prominent as a **sagittal crest,** that runs anteroposteriorly on the top of the cranium at the attachment of the **temporalis muscles** and that is caused in part by the stresses exerted by the action of those muscles.

**sagittal sinus:** large unpaired venous sinus found in the **dura mater** of the frontal, parietal, and occipital regions and that functions to drain blood from the brain.

‡ **sagittal suture:** articulation between the two parietal bones which runs medially, i.e. sagittally, along the skull.

*Saguinus* **Hoffmannsegg, 1807:** platyrrhine genus to which the tamarins belong; 10–14 species recognized. This genus is sometimes divided into sections based on face **pelage** or lack of face pelage. Distributed in tropical rain forests from Panama through the Amazon south to Bolivia. Arboreal; diurnal; arboreal quadrupedalism with leaping. Small body size ranging from 300 to 600 g; little or no **sexual dimorphism.** There is a wide variety of pelage color, facial markings, and accessory pelage structures such as tufts and moustaches in this genus. **Tegulae** on all digits except the **pollex** and **hallux,** which are nailed. Dental formula: 2.1.3.2; mainly **frugivorous** with insect or gum supplements. Unlike the marmosets, tamarins have larger canines relative to the incisors; the mandible is a rounded U-shape in contrast to the sharp V-shaped condition found in the closely related marmosets. In the past, tamarins were believed to live in monogamous groups, but this has been questioned in recent years; some tamarins are reported to live in groups of up to 40 individuals. Defended territories are typical of these species. Twin births are usual; male assistance in infant care is a characteristic of the genus. See **hairy-faced tamarin section, mottled-faced tamarin section,** and **bare-faced tamarins;** See Appendix 2 for taxonomy, Appendix 3 for living species.

*Sahelanthropus tchadensis* **Brunét et al. 2002:** fossil species composed of six specimens (a cranium, mandibular fragment, and four teeth); recovered from **Toros-Menalla** locality TM 266, Djurab Desert, northern Chad, in 2001. It has a combination of primitive and derived traits and, consequently, is proposed as a possible stem for the **hominid** lineage. The **holotype** is TM 266-01-060-1, a nearly complete, presumed male cranium that was recovered in a dorsoventrally flattened condition. Hominid traits include small canines, no evidence of a sectorial premolar or a diastema, and cheek teeth with an enamel thickness that is intermediate between those of later hominids and chimpanzees. Hominoid features are an elongated and small brain case (estimated volume 320–380 cm³) and apelike features of the basicranial skeleton and petrous portion of the temporal bone. Other traits include a massive single **supra-orbital torus**, small **sagittal crest**, large ovoid **foramen magnum** bordered by small **occipital condyles**, and a large pneumatized mastoid process. There is insufficient data to ascertain whether this species was a habitual biped. The small canine and large brow ridge (suggesting this is a male) implies there was very little **sexual dimorphism** in canine size. This fossil species suggests that the time period when the chimp–human divergence occurred should be reevaluated.

**Sahul shelf:** shallow shelf of land in southeast Asia, now at least 100 m deep under the sea, but exposed during the Pleistocene when more sea water was bound up in continental glaciers; the Sahul shelf would have united New Guinea with the Australian continent.

*Saimiri* **Vogt, 1831:** platyrrhine genus to which the squirrel monkeys belong; one to five species recognized depending on author. The systematics are complex and many workers simplify the matter by recognizing only one species with up to eight subspecies. Occupy a wide variety of forest types, although they prefer gallery and secondary forest, from southern Costa Rica into Panama, where their range breaks, and then from the Amazon side of central Columbia to Bolivia. Arboreal; diurnal; quadrupedal. Body mass ranges from 750 to 1100 g; males larger than females. Dental formula: 2.1.3.3; **frugivorous** with insect supplements. The brain to body ratio is second only to humans among the primates. Squirrel monkeys live in large troops that can have as many as 180 members; they frequently compete with larger-bodied primates through **mobbing** behavior, by which they can take over a fruiting tree. Squirrel monkey troops often form an **association** with capuchin monkeys for feeding and traveling. See Appendix 2 for taxonomy, Appendix 3 for living species.

**St. Acheul:** archaeological site found in 1854 near Amiens (Somme), in Northern France, that dates to the Middle Pleistocene and contains **artifacts** (**handaxes** and **flakes**); the original **type site** from which the description of the **Acheulean** tool industry was derived.

**Saint-Césaire:** archaeological site found in 1979 near Saintes in Charente-Maritime, France, dated to 42.4–29 kya or older (TL; radiocarbon), and that contains **Châtelperronian** points and back blades. Hominid remains include an incomplete cranium and mandible and some crushed postcranial bones assigned to *Homo neanderthalensis*. The relatively late date of the site led to the label **'last of the Neandertals'**. Occupation layers above the hominid remains contain **Aurignacian** I industry artifacts but no skeletal material. The Châtelperronian and Aurignacian strata overlay a deeper and clearly **Mousterian** horizon. Aka Pierrot's Rock. See **Vindija**.

**saki monkey:** any of the five platyrrhine species belonging to the genus *Pithecia*.

**Sala:** archaeological site found in 1861 in Czechoslovakia, dated to the Upper **Pleistocene**, and that contains hominid remains, including an adult frontal bone assigned to *Homo neanderthalensis*. Also spelled Sal'a.

**Salawusu:** archaeological site found in 1925 near Dagouwan in the Hetao (Ordos) region of Inner Mongolia (Nei Menggu), China, dated to 65–35 kya, and that contains miniscule flake tools made on small pebbles. Hominid remains include a parietal, other cranial elements, and a mandible, as well as a femur and other postcranial bones attributed to *Homo sapiens*. Aka Sjara-osso-gol, Hetao, Ordos Man.

**Saldanha:** see **Elandsfontein**.

**Salé:** archaeological site found in 1971 near Rabat, Morocco, dated to 400 kya; contains hominid remains including an 880 cm³ adult cranium, possibly female, with thick vault bones, a natural sandstone endocast, and a partial maxilla. Some researchers favor assignment to the **archaic Homo sapiens** group while noting several features also found in **erectines**; others favor a straight attribution to *Homo erectus*. The occipital features are damaged. Compares favorably with **Rabat** and **Sidi Abderrahman**.

**salenodont:** describes a low and flat, unpointed tooth cusp of the type found in omnivores and herbivores.

**salination:** deposit and concentration of salts in the soil arising from irrigation or periodic flooding.

**saline:** relating to or containing salt.

**saliva:** fluid mixture excreted from the **parotid gland**, the **sublingual gland**, the **submandibular gland**, and the mucous glands of the oral cavity. Saliva consists of salts and proteins, including mucins, amylase, and ptyalin, which function to begin the process of digestion. In humans, saliva contains **salivary amylase**. In addition, saliva functions to provide moisture to hold the masticated food together as a **bolus** and it provides lubrication for the bolus as it travels through the **esophagus.**

**salivary amylase:** see **amylase.**

**salivary gland:** one of three pairs of glands in the mouth that secretes **saliva** into the oral cavity. See **parotid glands, submandibular glands,** and **sublingual glands.**

**Salongo monkey:** vernacular for *Cercopithecus salongo.*

**salt:** 1. sodium chloride. 2. compound produced by the reaction of an acid with a base.

**saltation:** leaping. 1. mutation. 2. mode of locomotion. Adjective: saltatory. 3. see **saltational evolution or speciation.** 4. any sudden evolutionary change to DNA, such as a tandemly reduplicated evolutionary sequence.

**saltational evolution** or **speciation:** origin of a new taxon in a single step; rapid evolution of phenotypically similar **species** differentiated primarily by structural chromosome changes, often accompanied by **aneuploidy;** saltatory. Aka macrogenesis. See **stasipatric speciation.** Cf. **punctuated equilibrium** and **hopeful monsters.**

**saltationism:** evolutionary model of large-scale morphological change that occurs within a very short period of time because of major organismal reorganization.

**salt-gene hypothesis:** see **sodium hypothesis.**

**salt-washing behavior:** see **potato-washing behavior.**

**Salzgitter-Lebenstadt:** archaeological site found in 1956 in West Germany, dated to 55.6 kya, and that contains **Mousterian** artifacts and hominid remains, including adult occipital and parietal bones attributed to *Homo neanderthalensis.*

**samango:** vernacular for *Cercopithecus mitis.*

**sambaqui:** prehistoric kitchen midden found on the coast of Brazil.

**Sambungmacan** (SM): an archaeological site found in 1973 on the Solo River in central Java, originally dated to about 900–800 kya (**Kabuh Formation?**) and containing hominid remains (see box below) including partial (SM 1,3) and nearly complete calvaria (SM 4) attributed to *Homo erectus* (originally to *Pithecanthropus soloensis*). Later reassessment of matrix materials yielded a possible much younger estimated date of 100–27 kya. Aka Sambungmachan, Sambungmatjan. See also **Ngandong, Trinil, Solo** and **Sangiran.**

---

### Some fossil specimens from Sambungmacan

All specimens attributed to *Homo erectus* (originally to *Pithecanthropus soloensis*) unless specified otherwise.

**SM 1:** field number for hominid remains found in 1973; consists of a 1035 cm³ calvaria attributed to *Homo erectus* (originally to *Pithecanthropus soloensis*); one of the few hominid fossils in Southeast Asia to be excavated *in situ.* Aka Sambungmacan 1.

**SM 3:** field number for hominid remains found in 1997; consists of a 918 cm³ partial calvaria attributed to *Homo erectus.* Aka Sambungmacan 3.

**SM 4:** field number for hominid remains found in 2001; consists of a well-preserved, nearly complete 1006 cm³ platycephalic calvaria attributed to *Homo erectus.* The specimen could not be dated, but is remarkable in that it is one of the few *H. erectus* calvaria to possess a nearly complete cranial base; the **angle of the cranial base** is strongly flexed, a trait shared with modern humans (but not **Neandertals**). Aka Sambungmacan 4.

---

**Samburu Hills:** paleontological site found in 1984 in Northern Kenya, dated to about 9–7 mya (fauna, late **Miocene**), and that contains **hominoid** remains including a partial left maxilla (KNM-SH 8531) from the Namurungule Formation, attributed variously to the Hominoidea (*incertae sedis*) or to *Samburupithecus kiptalami.*

***Samburupithecus kiptalami* Ishida and Pickford 1998:** taxonomic designation for a **hominoid** partial left maxilla (KNM-SH 8531) from the **Samburu Hills.** The specimen possesses gorilloid features: expanded premolar crowns, reduced sectoriality, thick molar enamel, and elongated M3s.

**Sami:** foragers or hunter-gatherers in modern-day northern Scandinavia who have survived with a subsistence lifestyle in small-scale societies into the twenty-first century, considered by many to be a Caucasoid subgroup with Mongoloid elements. The word is the Sami name for themselves. Non-Sami outsiders previously used the term Lapps or Laplanders.

**sample:** any subset of a larger population.

**sampling:** process of selecting some, but not all, members of a population.

**sampling error:** 1. any **sample** that does not represent the population from which it is drawn. 2. in genetics, any change in allele frequencies within a population which is due to the small size of the effective breeding population; see **genetic drift, Sewell Wright effect.**

**sampling with replacement:** sampling method usually involving some variation of a sampling frame in which a subject, once chosen as a member of a sample, immediately becomes eligible to be chosen again. Cf. **sampling without replacement.**

**sampling without replacement:** sampling method usually involving some variation of a sampling frame in which a subject, once chosen as a member of a sample, becomes ineligible to be chosen again. Cf. **sampling with replacement.**

**sanction:** a social reaction to certain behaviors, either approval (**positive sanction**) or disapproval (**negative sanction**).

**Sandhoff disease:** autosomal recessive genetic disorder associated with a defect in production of hexosaminodase B, causing symptoms similar to those of **Tay–Sachs disease.**

**Sandia point:** spear tip found at Sandia Cave in New Mexico, dated to *c.* 10 kya; resembles the willow- and laurel-shaped points of the **Solutrean** peoples of Europe.

**sandstone:** composite rock composed of sand-sized grains of hard **quartz** cemented loosely together; a poor flaking material that tends to crumble and is not well suited to making tools.

**sandstone tool:** any implement made from **sandstone.**

**Sanfilippo syndrome:** see **mucopolysaccharidoses.**

**Sanford's brown lemur:** vernacular for the subspecies *Eulemur fulvus sanfordi.*

**Sangiran:** archaeological site found in 1937–41 on the upper Solo River in central Java and reworked in the 1960s, dating from 1.4 mya to 500 kya, and that contains multiple hominid remains attributed originally to *Pithecanthropus* sp. See individual specimens in box below.

---

### Some fossil specimens found at Sangiran

Pithecanthropus IX: see entry under **Pithecanthropus IX**.

Sangiran 2: field number for a hominid fragment found in 1937, dated to 750 kya (**Kabuh Formation**, above Grenzbank) but no older than 1.3 mya. Hominid remains include one **calotte** with a cranial capacity estimate of 815 cm³. Attributed to *Pithecanthropus* (= *Homo*) *erectus*. Aka Pith II, HE II, *Homo soloensis*.

Sangiran 4: field number for a hominid fragment found in 1938, dated to 1.0+ mya but no older than 1.3 mya (Pucangan Beds, above Tuff 10). Hominid remains include one **calotte** with an estimated cranial capacity of 908 cm³ assigned to *Homo erectus* (originally as *Pithecanthropus robustus*). Aka HE IV, *Pithecanthropus* IV.

Sangiran 5: field number for hominid remains found in 1939 (reworked in 1960), dated to 1.4 mya – 900 kya, and that contains two mandibles, S5 and S9, attributed to *Homo erectus* (originally as *Pithecanthropus dubius*). These mandibles have a 'swollen' inferior mandibular border, unknown in any other hominid.

Sangiran 6: field number for a hominid fragment found in 1941, dated to 900+ kya but no older than 1.3 mya (Pucangan Beds with Djetis fauna). Hominid remains include one exceptionally large partial right mandible assigned to *Homo erectus* (originally *Meganthropus paleojavanicus*). Aka HE VI.

Sangiran 8: field number for a hominid fragment found in 1941, dated to 900+ kya but no older than 1.3 mya (**Pucangan Formation** ). Hominid remains include an exceptionally large mandibular fragment assigned to *Homo erectus* (originally *Meganthropus paleojavanicus*). Like **Sangiran 5**, the mandible has a 'swollen' inferior mandibular border, a feature unknown in any other hominid. Aka HE VIII.

Sangiran 9: field number for a hominid found in 1937, dating to >1 mya and possibly as old as 1.6 mya, consisting of fragments assigned to *Pithecanthropus* (= *Homo erectus*) *modjokertensis*. From the same locality that yielded *Pithecanthropus* IX, a recently discovered 856 cm³ skull has also been recovered, tentatively, dated to 1.6 mya.

Sangiran 12: field number for a hominid found at **Sangiran** in 1965, dated to 800 kya (**Kabuh Formation**, Bed A) and consisting of one **calotte** (S12/P7) with a cranial capacity of 1004–1059 cm³, attributed to *Homo erectus* (originally as *Pithecanthropus* VII).

Sangiran 17: field number for a hominid fragment found in 1969, dated to 750–500 kya (**Kabuh Formation**; a more recent but controversial date places this hominid in Java by 1.7 mya; see **Bapang Formation**). Hominid remains include one **calotte** and face with an estimated cranial capacity of 1004 cm³ attributed to *Homo erectus*. This is the most complete cranium from Java. Aka *Pithecanthropus* VIII.

---

**Sangiran Dome sediments:** geoanticline located in central Java consisting of marine, terrigenous, and volcanic sediments; the stratigraphic units include the **Notopuro formation,** the **Kabuh formation,** the **Pucangan Formation,** and the **Kalibeng** formation. The total succession exceeds a thickness of 300 m.

**Sangiran Formation:** revised name proposed for the **Pucangan Formation** in central Java, a member of the Kendeng Group.

**Sangoan:** modified **Acheulean** culture of Central Africa in which the **hand-ax** became a pick.

**Sanmenian:** geological column in Northern China corresponding to the Lower Pleistocene (lower Sanmenian) and Middle Pleistocene (Upper Sanmenian).

**Sansan:** paleontological site found in 1834 near Auch (Gers), France, dated to 'Tertiary deposits', and that contains fossil hominoids that are attributed to *Pliopithecus* (1837) and *Dryopithecus* (1856).

**Santana do Riacho 1:** archaeological site found in 1994 in Brazil, South America, dating to 11–8 kya; containing artifact and hominid remains including 40 individuals interred in 28 graves assigned to **AMH.** Walter A. Neves has interpreted the morphology of some of the adult skulls as Australo-African.

**Santarem marmoset:** vernacular for *Callithrix humeralifer*.

*sapiens:* epithet for both the **species** and **subspecies** of living humans; derived from the Latin 'to be wise'. The proper use of these epithets is with their genus or the genus abbreviation; e.g. *H. sapiens* or *H. s. sapiens*.

**sarcoma:** cancer of connective tissue, sometimes associated with a retrovirus; e.g. **Kaposi's sarcoma.**

**sarcosome: mitochondrion** of muscle.

‡ **Sarich, Vincent M.** (1934–): US molecular bioanthropologist at Stanford and UC Berkeley; in the 1960s, he employed the **microcomplement fixation** technique to show that humans and apes are very closely related. He calibrated a serum albumin **molecular clock**, which suggested that the last **common ancestor** of **hominids** and **pongids** was much more recent than was then accepted. This work revolutionized paleontological models concerning where and when to look for fossil hominids. He co-authored the concept that **bonobos** are humans' closest living relative. Co-author (with F. Miele) of *Race: The Reality of Human Differences* (2004). See A. C. **Wilson** and **relative rate test.**

**Sarstedt:** archaeological site located near Sarstedt in the Liene River Valley, Germany, and dated possibly to the Weischel glaciation. The site contains Middle Paleolithic artifacts, and hominid remains from three individuals including an infant temporal bone, all assigned to *Homo neanderthalensis*.

**satellite:** 1. any outlier relative to some process or image, e.g. **satellite DNA**. 2. characteristic, densely staining blobs on the short arms of **acrocentric chromosomes.** Chromosomal satellites are thought to be involved in the formation of the nucleoli.

**satellite area:** peripheral areas of a **metapopulation's** range that contains fluctuating populations. In unfavorable years these populations may become extinct, but this area may be recolonized by migrants from the **core population.**

**satellite DNA:** minor buoyant density fractions of DNA that appear after appropriate centrifugation methods as 'satellites' to the main fraction of genomic DNA. Satellite DNA is characteristically simple sequence DNA that is highly repetitive.

**satellite male:** see **peripheral male.**

**saturated fatty acid:** long carbohydrate chain that contains triglycerides and whose carbon atoms are linked by single covalent bonds with no 'missing' hydrogen atoms; hence 'saturated'. Sources of saturated fatty acids include animal fat and certain plant oils (coconut and palm).

**savagery:** hypothetical culture stage in which there are no crops or language. Avoided by modern anthropologists, but widely used in **unilineal evolution** schemes in the nineteenth century anthropological literature to describe any cultural stage that was supposed to precede **barbarism.**

‡ **savanna:** type of vegetation zone characterized by grasslands with low shrubs and scattered trees. Food resources tend to be patchy in such zones. Low-latitude grasslands first became prolific during the **Miocene,** and were exploited by early apes such as *Proconsul.* Also spelled savannah.

**savanna mosaic:** term used by some researchers to emphasize the patchiness of resources in a grassland environment. During the **wet season,** fruits, nuts, berries, seeds, tubers, roots, eggs, birds, insects, and small animals would have been possible resources available to early hominids, but these would have been less abundant during the **dry season.**

**savannah chimpanzee:** vernacular for *Pan troglodytes schweinfurthii.*

**saw:** denticulated flake; aka scie.

**saw mark:** pattern on bone that is repetitive and parallel.

*Saxonella* **Russell, 1964:** archaic mammal of the **Plesiadapiformes** family **Saxonellidae** of the late Paleocene of Europe and North America containing two species; previously included in the family **Carpolestidae.** Known only from jaws and dental remains. Dental formula: 2.1.3.3/1.0.2.3; **plagiaulacoid dentition,** but it is the lower third premolar that is bladelike, rather than the lower fourth premolar as found in the carpolestids; body size and dentition suggests diet of some high-calorie food such as insects, seeds, or nuts. Body mass estimated to be between 60 and 90 g. See Appendix 1 for taxonomy.

**Saxonellidae:** family of the archaic mammal order **Plesiadapiformes** of the late Paleocene of Europe and North America containing only the genus *Saxonella* and two species.

**Sbakian:** Middle Paleolithic tool industry comprised of a variety of chipped stone implements intermediate in type between **Acheulean** and **Solutrean**, and discovered near Sbakia in North Africa.

**SCA:** abbreviation for **sickle cell anemia**.

*Scala Naturae:* medieval rationale for the organization of life, literally a 'scale of nature', in which all organisms were arranged from least complex (most imperfect) upwards to the most complex and perfect (humans, angels, archangels); the ordained categories of creatures were immutable, or unchanging, since their creation. Can be traced to Plato and **Aristotle**, but most fully developed by Gottfried von Leibniz (1646–1716), German philosopher and mathematician. Aka **ladder of nature** and **Great Chain of Being**.

**scaling:** see **behavioral scaling** and **allometry**.

**scan sampling:** sampling technique used in primate behavior studies in which the study group is rapidly scanned, or censused, at regular intervals; during this time the behavior of each individual is recorded by **instantaneous sampling**. This method of sampling limits the observer to only a few well defined behaviors and is biased towards conspicuous behaviors and individuals. Cf. *ad libitum* sampling, **behavior sampling**, **focal sampling**.

**Scandentia:** **monotypic** mammalian order to which the tree shrews (family **Tupaiidae**) belong. Consists of one family, five genera, and sixteen species; member of the grandorder **Archonta**. Tree shrews are located in Asia and, despite their name, contain some semiterrestrial genera; there are both diurnal and nocturnal species; body mass ranges from 100 to 400 g; quadrupedal. Dental formula: 2.1.3.3/3.1.3.3; diet is **insectivorous** and **frugivorous**. From the 1920s to the 1970s tree shrews were included in the order Primates by most authors; reevaluation in the late 1970s removed them from the primates and they were established as a separate order. Recent work indicates that this group is more closely related to primates than is any other mammal.

**scanning:** 1. process of minute examination. 2. memorization of a topography or traversed surface. 3. the movement of a **ribosome** along an RNA molecule.

**scanning electron microscope** (SEM): high-resolution technique in which specimens coated in carbon or gold can be magnified up to 100 000 times, permitting visualization of objects as small as a **plasmid**.

**scansorial:** pertaining to an arboreal mammal that is anatomically adapted for climbing in trees; scansorial mammals (e.g. **Callitrichidae**) generally have claws, and live on both the ground and in the trees (like many opossums and rodents).

**scaphocephaly:** condition in which there is a keel-like projection from the front to the back of the cranium.

**scaphoid:** 1. boat-shaped. 2. most lateral and largest bone of the proximal row of **carpals** articulating with the **radius** to help form that wrist joint and with the **lunate, trapezium, trapezoid,** and **capitate**. Aka navicular, cotyloid. 3. older term used for the **navicular** of the foot.

‡ **scapula:** shoulder blade; one of a pair of large flat bones (scapulae) that are on either side of the back of the **thoracic cage** in **hominoids**, rather than laterally placed as in quadrupedal primates. The scapula articulates with the **clavicle**, which connects the upper limb to the **axial skeleton**. It also articulates with the **humerus** and forms a freely movable joint held together principally by musculature.

**scat:** mammalian fecal droppings, often identifiable to genus and sometimes to species. Can be used as a **sign** that a particular mammal is in the area, and is also useful for nutritional analysis. See **coprolite**.

**scatology:** study of animal feces, or **scat**. Adjective: scatological.

**scatophagy:** see **coprophagy**.

**scattered repeat sequences:** scattered repeats of nucleotides in DNA of about 100 bps; probably originate by DNA transposition. Cf. **short tandem repeats** and **tandem repeat sequences**.

**scavenger:** 1. organism that feeds on carrion or organic refuse; scavenging. 2. one who scavenges. 3. See **free radical scavenger**.

‡ **scavenging hypothesis:** proposal that early **hominids** were opportunistic scavengers rather than systematic primary killers of savanna animals, and perhaps that hominids returned to **base camps** with portions of the scavenged carcass. Assemblages that contain disproportionately high numbers of bones from the neck, shoulders and forelimbs of certain game animals could be considered evidence that hominids were retrieving less desirable portions of animals previously killed by other predators. Cf. **schlepp effect**.

‡ **scavenging opportunity theory:** proposal that older scavenging models were too speculative and that evidence suggests that early hominid land use resulted in scavenging opportunities; evidence of scavenging episodes by hominids can be found in African Plio-Pleistocene sites where tools and bones are found *in situ*, and the bones possess evidence of defleshing such as **cut marks** and hammer-and-anvil signatures made during marrow extraction. Aka Blumenschine scavenging theory.

**SCD:** abbreviation for **sickle cell disease**.

**SCE:** abbreviation for **sister chromatid exchange**.

‡ **scenario:** historical narrative or interpretation of a given fossil record; any attempt to describe (1) phylogenetic relationships among taxa, (2) ecological circumstances, and (3) for example, the evolution of the hominid brain.

**scent:** any volatile organic substance deposited by a primate or other animal that contains information about the animal or its environment; see **pheromones**, **scent marking**.

**scent gland:** specialized gland that produces an odoriferous secretion. Scent glands are generally sweat, sebaceous, or a modified combination of these two types of glands. See **circumanal gland**, **carpal gland**, **throat gland**.

**scent marking:** act of placing an olfactory cue on elements of the environment within a territory, on a mate, or on the individual itself, to advertise the presence of the marker to **conspecifics**. Some of the lower primates have specialized scent glands used for such marking behavior. In some cases, as in the potto, the scent is used to navigate the home range. Scent marking may be accomplished by **scent glands** that secrete the odorous substance, by deposition of feces, or by urine; the last is the primary substance used by primates. See **marking** and **urine washing**.

**Schaaffhausen, Hermann** (1816–1893): German physician, anatomist, anthropometrist at Bonn and one of the founders of German physical anthropology; with Johann Fuhlrott, Schaaffhausen described the original **Feldhofer Grotto** Neandertal fossils, found in 1856. He defended their antiquity against the arguments for pathology lodged by R. **Virchow**. Schaaffhausen also described the **Šipka** and **Spy** remains, all of which he interpreted as earlier forms of modern humans. He was an ardent evolutionist, and Charles **Darwin** acknowledged him in the *Descent of Man* (1872). Schaaffhausen was instrumental in the acceptance of the 1882 **Frankfort Agreement** that standardized anthropometric landmarks and techniques.

**Scheie syndrome:** see **mucopolysaccharidoses**.

**schist:** a rock type that possesses a preferential cleavage plane that makes it difficult or impossible to control fractures and thus to produce a sharp-edged tool.

**schistocyte:** any fragment of a formerly intact **erythrocyte**. Aka schizocyte.

**schistosomiasis:** group of related diseases caused by parasitic microorganisms called schistosomes, or blood flukes; these agents are flatworms in the genus *Schistosoma* that cause symptoms in mammalian hosts, including humans, referable to (a) the intestine and liver, with concomitant dysentery, or (2) the bladder, resulting in blood passage into urine. The flukes are vectored by several species of snail. There are multiple clusters of endemicity, found worldwide; agents and vectors vary by region. Aka bilharziasis, snail fever.

**schizodactyly:** condition in some primates in which the thumb is reduced and the second and third fingers are used for holding objects.

**schizophrenia** (SCZD): constellation of similar disorders characterized by a debilitating loss of the ability to organize thoughts and perceptions, and that leads to inappropriate behaviors and a withdrawal from reality. An increased probability of recurrence among close relatives and high concordance between **identical twins** suggests a genetic component of large magnitude. Schizophrenia is possibly a genetically heterogenous, multifactorial and/or polygenic presentation. Alternatively, schizophrenia has been suggested to be due completely to environmental agents, caused, for example, by maternal influenza during the **second trimester**, when fetal brain cells are undergoing rapid hyperplasic growth and are susceptible to the effects of such a virus.

**schlepp effect:** artifact of a butchering process occurring as the result of meat being piled on butchered skins, and then being dragged home by using the still attached lower (posterior) limb bones; upper limb bones are thus discarded at the kill site, and lower limb bones are found more commonly at the habitation site.

**Schöningen:** archaeological site found in 1997 near Schöningen, Germany, dated to 400 kya; contains Lower Paleolithic artifacts including four heavy wooden javelins (throwing or thrusting spears).

**Schultz, Adolph Hans** (1891–1976): Swiss-American anatomist, physical anthropologist; Carnegie Institution (DC), then Johns Hopkins after 1925; editorial board of *Human Biology* (1929); president, **AAPA** (1932–4); 3rd Viking Fund medallist (1948). Supported the hypothesis that humans and apes were closely related, based on embryological evidence; published many papers on the comparative anatomy of primates. Author of '*The Life of Primates*' (1969). Co-founder of *Folia Primatologia*.

**Schwalbe, Gustav** (1844–1916): German physician, anatomist; Schwalbe turned from an early interest in histology to an increased contemplation of phylogenetic questions later in his career. Schwalbe was an enthusiastic Darwinist, and best known for his **unilinear** hypothesis that the Dubois' *Pithecanthropus erectus* and Neandertals were both direct antecedents of modern humans; in his late career, however, he concluded that these taxa may have represented side branches and in fact did not evolve directly into modern humans. He was one of the first to propose that *Homo primigenius* (his term for Neandertals) represent a distinct species. Schwalbe's student, Franz **Weidenreich**, carried these ideas forward into the well-known '**trellis model**'. Schwalbe was founder of *Die Zeitschrift für Morphologie und Anthropologie* (1899).

**sciatic notch:** see **greater sciatic notch**, **lesser sciatic notch**.

**SCID:** abbreviation for **severe combined immune deficiency (syndrome)**.

‡ **science:** method of inquiry about phenomena that requires the proposal, testing, and acceptance or rejection (see **falsification**) of **hypotheses**. See the **hypothetico-deductive approach** to science.

**scientific classification:** grouping of objects according to rules of **taxonomy** and other practices in accord with the **scientific method**. Compared to **folk taxonomy**, classification in science, while sharing ranks and morphological cues, tends to utilize **homology** rather than **analogy**, to have many more ranks, and to avoid the self-utility inherent in the lay procedure.

**scientific creationism:** proposal by creationists late in the twentieth century that the views held by them are not a religious but a scientific body of knowledge. This claim was tested and rejected in *McLean v. Arkansas Board of Education* (1982).

**scientific materialism:** view that all phenomena in the universe, including the human mind, have a material basis, are subject to the same physical laws, and can be most deeply understood by scientific analysis.

‡ **scientific method:** process of conducting scientific inquiry; the identification of a **problem**, the collection of relevant **data**, the formulation of an appropriate **hypothesis**, the empirical **testing** of each hypothesis, and the **interpretation** of the outcome. See **science** and the **hypothetico-deductive approach** to science.

‡ **scientific testing:** see **hypothesis testing**.

**Sciuridae:** rodent family that consists of the various genera of squirrels. Sciurids are used as models for early primates by some workers.

**Sclater's black lemur:** vernacular for the subspecies *Eulemur macaco flavifrons*.

**sclera:** in humans, the white, fibrous outer capsule of the eye, including the transparent cornea; it is composed of connective tissue and protects the eye. In most nonhuman primates the sclera is melanized.

**sclerophyllous:** refers to any vegetation that has adapted to dry conditions.

**sclerosis:** hardening of tissue; usually used in reference to bone or nervous tissue.

**scoliosis:** abnormal lateral curvature of the vertebral column, occurring most often in the **thoracic** region. Cf. **kyphosis** and **kyphoscoliosis**.

**Scopes Trial:** infamous and acrimonious 1925 confrontation between jurists William Jennings Bryan and Clarence Darrow over the 1923 Tennessee 'Monkey Law' which forbade the teaching in publicly-funded schools of biological evolution '...that denies the story of the divine creation of man as taught in the Bible, and to teach instead that man descended from a lower order of animals'.

**scramble competition:** in ecology, a form of **intraspecific** competition in which resources are distributed equally in the environment and every individual in a population has equal access to resources; this results in a contest in which some individuals obtain insufficient resources. Scramble competition can also lead to a population crash when there are insufficient resources to sustain all the individuals in the population. Cf. **contest competition**.

**scramble competition polygyny:** mating pattern in which males try to find receptive females and mate with them before other males can; there is no fighting among the competing males.

**scraper:** 1. any **stone tool** with a finished edge, sometimes polished by use, used or intended for scraping fat and soft tissue from skin and hide. Scrapers are usually retouched on one side only. 2. term sometimes used for any flint implement that is not otherwise classified. Examples of scraper types include: core, disk, end, keeled, **Levallois**, heavy duty, Mousterian side, notched and side.

**scrapie:** one of the **transmissible spongiform encephalopathies** (TSEs) of animals alleged to be caused by a **prion protein**. Currently, the ultimate reservoir is thought to be sheep and goats; transmission is by direct ingestion or contact with brain tissue. The transmissible form in sheep is denoted by PrPSc ('S' for sheep) and appears to have been transmitted horizontally from sheep to cows (BSE) to humans (nvCJD).

**screening:** 1. process of examining large groups of people for a given characteristic such as a disease. 2. survey of a specimen for certain substances. 3. physical sieving of archaeological debris through screens of sequentially smaller pore sizes.

**scrotum:** sac on male mammals, located in the anogenital area, that holds the **testes**. Adjective: scrotal. In humans the testes are in the scrotum during the entire year, but for most primates and mammals the testes only descend into the scrotum during the breeding season.

‡ **scurvy:** state of **malnutrition** caused by a reversible deficiency (**avitaminosis**) of **vitamin C**. The symptoms include general malaise and depression, debility, spongy gums, and tissue hemorrhaging; the final stages involve most systems. Scurvy is often fatal unless reversed. Aka scorbutus.

**SDY gene:** see **SRY gene**.

**s.e., se:** abbreviation for **standard error**.

**sea-floor spreading:** proposal that convective forces cause the extrusion of molten rock near oceanic ridges, and that the magnetite contained in such a relatively fluid medium is polarized during cooling by the earth's current magnetic orientation, thus explaining the deflections and deviations from the present alignment that can be observed in older rocks. Proposed in 1963 by British geographers Drummond Matthews (1931–) and F. J. Vine (1939–88), who acknowledged earlier contributions by Arthur Holmes (1890–1965) and Alfred **Wegener.**

**sea voyaging:** technology that permitted hominids to cross bodies of water that were barriers to earlier species; currently (2003) there is little evidence that species antedating **AMHs** had access to such technology, which first appears unequivocally about 55–50 kya, as early populations entered Australia and Papua New Guinea, probably utilizing **bamboo** rafts.

**search image:** 1. mental model against which a visual comparison is made. Search images are formed as animals search for food or mates and optimize behavior by allowing an animal to systematically choose certain resources or individuals and to ignore others. 2. in reference to an animal focusing on a particular item; for example, a primate looking for food may only give its attention to a particular type of fruit at one time as long as it is rewarding to do so; this term is used almost exclusively for selective **foraging.**

**seasonal isolation:** where mating or flowering episodes in closely related species occur at different seasons; a premating or **prezygotic mechanism.**

**seasonality:** 1. pertaining to a seasonal activity or trait, e.g. birth season. 2. estimate of the range of time during a year when an archaeological site was originally occupied.

**sebaceous gland:** holocrine gland associated with a **hair follicle** that secretes sebum, a liquid that helps to waterproof the skin and hair and keep them soft and pliable.

**Sebilian:** pertaining originally to the **Aurignacian tool tradition** when found in Egypt, but later used to identify an **Upper Paleolithic** flake industry there.

**seccotine:** temporary cement used in archaeological work.

**second Darwinian revolution:** so-called because of certain proposed 'solutions' to problems that Charles **Darwin** had admittedly left unsolved by his theory of **natural selection,** apparent solutions presented by William D. **Hamilton,** John **Maynard Smith,** Edward O. **Wilson** and their students, and the writer Richard **Dawkins.** Foremost among these 'solutions' was to the problem of **altruism.**

**second-degree relative:** see **relative, second-degree.**

**second glaciation:** see **Mindel glaciation.**

**second interglacial:** see **Mindel–Riss interglacial.**

**second polar body:** in females, a small, acytoplasmic cell that is the homologue of the ovum, both of which contain 23 chromatids; the second polar body is discarded from the ovum if pregnancy occurs.

**second premolar:** **premolar** that is posterior to the most anterior premolar of the four premolars in the primitive mammalian dentition. During the course of evolution primates have lost anterior premolars; thus, the second premolar may actually be the most anterior premolar in a species, such as in most lemurs. However, some workers number teeth by those actually present in a species; in such a case the second premolar is either the third or fourth premolar of the primitive condition. See **P1, P2, P3, etc.**

**second trimester:** second of the three **trimesters** of human gestation, consisting of months 4–6, and during which early fetal growth occurs, especially of the **central nervous system,** and differentiation diminishes in importance.

**secondary:** 1. sequential to something considered primary. 2. the second of several stages, as in certain diseases. 3. something superimposed upon an existing context, as ores and minerals that have percolated down into existing deposits.

**secondary burial:** final burial of a person's bones, after a first temporary or **primary burial** during which the flesh had decomposed. The deceased's bones are gathered, often compacted and wrapped in animal skin, and redeposited. Aka bundle burial.

**secondary calcaneus:** supernumerary bone that sometimes develops lateral and distal to the **calcaneus.**

**secondary (metabolic) compound:** substance produced that is not necessary for the normal metabolic activities of an organism; for example, plant **toxins** serve to protect a plant, but are not absolutely necessary for the functioning of the organism, and deter other organisms from consuming them. This term usually refers to plant **allochemicals** as it is used by primatologists and human biologists.

**secondary constriction:** unspiralized, lightly staining region in a metaphase **chromosome** that is not located near the centromere, and that may contain a **nucleolus organizer region.** Cf. **primary constriction.**

**secondary consumer:** any organism that survives through consumption of plant-eating organisms; secondary consumers are heterotrophs at the second trophic level.

**secondary contact:** reintroduction of interaction between two species by elimination of a geographic barrier; generally used of descendants after an **allopatric speciation** event.

**secondary cuboid:** supernumerary bone that sometimes develops between the **cuboid** and **navicular bones** on the **plantar** side of the foot.

**secondary immune response:** immune system's response to a foreign antigen that it has previously encountered. Aka booster response. See **primary immune response.**

**secondary nondisjunction:** production of aneuploid gametes as the result of **nondisjunction** in viable individuals who are already constitutionally aneuploid, e.g. production of 24,XY sperm from an XXY male. Cf. **primary nondisjunction**.

**secondary oöcyte: haploid** female cell produced by **meiosis** that will become a functional **gamete**, an **ovum**, and three **polar bodies**.

**secondary race:** race that results from commingling between members of two primary races.

**secondary rain forest: rain forest** characterized by immature stages of the succession cycle, commonly found on the edges of **forests**, along rivers, and around tree falls.

**secondary sex ratio:** see **sex ratio**.

**secondary sexual trait, character or feature:** external physical trait associated with the onset of sexual maturation, including the development of facial hair and muscularity in boys and the development of breasts and adult fat distribution in girls. Cf. **primary sexual trait, character or feature**.

**secondary speciation:** see **reticulate speciation**.

**secondary spermatocyte:** cell in the **testis** which undergoes **meiosis II**, producing two haploid **spermatids**. See **spermatogenesis**.

**secondary structure:** ($2°$) pleated or helical structure in a protein molecule that is brought about by the formation of bonds between amino acids; see **protein structure**.

**secondary succession:** sequence of communities in a habitat where the **climax** community has been disturbed or completely removed. Cf. **primary succession**.

**secondary talus:** supernumerary bone that sometimes develops posterior to the **talus**.

**secretion:** any one of many fluids normally exuded from body cells in response to specific stimuli, including milk, **saliva**, urine, tears, and respiratory and digestive fluids; several types contain **antibodies**.

**secretor:** person who possesses water-soluble forms of antigens, used especially with respect to the A and B antigens in the **ABO blood group**; the antigens can be detected in secretions such as saliva.

**secretor locus:** genetic **locus** having a recessive **allele** that, when **homozygous**, prevents secretion of the A and B blood group antigens in sweat, saliva, intestinal, and other body fluids; the dominant allele permits secretion.

**secretory phase:** third phase of the **human uterine cycle**, encompassing days 14–27, and characterized by relatively low concentrations of the hormones **LH** and **FSH**, but rising concentrations of **progesterone** and **estrogen**. **Ovulation** normally occurs during the initial hours of the secretory phase. The corpus luteum grows dramatically, and the endometrium thickens. If fertilization does not occur, these structures begin to degenerate. Aka progestational phase.

**secretory vesicle:** membrane-bound vesicle produced by the **Golgi apparatus**; contains protein to be secreted by a cell.

**section:** 1. to cut into portions. 2. any of several segments of a structure or organism. 3. a subdivision within a taxon, especially a genus; or subgenus.

‡ **sectorial premolar:** in catarrhines, the lower third premolar that is elongated and laterally compressed, forming a scissor-like **honing facet** that occludes with large interlocking **canines**. Present in many cercopithecoids. Aka sectorial tooth.

**secular change:** change in the historically average pattern of growth in a population over several generations.

**secular radioactive equilibrium:** condition that is found in uranium-bearing material that has been undisturbed for millions of years, and in which various decay rates are equal.

**secular trend:** any trend continuing for a long term, or over the span of a generation.

**sedentary:** stationary; remaining within a core area or home range.

**sedente:** organism that remains behind in the region of birth when others migrate into another geographical area; nonmigrating individual.

**sediment:** 1. in geology, particulate matter transported by wind, water or ice, and deposited as a dune, loess, or other formation. 2. insoluble material, including both inorganic and organic matter, that settles to the bottom of a body of water. 3. any precipitate that settles to the bottom of a liquid; hypostasis.

**sedimentary nutrient cycle:** biogeochemical cycle in which the earth's lithosphere serves as the source for certain nutrients (such as minerals).

**sedimentary rock:** rocks formed by the settling of clays, silts, or sand that has become compacted into a hard material over a long period, or cemented by a congealing or crystallization process. See **cryptocrystalline siliceous rock**.

**sedimentation:** process of formation of **sedimentary rock**; settling.

**seed dispersal:** spreading of seeds throughout the environment by wind, water, or animals. In the latter case, this may be accomplished either by consuming fruit with the seeds which pass through the animal's **gastrointestinal tract**, or by carrying the seeds that stick to a mammal's fur. Primates are important seed dispersers.

**seed-eating hypothesis:** model of hominid evolution proposed by C. Jolly that adaptations for feeding on small food items such as seeds, grasses, and tubers provided the **selection pressures** for the evolution of **hominid** biological characteristics. According to this model, early hominids relied on small-object feeding, which cascaded into savannah adaptations and **bipedalism**. It is a referential model that exploits supposed morphological and behavioral analogies between **gelada baboons** and early hominids. See **T complex**.

**segment:** 1. any repeated subunit. 2. see **body segment**, **somite**, and **segmentation**.

**segmentation:** 1. process of being divided into similar parts; e.g. **dermal segmentation**. 2. **cleavage**, as of a fertilized ovum. 3. rhythmic contractions of rings of intestinal smooth muscle that mixes intestinal contents.

**segmentation nucleus:** fertilized ovum containing female and male **pronuclei**, and that will divide to form the **morula**.

**segregate:** 1. to separate or set apart. 2. to practice segregation, as among individuals. 3. to separate during **cell division**. 4. hybrid that resembles only one of its parents.

**segregation:** separation of gene pairs during **meiosis**; distribution of alleles to different daughter cells.

**segregation, law of:** see **Mendelian principle of segregation**.

**segregational load:** reduction of the mean fitness of a population owing to the segregation of alleles from favored heterozygotes into homozygotes with relatively lowered fitness. Aka balanced load. See **genetic load**.

**selectin:** any of several specific **cellular adhesion molecules** that bind to white blood cells or to capillary walls.

‡ **selection:** 1. a natural or artificial process that results or tends to result in the survival and propagation of some individuals but not of others, with the result that the inherited traits of the survivors are perpetuated. Selection involves an **agent of selection** and results in either **differential mortality** or **differential fertility** by **genotype**, hence, **net reproductive success**. 2. classic Darwinian or individual **natural selection** is measured by a **coefficient of selection** for each genotype. 3. see **anthropogenic selection, artificial selection, balancing selection, canalizing selection, counter selection, counteracting selection, cultural selection, cyclical selection, directed selection, directional selection, disruptive selection, epigamic selection, frequency-dependent selection, gene selection, group selection, habitat selection, hard selection, individual selection, interdemic selection, intrademic selection, intersexual selection, intrasexual selection, kin selection, maintenance selection, migrant selection, mutant selection, natural selection, negative selection, normalizing selection, orthoselection, reinforcing selection, relaxed selection, sexual selection, soft selection, species selection, stabilizing selection,** and **truncation selection**.

**selection coefficient** ($s$): see **coefficient of selection**.

**selectionism:** idea that the majority of molecular and phenotypic changes are genetic, and that the changes were brought about by **natural selection**.

**selection pressure:** any feature of the natural environment that results in natural selection such as food shortage, predators, or competition from other members of the same sex for a mate.

**selective advantage:** situation in which the fitness of a certain genotype is greater than that of another in a given environment. Cf. **selective disadvantage**, **heterozygote advantage**.

**selective breeding:** see **artificial selection**.

**selective disadvantage:** situation in which the fitness of a certain genotype is less than another in a given environment. Cf. **selective advantage**, **heterozygote advantage**.

‡ **selective pressure:** environmental agent that exerts influence on the reproductive success of individuals within a population.

**selective theory of antibody diversity:** refers to any of several theories of antibody formation in which pre-existing antibodies are thought to exist, and that these bind selectively to antigens.

**selective value:** reproductive success of an individual as measured by the mean value of its offspring with respect to a particular character. See **fitness**.

**Selenka Expedition:** expedition led by L. Selenka to Java in an attempt to recover fossils; the 1907–08 expedition located numerous mammal fossils, but failed to recover hominid material.

**self antigen:** receptor molecule on the plasma membrane surface of cells that the immune system uses to differentiate the body's own cells from foreign material; produced by a cluster of genes on human chromosome 6. See **MHC**.

**self-grooming:** grooming directed at one's own body; **autogrooming**. Cf. **allogrooming**.

**selfish act or behavior:** see **selfishness**.

**selfish DNA:** proposed name for functionless DNA that exploits a cell or an organism in order to replicate itself. Although originally proposed by August **Weismann** in different terms, the idea that selfish DNA behaves in this manner was popularized by Richard **Dawkins**, and remains controversial. Examples include: **pseudogenes** that arise by **endoreduplication**; repeated and dispersed elements that are generated during **unequal crossing over**. Aka junk DNA, parasitic DNA.

**selfish herd:** concept in **sociobiology** that explains the evolution of some social groups as an attempt by individuals in the unit to use other individuals as shields against predators; such a group is clumped together rather than spread out.

**selfish trait, character** or **feature:** any trait that benefits the individual organism at an expense to its conspecifics; the cost and benefit are measured in terms of genetic **fitness**.

**selfishness:** behavior that **benefits** an actor in terms of genetic **fitness** at a **cost** to the **reproductive success** of another or other members of the same species; selfish acts decrease **inclusive fitness**. One of W. D. **Hamilton's** and E. O. **Wilson's** three classes of social behavior; cf. **altruism** and **spite**.

**sella** (sl): mid-point of the **sella turcica** of the **sphenoid bone**; used in X-ray and **CAT scanning** analyses.

**sella turcica:** depression in the body of the **sphenoid bone** in which the pituitary gland sits.

**sellion** (se): **craniometric landmark:** deepest portion of the mid-sagittal depression inferior to the **glabella**.

**semelparity:** production of offspring all at the same time by organisms living in a group, and only once during a lifetime, as in certain species of salmon. Cf. **iteroparity**. See **parity**.

**semen:** thick whitish secretion of the reproductive organs of the male, consisting of spermatozoa and nutrients added by the **prostate** and seminal vesicles during male ejaculation.

**semiconservative replication:** synthesis of new **DNA** using opposite halves of the parental double helix which are therefore conserved as templates to construct two new strands or **sister chromatids**.

**semidominance:** intermediacy of the phenotype of the heterozygote between the phenotypes of the two homozygotes.

**semilethal gene:** any allelic mutation in a gene that causes the death of 50%–100% of a population that carries it. In reference to humans, initial expression of the gene after the age of one year is stipulated by some researchers. Aka quasilethal gene, semilethal mutation. See **genetic load**. Cf. **lethal gene** and **sublethal gene**.

**semilunar:** see **lunate**.

**semi-Mongoloid:** hypothetical Caucasoid–Mongoloid hybrid thought to have given rise to the Hmong and similar peoples.

**seminal fluid:** secretions of the prostate that facilitate sperm transport during male ejaculation.

**seminal vesicle:** either of a pair of accessory male reproductive organs, lying posterior to and inferior to the urinary bladder, that secrete additives to spermatozoa into the ejaculatory ducts. Cf. **germinal vesicle**.

**seminaturalistic field research:** studies in which animals have been transferred from their natural habitat to another outdoor habitat in which the animals are free-ranging. In many cases the animals are maintained by **provisioning**. The most prominent example in primatology is the rhesus macaque research at **Cayo Santiago Island**.

**seminiferous tubule:** any of numerous small ducts in the testes where spermatozoa are produced; contains **Sertoli cells**.

**seminiferous tubule dysgenesis:** see **Klinefelter syndrome**.

**semiotics:** scientific study of communication, signals, and signs.

**semipermeable membrane:** tissue with properties that permit passage of certain molecules or fluids but act as a barrier to others.

**semispecies:** populations that are completely isolated from each other (see **allopatry**), are evolving independently without **gene flow**, but which have not yet reached the status of distinct **species**; similar to a **geographical race**. Cf. **race**.

**semiterrestrial:** in reference to animals that spend a significant portion of their daily routine both on the ground and in the trees.

*Semnopithecus* **Desmarest, 1822:** 1. monotypic catarrhine genus to which the Hanuman, sacred, or common gray langur belongs. Found in wide variety of habitats in South Asia. Body mass ranges from 15 to 21 kg with slight body size **sexual dimorphism**. Dental formula: 2.1.2.3; **frugivorous** and **folivorous**. Social organization usually a **one-male unit**. These langurs were the first primate species observed practicing **infanticide**. See Appendix 2 for taxonomy, Appendix 3 for living species. 2. subgenus of *Presbytis* used in schemes that lump the langurs in that genus. The langurs in this group are South Asia species and include *P. (S.) entelllus, P. (S.) vetulus* (=*senex*), and *P. (S.) johnii*. The langurs are also divided into species groups by some workers as an alternative to subgenera.

**Senegal bushbaby:** vernacular for *Galago senegalensis*.

‡ **senescence:** last living stage in the human **life cycle** that manifests variably, but extending the stage of **old age** and before **death**. Characterized by marked loss of competence in many body functions in latest **adulthood**, most noticeably in profound memory loss and orientation, and an increased dependency upon others. See **cell senescence**.

**senescence gene hypothesis:** proposal in 1882 that a gene or genes for organismal degeneration exist, and that these can be modified by **natural selection**. First suggested by Ernst Mach (1838–1916). See **programmed aging**.

**senilicide:** killing of the aged. Aka geronticide.

**senility:** 1. state of mental infirmity in old age. Adjective: postreproductive, senile. 2. a level, featureless plain formed by extensive erosion.

**senior synonym:** in taxonomy, the first published name of two or more synonyms; the name that has historical priority. Cf. **junior synonym**.

**sensation:** feeling that results from the brain's interpretation of sensory nerve impulses without higher brain centers. Cf. **perception.**

**sense mutation:** any mutation that changes a termination codon (= **stop codon**) into one that codes for an amino acid; such mutations produce elongated proteins; may be either a **transition** or a **transversion.**

**sense RNA:** single-stranded polynucleotide that is complementary to a coding strand of DNA, e.g. **messenger RNA.** Cf. **antisense DNA/RNA.**

**sense strand:** DNA that is transcribed into mRNA. In duplex DNA, information proceeds from the 5′ to the 3′-end of the sense strand. Cf. **antisense DNA/RNA.**

**sensible temperature:** ambient temperature as perceived by an individual; aka effective temperature.

**sensitive growth period:** periods during the developmental life cycle when **catch-up growth** is not possible.

**sensitive phase:** period in the life history of an animal in which certain learning experiences are likely to have a very strong effect on its behavioral development. The sensitive phase varies between behavioral traits, between individuals within the same species, and between primate species. Aka sensitive period. Cf. **critical period.**

**sensitive tree ring:** in **dendrochronology,** a growth ring in a tree in which the width varies annually. Cf. **complacent tree ring.**

**sensitivity:** 1. ability to perceive stimuli with one or more of the senses. 2. in epidemiology, the successfulness of correctly identifying the proportion of individuals carrying a disease. 3. in immunology, the ability of an antibody to detect the presence of an antigen, particularly at low antigen concentrations; in the context of a test for diagnosing a disease condition, sensitivity is defined as the proportion of people with a disease who test positively for the disease.

**sensorimotor cortex:** areas of the cerebral cortex that play a role in skeletal-muscle control, including primary motor areas, somatosensory areas, and parts of the parietal-lobe association cortex and the premotor area.

**sensory:** pertaining to a sensation or sense organ.

**sensory exploitation:** hypothesis that the evolution of sexually selected traits is influenced by pre-existing biases, and which predicts that preferences (in one sex) evolve before sexually selected phenotypic traits (in the other sex).

**sensory receptor:** specialized dendrite that responds to specific stimuli by initiating an action potential towards the **central nervous system.**

*sensu* (*sens.*) (Latin): in the sense of. In taxonomy, used to indicate the author of a misapplied name.

*sensu lato* (*s.l.*) (Latin): in the broadest sense; term often applied to a group of specimens lumped into a taxon that is not well defined.

*sensu stricto* (*s.s., s. str.*) (Latin): in the strict, or narrow, sense; often applied to a **type species.**

**separate creation:** idea that species have separate origins and never changed after their creation, with the usual extension that creation occurred through supernatural action.

**separation syndrome:** set of abnormal characteristics resulting from social isolation in early infancy. These traits include inability to form social attachments, apathy, and **stereotypy.** See **deprivation study.**

**sepsis:** poisoning caused by a putrefactive process (infection with the formation of pus). Common forms include intestinal sepsis, post-childbirth (puerperal) sepsis, and oral sepsis. Adjective: septic.

**septal aperture:** foramen that is sometimes present in the region of the **ulna** of modern humans. It is more common in females than in males and may assist archaeologists or forensic workers with information regarding a recovered skeleton.

**septal region:** portion of the **limbic system** that is involved with sensations of pleasure, and that is connected to the **hypothalamus,** the **hippocampal formation,** and the **amygdala.**

**septic:** see **sepsis**

**septum:** 1. a partition. 2. forebrain area anterior to the hypothalamus involved in emotional behavior.

**sequence affinity:** similarities in gene sequences of two or more biological species that cause them to cluster in a portion of a phylogenetic tree.

**sequence analysis:** 1. see **DNA sequencing.** 2. analysis of the order in which behavior patterns occur. If behavior always occurs in the same sequence it is referred to as a deterministic sequence; if the behavior is variable, yet consistent enough to be predictable, it is called a stochastic or probabilistic sequence; if the behavior has no set order it is referred to as a random sequence and the probability that a given behavior will follow any other behavior is the transition probability. See **form analysis, situation analysis.**

**sequence tagged site** (STS): unique, unrepeated **DNA sequence** on a chromosome that can serve as a landmark during mapping or walking procedures.

**sequencing techniques:** see **DNA sequencing techniques.**

**Sera:** plural of **serum.**

**Sergi, Giuseppe** (1841–1936): Italian anthropologist who viewed anthropology as the holistic study of humans. Sergi was skeptical of anthropometry and utilized drawings and photographs to support his notion that the early races of Europe were displaced by Africans who were the ancestors of Mediterranean and Nordic Europeans. Author of *Origine e Diffusione* *della Stirpe Mediterranea* (1895). Sergi founded the first Italian anthropological society and was editor of its first journal. Erected three grades of human evolution: **protoanthropic, paleoanthropic,** and **neanthropic.**

**seriation:** 1. temporal ordering of artifacts based on the assumption that cultural styles change (fads) and that the popularity of a style or motif can thus be associated with a certain time frame. 2. **Piagetian** term for the cognitive ability to arrange objects in a sequence. Demonstrated, for example, in rhesus monkeys. 3. the ordering of a set of **operational taxonomic units** (OTUs) such that similar OTUs are adjacent.

**series:** 1. systematically related group of elements. 2. taxon between the section and species. 2. a sample available for study. 4. any major division.

**series mounters:** in reference to primate species in which the male must mount the female several times over about a half-hour in order to perform a successful copulation.

**serine** (Ser): an **amino acid**; one of the twenty building blocks of **proteins.**

**serine protease:** any of a number of homologous enzymes that have the same activity mechanism and that include serine in their active sites. Examples are enzymes for blood coagulation (thrombin), blood clot dissolution (plasmin), complement fixation (CI protease), digestion (chymotrypsin, elastase, **trypsin**), fertilization (acrosomal enzymes), and pain sensing (kallikrein).

**seroimmunity:** see **passive immunity.**

‡ **serology:** study of the properties and actions of blood **serum**; the study of **antigen–antibody** reactions *in vitro.*

**seropositive:** having a blood test result with an indication of infection (e.g. **HIV**). A test may detect antibodies to an organism (**antibody** positive), or the organism itself or its proteins (**antigen** positive).

**serotonin:** monoamine neurotransmitter found in the gastrointestinal mucosa (where it causes smooth muscle contraction), in blood platelets (secretion increases capillary permeability), and in the brain. Serotonin has different inhibitory roles in several parts of the brain, and serotonin concentrations have been reported to modify mood, appetite, memory, and learning ability. Aka 5-hydroxytryptamine, 5-HT.

**serotype:** any antigenic property of a cell (such as a red blood cell) that can be identified by means of serological methods.

**serrate:** pertaining to a structure that is notched or saw-tooth-shaped; aka serrated.

**Sertoli cell:** large amorphous cell intimately associated with developing male germ cells in the **seminiferous tubule**; secretes fluid into tubule, mediates

hormonal effects on tubule, and mediates the blood–testis barrier.

**serum** (S): clear fluid of blood remaining after removal of fibrinogen and cells, and that contains specific **immunoglobulins.** Plural: sera.

**serum albumin: albumin** that represents about half of the plasma protein in adult mammals, and that is related structurally to **alpha fetoprotein.**

**SES:** socioeconomic status; an indicator, often defined by measures of occupation and education, used as a proxy for the general quality of the environment for growth and development of an individual.

**sesamoid:** round bone found in tendons; some of these bones help influence the actions of muscles, whereas others are supernumerary. See **patella.**

**settlement pattern:** distribution of a population throughout its habitat.

**settlement types:** three campsite variants proposed by L. **Binford** *et al. c.* 1966–9 for the **Middle Paleolithic** based upon analysis of **Mousterian** assemblages: **base camps,** where food was prepared and consumed; work camps, where food and raw materials were obtained; and 'overnight stops'.

**seventy-five percent rule:** arbitrary rule propounded by amateur ornithologist Admiral H. Lynes, but accepted by many earlier taxonomists, that a **subspecies** designation is warranted for any **population** in which 75% of the members can be distinguished from 100% of the other populations of that species.

**severe combined immune deficiency syndromes** (SCID): group of inherited disorders characterized by mutations to genes involved in humoral and cellular immunity; often, a lack of certain immune system cells. See **adenosine deaminase deficiency.** Cf. **X-linked severe combined immune deficiency.**

**Sewall Wright effect:** see **genetic drift.**

‡ **sex:** 1. reproduction involving contribution of heritable elements from more than one parent. 2. classification of individuals into categories based on types of gamete production (males, females). 3. biological category based upon reproductive attributes and roles in sexually reproducing species; term often replaced by **gender** under certain circumstances. Outcome is dependent upon the circumstances of, and interactions among, factors that contribute to **genetic sex, chromosomal sex, phenotypic sex,** and **psychosocial sex.** See **intersexuality.**

**sex bias:** degree to which feminine or masculine potentials are expressed at a given time during development.

‡ **sex cell:** see **gamete, ovum, sperm.**

**sex chromatin:** ball-shaped staining body, or **Barr body,** in a treated cell. Identifies the usually single inactive **X chromosome** in female mammals. See **X inactivation**.

‡ **sex chromosome:** chromosome or chromatid that contains genes that determine sex. Mammalian males normally have one X and one **Y chromosome**, whereas females have no Y but two **X chromosomes**. Human sex chromosomes were first identified in 1902. See **sex determination** and **heterogametic sex**. Cf. **heterosome**.

**sex chromosome aneuploidy:** condition that gives rise to an individual that has more or fewer chromosomes than a species' standard or clinical standard. The error involves one or more sex chromosomes, as in **XXX**, XXXX, **XXY, XYY**, X—,... etc. See **primary nondisjunction, sex chromosomes, triplo-X syndrome, Turner syndrome, Klinefelter syndrome**, and **double-Y syndrome**.

**sex chromosome mosaic:** see **mosaic**.

**sex-controlled:** See **sex-influenced trait**.

‡ **sex determination:** 1. process by which the sex of an individual is achieved; for example, the presence of a **Y chromosome** (specifically, the **SRY gene**) in an embryo causes the fetus to develop into a male. In mammals, an individual without a Y chromosome will become a female by default. See **genetic sex, chromosomal sex, phenotypic sex**, and **psychosocial sex**. 2. the use of skeletal markers, dimensions, bone density, and similar variables to estimate biological sex in a skeletal population. See **skeletal sexing**. 3. the use of genetic markers to estimate biological sex in a fluid, bone or tissue sample. See **molecular sex determination**.

**sex-determining region of the Y chromosome** (SRY): among the very few genes which have been mapped specifically to the **Y chromosome**. SRY is a testis-determining transcription factor located on the **pseudoautosomal region**. The SRY gene product occurs in male gonadal tissue at the time of sex determination; in humans this is about the sixth week of development. SRY binds to DNA, distorting its shape, and alters gene expression at the binding site. It is suspected that this starts a cascade of activity in genes located on the autosomes; these are then expressed either differently (or only) in males than in females. All Theria (marsupials and placental mammals) have the SRY gene. When transferred into normal XX female mouse genomes by means of the new genetic technology (creating 'transgenic' species), SRY DNA fragments induce testis differentiation in those females. Aka TDF, or testis-differentiating factor. See **ambiguous genitalia, pseudohermaphroditism, XX male**, and **XY female**.

**sex differentiation:** development of male or female reproductive organs.

**sex hormones:** the **estrogens** and **androgens** considered together.

**sex-influenced trait, character** or **feature:** 1. trait produced by an autosomal gene and therefore present in both sexes but expressed more frequently in one sex than the other. 2. phenotypic outcome when an allele is recessive in one sex (usually the homogametic sex) but dominant in the other (usually the heterogametic sex), as in **male pattern baldness**. Aka sex-conditioned or sex-controlled trait.

**sex-limited inheritance:** sex-linked or autosomal gene which affects a structure or function of the body that is present in only males or only females. In humans, body hair, breast development, and other **epigamic** secondary sexual characteristics are examples.

**sex-limited trait, character** or **feature:** trait produced by an autosomal gene and therefore present in both sexes but expressed only in one sex and not the other. Such features depend on the presence of certain hormones. Aka sex limitation.

**sex linkage:** state or process by which a trait is physically linked or mapped to either an **X chromosome** or a **Y chromosome** linkage group.

**sex-linked:** see **sex-linked inheritance**

**sex-linked inheritance:** mode of trait transmission following the standard segregation patterns of genes located on the **sex chromosomes**; in mammals, the X and Y chromosomes. See **X-linked pattern of inheritance** and **Y-linked pattern of inheritance**.

**sex ratio:** ratio of males : 100 females in a population. The primary sex ratio is the ratio at conception; the secondary sex ratio is the ratio at hatching or birth (about 105 : 100 in humans); the tertiary sex ratio is the ratio in a population at a given age $x$.

**sex ratio adjustment:** any method that changes the ratio of males to females in a population; adjustments may be due to hormone concentrations, immunological effects, infanticide, asymmetrical weaning, asymmetrical benign neglect, and sex roles that asymmetrically increase or decrease in mortality.

**sex reversal:** apparent change to the opposite sex, as in certain pseudohermaphroditic individuals.

**sex trait, character** or **feature:** any feature exhibiting **sexual dimorphism**.

**sexing, skeletal:** see **skeletal sexing**.

**sexism:** any statement or position, implicit or explicit, that males are fundamentally superior to females (or vice versa); in many theoretical statements, sexism is implicit rather than overtly articulated.

**sexology:** study of sex and the evolution of sexual behavior.

**sexual-and-reproduction strategy model** (SRSM): model of human origins based upon the trend toward prolonged life span in the primate evolutionary record and its implications for primate physiology, population dynamics, and behavior.

**sexual asymmetry:** any situation in nature in which the values for a dimorphic character are unequal, such as the number of males and females in a population, the fertility or mortality rates for males and females, the amount of parental investment, reproductive success, etc. In most diploid species, including humans, asymmetry is more common than **sexual symmetry**.

**sexual characteristics** or **features:** see **primary sexual characteristics** and **secondary sexual characteristics**.

**sexual dichromatism:** form of **sexual dimorphism** in which males and females of a species differ in **pelage** colors, as in some *Eulemur* and *Alouatta* species. The pelage of the heterochromatic sex may fluoresce dramatically as the breeding season approaches; Aka dichromism.

‡ **sexual dimorphism:** existence of two different forms (as of color or size) between **male** and **female** of a sexually reproducing **species**, especially in the same **population**. Among primates, **arboreal** species tend to display minimal physical sexual dimorphism, whereas **terrestrial** species are often highly dimorphic. Cf. **sexual monomorphism**.

**sexual division of labor:** division of tasks based on sex; for example, in human hunter–gatherer societies males contribute game to the diet, whereas females contribute vegetable matter.

**sexual inheritance:** inheritance of traits by one organism from another (e.g. a child from a parent) by means of the **haploid** male and female **gametes** that have been produced by **meiosis** at fertilization. See **cytoplasmic inheritance, maternal inheritance, mitochondrial inheritance, paternal inheritance, sex-limited inheritance, sex-linked inheritance, X-linked pattern of inheritance, Y-linked pattern of inheritance**. Cf. **criss-cross inheritance, genomic imprinting,** and **pseudoautosomal inheritance**.

**sexual isolation:** condition where mutual attraction between the sexes of different species is weak or absent; a premating or **prezygotic mechanism**.

**sexual maturity:** see **onset of sexual maturity**.

**sexual mimicry:** physical structure on one sex that resembles the genitalia of the other; for example, in female squirrel monkeys, howlers, and muriquis, an enlarged **clitoris** resembles the male penis.

**sexual monomorphism:** condition in which the two sexes are morphologically similar (e.g., same body size, form, and **pelage** color), making it difficult to tell which sex a particular animal is unless the genitalia can be observed. This condition is present in gibbons and some other primates. Cf. **sexual dimorphism**.

**sexual reproduction:** production of offspring by the regular alteration of **gamete** formation, usually **haploid**, and the fusion of recombined gametes into a **zygote**, usually **diploid**. Cf. **asexual reproduction** and **haplodiploid hypothesis**.

‡ **sexual selection:** differential ability of individuals of variable **genotypes** to acquire mates; also, the process by which characters evolve in one sex only, to facilitate reproductive success as the result of competition among members of that sex for access to mating opportunities with the opposite sex, and the subsequent choices by members of that opposite sex among the competitors. A **mechanism of evolution** suggested by Charles **Darwin** in 1871. See **assortative mating, intrasexual selection, epigamic selection,** and **female mate choice**.

**sexual skin:** skin in the anal and genital regions of females in some cercopithecine species when they are ovulating. Sexual skin often turns red when it swells, advertising the female's **estrus** condition to males in the area. In some cases, such as in *Theropithecus*, the sexual skin is on the chest of the female. Aka sexual swelling.

**sexual symmetry:** any situation in nature in which the values for a dimorphic character are equal, such as the number of males and females in a population, the fertility or mortality rates for males and females, the amount of parental investment, etc. In most diploid species, symmetry is not the most common case; see **sexual asymmetry**.

**sexually receptive:** describes a female who is amenable to mating; in nonhuman primates this corresponds to the period of **estrus**.

**sexy son hypothesis:** argument from the sociobiology literature that a female who is secondary in a polygynous relationship benefits if her sons inherit their father's propensity for **polygyny** in that they produce more grandchildren (increasing their mother's alleles) than if they were **monogamous**.

**s-g., subgen.:** see **subgenus**.

**SH site:** see **Sima de los Huesos**.

**shadow child:** child of parents from different, culturally defined ethnic groups or races, especially a child of a European father and slave mother during the US colonial period.

**shaft:** 1. middle portion of a pole. 2. a vertical passage or excavation.

**shaft straightener:** artifact manufactured from a coarse stone (often volcanic), with a groove used as a rasp to finish spears and arrow shafts.

**Shanidar Cave:** archaeological site excavated 1953–60, located above the Greater Zab River (a tributary of the Tigris) in the Zagros Mountains, Iraq, dated to 51–27 kya ($^{14}$C), and that contains associated **Mousterian** artifacts. Hominid remains (see p. 484) include four individuals crushed by rockfalls, and five intentional burials, of which two are infants, all attributed to

*Homo neanderthalensis* (a few researchers have questioned this assignment). Some skulls exhibit **cranial deformation**, possibly due to head binding. One skeleton has a possible intentional amputation. The popular 'flower burial' **hypothesis** has also been questioned. There are in addition 28 modern human burials in the 'upper' cave at Shanidar, some possibly associated with the **Baradostian** industry. Aka Baradost Mountain. Cf. **Zuttiyeh**, **Amud**, and **Tabūn**.

---

**Some of the Neandertal material from Shanidar**

Shanidar 1: field number for a male skeleton recovered from **Shanidar Cave**. This specimen is of interest because of the evidence of extreme trauma experienced by this individual with a cranial capacity of 1600 cm$^3$. Before his death at age 35–40, he had experienced a blow to the left side of his head and was probably blind in his left eye, another blow to the right side of the body that left him with an atrophied shoulder blade, collar bone and withered right arm probably amputated later, and he has still more **pathology** in his right knee and left leg. The extent of his injuries suggests that he may have been cared for by others.

Shanidar 4: one of five intentional burials found at **Shanidar Cave**; burial 4 apparently contained pollen and other indications that the individual had been covered with flowers at the time of burial, although some now dispute this interpretation. Archaeologist Ralph Solecki's view of this burial is found in *Shanidar, the First Flower People* (1971).

---

**Shapiro, Harry Lionel** (1902–90): US physical anthropologist; educated at Harvard (PhD, 1926) under Kluckhohn and E. A. **Hooton**. Worked at the Bishop Museum (Hawaii) and American Museum of Natural History. Chair at Columbia, president of the AAA, Eugenics Society, Ethnological Society. Specialist in human biology and racial variation of Pacific island populations, especially **gene flow** as regards the descendants of the H.M.S. *Bounty* mutineers on Pitcairn and Norfolk Islands. Author of *The Heritage of the Bounty* (1936) and *Migration and Environment* (1939); the latter of these volumes offered support for the Boasian thesis that even hereditary characters such as the **cephalic index**, were unstable. He was also one of five prominent physical anthropologists asked to participate in the identification of American casualties after World War II. Late in his career, Shapiro was involved in attempts to recover the **Zhoukoudian** material lost during the Sino-Japanese War; these latter events were recounted in his book *Peking Man* (1974).

‡ **shared derived trait, character** or **feature:** referring to any character shared in common by two individuals or groups and considered useful for making evolutionary interpretations; a **synapomorphy**. See **cladistics**.

**shared DNA:** common phrase that refers to the percentage of DNA shared between two organisms. All humans share 99.9% of their DNA; a comparison of human and chimpanzee **DNA sequences** indicates that these share 98.4% of their DNA sequences.

**shared environments:** experiences that family members have in common that contribute to similarities in behavior.

**Sheldon, William Herbert** (1898–1977): US psychometrist, somatologist; advocate of **constitutional typology**, aka biotypology. Author of *Varieties of Delinquent Youth* (1949).

**shell:** bivalve exploited as a food resource whose hard exoskeleton is also used as raw material for the manufacture of scrapers, beads, and so forth.

**shell bed:** geological stratum that is rich in fossil fragments; cf. **bone bed** and **midden**.

**shell midden: Upper Paleolithic** mound consisting primarily of ashes and snail shells, indicating snails as an important food source to the former occupants. Aka escargoterie.

**shelter:** protection of refuge afforded by a person, place or thing; in anthropology, the term usually applies to natural or constructed structures that provide relief from weathering elements in the environment, e.g., **rockshelter**.

**Sherman paradox:** phenomenon in which the **fragile X syndrome** is transmitted via nonmanifesting male carriers to their daughters, who have affected offspring. Due to **premutation**.

**shifting balance theory (of evolution):** metaphorical proposal that certain combinations of **alleles** at different loci produce positive **fitness** effects in an organism, and that these same alleles in other - combinations may in some cases lower another organism's fitness. Suggested by Sewall **Wright** in conjunction with his **adaptive landscape** metaphor. Cf. **Fisher's fundamental theorem of natural selection**.

**shifting cultivation:** see **swidden agriculture**.

**shivering thermogenesis:** increase in the rate of heat production during cold exposure due to increased contractile activity of skeletal muscles not involving voluntary movements and external work. See **hypothermia.**

**Shiyu:** archaeological site located near Shiyu, Shuoxian county, Shanxi province, China, dated to 28 kya, and that contains hominid remains that include an occipital bone attributed to *Homo sapiens* (**AMH**). Aka Shuoxian.

*Shizarodon dhofarensis* **Gheerbrandt, Thomas, Sen, and Al-Sulaimani, 1993:** adapoid **prosimian** from the early Oligocene of Arabia and belonging to the notharctid subfamily **Cercamoniinae; monotypic;** known only from dentition. Estimated body mass around 200 g. See Appendix 1 for taxonomy.

**Shiziyan Hill:** Aka Shizi Hill; see **Maba.**

**SHK:** Sam Howard's **Korongo** at Olduvai Gorge.

**short bones:** one of the four types of bone as classified by their shape; short bones are characterized by thin **compact bone** covered by **periosteum** with **endosteum**-covered **cancellous bone** inside; these bones are roughly cube-shaped. Examples are some of the bones of the wrists and ankles. Short bones undergo **endochondral ossification.** Cf. **long bones, flat bones,** and **irregular bones.**

**short chronology model:** model for the human occupation of Europe proposed by Dutch prehistorians W. Roebroeks and T. van Kolfschoten in 1994, which posits that hominids did nor inhabit Europe prior to 500 kya. This discovery of human species at **Gran Dolina** and **Ceprano** that date to older than 500 kya, however, falsified this model and resulted in an alternative form called the **two-phase model.**

**short interspersed nucleotide element** (SINE): one of the nonviral type **retroposons** found dispersed throughout eukaryotic genomes, such as the Alu-like elements. Cf. **long interspersed nucleotide element.**

**short tandem repeats** (STRs): short, repeated sequences of 2–5 base pairs; when expanded, STRs can cause diseases called **expanding triplet repeat** disorders. STRs are also individually specific, and can be used to obtain **DNA fingerprints** of individuals for forensic applications. Aka microsatellites. Cf. **scattered repeat sequences** and **tandem repeat sequences.**

**short-term memory:** see **memory.**

*Shoshonius* **Granger, 1910:** genus of tarsiiform primate from the early and middle Eocene of North America belonging to the omomyid subfamily **Anaptomorphinae;** two species; one of the best known omomyids represented by several skulls and **postcrania.** *Shoshonius* shows a number of affinities with *Tarsius*, including large orbits and morphology of the **auditory bulla;** it is purported to also have **anthropoid** features and argued as a candidate for anthropoid origins. Estimated body mass around 160 g. Dental formula: 2.1.3.3/2.1.3.3. See Appendix 1 for taxonomy.

**shotgun:** referring to cloning experiments where an entire genome is snipped into fragments by using multiple **restriction enzymes** before cloning.

**shotgun approach:** see **contig map.**

**shoulder:** region of junction between the forelimb (or upper arm) and the trunk of the body.

**shoulder blade:** vernacular for **scapula.**

**shoulder breadth:** when a subject is standing normally, the distance between the acromial points.

**shoulder circumference: anthropometric** measurement; distance around the upper **torso** at shoulder level. The subject is standing erect with shoulders back; a tape measure is placed on one of the **deltoid muscles** just inferior to the **acromion process** and passed around the body at the same level. The measurement is taken after a normal expiration. Shoulder circumference reflects muscular development and, consequently, is important in studies of lean body mass, strength training, and **human engineering.**

**shoulder–elbow length: anthropometric** measurement; distance between the superior/lateral surface of the **acromion process** of the scapula and the posterior surface of the **olecranon process** of the ulna as measured with an **anthropometer;** the subject is standing erect with the forearm flexed, thereby placing the olecranon process and the hands in the horizontal plane. Used in **human engineering** and biomechanical analyses of range of motion.

**shouldered projectile point:** Upper Paleolithic **artifact** dated roughly 23–21 kya, found in Kostenki, Spadzista Street (Cracow), and at **Willendorf.**

‡ **shovel-shaped incisor: incisor** whose lingual surface is characterized by a scoop reminiscent of a coal shovel. This scoop is formed by lingual extensions of the enamel from the mesial and distal sides of the tooth, or inrolling of the lateral borders. This tooth form is characteristic of certain **Mongoloid** populations first described in the literature by A. **Hrdlicka** in 1907. There is also a variant in which, additionally, a labial extension of enamel forms a scoop on the labial surface of the incisor. Cf. **barrel-shaped incisor.**

**Shungura Formation:** Plio-Pleistocene sedimentary unit found in the Lower **Omo Valley** of East Africa; 13 dated tuffs (basal, then lettered A, the oldest, through L) with intercalated sediments comprising the various members, which span 3.3 mya – 800 kya. The **Omo** localities and most of the **Omo hominids** come from the Shungura formation. The 1.88 mya marker bed known as Tuff H2 may be the same as the **KBS tuff** at Koobi Fora.

**siamang:** vernacular for *Hylobates syndactylus.*

‡ **Siamese twins:** see **conjoined twins.**

‡ **sib:** 1. abbreviation for **sibling.** 2. in some cultures, an extended lineage group, a general term for both **clan** and **gens.**

**sib-pair method:** method of detecting autosomal linkage in which siblings are compared pairwise with respect to the concordance and discordance of two trait states. See **concordan trait.**

**sibling:** close kin, usually a full brother or sister issued from the same two biological parents. See **half-sibling, cousin,** etc.

**sibling cell:** one of two cells that result from a single cell following **cell division.**

**sibling competition:** struggle for dominance between littermates or other brothers and sisters.

**sibling species:** pairs of closely related, usually sympatric but reproductively isolated species that are closely related and morphologically indistinguishable. Aka twin species, espèces jumelles.

**sibship:** family of brothers and sisters. See **sibling** and **half-sibling.**

‡ **sickle cell allele:** one of the many **alleles** of the hemoglobin locus (HbS); if two such alleles are present in one individual, that **homozygous** individual has **sickle cell disease.**

‡ **sickle cell anemia:** anemia due to **sickle cell disease.**

‡ **sickle cell disease** (SCD): heritable autosomal condition caused by homozygosity for the mutant hemoglobin S allele (HbS). SCD is found in populations where malaria is endemic, and is characterized by anemia caused by a culling of red blood cells (RBC) possessing an altered morphology due to defective hemoglobin in the RBC wall that crystallizes under conditions of dehydration or low oxygen tension, deforming them into a characteristic sickle shape; the deformed corpuscles block capillary blood flow (thrombosis). Symptoms of a sickling crisis include external manifestations of thromboses and ulceration of limb tissues (internal lesions also occur), bone and joint pain, infections and anemia. A substitutional mutation of the glutamic acid for the normal valine amino acid at position six in the beta chain of the more common form (HbS) of the adult **hemoglobin** molecule is the cause of clinical problems. The marrow and spleen are stressed to produce more RBCs; too few RBCs causes anemia and too few white blood cells (WBCs) impairs immunity. Sickle cell disease usually limits life to 10 years or less in countries where incidence is high. SCD-affected individuals are homozygous (SS), with an estimated direct fitness lowered to 10% or less. Carriers of the allele (AS) enjoy the maximum relative fitness (100%) due to heterozygote advantage, and are said to carry the **sickle cell trait.** Originally treated as a recessive genetic condition, since heterozygotes can now be identified electrophoretically, SCD is treated as a **codominant.** Although the cause of SCD is known, prophylaxis had been limited to transfusions until recently. The stimulation of fetal hemoglobin synthesis by administration of **hydroxyurea** has been successful. Worldwide, the HbS allele is found in Africa, South America, in the Australasian and Indian subcontinents, in the Mediterranean region, and in the Caribbean. See **hemoglobin alleles.** Aka Dresbach's anemia, Herrick's anemia, sicklemia, and sickle cell anemia, SCA.

‡ **sickle cell trait:** relatively minor blood disorder caused by the possession of the **hemoglobin S** allele, a mutant form of a critical metabolic protein possessed by some individuals in one copy or dose; a heterozygote. The trait enhances the **fitness** in heterozygous **carriers** of the trait (AS) in an environment in which **malaria** is **endemic,** but reduces the fitness of **homozygotes** (SS), who have **sickle cell disease.** In carriers, 20%–40% of total Hb is HbS, but carriers should avoid hypoxia and under certain conditions can experience a sickling crisis. See **genotype.**

**sicklemia index:** measure of the extent of sickled erythrocytes in the blood.

**sickness:** condition or episode characterized by any marked change from a normal healthy state; aka illness.

**side-chain theory:** first version of many subsequent **selective theories of antibody diversity,** now abandoned as originally proposed by German bacteriologist Paul Ehlich (1854–1915); specifically, that immunocytes develop groups of surface chemical receptors that are released upon interaction with an antigen, and that their release stimulates the production of more side-chain groups.

**Sidi Abderrahman:** archaeological site found in 1954 near Casablanca, Morocco, undated, containing artifacts called (Acheulean?) 'pebble tools' (galet aménagé) and hominid remains including mandibular fragments attributed to *Homo erectus,* found by Pierre Biberson. Cf. **Rabat** and **Salé.** Aka Littorina Cave, Cuvette de Sidi Abderrahman.

**Sidi Hakoma Member:** Member of the **Hadar Formation;** the hominid fossil-bearing sediments above and below the dated basalt (3.3 mya) are estimated to range from 3.6 mya (40 m below) to 2.6 mya (40 m above the basalt).

**Sidrón:** archaeological site found in 1994 located in Asturia, Piloña, northern Spain, as yet undated, and that contains lithic fragments assigned to the **Mousterian,** and hominid remains belonging to at least five individuals ranging in age from infants to adults, all attributed to *Homo neanderthalensis.* In 2000-01, more hominid remains and associated fauna were recovered from the site.

**SIDS:** sudden infant death syndrome, or unexpected death of an apparently healthy infant. Thought to be due to either immaturity of the respiratory system, sleeping position, falling into deep sleep (sleep apnea), or abuse by parents.

**sieve model:** simplest dynamic model in **population genetics:** chance **mutation** followed by **selection** at a single locus with two alleles. Considered incomplete and simplistic after 1930 by many, yet the model persisted in many countries through the mid-twentieth century.

**sifaka:** vernacular for species belonging to the genus *Propithecus.*

**sigma:** 1. the eighteenth letter of the Greek alphabet, ($\Sigma$, $\sigma$). 2. in statistics, letter that stands for the **standard deviation** ($\sigma$) or the process of summation ($\Sigma$).

**sigmoid:** pertaining to a shape like the (Greek) letter sigma ($\sigma$) or the letter S; e.g., the sigmoid notch of the mandible. Less frequently, shaped like the letter C.

**sigmoid colon:** fourth portion of the colon at the end of the **descending colon** that becomes a short S-shaped curve before becoming the **rectum**.

**sigmoid growth curve:** see **logistic growth curve**.

**sigmoid notch:** see **trochlear notch**.

**sigmoid sinus:** large bilateral venous sinus found in the **dura mater** of the inferior temporal region where it links the **transverse sinus** with the internal jugular vein and that functions to drain blood from the brain.

**sign:** 1. evidence that a particular animal is in the environment. Sign may include **scat**, physical evidence on plants (e.g., scratchings, gouges out of trees, bites out of leaves), openings to burrows, nests, etc. 2. objective evidence of a disease.

**sign language:** communication by stylized movements of the hand, or the use of smoke or other signaling devices; **pasimology**. See, for example, **American Sign Language**.

**sign stimulus:** key stimulus that elicits an immediate response from an animal even though it consists of a very small quantity of the total sensory input the animal is receiving. In a social context this stimulus may be scent, vocalization, or visual cues, and helps an animal to distinguish objects such as enemies, potential mates, and suitable nesting places. See **releaser**.

**sign vehicle:** that part of a signal that elicits a response; in many contexts the **sign stimulus**, but the sign vehicle may include longer term physiological effects.

**signal:** behavior that conveys **information** from one individual to another, regardless of whether the behavior serves other functions as well. A signal specially modified in the course of evolution to convey information is called a **display**. See **discrete signal**, **graded signal**, **honest signal**, **illegitimate signal**, **play signal**.

**signal transduction:** process of one or more steps through which receptor activation leads to a cellular response.

**significance:** in statistics, an outcome or measure of the robusticity of a test; the degree of importance of an outcome. Significance approaches zero asymptotically, i.e. large values ($>$ 0.10) are insignificant, values less than the **alpha level** (usually, $\alpha$ = 0.05 or 0.01) are significant, and values much less than the alpha level become increasingly significant. Aka statistical significance, significance level, *p* value.

**silent bared-teeth face:** primate facial expression in which the animal either stares blankly or its eyes evade an onlooker and the corners of the mouth are pulled back, exposing the teeth, in the social context of submission or a greeting.

**silent mutation:** base substitution in DNA that is transcribed into mRNA and results in a new codon, but translates into the same amino acid in a polypeptide chain due to the redundancy or degeneracy of the **genetic code**; may be either a **transition** or a **transversion**, and generally affects the third position in a codon. Aka same-sense mutation.

**silicification:** process in which silica replaces original organic material, as with silicified wood. See **permineralization**.

**silt:** loose sediment composed of fine particles of argillaceous (clayey) material less than 0.6 cm in diameter; silt is often suspended in a body of water.

**silverback:** term for an adult male gorilla (around age 16) that has a saddle of gray fur; the dominant animal in a gorilla group is a silverback male.

**silvered leaf monkey:** vernacular for *Trachypithecus cristatus.*

**silvery gibbon:** vernacular for *Hylobates moloch.*

**silvery marmoset:** vernacular for *Callithrix argentata.*

**Sima de los Huesos** (SH): archaeological cave site found in 1976 in the Sierra de Atapuerca, Ibeas, Spain, and dated to 325–205 kya (U series, Matuyama chron). At least 33 **Middle Pleistocene** individuals have been found (4,000+ specimens). Variation in cranial capacities (1125-1390 cm³) has been interpreted as representing extensive **sexual dimorphism**. The population is characterized by a **mosaic** of **erectine** and **neandertaloid** features (e.g. **Atapuerca 5**). A controversial new taxon, *Homo antecessor*, has been proposed for this material that other researchers recognize as *H. heidelbergensis*. In 1998, one unworn quartz hand-ax was found among the earliest fossils, and has been interpreted by some as evidence for burial ritual and symbolism. Aka **Atapuerca**, 'pit of bones', SH site. See **Gran Dolina**.

**Simakobu langur:** vernacular for *Simias concolor.*

**Simiae:** **hyporder** that consists of the catarrhine anthropoids.

**simian:** 1. (n.) an **ape** or **monkey**. 2. an older label for a superfamily within the Catarrhini containing monkeys with ape-like characteristics; Simia. 3. (adj.)

referring to apes or monkeys; any monkey- or ape-like condition. Cf. **prosimian**.

**simian crease:** fold in the hand extending completely across the palm.

**simian immunodeficiency virus:** see **SIV**.

**simian shelf:** see **mandibular torus**.

**simian sulcus:** furrow on the surface of the **cerebrum** forming a boundary to the visual cortex; Aka **lunate sulcus**.

*Simias* **Miller, 1903:** monotypic catarrhine genus to which the **simakobu langur** belongs. Some authorities include this species as a **subspecies of** *Nasalis larvatus*. Inhabits primary forests in the Mentawi Islands (near Sumatra). Arboreal, but will come to the ground to flee when threatened; diurnal; arboreal quadrupeds. Body mass ranges from 7 to 9 kg. Dental formula: 2.1.2.3; **folivorous**. Short tail. Live in **monogamous** social groups of around four individuals; not known to vocalize to any extent. Natural history poorly known and considered endangered. See Appendix 2 for taxonomy and Appendix 3 for species.

**Simiidae:** older term for the family containing the great apes, now replaced by **Pongidae**.

**similarity method:** method of ascertaining twin zygosity in which twin pairs are compared for concordance with respect to a large number of genetic traits. See **concordant trait**.

**simiolemuriform:** member of the taxon Simiolemuriformes. See **lemurophile hypothesis**.

*Simiolus* **Gitau, 1995:** genus of **hominoids** from the early Miocene of East Africa belonging to the catarrhine family **Proconsulidae**; two species recognized; previously included within *Micropithecus*. Estimated body mass around 7 kg. Dental formula: 2.1.2.3; dental morphology suggestive of **folivory**. Postcrania suggest this genus had more suspensory abilities than most other Miocene apes. See Appendix 1 for taxonomy.

**Simons, Elwyn L.** (1931–): US paleontologist at Yale, then at the Duke University Primate Center. In the 1960s, on the basis of reconstructed gnathic fragments, Simons and David **Pilbeam** suggested that *Ramapithecus* was an early tool-using **hominid** from the **Oligocene**; but when a more complete specimen was finally located, the genus compared more favorably to the **Sivapithecidae**, and *Ramapithecus* was removed from the **Hominidae**. More recently, Simons has located and described a dozen new early Oligocene primate fossils from the Egyptian **Fayum**, including *Aegyptopithecus*. Simons trained many students who conducted fieldwork during the 1970s–90s. Author of *Primate Evolution* (1972).

*Simonsius* **(=** *Parapithecus***) grangeri (Simons, 1972):** catarrhine from the early Oligocene of North Africa belonging to the **anthropoid** family **Parapithecidae; monotypic;** known from jaws and isolated teeth; relationship to later primates uncertain; synonym for *Parapithecus* grangeri, but separated from *Parapithecus* based on cladistic analysis, which is not accepted by most workers. Dental formula uncertain, but lower dentition may be 0.1.3.3; the canines are long and tusklike, the molars **bilophodont**. Diet uncertain, but both **folivory** and **granivory** have been suggested. Estimated body mass around 3 kg. See Appendix 1 for taxonomy.

*Simopithecus* **Andrews, 1916:** subgenus of fossil *Theropithecus* that consists of three species from Plio-Pleistocene Africa.

*Simopithecus jonathani* **Leakey and Whitworth, 1958:** synonym for the fossil gelada *Theropithecus oswaldi*.

**simotic index:** an index of facial flatness used primarily by Russian anthropologists: simotic subtense multiplied by 100 and divided by simotic chord. The simotic **subtense** is the point on the nasal suture that is between and in front of the nasal bones. The simotic chord is the minimum horizontal breadth of the two nasal bones. This index reflects the arch of the nasal bones at their root. See **frontal index, premaxillary index, rhinial index**.

**simple sib method:** technique for correcting the normal-to-affected ratio in pooled family data in which only sibs of the **propositi**, and not the **propositi** themselves, are included in the sample. See **ascertainment**.

**simplex uterus:** form of the uterus in which the two uterine horns have fused for much of their length creating a large single uterine body. The two **uterine tubes** are at the superior lateral aspect of the uterine body. This is the condition found in **anthropoids**. Aka unicornuate uterus, uterus simplex. Cf. **bicornuate uterus**.

**simpona:** vernacular for species belonging to the genus *Propithecus*.

**Simpson, George Gaylord** (1902–84): US paleontologist, mammalogist; known for the application of **population genetics** to analyze the consequences of **migrations** of **mammals** between continents, and like **Mayr** popularized the methodology of **neo-Darwinism**, in Simpson's case to early mammalian evolution. Worked at the American Museum of Natural History, Columbia, Harvard, and Arizona, where he described many new species. Author of *Tempo and Mode in Evolution* (1944) and *The Major Features of Evolution* (1953).

*Simpsonlemur citatus*: archaic mammal from the early Eocene of North America belonging to the family **Paromomyidae; monotypic.** Body mass estimated at around 170 g. See Appendix 1 for taxonomy.

**simulacrum:** representation; image.

**simulated altitude:** artificial environment in which the oxygen pressure has been reduced by lowering the barometric pressure in a chamber; less often, oxygen pressure is reduced by decreasing the oxygen concentration of a gas mixture at atmospheric pressure.

**simulation:** 1. an imitation or mimic. 2. malingering. 3. a model intended to mirror the behavior of a system.

‡ *Sinanthropus* **Black, 1927:** generic **nomen** applied to **hominid** fossils found at Zhoukoudian, China, in the 1920s, e.g. *Sinanthropus pekinensis*. Now referred to *Homo erectus*.

*Sinanthropus pekinensis* **Black, 1927:** see *Homo erectus pekinensis*.

**sinciput:** 1. region of the anterior cranium from the forehead to the crown. 2. **bregma.**

**SINE:** see **short interspersed nucleotide element.**

**sinew:** thread made from uncured animal tendon.

**Singa:** archaeological site found in 1924 located on the banks of the Blue Nile in the Singa district, Sudan, Africa, dated to $133 \pm 2$ kya (**ESR**), and that contains Middle Paleolithic artifacts and hominid remains including a late **archaic** *Homo* sp. calvaria and associated dental materials encased in calcrete limestone. The skull shows abnormal growth in the parietal and ear regions.

**single active X principle:** inactivation, soon after fertilization, of one and/or the other **X chromosome** in each cell of a female **zygote.** See **X inactivation.**

**single crystal laser fusion** (SCLF): advanced method of **potassium–argon dating** in which a laser is used to melt crystals to release argon gas; it is more accurate, and requires smaller samples, than older techniques.

**single-gene hypothesis:** any proposal that a specific structure, function, or behavior in an organism is the result of the action of DNA at one genetic locus; verification of many such hypotheses exists, whereas other putative single-gene effects have reverted to hypotheses invoking either **polygenic inheritance** or **multifactorial inheritance,** or have been shown not to have any genetic basis whatsoever.

**single-gene trait, character or feature:** any trait influenced by the expression of one gene, e.g. **phenylketonuria.**

**single-line evolution:** see **anagenesis.**

**single nucleotide polymorphism:** see **SNP.**

**single origin hypothesis:** see the **out of Africa II** model for **human origins,** aka the **monophyletic hypothesis of racial orgins,** the **mitochondrial 'Eve'** model, and the 'Noah's Ark' model.

**single species hypothesis:** theory that there has never been more than one **Plio-Pleistocene** hominid lineage at any given time because all **hominids** are characterized by **culture** and thus occupy the same

ecological niche; popularized in the 1960s by **Brace** and **Wolpoff** and at that time held to be true by many paleontologists; later fossil discoveries proved the untenability of this idea.

**single-stranded conformational polymorphism** (SSCP): method for identification of **DNA sequence** harboring a gene mutation, based on altered mobility of single-stranded sequences in **polyacrylamide gel electrophoresis** due to sequence-specific conformational change.

**sinistrality:** state of having the left side or its parts or members different from and usually more efficient than those of the right side, e.g. using and favoring the left hand, as opposed to **dextrality.** Adjective: sinistral.

*Sinoadapis carnosus* **Wu and Pan, 1985:** adapoid prosimian from the late Miocene of China belonging to the family **Sivaladapinae; monotypic;** known only from dentition. See Appendix 1 for taxonomy.

**Sinodont:** C. Turner's term for a suite of dental characteristics found in all Native Americans and northern Asians: incisor shoveling and double-shoveling, single-rooted upper first premolars, and three-rooted lower first molars.

**sinognathism:** S-shaped facial profile as the result of projecting teeth, a concave face, and a short and round brain case, as in an orangutan.

**sinus, sinuses:** cavity or cavities in bone or other tissue; in living bone they are lined with epithelium. Examples of sinuses in bone include: **ethmoidal sinus, frontal sinus, maxillary sinus, paranasal sinus,** and **sphenoidal sinus.** Examples of sinuses in the brain include: **dural venous sinus, marginal sinus, occipital venous sinus, sagittal sinus, sigmoid sinus, straight sinus,** and **transverse sinus.** Examples of sinuses in other tissues include: **carotid sinus.** See **pneumatization.**

**Šipka Cave:** archaeological site found in 1880 near Stramberk, Moravia, Czechoslovakia, dated to 32–28 kya, and that contains **Mousterian** artifacts and hominid remains found in the 'badger hole' side passage, including a partial juvenile mandible attributed to *Homo neanderthalensis*.

**sister:** female in a sibship; a kinship term that identifies a genealogical or fictive degree of relationship in a **nuclear family** or **extended family.** See **father, mother, brother, uncle, aunt, cousin.**

**sister chromatid cohesion protein:** molecule that holds sister chromatids together during the metaphase and anaphase stages of meiosis I. The protein is inactivated during meiosis II so that sister chromatids can separate normally at anaphase. Mutations in this protein can result in premature separation of sister chromatids and result in malsegregation aneuploidy. A candidate gene maps to HSA

14q11.2 (8rech or Rec8p), a phosphoprotein of the rad21p family. Aka velcro protein.

**sister chromatid exchange** (SCE): recombination between the identical **chromatids** comprising a chromosome, i.e. the two chromatids resulting from **DNA replication** and attached at the **centromere**. In theory, crossing over between sister chromatids is of no consequence, but see **unequal crossing over**.

‡ **sister chromatids: chromosome**; identical chromatids attached by a **centromere** after S-phase **DNA replication**. Attached sister chromatids exist only during the early phases of **cell division**, the object of which is the normal **disjunction** and **segregation** of the condensed **chromatids** into the daughter cells. Although genetically identical, one chromatid is not exactly a 'copy' of its sister, owing to **semiconservative replication** of **DNA**.

**sister group (taxon):** either of two groups or taxa that result from a single split of a clade, i.e. they (and only they) share the same **common ancestor**. Aka sister taxa, sister species.

‡ **site:** location or place, e.g. a specific fossil site. 2. **locus**. 3. location of a **mutation** in DNA.

**site-directed mutagenesis:** technique that alters the sequence of a structural gene by insertion of a specific **point mutation**.

**site 50:** see **FxJj 50**.

**site catchment analysis:** evaluation of resources within the exploitable range of a site.

**sitting height: anthropometric** measurement of an individual that is sitting on a table with legs dangling and the head held in the **Frankfort horizontal**. The individual is measured with an **anthropometer** from the base of the sacrum to the **vertex** of the head. A very important measurement in **human engineering**.

**site-name principle:** practice of designating archaeological materials by the site in which they were found, e.g. **Aurignacian, Mousterian, Perigordian**, etc.

**site transformation process:** ways in which n-transforms (*n*atural processes such as wind and rain) and c-transforms (*c*ultural formation processes) affect archaeological remains. Excavation of a site is itself a c-transform process.

**sitting pads:** see **ischial callosities**.

**sitting vertex height:** on a sitting subject, the distance from the sitting surface to the highest point of the head.

**situation analysis:** analysis of behavior in the context under which it occurs with the intent of deducing its evolutionary origins. Situation analysis is used in conjunction with both **form analysis** and **sequence analysis**.

**situs inversus viscerum:** failure to establish normal left–right asymmetry during embryonic development results in heterotaxy (reversed asymmetry); the usual case is a complete mirror image of normal internal visceral orientation, with the heart in the right lung cavity, etc. Most cases are familial and segregate as an autosomal recessive, although X-linked forms have been reported. There is suspicion of a **paternal age effect**.

**SI unit:** Systéme international d'Unites (International System of Units), a coherent system accepted in nearly all countries for technical work. Base units include the meter (metre), kilogram, second, ampere, kelvin, mole, and candela.

**SIV:** simian immunodeficiency virus, a DNA virus hosted by the African green monkey, and that has a sequence homology with **HIV**, suggesting a common ancestry (Herpesviridae; Herpes B; herpesvirus simiae). SIV can affect humans that handle primates.

**Sivaladapidae:** family of adapoids known from the late Miocene of South Asia and China; three genera and four species; latest adapoids. Body mass ranged from 2 to 4.5 kg. Dental formula: 2.1.3.3/2.1.3.3; shearing crests on cheek teeth suggestive of **folivory**. See Appendix 1 for taxonomy.

**Sivaladapinae:** subfamily of adapoids previously included in the family **Adapidae**. Following revision of the adapids, a separate family was erected for this group of prosimians. See **Sivaladapidae**.

*Sivaladapis* **Gingerich and Sahni, 1979:** adapoid prosimian from the late Miocene of South Asia belonging to the family **Sivaladapidae**; two species. Body mass estimated for the two species between 2.5 and 4.5 kg. Dental formula: 2.1.3.3/2.1.3.3; shearing crests on cheek teeth suggestive of **folivory**. See Appendix 1 for taxonomy.

**Sivapithecidae:** little-recognized family of **hominoids** of the middle and late Miocene, usually included within either the **Pongidae** or the **Hominidae** by most authors.

‡ *Sivapithecus* **Pilgrim, 1910:** genus of **hominoids** from the late Miocene of Asia, belonging to the family **Pongidae** (depending on authority); currently, three species generally recognized. Major revisions in the 1960s reduced the number of previously recognized species; in the 1980s the genus *Ramapithecus* was referred to *Sivapithecus* as the female representative of the genus; this makes this genus **sexually dimorphic** in body size (although not in canine size). Known mainly from cranial elements and only a few postcrania. Estimated body mass from 40 to 100 kg. Dental formula: 2.1.2.3; molars characterized by a thick cap of enamel; large canines. The mandibles are robust and deep. It appears the diet consisted of hard and gritty morsels. Postcrania that are known suggest quadrupedalism as the form of locomotion. *Sivapithecus* bears a very strong cranial resemblance to the living orangutan and most paleoprimatologists

view this genus as giving rise to *Pongo*. This genus appears to be associated with open forest areas. See Appendix 1 for taxonomy.

**Siwalik group:** thick sequence of fossil-bearing sediments in Pakistan, deposited in the Potwar Plateau at the base of the still-rising Himalayan mountains.

**Siwalik Hills:** paleontological region found in 1910 in Pakistan, dated to 15–10 mya (middle/late **Miocene**), and that contains **hominoid** remains, including those of *Ramapithecus*, *Sivapithecus*, and *Gigantopithecus*.

**size bias:** acknowledgement that small and large organisms can be differentially preserved, with large animals overrepresented and smaller animals underrepresented in the fossil record; in human paleontology, females and infants tend to be underrepresented in burials.

**size rule:** see **Bergmann's rule**.

**SK:** see **Swartkrans**.

**skeletal:** Pertaining to the **skeleton**.

**skeletal age:** measure of biological maturation based on stages of formation of the bones, as distinguished from **chronological age**. Aka bone age. See **Tanner stage**.

**skeletal biology:** field of study that focuses on the structure and function of the bones as well as other aspects of the skeleton such as **taphonomy**; aka osteology.

**skeletal decomposition: postmortem** loss of water and collagen in bone. This changes the characteristics of bones and they become harder, stiffer and, consequently, more brittle than living bone. Given sufficient time **permineralization** will occur, replacing organic materials, with inorganic material, leading to **fossilization**.

**skeletal muscle:** grossly, a collection of striated muscle fibers, a type of contractile tissue found in muscle organs and attached to the bony framework of the body. Histologically, a diagnostic characteristic of skeletal muscle is the presence of transverse **striations** and multinucleated fibers (cells) together with connective tissues, blood vessels, and nerves. Skeletal muscle is **voluntary** and is involved with body movement as well as such actions as facial expressions, mastication, breathing, etc. See **abductor, adductor, extensor, fixator, flexor, intrinsic, sphincter,** and **synergist**. Cf. **cardiac muscle, smooth muscle**.

**skeletal pathology:** anomaly or malformation of skeletal elements, such as arthritis or osteoporosis.

**skeletal position:** see **burial**.

‡ **skeletal sexing:** 1. procedure by which skeletal remains can be identified as to sex. The best source for identification is the adult **pelvis** because it is highly **sexually dimorphic**. Differences between males and female pelves include the shape of the **obturator** foramen, angle of the **pubic arch**, shape of the **pelvic inlet,** width of the **greater pelvis, acetabulum,** and several other features. The skull can also be used for sexing in that males tend to have more heavily built (i.e. more robust) skulls , but this is only about 80% accurate. 2. sexing of skeletal material can also be attempted by **molecular sex determination**, utilizing an assay for the **amelogenin** gene.

**skeletal system:** body system that supports the body, provides framework, and is involved with movement (in concert with the muscular system). The organs of the skeletal system are the bones, ligaments, and cartilages.

**skeletal variation:** plasticity in osseous tissue resulting from behavioral stress placed upon developing skeletal and dental tissues through the influences of culture and environment.

‡ **skeleton:** structure that supports and maintains the shape of an organism. Humans, as vertebrates, possess an **endoskeleton** composed of bone and cartilage. Adjective: skeletal.

**Skhūl:** archaeological site worked 1929–34 in Mount Carmel, near Haifa, Israel (then Palestine), dated to 90 ± 25 kya (minimum dates 55–33 kya), and that contains **Levalloiso-Mousterian** artifacts. Hominid remains were originally attributed to neandertaloid *Homo sapiens* but were more recently assigned to early **AMH**. Remains of at least ten intentionally buried individuals were found. The Skhūl 5 adult male's cranial capacity has been estimated at 1450–1518 cm³, and he was buried with the jaw bone of a wild boar clasped in his hand. Aka es-Skhūl, Mugharet es-Skhūl, 'cave of the kids'. Cf. **Qafzeh**.

**skin:** outer covering of an animal's body; integument. In mammals the skin is composed of two layers, the superficial **epidermis** and the deeper **dermis**. Cf. **integumentary system**.

**skin color:** in humans, perceived **reflectance** of the **epidermis**; skin color involves the blending of three or more **chromoproteins: melanin, heme** (in **hemoglobin**), **carotene,** and other **porphyrins** such as **metmyoglobin** and laminin. Skin color is a **polymorphism** in most species, including humans, and maintained by **natural selection** chiefly in response to **ultraviolet radiation,** but **camouflage coloration** maintenance in response to predator pressure is also a factor. Although **heritability** is significant, skin color is a **multifactorial trait**.

**skinfold calipers: anthropometric** instrument that consists of two spring-loaded jaws that exert standardized pressure per unit of caliper jaw surface area. The instrument provides a dimension datum that can be read on a digital or scaled dial. See **skinfold thickness**.

**skinfold measurements:** any of several anthropometric dimensions that yield estimates of **skinfold**

thickness. These include **abdominal skinfold, biceps skinfold, forearm skinfold, medial calf skinfold, mid-axillary skinfold, pectoral skinfold, subscapular skinfold, suprailiac skinfold, suprapatellar skinfold, thigh skinfold,** and **triceps skinfold.**

**skinfold thickness:** measurement of the double folds of skin and subcutaneous adipose tissue that develop as the result of a measurer pinching a particular area of the body. **Skinfold measurements** are taken with **skinfold calipers** and the data obtained are used to estimate body fat composition, blood pressure, and lipids of an individual.

‡ **skull:** strictly applied, the bones of the **cranium, facial skeleton,** and **mandible;** however, the term skull is often loosely used for the cranium and facial skeleton alone.

**Skull II:** second in a well-known series of crania found at **Zhoukoudian.**

**skull base:** see basicranium.

**skullcap:** see calotte.

**SKX:** see Swartkrans.

‡ **slash-and-burn agriculture:** see swidden agriculture.

**sleep:** see sleeping behaviour.

**sleep center:** neuron cluster in the **brainstem** whose activity periodically opposes the awake state and induces cycling of **slow-wave sleep** and **paradoxical sleep.**

**sleep response:** behavior mediated by the **reticular activating system** seated primarily in the **reticular formation** located in the **hindbrain** and lower **brainstem,** but with portions also located in the **spinal cord, pons, limbic mid-brain,** and parts of the **thymus** and **hypothalamus.** See **sleeping behavior.**

**sleeping behavior:** periodic state of temporary unconsciousness from which an individual can be aroused, and during which sensory activity is depressed, muscles become inactivated, **basal metabolism** is lowered, and the ability to regulate body temperature is suspended. The exact purpose of the **sleep response** is unknown, but most workers believe it serves an important role in maintenance; for example, sleep stimulates secretion of **growth hormone,** important in tissue repair and **protein synthesis.** See **paradoxical sleep, sleep center,** and **slow-wave sleep.**

**sleeping platform:** structure built in trees by orangutans and chimpanzees from branches and leaves. Generally these structures are abandoned after a day, but these species sometimes occupy a sleeping platform abandoned by a **conspecific.** This is essentially the same as a sleep nest from the bird literature.

**slender loris:** vernacular for *Loris tardigradus.*

**sliding caliper:** instrument consisting of a pair of jaws (arms) that can move apart from one another at a known distance; a sliding caliper is used to measure linear distances or thickness. In anthropological studies, it is used primarily for measuring the face or mandible when the contour of the skull does not interfere.

**slippage:** imperfect DNA duplication such that there is either partial duplication or deletion, often resulting in short repeats, and thought to be the result of loops in DNA during replication.

**slope:** see **regression coefficient.**

**sloth lemur:** vernacular for the four genera belonging to the recently **extinct subfossil Malagasy prosimian** family Palaeopropithecidae.

**slow fiber:** muscle fiber whose myosin has low ATPase activity.

**slow loris:** vernacular for *Loris tardigradus.*

**slow virus:** any virus that produces symptoms of disease long after it first enters a host cell; such viruses may reproduce at a low rate during their cryptic period, and cell damage is not detectable. Many formerly 'slow viruses' are now thought to be **prion protein.**

**slow-wave sleep:** state of sleep associated with large, slow **EEG** waves and considerable postural-muscle tone but in which dreams do not occur. See **sleeping behavior.**

**small-but-healthy hypothesis:** argument that small body size, owing to slower growth rates, in Third World countries is an adaptation for nutrient deficiencies.

**small-eared greater bushbaby:** vernacular for *Galago garnettii.*

**small-for-gestational age:** describes a fetus that is below average size for its growth stage. Aka **intrauterine growth retardation.**

**small intestine:** proximal portion of the **intestine** that is between the stomach and the cecum. The small intestine receives its name from the smaller diameter (relative to the **large intestine**), although its length is greater than that of the large intestine, about 5.5 m long in the adult human. It consists of three regions, the **duodenum, jejunum,** and **ileum.** It is in the small intestine that most nutrients are absorbed.

**smallpox:** acute, highly contagious infection caused by variola, one of a group of Old World DNA poxviruses. Occurred in three forms of increasing severity: varioloid, variola minor, and variola major. Symptoms included an initial stage characterized by high fever, headache, and vomiting, and a second stage marked by the formation of disfiguring lesions; encephalitic involvement and death was a common outcome. Variola is molecularly related to other Poxviridae that cause similar diseases in domestic animals such as cows (cowpox), sheep, goats, horses and pigs. Some researchers speculate that the human form developed after domestication, and is possibly a simple mutant of the wild form. The last case of smallpox occurred in Somalia on October 26, 1977;

the virus has been preserved in laboratories, however. Aka variola.

**small RNAs:** class of short RNA molecules of 21–28 nucleotides that have inhibition and tagging roles related to routine **epigenetic** cellular housekeeping. Inhibition, aka RNA interference (RNAi), results in gene silencing, and seems to involve small interfering RNAs (siRNAs). MicroRNAs (miRNAs) seem to inhibit translation of RNA into protein. The source of small RNAs seems to be degradation of larger RNA molecules with completely different functions, facilitated by an enzyme called DICER and an enzyme complex called RISC.

**smell:** to perceive an odor or scent through the nose via the olfactory nerves; see **olfaction.**

*Smilodectes* Wortman, 1903: adapoid **prosimian** from the early and middle Eocene of North America belonging to the notharctid subfamily **Notharctinae;** three species. Appears to be descended from the earlier *Cantius*, although it is also suggested that *Copelemur* is the ancestor of this genus. Diurnal. Dental formula: 2.1.4.3/2.1.4.3; dental morphology suggests **folivory.** Unlike that of living prosimians, the mandible is fused. Body mass estimated to range from 2 to 3 kg. Well-preserved **endocasts** reveal an increased reliance on vision and a decreased dependence on smell. Locomotion appears to be leaping and quadrupedalism when the animal was on the ground. See Appendix 1 for taxonomy.

**Smith, Grafton Elliot** (1871–1937): Australian-born British comparative anatomist; Smith was a recognized authority on primate brain evolution; named the **lunate sulcus.** His preference for cranial preeminence led him to support the **Piltdown hoax.** Both Raymond **Dart** and Davidson **Black** were among his students. Smith also supported the **arboreal theory of primate evolution** as an explanation of primate origins. Author of *Human Nature* (1927) and a number of lesser books on diffusionism and embalming.

**Smith, Samuel Stanhope** (1750–1819): US minister, moral philosopher, and educator; a biblical **monogenist** who supported the adaptive arguments of **Blumenbach.**

**Smith, William ('Strata'):** (1769–1839): English engineer; remembered by some as the 'father of English geology', Smith was a surveyor of coal mines, drainage systems and canals, from which his observations concerning **stratigraphy** and **faunal assemblages** emanated. He is known for detailed stratigraphic and geological maps of England, and for using **fossils** to demonstrate the correlated ages of rock **strata.**

**smooth-ear marmoset:** vernacular for *Callithrix argentata.*

**smooth endoplasmic reticulum:** see **endoplasmic reticulum.**

**smooth muscle:** type of contractile tissue found in hollow organs such as bladders, blood vessels, and the **gastrointestinal tract,** as well as in a few other structures; histologically, a diagnostic characteristic of skeletal muscle is the lack of **striations** and fibers (cells) with a single nucleus. Smooth muscle is **involuntary** and is associated with autonomic activities involved with basic body maintenance. Cf. **cardiac muscle, skeletal muscle.**

**smorgasbord feeder:** term used by a few authors in reference to cercopithecines that forage by stuffing a variety of food into their **cheek pouches** as they travel along their **foraging range.** Cf. **banquet feeder.**

**Smuggler's Cave:** archaeological site found in Morocco a short distance from **Sidi Abderrahman,** undated, that contained hominid remains including a small mandible attributed to the **archaic *Homo sapiens*** group; others favor a straight attribution to *Homo erectus*. Aka Grotte des Contrabandiers.

**sneaking:** see **cuckoldry.**

**Snethlage's marmoset:** vernacular for *Callithrix emiliae.*

**snout:** elongated nose of some mammals; among the primates, those with the longest snouts are found among some of the prosimians (especially the lemurids) and some of the cercopithecids (especially among the baboons). Aka muzzle.

**Snow, Clyde C.:** (1928–) US physical anthropologist at the University of Oklahoma. Snow began his career with an interest in archaeology but completed a dissertation on baboon skeletal growth. He joined the Federal Aviation Administration as a forensic pathologist, and received media attention for his work identifying plane crash victims, Nazi war criminal Josef Mengele, and serial killer victims. Later in his career Snow applied his skills to human rights abuse cases in Argentina and Central America. Co-author of 'The investigation of the human remains of the 'disappeared' in Argentina', *Amer. J. Forensic Med. Pathol.* (1984), 5(4): 297.

**SNP:** single nucleotide polymorphism; any location in DNA where there is variation for a nucleotide pair within a species; pronounced 'snip'. Synonymous (sSNP) and nonsynonymous (nsSNP) nucleotide polymorphisms have been described.

**SNP map:** haplotype or portion of a chromatid that contains a **SNP.**

**snub-nosed monkeys:** term used for the Asian colobine monkeys that belong to the genera *Pygathrix* and *Rhinopithecus*. Noses of these monkeys vary from a small upturned nose (*Pygathrix*) to a nose set in a concave cavity with large nares in which the **septum** is visible.

**Soan:** chopper culture found in the Punjab region of India and dated to the second interglacial period.

**social behavior:** interaction between **conspecifics;** this includes **agonistic** encounters, parental care, division of labor, courtship, mating, etc. One of the hallmarks of the primate order is the sociality of this group of mammals.

**social carnivores:** animals that hunt in groups, e.g. wolves, lions, African dogs, hyenas, and humans. See **Carnivora.**

**social Darwinism:** proposed application of **Darwin's** mechanism of natural selection to social policy, especially in Europe and America at the end of the nineteenth century. According to this application, only the administration of social services allowed the least fit to survive, thus perpetuating their negative characters and behaviors in their children. In its extreme manifestation, it became the core of the **eugenics** movement.

**social drift:** random divergence in the behavior and the mode of organization of societies.

**social dynamics:** activity involved with the maintenance of social structure.

**social evolution:** term loosely used to refer to the sequential accumulation of information, knowledge of historical events, and wisdom by human societies. In some applications this knowledge is viewed as being culled or amplified by each human generation, depending on its current utility, and in some sense as analogous to Darwinian natural selection.

**social facilitation:** ordinary pattern of behavior that is initiated or increased in pace or frequency by the presence or actions of another animal.

**'social glue' hypothesis:** outmoded hypothesis proposed by primatologist Solly **Zuckerman** in the 1930s, in which he proposed that sexual activity was the primary cohesive force of **sociality** in **primates;** the fact that a female primate only spends about one-fifth of adulthood in estrus was used to discredit this hypothesis.

**social grooming: grooming** done for pleasure; a common behavior among primates which reinforces social relationships.

**social group:** cooperatively assembled group of individuals of the same species.

**social inheritance:** see **cultural inheritance.**

**social inhibition:** situation in which the behavior of one individual curtails the actions of other individuals; for example, **appeasement** by a subordinate inhibits aggression from an animal that might attack it.

**social intelligence hypothesis:** proposal by psychologists A. Whiten and R. W. Byrne that the primate brain, and consequently primate intelligence, evolved as adaptations to the requirement to operate in large groups where a detailed understanding of group members is a fundamental datum ('tertiary relationships'). In addition, the acquisition of complex social skills and strategies, including **tactical deception, alliance** formation, and the manipulation of other members of a group led, researchers speculate, to increased brain size and complexity in primates. Aka social brain hypothesis, Machiavellian intelligence hypothesis. See **Machiavellian intelligence** and **deceit.** Cf. **cognitive ecology.**

**social learning:** see **observational learning.**

**social network:** pattern of sustained interactions between members of a primate group.

**social organization:** structure of a society including the interactions between all members, interactions between the sexes, stability of the group, immigration–emigration patterns, land use, etc. The pattern of social organization is strongly tied to environmental and ecological conditions.

**social recognition:** ability to discriminate between individuals; this is essential for a complex **social organization,** as is found in primates.

**social strategy:** behavior employed by an individual to build relationships and increase rank in its social group.

‡ **social structure:** composition of a social group and the way it is organized, including factors of size, age structure, and the number of individuals of each sex.

**social system:** see **social organization.**

**social theory:** application of the principles of evolution to the organized behavior of organisms in groups. See **sociobiology.**

‡ **sociality:** tendency to associate in or to form social groups.

**socialization:** total modification of behavior in an individual owing to its interaction with other members of a society, including its parents. Cf. **enculturation.**

**society:** group of individuals belonging to the same species and organized in a cooperative manner. The diagnostic criterion, according to E. O. **Wilson** (1975), of a society is reciprocal communication of a cooperative nature, extending beyond mere sexual activity. See **foraging group pattern.**

**society, fission–fusion:** see **fission–fusion society.**

**Society for American Archaeology** (SAA): Founded in 1934, the SAA is an international organization dedicated to research, interpretation, and protection of the archaeological heritage of the Americas. Its 6,600 members consist of students and archaeologists who work in museums, and the academic and/or private sectors.

**society, fusion:** see **fission–fusion society.**

‡ **sociobiology:** according to E. O. **Wilson,** the scientific, systematic study of the biological basis of all forms of social behavior in all kinds of organisms, including humans, and focusing on the potential role of **natural selection** in behavior maintenance. See **second Darwinian revolution.** Cf. **Standard Social Science Model.**

**sociocline:** series of different social organizations observed among related species and interpreted to represent stages in an evolutionary trend.

**sociocultural adaptation:** nongenetic adaptation; occurs when any cultural trait (e.g. a tool or a concept) offers survival advantages in a given environment.

**sociocultural evolution:** development of a society and its culture over time.

‡ **socioecology:** study of patterns of relationships among variables in the environment, and the biological needs and social behaviors of animals.

**socioeconomic group:** set of people classified as similar based upon variables such as income level, education, livelihood, and so forth.

**socioeconomic status:** see **SES**.

**socioendocrinology:** interaction between hormones and behavior in animals that reside in small groups.

**sociogram:** full description, taking the form of a catalog, of all the social behaviors of a species, including a specification of the forms and frequencies of interactions. Cf. **catalog of behavior**, **ethogram**, and **repertoire**.

‡ **socionomic sex ratio:** see **tertiary sex ratio**.

**SOD:** see **superoxide dismutase**.

**sodium hypothesis:** controversial proposal that **hypertension** can be caused by a high salt (sodium) intake in the diet. Attributed to suggestions in 1904 by French physicians L. Amberd and E. Beaujard, the hypothesis has recently been resurrected by certain researchers who have speculated that the prevalence of hypertension in Americans of African ancestry is a function of a genetically mediated salt retention mechanism present in slave ancestors who survived the voyage from Africa to the New World. Aka salt-gene hypothesis, salt hypothesis.

‡ **soft hammer technique:** see **soft percussion**.

**soft inheritance:** inheritance during which the genetic material is not constant from generation to generation but may be modified by the effects of the environment, by use or disuse, or other factors. Cf. **hard inheritance**.

**soft palate:** posterior portion of the **palate** of the oral cavity that is a muscular extension from the palatine bones. It terminates posteriorly in the uvula. During swallowing the soft palate raises, closing the opening to the nasal cavity and preventing food from entering.

‡ **soft percussion:** later **Acheulean** tool-making technique that substituted softer materials such as wood, bone or antler for a hammerstone in order to chip smaller **flakes** from a **core**.

**soft release:** reintroduction of animals that are carefully monitored after their release and are assisted if needed. This approach has been used with released golden lion tamarins (***Leontopithecus rosalia***). Cf. **hard release**.

**soft selection:** reduced selection intensity associated with cultural buffering from environmental stress. See **relaxed selection**.

**soft tissues:** term applied loosely to those elements that are degraded early in the process of decay of an organism, and rarely preserved during fossilization except in rare cases of tissue **permineralization**, natural cryogenesis or desiccation, or intentional **mummification**. Cf. **hard tissues**.

**soft-wired:** in reference to behavior that predominantly results from experience and learning. Cf. **hard-wired**. See **program**.

**soil:** any unconsolidated materials found above **bedrock**.

**soil horizon:** product of the natural weathering of geological and archaeological surfaces.

**soil profile:** vertical section of soil through the **soil horizons**.

**solar radiation:** radiant energy emitted by the sun; after filtration by the atmosphere, the earth's surface receives solar radiation at wavelengths that range from about 290 nm to about 3000 nm. See **ultraviolet light**.

**solar radiation hypothesis:** proposal that the Great Ice Age resulted from variations in the solar radiation reaching the earth's surface, and usually linked to the **Milankovich orbital forcing hypothesis**.

**sole:** **plantar** surface of the foot; bottom of the foot.

**soliciting behavior:** female primate behavior that invites a male to copulate; in many species this includes **genital display**.

**solitary behavior:** see **noyau**.

**solitary group:** smallest primate social group, consisting of a mother and her dependent offspring; also known as **noyau**.

**Solo Man:** designation for a hominid specimen found in 1931–3 near Ngandong on the upper terrace of the Solo River. One of eleven hominid skulls and two tibia collectively called **Solo Man** and inadvertently labeled 'tiger skulls'. Recent dating (thorium--uranium) suggests that these specimens have a date less than 100 kya. These specimens have been considered as 'tropical Neandertals' or 'proto-Australian'; recent attributions place then with other Asian examples of ***Homo erectus***. See **Ngandong**.

**Solo River:** see **Ngandong**, **Trinil**, and **Java man**.

**soluble RNA** (sRNA): transfer RNA.

**solution:** 1. homogenous mixture of two or more substances, without chemical change, although one substance may be dissolved (the solute) in another (the solvent). 2. a **weathering** process involving **groundwater** that results in the reduction of **fossil** tissues during **permineralization**; the removal of organic elements and molecules and their replacement by inorganic entities is typical of this action; see **fluorine dating** and **diagenesis**. 3. the act of solving a **problem** or answering a question; or, the answer itself. 4. termination of a **disease** state.

**Solutré:** extensive archaeological site found in 1866 in southeastern France, on a bluff above the river Saône, dated to 20–17 kya, and that contains Solutrean artifacts including fine willow- and laurel-shaped spear tips. Hominid remains found in 1923 include two males and one female attributed to *Homo sapiens* (Cf. **Cro-Magnon**). Type site for the **Solutrean tool tradition**. Aka Crot-du-Charnier, La Solutré.

**Solutrean–Clovis similarity hypothesis:** proposal in the 1930s by archaeologist Frank Hibben that some of the first Native Americans came from Iberia, based on the observation that both Solutrean points (from Iberia) and Clovis points (from New Mexico) are similarly thin and skinny and have concave bases. The hypothesis diminished in popularity when radiometric dating techniques showed that the end of the Iberian **Solutrean tool tradition** at 18–15 kya antedated the first **Clovis** events at 11.5 kya by 5,000 years. Aka the 'Iberia not Siberia' hypothesis.

‡ **Solutrean tool tradition: Upper Paleolithic** stone tool **assemblage**, dated to around 21–15 kya; considered to be the most highly developed stone tool industry, and is characterized by its pressure-flaked, laurel-leaf blades. Found in southwestern France and Spain. See **Solutré**.

**soma:** body; see **somatic**.

**Somali bushbaby:** vernacular for *Galago gallarum*.

**somatic:** of or pertaining to the nonvisceral parts of the body, the body's framework and outer walls; skin, skeletal muscle, tendons, cartilage, joints.

‡ **somatic cell:** any of many body cells in an organism that are usually diploid; somatic cells do not include the germinal tissues nor their products the haploid **gametes**, or sex cells.

**somatic cell gene therapy:** see **somatic gene therapy**.

**somatic cell hybridization:** method of mapping human genes that uses hybrid cells produced by fusing together cells from two different organisms, usually human–rodent; the hybrids selected contain only one human chromosome and are thus useful for localizing probes to specific chromosomes.

**somatic embryo:** embryo that develops from a somatic cell. The phenomenon is common in plant biotechnology, but rare in mammals. See **clone**.

**somatic gene therapy** (SomGT): nonheritable modification of somatic cell genomes to cure or prevent **deleterious** conditions, without simultaneous modification of gametes or the germ-line. Typically, body cells are removed from an individual, genetically modified or engineered, and replaced again within the soma of the same individual; the result is an altered function or clinical result. Aka nonheritable somatic cell gene therapy. See **substitutional gene therapy** and **gametic gene therapy**.

**somatic growth:** growth of the body; trophic growth.

**somatic mutation:** mutation that occurs in a somatic or nonsex cell or cell line, and can be transmitted to daughter cells or clone lines but cannot be transmitted from parent to offspring. Cf. **germinal mutation** or constitutional mutation.

**somatic mutation hypothesis** or **theory:** proposal that cancer is caused by one or more mutations in body cells; the mutations may be either chromosomal, or in an updated version of the hypothesis, in DNA. Originally suggested in 1914 by German zoologist Theodor Boveri (1862–1915), the theory has enjoyed widespread support with specific additions and modifications.

**somatic mutation theory of aging:** intracellular, stochastic model of aging in which the major premise is that mutations to stem cell DNA alter genetic information and decrease cellular efficiency to a subvital level. The proposal that aging is due to an accumulation of mutations in somatic cells was first made in 1959 by American physicist Leo Szilard; aka the random hits theory of aging. Cf. **chromosome theory of cancer**.

**somatic nervous system:** component of efferent division of the peripheral nervous system that innervates skeletal muscle.

**somatic recombination:** crossing-over during **mitosis** of somatic cells that leads to the segregation of heterozygous alleles. Rare. Aka mitotic recombination, mitotic crossing-over.

**somatic synapsis:** fusion of chromosome pairs in body cells.

**somatically transmitted system of behavior:** proposal for a noncultural form of adaptation that is tool-assisted, erected to explain the artifact assemblages at **Zhoukoudian**.

**somatogenic variations:** pertaining to characteristics that are acquired and not inherited.

**somatology:** study of the body of an organism, usually taken to mean the fluids and other soft tissues rather than the skeleton. Somatology thus includes the measurement and/or descriptions of skin color, hair form and distribution, the shape of features such as the eyes and nose, dermatoglyphics, and features of blood such as blood types, taster/non-taster determination, presence/absence of sicklemia, measurements of body parts and proportions, etc. Although somatologists may be involved with investigating the relationships of such information with environmental variables, somatologists in general do not involve themselves with the identification of a limited number of **morphological types**, i.e. they are not aligned with the principles of **biotypology**. See **constitutional typology, Bergmann's rule, Gloger's rule, Allen's rule.**

**somatomedin:** see **insulin-like growth factor.**

**somatometry:** measurement of the human body with the soft tissues intact; normally performed on the living body.

**somatosexual:** relating to both physical and sexual characteristics; usually refers to physical manifestations of sexual development.

**somatostatin** (SS): 1. any of several cyclic tetradecapeptides elaborated primarily by the median eminence of the hypothalamus and by the delta cells of the pancreas. The somatostatins inhibit release of **growth hormone, thyrotropin,** and **corticotropin** by the **adenohypophysis,** of **insulin** and glucagon by the pancreas, of gastrin by the gastric mucosa, of secretin by the intestinal mucosa, and of renin by the kidney. Aka growth hormone release-inhibiting hormone, somatotropin release-inhibiting hormone. See **insulin-like growth factor I.** 2. a recombinant (genetically engineered) gene product. SS was spliced into the **plasmid** of *E. coli* in 1977, and became the first commercially produced human protein, followed shortly by **insulin.**

**somatotropin:** see **human growth hormone.**

**somatotype:** body form associated with **constitutional typology** in which body shape is evaluated and rated on a 1 to 7 scale. The three principle somatotypes are **ectomorphy, endomorphy,** and **mesomorphy,** although an individual can be a mosaic of all of these somatotypes.

‡ **somite:** one of any similar segmental units that are arranged along the length of the body of a metameric animal (such as a vertebrate). Now more frequently referred to as a metamere within biology.

**son:** male offspring; a kinship term that identifies a genealogical or adopted degree of relationship in a **nuclear family** or **extended family.** See **father, mother, brother, sister, daughter, aunt, uncle, cousin.**

**song:** any elaborate vocal signal.

**Songhor:** paleontological site found in the 1920s near Lake Victoria in Kenya, dated to *c.* 20 mya (early **Miocene**), and that contains primate remains including *Proconsul, Dendropithecus, Rangwapithecus,* and *Nyanzapithecus.*

**sonogram:** see **sound spectrogram.**

**sooty mangabey:** vernacular for *Cercocebus torquatus atys.*

**sororate:** institutionalized pattern in which a woman marries her sister's husband.

**sorority:** 1. sisters. 2. a society of women. Cf. **fraternity.**

**sorting criterion:** one of a set of morphological features or metric traits used to create subsets in a database.

**SOS polymerase:** specific enzyme, DNA polymerase IV; it has been suggested that this molecule produces error-prone replication during DNA repair. See **directed mutation** and **hypermutation.**

**sound:** 1. noise. 2. healthy.

**sound spectrogram:** two-coordinate graphical representation of sound frequencies produced by animals and recorded by an instrument called a sound spectrograph (more recent technology has produced spectrum analyzers) used in the study of **bioacoustics;** this type of instrument can pick up frequencies within the human **hearing range** as well as sounds being emitted by animals that the human ear cannot detect. Aka sonograph.

**South African hominids:** see entries beginning with **SK, Sts, Stw** and **TM.**

**South African lesser bushbaby (galago):** vernacular for *Galago moholi.*

**South African sites:** see **Taung, Sterkfontein, Kromdraai, MAkapansgat, Swartkrans, Gladysvale,** and **Drimolen;** see also **Die Kelders Cave, Equus Cave, Border Cave, Klasies River,** and **Florisbad.**

**South Turkwel River:** archaeological site near the South Turkwel River, Kenya, dated to *c.* 3.5 mya (Middle Pliocene); contains a faunal sample that suggests the environment was bushland, and hominid remains including fragments of a mandible and wrist bones comparable to *Australopithecus.*

**Southern blot analysis:** method of identification developed by E. M. Southern in which DNA fragments are cleaved by a restriction enzyme, separated by **electrophoresis,** electroblotted onto a suitable nitrocellulose or nylon membrane, denatured, and hybridized with a labeled **cDNA** acid probe. Aka Southern blotting, Southern hybridization. See **blot.**

**southern night monkey:** vernacular for *Aotus azarai.*

**SOX:** acronym for **SRY box.**

**SOX9:** one of the **SRY box** variants, with a length of about 80 amino acids located on human chromosome 17 with great homology to the SRY, aka the high-mobility group domain, and believed to be involved with the gonad formation cascade.

**SOX*n*:** acronym for **SRY box.**; the '*n*' as in **SOX9** refers to a specific SRY box variant, number *n*.

*sp.***:** see entries under **species.**

**spacer DNA:** untranscribed **junk DNA.**

**spacer region:** any sequence of nucleotides in the DNA between coding genes.

**spall:** to break around or into small pieces; used of a piece broken off in making a core tool; a flake, fragment, or chip.

**span:** 1. see **arm span**. 2. distance separating the tips of the little finger and thumb of one hand with the fingers outstretched; finger span.

**spatial memory:** term often used instead of **cognitive map** in primatology; refers to an animal's capacity to remember locations and return to valuable resources. It has been argued that **frugivores**, which have to search for rare food items, should have better spatial memory than **folivores**, whose food source is more evenly distributed in the environment.

**spatial variation:** pattern of variation among organisms in space. See **cline**.

**spatulate:** spoonlike; e.g. spatulate incisors.

**spear:** tool present in **Upper Paleolithic** and later tool kits; used primarily as a projectile or thrusting weapon, and may have had either a stone or burnished tip.

**Spearman's hypothesis:** argument proposed by psychologist Arthur Jensen that **IQ** scores reflect general-purpose problem-solving skills on which we all differ, but that humans also have general-purpose associative learning systems, largely independent of testing, on which individuals do not differ, and that is measured by the so-called 'Spearman's *g*'. Aka Level I – Level II theory.

**spearthrower:** device present in **Magdalenian** Upper Paleolithic and later tool kits designed to enhance the power and distance of a hurled spear; developed by the Cro-Magnons and providing the user with the equivalent of an extra segment on the throwing arm. Made of bone, antler or wood, it consists of a grip at one end and a hook or notch at the other. Aka an atlatl in central America, woomera in Australia.

**Special Creation:** belief that the earth and its creatures were specially created by God. This sometimes includes the additional beliefs that the earth was created in 4004 BC and that other species were created for the dominion and special use of Mankind.

**specialist:** organism that displays a narrow pattern of resource usage. Cf. **generalist**.

**specialized:** 1. having a unique attribute, a specialty. 2. possessing a unique adaptation(s) to a particular **ecological niche**, sometimes highly diverged from an ancestral form, and unable to live in an ancestral niche. Cf. **generalized**.

**specialized cell:** differentiated cell committed to specific activities and functions within a tissue, and thought unable to revert to a more generalized state. A **restricted** cell that has been derived from a **totipotent** or pluripotent stem cell.

‡ **specialized trait, character** or **feature:** any biological structure adapted to a narrow range of conditions and used in specific ways; the hooves of horses are specialized structures, for example, that allow for movement over hard and flat terrain.

‡ **speciation:** development of new species; the process of genetic diversification that results in the appearance of new **species**. Aka **primary speciation**. See **microevolution** and **macroevolution**.

**speciation modes:** any of the empirical or theoretical models of species-splitting. See **allochronic speciation, alloparapatric speciation, allopatric speciation, anagenetic speciation, centrifugal speciation, gradual speciation, parapatric speciation, peripatric speciation, peripheral isolate speciation, reticulate speciation, saltational speciation, stasimorphic speciation, stasipatric speciation,** and **sympatric speciation**. See also **primary speciation** and **secondary speciation**.

**speciation, theory of:** theory regarding the formation of distinct daughter taxa from a single parent or ancestral taxon; usually taken to mean geographical speciation, specifically **allopatric speciation**. Associated most strongly in the twentieth century with biologist Ernst **Mayr**, who incorporated the principles of **neo-Darwinism** into previously understood principles, such as **gradualism**.

**speciational evolution:** see **punctuated equilibrium**.

*species* (*sp.*) (Latin): species.

‡ **species:** 1. a group of individuals having common attributes and designated by a common name. 2. in biological **taxonomy**, the basic lower unit of **classification**, consisting of a population or series of populations (**demes**) of closely related and similar organisms capable of interbreeding freely with one another, and which produce **viable** and **fertile** offspring. 3. the second name in a **binomen**, which follows the **genus** name. See **species concepts**.

**species-advantage reasoning:** see the **group selection fallacy**.

**species–area relationship:** rule from the **island biogeography model** that islands with larger area have more species diversity than do smaller islands.

**species concepts:** see **biological species concept, cladistic species concept, ecological species concept, evolutionary species concept, isolation species concept, morphological species concept, phenetic species concept, recognition species concept,** and **reproductive species concept**.

**species drift:** increases and decreases in the number of species in a higher taxonomic group (such as a genus) owing to random processes.

**species essentialism:** idea based on the ideas of **Aristotle** and practiced by **Linnaeus**, that members of a **species** share a common natural inner state or essence that is different from other species, that each individual is capable of attainment of the perfect state (a **type specimen**), but that outside forces interfere with its attainment, producing observed individual variations. See **fixity of species** and **essentialism**.

*species indeterminata* (*sp. indet., sp. ind.*) (Latin): indeterminate species. The abbreviation follows the **genus** nomen when an organism's species is not certain, e.g. *Homo sp. indet.* See *incertae sedis*.

**species naming rules:** see entries following **nomen**.

*species nova* (*sp. n., sp. nov.*) (Latin): new species.

**species replacement:** turnover of species in time owing to species extinction of some and the origin of others. Aka species selection.

**species resistance:** condition in which a species is not affected by a particular pathogen, although it may be virulent to another species. Examples are the susceptibility of canids to distemper, which does not affect humans; and the fact that humans are susceptible to common cold viruses, which do not affect chimpanzees.

*species revivisco* (*sp. rev.*) (Latin): species revived.

**species selection:** process of selection in which some species are more likely to survive and/or develop into new species; species selection, which is not recognized by all evolutionary biologists, is essentially the differential survival and reproduction of species. Certain species develop mechanisms that result in lower extinction and higher speciation rates (such as primates, and mammals in general); such species will display frequent adaptive radiations. Certain other species develop mechanisms that result in higher extinction and lower speciation rates; such species will display infrequent adaptive radiations.

**species stasis:** apparent lack of change in the morphology of a species during its history.

**specific:** 1. pertaining to a particular element, especially of a species. 2. free from ambiguity.

**specific immune response:** response that depends upon the recognition of a specific foreign material for reaction to it.

**specific trait, character** or **feature:** any feature that is diagnostic for a species.

**specificity:** 1. selectivity; inability of an antibody to detect the presence of unrelated antigens, even at low antigen levels. 2. in the context of a test for diagnosing a disease condition, specificity is defined as the proportion of people without a disease who test negatively for the disease. 3. in serology, the capacity of an antigen to react exclusively with red cells that have the corresponding antigenic determinants in common.

**specimen:** part or an entire individual that is taken to represent the whole. 2. any typical instance. 3. a sample taken for examination or study, e.g., tissue specimen.

**spectral tarsier:** one of the vernaculars for *Tarsius spectrum*.

**spectrograph:** instrumentation that measures the response of a specimen to selected frequencies of the light spectrum.

**spectrographic analysis:** use of a spectrograph to identify specific chemical elements in a given specimen.

**spectrum hypothesis:** model attempting to explain the position of the Neandertals proposed by J. S. **Weiner** and B. **Campbell**, who argued that the variation in past species would have been as extensive as in *Homo sapiens* today, and that **Neandertals** and certain archaic groups should thus be sub-specific variants of humans, e.g. *Homo sapiens neanderthalensis*.

**speculum:** white or colored patch on the **pelage** of a primate, often at the rump.

**speech:** actual acts of auditory communication in humans. Cf. **language**.

**speech apparatus:** portions of the body used to produce vocal sound: lips, teeth, soft and hard palate, tongue, nose, larynx, and vocal folds.

**speech centers:** those portions of the human cerebral cortex concerned with the formulation and use of linguistic utterances; included among these are the **motor speech area** (Broca's area) and **Wernicke's area**.

**speleology:** science of cave exploration; a spelunker is someone who practices speleology.

**speleotherm:** any of a number of mineral deposits with characteristic shapes; deposits formed in caves through the action of water (**stalactites, stalagmites,** flowstones).

**Spencer, Frank** (1941–1999): British-born physical anthropologist and historian at Queens College, NY; trained as a microbiologist, Spencer worked in Canada at that profession before receiving a PhD at Michigan. He is known for papers assessing the work of Aleš **Hrdlicka** and several papers on the early history of physical anthropology. Author of *Piltdown, A Scientific Forgery* (1990), and *The Piltdown Papers* (1990), and editor of a respected two-volume historical work, *History of Physical Anthropology* (1997).

**Spencer, Herbert** (1820–1903): social scientist; anticipated **Darwin** in an essay 'A theory of population deduced from the general law of human fertility' (1852) in which he first used the phrase 'survival of the fittest'. Considered by some as perhaps 'the greatest evolutionist of them all'. Spencer embraced a form of cultural evolution similar to that held by Tylor and Morgan called unilineal cultural evolution. Author of *The Principles of Biology* (1863–67).

‡ **sperm:** haploid male **gamete**, specialized for motility, rather than for storage of nutrients; a **spermatozoon**, the end product of **spermatogenesis**. Consists of a head, mid-piece, and motile tail segment.

**sperm bank:** location where sperm is preserved frozen for future use in artificial insemination. See **germinal choice**.

**sperm capacitation:** see **capacitation**.

**sperm competition:** 1. any male–male **competition**. 2. hypothesis that because the first ejaculate often incurs greater sperm mortality, various sperm morphologies have developed to block sperm in subsequent ejaculates.

**sperm dilution effect:** condition that occurs after a male has had repeated copulations over a given period of time, such as when females in a primate society are in **estrus**; the amount of sperm contained in the semen is reduced after each ejaculation, making his chances of producing a conception less with each additional female he copulates with during a given period of time; it is to his advantage to have fewer copulations in order to have a sperm-rich ejaculate.

**sperm head:** portion of a spermatozoon that contains the heritable male nDNA. The anterior portion is called the **acrosome**.

**sperm mid-piece:** central portion of a **spermatozoon**, located between the enucleated head and a motile tail; the mid-piece contains the male **mitochondria**, which produce energy for flagellation.

**sperm polymorphism:** production of both normal as well as large numbers of abnormal sperm lacking a head, lacking a tail, or multi-headed or -tailed. Some researchers think that such polymorphisms are a consequence of **sperm competition**.

**sperm scarcity hypothesis:** argument that it is advantageous for a female to copulate with multiple partners in order to provide sufficient sperm to ensure conception.

**sperm typing:** technique used to develop linkage maps during which allele configurations in sperm are compared with those in a male's somatic cells. See **recombination frequency**.

**spermatic cord:** developmental tissue in males that consists of the ductus deferens, testicular vessels and nerve, a portion of the internal oblique muscle, and lymph vessels; see **descent of the testes**.

‡ **spermatid:** immature **spermatozoon**. See **spermiogenesis**.

**spermatocyte:** cell in the **testis**, either a **primary spermatocyte** or a **secondary spermatocyte**.

**spermatogenesis:** production of male sex gametes. **Spermatogonia** divide mitotically and give rise to **primary spermatocytes** during meiosis I, which give rise to **secondary spermatocytes** during meiosis II, producing **spermatids**. See **spermiogenesis**.

**spermatogonium:** mitotically active cell in the gonad which gives rise to **primary spermatocytes**. Plural: spermatogonia.

‡ **spermatozoon:** mature male gamete or germ cell produced in the **testes** that is expelled from the male urethra during ejaculation; male gamete. It consists of the **sperm head**, **sperm mid-piece**, and flagellating tail. Plural: spermatozoa.

**spermiogenesis:** maturation of a **spermatid** by the addition of a mid-piece and flagellating tail, and further modifications to the nucleus the acrosome; the result is a **spermatozoon**. Nurse cells play an active part in this process.

*Sphacorhysis burntforkensis* **Gunnell, 1995:** tarsiiform primate from the middle Eocene of North America belonging to the omomyid subfamily **Anaptomorphinae; monotypic**. Estimated body mass around 150 g. See Appendix 1 for taxonomy.

**S phase:** stage of interphase in the cell cycle when DNA replicates. See **gap1 phase** and **gap2 phase**.

**sphenion:** **craniometric** landmark; tip of the sphenoidal angle of the parietal bone.

**spheno-frontal suture:** articulation between the **sphenoid bone** of the **facial skeleton** and the **frontal bone** of the **cranium** that courses laterally and into the **orbit**.

**sphenoid bone:** one of a pair of wedge-shaped bones that help make up the facial skeleton. The sphenoids help to form the floor and lateral walls of the cranium and sides and floor of the orbits.

**sphenoidal sinus:** one of a pair of air-filled cavities lined with mucous membrane located inside the **sphenoid bone** above the superior portion of the nasal cavity.

**spheno-parietal suture:** articulation between the sphenoid bone of the **facial skeleton** and the **parietal bone** on the lateral region of the **cranium**.

**spheno-temporal suture:** articulation between the **sphenoid bone** of the **facial skeleton** and the **temporal bone** on the lateral side of the **cranium**.

**spherocyte:** **erythrocyte** that appears circular rather than button-shaped as in normal red blood cells, and characteristically found in individuals diagnosed with certain hereditary anemias.

**sphincter:** circular muscle that functions to constrict a body opening or the lumen of a tubular structure.

**spicule:** spikelike or needlelike structure.

**spider monkey:** general vernacular for any of the four platyrrhine species belonging to the genus *Ateles*.

**spina bifida:** failure of the neural tube to close during fetal development. It is a congenital disorder that occurs when one or more vertebrae do not develop properly from the neural tube; a portion of the spinal cord and nerves also fail to develop properly. It is usually an isolated birth defect. It usually occurs within the first month of pregnancy, and affects 0.5–1 out of 1,000 infants born in the USA. Aka cleft spine, myelomeningocele. See **neural tube defect**.

‡ **spinal column:** see **vertebral column.**

**spinal cord:** portion of the **central nervous system** that extends downward from the **brain stem** through the vertebral canal.

*sp. indet:* see *species indeterminata.*

**spindle:** see **meiotic spindle** and **mitotic spindle.**

‡ **spindle fiber:** 1. a nexus of fine contractile fibers or **microtubules** that appear to tether chromosomes and/or chromatids during **cell division.** 2. a modified skeletal muscle fiber in muscle spindle.

**spine:** sharp-pointed process, e.g. the spinous process of some vertebrae.

**spirochete:** spiral-shaped category of bacterial pathogen; examples are the organisms responsible for **Lyme disease** and **syphilis.**

**spite:** see **spiteful act, trait, character** or **feature.**

**spiteful act, trait, character** or **feature:** behavior that incurs a cost to both actor and recipient, measured as a quantitative devaluation of **reproductive success.** One of W. D. **Hamilton's** and E. O. **Wilson's** three classes of behavior. Aka spite. See **altruism** and **selfishness.**

**splanchnocranium:** portion of the cranium that forms the **facial skeleton** including the **nasal, lacrimal, zygomatic, palatine, maxilla, mandible, vomer,** and **nasal conchae bones.** These bones develop by both **intramembranous ossification** and **endochondral ossification.** These portions of the skull are derived from the primitive skeleton of the gill apparatus, i.e. the bony face. Aka viscerocranium. See **cranium.**

**spleen:** large blood-filled, glandular organ located in the upper left quadrant of the abdomen and attached by mesenteries to the stomach; the largest organ of the **lymphatic system.**

**splice acceptor:** sequence at the 3′ border of an **intron.**

**splice donor:** sequence at the 5′ border of an **intron.**

**spliceosome:** complex of small nuclear **ribozymes** and small nuclear **ribonucleoproteins** that excise introns from genes and splice the exon tails together during **RNA processing.**

**splicing:** see **RNA splicing** and **alternative splicing.**

**splicing mutations:** mutations that change the patterns of RNA splicing, usually by altering splice donor or acceptor sites.

**split-base bone-lance point:** slender point of which the butt end is split upward for a short distance, probably for **hafting.** The split-base dates from the Middle **Aurignacian tool tradition.**

**split gene:** cistron (gene) that has its coding sequence interrupted by **introns.** Aka interrupted gene. See **cistron.**

**splitter:** taxonomist who tends to erect relatively more taxa than others when examining a set of specimens. By the late 1950s some 29 genera had been erected to describe hominid fossils; Wenner-Gren conferees in 1962 collapsed these into fewer than half the former number Cf. **lumper.**

**spondylitis:** inflammation of one or more vertebrae; Aka Pott's disease.

**spongy bone:** see **cancellous bone.**

**spontaneous abortion:** see **abortion.**

**spontaneous fission:** scars or damage tracks left within rock crystals as the result of the fission of particles within the nucleus of $^{238}$U.

**spontaneous generation:** archaic proposal that living things arise from nonliving elements by natural processes, and without the intervention of supernatural power; aka abiogenesis, xenogenesis.

**spontaneous mutation:** rare, random, and unpredictable change in a gene; occurs naturally and without the application of any known mutagenic agent.

**spontaneous mutation rate :** frequency of the occurrence of natural gene mutations in a particular organism when no **mutagenic agents** have been employed.

**sporadic cancer:** any cancer not transmittable through a germline or constitutional mutation; non-familial cancer; cancers caused by triggers and agents in the environment and thus related to the distribution and intensity of the agents themselves.

**sporozoite:** stage in the life cycle of the *Plasmodium* parasite when it lives in the salivary glands of the *Anopheles* mosquito and invades humans and other primates. The sporozoite can produce **immune decoy proteins.** See **merozoite.**

**sport:** 1. any organism that shows a 'major' mutation. 2. the mutation itself. Usage of the term was common in the nineteenth century, but has largely been replaced by the term **mutation.** Aka monster, freak, rogue. Cf. **atavism.**

**sportive lemur:** vernacular for the species in the genus *Lepilemur.* Prior to 1977, and reorganization of the genus, this name applied to *L. mustelinus.* Aka weasel lemur.

**sports:** see **lusus naturae.**

**spot-nosed guenon:** vernacular for *Cercopithecus nictitans.*

*spp.:* see *species,* *subspecies.*

**spreading caliper:** instrument consisting of two pivoted legs that are adjustable for distance; used for measuring linear distance or thickness when it is not possible to obtain straight line measurement. For example, the distance between craniometric points on opposite sides of the skull can be measured using a spreading caliper; aka hinge caliper.

**spreading position effect:** referring to observations that many genes in the region of an inversion or translocation seem to become inactivated. See **position effect.**

**spurious correlation:** apparent relation between two variables that results from factors other than those to which the relation is mistakenly attributed.

**Spy Caves:** archaeological site found in 1886 near Namur, Belgium, dated to the **Pleistocene** (early Würm, estimated age about 60 kya), and that contains **Mousterian** artifacts and hominid remains including two nearly complete male skeletons, possible burials, attributed to *Homo neanderthalensis*, Spy 1 and 2, with estimated cranial capacities of 1553 and 1305 cm³, respectively. The linear builds of these skeletons was the first sound evidence that the reconstruction of the 'Old Man' of **La Chapelle** was a pathological specimen. Aka Spy d'Orneau, Betcheaux-Rotches Cave.

**squama:** any concave, shell-shaped bone, e.g. the **parietal bone.**

**squamosal:** pertaining to the region of the **temporal** bone in primates that is a separate platelike bone in lower vertebrates.

**squamosal suture:** articulation between the **temporal bone** and the **parietal bones.**

**square orbit:** subjective assessment of the shape of the eye sockets, which appear squarer in **AMH** compared with earlier species.

**squirrel monkey:** general vernacular for two to five platyrrhine species belonging to the genus *Saimiri*.

**Sr/Ca ratio:** see **strontium/calcium ratio.**

**sRNA:** abbreviation for **soluble RNA.**

**SRY box:** set of homeotic genes (**SOX***n*) affected by the presence of the *SRY* gene on the **Y chromosome** in mammals.

**SRY gene:** gene located in the 'sex determining region of the Y' chromosome. The *SRY* encodes an **SRY box** factor; mutations in this gene result in **XY females** with **gonadal dysgenesis**; translocation of this portion of the Y chromosome gives rise to **XX males**. Aka SDY. See *TDF* **gene.**

**S-shaped growth curve:** see **logistic growth curve.**

*ssp.:* abbreviation for **subspecies.**

**S-strategist:** stress-tolerant species, characterized by small body size, slow growth, extended life span, minimum dispersal attributes, tolerance to environmental stress, and minimum parental investment. See **C–R–S triangle** of ecological strategies.

**stabilizing selection:** 1. selection that operates against the extremes of variation and thus tends to stabilize the distribution of a population around the mean. Occurs when individuals with intermediate values for a phenotypic trait have higher fitness values. Aka maintenance selection. Cf. **directional selection** and **disruptive selection.** 2. less well-known (nor accepted) extension by Schmalhausen that a process exists whereby favorable adaptabilities caused by the environment eventually become genetically assimilated adaptations. Cf. the **Baldwin effect.**

**stable age distribution:** condition in which the - proportions of individuals belonging to different age groups remain constant for generation after generation.

‡ **stable carbon isotope:** see **carbon 13.**

**stable equilibrium:** see **balanced polymorphism.**

**stable isotope:** naturally occurring nonradiogenic isotope of an element. Many elements have several stable isotopes, e.g $^{13}$**C** and $^{12}$**C**. Cf. **unstable isotope.**

**stable isotope analysis:** technique for reconstruction of past diets by analyzing **isotope** ratios obtained from bones and **tooth enamel**. Among elements analyzed are carbon, nitrogen, and oxygen. **C$_3$ and C$_4$ vegetation consumers** have different $\delta^{13}$C ratios ($^{13}$C : $^{12}$C) in their **hard tissues**, whereas carnivores have values similar to those of their prey. **Mass spectrometry** is used to obtain the data upon which the ratios are constructed.

**stable population:** population that contains constant **age-specific vital rates**, which may be increasing or decreasing in size.

**stadia:** series of variations in climate.

**stadial:** one of two or more peaks (or maxima) within a single **glaciation.**

**stadiometer:** instrument for measuring height that consists of a vertical board with an attached metric rule and horizontal board that is brought into contact with the superior point of the head.

**stage:** 1. discrete growth or developmental phase of an organism. 2. biostratigraphic unit distinguished by the presence of particular fossil taxa.

**stages of the human life cycle:** conventional ontogenetic phases expressed as genotypes and serial phenotypes and the social roles that accompany each phase, from **conception** to **death**. See individual stages and events: **fertilization, preimplantation stage, preembryonic stage, embryonic stage, fetal stage, birth, neonatal stage, infancy, childhood, juvenile growth stage, menarche** and **puberty, adolescent stage, adulthood, middle age, menopause, transition to full maturity,** full **maturity, old age, senescence,** and **death.**

**stalactite:** conical or irregular deposit of **calcite** that hangs like an icicle from the roof of a cave; formed by the precipitation of **calcium carbonate** from drops of lime-saturated water. Cf. **stalagmite.**

**stalagmite:** compact, hard material composed of **calcium carbonate** that may form on the walls of rockshelters during times of dampness, and may become redeposited on the floor, resembling an inverted icicle. Cf. **stalactite.**

**standard:** established rule of comparison for a value or state; standardization. Cf. **gold standard.**

‡ **standard deviation** ($\sigma$, s.d.): summary statistic that measures within-group variation. Returned by $\sigma = (x_i - \mu)^2/n$.

**standard erect position:** posture during the taking of somatic measurements in which a subject stands erect with arms hanging loosely with palms inward and the heels are in contact at an angle of about 45°. The head is held in the **Frankfort horizontal**.

**standard error** (s.e.): measure of the dispersion of the means or mean differences expected due to sampling variation; used in the calculation of the $t$ statistic.

**standard karyotype:** graphic arrangement of a species' **chromosomes** in order of decreasing size and position of the **centromere**. Used to identify any visible **chromosome mutation** when compared with individual variants, such as humans born with **Down syndrome**, or to identify chromosome mutations that have become fixed during the course of **chromosome evolution** when compared with the standard karyotype of another species. See **major chromosome anomaly**.

**standard score:** see **z score**.

**standard sitting position:** posture during the taking of somatic measurements in which a subject sits erect with knees at a right angle, thighs parallel, hands on thighs, and with upper arms along the rib cage. The head is held in the **Frankfort horizontal**.

**Standard Social Science Model** (SSSM): hypothesis that the neonate brain is a blank slate, a *tabula rasa*, and shaped almost entirely by learning and experience as an organism grows. Aka Skinnerian behaviorism. Cf. **sociobiology** and **evolutionary psychology**.

**standing erect posture:** position in which the individual is standing with the heels together and the arms hanging at the sides; some variations of this posture require the head to be oriented in the **Frankfort horizontal**. Aka military position. Cf. **anatomical position**.

**standing height:** on a standing subject, the distance from the floor to the highest point of the head.

**Stanley's rule:** 1973 modification of **Cope's law** that the perceived tendency toward increases in body size is due to sorting from initial small sizes.

**stapedial artery:** one of the two branches of the internal carotid artery in the middle ear of certain primates, the other being the **promontory artery**. It supplies the middle ear cavity of **prosimians**, but is absent in anthropoids.

**staphylion** (sta): **craniometric landmark**; distal midsagittal point on the hard palate. See Appendix 7.

**staring bared-teeth scream face:** primate facial expression in which the eyes are fixed in a wide stare, the corners of the mouth are pulled back, and the teeth are exposed; an expression of fear.

**staring open mouth face:** primate facial expression in which the eyes are fixed in a wide stare and the mouth is opened wide; a threat gesture.

**stasigenesis:** pertaining to a period of an evolutionary lineage in which little or no measurable phenotypic evolution occurs. See **punctuated equilibrium**.

**stasimorphic speciation:** formation of new species without morphological differentiation.

**stasipatric speciation:** special case of **sympatric speciation** by chromosomal mechanisms in which new chromosomal variants occur within the range of a parent species but are buffered from the parent species by **hybrid inviability**, **hybrid sterility** or **hybrid breakdown**. See **transilience mechanisms of speciation**.

‡ **stasis:** equilibrium, inactivity or stoppage; in biology, the view that nature and all of its organisms are unchanging (e.g. held by **Linnaeus** *c.* 1758); recently, the hypothesis that **species** exist for relatively long periods without morphological change, then evolve rapidly for short periods in response to environmental pressure. Cf. **punctuated equilibrium**.

**state:** 1. the contextual condition of an organism or object. 2. society with a strong central government and professional ruling class not based on kinship affiliation. 3. in behavioral studies, the behavior that an animal is involved in; for example, a baboon walking is a state of ongoing behavior. Cf. **event**.

**state of preservation:** assessment of chemical and mechanical wear on fossils and artifacts. See **taphonomy** and **differential preservation**.

**stationary growth phase:** see **growth curve and logistic growth curve**.

**stationary population:** population that is neither increasing or decreasing in size.

**statistic:** any numerical fact or **datum**.

**statistical:** 1. pertaining to, of, or based on **statistics**. 2. in **anthropology**, refers to the occurrence of actual practice in a culture, in contrast to 'normative' or ideal practices that people strive to follow.

**statistical cycle:** model or approach to science used by many researchers that combines an inductive phase that leads to theory and hypotheses, followed by a deductive phase in which data are collected and hypotheses are tested (usually by the **hypothetico-deductive approach**). The cycle is repeated as necessary.

**statistically significant:** claim for which there is some degree of evidence in the data used. A result is considered significant by **Fisher's** convention if the probability ($\alpha$) is $\leq 0.05$ that the observed violation of the **null hypothesis** is due to chance effects. See **alpha level**.

**statistics:** science that deals with the collection, **classification**, **analysis**, and **interpretation** of numerical facts or data by using mathematical theories of **probability**.

**stature:** standing height; stature is polygenic and multifactorial, but its heritability is relatively high (about 70%).

**status:** see **rank**.

**status signal:** indicator to **conspecifics** of an individual's rank, e.g. the gray back of a **silverback male** gorilla. The status signal is believed to help keep order within a primate group.

**steady state:** any apparently unchanging condition due to a balance between the synthesis (or arrival or birth) and degradation (or departure or death) of all relevant components of a system. Aka equilibrium, steady-state system.

**steatite:** soapstone used to make stone bowls, especially in eastern North America.

**steatopygia:** condition in several human populations in which there is a marked deposition of fat over the female buttocks regardless of the amount of body fat distributed over the rest of the body. This is most pronounced in the desert-adapted Khoisan **!Kung**, Hottentots, and some of the pygmy peoples of the Malayo-Indonesian area. Aka steatopygy. See **Venus figurines**. Cf. **Rensch's desert rule**.

**Steinheim:** archaeological site found in 1933 in a gravel quarry near Steinheim, Germany, dating estimated from >200 kya (>**Mindel–Riss interglacial**) to as recent as 100 kya; contains hominid remains consisting of a distorted gracile **calvaria**, probably female, with a cranial capacity of 1100 cm³, small mastoid, broad nose, double-arched supra-orbital torus, suprainiac fossa, high parietal width and no bun. Assigned to the later '**anteneandertal**' or archaic *Homo sapiens* group. Aka Sigrist gravel pit.

***Steinius*** **Bown and Rose, 1984:** genus of tarsiiform primate from the early Eocene of North America belonging to the omomyid subfamily **Omomyinae**; two species. Estimated body mass between 300 and 400 g. Dental formula: 2.1.3.3/2.1.3.3; dental morphology suggestive of either **granivory**, **insectivory**, or **frugivory** (or a combination of at least two). See Appendix 1 for taxonomy.

**stem cell:** cell that can proliferate in an undifferentiated state, as well as give rise to differentiated cell lines. Aka formative cell. See **totipotent**, **pluripotent**, **specialized cell** and **restriction**.

**stem group:** taxa in a clade prior to a major cladogenetic event such as an adaptive radiation; see **stem lineage**. Cf. **crown group**.

**Stem–leg length index:** see **Manouvrier's skelic index**.

**stem lineage:** all the fossils in a clade since its origin; see **stem group**.

**stenion:** craniometric landmark: linear measurement obtained with **spreading calipers** that is the shortest distance between the two temporal fossae.

**stenogenic gene control:** limited patterns of transcriptional gene expression. Cf. **eurygenic gene control**.

**Steno's law:** empirical observation in the seventeenth century that **fossils** appearing in geological strata are organic in origin, and were therefore once living organisms.

**step cline:** relatively abrupt change in a small geographic distance as compared to the relatively smaller changes in the same distance on either side of the step. Aka stepped cline.

**steppe:** extensive plain, especially one without trees.

**stereoscopic vision:** ability to see in three dimensions. The condition is due to **binocular vision** and overlapping visual fields, and is found especially in **primates**, in whom visual images are superimposed upon one another in real time and interpreted by the **visual cortex** of the **brain** as having depth. Aka stereopsis, stereoscopy.

**stereotype:** 1. set form or convention. 2. simplified, standardized image used as a reference by a closed group, e.g. 'cowboy'. 3. any fixed form.

**stereotypy:** repetitive movements or vocalizations in an animal. This may be characteristic of the species in the wild, such as a distinctive call; however, captive animals, particular social mammals and primates in an unenriched environment, exhibit motor patterns that are not natural, such as ceaseless pacing.

**sterile:** 1. without life. 2. any individual unable to produce normal **gametes**. Caused by dysfunction in genetic and/or cytogenetic pathways.

**sterile layer:** **soil** deposit lacking evidence of human occupation.

**sterility:** inability to produce normal **gametes**. Cf. **fecund**.

**sterilization:** surgical interruption of gamete development or passage, such that an organism is rendered infertile; see **eugenic sterilization**.

‡ **Sterkfontein** (Sts, Ste, SE, Stw, Stx): archaeological site found in 1936 by R. **Broom** in Gauteng Province, Transvaal, South Africa, with six depositional members dating from more than 3.0 mya to as recently as 1.5 mya. Contains both **Oldowan** and proto-**Acheulean** artifacts. **Hominid** remains, including fragments from between 50 and 600 individuals from several species and at least two genera, have been found at the site (see boxes below). The lowest, earliest hominid-bearing depositional Member 2 contains the foot bones of 'little foot' (**Stw 573**). Those Members that date from 3.0–2.4 mya contain the fossils of **gracile australopithecines**, including **Sts 5**. The youngest Members date from 2.1–1.5 mya and include the remains of **robust australopithecines**, **habilines**, and **tools**, including possible bone tools, and animal bones possessing alleged cut marks. In South African sites, all

Pliocene australopithecines appear to be gracile, whereas all robust forms and habilines appear to be Pleistocene in age. The Pliocene paleoenvironment seems to have been forested, with savanna increasing dramatically after 2.5 mya.

Sterkfontein Valley: region located about 80 km north of Johannesburg, South Africa, known locally as the 'Cradle of Mankind', that contains 13 excavated fossiliferous sites and another 30 that have not yet been touched. The best known of these are Sterkfontein

---

### Some fossil hominids found at Sterkfontein (Sts Series)

**Sts 5:** field number for a well-known partial hominid cranium discovered in 1947, the first example of an adult *Australopithecus africanus* ever found. The remains date to between 2.8 and 2.4 mya. Cranial capacity estimated at 485 cm$^3$. first assigned to *Plesianthropus* but later collapsed into *Australopithecus africanus*. Aka 'Mrs. Ples', although there has been a proposal that the specimen is male.

**Sts 7:** field number for a partial hominid consisting of a scapula and humerus belonging to the same individual and attributed to *Australopithecus africanus*.

**Sts 14:** field number for a partial hominid consisting of two nearly complete hip bones and associated left femur. The pelvis was badly crushed. Attributed to *Australopithecus africanus*.

**Sts 52b:** field number for a partial hominid consisting of a robust mandible attributed to *Australopithecus* sp.

**Sts 60:** field number for a hominid, dated to between 2.8 and 2.4 mya, consisting of a gracile partial cranium assigned to *Australopithecus* sp. Cranial capacity estimated at 428 cm$^3$.

---

### Some fossil hominids found at Sterkfontein (Stw Series)

**Stw 13:** field number for a partial hominid, consisting of craniofacial fragments assigned to *Australopithecus africanus*.

**Stw 53:** field number for a partial hominid found by Alun Hughes in 1976, dated to 2.0–1.5 mya, and consisting of a mesati-cephalic cranium and some teeth, with a large brain size for an australopithecine. At first attributed to *Australopithecus africanus*, later attributed by many to *Homo habilis* and thought to be a South African equivalent of *H. habilis* known from East Africa (OH 24). Many stone tools were found in the same stratum.

**Stw 431:** field number for a fossil hominid, dated to 2.8–2.6 mya (Member 4 breccia) and that consists of several postcranial fragments. This hominid is attributed to *Australopithecus africanus*.

**Stw 505:** field number for a fossil male hominid found in 1989 at Sterkfontein, dated to 2.8–2.6 mya (Member 4 breccia) and that has a cranial capacity of 515 cm$^3$. The hominid is attributed to *Australopithecus africanus*.

**Stw 573:** field number for an australopithecine found in 1994–97 at sterkfontein, which has several depositional Members dating from 3.3 mya. The lowest and earliest, Member 2, contained the foot bones of 'little foot', Stw 573. The rest of this individual, now almost a complete skeleton, was recovered after 1998. Provisional dates range from 3.6 to 3.01 mya (but may be younger).

---

and **Swartkrans**, although nonhominid sites include Bolt's Farm (contains fossilized sabre-toothed cats), Haasgat (contains 1.3 mya primate fossils) and Gondolin (contains 90,000 fossil specimens including 1 hominid tooth).

**sternal rib:** true **rib**

**sternal scent gland: scent gland** located on the chest of some **prosimians** and callitrichids.

**sternum:** flat elongated bone located at the mid-line of the **thoracic cage**; it articulates with some of the ribs and the clavicles. In **hominoids** the sternum develops in three parts (sternebrae) and is broad, giving considerable support to the **pectoral girdle,** in contrast to the sternebrae of other mammals and primates.

**steroid:** subclass of **lipids**; any molecule consisting of four interconnected carbon rings to which polar groups may be attached. Examples of steroids include the adrenocortical hormones, gonadal hormones (**estrogens** and **androgens**), digitalis, **vitamin D,** and bile acids. Certain **carcinogens** (carcinogenic hydrocarbons) are also steroids or steroid mimics.

**Stewart, Thomas Dale** (1901–97): US physician, physical anthropologist at the US National Museum; an internationally recognized authority on human comparative osteology, skeletal growth, paleopathology, human identification, and forensic anthropology. Stewart also published numerous descriptions of fossil **AMHs** in both the Old and the New Worlds. Editor of the **AJPA** (1942–9); president, **AAPA** (1949–51); Viking Fund medallist (1953). Stewart was one of five physical anthropologists who participated in the identification of American war dead at Oahu, Hawaii, after World War II. Editor of *Personal Identification in Mass Disasters* (1970), and of *Hrdlicka's Practical Anthropometry* (1947).

**'sticky':** vernacular term referring to the behavior of chromosomes that have failed to separate normally (**nondisjunction**) during **cell division.**

**stigmata:** 1. plural of stigma. 2. physical abnormalities believed to be associated with abnormal behavior. Now largely unaccepted, stigmata were once used to identify criminal personalities *c.* 1876-1910. See Cesare **Lombroso.** 3. spot(s) on the skin that bleeds during certain mental states.

**stillbirth:** 1. a dead fetus at birth. 2. delivery of a dead child or organism at term. Aka stillborn. See **abortion.** Cf. **miscarriage** (2).

**stimulus:** change in the environment that is met with by a **response** from a healthy organism. Plural: stimuli.

**stink fight:** term used for territorial display between male **ring-tailed lemurs** that involves applying **pheromone** from the **carpal glands** to the tail. During a stink fight the tail is held upright and pheromone is wafted towards the opponent. Stink fights have been described as restoring boundaries and avoiding physical fighting.

**stochastic:** pertaining to a process involving a randomly determined sequence of observations, each of which is considered as a sample of one **element** from a probability distribution.

**stochastic model:** dynamic mathematical model that includes variable probabilities such that a given input results in more than one output value, and usually many more than one. Cf. **deterministic model.**

**stock:** line of descent; a tribe, race or ethnic group; trunk or main stem.

***Stockia powayensis* Gazin, 1958:** tarsiiform primate from the late Eocene of North America belonging to the omomyid subfamily **Omomyinae; monotypic;** closest relationship appears to be with ***Utahia***, although dentally distinct. Estimated body mass around 500 g. Dental formula uncertain; mandibular and dental morphology suggestive of **frugivory** or, perhaps, **nectarivory.** See Appendix 1 for taxonomy.

**stomach:** hollow muscular organ that lies between the esophagus and small intestine. In primates it serves as a temporary storage area for food as well as the site of initial food breakdown. The **colobines** have a specialized sacculated stomach with an alkaline environment that retains high-fiber food, which is broken down by symbionts. In humans the stomach contains an acid environment and is principally the site of protein digestion.

**stomion:** mid-point of the oral fissure when the lips are closed.

**stone:** 1. polished concretion of hardened sediment, one of the raw materials exploited by Paleolithic peoples, of which **rocks** consist. 2. a nonmetric unit of weight (body mass). 3. rarely, in various (but not all) geological classification systems, a particle of sediment about 60 ± 40 mm in diameter, larger than a **pebble** but smaller than a **cobble.**

**Stone Age:** earliest period of human material **culture,** from roughly 2.4 mya until the earliest use of metal objects about 5 kya; divided into the **Old Stone Age,** the **Middle Stone Age,** and the **New Stone Age.**

**stone chipping:** shaping stones by the removal of flakes. See **knapping.**

**stone circle:** see **DK,** a site at **Olduvai Gorge,** and Guattari Cave.

**stone-knapper:** one who makes or retouches stone tools; see **knapping.**

**stone tool:** any **tool** constructed of **stone** or other lithic material.

**stone tool typology:** classification of lithic implements based upon shape, size, composition, and perceived use.

**stop codon:** codons present in mRNA which signal the end of a growing peptide chain; the codons UAA, UGA and UAG function as stop codons. Cf. **terminator.**

**straight sinus:** large bilateral venous sinus found in the **dura mater** of the frontal, parietotemporal, and occipital regions and that functions to drain blood from the brain. In modern humans, joins with the **transverse sinus** in the occipital region.

**strain:** in a physiological context, condition of an animal body resulting from exposure to **stress** accompanied by reversible or irreversible changes in performance, physiological, or biochemical characteristics.

**strata:** plural of **stratum.**

**strategic model:** employing evolutionary theory to predict how species will be similar or different based on ecological niches and environment.

**strategy:** 1. any plan, method or model utilized in order to cope with a specific set of conditions; see, for example, **reproductive strategy.** 2. set of behaviors for decision making exhibited by individuals that affects their fitness. See **conditional strategy, evolutionarily stable strategy.**

**stratification:** concordance of traits due to homogeneity of the gene pool rather than because of linkage. See **concordant trait.**

**stratigraphic context:** geographic context in which a fossil is found.

**stratigraphic column:** 1. succession of rocks laid down during a specific interval. 2. the whole of geologic time. 3. a simplified columnar diagram of lithostratigraphic units.

‡ **stratigraphy:** study of the geologic **strata** in the earth's crust and of the **fossils** and other items embedded within them. See **biostratigraphy** and **superposition of strata.**

**stratum:** 1. any layer. 2. a layer of sediment, basalt, or other material of a perceived thickness, defined by characteristics that distinguish it from those layers immediately above and below it in a **stratigraphic column.** Plural: strata. See **stratigraphy.**

**stratum basale:** deepest layer of the **epidermis** where mitosis occurs in order to produce new epidermal cells; about ten per-cent of the basal layer's cell population are **melanocytes.** Aka stratum germinativum, basal layer.

**stratum corneum epidermis:** outer and fully **keratinized** layer of the **epidermis;** the stratum corneum is the pigmented portion of the skin. Peoples of the Far East have a thicker stratum corneum than is found in other human populations; this results in a yellowish hue being imparted to the skin and also prevents the fine wrinkles associated with advancing age of European populations.

**stratum coreum unguis:** outer layer of the nail; aka nail plate.

**stratum granulosum:** layer of the epidermis deep to the **stratum corneum epidermis** in most skin; it consists of two to five layers of cells containing dark-staining keratohyalin granules.

**stratum lucidum:** clear thin layer of epidermis deep to the **stratum corneum epidermis** when present; this layer is found in thick skin only, such as is found on the palms or the soles of the feet.

**strepsirhine:** primate belonging to the suborder **Strepsirhini.**

‡ **Strepsirhini:** one of two suborders of primate classification (the other is the **Haplorhini**) suggested to replace the older **Prosimii/Anthropoid** dichotomy; strepsirhines are primates with a moist rhinarium (e.g. lemurs and lorises).

‡ **stress:** in a physiological context, any factor that acts to disrupt **homeostasis;** stress may be caused by pathogens, extremes of environment to which an organism has not adapted, or psychological factors. See **strain.**

**stress hypothesis:** proposal that population size is self-regulatory. The internal dynamics of populations in a growth phase lead to phenotypic physiological changes that eventually decrease the birth rate and increase the death rate.

**stress indicator:** **stress**-induced growth disruption manifesting as **strain** in the skeleton and dentition. Example are, **Harris lines, fluctuating (dental) asymmetry,** enamel defects (**Wilson bands**), enamel **hypoplasias,** and enamel **hypocalcifications.**

**stria:** 1. anatomical term meaning furrow, line, or streak; especially, parallel strips or bands. Adjective: striate; plural: striae; aka striation. 2. small groove or channel in obsidian or other stone that radiates outward from the **bulb of percussion** from which striae converge, and which can be used to determine the percussion point on many stone artifacts.

**stria of Retzius:** microscopic increment of enamel deposited weekly as teeth are formed, and which may also show seasonal patterns indicative of dietary **stress.** See **perikymata.**

**striated muscle:** see **skeletal muscle.**

**striation:** microscopic scratch or abrasion on stone tools that reveals the direction of force and, possibly, the nature of tool use. 2. alternating light and dark cross-markings; in anatomy this is often in reference to muscle tissue.

**striding gait:** bipedal **locomotion** involving extension of the leg to a position behind the vertical axis of the **spinal column,** achievable only if the **ischium** is short, as in the pelvis of modern man. See **habitual bipedalism.**

*Strigorhysis* **Bown, 1979:** genus of tarsiiform primate from the middle Eocene of North America belonging to the omomyid subfamily **Anaptomorphinae;** three species. Estimated body mass ranges between 300 and 600 g. See Appendix 1 for taxonomy.

**striker:** hard, circular stone, often with a flat lateral surface, and used for a hammer or a weight. See **hammerstone.**

**striking platform:** surface where the hammer struck a **core** and knocked off the flake; one of the diagnostic features that archaeologists use to distinguish a stone **tool** from a naturally occurring **geofact.** Aka plan de frappe.

**Stringer, Christopher B.:** (1947- ) British paleontologist, director of the Human Origins Group at the Natural History Museum in London. Challenged the theory proposing a European origin for *Homo sapiens* and that **Neandertals** are ancestral to **AMHs.** Stringer collaborates at numerous sites, and currently directs the Ancient Human Occupation of Britain project. Co-author (with Clive Gamble) of *In Search of the Neanderthals* (1993); (with Robin McKie) *African Exodus: The Origins of Modern Humanity* (1997); and (with J. Weiner) *The Piltdown Forgery* (2003). See the **Out of Africa II model** of **human origins** and **Günter Bräuer.**

**strontium:** trace dietary element similar to **calcium; stable isotope** used in determining nutritional states of prehistoric populations, measured as a strontium/calcium ratio; see **paleonutrition** and **strontium/calcium ratio.**

**strontium/calcium ratio** (Sr/Ca): ratio of **strontium** to **calcium;** used in determining nutritional states of prehistoric populations. Sr/Ca ratios are usually lower in carnivores than in folivores. See **paleonutrition**.

**STRs:** abbreviation for **short tandem repeats**.

‡ **structural gene:** any gene that codes for the production of protein contributing directly to a feature. Cf. **regulatory gene**.

**structural genomics:** collection of data informative of the structure of biological molecules, including protein-folding assignment, model building, and function prediction. Tools used in structural genomics include the synchrotron, **magnetic resonance imaging** instrumentation, and the multi-wavelength anomalous diffraction method of phase determination.

**structural heterozygote:** pertaining to homologous chromosomes in a cell or organism in which one contains a structural defect such as an insertion, deletion, inversion, or translocated fragment.

**structural homozygote:** pertaining to homologous chromosomes in a cell or organism that both contain a structural defect such as an insertion, deletion, inversion, or translocated fragment, relative to the standard karyotype for a species.

**structure:** any nonrandom material or nonmaterial accumulation of resources or features; evidence of human manipulation or occupation; commonly, a dwelling or other architectural edifice.

**'struggle for existence':** competition between members of a population for limited resources that results in differential survival, a phrase implied by Thomas **Malthus** in 1798, and later adopted by Charles **Darwin** in the sixth edition of his *Origin of Species*.

**STS:** see **sequence tagged site**.

**Sts:** see **Sterkfontein**.

**Student's *t*-test:** see *t*-test.

**study group:** animal social unit that is the center of interest in **ethological** studies.

**stump-tailed macaque:** vernacular for *Macaca arctoides*.

**Stw:** see **Sterkfontein**.

**stylar shelf:** flattened accessory development of enamel on the buccal side of a molar of some primates. Aka external cingulum.

**style:** accessory fold of enamel that develops from the **cingulum** on the buccal surface of a molar.

**stylion: anthropometric** landmark; most distal point on the lateral margin of the styloid process of the **radius**.

*Stylohipparion*: Pliocene-aged, three-toed grazing horse-like mammal found at **Olduvai Gorge** in Bed IV deposits dating 1 mya to 500 kya, and useful for **faunal correlation**.

**styloid:** describes a slender projection, i.e. styluslike; long and pointed, e.g. styloid processes of the **temporal bone**, of the **radius**, of the **ulna**, etc.

**styloideum:** supernumerary bone that sometimes develops in the **carpus**, found near the **trapezoid bone**.

**Suard:** see **Abri Suard**.

**subacute infantile mountain sickness:** condition found in some infants that are born or brought into a high-altitude environment; signs include low circulating oxygen concentrations and elevated incidence of polycythemia. Infants suffering from this condition have high mortality risks.

**subacute mountain sickness:** condition caused by exposure to high altitude in which milder symptoms appear in a few hours, symptoms are similar to those of **acute mountain sickness** but are more persistent. Cf. **chronic mountain sickness**. See **altitude sickness**.

**subaurale:** low point on the inferior border of the ear lobule with the head held in the **Frankfort horizontal**.

**subbrachyskelic:** pertaining to a stem–leg length index of between 80 and 84.9.

**subchondral:** underneath cartilage.

**subchron:** a magnetic reversal of relatively short duration within a **chron**. Aka polarity event. See **paleomagnetism**.

**subclass:** in hierarchical taxonomy, the category ranked below the **class** and above the **order**; a set of such categories within the former taxon.

**subclavius muscle:** small muscle that originates in the first rib and inserts into the collarbone. In humans, presence of this muscle is polymorphic: **AMHs** can have either none, one or two of these muscles. See **vestigial trait**.

**subcutaneous fat:** adipose tissue located beneath the skin.

**subcutaneous layer:** loose connective and adipose tissues beneath the **dermis** that binds it to the deeper organs. Aka hypodermis.

**subduction:** in **plate tectonics**, process of one **plate** descending beneath another, as in the case of the subduction of North Africa under the European plate.

**subfamily:** in hierarchical taxonomy, the category ranked below the **family** and above the **genus**; a set of such categories within the former taxon.

**subfossil:** any fossil of a recently **extinct** species whose remains have not yet become fully transformed by **permineralization**; e.g. **subfossil Malagasy prosimian**.

**subfossil Malagasy prosimian (lemur):** any of about eight species of lemurs in four families that became extinct in recent times, most likely as a result of human intervention. These lemurs were quite different from **extant** forms; large (ranging in size from that of the largest living prosimians to the size of an adult male gorilla), diurnal, with some species terrestrial; with fused mandibles; and occupying diverse ecological niches. See *Pachylemur*, **Archaeolemuridae**, **Palaeopropithecidae**, and *Megaladapis*.

**subgenus** (s-g.): in hierarchical taxonomy, the category ranked below the **genus** and above the **species**; a set of such categories within the former taxon. Plural is subgenera (sgg.).

**subischial height: anthropometric** measurement; distance between the hip joint and floor when an individual is standing erect; the measurement obtained should be considered to be only an estimate in a living person. Used in studies of body proportions, athletic performance, and in various areas of **human engineering**. Aka lower extremity length.

**subject:** anything under examination, treatment or experimentation (noun).

**subjective:** 1. assessed as a matter of opinion. 2. **symptom** perceived by a patient but not by a healer. 3. lacking reality. Cf. **objective**.

**sublethal:** not causing death by direct action, but causing cumulative effects that adversely affect **fitness**.

**sublethal gene:** any noncommunicable factor that kills less than 50% of its carriers before **reproductive age**. Aka subvital mutation. See **genetic load**. Cf. **lethal gene, semilethal gene**.

**sublingua:** cornified serrated structure underlying the tongue in **prosimians** and *Tarsius*; this type of structure is also found in other mammals such as marsupials. Adjective: sublingual. In primates the sublingua is used to keep the **dental comb** (when present) or other lower anterior teeth clean. Some workers have described a remnant sublingua in platyrrhines.

**sublingual gland:** salivary gland located below the tongue; its duct opens to the side of the lingual frenulum. One of three pairs of **salivary glands**.

**submacroskelic:** pertaining to a stem–leg length index of between 90 and 94.0.

**submandibular gland:** one of a pair of **salivary glands** located on the floor of the mouth and on the inside surface of the **mandible**. The submandibulars secrete a serous **saliva** that contains some **mucus**.

**submetacentric:** pertaining to or being a **chromosome** with a **centromere** located off center, closer to one end than to the other. See **telocentric**.

**submission: appeasement;** one animal showing a dominant animal that it is no threat in any way. This behavior can inhibit aggression from the dominant animal and avoid serious injury to both.

**submissive display:** ritualized form of **submission**, such as presenting the rump to a dominant animal.

**subnasal:** inferior to the nasal cavity.

**subnasal alveolar process:** see **premaxilla**.

**subnasal prognathism:** forward projection of the jaws, or prominence of the snout.

**subnasale:** craniometric point at which the nasal septum merges with the upper cutaneous lip on the mid-sagittal plane.

**suborder:** in hierarchical taxonomy, the category ranked below the **order** and above the **family**; a set of such categories within the former taxon.

**subordinate:** low in the order of social rank; not dominant.

**subordination of characters, theory of:** in Aristotelian taxonomy, principle that a given character is universal to those subordinate to it, but is itself particular to a higher category; for example, a species is universal to its subspecies and particular with respect to its genus.

**subperiosteal:** pertaining to the area underneath the **periosteum** of bone.

‡ **subphylum:** in taxonomy, a high-level category just beneath the **phylum** and above the **class**. Vertebrata, for example, is the subphylum that contains all vertebrates, and other forms with a chordate nervous system.

**subplatyhieric:** pertaining to a length–breadth sacral index of between 100 and 105.9.

**subpubic concavity:** depression present on the inferior border of the adult female pubic bone that aids in assessment of a recovered skeleton, such as **skeletal sexing**.

**subrotundrum:** see **pisiform**.

**sub-Saharan theory:** antiquated proposition that the ancestors of present-day Europeans had occupied the milder regions of Africa during the **Pleistocene** glacial periods, and had simply returned to Europe after the glaciers melted; the morphology of these ancestors was thought by the theory's supporters to have been **Caucasoid** rather than **Negroid**.

**subscapular:** of or pertaining to the region of the back directly below the **scapula**. This is an area where **subcutaneous fat** is often measured. See **subscapular skinfold**.

**subscapular skinfold: anthropometric** measurement; skinfold measured just inferior to the inferior angle of the **scapula**. Used for assessment of nutritional status and, in combination with other **skinfold measurements**, to estimate body fat composition, blood pressure, and blood lipids of an individual.

‡ **subsistence:** any means of supporting life or providing a livelihood; techniques and **strategies** for insuring a supply of food.

**subsistence agriculture:** see **swidden agriculture**.

*subsp.:* see *subspecies*.

**subspeciation:** initial stages of most gradual modes of speciation such as **allopatric speciation** that involves the clustering of demes into regional populations and the reduction of **gene flow** that produces varieties.

‡ **subspecies:** subdivision of a **species** (first used by Schlegel, 1844), usually narrowly defined as a

**geographical race**; a population or series of populations occupying a discrete range and differing genetically from other geographical races of the same species; discrete populations for which between-population variation is high relative to within-population variation. Cf. **semispecies**. Abbreviated *ssp.*, *subsp.*

**subspinale:** point of the nasal aperture below the nasal spine.

**substitution:** 1. replacement of one or more atoms of one element by those of another. 2. replacement of one nucleotide by another in a DNA molecule, aka **nucleotide substitution.** 3. replacement of one amino acid by another in a polypeptide chain, aka **amino acid substitution.** Aka substitutional mutation (2,3).

**substitutional gene therapy** (SubGT): nonheritable replacement or augmentation of a working product for a null gene product, typically a deleterious mutation. The use of recombinant human insulin by **insulin-dependent diabetics** as a replacement for genetically defective insulin is an example of SubGT. See **somatic cell gene therapy, gametic (germline) gene therapy, proximate** and **ultimate effect.**

**substitutional load:** reduction of the mean fitness of a population owing to the replacement of one allele by another. Aka transitional load. See **genetic load.**

**substitutional mutation:** see **point mutation.**

‡ **substrate:** 1. supporting surface. 2. something spread or laid under something else; see **substratum.** 3. reactant in an enzyme-mediated reaction.

**substratum:** ground or other surface upon which organisms exist, or are active.

**subtalar joint:** articulation of two to three facets (due to within-species variation) of the **talus** with the **calcaneus** of the ankle; there are actually two separate joints that comprise the subtalar joint, an anterior talocalcaneal joint and a posterior talocalcaneal joint.

**subtelomere:** unique region of the genome located between the chromosome-specific sequence and the **telomere** that caps each chromosome end. Subtelomeres consist of patches of duplicated blocks of DNA that exhibit homology with similar regions on nonhomologous chromosomes. Subtelomeres are involved in ectopic **recombination** and play a central role in abnormal **translocation.**

**subtense:** line that divides an isosceles triangle into two equally sized areas. A subtense is used in some anthropometric indices.

**subterminal:** pertaining to a chromosome in which the centromere is located between the middle and one end.

**subtractive technology:** process in which artifacts take form as material is removed from an original mass, such as stone-knapping.

**subtribe:** in hierarchical taxonomy, the category ranked below the **tribe** and above the **genus**; a set of categories within the former taxon.

**subtrochanteric:** area located inferior to one of the **trochanters.**

**succession:** 1. in anthropology, the passage of rights and/or status from one person or group to another person or group, often by means of descent or marital ties, but sometimes through institutions and certification. 2. in ecology, the changes in the nature of an ecosystem that take place until a climax is attained.

‡ **sucking reflex:** instinctive behavior found in mammal neonates to put their mouths on the mother's **areolae** (nipples or teats) in order to stimulate **lactation.**

**sucrose:** white, crystalline **disaccharide** composed of glucose and fructose; usually obtained from sugar cane, sugar beet, and maple, and used as a sweetener and preservative. Aka cane sugar, saccharose, table sugar. Cf. **fructose.**

**sudden infant death syndrome:** see SIDS.

**sudor:** pertaining to sweat.

**sudoriferous:** pertaining to a gland that produces **sweat** or a duct that conveys sweat to the surface of the skin. See **apocrine sweat gland, eccrine sweat gland, sudoriparous gland.**

**sudoriparous gland:** aggregation of cells that secrete or produce **sweat.** Two of the most important are **apocrine sweat glands** and **eccrine sweat glands.** Archaic for **sudoriferous** gland.

**sugar:** kind of carbohydrate, many with a sweet taste; in common usage, any simple hexose sugar of the general form $C_6H_{12}O_6$; **monosaccharides** and **disaccharides.**

**suid:** any member of the family Suidae, the family of mammals that includes pigs and boars.

**Sulawesi black macaque:** vernacular for *Macaca nigra.*

**sulcal pattern:** configuration of the grooves and fissures on the surface of a brain. In fossils, **endocasts** often reflect these patterns, preserved as imprints on the internal surfaces of skulls.

**sulcus:** groove, furrow or depression.

**Sumatran orangutan:** vernacular for the orangutan subspecies *Pongo pygmaeus abelii.*

**Sunda Island leaf-monkey:** vernacular for *Presbytis aygula* (= *comata*).

**Sunda shelf:** shallow shelf of land in southeast Asia, under less than 100 m of sea water but exposed during most of the **Pleistocene** when sea water was extensively bound up in continental glaciers; the Sunda shelf would have tied the Malayan peninsula to the (now) islands of Sumatra, Borneo and Java, making them one large peninsula accessible to early hominids, as well as to other flora and fauna. See **Sunda trench.**

**Sunda trench:** undersea channel in southeast Asia, deeper than 100 m and therefore a continuous body of water during most of the **Pleistocene** when more sea water was bound up in continental glaciers; the Sunda trench would have delimited the **Sunda shelf.** The trench itself would have presented a continuous water barrier, navigable only with rafts or boats. See **Wallace's line.**

**Sungir:** a periglacial archaeological site found in 1955 on the Klyaz'ma River north of Moscow in Russia dated to 24–22 kya; contains Upper Paleolithic artifacts (3500 bead ornaments, weapons, and carvings) including carved mammoth ivory spears. Hominid remains include an adult (buried with the spears), and two boys (ages 7–9, and 10–12), all **AMHs.** Aka Sunghir.

**superaurale:** apex on the superior border of the **helix.**

**superciliary arch:** faint ridge of bone above the **orbits** to which the corrugator supercilii muscle originates; this muscle depresses the eyebrows and draws them closer together. Aka superciliary ridge, brow ridge.

**superclass:** in hierarchical taxonomy, the category ranked below the **subphylum** and above the **class;** a set of categories within the former taxon.

‡ **superfamily:** in taxonomy, the category between the **family** and the **order,** and thus consisting of a group of related families. The superfamily **Hominoidea,** for example, contains the families **Hylobatidae, Pongidae,** and **Hominidae.**

**superfecundation:** fertilization of two or more eggs by an equal number of spermatozoa at different times within the same menstrual cycle. This may produce **twins** or other **higher-order multiples** conceived at different times, sometimes by different fathers.

**superfemale:** female who has a greater dose of female **sex determination** factors than normal females in a species have. In most mammals, females have two X chromosomes, whereas individuals with more than two X chromosomes have additional copies of all the genes on those X chromosomes or chromatids. Aka **metafemale.** See **dosage compensation** and **X inactivation.**

**superfetation:** release of two or more eggs several weeks apart, and their fertilization by separate spermatozoa. This is thought to produce **fraternal twins** that differ markedly in their maturity.

**superficial:** anatomical term of relative position meaning on the surface or towards the surface.

**supergene:** any set of genes so tightly linked that they behave during recombination like a single locus.

**supergene family:** group of genes that have a common sequence homology such that common ancestry is implied.

**superior:** anatomical term of relative position meaning that a structure is positioned above another structure; towards the head. **Cranial** is used as a synonym.

**superior colliculus:** structure within the mid-brain or **mesencephalon** that functions to control visual reflexes (hand–eye coordination). Cf. **inferior colliculus.**

**superior frontal gyrus:** major convolution located on the superior and medial surface of the **frontal lobe** of the brain.

**superior frontal sulcus:** cleft in the **frontal lobe** lateral and inferior to the **superior frontal gyrus.**

**superior transverse torus:** faint bar of bone on the posterior portion of the mandibular symphysis. See **mandibular torus.**

**supermale:** male with more than one **Y chromosome;** see **double-Y syndrome.**

**supermethylation:** addition of methyl groups to cytosine bases (usually at CpG dinucleotides). The extra methyl groups can inactivate a gene's promoter region, causing an effect similar to mutation in the structural portion. Supermethylation has been implicated in 20–50% of women with certain breast cancers but without a mutated *BRCA1* gene. See **DNA methylation.**

**supernumerary:** extra; additional.

**supernumerary bone:** extra or additional bone such as a finger in **polydactyly** or growth island in a cranial suture; see **sutural bone.**

**supernumerary chromosome:** any chromosome or fragment that causes the karyotype of an organism to be different from the modal **karyotype** for a species. Aka B-chromosome.

**supernumerary mammae:** additional **mammae** in humans, usually pairs of vestigial nipples extending onto the stomach area.

**supernumerary tooth:** additional tooth, usually an underformed duplication of another tooth present in the normal dentition.

**superorder:** in hierarchical taxonomy, the category ranked below the **subclass** and above the **order;** a set of such categories within the former taxon.

**superorganic:** term used by some cultural anthropologists to describe that which is literally 'above the organic', i.e. culture; that which is nurture rather than nature.

**superovulation:** simultaneous release of more than the normal number of eggs.

**superoxide dismutase** (SOD): antioxidant enzyme found in both prokaryotes and eukaryotes. Mammals have one form coded for by a nuclear gene (*SOD1*, which maps to HSA 21q22.1) and another mitochondrial form (*SOD2*). SODs are anti-oxidant enzymes that convert cellular **superoxide anions** ('free radicals') to nontoxic chemicals by conversion to hydrogen peroxide and water. Aka indolophenoloxidase. See **amyotrophic lateral sclerosis.**

**superoxide anion: free oxygen radical** generated by the loss of one electron to an oxygen molecule ($O_2^-$).

**superposition of strata, rule** or **law of:** one of the principles or rules in geology, which states that (usually) a sedimentary layer that is currently situated below another such layer, is older than the layer(s) above it. This principle assumes that gravity has always operated in the same way that it does today, and that it would be unlikely therefore that a complete sedimentary layer (or volcanic layer) to be inserted between two preexisting geological strata. first proposed by N. Steno.

**superspecies: allopatric, monophyletic** group of morphologically distinct species; this distinctiveness precludes them from being included in a single species. Among the primates, it has been suggested that the species included within *Papio* constitute a superspecies.

**supersternale:** point at the top of the **sternum** used as a landmark when measuring living people; Aka suprasternal notch.

**supertroop:** formation of a larger group by two separate primate social units without fighting; this group stays together for a short period of time, but may do so on a regular basis. This is not a **fission-fusion group.**

**supertwins:** see **higher-order multiples.**

**supervital mutation:** any alteration to a gene or chromosome that increases the viability of the affected individuals relative to the rest of the population. Some hemoglobin mutants are suspected to function as supervitals.

**supination:** lateral rotation of the forearm which results in the palms of the hands facing anteriorly (in reference to **anatomical position**). Cf. **pronation.** See **eversion** and **inversion.**

**supinator ridge** or **crest:** elongated feature on the inside of the ulna that provides attachment for the supinator muscle.

**supplantation:** action in which an individual moves away from its previous location in order to avoid confrontation with another individual.

‡ **suppressor T cell:** white blood cell that inhibits antibody production and cytotoxic T cell function.

**suppressor tRNA:** altered **tRNA** that inserts an amino acid at a **stop codon.**

**supracondyloid process:** small process that occasionally occurs on the medial surface of the human **humerus.** Some comparative anatomists consider this process to be an **atavism.**

**supraglabella:** area above the **glabella.**

**suprailiac skinfold: anthropometric** measurement; skinfold measured in the mid-axillary line immediately superior to the iliac crest of the **pelvis.** Used in combination with other **skinfold measurements** to estimate total body density. See **skinfold thickness.**

**suprainiac fossa:** mid-sagittal depression on the **occipital bone** characteristic of **Neandertals.**

**supramastoid crest:** horizontal ridge of bone that extends backwards from the **zygomatic process.** It serves as a site of attachment for the lowermost fibers of the **temporalis muscle.** It is present in several extinct hominids, namely *Paranthropus, Australopithecus,* and *Homo erectus.*

**supraorbital:** above the eyes.

‡ **supra-orbital torus, tori:** heavy ridge of bone above each **orbit** that forms a brow ridge in many hominid fossil species. In most of these species the **glabella** unites the two sides of the brow ridge; in such cases the glabellar torus unites the two **superciliary arches** into a continuous bar of bone, as in *Homo erectus,* and is termed the **frontal torus.** Absence of the glabellar aspect results in a **double-arched supra-orbital torus,** as in **Neandertals.** Aka supra-orbital arch or ridge.

**supraorganic evolution:** doctrine that societies and cultures grow in a manner analogous to the evolution of organisms. First suggested by H. **Spencer** (see **social Darwinism**) and later promulgated by E. B. **Tylor** (see **unilineal evolution**) and other evolutionary anthropologists.

**suprapatellar skinfold: anthropometric** measurement: skinfold measured on the mid-line of the anterior surface of the thigh 2 cm above the proximal border of the knee. Used in combination with other **skinfold measurements** to estimate body composition. See **skinfold thickness.**

**suprasternal height:** on a standing subject, the distance from the floor to the center of the anterior–superior border of the manubrium sterni.

**supratoral sulcus:** shallow groove behind the **supra-orbital torus** in *Homo erectus.*

**sureli:** vernacular used for the leaf monkeys belonging to the genus *Presbytis*; authors using this term generally use the term langur for the alternative genera *Semnopithecus* and *Trachypithecus.*

**surface archaeology:** recovery and analysis of unburied material culture produced by human activity.

**surface area:** free surface in organisms that is available for physiological exchanges, such as the alveoli in the lungs or the villi in the small intestine.

**surface–mass law:** empirical observation that the surface area of a spherical object doubles as its mass triples. Since animals lose body heat roughly in proportion to the combined surface area of their bodies and lungs, an animal with a circular or thick body will have a minimal surface area for its mass, and therefore retain heat, while another animal of equal mass but with a lineal body build will lose heat more rapidly. See **Bergmann's rule** and **Allen's rule**.

**surface pheromone:** substance that has a limited active space such that a recipient must be in direct contact, or nearly so, for it to take effect. See **pheromone**.

**surface site:** area in which artifacts and structures remain on stable ground surfaces.

**surrogate:** term from primate laboratory experiments that refers to a wire or cloth dummy that substitutes for the mother; this term is rarely used in this context outside of primatology. Cf. **surrogate mother**.

**surrogate mother:** woman who carries an embryo and fetus to term on behalf of another person or couple; the surrogate may or may not have donated the oöcyte, as well. Aka surrogate motherhood.

**survivability:** probability of survival of a certain genotype in a population given as a function of its associated selection coefficient.

**survival:** endurance under adverse conditions or remaining alive longer than expected.

‡ **'survival of the fittest':** phrase coined by Herbert **Spencer** in 1864, and later adopted by Charles **Darwin** in the 6th edition of his *Origin of Species*. Idea that individuals better adapted to their environment are those most likely to reproduce. The idea was later co-opted by the supporters of **social Darwinism** to justify *laissez-faire* capitalism and colonial expansionism.

**survival value:** measure of the effectiveness of a trait in conferring **fitness** on an individual.

**survivorship:** proportion of individuals from a given **cohort** that survive to a given time. See **survivorship curve**.

**survivorship curve:** graphical representation of **life table** data of survivorship which produces three different curves. Type I represents an organism in which offspring survival is high and mortality increases as individuals age; modern humans in developed nations fit this curve. Type II represents an organism in which death may occur at any stage of the life cycle. Type III represents an organism in which there is early mortality with few individuals reaching adulthood and reproductive age. Such an organism produces large numbers of progeny.

**suspended animation:** temporary suspension of life processes. A vernacular term for phenomena such as hibernation and the **dictyotene stage** of oogenesis.

**suspensory climbing:** ability to raise the arms above the head and to hang from branches, and to climb while in such a position; hominoids are suspensory climbers.

**suspensory locomotion:** see **brachiation**.

**suspensory posture:** locomotor position in which the body is suspended below a branch(es) that the hands are holding onto; such posture distributes the weight of animals that would be too large to balance on smaller supports. See **brachiation**.

**sustainable development:** development that does not destroy resources and enables the resource to be harvested into the foreseeable future, e.g. logging selected trees in a forest and preserving the future by not clear-felling.

**sustentacular cell:** 1. cell in the fetal testes that secretes **Müllerian-inhibiting hormone**. 2. specialized cell in the mature testes that supplies nutrients to developing spermatozoa; Aka Sertoli cell or nurse cell.

**sustentaculare:** supernumerary bone of the foot that sometimes develops near the dorsal surface of the head of the **talus**.

**sutural bone:** small supernumerary bone occasionally found near the site of cranial sutures; these bones often are named after the suture they are closest to (e.g. **asterionic bone**, **epiteric bone**). Aka Wormian or Inca bone (because they were observed in Peruvian skulls).

**suture:** fibrous articulation between **flat bones** of the skull. There are three types of suture: a serrate suture is connected by interlocking teeth at the articulation; a lap suture is an articulation of bones that are beveled so they overlap and appear smooth; a plane suture is an articulation of two bones that simply abut against one another.

**Swanscombe:** archaeological site found in 1935 and reworked in 1955 in the Thames Valley in Kent, England, dating to 400–225 kya (**Mindel–Riss**, or second interglacial), and that contains thousands of Middle **Acheulean** flint handaxes and worked bones. Hominid remains include a partial face and three separate parietal fragments of a variety of archaic *Homo* sp. (see *Homo swanscombensis*), including that of a possible female, with a 1325 cm³ cranial capacity and with a **suprainiac fossa** but no bun. Aka Barnfield Pit, presapiens man.

‡ **Swartkrans** (SK): archaeological site found in 1948 by **Broom** near Johannesburg, South Africa. Consists of five major rock units (known as Members 1–5) dating from about 1.8 (Member 1) to <1.0 mya (Member 3), and contains artifacts (developed **Oldowan** tools) and **hominid** remains (see box below) that include 98 individuals from Member 1, 17 from Member 2, and 9 from Member 3, all assigned to *Paranthropus* (= *Australopithecus*) *robustus* (e.g. **SK 48** and **SK 1585**). The hominids are expected to date to the younger portion of the deposition interval, however. In 1949, other fragments, dated to about 1.5 mya, were found. These

fragments included bone artifacts and several hominid remains from Members 1 and 3, and two mandibles and a partial skull attributed to *Telanthropus capensis* (= *Homo erectus*) from Member 2. Tools found at the site in 1970 and associated with hominid remains have been described as similar to **Oldowan**, but larger. The site was actively excavated through 1987, and some 90+ individuals were finally recovered from the site. No hominids are reported from Members 4–5.

---

**Some hominid fossils found at Swartkrans**

All except **SK847** are assigned to *Paranthropus* (= *Australopithecus) robustus*.

**SK 23**: field number for a fossil hominid consisting of a well-preserved mandible.

**SK 48**: field number for a fossil hominid recovered in 1950 consisting of an almost complete cranium of an adult female, dated to 2.0–1.5 mya.

**SK 56**: field number for a fossil hominid recovered from **Swartkrans**, South Africa, consisting of a partial innominate.

**SK 82**: field number for a fossil hominid consisting of a femoral head fragment.

**SK 97**: field number for a fossil hominid consisting of a femoral head fragment.

**SK 847**: field number for a separate cranium and palate found decades earlier but only fully articulated in 1969 by Ron Clarke and assigned to the genus *Homo sp. indet.* Recovered from the older pink breccia at **Swartkrans**, which is thought to date to >1 mya and contemporary with the **australopithecine** fossils found at the same site. Aka *Telanthropus capensis*.

**SK 1585**: field number for a fossil hominid consisting of a natural cranial endocast with an estimated cranial capacity of 530 cm$^3$, and dating from 1.8–1.6 mya.

---

**Swartkrans pink breccia:** orange or pink **breccia** that corresponds to Member 1 (see **Swartkrans**).

**sweat:** perspiration. Clear liquid exuded from **apocrine sweat glands** and especially **eccrine sweat glands** or **sudoriferous glands**. Sweat contains water, sodium chloride, cholesterin, fats and fatty acids, and traces of albumin, urea, and other minor compounds. In addition to clearing the body of these components, eccrine sweat facilitates **thermoregulation** in some mammals, such as humans and horses. See **thermal sweat** and **nonthermal sweat**.

**sweat gland:** see **apocrine sweat gland**, **eccrine sweat gland**, and **sudoriferous gland**.

**sweating:** act of perspiring. See **thermal sweat** and **nonthermal sweat**.

**sweepstakes bridge** or **route:** difficult dispersal or migratory path along which chance events dramatically decrease the chance of survival for many individuals.

‡ **swidden agriculture:** type of hoe agriculture in which an area of natural vegetation is cut, dried and burned; the nutrient-containing ashes are then mixed into the soil, and small plots containing a complex mixture of crops are planted; after a period, when nutrients are selectively exhausted, the plot is allowed to lie fallow and overgrow with 'natural' vegetation; the process is then repeated in a new location. This mode of subsistence farming usually provides for the basic needs of the group, with little surplus for marketing. Aka shifting cultivation, slash-and-burn, milpa, chitimeme.

**switch gene:** gene that selects for a different developmental pathway; see **epigenotype**.

**Syke's monkey:** vernacular for *Cercopithecus mitis albogularis*.

**sylvan:** pertaining to a wooded region; from the (Latin) term *silva*.

**sylvian crest:** ridge found on the internal surface of the parietal bone of some primitive hominid skulls; it occupies the **sylvian sulcus** or fissure of the brain.

**sylvian fissure:** see **sylvian sulcus**.

**sylvian sulcus:** groove on the brain on the lateral side of each cerebral hemisphere that separates the temporal lobe from the frontal and parietal lobes; Aka **lateral sulcus**.

**symbiont:** member of one of the species in a symbiotic relationship.

**symbiosis:** interrelationship, often obligate, between two organisms that live together; symbiotic. Aka consortism. See **commensalism, mutualism, parasitism**.

**symbol:** feature of behavior or language that conveys meaning.

**symbolic communication:** any communication system utilizing arbitrary but conventional sounds and signs for meaning; referential. Cf. **vocalization**.

**symmetry:** arrangement of organs and other structures of the body relative to imaginary planes and axes. Adjective: symmetrical.

**sympathetic division:** one of the two divisions of the **autonomic nervous system**. The sympathetic division arises from the thoracic and lumbar regions of the spinal cord and consist of those nerve fibers that are involved with unconscious preparation for energy-expending, stressful, or emergency situations; colloquially referred to as the 'fight or flight' division. The sympathetic division **innervates** the same effectors as the **parasympathetic division**, but the effects are generally **antagonistic**. Aka sympathetic nervous system.

**sympathetic nervous system:** see **sympathetic division**.

**sympathomimetic:** describes any substance with activity that activates the portions of the nervous system that induce moods, emotions, or emotional behavior. **Serotonin, dopamine,** the **endorphins,** and **phenylethylamine** are examples.

**sympatric:** occurring together in the same geographic area; used of related taxa that compete in the same or nearby habitats.

**sympatric speciation:** speciation by populations with overlapping geographic ranges.

**sympatry:** 1. condition when two or more populations occupy the same habitat but do not interbreed. Adjective: sympatric. 2. overlap in the geographical range of two species or nonbreeding populations. Cf. **allopatry**.

**symphalangism:** condition characterized by **ankylosis** of the finger and toe joints.

*Symphalangus* **Gloger, 1841:** subgenus within *Hylobates*. This subspecies consists only of *H. syndactylus*.

*Symphalangus syndactylus* **(Raffles, 1821):** siamang; synonym for *Hylobates syndactylus*.

**symphyseal angle:** angle made by the horizontal lower border of the body of the **mandible** and its intersection with a line tangent to the anterior teeth and chin (or mandibular symphysis).

**symphyseal face:** articular surface of the **pubic bone**.

**symphyseal fusion:** closure and ossification of a **symphysis**.

**symphyseal rim:** elevated margin that develops on the edge of the **symphyseal face** of the **pubic bone**. Used in age estimation.

**symphysion:** anthropometric landmark at the upper and outer border of the symphysis pubis.

**symphysion height:** measure taken on a standing subject, the distance from the floor to the **symphysion**.

**symphysis:** type of **cartilaginous joint** found in several locations along the mid-line of the body in which hyaline cartilage is attached to the articulating surfaces; a pad of springy fibrocartilage is situated between the hyaline cartilages, providing a limited amount of movement; an example is the pubic symphysis.

**symphysis, mandibular:** see **mandibular symphysis**.

**symplesiomorphy, symplesiomorphies:** referring to **traits** that are co-inherited from a **common** ancestor within a group of organisms; aka **primitive** or general traits. See **plesiomorphy**.

**sympodial:** pertaining to the nonlinear, meandering nature of evolution. Cf. **progressive evolution**.

**synapomorphy:** new trait, shared between two or more **sister groups** in an evolving lineage that signifies their close relationship; synapomorphic. Aka **derived** trait, **homology**. See **advanced** and **apomorphy**.

**symptom:** phenomenon that arises as the result of a particular disease or disorder and that serves as in indicator of it. Cf. **sign** (2).

‡ **synapse:** minute space between the axon terminal of a presynaptic neuron and a dendrite of a postsynaptic neuron, into which neurotransmitters are released that allow the continuation or inhibition of an action potential.

‡ **synapsis:** point-for-point pairing of **homologous chromosomes** in the early **prophase** of **meiosis** due to the construction of a **synaptonemal complex**, and during which **crossing over** also occurs; a prerequisite to normal **anaphase I** assortment.

**synaptonemal complex:** paired homologous chromosomes of a **pachytene** bivalent, along with several maintenance substructures and proteins, and that serves to maintain the proper parallel configuration of the synapsed chromatid arms. See **synapsis**.

**synarthrotic joint:** immovable joint or articulation. A **suture** is an example of such a joint. Cf. **amphiarthrotic joint, diarthrotic joint**. See **joint**.

**synchondrosis:** type of **cartilaginous joint** in which bones are connected by bands of hyaline cartilage; often this cartilage is replaced by bone as the individual grows. Examples are the sutures of the skull, which may become completely obliterated with age.

**synchronic:** existing or occurring at the same time as something else. Cf. **diachronic**.

**syndactyly:** fusion or growing together of two or more fingers or toes; web fingers or web toes. Syndactyly is normal in many species, but in humans is inherited as an abnormal Mendelian recessive, and is common in **triploid** fetuses. Aka syndactylia.

**syndesmosis:** type of fibrous joint in which the bones are joined by connective tissue that forms an interosseous ligament which allows limited flexibility, e.g. the tibiofibular articulation. Cf. **synostosis**.

**syndrome:** group of symptoms occurring with sufficient regularity to be considered characteristic; commonly used to refer to collections of symptoms that do not have an easily identifiable cause. Cf. **disease**.

**syndromic deafness:** genetic defect in a single gene that causes a single medical problem, **deafness**; e.g. **Pendred syndrome**. 70% of cases of **inherited deafness** are syndromic. See **nonsyndromic deafness**.

**synecology:** study of whole organismic communities rather than individual species. Cf. **autecology**. See **community ecology**.

**synergism hypothesis:** recent manifestation of meaningful **directional selection**, and based upon cooperation and **mutual aid** rather than competition; see **progressive evolution**.

**synergist:** muscle that acts to assist a **prime mover**.

**syngamy:** final step in fertilization, in which the nuclei of the sex cells (gametes) meet and fuse. Encompasses both **plasmogamy** and **karyogamy**.

**syngeneic:** relating to genetically identical or near-identical mammals such as **twins** or highly inbred lines; isogenic.

**synonym:** one of two of more names used for the same **taxon**.

**synonymous mutation:** base substitution in DNA in which exactly the same nucleotide is supplied during DNA repair, resulting in no change in a polypeptide chain after synthesis; may be either a **transition** or a **transversion**.

*synonymum novum* (*syn. nov.*) (Latin): new synonymy.

**synostose:** to fuse together. See **ankylosis**.

**synostosis:** bony articulations that becomes ossified with time; the **metopic suture** of the frontal bones in anthropoids is one example, sutures of the human cranium that become completely obliterated with old age is another; aka bony joint. Plural: synostoses. Cf. **syndesmosis**.

**synovial fluid:** viscous lubricating fluid secreted into the **joint cavity** by the **synovial membrane**; this fluid also helps to nourish the **articular cartilage** with nutrients obtained from the vascular lining of the **synovial membrane**.

**synovial joint:** freely movable joint with **hyaline cartilage** on the articular surfaces, an **articular capsule**, and a **synovial membrane** which secretes **synovial fluid**. The six types of synovial joint are **ball-and-socket joint, condyloid joint, gliding joint, hinge joint, pivot joint,** and **saddle joint**. See **joint**.

**synovial membrane:** vascular lining of loose connective tissue that covers the surfaces contained within an **articular capsule** except that portion covered by **articular cartilage**. This membrane has specialized cells that secrete a thick lubricating **synovial fluid**. It also takes up excess fluid, stores **adipose tissue**, and forms movable fatty pads for use in the joint.

**synteny:** correspondence of genes located on comparable **chromosomes** in several **species**.

**synthesis:** in science, a complex whole formed by combining elements. Cf. **analysis**.

**synthetic theory of evolution:** see **neo-Darwinism**.

**syntype:** in the absence of a designated **holotype**, any of two or more specimens described in the original document that described a new taxon.

**syphilis:** 1. nonvenereal, or endemic form of syphilis; see **bejel**. 2. common chronic, infectious congenital or sexually transmitted disease (STD) caused by a **spirochete** (*Treponema pallidum pallidum*); affects any tissue or vascular organ and may persist for years without symptoms. May also be contracted at a **nosocomial** source. Four progressive stages are recognized: primary (infection followed by an incubation period of 3-8 weeks), secondary (characterized by the eruption of chancres and lesions), latent (remission of symptoms but seropositivity is maintained), and late (formerly the tertiary; noninfectious stage that results in the reemergence of lesions, and irreversible organ damage that results in death). Skeletal manifestations involve signature modifications to the shin and tibia. May be a New World mutation of **yaws**. Aka venereal syphilis. Cf. **nonvenereal treponematoses**.

**systadial:** pertaining to the same stage in an evolutionary sequence.

‡ **system:** 1. assemblage or complex of parts forming a unitary whole, such as a group of body organs that function together. 2. a set of variables that interact in such a way that a change in the state or value of one causes a cascade of changes in another or others. 3. rocks formed during a given geological episode.

**systematic:** 1. relating to a system. 2. arrangement in an ordered sequence according to a system.

‡ **systematics:** science of classifying organisms and the study of their genealogical relationships. A near synonym of **taxonomy**, as defined by **Simpson**, 'systematics is the scientific study of the kinds and diversity of organisms and of any and all relationships among them'.

**systemic:** relating to an entire organism rather than to individual parts.

**systemic lupus erythematosus** (SLE): connective tissue disorder characterized by facial rash, the destruction of heart, brain and kidney cells, and a persistent high fever. One of the **autoimmune diseases** in which antibodies are produced against one's own conservative elements in DNA, neurons and blood cells. HLA haplotypes containing the **HLA DR3** antigen predispose individuals to this condition.

**systemic mutations** or **macromutations:** R.B. **Goldschmidt's** term for his so-called **macromutations** that gave rise to the '**hopeful monsters**' that inspired his version of **macroevolution**, *c.* 1940.

*Szalatavus attricuspis* **Rosenberger, Hartwig, and Wolff, 1991:** platyrrhine from the late Oligocene of South America and placed in a category *incertae sedis*; **monotypic;** some workers think that this is a junior synonym for *Branisella boliviana*; one of the geologically oldest of the New World monkeys; phylogenetic relationship uncertain, but some workers think that this monkey is a callitrichid ancestor. Estimated body mass around 500 g. Dental formula: 2.1.3.3/2.1.3.3; dental morphology suggestive of **frugivory**. See Appendix 1 for taxonomy.

**Szeletian tool tradition:** 'transitional' tool industry found in eastern Europe, presumably carried by **Neandertals**, but like the **Châtelperronian** seems to be a mixture of Middle and Upper Paleolithic techniques and tool types. Cf. **Buhunician** and **Uluzzian**.

**t:** convertional symbol for selection coefficient. See **fitness, s**$_i$.

**T box gene:** part of the DNA structure of certain genes that contains a conserved **motif** that encodes a DNA-binding site.

**Tabarin:** see **chemeron Formation.**

*tabula rasa*: Latin for a blank tablet; in learning theory, the term has come to mean that at birth the brain contains neither knowledge nor innate programs of behavior. See **Standard Social Science Model.**

**Tabūn Cave:** archaeological site worked during 1929–34 in Mount Carmel near Haifa, Israel, dated to 105 ± 25 kya, and that contains **Levalloiso-Mousterian** artifacts. The hominid remains include a partly extended female skeleton, possibly representing a burial, with a cranial capacity of 1270 cm$^3$ (**Tabūn I,** aka Tabūn C1; some consider this specimen to be *c.* 70 kya), and a larger, possibly male, mandible (**Tabūn II,** aka Tabūn C2; some consider this specimen to be more modern-looking and considerably older, *c.* 125 kya, than the female skeleton), both attributed to *Homo neanderthalensis.* Older **Yabrudian** levels date to 213–151 kya and overlie an even older **Tayacian** assemblage. Aka Mugharet et-Tabūn, 'the oven'. See **Amud, Zuttiyeh, Shanidar,** and Dorothy **Garrod.**

**tachyauxesis:** growth in which a part or organ of interest grows faster than the organism as a whole. See **heterauxesis** and **allometry.**

**tachygenesis:** relatively accelerated ontogenetic development in a phylum; Cf. **bradygenesis.**

**tachytely:** Simpson's term for a rate of evolution that is relatively fast.

**tactical deception:** a form of **deceit** in which normal behavior(s) is employed such that another individual may misinterpret what the act(s) signify, to the advantage of the actor. See the **social intelligence hypothesis.**

**tactile communication:** portion of a complex signaling system utilized by many animals, and especially primates, by which information is exchanged by body contact, usually through the use of hands, e.g. by holding, touching, and grooming.

**tactile hair:** see **vibrissa.**

**tactile pad:** concentration of nervous tissue associated with dermal ridges on the palmar and plantar surfaces of primate paws (and those of some other arboreal mammals); these dermal ridges are sensitive to touch and also provide an uneven surface that helps grip the substrate. See **friction pads.**

**Taforalt:** archaeological site found in Morocco dating to 11 kya; contains **Ibero-Maurusian** artifacts and hominid remains including almost 300 'skeletally robust' individuals assigned to *Homo sapiens.*

**taiga:** Russian term for **boreal forest.**

‡ **tail:** 1. the last, rear or hindmost portion of anything. 2. distal portion of the vertebral column that extends externally beyond the trunk, located on the sagittal mid-line, and that arises just above the anus. The hindmost part of many animals, considered an appendage to the trunk, and consisting of the **caudal vertebrae.** Among the many functions of tails are balance, signaling, swatting, grooming, and locomotion. Among the primates, only the superfamily **Hominoidea** lack tails. Adjective: caudal.

**Taiwan macaque:** vernacular for *Macaca cyclopis.*

**talapoin monkey:** vernacular for *Miopithecus talapoin.*

**tali:** plural of **talus.**

**talocrural joint:** **hinge joint** formed between the **talus, tibia,** and **fibula** that permits dorsiflexion, plantar flexion, and a slight amount of circumduction.

**talon:** low cusp on the distal **occlusal surface** of a maxillary molar. Cf. **talonid.**

**talonid:** posterior region on the distal **occlusal surface** of a **mandibular** molar. Cf. **talon.**

*Talpohenach* (= *Plesiolestes*) *torrejonia* Kay and Cartmill, 1977: archaic mammal known from the middle to late Paleocene of North America, belonging to the **Plesiadapiformes** family **Palaechthonidae; monotypic.** Known only from dentition and mandibular remains. Dental formula probably 2.1.3.3; enlarged anterior dentition, enlarged third molars, low-crowned molars are suggestive of herbivorous diet, probably **frugivory.** Mandible unfused as in modern prosimians. Body size estimated at 300 g. Some authors include *Talpohenach* within *Plesiolestes.* See Appendix 1 for taxonomy.

**talus:** 1. one of the seven bones that make up the tarsus or ankle. The talus sits atop the **calcaneus,** and is freely movable where it joins with the **tibia** and **fibula.** In humans this is one of the two bones of the foot that bear most of our body weight, and is the only bone in the human body that does not have a muscle associated with it. This bone is referred to as the **astragalus** in nonprimates. Plural: tali. 2. fossil-containing sediment in a cave that has been deposited from the surface; aka presle.

**talus cone:** deposition at the base of a cliff where it has fractured from the exterior surface. Talus cones are formed through the action of water in rock fractures that expands upon freezing, cracking the cones away from the parent rock.

**tamarin:** vernacular for the small callitrichid monkeys belonging to the genus *Saguinus.* Tamarin is a word derived from a Caribbean language meaning squirrel-like monkey.

*Tamarin* Gray, 1870: recently discarded synonym for the genus *Saguinus.*

**Tana River:** research site located in Kenya where long-term field studies of red colobus monkeys (*Piliocolobus badius*) have been conducted for decades. Primatologists who have conducted field research at this site include T. H. Clutton-Brock, C. W. Marsh, and V. K. Bentley-Condit.

**Tana River mangabey:** vernacular for *Cercocebus galeritus*.

**Tana River red colobus:** vernacular for *Piliocolobus rufomitratus*.

**tandem duplication:** repetition of nucleotide sequences in adjacent sections of a DNA molecule. Aka tandem reduplication.

**tandem repeat sequences** (STRs): 1. repetitive DNA that probably originated by **unequal crossing over** and **slippage**, especially for short to medium repeats. 2. often refers to repeated blocks of 1,000 or more nudeotides in DNA that include **microsatellite DNA, minisatellite DNA**, and **satellite DNA** Cf. **scattered repeat sequences** and **short tandem repeat.**

**tang:** long, slender prong that forms part of an object; usually serves as a means of attachment of a handle.

**Tangshan Hill:** archaeological site found in 1993 near Nanjing, Jiangsu province, China, dating to 400–200 kya; contains hominid remains, including two partial crania attributed to *Homo erectus* and described as comparable to **Zhoukoudian** skull V. Aka Huludong Cave, Nanjing.

**Tanjung Puting National Park:** research site located in Central Kalimantan where long-term field studies of orangutans (*Pongo pygmaeus*) and proboscis monkeys (*Nasalis larvatus*) have been conducted for decades. Primatologists who have conducted field research at this site include B. M. F. **Galdikas**, J. W. Wood, C. P. Yeager, and S. C. Silver.

**Tanner, James M.** (1920–): British physician, auxologist, physiologist, and growth specialist at the University of London. Best known for his standards of skeletal maturation, attenuation of the so-called **Tanner stages** of pubertal development, a set of growth standards for several anthropometric measures, and studies of the physiques of Olympic athletes. He was also a pioneer in human growth hormone therapy. As a member of the **International Biological Programme**, he compiled and published comparative growth studies from around the world. He was a founding editor of the *Annals of Human Biology* and founding member of the International Association of Human Auxology. Author of 250 papers and 10 books, including *Growth at Adolescence* (1962), (with P. B. Eveleth) *Worldwide Variation in Human Growth* (1976, 1990), *A History of the Study of Human Growth* (1981), and (with R. H. Whitehouse) *Atlas of Children's Growth* (1982).

**Tanner stage:** any of several grades of human pubertal development devised by J. M. **Tanner** for children. Tanner growth distance and velocity charts also exist for body size, anthropometric traits, ossification centers, etc. Aka Tanner standard. See **Tanner–Whitehouse method** and **biometry.** Cf. **Greulich–Pyle method.**

**Tanner–Whitehouse method:** one of several techniques for the estimation of **skeletal age** that utilizes radiographs of various growth centers such as the ossification centers of the wrist, the epiphyses of long bones, and the sutures of the cranium. Cf. **Greulich-Pyle method.**

**tanning:** 1. a process of converting hides into leather. 2. a two-stage **acclimatization** response resulting in browning or darkening of the living **skin**, as by exposure to **UV radiation.** See **skin color, immediate tanning**, and **delayed tanning.**

**tantulus monkey:** vernacular for *Chlorocebus aethiops tantulus*.

**tapeinocranic:** pertaining to a cranial breadth–height index of less than 91.9.

**tapetum lucidum:** reflecting layer in the choroid coat of the eye wall behind the neural **retina**; the light reflected back out of the eye is believed to help the animal see better in low light conditions. The tapetum lucidum is characteristic of **nocturnal** mammals and is present in many **prosimian** species; it is lacking in all **anthropoids.** See **eyeshine.**

**taph-:** combining form meaning grave or burial.

‡ **taphonomy:** study of the processes that affect the remains of organisms from the death of the organism through its burial, process of **fossilization**, and collection; taphonomists determine explanations for the post-mortem distribution and condition of fossils. See **biostratinomy** and **diagenesis.**

**Tardenoisian culture:** transitional **Epipaleolithic** culture area in western Europe roughly contemporary with the **Azilian** period, found commonly in sandy soils. The type site is Fère-en-Tardenois but similar assemblages have been found in western Europe, North Africa, and Asia. The assemblage lacked hand-axes, and is characterized by many small flakes such as microgravers, and other chips thought to be components of composite tools. See **Mesolithic.**

**target site:** organ or site of action of a **hormone.** Aka target cell, target organ, target tissue.

**tarsal:** of or pertaining to the ankle.

**tarsal gland:** oil-secreting gland found in some mammals that opens on the exposed edge of each eyelid; aka Meibomian gland.

‡ **tarsier:** any of several small, nocturnal primates, the **extant** forms belonging to the genus *Tarsius*; historically, tarsiers were included in the suborder

**Prosimii,** but in recent years they have been placed in an alternative suborder, **Haplorhini,** owing to shared features with monkeys and apes. The name tarsier refers to the elongated tarsal (ankle) bones in this primate. Tarsier-like primates are found in the fossil record as far back as the early Eocene. See *Tarsius.*

**tarsifulcrumating:** form of **saltation** in which the push-off point is at the **distal** end of the **tarsals** rather than at the tip of the **metatarsals.**

**Tarsiidae:** monotypic family to which the **tarsiers** belong, consisting of *Tarsius* and five species. See Appendix 2 for taxonomy, Appendix 3 for living species.

**Tarsiiformes:** tarsierlike primates. The only living members of this group belong to the genus *Tarsius.* Historically an infraorder of the suborder **Prosimii;** if the tarsiers are recognized as a separate group among the primates there is no need for this division within the suborder **Tarsioidea;** in the more accepted recent classificatory scheme the tarsiiforms become an infraorder within the **Haplorhini.** See Appendix 1 for taxonomy.

‡ **Tarsioidea:** 1. suborder of order Primates that consists of the tarsiers and their extinct relatives; this suborder was established on morphological and chromosomal traits including features that are unique to this group and not shared with either prosimians or anthropoids; although recognized in this dictionary, it is not widely accepted. 2. superfamily within the prosimian infraorder **Tarsiiformes** when the tarsiers are included in the **Prosimii.** See *Tarsius.*

**tarsiphile hypothesis:** hypothesis of primate phylogeny that considers **tarsiers** to be the sister group of the platyrrhines and catarrhines. See **omomyophile hypothesis** and **lemurophile hypothesis.**

*Tarsius* **Storr, 1780: prosimian** (haplorhine) genus to which the tarsiers belong; five species described. Found in primary and secondary forests of the islands of Southeast Asia; also frequent in disturbed areas. This group of primates was problematic for systematicists because it shared traits with both prosimians and **anthropoids;** in addition, it was felt that a tarsiiform gave rise to the anthropoids. The solution to this problem was to abandon the traditional primate **suborders** and to resurrect two alternative suborders, the **Strepsirhini** and the **Haplorhini,** the tarsiers included with the anthropoids in the latter group. Arboreal; nocturnal; utilizes **vertical clinging and leaping,** but is **saltatory** on ground; short forelimbs, long hindlimbs, and elongated tarsal bones (giving name to this genus); tail longer than body, hairless and scaled in one of the species (*T. spectrum*) and tufted in all species. Striking anatomical features

are the large eyes (the two accounting for one-third of the animal's body mass) and the ability to rotate the head almost 359 degrees as a compensation for the inability to move the eyes. Digits two and three of the hind paw possess grooming claws. Mobile **pinnae** can focus on sounds; pinnae lined with **rugae;** hearing very acute. Body masses range from 80 to 170 g. Dental formula: 2.1.3.3/1.1.3.3; **faunivorous;** only **extant** primate never observed to consume plant matter, with one exception: Carlitos Pizarras of the tarsier sanctuary at Bohol (Philippines) reports that tarsiers medicate themselves with a local plant. Natural history poorly known. Social organization variable, depending on species. May be **monogamous** pairs or **noyau.** In some cases they mark (through scent and sound) and defend territories. **Infant parking** is characteristic of the females. Extant tarsiers are the remnants of a once widespread group of primates that were found in North America, Europe, Asia, and Africa. See Appendix 2 for taxonomy, Appendix 3 for living species.

**tarsus:** ankle, consisting of seven bones.

**Tarui disease: glycogen storage disease (VII).**

**tassel-ear marmoset:** vernacular for *Callithrix humeralifer.*

**taste aversion:** avoidance of food because of the way it tastes; taste aversion may be adaptive because it prevents ingestion of harmful substances which often have a bad taste. Taste aversion includes reactions, such as vomiting, where taste may not be the obvious cause; for example, a primate consumes a noxious insect, becomes ill, and avoids eating such an insect in the future.

**taste bud:** organ containing the chemoreceptors associated with the sense of taste.

**taste sensitivity:** the ability to detect substances such as phenylthiocarbamide; the ability is **polymorphic** in human populations. See **PTC taster–nontaster polymorphism.**

**taster:** person who perceives a bitter flavor when **PTC** is placed on the tongue; Cf. **nontaster.** See **PTC taster/nontaster polymorphism.**

*Tatmanius szalayi* **Bown and Rose, 1991:** tarsiiform primate from the early Eocene of North America belonging to the omomyid subfamily **Anaptomorphinae; monotypic.** Estimated body mass around 160 g. See Appendix 1 for taxonomy.

**Tatrot:** fossil-bearing geological formation in the Siwalik Hills of India, laid down during the early part of the first of four Himalayan glaciations, and thus early Lower Pleistocene in age.

**Tattersall, Ian** (1945–): British-born US physical anthropologist; curator at the American Museum of Natural History; adjunct, Columbia University.

Interests include primates, Malagasy ecology, human evolution, and science education. Author of many articles and books, including *The Last Neanderthal* (1999) and *The Primates of Madagascar* (1982). Coeditor (with E. Delson and J. Van Couvering) of *Encyclopedia of Human Evolution and Prehistory* (1988). Co-author (with J. Schwartz) of *Extinct Humans* (2000) and (with N. **Eldredge**) of *The Myths of Human Evolution* (1982).

**tau amyloid:** one of several proteins that accumulate in the brain tissue of people with **Alzheimers' disease.** Tau disrupts microtubules in neuron branches. See **beta amyloid** and **prion protein.**

**Taubach:** archaeological site found in 1887 in East Germany, dated to 116–110 kya, and that contains **Middle Paleolithic** (Taubachian) artifacts. The hominid remains include some isolated teeth attributed to *Homo neanderthalensis.*

‡ **Taung(s):** archaeological site found in 1924 in Bophythatawana, South Africa, dated to about 2.8–2.6 mya (see **Thabaseek deposits**), and that contains **hominid** remains encased in limestone **breccia**, including one juvenile demicranium assigned to *Australopithecus africanus*, better known as the **Taung child.** No artifacts were recovered from the quarry site. Aka Taungs, Buxton limeworks. See Raymond **Dart.**

‡ **Taung child:** hominid remains from **Taung** first described by Raymond **Dart** in a *Nature* article in 1925. The primary characteristics noted by Dart were a relatively small brain (405 cm³, and not expected to exceed 440 cm³ as an adult, estimated from a **fossil** hemi-**endocast**) and a hominid-like **deciduous dentition.** Perikymata aging technique suggests the child's age at death was about 3 years. These characters in Dart's *Australopithecus africanus* were diametrically opposed to **Keith** and others who then championed the **Piltdown** fragments (*Eoanthropus dawsonii*) with its alleged large brain but primitive teeth. **Tobias** suggested that the hominid was a raptor kill. Aka Taung 1.

‡ **taurodont:** literally, 'bull-toothed'; describes dentition in which the **pulp cavities** of **molar** teeth are enlarged and roots are fused. Noun: taurodontism. The condition is found in cattle, from which the term is derived. Some populations of *Homo erectus*, **Neandertals**, and even modern humans, e.g. **Arctic Inuit**, are taurodont. The condition may reflect tooth-use behaviors more than a genetic condition, although modern **poly-X females** also display the trait. Cf. **cynodont.**

**Tautavel Man:** see **Arago.**

**tautology:** 1. the unnecessary repetition of a word or statement, as in 'male father'. 2. any rule or law that excludes no logical possibilities; nondiscriminatory rule.

**tautomer:** either of two forms of a chemical in which one is stable and common, whereas the other is unstable and rare. See **racemization.**

**tautonym:** scientific name in which the generic and the specific names are the same, as in *Gorilla gorilla.*

‡ **tawny hair:** human **polymorphism** for hair color in central Australian aboriginals that includes a reddish-blonde variant of hair color in juveniles.

**taxa:** plural of **taxon.**

**taxol:** chemical first derived from the bark of the Pacific yew tree, and later synthesized and used as a cancer treatment. Taxol functions to alter cell division by preventing the disassembly of the tubulin protein subunits of the spindle assembly.

‡ **taxon:** any formally recognized and named group of organisms constituting a particular unit of **classification,** such as all the membership of a given species; organisms may belong to any particular rank within the **Linnaean hierarchy.** Plural: taxa.

**taxonomic rank:** position or rank of a category in the **Linnaean hierarchy: kingdom, phylum, class, order, family,** etc.

**taxonomically related discipline:** field of study that is unified only by the focus on a particular type of organism; thus **primatology** is unified by a focus on the members of the order **Primates,** but within primatology there are specialists in anatomy, behavior, ecological genetics, paleontology, reproductive physiology, etc.

‡ **taxonomy:** orderly **classification** of organisms according to their presumed natural relationships; defined by **Simpson** and **Mayr** as 'the theory and practice of delimiting kinds of organisms and of classifying them'. See **microtaxonomy, macrotaxonomy,** and **systematics.**

‡ **Tay–Sachs disease, infantile** (TSD): lethal autosomal **recessive** condition characterized clinically by a 'startle reaction' (due to nervous tissue degeneration), mental impairment, paralysis, blindness, and inevitable death in infancy. The defective gene, *hexA*, codes for the alpha chain subunit of beta-hexosaminosidase A, found in lysosomes; the mutant form interrupts **lipid** metabolism, causing irreversible problems in the **central nervous system.** Two common mutations account for more than 90% of all cases. Other variants of TSD exist, i.e. mutations in hexB. As many as 1 : 30 Jewish Americans of Eastern European ancestry may be carriers of an impaired TSD **allele.** Aka amaurotic, familial infantile idiocy, cerebromacular degeneration GM$_2$ gangliosidosis.

**Tayacian:** poorly defined flake culture found in Europe and the Near East, supposedly allied to the **Clactonian.** Type site: Tayac, Les Eyzies, Dordogne, France.

‡ **T cell:** white blood cell that originates in bone marrow but undergoes maturation in the thymus gland; associated with cell-mediated immunity. T cells attack antigen-bearing cells or substances and secrete **cytokines**. Aka T lymphocyte. Cf. **B cell**.

**T cell immunodeficiency:** any of several conditions characterized by complete lack of T cell immunity but normal B cell immunity; may be inherited as an autosomal recessive trait.

**T cell receptors:** peptides on T cells that bind foreign antigens, such as the CDn receptors.

*Tchadanthropus uxoris:* putative australopithecine found in Chad in 1961 that turned out to be a modern human skull weathered by wind-blown sand.

‡ **T complex:** series of traits associated with dentition and mastication which are an adaptation for consuming seeds and other small gritty objects. These traits include reduction in the length of **canine** teeth, mandibular buttressing (due to strenuous chewing forces), and thick enameled molars; this adaptation is used to explain dental **homoplasies** in *Gigantopithecus*, early **hominids**, and the panda. The T complex is named after the gelada baboon (*Theropithecus*), which has a **graminivorous** and **granivorous** diet. See **seed-eating hypothesis**.

*TDF* **gene:** testis-determining gene; see *SRY gene*.

**technology:** tools, tool-making techniques, products, and knowledge of how to use them. This includes everything from simple **tools** such as **Oldowan** tools or chimpanzee termite sticks to the complex technology of the modern world such as computers and lasers. Technology enables humans, e.g. the **Arctic Inuit**, to occupy environments to which they are not fully evolutionarily adapted. Technology is the cultural means and agency through which human societies cope with and transform the immediate material environments. According to Mumford's 1934 scheme, humans have experienced an **eotechnic phase**, a **paleotechnic phase**, and some societies are currently in a **neotechnic phase**.

**tectiform:** pertaining to triangular representations found in designs attributed to the **Magdalenian** period, and thought to represent the frameworks of dwellings or tents.

**tectonic activity:** distortions of the earth's crust that result in mountain-building, volcanic activity, the formation of rift valleys, and the movement of continental plates. See **plate tectonics**.

‡ **tectonic movement:** see **plate tectonics**.

**teeth:** plural of **tooth**.

**tegula, tegulae:** in reference to primates, term applied to the laterally compressed nails of platyrrhines, which form secondarily evolved claws. In the callitrichids there is extreme mediolateral compression, which produces functional claws (faculae).

**Teilhard de Chardin, Pierre** (1881–1955): French Jesuit, paleontologist, philosopher; a student in Paris of Marcellin **Boule**, found the infamous canine tooth at **Piltdown** while a student in Hastings, and has been implicated as a participant in the hoax, as well. As a missionary in China (1923–46), he was involved in the excavations at **Zhoukoudian** as interim director. Worked at the Wenner–Gren Foundation from 1951 until his death. Author of *The Phenomenon of Man* (1955), a work that attempted to reconcile evolution with deism. See **progressive evolution**.

*Teilhardina* Simpson, 1940: genus of tarsiiform primate from the early Eocene of North America belonging to the omomyid subfamily **Anaptomorphinae**; six species; earliest and most primitive member of the omomyoids and the probable ancestor to later families and subfamilies; systematics and taxonomic placement subject to debate. Small, with most species around 100 g. Dental formula: 2.1.4.3/2.1.4.3; primitive dental formula for the anaptomorphines, later members having reduced numbers of teeth; dental morphology, coupled with small body size, suggests **insectivory**. See Appendix 1 for taxonomy.

‡ **tektites:** glassy objects of supposed extraterrestrial origin; see **microtektites**.

**tektite fall:** presence of **tektites** over a considerable region; such a fall occurred across Southeast Asia *c.* 803 and 730–670 kya. See **microtektites**.

**tel:** large midden or mound; the result of repeated occupation of a favorable site during which gradually accumulated debris and structural reclamation progressively increased the size of the mound.

*Telanthropus* Broom and Robinson, 1949: generic nomen assigned to a group of South African fossil hominids known from **Swartkrans**; 'distant-man' or 'perfect-man'. South African specimens originally attributed to this genus were reassigned to *Homo erectus* by **Robinson** in 1961.

*Telanthropus capensis* Broom and Robinson, 1949: species proposed from material recovered from **Swartkrans**, South Africa. This material has also been attributed to *Homo erectus* as well as to *Australopithecus*. Best known specimen is a partial skull, **SK 847**. Dating from **index fossil** analysis places it in the 1 mya to 700 kya range. Not widely recognized as a separate **species**. Many authorities place it with *Australopithecus africanus*. LeGros Clark, F. Clark Howell and C. K. **Brain** (1970) refer to this material as *Homo* **sp. indet.**

**teleconnection:** process of correlation of annual layers or depositions over a wide region, on the basis of **varve** analysis, **dendrochronology**, or using an **index species**.

**telegony:** nineteenth century theory of heredity that inheritance is influenced by the father and also by all the previous mates of the mother, based on the incorrect notion that male fluids 'innoculated' the mother's blood and thus her whole being with the characteristics of the sire. This notion was discarded after the acceptance of **Weismann's barrier.**

**telencephalon:** anterior region of the forebrain or **prosencephalon** that contains the **cerebrum.**

**teleolith:** any deliberately shaped stone artifact.

‡ **teleology:** 1. any explanation of events in terms of an ultimate purpose served by them; any end-directed process. 2. within the context of anthropology, an approach to the explanation of human history that is often pseudoevolutionary and is always antievolutionary since it denies the opportunism of the evolutionary process; a teleological explanation explains history as the unfolding of a pre-ordained plan.

**teleomatic process:** any seemingly end-directed process that is strictly controlled by natural laws, e.g. by the law of gravity or the laws of thermodynamics.

**teleonomic process:** any goal-directed process; process that is preset or preordained.

**teleonomic selection:** alleged capacity for internally controlled, goal-directed behavioral changes. See **organic selection theory.**

**teleonomy:** proposition that all existing structures and functions have evolved and are maintained owing to the selective advantage they confer on their bearers.

**tell, tulul:** high, artificial mound containing the accumulated debris of one or more ancient settlements built on the same site. Cf. **funeral mound.**

**tellurism:** capacity of the earth or soil to produce disease.

**telocentric chromosome:** chromosome in which the **centromere** is located such that the size of the **p arm** is about half that of the **q arm.** See **submetacentric.**

**telomerase:** enzyme that adds characteristic DNA to **telomeres.** Telomerase activity has been implicated in **cell senescence.** See **Hayflick limit.**

**telomere:** chromosome end or tip, normally containing a specific repetitive nucleotide sequence of variable length. See **telomerase.**

**telomeric silencing:** repression of transcription of genes located near the **telomere** of a chromatid. Aka telomere-position effect.

‡ **telophase:** last stage of **cell division,** during which division of the cytoplasm occurs, the chromosomes of the daughter cells condense, and the nucleus reforms.

**telophase I:** stage during **meiosis I** in which the cytoplasm divides for the first time, producing two cells.

**telophase II:** stage during **meiosis II** in which the chromatids uncoil, the nuclear membrane reforms, the cytoplasm divides for the second time, producing four cells, and meiosis is complete.

**Témara:** archaeological site found in 1959 in Morocco, Africa, dated to >100 kya, containing **Aterian** artifacts and hominid remains including fragments of three individuals attributed to *Homo sapiens.* Aka Rabat.

**temperament:** unique and natural disposition of an individual; a characteristic manner of thinking, behaving and reacting.

**temperate forest biome:** mixed forest of conifers and broad-leafed deciduous trees, in which seasons are clearly defined, and further characterized by high rainfall and a rich trophic pyramid containing many bird species and large mammals including carnivores; found in temperate regions across the world.

**temperature regulation:** maintenance of the temperature or temperatures of a body within a restricted range under conditions involving variable internal and/or external heat loads, a homeostatic process. See **homeothermy.**

**template:** a pattern, mold, or guide.

**template DNA:** single-stranded DNA that serves to specify the nucleotide sequence of a newly synthesized polynucleotide strand; Aka template strand DNA, informational DNA, samesense DNA. See **cDNA.**

**template RNA:** macromolecular mold for the synthesis of a complementary polynucleotide molecule. Aka template strand RNA.

**tempo:** refers to the rate of evolution. See **bradytely, horotely,** and **tachytely.** Cf. **mode.**

**'tempo and mode':** phrase popularized by G. G. **Simpson** in a book of the same title: refers to the speed of evolution and to the various types of **speciation** and mechanisms of **adaptation.**

**temporal:** 1. of or relating to time as distinguished from space. 2. of or relating to the sequence of time or to a particular time; chronological. 3. of or relating to the **temporal bone.**

‡ **temporal bone:** one of two bones on either side that forms the lower side and anterior base of the cranium; the temporal bone articulates with three of the bones of the **cranium** and with the **mandible;** the temporal houses the inner ear structures.

**temporal crest:** ridge on the **temporal bone;** aka **temporal line.**

**temporal fossa:** depression formed by the confluence of the **parietal, temporal, frontal, sphenoid,** and **zygomatic bones** into which the fan-shaped **temporalis muscle** is seated; the temporal fossa includes the opening that is bordered by the **zygomatic arch.**

**temporal isolation:** where mating or flowering episodes occur at different seasons; a premating or **prezygotic mechanism.**

**temporal line:** faint anterior-to-posterior marking of bone extending along the frontal and parietal bones;

there are two such lines, the superior temporal line and the inferior temporal line; these structures serve as sites of origin for the **temporalis muscle**. Aka temporal crest.

‡ **temporal lobe:** portion in each cerebral hemisphere of the brain positioned inferior to the **lateral sulcus** and anterior to the **occipital lobe**. Functions include the interpretation of auditory sensations, and the storage of auditory and visual experiences. See **Wernicke's area**.

**temporal muscle:** see **temporalis muscle**.

**temporal polyethism:** synonym for **age polyethism**.

**temporal scope:** geologic time represented by a certain stratigraphic rock column.

**temporal stratigraphic completeness:** proportion of actual time represented by the preserved portion of a stratigraphic rock column.

**temporal type:** morphological motif that has stage value; aka 'time marker'.

**temporalis muscle:** muscle of mastication. The temporalis originates from the **temporal lines** of the **temporal bone** and **temporal fossa**; it inserts into the **coronoid process** and anterior **mandibular ramus**. Its action is to elevate the mandible. This muscle is particularly large and well developed in the genus *Paranthropus* and is associated with a **sagittal crest** in this taxon.

**temporomandibular joint** (TMJ): **synovial joint**(s) between the **mandibular condyle** and the **mandibular fossa** of the **temporal bone**. Three different types of joint are represented at this location: **hinge**, **gliding**, and **condyloid**, permitting the mandible to open and close, glide, and protract and retract.

**temporonuchal crest:** bony crest on the **cranium** which is the result of the convergence of the **temporal lines** (or **sagittal crest**) with the **nuchal crest** in the occipital region. This condition is found among the great apes and some fossil **hominid** species.

**tendon:** cord or band of white fibrous connective tissue that joins a muscle to a movable structure, such as bone or cartilage; transmits muscle contractile force to the bone.

**tension zone:** geographic zone in which two populations, formerly separated by geographic isolation, hybridize after the breakdown of the geographic barrier. Aka hybrid zone.

**tentorium cerebelli:** portion of the **meninges** that extends into the **transverse fissure** of the brain at the **internal occipital protuberance**.

**teosinte:** a wild grass, aka teocinte; see **maize**.

**Tepexpan:** archaeological site found in 1946 in the Valley of Mexico, dated to about 11 kya, containing flint artifacts and hominid remains including one complete skull of an **AMH** found in direct association with a fossil mammoth. Aka Tepexpan Man.

**tephra:** volcanic ash.

**tephrachronology:** stratigraphy and dating analyses of undisturbed beds of volcanic ash for which a temporal sequence can be constructed. Aka tephrochronology.

‡ **teratogen:** any substance or agent capable of disrupting genetic, cellular, or developmental processes in an embryo, typically, radiation or a chemical. Cf. **mutagen** and **carcinogen**.

**teratology:** 1. the study of abnormal development of an embryo or fetus; desmorphology. 2. with reference to the etiology of **congenital** malformations or monstrosities. See **monster**.

**teratoma:** tumor that consists of an aggregation of undifferentiated cell types.

**teratophobia:** 1. morbid fear of monsters. 2. morbid dread of giving birth to a child with a congenital defect.

**term:** 1. a definite period of time, as in the length of gestation. 2. a word designating a specific taxonomic rank in a hierarchical classification.

**terminal branch feeding:** refers to obtaining fruit or leaves from the end of branches, usually accomplished by hanging underneath the branch, rather than precariously from the top; seen in gibbons and spider monkeys.

**terminal branch feeding hypothesis:** see **angiosperm radiation hypothesis**.

**termination codon:** see **stop codon**.

**termination of parental investment:** in social theory, explanation of the window of weaning conflict as a discrepancy between a point where a parent's cost of continued investment increases, and the point, usually later, at which an offspring also realizes an increased cost. Cost and benefit are measured in terms of reproductive success. See **parental investment, parent–offspring conflict**.

**terminator:** nucleotide sequences in DNA that contain serial complementary sequences with an intervening noncomplementary region, a loop will be formed in **pre-mRNA** as it is being transcribed, and **transcription** will cease. Not to be confused with a **stop codon**, which terminates **translation**. Aka termination hairpin, termination sequence.

**terminalization:** movement of chiasmata toward the ends of chromosomes; occurs during the diplotene stage of prophase I in **meiosis**.

**termite stick:** 1. one of two sticks of different composition used by the Azande people to pose questions to termites, who eat one of the sticks. 2. tool produced by a chimpanzee by removing branchlets from a twig, and used to catch termites. See **termiting**.

**termiting:** tool-using behavior of chimpanzees in which they insert a **termite stick** into the entryway of a termite mound, catch the termites on the saliva-moistened tip, pull the stick out, and consume the insects. The observation of this behavior by Jane **Goodall** resulted in a re-evaluation of the definition of humans as the tool-using animal.

**Ternifine:** archaeological site found in 1872, reworked in 1954–55, located near Mascara, Oran, Algeria, dated to <700 kya (**Middle Pleistocene**), and that contains hundreds of **Acheulean** and **Clactonian** quartzite artifacts. The hominid remains include three chinless mandibles, some isolated teeth, and a cranial fragment of *Atlanthropus mauritanicus* (now attributed to *Homo erectus*). Often favorably compared with specimens from **Zhoukoudian** (Locality 1). Aka Tighennif, Pelikao.

**terra firme:** high ground that is spared from flooding during the rainy season; this term usually applies to forests of the Amazon basin. Many primate species are restricted to this zone. Cf. **flooded forest.**

‡ **terrestrial:** pertaining to the ground surface on land; term used for organisms that are habitually found on the ground.

**terrestrial quadrupedalism:** walking on all four limbs on the ground; terrestrial quadrupeds typically have equal limb proportions.

**territorial boundaries:** recognized lines of demarcation, the crossing of which is perceived as a violation; boundaries are often patrolled by the vigilant male(s) of a group.

‡ **territoriality:** defense of a space, either geographically defined or, as in the case of personal space, an area surrounding the defending individual and possibly others in a group.

‡ **territory:** bounded area occupied and used by an individual animal or a social group and that is defended against **conspecific** intruders by means of repulsion through overt defense or advertisements such as **aggression** or **display.** Cf. **defended territory** and **exclusive territory.**

**Terry, Raymond James** (1871–1966): US physician, osteologist at the Washington University Medical School (St. Louis); Terry was a renowned teacher and specialist in osteology, but who is best known for his accumulation of over 1,600 complete skeletons (the Terry Collection) later enlarged and donated to the National Museum of Natural History in Washington, DC.

**tertiary:** 1. third in a series. 2. a formation consisting of three elements. 3. in geology, the **Tertiary (period).**

‡ **Tertiary (period):** oldest **period** of the **Cenozoic era**, lasting from approximately 65 to 1.6 mya and consisting of the **Paleocene, Eocene, Oligocene, Miocene,** and **Pliocene** epochs. See **Quaternary period.**

**Tertiary–Quaternary boundary:** cusp between the **Pliocene** and **Pleistocene** epochs set officially at 1.8 mya (stratotype at Vrica, Italy). There is mounting

evidence for the rapid global buildup of glaciation *c.* 2.6 mya, however, and many scientists favor a recalibration of the traditional boundary to the older date. Aka Pliocene–Pleistocene boundary, Plio-Pleistocene boundary. See the **turnover-pulse hypothesis.**

**tertiary sex ratio:** see **sex ratio.** Aka socionomic sex ratio.

**tertiary structure** (3°): the three-dimensional structure of a protein molecule brought about as the result of a polypeptide folding on itself. See **protein structure.**

**tertiary tool:** implement that requires the use of primary and secondary tools during its construction; a tertiary tool is the final product, and is not used to shape other tools. The **spearthrower** is an example of a tertiary tool.

**Teshik-Tash:** archaeological site found in 1938 near Bajsuntau in the Turgan-Darya Valley in southern Uzbekistan, Iran, dated to *c.* 70 kya (130–45 kya, [14]C), containing a classic **Mousterian** tool assemblage and hominid remains including a 'deliberately buried' (i.e. with several ibex 'horn cores') 9-year-old boy(?) attributed to *Homo neanderthalensis.* This site may mark the easternmost limits of the Neandertal distribution. Aka 'rock with a hole in it', Tesik-Tas.

**test:** 1. set of standardized questions, problems, or tasks; see **choice test, open-field test.** 2. a critical examination, observation, or evaluation; trial. Specifically, the procedure of submitting a statement (**hypotheses**) to such conditions or operations as will lead to its proof or disproof or to its acceptance or rejection; see **chi-square test, *t*-test.** 3. process of detection of an ingredient or substance, e.g. a chemical test. See **Ames test, fluorine test, immunological diffusion test.** 4. detection of specific signs or symptons, as in a medical diagnostic test.

**test cross:** see **backcross.**

**testes:** plural of **testis.**

**test tube baby:** infant produced by an *in vitro* fertilization technique, including an embryo transplantation in order to complete normal gestation.

**testicle size:** see **sperm competition.**

**testicular feminization** (TF): see **androgen insensitivity syndrome (AIS).**

**testicular hormone, testis hormone:** any hormone secreted by the **testis.**

**testis:** gamete-producing organ of a male animal; aka male gonad, testicle. Plural: testes.

**testis determining factor** (TDF): a gene located near the end of the short arm of the Y chromosome that plays a major role in causing the undifferentiated gonad to develop into a testis. See *SRY* gene.

**testosterone:** steroid hormone formed in greatest quantities by the interstitial cells of the **testes,** and possibly also secreted by the **ovary** and **adrenal cortex**, and the most potent naturally occurring **androgen**. This naturally occuring sex **hormone** normally controls the masculinization of internal reproductive structures in the fetus, inhibits the development of female characters, and stimulates the development of male secondary sexual characteristics at puberty. In females, testosterone is a precursor for **estrogen** biosynthesis and induces follicular **atresia**. Synthetic testosterones are used in the treatment of hypogonadism, cryptorchism, certain carcinomas, and menorrhagia. Aka male gonadal hormone, testicular hormone. Cf. **estrogen, dihydrotestosterone.**

**Tethyan region:** area circumscribed by the ancient **Tethys Sea**, i.e. northern Africa, Arabia, and southern Europe.

**Tethys Sea:** broad Mesozoic waterway that once divided the northern from the southern supercontinents (**Laurasia** and **Gondwanaland**).

*Tetonius* **Matthew, 1915:** genus of tarsiiform primate from the early Eocene of North America, belonging to the omomyid subfamily **Anaptomorphinae**; three species; this genus may be the ancestor to *Absarokius*; known from jaws, isolated teeth, and some cranial material. Estimated body mass ranges from 100 to 300 g. Large orbits, but other characteristics make it difficult to say with certainty what the activity cycle was; short snout. Dental formula: 2.1.3.3/2.1.3.3; dental morphology interpreted as adapted for **frugivory**. See Appendix 1 for taxonomy.

*Tetonoides* (= *Anemorhysis*) **Gazin, 1962:** genus of tarsiiform primate from the early Eocene of North America, belonging to the omomyid subfamily **Anaptomorphinae**; two species described, but many workers include this genus within *Anemorhysis*. Estimated body mass ranges between 70 and 80 g. Dental formula: 2.1.3.3/2.1.3.3; small size and dental morphology suggestive of **insectivory**. See Appendix 1 for taxonomy.

**tetrad:** 1. set of four related things. 2. group of two chromosomes, i.e. four chromatids, formed during **meiosis**, unpaired chromosomes in a **secondary spermatocyte** or **secondary oöcyte**, just after the first meiotic division (anaphase I).

**Tetraploid:** cell with a chromosome number that is four times the **haploid** number, having four copies of all autosomes and four sex chromosomes. Aka 4N cell.

**tetrapod:** member of the four-limbed group of vertebrates made up of amphibians, reptiles, birds and mammals.

**tetrasomic:** having two or more chromosomes in excess of the normal number; see **aneuploidy.**

**Thabaseek deposit:** oldest **Taung** tufa. Although radioisotope dates suggest a young age for the tufa

(1.0 mya), more recent analysis suggest that younger uranium leaked into the older depositions, and that the earlier faunal date of 2.3 mya seems the more accurate. The Thabaseek deposit provided a maximum age for the Taung hominid deposits.

**thalamus:** structure in the diencephalon that functions as a relay center, channeling all sensory input except the olfactory impulses into the **cerebrum**; processes the initial autonomic response to pain.

‡ **thalassemia, alpha:** inherited autosomal **codominant** abnormality of blood, caused by an imbalance in the production of the subunits of hemoglobin. Symptoms range from mild to lethal anemia that results in stillbirth (hydrops fetalis), heart failure, and serous fluid accumulation. The cause of the *alpha* forms is inactivation of up to four loci (in various combinations) that produce the alpha globin chains. Some variants confer resistance to malaria in the heterozygous state in adults, although even heterozygotes have mild anemia (Mediterranean anemia). Highest frequencies of the alpha form are found in Persia, but it is also found in the Mediterranean region, Africa, Southeast Asia, the Philippines, New Guinea, and Japan.

‡ **thalassemia, beta:** inherited autosomal **codominant** abnormality of blood, divided into three clinical entities. (1) Thalassemia major is an often severe condition in which the amount of hemoglobin is decreased by the action of a recessive beta allele when in the homozygous condition; characterized by severe anemia and defects in bone, liver, and spleen that are ultimately fatal. (2) Thalassemia intermedia, characterized by mild anemia in persons heterozygous for the same autosomal recessive allele that, when homozygous, causes thalassemia major; t. intermedia also confers some resistance to malaria. (3) Thalassemia minor can be asymptomatic or result in mild anemia; this deficiency also confers some resistance to **malaria** (Aka Cooley's anemia). The beta form is found worldwide, and is common in Africa, the Caucasus, Asia, Europe, and the Americas.

**thalassemia major** and **thalassemia minor:** see **thalassemia, beta.**

**thalidomide:** sedative widely prescribed between 1959 and 1962, later shown to interfere with human limb bud development and to produce phenocopies of **phocomelia**; gave rise to a cohort of children known as the 'thalidomide babies'. Thalidomide is a known **teratogen.**

**thanatocenosis:** collection of organisms that coexisted at the same geological time and died at approximately the same time; the frequencies of species represented does not imply the actual proportions that existed when these organisms were alive. Aka death assemblage; taphocoenosis.

**thanatology:** study of dead organisms that are found together. Cf. **taphonomy.**

**thawing:** in an archaeological site, process precipitated by raising ambient temperature above 0 °C, and associated with a contraction or collapse of soil layers; the result is a new terrain (hilly thermokarst). Cf. **freezing.** See **cryogenic soil modification.**

**theca cell:** one of a cell layer that surrounds the ovarial-follicle granulosa cells, formed from the follicle and connective tissue cells. Aka theca folliculi.

**thecodont:** organism with a mechanism for tooth attachment directly to the skeletal system, and in which nerves and capillaries enter a pulp cavity at the open tips of hollow roots, as in primates.

**thegosis:** the act of tooth grinding in animals in order to sharpen teeth.

**theism:** belief in a personal God who is everywhere and forever present (omnipresent) and/or is able to affect any natural process at any time (omnipotent) and/or is all-knowing (omniscient).

**thelarche:** beginning of breast development in females, usually at puberty. See **premature thelarche.**

‡ **theory:** in **science** (including **human evolutionary biology**), any set of broad **hypotheses** that have been subjected to repeated **tests** and that currently have not been falsified and rejected; hypotheses informed by statistical trends. A 'good' theory stimulates further thinking and testing of propositions, and outweighs rival theories if it possesses 'robust' explanatory power, **veracity**, and **parsimony**, e.g. **evolutionary theory.** The term 'theory' sometimes has alternative meanings, however, in the literature of the social sciences and humanities.

**theory of parental investment:** see **parental investment.**

**theory of tribuberculy:** theory proposed by Cope and Osborn to account for the evolution of molar teeth. The proposal held that in the development from simple conical teeth, the molar crowns became **tritubercular** with the base of the triangle buccal in the mandible and lingual in the maxilla. The simple tritubercular molar then gave way to the more complex molars of placental mammals.

**Therapsida:** extinct order belonging to the subclass Synapsida, class Reptilia, that contains the suborder Cynodontia, considered to be the ancestors of all mammals; mammal-like reptiles; the therapsids consist of three suborders and 36 families. This group of reptiles had features that laid down the basic mammalian body plan, including more advanced terrestrial locomotion and masticatory apparatus. They existed from the Middle Permian to the Early Jurassic.

**Theria:** subclass of class **Mammalia** consisting of the two infraclasses **Metatheria** and **Eutheria.** This subclass is distinguished from the **Prototheria** principally by skull structure and dentition. Theria includes all extant mammals except for the prototherians. Adjective: therian.

**thermal agitation:** heat-induced movement of molecules.

**thermal conductivity:** rate of transfer of heat by conduction, through material of unit thickness.

**thermal cracking:** in an archaeological site, process caused by the **freezing** and expansion of water contained in rocks; when internal pressures are sufficiently great to exceed the strength of the rock, the rock ruptures. See **cryogenic soil modification.**

**thermal equilibrium:** condition under which the rate of heat production of an animal is equal to the rate of heat loss such that body temperature does not change.

**thermal sweat:** loss of body heat through water diffused through the **eccrine sweat glands** in response to ambient temperature stress, and regulated by the hypothalamus. Cf. **nonthermal sweat.**

**thermogenesis:** heat generation. See **shivering thermogenesis** and **nonshivering thermogenesis.**

**thermoluminescence dating:** see **TL dating.**

**thermoneutral zone:** range of ambient temperature within which metabolic heat production equals heat loss, and within which temperature regulation is achieved by nonevaporative physical processes alone.

**thermoreceptor:** sensory cell in the skin stimulated by changes in temperature.

‡ **thermoregulation:** maintenance or regulation of temperature. In physiology, thermoregulation results from the sum of factors that contribute to **homeostasis** with respect to an organism's thermal well-being. These factors include internal temperature adjustment in **homeotherms** or behavioral location adjustment in **poikilotherms**, as well as many factors that contribute to heat gain and loss during exercise, such as breathing rate, **surface area** of heat-dissipating tissues, and the rate of moisture loss from those tissues and surfaces. Thermoregulation permits essential processes to occur while avoiding destruction of tissue. See **partitional calorimetry.**

***Theropithecus* I. Geoffroy, 1843:** monotypic catarrhine genus to which the gelada baboon belongs. Found in open areas and rocky gorges in the mountains of northern and central Ethiopia. Considered the most terrestrial of the nonhuman primates; diurnal; quadrupedal. Marked **sexual dimorphism** in teeth, body size, and other superficial features such as whiskers and a shoulder cape on the males. Body mass range 10–13 kg for females, 18–21 kg for males. Dental formula: 2.1.2.3; only primate considered to be **graminivorous.** They sit on their haunches while feeding; both sexes have patches of skin on the chest, but the female's skin becomes bright pink during **estrus;**

this signaling of **estrus** may be the result of the gelada feeding posture, which would hide sexual skin on the **ischial callosities**. Social organization consists of **one-male units**, which fuse into larger cliff-sleeping troops at night, sometimes numbering 400 animals; unattached males live in **bachelor herds** within this larger group. See Appendix I for taxonomy.

**theta:** 1. the eighth letter of the Greek alphabet ($\Theta$, $\theta$). 2. see **recombinant fraction**.

**theta waves:** electrical activity emanating from the temporal and occipital lobes of the cerebral hemispheres, normally detected as rhythmic oscillations of about 5–8 cycles per second. Theta waves are normal and common in newborns, but their presence in an adult indicates severe emotional stress. See **electroencephalogram**.

**thiamine:** see **vitamin**.

**Thibetan macaque:** vernacular for *Macaca thibetana* (= *arctoides*).

**thigh:** in anatomy, the segment of the lower limb between the hip above and the knee below. Cf. **leg**.

**thigh bone:** see **femur**.

**thigh circumference:** see **distal thigh circumference, mid-thigh circumference, proximal thigh circumference**.

**thigh length: anthropometric** measurement; distance between the hip joint and the knee joint as measured with a tape measure; this measurement is only an estimate because of the difficulty in locating these joints. Used in studies of body proportions and in various areas of **human engineering**.

**thigh skinfold: anthropometric** measurement; skinfold measured on the mid-line of the anterior surface of the thigh mid-way between the inguinal crease (between the groin and the thigh) and proximal border of the knee. Used in combination with other **skinfold measurements** to estimate body composition. See **skinfold thickness**.

**thinking:** see **problem solving** and **cognition**.

**third-degree relative:** see **relative, third-degree**.

**third gonad:** adrenal gland, so called because of its hormonal relationship with the sex glands, or **gonads**.

**third molar agenesis:** absence, failure, or defective development of the third molar or 'wisdom' teeth. Humans populations vary with respect to the degree of this trait.

**third premolar:** premolar that is posterior to the first two premolars in a mammal. During the course of evolution primates have lost anterior premolars; thus, the third premolar may actually be the most anterior premolar in a species, such as in humans. However, some workers number teeth by those actually present in a species; in such a case humans would not have a third premolar. See **P1, P2, P3, etc**.

**third trimester:** third of the three **trimesters** of human gestation, consisting of months 7–9, which includes the latter half of the fetal period, and during which differentiation continues to diminish in importance relative to growth of the fetus. By the middle of the third trimester a fetus could survive independently if born prematurely (weeks 26–38); the trimester ends upon **parturition**.

**third ventricle:** cavity located in the **diencephalon** of the forebrain, between the thalami; it is filled with **cerebrospinal fluid** and is connected to the **lateral ventricles** by the interventricular foramen, and to the **fourth ventricle** by the mesencephalic aqueduct.

**thirteenth rib:** most humans lack this accessory set of **ribs**, but 8% of adults possess this extra set of **floating ribs**. See **vestigial trait**.

**Thomas' bushbaby:** vernacular for *Galagoides thomasi* (*demidoff*).

**Thomas' leaf monkey:** vernacular for *Presbytis thomasi* (= *comata*).

**Thompson, D'Arcy Wentworth** (1860–1948): Scottish mathematician and biologist, Chair of Natural History in St. Andrews. Following **Buffon**, he raised biomathematics to a new level in his attempts to understand morphology in terms of reflexive, universal mathematical patterns. Authored over 300 scientific papers; his most famous book was *On Growth and Form* (1917). Awarded the Darwin Medal of the Royal Society in 1946.

**thoracic:** of or pertaining to the chest.

**thoracic breadth index:** breadth of the chest $\times$ 100, then divided by the anterior trunk length.

**thoracic cage:** skeletal structure of the **axial skeleton** that consists of the ribs, costal cartilages, sternum, and thoracic vertebrae. The thoracic cage protects the vital organs of the thorax and supports the **pectoral girdle** as well as serving as a site for muscle attachments for the upper limbs, shoulder, back, and chest. Aka bony thorax.

‡ **thoracic cavity:** chest cavity.

**thoracic curve:** concave anterior (primary) curvature of the **vertebral column** corresponding to the region of the thoracic vertebrae; one of the four curvatures of the vertebral column that help distribute the body's weight over the center of gravity and provides resiliency.

**thoracic duct:** major lymphatic vessel of the body that drains lymph from the entire body except the upper right quadrant and returns it to the left subclavian vein.

**thoracic index:** depth of the chest $\times$ 100 and then divided by the breadth.

**thoracic vertebra:** any one of the twelve vertebrae inferior to the **cervical vertebrae** and superior to the

**lumbar vertebrae.** Each thoracic vertebra articulates with a rib.

**thorax:** portion of the body superior to the **respiratory diaphragm**, but inferior to the neck. See **thoracic cage.**

**Thorne, Alan G.** (1943–): Australian journalist, archaeologist, and physical anthropologist who excavated the **Mungo** remains. Thorne is a supporter of the 'center and edge' version of the **multiregional continuity model**, with views similar to those of **Wolpoff** on the Neandertal question. Coeditor (with R. L. Kirk) of *The Origin of the Australian* (1976), and coauthor (with R. Raymond) of *Man on the Rim* (1989).

**threat display:** behavior meant to intimidate a rival. This varies among primates and may include bristling of hair, tearing up vegetation, yawns that expose the canine teeth, vocalizations, stares, etc.

**threat face:** facial expression meant to intimidate a rival, ward off another animal, or restore order in a group; made possible by the development of facial musculature that has evolved independently in three mammalian orders: carnivores, cervids (deer), and primates.

**three age system:** any tripartite division of prehistoric/historic periods; the most common is Christian Thomsen's Copper Age, Bronze Age, and Iron Age. An older partition includes stone, bronze and iron; a later one is aka the Three Ages of Man.

**three cusp molar pattern:** pattern found variably in humans on the **occlusal surface** of **maxillary** molars in which there are only three well-defined cusps.

**threonine** (Thr): an **amino acid** present in most **proteins** and an essential ingredient in the diet of humans and other mammals.

**threshold:** 1. that value at which a stimulus just produces a sensation, is just appreciable, or comes just within the limits of perception. 2. a hypothetical barrier that stimuli must pass to be detected; see **threshold limit value.** 3. that degree of concentration of any of specific substances (threshold substances) in the blood plasma above which the substance is excreted by the kidneys and below which it is not excreted. 4. the minimum level of input required to cause some event to occur.

**threshold limit value** (TLV): minimal value at which a particular effect or response is produced.

**threshold model:** model of multifactorial inheritance stating that a trait occurs when liability exceeds a threshold produced by the combined effects of both genetic and environmental influences.

**thrifty genotype hypothesis:** argument that fat storage capabilities under genetic control increase adaptation of certain human populations to unstable foraging circumstances: periods of plentiful food supply followed by periods of famine. Today, when presented with a stable high caloric diet without intervening periods of food deprivation, there is a tendency for people with this adaptation to become obese. Best known from the Pima Indians of the American southwest. **Neel**'s original concept has recently been challenged by a 'thrifty phenotype' hypothesis that invokes poor fetal and neonatal nutritional factors. See **diabetes mellitus, type II** and **New World syndrome.**

**throat glands: scent glands** located on the throat of some prosimians and platyrrhines.

**throat sac:** see **laryngeal sac.**

**thrombin:** enzyme that catalyzes the conversion of **fibrinogen** to fibrin, the basic component of a blood clot. Aka coagulation **factor** II.

**thrombocyte:** fragment that develops from a **megakaryocyte** and constitutes a formed element of blood. Thrombocytes are involved with blood clotting; aka blood platelet.

**thrombosis:** clot formation in the body; aka thrombus.

**throwback:** vernacular label for an individual believed to be the result of a single act of **miscegenation** and that resembles the minority variety that formed an original hybrid in a much earlier generation. Geneticists have found little evidence for this supposed phenomenon, and often ascribe it to a sanctioning system in which miscegenation is discouraged. Cf. **atavism** and **segregation.**

**throwing:** act of propelling, casting, hurling or projecting; some paleontologists believe that stone-throwing behavior, also observed in chimpanzee troops, was characteristic of early hominids, and may have spurred a connection between the available tool and the later cutting task.

**throwing behavior:** motion made possible by the freely movable **glenohumeral joint** held together by the rotator cuff muscles in which the arm extends over the head and then rotation allows an object in the hand, such as a spear or a baseball, to be flung forward. A physical characteristic prerequisite for much of human cultural behavior.

**throwing technique:** method of manufacturing a stone **tool** in which a core is thrown forcefully against a large, stationary **anvil stone** in order to produce a fracture in the core.

**Th/U:** see **uranium series dating.**

**thumb:** see **hallux.**

**thumb scraper: round scraper.** See **scraper.**

‡ **thymine** (T): one of the two **pyrimidine nucleosides** found in **DNA**, composed of one carbon–nitrogen ring. Thymine is replaced by **uracil** in **RNA**.

**thymine dimer:** molecular lesion produced by **ultraviolet light** in which abnormal chemical bonds form between a pair of adjacent **thymine** bases in a DNA molecule. Such dimers are highly mutagenic unless repaired. See **xeroderma pigmentosum**.

**thymocyte:** **lymphocyte** that originated in the **thymus gland**.

**thymosin:** one of several humoral polypeptide factors secreted by epithelial cells of the **thymus gland**, the most active being thymosin $\alpha_1$. Thymosin functions to stimulate **white blood cell** production, maintains immune-system function, and can restore **T cell** function in animals who have had thymectomies. See **thyroxines**. Aka thymopoietin.

**thymus gland:** bilobed lymphoidal organ positioned in the upper mediastinum, posterior to the sternum and between the lungs; part of the **lymphatic drainage** subsystem. The thymus secretes **thymosin** and is the site of T lymphocyte differentiation.

**thyroglobin:** large protein to which **thyroid hormones** bind in the **thyroid gland**; the storage form of the thyroid hormones.

**thyroid gland:** an organ positioned just below the larynx; it is U-shaped and has two major lobes on either side of the **trachea**. It is the largest of the **endocrine glands** and secretes **thyroid hormones**.

**thyroid hormones** (TH): collective term for amine **hormones** released from the thyroid gland, i.e. **thyroxine**, triiodothyronine, and **calcitonin**.

**thyroid-stimulating hormone** (TSH): Aka See **thyrotropin**.

**thyrotropin:** a glycoprotein **hormone** of the **adenohypophysis** that promotes the growth of, sustains, and stimulates the hormonal secretion of the **thyroid gland**. Aka thyroid-stimulating hormone, thyrotropic hormone.

**thyrotropin-releasing factor** (TRF): former name for **thyrotropin-releasing hormone**.

**thyrotropin-releasing hormone:** a **hormone** from the **hypothalamus** that stimulates the anterior lobe of the **pituitary gland** to release **thyrotropin**. Aka thyroid-stimulating hormone-releasing factor, thyroliberin.

**thyroxine:** the major **hormone** elaborated by the **thyroid gland** follicular cells, formed from **thyroglobulin** and transported mainly in the blood serum thyroxine-binding globulin. Its chief function is to increase the rate of cell metabolism; it is also essential for maturation of the **central nervous system** and the regulation of a number of other functions. Also spelled thyroxin.

**Tianshuigou:** see **Dali**.

**tibale externum:** supernumerary bone of the foot that develops as a result of abnormal ossification of the **navicular** in which the tuberosity of that bone ossifies separately. Also referred to as the **prehallux**.

‡ **tibia:** larger of the two lower leg bones, located on the medial side; aka shinbone. Of the two bones of the lower leg, only this bone is weight-bearing; it receives weight from the **femur** and transfers it to the foot. The **proximal** end helps form the **knee joint**; the **distal** end articulates with the **talus** and helps form the ankle joint.

**tibial malleolus:** see **malleolus**.

**tibio-femoral index:** lower leg length × 100, divided by the length of the thigh.

**tibio-radial index:** length of the forearm × 100, divided by the length of the lower leg.

**tidal cycles:** rhythmic minima and maxima of tides caused by three gravitational phenomena: perigee of the moon (i.e. when it is nearest to the earth; every 411 days), the perigee of the earth (when it is nearest to the sun), and the alignment of the earth, moon and sun that causes a lunar eclipse. These three events are synchronous approximately once every 1.8 kya; it has been suggested that this synchronicity could cause powerful tides that may cause deep cooling in the Atlantic, and trigger global cooling, including the 'Little Ice Age' 500 years ago.

‡ **tidal volume:** air volume entering or leaving the lungs with a single breath during any state of respiratory activity. Aka tidal air.

**Tighennif:** see **Ternifine**.

**Tiglian:** cool interglacial interval of the Lower Pleistocene in Western Europe that preceded **Günz I**.

**Tigoni Primate Research Centre:** facility established near Nairobi, Kenya, in 1958 by Louis Leakey for studying the behaviors of captive monkeys; renamed the **Institute for Primate Research** in 1974.

**till:** stratified layers of glacial drift.

**time-energy budget:** amounts of time and energy allotted by animals to various activities.

**time minimizing foraging strategy:** technique by which an adequate amount of nutrients is gathered in as short a time as possible per 24 h; this type of **foraging strategy** is found among many small mammals, including small primates such as callitrichids, and is advantageous because it limits amount of time the animal is exposed to predators. An animal adopting such a strategy is called a time minimizer. Cf. **energy maximizing foraging strategy**.

**time sampling:** behavioral observation recording rule in which observations are recorded periodically; this method provides a less exact record of behavioral patterns because less information is preserved. There are two different forms of time sampling, **instantaneous sampling** and **one–zero sampling**. Cf. **continuous recording**.

‡ **time scale:** estimation of the age of the several 'ages' of the earth's history. Prior to **Buffon**, the earth was considered to be less than 6,000 years old; by 1925, scientists reckoned that age to be 65 **my**

(with the **Age of Mammals** and the **Pleistocene** then set at 3 mya and 500 **kya**, respectively); today, with the discovery of **absolute dating** techniques, each of these episodes had been expanded considerably. See **geological time scale**.

**time series:** in behavioral studies, a series of behaviors that occur over a period of time.

**time-stratigraphic unit:** body of rock strata unified by having been formed during a specific interval of geologic time; represents all the rocks (and only those rocks) formed during a certain time span of earth's history; the units are erathem, system, series and stage.

***Tinimomys graybulliensis* Szalay, 1974:** archaic mammal known from the early Eocene of North America belonging to the **Plesiadapiformes** family **Micromomyidae; monotypic.** Dental formula probably 2.1.2.3/2.1.3.3; small body size strongly suggestive of **insectivory**; unique among mammals related to primates in that the fourth upper premolar is semimolarized; however, other traits clearly indicate this is a plesiadapiform. Body size of the species very small; estimated at 15 g. It has been suggested that *Tinimomys* was a gliding mammal. See Appendix 1 for taxonomy.

‡ **tissue:** group of similar cells and their binding intercellular substances, which work together to perform a specific function; the general cellular fabric of a given organ.

**tissue culture:** maintenance *in vitro* of tissue growth such that differentiation and preservation of both function and architecture occurs.

**tissue rejection reaction:** destruction of transplanted tissue by a responsive immune system.

**tissue typing:** serological testing of tissues for histocompatibility haplotypes in the **major histocompatibility complex.** Tissue typing is a prerequisite to grafting procedures.

**tit-for-tat strategy:** behavioral rule in **game theory** in which one player utilizing the rule always reciprocates another player's move. This strategy has been shown to optimize outcomes in most simple situations.

**titer:** strength of a solution as compared to a standard.

**titi monkey:** any of the three to thirteen platyrrhine species belonging to the genus ***Callicebus***.

**tjaele:** permanently frozen subsoil, as in Lapland; **alpine tundra.**

**TL dating:** thermoluminescence dating, a **chronometric dating** method that exploits the fact that certain heated objects accumulate trapped electrons over time, which permits a date estimation to be made of the time an object was last heated. The greater the measured thermoluminescence, the older the object. Used to date **pottery** and fired clay. A variant, **optically stimulated luminescence**, can be used on sediments.

**TM:** 1. abbreviation for Transvaal Museum. For specimens, see box below; see also **Kromdraai**. 2. abbreviation for **Toros–Menalla**.

---

**Some Kromdraai specimens in the Transvaal Museum**

See also KB 5223.

TM 1512: partial cranium with an estimated cranial capacity of 650 cm³, together with a face and maxilla attributed to *Paranthropus* (= *Australopithecus*) *robustus*.

TM 1517: partial cranium, face and maxilla with 5 teeth, the first *Paranthropus* (= *Australopithecus*) *robustus* ever found.

TM 1517a and b: craniofacial fragment of one robust individual with an estimated cranial capacity of 650 cm³ attributed to *Paranthropus* (= *Australopithecus*) *robustus*; dated from 1.7 mya (or earlier) to about 1.0 mya.

TM 1517c–g: hominid remains including miscellaneous postcranial bones, dated from 1.7 mya (or earlier) to about 1.0 mya.

TM 1517h–o: primate remains including baboon extremities that were formerly grouped with the type specimen of *Paranthropus* (= *Australopithecus*) *robustus*, dated from 1.7 mya (or earlier) to about 1.0 mya.

TM 1536: hominid juvenile mandible, dated from 1.7 mya (or earlier) to about 1.0 mya.

---

**TM 266-01-060-1: holotype** of *Sahelanthropus tchadensis* found at **Toros–Menalla**.

**Toba eruption:** very large volcanic eruption that occurred on the island of Sumatra 74 kya; this **caldera** is the most recent example of an **ultra-Plinian eruption**, the most violent of the known eruption types. Some researchers have suggested that this eruption caused a 'volcanic winter' that

interrupted photosynthesis for a decade or more, and resulted in a minor episode of mass extinction, and may have increased the extent of **Pleistocene glaciation**. Aka Toba event.

**Tobias, Phillip Vallentine** (1925–): South African geneticist, anatomist, and paleontologist; trained as a geneticist, he established the first genetic counseling program in South Africa. Because of this training,

Tobias understood the genetic homogeneity of humanity, and was active in anti-apartheid organizations as a student; he later published several papers on this theme, and a monograph, *The Meaning of Race* (1961). He was placed under house arrest because of his activism. As a student, he led surveys at **Kromdraai**, **Gladysvale**, Mwulu's Cave, Buffalo Cave, and **Makapansgat**. Appointed lecturer in the anatomy department, Tobias became **Dart**'s successor at the University of Witwatersrand. Tobias is known for his digs at virtually all South African sites, but especially at **Sterkfontein**. He has been instrumental in hominid taxonomic studies. During his tenure, more than 500 hominid specimens were catalogued, and he traveled ceaselessly during his career, lecturing worldwide, and promoting the South African collections, which became world famous. He established the Institute for the Study of Man in Africa, guided 50 graduate students to degrees, is a member of numerous professional societies, has received numerous honors including 22 medals (that include the Balzan International Prize in 1987 and the Huxley Medal in 1996), and ten honorary degrees. Tobias was nominated for the Nobel Prize three times. In addition to over 900 scholarly journal publications, he has produced several films and is the author of some 15 books, including *Olduvai Gorge*, Vol. 2 (1967) and *The Brain in Hominid Evolution* (1971).

**Todd, Thomas Wingate** (1885–1938): English-trained physician and anatomist at (Case) Western Reserve University from 1912–38. Todd was a distinguished osteologist and skeletal pathologist, and amassed one of the largest skeletal research collections in the USA, the Todd Collection. Todd published careful studies of skeletal growth and maturation, especially of the pubic region; his guidelines are still used by forensic anthropologists. Founding member and later president of **AAPA** (1938). Author of *Atlas of Skeletal Maturation* (1932), among other works.

**toe:** any one of the five digits of the primate foot or hind paw; **phalanx.**

**toilet claw** or **digit:** see **grooming claw.**

**tolerance:** condition in which increasing drug doses are required to achieve effects that initially occurred in response to a smaller dose.

**tomography:** see **CAT scanning** and **PET imaging.**

**Tongtianyan:** archaeological site found in 1957 in Liujiang County, Guangxi Province, China, dated to the late **Pleistocene** (consistency of dates of 153–67 kya, U-series, is questionable), and that contains hominid remains, including a cranium and nearly complete axial skeleton attributed to *Homo sapiens*. Aka Liukiang (Kwangzi), Liujiang.

**Tonkenese macaque:** vernacular for *Macaca tonkeana* (= *nigra*).

**Tonkin snub-nosed langur:** vernacular for *Rhinopithecus avunculus*.

**tonsils:** aggregations of lymphatic tissue in the throat. There are three pairs of tonsils. The palatine tonsils are a common site of infection and are located laterally beneath the epithelial lining of the mouth; the pharyngeal tonsils (adenoids) are on the posterior wall of the pharynx; the lingual tonsils are at the posterior of the tongue. All help the body fight infections and are part of the **lymphatic system.**

‡ **tool:** object used for some purpose outside the individual that is used to modify or manipulate something else in the environment; precludes simple environmental shaping. Any object that aids in the accomplishment of work; typically, an implement makes a task more efficient. Diagnostic features of a **flake** tool — as opposed to a **geofact** — include the **striking platform**, the **bulb of percussion**, the **bulbar scar**, **ripple marks**, **fissures**, and **dorsal scars.** Among the telltale features of a **core** tool are the **cortex**, the **flake scars**, and the **negative bulb.** Cf. **implement.**

**tool composite:** condition in which two or more tools are used for different purposes and in sequence to achieve an overall goal. See the **tool-feedback hypothesis.**

**tool-feedback hypothesis:** proposal by Charles **Darwin** in *The Descent of Man* which stated that small canines, bipedalism, and large brain size in hominids evolved together in a positive **feedback** mechanism in which tool use was the primary catalyst. According to this scenario, as proto-hominids began to use tools they had to stand upright when carrying the tools; canine teeth, previously large and used as tools, were reduced owing to disuse; the brain enlarged because tool use required elaborate hand-eye coordination. When Darwin proposed this hypothesis there was very little supportive evidence from the fossil record. When hominid fossils became more extensive in the twentieth century, the tool-feedback hypothesis was rejected, as the new fossils indicated that **bipedalism** preceded increased **brain size.** Cf. Washburn's **biocultural feedback model.**

**tool kit:** spatially or functionally patterned combination of artifacts.

‡ **tool use:** manipulation of the environment with objects (tools) constructed by humans or other animals. See **technology.**

**tool use in primates:** both common chimpanzees and bonobos have been observed using tools such as hammerstones and platform rocks (anvils); females have been observed using tools more frequently than males. See **leaf-sponge**, **potato-washing behavior** and **rice-washing behavior**, and **termite stick.**

**tool use model:** see **tool-feedback hypothesis.**

**toolmaking by chimpanzees:** see **termite stick.**

**toolmarks identification:** pattern made by various tools on bones processed at an archaeological site.

‡ **tooth:** enamel projection that grows out of the jaws of vertebrates. Plural: teeth. Teeth usually consist of enamel, dentine, cementum, and a pulp chamber or cavity. Anatomically, a tooth is divided into a crown, a neck, and roots. It functions in mastication, speech, and swallowing. Humans develop two sets of teeth: the infant set of 20 **teeth** (the **deciduous dentition**) are replaced beginning at about six years by a permanent set of 32 in the **adult dentition.** See **dental formula.** Although many primates, including humans, have generalized teeth, for the most part mammal teeth are highly specialized to perform particular functions, unlike the teeth of other vertebrates.

**tooth abrasion:** grinding or wearing away of enamel from gritty food, use of teeth as tools, or other external factors.

**tooth avulsion:** removal of a tooth for reasons other than tooth disease, usually associated with an initiation ceremony.

**tooth bud:** germ tissue from which a tooth develops.

**tooth comb:** see **dental comb.**

**tooth crown:** see **crown.**

**tooth enamel:** ectodermal derivative that forms on the crown of a tooth; see **enamel.**

**tooth eruption sequence:** see **dental eruption sequence.**

**tooth nodule:** measure of tooth size in which the nodule is given as {(length × breadth)/2}. A measure often used in **discriminant function** analyses.

**tooth row:** pertaining to two or more adjacent teeth in the same individual.

**tooth wear:** see **dental wear.**

**top predator:** species inhabiting the highest **trophic level** in the food chain of a given habitat.

**Topinard, Paul** (1830–1911): French physician, craniometrist; disciple of Paul **Broca**, and known for his work on racial taxonomy using primarily **hair form** and nose shape to classify humans. Author of the first anthropological textbook, *Eléments d'Anthropologie générale* (1895), in which he divided French anthropology into the study of humans and evolution, and the study of his trifurcate racial division of European peoples.

**topology:** surface morphology of a structure; topology is sometimes modeled by using a computer and software that can measure surface tension.

**Topper:** archaeological site located on the Savannah River near Allendale, South Carolina, dated to >12 kya, and that contains artifacts (stone blades, flakes). Cf. **Meadowcroft rockshelter** and **Cactus Hill.**

**toque macaque:** vernacular for *Macaca sinica.*

**Toros–Menalla:** archaeological site (locality **TM 266**) found *c.* 1970 on the ancient shoreline of Lake 'Mega' Chad in the Djurab Desert, northern Chad, possibly dating to the late **Miocene** (deposits estimated at 7–6 my based on **faunal correlation** with East African sites that have known dates; see **A.3 date**). The site finally produced at least six hominid specimens found in 2001, including a nearly complete cranium attributed to *Sahelanthropus tchadensis*, and expands the geographical distribution of Miocene/Pliocene hominids, previously centered in East Africa.

**torpor:** dormant condition into which some mammals enter in order to conserve energy; aka torpidity. Torpor is accompanied by a lower metabolic rate and concomitant physiological changes as the animal's body temperature drops in conformity with the ambient temperature of the environment; technically, such a mammal is **poikilothermic** during this period. Several cheirogalids enter varying degrees of torpor. See **estivation** and **hibernation.**

**Torralba:** archaeological site found in 1960 near Torralba in Spain, dated to 400–200 kya, and that contains **Acheulean** artifacts and disarticulated bones from the left side of an elephant, but no hominid remains. It was a butchering site and it has been suggested by F. Clark Howell that there is evidence of the controlled use of fire by hominids. See **Ambrona.**

*Torrejonia wilsoni* **Gazin, 1968:** archaic mammal known from the middle to late Paleocene of North America belonging to the **Plesiadapiformes** family **Palaechthonidae; monotypic.** Known only from dentition and mandibular remains. Dental formula: 2.1.3.3/2.1.3.3; enlarged anterior dentition, enlarged third molars, low-crowned molars all suggestive of a herbivorous diet, probably **frugivory.** Mandible unfused as in modern prosimians. Body size estimated at 575 g. Some authors include *Torrejonia* within either *Palaechthon* or *Plesiolestes.* See Appendix 1 for taxonomy.

**Torres Straits Expedition (of Cambridge University):** first major interdisciplinary field investigation in 1898–9 which resulted in several major publications and that set high scientific standards for the future within anthropology. Led by A. C. Haddon, the team of anthropologists included C. S. Myers, C. G. Seligman, W. H. R. Rivers, and A. Wilken.

**torso:** trunk of the body; body without the head and appendages.

**tortoise core:** nodule of flint prepared to form a core and resembling a tortoise, from which flakes are struck, and characteristic of the **Levalloisian** culture.

**torus:** protuberance or eminence; in physical anthropology, a torus generally means a bar of bone, e.g. **supraorbital torus.** Plural: tori.

**torus angularis:** see **angular torus**.

**torus mandibularis:** see **mandibular torus**.

**total arm length:** measured with the subject standing naturally, with the palm facing the body, the distance from the **stylion** to the acromiale.

**total biomass growth** (*G*): sum of the masses of the living organisms of a species or a trophic level in a particular region per unit of time.

**total body surface area:** sum of the outer surface of a body, assumed smooth; surface area is usually measured from a formula such as that of DuBois, aka the **Meeh–Dubois formula**.

**total energy expenditure:** sum of external work done plus heat produced plus energy stored by the body.

**total facial height** (gn–n): craniometric measurement: distance from the **gnathion** to the **nasion** measured with spreading calipers. See Appendix 7 for an illustration of the landmarks used.

**total facial index:** ratio of facial height to facial width; **total facial height** divided by **bizygomatic breadth** multiplied by 100. See **hypereuryprosopic, mesoprosopic, leptoprosopic**.

**total jaw height:** with the jaws closed normally, the distance from **gnathion** to **subnasale**.

**total leg length:** measured in the standing position, the distance from the upper edge of the greater trochanter to the floor.

**total lung capacity:** amount of air in the lung, usually measured as the sum of **forced vital capacity** and residual lung volume.

**total morphological face height:** gnathion–nasion distance in the median sagittal plane.

**total morphological pattern:** pattern that is a combination of anatomical traits, the sum of which provides evidence of functioning as an adaptive complex.

**total phenotypic variance** ($V_T$): the **variance** of a quantitative character in a population; can be divided into components due to genetic differences and to environmental differences between individuals. See **heritability**.

**total range:** entire area covered by an individual in its lifetime.

**total sagittal arc:** craniometric measurement: distance of the curve from one **nasion** to **opisthion** as measured by a flexible tape measure. It includes the **frontal arc** (nasion to bregma), **parietal arc** (bregma to lambda), and **occipital arc** (lambda to opisthion).

**total upper extremity length:** measured with the subject standing, the distance from the **dactylion** to the acromiale, (shoulder joint).

**totipotent:** cellular characteristic involving the retention of the potential to form any derivative cell type in the body; a characteristic of cells in the inner cell mass of a **blastocyst**. Aka equipotentiality, blank slate. Cf. **pluripotent**. See **stem cell**.

**touching behavior:** physical contact between **conspecifics**. See **grooming**.

**Toumai:** nickname for a hominid fossil, *Sahelanthropus tchadensis*, found at the site of **Toros–Menalla**.

**Tourette syndrome** or **disorder:** see **Gilles de la Tourette syndrome**.

**toxemia:** condition caused by the presence in the blood of poisonous metabolic end-products of bacteria formed at a local infection site.

**toxemia of pregnancy:** condition occurring in pregnant women and associated with fluid retention, urinary protein, hypertension, and possibly convulsions; aka eclampsia.

**toxicogenomics:** branch of **biotechnology** that identifies DNA that codes for certain enzymes, receptors, and other immune system components, and that can be used to model and predict people's responses to particular environmental toxins.

**toxin:** substance that has a poisonous effect on living tissue.

**trabecula, trabeculae:** 1. bar, band, or septum that forms the framework of an organ or structure. 2. branching struts of bone that provide the framework to **cancellous bone** and enable the bone to be lighter and strong.

**trace element:** mineral present in a body in extremely small quantities.

**trace fossil:** sedimentary structure that reflects the activity of a previously living animal; a track, footprint, burrow, etc. of a **fossil**. Aka vestigiofossil, ichnofossil.

‡ **trachea:** tubular airway through which air travels to and from the larynx to the bronchi of the lungs; composed of cartilaginous rings and internally lined with ciliated mucosa; commonly called the windpipe.

*Trachypithecus* **Reichenbach, 1862:** 1. colobine genus to which the brow-ridged langurs belong; nine species recognized that were formerly included in *Presbytis*. Distributed from South Asia into Southeast Asia. Arboreal; diurnal; arboreal quadrupeds that employ leaping. Body mass ranges from 4–15 kg. Dental formula: 2.1.2.3; diet predominantly **folivory**. Dietary adaptations for folivory include specialized dentition, large **salivary glands**, and a large **sacculated stomach. One-male units,** with the presence of **bachelor herds,** are the usual social organization. See Appendix 2 for taxonomy, Appendix 3 for living species. 2. subgenus of *Presbytis* used in schemes that lump the brow-ridged langurs in that genus. The langurs in this group are Southeast Asia species and include *P. (T.) obscura, P. (T.) phayrei, P. (T.) cristata, P. (T.) pileata, P. (T.) geei,* and *P. (T.) francoisi.*

‡ **tract:** bundle of nerve fibers within the **central nervous system.**

**tradition:** specific form of behavior, or a particular site used for breeding or some other function, passed from one generation to the next by learning in the present to add value for the future. See **enculturation.**

**traditional medicine:** any ethnomedical system that holds to a perceived balance between fundamental qualities and forces of nature. Traditional medical healers frequently employ superorganic as well as organic models of sickness and disease, and may seek to restore humoral equilibrium within a body through the use of nutrition, herbs, or ritual magic.

**tragion:** notch just above the **tragus** of the ear.

**tragus:** small projection of cartilage in front of the opening of the external ear.

‡ **trait (character** or **feature):** 1. any characteristic or property of an organism. 2. in genetics, a variant of a character: an inheritance of flower color is a character, whereas the trait is the variation of color such as purple or white. Cf. **character.**

**trait association:** manifestation in an individual of two or more traits for reasons other than genetic linkage.

**trait group (character group):** group of individuals that exhibit specific and predictable interactions with respect to behavior traits; such traits may include competition, aggression, sex, defense, or other behavior, especially those mediated by the **limbic system.**

**tranchet:** quadrangular, hatchet-like blade or flake that is an outgrowth of the side **scraper.** Aka coupoir.

**tranchet technique:** use of a transverse blow to produce an edge on flint implements.

**trans phase:** see **repulsion linkage.**

**transad:** flora found on both sides of a current barrier, an indication that the range was probably continuous in the past.

**transcarbamylase deficiency:** see **ornithine carbamoyl transcarbamylase deficiency.**

**transconformational DNA:** polynucleotides that function to bring about the regional condensation and decondensation of **chromatin.**

‡ **transcription:** see **genetic transcription.**

**transcription factor:** any protein that activates or deactivates the transcription of other genes, by binding to the regulatory region of a gene.

**transcription unit:** see **cistron.**

**transcriptional gene silencing:** inactivation of a gene, portion of a chromosome, or an entire chromosome by **epigenetic reprogramming,** during **transcription.** See **posttranscriptional gene silencing** and **gene silencing.**

**transcriptome:** entire complement of genes, or **mRNAs,** or transcripts, activated in a specific tissue at a particular time. Cf. **genome** and **proteome.**

**transduction:** 1. transfer of donor to a recipient microorganism, especially the viral transfer of DNA into a new host. 2. conversion of energy from one form to another.

**transfection:** introduction of a functional segment of foreign DNA into a cell. In older usage, the source of the DNA was always viral, but recent usage applies to the transfer of DNA from any source. Aka transgenesis. Cf. **transformation.**

**transfer:** See **intergroup transfer.**

‡ **transfer RNA:** see **tRNA.**

**transferrin:** any of a group of serum proteins with iron-binding properties.

**transformation:** 1. change in form, appearance, and/or structure; makeover; metamorphosis. 2. in genetics, process of transferring genetic information between cells by means of DNA, common among certain prokaryotes. Cf. **transposon** and **transfection.** 3. in statistics, the creation of a new variable from the values of an old variable by systematically changing all the old values by some constant coefficient or offset.

**transformation grids:** method used to describe two-dimensional changes in growth and form, both within and between populations of organisms; developed by D'Arcy Thompson (based on drawings of the artist Albrecht Dürer).

**transformational evolution:** belief in the gradual change of an organism from one state into another, e.g. **Lamarckism,** and usually accompanied by a belief in progress, or change from a lower to a higher state, from less to more perfect. Aka variational evolution, transformationism.

**transformism:** Lamarckian version of evolution; see **acquired characteristics** and Geoffroy **Saint-Hilaire.**

**transfusion syndrome:** transfer of blood from one twin to another, due to a **monochorionic placenta** and the **anastomosis** of arterial blood from one twin with venous blood of the other; the clinical result is one twin that is anemic and a second that has too much blood.

**transgene:** exogenous gene introduced into the genome of another organism by **transfection.**

**transgenesis:** see **transfection.**

**transgenic:** pertaining to a **transgene** or a **transgenic organism** or species.

**transgenic organism** or **transgenic species:** any organism whose genome has been modified by the artificial introduction of external **DNA sequences** into its germ line DNA, leading to the growth and development of an individual with the desired modification in every cell; inbred mouse lines are common transgenic organisms. Some transgenic organisms have been patented.

**transgressive variation:** phenotypes in progeny that are outside the range predicted by the phenotypes of the parents. Transgressive variants (TVs) are often suggested to be the result of polygenes.

**transhumant:** semi-nomadic human that grows crops during part of the year, but whose seasonal living pattern is governed by the resource requirements of animals; one who practices transhumance.

‡ **transient polymorphism:** genetic polymorphism that occurs as one allele goes to fixation while a second becomes extinct owing to either **natural selection** or **neutral evolution.**

**transilience:** 1. leaping from one state to another. 2. change due to the rapid shift of a population(s) from one adaptive peak to another across an adaptive valley.

**transilience mechanisms of speciation:** factors that involve changes in genetic organization, such as polyploidy or chromosome **inversion.**

**transition:** 1. movement or passage from one state to another. 2. a **substitutional mutation** in DNA in which a **purine** has been replaced by another purine, or a **pyrimidine** by another pyrimidine. Cf. **transversion.**

**transition probability:** estimation of the likelihood that, given that behavioral event A has occurred, it will be followed by behavioral event B. See **sequence analysis.**

**transition to full maturity:** In the human **life cycle**, the period between **middle age** and full **maturity.**

‡ **transitional form:** fossil that is thought to have both primitive and derived features; not fully either one form or another, but rather exhibiting traits from two different species, such as *Homo erectus*/*H. sapiens* or Neandertal/modern. The term tends to be used by researchers who prefer the **polyphyletic hypothesis** of modern human origins, as opposed to the use of **archaic** forms. See **monophyletic hypothesis.**

‡ **translation:** see **genetic translation.**

**translation elongation:** cytoplasmic process involving the binding of ribosomes to an mRNA initiation complex, and translation of codons.

**translation initiation:** initial assembly of all components required for protein synthesis, including mRNA, tRNAs, ribosomes, and energy-storage molecules.

‡ **translocation:** 1. repositioning of portions or chromosome segments between nonhomologous chromosomes, and hence of the genes from one **linkage group** to within the context of another. Aka chromosomal interchange. See **reciprocal translocation** and **Robertsonian translocation.** 2. movement of a primate population from one site to another. See **seminaturalistic field research.**

**translocation carrier:** individual with exchanged nonhomologous chromosomes but no clinical symptoms.

The carrier has the normal amount of genetic material, but it is rearranged in a balanced manner. **Zygotes** resulting from the recombined **gametes** of such an individual, however, may contain **duplications** or **deletions**, and recurrent spontaneous **abortion** is indicative of such an individual.

**translocation Down syndrome:** alternate mode of **Down syndrome** in which **trisomy** is produced by a **translocation** (rather than by **nondisjunction**), usually involving chromosomes 14 and 21 (t14;21). Aka familial Down syndrome, because the cause can be hidden in a **translocation carrier** and passed from generation to generation.

**transmissible neurodegenerative disease** (TND): see **transmissible spongiform encephalopathies.**

**transmissible spongiform encephalopathies** (TSE): any of several fatal degenerative diseases, allegedly caused by a **prion**, which create spongiform abscesses in brain tissue, and accompanied by progressive muscular and cognitive impairment. The human diseases in this group include **kuru**, new variant **Creutzfeldt–Jakob disease** (nvCJD), **fatal familial insomnia** (FFI), and **Gerstmann–Straussler–Scheinker syndrome** (GSSS). The **prion protein gene** (*PRNP*) on chromosome 20 is responsible. Analogous animal diseases include scrapie, transmissible mink encephalopathy, chronic wasting of deer and elk (wapiti), bovine spongiform encephalopathy ('mad cow disease'), feline spongiform encephalopathy, and exotic ungulate encephalopathy. These appear to be limited to regions where certain varieties of sheep reside, and to countries where these same sheep varieties (or, subsequently, cattle) have been exported. The potential for similar prion diseases in humans exists wherever prion-infected animals are consumed, e.g. deer and elk. See the **protein-only hypothesis** and **prion protein.**

**transmission genetics:** study of the manner by which traits are passed from one generation to the next.

‡ **transmutation:** term applied by **Darwin** and subsequent nineteenth-century naturalists to account for changes in **species** over time; a term that pre-dated the English sense of **evolution.**

**transpiration:** passage of watery vapor or sweat through a porous membrane such as skin or lung tissue; evapotranspiration.

**transplant:** 1. to move from one place to another. 2. in medicine, to move tissue from one organism to another; **graft.**

**transposable genetic element:** DNA sequence capable of moving from one site in nuclear DNA to another, or capable of producing a replicate that can do so. Aka duplicative transposition, transposable element. See **transposon.**

**transposition:** see **DNA transposition.**

**transposon:** DNA segment capable of moving spontaneously up or down a chromosome, into a different chromosome, from mitochondrial DNA into nuclear DNA, or even into another genome. Transposons contain genes that facilitate their insertion into host cell DNA. Aka transposable genetic element.

**transsexual:** individual whose psychosocial sex does not coincide with their phenotypic sex.

**transthyretin** (TTR): transport protein for both thyroxine and vitamin A$_1$ (retinol). Mutations in TTR are the cause of several heritable types of **amyloidosis**, one class of the **protein misfolding disorders**. Aka prealbumin.

**Transvaal Museum** (TM): see entries under **TM.**

**transverse arc** (po–b): **craniometric** measurement: distance of the curve from one **porion** to another, passing by the **bregma**, as measured by a flexible tape measure.

**transverse colon:** second portion of the **colon** that begins when the **ascending colon** flexes to the left, crosses the abdominal cavity, and then turns abruptly downward as it becomes the **descending colon**.

**transverse fissure:** prominent cleft that separates the **cerebellum** from the overlying **cerebrum**.

**transverse fronto-parietal index: frontotemporale–** frontotemporale distance divided by the **euryon–** euryon distance, × 100.

**transverse occipital torus:** buttressed horizontal ridge of bone on the occipital region for attachment of powerful neck muscles; present in the great apes and many fossil **hominid** species, this structure is reduced in modern humans and is referred to as the superior nuchal line.

**transverse plane:** plane or line of anatomical orientation that divides a bilateral organism into any number of superior and inferior halves. Aka horizontal plane or cross section.

**transverse process:** 1. projection that extends laterally and posteriorly from the arch of a vertebra; in life, ligaments and muscles attach to these structures. 2. synonym for the lateral crest of the sacrum.

**transverse sinus:** in **AMHs**, a large venous sinus found in the **dura mater** of the occipital region superior to the nuchal region and that functions to drain blood from the brain. In the **Hadar** hominids and **australopithecines**, this function is accomplished by the **occipital–marginal venous system**.

**transverse torus:** see **inferior transverse torus** and **superior transverse torus**.

**transversion: substitutional mutation** in DNA in which a **purine** has been replaced by a **pyrimidine**, or vice-versa. Cf. **transition.**

**trapezium:** most lateral bone in the distal row of **carpals**, articulating with the **trapezoid, scaphoid**, and **metacarpals** I and II. Aka rhomboides, greater multangular.

**trapezoid:** bone of the **carpus** located in the distal row of carpals articulating with the **trapezium, capitate, scaphoid**, and **metacarpal** II; Aka lesser multangular, pyrimidale.

**traplining:** feeding strategy by which an organism obtains a small portion of its daily nutritional requirements by exploiting a sequence of widely dispersed resources.

**trauma:** injury that results from an external agent such as violent force, or thermal or chemical factors.

**travertine:** almost pure crystalline calcium carbonate deposit precipitated in solution by inorganic chemical processes; deposited around lime-rich springs and lakes; can be utilized as a medium for dating (see **uranium-series**). Travertines are used as a building material. See **stalactite** and **stalagmite**.

**treatment:** independent variable that a researcher manipulates to assess the effect (if any) on the dependent variable(s).

**treatment group:** in experimental design, the experimental group; in contrast to the **control group**, which is exposed to all the conditions affecting the experimental group except one—the potential causative agent of interest — to which only the treatment group is exposed.

‡ **tree:** 1. perennial woody plant that is at least six meters high at maturity. Trees have a vertical central stem (or trunk) with side branches that lead to a well-developed crown or leafy canopy. 2. diagram with a branching pattern resembling that of a tree that illustrates the hypothetical ancestry of a set of taxa.

**tree-ring chronology:** local map of annual growth rings obtained from deciduous trees for the purpose of dating; see **dendrochronology**.

**tree-ring dating:** see **dendrochronology**.

**tree shrew:** vernacular for the mammals belonging to the Order Scandentia, consisting of one family, the Tupaiidae, five genera, and between sixteen and nineteen species. Tree shrew is also the common name of the eleven species of *Tupaia*. Used as models of the earliest primates. See **Tupaiidae**.

**trellis model:** early hypothetical scheme of **hominid evolution** proposed by **Weidenreich** in the 1930s in which hominid lineages in Europe, Asia, and Africa are supposed to have evolved independently during the past 1 my, but with some gene flow acknowledged among these regional populations. This model is essentially the current **multiregional continuity model** supported by **Wolpoff, Thorne**, J. Relethford, A. R. Templeton, and others. See the **out of Africa again and again model**.

**trend:** 1. an apparent direction of change. See **evolutionary trends** and **secular trend**. 2. **orthogenesis**.

**trepanation:** intentionally bored hole found in the skulls of some archeological specimens; differs from

**trephination** in that a section of the skull is not removed, only a hole is drilled; Aka trepanning.

**trephination:** intentional removal of a small section of the skull vault without damaging the underlying tissues. This is found in many different cultures, beginning during the Neolithic, but was particularly prominent in Peru. Trephination was performed on living subjects, who recovered from this operation (based on evidence of healing). Based on the historical literature and ethnographic data of recent peoples, trephination was performed for a variety of reasons, including relieving pressure from head injury, and an attempt to treat pathological conditions such as chronic headaches or epilepsy. In modern medical terminology, trephination refers to a circular piece of tissue being removed; when the term is applied to archeological specimens it does not necessarily imply a circular shape. Cf. **trepanation.**

**treponemal disease:** condition caused by one of the flagellated **protozoa.**

**triadic awareness:** awareness by an individual of its social position and situation relative to other members of the group.

**trial and error learning:** development and maturation of an association between a stimulus and an appropriate response as the result of positive or negative reinforcement. See **play behavior.**

**triangle inequality:** statement that $d_{AB} \geq d_{AC} + d_{BC}$, where A and B are two polynucleotide or amino acid sequences descended from a common ancestral sequence C, and $d$ is any well-defined metric measure of distance. Aka the **relative rate test.**

**triangular (of the carpus):** see **triquetral.**

**tribe:** 1. in anthropology, a distinct social or political group that is autonomous, and claims a particular territory as its own. 2. in taxonomy, a level of classification ranking just below the **subfamily** and above the **genus.**

**triceps skinfold: anthropometric** measurement: mid-point between the **acromion process** of the scapula and the **olecranon process** of the ulna, at which point the **skinfold thickness** is measured. Used in combination with other **skinfold measurements** to estimate body composition.

**trichinosis: helminthic disease** resulting from infestation of *Trichella spiralis*, caused by ingestion of another infested species (usually porcine), and characterized by muscle weakness, diarrhea and fever.

**trichion:** border of the scalp where the hair begins; the center of the hairline on the forehead.

**trichotomy:** evolutionary split involving three lineages; trifurcation; e.g. the gorilla–chimp–human trichotomy.

**trichromatic vision:** color vision made possible by light receptors that are maximally sensitive to three different light wavelengths (and white light) that are combined to form various hues. This type of color vision is characteristic of the **anthropoids.** See **color vision.** Cf. **monochromatic vision, dichromatic vision.**

**tricuspid:** tooth with three cusps.

**trigger:** in common usage, any agent that causes a certain result.

**trigon:** triangular region of a mammalian upper molar that contains the first three cusps. Also spelled trigone. See **paracone, metacone, protocone.** Cf. **trigonid.**

**trigonid:** triangular region of a mammalian lower molar that contains the first three cusps. See **paraconid, metaconid, protoconid.** Cf. **trigon.**

**trigonocephaly:** malformation of the **cranium** that results from premature fusion of the metopic suture and other cranial bones, it produces a triangular configuration to the cranium and compresses the cerebral hemispheres.

**trigonum:** supernumerary bone of the foot that sometimes develops as a result of abnormal ossification of the **talus.**

**trihybrid hypothesis:** J. B. **Birdsell**'s proposal that the aboriginal people of Australia are hybrids and descendants of three waves of immigrants from mainland southeast Asia. He called these waves of people the Barrineans, the Murrayians, and the Carpentarians. Birdsell also thought that Native Americans were composed of three waves of hybrids (that originated in Siberia).

**trimester:** one-third of the human gestation period, consisting of three months. A clinical, rather than a developmentally defined interval, and related more to events that occur in the mother, than to events in the developing fetus. See **first trimester, second trimester,** and **third trimester.**

**Trinchera del Ferrocarril sites:** series of sites in Spain, dated to about 780 kya, among which is **Gran Dolina.** Aka Trinchera Dolina.

‡ **Trinil:** archaeological site found in 1891 in the Ngawa district on the Solo River in Central Java, dated to 750–500 kya (the 'lapilli stratum' of the **Kabuh Formation**), and that contains **hominid** remains that included the 850–940 cm³ Trinil 2 **calotte** (1891), a few teeth, and the pathological Trinil 3 femur (1894), that were located by Eugene **Dubois** and assigned to *Pithecanthropus* (= *Homo*) *erectus* (originally *Anthropopithecus*). The teeth 'associated' with Trinil 2 may belong to an orangutan. The pathological Trinil femur (presents **exostosis** and possibly **myositis ossificans**) found in 1894 remains controversial; some scientists now think that this femur may be modern, and not associated with the Trinil 2 calotte, found only 10 m away. See **Sambungmacan, paleopathology.**

**Trinil fauna:** fossil animals from the Indonesian site of **Trinil;** this is not a collection of animals that form a distinctive unit, but originating from different stratigraphic layers.

**Trinkaus, Erik** (1948–): US physical anthropologist at the University of New Mexico; has written over 100 scientific papers on the anatomy and adaptations of the **Neandertals;** he supports the **assimilation model of human origins.** Author of *The Shanidar Neandertals* (1983); co-author (with Pat Shipman) of *The Neandertals* (1992); editor of *The Emergence of Modern Humans* (1989).

**trinomen:** three-word scientific designation of a **subspecies,** consisting of the genus and species names plus the subspecies epithet. For example, the trinomen of the savannah chimpanzee is *Pan troglodytes schweinfurthii*; of modern humans, *Homo sapiens sapiens.* The need for trinomial nomenclature first arose among ornithologists in 1844. See **binomial nomenclature.**

**trinucleotide expansion disorder:** any condition characterized by a heritable **trinucleotide repeat mutation** in which a DNA triplet, that normally repeats only about 10–30 times, expands beyond the range of normal variation (60–3000 times). The numbers of expansions apparently increases with each generation and the severity of symptoms increase proportionally. Examples are **Fragile X syndrome, Huntington disease,** and **myotonic dystrophy.**

**trinucleotide repeat mutation:** form of **mutation** associated with the regular expansion in the numbers of a specific nucleotide triplet (that always begins with C and ends with G) in or near a functioning gene. See **trinucleotide expansion disorder.**

**tripartite:** having three parts or aspects.

**tripartite brain:** superior portion of the **central nervous system,** subdivided into three functional lobes, the **forebrain, mid-brain** and **hindbrain.**

‡ **triplet:** 1. chain of three nucleotides in a **cistron** in DNA that when transcribed are represented by a complementary **codon** in **mRNA.** AKA codin. 2. one of a **litter** or sibship set of size three; the three may be any combination of genetic identity: either two or three may be genetically identical, or all three may be fraternal; an instance of **higher-order multiples.** See **polyembryony.**

**triploblastic:** referring to tissue derived from all three layers of the developing embryo.

**triploid:** having three complete **haploid** sets of **chromosomes** or **chromatids.** In humans, the result is 69 chromosomes (3N). Usually not compatible with full-term **pregnancy** if many cells in an **embryo** or **fetus** are affected. Noun: triploidy. See **abortion.**

**triplo-X syndrome:** major chromosome anomaly (48,XXX) characterized by amenorrhea in tall, thin

females; otherwise phenotype is normal; slightly lowered IQ in some reports. Affects 1 : 1,500 live born females (Aka 'superfemale' syndrome). See **X inactivation, X-polysomy,** and **primary nondisjunction.**

**triquetral:** most medial bone in the proximal row of carpals, articulating with the **radius, pisiform, lunate,** and **hamate;** Aka cuboid bone. Also spelled triquetrum.

**triradius:** in dermatoglyphics, the tiny triangle made by lines that meet at the corners in some fingerprints.

‡ **trisomy:** form of **aneuploidy** in which one chromosome is present in three rather than the normal two copies as in the other chromosomes, resulting in an **aneuploid** count of 47 instead of the normal 46. Adjective: trisomic. An example in humans is **trisomy 21 (Down syndrome).**

**trisomy 13:** see **Patau syndrome.**

**trisomy 18:** see **Edward syndrome.**

‡ **trisomy 21:** see **Down syndrome.**

**trisomy 22: major chromosome anomaly.** Very rare condition in humans. There has been some confusion with **trisomy 21.** Affected individuals have large ears and nose, a small jaw, and a narrow face. Trisomy 22 in great apes results in 49 chromosomes instead of the normal 48, but the characteristic facies of **Down syndrome** in chimpanzees is clearly homologous with the human syndrome.

**trisomy X:** see **triplo-X syndrome.**

**tritanopia:** form of partial color blindness caused by any defect in the gene located on chromosome 7, resulting in blue **color blindness.** Aka the blue opsin defect. See **protanopia** and **deuteranopia.**

**tritiated thymidine:** amino acid thymidine that has been labeled by the addition of radioactive hydrogen ($^3$H); used to trace the uptake of amino acids *in vivo.*

**tritubercular:** triangular **cusp** pattern on the molars of archaic mammals on which later elaborations are based; primitive mammalian molar cusp pattern.

**Trivers, Robert** (1943–): US sociobiologist. A student of W. D. **Hamilton,** Trivers published early on sociobiological themes, developing mathematical models that indicated how behaviors such as **altruism** could be gene-based. Author of *Social Evolution* (1985) and *Natural Selection and Social Theory: Selected Papers* (2002).

**Trivers–Willard hypothesis:** proposal from proponents of **sociobiology** that the fittest females in some species give birth to more male offspring, whereas the least fit females give birth to more female offspring.

**trivial name:** in a **binomen,** the species epithet or **nomen triviale;** e.g. the *sapiens* portion of *Homo sapiens.*

**trivial trait, character** or **feature:** any characteristic that has no obvious or immediate impact on reproductive success, hence no apparent contribution to the adaptation of an organism or species.

‡ **tRNA:** transfer RNA; short, folded molecule of **RNA**; its three-base **anticodon** specifies amino acids to be transferred to a growing polypeptide chain on the ribosomes for incorporation into **proteins** during **polypeptide synthesis.** See **translation.**

**trochanter:** one of two broad processes on the **femur** that serve as sites for attachments of muscles, i.e. the **greater** and **lesser trochanters.**

**trochlea:** any smooth, saddle-shaped bony surface that resembles a pulley as it articulates with other bones; found in the elbow, knee and ankle joints. Can be applied to other tissues, as well.

**trochlear notch (of the ulna):** crescentlike opening in the **proximal** end of the **ulna** that articulates with the **trochlea** of the humerus, helping to form the elbow joint. Aka sigmoid notch.

**trochlear ridges:** raised margins surrounding any **trochlea.**

**troglophile:** any frequent denizen of caves or passages but not confined to them; aka troglodyte.

*Trogolemur* **Matthew, 1909:** genus of tarsiiform primate from the middle to late Eocene of North America, belonging to the omomyid subfamily **Anaptomorphinae;** two species described; poorly known from jaw fragments. Very small, with estimated body mass around 75 g. Dental formula: 2.1.?2.3/2.1.2.3; dental morphology and small size suggestive of **insectivory.** See Appendix 1 for taxonomy.

**troop:** group of primates. See **foraging group pattern.**

**troop transfer:** emigration of a primate from one social group to another.

**trophectoderm:** outer, epithelial layer of the **blastocyst**, but still circumscribed by the **cytotrophoblast.**

**trophic level:** position of a species in a food chain, determined by which species it consumes and which consume it.

**trophic species:** group of organisms occupying the same **tropic level** in the trophic pyramid. These species feed on the same set of organisms and are preyed upon by the same set of organisms at a higher trophic level. Aka trophic unit.

**trophoblast:** post-implantation derivatives consisting of a nonembryonic, single outer layer of cells of the developing **blastocyst**; gives rise to placental tissues. It is these tissues that contain only a maternal activated X chromosome. See **paternal X inactivation, hypoblast, extraembryonic mesoderm, trophoectoderm,** and **cytotrophoblast.** Cf. **embryoblast.**

**trophoblastic invasion:** developmental process of invagination of uterine tissues by an **embryo** during **implantation.**

**tropic hormone:** any substance, especially those produced by the anterior **pituitary gland**, that stimulates the secretion of another **hormone,** or that

affects the growth, nutrition, or function of other **endocrine glands.** Aka trophic hormone.

**tropical:** region where climates display little seasonality, primarily between 30 degrees north and south of the equator.

**tropical rain forest (TRF): forest** located near the equator where rainfall is abundant; Earth's most complex biome that contains the largest biodiversity.

**Trotter, Mildred** (1899–1991): US physical anthropologist at Washington University Medical School (St. Louis); a specialist in **skeletal biology,** Trotter made significant contributions to the methodology of stature estimation from long bones; was one of five physical anthropologists who participated in the identification of American war dead at Oahu, Hawaii, after World War II. President, **AAPA** (1955–7); Viking Fund medalist (1956). Co-author (with T. Dale **Stewart**) of *Basic Readings on the Identification of Human Skeletons: Estimation of Age* (1954).

**true breeding:** describes a group of individual organisms identically homozygous at a given locus, and that when crossed sexually always produce progeny that are homozygous.

**true pelvis:** see **lesser pelvis.**

**true rain forest:** tropical rain **forest** with an annual rainfall of at least 100 in, (250 cm) per year, and in which there is some rain every day of the year.

**truncate distribution:** atypical sample due to the omission of certain values or individuals.

**truncation selection:** mechanism that eliminates all individuals with a phenotype beyond a certain threshold value.

**trunk:** 1. main stem of a blood vessel, nerve, or other structure before it begins to form branches. 2. see **torso.**

**trunk height:** on a standing subject, the straight distance from the suprasternal notch to the upper edge of the pubic symphysis.

**trunk index:** biacromial breadth × 100, divided by the sitting suprasternal height.

**truth:** actual state, truth or conformity with reality; verity, verified fact or empirical observation obtained through an *a posteriori* analysis.

**'Truth':** proposition, opinion or belief obtained through an *a priori* method.

**trypanosome:** any of the flagellated **protozoan** parasites which cause several diseases in humans, and similar conditions in cattle and other animals. See **Chagas' disease.**

**trypsin:** enzyme secreted by the pancreas that functions to convert proteins into amino acids during **digestion;** a protease.

**tryptophan** (Try): an essential **amino acid;** one of the twenty building blocks of **proteins** and a precursor of **niacin** and **serotonin.** See **pellagra.**

**TS/TV ratio:** proportion of **transitions** to **transversions** that occur in a given evolutionary lineage.

**tschum:** seasonal dwelling constructed by hunting peoples.

**TSE:** see **transmissible spongiform encephalopathy**.

**t-test:** test to assesses the statistical significance of the difference between two sample means for a single dependent variable.

**tuber:** underground stem modified to store nutrients in a plant; e.g. a potato.

**tubercle:** small rounded knoblike process on a bone; aka **tuberculum**.

**tuberculare:** tubercle on the upper portion of the helix.

**tuberculosis** (TB): infectious respiratory disease endemic to both the Old (first described about 650 BCE) and New Worlds. Identified in 1882 by R. Koch, the agent is a bacillus, *Mycobacterium tuberculosis*, historically the first direct link of a specific germ with a disease. Tubercles form in bone and other tissues. Aka 'TB', 'summer fever', and 'consumption'. The antibiotic streptomycin, developed in 1943, is initially effective. Drug-resistant forms of TB began to appear in the 1980s. The term 'tubercle bacillus' also refers to *Mycobacterium bovis*.

**tuberculum:** nodule or eminence; tubercle.

**tuberosity:** knoblike process or protuberance on a bone that is usually larger than a **tubercle**.

‡ **tufa:** chemical sedimentary deposit, spongy in texture and rich in calcium carbonate; occurs typically as encrustations around the mouths of lime-rich springs and rivers.

‡ **tuff:** consolidated deposit of volcanic ash, often laid down in water.

**tufted capuchins:** morphological grouping of the monkeys within the genus *Cebus*; the tufted capuchins are characterized by a thick mat of stiff erect brown hairs on the crown; this tuft sometimes forms horns at the side of the head. Only *C. apella* belongs to this group.

**tufted-ear marmoset:** vernacular for *Callithrix jacchus*.

**Tugen Hills:** conspicuous north–south topographic feature in the **Baringo** district, Rift Valley Province, Kenya. The hills have steep slopes with prominent ridges, and rivers flow in deep gullies. Escarpments dominate the eastern and western limits. The feature contains several hominoid-yielding sites that date from 15 to 1.5 mya. See **Chemeron, Lukeino, Mabaget, Muruyur,** and **Rondinin**.

**Tulu Bor tuff:** Pleistocene volcanic deposit at Koobi Fora, **Lake Turkana**, dated by K/Ar to 3.2 mya (3.32–3.06).

**tumescence:** swelling, as when the sexual skin of a female cercopithecine becomes engorged with blood. Adjective: tumescent.

**tumor:** abnormal proliferation of cells.

**tumor antigen:** antigen or molecule that is predominantly expressed in tumor tissues.

**tumor necrosis factor** (TNF): **monokine** that kills cells, stimulates inflammation, and mediates many systemic acute-phase responses.

**tumor suppressor gene** (TSG): any **wild type** recessive gene that normally functions to limit or suppress the number of cell divisions; e.g. the gene that codes for *p53* **tumor suppressor protein**. AKA antioncogene.

**tumorigenesis:** induction of neoplastic growth. Adjective: tumorigenic.

**tumpline:** corded device slung over the forehead to support burdens carried on the back. The tumpline is a widely used device, even today. Aka mecapal.

**tumpline deformation:** acquired impression in the forehead of modern peoples who utilize a **tumpline** to support burdens carried on the back.

**tundra:** see **alpine tundra**.

*Tupaia* Raffles, 1821: genus in the order **Scandentia**, to which the tree shrews belong; eleven species recognized. Distributed from South Asia to the islands of Southeast Asia. Semi-terrestrial, although a few species are mostly arboreal; diurnal; quadrupedal. Body mass 100–300 g. **Insectivorous** with fruit and seed supplements. See **Tupaiidae**.

**Tupaiidae Gray, 1825:** only family contained within the mammalian Order **Scandentia**. The general vernacular for these animals is tree shrews; five genera and sixteen species. Historically the tupaiids were included within the Insectivora and then **Primates**; they are considered to be very primitive mammals and serve as basal models for both the mammals and the primates. Current evidence suggests a very long lineage for these animals; they may have separated from other mammals as far back as the Cretaceous. Some members are highly arboreal; others spend most of the time on the ground; most diurnal; quadrupedal. Small, mass 400 g or less. Dental formula: 2.1.3.3/3.1.3.3; primarily **faunivorous** with insects being the main prey taken; supplement with fruit, flower, and leaves. Territories and **monogamy** appear to be the rule.

**turbinate bone:** see **nasal concha**.

**Turkana:** 1. one of the fourteen districts in Rift Valley Province, Kenya. 2. a lake in the Turkana district. 3. an archaeological region identified in 1967 near **Lake Turkana**, then Lake Rudolf.

‡ **'Turkana boy':** popular name for **KNM-WT 15000**, found by Kamoya **Kimeu**, an almost complete skeleton of a 11–12-year-old boy from West **Lake Turkana**, Kenya, and attributed to either *Homo ergaster* or *Homo erectus*. The site, found in 1984, is dated to about 1.6 mya. The boy was about 160 cm tall (5'3") at

the time of his death, with a cranial capacity of 884 $cm^3$; as an adult he would have been about 185 cm tall (6'1"), with a cranial capacity of about 910 $cm^3$. Like some of the **australopithecines**, he also possessed six lumbar vertebrae, instead of five as in modern humans. A suggested cause of death is septicemia secondary to dental abscess. See **Nariokotome III**.

***Turkanapithecus kalakoensis* Leakey and Leakey, 1986:** monotypic genus of **hominoids** from the early Miocene of Kenya; phylogenetic relationships uncertain, but often placed with the **Proconsulidae**. Estimated body mass around 10 kg. Dental formula: 2.1.2.3; dental morphology suggests **frugivorous** diet. Appears to have been an arboreal quadruped with some suspensory abilities. See Appendix 1 for taxonomy.

**Turkwel:** see **South Turkwel River**.

**Turner, Christy G. II** (1922–): US physical anthropologist at Arizona State and the University of Arizona. A specialist in dental variation, he has worked in the field for nearly 40 seasons on six continents; other interests include **taphonomy** and the peopling of the Americas and the Pacific Basin. Co-author (with G. R. Scott) of *The Anthropology of Modern Human Teeth* (1997); author of *The Dentition of Arctic Peoples* (1991); author (with Jacqueline Turner) of *Man Corn: Cannibalism and Violence in the Prehistoric American Southwest* (1999).

‡ **Turner syndrome:** nonfamilial aneuploid condition (2N = 45, Xo); clinical symptoms in these females include low birth weight, swelling in hands and feet, webbing of the neck, coarse facial features, nail hypoplasia, and a very low hairline in childhood; there is no sexual maturity (gonadal dysgenesis and sterility are nearly universal). Further symptoms include a short adult stature, wide-spaced nipples, broad chest, and pigmented moles; hearing impairment prevalence ranges from 50 to 100%. There is an excess of lymphocytes at all stages of cases. There is no reported parental age effect. Rare cases of phenotypic sex discordance sometimes involve originally male **MZ twins** with subsequent somatic nondisjunction in one of the pair that produces a 45,Xo female phenotype; the other twin remains a normal male. Recently developed hormonal therapy techniques can produce a near-normal **phenotype**. Turner syndrome exhibits evidence for genomic imprinting; it is usually the father's X chromosome that is lost. 1 : 2,500 live-born females affected; 1% of all conceptions are 45,Xo, but 98% of all Xo conceptuses are spontaneously aborted, which indicates that the condition is frequent at conception (1 : 250). See **primary nondisjunction**.

**turnover-pulse hypothesis:** proposal that a dramatic cooling event occurred between 2.8 and 2.4 mya that precipitated minor glaciation in the northern hemisphere, and simultaneously reduced the area of moist woodlands in Africa, replacing it with drier and more open **savannas** about 2.5 mya. This event seems to be correlated with an episode of rapid evolution in plants, hominoids, antelopes, rodents, and certain marine invertebrates. Among the new species of hominoids were several in the genera *Australopithecus* and *Homo*.

**Turolian:** European land-mammal age (late Miocene, approximately 6–9 mya).

**turricephaly:** condition of having a short skull that results from early **synostosis** of the coronal and lambdoid sutures.

‡ **twin(s):** 1. either of two offspring produced at one birth (**parity** event); the product of a litter of size two. 2. one of two individuals closely related or resembling each other. Twins may be either (a) identical and always same-sexed, or (b) fraternal, in which case the pairs may be either same- or opposite sexed. Technically, the former are termed **monozygotic twins** and the latter **dizygotic twins**. Twins are normal in tree shrew, mouse lemur, dwarf lemur, slender loris, marmoset, and tamarin births, but are the exception among humans and most other higher primates. A female marmoset may have up to two litters per year, a total of four offspring annually. See **chimeric twin, fraternal twins**, and **identical twins**. See **multiple births** for incidences of higher-order births.

**twin method:** strategy for estimating complex trait **heritability** in humans by comparing **total phenotypic variances** of **monozygotic twins** (MZT) against **dizygotic twins** (DZT), under the expectation that the variances will be equal in those traits that have no genetic contribution. The estimated heritability increases in proportion to the relative decrease in MZT twin variance as compared to DZT twin variance for the trait. See F. **Galton** and **Holzinger's *H***.

‡ **twins, dizygotic** (= fraternal twins, DZT): DZTs are siblings thought to be the result of two simultaneous pregnancies such that a pair (or more) of individuals reside in a womb. There are two placentas, and twin pairs can be the same sex or opposite-sexed. Genetically, DZTs are only as similar as ordinary pairs of **siblings**; they may be **discordant** for many character states. These twins share half their genes, on average, by descent from the same parents. There is a strong maternal age affect, with the probability of dual conception rising sharply in the latter portion of the 4th maternal decade (Aka binovular twinning). The DZ twin rate varies by geographic region: overall number of DZ twins per 1,000 live births is 2–7; in North America, 7–11; in Europe, 9–20; in Africa,

45–50. Cf. **twins, monozygotic, uniovular dispermatic twins**, and **half-siblings**.

‡ **twins, monozygotic** (= identical twins, MZT): MZTs are siblings thought to be the result of a single conception, with cleavage of the fertilized **ovum** occurring (sometimes asymmetrically) while the preimplantation cells of the morula are still **totipotent**; hence monozygous. MZT pairs are 'always' of the same sex, except in very rare cases of discordant gonadal dysgenesis caused by epigenetic factors. Genetically, MZTs are identical sib pairs; they must be **concordant** for genotypic character states, and must also be of the same sex. There are no demonstrable parental age effects in MZ twinning. Whether MZ twinning is familial is still an open research question (Aka uniovular twinning). The MZ twin rate is about the same worldwide: 3–4 per 1,000 live births (1 : 240 full-term pregnancies is a frequently cited figure). Of all twin conceptions, however, about 70% result in singleton births, a result of the '**vanishing twin**' phenomenon; the actual MZ twinning rate may thus be as high as 1 : 80. See **polyembryony**. Cf. **twins, dizygotic** and **half-siblings**.

**twin study:** any of a series of research projects carried out since the nineteenth century work of Francis **Galton** that attempt to estimate the **heritability** of a complex phenotypic trait. Such studies operate under the assumption that all twin pairs are of only two modalities (**monozygotic twins**, MZT, or **dizygotic twins**, DZT), that twin **zygosity** can always be correctly ascertained, and that the average proportion of genes shared by MZT twins is 100% whereas for DZT twins it is 50%.

**two-hit hypothesis:** hypothesis formulated by A. Knudsen, postulating that malignant transformation occurs following a two-step process.

**two-hominid theory:** idea proposed by Mary **Leakey** that **habilines**, who made **Developed Oldowan** tools (according to Leakey), and **erectines**, who made **Acheulean tools**, lived contemporaneously at **Olduvai Gorge** between 1.5 and 1.2 mya, based on excavations of both tool traditions in the same strata a few hundred meters apart.

**2.1.2.3/2.1.2.3:** see **dental formula**.

**two-phase model:** proposed modification of the **short chronology model** for the human occupation of Europe. This model proposes that hominid species inhabited the Mediterranean regions of Europe intermittently, from perhaps 1.2 mya, with continuous colonization of the circum-Mediterranean region followed by phased migration and occupation of areas north of the Alps and Pyrenees mountains between 600 and 500 kya.

**Tylor, Edward Burnet** (1832–81): British anthropologist; Tylor constructed the theory of animism and promulgated a school of cultural evolutionism called **unilineal evolution**; among the first to 'quantify' (typologize) cultural phenomena as data for comparative analysis; culture was unilineal and progressive, from **savagery** to **barbarism** to **civilization**; author of *Primitive Culture* (1871). Although ethnology already existed, Tylor is considered by many historians to be the founder of cultural anthropology.

**tympanic bone:** see **tympanic region of the temporal bone**.

**tympanic bulla:** see **auditory bulla**.

**tympanic membrane:** thin membrane that covers the auditory canal where it separates the external ear from the middle ear. The tympanic membrane vibrates when sound waves impinge upon it and this vibration is transmitted to the **auditory ossicles**. One of these tiny bones, the malleus, is attached to the tympanic membrane. Aka tympanum, eardrum.

**tympanic region of the temporal bone:** bony ring that develops from dermal bone and supports the **tympanic membrane** in mammals; in primates a ringlike ectotympanic is found among some lemurs, whereas a tubular ectotympanic is present among the **anthropoids** and some prosimians. In catarrhines this bone becomes elongated, fuses with the tympanic plate, and forms a tube that helps form the **external acoustic meatus**. Because a tubular tympanic region is present in some of the basal primates, it is uncertain which trait is primitive. Sometimes referred to as the ectotympanic or tympanic bone.

**tympanic ring:** bony ring of dermal origin that supports the tympanic membrane in mammals. See **tympanic region of the temporal bone**.

**type:** 1. a kind, class, or group distinguished by a particular key or set of key characteristics; cf. **archetype**. 2. in systematics, the single specimen that serves as the basis for the name of a taxon. See **type specimen, holotype**. 3. location, the **type locality**, where a holotype was found. 4. one of a noncontinuous series, as in **genotype; albinism, type II**; or **type 1 error**. 5. commonly appended as a suffix (-type) in all senses (1–4).

**type I diabetes:** see **diabetes mellitus, type I**.

**type II diabetes:** see **diabetes mellitus, type II**.

**type 1 error:** probability of rejecting a **null hypothesis** incorrectly (i.e. when it is true); the probability of committing such an error is set by a researcher at the **alpha level** ($\alpha$). Typical levels are 5 or 1 percent, termed the 0.05 or 0.01 levels, respectively.

**type 2 error:** probability of incorrectly failing to reject a **null hypothesis** (i.e. accepting it when it is false); the probability of committing such an error is conventionally set at the **beta level** ($\beta$). Beta is related inversely to a **type 1 error**, and $(1-\beta)$ is defined as **power**.

**type culture:** totality of qualitatively similar characteristics that distinguish a given culture. In archaeology, a type culture is usually characterized and named on the basis of a site with historical priority, regardless of its eventual place in the spectrum of similar sites.

**type locality:** site from which the type specimen for a particular species or rock unit was taken.

**type site:** archaeological location considered to be typical of a unit such as a focus, aspect, culture, etc., and often also the source of the name for that unit, e.g. La Soultré. The term type station is synonymous.

**type species:** single designated species of a genus, which serves as the basis for the original name and description of a **genus** or **subgenus.**

‡ **type specimen:** single designated individual of an organism which serves as the basis for the original name and description of the **species.** Aka *fossile directeur.*

**type station:** see **type site.**

**typhus:** severe form of infection characterized by malaise, severe headache, sustained high fever, and accompanied by skin discoloration and lesions in the 3rd to 7th days. Such infectious 'plagues' associated with rats, lice, and fleas caused 'battlefield typhus' during European wars from the sixteenth through the twentieth centuries. The agent of typhus is a bacteria-like organism, *Rickettsia prowazekii.* Common names include louse-borne typhus, scrub typhus, India tick typhus, Kenya tick typhus, and murine typhus.

**typing:** determination of the category to which any discrete entity belongs, as in the determination of an individual's **blood type.**

**typological race concept:** idea that race is a real taxonomic category. Cf. **nominalistic race concept.**

**typological seriation:** study of the chronological development of a morphological element, a kind of artifact, or an art form.

**typological species concept:** see **phenetic species concept.**

‡ **typology:** 1. set of discrete groupings in **classification;** typologies emphasize average tendencies within a data set, and usually ignore variation within groups. **Racial classifications** are a form of typological construct. See **folk taxonomy.** 2. classification of artifacts by families and groups on the basis of their form and mode of manufacture; e.g. **stone tool typology.** 3. the taxonomic and evolutionary phases (stages) of archaeological research.

**tyrosinase:** enzyme that converts **tyrosine** to **dopa** and dopa to dopaquinone as a precursor to the production of **melanin.** Tyrosinase deficiency results in **oculocutaneous albinism.** More than 60 mutations in tyrosinase have been identified.

**tyrosine** (Tyr): a crystalizable, essential **amino acid;** one of the twenty building blocks of **proteins.** Tyrosine is a precursor of **melanin, thyroxines,** and **dopamine.**

**tyrosinemia, Type II:** hereditary autosomal recessive form of abnormal tyrosine accumulation that causes liver and kidney damage; occurs when the amino acid **tyrosine** fails to be degraded by a defective enzyme. Rare.

**Tyson, Edward** (1650–1708): British physician touted as the 'father of primatology' because he was the first to dissect and describe a great ape, the common chimpanzee; author of *Orang-Outang, Sive Homo Sylvestris* (1699). Tyson's 'Orang-Outang' may actually have been the first dissection of an infant chimpanzee.

**uakari:** vernacular for the two or three platyrrhine species belonging to the genus *Cacajao*.

**'Ubeidiya:** archaeological site found in 1959, in the Jordan Valley of Israel, dated to 1.5–1.2 mya ('Ubeidiya Formation); containing artifacts similar to those found at **Olduvai Gorge**, both **Developed Oldowan** and **Acheulean**. Several hominid teeth found at the site were reported in 2002.

**ubiquitin** (ub): an evolutionarily conservative protein molecule consisting of 76 nearly invariant amino acid residues found in all prokaryotic and eucaryotic cells, both as a free molecule and conjugated to other molecules. Among other suggested functions, cells use ubiquitin to tag molecules and organelles for recycling. See **mitochondrial DNA**, and **ubiquitination**.

**ubiquitination:** attachment of **ubiquitin** to other molecules, thus flagging them for proteolytic recycling, kinase activation, and other molecular trafficking.

**Uintanius Matthew, 1915:** genus of tarsiiform primate from the early to middle Eocene of North America, belonging to the omomyid subfamily **Omomyinae**; two species; most primitive omomyine, with a recent ancestry from one of the anaptomorphines, and some workers place this genus within that group. Estimated body mass around 160 g. Dental formula: 2.1.3.3/2.1.3.3; dental morphology has been variously interpreted by different authors as adapted for **gummivory**, **granivory**, or a compromise between **frugivory** and **insectivory**. See Appendix 1 for taxonomy.

**Uintasorex parvulus Matthew, 1909:** archaic mammal of the middle and late Eocene of the Rocky Mountain region of North America, belonging to the plesiadapiform family **Microsyopidae; monotypic;** some authorities assign this genus to the order Insectivora. Maxillary dental formula uncertain, mandibular formula = 1.0.3.3. Estimated body mass around 45 g. Small body size and dentition suggests **insectivory**. See Appendix 1 for taxonomy.

**ulcer:** depressed lesion, erosion or sore, as in the stomach or intestinal wall. One of the major contributing factors to gastric ulcers is the organism *Helicobacter pylori*.

‡ **ulna:** medial bone of the forearm when the skeleton is viewed from **anatomical position**. Its **proximal** end helps form the elbow; its **distal** end articulates with the distal end of the **radius**, where the ulnar **styloid** process provides attachments for ligaments of the wrist.

**ulnar:** 1. of or pertaining to the elbow or **ulna** bone. 2. referring to the little finger.

**ulnar loop: dermatoglyphic** pattern in which the ridges of fingerprints swirl around one head and toward the margin and open toward the outside of the hands. See **loop** and **radial loop**.

**ulnar–radial deviation:** side-to-side motion at the wrist joint; only the **ulna** articulates with the **carpus** among the **hominoids**, providing more lateral range of motion than is found in monkeys, whose carpus articulates with both the ulna and the **radius**.

**ulotrichous:** pertaining to the possession of woolly hair.

**ultimate causation:** conditions of the environment that render certain traits adaptive and others non-adaptive; the adaptive traits tend to be retained in the population and are 'caused' in this ultimate sense. Aka evolutionary causation. Cf. **proximate causation**.

**ultimate effect:** long-term effect or consequence of conditions brought about by change in a variable or variables. Medicine, for example, often has the **proximate effect** of lowering **mortality rates**, and the ultimate effect of increasing absolute population size and disease **incidence**.

**ultimate glaciation:** fourth and last glaciation of the Pleistocene; see **Würm glaciation**.

**ultrabrachycranic:** in reference to the **cranial index**, with an index of 90.00 or greater; such an individual is considered to be very broad-headed. See **hyperbrachycranic**.

**ultradian rhythm:** cycle that occurs in a period shorter than 24 h. Cf. **infradian rhythm**, **periodic behavior**. See **circadian rhythm**, **rhythmic behavior**.

**ultradolichocranic:** in reference to the **cranial index**, with an index of 64.99 or less; such an individual is considered to be ultranarrow- or long-headed. See **dolichocranic**.

**ultra-Plinian eruption:** very large volcanic eruption, as defined by measures on the Dust Veil Index and the Volcanic Explosivity Index; the **Toba eruption** on the island of Sumatra 74 kya was an example. Such eruptions are thought to reduce the amount of solar radiation that reaches the earth by more than 20% for a decade or more, and to have a significant cooling effect on the earth's climate. Smaller eruptions are termed Hawaiian, Strombolian, Vulcanian, and **Plinian eruptions**.

**ultrasonic:** having a frequency above the human audible range; sound waves above 30,000 cycles per second.

**ultrasound scanning:** technique utilizing high-frequency sound waves that can be focused to obtain pictures of tissues, organs, structures and tumors within a body. Because it is noninvasive, ultrasound is especially useful for fetal examinations *in utero*.

**ultrastructure:** structure at the cellular level that is observed with a transmission electron microscope.

**ultraviolet, ultraviolet light,** or **ultraviolet radiation:** see **UV radiation**.

**Uluzzian tool tradition:** 'transitional' tool industry found in Italy, presumably carried by **Neandertals**, but like the **Châtelperronian** seems to be a mixture of Middle and Upper Paleolithic techniques and tool types. Cf. **Szeletian** and **Buhunician.**

**umbilical cord:** embryonic and fetal structure containing primarily blood vessels and extending from the placenta to the embryo or fetus.

**umbilicus:** site in the umbilical region where the **umbilical cord** was attached; aka navel.

**umbrella hypothesis:** scenario in which apparently unrelated phenomena and data are organized according to a perceived theme in an attempt to explain or unify them according to a central scheme or process. Umbrella hypotheses are characterized by a large number of untested and sometimes untestable assumptions. See the **aquatic theory of human evolution.**

**unciform:** see **hamate.**

**uncle:** brother of one's mother or father; a kinship term that identifies a genealogical or adopted degree of relationship in a **nuclear family** or **extended family.** See **father, mother, brother, sister, aunt, cousin.**

**underarm skin color:** color of skin in the **axillary** region, where the least amount of sunlight penetrates the body; used for measuring skin color because this area is considered to be least affected by the environment.

**underdominance:** rare instance when the **fitness** of a **heterozygote** is less than that of both **homozygotes** in a case of **Mendelian inheritance.** Cf. **overdominance.**

‡ **undernutrition:** inadequate **nutrition** due either to scarcity of resources or to failure to ingest, absorb, or adequately convert necessary food elements. See **protein–calorie malnutrition, marasmus,** and **kwashiorkor.**

**understory:** that part of a forest that lies below the upper **canopy** layers. Also spelled understorey.

**underwater excavation:** exploration or uncovering of an object or site that is covered with water; see **excavation** and **marine archaeology.**

**undifferentiated:** describes an *in vitro* state in animal cells in which a cell in a culture medium lacks the function and/or architecture of that specialized cell type when *in vivo.*

‡ **unequal crossing over: crossing over** in which the two **chromatids** do not exchange equal lengths of DNA. See **sister chromatid exchange.**

**UNESCO Statement on Race:** formal statement concerning **race** signed by many prominent biologists in 1950; the original statement rejected the existence of racial hierarchies and the notion of pure human races, and stated that the mental aptitudes of human races are similar and that no evidence suggested that **miscegenation** resulted in

deterioration, that no correlation existed between emotional temperament or personality and race, and that 'race is not so much a biological phenomenon as a social myth'. A revised 'Statement on the Nature of Race and Race Differences by Physical Anthropologists and Geneticists' appeared (1951) in which signatories agreed to retain the term **race** as a biological entity, and omitted previous statements regarding both temperament and intellectual capacity, while essentially retaining the remainder of the original document.

**ungual phalange:** distal or terminal **phalange** modified to support nails, claws, or hooves.

**unguarded X chromosome:** hemizygosity in species such as primates in which males are the **heterogametic sex** that causes the expression of all deleterious recessives on a male's X chromosome and that results in higher average mortality in males than in females. See **differential male mortality.**

**Unguiculata:** cohort presented by Simpson in 1945 that consisted of eight mammalian orders considered to be closely related evolutionarily. Four of these orders comprise the grandorder (or superorder) **Archonta.**

**ungula:** in primatology, the broad flattened nail found on the terminal or ungual digits of primates; in other areas of zoology, this term applies to claws and hooves.

**ungulate:** referring to a mammal that has hooves; originally a taxonomic group (Ungulata), but today the members are in different orders and ungulate is merely a descriptive term with no formal taxonomic meaning. See **artiodactyl** and **perissodactyl.**

**ungulicutate:** describes a mammal that possesses nails or claws.

**unicuspid:** tooth that has only one cusp.

**uniface:** stone tool that has been flaked on one side only; often a **chopper.**

**uniform convergence hypothesis:** statement that convergence in all regions of a phylogenetic tree proceeds at a uniform rate.

**uniform dispersion:** in ecology, pattern of spatial distribution of individual members of a species within their geographic range. Uniform dispersion refers to individuals that are evenly spaced from one another. Cf. **clumped dispersion.**

**uniform rate hypothesis:** statement that divergence of any two lines of descent in an evolutionary tree takes place at a constant rate with respect to each other. See **unweighted pair group method.**

‡ **uniformitarianism:** theory that the earth's geological features are the result of long-term processes, still visible, that require immense geologic time; although there were antecedents, the term's modern sense is attributed to Charles **Lyell** *c.* 1830. Aka fluvialism.

**unilateral:** occurring on one side. See **unilinear**.

**unilinear:** pertaining to descent, inheritance, or descent through either the mother's or the father's line alone; aka unilateral descent.

**unilinear evolution:** theory of **cultural evolution** which asserts that the whole of human history can be understood as a sequence of **evolutionary stages** through which all human cultures have passed or will pass during their cultural development; contradicts the basic biocultural evolutionary perspective because it is **teleological**; sometimes termed unilineal evolution. Cf. **multilinear evolution**.

**uni-male group (polygyny** or **society):** see **one-male unit**.

**unineme hypothesis:** confirmed hypothesis that a newly formed **chromatid** consists of only one DNA complex, and that it is unbroken as it passes through the **centromere**. The competing polyneme hypothesis was falsified experimentally.

**uniovular dispermatic twins:** rare mode of twinning that may result from the simultaneous fertilization of an ovum and **polar body** by two spermatozoa. Polar bodies are usually not fertilized. Aka polar body twinning. See **twin method**. Cf. **monozygotic twins** and **dizygotic twins**.

**uniparental disomy** (UPD): unusual inheritance of two copies of a gene from one parent, and none from the other. One of the forms of **non-Mendelian inheritance**. There are two classes of UPD: **isodisomy** and **heterodisomy**.

**uniparental embryo:** embryo created *in vitro* from two haploid genomes from the same parent, and utilized in **biotechnology** and medical research.

**uniparity:** 1. state of having had only one **litter** or brood during a life cycle. 2. production of a single offspring at each birth event. Adjective: uniparous. Cf. **primiparity**. See **parity**.

**unipolar disorder:** emotional disorder characterized by long bouts of depression. Cf. **bipolar affective disorder**.

**unipotent:** capable of developing into only one kind of cell; committed.

**unisexual:** 1. said of a population composed of one sex only. 2. said of an individual having either male or female reproductive organs and that produces only male or female gametes, respectively. Cf. **bisexual**.

**unit:** 1. a single thing or organism. 2. a set considered as a single entity. 3. a certain magnitude; aspect of a measure.

**unit of evolution:** the level at which evolution occurs; the **population** or **deme** is considered the unit of evolution. Cf. **unit of selection**.

**unit of selection:** the level at which selection occurs; the **organism** is considered the unit of selection. Cf. **unit of evolution**.

**unit trait, character** or **feature:** 1. any feature transmitted as a hereditary unit, and controlled by a single allele. 2. in taxonomy, any feature that cannot be subdivided.

**univariate analysis:** analysis of **variation** that focuses on one trait or **variable** at a time.

**universal:** 1. characteristic of the whole; general. 2. pertaining to behavior characteristic of all the members of a society.

**universal code theory:** assumption that the **genetic code** is used by all forms of life. The near-corollary that all the triplets in the vertebrate **lookup table** are also universal has fewer than half a dozen exceptions.

**universal donor:** in the human **ABO blood group** system, individuals with blood type O, the null peptide that cannot produce an antigenic response in most humans; type O individuals can donate blood to nearly all other persons.

**universal evolution:** proposal that there is a trend toward development and an unfolding generally characteristic of all life.

**universal law of learning:** position held by Skinner and other behaviorists that learning is an evolved trait, and that all animals learn in essentially the same manner. This implies that principles of learning discovered in one species in a particular situation can be generalized to all types of learning; unproven and controversial.

**universal recipient:** in the human **ABO blood group** system, individuals with blood type AB, the only genotype lacking the ability to produce both anti-A and anti-B antibodies; type AB individuals can receive blood from nearly all other persons.

**unreplicated chromosome:** 'I'-shaped chromatid; one **chromatid** before DNA replication has occurred. Conventionally, a **chromatid**.

**unrooted cladogram:** **cladogram** in which genealogy is unassumed, prior to assumption of a root node.

**unsaturated fatty acid:** long carbohydrate chain that contains triglycerides and with more than one double bond with 'missing' hydrogen atom(s). See **monounsaturated fatty acid** and **polyunsaturated fatty acid**. Cf. **saturated fatty acid**.

**unscheduled cell division:** abnormal increase in the rate and number of cell divisions, usually caused by loss of function of a **housekeeping gene** such as a **tumor suppressor gene**.

**unscheduled DNA synthesis:** activity that does not occur during the **S phase**, and that usually indicates repair of DNA.

**unstable isotope:** radiogenic isotope of an element. Many elements have unstable isotopes, e.g. $^{14}$C. Cf. **stable isotope**.

**untufted capuchins:** morphological grouping of the monkeys within the genus *Cebus*; characterized by a dark 'skullcap' (reminiscent of the caps worn by capuchin monks) with a peak at the forehead that contrasts with a light face. The members of this group are *C. capucinus*, *C. albifrons*, and *C. olivaceus* (= *nigrivittatus*).

**unweighted pair group method:** clustering procedure that results in an evolutionary tree that first joins the smallest branches of a dendrogram and proceeds until the two largest branches are joined.

**unweighted trait, character** or **feature:** character that has been added to an analysis, and considered to be no more or less important than any other character. Cf. **weighted character.**

**U/Pb:** abbreviation for **uranium-lead dating.**

**upper arm length:** measured with the subject standing, and with the arm hanging naturally and with the palm facing the body, the distance from the **radiale** to the **acromiale.**

**Upper Cave:** archaeological site found in 1933 at **Zhoukoudian**, near Beijing, China, dated to 25–18 kya, and that contains stone artifacts, ornaments, a bone needle, and hominid remains, including three crania and bones from several other individuals. The cranium of an older male has a capacity of 1500 cm³ and that of a young female has a capacity of 1380 cm³. All attributed to *Homo sapiens*. Authorities are divided regarding the similarity of these fossils to existing people; some see affinities with **Cro-Magnon** rather than with modern Asians. See **locality 1.**

**upper facial height** (ids–n): craniometric measurement: distance from the **alveolare** to the **nasion** measured with spreading calipers. See Appendix 7 for an illustration of the landmarks used.

**upper facial index:** ratio of upper facial height (i.e., the mandible is excluded) to facial width; **upper facial height** divided by **bizygomatic breadth** multiplied by 100. See **hypereuryenic, euryenic, mesenic, leptenic, hyperleptenic.**

**upper facial length:** nasion–endobasion distance, measured in the median sagittal plane.

**upper limb:** term in human and ape anatomy for the superior appendage, i.e. the **pectoral girdle**, arms, and wrist; the upper limb corresponds to the forelimbs of quadrupeds.

**upper morphological facial height:** nasion–prosthion distance in the median sagittal plane.

‡ **Upper Paleolithic Age** (UP): the Upper **Old Stone Age**; refers to a cultural period of early modern humans and distinguished by innovative stone tool technologies; the series dates from around 40,000 to about 14,000 years ago, and before any evidence of **domestication** of plants and animals. The UP is conventionally divided into five **assemblages** from the oldest to the most recent: **Châtelperronian, Aurignacian, Gravettian, Solutrean,** and **Magdalenian.**

**Upper Pleistocene:** see **late Pleistocene.**

**upper temperature survival limit:** environmental temperature above which thermal balance cannot be maintained for a long period, and that causes animals to become progressively hyperthermic.

**upright posture:** see **bipedalism.**

**upstream:** on a chromosome, the nucleotide sequences 5′ to the end of the last **exon** of a gene. See **flanking sequence.** Cf. **downstream.**

**upward causation:** proposition that changes that occur at one hierarchical level cause concomitant changes at a higher hierarchical level.

‡ **uracil** (U): one of the **pyrimidine nucleosides**; found only in **RNA**; composed of one carbon–nitrogen ring. **Thymine** replaces uracil in **DNA**. Uracil differs from thymine only in the substitution of a single radical.

**Uraha:** archaeological site found in 1991 near Uraha in northern Malawi, dated to 2.5–2.3 kya (Chiwondo Beds), and that contains hominid remains including a partial hominid mandible (UR 501) assigned to Cf. *Homo rudolfensis.*

**uranium fission track:** see **fission track dating.**

**uranium–lead dating** (U/Pb): **radiometric dating** technique that measures the decay of uranium ($^{238}$U) into lead (Pb); the half-life of $^{238}$U is 4.5 billion years.

**uranium-series dating** (U/Th): radiometric dating technique that measures the decay of uranium ($^{238}$U) into thorium ($^{230}$Th).

**urea:** major nitrogenous waste product of mammalian protein breakdown and amino acid catabolism; formed in the liver. A normal person excretes about 30 g of urea per day.

**urea-cycle defect:** any heritable condition that results from one or more defective enzymes in the metabolic pathway that removes nitrogen from one source to another. Urea-cycle defects include argininosuccinicaciduria, ornithinuria, and citrullinuria.

**urethra:** tube that transports urine from the urinary bladder to the outside of the body; also transports semen during ejaculation in males.

**urinary bladder:** thick-walled sac composed of smooth muscle; stores urine prior to micturition.

**urination:** act of voiding urine; micturition.

**urine washing:** form of **scent marking** in which the animal urinates on the paws and then leaves the scent of its urine through the territory or range; found among the **prosimians** and **platyrrhines.** Aka urine marking.

**urogenital triangle:** region of the pelvic floor containing the external genitalia.

**use and disuse, theory of:** see **Lamarckism.** Aka use inheritance.

**U-shaped dental arcade:** see **parabolic dental arcade.**

**Usno Formation:** late Pliocene sedimentary unit found in the Lower **Omo Valley** in East Africa, dated to 3.3–2.97 mya.

‡ **Ussher, James** (1581–1656): Archbishop of Armagh, Ireland, and scriptural chronologist who counted the number of generations named in the Old Testament of the Judeo-Christian Bible, arriving at a total of about 220 generations having occurred from Adam and Eve to his generation in AD 1646. By estimating the length of each generation, Ussher was able to calculate that the creation cited in the Old Testament had occurred in exactly 4004 BC. Others made similar attempts at calculating the age of the earth (e.g. Lord Kelvin), but Ussher's estimate (published 1650) was the most widely accepted in the eighteenth and nineteenth centuries. See **Lightfoot.**

**usurper:** outside male primate that overthrows the male controlling a group of females.

**usurper strategy:** infanticide performed by a male (the usurper) who has overthrown a **harem** male in order to speed up **estrus** in group females; term originally coined by **Hrdy** based on an observation of Hanuman langurs.

*Utahia kayi* **Gazin, 1958:** tarsiiform primate from the late Eocene of North America, belonging to the omomyid subfamily **Omomyinae; monotypic.** Estimated body mass around 100 g. Dental formula uncertain. Small body size and known dental morphology suggest **insectivory.** See Appendix 1 for taxonomy.

**uterine:** of or pertaining to the **uterus.**

**uterine cycle:** monthly female sexual cycle characterized by repetitive shedding, regeneration, and enrichment of the **endometrium,** and described by four temporal phases: **menstrual phase, proliferative phase, secretory phase,** and **ischemic phase.** In fecund human females, the cycle is completed every 28 days. This term is preferred over 'menstrual cycle' because it reduces confusion with the menstrual phase of the cycle. It is modified from the **estrous cycle** of female primates. Aka human female reproductive cycle.

**uterine descent:** see **matriline.**

‡ **uterine tube:** one of two symmetrical slender tubes leading from the uterus to the region of the **ovary.** The uterine tube is where conception (fertilization) usually occurs, after which it conveys the fertilized **zygote** to the **uterus.** Aka oviduct, Fallopian tube.

**uterus:** hollow, muscular organ in which a fetus develops; located within the female pelvis between the urinary bladder and the rectum. Aka womb.

**U/Th:** abbreviation for **uranium/thorium.** See **uranium-series dating.**

**utilized bone:** bison or horse toe bone that was cut and used as an anvil during the Middle Paleolithic.

**utilized flakes:** stone **débitage** used for cutting or slicing; edge wear is from use rather than from deliberate modification.

**utilized piece:** byproduct of the tool-making process, material not intended as a tool; hammers, anvils, utilized flakes.

**UV radiation:** invisible (ultraviolet) region of the spectrum of electromagnetic radiation with wavelengths shorter than those of visible light (about 10–400 nm), i.e. above the violet end, and thus too short to be seen by the human eye. The ultraviolet band extends to the lower limit of the X-ray portion of the spectrum. Other species such as birds and bees can see in the ultraviolet range, and are able to detect morphological patterns in flowers and eggs normally undetectable to humans. UV radiation is divided into three regions: UV-A, UV-B, and UV-C. Aka actinic rays, ultraviolet light. See **melanin, photolysis, rickets,** and **vitamin D.**

**V:** abbreviation for **vitamin**.

**V$_g$:** symbol for **genetic variance**.

**vaccination:** see **inoculation**.

‡ **vaccine:** inactivated or partial form of a pathogen artificially introduced into an immune system to pre-produce antibodies against the event that the virulent form of the pathogen is encountered.

**vagile:** endowed with freedom of movement. Noun: vagility.

**vagina:** tubular canal that leads from the **uterus** to the vestibule of the female reproductive tract and receives the male penis during coitus. Aka birth canal.

**valgus:** bent outward, twisted; denoting a deformity in which the angulation of the part is away from the midline. The term valgus is an adjective and should be used only in connection with the noun it describes, as in **genu valgum**. The meanings of valgus and **varus** are often reversed.

**valine** (Val): an essential **amino acid**; one of the twenty building blocks of **proteins**. Valine is an important constituent for optimal growth in infants and for nitrogen equilibrium.

**valine homozygosity:** genotype of individuals susceptible to acquiring **Kuru** and **Creutzfeldt–Jakob disease**. The individuals are homozygous for valine at amino acid position 129 of the **prion protein**, as well as for another mutation at position 178.

**Vallesian:** European land-mammal age (late middle Miocene, approximately 10–12 mya).

**valley fever:** see **coccidioidomycosis** and **San Joaquin Valley fever**.

**Valley of the Caves:** see **Vézère Valley**.

**Vallois, Henri Victor** (1889–1981): French anatomist and paleontologist. Vallois, after the death of his mentor Marcellin **Boule**, became the main proponent of the **presapiens hypothesis** of human evolution in which Neandertals were considered to be an offshoot of the human species that became extinct without descendants. Examination of Neandertal **mtDNA** and the recent discovery of *Homo antecessor* has supported his and Boule's early views. Author (with Boule) of *Les Hommes fossiles: Elements de paléontologie humaine* (1952).

**value:** 1. relative worth or importance. See **selective value, phenotypic value, reproductive value, marginal value theorem**. 2. worth compared to other things with which it can be exchanged; utility. See **cost : benefit analysis, direct value, indirect value, option value, threshold limit value**. 3. significance; **intrinsic value**; values. 4. in statistics, a numerical quantity that is assigned or is determined by calculation or measurement. See **critical value, expected value, observed value**.

**vanishing twin phenomenon:** controversial hypothesis that as many as 12% of all conceptions may have originated as identical **twin** pregnancies, but that competition for maternal resources resulted in resorption of one of the two fetuses. The hypothesis arose in an attempt to explain **left-handedness** as a relict of mirror-image twins, and from the clinical manifestation of embedded twins. Aka vanishing twin syndrome. See **mericlinal chimera** and **twins, monozygotic**.

**Vanzolini's squirrel monkey:** vernacular for *Saimiri vanzolinii*.

**var., v.:** see *varietas*.

***Varecia* Gray, 1863:** monotypic **prosimian** genus to which the ruffed lemur belongs; Aka variegated or black-and-white lemur; two **subspecies** recognized; previously included in *Lemur*. Occupies tropical rain forest running parallel to the east coast of Madagascar. Arboreal; **crepuscular**; quadrupedal. Body mass 3–4.5 kg; this is the largest of the 'true' lemurs. A characteristic that distinguishes it from *Lemur* and *Eulemur* is the three pairs of **mammae** instead of the one pair found in the other two genera. Dental formula: 3.1.3.3; **frugivorous**. Social organization varies depending on environment; small **monogamous** family units are reported as well as larger groups of 8–16 animals. Territorial with a number of vocalizations, including alarm calls and territorial markers. See Appendix 2 for taxonomy and Appendix 3 for species.

**variability:** state of existing **variation** in a population or set.

**variability, genetic:** see **genetic variability**.

**variability selection:** term coined by Richard Potts that refers to the human ability to behaviorally adapt to change that requires the cognitive skills of the modern human mind; this is not simply adaptation to the physical environment, but the ability to make reasoned choices.

**variable:** quantity or function that may assume any given **value**, range, or set of values; a representative symbol, such as $x$ or VAR001.

**variable expressivity:** condition in which individuals who possess the genotype for a particular **trait** do not always exhibit the trait to the same degree. See **expressivity**.

**variable number tandem repeats** (VNTRs): long sequences of repeated nucleotides in DNA; such repeats are frequently polymorphic, and can be used in **DNA fingerprinting**.

**variable regions** (V): portions of antibodies that differ among individuals. See **light chain**; Cf. **heavy chain**.

**variable trait, character** or **feature:** any feature in a taxon that has more than one state, either a **discrete trait** or a **continuous trait**.

**variably expressive:** describes a genotype that yields several phenotypes in individuals, due either to the

**epistatic** context of the alleles, or to effects of the environment, or both.

‡ **variance** ($\sigma^2$): the measure of variation (dispersion) of a trait within a population; the mean squared deviation of all cases from the sample mean; the value of the square of the **standard deviation**. Aka mean square, sum of squares. Cf. **environmental variance** and **genetic variance**.

**variance in reproductive success:** range in differential reproductive success among individuals.

**variant:** 1. tending to deviate from a standard; phenotypic variant. 2. in cell culture, cells exhibiting a stable phenotypic change regardless of the source.

‡ **variation:** 1. process of varying in condition, kind, or degree. 2. in morphology, the divergence of characters in a population not due to sexual dimorphism or ontogeny. 3. in anthropology, real or perceived differences that exist among individuals or populations. Anthropologists study both physical and cultural **human variation**. See **ethnicity** and **race**. Cf. **coefficient of variation**, **interspecific variation**, and **intraspecific variation**.

**variational evolution:** type of change promoted by Charles **Darwin**, that change occurs in every generation through the production of a large amount of new genetic variation, and thence through the survival (selection) of a small percentage of the variants who serve as progenitors of subsequent generations.

**variegated lemur:** vernacular for *Varecia variegata*.

*varietas (v., var.)* (Latin): variety.

**variety:** ambiguous taxonomic level below the **species** and above the **form**; aka varietas, cultivar. Includes certain morphological clusters within subspecies, including nongenetic variants and microclimatic races, but not applied in a consistent manner in the literature.

**variogram:** graph, similar to a scatterplot, in which **genetic distance** is on the $Y$ axis, and geographic distance is on the $X$ axis. This method permits comparison among regions. Europeans, for example, tend to be more similar over broad geographic regions (mean genetic distance = 0.007), whereas other populations tend, in the following rank order, to show increased genetic distance for the same spatial unit (i.e. 1000 miles): Asia (0.009), Africa (0.014), New Guinea (0.023), Australia (0.027), and America (0.040).

**variola:** see **smallpox**.

**varion:** any specific nucleotide or amino acid that has changed in either of two sequences that have diverged since sharing a last common ancestor. Cf. **covarion**.

**varus:** bent inward; denoting a deformity in which the angulation of the part is toward the midline of the body. The term varus is an adjective and should be used only in connection with the noun it describes, as in **genu varum**. The meanings of varus and **valgus** are often reversed.

**varve:** layer of glacial till that reflect patterns of annual cycles of summer melt-off; varves appear as laminated couplets (summer and winter, representing one year), and have been used for dating purposes since 1878.

**varzea forest:** Brazilian term for Amazonian **forest** that is seasonally flooded by **whitewater** for long periods during the year. Cf. **igapó forest**.

**vas deferens:** see **ductus deferens**.

**vascular marking:** impressions of blood vessels that are left on bone.

**vascularized:** well endowed with blood vessels.

‡ **vasoconstriction:** decrease in the diameter of blood vessels; this permits reduced blood flow to the skin. Vasoconstriction is an involuntary response to cold stress and reduces heat loss at the skin's surface. Cf. **vasodilation**.

‡ **vasodilation:** involuntary increase in the diameter of blood vessels, permitting increased blood flow to the skin; vasodilation permits warming of skin surfaces and facilitates radiation of heat as a means of cooling when an organism is too warm. The state of increase in diameter is known as vasodilatation. Cf. **vasoconstriction**.

**vasopressin:** one of two **hormones** produced by neuronal cells of the **hypothalamus** but stored and secreted by the **pituitary gland**; it acts on the kidneys and the brain, among other tissues. It stimulates contraction of capillaries (thus raising blood pressure), exerts a contractile influence on the **uterus**, and concentrates urine in the water transport pathways of the kidneys. Vasopressin variation has been implicated as a genetic contributor to 'typical male behavior' in mammals. Aka antidiuretic hormone. See **diabetes mellitus**. Cf. **oxytocin**.

**vault:** see **cranial vault**.

**Vavilov center:** see **center of origin**.

**vDNA:** viral **DNA**.

‡ **vector:** 1. a mathematical quantity possessing both magnitude and direction. In **growth and development** studies, any size variable, such as **body size**. 2. any organism, such as a mosquito, that transmits a **pathogen** from one **host** to another. 3. in **recombinant DNA** technology, a self-replicating DNA molecule such as a **plasmid** or **virus** that is used to transfer foreign DNA segments between host cells. A DNA segment of interest can be spliced into e.g. a **plasmid**, and then the plasmid can be inserted into the host cell, which then divides, replicating or cloning the foreign DNA along with the host cell's normal DNA.

**Veddoid:** hypothetical population in ancient Southern Asia characterized by some prognathism, moderate melanization, short stature, wavy hair including moderate body hair, and a narrow head. The Veddoids were supposedly hybridized by the Caucasoids, Pre-Dravidians, and Indo-Australians.

**vegetarian dietary hypothesis:** proposal by R. Wrangham and G. Laden that about 1.9 mya early hominids cooked and consumed vegetables, increasing the available dietary calories. As a consequence, they suggest that this behavior resulted in a decrease in the size of jaws and teeth, that females increased in size relative to males, and that, because cooking created a delay between harvesting and processing, theft became more likely. This possibility promoted cooperative alliances between males and females, 'to prevent males from stealing food from females'. Cf. *Australopithecus garhi* **dietary hypothesis.**

**vegetation:** totality of plant life that covers a region or habitat; a plant assemblage.

‡ **vein:** blood vessel that carries blood towards the heart. See **emissary vein.** Cf. **artery.**

**VEK:** archaeological site at **Olduvai Gorge.**

**veldt grasslands:** savanna regions found in the Transvaal, South Africa, where several hominid-bearing sites such as **Taung** are located.

**Velika Pecina (Cave):** archaeological site found in 1948 near Zagreb in the Hrvatsko Zagorje (northwestern Croatia), dating to >33 kya (level i, radiocarbon), and that contains Middle to Upper Paleolithic artifacts and hominid remains from level j that include a partial frontal bone assigned to *Homo sapiens.* Cf. **Vindija, Veternica.**

**vellus:** short, downy hair found on the scalp, forehead and face.

**velocity curve:** measure of the rates of change in some variable over time. A chart of the rate of growth at different ages is an example. Cf. **distance curve.**

**venereal syphilis:** see **syphilis** (2).

**venous return** (VR): blood volume flowing toward the heart per unit of time.

**Venta Micena:** see **Orce Ravine.**

**ventifact:** stone that has been faceted by sandstorms, rather than by human activity.

**ventilation:** cyclic **inspiration** and **expiration** that results in air exchange between the atmosphere and lung alveoli. Aka alveolar air flow.

**ventilation rate:** volume of air breathed in and out of lungs per minute.

‡ **ventral:** anatomical term of relative position referring to the side of a vertebrate that is closest to the substrate or that part that is farthest away from the **notochord.** Whereas ventral is normally used in primate biology, the term **anterior** is more common in human anatomy. Cf. **dorsal.**

**ventral pallidum:** portion of the basal forebrain that receives information from the **ventral striatum** and

regulates complex motor activity and cognitive aspects of motor control; a part of the **limbic system.**

**ventral rampart:** concave outer surface of the **symphyseal face** of the **pubic bone,** which is used to help assess age in a recovered skeleton.

**ventral striatum:** portion of the **basal forebrain** that receives input from other limbic areas and relays it to the **ventral pallidum.** Often referred to as the 'crossroads' between emotional and motor information; a part of the **limbic system.**

**ventricle:** fluid-filled cavity, e.g. the **lateral ventricles** of the brain, which are filled with cerebrospinal fluid.

**venule:** small vessel that carries blood from the capillary network to a vein. Cf. **arteriole.**

**Venus figurines:** anthropomorphic **Aurignacian** 'sculptures' dated to 23–21 kya, usually of females depicted with explicit genitalia. These objects are found at about a dozen European sites including **Willendorf** and **Dolni Vestonice.** The sculpted figures display a hair form that is possibly African in origin, and several of the full statuettes also depict **steatopygia,** such as the steatite figurine from the **Grimaldi** caves.

**veracity, principle of:** see **principle of veracity.**

**Verdouble valley:** see **Arago.**

**verifiability principle:** statement that to be meaningful a sentence or proposition must be verifiable either by means of the five senses or by a tautology of logic. A central tenet of **logical positivism.**

**verisimilitude:** 1. the semblance of truth. 2. the mere appearance of truth. 3. in the philosophy of Karl **Popper,** the acceptance of 'truthlikeness'. Any theory thus has (1) truth-content (a class of true propositions), and (2) falsity-content (a class of the theory's false consequences). A good **theory,** according to Popper, has a large body of the former while the latter class is empty. Cf. **principle of veracity.**

**vermiform appendix:** tubular structure located on the **cecum** that contains lymphatic tissue; actual function unknown, but may have an immune function; does not have a digestive function. Found in the great apes and humans; commonly referred to as simply the appendix.

**vermis:** coiled middle lobular structure that separates the two cerebellar hemispheres.

**vernacular:** name for a species, organism, or group of organisms that is native or common to a group of people or to a region, as opposed to the formal **binomial nomenclature** for that **species.**

**Verreaux's sifaka:** vernacular for *Propithecus verreauxi.*

‡ **vertebra:** irregular bone that is one of the members of the **vertebral column.** Plural: vertebrae. Adjective: vertebral.

**vertebral canal:** passageway through the vertebral column in which the spinal cord passes.

**vertebral column:** backbone or spine; series of articulated bones (**vertebrae**) that surround and protect the **spinal cord.** The vertebral column forms the central axis of the skeleton. In primates, five vertebrae fuse to form the **sacrum** which becomes part of the **pelvis.** In adult humans, the four most inferior vertebrae are fused to form the **coccyx**; in other primates these four bones are part of the **caudal vertebrae** that form the tail. The human vertebral column reflects the **bipedal** adaptation in that it has four curves, which help redistribute the weight of the body over a center of gravity.

**Vertebrata: subphylum** of the phylum **Chordata.** Vertebrates are characterized by the presence of an **endoskeleton,** including a protective segmented column of bone that surrounds the spinal cord, bilateral symmetry throughout life, a well-differentiated head that contains a brain, and internal organs. Bone, as a chemical substance, is unique to vertebrates. Among the vertebrates, primates belong to the Class **Mammalia.** In the past this group has been referred to as the Craniata.

**Vértesszöllös:** archaeological site found in 1964 near Budapest, Hungary, dated to 475–185 kya (210–160 kya, U series on travertines), and that contains chopper/chopping tool and microlith artifacts attributed to the Buda industry. The hominid remains from at least two individuals include juvenile teeth and an adult occiput with thin bones but also with a sharp nuchal angle, possibly male, having a cranial capacity of 1300 cm$^3$, and attributed to the **earlier archaic *Homo sapiens*** group. Cf. ***Homo heidelbergensis.***

**vertex** (v): 1. apex; top of a structure. 2. **cephalometric landmark;** superior point of the head on the midsagittal plane. Vertex is not a synonym for **apex,** but it sometimes coincides with the apex. It is used by both cephalometrists and **craniometrists.** Cf. **bregma,** which is used on skeletal specimens.

**vertical auricular height:** porion–apex vertical distance; or the apex–biporionic axis distance.

**vertical clinging and leaping** (VCL): type of locomotion and posture in which animals cling to vertical supports and move by leaping between these vertical supports.

**vertical dental impaction:** condition in which a tooth is placed low in the alveolus and in contact with an adjacent tooth or teeth so as to be incapable of complete eruption. See **dental impaction.**

**vertical lumbar index:** sum of the dorsal vertical diameters of the centra (vertebral bodies) × 100, divided by the sum of the ventral vertical diameters. See **koilorachic, kurtorachic,** and **orthorachic.**

**vertical ramus:** see **mandibular ramus.**

**vertical stratification:** horizontal layers of organisms of a community superimposed onto a vertical structure. The vertical structure, as an example, may be the height of plants in a forest or the depth of an aquatic environment.

**vertical transmission:** transmission of an infectious disease from mother to child. Cf. **horizontal transmission.**

**vervet:** vernacular for *Chlorocebus aethiops aethiops.*

**very low density lipoprotein:** see VLDL.

**vesalianum:** supernumerary bone of the foot that sometimes develops near the distal portion of the fifth **metatarsal.**

**Vesalius, Andreas** (1514–c.1564): Belgian dissectionist, surgeon at Padua, and considered the founder of modern anatomy. He was the personal physician to Charles V and author of *De humani corporis fabrica, libri septem* (seven volumes, Basel, 1538). Through direct observation by dissection of human cadavers, Vesalius discovered errors in Galen's anatomy, which he showed to be that of an ape rather than of man. In book seven, on the brain, Vesalius noted that there existed globular, flattened and oblong skulls, and he was therefore the earliest craniometrician. He attributed the variation to artificial deformation.

**vespertine:** pertaining to the evening; aka **crepuscular.**

**vestibular folds:** horizontal fold of muscle and connective tissue covered by mucosa and located in the larynx and covering a similar structure, the **vocal cords.** The vestibular folds function to close the larynx during swallowing. They do not function in speech. Aka false vocal cords.

**vestige:** atrophied structure that is usually reduced in size and function over the course of evolution; e.g., the fat-filled nonfunctional lung in the coelacanth, which was fully functional in its ancestors. Adjective: vestigial. Aka relict.

**vestigial trait, character** or **feature:** any feature that is imperfect or poorly developed. Used especially of features that have become reduced or diminished during the course of evolution or individual maturation and aging. Examples of vestigial tissues in humans include body hair, **cervical rib, female vas deferens,** male **nipples, male uterus, palmaris muscle, plantaris muscle, polymastia, pyramidalis muscle, subclavius muscle, thirteenth rib, vermiform appendix, vomeronasal organ,** and **wisdom teeth.**

**vestigiofossil:** see **trace fossil.**

**Veternica (Cave):** archaeological site excavated since 1953 near Zagreb in the Hrvatsko Zagorje (northwestern Croatia), dating to the late Pleistocene, and that contains 'Mousterian' artifacts. Hominid remains including a partial human skull were initially attributed to ***Homo neanderthalensis,*** but have also been interpreted as early **AMH**. Cf. **Vindija, Velika Pećina.**

**Vézère Valley:** river valley in south-central France; a tributary of the **Dordogne**. Rich in late Pleistocene Middle and **Upper Paleolithic** cave sites such as **Abri Pataud, Cro-Magnon, Le Moustier, Lascaux,** la Grèze, Cap Blanc, Laussel, Commarque, Combarelles, Font de Gaume, la Mouthe, Laugerie Basse, and la Micoque. Aka Valley of the Caves.

**viability:** measure of the proportion of surviving individuals in a given **genotype** or **phenotype**.

**viable:** pertaining to or having the capacity to develop, grow, and live. Cf. **nonviable.**

**vibrissae:** long stiff hairs that are associated with sensory receptors in the skin and provide a mammal with a tactile sense that helps it detect physical objects in the environment. In most mammals vibrissae are located in the snout, as they are in some prosimians, but in most primates they are also located on brows, cheeks, lips, and chin. Notably absent in humans, although the nose hairs are referred to as vibrissae (Aka sinus hairs) in human anatomy. Also referred to as whiskers and tactile hairs. Singular: vibrissa.

**vicariance:** any event that results in the geographic isolation of **allopatric** populations that were once **sympatric**; vicariance events include the separation of continents during drift, the formation of mountain ranges, volcanic action, the change in the course of a river, the rise of sea level to form islands of a formerly hilly peninsula, etc.

**vicariance model:** theory that components of **ecosystems** evolve in unison and are mutually subject to the effects of climatic and geographical fluctuations. Current biogeographical distributions therefore are the result of the division of ancestral ecosystems by the formation of natural barriers, or **vicariance** events.

**Victoriapithecidae:** family of catarrhines known from the Miocene of Africa; two genera and three to four species. The most primitive cercopithecoid monkeys known; precede the divergence of the cercopithecines and colobines. Estimated body mass ranges between 7 and 25 kg. Dental formula: 2.1.2.3/2.1.2.3; **sexually dimorphic** canines; possess **bilophodont** molars, but in general the dental morphology is much more primitive (sharing traits with the **hominoids**) than found in living cercopithecoids. Recovered **postcrania** indicate quadrupedalism and it appears these monkeys were **semiterrestrial**; some workers think that these animals were terrestrial and over time evolved towards a more arboreal habit. See Appendix 1 for taxonomy.

**Victoriapithecinae:** as used in some classificatory schemes, a subfamily of the extinct catarrhine family **Victoriapithecidae**; a group of middle Miocene (12–8 mya) East African colobines that may be ancestral to cercopithecines and colobines. Consists of the two genera **Victoriapithecus** and **Prohylobates**. Dental morphology suggests a primary diet of hard fruit.

**Victoriapithecus macinnesi von Koenigswald, 1969:** cercopithecoid from the early to middle Miocene of East Africa; currently only one species is recognized. Estimated body mass around 7 kg. Dental formula: 2.1.2.3/2.1.2.3; **sexually dimorphic** canines, **bilophodont** molars. Traits intermediate between parapithecids and modern Old World monkeys; in particular, very small brain compared with modern cercopithecids. Limb bones indicate **semi-terrestrial** habits. See Appendix 1 for taxonomy.

**view:** anatomical orientation that describes a visual perspective of a specimen. See Appendix 7.

‡ **Villafranchian:** distinctive mammalian fauna of Europe, which appeared suddenly in the Lower Pleistocene, and that includes animals found in highly seasonal, drought-resistant grasslands: elephants (*Archidiskodon*), true bovines (*Leptobus*), camels (*Camelus*), and one-toed horses (*Equus*). Type site: Villafranca d'Asti, Italy.

**village:** small cluster of dwellings and probably the most ancient type of settlement. The dwellings are separate but mutually dependent homesteads, and the community is sufficiently small that inhabitants know one another. The village arose in Neolithic times, probably before 10 kya. Aka community.

**villus, villi:** very small fingerlike projection emanating from a surface; villi often serve to increase surface area, such as the villi of the small intestine, fallopian tubes, and other epithelial tissues.

**Vindija (Cave):** archaeological site found in 1928 near Zagreb in the Hrvatsko Zagorje region, Croatia, dated to 130–114 kya (vertebrates, level k) and 33–28 kya for the G1 occupation layer (AMS radiocarbon). An **amino acid racemization** date of 42 kya for the G3 level is tentative. The G3 (lower) and G1 (upper) levels contain artifacts that are **Mousterian** or 'Moustero-Levalloisian' in character; a carved bear **baculum** from level G1(?) suggests the presence of at least one proto-**Aurignacian** implement. The hominid remains from levels G3 and G1 include fragments from at least six individuals attributed to *Homo neanderthalensis*. Some of the hominid fragments are burned and display cut marks that have been cited as evidence of **cannibalism**. Three **AMH** specimens can be found in the more recent Vindija upper levels (F complex). See **last of the Neandertals, Mezmaiskaya Cave,** and **Abrigo do Lagar Velho rockshelter.** Cf. **Velika Pećina, Veternica.**

**vine titi:** vernacular for *Callicebus oenanthe*.

**Virchow, Rudolf Ludwig Karl** (1821–94): German physician, statesman, anthropologist, founder of cell pathology; demonstrated that the cell is the location of **disease** processes, displacing the ancient 'humoral' theory of disease; showed that new cells are generated by **cell division**, and not **spontaneous generation**; he was incorrect in his interpretation of the Feldhofer **Neandertal** as pathological (he suggested **giantism** and/or **rickets**); was influential in the founding of German anthropological societies in the 1860s; opposed **Darwinism**, arguing that the argument itself was not robust; opposed **Haeckel**, particularly concerning ideas about **race**.

**virgin:** 1. an animal that has not copulated. 2. pertaining to a native habitat unaffected by **anthropogenic** activity. 3. any naive entity.

**virgin soil epidemic:** high morbidity to an infectious disease in a population that has never been exposed to the disease and in which, consequently, none of the members has developed immunity.

**virion:** completed virus particle that consists of a glycoprotein coat and a core containing nucleic acid. Not to be confused with a viroid, a virus of plants.

‡ **virulence:** 1. quality of being infectious. 2. quantitative measurement of the strength of infectiousness of a microorganism calculated by dividing the number of individuals incapacitated by the number of individuals infected, as determined by immunoassay.

**virulent phage:** any **bacteriophage** that lyses the cell in which it has reproduced.

**Virunga mountain gorilla:** see *Gorilla gorilla*.

‡ **virus:** noncellular infectious agent regarded either as the simplest microorganism or as an extremely complex molecule, and that requires other cells or organisms in order to reproduce. A virus typically consists of a protein coat surrounding **DNA** or **RNA** (but not both). Examples are **measles** virus and **human immunodeficiency virus**. Some become **endogenous viruses**, and are capable of both **horizontal transmission** and **vertical transmission**.

**viscera:** internal organs found within the body cavities of an organism. Adjective: visceral.

**viscosity:** 1. property of fluid that makes it resistant to flow; fluid thickness. 2. relating to the slowness of individual dispersal and therefore the slow rate of **gene flow.**

**vision:** sense that results from the interpretation of light waves into forms, shape, movement, distance, color, etc.

**visual communication:** see **facial expression** and **body language.**

**visual cortex:** region of the neocortex at the rear of the brain which processes visual information; enlarged in the anthropoid primates compared with the prosimians. Aka higher visual cortex. See **primary visual cortex.**

**visual field:** that part of the world being viewed at a given time.

‡ **visual predation model: hypothesis** of **primate origins** that proposes that **stereoscopic vision** and **prehensile** hands first evolved as **adaptations** for hunting insects on tree branches. See M. **Cartmill.** Cf. **arboreal theory of primate evolution.**

‡ **vital capacity:** maximum amount of air that can be forcibly expelled from a subject's lungs following maximum inspiration, regardless of time required; measured with a spirometer. Cf. **forced vital capacity.**

**vital index:** number of births in a population multiplied by 100 and then divided by the number of deaths in a given unit of time. If greater than 100, the population is growing; if less than 100, the population is decreasing in size.

**vital statistic(s):** in demography, quantitative data on a population concerning life events, and that are characteristic of that population. Vital refers especially to the rates of birth, death, and fertility.

**vitalism:** view that life involves a special supernatural force and cannot be explained in terms of physical and chemical mechanisms and properties alone; in an extreme proposition, life may take the form of 'entelechies' within living things, responsible for their growth and development.

**vitamin** (V): any of a heterogenous class of organic compounds that in small quantities are essential for life; originally spelled vitamine. See box below.

**vitamin-dependent genetic disease:** any morbid condition caused by a molecular defect and that

---

### Some vitamins important to human health

**vitamin A:** a fat-soluble compound required for normal growth and maintenance of tissues such as the retina. Abundant in liver, eggs, dairy products and some vegetables. **Avitaminosis** A causes **nightblindness** and **xerophthalmia**. Vitamin $A_1$ is known as retinol.

**vitamin B:** **folate** (folic acid), a water-soluble molecule of the B-complex group of vitamins that is necessary for nucleotide formation. Abundant in liver. **Avitaminosis** B causes **anemia**.

**vitamin $B_1$:** thiamine, a water-soluble compound required for carbohydrate metabolism; one of the essential nutrients of the human diet. Abundant in yeast, meat, and cereal bran. **Avitaminosis** $B_1$ causes **beriberi**. Aka thiamin, aneurin, the anti-beriberi factor. (cont. overleaf)

---

**Some vitamins important to human health (*cont.*)**

vitamin B$_2$: riboflavin, a compound required for hydrogen transfer. Abundant in egg yolks and meat. Avitaminosis B$_2$ causes abnormal **angiogenesis** in facial tissues. (Formerly called vitamin G.)

vitamin B$_6$: pyridoxine, a water-soluble compound required for protein metabolism. Abundant in meat and vegetables. Avitaminosis B$_{12}$ causes convulsions and dermatitis.

vitamin B$_{12}$: a protein required for nucleic acid metabolism. Abundant in foods from animal sources. Avitaminosis B$_{12}$ causes pernicious **anemia**.

vitamin C: **ascorbic acid**, a water-soluble compound required for many metabolic activities; one of the most essential nutrients of the human diet. The ability to synthesize vitamin C is present in most animals, having been lost in guinea pigs and all **primates**. It was first identified and dietarily reversed in guinea pigs in 1907. Humans require large amounts daily (70 mg). Abundant in citrus fruits, where it prevents browning. Avitaminosis C causes **scurvy**.

vitamin D: a fat-soluble compound required for formation of bone; one of the most essential nutrients of the human diet. Abundant in fish liver oil. Avitaminosis D causes **rickets** in children, **osteomalacia** in adults.

vitamin E: a fat-soluble compound required for removal of **free oxygen radicals**. Abundant in green vegetables, wheat germ and rice. Avitaminosis E causes abnormal fat absorption.

vitamin K: a fat-soluble compound required for proper blood clotting. Abundant in fish and cereals. Avitaminosis K causes hemorrhaging.

---

can be resolved by the administration of a specific **vitamin.**

**vitrification:** process of forming stone from some other material; see **ignimbrite** for an example.

‡ **viviparity:** live birth; producing living offspring from within the body of the parent, a characteristic of **mammals.** Adjective: viviparous. A female producing live young is called a vivipara. See **parity.**

**VLDL:** very low density lipoprotein, a lipid–protein aggregate having a high proportion of fat.

**VNTR:** see **variable number tandem repeats.**

**vocal communication:** meaningful sound produced by passage of air over the vocal cords. Human speech is the most complex form of vocal communication, with vocalizations of birds second, and some other primate species third. Primate vocal communication has been studied in the wild and some basic meanings discerned.

**vocal cords:** horizontal fold of muscle and connective tissue covered by mucosa and located in the larynx inferior to a similar structure, the **vestibular folds.** The vocal cords function in producing vocal sounds as air is forced between these folds, causing them to vibrate from side to side. The resulting sound waves are formed into words through shape changes in the pharynx and oral cavity and by actions of the tongue and lips. Aka vocal fold.

**vocal fold:** the true **vocal cords.** Cf. **vestibular folds.**

**vocalization:** 1. act of making sound by pushing air past the vocal apparatus in the throat. 2. sound evoked by a primate, which emanates not from the **neocortex** (that is, from **Broca's area** and **Wernicke's area**), but from the lower forebrain, whose centers are part of the **limbic system.**

Nonhuman primate vocalizations are said to be 'emotional' rather than 'referential' (i.e. they are nonsymbolic). Primates such as vervets, however, do have discrete **warning calls** for various predators, which may be neocortical in origin.

**Vogel River series:** see **Laetoli.**

**Vogelherd Cave:** archaeological site found in 1931 in the Swabian Jura near Stetten, Germany, dated stratigraphically to 36–30 kya, and that contains **Aurignacian** artifacts (including carved ivory sculptures of horses) and hominid remains (Stetten 1–5) including a cranial vault (1) and a robust humerus (3) assigned to *Homo sapiens* (cf. **Cro-Magnon**). Although this site had been used to confirm that **AMHs** were the bearers of the **Aurignacian** tools, recent $^{14}$C direct dating of the skeletal material (5–3.9 kya) suggests that they may be intrusive, and not associated with the artifacts. Aka Stetten, Vogelherdhohle.

**volar:** describes the palm surface of the hand or sole surface of the foot. Also referred to as **palmar** and **plantar**, respectively.

**volcanic:** pertaining to igneous rocks that cool on the surface of the earth; because cooling is rapid, volcanic rocks contain characteristic small crystalline structures; extrusive.

**volcanic eruption:** see **eruption** and **ultra-Plinian eruption.**

**voluntary:** 1. brought about by choice or free will. 2. pertaining to organs that can be consciously controlled.

**voluntary muscle:** term sometimes used for **skeletal muscle**, which is under voluntary control. Cf. **involuntary muscle.**

**vomer:** thin flat bone situated along the mid-sagittal plane within the nasal cavity. It joins the perpendicular plate of the **ethmoid bone** posteriorly and together these two structures form the **nasal septum.**

**vomeronasal organ** (VNO): olfactory canal in the nasal mucosa that ends as a blind pouch in the anterior portion of the **palate** of many mammals. It appears to be sensitive to female **pheromones** and allows males to assess the reproductive status of a female. Present in prosimians, tarsiers, and platyrrhines, but not among the Catarrhini. Aka Jacobsen's organ.

**vomiting center:** neurons in the **medulla oblongata** that coordinate the vomiting reflex.

**von Baer's law:** empirical observation that the embryonic stage is derived from three germ layers (the **ectoderm, endoderm,** and **mesoderm**); further, speculation that the younger is the embryo of a species, the stronger the resemblance between the embryo of that species and the embryo of other vertebrate species. Aka law of corresponding stages. See **epigenesis.**

**von Dungern–Hirszfeld hypothesis:** hypothesis that red blood group antigens A and B are inherited as the result of two pairs of genes that undergo independent assortment.

**Von Gierke disease:** see **glycogen storage disease (I).**

**von Koenigswald, G. H. R.:** see **Koenigswald, Gustav Heinrich Ralph von.**

**von Willebrand disease:** heritable disease in which a missing blood clotting factor causes hemorrhaging and bruising.

**Vrba, Elizabeth S.** (1942– ): US geophysicist and taphonomist at Yale. Known for proposals of the **effect hypothesis, habitat hypothesis,** and **turnover-pulse hypothesis.** Author of *Turnover Pulses, the Red Queen, and Related Topics* (1993), and co-editor (with G. H. Denton and T. C. Partridge) of *Paleoclimate and Evolution* (1994).

**V-shaped dental arcade:** see **convergent dental arcade.**

**V28-238 deep sea core sequence:** see **Emiliani–Shackleton glacial sequence.**

**vulcanism:** proposal that the earth's heat is very old, and that granites crystallized from molten rocks. Once the granites had formed, according to this theory, the heat also uplifted the land; volcanoes were considered escape valves, and were correctly proposed as the source of **basalts.** Weathering and deposition led to renewed heat accumulation which in turn led to the production of new continents. One of the chief advocates was James **Hutton.** Aka plutonism. Cf. **neptunism.**

**vulnerable species:** one of the five conservation categories established by the **International Union for the Conservation of Nature.** This category includes those species that may become endangered in the very near future based on decreases in population size throughout their range. Some primate species are in this category, especially Malagasy prosimians. See **extinct species, endangered species, rare species, insufficiently known species.**

**vulva:** external genitalia of the female that surround the opening of the vagina; consists of the mons pubis, labia majora, labia minora, clitoris, vestibule of the vagina, and vestibular glands. Aka pudendum.

**W:** symbol for mean Darwinian fitness; measure of mean survivability in comparison of one **genotype** to other genotypes at a specific **locus**. See **mean fitness.**

**Waagenon:** diachronic subspecies; phyletic subspecies, temporal subspecies.

**Waardenburg syndrome, type 1** (WS1): heritable autosomal dominant defect characterized by wide-set eyes, wide nose, displacement of the epicanthic fold, pigment anomalies such as eyes that differ in color, white forelock and eyelashes, and variable hearing loss. Defect is in paired box gene 3 (PAX3). **Homeobox genes** regulate structural development in embryogenesis. Indications of a paternal age effect. There are several other forms of WS, all inherited in an autosomal dominant fashion. Rare.

**wadi:** gully or valley formed in the desert by seasonal precipitation; aka oued.

**Wadi Amud** ('Valley of the Pillar'): see **Amud Cave** and **Zuttiyeh.**

**Wadi el-Mughara:** 'valley of the caves', **Mount Carmel**; see **Kebara**, **Tabūn** (Mughäret et-Tabūn), and **Skhūl** (Mughäret es-Skhūl). Aka el-Mughara, Nahel Me'arot.

***Wadilemur elegans*** Simons, 1997: adapoid **prosimian** from the late Eocene of North Africa, belonging to the notharctid subfamily **Cercamoniinae.** See Appendix 1 for taxonomy.

**Wadjak:** see **Wajak.**

**Wahlund effect:** empirical deficiency of heterozygotes as compared with the proportion expected based upon a **Hardy–Weinberg equilibrium.** The effect occurs when two previously isolated populations with different allele frequencies at a given locus become sympatric and are sampled as a single population.

***Wailekia orientale*** Ducroq, Jaeger, Chaimanee, and Suteethorn, 1995: fossil primate from the Eocene of eastern Asia; phylogenetic relations uncertain and assigned by most workers to ***incertae sedis***; the original investigators believed this primate was an anthropoid, but others think that it may be a cercamoniine. Body mass around 2 kg. See Appendix 1 for taxonomy.

**waist circumference: anthropometric** measurement: distance around the waist as measured with a tape measure placed at the narrowest part of the **torso** passed horizontally around the body. The measurement is taken after a normal expiration. Used for various body indices pertaining to adipose distribution and for various applications in **human engineering.** Cf. **abdominal circumference.**

**Wajak:** archaeological site found c. 1889 in Java by B. D. von Rietschoten and later explored by E. **DuBois**; ambiguous dating, contains hominid remains including two skulls, one with a cranial capacity of 1650 cm³, and that resemble living Australian aboriginals; originally attributed to ***Homo wadjakensis***. The site was not described until 1930. Aka Wadjak.

**walk, walking:** see **striding gait.**

**Walker, Alan** (1938– ): British born US paleontologist at Penn State; educated at Cambridge. Located and/or co-described several of the hominid fossils in the **Koobi Fora** region of East Africa, including the 'Turkana boy' from Nariokotome (**KNM-WT 15000**). Author (with R. Leakey) of *The Nariokotome Homo Erectus Skeleton* (1993), and (with Pat Shipman and D. Bichell) of *The Human Skeleton* (1985).

‡ **Wallace, Alfred Russel** (1823–1913): Welsh field naturalist and correspondent with several scientists including **Bates** and **Darwin.** Independently, he co-developed **evolutionary theory**; in a letter that Darwin received in 1858 Wallace described, in effect, Darwin's own theory of **'natural selection'**, as Wallace had visualized it shortly after reading **Malthus.** Among other achievements, Wallace surveyed the entire southeast Asian archipelago and described an eastern limit of mammalian **dispersion**, still known as **'Wallace's line'**. Author, among other works, of the so-called 'Sarawak law' in 'On the law which has regulated the introduction of new species' (1855); also author of 'On the tendency for varieties to depart indefinitely from the original type' (1858) and ***Darwinism*** (1889). A socialist, in his later years Wallace was also a strong spiritualist. Winner of the Royal Society's Darwin Medal (1890).

**Wallace effect:** development and evolution of mechanisms that increase population isolation by selecting against hybrids, after the populations have reached the level of subspecies ('elementary biological species'). Reproductive isolation in which hybrids have a lowered fitness or are sterile eliminates these individuals from competition for resources. Aka Wallace's hypothesis.

**Wallacea:** combined land masses of the present islands of Sulawesi, Lombok, Flores, and Timor, much larger during the **Pleistocene** when sea levels were 100–250 m lower than at present; centrally located between the now sunken **Ice Age** continents of the **Sunda shelf** and the **Sahul shelf.**

**Wallace's Line:** imprecise boundary between the Philippines and the Moluccas, Sulawesi and Borneo, Bali and Lombok, and other points north and east; transition zone that divides the Oriental fauna from the Australian fauna. See **Sunda trench.**

**Wanlongdong:** archaeological site found in 1956 in Wanlongdong, Changyang County, Hubei Province, China, dated to 220–170 kya; contains hominid remains, including an orthognathic maxilla attributed to **archaic *Homo sapiens***. Aka Changyang.

**wanton extinction:** term coined by D. M. Raup to describe a highly selective extinction that only affects a particular **taxon; natural selection** is not a part of this type of extinction.

**warm-blooded:** see **endothermy.**

**warning call:** see **alarm response.**

**wart:** see **papilloma.**

**Warthian glaciation:** third major glaciation of the Pleistocene in the Poland/German sequence; see **Riss glaciation.**

*Washakius* **Leidy, 1873:** genus of tarsiiform primate from the middle and late Eocene of North America, belonging to the omomyid subfamily **Anaptomorphinae;** four species; some workers think that at least one of the species shares a more recent common ancestor with *Dyseolemur* than with other species of *Washakius*, and future revision may be in order. Estimated body mass for all species around 150 g. Dental formula: 2.1.3.3/2.1.3.3; dental morphology suggests dietary diversity among the different species including one that appears to be slightly **folivorous.** See Appendix 1 for taxonomy.

**Washburn, Sherwood L. ('Sherry')** (1911–2000): physical anthropologist at Chicago and UC Berkeley. Washburn trained at Harvard (PhD, 1940) under E. A. **Hooton;** worked in southeast Asia (1937, see the **Asiatic Primate Expedition**), and studied baboon behavior in the 1950s. Washburn was a central figure in the refocusing of physical anthropologists on evolutionary studies rather than on racial studies, on observational of primates in natural rather than captive settings, and on functional rather than on descriptive anatomy. Washburn mentored more than 35 PhD students, many of whom were leaders in the subdiscipline during the next few decades. He was the recipient of many awards, was president of the **AAPA** (1951–2); editor of the *AJPA* (1955–7); president of the **AAA** (1961), and a Viking Fund medalist (1960). In *Classification and Human Evolution* (1963), Washburn was an early supporter of a knuckle-walking, chimpanzee-like recent common ancestor of humans. He was author of many other scholarly publications, including 'the new physical anthropology' (*AJPA*, 1950, 1951); editor of *The Social Life of Early Man* (1961), and (with Phyllis Jay) of *Perspectives in Human Evolution* (1968, 1972).

**waste accumulation theory of aging:** intracellular, stochastic model of aging in which the major premise is that the cellular mechanisms that remove metabolic byproducts become less efficient over the life of an organisms, and that waste products accumulate within a cell, diminishing its efficiency to a subvital level.

**'wastebasket' taxon:** in classification, category that contains problematic members or disputed assignment criteria, e.g. the fossil taxon **Plesiadapiformes.**

**'watchmaker' argument:** see **Paley's watchmaker argument.**

**water** ($H_2O$): transparent, colorless, tasteless liquid, a compound of **hydrogen** and **oxygen.** Water is the main constituent of rain, rivers, lakes and oceans, and is essential to life for most organisms, including **primates.** Cf. **saline.**

**water barrier:** body of water of any size that prevents organisms from reaching the other side; this is an effective impedance to **gene flow.**

**water-soluble vitamin:** any of the vitamins that dissolve in water, i.e. **vitamin C** and the B complex vitamins.

**Watson–Crick hypothesis** or **model:** see **DNA** and **double helix.** Cf. **Rosalind Franklin.**

**Watson, James Dewey** (1928–): US biochemist and Nobel laureate; with F. **Crick** at Cambridge, deduced the structure of DNA from R. **Franklin's** X-ray crystallography data; with others, broke the **genetic code** in the 1960s. Perennial leader of American biological science policy at Cold Spring Harbor, and co-founder of the **Human Genome Project** in 1989. Winner of the Royal Society's Copley Medal (1993).

**wavelength:** distance between two wave peaks in an oscillating medium.

**WBC:** white blood cell, a vernacular for **leukocyte.** See **basophil, eosinophil, neutrophil, monocyte** and **lymphocyte.**

**wean:** to terminate feeding by lactation; to reduce **parental investment.**

**wear-and-tear theory of aging:** proposal that ordinary insults to the tissues of an organism encountered during daily living accumulate with age and eventually reduce in efficiency to a subvital level. At the level of tissues, loss of teeth and hair with age are examples. This theory has been reformulated to incorporate new molecular data, and now exists in reformulations such as the **DNA damage and repair theory of aging,** and similar theories.

**wear facet:** flat smooth polished surface on a tooth that develops as a result of continual contact between teeth.

**weasel lemur:** vernacular for the species that comprise the genus *Lepilemur.* Prior to 1977, and reorganization of the genus, this name applied to *L. mustelinus.*

**weathering:** one of the processes that affect the condition and distribution of **fossil** bones; typically, after scavengers are finished with a carcass, most bones will 'weather' into a fine calcium dust owing to the combined action of sunlight and microorganisms, unless rapidly buried. Cf. **fossilization.** See **diagenesis, weathering stage,** and **taphonomy.**

**weathering stage:** series developed by **Behrensmeyer** to describe taphonomic effects of weather on skeletal elements at paleontological or archaeological sites, as follows: 1. some longitudinal cracking on the surface; 2. cracks more pronounced with flakes separated from the surface; 3. exterior surface roughened; 4. deep cracks with extensive flakes; 5. bone disintegration. See **diagenesis, weathering,** and **taphonomy.**

**web foot:** sex-linked condition affecting males, characterized by a bridge of skin between the toes.

**webbed fingers:** congenital anomaly in which two or more fingers are fused to a varying degree by a fold of skin.

**Weber's line:** imaginary line of faunal balance between **Wallace's line** and the boundary of the Australian Region.

**Weddell's tamarin:** vernacular for *Saguinus fuscicollis weddelli.*

**wedge-capped capuchin:** vernacular for *Cebus olivaceous* (= *nigrivittatus*).

**weeper capuchin:** vernacular for *Cebus olivaceous* (= *nigrivittatus*).

**Wegener, Alfred Lothar** (1880–1930): German geographer and geologist; Wegener proposed that original continental masses had drifted apart, causing eventual formation of modern continents by **continental drift** (1912). Wegener's major contribution translated as *Origin of Continents and Oceans* (1924). He perished on the Greenland ice pack.

**Weichselian glaciation:** fourth major glaciation of the Pleistocene in the Poland–German sequence; aka Weichsel. See **Würm glaciation.**

**Weidenreich, Franz** (1873–1948): German physician and paleontologist; continued the excavations at **Zhoukoudian** during the 1935–8 seasons, until Japan invaded China; it was Weidenreich's casts and measurements of these lost fossils that were preserved; he did similar work in Java. Known for his 1943 **trellis model** of **hominid evolution,** which depicted **Neandertals** as ancestral to modern humans (see the **Neandertal phase of man hypothesis**), a modified form of **polygenism.** President, **AAPA** (1944–5); first Viking Fund medalist (1947). Author of *Apes, Giants and Man* (1946).

**weight-bearing:** pertaining to any structure in an organism that is adapted for holding the bulk of the body mass; in humans, the main weight-bearing structures are the **pelvis** and lower limbs.

**weighted trait, character** or **feature:** some feature such as the neocortex in humans that is thought by some to be unique, and given emphasis in an analysis. Cf. **unweighted character.**

**Weinberg, Wilhelm** (1862–1937): German physician and mathematician; in 1908, independently derived the principle known today as the **Hardy–Weinberg law.** In subsequent papers, Weinberg made significant contributions to equilibrium, random mating, methods of partitioning genetic and environmental

variance (in advance of R. A. **Fisher**), ascertainment bias, and ratios of expected twin births.

**Weiner, Joseph Sydney** (1915–82): South African-born British physical anthropologist at Oxford; remembered popularly for initiation of the **fluorine test** of the **Piltdown hoax** (1953, with Le Gros Clark and K. Oakley). Weiner was better known for his adaptation studies; see the **spectrum hypothesis.** Co-author of *An Introduction to Human Evolution, Variation and Growth* (1964) (with G. A. Harrison, J. M. Tanner, and N. A. Barnicot), and of an influential laboratory field manual, *Practical Human Biology* (1981). See the **International Biological Programme.**

**Weismann, August** (1834–1914): German cytologist and physician; described the complex hierarchy of particles and particle groups in explaining heredity (1892); postulated a barrier which forbade the flow of genetic information from somatic cells to germ cells (**Weismann's barrier**); author of *Essays Upon Heredity and kindred Biological Problems* (1891–2, 2 vols.) and *The Germ-Plasm: Theory of Heredity* (1893). See **Weismannism.**

**Weismannism:** set of assumptions by August **Weismann** that (a) the **germ-plasm** consists of biophors (ultimate life units) that determine all the physical characters of a developing organism; (b) the germ-plasm is continuous from one generation to the next and is isolated from the soma (see **Weismann's barrier**); and (c) **natural selection** is the overarching method by which congenital variations to the germ-plasm contribute to the formation of new species. Originally termed **neo-Darwinism** in the late nineteenth century, Weissmannism was 'Darwinism' without the mechanism of acquired characters, and with a strong emphasis on **natural selection.** The term neo-Darwinism came to refer to the beginnings of the Grand Synthesis in the 1930s and 1940s.

**Weismann's barrier:** speculative membrane that prevents the flow of genetic information from somatic to germ cells; the primary theoretical refutation of **Lamarckism.** Demonstrated experimentally by August **Weismann** in 1892. See **germ-plasm theory.**

**wellborn science, the:** see **eugenics.**

**Werner syndrome** (WRN): one of the **progerias,** or autosomal recessive syndromes in which the rate of 'aging' is increased, or at least mimicked. In WRN, onset is in the second or third decade of life; by age 40 an affected individual has premature wrinkles, baldness, cataracts, muscular dystrophy, and diabetes. Lifespan is truncated. The defective gene is WRN, probably a helicase in the RecQ family that normally unwinds **dsDNA.**

‡ **Wernicke's area** (WRN): region of the brain located in the superior gyrus of the **temporal lobe** responsible for the perception and interpretation of speech.

**West Turkana** (WT): refers to a number of sites found on the west side of **Lake Turkana**, Kenya. See **Nariokotome** and **Lomekwi localities**.

**Westermarck effect:** proposal that childhood familiarity lessens sexual desire between individuals, and that this behavioral mechanism evolved to prevent the deleterious consequences of inbreeding. According to some primatologists, nonhuman primates are subject to the same mechanisms.

**western black-and-white colobus:** vernacular for *Colobus* polykomos.

**western blot analysis:** method of identification in which whole proteins are separated by **electrophoresis**, electroblotted onto a suitable nitrocellulose or nylon membrane, denatured, and hybridized with a labeled antibody to the protein. See **blot**. Aka western blotting.

**western fat-tailed dwarf lemur:** vernacular for *Cheirogaleus* medius samati.

**western gray mouse lemur:** vernacular for *Microcebus* murinus murinus.

**western lowland gorilla:** see *Gorilla gorilla*.

**western needle-clawed bushbaby (galago):** vernacular for *Euoticus* elegantulus.

**Western Negrillo:** traditionally, one of the three geographic divisions of **Negrillo** peoples in Africa. Included in this group are the Bagielli, Babongo, and Babinga or Baka; aka Babinga, as a whole.

**western Olduvai Gorge:** archaeological site(s) found in 1911 on the Serengeti plain in northern Tanzania, Africa, dating to <1.85 mya (Tuff 1B, Ar/Ar). The western portion of the gorge is a 5 km extension of the main channel (see **Olduvai Gorge**), and is situated between the perennial and maximum shorelines of **paleo-Lake Olduvai**, i.e. the paleolake margin zone, just north of Naisiusiu Hill. The fossiliferous sediments overlie Tuff 1B. Remains of freshwater clams, fish, and reptiles suggest that the locality was a stream incised into the western margin. Fossils of terrestrial mammalian herbivores grazed on $C_4$ **vegetation** interspersed with a gallery woodland. Over 200 **Oldowan** core tools excavated from the channel were fashioned from local quartzite but three lava tools were apparently imported from over 15 km distant, beyond the main channel of the gorge to the southeast. The first hominid, **OH 65**, was recovered from the region in 1995.

**western woolly lemur:** vernacular for *Avahi* occidentalis.

**wet season:** in seasonal **ecozones**, the time of the year when the most moisture is available and resources are abundant. Cf. **dry season**.

**wetland:** see **flooded forest**.

**wetted area:** entire area of the **skin** that is covered with **perspiration** and is available for evaporative cooling. Wetted area is not considered measurable by most physiologists. Aka wettedness.

**wheat:** *Triticum*, foremost of the four most important food crops in the world, a domesticated plant food item that originated in the Fertile Crescent and Canaan (present-day Israel) *c.* 9 kya. Durum, (wild) einhorn, (wild) emmer, and spelt are the most common varieties.

**white blood cell:** see **WBC** or **leukocyte**.

**white-cheeked gibbon:** vernacular for *Hylobates concolor*.

**white-collared brown lemur:** vernacular for the brown lemur subspecies *Eulemur fulvus albocolaris*.

**white-collared mangabey:** vernacular for *Cercocebus torquatus*.

**white-faced capuchin:** vernacular for *Cebus capucinus*.

**white-faced marmoset:** vernacular for the subspecies *Callithrix jacchus geoffroyi*. Some workers give this monkey specific status as *C. geoffroyi*.

**white-faced saki:** vernacular for *Pithecia pithecia*.

**white-footed capuchin:** vernacular for *Cebus albifrons*.

**white-footed sportive lemur:** vernacular for *Lepilemur leucopus*.

**white-footed tamarin:** vernacular for *Saguinus leucopus*.

**white-fronted brown lemur:** vernacular for the brown lemur subspecies *Eulemur fulvus albifrons*.

**white-fronted capuchin:** vernacular for *Cebus albifrons*.

**white-fronted leaf-monkey:** vernacular for *Presbytis frontana*.

**white-handed gibbon:** vernacular for *Hylobates* lar.

**white-lipped tamarin:** vernacular for *Saguinus labiatus*.

**white matter:** second layer of the **neocortex** of the **cerebrum** of the brain, underlying the **cerebral cortex**, or **gray matter**; contains primarily myelinated nerve fibers.

**white-nosed guenon:** vernacular for *Cercopithecus nictitans*.

**white-nosed saki:** vernacular for *Pithecia albicans*.

**white race:** see **Caucasoid**.

**white saki:** vernacular for *Pithecia albicans*.

**white sifaka:** vernacular for *Propithecus verreauxi*.

**white tamarin:** vernacular for the subspecies *Saguinus fuscicollis melanoleucus*.

**white-throated capuchin:** vernacular for *Cebus capucinus*.

**white-tufted-ear marmoset:** vernacular for *Callithrix jacchus*.

**White, Timothy D.** (1950–): US osteologist and paleoanthropologist at UC Berkeley; PhD (Ann Arbor): has been an active field worker in Kenya and

Ethiopia. White has co-described several fossil hominids, and has been a leader in the training of East African students in paleontology. Co-author (with P. A. Folkens) of *Human Osteology* (1991). See **Bouri formation**.

**whitewater:** Amazonian waterways that contain rich alluvial mud deposited from the sediments that flow from more fertile soils from tributaries. See **varzea forest**. Cf. **blackwater**.

**white uakari:** vernacular for the subspecies *Cacajao calvus calvus*.

**WHO:** abbreviation for the **World Health Organization**.

**whorl:** 1. pattern of concentric loops around a core found in **dermatoglyphics**. 2. any concentric or spiraling pattern of growth found on fingers or in hair.

**widow titi:** vernacular for *Callicebus torquatus*.

**Wied's (black-tufted) marmoset:** vernacular for *Callithrix kuhli* (= *penicillata*).

**wild type:** phenotype, genotype or allele most commonly found in natural populations.

**Wildscheuer:** archaeological site found in 1953 in West Germany, dated to the **Pleistocene** (early Würm), and that contains **Mousterian** artifacts. The hominid remains include cranial fragments attributed to *Homo neanderthalensis*.

**Willandra Lakes** (WLH): semi-arid region about 1000 km west of Sydney in southwest New South Wales, that contains significant archaeological material pertaining to the settlement of Australia by **AMHs**. During the **Pleistocene epoch** (between 45 and 25 kya) the region consisted of 17 lakes, all of which dried up *c*. 14 kya. One of the largest of these lakes was located with others along Willandra Creek, a tributary of the Lachlan River; freshwater Lake Mungo covered about 135 km². Its desiccated lake bed and landforms are a rich source of Pleistocene-age fossils, including hominids, who occupied the site by at least 40 kya, coincident with flake tools and, later, grinders. The region became a World Heritage Site in 1981. See **Mungo**.

**Willendorf:** archaeological site found in 1884 in Austria, dated to 23–21 kya, and that contains artifacts including the Venus of Willendorf, a figurine carved in limestone. See **venus figurines**.

**Williams, George C.** (1926–): ichthyologist, ecologist, and theoretical evolutionary biologist at SUNY (Stony Brook); coincident with W. D. **Hamilton**, reduced **natural selection** to the level of the individual (see **adaptationist program**) in the 1960s. Author of *Biology of Aging* (1957), the classic *Adaptation and Natural Selection* (1966), *Sex and Evolution* (1975), and with R. M. Nesse, *Evolution and Healing: New Science of Darwinian Medicine* (1996), and other works. Member of the National Academy of Sciences: winner of the NAS Elliot Medal.

**Williston's law:** observation that with specialization the number of parts of an organism involved with that specific function will decrease in number.

**Wilms' tumor:** autosomal dominant inherited form of kidney cancer in children. Exhibits evidence for **genomic imprinting**.

**Wilson, Allan Charles** (1934–91): New Zealand born-US molecular biologist at UC Berkeley; with his students Vince **Sarich** (using **serum albumin**) and Rebecca **Cann** (using **mitochondrial DNA**), Wilson shocked the field of **paleontology** twice, first by predicting that the most recent ape–human ancestor was likely to be found in fossiliferous strata dating closer to 5 than to 15 mya (1967), and second, that the most recent ancestor of all **AMHs** was likely to be found closer to 200 kya than to 2 mya (1989). Wilson and his students were involved with the development of **molecular clock(s)** and the validation of such devices by means of, for example, the **relative rate test**. See *Ramapithecus* and **mitochondrial Eve**.

**Wilson bands:** stress-induced growth disruption manifesting in defective tooth enamel. Similar examples are **Harris lines**, **fluctuating (dental) asymmetry**, enamel **hypoplasias**, and enamel **hypocalcifications**.

**Wilson disease** (WND): inherited autosomal recessive condition that manifests by the second decade of life, characterized by liver disease in children and by neurological difficulties in young adults. Other symptoms include headache and stomach ache, loss of balance, gravelly voice, handwriting abnormalities, drooling, and uncontrolled facial expression. Defects in copper metabolism cause damage to the liver and CNS, a diagnostic ring around iris, tremors, and emotional changes. The defective gene is ATP7B. Rare.

**Wilson, Edward Osborne** (1929–): US entomologist and sociobiologist. Wilson's empirical work was with haplo-diploid insects; he described communication by pheromones and the caste system, and he explained their relationship to observed behaviors. His empirical and theoretical work culminated in the monumental synthetic work now considered to be a classic of genetic-behavior analysis, *Sociobiology: The New Synthesis* (1975); the book included a final chapter in which he suggested that, as in ants, social behaviors have a genetic basis in mammals and primates, including humans. This extrapolation from ants to humans evoked criticism from many social scientists. Wilson subsequently published several popular works with sociobiological themes, most notably the Pulitzer Prize-winning *On Human Nature* (1978), which hypothesized that many cultural behaviors are gene-based. He has also published *The Diversity of Life* (1992), as well as several more controversial works co-authored with Charles J. Lumsden such as *Genes, Mind and Culture*

(1981); Wilson's autobiography was *Naturalist* (1996). Wilson's work has become central to anthropology because of these proposed gene– behavior connections; several of his students favor similar hypotheses, especially with respect to behaviors mediated by the **limbic system**. See **sociobiology, evolutionary psychology,** W. D. **Hamilton,** R. **Trivers,** and G. C. **Williams.** Cf. **environmental determinism.**

**Wiltonian:** Upper Paleolithic tool tradition found in South Africa.

**Wisconsin glaciation:** second of two major episodes of the fourth major glaciation of the Pleistocene in the North American sequence; see **Würm glaciation.**

**wisdom teeth:** vernacular label used for the third molars of the modern human dentition. These teeth erupt between ages 17 and 23. If there is insufficient space for these teeth, they may turn and become impacted into the ramus of the mandible; in developed nations, it is routine to have such teeth extracted.

**Wiskott–Aldrich syndrome** (WASP): an X-linked recessive hereditary condition; symptoms include thrombocytopenia, eczema, and immunodeficiency. Death by age 10. The WASP protein binds to a GTPase (Cdc42), which undergoes a dramatic allosteric morphological change.

**WK:** Wayland's **Korongo** at **Olduvai Gorge** in Tanzania.

**WLH:** abbreviation for **Willandra Lakes.**

**wobble:** ability of the third base in some tRNA anticodons to pair with more than one kind of base in the mRNA codon.

**wobble hypothesis:** proposal to explain major elements of redundancy in the genetic code in terms of the third base in the triplet sequences that specify amino acid transcription; since a majority of codons that specify the same amino acid differ in the third position only, Francis **Crick** suggested that the first two bases are necessary, allowing for a certain degree of 'wobble' in the third base position.

**wolf-man syndrome:** see **hypertrichosis.**

**Wolffian bodies: primordium** of the urinary system in the embryo; aka mesonephros.

**Wolffian ducts:** unspecialized tissue in an early embryo that can develop into a male reproductive tract; the Wolffian ducts normally degenerate in female embryos. Aka mesonephric ducts. Cf. **Müllerian ducts.**

**Wolff's law:** empirical statement of the observation that the external form and internal architecture of a bone are related to the forces that act upon it. In a more general sense, an organ is enlarged when its functions increase, and smaller when its functions decrease. Aka the law of atrophy and hypertrophy.

**Wolf's monkey:** vernacular for *Cercopithecus wolfi.*

**Wolpoff, Milford H.** (1942–): US paleoanthropologist. Wolpoff is the main spokesperson for the **multiregional continuity model.** He argues that *Homo erectus* left Africa one million plus years ago and that this species populated the Old World from Europe to Asia and the islands of Southeast Asia. These populations remained in place and evolved together through gene flow; the modern populations of various geographical regions are the descendants of these ancient populations. Wolpoff has also argued that *Homo erectus* should be included in *Homo sapiens*. Author of *Paleoanthropology* (1980, 1999).

**Wolstonian glaciation:** third major glaciation of the Pleistocene in the British Isles sequence; see **Riss glaciation.**

**woman: female** human being; usually, an adult. Cf. **man.**

**'woman the gatherer' model:** see **gathering hypothesis.**

**wood technique:** production of flakes from obsidian or other stones by striking them with hard wood or bone.

**woodland:** vegetation type characterized by discontinuous strands of relatively short trees separated by strands of grassland (savanna).

**Woodward, Arthur Smith** (1864–1944): British paleontologist at the British Museum of Natural History; Woodward's specialty was fossil fishes but he is best remembered for his reconstruction of the **Piltdown** fragments presented to him by Charles **Dawson**, after which Woodward 'authenticated' the finds at formal meetings in 1912.

**woolly monkey:** general vernacular for the two to three platyrrhine species belonging to the genus *Lagothrix.*

**woolly spider monkey:** vernacular for *Brachyteles arachnoides.*

**working definition:** see **operational definition.**

**working hypothesis:** rough statement of an idea; any proposition that can serve as one of the alternatives in future testing and experimentation.

**working side:** side of the mouth in which the teeth are occluding during **mastication.** Cf. **balancing side.**

**workshop:** any archaeological site where tools have been made and that contains numerous stone flakes, rejects, and blanks.

**world geomagnetic polarity column:** magnetographic profile of the world. See **paleomagnetism.**

**World Health Organization** (WHO): agency of the United Nations, established in 1948, that is concerned with improving health and living conditions of people worldwide, and with the prevention and control of **communicable diseases.** Cf. **CDC.**

**world oxygen isotope stage column:** stratigraphic profile of the world constructed based on data from deep-sea cores. See **Emiliani–Shackleton glacial sequence** and Appendix 6.

**world prehistory:** that portion of human history that extends back some 2.5 my before the time of written documents and archives, not from the perspective of a single region such as the Near East, but from a global viewpoint; the **prehistory** of all cultures on all continents.

‡ **world view:** broad concept referring to a people's concept of their environment, the place or role of human beings, social systems, and systems of cultural ideas their culture creates; a world view is characterized by such a hierarchy of deep patterns that certain elements are likely to be expressed in all parts of it. See **paradigm**.

**Wormian bone:** see **sutural bone**.

**Wright, Sewall** (1889–1988): US population geneticist at Chicago and Wisconsin. PhD (Harvard) under William **Castle**. With **Chetverikov**, **Fisher**, and **Haldane**, Wright co-promoted the early stages of the **modern synthesis** of **Darwinism** and post-**Mendelism** in the 1930s ('**neo-Darwinism**'). Wright developed the relationship between **microevolution** and **small population size**; aka **genetic drift**, or the **Sewall Wright effect**. He also advanced the concepts of inbreeding, isolation by distance, and gene flow. He differed with R. A. Fisher on the importance of genetic drift vs. selection. Wright viewed his central contribution to population genetics to be the **shifting balance theory**. He also contributed significantly to the development of path analysis. Author of 200+ research articles; author of *Evolution and the Genetics of Populations,* 4 vols. (1968–78). See also **adaptive landscape** and **multiple-peaked fitness surface**.

**Wright's inbreeding coefficient:** see **coefficient of inbreeding**.

**wrist:** region of the arm that joins the hand to the forearm. See **carpus**.

**wrist breadth: anthropometric** measurement: distance between the ulnar and radial **styloid** processes as measured with **spreading calipers**. Used for studies of body frame size and skeletal mass.

**wrist circumference: anthropometric** measurement: distance around the wrist as measured with a tape measure placed just distal to the **styloid** processes of the radius and ulna and passed around the wrist. Used in determining body frame size.

**wrist joint:** see **radiocarpal joint**.

**WT:** abbreviation for **West Turkana**.

**WT 15000:** see **KNM-WT 15000**.

**WT 17000:** see **KNM-WT 17000**, the **black skull**, and *Paranthropus aethiopicus*. Aka WT17k.

**Wu Rukang** (1916– ): Chinese paleoanthropologist; leader of the renewed excavations at Zhoukoudian since 1959, and known for a classic study of *Gigantopithecus* in the 1950s. Wu was instrumental in the recent surveys of China that led to the recent discover of sites such as **Hexian** and **Maba**; the relatively continuous fossil record in China led to Wu's subsequent support of the **multiregional continuity model**. Co-author of *Palaeoanthropology and Palaeolithic Archaeology in the People's Republic of China* (1985), and founder of the journal *Acta Anthropologica Sinica* in 1982.

**Wuguidong:** archaeological site found in 1978 at Wuguidong, Jiande County, Zhejiang Province, China, dated to 117–90 kya; contains hominid remains, including a canine tooth attributed to **archaic *Homo sapiens***. Aka Jiande.

**Würm glacial maximum:** fourth (and last) major glacial episode in the **Alpine glacial sequence** of the Pleistocene, which lasted from about 75 kya until about 10 kya. See **Günz**, **Mindel**, and **Riss** glacial maxima, and **Günz–Mindel** (Cromerian), **Mindel–Riss** (Holstein), and **Riss–Würm interglacials** (or interstadials).

‡ **Würm glaciation:** one of the four traditional periods of glaciation or ice ages that define the Pleistocene epoch during the past 1.8 million years BP. The fourth stage in the Quaternary sequence of the Alpine region, the Würm had a duration of about 70 ky and terminated between 40 and 10 kya.

**Wyman, Jeffries** (1814–74): US physician in Boston; one of the first five American scientists to produce work that can be said to have had a lasting effect on physical anthropology. Wyman was made a corresponding member of the Anthropological Society of London in 1867; ' . . . the leading anthropologist in America'; an early creationist who had accepted evolutionary theory by 1870. With T. Savage, published the first complete description of the **gorilla** (1847), to which Owen remarked he had 'very little left to add, and nothing to correct' (Packard).

*Wyomomys bridgeri* **Gunnell, 1995:** genus of tarsiiform primate from the middle Eocene, belonging to the omomyid subfamily **Omomyinae; monotypic**. Estimated body mass around 300 g. See Appendix 1 for taxonomy.

**45,X0 syndrome:** see **Turner syndrome.**

**46,XX male syndrome:** see **XX male syndrome.**

**46,XY female syndrome:** see **XY female syndrome.**

**47,X–, 13 + syndrome:** see **Patau syndrome.**

**47,X–, 18 + syndrome:** see **Edward syndrome.**

**47,X–, 21 + syndrome:** see **Down syndrome.**

**47,XXX syndrome:** see **triplo-X syndrome.**

**47,XXY syndrome:** see **Klinefelter syndrome.**

**47,XYY syndrome:** see **Double-Y syndrome.**

**x̄:** in statistics, the symbol for a sample estimate of the parametric **mean** ($\mu$) of a population.

**X0:** 'X null'; see **Turner syndrome.**

**xanthism:** pigment anomaly among sub-Saharan Africans and individuals of African ancestry that is expressed by a copper-red skin, red or reddish-blond hair color, and/or a reduction in pigmentation of the iris of the eye.

**Xanthochroi:** archaic term for blond-haired peoples; Cf. **Melanocroi.**

**xanthoderm:** yellowish skin. An archaic term sometimes used by physical anthropologists to denote a Mongoloid.

**xanthoma:** small, flat, yellow-colored deposit of **lipids** in the skin, characteristic of lipid storage diseases such as **diabetes** and **hyperlipoproteinemia.**

‡ **X chromosome:** one of two **sex chromosomes** in mammals, the segregational homologue of the **Y chromosome**; occurs singly in the heterogametic sex (males) and as a pair in the homogametic sex (females), and is associated with **sex determination.** The X chromosome has been highly conservative in mammalian **chromosome evolution**; that is, whereas many other chromosomes have undergone multiple **inversions** and **translocation** exchanges with other chromosomes, the X chromosome has remained morphologically stable across many species. Cf. **Y chromosome** and **autosome.**

**X chromosome DNA: genes, pseudogenes,** or **junk DNA** located specifically on the **X chromosome.**

**X chromosome genes:** genes located specifically on the **X chromosome.** So far 1,168 genes have been mapped to the human X chromosome, five times more than have been mapped to the human **Y chromosome.**

**X chromosome inactivation:** see **X inactivation.**

**xenograft:** transplant in which the donor and recipient are different species. Aka heterograft.

**xenology:** homologous variants of a single genetic locus in different, very unrelated species, i.e. a **DNA sequence** that has not been duplicated and has been **transfected** to another species, usually by a viral **vector.** Cf. **parology** and **orthology.**

‡ **xenophobia:** fear of and/or hostility towards strangers.

**xenophobic alliance:** coalition of members of a chimpanzee group against **conspecific** intruders that encroach on territorial boundaries.

*Xenopithecus:* defunct genus that has been sunk into *Proconsul heseloni.*

*Xenothrix* **Williams and Koopman, 1952:** Jamaican monkey; **monotypic** platyrrhine genus (*X. mcgregori* is the only recognized species); recently extinct. Postcrania and mandible recovered from archeological site dated to 2145 BP, but actual date of extinction uncertain (it has been speculated that this species survived up to the eighteenth century). Body mass around 2 kg. Dental formula: 2.1.3.2, which suggests affinities with the callitrichids; however, the structure of the molars is quite different from that of the living callitrichids; probably **frugivorous.** See Appendix 2 for taxonomy, Appendix 3 for living species.

**xeric:** describes conditions that are extremely dry. 2. adapted to dry conditions. Cf. **hydric** and **mesic.**

**xeroderma pigmentosum** (XP): autosomal recessive set of conditions (XPA, XPB, . . ., XPG) caused by deficient genes that are normally involved in DNA excision repair ('cut-and-patch repair'). XP is characterized by extreme sensitivity to **UV radiation** that results in unrepaired damage to fibroblast DNA and the formation of multiple pigmented spots that often become skin cancer. Onset in the first decade of life. Rare.

**xerophthalmia:** blindness caused by severe, chronic vitamin A deficiency; symptoms include keratinization and dryness of eye tissues. See **vitamin, hypovitaminosis, nightblindness,** and **malnutrition.**

**xerophytic forest:** type of **forest** that has well-defined seasons with thorny trees and shrubs that are adapted for water storage. This type of forest is found in Madagascar, where sifakas and other prosimians live.

**X-5 molar pattern:** pattern found variably in humans on the **occlusal surface** of **mandibular** molars in which a section of the fissure separating the five cusps forms an X pattern.

**Xg blood group:** polymorphism dependent upon a reaction to the red blood cell antigen Xgᵃ, an X-linked dominant allele. The gene (*XG*) for the antigen was the first X-linked human gene to be shown to escape **X inactivation.**

**Xiangfen:** see **Dingcun.**

**Xiaochangliang** (XCL): archaeological site found in 1979 in the Nihewan Basin, North China, dated to 1.36 mya; contains flaked **Paleolithic** artifacts. It is currently (2004) the oldest occupation site in the region.

**Xiaomei:** archaeological site found between 1988 and 1996, in the **Bose Basin** of the Guangxi Zhuang Autonomous Region of China, and, dated to 803 kya (associated tektites), and that contains many **mode 2** large cutting tools similar in complexity to those assigned to the **Acheulean tool tradition** at sites located west of **Movius' line**.

**X inactivation:** normal inactivation of one of two randomly selected **X chromosomes** in each cell of a female mammal. X inactivation happens early in embryonic development (in humans, during the third week). It occurs randomly in mammalian embryonic cells destined to become the individual, but nonrandomly in other tissues of the **conceptus**. See **mosaicism, heteropycnosis,** and **Barr body**. Aka random X inactivation. Cf. **paternal-X inactivation**.

**X inactivation center:** that part of the **X chromosome** that contains genes that inactivate the sex chromosome. See *XIST*.

**Xindong Cave:** See **New Cave**, Zhoukoudian. Aka Xingdong.

**Xinghuashan:** archaeological site found in 1982 in Nanzhao County, Henan Province, China, dated to about 550 kya; contains hominid remains, including assorted teeth attributed to *Homo erectus*. Aka Xichuan.

**xiphoid process:** inferior bone of the **sternum**. It begins as cartilage and usually fuses to the body of the sternum by middle age.

*XIST*: gene on an X chromosome believed to be involved in the **epigenetic** initiation of **X inactivation** in a female cell into an inactive **Barr body**. *XIST* is transcribed into **RNA** but not translated; the *XIST* RNA product appears to coat the entire X chromosome prior to X inactivation. **Genomic imprinting** of *XIST* accounts for the nonrandom X inactivation of the extraembryonic tissues; see **random-X inactivation**. In humans, *XIST* is located at Xq13. In other species the terminology is *Xist*.

**X-linked agammaglobulinemia** (XLA): rare, sex-linked recessive trait characterized by the total absence of immunoglobulins and B cells.

**X-linked hemophilia:** see **hemophilia**.

**X-linked locus or gene:** any **gene** located on the **X chromosome**; see **locus**.

**X-linked pattern of inheritance:** mode of inheritance displayed by genes located on the **X chromosome**.

**X-linked severe combined immune deficiency** (XSCID): form of **agammaglobulinemia** that differs from the less severe Bruton type by a complete absence of lymphocytes that results in a greater vulnerability to infections and a consequently earlier age at death. Intravenous Ig administration is not beneficial; hence the designation 'severe'. Much of the phenotypic constellation (e.g. absence of thymus tissue) of XSCID is due to infection-induced tissue degeneration prior to the time of presentation. The affected gene is the interleukin-2 gamma receptor chain (*IL2RG*); about 150 different mutations have been identified. About 50% of all SCID cases in the US are XSCID. Cf. **severe combined immune deficiency syndromes**.

**X-linked trait, character** or **feature:** trait produced by genes that are located on, and thus linked to, the X chromosome.

**Xp arm:** upper or p-arm of the conservative mammalian **X chromosome**. The Xp arm appears to have fused with the **Xq arm** at some point after the divergence of marsupials and placental mammals, as marsupials have unfused Xp and Xq chromosomes. The Xp arm has a larger proportion of genes that escape inactivation (estimated to be about 15%) than the Xq arm. See **X inactivation**.

**X-polysomy:** presence of more than the normal number of X chromosomes in the cells of an individual. All X-polysomic individuals risk the production of gametes with an unbalanced sex chromosome count. Males with 47,XXY have one **Barr body**, 48,XXXY have two Barr bodies, 49,XXXXY have three Barr bodies, etc. Females with 47,XXX have two Barr bodies, 48,XXXX have three Barr bodies, 49,XXXXX have four Barr bodies, etc., and progressively impaired intelligence proportional to the number of Barr bodies. See **trisomy X**.

**Xq arm:** lower or p-arm of the conservative mammalian **X chromosome**. The Xq arm appears to have fused with the **Xp arm** at some point after the divergence of marsupials and placental mammals, as marsupials have unfused Xp and Xq chromosomes. The Xq arm has a smaller proportion of genes that escape inactivation (estimated to be about 1%) than the Xp arm. See **X inactivation**.

**Xq–Yp region:** nonfunctional 4 mb length with high **DNA sequence** similarity located on the long arm of the human X chromosome (Xq) and the short arm of the human Y chromosome (Yp). Because homologous regions exist on ape X chromosomes only, researchers have surmised that a massive Y-to-X transposition occurred 4–3 mya in the hominid lineage, and the human Xq–Yp nucleotide sequence divergence began at that time. See **pseudogene**.

**X-ray:** short wavelength electromagnetic radiation emitted from the nucleus of an atom; X-rays are produced by the interaction of high-speed free electrons with atoms.

**X-ray painting:** style of art in which internal structures as well as external features of an animal are depicted.

**XSCID:** abbreviation for **X-linked severe combined immune deficiency**.

**Xujiafenshan:** archaeological site found in 1983 in Huanglong county, Shaaxi province, China, dated to the late **Pleistocene** <200 kya, and that contains small-tool industry artifacts and hominid remains, including a partial cranium attributed to *Homo sapiens*. Aka Huanglong.

**Xujiayao:** archaeological site found in 1976 in Yanggao County, Shanxi Province, China, dated to 125–104 kya, and that contains many artifacts. The hominids remains include bones of 11 individuals with broad, orthognathous faces attributed to **archaic *Homo sapiens***, and similar to modern populations there today, according to some authorities. Aka Yanggao.

**XX female:** normal condition in which two whole X chromosomes are present, resulting in a phenotypic female that is also chromosomally female. Cf. **XY male; XX male syndrome**. See **X inactivation**.

**XX male syndrome:** condition where an individual with a 46,XX chromosome constitution presents with a male phenotype owing to an abnormal translocation of portion of the Y chromosome that contains the **SRY gene** to the X chromosome. All such XX sex-reversed males are sterile; some exhibit features of **Klinefelter syndrome**. XX males may lead normal lives; many marry. Rare (1 : 9,000). Cf. **XY female syndrome**.

**XXX syndrome:** see **triplo-X syndrome**.

**XXY syndrome:** see **Klinefelter syndrome**.

**XY female syndrome:** condition where an individual with a 46,XY chromosome constitution presents with a female phenotype and gonadal dysgenesis, XY type (GDXY). All XY sex-reversed females are sterile. Although sterile, XY females may lead normal lives; many marry (AKA Swyer syndrome). Behaves like an X-linked recessive. Rare (1 : 20,000). Cf. **XX male syndrome**.

**X–Y homologues:** genes that are similar on both the X and Y chromosomes in a species, and that synapse in the heterogametic sex during meiosis.

**XY homology:** mammalian **X chromosome** and counterpart, the **Y chromosome**, are homologous in certain regions, primarily in the distal portion of the long arms, where synapsis and crossing over. Genes in this **pseudoautosomal region** do not exhibit **sex-linked inheritance**. The major portion of the Y chromosome, once homologous to the X, was inverted in its early evolutionary history. See **nonrecombining region of the human Y chromosome**.

**XY male:** normal condition in which a single, whole Y chromosome containing the **sex-determining region of the Y chromosome** is complemented by a single, whole X chromosome, resulting in a phenotypic male that is also chromosomally male. Cf. **XX female; XY female syndrome**.

**X/Y specific amelogenin test:** method of biological sex estimation; see **molecular sex determination**.

**XYY syndrome:** see **double-Y syndrome** and **primary nondisjunction**.

**45,Yo:** karyotype that is incompatible with life.

**Y-4 molar pattern:** occlusal surface pattern on some human mandibular molars in which there are four-well defined **cusps** with the fissures separating the cusps forming a Y pattern.

‡ **Y-5 molar pattern:** pattern present on **hominoid** molars in which there are five cusps separated by a Y-shaped fissure. This pattern is present on the molars of *Aegyptopithecus* and later hominoids including fossil humans; modern humans more commonly have a T-pattern based on four cusps. It is believed that the Y-5 pattern is primitive for catarrhines and that the cercopithecoid **bilophodont** condition derived from it. In the late 1980s some workers questioned whether the Y-5 pattern was actually present on most hominoid specimens. Also referred to as the **dryopithecine** pattern because these were the most ancient fossil hominoids when this pattern was first described.

**Y-6 molar pattern:** pattern found variably in humans on the **occlusal surface** of **mandibular** molars in which an additional cusp, an **entoconulid**, is added to the **Y-5 molar pattern.**

‡ **ya:** abbreviation for years ago.

**Yabrudian:** 'upper **Acheulean**' lithic assemblage found in certain African and Near Eastern sites (Malewa Gorge, El Kowm, **Tabūn**) dating roughly 225–150 kya.

**Yamashita:** archaeological site located near Yamashita-cho, Okinawa, dated to >32 kya; contains hominid postcranial remains including a juvenile (c. 6 year old) femur and tibia attributed to early modern humans on the basis of its femoral neck-shaft angle.

**Yangwu:** archaeological site found between 1988 and 1996, in the **Bose Basin** of the Guangxi Zhuang Autonomous Region of China, dated to 803 kya (associated tektites), and that contains many **mode 2** large cutting tools similar in complexity to those assigned to the **Acheulean tool tradition** at sites located west of **Movius' line.**

**Yanhuidong:** archaeological site found in 1975 at Yanhuidong, Tongzi County, Guizhou Province, China, dated to 191–102 kya; contains hominid remains, including assorted teeth attributed to **archaic *Homo sapiens*.** Aka Tongzi.

**Yanshan:** archaeological site found in 1986 in Yanshan, Chaoxian County, Anhui Province, China, dated to 220–160 kya; contains hominid remains, including an occipital and maxilla attributed to **archaic *Homo sapiens*.** Aka Chaoxian, Yenshan.

*Yaquius travisi* **Mason, 1990:** tarsiiform primate from the middle Eocene of North America, belonging to the omomyid subfamily **Omomyinae; monotypic.** Estimated body mass around 2 kg. Dental formula: 2.1.3.3/2.1.3.3. See Appendix 1 for taxonomy.

**yawn:** in primatology, the wide opening of the mouth in cercopithecine males to exhibit the large canine teeth. This serves as a threat to other individuals. Aka oscitatel yawn threat.

**yaws:** contagious, nonvenereal, chronic, relapsing infection in humans characterized by systemic lesions; caused by a spirochete (Treponema palladium pertenue). Worldwide distribution; occurs in tropical regions in populations where overcrowding and poor sanitation prevail. Route of infection is through direct person-to-person contact and predominantly affects children. Early yaws includes primary and secondary stages and is characterized by the presence of contagious skin lesions. Late yaws includes the tertiary stage, when lesions are not contagious. Untreated patients progressively develop destructive lesions involving bone (especially the hands and feet), cartilage, skin, and soft tissue (disfiguring growths near the nose known as gangosa), similar to those seen in tertiary **syphilis.** In contrast to venereal syphilis, cardiovascular and neurological abnormalities almost never occur with yaws. Has been identified in New World skeletons dated to at least 6 kya. Aka framboesia, frambesia tropica, parangi, paru, buba, pian, bouba, endemic treponema, endemic treponematoses. See **nonvenereal treponematoses.**

**Yayo:** archaeological site found in 1960 in Chad, Africa, dated to the Pleistocene, containing no artifacts, and hominid remains from one individual consisting of fragmentary frontal and facial bones attributed to the genus *Australopithecus*, but later reconsidered by some to be *Homo habilis*. Aka Koro Toro, the Chad australopithecine, KT 12-H1. See **Bahr El Ghazal.**

**ybp:** abbreviation for years before present; see **BP**, which is the more common designation.

‡ **Y chromosome:** one of two **sex chromosomes** in mammals, the segregational homologue of the **X chromosome.** A single Y chromosome (and X) is normally found in each diploid cell in the **heterogametic sex** (usually males, in mammals), who are **hemizygous** for each sex chromosome. Although much of the **Y chromosome DNA** is homologous with DNA on the **X chromosome**, only about 5% displays linear **synteny**, the **pseudoautosomal region**; the major interior block is the **male-specific region of the Y chromosome.** See **Y chromosome genes** and **H-Y antigen.** Cf. **X chromosome** and **autosome.**

**Y chromosome DNA: genes, pseudogenes,** or **junk DNA** located specifically on the **Y chromosome.** Much of the long-arm Y chromosome DNA in mammals appears to be **selfish DNA**, which is not maintained by **natural selection** and is therefore ideal for comparing rates of **molecular evolution** among individuals and between species. **Y chromosome DNA** can be used to identify groups of related males, and is thus useful for tracing **paternity** along male lineages. Cf. **mitochondrial DNA.**

**Y chromosome genes:** genes located specifically on the **Y chromosome**, such as the *SRY gene* that determines the male sex, and another that controls differentiation of the testes. Only 251 genes have been mapped to the human Y chromosome, the fewest of any chromosome. The **male-specific region of the Y chromosome** forms 95% of the chromosome, and contains about 78 mapped genes. Intrachromosomal repetitive sequences and **palindromes** are abundant in the Y; of about 800 sequence markers, about 20% have multiple locations. See **pseudogene** and **Y chromosome DNA**.

**yellow baboon:** vernacular for *Papio cynocephalus*.

**'yellow baby':** a **jaundiced** neonate, usually a morbid symptom of **hemolytic disease of the newborn**.

**yellow-handed titi:** vernacular for *Callicebus torquatus*.

**yellow marrow:** adipose tissue that occupies the **medullary cavity** in the **diaphysis** of a long bone. Many human hunter–gatherers found this tissue to be a delicacy.

**yellow ochre:** see **ochre**.

**Yerkes Regional Primate Centers:** first of several centers was established in Florida in 1924, and was dedicated to the study of learning and intelligence, mental abilities, and cognition of the apes. See R. M. **Yerkes**.

**Yerkes, Robert Mearns** (1876-1956): US psychometrician, comparative psychologist, and eugenicist. Harvard-trained, he went to Yale in 1924. Yerkes essentially had two careers. During the first, as a psychometrician and an Army colonel during WWI, he was a member of a team that developed and administered intelligence tests to 1.75 million soldiers. These tests were modified Binet instruments that later became the foundations of today's IQ tests, SATs, and GREs. His eugenic interpretations of the outcome of the WWI tests had a significant impact on public policy, culminating in the Immigration Restriction Act of 1924. Yerkes has been judged harshly by succeeding generations for this work. His second career, as a pioneering primatologist, was very different. In 1929 he founded the Yale Laboratories of Primate Biology that later became the **Yerkes Regional Primate Center**; he observed chimpanzees and sent students to the field in 1929–31 to study apes in their natural habitat. Yerkes' interest in primates was rationalized as a search for behaviors in common with humans that might be useful in human **eugenics** programs; he later viewed primate research as legitimate in its own right. His major work on primates was *The Great Apes* (1929), a compendium of extant knowledge about hominoids, and was co-authored with his wife, Ada W. Yerkes.

**Y-linked gene:** any gene that is located on the **Y chromosome**, especially on the portion that is not homologous to the **X chromosome**.

**Y-linked locus:** any gene located on the **Y chromosome**. See **locus**.

**Y-linked pattern of inheritance:** mode of inheritance displayed by genes located on the **Y chromosome**.

**Y-linked trait, character** or **feature:** genes or **DNA sequences** such as pseudogenes that are located on a **Y chromosome**.

**yolk sac:** an extra-embryonic structure originally associated with a yolk and which provided nutrients for a developing embryo; in higher vertebrates, which lack a yolk during embryonic life, the yolk sac is largely vestigial, although certain elements of the blood first appear there. See **hypoblast**.

**younger archaic group:** see **later archaic group**.

**Yuanmou:** see **Danawu**.

**Yunxian:** see **Longgushan Cave** and **Quyuanhekou**.

**Yiyuan:** see **Qizianshan**.

**Zafarraya Cave:** archaeological site located in Andalucia in southeastern Spain, dating to 27 kya, containing **Châtelperronian** artifacts and hominid remains from at least five individuals, including a mandible assigned to *Homo neanderthalensis*. Aka Zaffaraya Cave.

**Zahavi's handicap principle:** see **handicap principle** or **theory**.

**Zaire monkey:** vernacular for *Cercopithecus salongo*.

**Zaire River Basin:** research site located in Zaire, Africa, where long-term field studies of the lowland gorilla (*Gorilla gorilla gorilla*) have been conducted for decades. The primatologists who have conducted field research at this site include: M. J. Casimir and A. H. Harcourt.

**Zambian human:** see **Kabwe**.

***Zanycteris* (= *Picrodus*) *paleocenus* Matthew, 1917:** archaic mammal of the late Paleocene of the Rocky Mountain region of North America, belonging to the plesiadapidiform family **Picrodontidae; monotypic;** known from badly crushed cranium and isolated teeth. Dental formula probably 2.1.3.3/ 2.1.2.3; dental morphology suggestive of the **nectarivorous** living bats and has led to speculation that these animals were pollinators who fed on nectar. See Appendix 1 for taxonomy.

**Zanzibar bushbaby:** vernacular for *Galagoides* (= *Galago*) *zanzibaricus*.

**Z-DNA:** alternative form of **DNA** characterized by a left-handed helical conformation. Repetitive sequences with alternating purine–pyrimidine base pairs are elements of the genomes of both **eukaryotes** and **prokaryotes**. Cf. **B-DNA**.

**Zellweger syndrome:** an autosomal recessive condition characterized by prenatal defects of skull, face, ears, eyes, hands, feet, liver, and kidneys; fatal. Defective proteins fail to develop surface receptors on **peroxisomes**. Rare.

**zero population growth** (ZPG): condition of human **population equilibrium**, i.e. where the global **birth rate** is equal to the global **death rate**. ZPG has been a goal of some scientists in the fields of **demography** and **ecology**, who report that the human population is outstripping the earth's resources.

‡ **Zhoukoudian** (ZKD): archaeological site found in 1918 near Beijing (formerly Peking), China. The site represents a collapsed former rockshelter known as the 'lower cave', dating from about 590–128 kya (with recent occupation by *Homo sapiens* in the **Upper Cave**), and that contains over 100,000 **chopper/chopping tools** and other artifacts and **hominid** remains, (see box below) including parts of at least 32 *Homo erectus* individuals (called, *c.* 1930, *Sinanthropus pekinensis*). From the remains on the living floor, it appears that the users of the cave exploited resources such as meat, fruit, eggs, and seeds. Charcoal at the site has been interpreted as evidence for the **controlled use of fire**. The original fossil material was lost prior to World War II, but extensive castings were saved. An additional **calvaria**, known as the '1966 skull', was subsequently excavated. Cranial capacities range from 915 cm³ to

---

**Some hominid fossils recovered from Zhoukoudian**

**1966 skull:** cranial fragments from the 'lower cave' dating from 590–128 kya. These fragments were found to articulate with previously known cast material (i.e. found in 1934–6). The 1966 skull has a marked **supra-orbital torus** in which there are large frontal sinuses and with a cranial capacity of about 1140 cm³; the description otherwise conforms generally to other materials in **Weidenreich's** original monographs. Aka skull V. See **skull III**, etc.

**skull II:** sobriquet for a cranium found in 1929 at Locus D, dating from 590–128 kya. The cranium is from an adult with a marked **supra-orbital torus** in which there are large frontal sinuses; the cranial capacity is about 1030 cm³. Aka Zhoukoudian II.

**skull III:** sobriquet for a cranium found in 1929 at Locus E, dating from 590–128 kya. The cranium is from a juvenile yet has a marked **supra-orbital torus** in which there are large frontal sinuses; the cranial capacity is about 915 cm³. Aka Zhoukoudian III.

**skull V:** see the **1966 skull**. Aka Zhoukoudian V.

**skull X:** sobriquet for a cranium found in 1936 at Locus L, dating from 590–128 kya. The cranium is from an adult male with a marked **supra-orbital torus** in which there are large frontal sinuses; the cranial capacity is about 1225 cm³. Aka skull LI, Zhoukoudian X.

**skull XI:** sobriquet for a cranium found in 1936 at Locus L, dating from 590–128 kya. The cranium is from an adult female with a marked **supra-orbital torus** in which there are large frontal sinuses; the cranial capacity is about 1015 cm³. Aka skull LII, Zhoukoudian XI.

**skull XII:** sobriquet for a cranium found in 1936 at Locus L, dating from 590–128 kya. The cranium is from a subadult with a marked **supra-orbital torus** in which there are large frontal sinuses; the cranial capacity is about 1030 cm³. Aka skull LIII, Zhoukoudian XII.

1,225 cm³. Individual crania are known simply as **skull II**, etc. Aka Peking Man, Choukou'tien Man, Zhoukoudian Man, Bejing Man, Locality 1, and 'hills of the dragons'. See J. G. **Andersson**, Davidson **Black**, **Pei Wenzhong**, Franz **Weidenreich**, and **Wu Rukang**. Cf. **Locality 4**.

**ZIFT:** zygote intrafallopian transfer; the placement of a fertilized zygote into a female's fallopian tube after an **in vitro fertilization** procedure.

**Zihlman, Adrienne L.:** primatologist, evolutionary biologist at UC Santa Cruz. Specialist in primate behavior, primate evolution, human evolution, comparative anatomy, and anatomical bases of behavior (e.g. locomotion, sexual dimorphism, and sex roles). Has conducted fieldwork in Africa (Kenya, Uganda, South Africa) and Europe. Author of *The Human Evolution Coloring Book* (2nd edn, 2000) and many articles, especially the classic (co-authored) 'Pygmy chimpanzee as a possible prototype for the common ancestor of humans, chimpanzees and gorillas' (1978). See the **bonobo hypothesis**.

**zinc finger:** DNA-binding region of several proteins that consists of a finger-like loop of amino acids attached at a 'knuckle' containing zinc atoms.

***Zinjanthropus boisei* Leakey, 1960:** specific nomen for a robust fossil hominid based on a famous type specimen, **OH 5**, a skull recovered from **Olduvai Gorge** at a **Pleistocene** site named FLK in Bed I found by Mary **Leakey** in 1959; although the genus ('Zinj' is Kikuyu for 'east' and anthropus = 'man') has been sunk into either *Australopithecus* or *Paranthropus*, the specific **epithet** *boisei* has been retained (Boise was a benefactor of the Leakey family during times of lean funding). Aka 'Zinj', 'Nutcracker Man', and 'Dear Boy'. See *Paranthropus boisei*.

**Ziyang:** archaeological site found in 1951 near Huangshanxi in Sichuan Province, China, dated to the late **Pleistocene**, but the provenience of the site is poorly documented. The site contains artifacts called 'paleoliths' at Locality B, and hominid remains including a relatively archaic cranium and maxilla attributed to *Homo sapiens*. Aka Huangshanxi.

**ZKD:** abbreviation for **Zhoukoudian**.

**zona pellucida:** thick, clear layer separating the **ovum** from surrounding granulosa cells; consists of gel-like glycoprotein. The zona pellucida degenerates just prior to implantation in the endometrium.

**zonation:** 1. vertical (in trees or bodies of water) or horizontal layers characterized by a particular assemblage of plants and animals. 2. arrangement of organisms into biogeographical locations.

**zoo blot:** Southern blot containing DNA from several species, used to detect species variation; also used in **synteny** detection. See **blot**.

**zooanthroponosis:** any disease of vertebrates that can be naturally acquired from humans when they are the maintenance host. Cf. **anthropozoonosis**, **amphixenosis**.

**zooarchaeology:** see **archaeozoology** and **faunal analysis**.

**zoogenesis:** 1. the evolution of any species of animal. 2. the origin of animals.

**zoogeography:** study of the geographical distributions of animals and their habitats. Cf. **paleozoogeography**, **phytogeography**.

**zoology:** scientific study of animals.

**zoomorph:** animal form used as a symbol in art.

**zoomorphism:** viewing human behavior on strictly animal standards. **Sociobiology** has been criticized as zoomorphic because it reduces human behavior to biological constraints rather than morality and reason. Considered the opposite of **anthropomorphism**.

**zoonosis:** any disease that is transmitted from animals to humans, e.g. **measles**, **influenza**, **smallpox**, **AIDS**, **plague**, and **tuberculosis**. Aka zoonose. Adjective: zoonotic.

**zoophagy:** dietary category pertaining to an animal that consumes other animals; **faunivory**. Adjective: zoophagous. See **carnivory** and **insectivory**. Cf. **phytophagy**.

**zoopharmacognosy:** medicinal use of plants by animals; for example, chimpanzees are known to ingest particular plant species, apparently treating themselves for parasites.

**zoophorous:** describes the representation of humans and animals in relief on a frieze.

**z score:** standardized score; transformation of a raw value $x_i$ so that it is expressed in standard deviation units; calculated for each value as $z_i = (x_i - \xi)/\sigma$.

**z score distribution:** standardized distribution for a sample population after **z score** transformation; the *z* distribution has a mean of zero (0) and a standard deviation of one (1).

**Zuckerman, Solly (Lord)** (1904–93): South African-born physiologist at Oxford and Birmingham (England); policy advisor; pioneer of field studies of monkeys and apes. Zuckerman was author of over 1000 scientific papers, including studies on human ovulation, the function of the pituitary gland, and hominid biomechanics. Author of *The Social Life of Monkeys and Apes* (1932), *Functional Affinities of Man, Monkeys and Apes* (1933), and a two-part autobiography, *From Apes to Warlords: The Autobiography of Solly Zuckerman* (1978), and *Monkeys, Men and Missiles* (1966).

**Zuttiyeh Cave:** archaeological site found in 1925 near Tagbha, on Lake Galilee and **Amud** in the **Levant**, Israel (formerly Palestine), dated to 164–47 kya (U series), and that contains pre-Yabrudian **Acheulean** artifacts and hominid remains, including a male attributed to late **archaic Homo** sp., or pre-Neandertal. Found in 1927 by Flinders Turville-Petrie in the 'Valley of the Pillar', named after an unusual rock column. Cf. **Amud**, **Tabūn**, and **Shanidar**. Aka Galilee, Wadi Amud (but not the same cave as **Amud Cave**).

**zygion** (zy): **craniometric landmark:** most lateral point of the **zygomatic arch**. See Appendix 7.

‡ **zygomatic arch:** bone on the side of the skull that connects the zygomatic and temporal bones; aka the 'cheek' bone. This bone serves to anchor muscles used in chewing.

‡ **zygomatic bone:** one of a pair of bones of the facial skeleton that forms the cheek of the primate face. These bones form portions of the lateral walls and floors of the orbits. A process extends posteriorly and joins another process from the **temporal bone**, forming the **zygomatic arch**. Aka malar bone.

**zygomatic process:** bony process that projects anteriorly from the **temporal bone**; it joins the temporal process of the **zygomatic bone** to form the **zygomatic arch**.

**zygomaticus:** muscle of facial expression. The zygomaticus originates from the **zygomatic bone** and inserts into the **orbicularis oris**. Its action is to raise the corner of the mouth, as when smiling.

**zygomaxillare** (zm): **craniometric landmark:** most inferior point of the zygomaticomaxillary suture. See Appendix 7.

**zygomaxillare anterior:** surface where the **masseter muscle** attaches at the zygomaxillary suture of the **zygomatic arch**.

**zygoorbitale** (zo): **craniometric landmark:** point of articulation between the zygomaxillary suture and the lateral and inferior margin of the orbit. See Appendix 7.

**zygosity:** condition of being developed from one or more eggs; said of multiple births.

‡ **zygote:** cell that results from the fusion of two **haploid** gametes during **fertilization** and that normally possesses a complete **diploid** set of **chromatids**. The zygote exists until the first **cleavage**.

**zygote intrafallopian transfer:** see ZIFT.

**zygotene stage:** in meiosis, the second stage of prophase, in which homologous chromosomes approach each other and begin to pair. Aka zygonema.

# Appendix 1 A taxonomy of extinct primates

KINGDOM ANIMALIA
  PHYLUM CHORDATA
    SUBPHYLUM VERTEBRATA
      CLASS MAMMALIA
        GRANDORDER ARCHONTA
          ORDER SCANDENTIA
          ORDER CHIROPTERA
          MIRORDER PRIMATOMORPHA
          ORDER DERMOPTERA
          **ORDER *INCERTAE SEDIS***
    Family Purgatoriidae
      Genus and species:
        *Purgatorius*
          *P. unio*
          *P. titusi*
          *P. janisae*
        **ORDER PLESIADAPIFORMES OR
        PROPRIMATES**[1]
  Superfamily Plesiadapoidea
  Family Plesiadapidae
    Genera and species:
      *Pandemonium dis*
      *Pronothodectes*
        *P. matthewi*
        *P. jepi*
        *P. gaoi*
      *Plesiadapis*
        *P. praecursor*
        *P. anceps*
        *P. rex*
        *P. gingerichi*
        *P. churchilli*
        *P. fodinatus*
        *P. dubius*
        *P. simonsi*
        *P. cookeri*
        *P. walbeckensis*
        *P. remensis*
        *P. tricuspidens*
        *P. russelli*
      *Nannodectes*
        *N. intermedius*
        *N. gazini*
        *N. simpsoni*
        *N. gidleyi*
      *Chiromyoides*
        *C. campanicus*
        *C. caesor*
        *C. minor*
        *C. potior*

        *C. major*
      *Platychoerops*
        *P. daubrei*
        *P. richardsoni*
  Family Carpolestidae
    Genera and species:
      *Elphidotarsius*
        *E. florencae*
        *E. shotgunensis*
        *E. russelli*
        *E. wightoni*
      *Carpodaptes*
        *C. aulacodon*
        *C. hazelae*
        *C. jepseni*
      *Carpocristes*
        *C. nigridens*
        *C. dubius*
      *Chronolestes simul*
  Family Saxonellidae
    Genera and species:
      *Saxonella*
        *S. crepatirae*
        *S. naylori*
  Family Paromomyidae
    Genera and species:
      *Paromomys*
        *P. maturus*
        *P. depressidens*
      *Ignacius*
        *I. graybullianus*
        *I. frugivorus*
        *I. fremontensis*
        *I. mcgrewi*
      *Phenacolemur*
        *P. praecox*
        *P. simonsi*
        *P. pagei*
        *P. jepseni*
      *Elwynella oreas*
      *Simpsonlemur citatus*
      *Dillerlemur robinettei*
      *Pulverflumen magnificum*
      *Arcius*
        *A. rougieri*
        *A. fuscus*
        *A. lapparenti*
  Family Micromomyidae
    Genera and species:
      *Micromomys*

---

[1] The taxonomy here is problematic. Until the 1990s the Plesiadapiformes were included among the primates. Both Gingerich (1990, *J. Hum Evol* **19**: 821) and Beard (1993, *Mammal Phylogeny: Placentals*, p. 129) removed these animals from the primates, but beyond this there is no agreement. Gingerich proposed the order Proprimates and removed the Plesiadapiformes from the primates. He suggested that the modern Scandentians might also be included in the Proprimates. Beard proposed the mirorder Primatomorpha including the primates and the mammalian order Dermoptera. In this scheme the Plesiadapiformes are included within the Dermoptera as a suborder. Here Fleagle (1999, *Primate Adaptation and Evolution*) is followed and the plesiadapiforms are placed in a separate order.

M. silvercouleei
M. willwoodensis
M. vossae
M. fremdi
Tinimomys graybulliensis
Chalicomomys antelucanus
Myrmekomomys loomisi
Superfamily Microsyopoidea
Family Palaechthonidae
Genera and species:
Palaechthon
P. alticuspis
P. nacimienti
P. woodi
Plesiolestes
P. problematicus
P. sirokyi
Talpohenach (= Plesiolestes) torrejonia
Torrejonia (= Plesiolestes) wilsoni
Palenochtha minor
Anasazia williamsoni
Premnoides douglassi
Family Microsyopidae
Genera and species:
Navajovius kohlhaasae
Berruvius
B. lesseroni
B. gingerichi
Niptomomys
N. doreenae
N. thelmae
Uintasorex parvulus
Avenius amatorum
Microsyops (= Cynodontomys)
M. angustidens
M. latidens
M. scottianus
M. elegans
M. annectens
M. kratos
Arctodontomys
A. wilsoni
A. simplicidens
A. nuptus
Craseops sylvestris
Megadelphus lundeliusi
Superfamily incertae sedis
Family Picrodontidae
Genera and species:
Picrodus silberlingi
Zanycteris (= Picrodus) paleocenus
Draconodus (= Picrodus) apertus
Family Picromyomyidae
Genera and species:
Picromomys petersonorum

Alveojunctus minutus

**ORDER PRIMATES**

SUBORDER PROSIMII[2]
Family Incertae sedis
Genera and species:
Altanius orlovi
Altiatlasius koulchii
Infraorder Lemuriformes
Superfamily Adapoidea
Family Notharctidae
Subfamily Notharctinae
Genera and species:
Cantius (= Pelycodus)
C. torresi
C. ralstoni
C. mckennai
C. trigonodus
C. abditus
C. angulatus
C. frugivorus
C. venticolis
C. eppsi
C. savagei
Pelycodus (= Cantius)
P. jarrovii
P. danielsae
Copelemur (= Pelycodus)
C. australotutus
C. tutus
C. feretutus
C. consortutus
C. praetutus
Smilodectes
S. gingerichi
S. mcgrewi
S. gracilis
Notharctus
N. robinsoni
N. tenebrosus
N. pugnax
N. robustior
Hesperolemur actius
Subfamily Cercamoniinae (= Protoadapinae)
Genera and species:
Donrussellia
D. gallica
D. provincialis
D. magna
Protoadapis
P. curvicuspidens
P. filholi
P. lemoinei
P. recticuspidens

---

[2] Many authorities have replaced this category with the Suborder Strepsirhini. However, paleontologists appear to prefer the grade Prosimii. One of the problems with the strepsirhines is that, until recently, diagnostic characteristics were based on soft tissue that does not fossilize.

P. russelli
P. louisi
P. weigelti
P. ulmensis
P. ignoratus
P. muechelnensis
Djebelemur martinezi[3]
Panobius afridi
Europolemur
  E. klatti
  E. koenigswaldi
  E. dunaefi
  E. collinsonae
Periconodon
  P. helveticus
  P. huerzleri
  P. roselli
  P. lemoinei
  P. jaegeri
Anchomomys
  A. gaillardi
  A. pygmaea
  A. crocheti
  A. milleri
Huerzeleria quercyi
Pronycticebus
  P. gaudryi
  P. neglectus
Buxella
  B. prisca
  B. magna
Agerinia roselli
Caenopithecus lemuroides
Cercamonius brachyrhynchus
Mahgarita stevensi
Aframonius dieides
Omanodon minor
Shizarodon dhofarensis
Wadilemur elegans
Family Incertae sedis
  Genera and species:
    Azibius trerki
    Hoanghonius stehlini
    Lushius qinlinensis
    Rencunius zhoui
    Wailekia orientale
Family Adapidae
  Genera and species:
    Adapis
      A. betillei
      A. parisiensis
      A. sudrei
      A. laharpei
    Cryptadapis tertius

Microadapis sciureus
Leptadapis
  L. magnus
  L. assolicus
  L. capellae
  L. priscus
  L. ruetimeyeri
Adapoides troglodytes
Family Sivaladapidae
  Genera and species:
    Indraloris himalayensis
    Sivaladapis
      S. nagrii
      S. palaeindicus
    Sinoadapis carnosus
Superfamily Lorisoidea
Family Galagidae
  Genera and species:
    Progalago
      P. dorae
      P. songhorensis
    Komba
      K. robusta
      K. minor
      K. winamensis
    Galago (see Appendix 2 for extant members)
      G. howelli
      G. sadimensis
Family Lorisidae
  Genera and species:
    Mioeuoticus
      M. bishopi
      M. spp.
    Nycticeboides simpsoni
Family Plesiopithecidae
    Plesiopithecus teras
SUBORDER TARSOIDEA[4]
Infraorder Tarsiiformes
Superfamily Omomyoidea
Family Microchoeriidae[5]
  Genera and species:
    Nannopithex
      N. pollicaris
      N. raabi
      N. fiholi
      N. quaylei
      N. abderhalderi
      N. barnesi
      N. humilidens
      N. zucolae
    Necrolemur
      N. zitteli
      N. antiquus

---

[3] Godinot (1994, *Anthropoid Origins*, p. 235) feels that this fossil has simian traits and is closely related to *Algeripithecus* and the parapithecids.
[4] Napier and Napier (1967, *A Handbook of Living Primates*) and Mai (1984, *J. Hum. Evol.* **14**: 229) are followed here in placing the tarsiers in a separate suborder. Most authorities place them among the Prosimii or, more recently and especially among neontologists, Haplorhini.
[5] Many workers include this family as a subfamily of the Omomyidae.

*Pseudoloris*
  *P. parvulus*
  *P. isabenae*
  *P. crusafonti*
  *P. requanti*
  *P. saalae*
*Microchoerus*
  *M. erinaceus*
  *M. edwardsi*
  *M. ornatus*
  *M. wardi*
  *M. creechbarrowensis*
Family Omomyidae
Subfamily Anaptomorphinae
Tribe Anaptomorphini
Genera and species:
  *Teilhardina*
    *T. belgica*
    *T. brandti*
    *T. americana*
    *T. crassidens*
    *T. tenuicula*
    *T. demissa*
  *Anaptomorphus*
    *A. aemulus*
    *A. wortmani*
    *A. westi*
  *Gazinius*
    *G. amplus*
    *G. bowni*
  *Tetonius*
    *T. homunculus*
    *T. mckennai*
    *T. mattewi*
  *Pseudotetonius (= Tetonius) ambiguus*
  *Absarokius*
    *A. abbotti*
    *A. noctivagus*
    *A. witteri*
  *Tatmanius szalayi*
  *Strigorhysis*
    *S. bridgeriensis*
    *S. rugosus*
    *S. huerfanensis*
  *Acrossia lovei*
Tribe Trogolemurini
Genera and species:
  *Trogolemur*
    *T. myodes*
    *T. amplior*
  *Sphacorhysis burntforkensis*
  *Anemorhysis*
    *A. sublettensis*
    *A. natronensis*
    *A. wortmani*
    *A. pattersoni*
    *A. savagei*
  *Tetonoides (= Anemorhysis)*
    *T. pearcei*
    *T. coverti*

*Arapahovius*
  *A. gazini*
  *A. advena*
*Chlororhysis*
  *C. knightensis*
  *C. incomptus*
Tribe Washakiini
Genera and species:
  *Washakius*
    *W. insignis*
    *W. woodringi*
    *W. izetti*
    *W. laurae*
  *Shoshonius*
    *S. cooperi*
    *S. bowni*
  *Dyseolemur pacificus*
  *Loveina*
    *L. zephyri*
    *L. minuta*
    *L. wapitiensis*
Subfamily Omomyinae
Tribe Uintaniini
Genera and species:
  *Uintanius*
    *U. ameghini*
    *U. rutherfurdi*
  *Jemezius szalayi*
Tribe Omomyini
Genera and species:
  *Omomys*
    *O. carteri*
    *O. lloydi*
  *Chumashius balchi*
  *Steinius*
    *S. vespertinus*
    *S. annectens*
Tribe Ourayini
Genera and species:
  *Ourayia*
    *O. uintensis*
    *O. hopsoni*
  *Wyomomys bridgeri*
  *Ageitodendron mattewi*
  *Utahia kayi*
  *Stockia powayensis*
  *Chipetaia lamporea*
  *Asiomomys changbaicus*
Tribe Macrotarsiini
Genera and species:
  *Macrotarsius*
    *M. seigerti*
    *M. montanus*
    *M. jepseni*
    *M. roederi*
    *M. macrorhysis*
  *Hemiacodon gracilis*
  *Yaquius travisi*
Subfamily Ekgmowechashalinae
Genera and species:

Ekgmowechashala philotau
Family *Incertae sedis*
  Genera and species:
    Rooneyia viejaensis
    Kohatius coppensi
Superfamily Tarsoidea
  Family Tarsiidae (see Appendix 2 for extant members of this family)
    Genera and species:
      Afrotarsius chatrathi
      Tarsius
        T. eocaenus
        T. thailandica
      Xanthorhysis tabrumi
SUBORDER ANTHROPOIDEA[6]
  Infraorder *Incertae sedis*
    Family Eosimiidae
      Genera and species:
        Eosimias
          E. sinensis
          E. centennicus
    Family *Incertae sedis*
      Genera and species:
        Amphipithecus mogaungensis
        Pondaungia cotteri
        Siamopithecus eocaenus
        Proteopithecus sylviae
        Arsinoea kallimos
        Algeripithecus minutus
        Tabelia hammadae
    Family Parapithecidae
      Genera and species:
        Biretia piveteaui
        Serapia eocaena
        Qatrania
          Q. wingi
          Q. fleaglei
        Apidium
          A. phiomense
          A. moustafai
          A. bowni
        Parapithecus fraasi
        Simonsius (=Parapithecus) grangeri
  Infraorder Platyrrhini
    Superfamily Ceboidea
      Family Atelidae
        Subfamily Atelinae
          Genera and species:
            Stirtonia
              S. tatacoensis
              S. victoriae
              S. sp.
            Protopithecus brasiliensis
            Caipora bambuiorum
        Subfamily Pitheciinae
          Genera and species:
            Soriacebus

S. ameghinorum
S. adrianae
Carlocebus
  C. carmenensis
  C. intermedius
Homunculus patagonicus
Cebupithecia sarmientoi
Nuciruptor rubricae
Propithecia neuquenensis
Family Cebidae
  Subfamily Aotinae
    Genera and species:
      Tremacebus harringtoni
      Aotus dindensis (see Appendix 2 for extant members of this genus)
  Subfamily Callitrichinae
    Mohanamico hershkovitzi
    Lagonimico conclutatus
    Micodon kiotensis
    Patasola magdalenae
  Subfamily Cebinae
    Genera and species:
      Dolichocebus gaimanensis
      Chilecebus carrascoensis
      Neosaimiri fieldsi
      Laventiana annectens
  Subfamily *Incertae sedis*
    Genera and species:
      Branisella boliviana
      Szalatavus attricuspis
      Mohanamico hershkovitzi
Infraorder Catarrhini
  Superfamily Propliopithecoidea
    Family Oligopithecidae
      Genera and species:
        Oligopithecus
          O. savagei
          O. rogeri
        Catopithecus browni
    Family Propliopithecidae
      Genera and species:
        Propliopithecus
          P. haeckeli
          P. chirobates
          P. ankeli
        Moeripithecus (= Propliopithecus) markgrafi
        Aegyptopithecus zeuxis
  Superfamily Cercopithecoidea
    Family Victoriapithecidae
      Genera and species:
        Prohylobates
          P. tandyi
          P. simonsi
        Victoriapithecus macinnesi
    Family Cercopithecidae
      Subfamily Cercopithecinae
        Genera and species:

---

[6] Many authorities have replaced this category with the Suborder Haplorhini.

*Macaca* (see Appendix 2 for extant
members of this genus)
  *M. prisca*
  *M. majori*
  *M. libyca*
  *M. anderssoni*
  *M. palaeindica*
  *M. jiangchuanensis*
*Procynocephalus*
  *P. wimani*
  *P. subhimalayensis*
*Paradolichopithecus*
  *P. arvernensis*
  *P. sushkini*
*Papio* (see Appendix 2 for extant mem-
bers of this genus)
  *P. robinsoni*
  *P. izodi*
  *P. quadratirostris*
*Dinopithecus ingens*
*Parapapio*
  *P. broomi*
  *P. jonesi*
  *P. whitei*
  *P. antiquus*
  *P. ado*
*Gorgopithecus major*
*Theropithecus* (see Appendix 2 for
extant members of this genus)
  subgenus *Simopithecus*
  *T. (S.) oswaldi*
  *T. (S.) delsoni*
  *T. (S.) darti*
  subgenus *Omopithecus*
  *T. (O.) brumpi*
  *T. (O.) baringensis*
Subfamily Colobinae
Genera and species:
  *Mesopithecus*
  *M. pentelici*
  *M. monspessulanus*
  *Dolichopithecus*
  *D. ruscinensis*
  *D. hanaumani*
  cf. *Semnopithecus sivalensis* (see Appendix
  2 for extant members of this genus)
  *Rhinopithecus lantainensis* (see Appendix
  2 for extant members of this genus)
  *Colobus* sp. (see Appendix 2 for extant
  members of this genus)
  *Colobus flandrini*
  *Libyapithecus markgrafi*
  *Microcolobus tugenensis*
  *Cercopithecoides*
  *C. williamsi*
  *C. kimeui*
  *Paracolobus*

  *P. chemeroni*
  *P. mutiwa*
  *Rhinocolobus turkanensis*
Superfamily Hominoidea
  Family Pliopithecidae
  Genera and species:
    *Pliopithecus*
    *P. antiquus*
    *P. vindobonensis*
    *P. platyodon*
    *P. priensis*
    *P. zhanxiangi*
    *Plesiopliopithecus* (= *Crouzelia*)
    *P. lockeri*
    *P. auscitanensis*
    *P. rhodanica*
    *Anapithecus hernyaki*
    *Laccopithecus robustus*
  Family Oreopithecidae
  Genera and species:
    *Mabokopithecus clarki* [7]
    *Nyanzapithecus pickfordi*
    *Oreopithecus bambolii*
  Family Proconsulidae
  Genera and species:
    *Proconsul*
    *P. africanus*
    *P. heseloni*
    *P. nyanzae*
    *P. major*
    *Rangwapithecus*
    *R. gordoni*
    *R. vancouveringi*
    *Dendropithecus macinnesi*
    *Micropithecus clarki*
    *Simiolus*
    *S. enjiessi*
    *S. leakeyorum*
    *Kalepithecus songhorensis*
    *Dionysopithecus* (= ?*Micropithecus*)
    *shuangouensis*
  Family *Incertae sedis*
  Genera and species:
    *Kamoyapithecus hamiltoni*
    *Afropithecus*
    *A. turkanensis*
    *A. leakeyi*
    *Morotopithecus bishopi*
    *Turkanapithecus kalakolensis*
    *Kenyapithecus*
    *K. africanus*
    *K. wickeri*
    *Otavipithecus namibiensis*
    *Samburupithecus kiptalami*
    *Platydontopithecus janghuaiensis*
  Family Pongidae [8]
  Subfamily Dryopithecinae [9]

---

[7] Some researchers include this species within the Proconsulidae. Others question whether it is a valid primate species.

Genera and species:
  *Dryopithecus*
    *D. brancoi* (= *carinthiacus*)
    *D. crusafronti*
    *D. fontani*
    *D. laietanus*
    *Lufengpithecus lufengensis*
Subfamily Ponginae
  Genera and species:
    *Griphopithecus*
      *G. alpani*
      *G. darwini*
      *G.* sp.
    *Khoratpithecus piriyai*
    *Sivapithecus* (= *Ramapithecus*)
      *S. sivalensis*
      *S. indicus* (= *sivalensis*)
      *S. punjabicus*
      *S. parvada*
    *Ankarapithecus meteai*
    *Gigantopithecus*
      *G. blacki*
      *G. giganteus* (= *bilaspurensis*)
    *Graecopithecus freybergi*
    *Ouranopithecus* (= *Graecopithecus*)
    *macedoniensis*
Family Hominidae
  Subfamily *Incertae sedis*[10]
    Genera and species:
      *Sahelanthropus tchadensis*

*Orrorin tugenensis*
*Kenyanthropus platyops*[11]
Subfamily Australopithecinae
  Genera and species:
    *Ardipithecus ramidus*
    *Australopithecus*
      *A. anamensis*
      *A. afarensis*
      *A. africanus*
      *A. bahrelghazali*
      *A. garhi*
Subfamily Paranthropinae
  Genus and species:
    *Paranthropus*
      *P. aethiopicus*
      *P. boisei*
      *P. robustus*
Subfamily Homininae
  Genus and species:
    *Homo* (see Appendix 2 for extant
      member of this genus)
      *H. habilis*
      *H. rudolfensis*
      *H. ergaster* (cf. *erectus*)
      *H. antecessor* (= *heidelbergensis*)
      *H. erectus*
      *H. rhodesiensis*
      *H. heidelbergensis*
      *H. neanderthalensis*

[8] Some authors place many, if not all, of the subfamilies that follow in the family Hominidae. A more conservative approach is adopted here. The hominids are restricted to bipedal hominoids while recognizing that the close relationship between humans and African apes warrants their inclusion within the same family.

[9] There is little agreement about the placement of this group of hominoids. Some (e.g. Groves 1989, *A Theory of Human and Primate Evolution*) recognize a family Dryopithecidae including only the genus *Dryopithecus*. Others simply include this group among the Pongidae without subfamily status. Still others (e.g. Szalay & Delson 1979, *Evolutionary History of the Primates*) include this group among the Hominidae.

[10] These are recent finds that have not been formally assigned to a subfamily.

[11] Leakey *et al*. (2001, *Nature* **410**: 433) have suggested that *Homo rudolfensis* be transferred to this species.

# Appendix 2 A taxonomy of recent and extant primates

KINGDOM ANIMALIA
  PHYLUM CHORDATA
    SUBPHYLUM VERTEBRATA
      CLASS MAMMALIA
        GRANDORDER ARCHONTA
          ORDER DERMOPTERA
          ORDER CHIROPTERA
          ORDER SCANDENTIA
          **ORDER PRIMATES**
SUBORDER PROSIMII[1]
  Infraorder Lemuriformes
    Superfamily Lemuroidea
      Family Cheirogaleidae[2]
        Genera and species:
          *Microcebus* (mouse lemurs)
            *M. murinus* (gray mouse lemur)
            *M. rufus* (brown mouse lemur)
            *M. myoxinus* (pygmy mouse lemur)
          *Mirza conquereli* (Conquerel's mouse lemur)[3]
          *Cheirogaleus* (dwarf lemurs)
            *C. major* (greater dwarf lemur)
            *C. medius* (fat-tailed dwarf lemur)
          *Allocebus trichotis* (hairy-eared dwarf lemur, recently found alive)
          *Phaner furcifer* (fork-marked dwarf lemur)
      Family Lemuridae
        Subfamily Lemurinae
          Genera and species:
            *Lemur catta* (ring-tailed lemur)
            *Eulemur* (true lemurs)[4]
              *E. fulvus* (brown lemur)
              *E. mongoz* (mongoose lemur)
              *E. macaco* (black lemur)
              *E. coronatus* (crowned lemur)
              *E. rubriventer* (red-bellied or red-fronted lemur)
            *Varecia variegata* (ruffed lemur)
            *Pachylemur insignis*
        Subfamily Hapalemurinae
          Genus and species:
            *Hapalemur* (gentle or bamboo lemurs)
              *H. griseus* (gray gentle lemur)
              *H. simus* (broad-nosed gentle lemur)
              *H. aureus* (golden lemur)
      Family Megaladapidae
        Subfamily Lepilemurinae
          Genus and species:
            *Lepilemur* (sportive or weasel lemurs)
              *L. dorsalis* (gray-backed sportive lemur)
              *L. edwardsi* (Milne-Edwards' sportive lemur)
              *L. leucopus* (white-footed sportive lemur)

              *L. microdon* (small-toothed sportive lemur)
              *L. mustelinus* (common sportive lemur)
              *L. ruficaudatus* (red-tailed sportive lemur)
              *L. septentrionalis* (northern sportive lemur)
        Subfamily Megaladapinae
          Genus and species:
            *Megaladapis* (koala lemurs)
              subgenus *Peloriadapis*
              *M. ewardsi*
              subgenus *Megaladapis*
              *M. madagascariensis*
              *M. grandidieri*
      Family Indriidae
        Genera and species:
          *Avahi* (woolly lemurs)
            *A. laniger* (eastern woolly lemur)
            *A. occidentalis* (western woolly lemur)
          *Indri indri* (indri)
          *Propithecus* (sifaka)
            *P. diadema* (diademed sifaka)
            *P. tattersalli* (golden crowned sifaka)
            *P. verreauxi* (white sifaka)
      Family Palaeopropithecidae (sloth lemurs)
        Genera and species:
          *Mesopithecus*
            *M. dolichobrachion*
            *M. globiceps*
            *M. pithecoides*
          *Babakotia radofilai*
          *Palaeopropithecus ingens*
          *Archaeoindris fontoynonti*
      Family Archaeolemuridae
        Genera and species:
          *Archaeolemur*
            *A. majori*
            *A. edwardsi*
          *Hadropithecus stenognathus*
      Family Daubentonidae
        Genus and species:
          *Daubentonia madagascariensis* (aye-aye)
    Superfamily Lorisoidea
      Family Lorisidae
        Genera and species:
          *Perodicticus potto* (potto)
          *Pseudoloris martini* (Martin's false potto)
          *Arctocebus callabarensis* (angwantibo or golden potto)
          *Loris tardigradus* (slender loris)
          *Nycticebus* (slow lorises)
            *N. coucang* (slow loris)

---

[1] Many authorities have replaced this category with the Suborder Strepsirhini.
[2] Some workers place the Cheirogaleidae within a superfamily Lorisoidea.
[3] This species is included in *Microcebus* by some authorities.
[4] Some workers recognize this taxon as the genus *Petterus*.

N. *pygmaeus* (pygmy slow loris)

Family Galagonidae
Genera and species:
*Galago* (bushbabies)
G. *gallarum* (Somali bushbaby)
G. *moholi* (South African bushbaby)
G. *senegalensis* (Senegal bushbaby)
*Otolemur* (= *Galago*) (greater bushbabies)
O. *crassicaudatus* (greater or thick-tailed bushbaby)
O. *garnettii* (small-eared greater bush-baby)
*Galagoides* (= *Galago*) (dwarf bushbabies)
G. *alleni* (Allen's bushbaby)
G. *demidoff* (dwarf galago, Demidoff's galago)
G. *zanzibaricus* (Zanzibar bushbaby)
*Euoticus* (= *Galago*) (needle-clawed bushbabies)
E. *elegantulus* (western needle-clawed galago)
E. *inustus* (= *matschiei*) (eastern needle-clawed galago)

SUBORDER TARSIOIDEA[5]
Family Tarsiidae
Genus and species:
*Tarsius* (tarsiers)
T. *bancanus* (Horsfield's tarsier)
T. *dianae* (Kamarora tarsier)
T. *pumilus* (pygmy tarsier)
T. *spectrum* (spectral tarsier)
T. *syrichta* (Philippine tarsier)

SUBORDER ANTHROPOIDEA[6]
Infraorder Platyrrhini
Superfamily Ceboidea
Family Cebidae
Subfamily Cebinae
Genera and species:
*Cebus* (capuchins)
C. *albifrons* (white-fronted capuchin)
C. *apella* (black-capped capuchin)
C. *capucinus* (white-throated capuchin)
C. *olivaceus* (= *nigrivittatus*) (weeper capuchin)
*Saimiri* (squirrel monkeys)
S. *boliviensis* (Bolivian squirrel monkey)
S. *oerstedii* (red-backed squirrel monkey)
S. *sciureus* (common squirrel monkey)
S. *ustus* (bare-eared squirrel monkey)
S. *vanzolinii* (Vanzolini's squirrel monkey)
Subfamily Aotinae
Genus and species:

*Aotus* (owl monkey, night monkey, douroucouli)
primitive grey-neck group
A. *lemurinus* (lemurine night monkey)
A. *brumbacki* (Brumback's owl monkey)
A. *hershkovitzi* (Hershkovitz's owl monkey)
A. *trivirgatus* (northern night monkey)
A. *vociferans* (Spix's night monkey)
derived red-neck group
A. *miconax* (Andean night monkey)
A. *nigriceps* (black-headed night monkey)
A. *nancymaae* (Ma's night monkey)
A. *infulatus* (feline night monkey)
A. *azarai* (Azara's southern night monkey)
Subfamily Callicebinae
Genus and species:
*Callicebus* (titi monkeys)[7]
C. *brunneus* (brown titi)
C. *calligatus* (booted titi)
C. *cinerascens* (ashy titi)
C. *cupreus* (red titi)
C. *donacophilus* (Bolivian gray titi)
C. *dubius* (Herkovitz's titi)
C. *hoffmannsi* (Hoffmann's titi)
C. *modestus* (Peurasaari's titi)
C. *moloch* (dusky titi)
C. *oenanthe* (Andean titi)
C. *olallae* (Beni titi)
C. *personnatus* (masked titi)
C. *torquatus* (collared titi)
Subfamily Pitheciinae
Genera and species:
*Pithecia* (sakis)
P. *aequatorialis* (equatorial saki)
P. *albicans* (white saki)
P. *irrorata* (bald-face saki)
P. *monachus* (monk saki)
P. *pithecia* (Guianan saki monkey)
*Chiropotes* (bearded sakis)
C. *albinasus* (white-nosed saki)
C. *satanus* (black-bearded saki)
*Cacajao* (uakaris, Eisenhower monkeys)
C. *calvus* (bald uakari)
C. *melanocephalus* (black-headed uakari)
C. *rubicundus* (red uakari)
Subfamily Alouattinae
Genus and species:

---

[5] Napier and Napier (1967, *The Natural History of Primates*) and Mai (1984, *J. Hum. Evol.* **14**: 229) are followed here in placing the tarsiers in a separate suborder. Most authorities place them among the Haplorhini or, historically, among the prosimians.

[6] Many authorities have replaced this category, considered a grade, with the Suborder Strepsirhini.

[7] Titi systematics are in a state of flux. Emmons and Feer (1998, *Neotropical Rainforest Mammals*) recognize only three species, but eight subspecies within *Callicebus*. Here Groves (1993, Order Primates, In: Wilson and Reeder, *Mammal Species of the World*) and Corbet and Hill (1991, *A World List of Mammalian Species*) are incorporated to provide additional species.

Alouatta (howler monkeys)[8]
  A. belzebul (black-and-red howler)
  A. caraya (black howler)
  A. sara (Bolivian red howler)
  A. fusca (brown howler)
  A. palliata (mantled howler)
  A. coibensis (Coiba mantled howler)
  A. pigra (=villosa) (Mexican (Guatemalan) howler)
  A. seniculus (red howler)
  A. arctoidea (bear howler)
Subfamily Atelinae
  Genera and species:
    Ateles (spider monkeys)
      A. belzebuth (long-haired spider monkey)
      A. fusciceps (brown-headed spider monkey)
      A. geoffroyi (Geoffroy's spider monkey)
      A. paniscus (black spider monkey)
    Brachyteles arachinoides (woolly spider monkey)
    Lagothrix (woolly monkeys)
      L. lagotricha (common woolly monkey)
      L. flavicauda (yellow-tailed woolly monkey)
Subfamily Incertae sedis
  Antillothrix bernensis (Hispaniolan monkey)
  Paralouatta varonai (Cuban monkey)
  Xenothrix mcgregori (Jamaican monkey)
Family Callitrichidae
  Genera and species:
    Callithrix (marmosets)
      Silvery marmoset group
        C. argentata (silvery marmoset)
        C. nigriceps (black-headed silvery marmoset)
        C. leucippe (white-headed silvery marmoset)
        C. melanura (black-tailed marmoset)
        C. intermedia (tassel-ear silvery marmoset)
        C. emiliae (Snethlage's marmoset)
        C. marcai (Marca's marmoset)
      Tassel-ear marmoset group
        C. humeralifer (tassel-eared marmoset)
        C. chrysoleuca (golden-white tassel-eared marmoset)
        C. mauesi (Rio Maués marmoset)
        C. saterai
      Callithrix jacchus group
        C. jacchus (common marmoset)
        C. penicillata (white-headed marmoset)
        C. kuhli (Wied's black-tufted-ear marmoset)

        C. geoffroyi (white-faced marmoset)
        C. flaviceps (buffy-headed marmoset)
        C. aurita (buffy tufted-ear marmoset)
    Cebuella pygmaea (pygmy marmoset)
    Saguinus (tamarins)
      S. bicolor (pied tamarin)
      S. fuscicollis (saddle-back tamarin)
      S. geoffroyi (Geoffroy's tamarin)
      S. graellsi (Rio Napo tamarin)
      S. imperator (emperor tamarin)
      S. inustus (mottle-face tamarin)
      S. labiatus (white-lipped tamarin)
      S. leucopus (white-footed tamarin)
      S. midas (golden-handed tamarin)
      S. nigricollis (black-and-red tamarin)
      S. mystax (mustached tamarin)
      S. oedipus (cottontop tamarin)
      S. tripartitus (golden-mantle tamarin)
    Leontopithecus (golden tamarins)
      L. chrysomelas (golden-headed tamarin)
      L. chrysopygus (golden-rumped tamarin)
      L. rosalia (golden lion tamarin)
    Callimico goeldi (Goeldi's marmoset)[9]
Infraorder Catarrhini
  Superfamily Cercopithecoidea
    Family Cercopithecidae
      Subfamily Cercopithecinae
      Genera and species:
        Macaca (macaques)
          M. arctoides (stump-tailed macaque)
          M. assamensis (Assamese macaque)
          M. brunescens (= nigra) (Muna-Butung macaque)
          M. cyclopis (Taiwan rock macaque)
          M. fascicularis (crab-eating macaque)
          M. fuscata (Japanese macaque)
          M. hecki (= nigra) (booted macaque)
          M. maura (= nigra) (Moor macaque)
          M. mulatta (Rhesus monkey)
          M. nemestrina (pig-tailed macaque)
          M. nigra (Sulawesi black macaque)
          M. nigriscens (= nigra) (Gorontalo macaque)
          M. ochreata (= nigra) (ochre macaque)
          M. radiata (bonnet macaque)
          M. silenus (lion-tailed macaque)
          M. sinica (toque macaque)
          M. sylvanus (Barbary macaque)
          M. thibetana (= arctoides) (Thibetan macaque)
          M. tonkeana (= nigra) (Tonkenese macaque)
        Cercocebus (mangabeys)
          C. agilis (agile mangabey)
          C. atys (sooty mangabey)
          C. galeritus (Tana River mangabey)

---

[8] Most workers recognize six species. Groves (1993, op. cit.) recognizes A. coibensis and A. sara; Nowak and Paradiso (1999, Walker's Primates of the World) recognize A. arctoidea.

[9] This genus is sometimes placed into its own family, Callimiconidae.

C. torquatus (white-collared mangabey)
*Lophocebus* (= *Cercocebus* ) (black mangabeys)
L. albigena (gray-cheeked mangabey)
L. aterrimus (black mangabey)
*Papio* (baboons)[10]
P. hamadryas (Hamadryas baboon)
P. anubis (savanna baboon)
P. cynocephalus (yellow baboon)
P. papio (guinea baboon)
P. ursinus (chacma baboon)
*Mandrillus* (mandrills and drills)
M. sphinx (mandrill)
M. leucophaeus (drill)
*Theropithecus gelada* (gelada)
*Allenopithecus* (= *Cercopithecus*) *nigroviridis*
(Allen's swamp monkey)
*Miopithecus talapoin* (talapoin
monkey)
*Cercopithecus* (guenons)
*Cercopithecus diana* group
C. diana (diana monkey)
C. dryas (Dryas guenon)
C. salongo (Zaire Diana monkey)
*Cercopithecus neglectus* group
C. neglectus (De Brazza's monkey)
*Cercopithecus hamlyni* group
C. hamlyni (Hamlyn's or owl-faced
monkey)
*Cercopithecus lhoesti* group
C. lhoesti (L'Hoest's monkey)
C. preussi (Preuss's monkey)
*Cercopithecus mitis* group
C. mitis (= albogularis) (blue monkey)
C. nictitans (spot-nosed guenon)
*Cercopithecus cephus* group
C. cephus (moustached guenon)
C. ascanius (redtail, Schmidt's guenon)
C. erythrogaster (red-bellied monkey)
C. erythrotis (red-eared monkey)
C. petaurista (lesser spot-nosed
guenon)
*Cercopithecus mona* group
C. mona (Mona monkey)
C. campbelli (Campbell's guenon)
C. denti (Dent's monkey)
C. pogonias (crowned guenon)
C. wolfi (Wolf's guenon)
*Chlorocebus* (savanna guenons)
C. aethiops (vervet, grivet)
C. sabaeus (green monkey)
*Erythrocebus* (=*Cercopithecus*) *patas* (patas
monkey)
Subfamily Colobinae[11]
Genera and species:
*Colobus* (colobus monkeys)

C. angolensis (Angolan black-and-white
colobus)
C. guereza (Abyssinian black-and-white
colobus)
C. polykomos (western black-and-white
colobus)
C. satanas (black colobus)
*Piliocolobus* (red colobus monkeys)
P. badius (= rufomitratus) (red colobus)
P. kirkii (Kirk's colobus)
*Procolobus verus* (olive colobus)
*Pygathrix nemaeus* (douc langur)
*Rhinopithecus* (snub-nose monkeys)
R. avunculus (Tonkin snub-nosed
monkey)
R. brelichi (Brelich's snub-nosed
monkey)
R. bieti (black snub-nosed monkey)
R. roxellana (golden monkey)
*Nasalis larvatus* (proboscis monkey)
*Simias concolor* (pig-tailed langur)
*Presbytis* (langurs)
P. comata (= aygula, hosei, thomasi)
(Sundra leaf-monkey)
P. frontata (white-fronted leaf-monkey)
P. melalophos (=femoralis) (banded leaf-
monkey)
P. potenziani (Mentawai leaf-monkey)
P. rubicunda (maroon leaf-monkey)
*Semnopithecus entellus* (Hanuman langur)
*Trachypithecus* (brow-ridged langurs)
subgenus *Kasi*
T. (K.) johnii (Nilgiri langur)
T. (K.) vetulus (= senex) (purple-faced
leaf-monkey)
subgenus *Trachypithecus*
T. (T.) cristata (silvered leaf-monkey)
T. (T.) fransoisi (= delacouri) (Francois'
monkey)
T. (T.) geei (= pileata) (golden
leaf-monkey)
T. (T.) obscura (dusky leaf-monkey)
T. (T.) phayrei (Phayre's leaf-monkey)
T. (T.) pileatus (capped leaf-monkey)
T. (T.) auratus (Lutong leaf-monkey)
Superfamily Hominoidea
Family Hylobatidae (gibbons and siamangs)
Genera and species:
*Hylobates* (gibbons and siamangs)
subgenus *Nomascus*
H. (N.) concolor (concolor gibbon)
H. (N.) leucogenys (Chinese white-
cheeked gibbon)
H. (N.) gabriellae (golden-cheeked
gibbon)

---

[10] Groves (1993, *op. cit.*) recognizes *P. hamadryas* as a superspecies and the only member of *Papio*. *P. anubis*, *P. cynocephalus*, *P. papio*, and *P. ursinus* are included as subspecies.

[11] Groves (1989, *A Theory of Human and Primate Evolution*) considers the colobines a full family, Colobidae, but later lists them as a subfamily (1993, *op cit.*).

subgenus *Bunopithecus*
    *H. (B.)hoolock* (Hoolock gibbon)
subgenus *Hylobates*
    *H. (H.) agilis* (agile gibbon)
    *H. (H.) klossi* (Kloss's gibbon)
    *H. (H.) lar* (common or lar gibbon)
    *H. (H.) moloch* (moloch gibbon)
    *H. (H.) muelleri* (gray gibbon)
    *H. (H.) pileatus* (pileated gibbon)
subgenus *Symphalangus*
    *H. (= Symphalangus) syndactylus*
    (siamang)[12]

Family Pongidae[13]
    Genera and species:
        *Pongo pygmaeus* (orangutan)
        *Gorilla gorilla* (gorilla)
        *Pan* (chimpanzees and bonobos)
        *P. troglodytes* (chimpanzee)
        *P. paniscus* (bonobo)
Family Hominidae[14]
    Genus and species:
        *Homo sapiens* (humans)

---

[12] Some workers separate this species into the genus *Symphalangus*.
[13] Some workers include only *Pongo* in the pongids and place *Gorilla* and *Pan* in either the Panidae or the Hominidae.
[14] Some workers include *Pan* and *Gorilla*.

# Appendix 3: Table of extant primate species

| Species | Common name | No. of sspp. | Pelage | Habitat | Mass | Other information |
|---|---|---|---|---|---|---|
| *Allenopithecus nigroviridis* (Pocock, 1907) | Allen's swamp monkey | monotypic | green–gray agouti dorsum, off-white or fulvous ventrum, white lower lip | swamp forest in TRF | F 3kg<br>M 7kg | found in C and W Africa. Natural history poorly known. Syns: *Cercopithecus nigroviridis, Lasiopyga (Chlorocebus) nigriviridis* |
| *Allocebus trichotis* (Günther, 1875) | hairy-eared dwarf lemur | monotypic | pale brown–gray, white ventrum | lowland TRF | 60–100g | found in E Madagascar. Believed to be extinct until recently. Appears to hibernate from May to October. Natural history virtually unknown. Syn: *Cheirogaleus trichotis* |
| Genus *Alouatta*<br>*A. arctoidea* (Humboldt, 1805) | howler monkey (h)<br>bear h | monotypic | reddish gold, head a darker red | primary and secondary forest | F 3.6–7kg<br>M 6–11kg | found in N Colombia and Venezuela. Most workers consider this howler to be a ssp. of *A. seniculus* |
| *A. belzebul* (Linnaeus, 1866) | black-and-red or red-handed h | 5 | completely black | primary and secondary TRF | F 4.8–6kg<br>M 6.5–8kg | ranges from C to E Brazil. Syns: *A. villosus, Mycetes rufimanus, M. discolor, Simia beelzebub, S. belzebul* |
| *A. caraya* (Humboldt, 1812) | black h, brown h<br>black-and-gold h | monotypic | M completely black;<br>F golden, black face | primary TRF, gallery forest, arid grasslands | F 4–5.5kg<br>M 5–8kg | found in central southern Brazil. Syns: *A. nigra, Simia caraya, Stentor niger* |
| *A. coibensis* (Thomas, 1902) | Coiba mantled h | up to 2 | pale brown dorsum, gold fringe, light ventrum | primary TRF, mangrove | F 3–7kg<br>M 4.5–10kg | many workers consider this howler to be a ssp. of *A. palliata*. Restricted to Coiba Island and the Azuero Peninsula of Panama |
| *A. fusca* (É. Geoffroy, 1812) | brown h | 2 | M variable, brown, deep red, or black, lighter ventrum, black face; F buff to dark brown, black face | primary and secondary forest, gallery forest | F 4–5kg<br>M 5–7kg | found in SE Brazil and east central Brazil, perhaps Bolivia. Sexually dichromatic with a great deal of color variation within the sp. Syns: *A. guariba, A. clamitans* |
| *A. palliata* (Gray, 1849) | (golden) mantled h | 3–7 | black with goldish fringe | primary and secondary TRF, montane forest, dry deciduous forest | F 3–7.5kg<br>M 4.5–10kg | ranges from E Mexico to N Peru. Syns: *A. aequatorialis, A. inclamax, A. mexicana, Mycetes palliata* |
| *A. pigra* (Lawrence, 1933) | Mexican/Guatemalan h | monotypic | completely black | prefers undisturbed primary TRF | F c. 6.5kg<br>M c. 12kg | ranges from S Mexico to Guatemala and Belize. Syns: *A. palliata, Mycetes villosus* |

NA, not available; TRF, tropical rain forest; M, male; F, female; Syn(s), synonym(s); sp, species (singular); spp, species (plural); ssp., subspecies (singular); sspp., subspecies (plural).

| Species | Common name | No. of sspp. | Pelage | Habitat | Mass | Other information |
|---|---|---|---|---|---|---|
| A. sara (Elliot, 1910) | Bolivian red h | monotypic | red body, buff ventrum, deep red head, dark brown face | NA | F 4–5.5kg M 5–8kg | known from Sara Province, Santa Cruz, in SE Bolivia. Many workers consider this howler to be a ssp. of A. seniculus |
| A. seniculus (Linnaeus, 1866) | red h | 7 | deep red dorsum, limbs, and head, lighter flanks and ventrum, dark brown face | variable forests | F 4–7 kg M 6–11 kg | found in N South America. Syns: A. macconnelli, Mycetes auratus, Simia seniculus, Stentor chrysurus |
| Antillothrix bernensis Arrendondo et al., 1995 | Hispaniolan monkey | monotypic | NA | TRF? | NA | Recently extinct (2 kya). Material recovered from the Dominican Republic and Haiti |
| Genus Aotus | owl (om) or night monkey (nm); douroucouli | | | | | |
| A. azarai (Humboldt, 1812) | Azara's southern om | monotypic | grizzled gray to brown dorsum, rusty ventrum, neck, and throat, black patch on forehead, face ringed by gray or white | variable, TRF, montane forest, scrub, often near human communities | 800–1200 g | ranges from Bolivia and Paraguay into N Argentina. Syns: A. boliviensis, A. miriquouina |
| A. brumbacki Hershkovitz, 1983 | Brumback's om | monotypic | grizzled gray to brown body and neck, gray ventrum and throat, white face | primary and secondary TRF | 800–1200 g | found in E Colombia. Some workers consider this sp. to be a ssp. of A. vociferans |
| A. hershkovitzi Ramirez-Cerquera, 1983 | Hershkovitz's om | monotypic | grizzled gray to brown body and neck, gray ventrum and throat, white face | primary and secondary forest | 800–1200 g | known only from Dept. of Meta, E Colombia |
| A. infulatus (Kuhl, 1820) | feline nm | monotypic | grizzled gray to brown dorsum, fulvous ventrum, neck, and throat, black patch on forehead, face ringed by gray or white | primary and secondary TRF | 800–1200 g | found in east-central Brazil. Some workers think this sp. should be treated as a ssp. of A. azarai |
| A. lemurinus I. Geoffroy, 1843 | lemurine nm | monotypic | grizzled gray to brown body and neck, gray ventrum and throat, white face | primary and secondary TRF | 800–1200 g | found in E Panama and N Colombia. Some workers consider this sp. to be a ssp. of A. vociferans. Syns: A. hirsutus, A. zonalis |
| A. miconax Thomas, 1927 | Andean nm, Peruvian nm | monotypic | grizzled gray to brown dorsum, rusty ventrum and throat, black patch on forehead, face ringed by gray or white | primary and secondary forest; montane forest | 800–1200 g | found in north-central Peru |
| A. nancymaae Hershkovitz, 1983 | Ma's nm | monotypic | grizzled gray to brown dorsum, rusty ventrum and throat, black patch on forehead, face ringed by gray or white. | primary and secondary TRF | 800–1200 g | found in NE Peru and W Brazil. Some workers thank this monkey should be treated as a ssp. of A. miconax |

| Species | Common name | No. of subspecies | Coloration | Habitat | Weight | Distribution/comments |
| --- | --- | --- | --- | --- | --- | --- |
| *A. nigriceps* Dollman, 1909 | black-headed nm | monotypic | grizzled gray to brown dorsum, rusty ventrum and throat, black patch on forehead, face ringed by gray or white. | primary and secondary forest | 800–1200 g | found in NE Peru and NW Brazil. Syn: *A. miconax* |
| *A. trivirgatus* (Humboldt, 1812) | northern om | monotypic | grizzled gray to brown body and neck, gray throat and ventrum, face ringed by white | primary and secondary forest | 800–1200 g | found in north-central Brazil. Systematics in flux. Several new *Aotus* species may be returned to this one. Syns: *A. duruculi, A. felinus, A. humboldtii* |
| *A. vociferans* (Spix, 1823) | Spix's nm | monotypic | grizzled gray to brown body and neck, gray throat and ventrum, face ringed by white | primary and secondary forest | 800–1200 g | found in NW Amazon basin. Some workers think that *A. lemurinus* and *A. brumbacki* should be considered sspp. of *A. vociferans*. Syn: *A. microdon* |
| *Archaeoindris fontoynonti* Standing, 1908 | sloth lemur | monotypic | NA | woodland? | 160–200 kg | recently extinct (8 kya?). Known only from C Madagascar in deposits dated at 8 kya, suggesting its extinction was not due to human Intervention |
| Genus *Archaeolemur* | baboon lemurs | | | | | |
| *A. majori* Filhol, 1895 | baboon lemur | monotypic | NA | dry open grassland? | c. 17 kg | recently extinct (c. 1 kya). Recovered from deposits in Madagascar |
| *A. edwardsi* Filhol, 1895 | baboon lemur | monotypic | NA | wet open grassland? | c. 22 kg | recently extinct (c. 1 kya). Recovered from deposits in Madagascar |
| *Arctocebus calabarensis* Gray, 1863 | golden potto or angwantibo | 2 | reddish-brown to yellowish-brown, lighter ventrum | understory of TRF | c. 300 g | found in west central Africa. Syns: *A. ruficeps, Perodicticus calabarensis* |
| Genus *Ateles* | spider monkey (sm) | | | | | |
| *A. belzebul* É. Geoffroy, 1806 | long-haired sm, white-bellied sm | 4 | variable, black to pale brown dorsum and flanks, black, off-white, fulvous, or light brown ventrum, black head | TRF, semi-deciduous forest | 6–10 kg | found in northern South America, east of the Andes, in Colombia, Venezuela, and NW Brazil. Syns: *A. bartlettii, A. braccatus, A. problema, Cebus brissonii* |
| *A. fusciceps* Gray, 1866 | brown-headed or Colombian black sm | 2 | black to brown body, brown or black head, depending on ssp. | TRF, montane rain forest | c. 9 kg | ranges from Panama to Ecuador, west of the Andes. Syns: *A. dariensis, A. robustus* |
| *A. geoffroyi* Kuhl, 1820 | black-handed, Central American, or Geoffroy's sm | 9 | variable, beige to black, lighter ventrum, black paws and face | TRF, semi-deciduous forest | 7–9 kg | ranges from S Mexico through Panama. Syns: *A. pan, A. rufiventris, A. vellerosus, Brachyteles frontatus* |

NA, not available; TRF, tropical rain forest; M, male; F, female; Syn(s), synonym(s); sp., species (singular); spp., species (plural); ssp., subspecies (singular); sspp., subspecies (plural).

| Species | Common name | No. of sspp. | Pelage | Habitat | Mass | Other information |
|---|---|---|---|---|---|---|
| A. paniscus (Linnaeus, 1758) | black sm | 2–16 | completely black except for pink eye mask and muzzle. | primary TRF | 8–14 kg | geographic distribution from NE Brazil to the Guianas, Bolivia, Venezuela, and Peru. Discontinuous range with populations split by A. belzebuth. Some authorities consider this to be the only sp. if Ateles and assign up to 16 sspp. to it; other workers name up to 4 spp. from the A. paniscus ssp. |
| Genus Avahi | woolly lemur (wl) | | | | | |
| A. laniger (Gmehlin, 1788) | eastern wl | monotypic | gray-brown to rust dorsum, gray ventrum, rusty tail, brown head | TRF | F 1300 g M 1030 g | inhabits E Madagascar. Syns: Lichanotus awahi, Habrocebus lanatus, Indri longicaudatus, Semnocebus avahi |
| A. occidentalis Lorenz, 1898 | western wl | monotypic | gray body and tail, lighter head | dry deciduous forest | c. 860 g | found in discontinuous range in NW and W Madagascar. Molecular evidence suggests the validity of this former A. laniger ssp. as a separate sp. |
| Babakotia radofilai Godfrey et al., 1990 | sloth lemur | monotypic | NA | NA | 15 kg | recently extinct (c. 1 kya). Material recovered from a site in far N Madagascar |
| Brachyteles arachnoides (É. Geoffroy, 1806) | muriqui, woolly spider monkey | 2 | yellowish gray to reddish, black or pink and black mottled face | primary or secondary semi-deciduous forest | 7.5–15 kg | restricted to coastal forests of SE Brazil. Syns: Ateles arachnoides, A. eriodes, Eriodes tuberifer |
| Genus Cacajao | | | | | | |
| C. calvus (I. Geoffroy, 1847) | uakari (u) bald, white, scarlet (-faced or -fever) or red-faced u, Eisenhower monkey | up to 2 | white body, brown paws, pink naked face and bald crown | permanently or semi-permanently flooded TRF, swamp forest | 2.3–3.5 kg | found in the upper Amazon of W Brazil, E Peru, and S Colombia. Most workers follow Hershkovitz and recognize two sspp.: others regard these sspp. as separate spp. Syns: C. rubicundus, Brachyurus calvus, Ouakaria calva, Pithecia alba |
| C. melanocephalus (Humboldt, 1811) | black, black-headed u | 2 | golden dorsum, brown shoulders with gold high-lights, black ventrum and limbs, black head with short hair on crown, rusty tail | permanently or semi-permanently flooded TRF, but also found in terra firme forest | 2.4–4 kg | ranges from central Colombia and S Venezuela to NW Brazil. Syns: Brachyurus ouakary, Ouakaria spixii |
| C. rubicundus (I. Geoffroy & Deville, 1848) | red uakari | monotypic | rusty red body, pink unfurred face, adult males with bald crown | swamp forest | 2.3–3.5 kg | found in upper Amazon basin. Many workers follow Hershkovitz and regard this sp. as a ssp. of C. calvus. Syn: Brachyurus calvus |

| Species | Common name | Subspecies | Pelage/description | Habitat | Weight | Distribution and notes |
|---|---|---|---|---|---|---|
| Genus *Callicebus* | titi monkey (t) | | | | | |
| *C. brunneus* (Wagner, 1842) | brown t | monotypic | brown, reddish-brown, or grizzled gray body, black face surrounded by variable lighter fur, black crown, black tail with a light tip | swamp forest, bamboo forest, riverine forest | c. 850 g | inhabits forests of SW Brazil, SE Peru, and N Bolivia. Syns: *C. cupres, C. moloch, Callithrix brunea* |
| *C. caligatus* (Wagner, 1842) | booted or chest-nut bellied t | monotypic | grizzled gray dorsum, rusty ventrum, throat, and forelimbs, dark black forehead, black face, gray tail grading into white | riverine TRF | c. 800 g | found in upper Amazon of Brazil. Sympatric with *C. cupres* in NW part of range. Syn: *C. moloch* |
| *C. cinerascens* (Spix, 1823) | ashy titi | monotypic | gray to black agouti body with tawny agouti middle back, black face | riverine TRF | c. 1 kg | found in SE Brazilian Amazon basin. Syns: *C. moloch, Callithrix cinerascens* |
| *C. cupreus* (Spix, 1823) | red t, coppery t | 0–3 | brown agouti dorsum, crown and tail, red ventrum, limbs, and throat, white brow line above black line, pale red eye-ring, gray muzzle | TRF | c. 1 kg | found in W Amazon basin of Brazil. Sympatric with *C. caligatus* in eastern portion of range. Syns: *C. moloch, C. dubius, Callithrix cuprea, C. discolor* |
| *C. donacophilus* (d'Orbigny, 1836) | Bolivian gray t, white-eared t | 0–2 | gray agouti to buffy orange agouti dorsum and head, orange ventrum white ear tuffs, eye mask and circum-muzzle fur, pinkish muzzle, tail buffy to black | TRF | 800–1000 g | occupies forests of N Bolivia and N Paraguay. Syns: *C. moloch, Callithrix donacophilus* |
| *C. dubius* Hershkovitz, 1988 | Hershkovitz's t | monotypic | gray rufous body and tail, black crown, white brow line above black line | primary lowland TRF | NA | found in central Brazil. Not widely recognized; may be a hybrid of *C. cupreus* and *C. caligatus*. Syn: *C. cupreus.* |
| *C. hoffmannsi* Thomas, 1908 | Hoffmann's t | monotypic | medium to dark brown agouti body, bright orange ventrum and throat, black face, black agouti tail with buffy tip | riverine TRF, swamp forest | c. 1 kg | found in central Brazil. Not widely recognized. Syn: *C. moloch* |
| *C. modestus* Lönnberg, 1939 | Rio Beni or Peurasaari's t | monotypic | grizzled brown body and head, reddish brown forehead and crown, black brow, white ear tuffs, black agouti tail | riverine TRF | NA | occupies forests of NW Bolivia. Not widely recognized; may be hybrid of *C. donacophilus* and *C. brunneus.* Poorly known. |

NA, not available; TRF, tropical rain forest; M, male; F, female; Syn(s), synonym(s) sp. species (singular); spp. species (plural); ssp., subspecies (singular); sspp., subspecies (plural).

| Species | Common name | No. of sspp. | Pelage | Habitat | Mass | Other information |
|---|---|---|---|---|---|---|
| *C. moloch* Hoffmannsegg, 1807 | dusky, red-bellied t | 7–10 | gray agouti to reddish-brown body, light gray to darker gray tail, black paws and forehead | riverine TRF | 928–1400 g | found in central Brazil. Systematics in flux; 7–10 sspp. described, but many of these have been reconsidered and placed into separate spp. However, some authorities think that molecular evidence does not show enough genetic difference between populations to warrant separate spp. |
| *C. oenanthe* Thomas, 1924 | Andean, vine, vine-leaf or Rio Mayo t | monotypic | agouti body and tail, orange ventrum and throat, off white circumfacial line | montane forests | NA | poorly known titi from the Rio Maya Valley of N Peru |
| *C. olallae* Lönnberg, 1939 | Beni, Lönnberg's dusky, or Olalla brother's t | monotypic | reddish-orange body, black face forehead, cheeks and throat, white ear tufts, gray agouti tail | TRF | NA | known from one location in NW Bolivia. Poorly known. Syn: *C. brunneus* |
| *C. personnatus* (É. Geoffroy, 1812) | masked or Atlantic t | 4 | variable, light brown to fulvous to gray body and tail, black paws and face with lighter fur on crown and surrounding face | littoral forest | 1–1.6 kg | found in E Brazil. Poorly known. Syns: *C. cupreus, Callithrix nigrifrons, C. gigot, Jacchus grandis, Simia personata* |
| *C. torquatus* (Hoffmannsegg, 1807) | collared, widow or yellow-handed t | 3–6 | reddish-brown to dark brown body, head, and tail, blue face framed by black fur, white band under throat from ear to ear, buffy forepaws | primary TRF | 800–1600 g | distributed from S Columbia and Venezuela into the Amazon basin of Brazil and Peru. Largest sp. of *Callicebus*. Sympatric with *C. moloch*, but the 2 spp. partition the resources with slightly different dietary choices and *C. torquatus* occupies the upper stories of the canopy. Syns: *C. lucifer, Callithrix torquata, Saguinus vidua, Simia lugens* |
| *Callimico goeldi* (Thomas, 1904) | Goeldi's marmoset | monotypic | completely black | secondary TRF | 393–505 g | ranges through the upper Amazon of S Colombia, Ecuador, Brazil, Peru and NW Bolivia. Some workers place this sp. in a monotypic family, Callimiconidae. Syns: *C. snethlageri, Callithrix goeldi, Midas goeldi (= weddelli)* |
| **Genus *Callithrix*** | | | | | | |
| *C. argentata* (Linnaeus, 1766) | marmoset (m) silvery, bare-eared, or black-tailed m | 5–6 | variable; five different color forms have been described. Body ranging from silvery white to black, face ranges from white to pink to brown | TRF, dry deciduous forest | c. 420 g | found in E. Brazil. Systematics in flux; some workers assign up to 5 sspp. to *C. argentata*, others separate them into full spp. Syn: *Simia argentata* |

| Species | Common name | Litter/social | Pelage | Habitat | Weight | Distribution and comments |
|---|---|---|---|---|---|---|
| *C. aurita* (É. Geoffroy, 1812) | buffy tufted-ear m | monotypic | black trunk with rusty speckling, rusty crown and ear tufts, grizzled white and rusty face | TRF | 400–450 g | found in E. Brazil. Some workers consider this marmoset to be a ssp. of *C. jacchus*. Syns: *Jacchus aurita, Hapale coelestis, H. petronius, H. caelestis* |
| *C. chrysoleuca* Wagner, 1842 | golden-white tassel-eared m | monotypic | golden-white body and head, white ear tufts, limbs deeper gold, banded tail | secondary TRF | 400–500 g | found in central Brazil. Considered by some to be a ssp. of *C. humeralifera* |
| *C. emiliae* (Thomas, 1920) | Snethlage's m, Emilia's m | monotypic | gray-brown back, lighter ventrum, forequarters lighter, black crown, pink face | TRF | c. 300 g | found in central Amazon basin of Brazil. sympatric with *C. argentata*, of which it is considered a ssp. by some authorities |
| *C. flaviceps* (Thomas, 1903) | buffy-headed, white-eared, black-plumed, or common m | monotypic | buffy and black dorsum and tail, rust ventrum, ocherous head and ear tufts, brown face, banded tail | TRF, semi-deciduous forest | c. 400 g | found in E Brazil. Considered by some workers to be a ssp. of *C. jacchus* |
| *C. geoffroyi* (Humboldt, 1812) | white-faced m | monotypic | variegated black, gray, and buffy body, black head, white blaze on medial forehead, white ear tufts, banded gray and white tail | secondary forest | c. 360 g | inhabits coastal forests of E Brazil. considered by some workers to be a ssp. of *C. jacchus*. Syns: *Hapale melanotis, Jacchus leucocephalus, J. maximiliani, Simia albifrons, S. geoffroyi* |
| *C. humeralifer* (É. Geoffroy, 1812) | tassel-eared, white-shouldered, or golden m, santarem | 2–3 | golden white body, silver gray forequarters, variegated black and yellow hindquarters, black head, gray face, white ear tufts, banded tail | secondary forest | 300–400 g | found in central Brazil. Syns: *C. chrysoleucos, Hapale chrysoleucos, H. humeralifer, Jacchus humeralifer, Mico sericeus, M. leucippe, Micoella chrysoleucos* |
| *C. jacchus* (Linnaeus, 1758) | common m | up to 6 | agouti black, gray, and buffy body, dark brown head, white face, blaze on medial forehead, ear tufts, banded gray and white tail | primary TRF, scrub, swamp forest, wooded savanna, disturbed forest | 210–323 g | distributed in SE Brazil. Systematics in flux; six sspp. are recognized by some authorities, while recent taxonomic revision have made these sspp. into separate spp. Syns: *Hapale jacchus, Jacchus vulgaris, Simia geoffroyi, S. jacchus* |
| *C. kuhli* (Wied-Neuwwied, 1826) | Wied's black-tufted-eared m | monotypic | agouti black, gray, and buffy body, buffy head, white face, blaze on medial forehead, black ear tufts, banded gray and white tail | secondary forest, semi-deciduous forest | c. 375 g | occupies coastal forests of SE Brazil. Considered by some workers to be a ssp. of *C. jacchus*. Syn: *Hapale penicillata* |

NA, not available; TRF, tropical rain forest; M, male; F, female; Syn(s), synonym(s); sp., species (singular); spp., species (plural); ssp., subspecies (singular); sspp., subspecies (plural).

| Species | Common name | No. of sspp. | Pelage | Habitat | Mass | Other information |
|---|---|---|---|---|---|---|
| *C. leucippe* (Thomas, 1922) | white-headed silvery or white m | monotypic | silvery white, pink face, no ear tufts | TRF | c. 350 g | inhabits rain forest of central Brazil. Considered by some workers to be a ssp. of *C. argentata*. Syn: *Mico leucippe* |
| *C. marcai* Alperin, 1993 | Marca's m | monotypic | brindled ochre and gray dorsum with chestnut mantle, lighter limbs, ocher ventrum, dark chestnut head, black face, no ear tufts | TRF | NA | known only from type locality in central Brazil. Considered by some workers to be a ssp. of *C. argentata* |
| *C. mauesi* Mittermeier et al., 1992 | Rio Maues or Maues m | monotypic | banded brown to black dorsum, fulvous ventrum, silvery haunch stripe, black and brown banded tail, face framed by brown, erect brown–black ear tufts | primary TRF | 300–400 g | known only from a few specimens collected in dense tropical rain forest in the state of Amazonas, central Brazil. Considered by some workers to be a ssp. of *C. humeralifer* |
| *C. melanura* (É. Geoffroy, 1812) | black-tailed m | monotypic | dark brown with white haunch stripe. | TRF | c. 350 g | occupies forests in SW Brazil, E Bolivia, and NE Paraguay. Some workers consider this marmoset to be a ssp. of *C. argentata* |
| *C. nigriceps* Ferrari & Lopes, 1992 | black-headed silvery or black-headed m | monotypic | brown-gray dorsum, buff to fulvous hindquarters and ventrum, black crown and face | TRF | c. 400 g | inhabits forests in west-central Brazil. Some workers consider this marmoset to be a ssp. of *C. argentata* |
| *C. penicillata* (É. Geoffroy, 1812) | white-headed, black tufted-ear, or black-plumed m | monotypic | variegated black, gray, and buffy body, banded dark brown head, white face and medial forehead spot, black ear tufts, brown face, banded gray and white tail | secondary TRF | 300–350 g | found in SE Brazil. Some workers consider this sp. to be a ssp. of *C. jacchus*. Syns: *Hapale melanotis, H. trigonifer, Jacchus penicillatus* |
| *Cebuella pygmaea* (Spix, 1823) | pygmy marmoset | 2 | tawny agouti body, tawny golden-gray head, banded tail | secondary TRF | 70–141 g | ranges from S Colombia through the Amazonian regions of Ecuador, Peru, W Brazil and Bolivia. Some workers think, based on DNA evidence, that pygmy marmosets should be placed in the genus *Callithrix* |

| Taxon | Common name(s) | Subspp. | Description | Habitat | Weight | Distribution / notes |
|---|---|---|---|---|---|---|
| **Genus *Cebus*** <br> *C. albifrons* (Humboldt, 1812) | capuchins (c) white-fronted (or -throated), brown pale-fronted c, cinnamon ringtail | 11–13 | variable, gray-brown, buffy, or rufous dorsum, buff or rust ventrum, dark brown crown (cap) over white forehead | primary deciduous forest, mangrove | F c. 1.8 kg <br> M c. 2.5 kg | discontinuous range from N Colombia and Venezuela, jumping to W Ecuador, where the range again breaks with northern Peru and the Amazonian regions of Colombia, Ecuador, Peru, Brazil, and Venezuela. Live in overlapping home ranges. Sympatric with *C. nigrivittatus* in part of Venezuelan Amazon range. Syns: *C. unicolor, C. aequatorialis, Simia albifrons, S. hypoleuca* |
| *C. apella* (Linnaeus, 1858) | black-capped, brown, tufted, hooded or large-headed c, ringtail monkey | 10–11 | variable, buffy to dark brown trunk, shoulder lighter than trunk, ventrum often rufous, black crown tufts, face dark brown, mottled brown, or pink, dark brown or black tail | primary and secondary TRF | F c. 1.7 kg <br> M c. 2.4 kg | distributed in variable forests of central South America. Diet differs from other members of *Cebus* and includes seeds, palm nuts, and insects, as well as fruit. Sympatric with *C. albifrons* and *C. nigrivittatus* in some parts of its range that is facilitated by resource partitioning. Syns: *C. baratus, C. griseus, Simia apella, S. fatuellus* |
| *C. capuchinus* (Linnaeus, 1858) | white-throated, white-faced, white-headed or sanjou c | 4–5 | black dorsum and tail, white chest, shoulders, throat and face, black crown | primary and secondary TRF | F c. 2.5 kg <br> M c. 3.5 kg | ranges from Honduras and W of the Andes in Colombia and Ecuador. Unlike other capuchins, this sp. may defend home ranges |
| *C. olivaceus* Schomburgk, 1848 | weeper or wedge-capped c | 5 | tawny brown body and tail, buffy shoulders and chest, buffy head, brown crown | TRF | F c. 2.2 kg <br> M c. 2.9 kg | distributed in rainforests of N and NE South America. Sympatric with *C. albifrons* in part of its Venezuelan range. Syn: *C. apella, C. capuchinus, C. nigrivittatus* |
| **Genus *Cercocebus*** <br> *C. agilis* (Milne-Edwards, 1886) | mangabey (m) agile m | 2 | olivaceous dorsum and head, fulvous chest, white eyelids, olive muzzle | TRF | F c. 6 kg <br> M c. 11 kg | found in W equatorial Africa. Included in *C. galeritus* by some workers |
| *C. atys* (Audebert, 1797) | sooty m | monotypic | brown-grey body with white ventrum, pink or gray face | primary and secondary TRF, swamp, mangrove, and gallery forest | F c. 6 kg <br> M c. 11 kg | found in W. equatorial Africa. Some workers consider this mangabey to be a ssp. of *C. torquatus*. Syn: *Simia atys* |
| *C. galeritus* Peters, 1879 | Tana River m | monotypic | brindled gray dorsum, white to buff ventrum, light gray crown, black face | diverse forest and wooded habitat | F c. 5 kg <br> M c. 10 kg | found only in 2000 ha along Tana R of Eastern Kenya |

NA, not available; TRF, tropical rain forest; M, male; F, female; Syn(s), synonym(s); sp., species (singular); spp., species (plural); ssp., subspecies (singular); sspp., subspecies (plural).

| Species | Common name | No. of sspp. | Pelage | Habitat | Mass | Other information |
|---|---|---|---|---|---|---|
| C. torquatus (Kerr, 1792) | white-collared, cherry-crowned, or red-capped m | 2 | dark brown to black dorsum, white ventrum and collar, rusty crown, black face with white sides, white eyelids | dry, swamp, and mangrove forest | F c. 6 kg<br>M c. 11 kg | found in far W equatorial Africa. Syns: C. aethiopicus, C. collaris, Simia aethiops |
| Genus Cercopithecus<br>C. ascanius (Audebert, 1799) | guenon (gn)<br>redtail, Schmidt's, coppertail, or black-cheeked white-nosed monkey | up to 5 | agouti brown with whitish ventrum, black crown, blue eye mask, white cheeks, lower end of tail is rusty | primary and secondary TRF, woodland, swamp, gallery, and montane forest | F c. 3 kg<br>M c. 3.5 kg | found in Congo basin. Syns: C. melanogenys, C. picturatus, Simia ascanius |
| C. campbelli Waterhouse, 1838 | Campbell's or Lowe's gn | 2 | yellow-gray dorsum, gray rump, white ventrum, speckled tawny crown, white or tawny brow line, black eye mask, speckled tawny cheeks | primary and secondary TRF, gallery forest | F c. 3 kg<br>M c. 5 kg | found in W. equatorial Africa. Natural history poorly known. Syns: C. burnetti, C. mona, C. monella, C. temminckii |
| C. cephus (Linnaeus, 1758) | mustached gn | 0–2 | rufous body and crown, gray ventrum, blue eye mask, white mustache bar, rusty tail | primary and secondary TRF, gallery forest | F c. 3 kg<br>M c. 4 kg | inhabits forests of W central Africa. Found in association with C. pogonias and C. nictitans. Syns: C. buccalis, C. pulcher, C. inobservatus, Simia cephus |
| C. denti (Thomas, 1907) | Dent's mona or monkey | monotypic | brown dorsum, gray–black flanks and legs, white ventrum, agouti yellow and black head, gray eye mask, tail becomes rusty distally | TRF | F c. 3 kg<br>M c. 5 kg | inhabits forests of the Congo basin. Syn: C. mona. Some consider this guenon to be a population of C. mona rather than a separate sp. |
| C. diana (Linnaeus, 1758) | diana monkey, roloway | 2 | agouti gray trunk with rufous back, white to buffy haunch stripe, rusty rump, agouti gray head, black face, white beard and chest | primary and secondary TRF, gallery forest, semi-deciduous forest | F c. 4 kg<br>M c. 5 kg | found in far W equatorial Africa. Syn: C. roloway, C. dryas, Simia diana, S. faunus, S. rolloway |
| C. dryas Schwarz, 1932 | Dryas or salongo gn | monotypic | agouti brown dorsum, white ventrum, black limbs, black face encircled by white, white ear tufts. Striking color differences between juveniles and adults | TRF | F c. 2 kg<br>M c. 3 kg | found in central Zaire. Syns: C. diana, C. salongo. Some workers believe this guenon belongs in the genus Chlorocebus |

| Species | Common name | Number of offspring | Coloration | Habitat | Weight | Distribution and notes |
|---|---|---|---|---|---|---|
| *C. erythrogaster* Gray, 1866 | red-bellied monkey, Jentink's or white-throated gn | 0–2 | variable, agouti brown dorsum and legs, ventrum gray or red, black crown with agouti buff and black forehead triangle, white beard, white or rusty chest and throat | primary and secondary TRF, littoral forest, semideciduous forest | F c. 2.5 kg M c. 4 kg | inhabits variable forests of SW Nigeria. Syns: *C. signatus, Lasiopyga erythrogaster* |
| *C. erythrotis* Waterhouse, 1838 | red-eared (nose-spotted) monkey, russet-eared gn | up to 3 | gray-brown agouti dorsum, ventrum gray, rusty tail, agouti buff and black crown, pinkish red eye mask, muzzle, and ears, white and buff cheeks, white beard, tail becomes red distally | prefers primary and older secondary TRF | F c. 3 kg M c. 3.5 kg | discontinuous range in S Nigeria and W Cameroon. Syns: *C. cephus, C. sclateri, Lasiopyga erythrotis* |
| *C. hamlyni* Pocock, 1907 | Hamlyn's monkey, owl-faced monkey | monotypic | dark olive-gray, limbs, ventrum, and tail black, yellow ticking on a black head, yellow and white brow line, white nose stripe | variable forest above 1000 m | F c. 3 kg M c. 5.5 kg | found in the eastern Congo basin. Natural history poorly known, but appears to prefer lower levels of forest. Syns: *C. leucampyx, Rhinostigma hamlyni* |
| *C. lhoesti* Sclater, 1839 | L'Hoest's monkey, mountain monkey or gn | 2 | dark gray with brindled yellow flecks, rust saddle, light eye mask, white throat ruff | wet primary montane forest | F c. 3.5 kg M c. 6 kg | inhabits wet high primary forest of the E Congo basin. Some workers separate one of the sspp. as *C. preussi*. Syns: *C. thomasi, Lasiopyga insolita, L. thomasi* |
| *C. mitis* Wolf, 1822 | blue, Sykes's, mitis, diademed, or white-throated monkey | 20–25 | extremely variable depending on population, but generally olivaceous or speckled blue-gray, black limbs | various types of forest including TRF, semideciduous, montane, bamboo forest, and scrub | F c. 4 kg M c. 8 kg | discontinuous distribution throughout W and E Africa as far N as Ethiopia and S into the Republic of South Africa. Syns: *C. albogularis, C. diadematus, Lasiopyga leucampyx, Simia leucampyx* |
| *C. mona* (Schreiber, 1774) | Mona monkey | 7–11 | brown dorsum, gray-black flanks and legs, white ventrum, agouti yellow and black head, gray eye mask | variable habitats including primary and secondary TRF, riverine forest, mangrove | F c. 3 kg M c. 5 kg | ranges from W equatorial Africa into the Congo basin. Some workers remove some of the ssp. and place them into separate spp. within the *C. mona* group. Syns: *C. campbelli, C. denti, C. pogonias, C. wolfi, Lasiopyga mona, Simia mona, S. monacha* |

NA, not available; TRF, tropical rain forest; M, male; F, female; Syn(s), synonym(s); sp., species (singular); spp., species (plural); ssp., subspecies (singular); sspp., subspecies (plural).

| Species | Common name | No. of sspp. | Pelage | Habitat | Mass | Other information |
|---|---|---|---|---|---|---|
| C. neglectus Schlegel, 1876 | De Brazza's or neglectus monkey, Schlegel's gn | monotypic | gray agouti body with rufous dorsum, dark limbs, white haunch stripe, black crown, ocherous forehead, black eye mask, white eyelids, muzzle, and beard. Striking color differences between juveniles and adults | prefers flooded forest and swamp | F c. 4 kg<br>M c. 7 kg | ranges from W equatorial Africa to the Congo basin. Syns: C. brazzae, C. brazziformis, C. ezrae, C. leucampyx, Lasiopyga brazzae |
| C. nictitans (Linnaeus, 1758) | spot-nosed, white-nosed, or putty-nosed gn, Hocheur monkey | 3 | brindled olive-gray with yellow tips; white ventrum, large oval white nose spot | primary TRF, old secondary forest | F c. 4 kg<br>M c. 7 kg | discontinuous range in west and central Africa. Found in association with C. cephus and C. pogonias. Syns: C. schmidti, C. signatus, Lasiopyga nictitans, Simia nictitans |
| C. petaurista (Schreiber, 1774) | lesser spot-nosed gn | 2 | olivaceous dorsum and crown, white ventrum and throat, black face, large oval white nose spot | variable forest types, including swamp and shrub forest | F c. 3 kg<br>M c. 4 kg | found in far W equatorial Africa. Found in association with C. campbelli, C. diana, and Procolobus verus. Syns: C. buttikoferri, C. fantiensis, Simia albinasus, S. petairosta |
| C. pogonias Bennett, 1833 | crowned gn, golden bellied monkey, crested mona | 3–4 | rusty agouti dorsum and flanks, white or buff ventrum and throat, speckled gray forelimbs, black paws, gray agouti crown with black stripes on either side, white forehead and a black medial stripe, blue eye mask, pink muzzle, white ear tufts | prefers primary TRF | F c. 3 kg<br>M c. 4 kg | found in W equatorial Africa. Found in association with C. nictitans and C. cephus. Some workers include this sp. as a ssp. of C. mona. Other syns: C. nigripes, Lasiopyga pogonias |
| C. preussi Matschie, 1898 | Preuss's or Cross' monkey | 2 | gray agouti body, red saddle, dark gray head, white throat and chest | primary montane forest | F c. 3.5 kg<br>M c. 6 kg | found in montane forest of W Cameroon. Many workers consider this guenon to be a ssp. of C. l'hoesti. Other syns: C. crossi, Lasiopyga preussi |
| C. salongo Thys van den Audenaerde, 1977 | Zaire Diana monkey, Salongo gn | monotypic | agouti brown dorsum, white ventrum, black limbs, black face encircled by white, white ear tufts | TRF | NA | found in central Zaire. Some workers think this sp. is an age variant of C. dryas. Natural history poorly known |
| C. wolfi Meyer, 1891 | Wolf's gn or mona | up to 3 | dark gray dorsum with red saddle, white or buff ventrum, black forelimbs, rufous hindlimbs, dark gray crown, pale brow band, dark gray eye mask, buff cheeks, pink muzzle | primary and secondary TRF, swamp | F c. 3 kg<br>M c. 4 kg | found in the Congo basin. Found in association with Lophocebus aterrimus, C. ascanius, Colobus angolensis, and Allenopithecus nigroviridis. Often considered a ssp. of C. mona. Syn: Lasiopyga wolfi |

| Genus / species | Common name | Subspecies | Coloration | Habitat | Body mass | Distribution and notes |
|---|---|---|---|---|---|---|
| *Genus Cheirogaleus* *C. major* É. Geoffroy, 1812 | dwarf lemur (dl) greater or eastern dl | up to 2 | rufous or brownish gray with white ventrum | evergreen rain forest | 350–600 g | found in E Madagascar with one small pocket in west-central Madagascar. Syns: *C. milli, C. typicus, Lemur commersonii, Mioxicebus griseus, Myspithecus typus* |
| *C. medius* É. Geoffroy, 1812 | fat-tailed or western dl | 0–2 | rufous or gray with white ventrum | dry deciduous forest | 140–230 g | found in W and S Madagascar. Body mass varies seasonally. Syns: *C. minor, C. samati, Altililemur medius, Microcebus samati, Opolemur samati* |
| *Genus Chiropotes* *C. albinasus* (I. Geoffroy & Deville, 1948) | bearded saki white-nosed bearded saki | monotypic | completely black with pink nose and upper lip | primary TRF | 2.2–3.6 kg | found in central Brazil south of the Amazon River. Occasionally found in association with *C. apella*. Syn: *Pithecia albinasa* |
| *C. satanas* (Hoffmannsegg, 1807) | black or brown bearded saki, black or red-backed saki, saki capuchin, or jacketed monkey | 2 | black with an ocherous to brown dorsum | TRF | 2–4 kg | ranges from S Venezuela into the Guianas and N Brazil. Some individuals with white eye sclera visible. Syns: *C. ater, C. chiropotes, Cebus satanas, Pithecia chiropotes, P. satanas, Simia satanas* |
| *Genus Chlorocebus* *C. aethiops* (Linnaeus, 1758) | savanna guenons vervet, grivet | up to 21 | pale olivaceous agouti dorsum, limbs, and crown, white ventrum, black face and paws, white brow line and cheeks | primarily savanna woodland | F c. 3 kg M c. 4 kg | ranges from W to E and S Africa; 21 ssp. have been described, but most workers believe there are at least four separate spp. represented in the sspp. Syns: *C. aethiops, C. griseus, C. matschie, Simia aethiops* |
| *C. sabaeus* (Linnaeus, 1758) | green monkey, savanna monkey | monotypic | grizzled olivaceous and golden dorsum, limbs, and tail, pale paws, white ventrum, speckled olivaceous crown, black face, buff brow line and cheeks. | savanna woodland | F c. 3 kg M c. 4 kg | found on the savannas of W Africa; most workers include this monkey as a ssp. of *C. aethiops*. Syns: *C. callithrichus, C. werneri, Simia sabaea* |
| *Genus Colobus* *C. angolensis* Sclater, 1860 | colobus (co) Angolan black-and-white co | up to 8 | black except for white circumfacial hair, ear tufts and long shoulder epaulettes | lowland and montane rain forest, patchy dry forest | c. 10 kg | major range in the Congo basin, then discontinuous pockets to the Tanzanian coast. Unlike other colobines, this species rarely utilizes suspensory locomotion. Syns: *C. abyssinicus, C. palliatus, Lemur abyssinicus* |

NA, not available; TRF, tropical rain forest; M, male; F, female; Syn(s), synonym(s); sp, species (singular); spp., species (plural); ssp, subspecies (singular); sspp, subspecies (plural).

| Species | Common name | No. of sspp. | Pelage | Habitat | Mass | Other information |
|---|---|---|---|---|---|---|
| C. guereza Ruppel, 1835 | Abyssinian black-and-white co, mantled guereza | 8 | black except for white circumfacial hair, cheeks, mantle, and often tail | primary TRF, but does occupy some other types of forest | 13–25 kg | ranges from W to E Africa with isolates separated from the metapopulation. Can brachiate, but rarely does so. One-male units the norm, with territories delineated by sound. Syns: C. abyssinicus, C. gallarum, Guereza occidentalis, Lemur abyssinicus |
| C. polykomos (Zimmermann, 1780) | western black-and-white, king, black, or pied co, full-bottom monkey | 3 or more | black except grayish white circumfacial hair, mantle, and tail | variable, different types of closed forest including primary and secondary TRF, riparian forest, open woodland | 13–23 kg | found in far W equatorial Africa. Can brachiate but rarely does so. Syns: C. vellerosus, C. satanas, Cebus polykomos, Semnopithecus villerosus, Simia polycomos, S. regalis |
| C. satanas Waterhouse, 1838 | black colobus | monotypic | completely black | primary and secondary TRF | c. 10 kg | located in W equatorial Africa. Consumes seeds with high levels of allo-chemicals: able to detoxify them. Molar structure (flat and larger) differs from other spp., apparently an adaptation to granivory. Live in mixed-sex groups |
| Daubentonia madagas-carensis (Gmelin, 1788) | aye-aye | monotypic | black body brindled with gray and white, lighter face (pink in some places) fine black eye rings, rodent-like tail | variable, including primary and secondary TRF, spiny forest, dry forest | 2.5–3.0 kg | near extinction, formerly found in N and E Madagascar. Syn: Tarsius daubentonii |
| Erythrocebus patas (Schreiber, 1775) | patas, red, red hussar, or military monkey | 4 | rufous dorsum and flanks, grayish-white ventrum, limbs, and muzzle, fulvous crown, black brow line | savanna, acacia woodland | F c. 6 kg M c. 12 kg | broad distribution across sub-Saharan equatorial Africa. Syns: Cercopithecus patas, Simia patas, S. ruber, S. rufra |
| Genus Eulemur E. coronatus (Gray, 1842) | true lemur (l) crowned l | monotypic | M dark gray-brown. F light gray. Both sexes have orange V on the crown | dry deciduous forest | c. 2 kg | found in N tip of Madagascar. Sympatric with E. fulvus, but avoids competition by partitioning the environment. Syns: Lemur coronatus, L. chrysampyx |
| E. fulvus (É. Geoffroy, 1796) | brown l | 7 | variable gray to rufous body and tail, black face and crown | prefers primary TRF | 2–3 kg | discontinuous distribution along the W and E coasts of Madagascar. the different ssp. possess different chromosome numbers, but appear to be capable of interbreeding and producing viable and fertile offspring. Syns: L. fulvus, Prosimia macromongoz |
| E. macaco (Linnaeus, 1766) | black l | 2 | M completely black. F rusty with black face | TRF | 2–3 kg | found in NW Madagascar and its coastal islands. Sympatric with E. fulvus over some parts of its range. Syns: L. macaco, Prosimia flavifrons |

| Species | Common name | Subspecies | Description | Habitat | Weight | Distribution / Notes |
|---|---|---|---|---|---|---|
| *E. mongoz* (Linnaeus, 1766) | mongoose l | monotypic | M gray-brown body, gray face, white muzzle, rusty beard. F gray to brown body, black face, gray-white muzzle, white beard | humid forest | c. 2 kg | found in dry forest of Madagascar and humid forest on Moheli and Anjouan, where it they appears they were introduced by humans. Sympatric with *E. fulvus* over some of its range. Social groups vary between habitats, but include small monogamous families. Syns: *L. mongoz, Prosimia micromongoz, P. ocularis* |
| *E. rubriventer* (I. Geoffroy, 1850) | red-bellied or red-fronted l | monotypic | M dark chestnut, black face with white spot below eyes. F dark chestnut dorsum and flanks, buff ventrum | primary TRF | 2–3 kg | found along a narrow strip of rain forest about 50 km inland running S to N in E Madagascar. Natural history poorly known. Syns: *E. flaviventer, L. rufiventer, Prosimia rufipes* |
| **Genus *Euoticus*** | | | | | | |
| *E. elegantulus* (Le Conte, 1857) | needle-clawed bushbaby/galago (ncb), western ncb, elegant galago | 2 | cinnamon except for gray-white ventrum and gray face | primary and secondary forest | c. 250 g | distributed in W equatorial Africa. Syns: *Galago elegantulus, Microcebus elegantulus, Otolicnus apicalis* |
| *E. inustus* Schwarz, 1930 | eastern or Matschie's ncb, spectacled galago | monotypic | dark brown, black eye rings, white vertical nose stripe | primary and secondary forest | c. 200 g | found in dense forest of NE Zaire and SW Uganda. Taxonomic status in dispute, many workers include this sp. with *Galago*. Syns: *E. matschiei, Galago matschiei, G. senegalensis* |
| **Genus *Galago*** | | | | | | |
| *G. gallarum* Thomas, 1901 | bushbaby/galago (bb) Somali bb | monotypic | brownish buff dorsum and flanks, whitish ventrum, buff tone to limbs, browneye-rings that are incomplete laterally white nose stripe, muzzle, and throat | savanna, open woodland | c. 200 g | found in Kenya and Somalia. Sympatric with *G. senegalensis* over part of range. Syn: *G. senegalensis* |
| *G. moholi* A. Smith, 1836 | South African or Southern lesser bb | monotypic | gray-brown with white ventrum, buff on lower legs, dark brown eye-rings and eye spots above eye | thorn bush | 200–300 g | ranges from South Africa into SW Tanzania and E Zaire. Many workers consider this sp. to be a ssp. of *G. senegalensis* |
| *G. senegalensis* É. Geoffroy, 1796 | Senegal or lesser bb | at least 9 | gray-brown to brown dorsum, buff flanks, whitish gray ventrum, white nose stripe, buffy and white throat and chest | savanna woodland | 200–300 g | widespread distribution throughout sub-Saharan Africa. Insectivorous, but switches to gummivory during the dry season. Twin births the norm. Syns: *G. braccatus, G. murinus, Lemur galago, Otolicnus teng* |

NA, not available; TRF, tropical rain forest; M, male; F, female; Syn(s), synonym(s); sp., species (singular); spp., species (plural); ssp., subspecies (singular); sspp., subspecies (plural).

| Species | Common name | No. of sspp. | Pelage | Habitat | Mass | Other information |
|---|---|---|---|---|---|---|
| **Genus *Galagoides*** *G. alleni* Waterhouse, 1837 | bushbaby (bb)/galago Allen's or black-tailed bb | monotypic | grey to grey-red, whitish gray ventrum | primary TRF | 250–300 g | found in W equatorial Africa. Diet variable between habitats and seasons, but includes frugivory and insectivory; gummivory is also important. Syns: *Galago alleni*, *G. batesi*, *G. cameronensis*, *G. gabonensis* |
| *G. demidoff* (Fischer, 1806) | dwarf, Demidoff's pygmy, or Thomas's bb | 7 | reddish gray dorsum and flanks, fulvous ventrum, brown eye-rings, truncated buffy vertical nose stripe | prefers dense forest | 70–80 g | found in a broad band of rain forest from Senegal to Zambia. Often known as *G. demidovii*, but *G. demidoff* has precedence. Syns: *Galago murinus*, *G. demidovii*, *G. thomasi*, *Otolicnus peli* |
| *G. zanzibaricus* (Matschie, 1893) | Zanzibar bb | 2–3 | ticked buffy gray, lighter gray ventrum, pale vertical nose stripe, buffy cheeks and throat | secondary rain forest dry littoral & montane forest | c. 150 g | distribution along E African coast from S Kenya through Mozambique and on Zanzibar. Some workers consider this bushbaby to be a ssp. of *Galago senegalensis*. Syn: *Galago zanzibaricus* |
| *Gorilla gorilla* (Savage & Wyman, 1847) | gorilla | 3 | completely black | prefers dense secondary forest & woodlands; also found in montane & bamboo forest | F 70–100 kg M 150–200 kg | discontinuous distribution, W equatorial Africa and central Africa. Syns: *Pan gorilla*, *Troglodytes savagei* |
| ***Hadropithecus stenognathus*** Lorenz von Liburnau, 1899 | | monotypic | NA | NA | 28 kg | recently extinct (1–2 kya). Recovered from sites located in central, SW, and S Madagascar |
| **Genus *Hapalemur*** *H. aureus* Albignac et al., 1987 | gentle/bamboo lemur (gl) golden (bamboo) lemur or golden gl | monotypic | rufous to dark brown with fulvous ventrum, black muzzle, gold eye spots above eye, short ear tufts | prefers bamboo forest | c. 1.5 kg | discovered in the 1980s in SE Madagascar, where it is sympatric with *H. griseus* and *H. simus*. Consumes parts of bamboo not eaten by the other two spp. Consumes large amounts of cyanide in its diet, but the exact mechanism by which it handles these toxic doses is unknown |
| *H. griseus* (Link, 1795) | gray gl, lesser bamboo lemur | 3 | olivaceous dorsum, flanks, and crown, silvery gray ventrum, pinnae, face, throat, and chest | bamboo thickets | c. 800 g | found in E Madagascar. Sympatric with *H. aureus* in some parts of its range. Specializes on leaves and new shoots of bamboo. Syns: *H. olivaceus*, *H. schlegeli*, *L. griseus* |
| *H. simus* Gray, 1870 | broad-nosed gl greater gl | monotypic | reddish gray, black face, white ear tufts | bamboo forest | 2.5 kg | found in E central Madagascar. Sympatric with *H. aureus* in some parts of its range. Specializes on soft pith inside bamboo stalks. Syn: *Prolemur simus* |

| Species | Common name | Subspecies | Description | Habitat | Weight | Distribution/Notes |
|---|---|---|---|---|---|---|
| *Homo sapiens* Linnaeus, 1758 | human | | sparse body hair, integument ranges from alabaster to very dark brown. Facial hair (M only) and head hair ranges from buff to brown to red to black, grays in elderly | variable environments | F 35–75 kg M 40–80 kg | found worldwide |
| Genus *Hylobates* | gibbon (gb) | | | | | |
| *H. agilis* F. Cuvier, 1821 | agile or dark-handed gb | 3 | variable, from buff to brown to black, white brow line, M and juveniles with white cheek and beard | TRF | c. 6 kg | found in Malaysia, Sumatra and Borneo. Some workers consider this gibbon to be a ssp. of *H. lar*. Syns: *H. albo. H. raffiei* |
| *H. concolor* (Harlan, 1826) | concolor, crested, black, or white-cheeked gb | 6 | M and juveniles completely black, F change to golden, brown, or gray, crown tuff on both sexes | TRF, montane forest | c. 6 kg | range from S China into S Vietnam, Syns: *H. harlani, H. niger, Nomaseus concolor, Simia concolor* |
| *H. gabriellae* Thomas, 1909 | golden-cheeked or red-cheeked gb | monotypic | M and juveniles black, fulvous cheek whiskers, F golden with black face and black peak on crown | TRF | c. 6 kg | occupies TRF of Indochina |
| *H. hoolock* (Harlan, 1834) | Hoolock gb | 2 | M black with two distinct white eyebrows. F golden brown with a single white brow line that thins medially. Juveniles of both sexes black with separate white eyebrows | variable, from primary TRF to scrub forest | 4–8 kg | distribution from E India and Bangladesh into Myanmar and S China. Syns: *H. fusca, Simia golock, S. hoolock* |
| *H. klossi* (Miller, 1903) | Kloss's, dwarf, pygmy or Mentawai Island gb, bilou, beeloh | monotypic | completely black, bare area on throat | primary and secondary TRF | 4–8 kg | only found on the Mentawai Islands. Syns: *H. sericus, Symphalangus brachytanites, S. klossii* |
| *H. lar* (Linnaeus, 1771) | common, lar, or white-handed gb | up to 9 | black body with a white face ring and white paws | primary and secondary TRF | 4–8 kg | wide range throughout SE Asia from S China and Burma to Borneo. Systematics in dispute with as many as 9 sspp. described; however, many workers consider some of the races to be separate spp. Syns: *H. pileatus, Homo lar, Pithecia variegatus, Simia longimana* |
| *H. leucogenys* Ogilby, 1840 | Chinese white-cheeked or northern white-cheeked gb | 2 | M black with white cheeks. F buff to golden, black face, deep brown cap | primary and secondary TRF | c. 5.7 kg | occupies TRF along the Chinese–Vietnamese border. |

NA, not available; TRF, tropical rain forest; M, male; F, female; Syn(s), synonym(s); sp, species (singular); spp., species (plural); ssp. subspecies (singular); sspp., subspecies (plural).

| Species | Common name | No. of sspp. | Pelage | Habitat | Mass | Other information |
|---|---|---|---|---|---|---|
| *H. moloch* (Audebert, 1797) | moloch, silver, silvery, or Sunda Island gb | monotypic | gray brown with a dark brown or black cap, buff brow line, buff or white beard | primary and secondary TRF | c. 6 kg | located in W Java. Some authorities consider this gibbon to be a ssp. of *H. lar*. Syns: *H. funerus, H. muelleri, Pithecia leuciscus, Simia moloch* |
| *H. mulleri* Martin, 1841 | gray, Mueller's (Bornean) (Gray) gb | 3 | gray to brown, darker ventrum and crown-cap, poorly delineated brow line | primary and secondary TRF | c. 6 kg | found in E Borneo. Some authorities consider this gibbon to be a ssp. of *H. lar*. Syn: *H. agilis* |
| *H. pileatus* (Gray, 1861) | pileated or capped gb | monotypic | M black, white toes, facial ring, long silvery hairs on side of black crown-cap, scant white facial ring, white brow line; F and juveniles, silver buff, black ventrum and crown-cap, white facial ring, buff crown side hair | primary TRF | 6–10 kg | distribution from Thailand to Laos and Cambodia. Syn: *H. lar* |
| *H. syndactylus* (Raffles, 1821) | siamang | 2 | completely black except for naked laryngeal sac | TRF | c. 11 kg | found in Malaysian peninsula and Sumatra. Possesses throat sac, which enables this ape to produce very loud calls. Sympatric with *H. lar*. Some workers place the siamang in *Symphalangus syndactylus* |
| *Indri indri* (Gmelen, 1788) | indri, babakoto, dog-faced lemur, short-tailed indri | monotypic | variable, black or white body, gray or white limbs, often a gray collar, black ear tufts, white or gray crown cap, sometimes a thin white facial ring | coastal and montane forest | 7–11 kg | inhabits east-central Madagascar. Syns: *Indris brevicaudatus, I. niger, I. ater, Lemur indri, Lichanotus mitratus* |
| Genus *Lagothrix* | woolly monkey (wm) | | | | | |
| *L. flavicauda* Humboldt, 1812 | yellow-tailed or Hendee's yellow-tailed wm | monotypic | deep brown, buff on the underside of the tail | montane forest | c. 10 kg | restricted to montane forest above 1800 m in the Andes of N Peru. Thought to be extinct until a Peruvian soldier was found to have one as a pet in 1974. Syn: *L. hendei, Oreonax flavicauda, Simia flavicauda* |
| *L. lagotricha* (Humboldt, 1812) | common, Humboldt's, or brown wm, gray barrigudo | 4 | variable, rusty brown, dark brown,gray to black. Neonatal color lighter, often buff | primary TRF | F 3.5–6.5 kg M 3.6–10 kg | principal range in upper Amazon basin, with some separate isolated pockets in N Colombia. Syns: *L humboldtii, L. geoffroyi, Cebus canus, Simia lagotricha* |
| *Lemur catta* Linnaeus, 1758 | ring-tailed lemur | monotypic | grayish-brown, lighter ventrum, white head, black crown, eye-rings, and muzzle, short white ear tufts, black and white banded tail | variable from dry deciduous to scrub forest | 1.5–3.0 kg | located in S and SW Madagascar. Syns: *L. macoco, Maki macoco, Prosimia catta* |

| Species | Common name | Subspecies | Pelage | Habitat | Weight | Comments |
|---|---|---|---|---|---|---|
| **Genus *Leontopithecus*** | golden tamarins (t) | | | | | |
| *L. chrysomelas* (Kuhl, 1820) | golden-headed or gold-and-black t | monotypic | black with golden limbs, mane, and upper portion of tail, black face, white brow line | TRF, swamp and semideciduous forest | c. 560 g | found in SE Brazil. Many authorities consider this lion tamarin to be a sssp. of *L. rosalia*. Syns: *L. ater, Hapale chrysomelas, Jacchus chrysomelas, Leontideus chrysomelas, Leontocebus ater, Midas chrysomelas* |
| *L. chrysopygus* (Mikan, 1823) | golden-rumped, black lion, or black-faced lion t | monotypic | completely black except for a golden patch on the rump | semideciduous riparian forest | 500–700 g | located in SE Brazil. Some authorities consider this lion tamarin to be a sssp. of *L. rosalia*. Syns: *L. ater, Jacchus chrysopygus* |
| *L. rosalia* (Linnaeus, 1766) | golden lion t | 0–4 | variable, orange to gold | primary and secondary TRF | c. 640 g | found in SE Brazil. Some workers consider this sp. to contain 3–4 sssp., while others separate these populations into separate spp. Syns: *L. marikina, Hapale rosalia, Jacchus rosalia, Midas leoninus, M. rosalia, Simia leoninus, S. rosalia* |
| **Genus *Lepilemur*** | sportive/weasel lemur (sl) | | | | | |
| *L. dorsalis* Gray, 1870 | gray-backed, back-striped, or Nosy Be sl | monotypic | brown with a medial dorsal stripe, gray or brown face, thin black eye-rings | gallery forest, scrub | 600–900 g | found in NW Madagascar. Syn: *L. grandidieri* |
| *L. edwardsi* (Forbes, 1894) | Milne-Edwards sl | monotypic | brownish gray dorsum and flank, gray ventrum, medial dorsal stripe | deciduous dry forest | c. 900 g | found in NW Madagascar. Syn: *L. rufiscens* |
| *L. leucopus* (Forsythe-Major, 1894) | white-footed sl | monotypic | brownish gray dorsum and flank, lighter gray or white ventrum, thin black eye-rings | gallery, riparian, and spiny forest | c. 550 g | found in S. Madagascar. The way this animal digests its food is in dispute. Charles-Dominique & Hladik described it as a coprophage, while R.J. Russell and others deny this. Syn: *L. globiceps* |
| *L. microdon* (Forsythe-Major, 1894) | small-toothed sl | monotypic | gray-brown dorsum and flanks, chestnut forelimbs, dark medial dorsal stripe, black eye-rings, blackish muzzle | secondary gallery and bamboo forest | c. 1 kg | found in NW Madagascar. As the name implies, the cheek teeth are small in comparison to other *Lepilemur* sp. Natural history poorly known. Syn: *L. mustelinus* |
| *L. mustelinus* I. Geoffroy, 1851 | common sl | monotypic | brown dorsum and flanks, black medial stripe extending from crown along length of back, gray ventrum, gray or brown head, thin black eye-rings | TRF | c. 1 kg | found in S and C Madagascar. Until 1977 this was the only recognized sp. of *Lepilemur* and has since been partitioned into 7 different spp. Sympatric with *L. leucopus* in southern part of its range and with *L. microdon* in northern part of range |

NA, not available; TRF, tropical rain forest; M, male; F, female; Syn(s), synonym(s); sp., species (singular); spp., species (plural); ssp., subspecies (singular); sspp., subspecies (plural).

| Species | Common name | No. of sspp. | Pelage | Habitat | Mass | Other information |
|---|---|---|---|---|---|---|
| *L. ruficaudatus* (Grandidier, 1867) | red-tailed sl | monotypic | brownish gray dorsum and flanks, light gray ventrum, side, gray face, black eye-rings and muzzle, rusty throat and chest | deciduous dry forest | 900 g | found in W Madagascar. Natural history poorly known. Syns: *L. mustelinus, L. pallidicauda* |
| *L. septentrionalis* (Rumpler & Albignac, 1975) | northern sl | monotypic | gray with brown highlights, medial dorsal stripe, thin black eye-rings | deciduous forest | 600 g | found in far N tip of Madagascar. Natural history poorly known. Syn: *L. mustelinus* |
| **Genus *Lophocebus*** | | | | | | |
| *L. albigena* (Gray, 1850) | black mangabey gray-cheeked, white-cheeked, crested mantled, or black mangabey | 3 | blackish dorsum, dark brown cape on M whitish or gray cheek hairs, often a crown tuft | primary TRF | F 6 kg M 9 kg | ranges from W Africa through central Africa into W Kenya. Strictly an arboreal sp. that prefers the upper canopy. Syn: *Cercocebus albigena* |
| *L. aterrimus* (Oudemans, 1890) | black mangabey, black crested mangabey | 2 | completely black with prominent medial crown tuft | primary and secondary TRF, swamp and gallery forest. | F 6 kg M 8 kg | found in Zaire and NE Angola. Strictly an arboreal sp. that prefers closed canopy. Syn: *Cercocebus aterrimus, C. congicus, C. hamlyni, Semnopithecus albigena* |
| *Loris tardigradus* (Linnaeus, 1758) | slender loris | 6 | variable: reddish, golden-brown, gray, may have dorsal stripe | variable from dry deciduous forest to scrub to montane forests to swamps | 250–300 g | found in S India and Sri Lanka. It has been suggested that more than one sp. may be contained within *L. tardigradus*. Syn: *L. gracilis* |
| **Genus *Macaca*** | | | | | | |
| *M. arctoides* (I. Geoffroy, 1831) | macaque (mq) stump-tailed or bear mq | 3 | brown, hairless face mottled with pink, red, or brown, short relatively hairless tail. Infant completely white | TRF, deciduous forest | F c. 8 kg M c. 10 kg | ranges throughout S. China, Indochina, and into the Malay peninsula. Syns: *M. brunneus, M. speciosus, M. hibetanus, M. ursinus, Papio melanotus* |
| *M. assamensis* (M'Clelland, 1840) | Assamese mq | 2 | variable, buffy brown to dark brown, pinkish skin forms eye mask surrounded by prominent lighter ticked cheek and chin whiskers | deciduous dry forest, bamboo thickets, montane forest. | F c. 6 kg M c. 9 kg | ranges from NE India through Nepal and into Indochina. Primarily terrestrial. Syns: *M. problematicus, M. rheosimilis* |
| *M. brunescens* (Matschie, 1901) | Muna-Butung mq | monotypic | brown | TRF | 5–10 kg | inhabits the islands of Muna and Buton. Syns: *M. nigra, M. ochreata* |
| *M. cyclopis* (Swinhoe, 1862) | Taiwan or Formosan rock mq | monotypic | brown, silver fringe surrounding naked pink face, very short tail | temperate forest | 5–6 kg | occupies mountains and highlands of Taiwan. Syn: *M. radiatus* |
| *M. fascicularis* (Raffles, 1821) | crab-eating, long-tailed, or common mq, cynomolgus, Java or Kra monkey | up to 21 | gray to rusty brown, lighter ventrum, pale brown eye mask, some with a whitish mustache, often a medial crown crest | very adaptable sp. that inhabits variable environments | 3–5 kg | ranges from Myanmar through the islands of SE Asia. Good swimmer and supplements diet with crustaceans and other littoral animals. Syns: *M. aurea, M. cynomolgus, M. irus, Cynomolgus cagayanus, Pithecus bintangensis* |

| Species | Common names | Subspecies | Pelage | Habitat | Weight | Comments |
|---|---|---|---|---|---|---|
| *M. fuscata* (Blythe, 1875) | Japanese mq, snow monkey | 2 | thick brown to gray pelage with silver highlights, pinkish red naked face | variable including subalpine zone | 10–18 kg | located on the 3 S islands of Japan. Consumes tree bark in winter when food is scarce. Good swimming abilities. Syns: *M. speciosus, Inuus speciosus* |
| *M. hecki* (Matschie, 1901) | booted, Celebes, or Heck's mq | monotypic | black dorsum and flanks, brown ventrum, gray rump patch, grayish brown cheeks, whitish gray brow line | TRF | 5–10 kg | found in NW Sulawesi. Syn: *M. nigra* |
| *M. maura* F. Cuvier, 1823 | Moor, booted, or Heck's mq | monotypic | dark brown or black back, gray rump patch | TRF | 5–10 kg | located in SW Sulawesi. Syns: *M. nigra, M. brunescens, M. fascicularis, Macacus fuscoater, Simia curvieri* |
| *M. mulatta* Zimmerman, 1780 | Rhesus mq | 4 | brown, reddish pink face | variable, highly adapted to many different habitats including TRF, dry deciduous and temperate forest | 5–11 kg | ranges from Afghanistan to China and SE Asia. Anatomy and physiology of these monkeys well known because of their extensive use in medical research. Introduced populations exist in Central America and the Caribbean. Good swimming abilities. Often found in human habitats. Hybridizes with *M. fascicularis* where ranges overlap |
| *M. nemestrina* (Linnaeus, 1766) | pig-tailed mq, giant rhesus | 4 | olivaceous agouti dorsum and flanks, whitish ventrum, black crown, white brow line, grizzled white chin whiskers, olivaceous cheeks | primary and secondary TRF, littoral and montane forest, swamp | 6–10 kg | ranges from NE India into the Malay peninsula and the islands of SE Borneo. Short tail. Forms associations with *Nasalis and Presbytis potenziani*. Syns: *M. brachyurus, M. pagensis, Simia nemestrina* |
| *M. nigra* Desmarest, 1822 | Sulawesi (Celebes), black, or Sulawesi crested mq | up to 7 | completely black with a prominent tuft of hair on the crown forming a backward directional crest | primary and secondary TRF | 5–10 kg | found on Sulawesi. Because the tail is absent, this macaque has erroneously been called an ape. Taxonomy equivocal: many of the sspp. may be distinct spp. Syns: *Cynocephalus niger, Inuus niger, Papio niger* |
| *M. nigrescens* (Temminck, 1849) | Gorontalo mq | monotypic | brown with black dorsal stripe, black limbs and crown, prominent tuft of hair on the crown forming a backward directional crest | primary and secondary TRF | 5–10 kg | located on Sulawesi. Syn: *M. nigra* |

NA, not available; TRF, tropical rain forest; M, male; F, female; Syn(s), synonym(s); sp., species (singular); spp., species (plural); ssp., subspecies (singular); sspp., subspecies (plural).

| Species | Common name | No. of sspp. | Pelage | Habitat | Mass | Other information |
|---|---|---|---|---|---|---|
| M. ochreata (Ogilby, 1841) | ochre or booted mq | 2 | black with gray rump patch and limbs, gray cheeks and throat | TRF | 5–10 kg | found on Sulawesi. Syn: *M. nigra* |
| M. radiata (É. Geoffroy, 1812) | bonnet mq | 2 | gray brown, white ventrum, reddish pink face | TRF, gallery forest | 4–6 kg | occupies forests of S India. Syn: *Cercocebus radiatus* |
| M. silenus (Linnaeus, 1758) | lion-tailed mq | monotypic | black with gray mane encircling face | deciduous and evergreen forest | c. 7 kg | inhabits the Western Ghats Mountains of S India. Syns: *Cercopithecus veter, Simia silenus* |
| M. sinica (Linnaeus, 1771) | toque mq | 3 | brown to tawny | variable habitats, including TRF, gallery forest | 2.5–6 kg | found throughout Sri Lanka. Spends 75% of time in trees. Smallest macaque |
| M. sylvanus (Linnaeus, 1758) | Barbary mq | monotypic | brown to fulvous | variable habitats including deciduous forest | c. 11 kg | discontinuous range in variable habitats of W N Africa and Gibraltar. Lacks tail, hence previous name of Barbary ape. Unknown whether the population on Gibraltar is the result of a previously widespread macaque population (there are Pleistocene fossils of *M. sylvanus* from elsewhere in Europe). Syns: *Inuus sylvanus, Magus sylvanus* |
| M. thibetana (Milne-Edwards, 1870) | Thibetan or Milne-Edwards' mq | monotypic | black, brown crown, gray cheeks and beard | temperate forest | F c. 8 kg, M c. 10 kg | found in central China. Syn: *M. arctoides* |
| M. tonkeana (Meyer, 1870) | Tonkenese mq | monotypic | black back and flanks, brown ventrum, gray rump patch, grayish brown cheeks, whitish gray brow line | TRF | 5–10 kg | found on Sulawesi. Syn: *M. nigra* |
| Genus *Mandrillus* | | | | | | |
| M. leucophaeus (F. Cuvier, 1807) | drill | 2 | olivaceous, black face, white cheek and beard | TRF | F c. 10 kg, M c. 20 kg | inhabits forests of W equatorial Africa. Syn: *Simia sylvicola* |
| M. sphinx (Linnaeus, 1758) | mandrill | monotypic | grizzled brown with fulvous highlights, bright red and blue muzzle, more pronounced in M, tawny cheeks and beard | TRF | F c. 12 kg, M c. 26 kg | found in W equatorial Africa. Syns: *M. schreberi, Papio planirostris, Simia sphinx* |
| Genus *Megaladapis* | | | | | | |
| M. edwardsi | koala lemur (kl) Edwards' kl | monotypic | NA | NA | c. 80 kg | recently extinct (3000–600 ya). Recovered from sites in N Madagascar |
| M. madagascariensis | koala lemur | monotypic | NA | NA | c. 40 kg | recently extinct (3000–600 ya). Recovered from sites in N Madagascar |
| M. grandidieri | Grandidier's kl | monotypic | NA | NA | c. 65 kg | recently extinct (3000–600 ya). Recovered from sites in N Madagascar |

| Taxon | Common name | Subspecies | Pelage | Habitat | Mass | Comments |
|---|---|---|---|---|---|---|
| Genus *Mesopithecus*<br>*M. dolichobrachion* | sloth lemur<br>sloth lemur | monotypic | NA | NA | c. 12 kg | recently extinct (500 ya?). Recovered from sites in N Madagascar |
| *M. globiceps* | sloth lemur | monotypic | NA | NA | c. 10 kg | recently extinct (500 ya?). Known only from materials recovered from the type locality in C Madagascar |
| *M. pithecoides* | sloth lemur | monotypic | NA | NA | c. 11 kg | recently extinct (500 ya?). Recovered from sites in N, central, W, and SW Madagascar |
| Genus *Microcebus*<br>*M. murinus*<br>(J.F. Miller, 1867) | mouse lemur (ml)<br>gray ml | monotypic | brownish gray dorsum, flanks, and head, white ventrum and throat, short white medial nose stripe | secondary wet or dry deciduous forest, shrub | 50–90 g | located in the deciduous forests and spiny desert of W Madagascar. Body mass fluctuates, with season. Fat is stored in the tail, and this sp. enters estivation. Syns: *Galago murinus, G. minor* |
| *M. myoxinus* Peters, 1852 | pygmy ml | monotypic | rufous brown with short dark medial dorsal stripe, ventrum white, short white nose stripe | dry deciduous forest | 24–38 g | found in a small area of dry deciduous forest of W Madagascar. Smallest living primate. Sympatric with *M. murinus* |
| *M. rufus* É. Geoffroy, 1834 | (eastern) brown ml | monotypic | rufous brown, grayish white ventrum, white medial nose stripe | primary and secondary forest | c. 60 g | occurs in variable habitats in E Madagascar. Syns: *Chirogaleus smithii, Gliscebus rufus* |
| *Miopithecus talapoin* (Schreber, 1774) | talapoin monkey, dwarf guenon | 3–4 | olivaceous, white ventrum, fulvous cheeks | primary and secondary TRF, gallery forest, mangrove, and swamps | 750–1400 g | distributed in the forests of W equatorial Africa. Syns: *Cercopithecus talapoin, Simia talapoin* |
| *Mirza coquereli* Grandidier, 1867 | Coquerel's or giant ml | monotypic | brown or gray brown, grayish white underside, tail mixed brown and black | dry deciduous forest | 270–300 g | discontinuous range along the coast of W Madagascar. Taxonomy equivocal: many workers assign this sp. to *Microcebus*. Syn: *Cheirogaleus conquerelli* |
| *Nasalis larvatus* (van Wurmb, 1781) | proboscis monkey | monotypic | golden, legs, rump patch, and tail white, venter mixed white, gray, and gold | mangrove and swamp forests | F c. 10 kg<br>M c. 20 kg | found on Borneo and 2 NE islands. Reported to dive from trees into rivers where they swim. Known to form associations with macaques and *Presbytis potenziani*. Syns: *Cercopithecus larvatus, Simia capistratus* |

NA, not available; TRF, tropical rain forest; M, male; F, female; Syn(s), synonym(s); sp., species (singular); spp., species (plural); ssp., subspecies (singular); sspp., subspecies (plural).

| Species | Common name | No. of sspp. | Pelage | Habitat | Mass | Other information |
|---|---|---|---|---|---|---|
| Genus *Nycticebus* | slow loris (sl) | | | | | |
| N. coucang (Boddaert, 1783) | common sl | 4–10 | light brown to gray, often white underside, dark ears surrounded by lighter fur, dark brown or black medial dorsal stripe, dark eye rings, medial white nose stripe | variable forests | c. 900 g | ranges from E India through Indochina. Syns: *N. sumatrensis*, *N. tardigradus*, *Lemur tardigradus*, *Tardigradus coucang* |
| N. pygmaeus Bonhote, 1907 | lesser or pygmy sl | monotypic | fulvous with white hairs intermixed, faint medial dorsal stripe, brown ears and eye rings, medial white nose stripe | secondary TRF | c. 300 g | located in E Indochina. Syn: *N. intermedius* |
| Genus *Otolemur* | greater bushbaby (bb) | | | | | |
| O. crassicaudatus (É. Geoffroy, 1812) | greater, thick-tailed, or fat-tailed bb, grand galago, gray night ape, rat of the coconut palm | 10–11 | gray to black, lighter ventrum | open forest, woodland savanna | 1–1.2 kg | distribution in E and SE Africa. Largest of the galago sp. Partly sympatric with *O. garnettii*. Syn: *Galago crassicaudatus* |
| O. garnettii (Ogilby, 1838) | small-eared greater bb | 4 | reddish to gray brown, whitish gray ventrum | littoral and riparian forest | c. 800 g | ranges from S Somalia to SE Tanzania and Zanzibar. Partly sympatric with *O. crassicaudatus* over part of range. Syn: *Galago garnettii* |
| Pachylemur insignis Lamberton, 1948 | | monotypic | NA | NA | c. 10 kg | recently extinct (2–1 kya). Recovered from sites in N, central, and S Madagascar |
| Palaeopropithecus ingens Grandidier, 1899 | sloth lemur | monotypic | NA | NA | 40–60 kg | recently extinct (c. 1kya). Recovered from sites in central, SW, and S Madagascar |
| Genus *Pan* | | | | | | |
| P. paniscus Schwarz, 1929 | bonobo, pygmy chimpanzee | monotypic | black | TRF | F c. 33 kg M c. 45 kg | restricted distribution in the tropical forests of Zaire, S of the Zaire River. Syn: *Pan satyrus* |
| P. troglodytes (Blumenbach, 1775) | chimpanzee | 3 | black, deep brown face, may have white chin hairs, infants have a white tail and lighter face that gets darker with age | variable, from savanna to TRF | F 45–68 kg M 56–80 kg | found throughout W and central Africa. Makes and uses tools. Can learn language in a laboratory situation. Males hunt small mammals; food sharing occurs through begging |
| Genus *Papio* | baboon (b) | | | | | |
| P. anubis (F. Cuvier, 1825) | olive, savanna, anubis, or doguera b | 4–7 | agouti olivaceous, black face, M have short mane | open areas within short distance of water | F 11–15 kg M 22–50 kg | distributed in a wide belt across Sub-Saharan and Saharan Africa from small Mauritania to Ethiopia. Mammals opportunistically seized and consumed. Lives in mixed sex troops of up to 200 individuals. Syns: *P. doguera*, *Simia anubis* |

| Species | Common name(s) | Subspecies | Pelage | Habitat | Weight | Notes |
|---|---|---|---|---|---|---|
| *P. cynocephalus* (Linnaeus, 1766) | yellow or long-legged b | 3–4 | buffy to buffy gray, white ventrum, dark brown face, M have short mane | savanna, open woodland. | F 11–30 kg M 22–50 kg | live in mixed-sex troops of up to 200 individuals. Syns: *P. strepitus, Cynocephalus babouin, C. ochraceus* |
| *P. hamadryas* (Linnaeus, 1758) | hamadryas, sacred, or mantled b | monotypic | M gray with long mane, F olivaceous | prefers arid semi-desert interspersed with *Acacia* trees. Also found on savanna or scrub grass | F 10–15 kg M 20–30 kg | found in E Africa and SW Arabia. When 5 *Papio* spp. are recognized, this is a monotypic sp.; however, some workers consider *P. hamadryas* to be a supersp. in which the other *Papio* spp. are included as sspp. Live in one-male units that congregate at night into sleeping troops of up to 800 animals. Unattached males live in bachelor herds. OMU males 'herd' females by biting them on the neck |
| *P. papio* Desmarest, 1820 | guinea or western b | monotypic | rufous brown, M have short mane | open country | F *c.* 15 kg M *c.* 20 kg | found in far W Africa. Natural history poorly known. Syns: *P. rubescens, Cynocephalus papio* |
| *P. ursinus* (Kerr, 1792) | chacma or pig-tailed b | 8 | buffy gray to very dark brown, whitish ventrum and hair running alongside of muzzle, black face | open woodlands | 14–41 kg | located in S Africa. Some workers treat *P. ursinus* as a ssp. of *P. cynocephalus*. Syns: *P. comatus, P. porcarius, Cynocephalus ursinus, Simia porcaria* |
| *Paralouatta varonai* Rivero & Arredondo, 1991 | Cuban monkey | monotypic | NA | TRF | NA | recently extinct (5 kya?). Recovered in W Cuba |
| *Perodicticus potto* (Mueller, 1766) | potto, Bosman's potto, half-a-tail | *c.* 5 | brown, lighter ventrum; the pelage changes from gray to brown with age | primary and secondary TRF, savanna woodland | 850–1600 g | distribution from extreme W equatorial Africa into central Africa. Sympatric with *Arctocebus* in some parts of range, but resource partitioning prevents competition. Occupies canopy level. Syns: *Lemur potto, Nycticebus potto* |
| *Phaner furcifer* (de Blainville, 1839) | fork-marked (crowned) dwarf lemur, fork-tailed mouse lemur | 4 | brown with a black dorsal stripe that bifurcates on the crown terminating at the eyes, ventrum grayish, paws black | primary and secondary deciduous forest | 350–500 g | found in discontinuous distribution around the peripheries of Madagascar with the exception of the E coast. Syns: *Cheirogaleus furcifer, Lemur furcifer, Microcebus furcifer* |
| **Genus *Piliocolobus*** *P. badius* (Kerr, 1792) | red colobus monkey red or bay colobus | up to 3 | gray or black dorsum, upper portion of limbs, crown and tail, rest of body reddish | variable, primary and secondary TRF, dry deciduous and gallery forest, open woodland | 7–13 kg | distribution discontinuous with separated populations ranging from in far W Africa to central Africa. Sympatric with the various black-and-white guereza colobus spp. Live in troops up to 100 individuals. Syns: *Colobus badius, C. rufomitratus, Simia ferruginea* |

NA, not available; TRF, tropical rain forest; M, male; F, female; Syn(s), synonym(s); sp., species (singular); spp., species (plural); ssp., subspecies (singular); sspp., subspecies (plural).

| Species | Common name | No. of sspp. | Pelage | Habitat | Mass | Other information |
|---|---|---|---|---|---|---|
| P. kirkii (Gray, 1868) | Kirk's colobus, Zanibar red colobus | monotypic | anterior portion of dorsum, ventrum, and shoulder, grayish white, remainder of dorsum and crown red, black face, pink nose, lips, and chin, ashy gray circumfacial hair | primary and secondary TRF | 7–13 kg | found in W and central Africa. Not universally recognized; many authorities consider Kirk's colobus to be a ssp. of C. badius. Syn: Colobus kirkii, Procolobus kirkii |
| **Genus Pithecia** | saki(s) | | | | | |
| P. aequatorialis Hershkovitz, 1987 | equatorial s | monotypic | black agouti, brown flanks, mixed white and gold ring around a black face | TRF | 2–2.5 kg | found in upper Amazon basin of Ecuador and Peru. Not a widely recognized sp. and is based on specimens included in P. monachus |
| P. albicans Gray, 1860 | white or buffy s | monotypic | black dorsum and tail, buff to gold flank, ventrum, and head | primary TRF | c. 3 kg | distributed in the Amazon basin of Brazil. Largest of the Pithecia spp. |
| P. irrorata Gray 1842 | bald-face or Rio Tapajós s | 2 | grizzled black, olive, and white, silver paws, black face | lowland TRF | 2–3 kg | located in Amazon basin. Some workers include this monkey as a ssp. of P. monachus |
| P. monachus (É Geoffroy, 1812) | monk, hairy, or whitish s | 2 | grizzled black and gray, white stripe running alongside muzzle, white mustache | primary TRF | 2.2–2.5 kg | found in upper Amazon basin of Ecuador. Sometimes found in association with S. nigricollis. Syns: P. hirsuta, P. inusta, Simia monacha |
| P. pithecia (Linnaeus, 1766) | Guianan, white-, or pale-faced s | 2 | M black with white face and black muzzle; F agouti black and brown, black face with white stripe running along-side muzzle | TRF | 1.5–2.4 kg | distribution in NE South America. Males larger than females. Syns: P. pogonias, Simia Pithecia |
| Pongo pygmaeus (Linnaeus, 1760) | orangutan | 2 | reddish shag, brown to maroon face | primary TRF, montane forest | F 35–50 kg M 80–90 kg | inhabits forests of Borneo and Sumatra Syn: Pithecus satyrus |
| **Genus Presbytis** | leaf-monkey (lm) | | | | | |
| P. comata (Desmarest, 1822) | Sundra or grizzled lm | 2 | gray dorsum and flanks, white ventrum, black head and crest, tan face, gray cheeks and jaws | montane forest | 5–7 kg | located in the forests of the islands of SE Asia. Many workers include P. aygula, P. hosel, and P. thomasi in this sp. |
| P. frontata (Mueller, 1838) | white-fronted or bald lm | 2 | gray dorsum and flanks, white ventrum, black head with white patch on the forehead | lowland TRF | 5.5–7 kg | inhabits forests of E Borneo. Natural history poorly known |
| P. hosei (= comata) (Thomas, 1889) | Hose's or Everett's lm | 3 | dark gray with lighter gray ventrum, black hands and feet, crown and crest black, pink to red face | lowland and montane TRF | c. 6 kg | found in N and E Borneo. Sympatric with P. rubicunda, with which it forms associations |

| Species | Common name(s) | Subspecies | Coloration | Habitat | Weight | Distribution and notes |
|---|---|---|---|---|---|---|
| *P. melalophos* (= *femoralis*) (Raffles, 1821) | banded or mitered lm, surili | 4–17 | highly variable; brown to fulvous, often with white ventrum, cheeks, and forehead, brown to black crown crest | prefers secondary forest | 5–10 kg | distributed in Thailand, Malaysia, and Sumatra. Appears to live in groups numbering less than 10; often one-male units. Sympatric with *Trachypithecus obscura* |
| *P. potenziani* (Bonaparte, 1856) | fulvous, Mentawai lm, langur, or joja | 2 | black back, flanks, crown, face, and tail, reddish underside, white brow line, cheeks, and throat | primary and secondary TRF | 5–7 kg | found on all four islands of the Mentawai Islands. Reported to live in monogamous social groups in which the males and females vocalize together, similarly to gibbons. Forms associations with *Nasalis* and *Macaca nemestrina* |
| *P. rubicunda* (Mueller, 1938) | maroon lm | 5 | highly variable; dark maroon to red to fulvous, buff ventrum, bluish gray face | lowland TRF | c. 6 kg | found in Borneo except for the NW corner of the island. Sympatric with *P. hosei*, with which it forms associations |
| *Procolobus verus* (van Beneden, 1838) | olive colobus, magic or van Beneden's monkey | monotypic | olivaceous, white ventrum, white circumfacial fur | variable, TRF, dry deciduous forest, swamp | 3–5 kg | found in far W equatorial Africa. Only cercopithecoid in which the females carry the offspring in their mouths. Syn: *Colobus verus* |
| **Genus *Propithecus*** | | | | | | |
| *P. diadema* Bennett, 1832 | sifaka (sk); diademed or Milne-Edwards's sk, simpona | 4–5 | highly variable, dependent on ssp.,almost all white to gold to completely black | TRF, deciduous forest | c. 6.5 kg | discontinuous range in E Madagascar. Largest of the *Propithecus* spp. |
| *P. tattersalli* Simons, 1988 | golden crowned or Tattersall's sk | monotypic | white body with gold forearms and chest, rufous crown, black face, white ear tufts | TRF, deciduous forest | c. 3.5 kg | very restricted range in the extreme N of Madagascar. Diet may be more granivorous than other sifaka sp. Highly endangered |
| *P. verreauxi* Grandidier, 1867 | Verreaux's or white sk | 4–5 | white body with reddish brown crown and nape of neck, black face, white brow line | TRF, deciduous forest, scrub | c. 3.7 kg | found in W and S Madagascar. Syn: *P. majori* |
| *Pygathrix nemaeus* (Linnaeus, 1771) | douc langur | 2 | grizzled gray body, brown head with chestnut face, white ruff around face | primary and secondary TRF | 8–11 kg | inhabits forests of Indochina. Natural history poorly known. Social groups reported to consist of 4–15 individuals |
| **Genus *Rhinopithecus*** | | | | | | |
| *R. avunculus* Dollman, 1912 | snub-nosed monkey (snm); Tonkin snm or langur | monotypic | dark brown to black back and flanks, whitish underside and head | TRF | F c. 9 kg M c. 14 kg | occupies forests of N Vietnam. Natural history poorly known |
| *R. bieti* Milne-Edwards, 1897 | black, Yunnan or cow-tailed snm | monotypic | black upper back, limbs, and crown crest, white ventrum, lower back, and throat, pink or red muzzle and lips | temperate forest | F c. 10 kg M c. 15 kg | found in forests of E Tibet and SW China (Yunnan province). Natural history poorly known |

NA, not available; TRF, tropical rain forest; M, male; F, female; syn(s), synonym(s) sp., species (singular); spp., species (plural); ssp., subspecies (singular); sspp., subspecies (plural).

| Species | Common name | No. of sspp. | Pelage | Habitat | Mass | Other information |
|---|---|---|---|---|---|---|
| *R. brelichi* Thomas, 1901 | Gray, Guizhou, or Brelich's snm | monotypic | gray brown dorsum and flanks, gray to rusty ventrum, orange shoulders and forehead patch, white face | deciduous and coniferous forest | F *c.* 9 kg M *c.* 16 kg | inhabits south-central China. Natural history poorly known. Syn: *R. roxellanae* |
| *R. roxellana* Milne-Edwards, 1871 | golden monkey or golden snm or langur | 2 | dark brown to gold, light blue around eyes, white muzzle | coniferous and bamboo forest | 6–20 kg | located in mountains of south-central China. Leafy diet includes needles from fir trees; these animals also consume lichens, particularly during the winter when food sources are scarce |
| Genus *Saguinus* | tamarin (t) | | | | | |
| *S. bicolor* (Spix, 1823) | pied or Brazilian barefaced t | 3 | anterior portion of body white, posterior agouti brown, black face, ears, and tail | primary and secondary TRF, disturbed and urban areas | *c.* 400 g | restricted to central Brazil N of the Amazon River. Reported to be sympatric with *S. midas* in a forest outside the city of Manaus. Syn: *S. martinsi* |
| *S. fuscicollis* (Spix, 1823) | saddle-back, brown-headed, red-mantled, Deville's, Illiger's, golden-mantled, Weddell's, or white t | 13 | highly varied dependent on ssp.; back mottled brown or orange saddle, rest of body tends to be ticked brown, face and or muzzle often white. | primary and secondary TRF | 340–440 g | found in W Amazon basin. Often found in association with other tamarins (*S. labiatus, S. imperator, S. mystax, S. nigricollis*) that are sympatric in a particular part of its range. During the dry season it switches to nectarivory. Syns: *S. devillei, S. fuscus, S. illigeri, S. lagonotus, S. melanoleucus, S. weddelli* |
| *S. geoffroyi* (Pucheran, 1845) | Geoffroy's, red-napped, or red-crested t | monotypic | mottled black and light brown, white chest and forelegs, naked black face and ears, white crown crest | secondary forest and disturbed areas | 450–520 g | ranges from S Costa Rica to NW Colombia. Prefers the shrub layer of the forest understory |
| *S. graellsi* Espada, 1870 | Rio Napo t | monotypic | black anterior that grades into rusty brown posteriorly and base of tail, rest of tail black, white muzzle | primary and secondary TRF | 270–400 g | found in Amazon basin of Colombia, Ecuador and Brazil. Most authorities regard this monkey as a ssp. of *S. nigricollis*. Syn: *S. nigricollis* |
| *S. imperator* (Goeldi, 1907) | emperor t | up to 2 | gray brown agouti body, black face, white mustache, rust tail | TRF | *c.* 400 g | inhabits forests of SW Amazon basin of Peru, Bolivia, and Brazil. This monkey has a long mustache reminiscent of that of Austrian Emperor Franz Joseph, who became the tamarin's namesake. Frugivorous during the wet season, but switches to nectarivory during the dry season. Sympatric in some parts of its range with *S. fuscicollis*, with which they often travel in association |
| *S. inustus* (Schwartz, 1951) | mottle-face or inustus t | monotypic | black, with mottled black and white face | TRF | *c.* 700 g | occupies forest of NW Amazon basin. Natural history poorly known |

| Species | Common names | No. sspp. | Coloration | Habitat | Weight | Distribution/notes |
|---|---|---|---|---|---|---|
| S. labiatus (É. Geoffroy, 1812) | white-lipped, red-bellied, or red-crested mustached t | 2 | dorsum, flanks and tail black with gray highlights, rusty ventrum, black head with white nose and upper lip | TRF | 265–580 g | located predominantly in W Brazil. Utilizes middle levels of the forest. Sympatric with S. fuscicollis, with which it often travels in association |
| S. leucopus (Gunther, 1877) | white-footed or silvery brown barefaced t | monotypic | buffy brown dorsum and sides, rusty ventrum, white limbs, black naked face, brown tail | forest fringes and secondary forest, disturbed areas | c. 500 g | narrow range in N Columbia. Syns: Hapale leucopus, Seniocebus pegasis |
| S. midas (Linnaeus, 1758) | golden-handed, midas, rufous-handed, red-handed, or black t | 2 | black with variegated rust on back, rusty paws | TRF | 400–600 g | occupies forest from E Columbia into the Guianas and N Brazil. Syn: S. tamarin |
| S. mystax (Spix, 1823) | black-chested mustached t | 3 | black with dorsum mottled with rust, nose and chin white forming a mustache | primary TRF | 530–700 g | ranges from NE Peru to NW Brazil. Sympatric with S. fuscicollis, with which it is often found in traveling association; the sp. partition resources by S. mystax utilizing higher levels of the forest. Small social units with one breeding female and several reproductively active males with helpers of both sexes; membership is fluid. Syns: S. pileatus, S. pluto |
| S. nigricollis (Spix, 1823) | black-and-red or black-mantle t | 2 | black anterior that grades into rusty brown posteriorly and base of tail, rest of tail black, white muzzle | TRF | 420–500 g | found in Amazonian Colombia, Ecuador, Peru, and Brazil. Sympatric with S. fuscicollis in some parts of range. Small basic social units fuse with other small social units to produce larger troops of up to 40 animals |
| S. oedipus (Linnaeus, 1758) | cotton-top or crested t, pinche | monotypic | brown to gray dorsum, white ventrum, black head with striking white crest, dark brown tail | primary and secondary TRF, disturbed areas | 350–500 g | found in N Colombia |
| S. tripartitus (Milne-Edwards, 1878) | golden-mantled t | monotypic | buff dorsum, ventrum fulvous to orange, golden limbs and shoulders, black head with gold forehead patch, black tail dorsally, red ventrally | lowland TRF | NA | only occurs in Ecuadorian Amazonia. Natural history poorly known. Sympatric with S. fuscicollis in part of range, but utilizes different parts of the habitat |
| Genus Saimiri | | | | | | |
| S. boliviensis (I. Geoffroy & de Blainville, 1834) | squirrel monkey (sq) Bolivian sq | 4? | buffy agouti, some sspp. with golden back light ventrum, white eye mask, small white ear tuft, black muzzle | primary and secondary TRF | c. 1 kg | found in upper Amazon of Bolivia, Peru, and Brazil. May be a ssp. of S. sciureus |

NA, not available; TRF, tropical rain forest; M, male; F, female; Syn(s), synonym(s); sp., species (singular); spp., species (plural); ssp., subspecies (singular); sspp., subspecies (plural).

| Species | Common name | No. of sspp. | Pelage | Habitat | Mass | Other information |
|---|---|---|---|---|---|---|
| *S. oerstedii* (Reinhardt, 1872) | red-backed, Central American, or black-headed sq | 2 | golden to rufous dorsum and paws, olivaceous upper legs and tail, black crown, white eye mask that arches into crownforming a widow's peak, black muzzle | remnant forest | c. 1 kg | found in remnant forests of Costa Rica and Panama in a discontinuous range. Some workers think these monkeys were introduced into Central America by humans. Syn: *S. sciureus* |
| *S. sciureus* (Linnaeus, 1758) | common, golden-backed, short-tailed, or Geoffroy's sq; common titi monkey | up to 8 | olivaceous to rufous dorsum, buff ventrum, rusty lower limbs, agouti gray shoulders and crown, whitish eye mask that arches into crown forming a widow's peak, black muzzle, white ear tufts, olivaceous tail | wide variety of forested habitats | 600–1400 g | found throughout the Amazon basin. Males heavier than females |
| *S. ustus* (I. Geoffroy, 1843) | bare-eared or golden-back sq | monotypic | goldish agouti dorsum, grayish white ventrum, white eye mask that arches into crown forming a slight widow's peak, black muzzle | lowland TRF | c. 1 kg | located only in central Amazon basin. Sympatric with *S. sciureus* at several locales. Syn: *S. sciureus* |
| *S. vanzolini* Ayres, 1985 | black, Vanzolini's, or Jeanne-Marie's sq | monotypic | agouti with black stripe running sagittally from crown to tip of tail, agouti gray flanks, shoulders, and thighs, white eye mask, black muzzle | TRF | c. 1 kg | found in central Amazon basin. Natural history poorly known. Sp. validity based on chromosomal differences from other squirrel monkeys |
| *Semnopithecus entellus* Dufresne, 1797 | Hanuman or common langur | up to 15 | dependent on subspecies; gray to golden, whitish, ventrum, black face and ears | wide variety of habitats, including semidesert and urban areas | 15–21 kg | found in S Asia. This was the first primate sp. observed practicing infanticide. Social organization is often a one-male unit |
| *Simias concolor* Miller, 1903 | pig-tailed, Mentawai Islands, or Pagai langur; Simakobu | 2 | two morphs exist; one is creamy buff, the other is a black brown | primary forest | 7–9 kg | found in hilly areas of the Mentawai Islands. Only colobine monkey with a short tail. Live in monogamous social groups of around 4 individuals; not known to vocalize to any extent |

| Genus / Species | Common name | Number | Color | Habitat | Weight | Range / Natural history |
|---|---|---|---|---|---|---|
| Genus *Tarsius* | | | | | | |
| *T. bancanus* Horsfield, 1821 | tarsier (t), Horsfield's, Borneo, western, Malaysian, or Raffle's t | 4 | ssp. dependent; light gray buff to fulvous | prefer forest edge and secondary growth; found in disturbed areas | c. 120 g | occurs in Indonesia and Borneo. Appears to have noyau social pattern organized into 'neighborhood' of overlapping male and female home ranges |
| *T. dianae* Niemitz, Warter & Rumpler, 1991 | Kamarora or Dian's t | monotypic | grayish brown | primary TRF | 75–110 g | located in central Sulawesi. Natural history poorly known |
| *T. pumilus* Miller & Hollister, 1921 | pygmy t | monotypic | grayish buff | montane forest | c. 80 g | occupies forests of central Sulawesi. Natural history virtually unknown. Syn: *T. spectrum* |
| *T. spectrum* (Pallas, 1778) | spectral, eastern or Celebesian (Sulawesian) t | up to 5 | grayish buff | secondary growth and lowland scrub | c. 120 g | found in Sulawesi lowlands. Natural history poorly known. Social organization described as monogamous pairs that delineate territories by both scent and vocalizations |
| *T. syrichta* (Linnaeus, 1758) | Philippine t | 3 | ticked gray | primary and secondary TRF | c. 120 g | inhabits S Philippines. Natural history poorly known |
| *Theropithecus gelada* (Ruppell, 1835) | gelada baboon | 2 | buff to dark brown, naked pink pectoral hour-glass-shaped patch, black forelimbs, black face, M with cape | open areas and rocky gorges | F c. 10 kg M c. 20 kg | inhabits mountains in N and central Ethiopia. Social organization consists of one-male units |
| Genus *Trachypithecus* | brow-ridged langurs | | | | | |
| *T. auratus* (É. Geoffroy, 1812) | Lutong leaf-monkey or ebony langur | up to 3 | completely black | littoral, mangrove, or gallery forest | 4–14 kg | found in Indonesia. Social organization appears to be one-male units |
| *T. cristata* (Raffles, 1821) | silvered leaf-monkey, negro or crested langur | 4–8 | dark brown with silver tips | littoral, mangrove, or gallery forest | 4–14 kg | ranges from Myanmar into Indochina and Borneo. Social organization appears to be one-male units |
| *T. fransoisi* Pousargues, 1898 | Francois' leaf-monkey or Tonkinese lugong | 4 | black, prominent crown crest, white strip of hair from chin to pinna | rocky areas | 3.5–14 kg | reported to occupy rocky areas of SE China into Vietnam and Laos. Natural history poorly known. Syn: *T. delacouri* |
| *T. geei* Khajuria, 1956 | golden langur or leaf-monkey | monotypic | golden orange, black face | highland TRF | 3.5–13.6 kg | occupies forests of NE India and S central Bhutan. Natural history poorly known. Syn: *T. pileata* |
| *T. johnii* (Fischer, 1829) | Niligiri or John's langur or leaf-monkey | monotypic | black, pale brown neck and crown, black face | upland forests | 4–13 kg | inhabits upland forests of S India. One-male units appear to be the most common social group. Maintain territories via vocalization, male displays, and visual vigilance |

NA, not available; TRF, tropical rain forest; M, male; F, female; Syn(s), synonym(s); sp., species (singular); spp., species (plural); ssp., subspecies (singular); sspp., subspecies (plural).

| Species | Common name | No. of sspp. | Pelage | Habitat | Mass | Other information |
|---|---|---|---|---|---|---|
| T. obscura (Reid, 1837) | dusky, spectacled, or Brillen leaf-monkey or langur | 7 | dark brown or black, gray ventrum, pinkish white incomplete eye rings and upper and lower lips | upland primary and secondary TRF | 4–14 kg | found on the Malay peninsula. Sympatric with Presbytis melalophos. Occupies canopy level of forest. Social organization is mixed-sex troops which split into smaller foraging units |
| T. phayrei (Blythe, 1847) | Phayre's leaf-monkey | 4 | black with gray highlights, pinkish white complete eye rings and upper and lower lips | TRF | 6–13 kg | distributed in SE Asia from Bangladesh to Indochina |
| T. pileatus (Blythe, 1843) | capped or bonneted langur | 5 | gray to black dorsum, cream to orange ventrum, black crown and face, buffy to red cheeks and beard, tail dark brown | TRF | 5–11 kg | inhabits forests of E India, Bangladesh, and W Burma. Said to be extremely arboreal |
| T. vetulus (Erxleben, 1777) | purple-faced leaf-monkey | 5 | black or dark brown, brown crown cap, dark brown (purplish) face, off-white cheeks and beard, tail black or brown terminating in white tip | TRF | 5–10 kg | found throughout Sri Lanka with the exception of the SE. Highly arboreal and among the most folivorous of the langurs. Highly territorial with territories delineated by loud vocalizations and displays by the males. Live in one-male units in which the harem male is periodically deposed; following such a takeover, the new male commits infanticide of the previous male's offspring. Syn: T. senex |
| Varecia variegata (Kerr, 1792) | ruffed, variegated, or black-and-white lemur | 2 | dependent on population, a black and white form varies in the distribution of white, while another population is predominantly red | TRF | 3–4.5 kg | occupies forest running parallel to the E coast of Madagascar. Largest of the true lemurs. Syn: Lemur variegata |
| Xenothrix mcgregori Williams & Koopman, 1952 | Jamaican monkey | monotypic | NA | NA | c. 2 kg | Recently extinct. Recovered from Jamaica |

# Appendix 4 A geological time scale

Adapted from Lincoln, R., G. Boxshall and P. Clark (1998). *A Dictionary of Ecology, Evolution and Systematics*. Appendix 1, p. 325. Cambridge: Cambridge University Press. Used with permission.

| Eon | Era | Period | Duration (My)[a] | Time (Mya)[b,c] | Epoch |
|---|---|---|---|---|---|
| Phanerozoic | Cenozoic | Quaternary | 0.008 | | Holocene |
| | | | | 0.008 | |
| | | | 1.792 | | Pleistocene[d] |
| | | | | 1.8 | |
| | | Tertiary | 5 | | Pliocene |
| | | | | 5.3 | |
| | | | 18.5 | | Miocene |
| | | | | 23.8 | |
| | | | 9.9 | | Oligocene |
| | | | | 33.7 | |
| | | | 21.8 | | Eocene |
| | | | | 55.5 | |
| | | | 9.5 | | Paleocene |
| | | | | 65 | |
| | Mesozoic | Cretaceous | 70 | | |
| | | | | 145 | |
| | | Jurassic | 68 | | |
| | | | | 213 | |
| | | Triassic | 35 | | |
| | | | | 248 | |
| | Paleozoic | Permian | 38 | | |
| | | | | 286 | |
| | | Carboniferous | 74 | | |
| | | | | 360 | |
| | | Devonian | 50 | | |
| | | | | 410 | |
| | | Silurian | 40 | | |
| | | | | 440 | |
| | | Ordovician | 65 | | |
| | | | | 505 | |
| | | Cambrian | 39 | | |
| | | | | 544 | |
| Proterozoic | Precambrian | Algonkian | | | |
| | | | | 2500 | |
| Azoic | | Archaean | | | |
| | | | | 4500 | |

[a] my, millions of years.
[b] mya, millions of years ago.
[c] Source: United States Geological Survey web site (2003).
[d] See Appendixes 5–6 for glacial divisions within the Pleistocene.

# Appendix 5 Terrestrial chronology of the Pleistocene 'ice age' in the Northern Hemisphere

Modified from Lincoln, R., G. Boxshall and P. Clark (1998). *A Dictionary of Ecology, Evolution and Systematics*, 2nd edition, p. 326. Cambridge: Cambridge University Press. Used with permission.

| kya | Duration | Alpine Sequence | British Isles | Northern Europe | North America |
|---|---|---|---|---|---|
|  | *(Interglacial)* |  | *Holocene* |  |  |
| 10 |  |  |  |  |  |
|  |  | Würm 3 |  | Pomeranian | Wisconsin |
|  | 70,000 years | Würm 2 | Devensian | Frankfurt |  |
|  |  | Würm 1 |  | Brandenburg | Iowan |
| 80 |  |  |  |  |  |
|  | *(Interglacial)* | *Riss–Würm* | *Ipswichian* | *Eemian* | *Sangamonian* |
| 110 |  |  |  |  |  |
|  | 100,000 years | Riss | Wolstonian | Warthe Saale | Illinoian |
| 210 |  |  |  |  |  |
|  | *(Great Interglacial)* | *Mindel–Riss* | *Hoxnian* | *Holsteinian* | *Yarmouthian* |
| 310 |  |  |  |  |  |
|  | 90,000 years | Mindel | Anglian | Elsterian | Kansan |
| 400 |  |  |  |  |  |
|  | *(Interglacial)* | *Günz–Mindel* | *Cromerian* |  | *Aftonian* |
| 420 |  |  |  |  |  |
|  | 100,000 years | Günz | Beestonian | Elbe | Nebraskan |
| 520 |  |  |  |  |  |
|  | *(Interglacial)* |  | *Pastonian* |  |  |
|  | 260,000 years | Donau | Baventian |  | Pre-Nebraskan |

The Terrestrial Chronology has now largely been replaced by the **Marine Oxygen Isotope Chronology** (see Appendix 6).

# Appendix 6 The Marine Oxygen Isotope Chronology

Modified from Lincoln, R., G. Boxshall and P. Clark (1998). *A Dictionary of Ecology, Evolution and Systematics*, 2nd edition, p. 327. Cambridge: Cambridge University Press. Used with permission.

| Age (kya) | OIS[a] | Relative temp. | Polarity epoch |
|---|---|---|---|
| 13 | 1 | warm | |
| 24 | 2 | ice increases | |
| 59 | 3 | cool/temperate | |
| 71 | 4 | ice increases | |
| 128 | 5 | warm | |
| 186 | 6 | ice increases | |
| 245 | 7 | warm | |
| 303 | 8 | ice increases | |
| 339 | 9 | warm | |
| 362 | 10 | ice increases | Brunhes (Normal) |
| 423 | 11 | warm | |
| 478 | 12 | ice increases | |
| 524 | 13 | warm | |
| 565 | 14 | ice increases | |
| 620 | 15 | temperate | |
| 659 | 16 | ice increases | |
| 689 | 17 | temperate | |
| 726 | 18 | ice increases | |
| 780 | 19 | warm | |
| 800 | 20 | ice increases | .................... |
| | 21 | temperate | Matuyama (Reversed) |
| | 22 | ice increases | |
| c.900 | 23 | temperate | |

[a] OIS, Oxygen Isotope Stage; the even numbered stages are interpreted as periods of increasing continental ice masses. Aka the **Emiliani–Shackleton Glacial Sequence**.

# Appendix 7 Anatomical landmarks, postcranial bones, and major muscle groups

Abbreviations for craniometric landmarks (Figures 7a–7d)

| | | | | |
|---|---|---|---|---|
| al | alare | inc | incision |
| alv | alveolon | la | lacrimale |
| ap | apex | mf | maxillofrontale |
| b | bregma | n | nasion |
| ba | basion | ns | nasospinale |
| CA | Broca Horizontal | o | opisthion |
| cdl | condylion laterale | ol | orale |
| ec | ectoconchion | op | opisthocranion |
| ecm | ectomolare | or | orbitale |
| endoba | endobasion | pg | pogonion |
| enm | endomolare | po | porion |
| eu | euryon | pr | prosthion |
| FH | Frankfort Horizontal | pt | pterion |
| ft | frontotemporale | se | sellion |
| g | glabella | sta | staphylion |
| gn | gnathion | v | vertex |
| go | gonion | zo | zygoorbitale |
| i | inion | zm | zygomaxillare |
| idi | infradentale | zy | zygion |
| ids | alveolare | | |

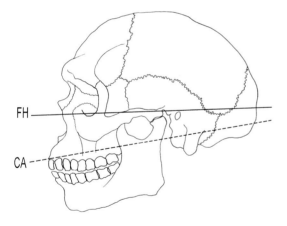

**Figure 7a** Modern human cranium: lateral/side view showing planes of orientation. See above for abbreviations used.

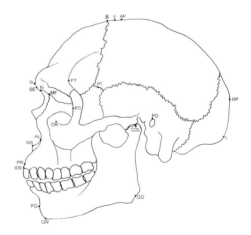

**Figure 7b** Modern human cranium: lateral/side view showing anatomical landmarks. See above for abbreviations used.

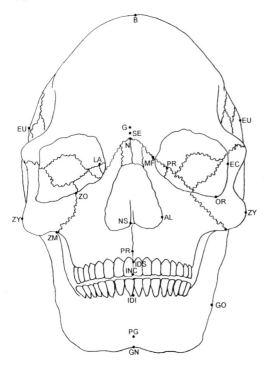

**Figure 7c** Modern human cranium: front view showing anatomical landmarks. See p. 621 for abbreviations used.

**Figure 7d** Modern human cranium: inferior view showing anatomical landmarks. See p. 621 for abbreviations used.

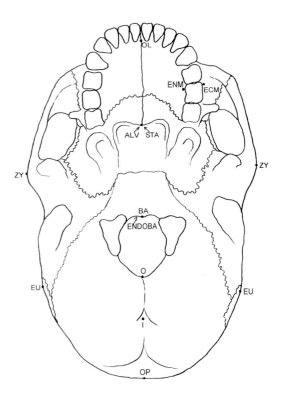

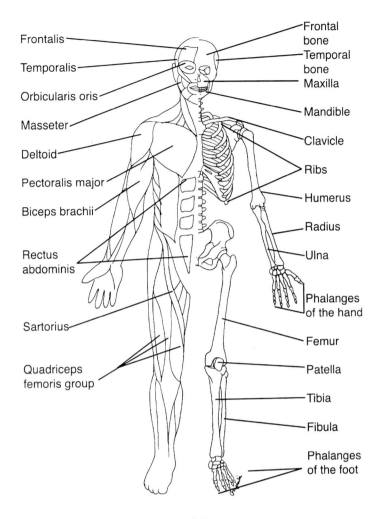

Frontalis

Temporalis

Orbicularis oris

Masseter

Deltoid

Pectoralis major

Biceps brachii

Rectus
abdominis

Sartorius

Quadriceps
femoris group

Frontal
bone

Temporal
bone

Maxilla

Mandible

Clavicle

Ribs

Humerus

Radius

Ulna

Phalanges
of the hand

Femur

Patella

Tibia

Fibula

Phalanges
of the foot

**Figure 7e** Modern human skeleton in ventral view: some
important postcranial bones and muscle groups.

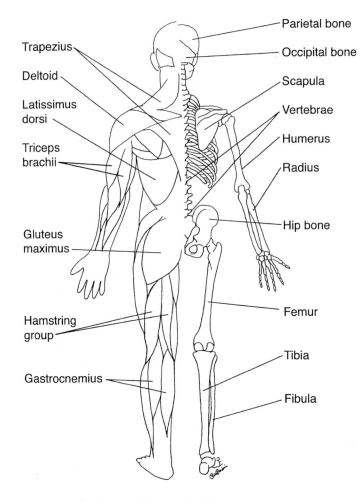

Trapezius
Deltoid
Latissimus dorsi
Triceps brachii
Gluteus maximus
Hamstring group
Gastrocnemius

Parietal bone
Occipital bone
Scapula
Vertebrae
Humerus
Radius
Hip bone
Femur
Tibia
Fibula

**Figure 7f** Modern human skeleton in dorsal view: some important postcranial bones and muscle groups.

# Appendix 8 Event timeline of human biology and evolution

**BCE:**

480  Hanno has the first recorded encounter with 'gorilloi'.

450  Empedocles speculates on changes in animal forms, is the 'father of the evolution idea'.

425  Herodotus describes peoples according to physical characteristics (*Historiae*, Book IX); observes that land is shaped by water that may have once covered the earth; postulates that Europe, Asia and Africa are separate continents.

250  Alexandrian astronomer Aristarchus proposes that the sun is at the center of the solar system.

**CE:**

140  Claudius Ptolemy, geographer and astronomer, says the earth is at the center of the universe.

180  The Roman physician Galen practices dissections exclusively on apes.

1080  Chinese scientists propose that fossil plants prove that climate changes have occurred throughout history.

1328  Excommunicated monk William of Ockham proposes a 'principle of parsimony'.

1501  The word 'anthropology' first appears in the literature, used by M. Hundt.

1515  L. da Vinci proposes that fossil marine shells have neither been carried to their present locations by a deluge, nor created on the spot.

1543  A. Vesalius publishes *De Humani Corporis Fabrica*, the first accurate human anatomy, accomplished through first-hand observations and dissection, during which he discovered Galen's anatomical errors.

1607  Reports of great apes begin to arrive in Europe; S. Purchas reports that an English sailor, taken prisoner by the Portuguese in Angola, told of two half-human 'monsters' — Pongo and Engeco — the gorilla and the chimpanzee.

1642  Vice-Chancellor of Cambridge Dr J. Lightfoot calculates the date of creation at 23 October 4004 BC; he fixes the exact time at 9 am on Sunday, 23 October. Lightfoot's estimate may contain no little irony, as the time and day are the start of the Fall term at Cambridge University.

1650  Archbishop of Armagh J. Ussher adopts Lightfoot's date of creation. Ussher's *Annals of the Ancient and New Testament* so impresses the establishment that the Protestants' King James Bible prints the date of 4004 BC in the margin of the Authorized Edition. Freemasons begin the convention of adding 4004 to the current calendrical year, stipulating the initials A.L., for *Anno Lucis*, in the Year of Light.

1661  S. Pepys speculates that chimpanzees 'might be taught to speak or to make signs'.

1686  J. Ray is the first to define a species as reproductive individuals.

1698  The Royal Society of London is founded on the Baconian tradition of description and discussion, having grown out of the Temple Coffee House. Its members are Fellows, and include many colonials in India and America.

1699  The first monograph appears that compares the anatomy of man with that of an ape, by E. Tyson, who performs the first dissection of a chimpanzee; he notes strong similarities with humans, especially in the brain.

1735  C. v. Linné (Linnaeus) publishes the first edition of *Systema Naturae*. He will publish sixteen editions of this work on taxonomy during his lifetime. It is the 10th edition of this work, published in 1758, that serves as the starting point for the modern scientific naming of animals — binomial nomenclature — later known as the 'Linnaean system', still utilized today. In this work he also proposes that species are constant and immutable, and can be objectively classified.

1740  Haller uses the word 'evolution' to describe the supposed unfolding of the preformed homunculus (=ontogeny).

1745  M. Lomonosov, on the basis of geological evidence, proposes that the earth must be hundreds of thousands of years old.

1746  P. L. Maupertuis analyses pedigrees of polydactyl families, implicitly falsifies preformationism.

1771  G.-L. L. de Buffon publishes *Les Epoques de la Nature*, in which he asserts that the earth is a staggering 75,000 years old, and that it existed long before the arrival of humans or any other form of life. Esper finds bones of humans and extinct animals at Gaillenreuth.

1775  Blumenbach publishes *On the Natural Varieties of Humans*, in which he describes five races of humans. This work was a rebuttal to the polygenist thesis of Henry Home, Lord Kames, in 1774.

1794  E. Darwin (grandfather of C. R. Darwin) publishes a poetical narrative, *Zoonomia*.

1797  Frere finds a Paleolithic axe with bones of extinct animals at Hoxne.

1798  T. Malthus publishes a pamphlet, *Essay on the Principle of Population*, in which he posits that there is a struggle for existence. This work will be a major influence on both Darwin and Wallace.

1800  The *Societe des Observateurs de l'Homme* becomes the world's first anthropological society. The membership includes the biologists Cuvier, Lamarck, Jussieu, and Geoffroy Saint-Hilaire; the explorers Bougainville and Levaillant; other physicians, chemists, and linguists.

| | |
|---|---|
| 1802 | Theologian W. Paley argues that every watch must have a Maker. |
| 1803 | An accurate description of a hemorrhaging disease that affects only males, hemophilia, is published by J. C. Otto of Philadelphia, but the genetic implications are ignored for over a century. |
| 1804 | G. Cuvier suggests that fossils found in the area around Paris are 'thousands of centuries old', a suggestion that pushes the age of the earth far beyond then accepted limits. Cuvier also publishes a paper explaining that the fossil animals that he has studied bear no resemblance to anything still living, suggesting either extinction or, as Cuvier prefers, catastrophism. |
| 1806 | French chemists Fourcroy and Vauquelin claim that buried ivory and fossil bones contain accumulated fluorine in precise proportion to their antiquity. |
| 1809 | J.-B. de Monet Lamarck publishes the first fully modern, systematic description of evolution, *Philosophie Zoologique*. His proposed 'mechanisms' for evolution are 'acquired characters' and a 'universal creative principle'. Lamarck is openly ridiculed by Georges Cuvier. |
| 1812 | G. Cuvier correctly identifies pterosaurs as flying reptiles; his conclusions will be ignored for decades. Twelve-year-old Mary Anning discovers the first fossil ichthyosaur. |
| 1818 | W. C. Wells describes natural selection when he suggests that human populations in Africa have been selected for their resistance to local diseases. |
| 1820 | C. F. Nasse describes the sex-linked mode of inheritance of hemophilia in humans. |
| 1821 | The Catholic Church lifts its ban on the teaching of the Copernican system. |
| | I. Venetz is the first to propose that glaciers once covered much of Europe. |
| | M. Anning discovers the first fossil plesiosaur; she is then twenty-one years old. |
| | L. de Mortillet separates the Paleolithic into the Acheulean and Mousterian, based on the different tool kits used in the different periods. |
| 1822 | J.-B. de Monet Lamarck's work, *Histoire naturelle des animaux sans vertèbres* ('The Natural History of Invertebrates'), is published; it is the first work to distinguish between vertebrates and invertebrates. |
| | W. Buckland publishes an account of how ancient hyenas lived and fed, a study based on their fossil remains. This study is one of the first descriptions of behaviors based on the study of fossil remains. |
| 1823 | W. Buckland discovers 'Red Lady of Paviland', who he assumes was a prostitute in service to a Roman encampment (hence the red ochre); actually a male dated to about 25–18 kya, possibly a Cro-Magnon. These are the earliest discovered fossil human remains then known to science. |
| 1825 | G. Cuvier formally announces his theory of catastrophism, in which he proposes that violent catastrophes have caused the extinction of large groups of animal species, and also have altered the Earth. |
| 1826 | Tournal attributes human bones from Bize to 'antehistoric' time. |
| | R. Jameson may have written a controversial essay, 'Observations on the nature and importance of geology', in which he questions the young-earth idea. |
| 1829 | A child's skull is found by P.-C. Schmerling at Engis in Belgium. Recognized a century later as a Neandertal, the initial systematic significance of the find goes unnoticed. Its apparent antiquity is convincing and helps C. Lyell, who views the material in 1833, to begin serious consideration of the antiquity of man. |
| 1830 | C. Lyell publishes volume 1 of his classic *Principles of Geology*, in which he focuses on the principle of uniformitarianism. C. R. Darwin will take a copy of this work on board HMS *Beagle* the following year. |
| | P.-C. Schmerling finds a Neandertal child in Engis Cave. |
| 1831 | C. R. Darwin embarks upon a five-year circumnavigation of the world |
| 1834 | C. J. Thomsen of the Danish National Museum divides the times that people have produced tools into a Stone Age, a Bronze Age, and an Iron Age. |
| 1835 | L. A. J. Quetelet publishes *Anthropométrie*, in which he measures several aspects of the human body and determines that physical sizes fall into a distribution later recognized as the normal curve. |
| | In September, HMS *Beagle* arrives at the Galápagos; C. R. Darwin observes land tortoise, iguanas, and on each island shoots local varieties of small birds known as finches. |
| 1836 | C. R. Darwin arrives back in Britain after spending five years on the *Beagle*. |
| 1837 | J.-L. R. Agassiz uses the term 'die Eiszeit' ('Ice Age') to describe his idea that all of Europe was once covered with glaciers at some time in the past. |
| | J. van Hoeven applies eleven measures to compare human crania. |
| | E. Lartet describes fossil ape designated *Pliopithecus*. |
| | In July, C. R. Darwin begins the first of his secret 'transmutation' notebooks while working in London on his *Journal of Researches* and the geology of the voyage of the *Beagle*. |
| 1838 | Through 1839, M. J. Schleiden and T. Schwann develop the cell theory, a great generality of biology equaled only by the theory of evolution; Schleiden also notes nucleoli within nuclei. |
| | On September 28, C. R. Darwin writes in his 'transmutation notebook' D, page 134: 'We ought to be far from wondering of changes in number of species, from small changes in nature of locality. Even the energetic language of (de Candolle) does not convey the warring of the species as inference from |

Malthus . . . . One may say there is a force like a hundred thousand wedges trying to force every kind of adapted structure into the gaps in the oeconomy of nature, or rather forming gaps by thrusting out weaker ones'. Darwin had just read Malthus' *Essay on the Principles of Population*.

1839    The *Société Ethnologique de Paris* is founded, and will exist until 1848. It had been preceded by the *Société des observateurs de l'homme* in 1800, and will be succeeded by the *Société d'Anthropologie de Paris* after 1859. American physician S. G. Morton publishes *Crania Americana*, in which he ranks human races by brain size.

1840    J.-L. R. Agassiz publishes *Études sur les glaciers* ('Study of Glaciers'), in which he describes glacial motion, confirming his theories concerning the ice ages.

1843    The *Ethnological Society* (of Great Britain) is formed. Also known as the 'ethnologicals', it includes Lane Fox, Pitt Rivers, T. H. Huxley, C. R. Darwin, A. R. Wallace, F. Galton, Busk, Lubbock, Evans, etc.

1844    R. Chambers anonymously publishes *Vestiges of the Natural History of Creation*. Although it contains many errors and does not suggest a mechanism for evolution, it is an important antecedent to Darwin, and clearly influences both Darwin's and Wallace's thinking, and promotes the evolution concept.

1847    Stories and rumors of 'gorillas' lead to new reports of their existence to western science by T. Savage and J. Wyman.
C. Bergmann proposes his 'rule' that body size follows a gradient, with thicker bodies found in colder regions.

1848    The American Association for the Advancement of Science is founded in Philadelphia, modeled on the British AAS.
A woman's skull is found at Forbes' Quarry in Gibraltar. Later recognized as a Neandertal, the initial significance of this find also goes unrecognized until discovered by scientists in a small local museum in 1864.

1849    The British Admiralty issues *Manual of Scientific Inquiry* as a guide for scientists, practitioners and cultivators of science traveling abroad. It is reissued in 1851 and 1859.

1852    A theory of encephalization is proposed by J. Gana.

1853    The term 'human paleontology' is first used for fossil men, by M. Serres.
Handaxes are found associated with bones of extinct mammals at St. Acheul, in France.

1855    A. R. Wallace formulates his Sarawak Law, in which he declares that 'Every species has come into existence coincident both in time and space with a pre-existing closely allied species'.

1856    E. Lartet describes a fossil ape from the Miocene beds of France, *Dryopithecus*.
A skullcap is found at Feldhofer cave in the Neander valley, Germany, which is different from that of 'normal' humans. Because its antiquity is not suspected, several anatomical interpretations are offered by Virchow and others.
Gregor Mendel, a monk at the Augustinian monastery of St. Thomas in Brünn, Austria (now Brno, Czechoslovakia), begins breeding experiments with the garden pea, *Pisum sativum*.

1858    A. R. Wallace posts his manuscript *On the Tendencies of Varieties to Depart Indefinitely from the Original Type* to C. R. Darwin, which arrives in June.
On July 1, Lyell and Hooker read Darwin's and Wallace's papers to the Linnaean Society.
C. R. Darwin begins to write an abstract of 'Natural Selection'.

1859    The antiquity of humankind is established through Boucher de Perthes' discoveries at Abbeville. At the suggestion of English paleontologist H. Falconer, an English group visits the Abbeville beds explored by Boucher de Perthes in 1846, essentially approving the antiquity of the stone tools. The group included J. Prestwich, J. Evans, C. Lyell and A. J. Evans.
P. Broca founds the Anthropological Institute (*Société d'Anthropologie*, Paris).
In November, the first edition of C. R. Darwin's *On the Origin* is published. Within ten years this work convinces most life scientists that organisms on the earth are the product of a long history of evolution.

1860    At the BAAS meeting in Oxford, responding to 'Soapy Sam' Wilberforce's question as to whether it was through his grandfather or grandmother that he claimed to be descended from the apes, T. H. Huxley states in effect that he would prefer to be descended from an ape rather than from any cultivated man who prostituted the gifts of culture and eloquence to the service of prejudice and falsehood.

1861    The 3rd edition of the *Origin* is completed. In it, Darwin acknowledges those he called his 'precursors', who had touched on critical elements of his thesis; these included: von Buch, d'Halloy, Kaup, Nägeli, Blainville, Wells, Prichard, Geoffroy St.-Hilaire, Matthew, Rafinesque-Schmaltz, Herbert, Haldeman, Chambers, and Wallace.

1863    G. de Mortillet classifies periods of the Stone Age based upon technology, utilizing a site that typifies each of the proposed industries such as Abbevillean, Mousterian, Aurignacian and Magdalenian.
C. Lyell publishes *Geological Evidence as to the Antiquity of Man*, in which he admits that the evidence for human antiquity is finally compelling, and that humans may have evolved from a simpler form of life.
T. H. Huxley publishes *Evidence as to Man's Place in Nature*, the first book specifically on human evolution.

É. Lartet excavates at La Madeleine; he finds a mammoth tooth engraved with a sketch of a mammoth and is convinced that the artist had actually seen a live mammoth.

W. King proposes a separate species, *Homo neanderthalensis*, for all Feldhofer-like specimens.

The *Anthropological Society* (of Great Britain) is formed, also known as the 'anthropologicals'.

1865    Lubbock's *Pre-Historic Times* is published; he uses the designations Neolithic and Paleolithic for the first time to distinguish two stages of stone working.

E. Dupont discovers a Neandertal mandible at Trou de La Naulette in Belgium.

Abbé G. Mendel presents the results and interpretations of his genetic studies on the garden pea at the Brünn Society for the Study of Natural Science at their monthly meetings held in February and March.

1866    G. Mendel publishes *Versuche über Pflanzenhybriden* ('Experiments in Plant hybridization') in a small journal, the local *Transactions*, but his work will be cited only twice during the next 35 years.

1868    German zoologist E. Haeckel publishes *Natürliche Schöpfungsgeschichte*, in which he divides humanity into 12 separate species, including the hypothetical *Pithecanthropus alalus*.

F. Galton, a cousin of C. R. Darwin, measures the mental abilities of human populations, and shows that these form a normal distribution, the bell-shaped curve.

T. H. Huxley publishes *On the Animals which are Most Nearly Intermediate Between Birds and Reptiles*, arguing that birds are descendants of dinosaurs, a suggestion that will be ignored for another century.

The first edition of C. R. Darwin's *The Variation of Animals and Plants under Domestication* is published.

L. Lartet excavates five Paleolithic burials at Cro-Magnon.

1869    F. Galton publishes *Hereditary Genius*, in which he emphasizes the genetic basis of intelligence, and is the first to compare mental traits in twins.

G. Mendel publishes a 2nd and final paper on garden peas before retiring from experimental life and assuming duties as the Abbot at the Brünn Monastery.

F. Miescher isolates 'nuclein' (DNA) from soiled bandages.

1870    E. Cope uses term 'evolution' in an article; it is the first English use of the term in its modern sense.

1871    The first edition of *The Descent of Man and Selection in Relation to Sex* is completed by C. R. Darwin. In this work Darwin connects man to the apes and monkeys in an evolutionary diagram, and states that 'Man is descended from a hairy, tailed quadruped, probably arboreal in its habits'. He also introduces the mechanisms of sexual selection (to explain hairlessness) and group selection (to explain humanity's lack of natural weapons).

1872    P. Gervais describes a new fossil primate from Monte Bamboli in Italy; he calls it *Oreopithecus bambolii*.

1873    Sections D and E of the BAAS are amalgamated as membership in the Anthropological Society of London falls off dramatically and its members join the alternative, the Ethnological Society. In 1872 Lane Fox states publicly that certain major issues in the anthropological societies have been resolved: (1) that the antiquity and descent of man is now an established fact; (2) that humans are ultimately monogenic in origin, and (3) that there is a progressive character to the growth of civilization. The joint membership becomes the Royal Anthropological Institute.

1874    The BAAS publishes an instruction manual conceived and edited predominantly by E. B. Tylor, called *Notes and Queries on Anthropology for the Use of Travellers and Residents in Uncivilized Lands*. This manual covers most of the major subjects that are to dominate anthropology in its early stages, such as what questions to ask about pedigrees, religion, food, sex roles, etc., as well as how to pose 'natives' for photographic purposes, etc.

More Neandertals are found at Pontnewydd (1874), Rivaux (1876), and Šipka (1880).

1877    Father of American Anthropology L. H. Morgan publishes *Ancient Society*, an early example of American evolutionism.

J. Allen modifies Bergmann's Rule; his exceptions constitute Allen's rule.

1879    M. de Santuola discovers the cave art of Altamira, in France; the painting is thought to be a hoax.

The Anthropological Society of Washington is established. Its publishes *Abstracts of Transactions* (1881–5) and the *American Anthropologist* (1888), which is subsumed by the AAA after 1902.

The US Congress creates the American Bureau of Ethnology at the Smithsonian, with J. W. Powell named as its first director. Later renamed the Bureau of American Ethnology, it becomes the repository of the 'archives, records, and material relating to the Indians of North America, collected by the geographical and geological survey of the Rocky Mountains'.

H. Spencer publishes *Principles of Sociology*, in which he applies Darwin's mechanism of natural selection to social life; this application becomes known as both Spencerism and Social Darwinism.

1882    C. R. Darwin dies and is buried in Westminster Abbey; among his pall-bearers are Huxley, Hooker, and Wallace. He had worked on new manuscripts until the end.

1883    E. van Beneden discovers that haploid cells are formed during the cell division of sperm and ova.

F. Galton coins the term 'eugenics' in his publication *Enquiries into Human Faculty*, and suggests that human beings can be improved by selective breeding.

1884    H. Spencer suggests that the principle of survival of the fittest implies that people who are burdens on society should be allowed to die rather than be helped by society.

1886    More discoveries of skeletons of the Neandertal type occurs in Belgium, at Spy.
T. H. Huxley publishes *Evolution and Ethics*, in which he addresses the possibility of the evolution of morality.

1887    E. van Beneden discovers that each species has a fixed number of chromosomes.
A. Weismann postulates that periodic reduction in chromosome number must occur in all sexual organisms.

1888    F. Galton introduces the concept of statistical correlation.

1889    Galton publishes *Natural Inheritance*, reporting on his research in quantitative genetics, including the concept of the correlation coefficient and a formula for standard error.

1890    A. Holmes uses radioactivity to date various rock formations; he establishes that the earth is about 4.6 billion years old.

1891    *Pithecanthropus erectus* remains ('Java Man') are found at Trinil in Java by E. Dubois.

1892    A. Weismann stresses the independence of the germ plasm from the body proper. He contradicts Lamarck's views on the heredity of acquired characters by asserting that the only inherited variations arise in the germ plasm.
F. Galton publishes *Fingerprints*, a practical study of the differences in fingerprints and the potential for their use in identification and criminology.

1894    E. Dubois discovers more examples of 'Java Man', and publishes his initial descriptions of *Pithecanthropus erectus*.

1895    Four boys discover cave paintings at La Mouthe; a previous finding of similar painting at Altamira is vindicated.
E. Dubois brings his new 'Java ape-man' fossils to Europe; his explanations meet with considerable resistance.

1896    K. Jordan is the first to state clearly that speciation is a product of both 'transmutation factors' and geographic isolation.

1897    R. Ross locates the malaria parasite in the *Anopheles* mosquito; he determines that it is the mosquito that transmits the parasite from one human to another. He will publish *Researches on Malaria* in 1904.
C. Ejikman demonstrates a relationship between the occurrence of beriberi and the consumption of polished rice; however, he does not attribute the disease to the absence of a vitamin.

1898    P.-L. Simond proposes that it is the fleas on rats that transmit the bubonic plague to humans.

1899    M. Beijerinck finds the smallest form of 'life', which he calls a 'virus'.
K. Pearson extends Galton's formulae to include a product-moment correlation.
K. Gorjanovic-Kramberger finds a Neandertal at the Krapina Rock Shelter in Croatia; he publishes in 1906, claiming great antiquity (100 kya).

1900    H. de Vries, K. Correns and E. Tschermak independently rediscover Mendel's papers and recognize their importance. W. Bateson stresses the importance of Mendel's contribution in an address to the Royal Society of London.
W. Reed, J. Carroll, J. W. Lazear, and A. Agramonte establish that the disease yellow fever is transmitted by mosquitoes of the genus *Aedes*.
K. Landsteiner discovers the blood agglutination phenomenon in man and names the blood factors A, B, and O.

1901    H. de Vries adopts the term 'mutation' to describe sudden, spontaneous alterations in hereditary material, in *Die Mutationstheorie*.
A. Windhaus shows that molecules of vitamin D can be affected by sunlight.

1902    G. Yule proposes a theory of population genetics, anticipating Castle (see 1903).
W. S. Sutton proposes that the independent assortment of gene pairs stems from the behavior of synapsed chromosomes during meiosis. He publishes *The Chromosome Theory of Inheritance* in 1903.
The American Anthropological Association is founded, and soon assumes publication of the *American Anthropologist*, which had first appeared in 1888 as an organ of the ASW.
C. E. McClung suggests that an 'accessory chromosome' is a sex determinant, and argues that sex must be determined at the time of fertilization, not just in insects, but perhaps in other species, including man. N. Stevens independently discovers sex determination in 1905.
P. Kropotkin challenges Darwin's doctrine, addressing the issue of cooperation (altruism).
K. Landsteiner discovers a 4th blood type in man and names the new factor AB.

1903    H. Poincaré realizes that small inaccuracies in initial conditions can lead to significant differences when cascaded through a system; this work becomes the foundation of chaos theory.
W. Castle says Mendel's 'factors' behave randomly; he anticipates the work of Hardy and Weinberg by five years.

1904    G. H. F. Nuttall uses blood groups and other serological factors to classify organisms into phyla, classes, orders, and genera.

W. Bateson coins the term 'genetics'.

1905    E. Wilson independently discovers the X and Y chromosomes.

A. Binet, V. Henri and T. Simon develop the intelligence test in France in order to identify students who require tutoring.

The *International Rules of Zoological Nomenclature* is published; it is the first attempt at bringing worldwide standardization to the classification of animals.

1906    B. Brunhes discovers that lava contains residual magnetism that reflects the earth's magnetic field at the time of cooling, and retains this information even after the lava has hardened, a fundamental principle of paleomagnetism.

W. Bateson and R. C. Punnett report the first case of gene linkage.

1907    B. Boltwood demonstrates that radioactive decay in rocks is independent of chemical or mechanical processes, and that the ratio of uranium to its final decay product, lead, can be used to determine its age. Workmen uncover a massive fossil jaw in the Rösch sandpit, near Mauer, Germany; O. Schoetensack attributes the specimen to *Homo heidelbergensis*.

1908    G. Hardy studies Mendelian proportions in mixed populations. *Uber den Nachweis der Vererbung bein Menschen* is published by W. Weinberg, and, independently, they formulate the so-called Hardy–Weinberg law of population genetics.

The Le Moustier 1 Neandertal is found in France; Le Moustier 2 is discovered in 1914 (and then misplaced). The Ehringsdorf Neandertal is found in Germany.

Buried in the floor of a small cave near the French village of La Chapelle-aux-Saints, A. Bouyssonie, J. Bouyssonie and L. Bardon discover a nearly complete skeleton which they forward to M. Boule for analysis. Boule attributes it to *Homo neanderthalensis*.

1909    C. E. Little initiates a breeding program that produces the first inbred strains of mice; the first strain is today called DBA, and is among several that have survived for nearly a century.

A. E. Garrod publishes *Inborn Errors of Metabolism*, the earliest study of the biochemical genetics of man (or any other species).

W. Johannsen's work on the inheritance of seed size in beans lead him to realize the necessity of distinguishing between the appearance of an organism and its genetic constitution. He invents the terms 'phenotype' and 'genotype' to serve this purpose, and he also coins the term 'gene'.

At La Ferrassie, in the Dordogne, R. Capitan and D. Peyrony report finding several Neandertals buried in a 'family cemetery'.

1910    L. Dollo's 'Law' proposes evolutionary irreversibility for complex traits.

T. H. Morgan discovers the first mutant in *Drosophila*, the white-eyed fly (the normal color is red), and consequently sex-linkage.

1911    The first 'human fossils' are found at Piltdown, a site excavated since 1908 in southern England, by amateur archaeologist C. Dawson; these are attributed to *Eoanthropus dawsonii* (see 1950).

C. Davenport declares that only breeding programs can save mankind.

The La Quina Neandertal is found in France; M. Boule publishes his monograph on the La Chapelle Neandertals, characterizing them as brutish.

R. C. Punnett publishes *Mendelism*, in which his famous diagram for showing heredity, the Punnett square, is illustrated.

A. Krober befriends Ishi, the last Yahi Indian in California.

1912    C. Dawson finds further specimens of 'Piltdown Man'; the mandible possesses the characteristics of an ape, while the skull appears to be more like a modern human. The find is accepted as genuine by A. Keith and others. A. Woodward says the Piltdown brain is above the 'cerebral Rubicon'.

F. Boas compares the cephalic indices of American-born children to their parents of European ancestry, and concludes that cranial plasticity, rather than heritability, explains the observed variation. His work will be frequently cited as an example that data from craniometry studies cannot be used to characterize populations nor to construct racial categories based on such data (see 2002).

A. Wegener first suggests his 'displacement theory' (continental drift); his ideas will be ignored until the late 1960s (see 1915).

1913    A. H. Sturtevant, in T. H. Morgan's lab, provides the experimental basis for linkage concept in *Drosophila* and produces the first genetic map, of the X chromosome.

1914    C. B. Bridges discovers meiotic nondisjunction in *Drosophila*.

1915    J. B. S. Haldane, A. D. Sprunt, and N. M. Haldane describe the first example of linkage in a vertebrate, in mice.

A. Wegener publishes *Die Entstehung der Kontinente und Ozeane* ('The Origin of Continents and Oceans') in which he elaborates his theory of continental drift and imagines the supercontinent of Pangaea (see 1912).

G. E. Pilgrim describes several fossil primates from the Miocene of the Siwaliks in India.

1917    Scottish biologist and mathematician D'Arcy Wentworth Thompson publishes *On Growth and Form*.

1918    The first issue of the *American Journal of Physical Anthropology* appears, edited by A. Hrdlička.

H. M. Evans incorrectly reports that human cells contain 48 chromosomes (see 1956).

J. G. Andersson discovers Chou K'ou Tien (Zhoukoudian) near Peking, China; he shows the site to O. Zdansky in 1921.

1919    T. H. Morgan calls attention to the equality in *Drosophila melanogaster* between the number of linkage groups and the haploid number of chromosomes.

F. Wood Jones publishes *The Origin of Man*, in which he argues that humans and the great apes diverged from a common ancestor similar to the modern tarsier, and like neither a monkey nor an ape.

1920    Russian population geneticist S. Chetverikov elucidates basic principles of populations genetics; his unpublished manuscript will greatly influence British biologists, notably J. B. S. Haldane.

Cave 'writing' is 'explained' and dated in France by Henri Breuil.

F. G. Banting and C. H. Best isolate insulin and study its physiological properties. Soon, diabetics will begin to inject animal analogues of human insulin, relieving their symptoms.

Chinese philosopher Lu Xun regards evolutionary theory as a serious pursuit.

1921    T. Zwigelaar finds the crania of a robust male hominid at the Broken Hill Mine, Kabwe, Zambia.

J. G. Andersson discovers fossil fauna at Chou K'ou Tien (Zhoukoudian).

R. B. Goldschmidt publishes the first genetic analysis and discussion of the evolutionary implications of industrial melanism.

1923    O. Zdansky finds humanlike teeth at Chou K'ou Tien (Zhoukoudien).

1924    The Kiik Koba Neandertal is found in the Crimea by G. A. Bonch-Osmolovsky.

The U. S. Congress passes the Immigration Restriction Act of 1924 that places limiting quotas on certain countries, e.g. Poland. It is heavily supported by eugenicists and lobbied for by Goddard, Yerkes, and others.

R. Dart discovers a fossil brain cast and the face of the Taung child in two boxes from the Taung Quarry. He names a new species of hominid, *Australopithecus africanus*.

1925    C. B. Bridges completes a cytogenetic analysis of the aneuploid offspring of triploid *Drosophila* and defines the relationship between the sex chromosomes and autosomes that control sexual phenotype.

D. Garrod directs the excavation of Devil's Tower Cave, a Neandertal archaeological site in Gibraltar.

In *Almost Human*, R. Yerkes suggests that great apes might acquire a simple, non-vocal, 'sign language'.

The 'monkey trial' occurs in Dayton, Tennessee. J. Scopes, a teacher, admits to having taught evolution, and is arrested and convicted for breaking a state law prohibiting the teaching of evolutionary theory.

F. Bernstein suggests that the ABO blood group is determined by a series of allelic genes.

1926    E. Hooton encourages his Harvard students to undertake field studies.

W. K. Gregory and M. Hellman describe the many fossil primates from the Miocene of Kenya, including *Dryopithecus*.

S. S. Chetverikov initiates the genetic analysis of wild populations of *Drosophila*.

A. H. Sturtevant finds the first chromosome inversion in *Drosophila*.

1927    J. B. S. Haldane suggests that genes known to control certain coat colors in various rodents and carnivores may be evolutionarily homologous.

D. Black discovers a single molar at Locality 1, Chou K'ou Tien (Zhoukoudian); he names the new species *Sinanthropus pekinensis*. Paleontologist Pei Wenzhong begins extensive exploration at the site.

P. Teilhard de Chardin describes *Omomys* (later, *Teilhardina*).

A. Hrdlička suggests that Neandertals are a successional stage in the human lineage.

H. J. Muller reports the artificial induction of mutations in *Drosophila*, by X-ray bombardment.

1928    T. D. Lysenko gains control of Soviet biological research under Stalin; through 1965, Russian biological and agricultural programs will labor under the neo-Lamarckian delusion that acquired characteristics can be inherited.

1929    The Saccopastore Neandertal is found in Italy; excavations continue 1929–35.

M. Matuyama proposes that rocks of certain strata have reversed magnetic fields, and concludes that the earth's magnetic field has reversed polarity several times in the past.

W. Cannon proposes that organisms return to a level state he calls homeostasis.

The Tabun Cave Neandertal is found at Mt. Carmel, Palestine (now Israel), by D. Garrod.

W. C. Pei (Pei Wenzhong) discovers the first nearly complete skull of *Sinanthropus pekinensis*. More than 40 individuals are eventually found at Chou K'ou Tien (Zhoukoudian), China.

P. Levene describes the four DNA bases: A, T, G, and C.

1930    K. Holzinger says IQs of foster children 'improve'; he reports new measure of heritability, *H*.

R. A. Fisher publishes *The Genetical Theory of Natural Selection*.

R. Yerkes becomes highly influential in promoting field studies of primates.

A. E. Douglas determines the date of an American archaeological site by using tree rings observed in artifacts found at the site, thus establishing the dating technique of dendrochronology.

D. Garrod excavates with T. McKown at Mt. Carmel (1930–2), finds 'Neanderthalians' (Keith).

The American Association of Physical Anthropologists (AAPA) is founded, and adopts the *AJPA* as its official organ, which had first appeared in 1918.

S. Wright calls some population-level genetic changes 'drift'. His mechanism becomes known as the Wright effect.

1931    C. Patterson establishes the exact age of the earth at 4500 million years, independently confirmed by Adolph Knopf.

S. Wright publishes a larger work, *Evolution in Mendelian Populations*. This work, together with Fisher's book (1930) and a series of papers by J. B. S. Haldane published between 1930–2 under the general title *A Mathematical Theory of Natural and Artificial Selection*, constitute the mathematical foundation of population genetics.

C. Stern, and independently H. B. Creighton and B. McClintock, provide the cytological proof of crossing over.

L. S. B. Leakey finds a perfect hand-ax within 24 hours of arriving at Olduvai Gorge. He names the gully in which finds it FLK after his wife Frida Leakey and the Swahili word for gully, 'korongo'.

W. Oppenoorth finds 'tropical Neanderthals' in the Solo River terraces, near Ngandong.

1932    G. E. Lewis discovers *Ramapithecus* in Miocene sediments of the Siwaliks in India.

L. K. Diamond (father of J. Diamond) describes hemolytic disease of the newborn (HDN).

J. S. Huxley publishes *Problems of Relative Growth*, in which he points out that the specific growth rates of organs exist in constant ratios to each other during embryogenesis, a fundamental allometric result.

Archaeologist T. McCown finds hominid skulls at Mugharet es-Skhūl, near Haifa.

1933    A. T. Hopwood describes the first fossil primates from the lower Miocene of Kenya.

Several skulls of *Homo erectus* are found in Java (1931–9) by G. Von Koenigswald.

K. Sigrist finds a calvaria washed downriver and deposited at Steinheim, Germany. It is described as *Homo steinheimensis*.

At Qafzeh, six more 'Neanderthalians' are excavated; publication is delayed until 1951.

1934    H. Fölling discovers phenylketonuria (PKU), the first hereditary metabolic disorder shown to be responsible for mental retardation.

P. L. Héritier and G. Teissier experimentally demonstrate the disappearance of a deleterious gene from populations of *Drosophila melanogaster*.

1935    G. H. R. von Konigswald buys teeth of a large fossil primate in drug stores in Hong Kong and Canton; he names the specimen *Gigantopithecus blacki*, the largest primate ever known.

L. Kohl-Larsen finds parts of a crania and maxilla, and an occiput from a 2nd individual, near Lake Eyasi, in then Tanganyika Territory; they are attributed to *Africanthropus njaransensis*.

J. B. S. Haldane is the first to calculate the spontaneous mutation frequency of a human gene. In *The Causes of Evolution*, he also notes that '. . . in so far as it makes for the survival of one's descendants and near relations, altruistic behaviour is a kind of Darwinian fitness, and may be expected to spread as a result of natural selection' (p.131).

M. D. Leakey begins a distinguished career in Tanzania and Kenya.

A. Blanc suggests the Neandertal he finds at Monte Circeo was ceremoniously cannibalized.

Skull fragments are found by A. T. Marston at Barnfield Pit, Swanscombe, Kent, England; they are attributed to *Homo swanscombensis*.

1936    F. Weidenereich begins exhaustive examinations of Chinese fossils.

A. H. Sturtevant and T. Dobzhansky publish the first account of the use of inversions in constructing a chromosomal phylogenetic tree.

Neandertals are not our ancestors, says H. Vallois, contradicting A. Hrdlička (see 1927).

A Neandertal child's crania from Engis is described by C. Fraipont.

R. Broom locates an almost complete endocast and adult skull of *Plesianthropus transvaalensis* at Sterkfontein.

1937    G. H. R. von Koenigswald discovers more erectine-like specimens at Sangiran, in Java.

T. Dobzhansky publishes a major work of 'evolutionary synthesis', *Genetics and the Origin of Species*.

1938    The Teshik Tash Neandertal is found in Central Asia by A. P. Okladnikov.

W. K. Gregory, M. Hellman, and G. E. Lewis describe new fossil primates from the Siwaliks of India, including *Bramapithecus* and *Ramapithecus*.

F. Kallman publishes *The Genetics of Schizophrenia*.

L. Penrose says mental deficiency is heritable.

1939    L. Kohl-Larsen finds parts of a maxilla containing premolars near Laetoli, in the then Tanganyika Territory; the specimen is attributed to *Meganthropus africanus*.

C. Coon publishes *The Races of Europe*.

Using new techniques, T. Painter identifies many bands on chromosomes.

J. S. Huxley coins the term 'cline' to describe certain patterns of spatial variation.

1940 Student of relative growth, size and scale in biology D'Arcy Wentworth Thompson, influenced by the art of Albrecht Dürer, uses transformation grids to illustrate changes in growth and form (see 1917).

Landsteiner and A. S. Weiner discover the *Rh* factor, common on the red blood cells of humans and rhesus monkeys.

Stress can affect the functions of the mammalian body, reports H. Selye.

R. Goldschmidt speculates that some 'hopeful monsters' are macromutations. Although he is heavily criticized, the discovery of HOX genes 50 years later partly explain his experimental observations.

Four boys discover the Lascaux cave art; the paintings are later dated to 17 kya.

1941 M. Milankovitch explains the Ice Age and cyclic fluctuations in climate.

G. W. Beadle and E. L. Tatum publish the one gene – one enzyme idea, later known as the central dogma.

1942 E. Mayr produces another tome of evolutionary synthesis, *Systematics and the Origin of Species*.

J. S. Huxley also publishes a major synthetic piece, *Evolution: the Modern Synthesis*, as well as *Problems of Relative Growth*.

C. H. Waddington proposes that 'genetics' (the study of inheritance or heredity) be distinguished from 'epigenetics', the study of the processes by which the genotype gives rise to the phenotype.

1943 At the early Pleistocene East African site of Olorgesailie, M. D. Leakey applies excavation techniques that expose Acheulean artifacts horizon by horizon, the first such approach to excavation of a Paleolithic site.

1944 T. Dobzhansky describes the phylogeny of the gene arrangements in the 3rd chromosome of *Drosophila*.

G. G. Simpson publishes *Tempo and Mode in Evolution*, another work on evolutionary synthesis.

Following Griffith's 1928–40 experiments, O. T. Avery, M. McCarty, and C. M. McLeod conclude that genes must consist of DNA, or deoxyribonucleic acid.

1945 R. Matthey counts the *nombre fondamentale*, homologous fragments of chromosomes, not whole chromosomes.

G. G. Simpson publishes 'The principles of classification and a classification of mammals' in *Bull. Amer. Mus. Nat. Hist.*

1946 The work of identifying World War II dead falls to several physical anthropologists, including T. D. Stewart.

E. Hooton separates Keith's 'Neanderthalians' into 'classics' and 'progressives'.

1947 The Center for Child Growth is established in Philadelphia by W. M. Krogman.

At Fontéchevade Cave, Charente, France, G. Henri-Martin finds portions of two skulls in association with Tayacian tools.

F. Weidenreich publishes a 'candelabra' model of recent human evolution known as multiregionalism.

1948 M. D. Leakey finds *Proconsul*, dated at 16 mya, on Rusinga Island, eastern Africa.

W. F. Libby *et al.* develop the radiocarbon dating method; soon, samples up to 100 ky BP can be dated by variations and enhancements to the original method.

A. Boivin *et al.* show that in different cells of an organism the quantity of DNA for each haploid set of chromosomes is constant.

Forgotten for almost 50 years, the fluorine method is refined by K. Oakley and is applied to the Galley Hill skeleton and the Swanscombe skull, confirming their antiquity.

1949 J. V. Neel provides genetic evidence that the sickle-cell disease is inherited as a simple Mendelian auto-somal recessive.

M. L. Barr and E. G. Bertram show that nuclei are different in the two sexes when they identify a het-eropycnotic body in female cats; this result was soon duplicated in many mammals. The diagnostic object in somatic cells subsequently becomes known as sex chromatin or a 'Barr body'.

L. Pauling *et al.* show that the HbS gene produces an abnormal hemoglobin, and they introduce the concept of genetically controlled molecular diseases.

1950 Anthropologists and biologists submit UNESCO amendment, the 'statement on race'.

S. L. Washburn publishes a classic paper, 'The new physical anthropology', that refocuses the discipline. In the 1950s, Washburn pioneers field studies of savannah baboons. I. DeVore studies dominance hierarchies in Kenya. C. Carpenter pursues early field studies of monkeys. Field studies by G. Schaller on mountain gorillas commence in Africa; field studies by P. Dolhinow of langurs are begun in India.

K. Lorenz suggests that aggression in animals is innate.

Tollund Man, a 2.4 kya 'bog man', is discovered.

R. Solecki begins work at Shanidar.

The Piltdown fossil is proved a fraud after it is established that the mandible and skullcap are of very different ages and cannot be from the same specimen (see 1911).

A. Hershey and M. Chase confirm that DNA is the genetic material.

Evidence for a case of observed speciation is documented after three domesticated species of the tuber *Trogopogon* become feral, spontaneously hybridize, and produce two new species within 125 years after being introduced to America from Europe.

1951    J. Mohr demonstrates linkage between the autosomal genes *Lutheran (Lu(a))* and *Lewis (Le(s))* in *Homo sapiens*.

W. E. Le Gros Clark and L. S. B. Leakey describe the many fossil primates from the Miocene of Kenya, including *Limnopithecus*, *Proconsul*, and *Sivapithecus*.

1952    Pioneering field studies of the Koshima troop of macaques are begun in Japan by S. Kawamura.

H. Vallois and W. Howells suggest that the spelling of 'Neanderthal' be modernized to 'Neandertal'.

E. Chargaff demonstrates that the amount of A=T, and G=C in DNA.

F. Sanger *et al.* work out the complete amino acid sequence for the protein hormone human insulin and show that it contains two polypeptide chains held together by disulfide bridges.

R. Franklin and R. Gosling's crystallography data are critical to DNA structure. Working in the laboratory of M. Wilkins, Franklin makes X-ray crystallography photographs of DNA that will permit J. D. Watson and F. H. C. Crick to suggest a structure for DNA in the following year. Franklin will die of cancer before her work can be properly recognized.

1953    Watson and F. Crick propose a model for DNA comprised of two helically intertwined chains tied together between the paired purines and pyrimidines in the journal *Nature*. They share the Nobel Prize for Chemistry with Wilkins 10 years later.

K. Mather agrees with C. H. Waddington on the potential for developmental stability, or canalization.

1954    A. C. Allison provides evidence that heterozygotes for the sickle-cell gene are at an advantage in a malarial environment.

A *Homo erectus* mandible is found at Sidi Abderrahman in Morocco by P. Biberson.

First explored in 1872, the Ternifine site in Algeria finally yields two mandibles and Clactonian tools to C. Arambourg and R. Hoffstetter; these are attributed to *Atlanthropus mauritanicus*.

1955    Kuru, a mysterious disease in Melanesia, is caused by a 'slow virus', reports D. C. Gajdusek (see 1982).

O. Smithies uses starch-gel electrophoresis to identify plasma protein polymorphisms.

C. Arambourg suggests that Boule's brutish interpretation of the La Chapelle skeleton was exaggerated; in 1957, others will demonstrate that the old man had arthritis.

1956    J. H. Tjio and A. Levan show that the correct diploid number of chromosomes for humans is 2N = 46, not 48 as had been previously reported (see 1918).

H. B. Kettlewell studies industrial melanism in the peppered moth. He demonstrates that moths that are conspicuous in their habitats are indeed eaten by birds more often than inconspicuous forms (see 1921).

R. Broom suggests robust and gracile australopithecine differences are dietary.

W. C. Pei *et al.* from the Academia Sinica discover animal bones and 47 hominoid teeth in apothecaries and caves in Kwangsi Province, China; later, a nearly complete jawbone of *Gigantopithecus* is located in a cave in the same Province.

1957    V. M. Ingram reports that normal and sickle-cell hemoglobins differ by a single amino acid substitution.

Since 1953, in the Shanidar Valley of the Zagros mountains north of Baghdad, Iraq, R. Solecki *et al.* excavate 9 Neandertal burials; these will become popularly known as the 'flower children', and give rise to J. Auel's fictional series.

1958    F. H. C. Crick suggests that during protein formation the amino acid is carried to the template by an adaptor molecule containing nucleotides and that the adaptor is the part which actually fits on the RNA template; Crick thus predicts the discovery of transfer RNA.

M. Meselson and F. Stahl show how DNA replicates.

W. L. Straus describes a nearly complete new specimen of a fossil primate from Baccinello, Italy, *Oreopithecus bambolii*.

1959    In *Mankind in the Making*, W. Howells uses multivariate statistics to classify skulls.

J. Lejeune *et al.* show that Down syndrome is a chromosomal aberration involving trisomy of a small acrocentric chromosome; that affected children have too many chromosomes, are 2N = 47.

P. A. Jacobs and J. A. Strong demonstrate that males suffering from Klinefelter syndrome are XXY and thus have one too many chromosomes.

S. Ohno proposes that the Barr body originates from one of the sex chromosomes, and proposes the $n-1$ rule for diploid mammal cells.

E. Freese proposes that mutations can occur as the result of single base pair changes. He coins the terms 'transitions' and 'transversions'.

C. E. Ford *et al.* discover that female *Homo sapiens* with Turner syndrome are Xo.

M. Chèvremont *et al.* demonstrate the presence of DNA in mitochondria.

M. D. Leakey finds a pneumatized skull eroding from the bed of the FLK site where stone tools had been found in 1931; the reconstructed 1.75 mya-old fossil is later named *Zinjanthropus boisei*.

1960 L. S. B. Leakey finds the first specimen of *Homo erectus* in East Africa at site LLK in Olduvai Gorge.

Encouraged by L. S. B. Leakey, J. Goodall takes up residence at Gombe Stream, Tanzania; she will spend the major part of the next 30 years observing chimpanzee behavior at the reserve.

J. Leakey finds the first habiline, *Homo habilis*, when he locates remains of one or more individuals scattered over a living floor 20 feet across. An almost complete foot shows that it had a free-striding gait, and its cranial capacity is estimated at 680 cm³.

Encouraged by L. S. B. Leakey, D. Fossey takes up residence at Karisoke, Rwanda; she will spend the major part of the next two decades observing gorilla behavior.

While exploring a cave near Petralona in eastern Greece, J. Malkotsis *et al.* find an archaic human embedded in a stalactite.

F. C. Howell suggests that the hominids have been split into too many taxa, and collapses them all into either *Homo* or *Australopithecus*.

1961 F. Jacob and J. Monod propose a new molecule, messenger RNA, that enters into temporary association with a ribosome and so confers upon it the ability to synthesize a given protein.

Messenger RNA is independently demonstrated empirically by S. Brenner *et al.*, and by F. Gros *et al.*

V. M. Ingram presents a theory explaining the evolution of the four known kinds of hemoglobin chain from a single primitive myoglobin-like heme protein, by way of gene duplication and translocation.

E. Chu and M. A. Bender demonstrate that primate evolution is also chromosomal.

M. F. Lyon and L. B. Russell independently provide evidence suggesting that in mammals one X chromosome is randomly inactivated in some embryonic cells and their descendants, that the other is inactivated in the remaining cells, and that females are subsequently X-chromosome mosaics.

F. H. C. Crick *et al.* show that the genetic code is made up of three-letter words.

In a cave on the lower course of the Wadi Amud, near Haifa, the Tokyo University Scientific Expedition finds a Neandertal with the largest cranial capacity of any known fossil hominid.

1962 F. French and J. M. Bierman publish startlingly high probabilities of first trimester fetal mortality in humans.

M. D. Leakey's team excavates the site known as the 'stone circle', a possible hominid living floor, at site DK in Olduvai Gorge.

E. Zuckerkandl and L. Pauling propose that molecular changes that accumulate over time can be used as a 'molecular clock' to estimate the time since the two species shared a common ancestor.

C. Coon states in *The Origin of Races* that he has evidence that human races have evolved separately, and without significant gene flow. Reviewers disagree. C. L. Brace offers an alternative scenario in *Refocusing on the Neanderthal Problem*, but repeats Hrdlička's claim that Neandertals gave rise to modern humans.

1963 E. Simons and D. Pilbeam revise the current Miocene primate taxonomy, lumping many genera from East Africa and India/Pakistan, and sinking genera such as *Kenyapithecus* and *Proconsul* into the Sivapithecidae.

Lascaux Grotto is closed to the public; increased humidity and microorganisms brought in by tourists have started to damage the 17 kyold cave art.

N. Mbuika finds the skull of 'Cinderella', a *Homo habilis* specimen, at site MNK in Olduvai Gorge.

1964 W. D. Hamilton publishes 'The genetical evolution of social behavior'. He uses the haplo-diploid system found in social insects to argue that haploid female workers benefit more by encouraging the queen to reproduce than by themselves reproducing; this ethological concept, kin selection, later becomes a central principle of sociobiology.

J. G. Gorman, V. J. Freda, and W. Pollack demonstrate that the sensitization of Rh-negative mothers can be prevented by administration of Rh antibody immediately after delivery of the mother's first Rh-positive baby.

F. Bordes reproduces a sophisticated experimental tool sequence in France.

P. Nzube finds the crushed but reconstructable crania of 'Twiggy', a fossil hominid attributed to *Homo habilis*, at site DK in Olduvai Gorge.

Volume 4 of the *Handbook of Physiology* is published as *Adaptation to the Environment* (D. B. Dill *et al.*, eds.), which contains reports of most of the major acclimation and acclimatization studies on indigenous peoples conducted to that date. The studies attempt to categorize the adaptive responses of populations to extreme stress.

1965 Swedish photographer L. Nilsson takes the first pictures of a human fetus *in utero*; his visual documentation of the development and growth process will result in a Nobel Prize.

Anthropologist N. Chagnon works at field sites in Venezuela, among the Yanomamo, whom he will call *The Fierce People*.

Between 1966 and 1980, B. Vandermeersch finds two dozen more individuals at Qafzeh, which he suggests are 'proto-Cro-Magnon' rather than Neandertals.

Near the village of Vértesszöllös, near Budapest, Hungary, L. Vértes and his team report two new specimens of archaic *Homo heidelbergensis*.

1966    V. A. McKusick publishes the first edition of *Mendelian Inheritance in Man* (MIM), a catalog listing some 1,500 genetic disorders of *Homo sapiens*. The catalog will be updated regularly for the next two decades. Eventually it will list over 10,000 conditions, and become a standard internet tool (see 1987).

F. H. C. Crick puts forward the wobble hypothesis to explain the general pattern of degeneracy found in the genetic code.

R. C. Lewontin and J. L. Hubby use electrophoretic methods to survey gene-controlled protein variants in natural populations of *Drosophila pseudoobscura*. They demonstrate that 8–15% of all loci in the average individual genome are in the heterozygous condition. Using similar techniques, H. Harris demonstrates the existence of extensive enzyme polymorphisms in human populations.

At Reno, Nevada, a ten-month-old female chimpanzee named *Washoe* begins to live in the backyard of psychologists B. and A. Gardner, where the young chimp is tutored in American Sign Language.

G. C. Williams publishes *Adaptation and Natural Selection*.

1967    *Aegyptopithecus zeuxis*, the oldest known hominoid primate, is excavated at a site in the Fayum depression, Egypt, by E. Simons *et al.*; the age is estimated to be 30 my.

F. Livingstone reports that the incidence of malaria and genetic disease is related to the slash-and-burn technique.

C. B. Jacobsen and R. H. Barter report the use of amniocentesis for intrauterine diagnosis and management of genetic defects.

A. Wilson and V. Sarich develop a then-primitive 'molecular clock' and propose the last common ancestor of the human and chimpanzee lived between 3 and 6 mya, contradicting current dogma that *Ramapithecus* was the common ancestor, which was considered more than 15 my old.

H. G. Khorana and coworkers use polynucleotides with known repeating di- and trinucleotide sequences to solve the genetic code.

1968    The *Glomar Challenger* commences a 15-year Deep Sea Drilling Project, collecting thousands of cores from the Atlantic Ocean. Analysis will show that the floor of the Atlantic is too young to yield substantial oil, and is also symmetrical on either side of the Mid-Atlantic Ridge, supporting the hypothesis of continental drift.

R. P. Donohue, W. B. Bias, J. H. Renwick, and V. A. McKusick assign the Duffy blood group locus to chromosome 1 in *Homo sapiens*. This is the first human gene localized to a specific autosome.

R. B. Lee, working in the Kalahari among the Dobe !Kung, a hunter-gathering population, concludes that in the long run the majority of digestible calories are harvested by women who gather, rather than by men who hunt.

K. Popper formalizes the 'hypothetico-deductive' method.

W. Arber, H. Smith, and D. Nathans describe 'restriction enzymes' that attach to DNA and cut both strands at sites of specific base sequences. One of the first restriction enzymes characterized comes from *E. coli*, and is designated *Eco*RI. Many similar restriction enzymes are soon characterized.

1969    C. Boon and F. Ruddle correlate the loss of particular chromosomes from a somatic hybrid cell line containing both human and mouse chromosomes with the loss of specific phenotypic characters. This approach permits assignment of specific loci to certain human chromosomes.

J. L. King and T. H. Jukes allege that not all molecular evolution is selection, that some may be neutral.

World's largest prehistoric cremation is found at Lake Mungo in Australia.

1970    Nobel laureate W. Shockley, the inventor of the transistor, suggests that humans with an IQ less than 85 should be sterilized.

Pioneering field work with orangutans in Sumatra and Borneo is begun by B. Galdikas.

R. Trivers claims that humans, like other animals, behave economically, and he introduces the concept of reciprocal altruism to explain certain behaviors.

G. Isaac *et al.* apply taphonomic principles to show that many bones in Pleistocene sites have been worked by hominids rather than gnawed by animals.

Pioneering field studies with hamadryas baboons in Africa begun by ethologist H. Kummer.

D. Pilbeam finds fossil apes at sites in Pakistan.

D. Baltimore and H. M. Temin report the existence of an RNA-dependent DNA polymerase in two oncogenic RNA viruses.

The brain and body have co-evolved and the encephalization quotient is related grossly to animal intelligence, and scale allometrically at 2/3, according to H. Jerison.

J. Mayanard Smith incorporates the principles of game theory, incorporating the ideas of J. von Neumann and O. Morgenstern (1944), J. F. Nash (1950), R. Selten (1965), and J. C. Harsanyi (1967), to promote ideas concerning behavior optimization.

T. Kuhn outlines a process of scientific 'paradigm shifts'.

1971    M. L. O'Riordan, J. A. Robinson, K. E. Buckton, and H. J. Evans report that all 22 pairs of human autosomes can be identified visually after staining with a new technique. They demonstrate that the Philadelphia chromosome is a deleted chromosome 22.

At the 1971 Paris Conference on Human Genetics, recent chromosome banding pattern technologies lead to the need for standardization in banding pattern for humans. By 1973 there are several positive or negative banding techniques.

D. Brose and M. Wolpoff commit to a polyphyly model for hominids, and place Neandertals directly on the line to modern humans.

M. Kimura and T. Ohta propose that the rate of molecular evolution is relatively constant when mutations are neutral (see 1983).

1972    P. Berg *et al.* make the first recombinant DNA molecule by using restriction enzymes; the result is a vital first step toward genetic engineering.

S. J. Gould and N. Eldridge publish a theory of punctuated equilibrium, in which evolution occurs in short bursts, followed by long periods of stasis, or evolutionary stability.

M. Nei calculates genetic distance between populations, and suggests distance is proportional to time. The California State Board of Education rules that biblical accounts of Special Creation can receive attention in public school texts equal to time spent on Darwinian theory (see 1987).

B. Ngeneo locates the first fragments of the skull KNM-ER 1470, from East Turkana. R. Leakey, M. G. Leakey, B. Wood, and A. Walker reconstruct the skull, later named *Homo rudolfensis*.

1973    S. Ohno proposes a theory of macroevolution by linkage and polyploidy, nicknamed 'frozen accidents'.

In S. H. Cohen and Herbert Boyer's lab, A. Chang transfers a gene, 'cut' from the plasmid of another strain, into the plasmid of a different strain of *E. coli*. Some of the *E. coli* reabsorb recombinant plasmids, and eventually express the gene as recombinant DNA.

1974    M. Nei and A. Roychoudhury, using proteins coded by nuclear DNA, propose a close genetic affinity for all modern human populations, and suggest a date for the common ancestor of 110 kya.

R. Alexander proposes that kin selection initiated haploidy, and that social behavior evolves.

B. Ngeneo locates new East African fossils, including KMN-ER 3733, an erectine-like cranium that some attribute to *Homo ergaster*.

Based on quantitative analyses, C. Stringer suggests that Neandertals cannot be ancestral to modern humans.

Led by Stanford's P. Berg, a large group of scientists meets at Asilomar, in California, to place a moratorium on certain types of recombinant DNA experiment considered potentially too hazardous to be conducted.

The American Academy of Arts and Sciences sponsors workshops in which the 'modern synthesis' is explored by many of those who had been directly involved in making that history; it is published as *The Evolutionary Synthesis*.

T. Gray and D. Johanson report on the fragmentary remains of 'Lucy', an australopithecine dated to 3+ mya in the Afar, Ethiopia. The fossil is attributed to a new species, *Australopithecus afarensis*.

1975    B. Dutrillaux publishes major works on primate chromosomal evolution.

A. Jeffreys develops a high-resolution version of RFLP mapping which detects human variation in short repeated DNA sequences termed 'variable number tandem repeats' (VNTRs); he reports that the number of repeats at each locus is unique to each individual (except twins) and coins the term 'DNA fingerprint' to describe the individual patterns.

R. Solecki suggests that Neandertals had religion; E. Trinkaus suggests they had modern human locomotor abilities.

E. O. Wilson publishes the controversial volume on ant behavioral genetics, *Sociobiology*; the last chapter suggests that humans may be as 'wired' as his ants. Although severely criticized for his deterministism, the work stimulates much research and theory.

E. Southern devises DNA hybridization analysis.

F. Sanger develops enzymatic chain termination sequencing.

M.-C. King and A. Wilson visualize evolution at both molecular and chromosomal levels; they suggest that, although the human and pongid genomes are 98.4% identical, differences in gene expression may explain the phenotypic disparities.

1976    After an examination of early fossil humans in Africa, G. Bräuer publishes the first 'out of Africa' model of hominid origins (see 1988).

E. Trinkaus proposes that Neandertal pregnancies were longer than those of modern humans. F. Smith, after studying Krapina, joins Wolpoff, Coon, and Hrdlicka, placing Neandertals on the direct line to humans.

A special strain of *E. coli*, x1776, is developed for use in recombinant DNA experiments. It perishes if exposed to sunlight or soap and is dependent upon certain nutrients available only in the laboratory. Genentech, a commercial biotech company, is formed to develop applications of recombinant DNA technology. It goes public in 1980.

R. Dawkins suggests that *The Selfish Gene* co-opts the entire organism to its ends, and shifts the unit of selection from the individual to the gene; he popularizes the approach of evolutionary psychology.

1977      Rapid evolution associated with chromosomal mutations is reported by G. Bush.

W. Gilbert and A. Maxam devise a chemical method for sequencing DNA.

Two homosexual men die of Kaposi's sarcoma in New York City, early victims of the AIDS epidemic that will not be officially recognized until 1981.

D. Barash publishes *Sociobiology and Behavior*, a textbook about evolutionary psychology.

1978      A. Zihlman *et al.* suggest that the bonobo is the best morphological prototype for the common ancestor of humans and chimpanzees.

J. Yunis' laboratory publishes high-resolution human chromosome bands.

M. D. Leakey exposes Laetoli footprints, demonstrating that hominids walked bipedally 3.6 mya.

Baby Brown is born in Great Britain, the first reported child successfully conceived after an *in vitro* fertilization.

E. O. Wilson publishes *On Human Nature*.

Researchers show that the *E. coli* strain K12 is much safer than originally assessed, and the specific use of the x1776 strain is relaxed. Researchers begin to use the K12 strain, and others, for recombinant DNA research.

1979      T. White and D. Johanson suggest that the newly discovered species *Australopithecus afarensis*, dated in the range of 3–4 mya, gave rise to all later species of African hominids (both gracile and robust forms) as well as to *Homo habilis*.

An adult male Neandertal is found at Saint Césaire, in France, in direct association with Châtelperronian tools previously thought to be a tool kit only of modern humans.

R. Alexander publishes a work on evolutionary psychology, *Darwinism and Human Affairs*; one of the theses of this work is that culture is an accretion of individuals seeking to maximize their separate inclusive fitness.

1980      The US Supreme Court rules that a recombinant microbe developed by General Electric for the digestion of oil spilled in the ocean can be patented as a new life form.

L. W. Alvarez *et al.* publish the asteroid impact theory of dinosaur extinction in *Science*. The theory is initially criticized, but gradually gains acceptance in the scientific community.

H. Terrace reports his failure to find language and communication in a chimpanzee, Nim Chimpsky, at a conference entitled 'The Clever Hans Phenomenon: Communications with Horses, Whales, Apes and People'.

M. Skolnick, R. White, D. Botstein, and R. Davis publish an RFLP marker map of the human genome.

1981      The US CDC officially recognizes acquired immune deficiency syndrome (AIDS) as a disease. (See 1977).

A. H. Harcourt *et al.* measure body and organ masses in primates and attempt to relate size to social structure; they report that species with males that have testes that are large for body size are more likely to be promiscuous.

Following C. Coon's thesis, A. Thorne and M. Wolpoff propose that human races evolved separately, an older concept they now call multiregional continuity (see 1971).

A study of sedimentary levels at Qafzeh suggests that modern humans may predate Neandertals found at other sites in the region; these findings will be reinforced by TL (1987) and ESR dating (1991).

J. D. Clark and T. D. White find fossil bones at Maka, Awash River valley, Ethiopia, dating to 4 mya. They assign the fragments to *Australopithecus afarensis*.

C. G. Sibley and J. E. Alquist use DNA to study the evolutionary relationships among birds, which results in a revised taxonomy; this is the first extensive use of DNA to revise a major taxonomy (see 1984).

Baby Carr is born, the first reported child successfully conceived after an *in vitro* fertilization in the USA.

Paleoanthropologist D. Pilbeam determines that *Ramapithecus* is most likely related to an ancestor of the orangutan, and is not an early hominid.

DNA *in situ* hybridization becomes a standard research method.

C. J. Lumsden and E. O. Wilson publish *Genes, Mind and Culture*, in which they propose that social behaviors are shaped by natural selection, and that all altruistic behavior is in fact genetically selfish behavior. By the end of 1981, 579 human genes have been mapped to specific chromosomes.

1982     With A. Levine, D. Lane describes a protein, *p53*, that is implicated in mouse cancers. It is described in 1992 as 'the Guardian of the Genome', after its vigilant behavior during mitosis is discovered, which prevents many human cancers.

GenBank is established as a public database managed by the US National Center for Biotechnology Information (NCBI); it already contains the complete or partial gene sequences of over 30 organisms, including humans.

The NIH issues a new set of Guidelines for recombinant DNA research that eliminates most of the restraints issued in the 1970s. Even the moratorium on specific experiments is lifted, but the NIH must be notified in the event that such experiments are ever planned.

Eli Lilly and Co. acquires that portion of Genentech's intellectual property which had resulted in the successful production of human insulin in *E. coli* plasmids. Recombinant human insulin becomes the first human gene cloned commercially in bacteria and the result of genetic engineering. Recombinant human insulin becomes available to people with insulin-dependent diabetes mellitus (IDDM).

Prions, short for 'proteinaceous particles', are proposed by S. B. Prusiner. They will later be shown to be the agents responsible for kuru (see 1955) and other transmissible spongiform encephalopathies, according to the protein-only hypothesis.

H. J. Landy *et al.* report the 'vanishing twin' phenomenon.

1983     M. Kimura proposes that the majority of mutations that occur in DNA are by definition 'neutral' and cannot be detected by natural selection since there is no net effect on the fitness of the organisms in which they occur (see 1971).

J. Gusella demonstrates that Huntington's Disease is on chromosome 4.

The first reported, successful mother-to-mother embryo transfer is achieved.

W. Stokoe states that signing chimpanzees '. . . have well-developed abilities to communicate using signs'.

M. G. Leakey finds a fossil ape at the site of Buluk, Kenya, dating to > 17 mya, it is first attributed to *Sivapithecus* but later removed to *Afropithecus*.

L. Smith, M. Carruthers, and L. Hood invent a method for automated DNA sequencing.

A method for dating objects based on chemical changes in obsidian is developed; the new technique is termed obsidian hydration.

1984     A. Hill *et al.* discover a 5 my-old mandible of *Australopithecus afarensis* in Kenya; it appears to be the oldest specimen of that species known to date.

M. G. L. Baillie and others establish an unbroken dendrochronology sequence of 7,272 years, based on Irish Oak trees.

The complete genomic sequence of the Epstein–Barr virus is published in *Nature*.

The nearly complete skeleton of 'Turkana boy' is discovered by K. Kimeu at Nariokotome.

C. G. Sibley and J. E. Ahlquist use DNA hybridization to estimate genetic relationships among the great apes and humans; they conclude that humans and chimpanzees share 98.4% of their DNA, and diverged from a common ancestor about 5 mya (see 1981).

'Lindow Man' is discovered.

Scientists at A. Wilson's lab extract 'ancient DNA' from the skin of an extinct equid, the quagga.

1985     K. Mullis at the Cetus Corporation conceives a technique that produces large amounts of specific DNA sequences, called the Polymerase Chain Reaction (PCR).

S. Pääbo extracts DNA from an ancient Egyptian mummy.

R. Brinster reports transgenic pigs that produce human growth hormone (HGH).

The US Congress amends the Animal Welfare Act, ordering laboratories to provide 'a physical environment adequate to promote the psychological well-being of primates'.

1986     T. White and D. Johanson find a fragmented specimen of a 1.8 my old hominid (the 'Dik-dik' hominid) near Olduvai Gorge. They assign it *Homo habilis*; the limb bones are more apelike than expected.

1987     DNA fingerprinting is entered as legal evidence for the first time, and a conviction is obtained.

The US Supreme Court rejects the equal-time concept for teaching 'Creation Science' along with Darwinian theory, thus overturning a school board decision made in California in 1972.

R. Cann, M. Stoneking, and A. Wilson allege that the 'Mitochondrial Eve' of all modern humans is less than 200,000 years old.

Field testing begins on a genetically engineered strain of *Pseudomonas* sp. to which has been added the 'ice minus' gene.

*Online Mendelian Inheritance in Man* (OMIM) goes online (see 1966). Management will pass to the US NCBI in December 1995.

1987     R. Holliday refers to genetics as the study of mechanisms of transmission of structural elements from generation to generation, and 'epigenetics' as the mode of action of genes during the development of an organism from the fertilized egg to adult (see 1994).

The US Congress authorizes funds for the Human Genome Project (HGP). A joint effort of the National Institutes of Health (NIH) and the Department of Energy (DOE), it has as its initial goals the identification of all genes in the human genome, and the sequencing of all loci.

1988    C. Stringer and P. Andrews publish the second — and now better-known — 'out of Africa' model of human origins (see 1976).

The US NIH creates an Office of Human Genome Research (OHGR) and assumes administration of the HGP. James D. Watson is named Associate Director.

T. D. Dillehay and M. B. Collins report that radiocarbon dating of charcoal artifacts found at Monte Verde in southern Chile indicates that humans have been living in the Americas for at least 33 kya, more than twice the previously accepted estimate (see 1997).

French and Israeli archaeologists announce that fossils found in a cave in Israel are the 92 kya old remains of anatomically modern-looking *Homo sapiens*; this find more than doubles the length of time that modern humans are known to have existed in the fossil record.

A telomere (chromosome end) sequence having implications for aging and cancer research is identified. HUGO is founded by scientists to coordinate international genome research efforts.

The US Patent and Trade Office issues patent No. 4,736,866 to Harvard Medical School for a mouse developed by P. Leder and T. A. Stewart, and created by genetic engineering; it is the first US patent issued for a vertebrate.

H. A. Erlich and coworkers announce that they have developed a method that can identify (or exclude) a given individual in forensics cases, using a single hair; the 'DNA fingerprinting' method is possible because of DNA amplification using PCR.

1989    The US NIH establishes the National Center for Human Genome Research; the joint Ethical, Social and Legal (ELSI) working group is formed.

B. Sykes *et al*. extract ancient DNA from the bones of a Paleolithic skeleton.

J. M. Bishop and H. Varmus describe the cellular origins of the *ras* retroviral oncogene.

1990    At 12:52 pm, September 14, Ashanti DaSilva, a 4-year-old girl with severe combined immunodeficiency syndrome (ADA deficiency) is given an autologous transfusion of T cells transfected with a modified virus carrying a 'good' human ADA gene. The viral vector transfers the gene to nuclear DNA in the girl's isolated lymphocytes. Ashanti was doing fine as of 2003, but the process has to be repeated every 3–5 months because of the limited life span of T cells.

The US DOE and NIH present a joint five-year US HGP plan to Congress. The fifteen-year project (1990–2005) formally begins in October.

By late 1990, the US FDA has approved 12 drugs produced by recombinant DNA technology, and 18 more are under review.

1991    D. Haig and T. Moore propose the asymmetrical genetic conflict hypothesis.

J. Diamond popularizes bioculture and the natural side of humanity in *The Third Chimpanzee*.

J. C. Venter and colleagues create expressed sequence tags (ESTs).

Ötzi, the 5.3 ky-old 'Alpine Iceman', the oldest intact human, is found in the Similaun Pass glacier in Italy's Ötztal Alps.

M. Stoneking and L. Vigilant increase the world mtDNA sample from humans and confirm Cann's earlier result (see 1987); others find the mtDNA studies problematical.

The Chicxulub crater is discovered in the Caribbean and on the Yucatan Peninsula of Central America, supporting the Alvarez asteroid impact theory suggested around 1980.

By the end of 1991, 1879 human genes have been mapped to specific chromosomes.

1992    The first genetic linkage map of the human genome is published by NIH/CEPH.

T. Adefris reinterprets the 'archaic' Bodo skull; F. Smith and E. Trinkaus re-examine 'AMHs' from Africa and conclude that many are not actually 'modern'.

The first human chromosome physical maps are published, for chromosomes Y and 21.

The US FDA rules that genetically engineered foods are to be regulated similarly to foods produced by conventional Mendelian crosses.

Barkow, Cosmides, and Tooby edit *The Adapted Mind: Evolutionary Psychology and the Generation of Culture*. The central tenet of evolutionary psychology becomes: humans are adaptation executors rather than fitness maximizers.

1993    A human embryo is cloned, but the experiment is voluntarily terminated. What is not widely reported is that the cloned tissue was intentionally triploid, to preclude ethical issues.

J. W. Schopf describes microfossils from the Apex Basalt in Australia, making the 3.5 By old fossils the oldest known.

Cai *et al*. and Fujiwara *et al*. independently report that a retroviral expression vector delivers wild-type **p53** *in vivo* to lung cancer cell lines and spheroids and induces apoptosis and 'bystander' effects in tumors with **p53** mutations.

1994   The Genetic Privacy Act, the first US HGP legislative product, is proposed to regulate collection, analysis, storage, and use of DNA samples and genetic information obtained from them; it is endorsed by the ELSI Working Group.

Y. Miki and colleagues identify the first breast cancer gene, *BRCA1*.

In *Chimpanzee Cultures* by R. Wrangham *et al.*, primatologists announce a list of 39 learned behaviors in chimpanzees; the use of the term 'chimpanzee culture' begins to replace 'protoculture' among primatologists.

T. D. White, G. Suwa, and B. Asfaw find oldest hominid yet identified, dated to 4.4 mya, in Ethiopia. They name the specimen *Ardipithecus ramidus*.

J.-M. Chauvet discovers 30 ky old cave paintings in Grotto Chauvet.

R. Holliday suggests two new variations on the term epigenetics: (1) changes in gene expression that occur in organisms with cell differentiation, and the mitotic inheritance of certain patterns of gene expression . . . including DNA-protein interactions, and (2) heritable changes in gene expression that can be reversed or deprogrammed at some later stage, sometimes after meiosis, i.e., nuclear inheritance not based on differences in DNA sequence (see 1987).

1995   The US FDA grants approval to terminate a phase III clinical study involving hydroxyurea to treat sickle cell disease. The treatment group is doing so much better than the placebo group that it is considered unethical to deny the control group the new treatment. By late 1995, the FDA has approved 24 drugs produced by recombinant DNA technology, and 161 more are in clinical trials.

England establishes a DNA database of every citizen convicted of a crime, as well as all suspects in unsolved cases.

The first complete genomic sequence of a free-living organism, *Haemophilius influenzae*, is published in *Science*.

The International HGP consortium decides to make genome sequences public property, and establishes the 'Bermuda rules'.

1996   EEOC guidelines extend ADA employment protection to cover discrimination based on genetic information related to illness, disease, or other conditions.

The *Methanococcus jannaschii* genome is sequenced, and confirms the existence of a 3rd major branch of life on earth.

M. Brunet *et al.* describe a fossil hominid dated to 3.5–3.0 mya from site KT 12 near Yayo, Chad, in central Africa. They assign it to a new taxon, *Australopithecus bahrelghazali*.

A baby gorilla, Timu, is born at the Cincinnati Zoo after a first-ever successful *in vitro* fertilization of that species.

The complete genomic sequence of a yeast, *Saccharomyces cerevisiae*, is published in *Science*.

1997   Généthon publishes the final version of the Human Genetic Map, which marks the end of the first phase of the HGP.

Oxford scientists extract mtDNA from a tooth cavity of the fossil known as Cheddar Gorge Man, a 9 kya old skeleton found in 1903 in the caves of Cheddar Gorge in southwest England, and match the sample to a history teacher living in present-day Cheddar village.

Mitochondrial DNA is extracted from the original Feldhofer Neandertal by S. Pääbo *et al.*; they suggest that AMHs and Neandertals last shared a common ancestor 690–550 kya (see 2002).

An international consortium of scientists agrees that a South American archaeological site, Monte Verde in Peru, has the earliest known human artifacts found in the Americas, and that the conservative radiocarbon date of 12.5 kya is accurate (see 1988).

I. Wilmut and colleagues at the Roslin Institute, England, announce the birth of Dolly, cloned from a single mammary gland cell obtained from an adult female Finn Dorset ewe (see 2003). Although somatic cloning by nuclear transfer has been possible since 1952, this is the first reported case of a reprogrammed adult cell used to obtain a clone.

R. Yanagimachi and his colleagues at the University of Hawaii clone Cumulina, 'The Mouse That Roared', from the nucleus of a cumulus cell, using the 'Honolulu technique'.

The complete genomic sequence of *Escherichia coli* is published in *Science*. Between 1995 and 2001, 60 microbial species are sequenced; 100 more will be sequenced by 2004.

1998   A 2nd ewe is cloned at Wilmut's lab; this lamb carries a recombinant gene that produces a blood-clotting factor in her milk.

The FBI establishes a DNA database of selected felons convicted of a crime (see 1995).

Cattle are cloned by Y. Kato *et al.*

The complete genomic sequence of *C. elegans* is published.

In December, the 10,000th entry to *Mendelian Inheritance in Man* is entered by V. McKusick (see 1966).

1999   A rhesus monkey, Tetra, is cloned at the Oregon Regional Primate Research Center by A. Chan *et al.*

Goats are cloned by A. Baguisi *et al.*

Scientists announce that pollen from potato plants with the *Bt* gene spliced into their genome has a negative effect on laboratory-raised rats fed exclusively on the potatoes; the rats exhibit retarded growth and lowered immune response. Laboratory-raised Monarch butterfly larvae fed on an exclusive diet of *Bt*-pollen-dusted milkweed are reported to eat less, grow more slowly, and have higher mortality rates than control larvae. The European Economic Union halts approvals of genetically altered crops on the grounds that they may be hazardous to human health.

More Feldhofer Grotto bones are recovered from a 2nd Neandertal skeleton found in a separate cave — Feldhofer Kirche — and dated to 44 kya. Mousterian tools are also found.

A transgenic sheep, Nancy, is genetically engineered to produce alpha 1-antitrypsin (AAT) in her milk.

J. Tsien recombines extra copies of the mouse NR2B gene into fertilized mouse eggs. The gene apparently enhances memory retention, and altered mice retain information up to 3 times longer than normal mice.

S. Ward *et al.* report 15–14 mya fossil hominoid fragments from the Tugen Hills, Kenya; they call the new genus *Equatorius*.

B. Asfaw *et al.* describe a new hominid species recovered from the Middle Awash, Bouri formation, Ethiopia, dated to 2.5 mya. They assign it to a new taxon, *Australopithecus garhi*.

J. Zilhão and E. Trinkaus conclude that proof of AMH–Neandertal hybridization resides in the skeleton of a young boy unearthed at Lagar Velho, Portugal.

Primatologists study intraspecific patterns of behavior at nine chimpanzee sites, find at least 39 examples of behaviors that are likely not gene-based, and conclude that culture in primates is probable.

The Kansas state Board of Education bans teaching evolution in public schools; within weeks, scholars ridicule the act. The ban is repealed in February 2001.

In Japan and Europe, citizens protest the use of genetically engineered crops. Food producers such as Heinz, Nestlé, and Gerber stop purchases of GM crops, including soy beans, potatoes and corn.

B. Buigues leads an expedition to recover a 23 kya adult male mammoth carcass encased in a 23-ton block of ice.

Members of HUGO announce that chromosome 22 is the first human chromosome to be completely sequenced; only 545 genes are found on the entire chromosome.

A patient undergoing recombinant DNA therapy in Philadelphia dies; trials are halted, and bioethicists suggest a reconsideration of the efficacy of such treatments.

2000     Rundle *et al.* report that parallel speciation has occurred in populations of threespine sticklebacks, *Gasterosteus* ssp., in freshwater lakes in British Columbia.

Teams led by M. D. Adams, E. W. Myers, and G. M. Rubin announce the complete sequencing of the 125 megabase euchromatic regions of the genome of the fruit fly, *Drosophila*. This is the 2nd successful sequencing of the genome of a metazoan.

A. Keyser announces the discovery in 1994 of two nearly complete skulls of *Paranthropus robustus* at Drimolen in South Africa. The 1.5+ my old pair of fossils are a male and a female. 'Eurydice' has the most complete female robust australopithecine crania discovered, and with 'Orpheus' provides information on the extent of sexual dimorphism in this species.

Monsanto, in collaboration with scientists at the University of Washington (Seattle), announces that it has completed a 'working draft' of the rice genome, and that it will share results with the 10-nation consortium that had been working toward the same goal.

R. Yanagimachi and colleagues announce the death of the cloned mouse Cumulina (see 1997), who died of natural aging, and lived 7 months longer than an average mouse of her species.

Members of HUGO based in Japan and Germany announce that a 2nd human chromosome, no. 21, the 'Down syndrome chromosome', has been completely sequenced; only 225 genes were found on the entire chromosome.

The complete genomic sequence of the fruit fly, *Drosophila melanogaster*, is published.

D. Lordikipanidze *et al.* describe Dmanisi, a site found in 1989 in southern Russia, dated to 1.75 mya. It yields choppers, chopping tools and their cores, animal bones of fauna found today only in Africa, and two partial hominid craniofacial specimens with cranial capacities of 650 and 780 cm³, provisionally attributed to *Homo ergaster* (see 2002).

A joint announcement is made by F. Collins (NIH) and J. C. Venter (PE-Celera Genomics) that a rough draft of the human genome has been completed. It will be published in February, 2001.

Mitochondrial DNA is extracted from the ribs of the fossil neonate from Mezmaiskaya Cave and is compared to mtDNA extracted in 1997 from the Feldhofer Neandertal. Both the Mezmaiskaya infant's and the Feldhofer adult's DNA are found to be equally distant from all modern human populations, but very similar to each other.

A green fluorescent protein gene obtained from a jellyfish is inserted into the sperm that fathered the first transgenic primate, ANDi, thus giving new meaning to the epithet 'green monkey'.

The StarLink variety of genetically modified corn, designed for use as animal fodder, is found to have accidentally made its way into taco shells distributed to a large chain of fast food stores.

The complete genomic sequence of a plant, *Arabidopsis thaliana*, is published.

2001    The HGP consortium (E. Lander and F. Collins) publishes its version of the working draft of the complete human genomic sequence in *Nature* on February 16, and Celera (J. C. Venter) publishes its version in *Science* on February 17.

Two groups of geophysicists agree that the Bapang formation in Java, from which some of the Sangiran fossils were recovered, is much older than suspected, and dates to 1.7–1.0 mya.

M. G. Leakey *et al.* describe a 3.5 my old fossil hominid found in 1999 at Lomekwi, Turkana district, Kenya. They name the specimen *Kenyanthropus platyops*.

B. Senut *et al.* describe a composite fossil specimen found in October 2000 near Rondinin, Tugen Hills, Kenya, dated to about 6.0 mya. They name it *Orrorin tugenensis* and attach the nickname 'Millennium Ancestor'.

Y. Haile-Selassie describes a new fossil hominid dating from 5.8–5.2 mya, represented by 11 specimens recovered from Alaya, Middle Awash, Ethiopia, in 1997; he calls the new subspecies *Ardipithecus ramidus kadabba*.

British geneticists announce that a 3rd human chromosome, no. 20, has been completely sequenced; only 727 genes were found.

Wu and Morris redefine epigenetics as changes in gene function that are mitotically and/or meiotically heritable, and that do not entail a structural change in DNA sequence.

Scientists at Advanced Cell Technology announce that they have produced a 6-cell human clone for the purpose of obtaining totipotent stem cells for research, rather than a complete organism.

2002    S. Pääbo *et al.* report that differences in the transcriptomes (gene transcription activity), rather than differences in linear sequences of DNA, may account for differences between humans and pongids in morphology and cognitive ability.

S. J. Gould finishes *The Structure of Evolutionary Theory* just months before his death.

The Daka hominid, a calvaria dated to 1.0 mya and recovered in 1997 from the Bouri formation, Middle Awash, Ethiopia, is described by B. Asfaw *et al.* It is attributed to *Homo erectus* and is cited as evidence that this taxon is not exclusively a far eastern species, and could therefore trigger a reconsideration of hominid taxa in Africa.

A. R. Templeton proposes an 'out of Africa again and again' model of early human origins; he argues that there were at least two major radiations of humanity from Africa into Eurasia subsequent to the original out of Africa I dispersal, and that the global replacement predicted by the mitochondrial Eve model is better explained by interbreeding (gene flow).

Scientists critique F. Boas' 1912 study that compared the Cephalic Indices of American-born children of European ancestry, and conclude that heritability, rather than cranial plasticity in response to new environments, explains the majority of the observed variation.

The team at Dmanisi (see 2000) reports a 3rd, more complete, and even smaller (600 cm³) crania, and attribute it to a new taxon, *Homo georgicus*. The smallness of the habiline-like specimen calls into question the idea that tall, large-brained erectines were the first to walk out of Africa.

M. Brunét *et al.* describe a new fossil recovered from Toros-Menalla, Djurab Desert, northern Chad, in 2001. The new taxon, *Sahelanthropus tchadensis*, has a combination of primitive and derived traits, and Brunét calls for a reevaluation of the chimp–human divergence period. Others suggest that the specimen has been misnamed, and should have been called *Sahelpithecus*.

Extrapolating from primate species diversity in the early Eocene (68 euprimate species), R. D. Martin *et al.* estimate that the last common ancestor of all primates must have lived more than 80 mya, in the Cretaceous. Bloch and Boyer describe a Paleocene carpolestid skeleton with an opposable hallux and nail, and rekindle the primate origins debate.

A consortium of geneticists use a world-wide sample to reaffirm that within-population differences account for over 90% of all genetic variation, and between population (3–5%) is even lower than earlier estimates (see 1966). Nevertheless, they identify six main clusters of humanity.

The complete genomic sequence of the malarial agent, *Plasmodium falciparum*, is published in *Nature*. Simultaneously, the complete genomic sequence of the malaria vector, *Anopheles gambiae*, is published in *Science*.

The complete genomic sequence of the mouse, *Mus musculus*, is published in *Nature*.

The 'Age of Omics' (genomics, proteomics, transcriptomics, etc.) is realized as researchers begin to piece together the complex epigenetic architecture of various genomes.

GM crops are reported growing in over 40 countries on six continents.

2003    Primatologists study intraspecific patterns of behavioral at six orangutan field sites, conclude that at least 24 examples of behaviors are unlikely to be gene-based, and reaffirm that culture in primates is a fact (see 1999).

The 2nd of 9 French children undergoing gene therapy for XSCID contracts leukemia, apparently the direct result of the procedure. The use of gene therapy in France continues to undergo the reevaluation begun in 2001.

A consortium based in France and the US announces that a 4th human chromosome, no. 14, has been completely sequenced. Only 1,050 genes were found on the chromosome.

Geneticists report the location of a chimeric (hybrid) gene *Tre2*, which occurs only in Hominids and that may have contributed to their unique evolution.

Dolly, the cloned Finn Dorset ewe, develops respiratory problems; she dies at age 6, at about half of the life expectancy for her breed.

Archaeologists find a *H. habilis* maxilla in the western portion of Olduvai Gorge, and conclude that *H. rudolfensis* is a questionable taxon.

Berkeley paleoanthropologist Tim White asserts that hominid fossils such as *Kenyanthropus platyops* appear divergent owing to postmortem distortion, rather that to morphology, and suggests that the hominid in question is most likely a variant of *Australopithecus afarensis*, thus potentially pruning one branch of the "bushy" hominid tree.

Italian Geneticists report the mtDNA extracted from Cro-Magnons, European *Homo sapiens* dated to 25–23 kya, show kinship to modern humans, but not to Neandertals.

Scientists report the first successful cloning of a mule, Idaho Gem.

Palaeoanthropologists report the remains of *Homo sapiens idaltu*, from Herto, Middle Awash, Ethiopia, dated to 155 kya, that they assert are too derived to have arisen from *Homo neanderthalensis*.

Scientists report the complete DNA sequence of 5th chromosome, the non-recombining portion of the Y chromosome genome. At least 78 genes were found in this portion of the chromosome, and 231 on the entire Y chromosome.

Scientists report the complete DNA sequence of a 6th human chromosome, no 7, and that 1,150 genes were found on the chromosome.

Scientists report that the first cloned horse, Prometea, is an identical twin of her mother (see goat, 2000).

Geneticists use a Y chromosome polymorphism, the M242 haplotype, to conclude that the first Native Americans reached the New World 18 kya.

Paleoanthropologists study 33 skulls from Baja California, and conclude that they resemble those from south Asian populations.

Primatologists report that when adult male savannah baboons intervene in fights between juveniles, the adults generally support their own offspring, suggesting that adult males use both indirect and direct cues to infer paternity.

Primatologists report that monkeys display knowledge of a sense of fairness in their behaviors.

Scientists report that a single-gene mutation can cause speciation in land snails when a mutation reverses shell chirality.

Investigators report finding red ochre in Qafzeh, an Israeli cave, dated to move than 90 kya, leading them to conclude that humans possessed symbolic thought by that time.

Consortium geneticists post the rough draft of the genome of the common chimpanzee, *Pan troglodytes*. In a related study, other researchers report that most of the genes studied thus far that are common to humans and chimpanzees and that have diverged rapidly during the past 5 my are involved in cell signaling; some changes were noted in genes that affect amino acid metabolism, hearing, olfaction, and speech.

Paleontologists report that fossil mammals from the Ethiopian site of Chilga confirm that migrations from the Northern Hemisphere were present in Afro-Arabia *c.* 27–24 mya.

In a survey of more than 10,000 human genes, geneticists report that most are interrupted by noncoding regions that can be variably spliced to yield diverse mRNAs.

2004    Soviet archaeologists report that AMHs occupied Arctic Siberia *c.* 30 kya, earlier than previously thought.

Chinese paleontologists report a new species of adapiform primate, *Teilhardina asiatica*, and suggest that the last common ancestor of all euprimates was a small, diurnal, visually oriented predator.

British scientists predict that 15%–37% of certain marker species will be 'committed to extinction' by 2050 CE, using climate-warming projections based upon current trends.

Geneticists report that a survey of more than 1000 global human mtDNA variants suggests that certain haplotypes distinguish African from Arctic variants, and that conserved Arctic mutants may have helped ancestral AMHs survive in higher latitudes.

Molecular biologists report the characterization of a gene in *Anopheles gambiae* that is a receptor for 4-methylphenol, a chemical component of human sweat.

Earth scientists report that simulations of Pleistocene proglacial lake environments suggests that these bodies accelerated ice sheet growth and delayed ice sheet decay *c.* 90 kya in Eurasia.

Chinese and French paleontologists describe a new genus and species of ancestral orangutan, *Khoratpithecus piriyai*, from Khorat, northeastern Thailand, that is similar to another specimen, *Lufengpithecus chiangmuanensis*, reported in 2003; *L. chiangmuanensis* is therefore referred to the new genus, as well.

EvoDevo geneticists report that X inactivation in eutherians is a two-stage process: (1) preferential inactivation of the paternal $X^P$ chromosome prior to fertilization via XIST (and which remains inactivated in blastocyst cells destined to become placental tissues), but (2) the imprinted paternal $X^P$ chromosome is then reactivated in cells within the inner cell mass (epiblast), and in these subsequent random X inactivation occurs.

Molecular biologists report the successful cloning of mice from post-mitotic olfactory neurons transferred into enucleated oocytes, demonstrating that post-mitotic cells can re-enter the cell cycle and be reprogrammed to totipotency.

Haile-Selassie *et al.* describe late Miocene fossil hominoid teeth from Ethiopia that are distinct from those of *Ardipithecus ramidus*, and assign the new specimens to *A. kadabba*; the new data question the authority of two other genera, *Sahelanthropus* and *Orrorin*.

Massachusetts biologists report the existence of proliferative germ cells that sustain oocyte and follicle production in the postnatal mammalian ovary, questioning the basic doctrine of reproductive biology that mammalian females have a fixed reserve of germ cells that is endowed at birth.

Physiologists in Philadelphia report that a gene encoding the myosin heavy chain and expressed only in masticatory muscles was inactivated by a frameshirt mutation in the hominid lineage an estimated 2.4 mya; they suggest that the mutation led to gracilization of masticatory muscles in certain early hominids.

The Rat Genome Sequencing Project Consortium announces the publication of the genome of the Brown Norway rat, in *Nature*, the third mammalian genome to be published (see Human 2001, Mouse 2002).

Consortium scientists report the complete DNA sequence of a seventh human chromosome, no. 13 and that 633 genes and 296 pseudogenes were mapped.

Consortium scientists report the complete DNA sequence of an eighth human chromosome, no. 19 and that 1,461 genes and 321 pseudogenes were mapped.

Primatologists report that young female chimpanzees learn tasks such as termite fishing from their mothers, and do so at a younger age than males; females spend more time watching their mothers perform tasks, whereas age-matched males prefer to play.

Archaeologists report on 41 perforated tick shell beads from Blombos Cave, South Africa, dated *c.* 75 kya, which are interpreted as 'unambiguous markers of symbolically mediated behaviour' and evidence in support of earliest examples of modern human behaviour earlier than 50 kya.

Asian scientists produce the first parthenogenetic mice that grow to adulthood and produce offspring by transferring two sets of identical haploid maternal genomes into an enucleated oocyte; the experiments suggests that paternal imprinting prevents parthenogenesis.

Statisticians examine recombination rate variation in the human genome and report that a minimum of 50% of recombination 'hotspots' exist in the genome. Conversely, they find that recombination occurs preferentially outside genes ('coldspots').

Two European scientists studying perikymata report that australopithecines developed nearly twice as fast as modern humans, or about the same rate as that seen in apes, and that *Homo neanderthalensis* developed at an intermediate rate, about the same rate as *Homo heidelbergensis*; members of these latter two species would have taken only about 15 years to reach adulthood, if rates of dental development reflect overall growth velocities.

Israeli archaeologists report the earliest controlled use of fire by humans nearly 790 kya at the site of Benot Ya'aqov.

Primatologists report that variation in the promotor region of monoamineoxidase A (MAOA) is correlated with reports of aggression in several species of primate, including humans.

Geophysicists report the rapid rise of sea level 19 kya in the Irish Sea basin, indicating a meltwater pulse from Northern Hemisphere ice sheets.

Biologists genotype microsatellite loci in purebred domestic dogs representing 85 breeds, and report that among-breed variation accounted for 30% of total variation, and that, using clustering methods, 99% were correctly assigned to their breeds. Nine breeds showed closest affinities to the wolf.

Consortium scientists report the complete DNA sequence of a ninth human chromosome, no. 9, and that 1,149 genes were mapped.

Consortium scientists report the complete DNA sequence of a tenth human chromosome, no. 10, and that 1,357 genes were mapped.

Consortium scientists report the complete DNA sequence of the first chimpanzee chromosome, no. 22, and that 231 coding sequences were found on the chromosome. Compared with its orthologue, human chromosome no. 21, only 1.44% of the alignable linear sequence of 33.3 megabases showed SNP-level differences; however, 68 k insertions or deletions were also reported, mostly (10:1) Alu-type insertions in the hominid lineage.

European scientists successfully insert a defective mtDNA polymerase in homozygous 'knock-in' mice that increased somatic point mutations $3\times$–$5\times$. This experimental genotype was associated with reduced lifespan and premature onset of aging-related phenotypes.

Members of the EPICA community report that the climatic record for the past 740 ky is reflected in a deep ice core from Dome C, Antarctica; the record agrees well with the previous deepest core, the 420 ky Antarctic Vostock ice core, and extends climatic knowledge back an additional 320 ky.

Using a viral vector, neuropsychologists insert a vasopressin gene allele (*V1aR*), thought to be crucial to pair bond formation, in the ventral forebrain of socially promiscuous meadow voles, and report profoundly altered behavior. They suggest that single gene variants provide a molecular mechanism for the rapid evolution of complex social behavior.

Psychobiologists report that mice lacking the μ-opioid receptor (experimental 'knockout' mice) exhibit a deficit in attachment behavior, and implicate a similar mechanism in human conditions such as autism or reactive detachment disorder.

Archaeologists report the first mid-Pleistocene hominin recovered from Olorgesailie, Kenya, dated *c.* 970 kya, associated with Acheulean handaxes.

Geneticists report that not all 'junk' DNA appears to be functionless: some untranslated RNAs seem to play editing and other roles.

Researchers report that indigenous peoples of the Americas carry a variety of louse that is different from those of other populations of *Homo sapiens*. Most controversial is the interpretation that the American lice lineage originally evolved in *Homo erectus*, and was transferred to AMH populations in Asia that later migrated to the Americas *c.* 25 kya.

Archaeologists discover a subfossil, a dwarf hominin species, *Homo floresiensis*, in a rock shelter on Flores, an island in eastern Indonesia.

Spanish paleontologists announce the discovery and reconstruction of a well-preserved 13 my old (middle Miocene) hominoid from a location near Barcelona, and name the new species *Pierolapithecus catalaunicus*.

Human biologists propose that sustained running, a special form of striding bipedalism, originated in hominids about 2 mya and may have been instrumental in the evolution of human body form.

# Appendix 9 Tentative hominid phylogeny

MYA, millions of years ago; horizontal lines indicate the Plio-Pleistocene (1.8 mya) and Mio-Pleistocene (5.0 mya) boundaries.

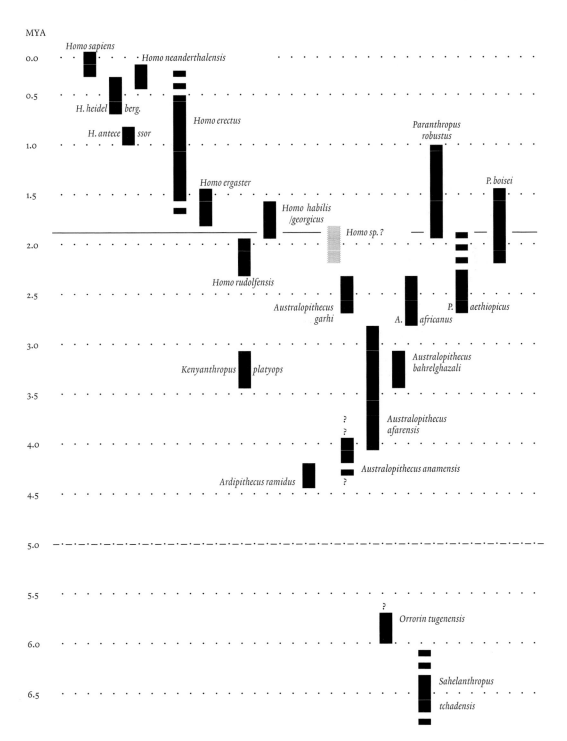

# Appendix 10 The Greek alphabet

A, α: 1st letter of the Greek alphabet; see **alpha**.
B, β: 2nd letter of the Greek alphabet; see **beta**.
Γ, γ: 3rd letter of the Greek alphabet; gamma.
Δ, σ: 4th letter of the Greek alphabet; see **delta**.
E, ε: 5th letter of the Greek alphabet; epsilon.
Z, ζ: 6th letter of the Greek alphabet; zeta.
H, η: 7th letter of the Greek alphabet; eta.
Θ, θ: 8th letter of the Greek alphabet; see **theta**.
I, ι: 9th letter of the Greek alphabet; iota.
K, κ: 10th letter of the Greek alphabet; see **kappa**.
Λ, λ: 11th letter of the Greek alphabet; see **lambda**.
M, μ: 12th letter of the Greek alphabet; see **mu**.
N, ν: 13th letter of the Greek alphabet; see **nu**.
Ξ, ξ: 14th letter of the Greek alphabet; xi.
O, o: 15th letter of the Greek alphabet; omicron.
Π, π: 16th letter of the Greek alphabet; see **pi**.
P, ρ: 17th letter of the Greek alphabet; rho.
Σ, σ: 18th letter of the Greek alphabet; see **sigma**.
T: τ: 19th letter of the Greek alphabet; tau.
Υ: υ: 20th letter of the Greek alphabet; upsilon.
Φ, φ: 21st letter of the Greek alphabet; phi.
X, χ: 22nd letter of the Greek alphabet; see **chi**.
Ψ, ψ: 23rd letter of the Greek alphabet; psi.
Ω, ω: 24th letter of the Greek alphabet; see **omega**.